Lecture Notes in Computer Science　　14399

Founding Editors

Gerhard Goos
Juris Hartmanis

Editorial Board Members

Elisa Bertino, *Purdue University, West Lafayette, IN, USA*
Wen Gao, *Peking University, Beijing, China*
Bernhard Steffen ⓘ, *TU Dortmund University, Dortmund, Germany*
Moti Yung ⓘ, *Columbia University, New York, NY, USA*

The series Lecture Notes in Computer Science (LNCS), including its subseries Lecture Notes in Artificial Intelligence (LNAI) and Lecture Notes in Bioinformatics (LNBI), has established itself as a medium for the publication of new developments in computer science and information technology research, teaching, and education.

LNCS enjoys close cooperation with the computer science R & D community, the series counts many renowned academics among its volume editors and paper authors, and collaborates with prestigious societies. Its mission is to serve this international community by providing an invaluable service, mainly focused on the publication of conference and workshop proceedings and postproceedings. LNCS commenced publication in 1973.

Sokratis Katsikas · Habtamu Abie ·
Silvio Ranise · Luca Verderame ·
Enrico Cambiaso · Rita Ugarelli · Isabel Praça ·
Wenjuan Li · Weizhi Meng · Steven Furnell ·
Basel Katt · Sandeep Pirbhulal · Ankur Shukla ·
Michele Ianni · Mila Dalla Preda ·
Kim-Kwang Raymond Choo ·
Miguel Pupo Correia · Abhishta Abhishta ·
Giovanni Sileno · Mina Alishahi ·
Harsha Kalutarage · Naoto Yanai
Editors

Computer Security

ESORICS 2023 International Workshops

CPS4CIP, ADIoT, SecAssure, WASP, TAURIN, PriST-AI, and SECAI
The Hague, The Netherlands, September 25–29, 2023
Revised Selected Papers, Part II

 Springer

Editors
Sokratis Katsikas (iD)
Norwegian University of Science and Technology
Gjøvik, Norway

Silvio Ranise (iD)
University of Trento
Trento, Italy

Enrico Cambiaso (iD)
Consiglio Nazionale delle Ricerche (CNR)
Genoa, Italy

Isabel Praça (iD)
Instituto Superior de Engenharia do Porto
Porto, Portugal

Weizhi Meng (iD)
Technical University of Denmark
Kongens Lyngby, Denmark

Basel Katt (iD)
Norwegian University of Science and Technology
Gjøvik, Norway

Ankur Shukla (iD)
Institute for Energy Technology (IFE)
Halden, Norway

Mila Dalla Preda (iD)
University of Verona
Verona, Italy

Miguel Pupo Correia
University of Lisbon
Lisbon, Portugal

Giovanni Sileno
University of Amsterdam
Amsterdam, The Netherlands

Harsha Kalutarage (iD)
Robert Gordon University
Aberdeen, UK

Habtamu Abie (iD)
Norwegian Computing Center
Oslo, Norway

Luca Verderame (iD)
University of Genoa
Genoa, Italy

Rita Ugarelli (iD)
SINTEF A.S.
Oslo, Norway

Wenjuan Li (iD)
Hong Kong Polytechnic University
Hong Kong, China

Steven Furnell (iD)
University of Nottingham
Nottingham, UK

Sandeep Pirbhulal (iD)
Norwegian Computing Center
Oslo, Norway

Michele Ianni (iD)
University of Calabria
Rende, Italy

Kim-Kwang Raymond Choo (iD)
The University of Texas at San Antonio
San Antonio, TX, USA

Abhishta Abhishta (iD)
University of Twente
Enschede, The Netherlands

Mina Alishahi
Open University in the Netherlands
Heerlen, The Netherlands

Naoto Yanai (iD)
Osaka University
Osaka, Japan

ISSN 0302-9743   ISSN 1611-3349 (electronic)
Lecture Notes in Computer Science
ISBN 978-3-031-54128-5   ISBN 978-3-031-54129-2 (eBook)
https://doi.org/10.1007/978-3-031-54129-2

Preface

The 28th edition of the European Symposium on Research in Computer Security (ESORICS) was held in The Hague, The Netherlands, September 25-29, 2023. In addition to the main conference, 12 workshops were organized and held in the same time period.

This volume includes the accepted contributions to 7 of these workshops, as follows:

- the 4th International Workshop on Cyber-Physical Security for Critical Infrastructures Protection (CSPS4CIP 2023).
- the 6th International Workshop on Attacks and Defenses for Internet-of-Things (ADIoT 2023);
- the 2nd International Workshop on System Security Assurance (SecAssure 2023);
- the Workshop on Attacks and Software Protection (WASP 2023);
- the Workshop on Transparency, Accountability and User Control for a Responsible Internet (TAURIN 2023);
- the International Workshop on Private, Secure, and Trustworthy AI (PriST-AI 2023); and
- the Workshop on Security and Artificial Intelligence (SECAI 2023).

While each of the workshops had a high-quality program of its own, the organizers opted to publishing the proceedings jointly; these are included in this volume, which contains 42 full papers. The authors improved and extended these papers based on the reviewers' feedback as well as the discussions at the workshops.

We would like to thank each and every one who was involved in the organization of the ESORICS 2023 workshops. Special thanks go to the ESORICS 2023 Workshop Chairs and to all the workshop organizers and their respective Program Committees who contributed to making the ESORICS 2023 workshops a real success. We would also like to thank the ESORICS 2023 Organizing Committee for supporting the day-to-day operation and execution of the workshops.

December 2023

Sokratis Katsikas
Habtamu Abie
Silvio Ranise
Luca Verderame
Enrico Cambiaso
Rita Ugarelli
Isabel Praça
Wenjuan Li
Weizhi Meng
Steven Furnell
Basel Katt
Sandeep Pirbhulal
Ankur Shukla
Michele Ianni
Mila Dalla Preda
Kim-Kwang Raymond Choo
Miguel Pupo Correia
Abhishta Abhishta
Giovanni Sileno
Mina Alishahi
Harsha Kalutarage
Naoto Yanai

Contents – Part II

ADIoT 2023

SecAssure 2023

Contents – Part I

CBT 2023

SECPRE 2023

CPS4CIP 2023

CPS4CIP 2023 Preface

CPS4CIP 2023 was a forum for researchers and practitioners working on cyber-physical security for critical infrastructures protection that supports finance, energy, health, air transport, communication, gas, and water. The secure operation of critical infrastructures is essential to the security of nations and, in an increasingly interconnected world, of unions of states sharing their infrastructures to develop their economies, and public health and safety. Security incidents in critical infrastructures can directly lead to a violation of users' safety and privacy, physical damage, interference in the political and social life of citizens, significant economic impact on individuals and companies, and threats to human life, while decreasing trust in institutions and questioning their social value. Because of the increasing interconnection between the digital and physical worlds, these infrastructures and services are more critical, sophisticated, and interdependent than ever before. The increased complexity makes each infrastructure increasingly vulnerable to attacks, as confirmed by the steady rise of cyber-security incidents, such as phishing or ransomware, and cyber-physical incidents, such as physical violation of devices or facilities in conjunction with malicious cyber activities. To make the situation even worse, interdependency may give rise to a domino effect with catastrophic consequences on multiple infrastructures.

To address these challenges, the workshop aimed to bring together security researchers and practitioners from the various verticals of critical infrastructures (such as the financial, energy, health, air transport, communication, gas, and water domains) to rethink cyber-physical security in the light of the latest technological developments (e.g., Cloud Computing, Blockchain, Big Data, AI, Internet-of-Things) by developing novel and effective approaches to increase the resilience of critical infrastructures and the related ecosystems of services.

The workshop attracted the attention of the critical infrastructures protection research communities and stimulated new insights and advances, with particular attention to the integrated cyber and physical aspects of security in critical infrastructures. The 4th International Workshop on Cyber-Physical Security for Critical Infrastructures Protection (CPS4CIP 2023) was held in hybrid form. The workshop was organized in conjunction with the 28th European Symposium on Research in Computer Security (ESORICS 2023), in The Hague, The Netherlands, September 28–29, 2023. The format of the workshop included technical presentations followed by presentations of preliminary project results from six ECSCI (European Cluster for Securing Critical Infrastructures) cluster member projects: HARPOCRATES by Antonis Michalas (TAU), ATL ANTIS by Christoforos Spartalis (ITI), PRECINCT by Jenny Rainbird (Inlecom Systems), SECANT by Christiana S. Kyperounta (8bellsresearch.com), HERON by Ilias Gkotsis (Satways Ltd), and eFORT by Alfonso Bernad Montenegro (FCIRCE).

The workshop received 15 submissions, which were sent for reviews, from authors in 9 distinct countries. After a thorough single-blind peer-review process, 9 papers were selected for presentation at the workshop. The review process focused on the quality of the papers, their scientific novelty, and their applicability to the protection of critical financial infrastructure and services, and the acceptance rate was 60%. The accepted articles represent an interesting mix of techniques for security risk assessment, intrusion and malware detection, XAI for security, privacy and attack detection, and digital twins' security challenges in healthcare.

The workshop was supported by projects of the ECSCI cluster, mainly (i) the ECSCI Running projects (AI4CYBER, ATLANTIS, CyberSEAS, DYNABIC, eFORT, EU-HYBNET, FeatureCloud, HARPOCRATES, IRIS, PRAETORIAN, PRECINCT, SUN RISE), (ii) the Horizon Europe project based on ECSCI (EU-CIP (European Knowledge Hub and Policy Testbed for Critical Infrastructure Protection)), (iii) the ECSCI ended projects supported by coordinators (FINSEC, ANASTACIA, CyberSANE, DEF ENDER, EnergyShield, ENSURESEC, IMPETUS, InfraStress, PHOENIX, RESISTO, SAFECARE, SAFETY4RAILS, SATIE, SealedGRID, SecureGas, SmartResilience, SOTER, SPHINX, STOP-IT, 7SHIELD), and (iv) three national projects: NORCICS (Norwegian Center for Cybersecurity in Critical Sectors) project funded by the Research Council of Norway under the Center for Research-based Innovation (SFI), RESTA-BILISE4.0 (Restabilise and Energy: Specialization of Enabling Technologies for Balancing Energy Infrastructures and Systems) project funded by START4.0 - Competence Center for security and optimization of strategic infrastructures, and CybAlliance (International Alliance for Strengthening Cybersecurity and Privacy in Healthcare) project funded by the Research Council of Norway under the INTPART International Partnerships for Excellent Education, Research and Innovation program. The organizers would like to thank these projects for supporting the CPS4CIP 2023 workshop.

Finally, the organizers of the CPS4CIP 2023 workshop would like to thank the CPS4CIP 2023 Program Committee, whose members made the workshop possible with their rigorous and timely review process. We would also like to thank the TU Delft in The Hague, The Netherlands for hosting the workshop, and the ESORICS 2023 workshop chairs for valuable help and support.

September 2023

Habtamu Abie
Silvio Ranise
Luca Verderame
Enrico Cambiaso
Rita Ugarelli
Isabel Praça

Organization

General Chairs

Habtamu Abie — Norwegian Computing Center, Norway
Silvio Ranise — University of Trento and Fondazione Bruno Kessler, Italy

Program Committee Chairs

Luca Verderame — University of Genoa, Italy
Enrico Cambiaso — National Research Council (CNR), Italy
Rita Ugarelli — SINTEF, Norway
Isabel Praça — GECAD/ISEP, Portugal

Program Committee

Dieter Gollmann — Hamburg University of Technology, Germany
Sokratis Katsikas — Norwegian University of Science and Technology, Norway
Fabio Martinelli — IIT-CNR, Italy
Einar Arthur Snekkenes — Norwegian University of Science and Technology, Norway
Stamatis Karnouskos — SAP Research, Germany
Reijo Savola — VTT Technical Research Centre of Finland, Finland
Alessandro Armando — University of Genoa, Italy
Alessio Merlo — University of Genoa, Italy
Cristina Alcaraz — University of Malaga, Spain
Giovanni Livraga — University of Milan, Italy
Shouhuai Xu — University of Texas at San Antonio, USA
Christos Xenakis — University of Piraeus, Greece
Mauro Conti — University of Padua, Italy
Denis Čaleta — Institute for Corporate Security Studies, Slovenia
Dušan Gabrielčič — Institute Jožef Stefan, Slovenia
Theodore Zahariadis — National and Kapodistrian University of Athens, Greece
Harsha Ratnaweera — Norwegian University of Life Sciences, Norway

Christos Makropoulos	National Technical University of Athens, Greece
Stefano Panzieri	Università degli Studi Roma Tre, Italy
David Tipping	DeftEdge, USA
Dionysis Nikolopoulos	National Technical University of Athens, Greece
Matteo Mangini	Network Integration and Solutions S.r.l., Italy
Corinna Köpke	Fraunhofer Institute for High-Speed Dynamics, Germany
Vasileios Kazoukas	Center for Security Studies (KEMEA), Greece
Matthias Eckhart	SBA Research, Austria
Johanna Ullrich	SBA Research, Austria
Muhammad T. Khan	University of Greenwich, UK
Sandeep Pirbhulal	Norwegian Computing Center, Norway
Ilias Gkotsis	Satways Ltd, Greece
Simon Hacks	KTH Royal Institute of Technology, Sweden
Joaquin Garcia-Alfaro	Institut Mines-Télécom, France
Nikos Passas	University of Piraeus, Greece
Frederic Guyomard	EDF, France
Basel Katt	Norwegian University of Science and Technology, Norway

External Reviewer

Ankur Shukla	Institute for Energy Technology, Norway

An Opportunity-Based Approach to Information Security Risk

Dinh Uy Tran$^{(\boxtimes)}$, Sigrid Haug Selnes , Audun Jøsang ,
and Janne Hagen

University of Oslo, 0373 Oslo, Norway
dinhut@ifi.uio.no

Abstract. The traditional approach to Information Security Risk Management (ISRM) is to assume that risk can only affect businesses negatively. However, it is interesting to notice that the latest edition of the standard *ISO/IEC 27005:2022 Guidance on managing information security risks* provides a definition of risk that covers both positive and negative consequences. Hence, present and future business leaders can expect information security professionals in their organisations to report on positive aspects of information security risk in addition to negative risk, which is a rather new and radical idea. Since information security risk assessment has traditionally focused on threats, no guidelines currently exist for how to identify, describe or assess positive risk in the context of ISRM. The aim of this study is to describe an opportunity-based approach to information security risk. In addition, this paper discusses some limitations of how ISO/IEC 27005:2022 defines risk, and hence this paper also proposes a definition of positive risk in the context of ISRM. Finally, some strategies to describe and assess positive risk are described.

Keywords: Positive Risk · Opportunity · Information Security Risk Management · Information Security Governance · Cyber Security

1 Introduction

Frameworks for Information Security Risk Management (ISRM) have traditionally focused on threats from a technological perspective. Standards, textbooks and industry certifications have mostly taken this perspective. In the last decade, however, information security has received increased attention from top-level management in organisations, due to the many distressing examples of cyberattacks seriously affecting businesses. As a result, standards and frameworks have evolved to include controls and policies to help information security gain management support and align with business objectives, where the standard *ISO/IEC 27001:2022 Requirements for Information Security Management Systems* is a prominent example ([4]). It is also noteworthy that the latest edition of

Supported by Sykehuspartner Trust.
Supported by the Raksha Project, funded by the Research Council of Norway.

S. Katsikas et al. (Eds.): ESORICS 2023 Workshops, LNCS 14399, pp. 7–25, 2024.
https://doi.org/10.1007/978-3-031-54129-2_1

the standard *ISO/IEC 27005:2022 Guidance on managing information security risks* ([7]) has expanded the definition of risk to include positive risk, which is a significant addition. This means that information security risk is not limited solely to negative risk, which is the traditional approach. There are three benefits of emphasising positive risk with regard to information security. The first benefit is that this could change the stereotypical assumption that information security practitioners tend to use fear to "sell" information security to managers, which is a negative way to communicate (Whitten, [3]). The second benefit is that this opens up new ways of communicate risk in the sense that it can be communicated both positively and negatively. The third benefit is that information security risk can be aligned with business risk, for which positive risk has been adopted since at least 2009, e.g. as described in *ISO 31000:2009 - Risk Management: Guideline.*

In a survey from ISO ([9]) the *ISO 9001 Quality Management* ([22]) management system standard was listed as the standard with the highest number of valid certifications, with 1,077,884 certified organisations worldwide, while *ISO 14001 Environmental management system* is the second most used, with 420,433 certified organisations. The standard *ISO/IEC 27001 Requirements for Information Security Management System* ([4]) is the fourth most used standard, with 58,686 certified organisations. These numbers do not include companies adopting these standards for their own benefit without seeking certification. This means that there is a high probability that a company will have designed its management system according to ISO 9001 ([8]), which also includes positive risk. Therefore, adopting a positive risk mindset for information security can help create a common understanding within the business, by using the same risk definition and principles. Even if these standards have added positive risk, a very limited body of literature discusses how to identify, describe or assess positive information security risk. Even the latest edition of ISO/IEC 27005:2022 ([7]) still mainly focuses on negative risks and threats, even though the definition of risk has been updated to cover positive risks. The aim of the present study is to review existing research papers, standards and related literature to understand the current state of research in this field. We then describe our findings and use this knowledge to propose principles that can be applied to identify and assess positive risks in an information security context.

This paper is structured as follows. The next section gives a summary of the current state of research and functions as a theoretical foundation for our research. The third section describes our research method. The fourth section presents our findings and critical analysis, as well as an example of use of proposed methods. The last section provides a summary and concluding remarks.

2   Related Research

This section gives a brief introduction to risk management and the current state of this field from a perspective that is relevant to our research and that discusses the research questions.

2.1   Risk Management

Risk is defined as *"the effect of uncertainty on objectives"* in the standards ISO/IEC 27000:2018, [6]; ISO/IEC 27005:2022, [7];ISO 31000:2018, [5]; ISO 9001:2015, [8], while NIST SP 800-37 ([11]) defines risk as *"A measure of the extent to which an entity is threatened by a potential circumstance or event, and typically is a function of: (i) the adverse impact, or magnitude of harm, that would arise if the circumstance or event occurs; and (ii) the likelihood of occurrence"*.

The definition of risk from NIST SP 800-37 ([11]) is similar to the previous version ISO/IEC 27005:2018 [15] which stated that *"risk is the potential that a given threat will exploit vulnerabilities of assets and thereby cause harm to the organization"*. Similar definitions of information security risk are expressed in mainstream textbooks for higher education and popular certifications such as CISM (Gregory, [14]) and CISSP (Harris & Maymi, [13]).

Risk management (RM) is a core component of information security governance. According to ISO 31000 [5], RM is defined as *"coordinated activities to direct and control an organization with regard to risk"*, while the RM process is defined as *"systematic application of management policies, procedures and practices to the activities of communicating, consulting, establishing the context and identifying, analysing, evaluating, treating, monitoring and reviewing risk"* (ISO/IEC 27000:2018, [6]). The importance of RM has led to the development of different standards and best practice approaches for implementing RM in an organisation, e.g., ISO/IEC 27005, ISO 31000, and NIST SP 800-37.

When surveying standards and guidelines for RM, researchers have identified a variety of limitations and challenges from both a theoretical perspective and for practical applications (Fenz et al. ([20]; Bergstrøm et al. [17]). For instance, frameworks are usually generic, with limited guidelines, and are not tailor-made for organisations (Mayer et al. [16]). ISRM frameworks tend to focus mostly on technological aspects, while the aspects of risk related to organisational aspects, human factors and processes are mentioned, but not elaborated on (Bergstrøm et al. [17]). This means that following the guidelines for ISRM might not cover risk at the organisational level, which could result in the organisation not having an oversight of the total risk and information security posture (Tran and Jøsang, [21]). This is a concern shared by Diefenbach et al. [18] and Abbass et al. [19].

By taking advantage of the relative flexibility of frameworks, as argued by Aleksandrov et al. ([22]), ISO/IEC standards can be integrated with other standards for management systems, which, when combined, provide a holistic approach to risk. This seems to be an approach adopted by many researchers, and many papers exist that propose a more holistic approach to RM by integrating different frameworks. For instance, the lack of guidelines for aligning ISRM holistically and providing an oversight of business assets has contributed to researchers such as Mayer et al. ([16]), Diefenbach et al. ([18]) and Abbass et al. ([19]) proposing a model for integrating the Enterprise Architecture Model (EAM) with risk management frameworks such as ISO/IEC 27005 and ISO 31000.

Shamala et al. ([23]) express concerns about the risk assessment methodology due to the huge amount of information that it is typically necessary to process, for reliable conclusions to be drawn. This is why they propose integrating relevant information quality attributes derived from quality management in the process of gathering and assessing risk. This proposal could contribute to more reliable, verifiable and objective, and more accurate assessments of risk, to become a reliable factor in the decision-making process. Webb et al. ([24]) proposed a similar model based on adapting Endsley's situation awareness model into ISRM, with the goal of improving the process of gathering quality information to facilitate more accurate risk assessments. They called this an intelligence-driven approach to ISRM.

Riesco and Villagrá ([25]) argue that current RM frameworks are too static, and do not apply well to a landscape where information security risks and threats are constantly evolving and dynamic. From this perspective, they propose to integrate near real-time cyber-threat intelligence information (CTI) into ISRM frameworks. Integrating CTI into ISRM frameworks could provide better up-to-date risk-level calculations due to automation. They tested this framework on a national CSIRT (Computer Security Incident Response Team), and found that they were able to advance from the original (static) risk assessment approach used by the organisation, to a more dynamic approach. Other researchers, such as Putra and Mutijarsa ([26]) have implemented the ISMR process by integrating ISO/IEC 27005 for establishing the RM process, and then supplementing it with the NIST standard SP 800-30 Rev.1, used specifically for its method of conducting risk assessments. This design was implemented at the Indonesian national police command centre, which reported that it met their organisational needs for managing risk.

These are several interesting studies that adopt the integration of different frameworks to establish a more holistic approach to ISRM. However, our observation is that they all tend to focus on negative risk and not on positive risk. Examples are well-recognised industry standards and methodology such as ITIL 4 and FAIR (Factor Analysis of Information Risk). ITIL 4 ([36]) on the other hand, states that risk is something to avoid, but also emphasises that failure to use an opportunity can be a risk, which implicitly acknowledges positive risk. ITIL 4 references and supports the ISO 31000:2018 [5] definition, but still does not specify how to assess positive risk. The popularity of the FAIR methodology ([37]) is increasing rapidly and some enterprises such as Netflix, Hewlett-Packard Enterprise (HPE), National Aeronautics and Space Administration (NASA) and many more, adopt this approach. However, FAIR has limited its methodology to negative risk, with its focus on threats, vulnerabilities and loss.

Le Grand ([27]) argues that ISRM tends to focus on threats without considering opportunities, which in brief means taking account of what can go wrong more than the benefits of information security. Therefore, they propose to shift the focus to opportunities to ensure that information security enables businesses to use new technology that keeps them innovative, while maintaining their competitive edge. Olsson ([29]) found empirical evidence showing that current information security risk management methodologies focus solely on negative risk, and that the absence of opportunity management is obvious, which is the same conclusion as from research conducted by Rajbhandari ([28]). Many years after the research conducted by Olsson ([29]) and Rajbhandari ([28]), the practice of assessing positive risk regarding information security has not gained much traction, even though the latest edition of ISO/IEC 27005:2022 ([7]) opens up for positive risk. This is also true for ISO 31010:2019 ([26]), which is a general guideline on risk assessment that focuses entirely on threats, with some mention of opportunities.

Our investigation found that there is limited research on assessment of positive risk. One of the few cases we have identified was by Ivascu and Cioca ([31]), who propose a risk model that consists of three components: the first component is to treat positive risk as opportunity management, the second component is to treat negative risk as hazard management, and the third component is control management, which is used to manage uncertainty. They also propose a model for risk treatment strategies specifically for opportunity, which was the inverse of the traditional risk treatment strategies. Hillson ([30]) argues that opportunities and threats do not differ, since both involve uncertainty, which affects the ability to achieve objectives. Hillson then proposed a double probability impact matrix for assessing opportunities and threats, and risk strategies similar to those of Ivascu and Cioca ([31]).

2.2   Research Questions

This study aims to answer the following three research questions. First, how should practitioners interpret the concept of risk as defined in ISO/IEC 27005:2022 ([7]) to make it more applicable to both positive and negative risks? Second, how should a definition of positive risk be articulated? Finally, how can the definition of risk be applied to describe and assess both positive and negative risks?

3   Research Method

This research started with a systematic literature review (SLR) procedure developed by Kitchenham [1]. However, by analysing the research data collected, we identified that there is limited research of positive risk and there was a need to choose a more appropriate research method. To answer the research questions, we needed to generate new theory due to limited research, but also manage our predetermined ideas and biases, because these issues have been identified from our practical experience. To address these issues, we found that grounded theory (GT) is an appropriate research method for this project. The aim of GT is to gain an understanding of the data and to use this knowledge to construct new theory, which means that this research method is appropriate when little is known about a research phenomenon. While constructing theory founded on the data, we can better manage our predetermined ideas and biases. There are many variations of GT, but we choose to combine different variations based on a framework described by Chun Tie et al. [38]], together with the main characteristics and guidelines described by Stol et al. [39] and Birks et al. [40], to match our research issues.

Our research started with SLR, but evolved over to GT, and to collect research data, we used purposive sampling from GT (Chun Tie, et al., [38]). The aim of purposive sampling is to select relevant data before further analysis. We decided that the most relevant digital libraries from which to collect research data were Web of Science, Scopus and Google Scholar because they cover a wide spectrum of research related to information security and risk management. However, due to limited research on this topic, we decided to collect relevant standards that are considered "best practice" by the industry, as well as mainstream textbooks used for industry certification programs, to understand how the industry applies risk management.

We then defined appropriate search keywords for a literature search. Our keywords consisted of strings that we considered relevant to the fields of study, as shown in the left-hand column of Table 1. We started with keywords related to information security, but surprisingly, there are limited papers discussing positive risks related to information security. We therefore decided to broaden the search by removing information security, with the intention of obtaining more papers related to positive risk. We decided not to collect papers from Google Scholar concerning the search string"Information Security Risk Management" because we encountered duplicate articles from other sources and found many entries other than research papers.

Table 1. Overview of relevant papers from research databases.

Search keywords	Web of Science	Scopus	Google Scholar
"Information Security Risk Management"	13	16	0
"Positive Risk Information Security"	3	3	1
"Opportunity Management"	3	6	1
"Positive Risk Management"	1	1	1
"ISO3100 Positive Risk"	2	4	1

We then applied constant comparison, which is used to analyse data from different viewpoints and help researchers understand their data and the gaps in their data, to generate new theory (Birks, et al., [40]). By constantly comparing data, we can use this for coding and categorisation, to generate more codes and different categories. Constant comparative analysis helps us find differences and consistencies/inconsistencies, to help us refine our theories or raise our understanding (Chun Tie, et al., [38]). The constant comparison helps us to collect data based on theoretical sampling, which constitutes collecting data to enrich the emerging theory or concepts until we reach theoretical saturation, when data ceases to give us new insight and we can predict what the analysis of the data is likely to describe (Birks, et al., [40]). In a way, this functions as constantly evolving inclusion and exclusion criteria similar to SLR, but in GT it is called theoretical sensitivity, which is knowing which theory is important to our own theory. We used an ever-evolving coding system as inclusion and exclusion criteria until we reached the point of theoretical saturation (Chun Tie et al., [38]).

Stol et al. [39] describe coding as an analytical method to label data according to its properties. The coding concepts we used were initial coding, core category and axial coding. At the initial coding level, the labels/codes are not categorised, but the main focus is to generate many codes, to give us an overview of the collected data. From the initial coding, we can then determine core concepts and use this data to generalise and categorise codes and then transfer the codes to respective categories. The final phase of coding is axial coding, of which the goal is to present interrelated codes or categories and explain relationships between the data, to ensure a better understanding of the data. To analyse and identify the interrelation between the codes and categories, we used diagramming tools to help us visualise and illustrate the complex interplay between codes and core categories (Mills, et al., [2]). The diagramming tool we used was Obsidian, which we used to develop codes, and then transferred the codes to their respective categories. Each code and category was marked and labelled with our interpretations and restructured to match similar codes. Obsidian can then illustrate how the codes are interrelated and give us a better overview, to generate more theory or collect more data to repeat this research process.

This resulted in 23 papers, and 32 codes are relevant for this study. The core categories are Industry standards (9 codes), Integration of RM (7 codes), Positive risk (2 codes), Risk challenge (5 codes), Risk communication (3 codes) and Standard risk (6 codes).

4   Results

Based on our research method, we observed two important findings. The first finding is related to the fundamental aspects of positive risk that need to be discussed and starts at a definition level. The second finding is that, to the best of our knowledge, there is limited research of how to conduct risk assessments of positive risk. These findings are described in separate subsections below.

4.1   Definition of Risk

Before we can propose a definition for positive risk, we need to address the limitations of the current risk definition from ISO/IEC 27005:2022 ([7]) and ISO 31000:2018 ([5]) to ensure consistency with these definitions. ISO/IEC 27005:2022 ([7]) and ISO 31000:2018 ([5]) state that risk is *"the effect of uncertainty on objectives"*, while the effect is a positive or negative deviation from the expected. The standards also described a note supporting the main definition that *"risk is usually expressed in terms of risk sources, potential events and their consequences and their likelihood"* (ISO 31000:2018, [5]). Our first observation is that the general definition of risk is too abstract for it to be applicable to describing information security risk. A similar statement is issued by Aven ([33]), who disagrees with the definition of risk from ISO 31000:2018 ([5]), arguing that it is inconsistent with the definition of "risk description" as *"Structured statement of risk usually containing four elements: sources, events, causes and consequences"*, where the uncertainty dimension is absent, and that to apply these elements, a risk analysis must first be conducted. We agree with Aven ([33]) to some degree, in the sense that describing all the elements generates too much information, because an important aspect of describing risk is to communicate risk simply to a recipient who is not necessarily an ISRM expert. This means that a risk description statement should be short, precise, easy to understand and tailored to the recipient.

The second limitation of the risk definition becomes evident on observing that risk can be identified from either a bottom-up or top-down approach (ISO 31010:2019, [12]). In our understanding, Aven ([33]) refers to a bottom-up approach and argues that a risk analysis is needed to include consequences and causes. We argue that it is possible to identify and describe risk first, then assess risk, and then refine the risk description afterwards, which is a top-down approach, and that both approaches have their pros and cons. To be clear, we could not find the definition of risk description in the new ISO 31000:2018 ([5]), ISO 31010:2019 ([12]) or ISO 27005:2022 ([7]). However, it still exists in *ISO Guide 73:2009 Risk management - Vocabulary* ([10]), but the issue remains because the definition is abstract and less applicable.

Our observation is that the main definitions from ISO 31000:2018 ([5]) and ISO/IEC 27005:2022 ([7]) are correct, depending on the stage of risk management that is applied. If risk management has not been applied, it makes sense to use the general definition, since it is abstract. This is similar to saying that uncertainty is classified in different categories, and Olsson ([29]) describes uncertainties as either aleatoric or epistemic. We argue that the general risk definition assumes aleatoric uncertainty whereby incidents cannot be foreseen in advance and could be random, so that the outcome could deviate from the expected. This is because when risk management has not been applied, risk is left to random outcomes and is unmanaged. In the next stage, when risk management has been applied, it makes more sense from a professional perspective to use a supplementary note on risk from ISO/IEC 27005:2022 ([7]), which states in brief that ISR is associated with potential threats that will exploit vulnerabilities which could cause harm to an organisation. Risk from a professional setting is like epistemic uncertainty, which derives from the lack of knowledge, where the goal is to precisely understand the knowledge gap, to be able to seek more knowledge to foresee risk and manage it so that the outcome is less random.

However, the risk analyst should focus on understanding the epistemic uncertainty and how to manage it, while acknowledging the aleatoric uncertainty in the sense that not all risk can be foreseen. The goal is to manage both types of uncertainty of risk to an appropriate level. Based on this, we recommend that

ISO standards clarify the distinct differences in the general and professional definition of risk. These notes from ISO/IEC 27005:2022 ([7]) can be used as a professional definition of risk and are practical. However, the notes are limited to negative risk and are inconsistent with the new definition. We will discuss five limitations of the current definition and propose an updated definition.

First, by saying "potential threats", the note implies that ISR is limited to negative events. We propose to use "events" instead of "threats", as both threat and opportunity are types of events. Second, the term "exploit" implies that an active entity is exploiting a vulnerability intentionally. Using "exploit" limits ISR to intentional exploiting and excludes accidental incidents or natural occurrences. Both unintentional incidents and natural occurrences affect information security objectives and we recommend removing "exploiting" from the note.

Third, the use of vulnerability makes sense when discussing technological risk. We argue that vulnerability is one of many causes, such as people or the process, and technological, economic and natural factors. It makes more sense to use "causes" instead of "vulnerabilities", where the term "cause" is equally relevant for both positive and negative risks. Fourth, the last phrase of the definition: *"cause harm to an organisation"*, should be changed to "could affect business objectives", since the goal of information security is to support business objectives and opens up for positive risk.

Finally, the general definition of risk implies that only the effect of uncertainty could be either positive or negative, which is the outcome. We argue that not only can the outcome be positive or negative, but the event itself can be framed as opportunity and/or threat, where the outcome could be either positive or negative. Based on these findings, we propose a supportive ISR definition to ISO/IEC 27005:2022 ([7]):

Definition 1. *"An information security risk is a possible security-related event that could affect business objectives."*

The first part of the definition emphasises "a possible event" since the event could materialise or not, which is why a likelihood assessment is needed. The second part of the definition is related to consequence in the sense that if the event materialises, then business objectives can be affected positively or negatively. The other benefit of this definition is that it can be used as a template for describing the risk discussed in Sect. 4.2. Now that we have defined general risk, which considers positive and negative risk, we can define positive risk as follows:

Definition 2. *"A positive information security risk is a possible security-related opportunity that could help businesses achieve their business objectives."*

We define opportunity as a type of event that is positive, such as process improvement, acquisition, upgrading, patching and building competence. The aim is to identify security-related opportunities to provide value or improve an organisation. We deliberately added "possible" before opportunity because we do not know whether the opportunity will materialise. If it does materialise, this will depend on whether implemented controls increase the likelihood of the opportunity materialising. The last phrase of the definition is related to the gains the identified opportunity could support in terms of how an organisation achieves its business objectives, such as increased income, reputation, optimised service and reduced workload. We have deliberately added "could" to the last part of the definition, since an opportunity could fail if it were not managed well, which means that positive risk should be managed.

4.2 Risk Description

By applying the proposed definition 1, it is possible to identify a possible event and outcome if the event materializes. The general template for describing a risk is as follows: *There is a possibility that <insert event> could result in <insert outcome>*. By assuming the possibility of an event as a threat/opportunity with a gain/loss as outcome, this template opens four ways to describe risk, as provided in Table 2. The aim of risk description strategies is to open up opportunities to apply risk framing, which is to communicate risk that is tailor-made for a specific recipient (Wangen and Snekkenes, [34]), since every recipient perceives risk differently, also known as risk perception (Lion and Meertens, [35]). Some decision-makers prefer positive information, while others can make effective decisions with negative information. Understanding the others' risk perception can help a risk analyst frame risk in a way that suits the recipient. Using the risk description strategies gives access to four alternative ways of communicating and describing risk, as shown in Table 2. In contrast to traditional ISRM, which only provides the first alternative.

Table 2. Risk description strategies.

Alternative	Risk description alternatives
1	There is a possibility that <insert threat> could result in <insert loss>
2	There is a possibility that <insert threat> could result in <insert gain>
3	There is a possibility that <insert opportunity> could result in <insert loss>
4	There is a possibility that <insert opportunity> could result in <insert gain>

A use case on the practical use of risk description strategies is provided in Sect. 4.3.

4.3 Sample Case - Use of Risk Description Strategies

The setting for this fictive case is a local private hospital that specialises in emergency healthcare. Medical doctors rely on advanced technology to perform emergency healthcare procedures. The top-level management has hired a risk analyst to perform a risk assessment because the technical system has been disrupted on several occasions, which has caused extensive loss of income and reputation. These disruptions have not impacted the patients, but top-level management is concerned about this scenario. Therefore, they require a risk assessment to determine whether to improve the system or acquire a new system. The risk analyst reviews the technical documentation and architecture description, and performs vulnerability scanning. The risk analyst also interviews key stakeholders, including the system owner, IT manager, top-level management and information security manager. The system owner wants to use the same system as before because they are accustomed to it, and the same applies to the IT manager, while only the information security manager wants a more robust system. The top-level management wants a solution that balances the needs of stakeholders, but also increases effectiveness and efficiency and provides a positive return on investment. From the interviews, the risk analyst has an idea of the stakeholders' risk perception.

The main findings are that the system is installed locally on different clients and servers spread across the hospital. There is no monitoring of the system, so the IT or security staff cannot detect potential incidents. When an incident occurs, the IT or security staff must be on-site to troubleshoot and fix the problem. It takes around 30 min for them to be on-site. Depending on the type of incident, it could take from one hour and up to two days to fix the issue. From these findings, the risk analyst concludes that there is a need for a centralised architecture with monitoring capabilities that could eliminate travel time, since IT and security staff would be able to troubleshoot offsite and fix problems before they occur, based on monitoring. The analyst's aim is to recommend the implementation of centralised architecture and monitoring capabilities. Since the risk analyst has mapped stakeholder risk perceptions, the analyst can use risk description strategies to match the different risk perceptions. The aim is to catch the stakeholders' attention and address their key concerns, so as to increase the likelihood of them listening to the assessment. The risk description serves as the first and fundamental line to catch the stakeholders' attention before presenting the assessment. In Table 3, we give examples of all four possibilities of framing risks based on strategies from Table 2, which will be discussed.

Table 3. Practical use of risk description strategies.

Examples
1. There is a possibility that malware can be installed without detection, which could cause business disruption
2. There is a possibility that malware can be installed without detection, which would not cause any business disruption
3. There is a possibility that acquiring updated infrastructure (centralised, monitoring capabilities) could cause business disruption
4. There is a possibility that by acquiring updated infrastructure detection of faults in the system (centralised, monitoring capabilities) could reduce the workload of the IT and security staff, and give a more reliable system

Alternative 1 from Table 3: *"There is a possibility that malware can be installed without detection, which could cause business disruption."* According to the risk description strategies provided in Table 2, the threat is that "malware can be installed" while the loss is related to "business disruption". Alternative 1 is suitable to communicate risk to security staff and top-level management. The security staff are accustomed to this rhetoric, since this is the traditional way of communicating risk from a threat-based approach. The top-level management might be interested in this approach because they care about the reputation of the hospital. However, this will depend on the person, since some might prefer solution-based rhetoric. Therefore, in this case, we know that malware cannot be detected, and at some point, malware can be installed, since this is a common attack vector. This could cause business disruption and it could take time to troubleshoot the issue, because the staff need to travel to the physical location. In this case, there is a high probability of not detecting malware, and the consequences can be high because this could affect patient safety.

Alternative 2 from Table 3: *"There is a possibility that malware can be installed without detection, which would not cause any business disruption."* According to the risk description strategies provided in Table 2, the threat is that "malware can be installed", while the gain is that, even though the threat materialised, it did not cause business disruption and revenue can still be generated. Alternative 2 is suitable for communication with the IT and security staff. By assuming that the IT and security staff can address the issue, they will probably receive praise for the way they handle the situation. This might increase the likelihood of them listening to the risk assessment, but if we frame the risk negatively, then the staff might feel humiliated and fail to support the risk assessment. Therefore, in this case, the malware cannot be detected, as in alternative 1, but the consequence assessment can be adjusted to the middle of the consequence scale. Here, we can acknowledge that IT and security staff can handle the situation, but that it can be handled better with appropriate tools.

Alternative 3 from Table 3: *"There is a possibility that acquiring updated infrastructure (centralised, monitoring capabilities) could cause business disruption."* According to the risk description strategies provided in Table 2, the opportunity is "updating the infrastructure", which could lead to loss related to"business disruption". Alternative 3 is suitable for top-level management and when the decision is made to acquire the new infrastructure. Successful acquisition does not equal a successful outcome because it depends on managing opportunities such as staff building, training and sufficient resources.

Alternative 4 from Table 3: *"There is a possibility that acquiring updated infrastructure detection of faults in the system(centralised, monitoring capabilities) could reduce the workload of the IT and security staff, and give a more reliable system."* According to the risk description strategies provided in Table 2, the opportunity is "updating the infrastructure", which gives rise to the gain that personnel's workload is reduced and a more reliable system can generate more income than an unstable system. Alternative 4 is suitable for all stakeholders, and especially those who prefer solution-based rhetoric. In this case, we emphasise improving the infrastructure so that it can detect faults. The IT and security staff can thereby fix a problem before it becomes an incident. We use infrastructure instead of system because it is easier for non-technicians to understand that changes do not affect the functionality of performing emergency healthcare procedures and that reduced workload is in the interest of all stakeholders. Therefore, communication based on alternative 4 will address everyone's concerns and support the overall goal of top-level management, which is to increase effectiveness, efficiency and return on investment. To address the return on investment, we develop measures or key performance indicators (KPI) related to every problem that is fixed before it becomes an incident, compared with the downtime before acquiring the system, and so on. It is easier to define measures with positive risk, while if we use alternative 1, we need to develop measures and KPIs related to malware attacks, and it is uncertain whether this specific scenario would occur enough to contribute a positive return on investment. Therefore, in this risk assessment, we need to address the measures needed to ensure successful acquisition and gain.

After the risk assessments are presented, the risk analyst recommends the acquisition of monitoring capabilities. The risk analyst presents an assessment of cost and benefit, return on security investment, and total cost of ownership, and concludes that the acquisition would most likely reach break-even. This means that this acquisition will generate neither profit nor loss; and therefore, if a malware attack occurs and the new system can detect and correct the incident without causing business disruption, technically the hospital will still not generate income directly.

However, the risk analyst recommends developing strategies to build business presence to improve business reputation and trust, which could indirectly generate more customers due to good information security, which in turn could generate income. The risk analyst gives an example where a hospital can handle a malware attack without business disruption, and then they need to go public and share lessons learned, which is one way of improving business reputation to show that this hospital has robust healthcare services. This could generate more interest and increase the likelihood of gaining more customers, which in turn could generate more income. The risk analyst presents a decision tree and possible scenarios of outcomes, depending on which decision is made, as shown in Fig. 1.

The best possible positive risk is not implementing the monitoring capabilities and where no malware attack occurs, but if an attack does occur, the likelihood of handling the incident without business disruption is low. It is naturally possible that the incident can be handled well, even without monitoring capabilities. The best possible positive risk when implementing the monitoring capabilities is that if a malware attack occurs and it causes no business disruption, the hospital can employ strategies to increase its business presence to build its reputation, which could lead to more customers in the future. Another positive risk is if a malware attack has not occurred, then it is important to emphasise that monitoring could provide other non-economic gains, such as reduced work-

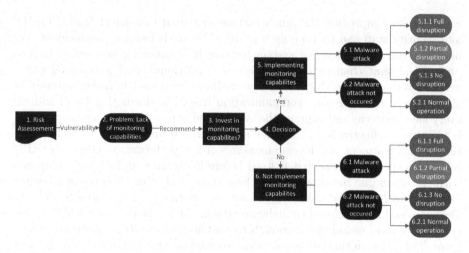

Fig. 1. Decision tree with possible outcomes

load and increased quality of their business services, which in turn could increase reputation and gain more customers.

This case presents different strategies to communicate risk based on recipients' risk perception, and in this case the goal was to propose a solution, but communicated as four different strategies, instead of being dependent on the traditional way, which is alternative 1, the threat-based approach.

4.4   Positive Risk Assessment

Before we can conduct a positive risk assessment, it is beneficial to have an idea of how these aspects fit the proposed definition from Sect. 4.1. Ivascu and Cioca ([31]) proposed a model for risk management that consists of three components: Hazard, Opportunity and Control Management. We will use this model as a basis and make some adjustments so that it fits into an ISRM context.

The use of hazard management focuses on negative events that could jeopardise business objectives. Hazard is not a familiar term used by information security professionals, and we recommend using threat because it is an established term in the information security community. Opportunity management is something we could keep, but we recommend that threat and opportunity are different types of events. We recommend adding a new component, objective, since it relates to consequences when a threat or opportunity is materialised, and the outcome could result in a loss or gain that affects the objective.

At the same time, we recommend removing control management because Ivascu and Cioca ([31]) consider this component to manage uncertainty that affects the outcome of the risk. We find it more logical to lift uncertainty as a component that surrounds both the event and the objective. This is also to emphasise that managing uncertainty is not only about the outcome, but also about managing events as well and is not limited to the outcome. It seems that the ISO/IEC 27005:2022 ([7]) definition can be interpreted to mean that just the outcome can be positive or negative, and we argue that uncertainty management also applies to assessing the likelihood of the event. The updated conceptualisation of risk is presented in Fig. 2.

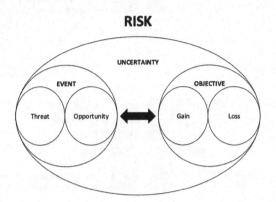

Fig. 2. Conceptualization of risk

Hillson ([30]) proposed a model for the double probability-impact matrix used for assessing opportunities and threats. The purpose of this matrix is to help professionals visualise and reflect on positive and negative risks. From this matrix, we propose some adjustments to fit our risk definition and description strategies. We propose to use likelihood instead of probability, since this is used in ISO/IEC 27005:2022 ([7]), and then we propose to use loss and gain instead of positive or negative impact. It makes more sense to determine a gain value instead of using positive impact. For instance, it is more intuitive to communicate a very high gain instead of a very high positive impact. The original model from Hillson ([30]) is a two-dimensional risk matrix, which we modified into a four-dimensional model so that it matches the four risk description strategies as provided in Table 2. The four-dimensional risk matrix model is presented in Fig. 3.

5   Summary and Conclusion

The aim of the present study has been to extended the understanding of positive risk in the context of information security. In particular, this paper proposes a business oriented definition of information security and positive risk that is applicable to describe risk. A strategy to describe and frame risk in four different ways then depends on the risk perception of decision-makers. Finally, we propose conceptual models for the information security risk definition, as a four-dimensional risk assessment matrix tailored for this study. To the best of our knowledge, this is the first study to propose strategies for risk description with a corresponding

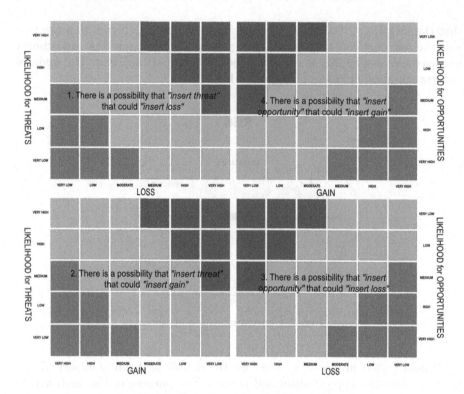

Fig. 3. Four-dimensional risk matrix

risk matrix to assess both positive and negative risks. Further research should be conducted to validate these concepts, and this could be done by applying these concepts in a professional business setting and then conducting interviews with security professionals to learn more about their experience. Even though this study offers a theoretical contribution, it still provides ideas on assessing positive risk and can give researchers and professionals ideas to reflect on threats and opportunities. Based on ISO 31000 ([5]) that since 2009 have incorporated positive risk, as well as on the recent ISO/IEC 27005:2022 ([7]), it is reasonable to assume that steering committees, stakeholders and business leaders will expect information security professionals to identify and assess positive information security risk opportunities. Since the risk management field is evolving, information security professionals should adapt to this change, which could also help them get a more holistic perspective in information security and speak the same language as management (Tran and Jøsang, [41]).

References

1. Kitchenham, B.: Procedures for performing systematic reviews. Keele, UK, Keele Univ. **33**(2004), 1–26 (2004)
2. Mills, J., Bonner, A., Francis, K.: The development of constructivist grounded theory. Int J Qual Methods **5**, 25–35 (2006)
3. Whitten, D.: The chief information security officer: An analysis of the skills required for success. Journal Of Computer Information Systems. **48**, 15–19 (2008)
4. Information Standardization: Information security, cybersecurity and privacy protection - Information security management systems - Requirements (2022)
5. Information Standardization: Risk management - Guidelines (2018)
6. Information Standardization: Information technology - Security techniques - Information security management systems - Overview and vocabulary (2018)
7. Information Standardization: Information security, cybersecurity and privacy protection - Guidance on managing information security risks (2022)
8. Information Standardization: Quality management systems - Requirements (2015)
9. International Organization for Standardization - 0. Explanatory note and overview on ISO Survey 2021 results. https://www.iso.org/the-iso-survey.html. Accessed 13 Jan 2023
10. Information Standardization: ISO Guide 73:2009, Risk management - Vocabulary (2009)
11. Technology Standardization: Technology risk management framework for information systems and organizations (2018). https://doi.org/10.6028/NIST.SP.800-37r2. Accessed 13 Jan 2023
12. Information Standardization: Risk management - Risk assessment techniques (2019)
13. Harris, S., Maymi, F.: CISSP All-in-One Exam Guide, 7 th edn. McGraw Hill LLC (2016)
14. Gregory, P.: CISM Certified Information Security Manager All-in-One Exam Guide. McGraw Hill LLC (2018)
15. Information Standardization: Information security, cybersecurity and privacy protection - Guidance on managing information security risks (2018)
16. Mayer, N., Aubert, J., Grandry, E., Feltus, C., Goettelmann, E., Wieringa, R.: An integrated conceptual model for information system security risk management supported by enterprise architecture management. Softw. Syst. Model. **18**, 2285–2312 (2019)
17. Bergström, E., Lundgren, M., Ericson, A.: Revisiting information security risk management challenges: a practice perspective. Inform. Comput. Secur. **27**, 358–372 (2019)
18. Diefenbach, T., Lucke, C., Lechner, U.: Towards an integration of information security management, risk management and enterprise architecture management-a literature review. In: 2019 IEEE International Conference on Cloud Computing Technology and Science (CloudCom), pp. 326–333 (2019)
19. Abbass, W., Baina, A., Bellafkih, M.: Improvement of information system security risk management. In: 2016 4th IEEE International Colloquium on Information Science and Technology (CiSt), pp. 182–187 (2016)

20. Fenz, S., Heurix, J., Neubauer, T., Pechstein, F.: Current challenges in information security risk management. Inform. Manage. Comput. Secur. **22**, 410–430 (2014)
21. Tran, D., Jøsang, A.: Information security posture to organize and communicate the information security governance program. In: Proceedings of the 18th European Conference on Management Leadership and Governance, ECMLG 2022, vol. 18, pp. 515–522 (2022)
22. Aleksandrov, M., Vasiliev, V., Aleksandrova, S.: Implementation of the risk-based approach methodology in information security management systems. In: 2021 International Conference on Quality Management, Transport and Information Security, Information Technologies (IT&QM&IS), pp. 137–139 (2021)
23. Shamala, P., Ahmad, R., Zolait, A., Sedek, M.: Integrating information quality dimensions into information security risk management (ISRM). J. Inform. Secur. Appl. **36**, 1–10 (2017)
24. Webb, J., Ahmad, A., Maynard, S., Shanks, G.: A situation awareness model for information security risk management. Comput. Security. **44**, 1–15 (2014)
25. Riesco, R., Villagrá, V.: Leveraging cyber threat intelligence for a dynamic risk framework. Int. J. Inf. Secur. **18**, 715–739 (2019)
26. Putra, I., Mutijarsa, K.: Designing information security risk management on bali regional police command center based on ISO 27005. In: 2021 3rd East Indonesia Conference on Computer and Information Technology (EIConCIT), pp. 14–19 (2021)
27. Le Grand, C.: Positive security, risk management, and compliance. EDPACS **47**, 1–10 (2013)
28. Rajbhandari, L.: Consideration of opportunity and human factor: required paradigm shift for information security risk management. In: 2013 European Intelligence and Security Informatics Conference, pp. 147–150 (2013)
29. Olsson, R.: In search of opportunity management: is the risk management process enough? Int. J. Project Manage. **25**, 745–752 (2007)
30. Hillson, D.: Extending the risk process to manage opportunities. Int. J. Project Manage. **20**, 235–240 (2002)
31. Ivascu, L., Cioca, L.: Opportunity risk: integrated approach to risk management for creating enterprise opportunities. Adv. Educ. Res. **49**, 77–80 (2014)
32. Purdy, G.: ISO 31000: 2009-setting a new standard for risk management. Risk Anal. An Int. J. **30**, 881–886 (2010)
33. Aven, T.: On the new ISO guide on risk management terminology. Reliab. Eng. Syst. Saf. **96**, 719–726 (2011)
34. Wangen, G., Snekkenes, E.: A taxonomy of challenges in information security risk management. In: Proceeding of Norwegian Information Security Conference/Norsk Informasjonssikkerhetskonferanse-NISK 2013-Stavanger, 18th-20th November 2013 (2013)
35. Lion, R., Meertens, R.: Security or opportunity: the influence of risk-taking tendency on risk information preference. J. Risk Res. **8**, 283–294 (2005)
36. Axelos. ITIL Foundation, ITIL (ITIL 4 Foundation). The Stationery Office (2020)
37. Measuring and Managing Information Risk: A FAIR Approach. Butterworth-Heinemann (2014)
38. Chun Tie, Y., Birks, M., Francis, K.: Grounded theory research: a design framework for novice researchers. SAGE Open Med. **7**, 2050312118822927 (2019)
39. Stol, K., Ralph, P., Fitzgerald, B.: Grounded theory in software engineering research: a critical review and guidelines. In: Proceedings of The 38th International Conference on Software Engineering, pp. 120–131 (2016)

40. Birks, D., Fernandez, W., Levina, N., Nasirin, S.: Grounded theory method in information systems research: its nature, diversity and opportunities. Eur. J. Inf. Syst. **22**, 1–8 (2013)
41. Tran, D., Jøsang, A.: Business language for information security. In: International Symposium on Human Aspects of Information Security and Assurance, pp. 169–180 (2023)

A Methodology for Cybersecurity Risk Assessment in Supply Chains

Betul Gokkaya$^{(\boxtimes)}$ ⓘ, Leonardo Aniello ⓘ, Erisa Karafili ⓘ, and Basel Halak ⓘ

University of Southampton, University Road, Southampton SO17 1BJ, UK
{betul.gokkaya,l.aniello,e.karafili,basel.halak}@soton.ac.uk

Abstract. Supply chain cyberattacks are on the rise as attackers are increasingly exploiting the intricate network of supplier connections between companies. Critical infrastructures too have been successfully targeted using this technique affecting their software and hardware estates, raising serious concerns due to the potential impact on public safety and the proper functioning of countries. This highlights the need to revise cybersecurity risk assessment strategies to stress the focus on threats originating from suppliers. This work proposes a novel supply chain cybersecurity risk assessment tailored for companies with limited cybersecurity expertise and constrained resources to execute risk assessment. Through a set of simple questions, this methodology first captures the perceived likelihood and impact of vulnerabilities and threats that derive from suppliers and target specific organisational assets and then generates cybersecurity risk scores for each relevant threat. A preliminary validation of the methodology is carried out, where generated risk scores are compared to evaluations provided by cybersecurity experts. The results show that the methodology produces risk scores that on average differ by 8% from those deriving from the experts' assessment, which corroborates the hypothesis that the methodology is reliable even though it does not require detailed information about the suppliers' cyber posture.

Keywords: Cybersecurity Risk Assessment · Supply Chain Risk · Threat Assessment · Vulnerability Assessment

1 Introduction

Global supply chains have become increasingly complex, with a large number of companies over multiple tiers, which makes it difficult for enterprises to have full visibility of their suppliers' networks. This complexity introduces significant challenges in maintaining robust security against cyberattacks in the supply chain [1], indeed, to target a specific company, cyber attackers are increasingly targeting its suppliers rather than the company itself because often suppliers have weaker cybersecurity measures in place; once the supplier has been compromised, the attackers can reach their actual target more easily. This cyberattack strategy is commonly referred to as a *supply chain attack*. Successful cyberattacks can have catastrophic consequences on a supply chain, as occurred in the SolarWinds attack [2], where critical infrastructures too were affected. In this incident, adversaries weaponized a network monitoring software developed by SolarWinds,

S. Katsikas et al. (Eds.): ESORICS 2023 Workshops, LNCS 14399, pp. 26–41, 2024.
https://doi.org/10.1007/978-3-031-54129-2_2

which was used by thousands of customers, including large companies, government entities, as well as critical infrastructures in the electric, oil, and manufacturing industries. This enabled the attackers to gain remote access to the IT networks of affected organizations.

To defend against supply chain cyberattacks, a company needs to carry out an accurate cybersecurity risk assessment focusing on threats that could derive from its suppliers. However, such an assessment is extremely challenging because of the intricate network of connections between organisations in a supply chain. Small and medium-sized enterprises (SMEs) are particularly susceptible to cybersecurity threats within the supply chain network, due to their limited resources and expertise in cybersecurity risk management compared to larger organizations [3]. Verbano and Venturini [4] argue that all enterprises, regardless of size, need to adopt a cybersecurity risk management strategy to identify, assess, and mitigate risks. However, while larger companies typically have well-developed cybersecurity risk management systems and apply risk-limiting instruments, SMEs are often unaware of those instruments [3,5] and therefore left in a vulnerable state where they are more likely to be targeted via a supply chain attack.

According to the Cybersecurity Breaches Survey 2023[1], conducted by the UK's Department for Science, Innovation & Technology, only about three in ten businesses have undertaken cybersecurity risk assessments in the last year (29% for businesses and 27% for charities). Remarkably, in the past year, 49% of medium and 37% of large businesses have failed to carry out cybersecurity risk assessments. Moreover, only about one in ten businesses review the risks posed by their immediate suppliers. This suggests a significant gap in assessing and managing supply chain cybersecurity risks, especially given that most of these businesses (55% of large businesses, up from 44% in 2022) have started to acknowledge the importance of reviewing supply chain risks. These statistics highlight the crucial need for an easy-to-apply methodology specifically designed to assist SMEs in managing their cybersecurity risks arising from supply chain connections.

The literature includes several works proposing approaches to assess risk in supply chains. However, many of them are specialized to particular supply chain markets (e.g., food), or assess the risk in general terms without sufficient focus on cybersecurity aspects, or look at specific angles of cybersecurity risk (e.g., information risk), or require complete and detailed knowledge about the company's assets and the cybersecurity posture and interconnections of its suppliers, which is usually very challenging to obtain, especially for SMEs.

This paper introduces a novel methodology for cybersecurity risk assessment in supply chains, which aims at bridging the gap between expert cybersecurity risk assessment and everyday organizational practices. Indeed, to be applied, this methodology does not require expert cybersecurity knowledge or detailed information about the suppliers' network. The main idea behind this methodology is to guide the users doing the assessment by asking them simple questions to gather basic information about the perceived likelihood and impact of threats that could originate from suppliers. Moreover, to simplify the process even further, this methodology does not require users to complete

---

[1] https://www.gov.uk/government/statistics/cyber-security-breaches-survey-2023/cyber-security-breaches-survey-2023.

any meticulous analyses to identify the company's assets, vulnerabilities, and threats; instead, it establishes predefined lists of general asset types, vulnerability types, and threat types that are relevant to most companies, and lets the users decide which ones are relevant for the company being assessed. The questions are designed in such a way to collect estimates on a 1-to-5 scale about the likelihood that an asset type presents a given vulnerability type or be targeted via a specific threat type, as well as the impact that this threat type would entail. This methodology then defines how to aggregate the provided estimates to produce risk scores for each threat type. This work provides the following contributions.

– The definition of general types of assets, vulnerabilities, and threats that are applicable to most organisations in a supply chain, based on the principles of NIST Special Publications 800-161[2] and insights from existing academic literature.
– A questionnaire with simple questions aimed at capturing the perceived likelihood of the above-mentioned vulnerability and threat types, as well as their impact on the above-mentioned asset types.
– An approach to compute cybersecurity risk scores for each threat type, based on answers to the above-mentioned questionnaire.
– A preliminary validation of the methodology, based on the comparison of risk scores provided by cybersecurity experts with those generated by the methodology itself; the results show that this methodology produces risk scores that on average differ by 8% from those given by experts, supporting the hypothesis that the methodology is reliable even without relying on detailed knowledge of suppliers' and company's cybersecurity postures.

This paper is structured as follows. Section 2 presents the related work. In Sect. 3, we present the supply chain cybersecurity risk assessment methodology. Section 4 details the preliminary validation carried out and discusses the results obtained. Finally, Sect. 5 concludes the paper.

2   Related Work

Traditional risk assessment standards aim to identify and manage business assets that may fail unexpectedly, leading to additional costs for interconnected systems, e.g., ISO 31000[3] and ISO 27005[4] offer guidelines for risk management in supply chain systems.

With increasing supply chain connectivity, cybersecurity risks (referred to as cyber risk hereinafter) may also threaten the supply chain's integrity. Standards such as NIST 800-161[5] and NIST SP 800-53[6] address security risk management within supply chains, offering guidelines for risk assessment and security and privacy controls. However, these standards do not explain how to practically implement the risk assessment [6].

---

[2] https://csrc.nist.gov/publications/detail/sp/800-161/rev-1/final.
[3] https://www.iso.org/iso-31000-risk-management.html.
[4] https://www.iso.org/standard/80585.html.
[5] https://csrc.nist.gov/publications/detail/sp/800-161/rev-1/final.
[6] https://csrc.nist.gov/publications/detail/sp/800-53/rev-5/final.

Although several research studies have been conducted in the field of supply chain risk assessment (e.g., Aqlan [8]), limited academic works exist that propose methodologies for cyber risk assessment of supply chains, which are discussed in this section.

For example, Creazza et al. [11] conducted an empirical analysis of the current practices in supply chain cyber risk management within the fast-moving consumer goods (FMCG) industry in Italy. Rather than proposing new supply chain risk assessment methodologies, they explore the perceptions of supply chain managers on the topic. As another example, Schauer et al. [6] propose MITIGATE, a cyber risk assessment methodology for maritime supply chains, which relies on the collaboration between companies within the supply chain. This methodology details the steps to: analyse the structure of the supply chain, identify threats and vulnerabilities, evaluate the impact, assess the risk, and, finally, identify suitable mitigation. Kieras et al. [7] focus instead on the assessment and mitigation of cyber risk in IoT networks deriving from information and communications technology (ICT) suppliers. Their approach uses minimal cutsets and importance measures to assess risk and relies on the complete knowledge of IoT components, their functional dependencies, and their suppliers.

Other works focus on the information risk, which is a subset of the cyber risk encompassing the likelihood and impact of loss due to incorrect, incomplete, or illegal access to information. For example, Faisal et al. [9] identify information risks that affect supply chains and create a theoretical structure to measure and reduce these risks. They employ graph theory for risk quantification and interpretive structural modelling (ISM) to comprehend the interconnections among information risk mitigation enablers. Similarly, Sharma et al. [10] have proposed a model for information management in supply chains. They employ a Bayesian belief network (BBN) to assess and quantify information risks. Their study highlights the potential drawbacks of information sharing, such as leakages and sharing incorrect data among suppliers, and presents a dynamic, probabilistic model that is continuously updated as new data arrives.

Current work focuses on a specific supply chain sector (e.g., maritime, IoT, FMCG) or on a specific type of cyber risk (e.g., information risk). Instead, the methodology we present is universal and can be applied to any sector and any cyber risk type. Also, the reviewed works that propose novel supply chain risk assessment methodologies assume a complete knowledge of interconnections among the companies within the supply chain, alongside further detailed information about suppliers. Rather, in our methodology, the risk for a company C derived from its suppliers is assessed solely based on the knowledge possessed by C, thereby reducing the complexity involved in gathering the data required to compute the risk. Furthermore, differently from existing work, our methodology does not require additional time-consuming and error-prone analyses to enumerate assets, threats, and vulnerabilities in detail; instead, it identifies the main types of assets, threats, and vulnerabilities relevant to cyber risk assessment and just ask users to decide which ones are pertinent to the company being assessed.

Although not considering both (i) the complete interconnections between companies within a supply chain and (ii) the distinguishing assets, threats, and vulnerabilities of a company, makes the cyber risk assessment process easier to complete, it also reduces its accuracy and might lead to unreliable results. In Sect. 4, we validate our methodology based on feedback from cybersecurity experts and show that the risk assessments it produces align with theirs.

3 Security Risk Assessment Methodology

Throughout this paper, we refer to supply chain risk assessment to indicate the estimation of the cybersecurity risk for a company due to its suppliers. This is a complex and multifaceted task, particularly given the interconnected structure of modern supply chains. Indeed, collecting accurate information about these inter-connections and the cybersecurity posture of all the upstream suppliers is a daunting, if not impossible, task. In this study, we overcome the lack of complete data about suppliers by proposing a methodology that solely relies on the suppliers information available at the company whose supply chain risk is being assessed.

Our methodology is universal and can be applied to any industry sector. To achieve that, we first determine the types of assets (Sect. 3.1), threats (Sect. 3.2), and vulnerabilities (Sect. 3.3) that are relevant to any company. Based on these, we propose a scoring mechanism to assess the supply chain risk for a company (Sect. 3.4). Finally, we present a questionnaire to gather all the data required to compute the risk score (Sect. 3.5).

3.1 Asset Types

Due to the broad range of assets within an organization, it can be challenging to identify and prioritize potential security risks for each asset [12]. To facilitate the identification of the assets to consider while ensuring a universal approach that can be applied to any company, we categorize assets in three main types: hardware, software, and users.

Information risk is a critical aspect of cybersecurity and we have incorporated it in this study within all the identified asset types, as information is pervasive across all assets in an organization - hardware, software, and users. Each of these asset types processes, stores, and transmits information, thus, incurring associated risks. Separating information risk into a distinct type could lead to unnecessary redundancies and potentially overlook the unique aspects of how information risk manifests in different types of assets. Furthermore, the classification of asset types we propose is general and suitable for any type of supply chain where cyberspace plays an important role (e.g., food supply chain, hardware supply chain).

Hardware Assets. Considering the diverse hardware assets that may exist across different organizations and industries, our methodology is designed with a broad scope. To ensure our risk assessment tool captures the majority of scenarios, we categorize hardware assets into three key sub-types:

User Electronics: This sub-type encompasses devices owned by individuals within the organization and used for daily operations, such as computers, mobile phones, tablets, or any personal devices utilized to access or manage supply chain resources. It is important to note that these devices, which are essential for day-to-day operations, are not directly controlled by the organization as they are owned by individual users. This lack of organizational control over such devices is a key consideration in the context of supply chain risks, as these devices have the potential to intentionally or unintentionally access, manipulate, or leak sensitive supply chain data.

Organizational Hardware: This sub-type encompasses the organization's enterprise-grade hardware infrastructure, including servers, desktop computers, network switches, routers, firewalls, and specialized equipment like industrial control systems. They are often the main points of communication with suppliers and could be targeted by attackers aiming to disrupt the supply chain.

Internet of Things (IoT) Devices: This sub-type comprises of IoT devices such as RFID tags, sensors, readers, and other connected devices involved in tracking, monitoring, and coordinating the supply chain process. These devices, often interconnected across multiple organizational and supplier systems, provide real-time visibility and control over the supply chain, making them attractive targets for attackers aiming to disrupt supply chain operations or gain access to sensitive information.

Software Assets. The proposed tool classifies software assets into two sub-types, i.e., third-party software and organizational software, based on their level of control, accountability, and implications for supply chain risk.

Third-party software: The organization may depend on an external entity for specific functionalities. These services can range from cloud storage providers to software-as-a-service (SaaS) applications like Customer Relationship Management (CRM) or Enterprise Resource Planning (ERP) systems. Importantly, this sub-type also includes any third-party software that organizations utilize, as such software constitutes a key aspect of many modern business operations. In these instances, the organization is heavily dependent on the third-party provider's security measures, necessitating careful evaluation of their trustworthiness, responsiveness, and regulatory compliance.

Organizational Software: This sub-type primarily includes software developed in-house, custom-made software solutions, and software specifically modified to suit the organization's needs. While organizational software assets are primarily controlled and managed by the organization itself, these assets play a crucial role in interfacing with suppliers, either directly or indirectly, in managing supply chain operations.

User Assets. User assets in a supply chain context predominantly refer to individuals who interact with the hardware and software components within the supply chain ecosystem. These can be the organization's employees, suppliers, partners, or even customers who have access to certain levels of the organization's digital systems. These user assets can either be internal (employees, contractors) or external (suppliers, partners, customers), and each group carries different risk profiles and requirements for risk management.

3.2 Threat Types

We determine threat types based on the NIST Special Publication 800-161, which identifies 20 security control families that should be considered to improve supply chain cybersecurity, such as access control, incident response, and supply chain risk management. We reviewed each control family to determine the underlying risks that each control is designed to mitigate. For example, when we consider the 'access control' family, we identify potential threats such as unauthorized access, privilege escalation, and insider threats. Moreover, within the context of supply chains, we extend our analysis to consider how these threats could emerge from various supply chain stages. As a result, we identify threats such as 'Malicious third-party software' and 'Supplier breach of contract or non-compliance', where vulnerabilities in access control at any point in the supply chain could lead to such threats.

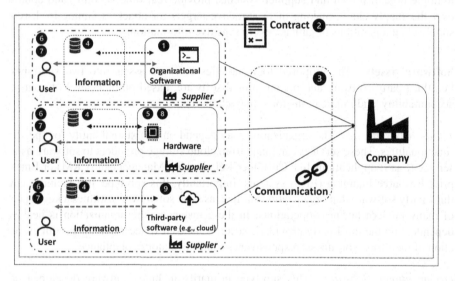

Fig. 1. Mapping SC threat types to SC asset types. Numbers identify the threat types listed in Table 1.

The identified threat types are listed in Table 1 and mapped to asset types in Fig. 1, to determine which threats are relevant for which assets. Although the 'Communication' and 'Contract' assets shown in Fig. 1 do not directly map to any asset type or subtype defined previously, they are two critical assets for the operations of any supply chain and need to be considered to identify all the relevant threats. Threats related to communication and supplier contracts are also considered, given their direct impact on the targeted organization and its supplier. In Fig. 1, the "Company" on the right is the organization for which the supply chain risk is being assessed, based on the threats derived from its suppliers.

Table 1. Supply chain security threats and vulnerabilities.

Threat type(s)	Associated Vulnerabilities
(1) Malicious third-party software	• Unsecured or poorly secured software systems • Insufficient access controls on software supply chain • Lack of secure development practices • Ineffective code review and auditing processes • Inadequate malware and intrusion detection systems
(2) Supplier breach of contract or non-compliance breach	• Lack of contractual safeguards or insufficient security vetting of third-party suppliers • Inadequate supplier vetting and management processes • Insufficient supplier oversight and performance monitoring • Failure to adhere to security regulations and standards • Insufficient IT system monitoring and auditing
(3) Supply chain communication breakdown or communication eavesdropping	• Insecure communication channels • Inadequate encryption of data in transit • Absence of strong authentication mechanisms • Lack of redundancy and disaster recovery planning
(4) Data breach, data loss incident, IoT data disclosure, or visual information leakage	• Insecure data storage and weak encryption • Insufficient training on data protection for employees • Weak or non-existent non-repudiation services • Inadequate software or hardware patching and vulnerability management • Weak access controls and password policies
(5) Tampering, sabotage with IoT devices or systems, or unauthorized access right usage	• Insecure IoT device firmware and hardware • Weak or default IoT device credentials • Lack of proper IoT device management and monitoring
(6) Insider threats	• Inadequate monitoring of employee activities and access
(7) Social engineering attacks	• Lack of employee security awareness training • Ineffective security policies and procedures • Weak email and communication security measures
(8) Counterfeit or substandard components	• Lack of secure supply chain traceability and visibility • Insufficient component validation and inspection
(9) Cloud security breaches	• Inadequate access controls and permissions management for cloud or SaaS applications • Insufficient data encryption in the cloud • Weak vendor security practices for cloud service providers or SaaS providers • Insufficient IT system monitoring and auditing or poorly managed SaaS application programming interfaces (APIs) and integrations • Dependency on a single SaaS provider without backup options • Inadequate service level agreements (SLAs) with SaaS providers
Not specified threat group	• Ineffective third-party risk assessment and management processes • Inadequate vendor access controls and monitoring • Poorly defined roles and responsibilities for vendor management

3.3 Vulnerability Types

Vulnerabilities refer to weaknesses or gaps in the security measures of an organization's assets [13], which attackers can exploit to gain unauthorized access to systems or data or to carry out other malicious activities [12]. We determine vulnerability types based on the NIST Special Publication 800-161 and on relevant literature on supply chain vulnerabilities [12–15,18,19]. We identify 37 supply chain vulnerability types and link them to threat types in Table 1.

3.4 Supply Chain Risk Assessment

The supply chain risk assessment consists in computing a score that reflects the perceived risk for an organisation to suffer a cyberattack because of misconduct or poor security practices of its suppliers. This process involves evaluating the probability and impact of a cybersecurity attack against an organization [15]. In security risk assessment, two types of analysis can be conducted: qualitative and quantitative [16]. The quantitative analysis employs numerical models and calculations to determine the probability and potential impact of identified risks. In contrast, qualitative analysis involves identifying factors, areas, and types of risks and typically involves human interaction, such as through workshops or interviews, to generate input data.

We employ a quantitative method, where a security employee (ideally, the employee who is the most knowledgeable about the security posture of the company and of its suppliers) provides ratings on a defined scale, indicating the likelihood of occurrence for each identified threat type and vulnerability type and the potential impact. The scale we use and the values and labels associated with each rating are defined as follows:

- very low (value: 1, label: VL)
- low (value: 2, label: L)
- medium (value: 3, label: M)
- high (value: 4, label: H)
- very high (value: 5, label: VH)

Let $R = \{VL, L, M, H, VH\}$ be the set of possible ratings, and let $value(r)$ be the value associated to rating r, with $r \in R$ (e.g., $value(M) = 3$). These ratings are then used to calculate the overall risk score for each threat type. The output of this process is a quantifiable risk score, allowing for clear comparisons and prioritization.

The formula we use in our study for risk assessment is provided in Eq. 1 and is widely supported by existing research and standards [6,8,16].

$$Risk = (Vuln\_likelihood \bullet Threat\_likelihood) \bullet Impact \qquad (1)$$

The terms in Eq. 1 represent the following:

(a) *Vuln_likelihood* represents the likelihood of any existing weakness or gap in the security measures that protect the organization's assets.
(b) *Threat_likelihood* is the likelihood that an event occurs that exploits a vulnerability in the organization's assets.

Table 2. Semantics of the ● operation.

VH	M	H	H	VH	VH
H	L	M	M	H	VH
M	L	M	M	M	H
L	VL	L	M	M	H
VL	VL	VL	L	L	M
	VL	L	M	H	VH

(c) *Impact* denotes the estimation of potential consequences or harm that could occur to the organization's assets as a result of a successful threat.

Each of the above terms can assume a value within R. Equation 1 is used to calculate the risk for each threat type, where the ● operation combines vulnerability and threat likelihoods to determine the *exploitation likelihood*, which represents the probability that a threat of a specific type successfully exploits a vulnerability. The ● operation is a binary commutative operation with $R \times R$ as domain and R as co-domain. Its semantics is defined in the matrix in Table 2; the result of $r_i ● r_j$ (with $r_i, r_j \in R$) is the value in the cell identified by row (column) r_i and column (row) r_j. The exploitation likelihood is a value in R.

As shown in Table 1, a threat of a specific type can exploit more than one vulnerability type. To account for this, the security employee is expected to provide *Vuln_likelihood* ratings for all the relevant vulnerability types associated with the threat type for which the risk is being assessed. The average of these *Vuln_likelihood* ratings is computed using their numerical values (i.e., using the *value*(·) function) and then combined with the *Threat_likelihood* using the ● operation to obtain the exploitation likelihood. The risk score for a threat type is determined by combining its exploitation likelihood with the impact rating using again the ● operation. The risk score is a value in R.

We explain below the link between asset types and vulnerability, threats, and impact.

3.5 Questionnaire

The questionnaire is meant to simplify the process of gathering from a security employee all the information required to assess the risk associated with each relevant threat type. All questions are Likert scale [17], with each question prompting the security employee to provide the rating in R that best reflects their perception of the likelihood of a vulnerability or threat type, or the impact of a threat type.

The first set of questions is to select those asset sub-types (Sect. 3.1) that are relevant for the company being assessed, to avoid including questions on types of asset that the company does not possess (e.g., Does your organization use IoT devices as a part of its infrastructure?).

For each relevant asset sub-type a, questions are included to obtain estimates about

- the likelihood of *a* presenting a vulnerability; one question is included for each vulnerability type relevant to *a* (e.g., How likely is it that your organization would lack a secure update mechanism for IoT devices?)
- the likelihood of *a* being targeted by a threat; one question is included for each threat type relevant to *a* (e.g., How likely is it that a cyber actor could compromise IoT devices used for tracking goods in your supply chain, potentially leading to inaccurate data or loss of visibility?)
- the impact of *a* being targeted by a threat; one question is included for each threat type relevant to *a* (e.g., If a cyber actor successfully compromises IoT devices used for tracking goods in your supply chain, what would be the potential impact on your organization's ability to manage its supply chain effectively?)

For example, the questionnaire contains 34 questions concerning IoT assets (under the hardware asset type), encompassing 16 questions related to vulnerability types, 9 to threat types, and 9 to impact.

When computing the risk score for a specific threat type *t* according to the methodology presented in Sect. 3.4, the ratings provided by the security employee are combined as follows:

- let A_t be the set of asset types that can be targeted by *t* (see Fig. 1);
- for each vulnerability type *v* associated to *t* (see Table 1), the ratings are considered from the questions asking the likelihood that the asset type *a* presents the vulnerability type *v*, $\forall a \in A_t$; these ratings are averaged based on their numerical values (i.e., using the *value*(·) function) to obtain the *Vuln_likelihood* rating for vulnerability type *v*;
- the ratings are considered of the questions asking the likelihood that the asset type *a* is targeted by the threat type *t*, $\forall a \in A_t$; these ratings are averaged based on their numerical values (i.e., using the *value*(·) function) to obtain the *Threat_likelihood* rating for threat type *t*;
- the ratings are considered of the questions asking the impact of asset type *a* being targeted by the threat type *t*, $\forall a \in A_t$; these ratings are averaged based on their numerical values (i.e., using the *value*(·) function) to obtain the *Impact* rating for threat type *t*.

Note that this risk assessment process is independent of the specific asset and threat types considered. Indeed, questions can be easily adapted to fit any set of asset and threat types, then the scores provided as answers can be then combined using the procedure described above. This ensures that our methodology remains valid in the ever-evolving threat landscape, as users simply need to incorporate new questions about newly identified threats.

4   Preliminary Validation of the Methodology

In this section, we describe the empirical validation of the methodology presented in the previous section. This is a preliminary validation based on feedback from three security experts. The aim of this validation is to compare the risk scores generated by our methodology with those provided by the security experts.

We consider a fictional scenario where three companies are interconnected via supplier relationships, i.e., each company acts as a supplier for either or both of the other companies. The description of the scenario provides these interconnections and information about the security posture of each company. Each security expert is given this description and asked to assess the risk for a number of specified threat types. The risk scores they provide are values in R (Sect. 3.4). The security experts are not given any information about our supply chain risk assessment methodology. We compute the risk score based on our methodology, for the same threat types for each of the three fictional companies and compare our scores for threat likelihood, impact, and risk with those produced by the three security experts.

We outline the profiles of the cybersecurity experts in Sect. 4.1, describe the fictional scenario in Sect. 4.2 and discuss obtained results in Sect. 4.3.

4.1 Security Experts

Our methodology aims to generate accurate cybersecurity risk scores for threats derived by the company's suppliers. Thus, for our validation, we selected cybersecurity experts with multi-year experience in performing risk assessments. We provide below the profiles of the selected cybersecurity experts, whose names and affiliations could not be disclosed for privacy-preserving reasons.

- Expert #1: chief of the cybersecurity department within a large UK-based institution, with more than 10 years of experience.
- Expert #2: cybersecurity consultant working at a large UK-based international enterprise, with more than 5 years of experience in the field of risk assessment.
- Expert #3: cybersecurity specialist in a small-sized UK-based company, with more than 20 years of experience in risk assessment and risk treatment planning.

4.2 Fictional Scenario

Company A, Company B, and Company C are interdependent, each serving a different role within the supply chain. Figure 2 illustrates the supplier relationships among those companies. The arrows represent the flow of supplied products or services; e.g., the arrow from Company A to Company B models the fact that Company A is a supplier of Company B. More details about each company are reported below[7].

This fictional scenario is loosely inspired by real-world supply chain cyberattacks; indeed, Company A resembles SolarWinds (see the SolarWinds attack [2]), while Company B and Company C mirror Supermicro and one of its customers, respectively, in the 'Big Hack' incident [20].

Company A is a business that provides a widely used network security management suite to other businesses, including Companies B and C. Despite handling sensitive customer data, Company A's security measures range from low to medium. They have

---

[7] Note that the security experts are provided with a much more detailed description of the security posture of each company.

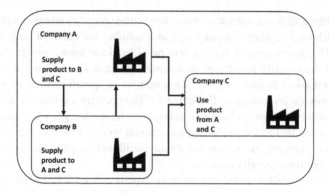

Fig. 2. Supplier relationships between the fictional companies.

an IT system where monitoring and auditing are inadequate, and there is also a lack of sufficient employee security awareness training. They rely heavily on cloud services for operations and data storage. However, Company A fails to implement any security configurations for the cloud services. Not only does this indicate a complete absence of protective mechanisms, but it significantly amplifies their vulnerability to cloud security breaches. Trust in suppliers like Company B is high, but this trust does not come with thorough security testing or code reviews, potentially exposing them to third-party software risks due to a lack of secure development practices.

Company B is a medium-sized enterprise that both develops software applications and manufactures hardware components. They provide system optimization and monitoring software to other businesses, and their hardware components could potentially have weak or default credentials. A breach in Company B's software could not only disrupt its operations but also complicate the supply chains of its users, namely Company A and Company C, potentially creating a cascade of vulnerabilities.

Company C is a large-scale enterprise that manufactures advanced hardware components for high-end servers and data centers. They use components and software from Companies A and B without conducting additional security checks, which can potentially introduce vulnerabilities into their systems. Incomplete checks may leave vulnerabilities that pose risks to the system's safety. Despite these potential weaknesses, they have robust internal security protocols and comprehensive employee training programs in place.

4.3   Result Discussion

As already mentioned in Sect. 4, not all the threat types we identify in Sect. 3.2 are relevant to all the fictional companies considered in this validation. Table 3 details the threat types applicable to each company. Each security expert is given the list of threat types that are relevant for each company, and asked to provide scores for each of them. Separate scores are produced for the likelihood, impact, and overall risk.

Table 3. Comparison between expert and methodology-based risk assessment scores.

Company	Threat Type	Expert #1			Expert #2			Expert #3			Expert Average			Proposed Methodology			Difference		
		Likelihood	Impact	Risk	Likelihood	Impact	Risk	Likelihood	Impact	Risk	Likelihood	Impact	Risk	Likelihood	Impact	Risk	Likelihood	Impact	Risk
Company A	Malicious third-party software	4	4	4	3	4	3	5	5	5	4	4.33	4	4	5	5	0	0.67	1
	Supplier breach of contract or non-compliance breach	4	4	4	4	5	5	3	3	3	4	4	4	4	4	4	0	0	0
	Data breach, data loss incident, or visual information leakage	4	4	4	3	4	3	4	4	4	3.67	4	3.67	3	5	4	0.67	1	0.33
	Insider threats	4	4	4	4	4	4	3	3	3	4	3.67	3.67	4	4	4	0	0.33	0.33
	Cloud security breaches	3	3	3	5	5	5	5	5	5	4.33	4.33	4.33	5	5	5	0.67	0.67	0.67
Company B	IoT data disclosure or visual information leakage	4	4	4	4	4	4	5	5	5	4.33	4.33	4.33	4	4	4	0.33	0.33	0.33
Company C	Malicious third-party software	1	4	2	5	5	5	4	4	4	3.33	4.33	3.67	4	4	4	0.67	0.33	0.33
	Cloud security breaches	2	4	3	3	3	3	4	4	4	3	3.67	3.33	3	4	3	0	0.33	0.33
	Counterfeit or substandard components (only IoT devices)	-	-	-	4	4	4	4	4	4	4	4	4	4	4	4	0	0	0
	Average difference																0.26	0.41	0.37
	Average difference (%)																5%	8%	7%

To enable a clearer comparison between the scores, their numerical values (i.e., 1, 2, 3, 4, 5) are used instead of their labels (i.e., VL, L, M, H, VH). For each relevant threat type of each company, we first compute the average likelihood, impact, and risk scores provided by the security experts, to obtain values that reflect their combined judgement and smooth out possibly varying scores. Then, we calculate the difference between our scores and these averages. Finally, we compute the average difference between those scores over all the threat types, both as an absolute value and in percentage with respect to the highest value (i.e., 5).

The results reported in Table 3 show that on average our scores differ by up to 8% from the average of the scores provided by the security experts, with our likelihood scores closer (5%) to theirs than the impact scores (8%). The highest differences in likelihood (0.67, 13.4%) are for data and cloud breaches at Company A, and for malicious third-party software at Company C. For the impact, the largest discrepancies are for Company A for malicious third-party software and cloud breaches (0.67, 13.4%) and for data breaches (1.00, 25%). The most relevant differences in the overall risk score are for Company A for malicious third-party software (1.00, 25%) and cloud breaches (0.67, 13.4%). Overall, these results are promising as they witness that our methodology produces scores that mostly align with the judgment of cybersecurity risk assessment experts, even though no details are required regarding the suppliers' cyber posture and the company's assets.

5   Conclusion

This paper presents a novel cybersecurity risk assessment methodology for supply chains, aimed at allowing SMEs and other organisations with limited cybersecurity expertise to evaluate the cybersecurity risk deriving from suppliers. To simplify the assessment process, users are asked simple questions to gather estimates about likelihood and impact of vulnerabilities and threats with respect to relevant assets. Although answering those questions does not require users to have accurate information about the company's assets or its supplier's cybersecurity level, the methodology generates risk scores that are close to those provided by cybersecurity experts.

As future works, we aim to further extend the validation of the methodology by involving a larger number of experts and different evaluation scenarios. We are implementing our methodology in a web-based tool that will allow us to collect the users' feedback and further improve our methodology and tool. Our focus will be to enhance the user experience and the reliability of the scores generated by the tool. Another interesting future work is the integration of our tool with other existing risk assessment tools. Furthermore, we plan to enable custom weighting for the impact of different assets, to let organisations tailor their risk assessments to their specific requirements and priorities.

References

1. Zhang, Y., Guin, U.: End-to-end traceability of ICs in component supply chain for fighting against recycling. IEEE Trans. Inf. Forensics Secur. **15**, 767–775 (2019)
2. Alkhadra, R., Abuzaid, J., AlShammari, M., Mohammad, N.: Solar winds hack: in-depth analysis and countermeasures. In: 2021 12th International Conference on Computing Communication and Networking Technologies (ICCCNT), pp. 1–7. IEEE (2021)
3. Ključnikov, A., Mura, L., Sklenár, D.: Information security management in SMEs: factors of success. Entrepreneurship Sustain. Issues **6**(4), 2081 (2019)
4. Verbano, C., Venturini, K.: Managing risks in SMEs: a literature review and research agenda. J. Technol. Manage. Innov. **8**(3), 186–197 (2013)
5. Belás, J., Macháček, J., Bartoš, P., Hlawiczka, R., Hudáková, M.: Business risks and the level of entrepreneurial optimism among SME in the Czech and Slovak Republic. J. competitiveness. Tomas Bata University in Zlín (2014)
6. Schauer, S., Polemi, N., Mouratidis, H.: MITIGATE: a dynamic supply chain cyber risk assessment methodology. J. Transp. Secur. **12**, 1–35 (2019)
7. Kieras, T., Farooq, M.J., Zhu, Q.: RIoTS: Risk analysis of IoT supply chain threats. In: 2020 IEEE 6th World Forum on Internet of Things (WF-IoT), pp. 1–6. IEEE (2020)
8. Aqlan, F.: A software application for rapid risk assessment in integrated supply chains. Expert Syst. Appl. **43**, 109–116 (2016)
9. Faisal, M.N., Kumar, D.K.B., Shankar, R.: Information risks management in supply chains: an assessment and mitigation framework. J. Enterp. Inf. Manag. **20**(6), 677–699 (2007)
10. Sharma, S., Routroy, S.: Modeling information risk in supply chain using Bayesian networks. J. Enterp. Inf. Manag. **29**(2), 238–254 (2016)
11. Creazza, A., Colicchia, C., Spiezia, S., Dallari, F.: Who cares? Supply chain managers' perceptions regarding cyber supply chain risk management in the digital transformation era. Supply Chain Manage. An Int. J. **27**(1), 30–53 (2022)
12. Garg, S., Singh, R.K., Mohapatra, A.K.: Analysis of software vulnerability classification based on different technical parameters. Inform. Secur. J. Glob. Perspect. **28**(1–2), 1–19 (2019)
13. Ganin, A.A., Quach, P., Panwar, M., Collier, Z.A., Keisler, J.M., Marchese, D., Linkov, I.: Multicriteria decision framework for cybersecurity risk assessment and management. Risk Anal. **40**(1), 183–199 (2020)
14. Zhang, X., Xie, H., Yang, H., Shao, H., Zhu, M.: A general framework to understand vulnerabilities in information systems. IEEE Access **8**, 121858–121873 (2020)
15. Cruz, S.T.: Information security risk assessment. In: Information Security Management Handbook, pp. 243–250 (2007)
16. Rot, A.: IT risk assessment: quantitative and qualitative approach. Resource **283**(March), 284 (2008)
17. Nemoto, T., Beglar, D.: Likert-scale questionnaires. In: JALT 2013 Conference Proceedings, pp. 1–8 (2014)
18. Figueira, P.T., Bravo, C.L., López, J.L.R.: Improving information security risk analysis by including threat-occurrence predictive models. Comput. Secur. **88**, 101609 (2020)
19. Khoury, R., Vignau, B., Hallé, S., Hamou-Lhadj, A., Razgallah, A.: An analysis of the use of CVEs by IoT malware. In: Nicolescu, G., Tria, A., Fernandez, J.M., Marion, J.-Y., Garcia-Alfaro, J. (eds.) FPS 2020. LNCS, vol. 12637, pp. 47–62. Springer, Cham (2021). https://doi.org/10.1007/978-3-030-70881-8_4
20. Mehta, D., et al.: The big hack explained: detection and prevention of PCB supply chain implants. ACM J. Emerg. Technol. Comput. Syst. (JETC) **16**(4), 1–25 (2020)

IM-DISCO: Invariant Mining for Detecting IntrusionS in Critical Operations

Guilherme Saraiva[1], Filipe Apolinário[1](✉) [iD], and Miguel L. Pardal[2] [iD]

[1] INOV INESC INOVAÇÃO, Lisbon, Portugal
{guilherme.a.saraiva,filipe.apolinario}@tecnico.ulisboa.pt
[2] INESC-ID Instituto Superior Técnico, Universidade de Lisboa, Lisbon, Portugal
miguel.pardal@tecnico.ulisboa.pt

Abstract. In today's interconnected world, robust cybersecurity measures are crucial, especially for Cyber-Physical Systems. While anomaly-based Intrusion Detection Systems can identify abnormal behaviors, interpreting the resulting alarms is challenging. An alternative approach utilizes invariant rules to describe system operations, providing clearer explanations for abnormal behaviors. In this context, invariant rules are conditions that must hold true for a system's different operational modes. However, defining these rules is time-consuming and costly. This paper presents IM-DISCO, a tool that analyzes operational data to propose inference rules characterizing different modes of system operation. Deviations from these rules indicate anomalies, enabling continuous monitoring with incident detection and response. In our evaluation, focusing on rail transportation, we achieved 99.29% accuracy in detecting and characterizing operational modes using real-world train data. Additionally, we achieved 99.86% accuracy in identifying anomalies during simulated attacks. Notably, our results demonstrate an average detection time of 0.026 ms, enabling swift incident response to prevent catastrophic events.

Keywords: Anomaly detection · Cyber-physical systems · Invariants · Intrusion detection systems

1 Introduction

Cyber-Physical Systems (CPS) monitor and control physical processes using embedded computers with sensor networks [20]. They are commonly found in Critical Infrastructures (CI) such as transportation networks and power grids. However, the growing complexity and interconnectivity of CPS make them especially vulnerable to cyber-physical attacks [16]. For instance, on October 29, 2022, a ransomware attack on a railway in Denmark caused a disruption on the train services. The attack was not directly targeted at the train systems but at a third-party IT service provider. The attack led to the shutdown of servers,

S. Katsikas et al. (Eds.): ESORICS 2023 Workshops, LNCS 14399, pp. 42–58, 2024.
https://doi.org/10.1007/978-3-031-54129-2_3

causing the mobile application used by train drivers to stop working. As a result, the trains came to a standstill for several hours.

Intrusion Detection Systems (IDS) for CPS have been developed throughout the years to prevent or mitigate cyberattacks [17]. An IDS passively collects and analyzes different data sources, such as network traffic and security logs. In particular, anomaly-based IDS establish a model of the system's normal behavior, and deviations from this model raise alarms [15]. Most analysis techniques are based on data mining and machine learning [25]. This type of IDS can detect novel attacks, but it is difficult to interpret the cause of its alarms, and occurrences of false positives are frequent.

An alternative approach is based on invariant rules [23]. An *invariant* is a physical condition that must be sustained in a certain operational mode, characterized by a unique combination of sensor readings and actuator states. In this approach, an "anomaly" corresponds to any physical process value that violates the rules. Invariant rules can be manually defined by CPS experts. However, manually defining invariants can be costly, time-consuming, and incomplete for complex CPS.

In this article, we present IM-DISCO (Invariant Mining for Detecting IntrusionS in Critical Operations), a tool that generates invariant rules for inferring operational modes and anomalies on CPS. This tool utilizes CPS log data as input to perform its analyses. Contrary to prior invariant rule mining approaches [10,11,27], IM-DISCO uses expert domain knowledge to define CPS operational modes and infers the invariants that describe the sensors and actuator conditions that best describe those modes. As a result, the invariant rules help to explain, based on observation, the current operational mode of a CPS. They can be used to monitor, in real-time, sensors and actuators, detect changes in CPS states, and identify anomalies. With IM-DISCO, experts are able to understand alerts and easily attest, based on the mode reported by IM-DISCO, the veracity of the alarm. Thus, IM-DISCO contributes to:

1. A novel approach for providing invariant rules for inferring operational modes within CPS;
2. An IDS method that allows the detection of anomalies in a timely way and that can be verified by human experts, as needed.

We performed an experimental evaluation with two real-world train datasets. The results of this evaluation showed that IM-DISCO can accurately detect operational modes. In addition, we used a simulated train ride containing attacks, during which IM-DISCO was able to identify them. We also showed that our solution maintained high accuracy even with low training data, demonstrating its agility in generating rules with limited input. Finally, we evaluated the performance of the different phases of our solution, and the results show fast rule generation and verification. This allows expert assessment for validation and implementation of suitable preventive actions.

2   Related Work

Detecting anomalies on CPSs is a topic of research that has been studied for many years in different industrial ecosystems [25]. We classify three different types of techniques used in Anomaly-based IDS: *Fingerprinting* [3,4,6], *Artificial Neural Networks (NN)* [12,13], and *Invariants* [1,5,10,11,23,26–28]. On the one hand, the initial two methodologies represent the system's behavior using black-boxes, which allows to accurately detect anomalies in high-dimensional datasets but are difficult to be interpreted by the system expert. On the other hand, invariant-rule-based anomaly detectors employ explicit rules that define the expected behavior of a system. These rules can be understood and interpreted by humans, as they represent specific conditions or thresholds that should be met. When an anomaly is detected, the violated rules can be used to explain the cause of the alarm. For this reason, we focus on invariant-based works.

Invariants are properties that must be held to maintain the normal behavior of the system. For instance, an invariant rule of an actuator A, a sensor S, and an operational mode M for a railway CPS can be:

$$A.doors{=}ON \land S.velocity{=}0 \implies M{=}\text{``}on\_station\text{''}$$

In this rule, each smallest subequation is a *predicate*. This rule states that if the doors of a train are opened and the velocity is equal to zero, then the train must be in the operational mode *on_station*.

Invariant rules can be derived from data logs and the system's design. Data-driven approaches rely on data mining and machine learning techniques to discover invariants. Typically, these approaches are divided into two steps: predicate generation and invariant rule mining. Some methods to generate predicates use the distribution of sensor value updates and estimate the parameters of this distribution [11]. Another set of predicates can be derived from sensor values that trigger changes in actuator states [11]. The manual definition of events with their associated data variables [5] and simple threshold calculations [27] represent other possible predicates. After obtaining sets of predicates, the goal is to find associations between them to generate invariants.

Association Rule Mining (ARM) is the technique most commonly used for this task [5,11,23,26]. ARM is a rule-based method to uncover relationships between multiple state variables [19]. These relationships represent the final invariant rules. General dynamic analysis-based tools can also be used to mine associations [10]. From the system's design, it is possible to derive invariants from Process and Instrumentation Diagrams (P&ID), State Condition Graphs (SCGs) [26], and Automata [1] or use axiomatic design theory to decompose functional requirements into invariants [28]. Table 1 depicts the various techniques found in the literature to generate invariant rules, and our proposal, IM-DISCO.

System design approaches have the advantage of deriving invariants directly from the architecture of the system. However, it can have extensive documentation, which makes the process of deriving invariants impractical, and sometimes the documentation does not follow the evolution of the system. Due to these limitations, we opt to follow a data-driven approach as an alternative.

Table 1. Key attributes of invariant-based anomaly detectors.

Related Work	Source	Predicate Generation	Invariant Mining	Knowledge-based
[27]	Data Logs	Thresholds	-	No
[11]	Data Logs	Distribution, Events	Association Rules	No
[10]	Data Logs	-	Dynamic Analysis	No
[23]	Data Logs	Manual Craft	Association Rules	Yes
[5]	Data Logs	Manual Craft	Association Rules	Yes
[1]	System's Design	Manual Craft	Hybrid Automata	Yes
[28]	System's Design	Manual Craft	Axiomatic Design	Yes
[26]	Data Logs, System's Design	Manual Craft	P&ID/SCGs, Association Rules	Yes
IM-DISCO	**Data Logs**	**Thresholds**	**Association Rules**	**Yes**

To the best of our knowledge, IM-DISCO is the first data-driven tool that generates predicates using out-of-bounds approaches, allowing the mining of invariants using Association Rule Mining to create understandable invariant rules that characterize operational modes that can be attested by CPS experts, optimizing the detection of anomalies, and improving CI protection.

3 IM-DISCO

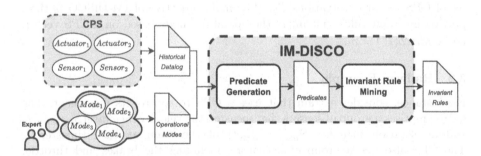

Fig. 1. Example of IM-DISCO generating invariant rules of a CPS with two actuators, two sensors, and four operational modes. IM-DISCO employs historical data logs encompassing CPS sensor and actuator values in distinct operational modes to create invariant rules.

As illustrated in Fig. 1, the goal of IM-DISCO is to provide *Invariant Rules* composed of *Predicates* that represent the physical conditions of system operation. These predicates will be extracted through the use of multiple techniques.

IM-DISCO uses a historical data log to generate invariant rules. This data log registers CPS sensors and actuator values while the system was operating in different modes. To generate invariant rules, IM-DISCO first calculates predicates that express the normal functioning of the CPS. These predicates are represented by statistical bounds of actuator and sensor values for each operational mode. Once the predicates are obtained, the tool finds associations between them to mine invariant rules. The final invariant rules can later be used by a detector to infer, based on sensor and actuator data, the current operational mode of the system and detect abnormal variances in the physical values.

3.1 Formalization of Concepts

A CPS comprises a group of $\mathbb{S}$ sensors that measure, at each timestep, some physical quantities of the environment (velocity, acceleration, position, etc.). Specifically, each sensor S_i performs $measure(S_i, t) = x$ where $x \in \mathbb{Q}$ and t is the respective timestep. Additionally, there is a group of $\mathbb{A}$ actuators that control physical processes, such as moving the wheels of a train or adjusting the flow rate of a fluid. The sensors in a CPS are responsible for collecting data from the physical environment and transmitting it to the control system. The control system processes this data and sends commands to the actuators to adjust the physical processes in response to changes in the environment. Specifically, each actuator A_k can change its state $state(A_k, t) = y$ at a certain timestep t according to the physical values measured by the sensors and that can cause a change in the system mode. At each timestep, a CPS can be represented as vector $\overrightarrow{C_m}$ of $|S| \times |A|$ dimensions, where each dimension is the value of a physical sensor/actuator. The CPS can operate in different modes m that belong to a set $\mathbb{M}$. These modes can be observed by an expert, and correspond to a given set of CPS vector observations $\mathbb{C}_M$. The main objective of IM-DISCO is thus, provide invariant rules that infers the operation mode based on a CPS vector, i.e., $imdisco(\overrightarrow{C}) = m$.

3.2 Railway Example

For instance, consider a train that uses a CPS to control its movement. The CPS comprises a group of sensors that measure the velocity $measure(S_{velocity}, t)$ and acceleration $measure(S_{acceleration}, t)$ of the train at each timestep t. The CPS also has a group of actuators, including the brakes and throttle, responsible for applying power to the train, making it go slower or faster. The system can operate in different modes: $m_1 = arriving\_station$, $m_2 = leaving\_station$, $m_3 = on\_station$, or $m_4 = riding$. To maintain the proper operation of the train, each mode has to respect a certain limit of velocity and acceleration, which are controlled by specific actuator state changes, such as $state(A_{brakes}, t) = ON$ to reduce the speed of the train when arriving at the station, $state(A_{throttle}, t) = ON$, to increase the speed of the train when leaving the station, or $state(A_{doors}, t) = OFF$ when the train is moving.

It is possible to establish relationships between the boundaries of the physical values and the corresponding states of the actuators for each operational mode of the CPS. This allows us to properly model the correct behavior of the CPS in the form of physical conditions. By incorporating these conditions into a detector, we can easily identify the current operational mode of the system and give context in the event of a detected anomaly.

3.3 Predicate Generation

The Predicates generated in IM-DISCO correspond to different types of boundaries for the sensor measurements and actuator states based on observation of previous runs of the CPS. The discovery of the CPS predicates will not only prevent malfunctions and attacks on the physical values, but will also constitute the sub-conditions of invariant rules. This approach is based on the fact that many values fall within safety limits, while others are binary in nature (i.e., ON/OFF switches).

Specifically, for each sensor S_i, actuator A_k, and mode m, we define a set of Predicates $\mathbb{P}_m$. To obtain these predicates, we applied techniques used by SIMPLE [27] in which different thresholds are defined for each sensor/actuator based on their characteristics. The difference between both systems is that SIMPLE models rules based on the individual actuator and sensor thresholds, while IM-DISCO uses them to uncover the CPS predicates and mine invariant rules. The approaches used by SIMPLE include: MinMax; Gradient; and SteadyTime.

MinMax extracts the minimum (Min) and the maximum (Max) values observed by each sensor. This approach is grounded on the premise that the physical values that constitute these systems are inherently constrained by well-defined limits. Consequently, measurements outside these limits have the potential to disrupt certain operations of the system. The resulting predicates are defined as $minmax : min(V_m) < measure(S_i, t) < max(V_m)$, in which V_m represents all the physical values captured in a certain mode m.

Gradient establishes the limits of each sensor's observed slope. Unlike the MinMax approach, the Gradient method is capable of detecting subtle attacks that aim to abruptly modify the physical values within operational limits. Such arbitrary changes to physical variables have the potential to cause critical disturbances to the system. The resulting predicates are defined as $gradient : min(G_m) < gradient(measure(S_i, t)) < max(G_m)$, in which G_m represents all the gradients of the physical values captured in a certain mode m, and $gradient(measure(S_i, t)) = measure(S_i, t) - measure(S_i, t-1)$.

Steadytime detects any instances wherein an actuator's value remains static for a duration shorter or longer than what has been previously observed. This approach is based on the observation that each actuator state should endure for a specific interval of time. The resulting predicates are defined as $steadytime : min(T_m) < (state(A_k, t) = y) < max(T_m)$, in which, T_m represents the totals of consecutive timesteps that the actuator A_k was in the state y in a certain mode m.

To complement these predicates, we can also define predicates of the form $state(A_k, t) = y$ for each timestep. This allows us to represent all the states that the actuator k can have during mode m.

With these techniques, we are able to extract predicates based on the physical values of the sensors and actuators. Associating these predicates allows the formation of invariant rules that characterize a certain mode. For instance, using the railway station example introduced earlier in Sect. 3.2, we can generate multiple predicates $\mathbb{P}_m$ for its sensors and actuators for when the train is leaving the station, i.e., $m = leaving\_station$. For example:

- $minmax : 0.0 < measure(S_{velocity}, t) < 29.9$. This predicate establishes the safety limits of the velocity of the train;
- $gradient : 0.0 < gradient(measure(S_{acceleration}, t)) < 2.42$. This predicate states that the acceleration slope of the train must be between 0.0 and 2.42;
- $steadytime : 90 < (state(A_{throttle}, t) = ON) < 142$. This predicate states that the throttle must be "ON" between 90 and 142 timesteps and only during this period;
- $state(A_{brake}, t) = OFF$. This predicate represents that the brake was "OFF" at a certain timestep.

3.4   Invariant Rule Mining

From the generated predicates, it is now possible to derive the invariant rules that characterize the operational modes of the CPS. The main goal is to identify the relationships that express the correct functioning of the CPS for each mode, which represent the rules that are critical for maintaining the infrastructure's normal operation. Specifically, from the sets of Predicates $\mathbb{P}_m$, we want to mine a set of Invariant Rules $\mathbb{I}_m$ in which each rule is of the form $A \implies C$, where A represents a subset of Predicates and C represents an operational mode m.

Invariant Rule Mining (IRM) is achieved through a data mining technique known as association rule mining, which discovers patterns and associations between variables in large datasets. ARM is typically divided into two phases: *Frequent Itemsets Extraction* (FIE) and *Association Rules Generation* (ARG).

Identifying *frequent itemsets* involves finding sets of items that commonly appear together - co-occur - in a dataset [2]. The most widely used algorithms to identify these itemsets are Apriori [22] and FP-Growth [18]. The items correspond to the predicates contained in $\mathbb{P}_m$.

The first step in identifying frequent itemsets is to define a *minimum support threshold*, which specifies the minimum proportion of entries that an itemset must appear in to be considered frequent [2]. After that, the algorithm scans the dataset to identify all the individual items and their support values. It then generates candidate itemsets, which are sets of items that have not yet been determined to be frequent. The algorithm then scans the dataset again to count the support of each candidate itemset. A candidate itemset is added to the list of frequent itemsets if its support is above the minimum support threshold. This process is repeated iteratively until no new frequent itemsets are found.

Given a dataset D, where each dataset entry d is a set of predicates $d \in \mathbb{P}_m$, and a minimum support threshold $minsup$, find all frequent itemsets F such that the support of I in D, denoted $supp(I)$, is greater than or equal to $minsup$ ca be expressed as: $F = \{I \subseteq \mathbb{P}_m | supp(I) \geq minsup\}$ where $\mathbb{P}_m$ is the set of all predicates in the dataset D, and $supp(I)$ is the proportion of entries in D that contain all the predicates in I, or $supp(I) = \frac{|\{d \in D | I \subseteq d\}|}{|D|}$.

After identifying the frequent itemsets, the next step is to generate *association rules*. Association rules are statements that describe the relationship between different items in the dataset. The process of generating association rules involves setting a minimum confidence threshold *minconf*. The confidence of an association rule measures how often the rule is valid for the entries in the dataset [2]. The minimum confidence threshold specifies the minimum level of confidence that an association rule must have to be considered significant.

Once the *minconf* is set, the algorithm generates all possible association rules from the frequent itemsets. Each association rule consists of an antecedent and a consequent, and the support and confidence of each rule are calculated. The algorithm then filters out the association rules that do not meet *minconf*.

The resulting set of association rules can be sorted by their support and confidence to identify the most significant rules. Other metrics can also be used to evaluate association rules, such as *lift*, which measures how much the presence of the antecedent increases the likelihood of the consequent, or *conviction*, which measures how much the absence of the antecedent decreases the likelihood of the consequent [8].

Hence, an association rule is an implication expression of the form $A \implies C$, where A is a subset of $\mathbb{P}_m$ and C is the respective operational mode, if and only if $conf(A \implies C) \geq minconf$, where $conf(A \implies C)$ is the respective confidence and can be calculated as:

$$conf(A \implies C) = \frac{supp(A \cup C)}{supp(A)}$$

In the end, we are able to derive invariant rules from the obtained predicates.

Considering again the railway scenario presented in Sect. 3.2. An example of an invariant rule for $m = leaving\_station$ would be:

$$minmax\!:\!0.0 < v_t < 29.9 \; \wedge \; steadytime\!:\!90 < (throttle_t = ON) < 142 \implies leaving\_station$$

By providing invariant rules, such as this one, our solution allows for straightforward interpretation and understanding of the system's behavior. The rule provides clear criteria for determining whether the system is operating correctly during the *leaving_station* mode in which the velocity of the train (v_t), given by $measure(S_{velocity}, t)$, can not be lower than 0.0 or higher than 29.9 units and the state of the throttle ($throttle_t$), given by $state(A_{throttle}, t)$, can not be "ON" less than 90 or more than 142 timesteps. Any deviation from these conditions would indicate the presence of a problem. By continuously monitoring the actuator states and comparing them to the defined rules, our solution can identify deviations or abnormal behaviors that may compromise the safety or efficiency of the system.

3.5 Summary

IM-DISCO is a tool that generates invariant rules composed of predicates to characterize the operational modes and detect anomalies in CPS. It utilizes historical sensor and actuator data to calculate predicates representing the normal functioning of the CPS. These predicates define the statistical bounds of physical values and actuator states for each operational mode.

IM-DISCO employs association rule mining to generate invariant rules. It extracts common co-occurring predicates and then finds relationships between them. The support and confidence of the generated rules are calculated, and the final rules are selected based on a minimum confidence threshold.

Overall, the use of easily understandable invariant rules facilitates effective preventive measures, enabling operators or experts to promptly respond to anomalies, mitigate risks, and ensure the smooth operation of the system.

4   Implementation

The IM-DISCO tool is composed of the phases presented in Fig. 1, namely: *Predicate Generation* and *Invariant Rule Mining*. We used Python programming language to develop our tool.

The *Predicate Generation* phase is responsible for generating predicates based on the input CPS data log, which includes telemetry from sensors and actuator states. To this data, the expert adds the observed operational modes. For each sensor and actuator, we calculate the appropriate thresholding approaches as described in Sect. 3.3. These thresholds determine the ranges of values that define different modes. Once the predicates are generated, they are combined to form itemsets, which are then used as input for the *Invariant Rule Mining* phase.

To associate the predicates and generate invariant rules, we used the *MLxtend* library [24], which offers a range of machine learning and data mining tools. We now describe the two subphases of the *Invariant Rule Mining* step: *Frequent Itemset Extraction* and *Association Rule Generation*.

The objective of FIE is to identify itemsets, which correspond to the generated predicates, that occur frequently in the dataset. First, we transform the dataset containing the predicates into a binary matrix representation using the MLxtend function $fit\_transform()$. This binary matrix indicates the position of each predicate in the dataset. We then apply the frequent itemset extraction algorithm. In our case, we utilized the FP-Growth implementation provided by MLxtend, which is reported to be approximately five times faster than the Apriori algorithm[1]. To capture the maximum number of frequent predicates, we set a *minsup* of 0.05, the minimum allowed value by the FP-Growth algorithm. Having a larger set of predicates enables us to generate a greater number of associations, resulting in more robust rules.

ARG aims to derive associations between the frequent predicates and generate invariant rules. We employed the $association\_rules()$ function from MLxtend, which takes the frequent predicates as input and returns the association rules that satisfy a certain confidence level. In our case, we set *minconf* to 1, ensuring that only rules with perfect confidence are generated. This choice minimizes the risk of false positives and ensures that the derived rules are highly significant.

---

[1]   https://rasbt.github.io/mlxtend/user_guide/frequent_patterns/fpgrowth/.

5   Evaluation

We performed several experiments using different train travel scenarios to evaluate the performance and efficacy of IM-DISCO in critical infrastructure. The evaluation aimed to answer the following research questions:

RQ.1) Can IM-DISCO infer the correct operational mode?
RQ.2) Can IM-DISCO be applied for anomaly detection?
RQ.3) How much time does IM-DISCO take to generate and verify rules?

By addressing these questions, we can obtain an understanding of the tool's accuracy, sensitivity to anomalies, and performance of rule generation and verification. The evaluation will provide insights into the practicality of the IM-DISCO tool and its ability to support anomaly detection in cyber-physical systems. The evaluation was performed on a computer with Intel Core i5-7300HQ CPU 2.50GHz processor, 16GB of RAM, and running Windows 10.

5.1   Data Collection and Experiment Setup

The datasets used to assess our solution correspond to two real-world suburban train rides on the same railway. The data, such as the geographic points and velocity, were collected at 1-second intervals using the *Strava* application running on a smartphone. This app is used to track physical exercise using Global Positioning System (GPS) data.

The first ride, or departure ride (R_d), was from Lisboa - Entrecampos to Portela de Sintra had a duration of 35 min and 22 s, and comprehended 12 stops until it arrived at the final one, which gives a total of 2122 datapoints. The second ride, or return ride (R_r), represents the return trip, had a duration of 34 min and 28 s, and comprehended the same number of stops totaling 2068 datapoints. The mean time between stops is approximately 3 min and the mean velocity of the train was 40.7 km per hour (km/h). From this data, we have derived other metrics, such as acceleration, the state of the brakes, and throttle (on and off). We have also annotated the state of the doors (opened or closed), and more importantly the operational mode of the train (*on_station*, *leaving_station*, *riding*, and *arriving_station*). From this scenario, we have modeled the train as a cyber-physical system with a set of actuators $\mathbb{A}$ and sensors $\mathbb{S}$ (recall Sect. 3.2). Actuators are the brakes, throttle, and doors. The sensors are the speedometer and accelerometer.

However, the collected datasets have limitations in representing the diverse conditions of real-world train operations; the sample size may not capture the full range of train behaviors and potential anomalies; and abnormal values were captured due to low GPS signals in tunnels. These values were used to assess IM-DISCO's detection capabilities in this specific scenario.

5.2 Evaluation Metrics

In the evaluation of our solution, we employed a set of commonly used metrics to assess its efficacy, namely: false positives (FP), false negatives (FN), true positives (TP), true negatives (TN), recall, precision, F1-measure, and accuracy. An FP is the number of instances that do not belong to a specific class but are incorrectly classified as belonging to that class. An FN is the number of instances that belong to a specific class but are incorrectly classified as not belonging to that class. A TP is the number of instances that are correctly classified as a specific class. A TN is the number of instances that are correctly classified as not belonging to a specific class. Recall measures the proportion of correctly classified instances out of the total instances that actually belong to a specific class and is computed as $\frac{TP}{(TP+FN)}$. Precision is calculated as $\frac{TP}{(TP+FP)}$ and measures the proportion of correctly classified instances out of the total instances predicted as belonging to a specific class. The F1-measure, also known as the F1-score, is the harmonic mean of precision and recall that determines the overall performance. Its formula corresponds to $\frac{2*Precision*Recall}{(Precision+Recall)}$. Accuracy measures the overall correctness of the classification model, and it is calculated as $\frac{(TP+TN)}{(TP+TN+FP+FN)}$. We consider this a multiclass classification problem [14] where the goal is to classify instances into multiple categories or classes. In this context, each class represents a specific operational mode or anomaly.

5.3 Operational Mode Inference (RQ. 1)

To evaluate the accuracy of our rules in correctly identifying the operational modes of the system, we conducted a training and testing process. Following the same approach of previous works [11,27], we have trained IM-DISCO with 80% of the dataset, and tested with 20%. Specifically, we used the data collected from the first 10 stops to generate invariant rules that characterize each mode. Then, we trained a detector with the resulting rules and tested it using the remaining data. Table 2 demonstrates the results of this experiment.

Table 2. Results of using invariant rules for detecting R_d and R_r operational modes.

	Precision		Recall		F1-score		Accuracy	
	R_d	R_r	R_d	R_r	R_d	R_r	R_d	R_r
arriving_station	100%	100%	98.53%	97.89%	99.26%	98.94%		
leaving_station	100%	43.75%	100%	100%	100%	60.87%		
on_station	100%	100%	100%	100%	100%	100%		
riding	99.60%	100%	99.60%	93.21%	99.60%	96.48%		
IM-DISCO	99.90%	85.94%	99.53%	98.22%	99.71%	89.07%	**99.29%**	**95.17%**

These results demonstrate that our solution can accurately detect the mode of the train using only two sensors and three actuators. The achieved high accuracy indicates the effectiveness of our approach. In addition, our solution successfully detected two out of the three abnormal datapoints caused by the low GPS signal. The third abnormal datapoint went undetected as the train maintained a constant movement during the interference.

However, we can observe by the precision metric in R_r that the *leaving_station* operational mode was wrongly inferred by the detector. This happened due to the overlapping of predicates in different invariant rules. Specifically, the *MinMax* predicate for velocity and acceleration overlapped between the *riding* and *leaving_station* states. For example, the predicates for *riding* were $29.452 \leq$ velocity ≤ 96.98 and $-13.676 \leq$ acceleration ≤ 21.078, while the predicates for *leaving_station* were $0.007 \leq$ velocity ≤ 29.974 and $-6.469 \leq$ acceleration ≤ 13.018. As a result, when the predicates of the two sensor values overlap, and the predicates for all actuators are the same, the detector chooses the first mode that meets its invariant rules. Having a larger set of sensors and actuators would significantly reduce the likelihood of this occurrence.

Moreover, to evaluate how well our solution maintains its high accuracy in detecting OMs, we use different training/testing split datapoints. Figure 2 displays a graph of the accuracy values for both rides for different training sizes. Our approach consistently achieves high accuracy, exceeding 95%, even with small training sizes. This shows that our solution effectively generates accurate rules despite limited data. The ability to achieve high accuracy with low training data is significant, as it allows our approach to be applied in challenging scenarios where obtaining large amounts of data is impractical. This is valuable in real-world situations with limited data collection due to constraints.

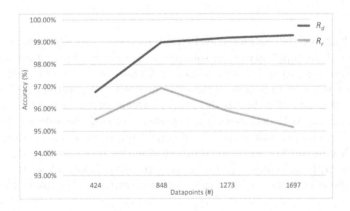

Fig. 2. Accuracy of IM-DISCO (y-axis) across different training sizes (x-axis).

5.4 Anomaly Detection (RQ. 2)

To evaluate the capability to detect anomalies, we developed a train ride simulator, since we could not implement attacks in the real-world datasets used before.

The simulated train ride uses the same operational modes as previously mentioned, comprising a throttle, a brake, and the doors that open when the train arrives at a station. Sensors were utilized to capture the velocity, acceleration, throttle force, and brake force at each second.

The resulting training dataset consisted of a 48-minute ride with 13 stops, providing substantial and representative data for training IM-DISCO. The testing dataset, obtained under the same conditions, encompassed a 12-minute ride with 3 stops. The stops were unevenly spaced to accurately replicate a real train ride. Additionally, an attack was introduced in the testing dataset, involving tampering with the brakes. The locomotive driver was unable to use the regular brakes and instead had to rely on an emergency brake that exerted a force 2.5 times stronger than the regular brake. This attack was enacted twice in the testing dataset. From this experiment, IM-DISCO generated a total of 76 predicates and 4 invariant rules, one for each operational mode.

Table 3. Results of using invariant rules for anomaly detection in a simulated ride.

	Precision	Recall	F1-score	Accuracy
anomaly	95.24%	100%	97.56%	
arriving_station	100%	99.56%	99.78%	
leaving_station	100%	100%	100%	
on_station	100%	100%	100%	
riding	100%	100%	100%	
IM-DISCO	99.05%	99.91%	99.47%	**99.86%**

Table 3 shows the obtained evaluation metrics. The experiment's results demonstrated the capability of our solution to accurately identify both anomalies and the other operational modes, achieving 99.86% accuracy in detection. This high accuracy was mainly due to the efficiency of the generated predicates and invariant rules, and also due to the good representativity of the training data. For instance, our tool detected an acceleration outside the values captured in training for each operational mode and considered it an anomaly. However, we got one FN inferring the mode *arriving_station* due to a velocity value that fell outside the range of values captured during training. Nonetheless, these results showcase the effectiveness of our approach in identifying abnormal situations.

5.5   Invariant Rules Verification and Validation (RQ. 3)

To evaluate the performance of rule generation and verification, we benchmarked the time taken to generate and validate invariant rules. We utilized different training/testing split datapoints and ran our tool 30 times to avoid skewed benchmarks. The duration of three key processes was recorded: predicate generation (Sect. 3.3), invariant rule generation (Sect. 3.4), and operational mode detection. By running our tool multiple times and calculating the means of the

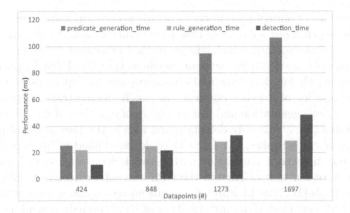

Fig. 3. Performance of our solution across different dataset sizes (x-axis, number of datapoints). The y-axis is the average performance in milliseconds (ms) of 30 executions.

duration for each process, we assess the average speed our solution performs. Figure 3 depicts the results of these experiments.

The results indicate that there is a direct relationship between the size of the training data and the time required for predicate and invariant rules generation. As expected, larger training datasets require more computational resources, leading to increased processing times in both processes. However, it is noteworthy that the rule generation process exhibits a lower rate of increase in processing time compared to the predicate generation process. This can be attributed to the fact that the number of sensors and actuators, and the number of predicates/itemsets remains constant throughout the experiments (2 sensors, 3 actuators, and 52 predicates). Despite this, we can observe that both processes are relatively fast, which will be advantageous in deploying the solution in a real-world scenario. Moreover, the low detection times, averaging around 0.026 ms per datapoint, further enhance the responsiveness of our solution, allowing prompt identification and preventive actions.

6   Conclusion

In this work, we described IM-DISCO, a solution for inferring the operational modes and detecting anomalies in cyber-physical systems using historical data. Our approach generates invariant rules based on different types of predicates that represent the physical conditions of the CPS. Through the evaluation of our solution, we have demonstrated its effectiveness, agility, and performance. The generated invariant rules exhibited an accuracy above 95% in detecting the correct operational modes with low training sizes. This indicates that our solution can reliably characterize and identify the different CPS operational modes even with limited training data available. In addition, we verified that the invariant rules are able to detect anomalies with 99.86% accuracy. We also assessed the performance of our solution in terms of rule generation and verification. The results showed that our solution is able to generate invariant rules in less than 150ms for 1697 datapoints, which can be verified in around 0.026 ms.

From the obtained results, we can conclude that IM-DISCO provides an effective approach for detecting and characterizing the operational modes or abnormal behavior of a cyber-physical system. It demonstrates high accuracy and agility in rule generation and fast detection of operational modes. Our solution facilitates timely anomaly detection and aids in the prevention of potential disruptions or catastrophes. IM-DISCO could be applied in infrastructures as an additive security tool: correlation with network detection tools [7], can reveal a network intrusion that originated the CPS anomaly; correlation with process monitoring tools [21], may identify anomalous processes; integration with impact assessment [9] may enable the investigation of CPS anomaly cascading effects.

Acknowledgement. Work supported by the European Commission through contract 101021797 (H2020 STARLIGHT https://www.starlight-h2020.eu/).

References

1. Adepu, S., Mathur, A.: From design to invariants: detecting attacks on cyber physical systems. In: 2017 IEEE International Conference on Software Quality, Reliability and Security Companion (QRS-C), pp. 533–540. IEEE (2017)
2. Agrawal, R., Imieliński, T., Swami, A.: Mining association rules between sets of items in large databases. In: Proceedings of the 1993 ACM SIGMOD International Conference on Management of Data, pp. 207–216 (1993)
3. Ahmed, C.M., et al.: NoisePrint: attack detection using sensor and process noise fingerprint in cyber physical systems. In: Proceedings of the 2018 on Asia Conference on Computer and Communications Security, pp. 483–497. ACM, Incheon ROK (2018)
4. Ahmed, C.M., Zhou, J., Mathur, A.P.: Noise matters: using sensor and process noise fingerprint to detect stealthy cyber attacks and authenticate sensors in CPS. In: Proceedings of the 34th Annual Computer Security Applications Conference, pp. 566–581. ACM, San Juan PR USA (2018)
5. Aliabadi, M.R., Kamath, A.A., Gascon-Samson, J., Pattabiraman, K.: Artinali: dynamic invariant detection for cyber-physical system security. In: Proceedings of the 2017 11th Joint Meeting on Foundations of Software Engineering (2017)
6. Apolinário, F., Escravana, N., Hervé, É., Pardal, M.L., Correia, M.: Fingerci: generating specifications for critical infrastructures. In: Proceedings of the 37th ACM/SIGAPP Symposium on Applied Computing, pp. 183–186 (2022)
7. Apolinário, F., et al.: COMSEC: secure communications for baggage handling systems. In: Katsikas, S., et al. Computer Security. ESORICS 2022 International Workshops. ESORICS 2022. Lecture Notes in Computer Science, vol. 13785, pp. 329–345. Springer, Cham (2022). https://doi.org/10.1007/978-3-031-25460-4_19
8. Brin, S., Motwani, R., Ullman, J.D., Tsur, S.: Dynamic itemset counting and implication rules for market basket data. In: Proceedings of the 1997 ACM SIGMOD international conference on Management of data, pp. 255–264 (1997)
9. Carvalho, O., Apolinário, F., Escravana, N., Ribeiro, C.: CIIA: critical infrastructure impact assessment. In: Proceedings of the 37th ACM/SIGAPP Symposium on Applied Computing, pp. 124–132 (2022)

10. Ceccato, M., Driouich, Y., Lucchese, M., Lanotte, R., Merro, M.: Towards reverse engineering of industrial physical processes. In: Katsikas, S., et al. Computer Security. ESORICS 2022 International Workshops. ESORICS 2022. Lecture Notes in Computer Science, vol. 13785. Springer, Cham (2022). https://doi.org/10.1007/978-3-031-25460-4_15

11. Feng, C., Palleti, V., Mathur, A., Chana, D.: A systematic framework to generate invariants for anomaly detection in industrial control systems. In: NDSS (2019)

12. Feng, C., Tian, P.: Time series anomaly detection for cyber-physical systems via neural system identification and bayesian filtering. In: Proceedings of the 27th ACM SIGKDD Conference on Knowledge Discovery & Data Mining. KDD 2021, Association for Computing Machinery, New York, NY, USA (2021)

13. Fung, C., Srinarasi, S., Lucas, K., Phee, H.B., Bauer, L.: Perspectives from a comprehensive evaluation of reconstruction-based anomaly detection in industrial control systems. In: Atluri, V., Di Pietro, R., Jensen, C.D., Meng, W. (eds.) Computer Security - ESORICS 2022, pp. 493–513. Springer Nature Switzerland, Cham (2022). https://doi.org/10.1007/978-3-031-17143-7_24

14. Grandini, M., Bagli, E., Visani, G.: Metrics for multi-class classification: an overview. arXiv preprint arXiv:2008.05756 (2020)

15. Hajj, S., El Sibai, R., Bou Abdo, J., Demerjian, J., Makhoul, A., Guyeux, C.: Anomaly-based intrusion detection systems: the requirements, methods, measurements, and datasets. Trans. Emerg. Telecommun. Technol. 32(4), e4240 (2021)

16. Huang, Y.L., Cárdenas, A.A., Amin, S., Lin, Z.S., Tsai, H.Y., Sastry, S.: Understanding the physical and economic consequences of attacks on control systems. Int. J. Crit. Infrastruct. Prot. 2(3), 73–83 (2009)

17. Kaouk, M., Flaus, J.M., Potet, M.L., Groz, R.: A review of intrusion detection systems for industrial control systems. In: 2019 6th International Conference on Control, Decision and Information Technologies (CoDIT), pp. 1699–1704 (2019)

18. Kiran, R.U., Reddy, P.K.: Novel techniques to reduce search space in multiple minimum supports-based frequent pattern mining algorithms. In: Proceedings of the 14th International Conference on Extending Database Technology (2011)

19. Kumbhare, T.A., Chobe, S.V.: An overview of association rule mining algorithms. Int. J. Comput. Sci. Inf. Technol. 5, 927–930 (2014)

20. Lee, E.A.: Cyber physical systems: design challenges. In: 2008 11th IEEE International Symposium on Object and Component-Oriented Real-Time Distributed Computing (ISORC), pp. 363–369 (2008)

21. Lima, J., Apolinário, F., Escravana, N., Ribeiro, C.: BP-IDS: using business process specification to leverage intrusion detection in critical infrastructures. In: 2020 IEEE International Symposium on Software Reliability Engineering Workshops (ISSREW), pp. 7–12. IEEE (2020)

22. Liu, B., Hsu, W., Ma, Y.: Mining association rules with multiple minimum supports. In: Proceedings of the Fifth ACM SIGKDD International Conference on Knowledge Discovery and Data Mining, pp. 337–341 (1999)

23. Pal, K., Adepu, S., Goh, J.: Effectiveness of association rules mining for invariants generation in cyber-physical systems. In: 2017 IEEE 18th International Symposium on High Assurance Systems Engineering (HASE), pp. 124–127. IEEE (2017)

24. Raschka, S.: MLxtend: providing machine learning and data science utilities and extensions to python's scientific computing stack. J. Open Source Softw. 3(24), 638 (2018)

25. Rubio, J.E., Alcaraz, C., Roman, R., Lopez, J.: Analysis of intrusion detection systems in industrial ecosystems. In: SECRYPT, pp. 116–128 (2017)

26. Umer, M.A., Mathur, A., Junejo, K.N., Adepu, S.: Generating invariants using design and data-centric approaches for distributed attack detection. Int. J. Crit. Infrastruct. Prot. **28**, 100341 (2020)
27. Wolsing, K., Thiemt, L., Sloun, C.v., Wagner, E., Wehrle, K., Henze, M.: Can industrial intrusion detection be simple? In: Atluri, V., Di Pietro, R., Jensen, C.D., Meng, W. (eds.) Computer Security - ESORICS 2022, vol. 13556, pp. 574–594. Springer Nature Switzerland, Cham (2022). https://doi.org/10.1007/978-3-031-17143-7_28
28. Yoong, C.H., Palleti, V.R., Maiti, R.R., Silva, A., Poskitt, C.M.: Deriving invariant checkers for critical infrastructure using axiomatic design principles. Cybersecurity **4**(1), 1–24 (2021)

Unravelling Network-Based Intrusion Detection: A Neutrosophic Rule Mining and Optimization Framework

Tiago Fontes Dias[1,2]([✉]) [ID], João Vitorino[1,2] [ID], Tiago Fonseca[1] [ID], Isabel Praça[1,2] [ID], Eva Maia[1,2] [ID], and Maria João Viamonte[1,2] [ID]

[1] School of Engineering, Polytechnic of Porto (ISEP/IPP), 4249-015 Porto, Portugal
{tiada,jpmvo,calof,icp,egm,mjv}@isep.ipp.pt
[2] Research Group On Intelligent Engineering and Computing for Advanced Innovation and Development (GECAD), 4249-015 Porto, Portugal

Abstract. The ever-increasing number of cyber-attacks thought the network is a real concern. It is of the utmost importance to reliably detect malicious network traffic, mitigating its impact on business continuity. Rule-based security measures are a very common security implementation that aims to protect critical infrastructure assets from cyber threats. However, it is extremely complicated to manage these systems, as one must identify the attacks signatures. This can be relatively easy if the threat is common, but unknown attacks require an expert analysis of the network's traffic, which is much more complex. Extracting accurate and comprehensible rules from multiple sources of authentic data is crucial to attaining reliable classification knowledge that can be applied to many real-life scenarios. This paper presents the Rule Generator (RUGE) framework, which automates the rule mining and selection process using a genetic algorithm with a single-valued neutrosophic cross-entropy fitness operator. The capabilities of the developed framework were evaluated using the network traffic flows of the CICIDS2017 dataset. The obtained results show that in a network-based context, intrusion detection systems may benefit from rule mining to automate the knowledge acquisition process, being able to keep the attack signatures up-to-date. Moreover, smaller groups of rules can be selected to achieve a good balance between performance and interpretability. Therefore, in the network-based intrusion detection context, optimizing the rules extracted from multiple machine learning models with a genetic algorithm using a neutrosophic logic can be significantly advantageous.

Keywords: rule mining · rule optimization · rule selection · neutrosophic logic · machine learning · intrusion detection

1 Introduction

The internet is at its core a constant flow of information, which is encoded and shared in the form of packets. The way these packets are switched is fundamental to the operation of networks. Internet protocols, software, hardware, commands, and similar functions

S. Katsikas et al. (Eds.): ESORICS 2023 Workshops, LNCS 14399, pp. 59–75, 2024.
https://doi.org/10.1007/978-3-031-54129-2_4

that support packet switching are modularized in protocol stacks, with each layer of the stack performing a specific and vital function [1]. Cybersecurity is the practice of protecting systems, networks, and programs, from failure and digital attacks. Cyber-attacks are usually aimed at accessing, changing, or destroying sensitive information, with multiple malicious intents. Therefore, due to the growing number and increasing complexity of cyber-attacks, the development of effective cybersecurity measures and systems is becoming more challenging every day.

Cyber-attacks are usually performed via the network or directly on the host. Intrusion detection is a cybersecurity technique used to safeguard exploitable systems from cyber-attacks, covering both network and host-based mediums. Typically, Intrusion Detection Systems (IDSs) use a knowledge base where attack signatures are described in form of rules that classify an attack. As such, their performance relies on the robustness of the knowledge base [2, 3].

Time and time again, many researchers have stated that rule-based approaches can be great for solving classification problems [4], such as the ones presented in the network intrusion detection field [5–7]. Their modular nature allows a knowledge-base to be constructed according to a specific domain, which enables an incremental development of the system. Rules can also be quite comprehensible because of their representational intuitiveness, which leads to more explainable and interpretable justifications [8]. A method of acquiring new rules is by meeting with one or more experts in the field. However, this can be both cost-expensive and time-consuming [4, 9] since an expert may not always be available and the domain may be too complex to easily identify rules. Moreover, expert systems are not usually able to self-update their knowledge-base, which may lead to inaccurate inferences, as the knowledge is stagnated [8, 10]. Therefore, the automation of the knowledge acquisition process is extremely important to ensure the continuity of these systems. One of the reasons, Artificial Intelligence (AI) is gaining momentum and is becoming more important in a set of diverse fields is because it enables automation [11–13]. Intrusion detection can benefit from this. However, the use of Explainable AI is desirable, to provide insight into the model's training and detections [14]. As such, the use of interpretable AI in this scenario can also be a benefit for the Security Operations Centre (SOC) operator, as it enhances technical support, whilst maintaining the transparency that these systems require [15].

The network domain is characterized by the constant flow of information which is not intuitively understood. Typically, when facing a cyber-attack, SOC operators have to analyse the data and deal with its high transmission. The large quantity and complex ontology make the data analysis extremely difficult. However, techniques such as Data Mining (DM) can be helpful to the operator, assisting in the extrapolation of meaningful knowledge from the malicious traffic. Therefore, DM is an area of interest for automating the knowledge acquisition process, as it provides the necessary data analysis tools to uncover previously unknown patterns in large datasets. There are several DM types, including classification, clustering, regression, and dependence modelling [16]. In the intrusion detection domain, one suitable approach to detect cyber-attacks is the application of classification techniques derived from DM mechanisms [17]. However, one of the major challenges of using a DM approach is the trade-off between the technique's explainability and accuracy [18].

This work presents the Rule Generator (RUGE), a neutrosophic rule mining and optimization framework, capable of extracting accurate and interpretable classification rules from malicious network traffic data whilst accounting for their uncertainty. The developed work tackles the difficulty of observing network data to infer new knowledge that a SOC operator has to go through, resorting to classification rule mining by combining the classification capabilities of accurate machine learning techniques with a rule extraction, optimization, and assessment phase. This work's goal is to be able to assist SOC operators to enhance security mechanisms, such as IDSs, by providing valuable network insight in form of rules that encode cyber-attacks. To the best of the authors knowledge, this approach has not yet been taken in the intrusion detection field and so this work is presented as a proof of concept to what could be integrated into a real-world environment and be used as an assistance tool to improve rule-based security mechanisms. To evaluate the usefulness of the framework in a network intrusion detection setting, the case study was conducted using the CICIDS2017 dataset [19] as testbed.

This paper is organized into multiple sections. Section 2 presents the state-of-the-art on classification rule mining, rule optimization techniques and rule mining in the context of intrusion detection, as well as approaches to deal with rule uncertainty. Section 3 overviews the proposed framework and describes the two phases of the workflow. Section 4 presents a case study scenario in the cybersecurity domain. Section 5 addresses the main conclusions and future work.

2 State-of-The-Art

Rule-based intrusion detection is naturally an interpretable technique that provides transparent reasoning behind a classification. As such, artificial intelligence methods for knowledge extraction should follow the same principle, so that it can be digested.

When considering the extraction of knowledge, one must evaluate its uncertainty, which reflects sureness and completeness. In cybersecurity, it is hard to be sure of every condition of each cyber-attack, as they may share some commonalities. As such, the uncertainty associated with the extraction of incomplete, erroneous or fuzzy knowledge must be assessed. It is especially concerning for the SOC operator, to know how certain a given rule is while assessing a problem.

This section details the challenges of reaching more explainable and accurate classification techniques and provides an overview of the current state-of-the-art of classification rule mining methods, as well as possible approaches to deal with the uncertainty associated with network-based intrusion detection.

2.1 Accuracy vs Explainability Dichotomy

Accuracy is the standard metric to evaluate how a result conforms to the expected outcome. In the intrusion detection field, one can define the accuracy of a detection model by the proportion of correctly classified network traffic [18]. Nonetheless, interpretability and explainability are as important as the accuracy of a classification model. Interpretability can be defined as the degree to which a human being can understand the cause of a decision made by a system, whereas explainability goes a step further by measuring the degree to which a system can provide a clear justification of the reasoning that led to a decision.

Focusing on the explainability of rule-based systems, the authors in [20] propose the analysis of a group of rules using the number of conditions in each rule and the total number of rules as the main indicators. However, the authors in [21] describe how challenging it can be to extract knowledge in the form of classification rules suitable for human interpretation and verification.

One of the main challenges of achieving explainability is the black-box problem. Black-box models are typically opaque to the user, preventing the understanding and tracing of the logic and most relevant attributes that contribute to a certain prediction. This lack of explainability and the difficulty in extracting rules suitable for human interpretation and verification are major limiting factors to the use of these techniques in scenarios where a system must be able to explain the reasoning behind a prediction, such as medical diagnosis or intrusion detection [22].

On the other hand, there are also other white-box machine learning techniques, mostly based on Decision Trees (DT), that provide clear explanations typically, at a cost of a lower accuracy [23, 24]. These tree-based algorithms are the most used method to extract classification rules. For that reason, rule-based classification systems, such as the ones used for network-based intrusion detection, are contingent on a trade-off between the explainability and accuracy of the applied rules.

2.2 Classification Rule Mining

Classification rule mining is used to extract rules from a large data sample. The interest in this area has been growing due to its wide applications in numerous areas where interpretability is a requirement, for instance in expert systems, decision support systems, document classifiers, fraud detection, performance prediction or medical diagnosis [25–27].

Han et al. [28] present a comprehensive review of some of the techniques used in classification rule mining. The authors explore algorithms such as DT, Random Forest (RF), Rough Sets, Support Vector Machines and Neural Networks. The authors also endeavour about the evaluation strategies applied to verify the accuracy, sensitivity, specificity, and precision of the extracted classification rules.

Some of the algorithms based on exhaustive searches of the domain space rapidly become computationally infeasible, due to the high number of combinations of parameters in the original data space. Therefore, many researchers have committed their efforts to applying evolutionary algorithms to find a "good enough" solution. Additionally, a set of nature-based and meta-heuristic approaches, such as Ant-Colony Optimization [29, 30], and Particle Swarm Optimization [31] algorithms were applied to find and extract the most significant classification rules.

Li et al. [32] further explore the optimization of classification rule mining by selecting a small subset of features as the most distinguishing characteristics among distinct types of data samples. The authors present a new classification rule mining approach that combines a feature selection technique, the Neighbourhood Preserving Embedding Algorithm, and a Genetic Algorithm (GA). The authors perform dimensionality reduction on the datasets via the embedding algorithm and then the GA is used to mine the classification rules. Their proposal shows much better performance when compared to other classification rule mining algorithms for its accuracy and the simplicity of the extracted rules. These authors approach might be the most similar to the one present in this paper, as GAs are also heavily relied on in this work. However, contrary to what is done in this work, the authors disregard the uncertainty associated with the data.

Considering the intrusion detection field, most approaches focus on using association rule mining. However, some works have also attempted classification rule mining for increasing detection capabilities of IDSs. Tsang et al. in [33] present a Multi-Objective Genetic Fuzzy IDS (MOGFIDS), which permits learning IF-THEN rules via learners by feeding a dataset to the system. Their work leverages an agent-based evolutionary computation to generate and evolve a fuzzy knowledge base for classification. To improve the generalization capability of the tool, it performs feature selection, resorting to search-based methods. The GA is used to select and mutate existing sets of fuzzy rules. The authors were able to detect cyber-attacks from the four main categories specified with a low false alarm rate. Similarly, Dartigue et al. [34] present an approach that performs feature selection to increase the accuracy of the classifier and multiboosting, which combines the outputs of multiple binary classifiers to decide on which class is most suitable, to alleviate the bias and variance. Their experiments were also conducted on KDD CUP-99 dataset [35], and their results showed that their results outperformed others by obtaining a 93% detection rate, with high detection rates especially for User to Root and Remote to Local categories of attacks. Although the authors deal with the uncertainty during the prediction phase of the model, neither approach translates the knowledge acquired from the model to produce interpretable rules in an IF-THEN format that can be added to an IDS. In fact, most approaches to the intrusion detection field attempt to use the learner itself as the IDS [23, 36–39], which in comparison to RUGE provides less explainability, interpretability and configurability, since most approaches utilize the algorithms with best accuracy which typically are black-box and the SOC operator has no possibility of editing the internal mechanisms of the trained model to alter the rules used to perform intrusion detection.

In summary, despite their apparent benefits, the approaches that do not tackle intrusion detection directly, do not take into consideration the uncertainty associated with the data. As such, their rules, which are mined from labelled datasets, might describe conditions that are common for more than one conclusion. This lack of sureness is especially concerning for network-based intrusion detection because of the ever-evolving nature of cyber-attacks. The approaches that fall within the context of intrusion detection use the learners as the IDSs which can be limiting regarding transparency and configurability. The proposed work attempts to tackle these issues by providing rules extracted from explainable AI models, whilst validating the uncertainty associated with the knowledge extracted.

2.3 Rule Uncertainty

One of the most pertinent concerns when performing classification rule mining is the quality and sureness of the utilized data. Regarding the intrusion detection field, the major drawback of relying only on known cyber-attack signatures for intrusion detection is that it leaves a computer network exposed to zero-day attacks until their signatures are detected and registered [40]. Therefore, a compromise must be reached to deal with the uncertainty associated with the detection of abnormal network traffic.

When analysing a dataset of network activity, the recorded data may not be the most reliable. The information can be incomplete, imprecise, or even contradictory, which leads to the existence of a degree of uncertainty [41]. To tackle this challenge, several approaches incorporate either Fuzzy or Neutrosophic logic [42] in the utilized rules. Many times, Fuzzy Logic serves as decision support, as it allows the introduction of truth values in an interval between 0 and 1. A truth value is a number that defines the membership of a certain proposition, similarly to a real-world, where it may not always be completely true [43]. Intuitionistic Fuzzy Logic works similarly, except that it contains an additional non-membership degree, and is therefore also capable of handling imprecise and incomplete information [41].

Neutrosophic logic is considered a generalization of other subtypes of Fuzzy logic [44]. It presents three membership values: Truthness, Indeterminacy and Falsehood (TIF). Therefore, it approximates human reasoning and is capable of dealing with a wide variety of deficient information problems [45]. Due to its effectiveness when dealing with several types of uncertainty, it is preferred for complex domains [43]. Table 1 summarizes the membership values and the uncertainty types that each logic takes into consideration.

Kavitha et al. [45] decided to deal with the uncertainty of rules by resorting to neutrosophic logic. After pre-processing the KDD Cup-99 dataset, they diminished the dimensionality of results by performing a Best-First Search method for finding the best potential features to extract resorting to a GA. The mined rules were then sent to a neutrosophic logic classifier, which classified the rules resorting to the TIF values and provided an atomic expression for the right-hand side of each rule, as well as a weight value. With this approach, the authors were able to account for the imprecision of the utilized knowledge.

Table 1. Summary of logic characteristics.

Logic Type	Membership Values	Uncertainty Types
Fuzzy	Truthness	Vagueness
Intuitionistic Fuzzy	Truthness Falsehood	Vagueness Imprecision
Neutrosophic	Truthness Falsehood Indeterminacy	Vagueness Imprecision Inconsistency Incompleteness

3 RUGE Framework

This section describes the RUGE framework and details the two phases of the workflow. It was developed to fully automate the rule mining and selection process of IF-THEN rules and can be divided into two phases, as shown in Fig. 1. In both, due to the promising results obtained in the surveyed work, a GA was used to find a good solution in reasonable time. In the rule mining phase, the framework uses a GA to optimize the hyperparameters of the chosen machine learning algorithms. Then, classification rules are extracted from these optimized models, creating a pool of initial rules. In the rule selection phase, the best group of unique rules is obtained by using another GA with a neutrosophic fitness operator.

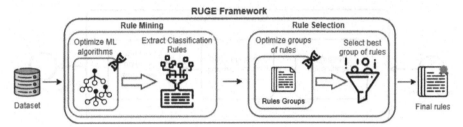

Fig. 1. Proposed framework workflow.

3.1 Phase 1: Rule Mining

This phase aims to extract optimized classification rules from a given dataset. At first, the hyperparameters of the chosen machine learning techniques are optimized by applying a GA. The algorithm searches the hyperparameter domain to optimize machine learning models and ultimately extract the best classification rules.

Initially, for each of the chosen algorithms, a solution space is given for each of its hyperparameters. Second, a set of candidate solutions are created with different hyperparameters inside the given solution space, and the first population is established. Then, the algorithm evolves from generation to generation, evaluating and selecting at each the best individuals based on their fitness. The crossover and mutation operators are used to, respectively, combine two individuals and apply random changes to individual parents, to create new individuals to be used in the next generation. The fitness operator is based on the performance of the algorithm. This operator begins by training a model with the given hyperparameters. Then, the resulting model is evaluated using a 5-fold cross-validation with a configurable metric. At the end of the optimization process, the best hyperparameters are used to train the machine learning techniques. Finally, classification rules can be extracted from the created models.

For the initial implementation of this framework, the rule extraction mechanisms were implemented for three machine learning algorithms: (i) DT, (ii) Skope-Rules [46] and (iii) RF. The first two algorithms were employed because they are highly explainable since their behaviour and prediction criteria are easily human-readable [47]. Even though

RF is black-box, meaning that it doesn't provide an explanation of how it works, it was also used because it is a well-established method with acknowledged performance in classification tasks [48].

To extract rules from a DT [10], taking advantage of its interpretability, a traversal of the tree is made by exploring its branches. Each path from root to leaf represents a rule that leads to a certain conclusion, fulfilling the Left-Hand Side and Right-Hand Side format, which represents conditions and conclusion, respectively. The Skope-Rules algorithm runs multiple DTs and is capable of extracting the best rules of each tree. Since the algorithm was intentionally developed for rule mining, it only has to go through a training phase to return very precise rules gathered from the multiple DTs using a threshold to filter the best ones (see Fig. 2).

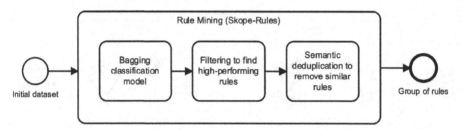

Fig. 2. Skope-Rules workflow.

Even though Skope-Rules is highly optimized for rule mining and therefore should be able to extract more powerful and precise rules than the DT and RF, the combination of all three models increases rule variety, which can significantly increase detection performance when properly combined.

After extracting rules from the three algorithms, duplicates are removed to avoid redundancy, and the remaining is aggregated to create an initial pool of rules. The outputted rules performance is as good as the initially provided dataset from where they are extracted, along with the parameterization of the models. As such, a well-processed and structured dataset can provide the needed information to obtain generalized rules regarding multiple attacks.

In the second phase of the workflow, the pool of initial rules incurs in a selection process to assemble the best group of rules.

3.2 Phase 2: Rules Selection

The second phase aims to select the best group of rules from those extracted at the previous step. Initially, the rules are randomly grouped, ensuring that every group has at least one rule of each target class. Due to the high number of rule combinations, it is computationally infeasible to apply algorithms based on exhaustive searches of the best solution. Therefore, another GA was also utilized in this phase.

The individuals (i.e., groups of rules) created by the GA have as many rules as the ones specified in the parameterization. At each generation, the best individuals are selected based on the neutrosophic cross-entropy fitness operator. The crossover operator mixes different parts of two individuals, combining rules from different groups to create new ones. Additionally, the mutation operator replaces one of the rules in a group with another from the pool of initially extracted rules.

To evaluate individuals, a neutrosophic fitness operator was developed. The neutrosophic approach was based on the equation proposed in [49], which converts the TIF values of multiple criteriums into a single-valued neutrosophic cross-entropy loss. It was applied considering each class as a different criterium and the final cross-entropy value was multiplied by the total number of conditions in the grouped rules, to prioritize small rules with a smaller size and a smaller cross-entropy loss. The fitness of a group of n rules is mathematically expressed as:

$$Fitness = \sum_{j=1}^{n} (C_j * [[\log_2 \frac{1}{\frac{1+Tj}{2}} + \log_2 \frac{1}{1-\frac{Ij}{2}} + \log_2 \frac{1}{1-\frac{Fj}{2}}]$$
$$+ [T_j \log_2 \frac{Tj}{\frac{1+Tj}{2}} + (1-T_j)\log_2 \frac{1-Tj}{1-\frac{1+Tj}{2}}] + [I_j + (1-I_j)\log_2 \frac{1-Ij}{1-\frac{Ij}{2}}] + [F_j + (1-F_j)\log_2 \frac{1-Fj}{1-\frac{Fj}{2}}]]) \quad (1)$$

where C_j is the total number of conditions of rule j and T_j, I_j, and F_j are the Truthness, Indeterminacy, and Falsehood values of that rule.

Each rule affects the TIF values of each class, according to the percentage of samples on the test set that correspond to its conditions. Therefore, if the class predicted by a rule is correct, its Truthness value is increased. On the other hand, if it is incorrect, either the Indeterminacy or Falsehood are increased, depending on the indeterminacy groups. It is pertinent to note that the fitness value calculated by this equation prioritizes groups of rules that contain multiple classes.

The indeterminacy groups are a pertinent aspect of the developed operator. These can be configured to consider incorrect class predictions as indetermined. Therefore, the rule evaluation process can benefit from the uncertainty associated with the similar characteristics of a specific group of classes. Table 2 provides a matrix showcasing the component of TIF increased for each combination of predicted and expected classes, in a scenario where class C2 and C3 belong to an indeterminacy group, being C2 and C3 different attacks of the same attack type family.

Table 2. Truthness, Indeterminacy and Falsehood Matrix.

Expected	Predicted		
	Class 1	Class 2	Class 3
Class 1	T	F	F
Class 2	F	T	I
Class 3	F	I	T

4 Intrusion Detection Case Study: A CICIDS2017 Testbed

As previously mentioned, intrusion detection is a field that has increased in popularity over the years, consequence of the rapid digital transformation. Many cyber-attacks exploit the vulnerabilities of systems that can be accessed via the network. However, the use of rule-based systems for intrusion detection has some disadvantages, one of them being that they require continuous improvement of the knowledge-base. This can be extremely challenging for a SOC operator, as there is a wide range of cyber-attacks, each with their own signatures. Zero-day attacks increase the complexity of this problem, due to their unknown nature.

To address this problem, this section evaluates the capabilities of the developed framework using as testbed the CICIDS2017 dataset, which contains cyber-attacks recorded in a network-based intrusion detection setting. The proposed framework was utilized to obtain classification rules from the initial dataset and find the best group of rules with a minimum of 50 and a maximum of 100 rules.

4.1 Dataset and Data Preprocessing

The CICIDS2017 dataset [19] was utilized because it contains a large quantity of labelled and up-to-date cyber-attacks, as well as benign network traffic. This dataset was published by Sharafaldin et al. and is publicly available at [50]. It contains seven captures of network activity, recorded in July 2017. The features of each recorded flow were extracted with CICFlowMeter and labelled as either benign or a specific malicious class. This dataset is known to have several issues related to traffic generation, flow construction, feature extraction and labelling that undermine its correctness [51]. However, it is still widely used across the scientific literature because it contains relevant network activity mixed with some noisy samples. Since these samples can occur in a real scenario because of erroneous packet captures or missing information in logging files, this dataset is relevant to address the uncertainty associated with network-based intrusion detection. Its usage was relevant to evaluate the performance of the extracted rules when the model is trained in a realistic and noisy environment. For this work, three captures were selected due to the types of cyber-attacks they contain. Table 3 provides an overview of each selected capture.

Table 3. Summary of select captures.

Capture	Attack Type	Attack Class
Tuesday	Brute-force	FTP-Patator; SSH-Patator
Wednesday	Denial-of-Service	GoldenEye; Hulk; Slowhttptest; Slowloris
	Exploit	Heartbleed
Friday	Port Scan	PortScan

The groups of classes of the same attack type correspond to the indeterminacy groups required for the neutrosophic fitness operator. Additionally, to adapt the dataset for this case study, a data preprocessing stage was performed to create training and evaluation subsets. First, the features that did not provide valuable information about a flow's benign or malicious purpose, such as origin and destination addresses, were discarded. Then, one-hot encoding was employed to convert the categorical features to numeric values. Due to their high cardinality, low-frequency categories were aggregated into a single category to avoid encoding qualitative values that had a small relevance. Finally, the data was randomly split into training and holdout sets with 70% and 30% of the samples, respectively. To preserve the imbalanced class proportions, the split was performed with stratification.

4.2 Scenario and Configuration

The proposed framework was applied to mine and select rules for the analysis of network traffic and the detection of cyber-attacks. A macro-averaged F1-Score was utilized to optimize the machine learning techniques on the training set. In the selection phase, the implemented neutrosophic cross-entropy fitness operator was utilized to optimize the rules. Then, using the evaluation set, a new macro-averaged F1-Score was calculated to assess the performance of the final selected group of rules.

During the rule mining phase, the pool of initial rules was created resorting to the three implemented algorithms: DT, RF and Skope-Rules. For the first two algorithms, the common parameters, the maximum depth and the minimum number of samples at a leaf were set to 10 and 2, respectively. This ensures that the pool of initial rules does not contain oversized rules and that a rule can be applied to multiple training samples. The remaining parameters were optimized by the GA to allow the extraction of better-performing rules, which were then used for the selection phase. To assess the effectiveness of the selected groups of rules, eleven iterations were performed, starting from groups of 50 rules and increasing the quantity up to 100, with a step of 5. Taking into consideration the type of data present on this dataset, which is common to the network intrusion detection field, the configuration parameters were chosen to allow for a better analysis of the framework's behaviour.

4.3 Results and Discussion

At the initial rule mining phase, the miners provided 983 rules, which obtained an evaluation score of approximately 99.92%. Despite achieving a high score, this large group of rules and the permutations between them can be extremely difficult for a human to understand, while also requiring great computational costs for the analysis of network traffic. Therefore, the rule selection phase was employed to reduce the number of utilized rules without significantly reducing the original score.

The obtained results indicate that a group with the 50 best rules reaches a significantly worse performance, compared to the initial 99.92%. Nonetheless, as the number of selected rules is increased, higher scores are gradually reached. The score increase starts stabilizing when groups of 90 to 100 rules are selected. Even though these groups still do not account for all the specific cases of the original rules, a score near 99% can be maintained (see Fig. 3).

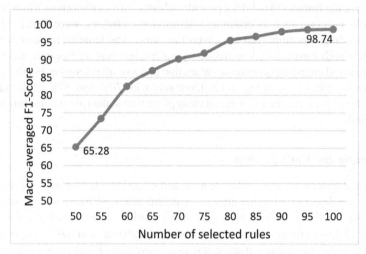

Fig. 3. Performance evaluation of rule groups.

Therefore, these groups achieve a good balance between detection performance and explainability, which can be verified by the human-readability of the final rules. Regarding computational costs, smaller groups of rules are permutated fewer times during selection, which decreases complexity. However, the selection of enormous groups can be very time-consuming. As previously mentioned, the final group contains at least one rule of each attack type. The most prevalent features which are present in the conditions of the rules are those that focus on the size of the packet, duration of the communication, destination ports, traffic direction flow and packet jitter, which make sense considering the attack types that are present in the dataset.

Whilst most rules that were considered part of the final group are small and concise, and therefore generalized, most of the discarded rules were bigger and had more specific conditions, meaning they had not generalized so well. Additionally, small rules that were not included displayed worst results, which could be caused by incomplete or erroneous knowledge.

The rule presented in Fig. 4 serves as an example of a rule selected for the final group after all the groups underwent the mutation and crossing processes. The described conditions of the rule are based on the features and the data collected on the used dataset, which are commonly known in the cybersecurity domain, making them highly interpretable. By analyzing this rule, the SOC operator is capable of understanding that the volume of a flow can be a cause of a *DoS_Hulk* attack, without the need to observe and correlate all flows captured during an attack. Moreover, the operator interacting with the framework may then decide whether the mined rule has value to the IDS's knowledge base or not. Nonetheless, it should be noted that rules are not meant to be used individually, as it is the whole group that is capable of obtaining a reliable classification.

Additionally, one must consider that over time, the rules may become brittle or inadequate regarding the current state of the network. Therefore, the tool should be used from time to time to update current rules and add new ones. The operator can do this by manually editing the rules or through the framework by parameterizing newly gathered interesting network data, which can be achieved by searching public datasets or monitoring the infrastructure's network. The last is ideally better since the rules would reflect best the current infrastructure, and therefore raise less false alarms which can become somewhat exacerbating.

```
If
    bwd_packet_length_std > 1494.157 AND
    fwd_packet_length_max <= 422.5 AND
    total_length_of_bwd_packets <= 11605.0 AND
    total_length_of_bwd_packets > 11565.5
Then
    DoS_Hulk
```

Fig. 4. Rule included in the final group.

Furthermore, by examining the machine learning techniques that provided each original rule, it can be observed that the selected rules were mostly extracted from the Skope-Rules algorithm, followed by RF and DT. This highlights the suitability of the Skope-Rules algorithm for rule mining tasks. Nonetheless, by also employing other algorithms, such as DT and RF, the proposed framework was able to benefit from a more diverse pool of rules to produce more valuable selections.

5 Conclusions

The developed work addresses the rule extraction problem in an intrusion detection setting by introducing an automated rule mining framework that aims to easily extract and select a group of accurate, interpretable, and simple IF-THEN rules. The proposed framework is based on a joint rule mining phase, where different algorithms can be used to obtain optimized classifiers, followed by a rule selection phase, where the best group of rules is selected. To preserve high levels of accuracy, the optimized selection uses a fitness operator based on a single-valued neutrosophic cross-entropy loss.

The results obtained in the case study demonstrate that the proposed framework can be significantly advantageous for knowledge acquisition by resorting to rule mining and selection processes when compared to the difficulties inherent to the traditional methods of gathering knowledge. Therefore, instead of meeting with an expert in the field, this framework automates the knowledge acquisition process by ingesting cyber-attack-related data from a dataset to produce very precise rules resorting to interpretable methods preserving the transparency required by IDSs. Additionally, it serves as an assistant to the SOC operator, who may not always be aware of certain conditions regarding cyber-attacks, due to the great volumes of data that travel through the networks and can be extremely hard to correlate.

In comparison to other attempts, RUGE stands out for its support on the uncertainty, which is important when the knowledge extracted is fuzzy and not 100% accurate. It reflects the completeness and sureness of the rule towards the cyber-attack it detected, which is disregarded in the literature. This way, the mined rules are capable of dealing with the instability characteristic of the cybersecurity domain, by considering uncertainty and assuring detection capability. Moreover, whilst most works on intrusion detection focuses on creating the models and using the learners directly, this does not provide the same level of transparency, explainability and configurability for the SOC operator who manages attacks signatures. RUGE provides the rules so that the operator can decide on which are best to keep and which can be discarded.

As future work, it is pertinent to augment the rule mining dataset with adversarial cyber-attack examples generated in a realistic attack scenario. By generating rules that account for the characteristics of these cyber-attack variations, the proposed framework may also be used to improve the robustness and reliability of an IDS. It could also be interesting to compare the performance of the rules extracted from the CICIDS2017 dataset against corrected versions of it, such as the ones presented in [51, 52] to test the framework's ability to mine generalized rules. Additionally, it could also be relevant to explore different dataset processing approaches, such as interpreting the problem as a time series to extract more context-aware rules.

Moreover, to validate this proof of concept, the proposed framework should be integrated with a network-based IDS handled by a SOC operator to understand how it behaves and how valuable the mined rules are in a real scenario. In this scenario, the rules could also be evaluated by a network analyst to evaluate their interpretability and understand their ability to characterize the threat. It is also essential to continue to expand the framework by employing more complex models and exploring the explainability of black-box techniques to be able to gather a wider range of neutrosophic rules.

Acknowledgements. The present work was partially supported by the Norte Portugal Regional Operational Programme (NORTE 2020), under the PORTUGAL 2020 Partnership Agreement, through the Fundo Europeu de Desenvolvimento Regional (FEDER), within project "Cybers SeC IP" (NORTE-01–0145-FEDER-000044). This work has also received funding from UIDB/00760/2020.

References

1. Zhang, Y., Breslau, L., Paxson, V., Shenker, S.: On the characteristics and origins of internet flow rates. In: Proceedings of the 2002 Conference on Applications, Technologies, Architectures, and Protocols for Computer Communications - SIGCOMM 2002 (2002). https://doi.org/10.1145/633025
2. Ozkan-Okay, M., Samet, R., Aslan, O., Gupta, D.: A comprehensive systematic literature review on intrusion detection systems. IEEE Access **9**, 157727–157760 (2021). https://doi.org/10.1109/ACCESS.2021.3129336
3. Khraisat, A., Gondal, I., Vamplew, P., Kamruzzaman, J.: Survey of intrusion detection systems: techniques, datasets and challenges. Cybersecurity **2**(1), 1–22 (2019). https://doi.org/10.1186/S42400-019-0038-7/FIGURES/8

4. Waltl, B., Bonczek, G., Matthes, F.: Rule-based Information Extraction: Advantages, Limitations, and Perspectives, vol. 24, no. 2, p. 26 (2007)
5. Fallahi, N., Sami, A., Tajbakhsh, M.: Automated flow-based rule generation for network intrusion detection systems. In: 2016 24th Iranian Conference on Electrical Engineering, ICEE 2016, pp. 1948–1953 (2016). https://doi.org/10.1109/IranianCEE.2016.7585840
6. Kong, H., Jong, C., Ryang, U.: Rare association rule mining for network intrusion detection, October 2016
7. Eesa, A.S., Sadiq, S., Hassan, M., Orman, Z.: Rule generation based on modified cuttlefish algorithm for intrusion detection S. Uludağ Univ. J. Faculty Eng. **26**(1), 253–268 (2021). https://doi.org/10.17482/uumfd.747078
8. Prentzas, J., Hatzilygeroudis, I.: Categorizing approaches combining rule-based and case-based reasoning. Expert. Syst. **24**(2), 97–122 (2007). https://doi.org/10.1111/j.1468-0394.2007.00423.x
9. Medsker, L.R., Bailey, D.L.: Models and guidelines for integrating expert systems and neural networks. In: Hybrid Architectures for Intelligent Systems, pp. 153–171 (2020). https://doi.org/10.1201/9781003068075-9
10. Dias, T., Oliveira, N., Sousa, N., Praça, I., Sousa, O.: A hybrid approach for an interpretable and explainable intrusion detection system. In: Lecture Notes in Networks and Systems, vol. 418 LNNS, pp. 1035–1045. Springer, Cham (2022). https://doi.org/10.1007/978-3-030-96308-8_96/COVER
11. Dash, B., Farheen Ansari, M., Sharma, P., Ali, A.: Threats and opportunities with AI-based cyber security intrusion detection: a review. Int. J. Softw. Eng. Appl. (IJSEA) **13**(5), 2022. https://doi.org/10.5121/ijsea.2022.13502
12. Sadiku, M.N.O., Fagbohungbe, O.I., Musa, S.M., Perry, R.G.: Artificial intelligence in cyber security. Int. J. Eng. Res. Adv. Technol. https://doi.org/10.31695/IJERAT.2020.3612
13. Smith, G.: The intelligent solution: automation, the skills shortage and cyber-security. Comp. Fraud Secur. **2018**(8), 6–9 (2018). https://doi.org/10.1016/S1361-3723(18)30073-3
14. Zhang, Z., al Hamadi, H., Damiani, E., Yeun, C.Y., Taher, F.: Explainable artificial intelligence applications in cyber security: state-of-the-art in research. IEEE Access **10**, 93104–93139 (2022). https://doi.org/10.1109/ACCESS.2022.3204051
15. Wang, M., Zheng, K., Yang, Y., Wang, X.: An explainable machine learning framework for intrusion detection systems. IEEE Access **8**, 73127–73141 (2020). https://doi.org/10.1109/ACCESS.2020.2988359
16. Fayyad, U., Piatetsky-Shapiro, G., Smyth, P.: From data mining to knowledge discovery in databases. AI Mag. **17**(3), 37 (1996). https://doi.org/10.1609/AIMAG.V17I3.1230
17. Mohan, L., Jain, S., Suyal, P., Kumar, A.: Data mining classification techniques for intrusion detection system. In: 2020 12th International Conference on Computational Intelligence and Communication Networks (CICN), Sep. 2020, pp. 351–355 (2020) https://doi.org/10.1109/CICN49253.2020.9242642
18. Cano, A., Zafra, A., Ventura, S.: An interpretable classification rule mining algorithm. Inf. Sci. (N Y) **240**, 1–20 (2013). https://doi.org/10.1016/J.INS.2013.03.038
19. Sharafaldin, I., Lashkari, A.H., Ghorbani, A.A.: Toward generating a new intrusion detection dataset and intrusion traffic characterization. In: ICISSP 2018 - Proceedings of the 4th International Conference on Information Systems Security and Privacy, vol. 2018-Janua, pp. 108–116 (2018). https://doi.org/10.5220/0006639801080116
20. García, S., Fernández, A., Luengo, J., Herrera, F.: A study of statistical techniques and performance measures for genetics-based machine learning: accuracy and interpretability. Soft. Comput. **13**(10), 959–977 (2009). https://doi.org/10.1007/s00500-008-0392-y
21. Lu, H., Setiono, R., Liu, H.: NeuroRule: a connectionist approach to data mining (2017)

22. Tsumoto, S.: Mining diagnostic rules from clinical databases using rough sets and medical diagnostic model. Inform. Sci. Inform. Comp. Sci. Intell. Syst. Appl. Int. J. **162**(2), 65–80 (2004). https://doi.org/10.1016/J.INS.2004.03.002

23. Vitorino, J., Andrade, R., Praça, I., Sousa, O., Maia, E.: A comparative analysis of machine learning techniques for IoT intrusion detection, pp. 191–207 (2022). https://doi.org/10.1007/978-3-031-08147-7_13

24. Pintelas, E., Livieris, I.E., Pintelas, P.: A grey-box ensemble model exploiting black-box accuracy and white-box intrinsic interpretability. Algorithms **13**(1), 17 (2020). https://doi.org/10.3390/a13010017

25. Gandhi, K.R., Karnan, M., Kannan, S.: Classification rule construction using particle swarm optimization algorithm for breast cancer data sets. In: 2010 International Conference on Signal Acquisition and Processing, ICSAP 2010, pp. 233–237 (2010). https://doi.org/10.1109/ICSAP.2010.58

26. Islam, N., Abu, Farid, T.: Crime Prediction Using Classification Rule Mining (2018)

27. Al-Diabat, M.: Arabic text categorization using classification rule mining. Appl. Math. Sci. **6**(81), 4033–4046 (2012)

28. Han, J., Kamber, M., Pei, J.: Data Mining. Concepts and Techniques, 3rd Edition (The Morgan Kaufmann Series in Data Management Systems) (2011)

29. Bo, L., Abbas, H.A., McKay, B.: Classification rule discovery with ant colony optimization. In: IEEE/WIC International Conference on Intelligent Agent Technology, 2003. IAT 2003, pp. 83–88 (2003) https://doi.org/10.1109/IAT.2003.1241052

30. Wang, Z., Feng, B.: Classification rule mining with an improved ant colony algorithm. In: Lecture Notes in Artificial Intelligence (Subseries of Lecture Notes in Computer Science), vol. 3339, pp. 357–367 (2004).https://doi.org/10.1007/978-3-540-30549-1_32

31. Wang, Z., Sun, X., Zhang, D.: Classification rule mining based on particle swarm optimization. In: Lecture Notes in Computer Science (including subseries Lecture Notes in Artificial Intelligence and Lecture Notes in Bioinformatics), vol. 4062 LNAI, pp. 436–441 (2006). https://doi.org/10.1007/11795131_63

32. Li, X., Qian, X., Wang, Z.: Classification rule mining using feature selection and genetic algorithm. In: PACIIA 2009 - 2009 2nd Asia-Pacific Conference on Computational Intelligence and Industrial Applications, vol. 2, pp. 107–110 (2009). https://doi.org/10.1109/PACIIA.2009.5406606

33. Tsang, C.-H., Kwong, S., Wang, H.: Genetic-fuzzy rule mining approach and evaluation of feature selection techniques for anomaly intrusion detection. Pattern Recogn. **40**(9), 2373–2391 (2007). https://doi.org/10.1016/j.patcog.2006.12.009

34. Dartigue, C., Jang, H.I., Zeng, W.: A new data-mining based approach for network intrusion detection. In: 2009 Seventh Annual Communication Networks and Services Research Conference, May 2009, pp. 372–377. https://doi.org/10.1109/CNSR.2009.64

35. Tavallaee, M., Bagheri, E., Lu, W., Ghorbani, A.A.: A Detailed Analysis of the KDD CUP 99 Data Set"

36. Almseidin, M., Alzubi, M., Kovacs, S., Alkasassbeh, M.: Evaluation of machine learning algorithms for intrusion detection system. In: 2017 IEEE 15th International Symposium on Intelligent Systems and Informatics (SISY), Sep. 2017, pp. 000277–000282. https://doi.org/10.1109/SISY.2017.8080566

37. Liu, H., Lang, B.: Machine learning and deep learning methods for intrusion detection systems: a survey. Appl. Sci. **9**(20), 4396 (2019). https://doi.org/10.3390/app9204396

38. Oliveira, N., Praça, I., Maia, E., Sousa, O.: Intelligent cyber attack detection and classification for network-based intrusion detection systems. Appl. Sci. **11**(4), 1674 (2021). https://doi.org/10.3390/app11041674

39. Carneiro, J., Oliveira, N., Sousa, N., Maia, E., Praça, I.: Machine learning for network-based intrusion detection systems: an analysis of the CIDDS-001 dataset (2022), pp. 148–158. https://doi.org/10.1007/978-3-030-86261-9_15

40. Hassan, M.M.M.: Current studies on intrusion detection system, genetic algorithm and fuzzy logic. Int. J. Distrib. Parallel Syst. (IJDPS) 4(2) (2013). https://doi.org/10.5121/ijdps.2013.4204

41. Abdalla, A.: Different methodologies in treating uncertainty. In: IMSCI 2018 - 12th International Multi-Conference on Society, Cybernetics and Informatics, Proceedings, vol. 1, no. July, pp. 59–64 (2018)

42. Jain, A., Pal Nandi, B.: Intuitionistic and neutrosophic fuzzy logic: basic concepts and applications. Stud. Comput. Intell. 827, 3–18 (2020). https://doi.org/10.1007/978-3-030-34135-0_1/COVER

43. Radwan, N., Senousy, M.B., Riad, A.E.D.M.: Neutrosophic logic approach for evaluating learning management systems. Neutrosophic Sets Syst. 11, 3–7 (2016)

44. Rivieccio, U.: Neutrosophic logics: prospects and problems. Fuzzy Sets Syst. 159(14), 1860–1868 (2008). https://doi.org/10.1016/j.fss.2007.11.011

45. Kavitha, B., Karthikeyan, D.S., Sheeba Maybell, P.: An ensemble design of intrusion detection system for handling uncertainty using Neutrosophic Logic Classifier. Knowl Based Syst. 28, 88–96 (2012). https://doi.org/10.1016/J.KNOSYS.2011.12.004

46. Gardin, F., Gautier, R., Goix, N., Ndiaye, B., Schertzer, J.-M.: Skope-Rules Algorithm. https://skope-rules.readthedocs.io/en/latest/. Accessed 30 Sep 2022

47. Loyola-Gonzalez, O.: Black-box vs. White-Box: understanding their advantages and weaknesses from a practical point of view. IEEE Access 7, 154096–154113 (2019). https://doi.org/10.1109/ACCESS.2019.2949286

48. Breiman, L.: Random forests. Mach. Learn. 45(1), 5–32 (2001). https://doi.org/10.1023/A:1010933404324

49. Ye, J.: Single valued neutrosophic cross-entropy for multicriteria decision making problems. Appl. Math. Model. 38(3), 1170–1175 (2014). https://doi.org/10.1016/J.APM.2013.07.020

50. Sharafaldin, I., Lashkai, A.H., Ghorbani, A.A.: IDS 2017 | Datasets | Research | Canadian Institute for Cybersecurity | UNB. Canadian Institute for Cybersecurity (2018). https://www.unb.ca/cic/datasets/ids-2017.html

51. Engelen, G., Rimmer, V., Joosen, W.: Troubleshooting an intrusion detection dataset: the CICIDS2017 case study. In: 2021 IEEE Security and Privacy Workshops (SPW), May 2021, pp. 7–12 (2021). https://doi.org/10.1109/SPW53761.2021.00009

52. Lanvin, M., Gimenez, P.-F., Han, Y., Majorczyk, F., Mé, L., Totel, E.: Errors in the CICIDS2017 dataset and the significant differences in detection performances it makes, pp. 1–16 (2023). https://hal.science/hal-03775466

Labeling NIDS Rules with MITRE ATT&CK Techniques Using ChatGPT

Nir Daniel[1,2]([envelope]) [ORCID], Florian Klaus Kaiser[3,4], Anton Dzega[1,2],
Aviad Elyashar[2,5] [ORCID], and Rami Puzis[1,2] [ORCID]

[1] Department of Software and Information Systems Engineering,
Ben-Gurion University, Beer-Sheva, Israel
[2] Cyber@BGU, Cyber Labs at Ben-Gurion University, Beer-Sheva, Israel
{nirdanie,dzega}@post.bgu.ac.il, aviadel2@ac.sce.ac.il, puzis@bgu.ac.il
[3] Institute for Industrial Production, Karlsruhe Institute of Technology, Karlsruhe,
Germany
florian-klaus.kaiser@kit.edu
[4] Institute of Information Security and Dependability,
Karlsruhe Institute of Technology, Karlsruhe, Germany
[5] Department of Computer Science, Shamoon College of Engineering,
Beer-Sheva, Israel

Abstract. A typical analyst spends much time and effort investigating
alerts from network intrusion detection systems (NIDS). Available NIDS
rules for enterprise and industrial control systems are not always accompanied by high-level explanations that allow for building valid hypotheses
about the attacker's techniques and intentions. The plethora of rules and
the lack of high-level information necessitates new automated methods
for alert enrichment. Large language models, such as ChatGPT, encompass a vast amount of knowledge, including cyber threat intelligence
such as ports and protocols (low-level) and MITRE ATT&CK techniques
(high-level). Despite being a very new technology, ChatGPT is increasingly used in order to automate processes that experts previously performed. In this paper, we explore the ability of ChatGPT to reason about
NIDS rules while labeling them with MITRE ATT&CK techniques. We
discuss prompt design and present results on ChatGPT-3.5, ChatGPT-4,
and a keyword-based approach. Our results indicate that both versions
of ChatGPT outperform a baseline that relies on a-priori frequencies of
the techniques. ChatGPT-3.5 is much more precise than ChatGPT-4,
with a little reduction in recall.

Keywords: Cyber threat intelligence · Alerts investigation · Natural
language processing

1 Introduction

Network Intrusion Detection and Prevention Systems (NIDS), such as Snort,
monitor network traffic and trigger alerts that need to be analyzed by security

Supported by the U.S.-Israel Energy Center managed by the Israel-U.S. Binational
Industrial Research and Development (BIRD) Foundation.

S. Katsikas et al. (Eds.): ESORICS 2023 Workshops, LNCS 14399, pp. 76–91, 2024.
https://doi.org/10.1007/978-3-031-54129-2_5

professionals to derive actionable insights into the current state of the ongoing attack. Diversity and a constantly growing number of attack procedures developed by perpetrators result in a plethora of rules operated by a typical NIDS. NIDS rules provide an efficient means of identifying specific attack procedures [3]. To mitigate the detected attacks a security analyst should construct valid hypotheses regarding the attacker's techniques and intentions [6]. However, a lack of links between Snort and comprehensive Cyber Threat Intelligence (CTI) requires the analyst significant skills, attention, and cybersecurity expertise to construct the hypotheses [15].

In order to reduce human effort and aid analysts to keep pace with malicious actors companies increasingly augment their security workflows with Artificial Intelligence (AI) methods [23]. Automation and scalability are the main advantages of AI when there is a need for timely insights derived from large volumes of security events. AI allows security professionals to devote more time to expert activities. In this paper, we utilize AI to enrich NIDS rules with relevant MITRE ATT&CK Techniques[1].

Today, rapidly developed Generative Pre-trained Transformers (GPT) aid in automating many processes formerly relying on human effort [16,28]. In this paper, we investigate the feasibility of using an open-accessible GPT to assist cyber security professionals. We use ChatGPT to automate the labeling of Snort rules with MITRE ATT&CK techniques, thereby suggesting information about the current state of a cyber attack.

Our main contributions are as follows:

- introduction of a workflow for employing a GPT to CTI labeling and generating an automated labeling procedure;
- evaluation of an open-accessible GPT on its potential to assist cyber security professionals by providing in-depth insights on cyber security.

Using ChatGPT for this task provides two main advantages: Firstly, it is possible to explain each technique suggestion. Explanations can be extremely beneficial, especially for new analysts with limited expertise in cybersecurity. Second, when using ChatGPT we utilize the knowledge base on which it is trained, which contains cyber-security knowledge from different data sources: incident reports, the MITRE ATT&CK framework, information on vulnerabilities, information on attack groups, etc.

While the labeling process takes place offline, its results can be used to aid the analyst during real-time attack incidents.

The rest of the paper is structured as follows. Section 2 gives relevant background. Section 3 presents related work. In Sect. 4 the method is presented. In Sect. 5 we evaluate the method. Section 6 contains a summary of the main insights and provides a research outlook.

---

[1] https://attack.mitre.org/.

2   Background

2.1   Cyber Threat Intelligence

CTI is a proactive measure of computer and network security [19], focusing on data collection and analysis in an effort of gaining useful insights on attacks, used for improving decision-making regarding the selection of appropriate defensive means [24]. According to Chismon et al. [4] CTI comprises insights that can be classified into four categories, depending on the focus and technical depth of the analysis:

- *Strategic CTI* is mainly addressed to a non-technical audience [8] and provides high-level information for the organization's board. Rather than being technical, it reflects the impact of cyber activity on the organization's state and the anticipated risks.
- *Operational CTI* details about impending attacks on the company, initially consumed by higher-level security staff, such as security managers or heads of incident response (IR) that are making day-to-day decisions. Most organizations do not have good operational CTI and in most cases, nations dominate the field.
- *Tactical CTI* is often referred to as Tactics, Techniques, and Procedures (TTPs) and describes information about how threat actors are conducting attacks. In order to test their methods of protection against such attacks, defenders and teams in Security Operation Centers (SOC) use tactical CTI.
- *Technical CTI* is information which considered more of a raw data, such as IP addresses or types of hash functions. This information needs to be used instantly as it can be changed frequently, and hence become useless in a short time.

Another categorization of CTI is given according to their source. Hereby two categories can be formed:

- Network-based CTI
- Non-network-based CTI

Especially the use of low-level CTI seems to be of practical use and a promising means of ensuring cyber security. Consistently, researchers (e.g., Daszczyszak et al. [5]) highlight CTI-based decision-making focusing on TTPs as an efficient means to improve decision-making in cybers security. The great potential is hereby inter alia based on its ability to enable greater levels of automation [10]. Threat Hunting (TH), Endpoint Detection and Response (EDR), or NIDS, for example, frequently take advantage of Technical or Tactical CTI (e.g., Indicators of Compromise - IoCs) [10]. Taken together, CTI is essential for organizations to gain visibility of the threat landscape, timely identification of attacks and the TTPs confronted with, as well as effectively respond to an attack [14] and can therefore be seen as an essential means in strengthening cyber-security within a corporation.

MITRE ATT&CK provides a curated knowledge base and model of cyber adversary behavior, incorporating a detailed understanding of the various phases of an adversary's attack life cycle and the platforms they have been known to attack [26]. According to Strom et al. [26], ATT&CK focuses on the way in which external adversaries compromise and operate within computer networks. MITRE ATT&CK hereby represents a comprehensive database on Tactical CTI, meaning that the database covers post-compromise adversary TTPs against Windows and Linux systems as well as macOS. Moreover, it also covers different technology-related domains, such as enterprise systems, mobile devices, cloud-based systems, and Industrial Control Systems (ICS). As of April 2023, MITRE ATT&CK describes 193 attack techniques and 401 sub-techniques, which belong to 27 different attack tactics for Enterprise, and 79 techniques which belong to 12 tactics for ICS.

Snort[2] is a lightweight NIDS based on Libpcap, which has fast packet filtering capabilities [20]. Snort describes single-line rules, that can be read, understood, and modified easily [11]. According to Khamphakdee et al. [11] Snort rules are divided into two logical parts (see Fig. 1):

- the header part, which consists of the fields: Action, Protocol, Source Address, Source Port, Direction, Destination Address, and Destination Port,
- the rules options part, which is found between a pair of parentheses and contains a list of keyword and argument pairs, separated by a colon.

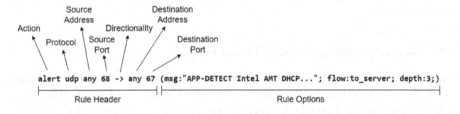

Fig. 1. Snort rule example

2.2 Generative Pre-trained Transformers

As one of the most sophisticated language models, this work relies on the use of GPT-4[3] taking advantage of the advanced reasoning capabilities of the model compared to its competitors. Several works have been conducted since the release of GPT-4 in order to automate processes that were previously performed by experts, in different fields. Törnberg [28] conducted a study that showed GPT-4

---

[2] https://www.snort.org/.
[3] https://openai.com/gpt-4.

outperforms both experts and crowd workers in the task of annotating political Twitter messages. Compared to human classifiers, GPT-4 achieved higher accuracy, higher reliability, and lower bias. Törnberg [28] also mentioned that GPT-4 is capable of annotating messages based on contextual knowledge and inferences about an author's intentions - both of which are traditionally regarded as uniquely human abilities. ChatGPT also concerns cyber security experts [27] and is frequently considered relevant for its use as a means of automating offensive actions (e.g. in generating sophisticated phishing mails). For example, Tod-Răileanu et al. [27] highlighted that ChatGPT gains growing attention from threat actors, it even mentioned that ChatGPT was used in various types of attacks. However, the fact that ChatGPT has general knowledge in the field of cyber security suggests that it may also be useful as a defensive means in cyber security. ChatGPT is hereby considered to contribute to automating processes and has the potential of support experts in different fields. In this study we will test the applicability of ChatGPT in performing cyber security experts' tasks with regard to the maintenance of an up to date CTI knowledge base and more specifically with regard to its potential to come up with reasonable attack techniques labels of NIDS rules.

3   Related Work on Language Models for CTI Labeling

The increasing capabilities of language models lead to rising adoption in different fields. Due to the high volume and speed of CTI sharing, automation of labeling can be considered a necessary means for staying on top of potential perpetrators of cyber attacks.

3.1   Non-networking-based CTI Labeling

Husari et al. [9] present TTPDrill, an automatic and accurate, context-aware method for extracting TTPs from unstructured text, it achieved more than 0.82 of precision and recall. As part of the extraction process, TTPDrill uses a text-mining approach that combines natural language processing and Information Retrieval (IR). Another tool for extracting ATT&CK tactics and techniques from reports named rcATT is introduced in Legoy et al. [12]. This tool is based on multi-class multi-label classifiers, trained on at least 80 reports mapped to TTPs, which are publicly available on MITRE ATT&CK. Mendsaikhan et al. [18] adopt the multi-label classification approach on a different CTI source. The work describes the extraction of vectors from vulnerability descriptions and the use of multi-layer perception as a base classifier for linking those vectors to adversary techniques. The training and evaluation were performed on a data set prepared by The European Union Agency for Cybersecurity (ENISA), containing mappings of Common Vulnerabilities and Exposures (CVE) to techniques, CVE is an industry standard for describing common vulnerabilities [29]. The proposed approach reaches an accuracy score of 0.7432. The above methods are providing a good basis for techniques extraction from reports. Extractor [22] furthermore is capable of extracting attack behaviors as provenance graphs from unstructured text. TIM [30], represents a threat context-enhanced TTP intelligence mining framework operating on unstructured data. It gains an accuracy of 0.941. However, it only supports six MITRE ATT&CK techniques. With AttacKG Li et al. [13] introduced a similar tool that extracts techniques from reports. It is superior to both TTPDrill and Extractor and provides a comparable technique knowledge graph as Extractor. Additionally, it is superior compared to Extractor by its ability to aggregate attack knowledge from multiple CTI reports. The most recent work on the extraction of TTPs from reports is TTPHunter [21] which targets APT reports. This work outperforms both rcATT and AttacKG while supporting 50 TTP classes.

All of the above methods share one major disadvantage - they are operating on offline CTI sources - reports, which limits their usage in real-time security processes, such as TH. In addition, the above methods are intended for unstructured text, so it is unclear how they will perform on structured CTI sources, such as NIDS rules.

3.2   Networking-Based CTI Labeling

According to McPhee [17], approaches for network-based detection of ATT&CK techniques based on network sensors, are focused only on Windows-specific protocols, and do not cover different types of systems (e.g., ICS). For this purpose, McPhee [17] demonstrated the use of the network monitoring system Zeek[4] for the detection of techniques in those environments. While this can be very useful, his approach involved manually defining the detection method for each individual technique, which requires expert knowledge and is a time-consuming task. Bagui et al. [2] also relies on the use of Zeek. Within the work, a network data set is crafted. Furthermore, the data set is labelled using the MITRE ATT&CK framework. This work is based on already labelled mission logs and does not describe the process of labeling it. In addition, 99.97% of the malicious traffic in the data set was identified as related to reconnaissance techniques. RADAR [25] can identify malicious behavior in network traffic. As part of its methodology, it detects TTPs from network traffic using both feature-based and heuristic-based detection rules. One of RADAR's limitations is that the feature-based rules are generated manually for every technique the system needs to support, which results in a small number of techniques currently supported by the system - only 17 techniques. Gjerstad [7] highlights the lack and motivates the generation of labeled data sets. The work presents an approach for labeling network data sets using MITRE CALDERA, a tool developed for experts to test the security of their systems. The approach is based on matching techniques already labeled in the CALDERA reports to attack traffic generated by simulations. To the best of our knowledge, the only work which specifically targets ICS environments is Arafune et al. [1]. They developed an automated TH, which detects attacks in network traffic using open-source tools. In their approach, they are linking

---

[4] https://zeek.org/.

network traffic to attack techniques, however, their method is signature-based, meaning that a human analyst still needs to perform the work of labeling at least one time for each signature, in order to be able to identify the techniques matching that signature. Lin et al. [15] propose a mechanism for linking NIDS rules to 12 attack tactics using text mining and machine learning, in order to aid experts during the threat-hunting process. Their method achieved an F1 score of over 0.9 and up to 0.96, which is superior to other TTP labeling tools, such as rcATT. However, it should be noted that labeling rules with tactics is easier than labeling rules with techniques, since currently, there are only 27 tactics, whereas there are at least 193 techniques (see Sect. 2.1).

Despite there is a plethora of different tools for labeling CTI, only a quite limited set of methods is focused on linking NIDS rules to TTPs. Furthermore, our work distinguishes itself from related work by relying on pre-trained and open-access language models and including explanations for each mapping.

4   Labeling NIDS Rules with MITRE ATT&CK Techniques

Figure 2 provides an overview of the rule labeling method. Each rule is labeled with techniques using two main methods: GPT-based labeling, and keyword-based labeling. The GPT-based labeling combines two methods - questioning ChatGPT while providing it the list of MITRE ATT&CK techniques, and questioning ChatGPT without providing it the list.

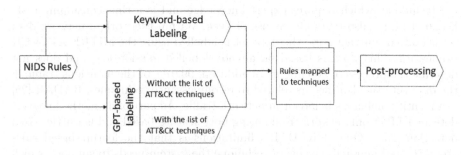

Fig. 2. Overview of the rule mapping approach

4.1   GPT-Based Labeling

Some rules do not explicitly refer to techniques, labeling those rules with techniques requires an in-depth analysis and understanding of the rules, as well as knowledge in different topics in cyber security. This method uses ChatGPT's capabilities to understand an NIDS rule as a whole. Using ChatGPT, we are able to explain each label, as well as utilize the knowledge base it is trained on, which includes knowledge of previous cyber security incidents.

Our GPT-based labeling method consists of two parts: questioning ChatGPT without providing it with the list of MITRE ATT&CK techniques, and questioning ChatGPT while providing it with the list of MITRE ATT&CK techniques. The exact prompts we used within this publication can be derived from the Appendix.

Questioning Without the List of Techniques (WLT): In this part of the method, ChatGPT is not guided towards specific fields of the rule, nor is it provided with any other information except the format of the answer. Additionally, we wish to provide the analyst with as accurate results as possible. Therefore, we request ChatGPT to categorize the techniques it provides into two categories. The first category contains techniques that are recognized as directly related to the rule, based on the type of data the rule detects. The second category contains techniques that are recognized as related indirectly to the rule, this can be based on the knowledge of ChatGPT on different subjects, such as unique actions that specific APT can perform, past experience, etc.

Questioning with the List of Techniques (LT): This iteration is intended to ensure that ChatGPT did not miss any important techniques. By providing ChatGPT with the complete list of MITRE ATT&CK techniques, we ensure that it is aware of all the techniques that exist, even if some of them appear infrequently in its knowledge base. During this part of the method, ChatGPT is asked the same question as in the previous part, with an addition at the beginning of the prompt that presents the current list of all MITRE ATT&CK techniques.

4.2   Keyword-Based Labeling (*KB*)

Often, the technique's names explicitly appear within the message field in Snort rules. However, ChatGPT tends to miss these techniques and focus on other related techniques. In these cases, the techniques can easily be identified without using ChatGPT. The KB method will label each rule with the techniques of which their names explicitly appear within the rule. For example, for every rule which contains the string "rootkit" in the message field, the KB method will label the rule with the technique Rootkit (T1014), as the string "rootkit" is the full name of technique T1014. The list of technique names the KB method uses can be derived from the repository[5].

---

[5] https://github.com/NirDaniel/Labeling-NIDS-Rules-with-MITRE-ATT-CK-Techniques-using-ChatGPT.git.

4.3   Post-processing

ChatGPT is trained on data until September 2021, which introduces a challenge as MITRE ATT&CK is consistently updated and techniques names and IDs are sometimes changed. Therefore, we perform post-processing which involves matching between the techniques ChatGPT outputted, and the most updated version of MITRE ATT&CK. As an example, the techniques Spearphishing Link (T1192) and Spearphishing Attachment (T1193) appeared in ChatGPT's answers, but in the most recent version of ATT&CK, these techniques have been added as sub-techniques under Phishing (T1566), whose IDs are T1566.002 and T1566.001. In addition, some techniques previously contained in ATT&CK were removed, then removing them from ChatGPT's answers is important to evaluate the method properly (see Sect. 5). Duplicate techniques are also removed during the post-processing phase. As we perform a few techniques labeling iterations in our method (Keyword-based and GPT-based), specific techniques may appear more than once, therefore it is important to remove these duplicates.

5   Evaluation

5.1   Evaluation Set

The evaluation process required us to define a set of ground truth mappings between NIDS rules and MITRE ATT&CK techniques. For this purpose, we extracted all Snort rules from the official repository, that provide a direct reference to MITRE ATT&CK techniques. A total of 162 annotated rules were extracted by manually examining the relationships between the rules and the referenced techniques. In the evaluation set, there are an average of 1.38 technique mappings per rule, out of a total of 30 unique techniques that are present in the entire evaluation set.

5.2   Performance Metrics

For evaluating our method, we are calculating the precision, recall and F1-score values for each rule, and averaging those values across rules.

$$Precision = \frac{TP}{TP + FP} \tag{1}$$

$$Recall = \frac{TP}{TP + FN} \tag{2}$$

$$F1 - score = \frac{2 \times Precision \times Recall}{Precision + Recall} \tag{3}$$

where TP are the true positives as the number of techniques labeled correctly, FN are false negatives describing the number of techniques not labeled by the method but are actually labeled according to the ground truth, and FP as false positives describing the number of techniques labeled by the method but are not labeled according to the ground truth.

5.3   Experimental Setup

For each NIDS rule in our evaluation set, we ask ChatGPT to label the rule from the 193 MITRE ATT&CK techniques. Furthermore, the evaluation is done for the KB method, as well as for the GPT-based association (LT and WLT). We perform the evaluation of the proposed GPT-based rule association approach based on ChatGPT-3.5 and ChatGPT-4. For both versions of ChatGPT, we run the labeling twice, where we apply the rule labeling with the WLT method, and another iteration where we use the LT method. As all approaches do have their specific pros and work best for labeling specific rules, we propose to unify the results to get the best out of each approach. Given the average number of labeled techniques within the evaluation set is quite low and we ask to label each rule from 193 techniques, the task is a hard problem i.e., randomly selecting the average number of linked techniques would basically come down to a recall of < 0.01. We compare rule labeling using ChatGPT to a frequency-based (FB) baseline which chooses the most common techniques regardless of the rule's content. For every number n of techniques between 1 and 30 (the number of techniques that exist in the evaluation set), we calculate precision and recall values for the approach of choosing the n-most frequent techniques.

5.4   Results

Figure 3 shows the precision and recall values for the rule labeling methods that we evaluated. Every point in the figure represents a combination of methods (KB, LT, and WLT). The different series represent ChatGPT versions. Green point refers to the keyword-based labeling (not using ChatGPT), red points refer to ChatGPT-3.5, blue points refer to ChatGPT-4, grey points refer to the FB baseline (not using ChatGPT). Similar combinations of methods applied to different ChatGPT versions are connected by a thin line to highlight the Precision-Recall trade-off.

All the different combinations of labeling methods perform better than the FB baseline. For the methods that do not include LT, ChatGPT-3.5 is always superior to ChatGPT-4. However, when the LT method is combined, there is a trade-off between precision and recall, and ChatGPT-4 achieves a better recall. In addition, it is always beneficial to combine the KB method, as it enhances both precision and recall.

Table 1 presents the precision, recall, and F1-score values for the various combinations of rule labeling methods.

The optimal F1-score value of the FB baseline is achieved by selecting the eight most frequent techniques in the evaluation set. The highest recall value is highlighted in Table 1 and is achieved by the combination of all three methods (WLT, LT, and KB) when using ChatGPT-4. Naturally, the KB method gained the highest precision value of one, as it detects explicitly mentioned technique names inside the rule and, therefore, never generates false positives. The second highest precision value is also highlighted and is achieved by ChatGPT-3.5 using the combination of two approaches, WLT and KB. The highest F1-score is also achieved by ChatGPT-3.5 using the WLT+KB method.

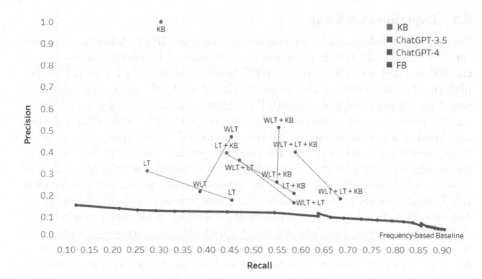

Fig. 3. Precision and recall

Table 1. Average Precision, Recall and F1-score values of each method.

Model	Method	Precision	Recall	F1-score
	FB baseline	0.117	0.637	0.191
	KB	1	0.304	0.304
ChatGPT-3.5	WLT	0.471	0.453	0.433
	WLT + KB	**0.514**	0.553	**0.492**
	LT	0.313	0.275	0.285
	LT + KB	0.396	0.443	0.397
	WLT + LT	0.363	0.47	0.382
	WLT + LT + KB	0.4	0.588	0.437
ChatGPT-4	WLT	0.218	0.387	0.247
	WLT + KB	0.263	0.549	0.317
	LT	0.179	0.454	0.241
	LT + KB	0.21	0.585	0.29
	WLT + LT	0.167	0.585	0.241
	WLT + LT + KB	0.185	**0.684**	0.271

5.5 Discussion

Comparing the different methods, KB labeling is able to label solely those techniques that are explicitly named within the rule. This approach is favorable in terms of precision generating no false positives. However, it is not able to provide an understanding and deeper analysis of the rules. The labeling of rules following

KB labeling furthermore focuses on a small set of techniques, e.g., brute force or rootkit.

GPT-based labeling is strong in providing deeper reasoning capabilities but misses obvious, i.e. explicitly named techniques in some cases. By providing a deeper understanding of the rule ChatGPT proposes reasonable labels to techniques. Furthermore, our implementation provides insights into those labels by presenting quotes on the rule (see Fig. 4).

```
1    {
2        "sid": 635,
3        "Technique id": "T1046",
4        "Technique name": "Network Service Discovery",
5        "Categorization": 1,
6        "Quotes": ["INDICATOR-SCAN XTACACS logout", "alert
             udp $EXTERNAL_NET any -> $HOME_NET 49"],
7        "Explanation": "The rule monitors for UDP traffic on
             port 49 which is associated with XTACACS, a
             network protocol used for remote administration.
             The 'INDICATOR-SCAN XTACACS logout' in the
             message indicates that the rule is designed to
             detect scanning activities, which is a clear sign
             of the Network Service Discovery technique (
             T1046)."
8    }
```

Fig. 4. ChatGPT example answer

We observe that ChatGPT-4 is more capable of performing the selection task of choosing between different provided techniques than ChatGPT-3.5. Providing the list of techniques to ChatGPT-3.5 (LT) is observed to worsen the results of the labeling, the decrease in recall might be explained by increasing the focus on selecting from the full set of techniques, rather than being biased towards more common techniques.

Comparing the different versions of ChatGPT, the results show that ChatGPT-4 achieved lower precision values and therefore also lower F1-score values than ChatGPT-3.5 consistently, this is due to the fact that ChatGPT-4 proposes on average more techniques labels than ChatGPT-3.5. This might be due to ChatGPT-4 having a larger limit on its answer size, compared to ChatGPT-3.5.

The experimental results show that ChatGPT-4 achieves better recall than ChatGPT-3.5 for labeling NIDS rules with ATT&CK techniques on the expanse of precision. The labels provided by ChatGPT-3.5 focus on more common techniques. Compared to that, ChatGPT-4 aims at providing more insightful results. While the labels provided by ChatGPT-4 seem to be insightful, it oftentimes misses the ground truth techniques for providing related techniques.

The results of the evaluation show interesting insights on the possibility of conducting automated labeling of NIDS rules with MITRE ATT&CK techniques. These labels can provide insights to security analysts and might be useful during alerts investigation.

6   Conclusions and Future Work

Within this work, we presented a proof of concept of using ChatGPT to label NIDS rules with ATT&CK techniques, while proposing the relevant prompt design. We evaluated both ChatGPT-3.5 and ChatGPT-4 with prompts containing (LT) or omitting (WLT) the list of techniques. Interestingly, providing ChatGPT-3.5 with the list of techniques weakened the results, whereas providing the list to ChatGPT-4 improved the results. Unifying the labels produced with the LT and WLT methods improved the recall with negligible reduction in precision in most cases. Furthermore, unifying ChatGPT results with keyword-based labeling improves both precision and recall. The evaluation results present promising insights into the feasibility of using ChatGPT to automate the labeling of NIDS rules with MITRE ATT&CK techniques.

The automation of the labeling process can aid junior analysts with limited experience in cyber security during alerts investigation. The explanations provided by ChatGPT for each mapping are also beneficial since they assist the analyst in understanding the rationale for each labeling. Providing security experts with those additional means can also be beneficial during the performance of other cyber security processes, such as threat-hunting.

The scope of the current work is limited to ChatGPT. Assessment using other large language models, as well as training specialized supervised models for this task, are important since ChatGPT is not open source. Future work may also combine large language models with classic supervised machine learning to label NIDS rules with MITRE ATT&CK Techniques or even use zero-shot classification to associate the rules with arbitrary CTI. Fine-tuning the language models to comprehend the syntax of Snort and Suricata rules can further increase the accuracy of the approach proposed in this paper.

A   Appendix: Chat-GPT Prompt Templates

- **ChatGPT-Prompt for the WLT method**
  "You are going to receive a Snort rule and your task is to find as many MITRE ATT&CK techniques as possible that are associated with the rule.
  Note: You should categorize the techniques to 1 or 2. Technique of type 1 is a technique that you can associate with the rule directly based on the rule. Technique of type 2 is a technique that can be associated with the rule indirectly, based on your knowledge and understanding. The categorization value should be the value 1 or 2, based on the explanation given above. The quotes field value should contain quotes from the rules data that are relevant to the technique mapped and they are the main reason you believe the

mapping to this technique is correct. The explanation's value should be your explanation for why you decided to give the technique and how it is associated with the rule. The technique id should be the official MITRE technique id. For each technique include the following information as JSON: sid, Technique id, Technique name, Categorization, Quotes, Explanation. After each rule I will provide you with, answer according to the provided format. Please do not write anything else but the JSON.
Rule: {Snort rule}"

– **ChatGPT-Prompt for the LT method**
"I will provide you with some knowledge now on MITRE ATT&CK techniques, then you are going to receive a task, you may use the knowledge below to perform the task:
{List of MITRE ATT&CK techniques IDs and names}.
You are going to receive a Snort rule and your task is to find as many MITRE ATT&CK techniques as possible that are associated with the rule.
Note: You should categorize the techniques to 1 or 2. Technique of type 1 is a technique that you can associate with the rule directly based on the rule. Technique of type 2 is a technique that can be associated with the rule indirectly, based on your knowledge and understanding. The categorization value should be the value 1 or 2, based on the explanation given above. The quotes field value should contain quotes from the rules data that are relevant to the technique mapped and they are the main reason you believe the mapping to this technique is correct. The explanation's value should be your explanation for why you decided to give the technique and how it is associated with the rule. The technique id should be the official MITRE technique id. For each technique include the following information as JSON: sid, Technique id, Technique name, Categorization, Quotes, Explanation. After each rule I will provide you with, answer according to the provided format. Please do not write anything else but the JSON.
Rule: {Snort rule}"

References

1. Arafune, M., et al.: Design and development of automated threat hunting in industrial control systems. In: 2022 IEEE International Conference on Pervasive Computing and Communications Workshops and other Affiliated Events (PerCom Workshops), pp. 618–623. IEEE (2022)
2. Bagui, S.S., et al.: Introducing UWF-ZeekData22: a comprehensive network traffic dataset based on the MITRE ATT&CK framework. Data **8**(1), 18 (2023)
3. Chakrabarti, S., Chakraborty, M., Mukhopadhyay, I.: Study of snort-based IDS. In: Proceedings of the International Conference and Workshop on Emerging Trends in Technology, pp. 43–47 (2010)
4. Chismon, D., Ruks, M.: Threat intelligence: collecting, analysing, evaluating. MWR InfoSecurity Ltd. **3**(2), 36–42 (2015)
5. Daszczyszak, R., Ellis, D., Luke, S., Whitley, S.: Ttp-based Hunting. Tech. rep, MITRE CORP MCLEAN VA (2019)

6. Elitzur, A., Puzis, R., Zilberman, P.: Attack hypothesis generation. In: 2019 European Intelligence and Security Informatics Conference (EISIC), pp. 40–47. IEEE (2019)
7. Gjerstad, J.L.: Generating labelled network datasets of APT with the MITRE CALDERA framework, Master's thesis (2022)
8. Haddad, A., Aaraj, N., Nakov, P., Mare, S.F.: Automated mapping of CVE vulnerability records to MITRE CWE weaknesses. arXiv preprint arXiv:2304.11130 (2023)
9. Husari, G., Al-Shaer, E., Ahmed, M., Chu, B., Niu, X.: Ttpdrill: automatic and accurate extraction of threat actions from unstructured text of CTI sources. In: Proceedings of the 33rd Annual Computer Security Applications Conference, pp. 103–115 (2017)
10. Kaiser, F.K., et al.: Attack hypotheses generation based on threat intelligence knowledge graph. IEEE Trans. Dependable Secure Comput. **20**, 4793–4809 (2023)
11. Khamphakdee, N., Benjamas, N., Saiyod, S.: Improving intrusion detection system based on Snort rules for network probe attack detection. In: 2014 2nd International Conference on Information and Communication Technology (ICoICT), pp. 69–74. IEEE (2014)
12. Legoy, V., Caselli, M., Seifert, C., Peter, A.: Automated retrieval of ATT&CK tactics and techniques for cyber threat reports. arXiv preprint arXiv:2004.14322 (2020)
13. Li, Z., Zeng, J., Chen, Y., Liang, Z.: Attackg: Constructing technique knowledge graph from cyber threat intelligence reports. In: Atluri, V., Di Pietro, R., Jensen, C.D., Meng, W. (eds.) Computer Security – ESORICS 2022. ESORICS 2022. Lecture Notes in Computer Science, vol. 13554, pp. 589–609. Springer, Cham (2022). https://doi.org/10.1007/978-3-031-17140-6_29
14. Liao, X., Yuan, K., Wang, X., Li, Z., Xing, L., Beyah, R.: Acing the IOC game: toward automatic discovery and analysis of open-source cyber threat intelligence. In: Proceedings of the 2016 ACM SIGSAC Conference on Computer and Communications Security, pp. 755–766 (2016)
15. Lin, S.X., Li, Z.J., Chen, T.Y., Wu, D.J.: Attack tactic labeling for cyber threat hunting. In: 2022 24th International Conference on Advanced Communication Technology (ICACT), pp. 34–39. IEEE (2022)
16. Long, C., et al.: Evaluating ChatGPT4 in Canadian otolaryngology-head and neck surgery board examination using the CVSA model. medRxiv pp. 2023–05 (2023)
17. McPhee, M.: Methods to employ zeek in detecting MITRE ATT&CK techniques, Tech. Rep. (2020)
18. Mendsaikhan, O., Hasegawa, H., Yamaguchi, Y., Shimada, H.: Automatic mapping of vulnerability information to adversary techniques. In: The Fourteenth International Conference on Emerging Security Information, Systems and Technologies SECUREWARE2020 (2020)
19. Palacin, V.: Practical Threat Intelligence and Data-driven Threat Hunting. Packt Publishing (2021)
20. Peng, Y., Wang, H.: Design and implementation of network instruction detection system based on snort and NTOP. In: 2012 International Conference on Systems and Informatics (ICSAI2012), pp. 116–120. IEEE (2012)
21. Rani, N., Saha, B., Maurya, V., Shukla, S.K.: TTPHunter: automated extraction of actionable intelligence as TTPs from narrative threat reports. In: Proceedings of the 2023 Australasian Computer Science Week, pp. 126–134 (2023)

22. Satvat, K., Gjomemo, R., Venkatakrishnan, V.: Extractor: extracting attack behavior from threat reports. In: 2021 IEEE European Symposium on Security and Privacy (EuroS&P), pp. 598–615. IEEE (2021)
23. Sentonas, M.: Crowdstrike introduces Charlotte AI, generative AI security analyst - crowdstrike (2023). https://www.crowdstrike.com/blog/crowdstrike-introduces-charlotte-ai-to-deliver-generative-ai-powered-cybersecurity/
24. Shackleford, D.: Who's using cyberthreat intelligence and how. SANS Institute (2015)
25. Sharma, Y., Birnbach, S., Martinovic, I.: Radar: Effective network-based malware detection based on the MITRE ATT&CK framework. arXiv preprint arXiv:2212.03793 (2022)
26. Strom, B.E., Applebaum, A., Miller, D.P., Nickels, K.C., Pennington, A.G., Thomas, C.B.: MITRE ATT&CK®: Design and philosophy (2020)
27. Tod-Răileanu, G., Axinte, S.D.: ChatGPT-information security overview. In: International Conference on Cybersecurity and Cybercrime, vol. 10 (2023)
28. Törnberg, P.: Chatgpt-4 outperforms experts and crowd workers in annotating political twitter messages with zero-shot learning. arXiv preprint arXiv:2304.06588 (2023)
29. Vulnerabilities, C.: Common vulnerabilities and exposures (2005). https://www.cve.org/About/Metrics
30. You, Y., et al.: TIM: threat context-enhanced TTP intelligence mining on unstructured threat data. Cybersecurity 5(1), 3 (2022)

User Behavior Analysis for Malware Detection

Valentina Dumitrasc[1] and René Serral-Gracià[2]([✉]) [iD]

[1] FSP Consulting Services, Reading, UK
tina.dumitrasc@fsp.co
[2] BarcelonaTech, Barcelona, Spain
rene.serral@upc.edu

Abstract. The rise in cyber-attacks and cyber-crime is causing more and more organizations and individuals to consider the correct implementation of their security systems. The consequences of a security breach can be devastating, ranging from loss of public confidence to bankruptcy. Traditional techniques for detecting and stopping malware rely on building a database of known signatures using known samples of malware. However, these techniques are not very effective at detecting zero-day exploits because there are no samples in their malware signature databases.

To address this challenge, our work proposes a novel approach to malware detection using machine learning techniques. Our solution provides a two-fold contribution, on the one hand, our training the model does not require any kind of malware, as it creates a user profile using only normal user behavior data, detecting malware by identifying deviations from this profile. On the other hand, as we shall see, our solution is able to dynamically train the model using only six sessions to minimize false positives. As a consequence, our model can quickly and effectively detect zero-day malware and other unknown threats without previous knowledge.

The proposed approach is evaluated using real-world datasets, and different machine learning algorithms are compared to evaluate their performance in detecting unknown threats. The results show that the proposed approach is effective in detecting malware, achieving high accuracy and low false positive rates.

Keywords: Machine Learning · Malware detection · User Behavior Analysis · Autoencoder

1 Introduction

The increase in cyber-attacks is a growing concern for individuals, organizations and governments as it leads to several problems, including: security breaches,

This work was partially funded by IRIS Artificial Intelligence Threat Reporting and Incident Response System (H2020-101021727).

S. Katsikas et al. (Eds.): ESORICS 2023 Workshops, LNCS 14399, pp. 92–110, 2024.
https://doi.org/10.1007/978-3-031-54129-2_6

financial losses, reputational damage, disruption to business operations and threats to critical infrastructure. This highlights the need for organizations to implement robust cybersecurity measures to protect against cyber attacks and minimise the risks associated with them.

Cybercrimes are constantly increasing. For example in 2020 [7], malware attacks increased 358% compared to 2019. From here, cyber attacks globally increased by 125% through 2021, while increasing volumes of such attacks continued to threaten businesses and individuals during 2022.

Apart from this increase in cyber-attacks, it is important to notice that these are normally focused on endpoints, such as computers, laptops, smartphones, etc. The reason behind this is that they are seen as the weakest link in an organization's security as they may have less security measures than other parts of the network, while providing a door for expanding to other assets of the victim, such as servers. By compromising an endpoint, attackers can steal sensitive information or spread malware to other parts of the network. Therefore it is important to detect a compromised device as soon as possible. This can be achieved through the deployment of intrusion detection systems, which focus on detecting multiple types of malware. Despite of this, none of them is fully prepared to detect new or unknown threats.

Nowadays, detecting malware relies on analyzing known malware code and behavior to build a database of signatures. But this approach has become limited in identifying new, quickly-evolving polymorphic and metamorphic malware, making it difficult to keep the database updated.

In order to mitigate this, we propose a novel Machine Learning based solution that is able to detect malware threats by modeling user behavior. In more detail, our proposal provides, as a first novelty, a solution which does not need actual malware samples or infected systems, on the contrary, we provide a real implementation of a system able to understand and profile user behavior, to then monitor, detect deviations and flag anomalous system behavior.

As a second contribution of this work, our model is able to converge to proper detection rates with a very short training period, which in most times is below 6 h, providing, as we will discuss later, very high accuracy in our real world testing scenario.

When dealing with machine learning models, the testing and the obtained results need to be trustworthy, as there is no perfect way to validate its full accuracy. To mitigate this uncertainty we installed our prototype in a couple of machines, which were used by real users in their day-to-day work and leisure time, in such an environment, we started gathering data for training, later in the process, we infected the machines with real malware and validated its proper detection.

The rest of the paper is structured as follows, in Sect. 2 we discuss about the related work and similar solutions found in the literature, later on, in Sect. 3 we outline our general solution and its architecture. Then, in Sect. 4 we dig into our Machine Learning model and evaluate its internal workings. This leads to our evaluation and analysis of the obtained solution in our real world scenario in Sect. 5. We finally conclude in Sect. 6 with a summary of our findings and outline of our future work.

2 Related Work

Historically, malware was analyzed by directly getting the malware binary file and analyzing its contents, this was, and still is, done mainly through Static and Dynamic code analysis. This approach, albeit if useful to understand how the malware works and to generate signatures [4] that allow fast and efficient malware detection, has been found unsuitable to detect the newest malware types present nowadays, such malware normally uses polymorphism or other well-known techniques to change its payload, thus rendering the signature matching unusable.

To overcome this limitation, malware analysis experts have devised other mechanisms for malware analysis, one of the most used has been Heuristic-based malware detection [10]. A technique based on identifying the characteristics and behavior of a piece of binary code, it relies on setting up a set of rules and heuristics to classify programs as malicious or non-malicious. The huge advantage of this solution over signature based detection is the fact that it allows the detection of polymorphic malware on top of the detection of previously unknown malware, i.e., 0-days. Despite of the benefits these solutions tend to have a relatively high rate of false positives due to the diversity of malware and legitimate applications.

On a different scope, we have observed other solutions, e.g., [6], that have decided to use a Machine Learning approach to malware analysis and detection, the outcomes of such alternatives is a better accuracy than Heuristic based detection.

All the discussed solutions so far are what is called malware centric, where the detection is based on the analysis of malware signatures, or in some cases on its behavior. Opposed to this, our approach, takes malware detection to a different level. Instead of focusing on a malware-centric approach, our contribution focuses on a user-centric approach in which user behavior is modeled into a profile, we leverage information such as system, network or file activities. Then, our model detects deviations from a baseline that could indicate malware. An important benefit of this approach is that our user-centric solution does not require any prior knowledge of a specific malware's behavior or signature. We solely rely on the user's normal behavior as a baseline.

The idea behind this technique is that normally when system's vulnerabilities are exploited, an abnormal use of the system is observed. As a result, abnormal patterns of system usage could detect security threats that would not be detected with other malware detection techniques.

Even if not common, this approach to the problem has already been studied in the literature, for example [8] the authors follow a similar approach, but the main difference in this case is the fact that the authors base their work by inspecting only the network traces, which greatly limits the type of malware they are able to detect. In [11] or [5] the authors follow a similar approach. The shortcomings we observe on such work is that they provide limited information about the features used and their results. Apart from that, the majority of these studies are based on statistical models, thresholds, and averages of a single metric and very few of them incorporate machine learning techniques into the profile creation. One exception to that is [9], where the used system information is very limited and only includes UNIX shell commands with their arguments, focusing only on detecting system intrusion.

3   Architecture

Given the heterogeneity of data sources, data gathering and normalization is a very well-known problem. In this section we describe the approach we propose to balance such complexity with the minimal data set necessary by our user behavior analysis system. This is specially important given that our system will be running on desktops, laptops or other appliances where resource consumption is important for the users.

In Fig. 1 we provide the different building blocks of our system. In a nutshell our proposal requires three different data sources:

- *System stats*: the gathered information, as we shall discuss in detail later on, refers to system metrics such as CPU usage, list of processes, ...
- *Network stats*: networking information is critical in nowadays systems. Despite of this, in this first iteration of the proposal we limit our analysis to amount of sent and received data and packets.
- *Audit Logs*: we leverage on auditing tools to receive insights about system status.

3.1   Enduser Host

Endpoint agent: is the agent used to obtain system information from the host. It is in charge of aggregating and buffering the different local events that will be

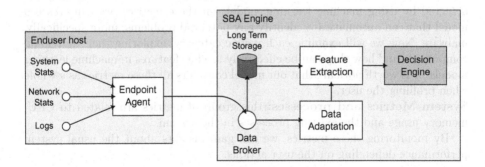

Fig. 1. Overall Architecture building blocks

sent to the Smart Behavior Analysis module. The recollected metrics, as already stated, are System, Network stats and audit logs. We defer the discussion about the different gathered stats to Sect. 3.3.

3.2 Smart Behavior Analysis (SBA)

This module is in charge of gathering all the different stats, to process them and to determine if the current state represents a potential anomaly due to malware activity.

Data Broker: When the information is extracted from the Endpoint Agent, it is reconciled into the Data Broker which has a three-fold goal, first coordinates the reception of data from different Endpoint Agents, second, it stores the raw information into persistent storage for later recovery in case of need, and third feeds the data to the data normalization module.

Data Adaptation: this module unifies the received data, scaling or transforming it when needed. This is necessary for some Machine Learning models improve the obtained results.

Feature Extraction: this module allows us to combine the historical information of this system and the current obtained data to extract the necessary processed metrics for the evaluation. We further discuss this logic in 3.3.

Decision Engine: By applying the ML algorithm, as described later in Sect. 4, the system is able to determine whether there is malware in action or not. In case of positive outcome, we leave as an important part of our future work to determine the mitigatory actions to perform.

3.3 Metrics

This section focuses on the system metrics used as features to train our model. The metrics are derived from the above-mentioned data sources, namely, system metrics and processes, network metrics, and audit logs. These metrics are periodically collected and assist in the detection of security risks when their values deviate from the normal behavior for an specific user. This deviation is detected by using machine learning models on these metrics, we can create a model that can automatically identify any potential problems, more specifically, malware. Now we will examine each metric category, exploring their individual components and how they can be effectively used as features in machine learning models. It is worth noticing that our model considers all these metrics as a whole when profiling the user.

System Metrics and processes: this group of metrics are related to CPU, memory usage and the existing processes in the system.

By monitoring these metrics, we can gain insights about the usual system performance depending on the user actions.

We consider the following metrics groups:

- **CPU usage**: This group of metrics provides information about CPU usage, which can help detect potential malware. The types of CPU usage we identify map to the classical metrics provided by nowadays systems. Hence, we analyze the CPU percentages of the following type:
  - **User**: Time running un-niced user processes, which are processes that have not been assigned a specific priority level or "niceness" value.
  - **System**: Time running kernel processes.
  - **Idle**: Time spent in the kernel idle handler.
  - **I/O Wait**: Time waiting for I/O completion.
  - **Nice**: Time running niced user processes.
  - **Software Interrupt**: Time spent servicing software interrupts.
  - **Harwdare Interrupt**: Time spent servicing hardware interrupts.
  - **Steal**: Time stolen from this VM by the hypervisor.
- **Memory usage**: This group of metrics provides information about memory usage, which can help identify potential malware. In this case we consider the following aspects of memory usage:
  - **Total memory**: Amount of physical memory in the system
  - **Used memory**: Amount of physical memory used in the system
  - **Free memory**: Amount of free physical memory in the system
  - **Buffer/Cache memory**: Amount of memory that is currently being used caching
  - **Total swap**: Amount of swap space in the system
  - **Used swap**: Amount of swap space used in the system
  - **Free swap**: Amount of free swap space in the system
- **Processes**: This section focuses on a set of metrics related to processes. In this case our goal is to analyze high level process statistics such as the amount of processes present on a system, but in the future we plan to use the process list names as it may prove a very good indicator of malware.

  Many types of malware may increase the number of running processes in the system, for example, File infecting viruses. These types of malware infect executable files on a victim's system and create multiple instances of themselves in memory, which can cause a significant increase in the number of running processes. Apart from that, any type of malware could increase the number of processes when performing their respective malicious activities.

  We identify the following metrics in this group:
  - **Total Processes**: Total number of running processes at a specific time.
  - **Userland Processes**: Total number of non kernel processes that are running at a specific time.
  - **Kernel Processes**: Total number of kernel processes that are running at a specific time.

Network Metrics: Nowadays almost all attacks use the network. As a consequence, this type of metrics are critical for our system. At a high level, network metrics such as the number of packets/bytes sent and received and the geographical location of new connections provide valuable information about the user. These metrics can be used to help detect various security threats, including DDoS.

Then, related with the network we identify the following metrics:

- **Amount of information**: This group of metrics is related to the amount of transmitted data over the network, specifically the number of bytes sent and received. These metrics can be used to detect unusual traffic patterns or abnormal levels of data transfer, which may indicate the presence of malicious activity.

  We distinguish in this group "amount of transmitted data" and "amount of packets per time unit". While both packet and byte metrics are useful in identifying potential security threats, they provide information that can be used in different ways. For example, the byte metrics may be more useful in identifying unusually large amounts of data being transferred, which could indicate data exfiltration. On the other hand, the packet metrics may be more useful in identifying unusual network traffic patterns, such as a sudden increase in the number of packets being sent from a particular source, which could indicate DDoS or command-and-control attacks.

- **Endpoint country**: This group of metrics provides information about the number of new network connections originating from each continent, which are well-known major sources of cyber-attacks such as China and Russia.

  The metrics included in this group are important in detecting potential security threats, as a sudden surge in new network connections from a particular region can indicate the presence of malicious activity.

Audit Logs: The audit logs provide information not present on other sources, in particular we consider:

- **Files**: This group of metrics provides information about the number of files that have been deleted, changed, or created during a period of time.

  The metrics in this group are the following, all provide values since last metric report:
  - **Files Write**: Number of files that have been written
  - **Files Read**: Number of files that have been read
  - **Files Created**: Number of files that have been created
  - **Files Deleted**: Number of files that have been deleted

  Many types of malware create, delete or modify a big number of files, for example:
  - **Viruses**: Viruses are a type of malware that infect executable files on a target's system. As the virus infects more files, it can create a large number of infected files on the system.
  - **Worms**: Worms are a type of malware that spread through computer networks, often by exploiting vulnerabilities in software. As worms spread to other systems, they may create copies of themselves or install additional malware on the victim's system. This can result in a large number of files being created, modified, or deleted on the victim's system. For

example, the Conficker worm, was known to create a large number of files on infected systems. Once it infected a system, it would create a large number of randomly named files in various directories to make it more difficult for antivirus software to detect and remove the worm.

- **Ransomware**: As just mentioned, ransomware attacks encrypt the victim's files. Therefore, a large number of files are modified.
- **Wiper Malware** [12]: Wiper malware is a type of malware that is designed to destroy or overwrite the victim's data. The malware may delete or modify a large number of files.

- **Commands**: In this case, there is only one metric related to commands: **Number of Commands**. This metric represents the number of commands that have been executed since the last set of metrics was obtained. As machine learning models are being used to detect malware behavior, metrics have to be static. Therefore, dynamic metrics can't be used in this case, which could have been used to create metrics related to the specific commands being executed. Nevertheless, the number of commands being executed is an indicative metric that can be used to detect different types of malware.

It's important to note that a single metric may not necessarily provide enough information to detect malware on its own, as certain metrics may have legitimate reasons for fluctuating or deviating from *normal* behavior. However, by analyzing a combination of metrics at a specific time, we can gain a more comprehensive view of the system and identify patterns that may indicate the presence of malware.

4 Machine Learning Model

In this section, we will discuss the performance of the different Machine Learning algorithms tested in this work, namely Autoencoders [16] and Kernel Density Estimation [15].

Following this, we will discuss the significance of features in detecting specific attacks, such as ransomware and denial of service. This preliminary result has the goal of understanding which of the models have the necessary features to be chosen. Subsequently, we will compare all the machine learning algorithms that were tested and determine which one works best for this project. Finally, we will examine how false positives evolve after collecting data over a few days.

It is important to note that the test data used was the same for all the algorithms. The models were trained using 481 min of normal behavior data and each test was performed with data ranging from 14 min to 1 h.

We leave out of this study algorithms such as One-class SVM and Local Outlier Factor models due to its poor performance.

4.1 Autoencoder Model

In the autoencoder model, we also present the he combination of parameter values that works best. In this case the layers are defined as follows:

- **Input layer:** Defined with the shape of the training data.
- **Encoding layer:** defined with 49 neurons, ReLU activation function, and L1 regularization with a coefficient of 0.00.
- **Decoding layer:** Defined with 49 neurons and ReLU activation function.
- **Output layer:** Defined with the same number of features as the input layer and sigmoid activation function.

Activation functions are used to introduce non-linearity into machine learning models. ReLU [3] is one of the most commonly used activation functions in deep learning models. It is a simple function that returns the input if it is positive and zero otherwise. ReLU activates/ignores certain neurons in the model, which can help learn complex patterns in the data. On the other hand, the sigmoid [14] activation function maps any input value to a value between 0 and 1, which is useful when the output needs to be either 0 or 1. In this case, we need to classify the output as normal behavior or security threat. Therefore, sigmoid function can be used to map the output reconstruction error to a value between 0 and 1, where values closer to 1 indicate a higher likelihood of a security threat.

L1 regularization [17] is a technique used to prevent overfitting in machine learning models. What it does it to add a penalty term to the loss function that forces the model to set many of the weights to zero, which will remove some features from the model. In this case, we don't want to remove any of the features as all of them were determined to have importance. Therefore, the coefficient is set to 0.00 as it is important to not remove features.

The model is compiled with the Adam optimizer [2] and mean squared error loss function. The optimizer is the algorithm used to update the weights of the neural network during training. The Adam optimizer is a commonly used optimizer that adapts the learning rate of the network during training. The loss function is a measure of how well the model is able to reconstruct the input data. Mean squared error is a commonly used loss function for autoencoders, which calculates the average squared difference between the input and the output of the model.

The *epochs* are set to 50, which is the number of times to iterate over the entire training dataset. The *batch_ size* is set to 32, which is the number of samples to be processed at once during each epoch. And the *validation_ split* is 0.2, which is the proportion of the data to use for validation during training (in this case, 20%).

Finally, the threshold for anomaly detection is set at 85% of the reconstruction errors. This means that any data point with a reconstruction error greater than the 85*th* percentile of all reconstruction errors is considered an anomaly. We performed different tests and decided that a lower threshold started to get false positives.

The model performed very well in general. However, it had trouble detecting ransomware attacks, so we extracted the important metrics for the model (normalized to 100 for readability) as shown in Fig. 2.

In this model, feature importance cannot be directly extracted. However, to understand which features are the most important we can examine the weights of the layers. This approach can be subjective, as the weights do not directly represent feature importance, and interpreting them can be challenging.

All features seem to have a similar importance, which may indicate that the features are not well differentiated and that they are not providing much information to the model. However, the performance of the model is good despite of this, which could mean that the dataset has a relatively simple structure and that the autoencoder is able to capture the important features with a similar level of importance. However, identifying and focusing on important features can improve the performance of the model. Not doing so, resulted in missclassifying the ransomware data in some cases that some of the metrics were similar to the normal behavior ones.

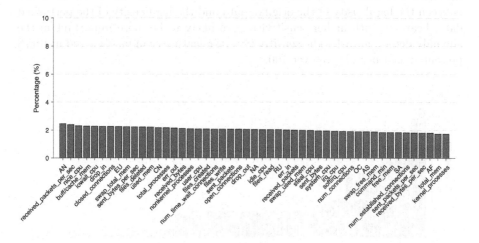

Fig. 2. Autoencoder feature importance

4.2   Kernel Density Estimation Model

This model has many different parameters that can be set to different values. In this particular case, several combinations of parameters have been tried, The combination of parameter values that works best is the one that is presented in this section.

The *kernel* is defined as *Gaussian*. A kernel is a weighting function that is used to estimate the probability density function of the underlying data.

The *Bandwidth* is set as 'Scott', which determines the width of the kernel function, and it affects the smoothness of the density estimation. The Scott [13] bandwidth is a method that estimates the bandwidth based on the data, which can help to avoid overfitting or underfitting the data.

Finally, the *threshold* is set to the 7th percentile of the log-densities of the test data. This means that any data points with a log-density below this threshold will be classified as anomalous, and any data points with a log-density above this threshold will be classified as normal. The threshold is chosen based on the assumption that anomalous data points will have a lower density than normal data points. This parameter was decreased until the normal behavior data started to give false positives as it is important to assure the lowest number of false positives.

This model was able to accurately pass half of the tests. However, it had trouble detecting botnet and ransomware data. To better understand where the model is failing, we analyzed the features used in the model.

Kernel density estimation does not directly provide information about the importance of individual features in the data. Therefore, the sensitivity of the features is extracted. To do this, features of the test data are perturbed and the density estimate is observed. The sensitivity is calculated as the difference between the log-density of the original data and the log-density of the perturbed data. Features with higher sensitivities are likely to be more important in the anomaly detection task. The sensitivity of the features can be observed in Fig. 3 presented as a percentage over 100.

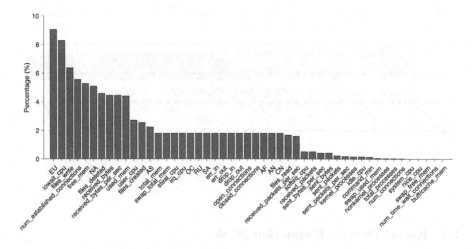

Fig. 3. Kernel Density Estimation feature sensitivities

Before applying the perturbation in this model, the features are first normalized. This is important because the range of values for each feature can be very different, so by normalizing, the same perturbation can be applied to each feature. If the perturbation was applied before normalization, it could result in inaccurate sensitivity calculations.

This model has identified certain features as being highly important, such as "EU", even though they should not have that level of importance. This can lead to incorrect classifications. The model's poor detection of ransomware attacks could be due to this incorrect feature importance. Some of the features that increase in ransomware attacks are the ones related to processes, which are not taken into account in this model. Due to all this we believe that this model is not suitable for our task.

5 Model Accuracy and Validation

This section focuses on the data used to train and test the machine learning models. Firstly, we will examine the data that represents the user's normal behavior, which is the training data. Next, we will move on to the data that was collected to test the performance of the different models. Finally we compare the studied models and analyze how the false positives are reduced as the system learns.

5.1 Training Data

In this section we take a look at the data that was generated to create the machine learning algorithms. Specifically, the data was collected by performing on a real system day-to-day activities such as:

- **Audiophile:** We profiled a person listening to music while idly performing other tasks.
- **Writer:** While working on this paper we created a writer profile.
- **Researcher:** To assess the behavior of a researcher, while processing the training data we also performed a profile of this workload.
- **Sys. Admin:** During the model debugging sessions using the Linux terminal we created this profile.
- **Journalist:** While searching for information related to this paper we performed long information search sessions.
- **Publisher:** As a backup and as work collaboration platform, publishing this paper to cloud facilities allowed us to create this profile.
- **Idle state:** This is not a profile per se, but in order to model the breaks and the system in idle state we created this profile as well.

5.2 Test Data

The test data used to validate our work was collected on different days from the training data to ensure a more accurate evaluation of the algorithms' performance. This was done to assess real-world scenarios and obtain results that better reflect the models' capabilities.

Each type of data was collected during multiple days to improve the results' accuracy. By collecting data over a longer period, the study was able to capture a more comprehensive picture of the malware's impact on the user's behavior and computer usage patterns. Particularly we checked our system using the following malware:

- **Ransomware:** To obtain precise results, an actual malware was utilized, specifically a ransomware sample obtained from MalwareBazaar [1]. The sample was executed simultaneously while the user was engaged in typical activities.
- **DoS:** It was also decided to collect Denial of Service data as this malware detection system can be applied not only to computers used by individual users but also to servers, which are frequently targeted by DoS attacks. In this case we used GoldenEye.

- **Botnet**: In this scenario the user's machine has been compromised and is being used as part of a botnet involved in a Denial of Service (DoS) attack on a remote server. We also leveraged GoldenEye but as generator of the attack.

In all cases the user was working as usual using one of the profiles previously generated.

In order to improve a little bit our model, we decided to also feed the system with similar load of malware but using legitimate applications. Particularly we used:

- **Backup**: Our model was trained both including and excluding the data collected while performing a backup in order to see the how this impacted the accuracy. The comparison can be found at Sect. 5.4. It is important to add that the backup data used for testing was taken in different days that the one used for training.
- **Software compilation**: We used a kernel compilation as baseline to see how the system detected high CPU usage, as before we trained the model with and without this information.
- **Normal behavior**: To make the tests completed we also checked the accuracy of the system through normal work sessions to see how it was detected by the system.

5.3   Metric Relevancy

In this part, the Random Forest machine learning algorithm was used to compare normal user behavior data with malware data to observe which metrics are the most significant in detecting the malware. Apart from that, we detected that some machine learning models used had issues identifying ransomware when high CPU usage was added to normal user behavior, we decided to analyze their difference in metrics.

It is worth noticing that the purpose of this comparison is to provide a general idea of the relevant features when it comes to differentiating normal behavior from security threats.

To make sure that only the key feature differences are extracted, the normal user behavior was the same in both malware and no malware data. Each feature's importance is presented as a percentage over 100 to make it easier to understand. This allows for a clearer visualization of the relative importance of each feature in the model.

DoS: the Random Forest model was trained with 2 labels, the normal behavior data and the malware data. The accuracy of the model was found to be 0.96296, which is very close to perfect accuracy. The metrics shown in Fig. 4a are the ones that were the most relevant for the malware classification.

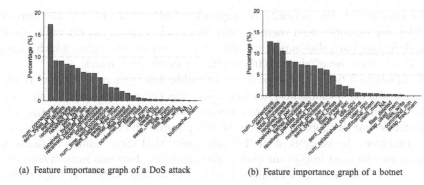

(a) Feature importance graph of a DoS attack   (b) Feature importance graph of a botnet

Fig. 4. xx

In this scenario, it is easy to differentiate between a Denial of Service (DoS) attack and normal user behavior. The most important metrics are related to the network, such as the number of connections and packets sent, which have higher values during a DoS attack.

Botnet: in this case the accuracy of the model to detect a botnet was 1, indicating perfect accuracy. The metrics shown in Fig. 4b are the ones that were the most relevant for the malware classification.

In this situation, the analysis is similar to the DoS case in that network features are crucial. However, in this instance, the number of processes is also significant because creating a DoS attack requires a large number of new processes. During the botnet collection data, the number of processes increased by approximately 150, which is noteworthy.

Ransomware: we observed that the accuracy assessing ransomware was 0.96. The metrics shown in Fig. 5a are the ones that were the most relevant for the malware classification.

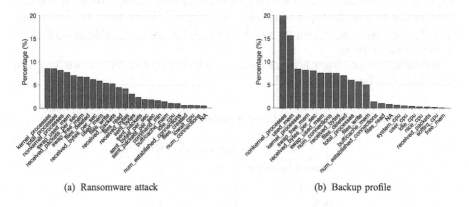

(a) Ransomware attack   (b) Backup profile

Fig. 5. yy

As anticipated, the majority of important features are related to memory and files, for example used memory and files read/created. Additionally, some network features are also important, like the number of sent bytes, which shows a significant increase of about 200% during a ransomware attack.

As mentioned before, as some models trouble detecting ransomware attacks when introducing backup data, a comparison was conducted using backup data as the "no malware" group and ransomware data as the "malware" group. The key features that distinguish between the two groups can be visualized in Fig. 5b.

In this case, the analysis of the features shows that those related to memory and files are the most important ones in distinguishing between ransomware and backup data. The amount of memory used by ransomware is slightly higher than that of backup data, but this can vary depending on the specific ransomware type. Additionally, the number of files written by ransomware is much higher than that of backup data since the ransomware encrypts the files, while in backup data, the files are not modified. On the other hand, the number of files read in backup data is much higher, reaching up to 1500 files per minute, compared to ransomware.

There are clearly various differences between the two datasets. However, the specific features that are considered important in the models will determine their ability to detect ransomware. For instance, if the important features are related to memory, then it may be difficult for the model to detect ransomware. Apart from that, when it comes to the models that use a threshold for detecting security threats, the value of the threshold can definitely change the result of the prediction. Therefore, an appropriate threshold that has both low false positives and high true positives should be found.

5.4   Models' Comparison

This section will focus on comparing all of the models, specifically their effectiveness in detecting malware and the number of false positives they generate. In addition, we will analyze how well the models perform when additional training data similar to specific types of malware attacks is incorporated. By evaluating these factors, we can determine which model is the most reliable and effective for detecting malware.

Initially, the precision level of each model is reviewed for various types of data. This can be seen in Table 1.

Table 1. Accuracy of different anomaly detection algorithms

	Autoencoder	KDE
Normal behavior	1	1
Botnet	1	0.9
DoS	1	1
Ransomware	0.71	0.42

After reviewing the table, it can be observed that the Autoencoder model is the most accurate in detecting both normal behavior and malware activity, achieving good accuracy in all tests. It is worth noting that models with precision scores different than 1 in detecting normal behavior should not be considered since the goal is to have the least amount of false positives. This is particularly important because false positives can increase when making live predictions, and thus minimizing their occurrence is crucial. Due to space limitations in this work we don't present some algorithms which proved inaccurate, i.e., One-class SVM and Local Outlier Factor.

DoS attacks and botnet behavior is accurately detected by the majority of the models. However, ransomware attacks are not properly classifieds by KDE as their feature importance is not properly defined. In terms of malware detection, low accuracy in detecting malware activity can have serious consequences as it can delay the detection of the threat, which is crucial for containing and mitigating the attack. While the models may eventually detect the threat, the delay in detection can result in a more severe impact on the system. Therefore, apart from the Autoencoder model which has the highest accuracy for detecting both normal behavior and malware activity, the KDE model can also be considered as it has relatively better accuracy than the other discarded models.

To assess the reliability of the models, we will evaluate their performance when additional data related to backup and kernel compiling is included. Backup data, which uses a considerable amount of memory and accesses many files, is similar to ransomware data. Additionally, we will incorporate kernel compiling data, which utilizes significant system resources, to observe any changes in model precision. Table 2 demonstrates the varying performance of each model when this data is added.

Table 2. Accuracy of different anomaly detection algorithms - 2

	Autoencoder	KDE
Normal behavior	1	1
Botnet	1	1
DoS	1	1
Ransomware	0.78	0.35

By reviewing the results, it was observed that most models had reduced accuracy in detecting ransomware attacks. However, the Autoencoder model showed an increase in accuracy after adding data that is similar to ransomware attacks. This could be due to a reconfiguration of feature importance. Nonetheless, the accuracy of detecting ransomware attacks is still not perfect, and is something we will study on our future work.

5.5 False Positive Reduction

Finally, to see how much time would it take the models to have enough training data to have a considerably low rate of false positives, we'll see how these false positives progress in the span 8 d. For this study, 1 h of normal behavior data was collected every day for the specified time period. Each day (excluding the first day), the new data was passed through the model to observe the false positive rate, then the data was added to the training set and the model was retrained. On the first day of data collection, the data was solely utilized to create the model, without performing any testing. The Autoencoder was employed for this study, as it demonstrated superior performance in comparison to all other algorithms that were tested. The outcomes of this study are presented in Fig. 6.

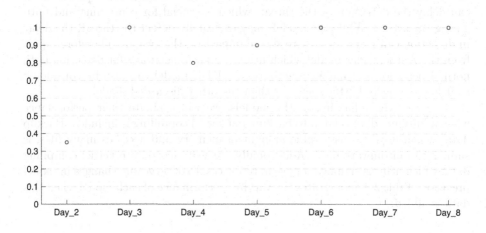

Fig. 6. False positive reduction

On the second day, which is the first day of predicting the data, the precision was quite low at 35%, but starting from the third day, it increased rapidly and stabilized at 100% on day 6. Therefore, it took a total of 6 h to achieve perfect precision in this particular study.

However, it should be noted that these results are specific to this study, and achieving perfect precision may vary in other environments depending on the diversity of normal behavior data for each user. Nonetheless, this study demonstrates that it is possible to achieve perfect precision.

This statement suggests that in a work environment where employees follow a routine and exhibit consistent web browsing behavior, the model would require less time to reach a stable and accurate prediction. This is because the model would have a more predictable and consistent set of data to learn from, leading to a faster convergence toward accurate predictions.

This also suggests that implementing the detection system on a server with highly automated and repetitive tasks would be beneficial. Not only would it achieve high accuracy with normal behavior quickly, but as the actions are automated, it would effectively detect any type of security threat.

6 Conclusion

In this paper we have shown that using user behavior analysis is a feasible mechanism to detect malware, in our case of all the tested models we found that autoencoders seem to be the most accurate of the tested models, as it can quickly adapt to changing user behavior, while effectively ruling out actual malware samples. We have also shown that our models show high accuracy in predictions in a matter of seconds, given the frequent collection of metrics, any possible security threats can be detected rapidly.

A very big advantage of these light-weighted models is the fact that they can adapt to the specific behavior of the user, which avoids the need of having a database with malware samples and could detect zero-day threats just by noticing a deviation of the user's normal behavior.

As previously mentioned, we believe that it would be wise to deploy our solution on a running server since its behavior is often very repetitive and predictable, and the models tested in the study performed well in such a context. To be more precise, utilizing the Autoencoder model would be an effective way to identify virtually any potential security threat on a system.

We leave as part of our future work several aspects that may be of interest, first we do believe that there is still room for improvement by performing more real tests of the system to be able to better tune the detection under a set of changing user behaviors. We also think that trying other machine learning models such as Isolation Forests may prove a valuable addition to the solution.

References

1. abuse.ch: Sha256 edfe81babf50c2506853fd8375f1be0b7bebbefb2e5e9a33eff95ec23e867 de1, https://bazaar.abuse.ch/sample/edfe81babf50c2506853fd8375f1be0b7bebbefb 2e5e9a33eff95ec23e867de1/
2. Brownlee, J.: Gentle introduction to the adam optimization algorithm for deep learning (2021). https://machinelearningmastery.com/adam-optimization-algorithm-for-deep-learning/
3. Brownlee, J.: A gentle introduction to the rectified linear unit (relu), https://machinelearningmastery.com/rectified-linear-activation-function-for-deep-learning-neural-networks/
4. Cyberwire, T.: signature-based detection. https://thecyberwire.com/glossary/signature-based-detection
5. Denning, D.: An intrusion-detection model (1987). https://ieeexplore.ieee.org/abstract/document/1702202
6. Gavriluţ, D., Cimpoeşu, M., Anton, D., Ciortuz, L.: Malware detection using machine learning. In: 2009 International Multiconference on Computer Science and Information Technology, pp. 735–741 (2009). https://doi.org/10.1109/IMCSIT.2009.5352759

7. Griffiths, C.: The latest 2023 cyber crime statistics (2023). https://aag-it.com/the-latest-cyber-crime-statistics/#
8. Hindy, H., Atkinson, R., Tachtatzis, C., Colin, J.N., Bayne, E., Bellekens, X.: Utilising deep learning techniques for effective zero-day attack detection. In: Electronics, vol. 9, p. 1684 (2020). https://doi.org/10.3390/electronics9101684
9. Lane, T., Brodley, C.E.: An application of machine learning to anomaly detection (1997). http://ftp.cerias.purdue.edu/pub/papers/terran-lane/brodley-lane-nissc97_paper.pdf
10. Miao, Y.: Understanding heuristic-based scanning vs. sandboxing (2015). https://www.opswat.com/blog/understanding-heuristic-based-scanning-vs-sandboxing
11. Ahmed, M.E., Nepal, S.,Kim, H.: Medusa: malware detection using statistical analysis of system's behavior (2018). https://ieeexplore.ieee.org/abstract/document/8537842
12. packetlabs: What is wiper malware and how does it work? (2022). https://www.packetlabs.net/posts/how-does-wiper-malware-work/
13. rdrr: bw.scott: Scott's rule for bandwidth selection for kernel density (2013). https://rdrr.io/cran/spatstat.core/man/bw.scott.html
14. Saeed, M.: A gentle introduction to sigmoid function (2021). https://machinelearningmastery.com/a-gentle-introduction-to-sigmoid-function/
15. sklearn: density (2023). https://scikit-learn.org/stable/modules/density.html
16. tensorflow: Intro to autoencoders (2023). https://www.tensorflow.org/tutorials/generative/autoencoder
17. Tyagi, N.: L2 and l1 regularization in machine learning (2017). https://www.analyticssteps.com/blogs/l2-and-l1-regularization-machine-learning

Balancing XAI with Privacy and Security Considerations

Christoforos N. Spartalis⬤, Theodoros Semertzidis$^{(\boxtimes)}$ ⬤, and Petros Daras⬤

Center for Research and Technology Hellas, Information Technologies Institute,
Thessaloniki, Greece
{c.spartalis,theosem,daras}@iti.gr

Abstract. The acceptability of AI decisions and the efficiency of AI-human interaction become particularly significant when AI is incorporated into Critical Infrastructures (CI). To achieve this, eXplainable AI (XAI) modules must be integrated into the AI workflow. However, by design, XAI reveals the inner workings of AI systems, posing potential risks for privacy leaks and enhanced adversarial attacks. In this literature review, we explore the complex interplay of explainability, privacy, and security within trustworthy AI, highlighting inherent trade-offs and challenges. Our research reveals that XAI leads to privacy leaks and increases susceptibility to adversarial attacks. We categorize our findings according to XAI taxonomy classes and provide a concise overview of the corresponding fundamental concepts. Furthermore, we discuss how XAI interacts with prevalent privacy defenses and addresses the unique requirements of the security domain. Our findings contribute to the growing literature on XAI in the realm of CI protection and beyond, paving the way for future research in the field of trustworthy AI.

Keywords: Trustworthy AI · Explainable AI (XAI) · Privacy · Security · Critical Infrastructures (CI)

1 Introduction

The incorporation of Artificial Intelligence (AI) into the operational procedures of Critical Infrastructures (CI) calls for enhancing both the acceptability of AI decisions and the efficiency of collaboration between AI and human operators. To this end, eXplainable Artificial Intelligence (XAI) becomes essential in creating a trustworthy and widely accepted AI workflow.

The main objective of XAI is to provide insights about the decision-making processes of AI models in a human-understandable manner. Furthermore, it can be applied at all stages of delivery process, including development, validation/verification, accountable prediction, and maintenance [32]. XAI can improve AI systems by revealing hidden facets of models and extracting new knowledge from underlying data correlations and learned strategies [2].

However, XAI methods unintentionally leak sensitive information about the training data and models at hand [48,58]. Moreover, adversaries can exploit these

S. Katsikas et al. (Eds.): ESORICS 2023 Workshops, LNCS 14399, pp. 111–124, 2024.
https://doi.org/10.1007/978-3-031-54129-2_7

methods to enhance privacy and security attacks [6,25,27,31,32,40]. Undoubtedly, highly accurate AI systems with explainability, privacy and security guarantees are complex but necessary, as emphasized by regulations [13], standards [18], and EU expert groups [17].

Hence, it is important to identify overlaps, conflicts, and trade-offs to explore the ideal compromise, particularly, when implementing AI systems in safety-critical domains with significant human impact. To this end, we review recent literature, categorize the findings, and present them in a comprehensive manner. We argue that our contribution attributes researchers and practitioners to design trustworthy AI systems that meet modern requirements.

In Sect. 2, we provide a concise overview of the fundamental concepts necessary for a comprehensive understanding of our findings. Then, in Sect. 3, we delve into the main analysis of the interplay between explainability, privacy, and security in AI. Finally, in Sect. 4, we consolidate our general conclusions.

2   Background

In this section, we aim to establish the background for a thorough understanding of our study. We do not intend to give an exhaustive analysis of all concepts, but rather to highlight those that are absolutely essential in supporting our findings (see Sect. 3). To this end, we start by constructing a partial taxonomy of XAI, focusing specifically on our areas of interest. We provide a conceptual representation of the classes pertinent to our study and briefly describe them. Furthermore, we address the evaluation of explainability in AI systems by enumerating qualitative indicators of explanations and outlining different levels of evaluations. Lastly, we succinctly describe the adversarial attack tests used to assess the robustness of AI systems.

2.1   XAI Taxonomy Classes

Constructing an XAI taxonomy is a complex task that requires a thorough and detailed analysis. A comprehensive work on this subject can be found in [8]. In our study, we selectively emphasize only on the classes presented in our findings (see Sect. 3); while excluding many others. Further, XAI methods with properties relevant to multiple general groups have been uniquely categorized based on the primary focus of the reviewed article in question.

Our XAI taxonomy, as illustrated in Fig. 1, offers a hierarchical conceptual representation of the different classes relevant to our study. It encompasses the scope of explanation methods, including *model-specific* and *model-agnostic* approaches, as well as the types of explained systems, such as *DL-based* and *feature-based* systems. Furthermore, it addresses the transparency of the explained models, distinguishing between *white-box* and *black-box* models. Additionally, we classify XAI methods into *intrinsic* and *post-hoc* categories, with the *post-hoc* methods further classified into *example-based, backpropagation-based, gradient-based*, and *perturbation-based* methods. For concise definitions of these taxonomy classes, please refer to Table 1.

Table 1. Definitions of XAI taxonomy classes.

Taxonomy Class	Definition
Model-specific	Methods exclusive to certain model classes that are highly relying on their internal parameters and mechanisms, such as weights and gradients [8]
Model-agnostic	Methods that maintain the ability to generalize across any *DL-based* system [58]
Deep Learning-based	Systems that process input data such as images, signals, or text with numerous features [32]
Feature-based	Systems that mainly process tabular data with a limited number of features, including numerical and categorical values [32]
Black-box	Models characterized by their complexity and obscurity, which pose interpretability challenges for stakeholders [16,52]
White-box	Models that are inherently interpretable and provide complete transparency, offering full access to their parameters and architecture [23]
Intrinsic	Methods that commonly impose constraints on model complexity during training to inherently increase interpretability; typically associated with model-specific methods [8]
Post-hoc	Methods applied after model training to clarify model decisions; typically associated with model-agnostic methods [8]
Backpropagation-based	Methods that leverage backpropagation to assess feature attribution in model decision-making [40]
Perturbation-based	Methods that involve querying the model with slightly modified inputs to determine feature attribution in model decision-making [6]
Example-based	Methods that use specific instances from the dataset to elucidate model behavior, without any manipulation of the features or the model itself [2]

2.2 Evaluation Criteria and Methods

In this section, we discuss the evaluation criteria and methods used to assess key aspects of trustworthy AI systems, including explainability, privacy, and security. Particularly regarding explanations, we also refer to the different levels at which evaluation can be conducted.

Explainability. Despite the absence of universally accepted evaluation criteria [6,8], we have identified a set of qualitative indicators that is referred to many recent studies, including [4,6,8,20,30,52]. In Table 2, we highlight the metrics relevant to our findings and provide concise definitions.

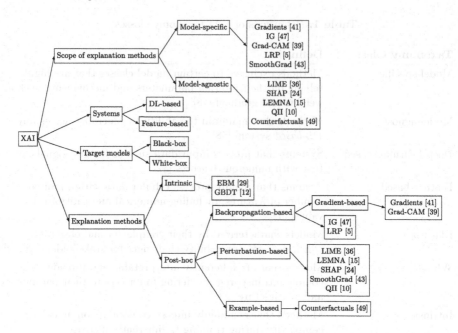

Fig. 1. A conceptual depiction of XAI taxonomy classes relevant to our findings.

Moreover, an intriguing aspect of this topic involves multi-level evaluation methods to assess explainability, as discussed in [6,8]. At the *functional-level*, quantitative measures are used as proxies for qualitative characteristics, eliminating the need for end-user experiments. However, solely relying on functional-level evaluation criteria can yield misleading results [6]. For a more comprehensive evaluation, it may be necessary to perform end-user experiments, involving domain experts at the *application-level* or laypersons at the *human-level* evaluation. By incorporating these different levels of evaluation, a more holistic understanding of the effectiveness and impact of explainability methods can be achieved.

Privacy and Security. Assessing privacy leakage in AI systems often involves taking the perspective of an adversary and measuring the success rate of the attack [40]. To this end, we enumerate and define popular privacy attacks discussed in the reviewed studies.

Attribute Inference refers to the disclosure of a sensitive attribute from a specific instance by utilizing the model's output and non-sensitive attributes [19,30].

Membership Inference involves querying a particular data point to the target model to verify its presence in the training dataset [7,9,40,59].

Property Inference confirms the existence of a data point with specific properties within the training dataset [59].

Table 2. Definitions of XAI evaluation criteria.

Criterion	Definition
Accuracy	The extent to which the features identified as relevant in unseen data are truly so [6,8,44,52]
Completeness	The extent to which the explanations are meaningful and consistent across all possible inputs [37,52]
Comprehensibility	The degree to which end-users understand the generated explanations [6,8]
Contrastivity	The degree of difference in feature attributions assigned to different classes [6]
Efficiency	Pertains to the computational complexity and runtime of the XAI method; it measures the extent to which the typical workflow of the explainee is disrupted [6,28,52]
Faithfulness	Closely related to *accuracy*; it measures the impact on model performance when the most important features are eliminated one by one [4,6]
Fidelity	It measures the approximation quality of the surrogate interpretable model [6,8]
Robustness	It measures the resilience to both random noise and adversarial attacks [6,52]
Sparsity	The extent to which the number of features considered important is kept to a minimum [6,37,52]
Stability	To what extent the generated explanations of the same instance remain consistent across multiple runs [6,52], or similar explanations are generated for similar instances [8]
Usability	The intersection of *comprehensibility* and *efficiency*, *ch7bhusalspssoksps2022*

Model Extraction (also known as *Model Stealing*) encompasses the construction of a surrogate model that mimics the behavior of the target model by creating a surrogate dataset and querying it to obtain the target model's decision boundaries [19,21,30,53].

Model Inversion involves reconstructing data from a private training dataset [30].

Furthermore, in Table 3, we categorize the corresponding reviewed studies based on the types of privacy attacks they employ, extending beyond the scope of explainability and security.

Table 3. Different types of privacy attacks featured in each reviewed study.

Reference	Authors	Attribute Inference	Membership Inference	Property Inference	Model Extraction	Model Inversion
[3]	Aivodji et al				✓	
[6]	Bhusal and Rastogi		✓		✓	
[7]	Carlini et al		✓			
[9]	Choquette-Choo et al		✓			
[19]	Izzo et al		✓			
[21]	Kariyappa and Qureshi				✓	
[27]	Milli et al				✓	
[28]	Miura et al				✓	
[30]	Oksuz et al				✓	
[40]	Shokri et al		✓			
[45]	Song and Shmatikov	✓				
[46]	Stadler et al	✓	✓			
[48]	Truong et al.				✓	
[51]	Wainakh et al					✓
[53]	Yan et al				✓	
[55]	Yin et al					✓
[58]	Zhao et al					✓
[57]	Zhao et al					✓
[59]	Zhu and Han		✓	✓		✓

Privacy and security attacks have different goals. Privacy attacks aim to leak sensitive information or violate the intellectual property of the target model, while security attacks focus on degrading the overall performance of the model [22]. However, the robustness of an AI system to both types of attacks is evaluated using the same approach [42,56]. Thus, as we have done for privacy attacks, we define the popular security attacks found in the reviewed literature:

Poisoning refers to manipulating training data or model parameters to degrade the model performance [50].
Evasion involves manipulating input data during inference to trigger incorrect model outputs with high confidence [56].

3   Findings

Our research aims to shed light on trade-offs, challenges, and opportunities that arise from the interplay of explainability, privacy, and security in AI. In this analysis, XAI serves as a cornerstone. This signifies that the identified aspects of this analysis are primarily examined from the angle of different XAI taxonomy classes or methods. Moreover, we approach privacy from two perspectives: potential attacks and prevalent defenses. Additionally, our security analysis takes into account two facets: the security of AI systems, focusing on the protection of the AI systems per se, and security enabled by AI systems, which seeks to enhance overall security measures in various domains and applications.

3.1   Privacy Attacks

AI models are already susceptible to inference attacks [7,40]. This vulnerability can be particularly relevant to specific architecture categories, such as those used in *DL-based* systems [21] or data properties such as underrepresented population groups [19,31,40]. However, privacy risks escalate when adversaries have explanations for decision-making at hand [6,25,27,31,32,40]. For example, *model-agnostic* explanation methods can be used in *black-box* models, which are inherently more resilient to privacy attacks [6,31], to mitigate their obscurity and thus increase their vulnerability [53,58]. Another method involves *model extraction, ch7truongspsdatafreesps2021.* Indeed, we argue that there is an intriguing reciprocal interaction between privacy and explainability; a privacy attack provides model interpretability and exposes it to higher risk for subsequent attacks.

In categorizing our findings into broader XAI taxonomy classes, we propose that *example-based* methods may be the most prone to privacy leakage. Comparing these with *backpropagation-based* and *perturbation-based* methods brings to light their distinctive risk profiles. The level of information leakage is so substantial that the models being explained become vulnerable not just to *membership inference* but also to *model inversion* attacks [40].

After *example-based, backpropagation-based* methods, particularly *gradient-based* ones, stand out as the next most significant source of privacy leak [40]. The variance of these explanations reveals statistical information on the decision boundaries of the model [6,40]. High variance indicates that a data point is close to the decision boundaries, which primarily suggests a lower probability of participating in the training set [40]. In fact, the correlation between variance and privacy leakage intensifies as the number of data features increases [40]. Based on a detailed analysis [58], *Grad-CAM* [39] is the most revealing method, followed by *Gradients* [41] and *LRP* [5]. This could be because *Class Activation Mapping (CAM)* explanations take into account a transformation of the original input, in addition to gradient information [58]. An additional justification could be that *backpropagation-based* methods, which are not *gradient-based*, such as *LRP* and *Integrated Gradients (IG)* [47], tend to lie near a low-dimensional manifold (i.e., they violate the data-manifold hypothesis) [31], and explanations with lower *fidelity* face less privacy risks [40]. Another general observation is that explanations focusing on neuron activations (like *Grad-CAM*) leak more privacy than those focusing on the model's output with respect to the input (like *Gradients, IG, LRP,* and *perturbation-based* methods) [58].

Perturbation-based methods, such as *LIME* [36] and *SmoothGrad* [43]), are found to be more resilient to *inference* and *model extraction* attacks [40,53]. This resilience may stem from their reliance on out-of-distribution (OOD) or off-manifold samples, resulting in lower *fidelity* and *stability* [31,40]. As mentioned previously, there is an underlying relation of explainability evaluation criteria and privacy leakage, as XAI methods that provide better explanations tend to leak more sensitive information [53]. Thus, a comparative analysis of *LIME, LEMNA* [15], and *SHAP* [24] is worth mentioning. This analysis [6] concludes that *LIME* achieves the highest *stability*, *SHAP* exhibits the lowest *faithfulness* and the highest *sparsity*, and all three methods demonstrate high scores in terms of *contrastivity* [6].

Remark 1. XAI methods "whiten" *black-box* models, increasing privacy risks.

Remark 2. Better explanations, higher exposure to privacy risks.

Remark 3. Order of XAI methods in terms of privacy leak (highest first):
Example-based > Gradient-based ≥ Backpropagation-based > Perturbation-based

3.2 Privacy Defences

Research in privacy-enhancing AI has converged on several prominent methods, including *Differential Privacy (DP), Federated Learning (FL), Homomorphic Encryption (HE),* and anonymization techniques such as generation of *synthetic data.*

DP introduces statistical noise into the data or the model [1], which can lead to extremely convoluted decision boundaries [31], hampering the *fidelity* and *comprehensibility* of explanations [38]. However, these explanations can reveal additional information about the data or the model, increasing the privacy budget to be spent by *DP* mechanisms [31].

It has been demonstrated that *perturbation-based* methods suffer less from the adverse impacts of *DP* [38]. When employed together, these techniques can strike a balance between explainability and privacy [10,31]. Furthermore, when *DP* is incorporated into inherently interpretable algorithms, such as *EMBs* [29], the objective extends beyond achieving high prediction accuracy and privacy [29]. The negative effects of noise can be mitigated post-training, and desirable constraints, like monotonicity, can be imposed. Moreover, it has been argued that the combination *DP* and *FL* could mitigate some of *DP*'s negative impacts [38].

FL is a collaborative learning process that offers a degree of privacy, as the model parameters or gradients shared by clients with the central server carry less sensitive information than raw data [26,54]. However, *model inversion* is possible using just publicly shared gradients [55,57,59], suggesting that *FL* is not foolproof in terms of privacy preservation, and *gradient-based* explanations can further worsen privacy leakage. Moreover, in this collaborative set up, clients can only make partial observations, potentially expressing doubts about model outputs or explanations [35]. We argue that resolving these conflicts might necessitate full information disclosure, which disregards privacy. On the other hand, such environments facilitate the provision of culture-based explanations that are tailored to individual clients [34].

HE allows computations on encrypted data without the need for decryption [33], and it has been effectively used in conjunction with XAI [14]. However, it comes with significant computational overhead and imposes limitations on the model architecture and types of operations, which complicates the integration with *intrinsic* constraints for interpretability [14]. Finally, the generation of *synthetic data* undermines interpretability, as it blurs the distinction between real and artificial information [46].

Remark 4. Each privacy-enhancing technique presents unique trade-offs with explainability, potentially varying across different XAI taxonomy classes.

Remark 5. Using a combination of privacy-enhancing techniques may better balance privacy and explainability.

3.3 Security Aspects

Each point discussed above is equally pertinent in the realm of security, as privacy concerns can trigger a cascading effect, thus escalating security risks. First, the data under consideration often contains sensitive information, the disclosure of which can critically compromise safety [11]. Second, if an adversary has already breached the privacy of an AI model, the process of crafting malicious samples is simpler [21].

Moreover, by revealing the inner-workings of AI systems, XAI methods can directly pose security risks [32]. The exploration of XAI in security is still not exhaustive; establishing robust defenses and defining additional prerequisites that need to be met remain open research questions [52]. The unique treatment this field necessitates arises from the participation of different stakeholders, the increased complexity of the systems, and the profound correlation between privacy and security concerns [6]. On this basis, the following evaluation criteria have been underscored as especially important: *accuracy, completeness, fidelity, robustness, stability,* and *usability* [6,52]. However, security-oriented explanations cannot yet achieve high *fidelity* and *stability* [6], perhaps due to the popularity of *DL-based* systems in the security domain [52].

Remark 6. Privacy concerns can lead to security risks.

Remark 7. The intersection of XAI and security presents unique characteristics which require further research.

4   Conclusions

Throughout our literature review, we identified numerous challenges involving explainability, privacy, and security within AI, and delved into the inherent trade-offs at their intersections. These findings were categorized according to the prevalent XAI taxonomy classes. To emphasize the contribution of our literature review, we consolidated our findings in the form of remarks in Sect. 3.

We underscored the significant role of XAI in bridging the vulnerability gap that exists between *black-box* and *white-box* models. Our study also emphasized the fundamental connection between explainability evaluation criteria and the success rate of adversarial attacks.

In the realm of privacy, we brought to light the potential risks induced by various XAI methods, highlighting the role of the quality of the explanations produced. *Example-based* methods pose the highest risk, followed by *Gradient-based*, other *Backpropagation-based*, and lastly, *Perturbation-based* methods. We also explored the intricate relationship between XAI and prevalent privacy defenses, highlighting the unique trade-offs associated with each privacy-enhancing technique. Moreover, we shedded light on promising results and future work directions.

Approaching the security aspects, we underlined the strong correlations of explainability and privacy vulnerabilities with security concerns. We elaborated on the additional challenges posed when incorporating XAI in security applications, emphasizing the urgent need for further research in this area.

In our future work, our aim is to implement these findings in actual use cases within CI, while exploring and taking into consideration the prioritization of requirements across different application domains.

In conclusion, we believe that our work enriches the expanding literature on XAI in the realm of CI protection and beyond. We provide a solid groundwork, supporting future research aimed at addressing challenges and balancing trade-offs inherent in trustworthy AI.

Acknowledgments. This work was partially supported by the EU funded project ATLANTIS (Grant Agreement Number 101073909).

References

1. Abadi, M., et al.: Deep learning with differential privacy. In: Proceedings of the ACM Conference on Computer and Communications Security, pp. 308–318 (2016). https://doi.org/10.1145/2976749.2978318
2. Adadi, A., Berrada, M.: Peeking inside the black-box: a survey on explainable artificial intelligence (XAI). IEEE Access **6**, 52138–52160 (2018). https://doi.org/10.1109/ACCESS.2018.2870052
3. Aïvodji, U., Bolot, A., Gambs, S.: Model extraction from counterfactual explanations. arXiv preprint arXiv:2009.01884 (2020)
4. Alvarez Melis, D., Jaakkola, T.: Towards robust interpretability with self-explaining neural networks. In: Advances in Neural Information Processing Systems, vol. 31. Curran Associates, Inc. (2018)
5. Bach, S., Binder, A., Montavon, G., Klauschen, F., Müller, K.R., Samek, W.: On pixel-wise explanations for non-linear classifier decisions by layer-wise relevance propagation. PLoS ONE **10**(7), e0130140 (2015). https://doi.org/10.1371/journal.pone.0130140
6. Bhusal, D., Rastogi, N.: SoK: modeling explainability in security monitoring for trust, privacy, and interpretability. arXiv preprint arXiv:2210.17376 (2022)
7. Carlini, N., Chien, S., Nasr, M., Song, S., Terzis, A., Tramèr, F.: Membership inference attacks from first principles. In: 2022 IEEE Symposium on Security and Privacy (SP), pp. 1897–1914 (2022). https://doi.org/10.1109/SP46214.2022.9833649
8. Carvalho, D., Pereira, E., Cardoso, J.: Machine learning interpretability: a survey on methods and metrics. Electronics **8**(8), 832 (2019). https://doi.org/10.3390/electronics8080832
9. Choquette-Choo, C.A., Tramer, F., Carlini, N., Papernot, N.: Label-only membership inference attacks. In: Proceedings of the 38th International Conference on Machine Learning, pp. 1964–1974. PMLR (2021)

10. Datta, A., Sen, S., Zick, Y.: Algorithmic transparency via quantitative input influence: theory and experiments with learning systems. In: 2016 IEEE Symposium on Security and Privacy (SP), pp. 598–617 (2016). https://doi.org/10.1109/SP.2016.42

11. De La Torre Parra, G., Selvera, L., Khoury, J., Irizarry, H., Bou-Harb, E., Rad, P.: Interpretable federated transformer log learning for cloud threat forensics. In: Proceedings 2022 Network and Distributed System Security Symposium. Internet Society, San Diego, CA, USA (2022). https://doi.org/10.14722/ndss.2022.23102

12. Dong, T., Li, S., Qiu, H., Lu, J.: An interpretable federated learning-based network intrusion detection framework. arXiv preprint arXiv:2201.03134 (2022)

13. European Commission: Regulation (EU) 2016/679 of the European Parliament and of the Council of 27 April 2016 on the protection of natural persons with regard to the processing of personal data and on the free movement of such data, and repealing Directive 95/46/EC (General Data Protection Regulation) (Text with EEA relevance) (2016). https://eur-lex.europa.eu/eli/reg/2016/679/oj

14. Franco, D., Oneto, L., Navarin, N., Anguita, D.: Toward learning trustworthily from data combining privacy, fairness, and explainability: an application to face recognition. Entropy **23**(8), 1047 (2021). https://doi.org/10.3390/e23081047

15. Guo, W., Mu, D., Xu, J., Su, P., Wang, G., Xing, X.: LEMNA: explaining deep learning based security applications. In: Proceedings of the 2018 ACM SIGSAC Conference on Computer and Communications Security, pp. 364–379. CCS 2018, Association for Computing Machinery, New York, NY, USA (2018). https://doi.org/10.1145/3243734.3243792

16. Gürtler, M., Zöllner, M.: Tuning white box model with black box models: transparency in credit risk modeling. Available at SSRN 4433967 (2023)

17. High-Level Expert Group on AI: Ethics guidelines for trustworthy AI. Tech. rep., European Commission, Brussels (2019). https://digital-strategy.ec.europa.eu/en/library/ethics-guidelines-trustworthy-ai

18. ISO, IEC: ISO/IEC 27001:2022(en), Information security, cybersecurity and privacy protection — Information security management systems — Requirements (2022)

19. Izzo, Z., Yoon, J., Arik, S.O., Zou, J.: Provable membership inference privacy. In: Workshop on Trustworthy and Socially Responsible Machine Learning, NeurIPS 2022 (2022)

20. Jiang, H., Kim, B., Guan, M., Gupta, M.: To trust or not to trust a classifier. In: Advances in Neural Information Processing Systems, vol. 31. Curran Associates, Inc. (2018)

21. Kariyappa, S., Qureshi, M.K.: Defending against model stealing attacks with adaptive misinformation. In: Proceedings of the IEEE/CVF Conference on Computer Vision and Pattern Recognition, pp. 770–778 (2020)

22. Liu, X., et al.: Privacy and security issues in deep learning: a survey. IEEE Access **9**, 4566–4593 (2021). https://doi.org/10.1109/ACCESS.2020.3045078

23. Loyola-González, O.: Black-box vs. white-box: understanding their advantages and weaknesses from a practical point of view. IEEE Access 7, 154096–154113 (2019)

24. Lundberg, S.M., Lee, S.I.: A unified approach to interpreting model predictions. In: Advances in Neural Information Processing Systems, vol. 30. Curran Associates, Inc. (2017)

25. Malek-Podjaski, M., Deligianni, F.: Towards explainable, privacy-preserved human-motion affect recognition. In: 2021 IEEE Symposium Series on Computational Intelligence (SSCI), pp. 01–09 (2021). https://doi.org/10.1109/SSCI50451.2021.9660129

26. McMahan, B., Moore, E., Ramage, D., Hampson, S., y Arcas, B.A.: Communication-efficient learning of deep networks from decentralized data. In: Proceedings of the 20th International Conference on Artificial Intelligence and Statistics, pp. 1273–1282. PMLR (2017)

27. Milli, S., Schmidt, L., Dragan, A.D., Hardt, M.: Model reconstruction from model explanations. In: Proceedings of the Conference on Fairness, Accountability, and Transparency, pp. 1–9. ACM, Atlanta GA USA (2019). https://doi.org/10.1145/3287560.3287562

28. Miura, T., Hasegawa, S., Shibahara, T.: MEGEX: data-free model extraction attack against gradient-based explainable AI. arXiv preprint arXiv:2107.08909 (2021)

29. Nori, H., Caruana, R., Bu, Z., Shen, J.H., Kulkarni, J.: Accuracy, interpretability, and differential privacy via explainable boosting. In: Proceedings of the 38th International Conference on Machine Learning, pp. 8227–8237. PMLR (2021)

30. Oksuz, A.C., Halimi, A., Ayday, E.: Autolycus: exploiting explainable AI (XAI) for model extraction attacks against decision tree models. arXiv preprint arXiv:2302.02162 (2023)

31. Patel, N., Shokri, R., Zick, Y.: Model explanations with differential privacy. In: 2022 ACM Conference on Fairness, Accountability, and Transparency, pp. 1895–1904. ACM, Seoul Republic of Korea (2022). https://doi.org/10.1145/3531146.3533235

32. Petkovic, D.: It is not "Accuracy vs. Explainability"—we need both for trustworthy AI systems. IEEE Trans. Technol. Soc. 4(1), 46–53 (2023). https://doi.org/10.1109/TTS.2023.3239921

33. Phong, L., Aono, Y., Hayashi, T., Wang, L., Moriai, S.: Privacy-preserving deep learning via additively homomorphic encryption. IEEE Trans. Inf. Forensics Secur. 13(5), 1333–1345 (2018). https://doi.org/10.1109/TIFS.2017.2787987

34. Raymond, A., Gunes, H., Prorok, A.: Culture-based explainable human-agent deconfliction. In: Proceedings of the 19th International Conference on Autonomous Agents and MultiAgent Systems, pp. 1107–1115. AAMAS 2020, International Foundation for Autonomous Agents and Multiagent Systems, Richland, SC (2020)

35. Raymond, A., Malencia, M., Paulino-Passos, G., Prorok, A.: Agree to disagree: subjective fairness in privacy-restricted decentralised conflict resolution. Front. Robot. AI 9, 733876 (2022)

36. Ribeiro, M., Singh, S., Guestrin, C.: "Why should I trust you?": explaining the predictions of any classifier. In: Proceedings of the 2016 Conference of the North American Chapter of the Association for Computational Linguistics: Demonstrations, pp. 97–101. Association for Computational Linguistics, San Diego, California (2016). https://doi.org/10.18653/v1/N16-3020

37. Saeed, W., Omlin, C.: Explainable AI (XAI): a systematic meta-survey of current challenges and future opportunities. Knowl.-Based Syst. 263, 110273 (2023). https://doi.org/10.1016/j.knosys.2023.110273

38. Saifullah, S., Mercier, D., Lucieri, A., Dengel, A., Ahmed, S.: Privacy meets explainability: a comprehensive impact benchmark. arXiv preprint arXiv:2211.04110 (2022)

39. Selvaraju, R.R., Cogswell, M., Das, A., Vedantam, R., Parikh, D., Batra, D.: Grad-CAM: visual explanations from deep networks via gradient-based localization. In: Proceedings of the IEEE International Conference on Computer Vision, pp. 618–626 (2017)

40. Shokri, R., Strobel, M., Zick, Y.: On the privacy risks of model explanations. In: Proceedings of the 2021 AAAI/ACM Conference on AI, Ethics, and Society, pp. 231–241. ACM, Virtual Event USA (2021). https://doi.org/10.1145/3461702.3462533

41. Simonyan, K., Vedaldi, A., Zisserman, A.: Deep inside convolutional networks: visualising image classification models and saliency maps. In: Proceedings of the International Conference on Learning Representations (ICLR). ICLR (2014)

42. Slack, D., Hilgard, S., Jia, E., Singh, S., Lakkaraju, H.: Fooling LIME and SHAP: adversarial attacks on post hoc explanation methods. In: Proceedings of the AAAI/ACM Conference on AI, Ethics, and Society, pp. 180–186. ACM, New York NY USA (2020). https://doi.org/10.1145/3375627.3375830

43. Smilkov, D., Thorat, N., Kim, B., Viégas, F., Wattenberg, M.: SmoothGrad: removing noise by adding noise. arXiv preprint arXiv:1706.03825 (2017)

44. Song, C., Shmatikov, V.: Overlearning reveals sensitive attributes. In: 8th International Conference on Learning Representations, ICLR 2020 (2020)

45. Song, Q., Lei, S., Sun, W., Zhang, Y.: Adaptive federated learning for digital twin driven industrial internet of things. In: IEEE Wireless Communications and Networking Conference, WCNC. vol. 2021-March (2021). https://doi.org/10.1109/WCNC49053.2021.9417370

46. Stadler, T., Oprisanu, B., Troncoso, C.: Synthetic data – anonymisation groundhog day. In: 31st USENIX Security Symposium (USENIX Security 22), pp. 1451–1468 (2022)

47. Sundararajan, M., Taly, A., Yan, Q.: Axiomatic attribution for deep networks. In: Proceedings of the 34th International Conference on Machine Learning, pp. 3319–3328. PMLR (2017)

48. Truong, J.B., Maini, P., Walls, R.J., Papernot, N.: Data-free model extraction. In: Proceedings of the IEEE/CVF Conference on Computer Vision and Pattern Recognition, pp. 4771–4780 (2021)

49. Wachter, S., Mittelstadt, B., Russell, C.: Counterfactual explanations without opening the black box: automated decisions and the GDPR. Harvard J. Law Technol. **31**, 841 (2017)

50. Wahab, O.A., Mourad, A., Otrok, H., Taleb, T.: Federated machine learning: survey, multi-level classification, desirable criteria and future directions in communication and networking systems. IEEE Commun. Surv. Tutorials **23**(2), 1342–1397 (2021). https://doi.org/10.1109/COMST.2021.3058573

51. Wainakh, A., Müßig, T., Grube, T., Mühlhäuser, M.: Label leakage from gradients in distributed machine learning. In: 2021 IEEE 18th Annual Consumer Communications & Networking Conference (CCNC), pp. 1–4 (2021). https://doi.org/10.1109/CCNC49032.2021.9369498

52. Warnecke, A., Arp, D., Wressnegger, C., Rieck, K.: Evaluating explanation methods for deep learning in security. In: 2020 IEEE European Symposium on Security and Privacy (EuroS&P), pp. 158–174 (2020). https://doi.org/10.1109/EuroSP48549.2020.00018

53. Yan, A., Huang, T., Ke, L., Liu, X., Chen, Q., Dong, C.: Explanation leaks: explanation-guided model extraction attacks. Inf. Sci. **632**, 269–284 (2023). https://doi.org/10.1016/j.ins.2023.03.020

54. Yang, Q., Liu, Y., Chen, T., Tong, Y.: Federated machine learning: concept and applications. ACM Trans. Intell. Syst. Technol. **10**(2), 1–19 (2019). https://doi.org/10.1145/3298981

55. Yin, H., Mallya, A., Vahdat, A., Alvarez, J.M., Kautz, J., Molchanov, P.: See through gradients: image batch recovery via GradInversion. In: Proceedings of the IEEE/CVF Conference on Computer Vision and Pattern Recognition, pp. 16337–16346 (2021)
56. Zhang, X., Wang, N., Shen, H., Ji, S., Luo, X., Wang, T.: Interpretable deep learning under fire. In: 29th {USENIX} Security Symposium ({USENIX} Security 20) (2020)
57. Zhao, B., Mopuri, K.R., Bilen, H.: iDLG: improved deep leakage from gradients. arXiv preprint arXiv:2001.02610 (2020)
58. Zhao, X., Zhang, W., Xiao, X., Lim, B.: Exploiting explanations for model inversion attacks. In: Proceedings of the IEEE/CVF International Conference on Computer Vision, pp. 682–692 (2021)
59. Zhu, L., Han, S.: Deep leakage from gradients. In: Yang, Q., Fan, L., Yu, H. (eds.) Federated Learning. LNCS (LNAI), vol. 12500, pp. 17–31. Springer, Cham (2020). https://doi.org/10.1007/978-3-030-63076-8_2

Utilizing the Ensemble Learning and XAI for Performance Improvements in IoT Network Attack Detection

Chathuranga Sampath Kalutharage[(✉)] [ID], Xiaodong Liu [ID],
Christos Chrysoulas [ID], and Oluwaseun Bamgboye [ID]

Edinburgh Napier University, Scotland, UK
{c.kalutharage,x.liu,c.chrysoulas,O.bamgboye}@napier.ac.uk
https://www.napier.ac.uk/

Abstract. As Internet of Things (IoT) networks continue to expand, it has become increasingly crucial to safeguard the security of these interconnected devices. This research study proposes a novel method for enhancing the effectiveness of IoT network threat detection by employing ensemble learning techniques and Explainable Artificial Intelligence (XAI).

The proposed method involves the utilization of an ensemble model combining an Autoencoder and eXtreme Gradient Boosting (XGBoost), a popular gradient-boosting algorithm. The workflow begins with quantizing the dataset to reduce computational complexity. Subsequently, the autoencoder is trained to learn a compressed representation of the quantized data, while XGBoost simultaneously performs classification tasks. To enhance the efficiency and accuracy of attack detection, feature importance analysis is conducted using XGBoost's `feature importance attribute`. This analysis enables the identification of the most influential features, which are then used to prepare a refined dataset, further reducing computational requirements. A Logarithmic layer is introduced within the autoencoder, enabling the linearization of relationships and handling of exponential characteristics.

The novel ensemble model, combining the Autoencoder's and XGBoost's strengths, is trained on the refined dataset. This unified model significantly enhances attack detection performance by leveraging the compressed representations learned by the autoencoder and the predictive power of XGBoost. Our proposed model is evaluated in the experiment on the CICIDS2017 data set. The evaluation metrics include accuracy, recall, precision, and runtime. For detection performance, our proposed model achieves an impressive 99.92% detection accuracy on the CICIDS2017 dataset, surpassing most state-of-the-art intrusion detection methods. Moreover, our proposed model exhibits the lowest runtime, further highlighting its efficiency.

Keywords: Attack detection · Ensemble learning · Explainable AI · XGBoost · Autoencoder

© The Author(s), under exclusive license to Springer Nature Switzerland AG 2024
S. Katsikas et al. (Eds.): ESORICS 2023 Workshops, LNCS 14399, pp. 125–139, 2024.
https://doi.org/10.1007/978-3-031-54129-2_8

1   Introduction

IoT devices run a significant risk of being the target of cyberattacks such as impersonation, interception, and unauthorised access by both people and viruses because of their connectedness via the Internet [23]. It is crucial to create a strong security system for these devices as a result. Due to the complexity of contemporary threats, traditional signature-based intrusion detection systems (IDS) have been inefficient in identifying these attacks [24]. As a result, the majority of current IoT security research focuses on using Artificial Intelligence (AI) techniques such as SVM [7], decision trees [17], neural networks [4], Autoencoder [15] and so on. AI systems present advanced solutions that exhibit improved capabilities in detecting and mitigating the impact of cyberattacks and potential threats on IoT data and infrastructures, particularly when countering modern attacks. The primary benefit of AI-based approaches is their ability to operate without seeking specific targets, eliminating the requirement to comprehensively define all known attack vectors and continuously update this attack dictionary [20]. AI systems are distinguished by their iterative and dynamic nature. IoT security measures may adapt to the changing threat landscape by utilising ML, providing improved defence and security capabilities [12].

IoT devices are characterized by limited resources, posing challenges when implementing traditional computing security solutions in IoT networks. The application of AI-based security mechanisms on IoT devices faces memory capacity limitations, necessitating the design of lightweight models [6]. However, many security datasets are complex and demand significant computational power. Data normalization serves as a necessary preprocessing step in numerous AI systems prior to feature engineering and classifier training. While this step can potentially improve model performance, it also carries the risk of diminishing data accuracy and detection accuracy, particularly in intrusion detection datasets. Furthermore, data normalization can introduce challenges when attempting to modify the dataset, as adding or removing data may necessitate a complete reconsideration of the training procedure, potentially resulting in increased runtime. In this study, we employ eXplainable Artificial Intelligence (XAI) technology to reduce the number of features by identifying the most influential ones for attack identification. This feature reduction process aims to refine the dataset, enhance performance, and achieve low computational power requirements while maintaining higher data accuracy and detection accuracy.

Machine learning-based detection techniques have yielded intriguing findings in the field of security. Among the available methodologies, binary detection techniques fall short in providing comprehensive security as they merely identify the presence of intrusions. Consequently, it is crucial to recognize the specific attack category to implement appropriate defences against each unique threat. This identification proves valuable for decision-making by network administrators, who can then take steps to address the vulnerabilities exploited by the attack. However, it is worth noting that existing multi-class detection techniques, aimed at categorizing attacks, often have lower hit rates compared to binary methods [2,31], which can make it challenging to detect certain types of attacks [13, 25]. Our work makes a significant contribution to the state of the art in attack detection and identification.

In this paper, the proposed approach is based on ensemble methods and a dual analytic architecture. Ensemble learning is used because there are machine learning scenarios where even the best model is not accurate enough. Hybrid methods are used to merge models to reduce model instability. State-of-the-art methods had several limitations in terms of identifying specific attacks. The ensemble method for IoT network attack detection combines an autoencoder as an anomaly detection model in the first stage and a multi-class detection method in the second stage. In the first stage, the autoencoder learns normal patterns during training and identifies anomalies by measuring the reconstruction error of input data during testing. Instances with high reconstruction error beyond a threshold are classified as potential attacks. In the second stage, a multi-class classifier, XGBoost utilizes features extracted from network traffic features to determine the specific attack type. The classifier is trained to classify the detected anomalies into different attack categories.

This ensemble approach leverages the strengths of both the autoencoder's anomaly detection and the multi-class classifier's attack type identification, resulting in a more comprehensive and accurate IoT network attack detection system. It enables a nuanced understanding of detected attacks and facilitates the implementation of appropriate defense strategies. Careful model training, feature selection, and threshold setting are crucial for the reliability and performance of the ensemble method. This paper makes several key contributions, which include the following:

- We proposed a new methodology for refining datasets in attack detection by reducing the features to include only the most influential ones. This methodology leverages the principles of XAI (Explainable Artificial Intelligence) to identify and prioritize the features that have the most significant impact on the detection of attacks.
- This paper presents a new ensemble approach for detecting IoT attacks. The approach combines unsupervised learning using an autoencoder with a multiclass classifier, XGBoost, to achieve higher accuracy in attack detection.
- We have developed a computationally efficient model, surpassing the state-of-the-art approach, and conducted a comprehensive evaluation of our proposed method using the CIC-IDS dataset

The paper is organized as follows: Sect. 2 provides an overview of the background and related work in the field. Section 3 presents a detailed description of the proposed method. The obtained results using the CIC-IDS benchmark dataset are discussed in Sect. 4. Finally, Sect. 5 concludes the paper, summarizing the findings and highlighting potential future research directions.

2   Related work

Extensive research has been conducted on the detection of IoT network attacks, as well as traditional network intrusion detection methods. Sumaiya Thaseen

Ikram et al. [14] proposed an ensemble intrusion detection model that merged different neural network types, such as Long Short-Term Memory (LSTM), Backpropagation Network (BPN), and Multilayer Perceptron (MLP). The proposed model consisted of two core modules: the learning algorithm module and the evaluation module. The learning algorithm module included LSTM, BPN, and MLP, which were utilized to generate training data as input. The outputs of these three models were then sent to XGBoost in the evaluation module for further analysis. However, the study did not employ explainability for feature selection, and it also omitted the use of feature reduction techniques to create a more lightweight model. Hagos et al. [10] proposed a detection strategy that utilizes Support Vector Machines (SVMs) and the l1-regularized method with Least Absolute Shrinkage and Selection Operator (LASSO). This strategy aims to achieve robust regression for binary and multiclass attack categorization in network intrusion detection. Chunhe Song et al. [29] proposed an intrusion detection system method that combines deep learning and feature-based techniques. The method uses a Bayesian approach to tune XGBoost's hyperparameters for maximum performance while minimizing performance loss due to incorrect parameter selection. Additionally, a genetic algorithm-based crossover technique is proposed to reduce the likelihood of the Bayesian algorithm becoming trapped in local optimization during the optimization phase. The final detection results are merged based on the outputs of both LSTM and XGBoost, which are used as detectors in the system. This method does not cater to the resource constraint demand of IoT networks, and it also lacks the utilization of explainability for achieving more precise results.

Vinayakumar et al. [31] also explored deep networks for intrusion detection. They proposed a Deep Belief Networks (DBN)-based approach. The authors in [21] proposed a new intrusion detection method based on Sequential Online Extreme Learning Machine (OS-ELM) for fog computing environments. ELM is a neural network that is known for its fast training speed and good generalizability. OS-ELM is a modification of ELM that can be used to handle online applications. The proposed method uses multiclass detection, but this makes it more difficult to identify attacks that involve privilege escalation and probing. Chaofei Tang et al. [30] proposed a network intrusion detection system based on LightGBM and autoencoders. The LightGBM method was used for feature selection, and the AE was then used as a classifier for training and detection. The authors in [35] introduced a novel model for intrusion detection system (IDS) that combines a deep neural network (DNN) with an enhanced conditional variational autoencoder (ICVAE). The ICVAE is employed to automatically learn potential sparse representations between features and classes in the dataset. This helps improve detection accuracy by balancing the training data and generating new attack samples based on the defined intrusion categories. Furthermore, the weights of the hidden layers in the DNN are initialized using the ICVAE encoder, simplifying the forward and backward propagation processes.

Blanco et al. [3] proposed a method for multi-class network attack classification that can be installed in a router. The method is based on a Convolutional

Neural Network (CNN), which is a type of neural network that was originally developed for image classification. The method was validated using two open datasets, UNSW-NB15 and NSL-KDD. However, the work did not consider the IoT setting. The authors in [28] proposed a lightweight machine learning-based intrusion detection system (IDS) that uses a new feature selection technique called Correlated-Set Thresholding on Gain-Ratio (CST-GR) and Decision Tree (DT). The IDS was implemented on a Raspberry Pi. The method was tested on the Bot-IoT dataset, but results for benign traffic classification were not provided. Xukui Li et al. [16] proposed an efficient deep learning technique that combines an autoencoder (AE) and random forest (RF). The model uses RF to select the most useful features from the dataset. The AP clustering algorithm is then used to divide the selected features into subgroups, which provides information for the AE to determine the root mean square error (RMSE). The network traffic is then classified as normal or abnormal using either K-means or the Gaussian mixture model (GMM), depending on the RMSE values. Shafiq et al. [25] introduced a novel feature selection technique called CorrAUC. This innovative approach efficiently filters features and selects significant ones for machine learning models using the Area Under the Curve (AUC) metric in conjunction with the wrapper technique. To validate their proposed methodology, the authors utilized the Bot-IoT dataset and evaluated four machine-learning algorithms. Among these algorithms, Random Forest (RF) demonstrated the highest performance, further confirming the effectiveness of the suggested approach. RFs are ensemble algorithms that use a collection of combined decision trees to improve generalization and robustness. Maniriho et al. [19] proposed an anomaly-based intrusion detection system (IDS) for IoT networks. The system uses a hybrid resource selection mechanism to select the most relevant resources and Random Forest to classify each stream of traffic as normal or abnormal. The system was evaluated using the IoTID20 dataset, which is one of the most recent datasets for anomaly detection in the IoT ecosystem. The results showed that the system was effective in detecting anomalies. However, the system has not been evaluated in the multi-class detection scenario.

Many approaches have been proposed for detecting and identifying network intrusions in this area. Some of these methods have used machine learning techniques, but they have not taken into account the specific context of IoT networks. Others have been able to identify certain types of attacks, but they have been difficult to use in practice. None of the existing methods have used XAI, ensemble methods, or been able to achieve the same level of accuracy as the proposed model with low computational power requirements.

3   Methodology

3.1   Overview of Approach

The increasing use of IoT-based systems, their security flaws, and research on attack detection in these settings all point to the importance of being able to identify the specific class of an attack. This is essential for implementing counter-measures and making decisions. However, current multi-class detection methods often have difficulty identifying specific attack types [8]. This paper presents an ensemble approach aimed at identifying and classifying attack types in IoT contexts. The proposed method involves several key steps. First, we employ XAI to refine the dataset and identify the most influential features for attack detection. Next, we train an XGBoost model exclusively using these selected features, focusing on the top 20 most influential ones. Additionally, an autoencoder model is trained using benign data. The CIC flow meter[1] is then utilized to extract features from PCAP files, which are subsequently preprocessed for inference using both the autoencoder and XGBoost models. Figure 1 illustrates the main steps of the engineering pipeline in our proposed method.

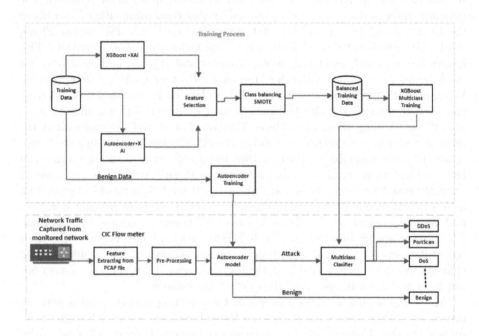

Fig. 1. Engineering pipeline of the proposed method.

3.2 Dataset Refinement with XAI

Many security datasets are large and complex, requiring a lot of processing power. Data normalization is a common preprocessing step used by many AI systems before feature engineering and classifier training. While this can improve model performance, it also risks reducing data accuracy and detection accuracy,

---

[1] https://www.unb.ca/cic/research/applications.html.

especially in datasets used for intrusion detection. Additionally, adding or removing data may require a complete re-evaluation of the training process, significantly increasing runtime. As a result, data normalization can present challenges when trying to adjust the dataset.

In this study, we use XAI technology to select the most important attributes for attack identification, thereby reducing the number of features. XAI is a type of AI that allows us to understand how models make decisions. This is important for intrusion detection, as it helps us to identify the specific features that are most indicative of an attack. By reducing the number of features, we can improve the performance of the model while also making it more interpretable. First, we trained both models and applied XAI techniques to identify the specific features that are most indicative of an attack. The steps for applying XAI are outlined in Algorithm 1 and Algorithm 2. We successfully reduced the dataset to 20 features while maintaining higher accuracy for each model. In addition, we conducted data type casting to determine the most efficient data type for the CIC-IDS dataset. Through our analysis, we found that utilizing a 32-bit data type proved to be the most efficient choice. This casting resulted in a significant reduction in memory usage, up to 48.75%, compared to the usage of the default 64-bit data type, while maintaining the same accuracy with less prediction time.

SHAP Values: In the realm of additive feature attribution techniques, the Shapley additive explanation (SHAP) approach encompasses previously introduced explanation methods like local interpretable model-agnostic explanations (LIME) and deep learning essential features (DeepLIFT) [18]. SHAP employs Shapley values to elucidate a particular prediction, with these values stemming from the principles of game theory. The SHAP framework introduces Kernel SHAP, which is a model-agnostic estimate of SHAP values. Kernel SHAP combines linear LIME with Shapley values to construct a localized explanation model. This model utilizes weighted linear regression and is established on a background dataset along with a sample from the potential group of data elements.

Algorithm 1. Finding Most Influential Features using SHAP Values with Autoencoder

---

Require: Autoencoder model, X test data
Ensure: Top features based on SHAP values
1: **function** FINDTOPFEATURES(autoencoder, x_{test})
2:    Create SHAP explainer object
3:    Compute SHAP values for the test data
4:    Compute mean absolute SHAP values for each feature
5:    Get indices of top features based on SHAP values
6:    Get top feature names
7:    **return** Top feature names
8: **end function**

Algorithm 2. Finding Most Influential Features using SHAP Values

---

Require: XGBoost model, X test data
Ensure: Top features based on SHAP values
 1: **function** FINDTOPFEATURES(xgb, x_{test})
 2:     Create SHAP explainer object
 3:     Compute SHAP values for the test data
 4:     Compute mean absolute SHAP values for each feature
 5:     Get indices of top features based on SHAP values
 6:     Get top feature names
 7:     **return** Top feature names
 8: **end function**

3.3 Attack Detection

The next step in the proposed approach is anomaly detection. An autoencoder is used to perform this task, which distinguishes between attack and benign traffic. Autoencoders are important tools for anomaly detection. Recent research has focused on anomaly-based attack detection for security systems [22,27]. Autoencoders are a type of neural network that can learn to reconstruct its input. This means that after training, an autoencoder can take an input and produce an output that attempts to replicate the input itself. Autoencoders are made up of two parts: an encoder and a decoder. The encoder takes the input and transforms it into a latent representation. The decoder then takes this latent representation and reconstructs the input. Autoencoder models were utilized to identify anomalous network traffic behaviours. To achieve this, we trained an autoencoder to reconstruct input data. Subsequently, we computed an anomaly score by calculating the difference between the input value and the reconstructed output value. Anomalies were identified as data points with high anomaly scores. In our study, the computation of the reconstruction error is presented in Eq. 1. We employ an anomaly detection model (F), where an input row (X) consists of an array of features (x_i), and its corresponding output row (X') contains reconstructed feature values (x'_i). The reconstruction error for a specific row is determined by summing the reconstruction errors for all features unique to that row. It is recognised as an anomaly if the reconstruction error is greater than the input value. Benign data was used to train the model. We employed a fully connected autoencoder model with a RELU activation function. To reduce the network load, we used only 2 hidden layers, with 10 and 32 neurons in each layer, respectively. The threshold for detecting anomalous data was determined by selecting the largest mean squared error (MSE) from the benign data.

$$F(X, X') = \sum_{i=1}^{n}(x_i - x'_i)^2 \tag{1}$$

3.4 Attack Identification

The subsequent stage in the proposed approach involves identification, which focuses on analyzing traffic that has been previously identified as an anomaly and determining the specific type of attack. This step employs a more robust method by utilizing XGBoost for the identification process. We first explain the gradient boosting decision tree (GBDT) before introducing XGBoost. In a nutshell, the classification and regression tree (CART) results are accumulated by GBDT to reach the conclusion. The fundamental principle is that every tree learns the difference between the true value and the predicted value of all prior CART results. However, each iteration of GBDT necessitates numerous traversals of the full data set. The size of the data can only be as much as what can fit in memory; otherwise, time-consuming read and write operations must be performed repeatedly. Therefore, GBDT is unable to satisfy its needs when presented with huge and highdimensional data. XGBoost was created to address GBDT's problem in handling big samples and high-dimensional data [5]. XGBoost is a powerful distributed gradient boosting library that excels in terms of performance, flexibility, and portability. It provides extensive support for various machine learning techniques within the gradient boosting framework. Compared to traditional gradient boosting methods like GBDT (Gradient Boosting Decision Tree), XGBoost offers several notable advantages:

- The algorithm introduces a distinct loss function and elevates the objective function from the first order to the second order
- The inclusion of the L2 regularization term on the number of leaf nodes and leaf weights effectively reduces the model's variance and prevents overfitting
- The base learner of the algorithm supports both CART
- To leverage the block structure and accurately locate data separation points, the method stores the presorted dataset in a sparse matrix storage format. This approach reduces the computational workload significantly, enabling more efficient calculations
- The introduction of sparsity-aware algorithms incorporates automatic handling of default values. This feature automatically splits samples with default values by evaluating the gain of default-valued samples in both left and right branches. The algorithm selects the branch with the highest gain, enabling effective division of samples with default values
- To mitigate overfitting and reduce computational complexity, the algorithm incorporates column sampling. This technique draws inspiration from the sampling process used in random forests. By randomly selecting a subset of columns (features) during the training process, the algorithm effectively reduces overfitting and computational requirements
- The shrinkage approach is presented. The weight of each leaf node of the tree is multiplied by the reduction weight in each iteration, which reduces the influence of each tree and increases the opportunity for optimisation of the subsequent trees

4   Results and Evaluation

In this section, we provide an overview of the methodology employed to evaluate the proposed approach. We discuss the key aspects of the evaluation process and present the results obtained from conducting experiments. Evaluating detection methods is crucial to assess their applicability in real-world scenarios. The primary objective is to obtain an estimation of the practical accuracy of the approaches under investigation.

4.1   Dataset and Experimental Environment

This paper conducted comparative experiments on the CICIDS2017 dataset to validate the simulation results in the field of network intrusion detection. The experiments were divided into two sets: an ablation experiment that compared the impact of each module on performance, and a comparison with other existing intrusion detection algorithms to evaluate the algorithm's overall performance. The simulations were implemented using Python 3.6 in a Windows environment. The experiments were conducted on an ASUS ZenBook equipped with a 2.30 GHz Intel Core i7 processor and 16 GB of RAM.

4.2   Performance Metrics

The evaluation of our proposed model relies on several key metrics: recall, precision, F1-score, and accuracy. These metrics can be calculated using the scikit-learn machine learning module in Python. See Eqs. 2, 3, 4, 5. Accuracy represents the percentage of accurately predicted samples out of the total samples. Precision measures the proportion of correctly predicted positive samples among all predicted positive samples, while recall measures the proportion of correctly predicted positive samples among all actual positive samples in the original sample. The F1-score is a weighted harmonic average of precision and recall.

$$\text{Recall} = \frac{\text{True Positives}}{\text{True Positives} + \text{False Negatives}} \tag{2}$$

$$\text{Precision} = \frac{\text{True Positives}}{\text{True Positives} + \text{False Positives}} \tag{3}$$

$$\text{F1} - \text{score} = 2 \times \frac{\text{Precision} \times \text{Recall}}{\text{Precision} + \text{Recall}} \tag{4}$$

$$\text{Accuracy} = \frac{\text{Number of correctly predicted samples}}{\text{Total number of samples}} \tag{5}$$

The datasets utilized in the studies were divided into training and testing sets, with a stratification ratio of 70% for training and 30% for testing. The metrics mentioned above were computed based on the predictions made by the models on the testing set.

4.3   Experimental Evaluation on CIC-IDS Dataset

The suggested method was evaluated using the CSE-CIC-IDS dataset[2], which was developed through a collaboration between the Canadian Institute for Cybersecurity (CIC) and the Communications Security Establishment (CSE). The objective of this project was to create a comprehensive dataset comprising diverse sets of instructional data. These datasets include user profiles with various events paired with network-observed behaviours. The CSE-CIC-IDS dataset serves as a valuable resource for assessing the proposed method. We chose this dataset due to its widespread use in the literature. This dataset consists of 13 classes including benign classes which are Benign, Bot, DDoS, DoS GoldenEye, DoS Hulk, DoS Slowhttptest, DoS slowloris, FTP Patator, Heartbleed, Infiltration, Portscan, SSH-Patator, Web Attack. The proposed approach demonstrated high detection rates for most types of attacks, surpassing or matching the detection rates achieved by current state-of-the-art methods. The results obtained by the proposed approach, along with the results from existing state-of-the-art methods, are summarized in Table 1. In this study, we specifically employ recall (REC) and precision (PRE) as evaluation metrics. Recall measures the proportion of true positive instances correctly identified out of the total actual positive instances (true positives and false negatives). It provides insights into the model's ability to capture positive instances and is particularly useful when identifying all positive instances is important. Precision, on the other hand, measures the proportion of true positive instances correctly predicted out of the total predicted positive instances (true positives and false positives). It assesses the model's ability to avoid false positives and is valuable when minimizing false alarms is a priority. By considering both recall and precision, we gain a more comprehensive understanding of the model's performance in correctly identifying positive instances and minimizing false positives. Further, all types of DoS attacks, including DoS GoldenEye, DoS Hulk, and DoS Slowhttptest, exhibit similar detection rates, we refer to them collectively as DoS attacks for the sake of brevity and clarity. With the exception of the BOTNET attack class, the proposed approach achieves higher detection rates for all other attack classes compared to the current state of the art. Notably, the detection rates for Infiltration and Web attacks are particularly higher than those reported in previous works. The effectiveness of the proposed approach in detecting these specific attack classes demonstrates its superiority over existing methods. Furthermore, the overall performance of the proposed model significantly outperforms the current state of the art, as demonstrated in Table 2. The comprehensive evaluation of the model across various metrics highlights its superior performance and effectiveness compared to existing methods.

---

[2] https://www.unb.ca/cic/datasets/ids-2017.html.

Table 1. Results of comparison of each attack type with current state of the art

	DNN [6]		RF [6]		ET+Multi Cla [6]		**Proposed model**	
	PRE	REC	PRE	REC	PRE	REC	PRE	REC
Benign	98.81	99.91	98.88	99.78	98.96	99.58	99.96	99.80
BOT	99.77	99.88	99.62	99.77	99.99	99.90	86.78	82.89
DDoS	99.47	99.88	99.91	99.91	99.99	99.94	100	100
DoS	95.32	89.61	96.35	89.26	97.38	88.13	100	100
FTP-Patator	–	–	–	–	–	–	100	100
Heartbleed	–	–	–	–	–	–	100	67.97
Infiltration	44.10	01.79	29.60	07.08	28.46	13.50	100	64.87
Portscan	–	–	–	–	–	–	99.77	100
SSH-Patator	–	–	–	–	–	–	100	100
Web Attack	100	39.29	92.31	42.86	39.34	85.71	99.92	99.23

Table 2. Overall model Performance

Detection Method	Accuracy	Time(s)
NB-SVM [9]	98.92	–
T-SNERF [11]	99.78	–
MTH-IDS [34]	99.89	478.2
LMDRT-SVM2 [32]	99.28	–
DT+rule-based model [1]	96.66	160.07
KNN [26]	96.30	152463.6
RF [26]	98.82	1848.3
LogAE-XGBoost [33]	99.92	1092.35
ET+MultiClass Clasi [6]	98.21	–
Proposed Model	**99.92**	**826.30**

5   Conclusions

This paper introduces a novel IoT network attack detection system that leverages XAI and ensemble learning techniques. The proposed model incorporates XAI to identify the most influential features for attack detection and to reduce the feature space for a lightweight model. An autoencoder is employed for anomaly detection in the first stage, allowing agile release of benign traffic and enabling more robust inspection using the XGBoost approach for unidentified events. Additionally, the identification of attack types provides valuable information for mitigation mechanisms and network management. The proposed approach demonstrates comparable or superior performance, highlighting its robustness. The initial experiments conducted on the CIC-IDS dataset have shown promising results. However, future work will focus on evaluating the proposed approach using additional benchmark datasets, such as BoT IoT[3] and the NSL-KDD[4] security dataset. This broader evaluation will ensure the approach's robustness and applicability across various network environments.

Furthermore, our plan includes simulating the system on real-world IoT and critical infrastructure networks to assess its effectiveness in real-time intrusion detection. This practical evaluation will provide valuable insights into the approach's performance in production settings. As a first step, we will deploy the approach on a Raspberry Pi device using TensorFlow Lite, allowing us to test it on a low-cost, embedded platform. Once successful on the Raspberry Pi, we will explore the potential of deploying the approach on other embedded systems or MCUs. This scalability investigation will help expand its reach and applicability. In addition to attack detection, future research will concentrate on developing countermeasure systems tailored to specific types of attacks. By incorporating targeted actions for each attack type, we aim to enhance the effectiveness of the proposed approach. The experiments and simulations we plan to conduct will serve as crucial steps in assessing the feasibility of the approach and identifying areas for improvement.

References

1. Ahmim, A., Maglaras, L., Ferrag, M.A., Derdour, M., Janicke, H.: A novel hierarchical intrusion detection system based on decision tree and rules-based models. In: 2019 15th International Conference on Distributed Computing in Sensor Systems (DCOSS), pp. 228–233. IEEE (2019)
2. Almiani, M., AbuGhazleh, A., Al-Rahayfeh, A., Atiewi, S., Razaque, A.: Deep recurrent neural network for IoT intrusion detection system. Simul. Model. Pract. Theory **101**, 102031 (2020). https://doi.org/10.1016/j.simpat.2019.102031, https://www.sciencedirect.com/science/article/pii/S1569190X19301625, modeling and Simulation of Fog Computing
3. Blanco, R., Malagón, P., Cilla, J.J., Moya, J.M.: Multiclass network attack classifier using CNN tuned with genetic algorithms. In: 2018 28th International Symposium on Power and Timing Modeling, Optimization and Simulation (PATMOS), pp. 177–182 (2018). https://doi.org/10.1109/PATMOS.2018.8463997
4. Canêdo, D.R.C., Romariz, A.R.S.R.: Intrusion detection system in ad hoc networks with artificial neural networks and algorithm k-means. IEEE Lat. Am. Trans. **17**(07), 1109–1115 (2019)
5. Chen, T., Guestrin, C.: XGBoost: a scalable tree boosting system. In: Proceedings of the 22nd ACM SIGKDD International Conference on Knowledge Discovery and Data Mining, pp. 785–794 (2016)
6. de Souza, C.A., Westphall, C.B., Machado, R.B.: Two-step ensemble approach for intrusion detection and identification in IoT and fog computing environments. Comput. Electr. Eng. **98**, 107694 (2022). https://doi.org/10.1016/j.compeleceng.2022.107694, https://www.sciencedirect.com/science/article/pii/S0045790622000155

---

[3] https://research.unsw.edu.au/projects/bot-iot-dataset.
[4] https://www.unb.ca/cic/datasets/nsl.html.

7. Deng, H., Zeng, Q.A., Agrawal, D.P.: SVM-based intrusion detection system for wireless ad hoc networks. In: 2003 IEEE 58th Vehicular Technology Conference. VTC 2003-Fall (IEEE Cat. No. 03CH37484), vol. 3, pp. 2147–2151. IEEE (2003)
8. Diro, A.A., Chilamkurti, N.: Distributed attack detection scheme using deep learning approach for internet of things. Future Gener. Comput. Syst. **82**, 761–768 (2018). https://doi.org/10.1016/j.future.2017.08.043, https://www.sciencedirect.com/science/article/pii/S0167739X17308488
9. Gu, J., Lu, S.: An effective intrusion detection approach using SVM with naïve bayes feature embedding. Comput. Secur. **103**, 102158 (2021)
10. Hagos, D.H., Yazidi, A., Kure, i., Engelstad, P.E.: Enhancing security attacks analysis using regularized machine learning techniques. In: 2017 IEEE 31st International Conference on Advanced Information Networking and Applications (AINA), pp. 909–918 (2017). https://doi.org/10.1109/AINA.2017.19
11. Hammad, M., Hewahi, N., Elmedany, W.: T-SNERF: a novel high accuracy machine learning approach for intrusion detection systems. IET Inf. Secur. **15**(2), 178–190 (2021)
12. Hussain, F., Hussain, R., Hassan, S.A., Hossain, E.: Machine learning in IoT security: current solutions and future challenges. IEEE Commun. Surv. Tutorials **22**(3), 1686–1721 (2020)
13. Ieracitano, C., Adeel, A., Morabito, F.C., Hussain, A.: A novel statistical analysis and autoencoder driven intelligent intrusion detection approach. Neurocomputing **387**, 51–62 (2020). https://doi.org/10.1016/j.neucom.2019.11.016, https://www.sciencedirect.com/science/article/pii/S0925231219315759
14. Ikram, S.T., et al.: Anomaly detection using XGBoost ensemble of deep neural network models. Cybern. Inf. Technol. **21**(3), 175–188 (2021)
15. Kalutharage, C.S., Liu, X., Chrysoulas, C., Pitropakis, N., Papadopoulos, P.: Explainable AI-based DDOS attack identification method for IoT networks. Computers **12**(2), 32 (2023)
16. Li, X., Chen, W., Zhang, Q., Wu, L.: Building auto-encoder intrusion detection system based on random forest feature selection. Comput. Secur. **95**, 101851 (2020)
17. Luna, J.M., et al.: Building more accurate decision trees with the additive tree. Proc. Natl. Acad. Sci. **116**(40), 19887–19893 (2019)
18. Lundberg, S.M., Lee, S.I.: A unified approach to interpreting model predictions. In: Advances in Neural Information Processing Systems, vol. 30 (2017)
19. Maniriho, P., Niyigaba, E., Bizimana, Z., Twiringiyimana, V., Mahoro, L.J., Ahmad, T.: Anomaly-based intrusion detection approach for IoT networks using machine learning. In: 2020 International Conference on Computer Engineering, Network, and Intelligent Multimedia (CENIM), pp. 303–308 (2020). https://doi.org/10.1109/CENIM51130.2020.9297958
20. Mitchell, R., Chen, I.R.: A survey of intrusion detection techniques for cyber-physical systems. ACM Comput. Surv. (CSUR) **46**(4), 1–29 (2014)
21. Prabavathy, S., Sundarakantham, K., Shalinie, S.M.: Design of cognitive fog computing for intrusion detection in internet of things. J. Commun. Networks **20**(3), 291–298 (2018). https://doi.org/10.1109/JCN.2018.000041
22. Rajapaksha, S., Kalutarage, H., Al-Kadri, M.O., Petrovski, A., Madzudzo, G.: Beyond vanilla: Improved autoencoder-based ensemble in-vehicle intrusion detection system. J. Inf. Secur. Appl. **77**, 103570 (2023). https://doi.org/10.1016/j.jisa.2023.103570, https://www.sciencedirect.com/science/article/pii/S2214212623001540
23. Samaila, M.G., Neto, M., Fernandes, D.A., Freire, M.M., Inácio, P.R.: Challenges of securing internet of things devices: a survey. Secur. Priv. **1**(2), e20 (2018)

24. Kalutharage, C.S., Liu, X., Chrysoulas, C.: Explainable AI and deep autoencoders based security framework for IoT network attack certainty (extended abstract). In: Li, W., Furnell, S., Meng, W. (eds.) Attacks and Defenses for the Internet-of-Things. ADIoT 2022. Lecture Notes in Computer Science, vol. 13745. Springer, Cham (2022). https://doi.org/10.1007/978-3-031-21311-3_8
25. Shafiq, M., Tian, Z., Bashir, A.K., Du, X., Guizani, M.: CorrAUC: a malicious bot-IoT traffic detection method in IoT network using machine-learning techniques. IEEE Internet Things J. **8**(5), 3242–3254 (2021). https://doi.org/10.1109/JIOT. 2020.3002255
26. Sharafaldin, I., Lashkari, A.H., Ghorbani, A.A.: Toward generating a new intrusion detection dataset and intrusion traffic characterization. ICISSp **1**, 108–116 (2018)
27. Singh, J., Nene, M.J.: A survey on machine learning techniques for intrusion detection systems. Int. J. Adv. Res. Comput. Commun. Eng. **2**(11), 4349–4355 (2013)
28. Soe, Y.N., Feng, Y., Santosa, P.I., Hartanto, R., Sakurai, K.: Towards a lightweight detection system for cyber attacks in the IoT environment using corresponding features. Electronics **9**(1), 144 (2020). https://doi.org/10.3390/electronics9010144, https://www.mdpi.com/2079-9292/9/1/144
29. Song, C., Sun, Y., Han, G., Rodrigues, J.J.: Intrusion detection based on hybrid classifiers for smart grid. Comput. Electr. Eng. **93**, 107212 (2021)
30. Tang, C., Luktarhan, N., Zhao, Y.: An efficient intrusion detection method based on lightGBM and autoencoder. Symmetry **12**(9), 1458 (2020)
31. Vinayakumar, R., Soman, K.P., Poornachandran, P.: Evaluating effectiveness of shallow and deep networks to intrusion detection system. In: 2017 International Conference on Advances in Computing, Communications and Informatics (ICACCI), pp. 1282–1289 (2017). https://doi.org/10.1109/ICACCI.2017.8126018
32. Wang, H., Gu, J., Wang, S.: An effective intrusion detection framework based on SVM with feature augmentation. Knowl.-Based Syst. **136**, 130–139 (2017)
33. Xu, W., Fan, Y., et al.: Intrusion detection systems based on logarithmic autoencoder and XGBoost. Secur. Commun. Networks **2022**, 9068724 (2022)
34. Yang, L., Moubayed, A., Shami, A.: MTH-IDS: a multitiered hybrid intrusion detection system for internet of vehicles. IEEE Internet Things J. **9**(1), 616–632 (2021)
35. Yang, Y., Zheng, K., Wu, C., Yang, Y.: Improving the classification effectiveness of intrusion detection by using improved conditional variational autoencoder and deep neural network. Sensors **19**(11), 2528 (2019)

Digital Twins in Healthcare: Security, Privacy, Trust and Safety Challenges

Cecilie Solberg Jørgensen[1], Ankur Shukla[2(✉)], and Basel Katt[3]

[1] Department of Information Security and Communication Technology (IIK),
Norwegian University of Science and Technology (NTNU), Trondheim, Norway
`cecilie98@gmail.com`
[2] Department of Risk and Security, Institute for Energy Technology, Halden, Norway
`ankur.shukla@ife.no`
[3] Department of Information Security and Communication Technology (IIK),
Norwegian University of Science and Technology (NTNU), Gjøvik, Norway
`basel.katt@ntnu.no`

Abstract. The health sector is a critical and vulnerable infrastructure, making it an easy target for hackers and attackers. Healthcare is also a highly trusted sector that contains sensitive and personal information; therefore, exploiting its vulnerabilities can lead to great financial and political gains. The digital twin is an emerging technology that could play a powerful role in the healthcare sector in the future, for example, offering customized diagnosis and treatment to each patient. Although digital twins come with several advantages, there are several challenges to implementing digital twins successfully in healthcare. In this paper, we have discussed the different challenges related to the security, privacy, trust, and safety of digital twins and its implementation in healthcare. We have also presented the comparative conflict analysis of implementing the security, safety, privacy, trust, and operational requirements for IoT digital twins.

Keywords: Security · Privacy · Digital Twins · IoT · Healthcare

1 Introduction

The digital twin is one of the basic key pillars of Industry 4.0 [15]. In the 1960s, NASA used technology that reminded of a digital twin for the Apollo 13 spacecraft [8]. However, with the rise of Industry 4.0, the digital twin has shown its true potential in recent years. This is due to huge advancements in important enabling technologies for the digital twin, such as artificial intelligence (AI), 5G, big data, cloud computing, and the Internet of Things (IoT). Digital twins are virtual simulations of real-world products, machines, systems, and processes based on sensor data. This allows businesses to understand better and maintain industrial systems and products. The digital twin can give an accurate and detailed representation of the physical counterpart using customized models with parameters such as time, position, location, processes, functions, and geometrical shapes. These factors contribute to distinguishing a digital twin from a normal simulation model.

© The Author(s), under exclusive license to Springer Nature Switzerland AG 2024
S. Katsikas et al. (Eds.): ESORICS 2023 Workshops, LNCS 14399, pp. 140–153, 2024.
https://doi.org/10.1007/978-3-031-54129-2_9

Digital twins are defined in many different ways in literature, but there seems to be a lack of a common understanding of what a digital twin is [23]. It is common knowledge that a digital twin system consists of three main components: a digital twin, a physical twin, and a communication link between these two [36]. Digital twins are enabled by several technologies, such as IoT, cloud computing, AI, augmented reality (AR), virtual reality (VR), and different modelling and simulation tools. Redelinghuys et al. [37] proposed a six-layer digital twin architecture as a means of properly integrating devices and their virtual replicas in the cyber-physical domain, as well as of effectively exchanging information and data among digital twins, physical twins, and the outside world as shown in Fig. 1.

The digital twin is a technology that has the potential to change the way of operation and management in highly trusted sectors, such as healthcare. However, implementing digital twins in this industry is confronted with several challenges regarding security, privacy, trust and safety [38]. However, digital twins can also be used in enhancing security and resilience, given their capability to identify malicious activities within a system. In the past, some research works have been done on the security and privacy of digital twins in healthcare [13,32–34,42,46]. Kuehner et al. [23] presented a review to address misconceptions and inconsistencies related to what is considered a digital twin and aimed to contribute to a common understanding of digital twins. Alcaraz et al. [6] conducted a comprehensive survey on security threats related to digital twins. The survey identifies threats to digital twins in four functional layers. Shaikh et al. [40] discussed the security challenges and possible countermeasures for a digital twin and suggested a security framework. The work used the end-to-end conceptual model for digital twins in the context of IoT presented in [5]. Suhail et al. [41]

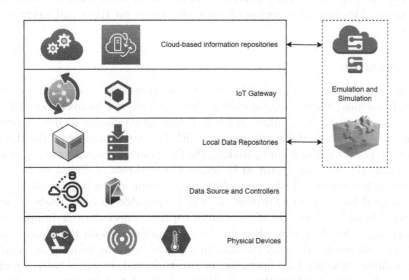

Fig. 1. Architecture of digital twins [37,47].

discussed the possible attacks towards digital twins and suggested mitigation to the identified attacks. The paper also considers information technology (IT)/ operational technology (OT) implications and control systems. E. Kaaralslan [21] presented security threats to digital twins and countermeasures in their work. Wang et al. [46] presented a review of the Internet of Digital Twins (IoDT) and discussed the security and privacy challenges of the IoDT, followed by a set of suggested countermeasures.

However, the existing works mainly focused on the security and privacy of the digital twins. There are several other challenges that need to be discussed, such as ethical considerations, trust, safety, and so on. On the other hand, there are conflicts between security, privacy, trust, and safety while implementation of digital twin technology that need to be addressed. Therefore, in this paper, we have provided a detailed discussion of the challenges associated with security, privacy, trust, and safety, as well as the conflict between these challenges.

The rest of the paper is organized as follows: Sect. 2 presents the different challenges related to the digital twins. In Sect. 3, a detailed discussion of the ethical concerns of digital twins and the threat landscape in healthcare have been discussed. In Sect. 4, we have discussed the challenges and conflict analysis of the different factors related to security, safety, privacy, operational requirements, and trust. Finally, Sect. 5 presents the summary and conclusion of the article.

2   Challenges of Digital Twins

Digital twins are relatively new and emerging technologies that have low maturity; therefore, they are accompanied by numerous challenges such as security, privacy, trust and data quality, safety, and missing standardization [16,47]. The focus of this paper is to discuss the challenges related to security, privacy, trust, and safety. We have also presented some discussion on trust and safety challenges.

2.1   Security

The use of digital twins can contribute to the automation process, making them critical systems. When a digital twin is implemented, it effectively doubles the attack surface as either the physical asset or the digital twin can be used as access points [3,6]. When digital twins are used with IT, they can increase the threats related to IT/OT integration by making the OT systems even more exposed and connected [47]. It is important to be aware of the threat of digital twins being connected to various IoT devices, which may inherit vulnerabilities [36,47]. In some digital twin implementations, it may be possible to manipulate or send control signals from the digital twin or to capture, inject data or tamper with sensory data [36]. This could lead to the compromise of both the physical and digital twins. Solely accessing the data in a digital twin can provide adversaries with valuable insights into operation in real-time and, in some cases, provide them with sensitive information [3]. However, the attack surface of a digital twin can vary greatly depending on the application and implementation [6].

2.2 Privacy

Digital twins pose several privacy challenges [6,36]. Privacy must be taken into account when considering entities and locations of assets [6]. As an example, the digital twin can be used by an attacker to extract and map out the whole system or a portion of it, extract private information, or determine patterns by analyzing the databases, states, configurations, and resources. As a result, privacy is compromised [6]. Therefore, the confidentiality and integrity of this privacy-sensitive data are crucial.

2.3 Trust

According to NISTIR 835 [45], trust is a "level of confidence in the probability that the intended and actual behavior are equivalent given a fixed context, fixed environment, and fixed point in time". Trust in the digital twins are related to whether digital twins will be able to provide operational functionality with an acceptable level of quality. On the other hand, NIST [30] defined the trustworthiness of a system as: "Trustworthiness expresses the degree to which information systems can be expected to preserve the confidentiality, integrity, and availability of the information being processed, stored, or transmitted by the systems across the full range of threats." NIST considered two factors for the trustworthiness of a system: security functionality and security assurance.

Several other works also mention challenges related to trust, and the challenges related to data quality are often highlighted [6,47]. It is important to consider these because they can be connected to the digital twin's accuracy, usefulness, and performance [45]. Then, it can also affect the overall security and safety of the digital twin. Many of these are also related to implementation, and since there is no current standard for digital twins, the challenges are even more significant.

2.4 Safety

Safety, which must not be confused with security, is defined by the NIST[1] as "freedom from conditions that can cause death, injury, occupational illness, damage to or loss of equipment or property, or damage to the environment." From this, we can see that safety includes damage to human beings, but it is not limited to that. However, the potential threats to human safety will be most critical in a healthcare setting. A digital twin may pose challenges related to healthcare, especially in the case where bi-directional communication capabilities are implemented.

3 Digital Twins in Healthcare

In the healthcare sector, the digital twin has the potential to be used for several different purposes, such as precision medicine [7,8,10,12,42], remote care

---

[1] https://csrc.nist.gov/.

[25,31,47] and for logistic purposes [9,14,19,22,26]. Digital twins can represent systems, processes, and products within this sector [14]. In spite of several potential applications, there are currently few real-world applications in the healthcare.

In healthcare settings, input data could include historical data, medical records, health prediction data, surgical simulation data, patient or healthcare personnel input, and virtual drug test data. [42,47]. However, in most cases, the primary data source is IoT, and this paper focuses on digital twins with IoT as the primary data source. Further details on implementing digital twins in healthcare would depend on the specific implementation.

3.1 Ethical Concerns of Digital Twins in Healthcare

There are several things to consider when it comes to the ethics regarding digital twins in healthcare. For example, ethical concerns can be related to ownership of the data extracted by digital twins not being addressed [14]. This relates to privacy, which is a risk and might be a disadvantage of digital twins [42]. In healthcare, if a digital twin is compromised so that, for example, sensitive healthcare data is leaked, it could lead to interference or discrimination related to a person's work and life [42]. Additionally, the high costs of digital twins could lead to inequality and injustice and thus widen the existing socioeconomic gap [42].

In healthcare, there are also ethical implications related to the possible bi-directional capabilities of a digital twin. Even though full automation is theoretically possible, it can be argued that there should always be a human in the control loop to ensure safety [11]. Ethical considerations like these are essential when designing and implementing digital twins for healthcare use cases.

3.2 Threat Landscape in Healthcare

The threat landscape in the healthcare sector is complex. It is challenging to provide a complete overview of the threat landscape in this sector; however, the most significant and relevant threats have been discussed in the paper. The relevance of threats may vary across different domains within the healthcare sector. The healthcare sector is considered a critical infrastructure sector, dependent on IT, OT, and human operation. One important factor distinguishing the healthcare sector from other critical infrastructures is the amount of privacy-sensitive data we can find [27]. The healthcare industry can be a good target for adversaries because of poor cybersecurity practices, poor sensitive data storage, and poor availability requirements [1].

Maintaining security, privacy, and safety in this sector is essential by maintaining good cybersecurity hygiene. In addition to providing the confidentiality and integrity of sensitive data, it is also crucial to provide availability so that patients can receive treatments whenever and wherever they need them. It can be said that cybersecurity in healthcare is considered an investment in patient safety as cyber-attacks disrupt healthcare personnel's ability to provide life-changing and life-saving acts [44]. In addition, privacy must be ensured by both general and sector-specific legal regulations. Lastly, safety becomes a high priority in a sector where human health is central and, in many cases, directly affected.

3.2.1   IoT and Edge Devices Vulnerabilities

In the healthcare sector, there are many use cases for edge devices such as IoT, industrial Internet of Things (IIoT), and the Internet of Medical Things (IoMT). In this paper, we have referred to these as IoT devices. These devices could gather and share health data and make healthcare information more accessible and portable [2]. Some typical IoT-related systems that we can find in healthcare include medical devices such as infusion pumps and respiratory ventilators, wearable devices, home medical equipment, and connected devices [2]. These devices support many functions in the healthcare industry, for example, monitoring through wearable devices. The growth of IoT and OT has played an increasingly important role in healthcare but has also increased the attack surface, making cybersecurity risks more complex and challenging [35]. In a report from 2022, [35], insecure medical devices and insecure mobile apps are identified to be among the top six cybersecurity threats to be concerned about in the healthcare industry, and there is a lack of preparedness for cyber incidents related to attacks on these devices [35].

Regarding IoT and edge devices, the threats could be many, and it is also the case that many healthcare facilities are using vulnerable old or non-renewable components. For example, in 2017, the pharmaceutical domain was affected by the NotPetya ransomware that targeted older unpatched Microsoft systems [17]. Several critical devices are running outdated Windows OS [4]. Such an attack could be critical in healthcare if critical systems become unavailable or store privacy-sensitive information [35]. There are also threats associated with the many heterogeneous devices in the sector, as it could be challenging to have a good overview of all assets, accesses, and communication flows. For example, if a huge amount of insecure IoT devices or non-compliant BYOD (Bring Your Own Device) is connected to a hospital network and proper network segmentation is not implemented. The impact of attacks on those devices could be increased as it would be easier for attackers to move laterally and for malware to spread through the network. Another important concern is that these devices would also be susceptible to threats from a poorly configured home network, depending on the security stance of users. There is, in other words, a huge responsibility of the user to properly secure these devices [2]. Default settings and credentials are the most common vulnerabilities of IoT [4].

Wearable devices are typically used to monitor patient's vital data in real time. For example, smartwatches collect heart rate, steps, and hours of sleep, and glucose monitors can collect data about a patient's glucose levels and alert when an insulin shot is needed. Threats related to IoT devices that can only monitor and collect data are mostly related to data theft and DDoS [2]. The threat of DDoS is primarily connected to IoT devices that, for example, can be infected by malware and forced part of a botnet that is targeting a server and forcing it offline [1]. DDoS is considered among the top threats to the healthcare sector [1].

3.2.2   Communication Network

The threat posed by edge devices is related to increased connectivity and attack surface in the healthcare sector [35]. The increase in remote care and associated remote devices have significantly risen after the outburst of COVID-19, and this trend is predicted to continue [39]. This trend of remotely and wirelessly connected devices results in more possible endpoints to attack and target sensitive data or critical operations. Attacks on healthcare can result in the unavailability of health records and medical devices, which in turn can cause unavailability in an emergency or life-saving care activity and end in loss of safety [18,44]. Most of these remote devices are IoT, which found [35] in 2022 to be the root of up to 12% of cyberattacks on healthcare.

3.2.3   Data Theft and Manipulation

Threats could also include data theft or manipulation that may result in inaccurate data and harm patients [2]. Data manipulation is an even more significant threat to devices interacting with patients. For example, if an insulin pump is vulnerable so that an attacker can manipulate its operation, the attack could lead to life-threatening situations. This is because if these devices work remotely, patients may be located far away from medical help [2].

3.2.4   Supply Chain and Third-Parties Attack

Cloud compromise, supply chain, and third-party/partner breach are among the top cybersecurity threats in healthcare [18,35], and between 60% and 70% of attacks on supply-chain and cloud compromise hurt patient care in the form of disruption. The disruptions could result in delays, increased patient transfer, more frequent medical complications, and even increased mortality rate [35]. Also, 60% of data breaches in the healthcare sector in 2022 occurred via compromised third parties [1]. Despite this, there is a lack of preparedness for cyber incidents in the healthcare industry, mainly related to the supply chain [35].

Attacking the supply chain can give an attacker access to the sensitive data of multiple victims and is, therefore, a valuable target. This is previously seen in, for example, the Solarwind attack in 2020 that affected around 18 000 organizations [20]. It is predicted that in the future, cloud providers will be even more targeted by adversaries for the same reasons [18]. In addition, it is predicted that OT will increasingly be targeted in supply-chain attacks via vendor updates or vulnerabilities in the programmable logic controller (PLCs), as ransom is more likely paid in OT as organizations do not want to shut down operations. It was also found by ENISA in 2021 that over 50% of supply-chain attacks originated from advanced persistent threats [24].

3.2.5   Social Engineering and Insider Threats

Insider threats and social engineering attacks such as variants of phishing and business email compromise (BEC) are among the highest risk threats to the healthcare industry [1,18,35,44]. According to a 2022 report from the U.S. Department of HSS [43], threats such as phishing will continue to pose significant threats to the healthcare industry in the future. [35] identified in 2022 that many healthcare organizations had experienced at least one social engineering attack in the last two years and that these attacks could disrupt patient care. Insufficient cybersecurity protection, awareness training, and data transparency are often seen, while PII is a high-value target for attackers. For example, when paper health records are shifted to electronic health records, PHI becomes more exposed and accessible to attackers [18]. Social engineering and insider threats are related to other threats and attacks, such as data breaches, which indicates the importance of the human element in cybersecurity [44]. A more organizational threat is the violation of cybersecurity policies. For example, missing expertise on premises may lead to unauthorized remote services being used, leaving the internal network more exposed. Future predictions for social engineering threats include techniques such as AI and deep fakes used by adversaries for criminal campaigns [18,29].

3.2.6   Loss, Damage or Theft of Data and Equipment

Related to all the threats already mentioned is the threat of data breaches. Either intentionally or unintentionally, this, alongside damage to or loss of equipment, is also considered among the most significant threats in the healthcare sector [44]. For example, [18] identifies nation-state threats of espionage, theft of intellectual property, and destructive attacks to be considerable and posing as advanced persistent threats (APT). Stakeholders in healthcare must understand the value associated with these threats. Such as adversaries selling personally identifiable information (PII), protected health information (PHI), or personal information (PI) to high values [43].

3.2.7   Ransomware

Another of the threats considered most significant to healthcare is ransomware [1,18,35,44]. Ransomware[2] is "a type of cyber extortion where a malicious actor infiltrates an environment and encrypts and exfiltrates files, denying access and threatening disclosure, unless the victim pays a ransom". According to [1], more than 1 out of 3 healthcare organizations globally were victims of ransomware

---

[2] https://www.gartner.com/en/information-technology/glossary/ransomware.

attacks in 2020. The sector is especially vulnerable to these types of attacks as victims often panic due to regulatory consequences that follow the theft of patient data and the strict goal to minimize operation disturbances as this could affect patient care negatively [1]. Also, a threat associated with ransomware is that ransomware as a service (RAAS) is becoming increasingly common.

4   IoT Digital Twins: Challenges and Conflict Analysis

There are several challenges to consider while considering the security assurance of IoT digital twins in healthcare. Many of these challenges do not have one correct answer, or they may even be paradoxes without any correct answer. The primary challenges relate to finding a balance between conflicting aspects. These include objectives related to privacy, ethics, safety, security, trust, and operational requirements. However, our main focus will be directed towards security-related challenges. This section provides an overview of how security may conflict with the other aspects.

4.1   Security vs. Safety

The conflict between safety and security in an IoT digital twin setting is primarily related to the OT environment. In healthcare, safety is mainly concerned with human safety and how this may be affected by human-machine interaction. Even though there are several overlaps between security and safety, it is essential to address and be aware of the conflicts and the challenges following the gaps and conflicts. A few of these challenges are discussed in this paragraph. While security is about protecting against malicious attacks, safety is more about hindering unintentional failures that result in harm [28]. Among common safety goals, there is a need for controllability and hindering unauthorized access. The two domains have become more connected after the increased IT/OT integration, as unsafe systems with undefined behavior are often also insecure [28]. This could pose a threat to both domains. When digital twin models represent physical systems, it is also important to remember that it is impossible to model every possible scenario that could go wrong from a safety perspective.

When it comes to conflicts in terms of security mechanisms, especially encryption, access control, and intrusion detection systems (IDS), it needs attention. Regarding encryption and access control, it is essential not to encrypt traffic or enforce too strict access mechanisms if it can hinder access to information or emergency services. It may be too high a risk if you cannot be sure who may need authorization in an emergency situation. While from a security point of view, you always want to hinder unauthorized access to information and assets. When safety is concerned, quick access should be possible for those who may need it in an emergency. If time is critical, strict access controls to either physical or digital assets could be hindering safety. Lastly, there are challenges related to safety and AI models, primarily when used in security mechanisms like IDS. Regarding safety, we wish to have complete knowledge of system components to avoid loss of control or unexpected behavior [28]; however, when it comes to AI, it is not known exactly how decisions are made. This results in less control over system behavior, and if security mechanisms placed in a control loop start acting unpredictably, this could pose a considerable threat to safety. As a result, several interviews stated that it is generally undesirable to place security mechanisms inside the control loop.

4.2   Security vs. Privacy

Challenges may arise regarding the balance between privacy and security when considering digital twins in healthcare. There are several overlaps between the two, especially between privacy and the security objective of maintaining confidentiality. However, privacy stretches beyond the scope of confidentiality, and it is crucial to be aware that you do not obtain privacy directly from security. The main challenges related to privacy that have been identified through the research for this paper are the vast amounts of sensitive personal data that will be present in a digital twin system. From a privacy point of view, it is crucial to keep the confidentiality of the data. Confidentiality is also important in security; however, other security objectives may need higher prioritization in a healthcare context. Looking beyond confidentiality, privacy concerns include the location of personal data, how long it is stored, how it is processed and collected, and for what reasons. An issue could be related to IDS systems in healthcare. To identify anomalies in privacy-sensitive data, you need to process the data. If this is not done correctly and with consent, it would lead to a breach of privacy. We also need to consider if traffic analysis or monitoring of routines can be used to deduce privacy data, even if the analyzed traffic is encrypted. Lastly, it is essential to consider AI models and privacy. When AI models use privacy-sensitive data, it is necessary to ensure that it cannot be extracted from the model or that membership can be deduced. It is also essential to know where the model processes that data, where it is transferred, and what usages have been consented to.

4.3   Security vs. Operational Requirements

Most payoffs regarding digital twins in healthcare have to be between security and operational requirements. This is because any security mechanism comes with overhead and may, to some degree, hinder system operation [6]. From a security point of view, it is easy to be blinded by the goal of a perfectly secure system and forget the importance of a proper balance between security needs and operational requirements. After all, security is about obtaining a residual risk lower than the accepted risk. The accepted risk should take into account operational needs as well as relevant threats. As stated by one interviewee, there is no point in a perfectly secure system if it does not work. Some examples of conflicts are related to time-sensitive operations, where security mechanisms like encryption or packet inspection could hinder the system from reaching critical deadlines. As mentioned by another interviewee, in control environments, end-to-end encryption could hinder legitimate monitoring of system health, and placing security mechanisms such as IDS inside the control loop could hinder critical system functionality.

4.4 Security vs. Trust

Trust is close to operational requirements; similar to functional requirements, trust objectives can conflict with security goals. For example, to have a model of proper fidelity and accuracy, a certain amount of data is needed, and the data needs to be adequately synchronized across components and between the physical and digital spaces [45]. Due to overhead from security mechanisms, this could be challenging. Regarding trustworthy decisions from the digital twin, it could be a challenge to verify the correctness of a decision. Because the cognitive functionality of a digital twin is enabled by AI, and as mentioned, we often need to learn how the decision from an AI model was reached. It is thus difficult to identify flaws in the model and invalid decisions. If a decision is entirely wrong, it would be easily detected, but it is much more challenging to detect if it is incorrect in the normal range.

5   Summary and Conclusion

Digital twins, as an evolving and developing technology, are still in their early stages of maturity. This brings about various challenges, including issues related to security, privacy, trust, data quality, safety, and a lack of standardization. When a digital twin is deployed, it amplifies the potential areas of attack since both the physical entity and its digital counterpart can become entry points. Utilizing digital twins alongside IT can heighten the risks associated with IT/OT convergence, further exposing and connecting OT systems. The digital twins also come with several privacy concerns. It is important to consider privacy when considering the entities and positioning of the assets. Trust in digital twins hinges on their ability to deliver operational functionality at a satisfactory quality level. This trust is intrinsically linked to the accuracy, utility, and performance of the digital twin. Nevertheless, the potential threats to human safety are paramount in a healthcare environment. Digital twins can introduce specific challenges in this context. Many of these challenges present dilemmas without a clear or single solution, often resembling paradoxes. The main difficulties lie in balancing opposing facets such as privacy, ethics, safety, security, trust, and operational needs.

The digital twins can serve various functions in the healthcare sector, including precision medicine, remote patient care, and logistics. The healthcare sector showcases a complex threat landscape. Notable and pertinent threats include data theft and manipulation, supply chain and third-party vulnerabilities, social engineering attacks, insider Threats, loss, damage, or theft of data and equipment, and ransomware.

Due to its critical and vulnerable infrastructure, the healthcare sector has been identified as an easy target for attackers or hackers. It is difficult for the healthcare sector to remain open to the public while protecting its own cybersecurity. As an emerging technology, digital twins may play an increasingly important role in healthcare in the future, for example, providing patients with customized diagnoses and treatments. In addition to simulating real-world conditions, digital twins can also be used to analyze how they respond to changes, allowing for better operations and assessment of significant changes. Digital twins' technology has many advantages, but it also faces several challenges related to security, privacy, trust, and safety. In order to successfully implement the digital twin technology in healthcare, it is important to consider these challenges. However, there are several conflicts between these challenges. We have discussed a number of challenges related to the implementation of digital twins in healthcare, including security, privacy, trust, and safety. Our study also presents a comparative conflict analysis of the requirements for implementing IoT digital twins, including security, safety, privacy, trust, and operational requirements.

References

1. Biggest Cyber Threats in Healthcare (Updated for 2023) — UpGuard — upguard.com. https://www.upguard.com/blog/biggest-cyber-threats-in-healthcare. Accessed 22 Aug 2023
2. Securing the Industrial Internet of Things: Addressing IIoT Risks in Healthcare - Security News — trendmicro.com. https://www.trendmicro.com/vinfo/us/security/news/internet-of-things/securing-the-industrial-internet-of-things-addressing-iiot-risks-in-healthcare. Accessed 22 Aug 2023
3. The cybersecurity challenges and opportunities of digital twins — csoonline.com. https://www.csoonline.com/article/574179/the-cybersecurity-challenges-and-opportunities-of-digital-twins.html. Accessed 22 Aug 2023
4. A cynerio research report: The state of healthcare IoT device security 2022 (2022). https://www.cynerio.com/landing-pages/the-state-of-healthcare-iot-device-security-2022
5. Al-Ali, A.R., Gupta, R., Zaman Batool, T., Landolsi, T., Aloul, F., Al Nabulsi, A.: Digital twin conceptual model within the context of internet of things. Future Internet **12**(10), 163 (2020)
6. Alcaraz, C., Lopez, J.: Digital twin: a comprehensive survey of security threats. IEEE Commun. Surv. Tutor. **24**(3), 1475–1503 (2022)
7. Aluvalu, R., Mudrakola, S., Kaladevi, A., Sandhya, M., Bhat, C.R., et al.: The novel emergency hospital services for patients using digital twins. Microprocess. Microsyst. **98**, 104794 (2023)
8. Attaran, M., Celik, B.G.: Digital twin: benefits, use cases, challenges, and opportunities. Decis. Anal. J. 100165 (2023)
9. Augusto, V., Murgier, M., Viallon, A.: A modelling and simulation framework for intelligent control of emergency units in the case of major crisis. In: 2018 Winter Simulation Conference (WSC), pp. 2495–2506. IEEE (2018)
10. Björnsson, B., et al.: Digital twins to personalize medicine. Genome Med. **12**, 1–4 (2020)

11. Chase, J.G., et al.: Digital twins in critical care: what, when, how, where, why? IFAC-PapersOnLine **54**(15), 310–315 (2021)
12. Díaz, R.G., Laamarti, F., El Saddik, A.: DTCOACH: your digital twin coach on the edge during COVID-19 and beyond. IEEE Instrument. Measur. Mag. **24**(6), 22–28 (2021)
13. El Saddik, A.: Digital Twin for Healthcare: Design, Challenges, and Solutions. Elsevier (2022)
14. Elkefi, S., Asan, O.: Digital twins for managing health care systems: rapid literature review. J. Med. Internet Res. **24**(8), e37641 (2022)
15. Fedorko, G., Molnar, V., Vasil', M., Salai, R.: Proposal of digital twin for testing and measuring of transport belts for pipe conveyors within the concept industry 4.0. Measurement **174**, 108978 (2021)
16. Fuller, A., Fan, Z., Day, C., Barlow, C.: Digital twin: enabling technologies, challenges and open research. IEEE access **8**, 108952–108971 (2020)
17. Greenberg, A.: The untold story of notpetya, the most devastating cyberattack in history. Wired, August 22 (2018)
18. H-ISAC, Hamilton, B.A.: Current and emerging healthcare cyber threat landscape executive summary. Technical report (2022)
19. Haleem, A., Javaid, M., Singh, R.P., Suman, R.: Exploring the revolution in healthcare systems through the applications of digital twin technology. Biomed. Technol. **4**, 28–38 (2023)
20. Hammi, B., Zeadally, S., Nebhen, J.: Security threats, countermeasures, and challenges of digital supply chains. ACM Comput. Surv. **55**, 1–40 (2023)
21. Karaarslan, E., Babiker, M.: Digital twin security threats and countermeasures: an introduction. In: 2021 International Conference on Information Security and Cryptology (ISCTURKEY), pp. 7–11. IEEE (2021)
22. Karakra, A., Fontanili, F., Lamine, E., Lamothe, J.: Hospit'win: a predictive simulation-based digital twin for patients pathways in hospital. In: 2019 IEEE EMBS International Conference on Biomedical & Health Informatics (BHI), pp. 1–4. IEEE (2019)
23. Kuehner, K.J., Scheer, R., Strassburger, S.: Digital twin: finding common ground-a meta-review. Procedia CIRP **104**, 1227–1232 (2021)
24. Lella, I., Theocharidou, M., Tsekmezoglou, E., Malatras, A., García, S.: ENISA Threat Landscape for Supply Chain Attacks. ENISA (2021)
25. Liu, Y., et al.: A novel cloud-based framework for the elderly healthcare services using digital twin. IEEE Access **7**, 49088–49101 (2019)
26. Madubuike, O.C., Anumba, C.J.: Digital twin-based health care facilities management. J. Comput. Civ. Eng. **37**(2), 04022057 (2023)
27. Markopoulou, D., Papakonstantinou, V.: The regulatory framework for the protection of critical infrastructures against cyberthreats: identifying shortcomings and addressing future challenges: The case of the health sector in particular. Comput. Law Secur. Rev. **41**, 105502 (2021)
28. Menon, C., Vidalis, S.: Towards the resolution of safety and security conflicts. In: 2021 International Carnahan Conference on Security Technology (ICCST), pp. 1–6. IEEE (2021)
29. Nguyen, T.N.: Toward human digital twins for cybersecurity simulations on the metaverse: ontological and network science approach. JMIRx Med **3**(2), e33502 (2022)
30. NIST, S.: 800–37 rev. 2 risk management framework for information systems and organizations: a system life cycle approach for security and privacy

31. Pavlov., V., Hahn., F., El-Hajj., M.: Security aspects of digital twins in IoT. In: Proceedings of the 9th International Conference on Information Systems Security and Privacy - ICISSP, pp. 560–567. INSTICC, SciTePress (2023)
32. Pirbhulal, S., Abie, H., Shukla, A.: Towards a novel framework for reinforcing cybersecurity using digital twins in IoT-based healthcare applications. In: 2022 IEEE 95th Vehicular Technology Conference:(VTC2022-Spring), pp. 1–5. IEEE (2022)
33. Pirbhulal, S., Abie, H., Shukla, A., Katt, B.: A cognitive digital twin architecture for cybersecurity in IoT-based smart homes. In: Suryadevara, N.K., George, B., Jayasundera, K.P., Mukhopadhyay, S.C. (eds.) ICST 2022. LNCS, vol. 1035, pp. 63–70. Springer, Cham (2022). https://doi.org/10.1007/978-3-031-29871-4_8
34. Piroumian, V.: Making digital twins work. Computer **56**(1), 42–51 (2023)
35. Ponemon institute: Cyber insecurty in healthcare: The cost and impact on patient safety and care. Technical report (2022). https://www.proofpoint.com/sites/default/files/threat-reports/pfpt-us-tr-cyber-insecurity-healthcare-ponemon-report.pdf
36. Qian, C., Liu, X., Ripley, C., Qian, M., Liang, F., Yu, W.: Digital twin-cyber replica of physical things: Architecture, applications and future research directions. Future Internet **14**(2), 64 (2022)
37. Redelinghuys, A.J.H., Kruger, K., Basson, A.: A six-layer architecture for digital twins with aggregation. In: Borangiu, T., Trentesaux, D., Leitão, P., Giret Boggino, A., Botti, V. (eds.) SOHOMA 2019. SCI, vol. 853, pp. 171–182. Springer, Cham (2020). https://doi.org/10.1007/978-3-030-27477-1_13
38. Segovia, M., Garcia-Alfaro, J.: Design, modeling and implementation of digital twins. Sensors **22**(14), 5396 (2022)
39. Seshadri, D.R., et al.: Wearable sensors for COVID-19: a call to action to harness our digital infrastructure for remote patient monitoring and virtual assessments. Frontiers in Digital Health 8 (2020)
40. Shaikh, E., Al-Ali, A., Muhammad, S., Mohammad, N., Aloul, F.: Security analysis of a digital twin framework using probabilistic model checking. IEEE Access **11**, 26358–26374 (2023)
41. Suhail, S., Jurdak, R., Hussain, R.: Security attacks and solutions for digital twins. arXiv preprint arXiv:2202.12501 (2022)
42. Sun, T., He, X., Li, Z.: Digital twin in healthcare: recent updates and challenges. Digital Health **9**, 20552076221149652 (2023)
43. U.S Department of health and Human Services: Health sector cybersecurity: 2021 retrospective and 2022 look ahead. Technical report (2022)
44. US Department of Health and Human Services and others: Health industry cybersecurity practices: managing threats and protecting patients. Technical report (2023)
45. Voas, J., Mell, P., Piroumian, V.: Considerations for digital twin technology and emerging standards. Technical report, National Institute of Standards and Technology (2021)
46. Wang, Y., Su, Z., Guo, S., Dai, M., Luan, T.H., Liu, Y.: A survey on digital twins: architecture, enabling technologies, security and privacy, and future prospects. IEEE Internet Things J. **10**, 14965–14987 (2023)
47. Warke, V., Kumar, S., Bongale, A., Kotecha, K.: Sustainable development of smart manufacturing driven by the digital twin framework: a statistical analysis. Sustainability **13**(18), 10139 (2021)

ADIoT 2023

ADIoT 2023 Preface

The 6th International Workshop on Attacks and Defenses for Internet-of-Things (ADIoT 2023) was held on 28 September with ESORICS 2023, in The Netherlands.

The Internet of Things (IoT) technology is widely adopted by the vast majority of businesses and is impacting every aspect of the world. However, the natures of the Internet, communication, embedded OS, and backend resources make IoT objects vulnerable to cyber attacks. In addition, most standard security solutions designed for enterprise systems are not applicable to IoT devices. As a result, we are facing a big IoT security and protection challenge, and it is urgent to analyze IoT-specific cyber attacks to design novel and efficient security mechanisms. This workshop focused on IoT attacks and defenses, and sought original submissions that discuss either practical or theoretical solutions to identify IoT vulnerabilities and IoT security mechanisms.

This year, ADIoT received 10 submissions, and each submission was single-blind reviewed by at least three reviewers. Based on their novelty and quality, 5 regular papers were accepted with 1 short paper, resulting in an acceptance rate of 50%. For the conference program, we had two paper sessions to present research on threat analysis, intrusion detection, DoS attacks, and malware detection in IoT domains.

For the success of ADIoT 2023, we would like to first thank the authors of all submissions and all the PC members for their great efforts in selecting the papers. We also thank all the external reviewers for assisting the reviewing process.

September 2023

Wenjuan Li
Weizhi Meng
Steven Furnell

Organization

General Co-chair

Anthony T. S. Ho   University of Surrey, UK

Program Co-chairs

Wenjuan Li   Hong Kong Polytechnic University, China
Weizhi Meng   Technical University of Denmark,
     Denmark
Steven Furnell   University of Nottingham, UK

Local Chairs

Niclas Finne   Research Institutes of Sweden (RISE),
     Sweden
Mohamed Abdelsalam   Robert Bosch GmbH, Germany

Technical Program Committee

Elena Doynikova   SPC RAS, Russia
Luca Ferretti   University of Modena and Reggio Emilia,
     Italy
Vincenzo Moscato   University of Naples, Italy
Jay Ligatti   University of South Florida, USA
Evgenia Novikova   Saint-Petersburg Electrotechnical
     University, Russia
Ioannis Stellios   University of Piraeus, Greece
Georgios Kambourakis   University of the Aegean, Greece
Xiaobo Ma   Xi'an Jiaotong University, China
Reza Malekian   Malmo University, Sweden
Jianming Fu   Wuhan University, China
Yunguo Guan   University of New Brunswick, Canada
Jun Shao   Zhejiang Gongshang University, China
Mohiuddin Ahmed   Edith Cowan University, Australia
Lei Wang   Shanghai Jiao Tong University, China
Gang Wang   University of Connecticut, USA
Bin Xiao   Hong Kong Polytechnic University, China
Xuyun Zhang   Macquarie University, Australia
Cong Zuo   Beijing Institute of Technology, China

Steering Committee

Steven Furnell	University of Nottingham, UK
Anthony T. S. Ho	University of Surrey, UK
Sokratis Katsikas	Norwegian University of Science and Technology, Norway
Weizhi Meng (Chair)	Technical University of Denmark, Denmark
Shouhuai Xu	University of Texas at San Antonio, USA

Subreviewer

Fei Zhu

C-TAR: A Compositional Threat Analysis and Risk Assessment Method for Infrastructure-Based Autonomous Driving

Mohamed Abdelsalam[1,2]([✉]), Simon Greiner[1], Oum-El-Kheir Aktouf[2], and Annabelle Mercier[2]

[1] Robert Bosch GmbH, Abstatt Robert-Bosch-Allee 1, Gerlingen, Germany
{mohamed.abdelsalam,simon.greiner}@de.bosch.com
[2] Grenoble University, 621 Avenue Centrale, Grenoble, France
{mohamed.abdelsalam,oum-el-kheir.aktouf,
annabelle.mercier}@lcis.grenoble-inp.fr

Abstract. Autonomous Vehicles rely heavily on their sensors' information to navigate correctly. Autonomous driving requires the support of infrastructure-based systems to provide extra sensor information, which cannot be collected by vehicles. We expect that such infrastructure-based systems are typically not provided by the same manufacturer as the vehicle using them. In this paper, we propose a first of its kind, compositional threat analysis and risk assessment method, called C-TAR, and illustrate the method using a simplified example from an autonomous driving context. The proposed method extends a common threat and risk analysis method by statements of dependency on interfacing systems and provides a compatibility check of two systems working together. C-TAR allows the user to identify whether two independently developed systems can interact together securely based on the extended threat and risk analysis.

Keywords: Automotive Security · IoT · Autonomous Vehicles · Smart Infrastructure · Compositionality · Threat Analysis and Risk Assessment · TARA · C-ITS

1 Introduction

Autonomous Vehicles (AVs) need to be aware of their surroundings to navigate streets safely. Sensing a vehicle's environment can be achieved by sensors inside a vehicle or sensor information provided by an IoT network in the infrastructure. Using infrastructure systems is one way of supporting AVs in particular in cases where the vehicle's sensors are limited, e.g., due to occlusions. The setup of infrastructure sensors can be optimized for a certain area, e.g., an urban intersection, such that the local geography is taken into consideration. We can expect that typically, such infrastructure systems are not provided by the same manufacturer or operator as the vehicles using the infrastructure systems.

S. Katsikas et al. (Eds.): ESORICS 2023 Workshops, LNCS 14399, pp. 159–175, 2024.
https://doi.org/10.1007/978-3-031-54129-2_10

The key problem in assessing the security of such IoT configurations of AVs connected to smart infrastructure systems is the large variety of different systems by different manufacturers which might be present on the roads. Currently available approaches for security analysis require the analysis of the overall system, in our case the combination of vehicle and infrastructure system. It is infeasible to provide this analysis for every combination of infrastructure systems and vehicles which may at some point in time decide to connect to them. The potential configurations an AV may assume over its lifetime are unknown and virtually infinite, meaning that the number of vehicle to infrastructure configurations is countless.

Usually, systems are developed independently from each other, either because one system existed before the other or because they were not developed cooperatively, manufacturers perform threat analysis and risk assessment (TARA) to help identify, assess, prioritize, and mitigate security risks of a given system. If each of these systems is secure in the sense that all risks identified are dealt with appropriately, this does not guarantee that this is also true when two systems are combined into a cooperative traffic system. This is due to the fact that, when two systems are connected, new attack paths and threats may arise which could not be covered by the original security analysis. Individual manufacturers cannot identify such threats as each individual system may not be subject to the respective threat.

In this paper, we propose the first of its kind compositional threat analysis and risk assessment method. We introduce C-TAR, a TARA method that starts with creating a TARA according to ISO 21434 [1] then introduces new elements for a TARA of distributed systems. Using these new TARA elements, C-TAR processes this information and checks the compatibility of the systems. Finally, C-TAR produces a compatibility statement about the overall security of two systems working together. This compatibility statement provides information on whether two systems can securely work together. In case of incompatibility, i.e. there are security threats that arose as a result of connecting the two systems, C-TAR provides the reasons of incompatibility. C-TAR allows independent development of systems, and checking compatibility of systems at runtime. We illustrate C-TAR by applying it on a simplified example for infrastructure-supported autonomous driving.

This paper is structured as follows: Sect. 2 gives an overview of some preliminaries on threat analysis and risk assessment, followed by related work in Sect. 3. In Sect. 4 we describe C-TAR and in Sect. 5 we provide an example to illustrate our method. Finally we conclude the paper in Sect. 6.

2   Preliminaries

In this section, we provide an overview of TARA according to the ISO/SAE 21434 standard [1]. The standard defines in Clause 15 the general requirements on an automotive TARA. The purpose of a TARA is to perform a systematic identification of threats which a system is exposed to and the risks associated with these threats. The result of a TARA then serves as the basis for decisions on how to deal with the identified risks.

After defining the system and describing its interfaces and functions, the *assets* of the system are identified. An *asset* can be anything worth protecting in the system, and typically includes information, data, functionality and other elements. For each asset, one or more *security properties* which have to be protected are identified. Typical security properties are confidentiality, integrity, and availability of an asset. A *threat* is defined as the non-fulfillment of a security property.

For each threat, a *damage scenario* is provided, which describes the consequences of what happens when a threat is realised. For each damage scenario, an *impact* rating is provided which quantifies the consequences of a damage scenario. This impact rating serves as the cost-part of the risk analysis for a particular threat.

In order to estimate the probability of a threat, i.e. how likely it is that a threat is realised, the standard follows an indirect approach. Instead of directly providing a probability, which for most threats is hard to quantify, the standard requires a rating of the effort an attacker has to invest in order to realise the threat, the so-called *attack feasibility rating* (AFR).

To provide the AFR for a threat, first the attack paths have to be identified, which an attacker could perform in order to realise a threat. An *attack path* is a sequence of actions which an attacker performs, which together lead to the realization of the related threat. After identifying the attack path, for each attack path an AFR has to be provided. Using the rating of an attack path, together with the other elements of the TARA, the overall risk of the system under evaluation can be calculated. The standard offers several methods to determine the AFR, while we limit the presentation here to the attack potential method. The attack potential method requires to rate each attack path with the five attributes of *Elapsed Time*, i.e., the time an attacker requires to perform the attack path, the amount of *expertise* required by the attacker, the level of *knowledge about the product*, the *window of opportunity* required to perform the attack, and finally the type of *equipment* the attacker has to have available.

The standard leaves open how the different categories are translated into an AFR, however, it provides a possible realization as an example in the informative Appendix. Our presentation here is based on that example. Each rated category of an attack path is translated into an attack potential value as shown in Table 1. The attack potential values of an attack path are then added and the resulting number is translated according to another table in the AFR values *High*, *Medium*, *Low*, and *Very low*. Finally, the AFR together with the impact of a threat can then be translated into a qualitative risk value.

Table 1. ISO 21434 Attribute Ratings Table [1]

Elapsed time		Specialist expertise		Knowledge of the item or component		Window of opportunity		Equipment	
Enumerate	Value	Enumerate	Value	Enumerate	Value	Enumerate	Value	Enumerate	Value
≤1 day	0	Layman	0	Public	0	Unlimited	0	Standard	0
≤1 week	1	Proficient	3	Restricted	3	Easy	1	Specialized	4
≤1 month	4	Expert	6	Confidential	7	Moderate	4	Bespoke	7
≤6 months	17	Multiple experts	8	Strictly confidential	11	Difficult/none	10	Multiple bespoke	9
>6 months	19								

3   Related Work

In this section we present and discuss some of the related work that we classify into four main classes: threat modeling, risk assessment, digital dependability identities and automotive security surveys.

3.1   Threat Modeling

According to the work of Casola et al. [5], IoT systems are characterized by the high heterogeneity of involved systems. Moreover, there is a lack of a comprehensive threat model for IoT systems. This makes performing effective security assessment of actual IoT deployments very difficult.

Casola et al. [5] and Rak et al. [17] propose methods to automate risk analysis for IoT systems to identify threats and their related countermeasures. The authors in [5] use the information stored in a security knowledge base which maps threats to assets to build a threat model. While the authors in [17] relies on an open catalogue, for gathering information about threats and vulnerabilities of the IoT system under analysis. The identified threats are then associated with a risk level and mapped to a set of suitable countermeasures. The authors of [17] applied their method on a case study where they were able to automatically build a custom threat model associated with the system where they reported the asset to protect, the associated threat and the security controls.

In the work of Kim et al. [12], they discuss the use of threat modeling method (TMM) to investigate the potential threats to AVs. Also, in their work of [13], they demonstrate how the threat modeling process used in the computer industry, can be adapted and applied in the automotive domain.

The discussed methods focus on performing risk analysis for single systems which results in identifying individual threats specific to each system. While in our work, we focus on threats that arise as a result of two independently developed subsystems working together and forming an overall system.

3.2   Risk Assessment

Automotive development is a highly distributed process with many organizations involved. Full sharing of information is neither desirable nor possible. However, TARA requires a holistic view to cover all potential attack vectors. To address such an issue, Kiening et al. [11] propose a method to allow organizations to perform TARA analysis according to ISO 21434 in a collaborative and joint way while performing partial risk assessments within their scope. They propose the use of *Cybersecurity Interface Agreement* for a TARA to enable sharing appropriate information among involved organizations. The proposed interface agreement is a contractual agreement that requires developing the systems at the same time. In comparison to our work, we present a TARA method to determine the compatibility of an overall system comprising of two subsystems, while not necessarily having the subsystems developed at the same time, but at different points in time.

Eichler et al. [7] propose a method for risk assessment that targets heterogeneous and complex environments. Similarly in our approach, we are targeting heterogeneous systems to perform threat analysis and risk assessment. However, the focus of our approach is on checking the compatibility of two heterogeneous systems working together. On the other hand, their work focus is on flexibility and scalable effort for risk assessment but not on heterogeneous subsystems forming an overall system.

The development of CPS requires interdisciplinary cooperation between different stakeholders to avoid unidentified security threats. Japs et al. [10] present the SAVE method that enables early identification of safety relevant security threats. SAVE supports stakeholders identify security hazards by creating a SysML system model. The main difference to our work is that they use model-based safety engineering (MBSE) to identify security threats. Moreover, their method is designed to be applied in workshops with an interdisciplinary team of stakeholders.

Standards such as ISO/SAE 21434 Road vehicles - Cybersecurity engineering [1] and ETSI [6], focus on engineering secure functions at the vehicle level or analysis of the threats and risks of an Information and Communications Technology (ICT) system. However, automotive engineering projects are highly distributed among many stakeholders. ISO/SAE 21434 introduces the concept of *Cybersecurity Interface Agreement* to address distributed engineering in automotive industry. However, the standard does not provide any guidance on how to perform activities such as TARA in a collaborative, joint way. Moreover, using cybersecurity interface agreement is not suitable to solve our problem as it is tied to developing the subsystems simultaneously. Looking at both standards, there is no clear guidance on how to address risk analysis of heterogenous systems connected together.

3.3   Digital Dependability Identities

The configurations Cyber-Physical Systems (CPS) may assume over its lifetime are unknown and potentially infinite which makes it difficult to assess the dependability of CPS. Hence, the authors of [2,4,18], proposed and worked with the concept of digital dependability identity (DDI) to work as medium for synthesis of heterogeneous dependability information collected from different systems.

Adler et al. [4] and Armengaud et al. [2] use DDIs to check whether autonomous vehicles that come together at runtime can cooperate dependably. DDI is used to monitor the runtime cooperation between the systems and adapt it so that it will remain dependable. Moreover, the DDI concept was applied to truck platooning use case where they make it possible to check which vehicles are permitted to form a platoon.

While their interest in heterogenous systems is a shared interest with our work, the main difference between our research and theirs, is their focus on the dependability property of safety while our focus is on security property. Another difference is their focus on runtime operation.

3.4 Automotive Security Surveys

Luo et al. [16] have conducted a survey on TARA methods in the automotive field such as STRIDE, EVITA, OCTAVE, and BRA. In the survey of Lamssaggad et al. [14], the authors give a short background on the main security issues that hinder Intelligent Transportation Systems (ITS) and they provide a comprehensive analysis of existing security solutions in the literature. Another survey conducted by Lu et al. [15] provides a comprehensive security analysis for vehicular networks. Similarly, Huang et al. [9] provide an in-depth review of the state-of-the-art solutions concerning security and privacy for V2X communications. Alnasser et al. [3] analyze the threats for V2X and some of the available security solutions. Hammi et al. [8] conducted an extensive survey on the different Public Key Infrastructure (PKI) architectures used in C-ITS environments.

Even though the aforementioned surveys discuss different aspects of automotive security, such as TARA methods, risks, threat assessment and security countermeasures, there are no proposed methods for a TARA method of heterogeneous subsystems forming an overall system. Plenty of the TARA methods proposed used in the automotive industry target only a single system for threat analysis and risk assessment. Hence, the main contribution of this paper is providing a TARA method which solves this problem through analyzing the threats and risks of two independent subsystems forming an overall system.

3.5 Insights from Literature Review

In this section we showcased the current state of the art and discussed the main differences between the proposed methods in the literature and the work presented in this paper. Automotive security is discussed at length in the literature from different perspectives and our work is aimed at the overall security of heterogenous subsystems. To the best of our knowledge, the literature does not have a lot of similar works to ours.

4   C-TAR Method Description

This section elaborates and discusses the developed C-TAR method and presents our contribution of the paper. An overview of the method description is shown in Fig. 1. The method consists of three phases, each of which is discussed in detail in the following subsections. The first phase of C-TAR starts from a TARA created according to ISO 21434 and identifying attack paths and extracting the needed information from such attack paths. Followed by that, is the processing phase and checking the compatibility conditions. Finally, the output phase which presents the compatibility statement stating whether two subsystems are secure to work together as an overall system or not.

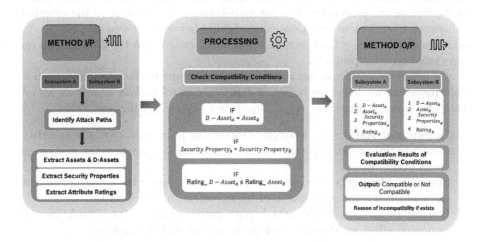

Fig. 1. C-TAR Method Overview

4.1   First Phase - C-TAR Input

When a manufacturer makes a TARA according to the common process described by ISO/SAE 21434 standard, the first phase of C-TAR is to identify the different attack paths for each subsystem under evaluation, in addition to the associated assets, assets security properties and attack path ratings. For every combination of an asset and its security property, the relevant attack paths are identified and given a rating, according to ISO 21434.

While conducting TARA analysis of a subsystem under evaluation, if the TARA of the subsystem under evaluation has a critical connection to another subsystem or dependent on another subsystem, knowledge about the subsystem under evaluation is not sufficient to rate all identified relevant attack paths while creating the TARA. The ISO 21434 standard does not define how to deal with the missing information in a TARA that is dependent on another subsystem's information.

Hence, we present *dependent attack path*. A *dependent attack path* allows to model parts of a subsystem under evaluation in a TARA, which are unknown or dependent on an external subsystem. To do this, an attack path, which is dependent on an external subsystem, is separated into two parts: A *partial attack path* and a *dependent attack path*. The *partial attack path* models the part of the attack path, which can be determined with knowledge about the subsystem under evaluation alone. This *partial attack path* is rated using the five attributes of AFR mentioned earlier in Sect. 2.

The second part is the *dependent attack path*, which depends on knowledge about the external subsystem. The dependent attack path acts as a placeholder for the part of the attack path which is dependent on the external subsystem information. The *dependent attack path* is given a rating in the subsystem under evaluation as an assumption, this rating becomes a requirement to the external subsystem to satisfy, to guarantee compatibility between the two subsystems. In addition to that, we extract from the *dependent attack path* the *D-asset* and its associated security property.

To reflect dependencies between a subsystem under evaluation and an external subsystem, we define the notion of *dependent attack path*. A *dependent attack path* $(D - asset_x, property_x, (r_{1x}, ..., r_{nx}))$ is a tuple consisting of:

- **Dependent Asset** $(D - asset_x)$: Is something to protect, typically an entity of information or data, this asset typically outside the control of the subsystem under evaluation.
- **Security Property** $(property_x)$: The security property of the dependent asset which has to be broken in order to realise an attack path,
- **Rating** $(r_{1x}, ..., r_{nx})$: The attack path rating given in the TARA for the estimated effort an attacker needs to break the security property,

where x is a notation for the subsystem under evaluation. While a partial attack path, is a set of actions that realizes a threat in conjunction with a dependent attack path.

4.2 Second Phase - Compatibility Conditions

Using the extracted information from the first phase of C-TAR, the second phase of the method is to process this input information and perform a compatibility check for the two subsystems. In order to identify if two subsystems, a subsystem under evaluation and an external subsystem, can be combined in a way that result in an overall system which has at most the risk of the two subsystems, we have to check whether the assumptions, modeled in a dependent attack path, of each of the subsystems, can be guaranteed. By combining the rating of the partial attack path and the dependent attack path, an overall rating of the attack path can be calculated. Using the rating of the attack path, together with the other elements of the TARA, the overall risk of the system under evaluation can be calculated. The risk is correct if all attack paths related to the dependent attack path are at least as hard as the dependent attack path rating assumption.

In the following, we describe how this compatibility check can be performed.

Two subsystems A and B are compatible, if for every dependent attack path $(D - asset_A, property_A, (r_{1A}, ..., r_{nA}))$ in the TARA of subsystem A:

- **Assets Condition:** There exists an asset $Asset_B$ in the TARA of subsystem B where $D - asset_A = Asset_B$, and
- **Security Property Condition:** There exists a security property $property_B$ for $asset_B$ in the TARA of B where $property_A = property_B$, and
- **Rating Condition:** For every attack path for $asset_B$ and $property_B$ with rating $(r_1B, ..., r_nB)$ it holds that $r_{iA} \leq r_{iB}$ for $1 \leq i \leq n$, and
- Vice versa with A and B exchanged in the conditions above.

Basically, the conditions above formalize that for two subsystems under evaluation, every attack on the D-asset assumed in one subsystem, is identified to require more effort in the TARA of the other subsystem, than assumed in the TARA of the first subsystem. As a result, the risk identified in the TARA of each subsystem reflects a risk which is at most as high as for the subsystem in combination with the other subsystem.

4.3 Third Phase - Compatibility Statement

Applying the aforementioned conditions enables C-TAR, in its third phase, to produce a compatibility statement about the risk assessment of the overall system. The compatibility statement presents an overview of the subsystems under evaluation, the identified and extracted information of a TARA, in addition to the verdict about the compatibility of the two subsystems. The statement starts with presenting one D-asset or several D-assets extracted from the corresponding dependent attack path, in addition to the asset or assets of each subsystem. Moreover, the associated security property of the D-asset and asset are included in addition to the attack paths ratings. Secondly, it presents each of the compatibility conditions and whether they were satisfied or not. Finally, it outputs a statement declaring whether the two subsystems are compatible or incompatible, i.e. whether they form an overall secure system or not. In case the subsystems are incompatible, the reasons of incompatibility are stated in the output.

5 Example

In this section we illustrate C-TAR by applying it to an exemplary development scenario. The given example consists of an AV system and a smart traffic light system (TL) communicating together. Both the AV and the TL are two heterogeneous systems that form an overall connected system. Whereafter, we would refer to the AV and the TL as subsystems while the overall aggregate of both of them as the system, (see Fig. 2). The given example is a simplification of a real use case TARA.

Operational Scenario: In the given example, the AV communicates with the TL exchanging information to help it navigate the road safely and to be aware of its surroundings. To initiate communication between the two subsystems, the AV sends a **REGISTER** message to register with the TL. While the TL sends a **SPATEM** message containing the TL status to the AV, which is either **RED** or **GREEN**. If it is **RED**, the AV brakes and if it is **GREEN**, the AV keeps moving. If the AV is within the range of the TL and it does not receive any signal from the TL it switches into safe mode and degrades its speed.

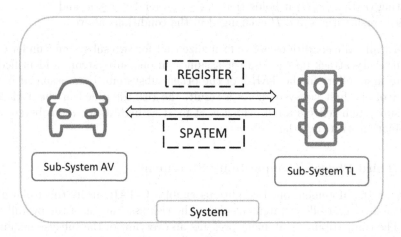

Fig. 2. Given Example Diagram

5.1   First Phase - C-TAR Input

The first phase of the method is creating a TARA according to ISO 21434 with the additional step of identifying attack paths, dependent assets, security properties and attack path rating to use in the second phase of C-TAR for processing. In this example, we have two TARAs for the respective subsystems, TARA_AV and TARA_TL.

TARA_AV

TARA_AV Elements:

- **Asset:** Vehicle ECU
- **Security Property:** Integrity
- **Threat:** Manipulate Vehicle ECU

AV Attack Paths: Typically, a TARA of a subsystem, has several attack paths that comprise this TARA. Such attack paths are depicted in Fig. 3. There are different types of attack paths shown in the figure. The first type we have is the *dependent attack path*, it contains one action in this example, which is *Steal*

Certificate. The second type is the *partial attack path*, it consists of action *Sign Message* and the action *Send message*. In order for an attacker to manipulate the vehicle behavior the following actions by two different attack paths are required. First, in the dependent attack path, in the action *Steal Certificate* an attacker steals the certificate from the traffic light. Second, in the partial attack path, in the first action *Sign Message* an attacker signs a message with the stolen certificate and the wrong traffic light status. The second action in the partial attack path is *Send message* where an attacker sends the signed message via ITS G5 to the vehicle. Since there is a dependent attack path, the next step of C-TAR is the identification of the D-asset, its associated security property and rating of the dependent attack path.

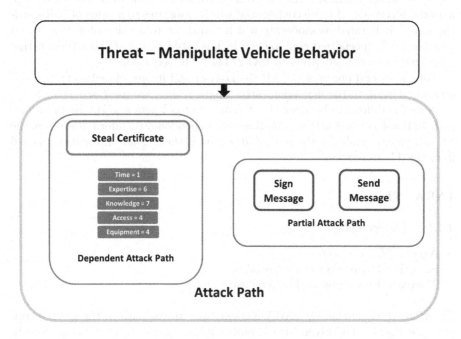

Fig. 3. TARA_AV Attack Paths and Threat

D-Asset: The action *Steal Certificate* is dependent on the TL subsystem. Therefore, the D-asset is identified as *TL Certificate*. Because from the perspective of the AV, the *TL Certificate* is an important asset that is worth protection as it could realise a threat of the AV TARA.

D-Asset Security Property: From the perspective of the AV, the certificate information need to be inaccessible by unauthorized parties, therefore, the security property of this D-asset would be confidentiality.

Rating: Referring to Fig. 3, the dependent attack path is given a rating based on assumptions by the AV subsystem about the TL subsystem. As previously mentioned in the method description, the ratings given are based on the ISO 21434 standard. These assumptions are then treated as requirements made by the AV subsystem that need to be satisfied by the TL subsystem. For simplicity reasons we refer to the five attributes of ISO 21434 for rating an attack path as following: "Elapsed time" as time, "Special expertise" as expertise, "Knowledge of the item or component" as knowledge, "Window of opportunity" as access and "Equipment" stays as equipment. The corresponding values for each of the attributes are shown in Fig. 3. We estimate less than a week needed by an attacker to perform the attack, this translates to a value of 1 for time. An attacker needs to be an expert which translates the expertise value into a value of 6. The knowledge required is considered to be confidential which translates to a value of 7. Regarding access, it is rated as moderate which translates to a value of 4. Finally, an attacker needs specialized equipment which is rated as 4. Note that these rating values were derived according to ISO 21434 AFR, see Table 1.

For the second phase of C-TAR the D-asset and its associated security property, in addition to the dependent attack path rating, are used, see Table 2.

Note the difference between the *dependent attack path* and the *partial attack path*. In the *dependent attack path*, there is a dependency on information from the TL subsystem, while for the *partial attack path*, there is no information needed from the TL subsystem.

TARA_TL

TARA_TL elements:

- **Asset:** *TL Certificate*
- **Security Property:** Confidentiality
- **Threats:** Extraction of TL Certificate

TL Attack Paths: The TL TARA has only one attack path in the given example, (see Fig. 4). The given attack path consists of the three actions given in the figure. In order for an attacker to extract the TL certificate the following actions are required. First, *Connect to Plug*: in which an attacker connects to the maintenance plug of the traffic light controller. Second, *Brute Force Controller*: an attacker brute forces the traffic light controller maintenance protocol. Third, *Read Certificate*: an attacker reads the certificate from the traffic light flash memory using the maintenance protocol. Since there is no dependent attack path, C-TAR does not identify in the TL TARA a D-asset nor the associated security property.

Rating: The rating values for the attack path according to ISO 21434 is shown in Fig. 4. We estimate the attacker to need less than one month in time which translates into a value of 4. For expertise, an attacker needs to be an expert which translates into a value of 6. The knowledge required by the attacker is considered to be restricted which translates to a value of 3. Regarding access, it is considered to be rated as easy, this translates to a value of 1. Finally, an attacker needs bespoke equipment which is rated as 7. Note that these rating values were derived according to ISO 21434 AFR, see Table 1.

For the second phase of C-TAR the asset and security property declared in the TL TARA, in addition to the attack path rating, are used, see Table 2.

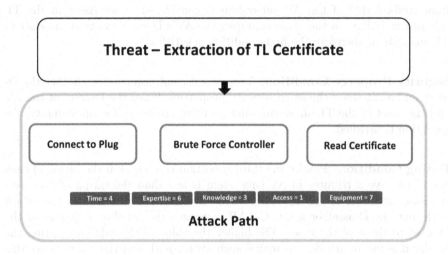

Fig. 4. TARA_TL Attack Path and Threat

Table 2. Generated Data of First Phase Used for the Second Phase of C-TAR

Asset Type	AV D-asset	TL Asset
Asset Name	*TL Certificate*	*TL Certificate*
Security Property	Confidentiality	Confidentiality
Attack Path Rating	**dependent**	**attack path**
Time	1	4
Expertise	6	6
Knowledge	7	3
Access	4	1
Equipment	4	7

5.2 Second Phase - Compatibility Conditions

In the second phase of C-TAR, we start processing the input and checking the conditions of compatibility, mentioned in Sect. 4.2, on the given input. There are three required conditions of compatibility:

1. **Assets Condition**: $D - asset_{AV} = Asset_{TL}$
2. **Security Property Condition**: $SecurityProperty_{AV} = SecurityProperty_{TL}$
3. **Rating Condition**: $Rating_{AV} \leq Rating_{TL}$

Assets Condition. The first condition checks if the D-asset "Steal Certificate from traffic light" of the AV subsystem is considered as an Asset in the TL subsystem TARA. In the given example, the AV's D-asset exists as an asset in TL subsystem, therefore the first condition is satisfied.

Security Property Condition. The second condition checks whether the D-asset and asset share the same security properties. Since the D-asset of the AV and the asset of the TL share the same security property of confidentiality, the condition is satisfied.

Rating Condition. Finally the third condition is to check if the rating of each one of the five attributes in AV subsystem is less than the rating of its corresponding attribute of the TL subsystem. Note that the rating rates the attack path, not the D-asset or asset. C-TAR compares the attributes ratings of the D-asset to those of the asset. The higher the value of the attribute rating the harder it is for an attacker to realise such attack path and the more secure this path is. The lower the value, the easier it is to perform an attack. Referring to Table 2, the attributes of time, expertise and equipment satisfy the third condition. Contrary to that, the rating of the attributes of knowledge and access in the AV subsystem dependent attack path are greater than that of the TL subsystem attack path. Hence, we conclude that the third condition is not satisfied.

Similar to attack potential or maximum likelihood methods to give a rating in a TARA based on personal evaluation, the dependent attack path is given a rating which might be different when given a rating by a different person.

5.3   Third Phase - Compatibility Statement

In the third phase of C-TAR, the method produces a compatibility statement as an output to the method, (see Fig. 5). The compatibility statement of the given example starts by presenting the D-asset of the AV subsystem and the asset of the TL subsystem which is *TL Certificate* for both subsystems. Moreover, it presents the associated ratings of $\{1, 6, 7, 4, 4\}$ for the AV subsystem and $\{4, 6, 3, 1, 7\}$ for the TL subsystem, in addition to the security property of confidentiality for the AV D-asset and the TL asset. Following that, the statement displays all needed conditions for compatibility and highlights the satisfied ones in green and the unsatisfied ones in red. Finally, it provides the verdict regarding the security compatibility of the two subsystems. The output declares the two subsystems incompatible due to not satisfying all of the necessary conditions. The reasons for incompatibility were the knowledge and access rating. In both cases, the AV attribute rating was less than the attribute rating of the TL subsystem, hence not satisfying the third condition.

In conclusion, we can summarize the process as follows: We create a TARA according to ISO 21434, C-TAR checks for attack paths. Then it extracts from the different attack paths; (1) D-asset, (2) associated security property of the different asset types and (3) rating of the attack paths. Afterwards, C-TAR checks conditions of compatibility, if satisfied or not, and finally produces a compatibility statement. For the given example the AV subsystem did not have its requirements satisfied by the TL subsystem guarantees, therefore the two subsystems would not be secure to work together due to not satisfying all conditions.

System Compatibility Statement:

Sub-System 1: AV

D-asset$_{AV}$: *TL Certificate*,
Security Property$_{AV}$: Confidentiality,
Rating$_{AV}$ = {1, 6, 7, 4, 4}

Sub-System 2: TL

Asset$_{TL}$: *TL Certificate*,
Security Property$_{TL}$: Confidentiality,
Rating$_{TL}$ = {4, 6, 3, 1, 7}

Compatibility Conditions:

Condition 1 (Assets Condition):
D-asset$_{AV}$ {TL Certificate} = D-asset$_{TL}$ {TL Certificate}
Condition 2 (Security Property Condition):
Security Property$_{AV}$ {Confidentiality} = Security Property$_{TL}$ {Confidentiality}

Condition 3 (Rating Condition):
Rating_Time$_{AV}$ {1} $\leq$ Rating_Time$_{TL}$ {4},
Rating_Expertise$_{AV}$ {6} $\leq$ Rating_Expertise$_{TL}$ {6},
Rating_Knowledge$_{AV}$ {7} $\leq$ Rating_Knowledge$_{TL}$ {3},
Rating_Access$_{AV}$ {4} $\leq$ Rating_Access$_{TL}$ {1},
Rating_Equipment$_{AV}$ {4} $\leq$ Rating_Equipment$_{TL}$ {7}.

Output:

Sub-Systems AV & TL are not compatible.

Reason(s) for incompatibility:

Rating_Knowledge$_{AV}$ > Rating_Knowledge$_{TL}$.
Rating_Access$_{AV}$ > Rating_Access$_{TL}$.

Fig. 5. Compatibility Statement Output

6   Conclusion

In this paper we presented C-TAR, a first of its kind method to help evaluate the threats and risks of an overall system, consisting of two connected heterogeneous subsystems. C-TAR is particularly useful in the automotive IoT domain where there is a network of connected vehicles and infrastructure-based systems communicating and sharing information.

The first step in our approach is to create a TARA according to ISO 21434, then identifies the TARA additional information of dependent attack paths with their attack potential rating and the dependent assets with the security property of these assets to be protected. Based on the dependent assets and attack paths, the compatibility of the two systems can be checked automatically based on well-defined conditions.

C-TAR allows to evaluate the maximum risks and threats for an overall system without actually conducting a TARA for the overall system. Instead, it is sufficient to analyze the constituent subsystems of the overall system separately. Thus, C-TAR is a compositional TARA method. Especially, if two subsystems are developed independently from each other, e.g. as expected for cooperative intelligent traffic systems, applying C-TAR to both subsystems allows to deduce whether the two subsystems are compatible. In case of incompatibility, the reasons provided by C-TAR helps to address the missed threats in the subsystem and provides an explanation why the two subsystems interacting could lead to an unacceptable risk.

In future work, we will apply C-TAR to industrial use cases, to further assess its suitability for larger applications and evaluate its performance. Furthermore, we would compare C-TAR to other methods in the literature in analyzing a specific example.

Acknowledgements. The authors would like to thank all partners within the Hi-Drive project for their cooperation and valuable contribution. [This project has received funding from the European Union's Horizon 2020 research and innovation programme under grant agreement No 101006664. The sole responsibility of this publication lies with the authors. Neither the European Commission nor CINEA - in its capacity of Granting Authority - can be made responsible for any use that may be made of the information this document contains.]

References

1. ISO/SAE 21434:2021 (Aug 2021). https://www.iso.org/standard/70918.html
2. Adler, R., Reich, J., Kaypmaz, C.: Dependable autonomous commercial vehicles. ATZheavy duty worldwide **14**, 50–54 (2021)
3. Alnasser, A., Sun, H., Jiang, J.: Cyber security challenges and solutions for v2x communications: a survey. Comput. Netw. **151**, 52–67 (2019)
4. Armengaud, E., et al.: DDI: a novel technology and innovation model for dependable, collaborative and autonomous systems. In: 2021 Design, Automation & Test in Europe Conference & Exhibition (DATE), pp. 1626–1631. IEEE (2021)

5. Casola, V., De Benedictis, A., Rak, M., Villano, U.: Toward the automation of threat modeling and risk assessment in IoT systems. Internet Things **7**, 100056 (2019). https://doi.org/10.1016/j.iot.2019.100056

6. CYBER, ETSI: Methods and protocols; part 1: Method and pro forma for threat, vulnerability. Risk Analysis (TVRA). Technical Specification TS 102, 165–1

7. Eichler, J., Angermeier, D.: Modular risk assessment for the development of secure automotive systems. In: Proceedings of the 31st VDI/VW Joint Conference Automotive Security, Wolfsburg, Germany, pp. 21–22 (2015)

8. Hammi, B., Monteuuis, J.P., Petit, J.: PKIS in C-ITS: security functions, architectures and projects: a survey. Veh. Commun. **38**, 100531 (2022)

9. Huang, J., Fang, D., Qian, Y., Hu, R.Q.: Recent advances and challenges in security and privacy for v2x communications. IEEE Open J. Veh. Technol. **1**, 244–266 (2020)

10. Japs, S., Anacker, H., Dumitrescu, R.: Save: security & safety by model-based systems engineering on the example of automotive industry. Procedia CIRP **100**, 187–192 (2021)

11. Kiening, A., Angermeier, D.: Trade-threat and risk assessment for automotive distributed engineering (2021)

12. Kim, S., Shrestha, R.: Security and privacy in intelligent autonomous vehicles. In: Automotive Cyber Security, pp. 35–66. Springer, Singapore (2020). https://doi.org/10.1007/978-981-15-8053-6_3

13. Kim, S., Shrestha, R.: AUTOSAR embedded security in vehicles. In: Automotive Cyber Security, pp. 97–120. Springer, Singapore (2020). https://doi.org/10.1007/978-981-15-8053-6_5

14. Lamssaggad, A., Benamar, N., Hafid, A.S., Msahli, M.: A survey on the current security landscape of intelligent transportation systems. IEEE Access **9**, 9180–9208 (2021)

15. Lu, Z., Qu, G., Liu, Z.: A survey on recent advances in vehicular network security, trust, and privacy. IEEE Trans. Intell. Transp. Syst. **20**(2), 760–776 (2018)

16. Luo, F., Jiang, Y., Zhang, Z., Ren, Y., Hou, S.: Threat analysis and risk assessment for connected vehicles: a survey. Secur. Commun. Networks **2021**, 1–19 (2021)

17. Rak, M., Casola, V., De Benedictis, A., Villano, U.: Automated risk analysis for IoT systems. In: Xhafa, F., Leu, F.-Y., Ficco, M., Yang, C.-T. (eds.) 3PGCIC 2018. LNDECT, vol. 24, pp. 265–275. Springer, Cham (2019). https://doi.org/10.1007/978-3-030-02607-3_24

18. Schneider, D., Trapp, M., Papadopoulos, Y., Armengaud, E., Zeller, M., Höfig, K.: WAP: digital dependability identities. In: 2015 IEEE 26th International Symposium on Software Reliability Engineering (ISSRE), pp. 324–329. IEEE (2015)

The VOCODES Kill Chain for Voice Controllable Devices

Sergio Esposito[1]([⊠]) [ID], Daniele Sgandurra[1] [ID], and Giampaolo Bella[2] [ID]

[1] Royal Holloway, University of London, London, UK
sergio.esposito.2019@live.rhul.ac.uk
[2] Università degli Studi di Catania, Catania, Italy

Abstract. In this paper, we introduce a formalisation of attacks on Voice Controllable Devices (VCDs), focusing specifically on attacks leveraging the voice command self-issue. The presentation starts from the seminal Lockheed Martin kill chain, which is used to derive a tailored kill chain with the necessary steps to perform self-activation attacks. Our new kill chain, termed the VOice COntrollable DEvice Self-issue (VOCODES) kill chain, is relevant to assess both ongoing and past attacks, enhancing analysis activities of both ethical adversaries and of defenders. To demonstrate VOCODES in practice, we use it to analyse a popular self-issue attack against Amazon Echo devices, that is, the AvA attack. We show that the VOCODES kill chain succeeds in the full description of the attack and all its nuances. Moreover, it is effective to quickly map out the attacker's malicious activities over specific attack steps, thereby favouring their interpretation. Finally, we show that, even if VOCODES is derived from the Lockheed Martin kill chain, VOCODES addresses some of the drawbacks of the seminal kill chain which have been pointed out over the years.

Keywords: Internet of Things · Kill Chain · Voice Personal Assistants

1 Introduction

In 2021, more than 258 million *smart homes* were counted worldwide, and this number continues to grow, indicating that an increasing number of people want to experience the new frontier of IoT commodities, fascinated by the possibility of a future where everything can be controlled using the voice channel only [27]. Smart commodities such as light bulbs, baby monitors, security cameras, TVs, ovens, and dishwashers are already available in physical and online stores, and they can all be controlled by issuing a simple voice command to a smart speaker, such as Amazon Echo [3] or Google Nest [12].

Unfortunately, to date, Voice Controllable Devices (VCDs) have very little or no means of authenticating the user who is interacting with them, making the processed sensitive information available to anyone who can issue commands to the device [9]. This includes smart speakers, but also personal computers, smartphones, game consoles, TVs, and more. While it is true that these sensitive features can be protected with a PIN number in some devices, it is also true that this PIN must be spoken aloud by the user when prompted to, making it lose its secrecy if someone is within earshot of the command [26].

The aforementioned lack of authentication and authorisation protocols on the voice channel lays the base for a multitude of security issues that have arisen in recent years. In fact, several attacks that undermine the safety, security, and privacy of smart speaker users have already been discovered, and most of these exploit that same voice channel that is the peculiarity of these devices, and that fascinates so many users with its unlimited possibilities. In particular, there is a class of attacks in which adversaries make use of audible commands to activate voice-controllable devices, and they do so from the victim device itself [2,8,10,15], exploiting the so-called *command self-issue* or *self-activation* vulnerability. This attack can be launched against all devices capable of accepting voice commands and playing audio files simultaneously. It simply consists of making the device play an audio file containing a malicious voice command: the microphone embedded in the voice controllable device will capture the command and the device will execute it as valid, as shown in Fig. 1. One of the peculiarities of the voice command self-issue is that of eliminating the need of placing rogue equipment in proximity of the target device for the attack to succeed, a constraint that many other attacks against voice controllable devices share [19,28,33].

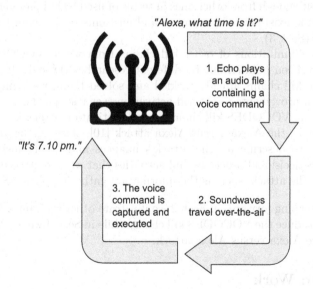

Fig. 1. Command Self-Issue on an Echo Device

For both offensive and defensive security researchers, defining and assessing environmental conditions before performing experiments is vital to allow their reproducibility, and attacks on the cyber-physical domain make no exception.

Contributions. The VOice COntrollable DEvice Self-Issue (VOCODES) kill chain that we introduce in this paper will allow future researchers and security analysts working on voice command self-issue to perform other experiments with an underlying strategy, and to better analyse and comprehend the flow of the attack. This also allows researchers to compare attacks and draw conclusions based on the performed comparison.

The VOCODES kill chain enables all of this by showing which steps an attacker has to perform to successfully execute a self-activation attack, and in which order. We show that the VOCODES kill chain builds upon existing literature in a tailored way, by excluding concepts that are not relevant in the self-activation context, modifying those elements that still make sense in such a context but that may need further customisation, and including new ideas that are applicable exclusively in this context. For example, in the creation of the VOCODES kill chain, we did not include any step that requires the *execution* of source code, which is a common step in other kill chains, then we revisited the meaning of other basic steps, such as the classical *reconnaissance*, and finally, we introduced new techniques such as the *audio weaponization.*

In summary, this paper brings the following technical contributions:

- It presents the VOCODES kill chain, a tailored model for analysing self-activation attacks, which stems from other relevant kill chains, with particular emphasis on the Lockheed Martin's one. We show that self-activation attacks are different enough from other ones in terms of used techniques and planning, to justify the existence of a separate and customised kill chain for this kind of attacks (Sect. 3).
- It addresses limitations of other kill chains from which VOCODES stems. These have been pointed out by different researches through the years, and while some kill chains already tackled and solved them, we bring the corresponding improvements to the self-activation scenario specifically (Sect. 3.2).
- It applies the VOCODES kill chain to a self-activation attack known in literature, that is, the Alexa versus Alexa attack [10], showing that VOCODES is suitable to describe all the attack's nuances and giving insight on the adversary's decisional processes and activities that were omitted in the paper describing the attack, such as the information gathering phase (Sect. 4).

Therefore, going forward, in Sect. 2 we illustrate other relevant kill chains, in Sect. 3 we introduce the VOCODES kill chain, while in Sect. 4 we use VOCODES to analyse the Alexa versus Alexa attack.

2   Related Work

"Kill Chains" refer to the steps an attacker needs to take to carry out a successful attack. This concept is essential for security researchers and analysts to predict and react to potential attacks. Kill chains allow researchers to visualise an attacker's possible actions, enabling them to understand the techniques used during an attack. Offensive researchers can also use kill chains to pinpoint where they are in the attack process, identify next steps, and evaluate previous attempts. In this section, we will examine essential kill chains discussed in the literature to understand the underlying concepts of these valuable tools.

Lockheed Martin's Cyber Kill Chain®. While the concept of kill chains was not new in the military context [30] and in general in the cyber-physical domain [31], Lockheed Martin's Cyber Kill Chain® (CKC) [14], or Intrusion Kill Chain, is the first work in the literature to formalise steps for a successful intrusion within a certain secured and trusted digital boundary. Authors describe kill chains as a *"systematic process to target and engage an adversary to create desired effects"* [14], and they are represented as a "chain" because a single failure in one of the steps will cause a failure in the entire process. The Intrusion Kill Chain has seven steps:

1. **Reconnaissance**: research and selection of targets to attack.
2. **Weaponization**: creating a deliverable that can be used to perform the intrusion, such as a file containing malware.
3. **Delivery**: actual delivery of the weapon within the target security boundary.
4. **Exploitation:** activation of the weapon, be it a Microsoft Word file with a malicious macro on it, or a SQL Injection within a website.
5. **Installation**: creation of a backdoor that enables the adversary to maintain persistent control of the target.
6. **Command and Control**: connection of the target to an attacker-controlled channel, to enable the adversary to remotely control one or more targets.
7. **Action on Objectives**: achievement of general mission goals: collection, exfiltration, and deletion of data, for example.

After detailing the seven steps, the authors explain how this information can aid security analysts in quickly identifying the current stage of a live attack, as well as efficiently categorising the different phases of security incidents or red-teaming activities during post-event analyses.

Derived Kill Chains. While the Intrusion Kill Chain certainly sets a milestone in the literature for both offensive and defensive security activities, the research community later identified two subtle issues within its structure [16].

The first problem is that kill chains in the digital domain are *not exactly chains*, for two reasons: (i) the adversary may fail one or more steps listed within the CKC, such as Installation or Command and Control, and be able to complete their mission nonetheless; (ii) during a real attack, the adversary might want to execute steps in a different order, or might need to "go back" and execute a previous step within the chain again—in other words, the CKC and other *linear* models do not allow for cyclicality of actions and do not show that some attacks, such as those performed by Advanced Persistent Threats (APTs), theoretically do not end if the threat (e.g., a malware) is not detected and removed.

The second problem with the Intrusion Kill Chain is that it has no depth, that is, it does not reflect the fact that some systems are not directly exposed to the adversary. This means that, if the attacker wants to target them, they need to breach another security boundary and execute a successful pivoting activity from there, before being able to breach the target.

Modified Kill Chain. The Modified Kill Chain (MKC) [16] tries to address both problems: authors start with an explanation of the two problems and a selection of *linear* and *circular* models derived from the CKC that fail to address them. Afterward, they present their solution as a model with two layers: an external one (External Threat Layer) and an internal one (Internal Threat Layer).

– **External Threat Layer**: consists of the seven steps found in the Intrusion Kill Chain, plus an Exit step.
– **Internal Threat Layer**: very similar to the previous one, consists of five steps: Internal Reconnaissance, Weaponization, Delivery, Exploitation, and Installation—all already known steps in this new internal context.

Note that this model also allows for cyclicality, although a somehow limited one: while Command & Control can lead to Reconnaissance, and (internal) Installation can lead to Internal Reconnaissance, creating some cycles, it is not clear why they could not lead to other steps as well.

Expanded Kill Chain. The Expanded Kill Chain (EKC) [20] proposes a solution to CKC's no-depth problem by treating the Intrusion Kill Chain as a process for gaining access to a secure perimeter that does not yet contain the target system. The adversary must perform additional actions before interacting with and breaching the system. Therefore, the Expanded Kill Chain divides the attack into three distinct parts: Legacy Kill Chain, Internal Kill Chain, and Target Manipulation Kill Chain

– **Legacy Kill Chain**: consists of the seven steps found within the Intrusion Kill Chain, in the same order. Because the adversary is trying to get access to the external perimeter, the *Exploitation* step is known as *External Exploitation* in the EKC.
– **Internal Kill Chain**: once the adversary gets access to the perimeter, they usually have to look for their target. Hence, the Internal Kill Chain consists of five steps: Internal Reconnaissance, Internal Exploitation, Enterprise Privilege Escalation, Lateral Movement, and Target Manipulation. While the first two steps are (again) clearly already known steps within a different context, Enterprise Privilege Escalation and Lateral Movement allow the adversary to perform horizontal and vertical movement within the network, to look for their target. Once found, the adversary can proceed with the Target Manipulation, that is, they can proceed with the final kill chain.
– **Target Manipulation Kill Chain**: at this point, the adversary only needs to gain access to the target system and complete the mission. The five steps of this final kill chain are: Target Reconnaissance, Target Exploitation, Weaponization, Installation, and Execution, with this last step being the one in which the adversary activates the malicious payload(s) to thwart system availability, steal or destroy data, etc.

While this work explains very well the differences between the actions that the adversary has to perform within the different environments, it does not address the problem of the cyclicality of actions.

The Unified Kill Chain. The Unified Kill Chain (UKC) [25] tries to combine the points of strength of the most used kill chains while also maintaining a practical and qualitative approach. The author describes the process for its creation, starting from a literature review of the most important kill chains and then going through a refinement process of the identified steps with the aid of different case studies. The output of this activity is a detailed kill chain consisting of 18 steps, divided into three different cycles: In, Through, and Out.

- **The In Cycle**: describes the activities that the adversary has to perform in order to enter a certain security boundary. Steps in this phase include Reconnaissance, Weaponization, Delivery, Social Engineering, Exploitation, Persistence, Defense Evasion, and Command & Control. While most of these are already known, Social Engineering separates the human contribution to the attack from the actual exploitation, while Defense Evasion gives further granularity on what is needed to gain access to the organisational perimeter.
- **The Through Cycle**: the adversary is now in the targeted network, but they do not have yet all the required privileges to access the target assets and complete the mission. This phase includes Pivoting, Discovery, Privilege Escalation, Execution, Credential Access, and Lateral Movement. While Privilege Escalation, Lateral Movement, and Execution are already known from the EKC, Pivoting and Discovery further detail how the adversary should explore and communicate with the other devices within the internal network.
- **The Out Cycle**: the adversary has now access to the target system and gains the privileges to execute the final tasks and complete the mission. Actions in this phase include Access, Collection, Exfiltration, Impact, and Objectives, giving granular detail over which actions on assets and data the adversary might want to perform.

By describing the different contexts in which the attack takes place as "cycles", this kill chain elegantly solves both problems of the CKC. Furthermore, the authors acknowledge that the adversary does not necessarily need to perform all the actions to succeed—they do not even need to follow the order in which they are presented, and one or more failures do not necessarily imply a mission failure. With its high level of detail and practical design, the Unified Kill Chain is currently considered the state-of-the-art regarding kill chains.

MITRE ATT&CK®. It is also worth mentioning the MITRE ATT&CK (ATT) matrix [29], although it is not considered a kill chain, but more of a knowledge base. This matrix lists all known adversary tactics and techniques observed in real-world attacks, divided into 14 different categories: Reconnaissance, Resource Development, Initial Access, Execution, Persistence, Privilege Escalation, Defense Evasion, Credential Access, Discovery, Lateral Movement,

Collection, Command and Control, Exfiltration and Impact. While these should all be familiar names for the reader by now, ATT&CK® goes the extra mile by presenting all known techniques to perform each step. For example, *Initial Access* might be performed via *Phishing*, the use of *Valid Accounts*, or because of a *Trusted Relationship*. The added value in this is that, for all of these techniques, ATT&CK® also provides all known related sub-techniques and tools for the purpose, making it a valuable reference for both red and blue teaming activities.

The PETIoT Kill Chain. Finally, another kill chain that is worth mentioning is PETIoT, which focuses on the penetration testing of IoT devices, with emphasis on the analysis of their network traffic [4]. PETIoT prescribes six steps:

1. **Experiment Setup:** the tester determines if the experiments will take place locally or remotely, and setups the network and the device to be tested.
2. **Information Gathering:** the tester attempts to get information on the device, similarly to the Reconnaissance step described in other kill chains.
3. **Traffic Analysis:** the tester analyses the traffic emitted and received by the tested device, to discover protocols used, actors involved, types of communications initiated, etc.
4. **Vulnerability Assessment:** the tester tries to discover vulnerabilities by using all information that was acquired during the previous steps, and by performing further actions at any hardware and software level.
5. **Exploitation:** the tester verifies if it is possible to exploit the identified vulnerabilities, similarly to the Exploitation step found in other kill chains.
6. **Fixing:** given that PETIoT is a kill chain for penetration testing, hence an ethical and authorised activity, the fixing step is a peculiarity of this kill chain, while being the natural conclusion of the penetration testing process. In fact, it allows the tester to formally specify how the identified vulnerabilities can be removed from the analysed system.

It can be noted that, instead of being an *attacker*, the actor who executes the actions is a *tester*, as the attacks are taking place in a sandbox and not in the wild. The strength in this kill chain is not the ability, for analysts, to quickly pinpoint at what stage a certain cyber attack is, or to perform post-attack analyses, but instead, PETIoT provides a tailored methodology for the ethical testing of these devices, laying out hints for specific actions in the IoT domain that traditional kill chains and methodologies do not give.

3   The VOCODES Kill Chain

While several kill chains have been discussed to comprehensively describe all the necessary steps for an attack, they may not always be the most suitable for certain attack scenarios. In the case of voice command self-issue attacks, we find that the Intrusion Kill Chain is the simplest way to describe all of their steps, although some links can be done in a somewhat broad way only. Therefore, we introduce the VOCODES Kill Chain, which tailors the Intrusion Kill Chain to the specific environment of voice controllable devices.

The VOCODES Kill Chain outlines the steps necessary to carry out self-activations on voice-controllable devices and incorporates modifications to the Intrusion Kill Chain to make it more relevant in this context. The changes made to the Intrusion Kill Chain dramatically aid in better formalising the requirements and objectives of each step in self-issue attacks on voice controllable devices, as we shall see below. Also, by using the VOCODES Kill Chain, security analysts can better understand and predict the actions of attackers targeting voice-controllable devices through self-issue attacks.

3.1 Steps

The VOCODES Kill Chain comprises six steps: Reconnaissance, Audio Weaponization, Initial Foothold, Exploitation, Persistence, and Actions on Objectives. While some of these steps retain the same names as in the Intrusion Kill Chain, VOCODES updates their interpretations and tailors these to the new context involving VPAs. Notably, (i) the term "Weaponization" has been updated to "Audio Weaponization", (ii) Installation, Delivery, and Command & Control have been excluded, while (iii) Initial Foothold and Persistence have been included. In the subsequent sections, we will elucidate the rationale behind these modifications.

Step 1. Reconnaissance. The reconnaissance (*recon*, for brevity) step starts by identifying and selecting targets for the attack. In the case of commercial voice-controllable devices, the adversary can obtain them by simply buying them online. However, this is not necessarily true for other devices running open-source Voice Personal Assistants. In fact, while some open-source VPAs such as MyCroft have their own commercial smart speaker [23], others such as Leon [13] do not. This means that while assessing the presence of the self-issue or other related vulnerabilities is relatively easy on commercial devices, as they share configuration and hardware, the adversary will have a harder time understanding if they can self-issue commands to an open-source voice-controllable device running on custom user-owned hardware. Hence, the attacker has to take this into consideration while listing the devices and the VPAs they want to attack.

The reconnaissance step does not terminate when the adversary has selected all target devices but continues with the identification of the related wake-words and possible actions the device can perform. For example, if the adversary wants to attack a device running the Alexa VPA, they have to know that possible wake-words include not only "Alexa", but also "Amazon", "Computer", and "Echo". Likewise, the context is also important. For example, if the adversary wants to attack the BMW Intelligent Personal Assistant [5], they need to know not only that "Alexa" is most likely not a valid wake-word[1] but also that "turn on the microwave oven" does not make much sense within a car (as of today, at least!).

From the above discussion, it is easy to see why recon in this environment is substantially different from the general strategy that consists of looking for machines on a subnet, scanning ports to check running services, obtaining operating system fingerprints, etc., because the component that we want to attack, that is, the input voice channel, is already known. Once the attacker knows how to activate such an input channel and what the set of valid commands is, they can proceed to the next step.

Step 2. Audio Weaponization. In the context of self-activation, weaponization does not involve writing code to exploit a vulnerability found in the recon step. Instead, the adversary's goal is to generate a malicious audio file containing a valid wakeword followed by an arbitrary voice command for the context.

However, simply generating an audio file with the desired contents may not reliably trigger the self-issue vulnerability. As shown in AvA [10], the voice profile used to generate the commands plays an important role in exploiting the self-issue vulnerability. Some voice profiles generate commands that are more easily recognised by certain Voice Personal Assistants.

Therefore, it is worth investigating the acoustic voice properties that characterise human voices and how an adversary can manipulate them to create audio files that are more easily recognised by the target VPA. According to the literature [7], the human voice has four main attributes: pitch, loudness (or sound pressure), timbre, and tone. Although speech rate is not among these attributes, it is useful for our purposes, as the time gaps between words can be used to detect human emotions. Thus, we summarise the five acoustic voice properties that an adversary should manipulate to generate voice command audio files:

- **Pitch**: the perceived frequency of vibrations emitted by a sound, in Hz.
- **Loudness**: strongly related to sound pressure, measured in dB.
- **Timbre**: the perceived quality of a sound, based on the type of sound production. It has no measurement unit, but a digital representation can be found by analysing the shape of a soundwave and its spectrum.
- **Tone**: the variation of pitch in language, used to distinguish or emphasise words. It has no measurement unit.
- **Speech rate**: the speed at which a sentence is pronounced, measured in words per second or as the average time gap between words, in seconds.

While an adversary could manually record their own voice commands, manipulate them with any audio editing software, and test their effectiveness on the target VPA, this approach is not scalable or easily automated. To generate malicious audio files, attackers can instead utilise various text-to-speech (TTS) services available online and adjust the five acoustic voice properties discussed

---

[1] Cunningly, BMW IPA allows the user to choose a custom wake-word, so "Alexa" could potentially be a valid wake-word.

earlier by modifying the parameters and variables exposed by the TTS service. For instance, Azure TTS [21] offers customisable settings such as:

- **Voice Profile**: a preconfigured voice that reads out the intended text.
- **Pitch**: the frequency of the voice used to read the text. It can be adjusted by the user and corresponds to the *pitch* property mentioned earlier.
- **Style**: the manner in which the text is spoken, with options like *cheerful, sad,* and *friendly*. It determines the *tone* of the voice.
- **Speed**: the playback speed of the text. The default speed is 1 but it can be increased or decreased by the user, corresponding to the *speech rate* property discussed earlier.

Using these TTS services to generate malicious audio files, attackers can experiment with different voice profiles and settings to craft voice commands that are more easily recognised by specific VPAs. While some TTS services only allow customisation of a limited set of voice properties, Azure TTS offers additional flexibility through the use of Speech Synthesis Markup Language (SSML) tags. By using SSML, users can customise voice properties in more detail:

- The **pitch** attribute of the `prosody` SSML tag allows for even more precise customisation of the *pitch* property, giving the user the option to choose between absolute values (in Hz), values relative to the current setting (specified as a variation in Hz or as a percentage), or preset values from a list.
- The **volume** attribute of the `prosody` SSML tag allows for customisation of the *loudness* property, allowing for an absolute value (with 0 being the quietest and 100 the loudest), a relative value, or a preset value.
- The **styledegree** attribute of the `mstts:express-as` SSML tag allows for the intensity of the chosen *tone* property to be adjusted. For instance, an utterance after `<mstts:express-as style='terrified' styledegree='3'>` will sound more scared than one after a tag with `style='terrified'` and `styledegree='1'`.
- The **rate** attribute of the `prosody` SSML tag allows for customisation of the *speech rate* property, which can be set to a relative value (with 0.5 indicating half the normal speed and 2 indicating double the normal speed), or to a preset value.

Note that some TTS services allow customisation of the *timbre* property as well: for instance, the `<amazon:effect vocal-tract-length>` SSML tag in Amazon Polly allows timbre modification for the standard TTS format. Once an attacker has crafted several payloads with customised voice properties, they must test them to ensure they trigger the self-activation of the target VPA. If the payloads are not successful, the attacker must adjust the parameters until a successful combination is found.

Step 3. Initial Foothold. This is the step in which the attacker gains the necessary privileges to play an audio file containing a voice command payload on a target voice-controllable device, thereby delivering it to trigger the self-issue. As previously mentioned, the self-activation vulnerability can only be exploited on devices that can play audio files and accept voice commands concurrently. Note that the initial foothold is a crucial requirement for all attacks on voice-controllable devices, such as needing to place a rogue speaker near the target device [22, 33] or a PZT transducer within the room [32], and not a constraint of the self-activation attack specifically. We identified two methods by which an attacker can obtain an initial foothold in the self-issue scenario: social engineering and temporary access.

In the case of *social engineering*, the attacker must trick the user into executing a malicious application that provides the attacker with the ability to play weaponized audio files. If the target VPA runs on a personal computer, social engineering tactics may include sending phishing emails, links to scam websites, or shipping malicious USB devices, with the expectation that the user will execute the malicious application or insert the USB device. However, if the user can only interact with the device via the voice interface, as with smart speakers, the social engineering strategy requires making the user run a malicious VPA application. There are two primary methods to do so:

- **Convincing the user to run the malicious application**: this approach might work with inexperienced users who may run the application for any reason, such as applications claiming to offer free "money" or "music".
- **Performing a Squatting Attack**: in this method, the attacker exploits the fact that ASR systems often misclassify one phoneme with a similar one, resulting in the transcription of a different word. The attacker deploys an application to intercept the misclassification of the application name by the VPA, which opens the malicious application instead of the intended one, such as PayPal/PayPaul [17].

In the case of *temporary access*, the attacker can use the device for a limited time, either with the user's permission or when the device is unattended. The attacker can then surreptitiously execute the malicious application. This is reminiscent of privilege escalation techniques in which temporary, unauthorised, or non-privileged access is utilised to gain higher privileges on the target. Moreover, if the attacker has temporary physical access to the target device, connecting a device they hold may be sufficient to play audio files without the need to execute an application on it. For instance, it is feasible to connect any Bluetooth device to a smart speaker and play any audio file.

Once the target device executes the malicious application or connects to the attacker's device, it is *de facto* connected to an audio C&C server that the attacker can use to issue voice commands to the target. Note that this operation generally does not require any user privileges on the target device, as playing audio files is usually permitted. Furthermore, identifying that the connection to the audio streaming service or the attacker's device is malicious would be challenging for antivirus software or any other protection mechanism. This is because these actions are innocuous in nature, and the malicious component is actually the voice command within the played audio files, which is challenging to fingerprint due to the variety of TTS services available on the internet and the possible customisation of the weaponized audio files seen in the previous step.

Step 4. Exploitation. In the context of VPA self-issue, the exploitation process is coherent with its classical interpretation. During this step, the audio payload sent via the C&C server is executed on the target device, exploiting the self-issue vulnerability. Once the payload is executed, any command contained within the audio files played by the voice-controllable device is captured by its microphone and executed successfully. As a result, the adversary gains the ability to issue any permissible voice command to the device through the remote or local audio streaming service.

However, if the target device gets disconnected from the malicious streaming server for any reason, the attacker would no longer be able to issue any more commands to the device, thus ending or pausing the attack. To avoid this, the attacker may try to establish persistent access to the device.

Step 5. Persistence. Similarly to the exploitation phase, the persistence step also shares some similarities with its classical interpretation, depending on the target device that the attacker wants to establish permanent access on. For instance, on a Windows device, the malicious application already running on the target device can use the Windows Service Control (`sc.exe`) to create a service containing the malicious application, which would run every time the machine is booted up. On Linux systems, a similar strategy involves using `systemctl`.

However, even if traditional malware cannot be executed, and the attacker is only capable of self-issuing voice commands, they can still achieve persistence on the victim device. For example, on Android systems, the attacker can use the Voice Access feature to perform any permissible operation, such as opening applications, tapping buttons on the screen, typing in search bars, visiting websites, and more. The attacker can then download and execute any rootkit available for the device to gain persistent root access to it.

While this is not possible with smart speakers, as their applications run on the cloud instead of the device, the attacker can protect the malicious audio streaming by running a silent application on top of it, or by running an application that performs a Voice Masquerading Attack to avoid detection by the user. For instance, if an Echo device is playing a malicious radio station and a skill is subsequently opened, if the user says "Alexa, stop", this command would only close the skill, but not the malicious radio station, enabling the attacker to retain control of the device.

Step 6. Actions on Objectives. Once the attacker gains the ability to issue any permissible voice command to the device and has possibly established permanent access to it, they can perform a range of malicious operations on the device itself, such as buying items, tampering with calendars and local files, sending emails, setting up or dismissing alarms, and more. If the target is a smart speaker, the attacker can also potentially control other connected smart appliances, allowing them to manipulate heating systems, operate smart locks, turn off lights, and perform actions that could put the user's physical safety at risk.

In the context of VCD attacks, attackers typically have one or more of these three objectives: (i) violating the user's privacy by obtaining sensitive information like passwords, PINs, or Personally Identifiable Information; (ii) executing malicious actions for financial gains, such as purchasing premium features from applications owned by the attacker or transferring funds to the attacker's account; (iii) undermining the user's physical safety, such as by opening their smart locks, turning on heating during a hot day, or turning off lights at night.

3.2   Discussion

Unlike the Lockheed-Martin kill chain, VOCODES does allow for cyclicality of actions. In fact, the attacker may need to repeat one or more steps from 3 to 6 in response to events that occurred during the attack. For instance, if the attacker failed to establish persistent access or skipped the persistence step for any reason, and the device gets disconnected from the C&C server, the attacker may need to restart the attack from step 3. This is also the case when the attacker wants to target multiple devices of the same family—they will need to repeat steps 3 to 6 for each device. Figure 2 illustrates the discussed steps and the possible cycles within the VOCODES kill chain. The related steps of other kill chains for each step of VOCODES are listed on the right.

The reader may have observed that not all steps of other kill chains are connected to a step of the VOCODES kill chain. This is because they do not fit into the structured process that the attacker must follow to execute a self-issue attack against a voice controllable device. We therefore set out to list the various steps of existing kill chains that VOCODES does not include because we deem them irrelevant to the focus of the new kill chain. Each such step is introduced below, along with the acronym (between square brackets) of the original kill chain it belongs to, as well as the applicable rationale for not including it in VOCODES. Such steps are:

- **Pivoting [UKC]**: even if the attacker can control smart appliances by self-issuing voice commands to a smart speaker, they cannot attack them or exploit their vulnerabilities. Moreover, the adversary does not have control over the tunneled traffic via such smart appliances or other connected devices. Hence, this differs significantly from a classic pivoting scenario.
- **Discovery [UKC, ATT]**: although the attacker can self-issue commands that prompt the user to disclose any smart appliances they have, such as setting up an application that intercepts all legitimate voice commands, this is a very limited internal reconnaissance tool that is closer to *social engineering* than *discovery*.

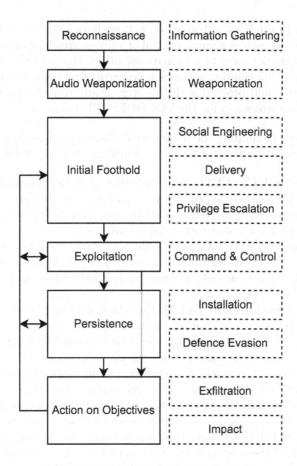

Fig. 2. The VOCODES Kill Chain

- **Lateral Movement [UKC, ATT, EKC]:** while the adversary can issue commands to smart appliances connected to the target device, this is not considered proper lateral movement since the adversary does not gain a shell or any access to them.
- **Collection [UKC, ATT]:** the adversary does not have to collect information before exfiltration since the attacker should always be listening to or recording the legitimate user's utterances, so any sensitive information is captured the moment it is spoken by the user.
- **Exit [MKC]:** the authors of the paper [16] where this step is presented unfortunately did not elaborate on its meaning. We can assume that it implies the adversary may want to stop the attack at some point, either because they achieved their mission goal or to avoid detection. However, this is not necessarily true: there are numerous attacks, especially those including C&C and zombie devices, where the attacker's goal is to gain control of as many devices as possible, and being detected is part of the game. In other words, the attack

never ends. In the VPA self-issue context, we have a similar scenario: assuming that the attacker is gaining control of voice-controllable devices remotely, they ideally do not want to terminate the attack since they would stop gathering sensitive information and give up control of all breached devices. While an adversary could proceed with this step at any time during the attack, it is not *ideal* or *necessary* for the VOCODES kill chain.

Furthermore, to simplify the model, we exclude several steps from other kill chains that bear redundancy with the terminology that VOCODES advances.

- **Execution [UKC, ATT]**: code execution can occur during the *initial foothold* or *persistence* phases, but we do not consider the exploitation of the self-issue vulnerability as code execution, as it involves executing an attacker-controlled *voice command* rather than *source code*.
- **Credential Access [UKC, ATT]**: the adversary can obtain any passwords or PINs entered by the legitimate user during the *action on objectives* phase. Additionally, this is already covered by the *exfiltration* step listed on the bottom right of Fig. 2 as well.
- **Resource Development [ATT]**: the adversary requires two resources for the attack: the malicious application and weaponized audio files. While developing the former is not explicitly mentioned in the VOCODES Kill Chain, because the adversary could use an existing solution to cast a radio station or use Bluetooth streaming to issue voice commands, the latter is already included in the *audio weaponization* step, making this step redundant.
- **Manipulation [EKC]**: manipulation includes further *reconnaissance, weaponization, exploitation, installation*, and *execution* on the main target. In the Expanded Kill Chain, this step was relevant because the adversary had performed these actions on other scopes (i.e. external, internal) and it was time to execute them on the target. However, this is redundant in the VOCODES kill chain, as there are no multiple scopes and the adversary is already executing all these actions on the target.

4   Applying VOCODES to Alexa vs Alexa

In this section, we study the Alexa vs Alexa (AvA) attack [10] through the steps of the VOCODES kill chain, to show how to use the new kill chain to analyse self-activation attacks. We chose to analyse AvA because it is a very recent attack that targets Amazon Echo Dot, one of the most widespread commercial smart speakers. AvA relies on the fact that, if the adversary manages to get the privilege of playing audio file on an Amazon Echo Dot device, then the adversary can also self-issue commands at will to that same device, by playing on it malicious audio files containing voice commands. The attack has serious impact on the users' safety, security and privacy, and its related CVE entry, CVE-2022-25809, was rated with Critical severity by the NIST.[2] The attack was partially fixed

---

[2] https://nvd.nist.gov/vuln/detail/CVE-2022-25809.

by Amazon, but the self-activation remains possible by streaming the malicious audio file via Bluetooth:[3] while countermeasures against self-issued commands existed before AvA [1,18,24], and others were designed after the attack [11], it is not clear if they were already in place before the partial fix by Amazon or not.

4.1 Reconnaissance

In the Reconnaissance step, the adversary tries to get as much information as possible on the target voice personal assistant, in this case, Amazon Alexa. The adversary can assess the devices on which Alexa runs to obtain a target voice-controllable device, finding that such voice assistant is embedded on lots of different devices such as smart TVs and headphones. However, Alexa also has a dedicated smart speaker that is largely deployed worldwide: Amazon Echo. Within the AvA paper, the 3rd Generation Echo Dot was chosen to test the self-activation attack, but it was later stated that it is also feasible on 4th Generation Echo Dot devices.

Afterwards, the adversary assesses the possible wake-words for the target device, discovering that the user is able to select between four of them: Alexa, Amazon, Computer, and Echo. They can be discovered from the Amazon Alexa Companion App, by entering the Echo device's settings and selecting "wake-word". As the set of wake-words is shared between all Echo devices, the adversary can get them from the control panel of their device, and then use them to generate valid commands for any other Echo device. However, these wake-words may change depending on the device's language and on its geographical position.

Then, the adversary assesses the possible commands that can be issued to the target smart speaker, discovering there are three main categories of commands:

- Commands that use internal functionalities of Alexa or of the Echo device. Examples: *"Alexa, what time is it?"*, *"Alexa, set a 10 min timer"*, *"Alexa, add tomatoes to my shopping list"*.
- Commands that control smart appliances within the household. Examples: *"Alexa, lights on in the living room"*, *"Alexa, make me a coffee"*.
- Commands that make use of third-party applications (skills) or services. Examples: *"Alexa, check my balance on Capital One"*, *"Alexa, play rock music from Spotify"*, *"Alexa, search who Ada Lovelace was on Wikipedia"*.

The adversary can also try to look for specifications or details on the implementation of the ASR system adopted by Alexa, however, Amazon has not disclosed them as of today, so the attacker will attempt AvA in a black-box scenario. Finally, the adversary can assess the possible conditions in which the device operates. The Echo device can be placed anywhere inside a house, however, as soundwaves emitted by Echo are reflected differently if there are obstacles nearby, three possible scenarios are considered [10]:

- **Open Scenario**: minimum soundwave reflection, no obstacles around Echo;

---

[3] https://www.ava-attack.org/.

- **Wall Scenario**: moderate soundwave reflection, Echo is placed near a wall;
- **Small Scenario**: massive soundwave reflection, there are at least 2 obstacles that are very close to Echo.

All the information that the adversary has gathered on the voice controllable device and on the voice personal assistant will be critical for the execution of the next step in the kill chain, the Audio Weaponization.

4.2 Audio Weaponization

In the AvA paper were identified three possible ways to generate audio files containing voice commands [10]:

1. **Text-To-Speech (TTS) Commands** created with the TTS technology.
2. **Adversarial Commands** working against Alexa *over-the-air*.
3. **Real-Voice Commands** featuring a real human voice.

The AvA attack was then mainly evaluated using Google TTS payloads, with pitch set to 0.00, speed set to 1.00, and no SSML tags that could affect the TTS pronunciation and timbre. To test the attack varying all five aforementioned voice properties (i.e., pitch, loudness, timbre, tone, and speech rate), in the AvA paper we can see that ten different Wavenet profiles were used to perform AvA, namely, from en-US-Wavenet-A to en-US-Wavenet-J.

Additionally, some adversarial commands generated using Devil's Whisper [6] were successfully self-issued, however, the success rate was rather low, hence, an attacker cannot reliably use them for a real attack. Finally, regarding real-voice commands, the adversary will not use their own voice for the attack, and performing replay attacks on other people's voices can be very impractical. However, this is theoretically possible, and the adversary could use audio editing software to manually edit voice properties.

4.3 Initial Foothold

After generating the weaponised audio files, the adversary will have at least one file for each command they would like to self-issue, and they now need to explore the potential methods for playing them on Echo. In the AvA paper, two valid approaches, or vectors, are discussed for playing audio on an Echo device [10]:

- **Vector 1 - Radio Station**: the Echo device tunes into a radio station. This can be done by means of Music and Radio skills;
- **Vector 2 - Bluetooth Audio Streaming**: another device, e.g. a personal computer or a smartphone, connects to Echo via Bluetooth and streams audio on Echo.

An interesting behaviour when reproducing audio files using these vectors is that when the Echo device receives a voice command, the audio streaming continues uninterrupted.[4] This allows commands to be correctly self-issued from

---

[4] Within the AvA paper, it is said that Echo reduces the playback volume upon hearing the wakeword. However, a bypass to this behaviour is also shown and it has not been fixed as of today.

beginning to end. Hence, if the adversary manages to get a connection to the target Echo device via one of these two vectors, then they will be able to self-issue voice commands to it.

4.4   Exploitation

If the adversary reaches the exploitation phase, regardless of the used attack vector, they can finally proceed to exploit the self-activation vulnerability and issue arbitrary voice commands to the attacked device. As it happens in more "traditional" offensive activities, this phase can feature the exploitation of multiple vulnerabilities at once, or in sequence. In the AvA paper, it is shown how another vulnerability can be chained to the self-activation one, to dramatically enhance recognition rates for the self-issued commands.

4.5   Persistence

In the AvA paper, it is described how the adversary can implement a Voice Masquerading Attack (VMA) [34] by exploiting a third vulnerability called the "break tag chain". Via this VMA strategy, the adversary can run a silent skill on Echo that intercepts all commands from the user and replies to them pretending to be Alexa. In the AvA paper, this skill is called "Mask Attack" and enables the adversary to [10]:

- **Get a further layer of intrusion on the device,** because instead of being solely able to issue commands thanks to the self-issue vulnerability, the adversary can now listen to commands given by the legitimate user and can tamper with the replies. This also allows the adversary to capture personal data that could be sent along with the voice commands, for example, the victim's home address.
- **Set up very realistic social engineering scenarios**, as the Mask Attack skill runs silently on the device, and the legitimate user will unknowingly interact with it, thinking they are talking with Alexa or with a certain skill. In fact, even commands that open other skills would be intercepted by Mask Attack instead. Additionally, as some sensitive actions require the user to say a PIN as a security measure, the adversary might attempt to steal it from the user by introducing a PIN request within a reply. Hence, this also means that a successful VMA attack can allow the adversary to know any secrets of the victim.
- **Get protection on the self-issue layer,** because any "Alexa, stop" command coming from the legitimate user would only terminate Mask Attack, but would not disconnect the Echo device from the attack vector, letting the attacker keep their foothold. In this way, the adversary gets Persistence for their self-issue foothold.

4.6   Actions on Objectives

The adversary can perform a variety of actions with different impact on the end user. Table 1 shows some of the possible actions the adversary might want to perform, and what are the affected user properties for each of them. The adversary may also choose to terminate the attack by issuing "Alexa, stop" (two times in a row if Mask Attack is being used), however, this is unlikely to happen in a real scenario, as the adversary would want to keep control of the target for as much time as possible to keep issuing and intercepting commands.

Table 1. Actions on Echo and their Impact

Action on Echo	Affected User Property
Control smart appliances	Physical safety
Capture commands	Confidentiality
Tamper with linked calendars	Integrity, Availability
Ask for personal data	Confidentiality
Reply to/delete emails*	Confidentiality, Integrity, Availability
Ask for passwords/PINs	Confidentiality
Call any phone number*	Confidentiality
Tamper with command replies	Integrity, Availability
Buy items on Amazon	Integrity
Infer user habits	Confidentiality, Physical safety

*This feature of Alexa is available only in certain countries.

5   Conclusions

In this paper, we discussed the existing kill chains for cyber attacks and derived a new kill chain that is tailored to the voice command self-issue scenario—the VOCODES kill chain. We discussed its six steps, detailing how the attacker must deal with them and how they differ from their most classical counterparts. We also briefly mentioned other steps of relevant kill chains and explained why they do not find a place within VOCODES. Finally, we analysed an attack already known in the literature, Alexa versus Alexa [10], under the new light of the VOCODES kill chain, finding that it can be profitably used to capture all the various steps and nuances of the attack with great accuracy.

Acknowledgements. Sergio Esposito's research was supported by a PhD studentship from Royal Holloway, University of London. Giampaolo Bella acknowledges financial support from: PNRR MUR project PE0000013-FAIR.

References

1. Adams, E.: Avoiding Wake-Word Self-Triggering (2018). https://patents.google.com/patent/US20190311719A1/en. Accessed 04 Dec 2020
2. Alepis, E., Patsakis, C.: Monkey says, monkey does: security and privacy on voice assistants. IEEE Access **5**, 17841–17851 (2017). https://doi.org/10.1109/ACCESS.2017.2747626
3. Amazon.com Inc.: Amazon Echo & Alexa Devices (2022). https://www.amazon.com/smart-home-devices/b?node=9818047011. Accessed 11 Aug 2022
4. Bella, G., Biondi, P., Bognanni, S., Esposito, S.: Petiot: penetration testing the internet of things. Internet of Things **22**, 100707 (2023). https://doi.org/10.1016/j.iot.2023.100707, https://www.sciencedirect.com/science/article/pii/S2542660523000306
5. BMW (UK) Limited: BMW Online Genius - What is Intelligent Personal Assistant? (2021). https://discover.bmw.co.uk/help/technology/what-is-ipa. Accessed 05 Dec 2022
6. Chen, Y., et al.: Devil's whisper: a general approach for physical adversarial attacks against commercial black-box speech recognition devices. In: 29th USENIX Security Symposium (USENIX Security 20), pp. 2667–2684. USENIX Association (2020). https://www.usenix.org/conference/usenixsecurity20/presentation/chen-yuxuan
7. Dasgupta, P.B.: Detection and analysis of human emotions through voice and speech pattern processing. arXiv preprint arXiv:1710.10198 (2017)
8. Diao, W., Liu, X., Zhou, Z., Zhang, K.: Your voice assistant is mine: how to abuse speakers to steal information and control your phone. In: Wang, C., Huang, D., Singh, K., Liang, Z. (eds.) Proceedings of the 4th ACM Workshop on Security and Privacy in Smartphones & Mobile Devices, SPSM@CCS 2014, Scottsdale, AZ, USA, November 03–07, 2014, pp. 63–74. ACM (2014). https://doi.org/10.1145/2666620.2666623
9. Edu, J.S., Such, J.M., Suarez-Tangil, G.: Smart home personal assistants: a security and privacy review. ACM Comput. Surv. **53**(6) (2020). https://doi.org/10.1145/3412383
10. Esposito, S., Sgandurra, D., Bella, G.: Alexa versus Alexa: controlling smart speakers by self-issuing voice commands. In: Proceedings of the 2022 ACM on Asia Conference on Computer and Communications Security, pp. 1064–1078 (2022)
11. Esposito, S., Sgandurra, D., Bella, G.: Protecting voice-controllable devices against self-issued voice commands. In: 2023 IEEE 8th European Symposium on Security and Privacy (EuroS&P), pp. 160–174 (2023). https://doi.org/10.1109/EuroSP57164.2023.00019
12. Google LLC: Compare the Google Nest family (2022). https://store.google.com/gb/magazine/compare_speakers. Accessed 11 Aug 2022
13. Grenard, L.: Leon - Your Open-Source Personal Assistant (2019). https://getleon.ai/. Accessed 05 Dec 2022
14. Hutchins, E.M., Cloppert, M.J., Amin, R.M., et al.: Intelligence-driven computer network defense informed by analysis of adversary campaigns and intrusion kill chains. Leading Issues Inf. Warfare Secur. Res. **1**(1), 80 (2011)
15. Jang, Y., Song, C., Chung, S.P., Wang, T., Lee, W.: A11y attacks: exploiting accessibility in operating systems. In: Proceedings of the 2014 ACM SIGSAC Conference on Computer and Communications Security. CCS 2014, New York, NY, USA, pp. 103–115. Association for Computing Machinery (2014). https://doi.org/10.1145/2660267.2660295

16. Kim, H., Kwon, H., Kim, K.K.: Modified cyber kill chain model for multimedia service environments. Multimedia Tools Appl. **78**(3), 3153–3170 (2019)

17. Kumar, D., et al.: Skill squatting attacks on amazon Alexa. In: 27th USENIX Security Symposium (USENIX Security 2018), Baltimore, MD, pp. 33–47. USENIX Association (2018), https://www.usenix.org/conference/usenixsecurity18/presentation/kumar

18. Lang, J.P.: Wake-Word Detection Suppression (2017). https://patents.google.com/patent/US10475449B2/en. Accessed 04 Dec 2020

19. Li, J., Qu, S., Li, X., Szurley, J., Kolter, J.Z., Metze, F.: Adversarial music: real world audio adversary against wake-word detection system. In: Wallach, H.M., Larochelle, H., Beygelzimer, A., d'Alché-Buc, F., Fox, E.B., Garnett, R. (eds.) Advances in Neural Information Processing Systems 32: Annual Conference on Neural Information Processing Systems 2019, NeurIPS 2019(December), pp. 8–14, 2019. Vancouver, BC, Canada, pp. 11908–11918 (2019). https://proceedings.neurips.cc/paper/2019/hash/ebbdfea212e3a756a1fded7b35578525-Abstract.html

20. Malone, S.: The Expanded Cyber Kill Chain Model (2016). https://www.seantmalone.com/docs/us-16-Malone-Using-an-Expanded-Cyber-Kill-Chain-Model-to-Increase-Attack-Resiliency.pdf

21. Microsoft Corporation: Text to Speech - Realistic AI Voice Generator | Microsoft Azure (2022). https://azure.microsoft.com/en-us/products/cognitive-services/text-to-speech/. Accessed 06 Dec 2022

22. Mitev, R., Miettinen, M., Sadeghi, A.R.: Alexa lied to me: skill-based man-in-the-middle attacks on virtual assistants. In: Proceedings of the 2019 ACM Asia Conference on Computer and Communications Security. Asia CCS 2019, New York, NY, USA, pp. 465–478. Association for Computing Machinery (2019). https://doi.org/10.1145/3321705.3329842

23. Mycroft AI Inc: Mark II - Mycroft (2021). https://mycroft.ai/product/mark-ii/. Accessed 05 Dec 2022

24. Pogue, M.A., Hilmes, P.R.: Detecting Self-Generated Wake Expressions (2013). https://patents.google.com/patent/US9747899B2/en. Accessed 04 Dec 2020

25. Pols, P., van den Berg, J.: The Unified Kill Chain. CSA Thesis, Hague, pp. 1–104 (2017)

26. Ponticello, A.: Towards secure and usable authentication for voice-controlled smart home assistants. Ph.D. thesis, Wien (2020)

27. Statista Inc.: Smart home - Statistics & Facts (2022). https://www.statista.com/topics/2430/smart-homes/. Accessed 11 Aug 2022

28. Sugawara, T., Cyr, B., Rampazzi, S., Genkin, D., Fu, K.: Light commands: laser-based audio injection attacks on voice-controllable systems. In: 29th USENIX Security Symposium (USENIX Security 2020), pp. 2631–2648. USENIX Association (2020). https://www.usenix.org/conference/usenixsecurity20/presentation/sugawara

29. The MITRE Corporation: MITRE ATT&CK (2013). https://attack.mitre.org/. Accessed 03 Jan 2023

30. U.S. Army: A Military Guide to Terrorism in the Twenty-first Century. Cosimo reports, Cosimo, Incorporated (2010). https://books.google.it/books?id=vmUjcAAACAAJ

31. Willison, R., Siponen, M.: Overcoming the insider: reducing employee computer crime through situational crime prevention. Commun. ACM **52**(9), 133–137 (2009)

32. Yan, Q., Liu, K., Zhou, Q., Guo, H., Zhang, N.: SurfingAttack: inter-active hidden attack on voice assistants using ultrasonic guided waves.

In: 27th Annual Network and Distributed System Security Symposium, NDSS 2020, San Diego, California, USA, February 23–26, 2020. The Internet Society (2020). https://www.ndss-symposium.org/ndss-paper/surfingattack-interactive-hidden-attack-on-voice-assistants-using-ultrasonic-guided-waves/

33. Zhang, G., Yan, C., Ji, X., Zhang, T., Zhang, T., Xu, W.: DolphinAttack: inaudible voice commands. In: Proceedings of the 2017 ACM SIGSAC Conference on Computer and Communications Security. CCS 2017, pp. 103–117, New York, NY, USA. Association for Computing Machinery (2017). https://doi.org/10.1145/3133956.3134052

34. Zhang, N., Mi, X., Feng, X., Wang, X., Tian, Y., Qian, F.: Dangerous skills: understanding and mitigating security risks of voice-controlled third-party functions on virtual personal assistant systems. In: 2019 IEEE Symposium on Security and Privacy (SP), pp. 1381–1396 (2019)

DETONAR-Light: An IoT Network Intrusion Detection Using DETONAR without a Sniffer Network

Victoria Bull[1], Niclas Finne[2(✉)], Andrea Agiollo[3], Pallavi Kaliyar[4],
Luca Pajola[5], Thiemo Voigt[1,2], and Mauro Conti[5]

[1] Uppsala University Sweden, Uppsala, Sweden
[2] RISE Computer Science, Stockholm, Sweden
niclas.finne@ri.se
[3] Università di Bologna, Bologna, Italy
[4] Norwegian University of Science and Technology, Trondheim, Norway
[5] University of Padua, Padua, Italy

Abstract. The Internet of Things is expanding and since IoT devices
and IoT networks are used in many crucial areas in modern societies,
ranging from security and military applications to healthcare monitoring and production efficiency, the need to secure these devices is of great
importance. Intrusion detection systems (IDS) play a significant role in
securing IoT networks as their goal is to detect intruders that have gained
access to one or several IoT nodes. While most IDS have been designed
to detect a specific or at most a few attacks, the DETONAR framework
detects multiple attacks. However, it is run on a designated sniffer network which adds additional cost in terms of hardware and maintenance.
In this paper, we propose *DETONAR-Light*, adapting DETONAR to
run using data collected at a border router rather than on sniffer logs.
Our experiments show that this is possible almost without any decrease
of detection and attack classification rate for many attacks.

1 Introduction

The Internet of Things (IoT) enables applications in domains of high industrial
and societal relevance such as healthcare, agriculture, aviation and aerospace,
civil infrastructure monitoring, and process control in industrial settings. The
underlying network is often a low-power wireless multi-hop network that we
call an IoT network. IoT networks are suspect to novel attack vectors due to
their resource constraints in terms of energy, computation power, memory, and
bandwidth [5,7,16]. Since they transmit with lower transmission power than
other networks, they are also exposed to different jamming attacks [14,26].

Due to their resource constraints, IoT networks require new routing protocols, amongst which the Routing Protocol for Low-Power and Lossy Networks
(RPL) represents a widely used solution [5]. While being energy-efficient, these
routing protocols expose novel security threats enabling new attacks [4,5,21].

S. Katsikas et al. (Eds.): ESORICS 2023 Workshops, LNCS 14399, pp. 198–213, 2024.
https://doi.org/10.1007/978-3-031-54129-2_12

Once attackers have been able to intrude into a system, they can start attacks, for example, denial-of-service attacks that can be performed on multiple layers in the IoT protocol stack including the routing layer [5]. Therefore, there has been a large amount of research to detect intruders [10, 12, 15, 18, 22, 24, 25]. Most of these studies enable the detection of one or a few attacks to enable secure deployment of RPL. Overcoming the state-of-the-art, DETONAR [2] represents the first framework capable of achieving attack detection and identification of compromised devices for a variety of RPL intruders, while keeping the computational and communication cost under control. To achieve low overhead in RPL communication, DETONAR makes use of a network of sniffers that overhear and collect all traffic in an IoT network in order to detect anomalies and identify attacks.

The introduction of sniffer networks to secure RPL communication represents a non-trivial requirement for many real-world scenarios, as it increases costs and maintenance requirements. To overcome this limitation, in this work, we investigate whether we can instead run the DETONAR framework using data based on nodes' statistics collected at the border router, the gateway between the IoT network and the Internet. We name this adaptation *DETONAR-Light*. Figure 1 shows a comparison between DETONAR and *DETONAR-Light* frameworks. For running *DETONAR-Light* using a border router, each node in the network collects statistics about routing changes and radio packets that are received and transmitted. The statistics are aggregated and periodically sent to the border router. In contrast to the information available to a sniffer network, only rough time estimates are available at the gateway, making anomaly and attack detection more difficult.

To validate *DETONAR-Light*, we create a new dataset since the original DETONAR's (named RADAR) cannot be utilized – i.e., it does not take into account information propagation to border routers. The original dataset consists of time-synchronized data from an additional network of sniffer nodes, while the data collected at a border router consists of statistics periodically sent by nodes in the network. The novel dataset is obtained using Multi-Trace [11] – an extension of Contiki-NG's [9, 19] Cooja simulator [20] – and contains eight attacks, each with 100 simulations, for a total of more than 5000 h of tests.

Contributions. Our contributions are summarized as follows:

- We propose *DETONAR-Light*, an adaptation of DETONAR making use of border routers instead of sniffer networks, making an IDS that can be easily installed in already existing networks without the acquisition of new equipment.
- We validate *DETONAR-Light* on a novel set of traces of RPL attacks with more than 5000 h – obtained using Multi-Trace –, showing almost no loss in attack detection and identification, and no increase in the false positives compared to the original DETONAR approach.

Organization. Section 2 presents some background on the RPL routing protocol and gives an overview of the DETONAR framework. The following section

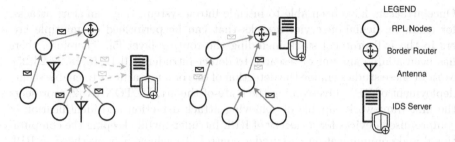

Fig. 1. Comparison between DETONAR (left) and *DETONAR-Light* (right). Here blue lines correspond to RPL routes, while dashed green lines correspond to wireless connections of the sniffing network used in DETONAR [2]. Here, black packets are normal RPL communications, while the orange packets transport *DETONAR-Light* packets to the border router.(Color figure online)

discusses design issues when adapting DETONAR to use data collected at a border router and on new data traces. Section 4 presents our experimental setup and the following section the results of our evaluation. After a section that discusses some limitations, Sect. 7 concludes the paper.

2   Background on RPL and DETONAR

2.1   RPL

The Routing Protocol for LLNs (RPL) is a standard routing protocol adopted in wireless networks containing low-power devices [27]. RPL networks utilize Destination-Oriented Directed Acyclic Graphs (DODAG), where the root node provides access to the Internet and serves as a gateway. To reach the border gateway, low-power devices rely on propagating packets to a preferred selected parent node. Thus, each node belonging to the DODAG is responsible for the propagation of messages toward the DODAG root, enabling an Internet connection at each node. To build and preserve DODAG structures, RPL protocol implements different types of communications among nodes, such as (1) DODAG Information Solicitation (DIS) packets, utilized by new nodes intending to join the network, (2) DODAG Information Object (DIO) packets, utilized by nodes to maintain the DODAG structure in terms of locating RPL instances, learning about DODAG configurations, or selecting a preferred parent, and (3) Destination Advertisement Object (DAO) packets, utilized for advertising backward route information by building upward and downward routes between nodes.

2.2   DETONAR

Thanks to its simplicity RPL enables Internet connection for low-power and constrained devices. However, the collaborative nature of DODAG enables the deployment of a set of attacks on RPL. Such attacks aim at disrupting RPL communication, targeting various components of its framework. A detailed analysis of all available attacks against RPL is out of the scope of this paper, and we refer interested readers to [6,23].

In order to deal with RPL's vulnerabilities several Intrusion Detection Systems (IDSs) have been recently proposed [3,22,24,25]. However, most such approaches suffer various drawbacks, such as *(i)* focusing on small subsets of available RPL attacks, *(ii)* the introduction of high communication overhead, and *(iii)* heavy computational requirements to be satisfied on RPL nodes, which are inherently constrained. Motivated by these severe drawbacks of defense mechanisms in RPL, Agiollo et al. [2] proposed DETONAR, an IDS for RPL networks which attempts to reliably detect and mitigate a large set of RPL attacks while adding virtually no communication overhead and keeping the computational costs under control. In particular, in designing DETONAR the authors rely on an ad-hoc sniffing network – separate from the RPL network – to sense the RPL traffic and propagate it to a central agent. The central server is in charge of detecting possible attacks, relying on a hybrid scheme mixing an unsupervised anomaly detection scheme and a rule-based attacker identification process. More in detail, DETONAR consists of the following steps: *(i) Traffic collection*, where a series of antennas collect RPL communications and forward them to a central server; *(ii) Feature extraction*, the collected traffic is transformed into a time series describing, for each node, the quantities of packets received and forwarded in the specific temporal interval; *(iii) Anomaly detection*, each time series is analyzed with ARIMA [8], an unsupervised model, attempting to spot inconsistencies between the observed and expected traffic; *(iv) Attack classification*, the raised anomalies are analyzed with a rule-based (signature) approach to identify the presence of a specific attack; *(v) Attacker identification*, if an attack has been detected, the IDS identifies compromised nodes with a rule-based (signature) mechanism.

DETONAR includes many desirable properties that an industrial IDS should have [28]: *sufficient*, as it can detect many attacks while preserving low-false positives; *independent*, since its hyperparameters are tuned during the set-up phase; *meaningful*, since it allows to understand which devices acted anomalously; *local* as it monitors single-devices activities; *efficient*, since its execution (training and testing phases) does not require many computational resources. Last, thanks to its simplicity of anomaly and rule-based mechanism, it provides an easy interpretation of classified anomalies and attacks, easing its usage by cybersecurity practitioners monitoring the traffic [17].

DETONAR is configured over the following properties: time window size to collect statics, size of the time series, and test significance. In this work, we utilized for both DETONAR and *DETONAR-Light* the optimal configuration found in the original paper [2].

2.3 RADAR

To test the performance of DETONAR over a broad set of attacks, Agiollo et al. [2] proposed RADAR, a novel Routing Attacks DAtaset for RPL. RADAR considers 14 popular attacks targeting RPL networks, e.g., blackhole, sinkhole, and wormhole. RADAR is collected using Netsim [1]. Here, the authors run five simulations for each of the selected attacks. The simulations consider rather simple but significant topologies, each of them containing 16 IoT devices and a single border router belonging to a single DODAG structure. Moreover, to allow for flexible usage, RADAR contains ten legitimate simulations. The output of each simulation is stored as NetSim packet trace files – which represent the content of the RADAR dataset –, enlisting details for each packet exchanged during the simulation. Overall, RADAR contains packet trace files of 80 different simulations (across 14 well-known attacks), amounting to a total of more than a million packets stored on average for each simulation. RADAR's networks contain a single DODAG structure obtained from 16 IoT devices and a single border router. Each simulation lasts for 1500 s. In attack simulations, the malicious behavior starts randomly between the second 500 and 700.

3 *DETONAR-Light* Design

This section introduces the design changes required to extend DETONAR to use data collected at a border router, thus introducing *DETONAR-Light* (Sect. 3.1). We also discuss the adaptation and modifications required to couple DETONAR, Contiki-NG, and Cooja (Sect. 3.2). Figure 1 shows how we modify the original DETONAR framework (left part of the figure). Rather than relying on a network of sniffers, nodes transmit collected statistics to the border router (orange packets). In our current implementation, these statistics are transmitted as separate packets but they could also be piggybacked on data packets (black packets in Fig. 1).

3.1 Running DETONAR Using Data Collected at a Border Router

For running DETONAR using a border router, each node in the network collects statistics about routing changes and radio packets that are heard and sent. The statistics are aggregated and sent to the border router every five minutes. We also include rough time estimates of rank and DODAG version changes as this is needed by DETONAR for attacker identification. Currently, only rough time estimates are available as we do not have any mechanism to synchronize the time in the network and each node has its independent system clock. This is different from the original DETONAR where data comes from a time-synchronised sniffer network. It may hence make it harder to identify the attacker for some of the attacks.

In our current implementation, the border router logs statistics received from the nodes, as well as statistics collected by the border router itself, to log files.

We modify DETONAR to support log files with aggregated statistics and run the modified DETONAR on these log files to detect and classify any network attacks.

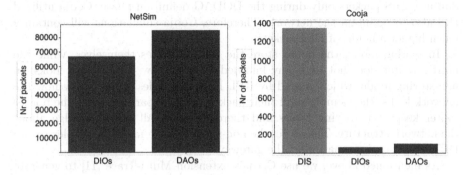

Fig. 2. The number of control packets in RADAR (generated using NetSim) and datasets generated using Cooja. The number of generated packets differs significantly (note the different scales on the y-axis).

3.2 DETONAR Adaptation to Contiki-NG and Cooja

The nodes simulated in Cooja are implemented using Contiki-NG. Since Cooja simulates deployable Contiki-NG code, this makes it easier to use *DETONAR-Light* in real testbeds and deployments. The RPL implementation in Contiki-NG has a number of differences compared to the RPL used by NetSim, that need to be addressed to use DETONAR together with Cooja.

1. Contiki-NG uses DIS broadcast packets to request routing information from nearby nodes. NetSim does not use DIS packets but instead relies on broadcast DIO packets being sent often enough for nodes to simply listen for information from nearby nodes.
2. Contiki-NG is optimized for low-energy applications and is much less aggressive than NetSim in regard to routing communication.
3. Contiki-NG uses the RPL Minimum Rank with Hysteresis Objective Function (MRHOF) to rank the nodes' path to the gateway. Meanwhile, NetSim assigns nodes' rank scores depending on link quality, which is defined as $L_q = 1 - \frac{P}{S_r}$, where P identifies the received power and S_r the receiver sensitivity. Both objective functions grade the quality of the path from a node to the sink node but use quite different rank values.
4. Contiki-NG uses non-storing RPL mode. NetSim uses storing RPL mode.

The first two points lead to the situation shown in Fig. 2. The figure compares the number of control packets in NetSim and in the traces generated by Contiki-NG's RPL implementation (RPL Lite) in Cooja. The numbers are from five simulations without attacks for each simulation tool, and correspond to the average total number of control packets for a whole simulation. The figure shows that NetSim does not include DIS messages but instead a very high number of DIO and DAO messages. This leads to different network behaviors: while Net-Sim uses DIS packets only during the DODAG definition phase, Cooja utilized DIS also to maintain the network. Therefore, Cooja simulations will contain a much higher amount of DIS packets.

In storing mode, the nodes store the routing tables themselves, while the border router does not have any knowledge about how the network looks. In non-storing mode, which is used by RPL Lite, the nodes do not know how the network looks, they simply send their packets to their parents, while the border router keeps the routing tables and therefore holds all the knowledge about the network structure. Therefore, the non-storing mode makes it simpler to run DETONAR on information at the gateway.

As mentioned above, we use Cooja's extension Multi-Trace [11] to generate the data traces on which we run *DETONAR-Light*. Multi-Trace enables us to quickly generate a large number of traces for a given number of nodes by varying the position of the nodes and hence generating different network topologies.

4   Experiments

This section presents the experimental setup used to validate *DETONAR-Light* and compares it against DETONAR. In detail, Sect. 4.1 describes the attack implementation, Sect. 4.2 the experiment setup, and Sect. 4.3 the metrics utilized to evaluate DETONAR and *DETONAR-Light*.

4.1   Attack Implementation in Contiki-NG

To analyze *DETONAR-Light* detection performance, we use Cooja to simulate eight different types of RPL attacks. We select these eight out of the 14 attacks implemented in DETONAR based on their realism and expected effectiveness. The eight attacks are the following: *(i) blackhole* and *(ii) selective forward* attacks, where an attacker drops application packets received from its children; *(iii) sinkhole*, and *(iv) continuous sinkhole* attacks, where the DODAG is modified via faked rank values; *(v) HELLO flooding*, and *(vi) DIS* attacks, where malicious device floods the network with forged control packets; *(vii) version*, and *(viii) local repair* attacks, where an attacker forges modified control packets to disrupt the DODAG.

The considered attacks are implemented leveraging the hook mechanism provided by Contiki-NG – in its network stack – to process, modify, and drop any incoming or outgoing IP packets. Using this mechanism, we implement a set of the network attacks available in DETONAR to, for example, modify outgoing DIO packets to include a fake routing rank, or drop application packets routed via the node. Therefore, the attack implementations are flexible as it is possible to configure different types of attacks with small effort. We include the attack implementation in all nodes of each simulation. Meanwhile, the simulation controls when and which nodes perform an attack by reconfigurating the nodes on the fly. We will make the attack implementations available.

4.2 Setup

For each of the experiments, we use topologies with 16 nodes, as originally done with DETONAR [2]. We run the experiments using the traces collected with Multi-Trace both for the sniffer – i.e., DETONAR – and for the border router – i.e., *DETONAR-Light* – approach. The results of DETONAR were originally achieved with another dataset, RADAR (see Sect. 2), based on traces acquired with the NetSim simulator, as discussed earlier. For both DETONAR and *DETONAR-Light* we use the size of the time window, the size of the time series, and test significance as in the original implementation [2].

We produce 100 different topologies where the 16 nodes are placed differently. While we started with totally random topologies, we placed some restrictions when generating the topologies using Multi-Trace [11]:

- We enforced a certain minimum distance between nodes (40 m in our Cooja simulations) to get a more realistic placement. Indeed, in real-world deployments, IoT devices would not be clustered together as they would be likely to measure the same phenomena.
- Some attacks require that the attacker node has children in the tree in order to be effective. For the Blackhole and Selective Forward attacks, we require that there is more than one node within the attacker node's transmission range and at least one of those nodes is further away from the sink than the attacker node.
- For the Sinkhole, Continuous Sinkhole and Local Repair attacks we require that there are more than two nodes within the attacker node's transmission range and at least one of those are further away from the border router than the attacker node. We also require that the border router must not be within range of the attacker.

We run 100 simulations per scenario with a simulation time of 24 000 s (400 min). The attacks start at 21 000 s (350 min).

To measure the robustness of *DETONAR-Light* against unreliable network communication, we consider an additional experiment setup where packet loss is artificially added to the RPL network. More in detail, we consider three levels of packet success rate probability: *(i)* perfect communication with a packet success rate of 100%; *(ii)* packet success rate of 99.5%, and *(iii)* packet success rate of 99%. To introduce loss in the networks, the success rate for each node can be configured in two ways within Cooja: the packet submission success rate and the packet reception success rate. Both of these rates were adjusted to the corresponding values of 100%, 99.5% and 99%. Over these setups, we investigate if and to what extent *DETONAR-Light* attack detection performance decreases.

4.3   Metrics

In the evaluation, we use four metrics:

- Alarm raised: The percentage of simulations in which *any alarm* was raised
  after the attack has taken place. This metric is mainly used to be able to
  distinguish between cases for which DETONAR completely misses that an
  attack is taking place, and cases where DETONAR recognizes that an attack
  is taking place, but fails to classify it correctly;
- Correctly classified: The percentage of simulations in which an alarm is raised
  after the attack has taken place is classified as the correct attack;
- Attacker identified: The percentage of simulations in which an alarm was
  raised *after* the attack has taken place and the attacker node is correctly
  identified;
- False positives: The percentage of simulations in which there are any alarms
  of attacks raised *before* the attack has taken place.

5   Results

In this section, we provide our experimental results. The focus is on attack
detection and classification accuracy.

5.1   Attack Detection and Classification for Networks Without
Packet Loss

Figure 3 shows the results when the network does not lose any packets. The top
of the figure shows the results achieved with a sniffer network while the bottom
shows the results with the border router approach when all packets are collected
by the border router where DETONAR is implemented. The results show that for
most of the attacks, an alarm is raised and the attacks are correctly classified.
For some of the attacks, i.e., Blackhole and Selective Forwarding attacks, the
results are worse, i.e., they have a detection (Alarm Raised) and classification
rate below of only around 80%. We believe that most of these cases are due to
topologies where the attack does not have any effect on the other nodes in the
network even though we try to avoid such cases as described above.

For some of the attacks, the attacker identification does not work as well
for the border router approach. For attacks on the rank which include sinkhole,
local repair, and continuous sinkhole, the attacker identification is based on
which node advertises a wrong rank first [2]. While the sniffer network is time-
synchronized, Contiki-NG nodes in Cooja simulations only have relative time-
synchronization, so it is not always possible for the border router to derive the
order in which packets have been sent. This makes attacker identification more
difficult for some attacks.

Figure 4 presents an aggregated view confirming that *DETONAR-Light* has
roughly the same performance as DETONAR. Overall, in our experiments, we
do not get any false positives when running DETONAR using data collected at

the border router while there is a small number of false positives when running it on the sniffer network. We believe that this difference would vanish with a larger number of experiments as we could not find any reason why they would differ between the two approaches. In general, the results are on par with that of other IDS such as SVELTE [24].

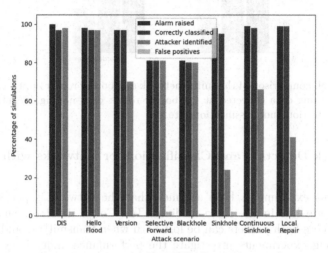

(a) DETONAR.

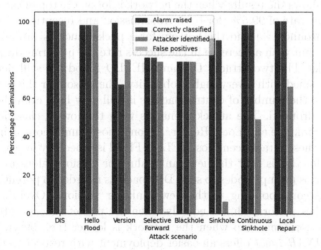

(b) *DETONAR-Light*

Fig. 3. Performance comparison between DETONAR and *DETONAR-Light* with no packet loss.

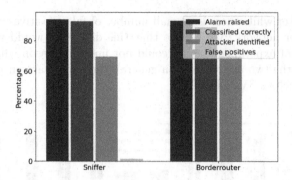

Fig. 4. Overall comparison of the sniffer network and border router approach. Running DETONAR using data collected at the border router does not significantly decrease the attack detection and classification rate.

5.2 Attack Detection and Classification for Networks with Packet Loss

The previous experiments have assumed that the network is perfect in that no packets are lost in the radio medium. The Cooja simulator enables lossy mediums where both packets can be lost both when transmitting and receiving. The following experiments investigate the performance under lossy networks. We focus on the border router approach but note that the performance for the sniffer approach is similar.

Figure 5 shows the results when the network is lossy: the top of the figure for a packet success rate of 99.5% (for both transmission and reception, so the overall loss rate is around 1%) and the bottom for a packet success rate of 99%. The figure shows that with a decrease in the success rate the performs drops for most of the attacks. The two attacks DIS and HELLO Flood are still detected and correctly classified with a very high probability. The reason for this is that under these attacks, the number of control packets is still very high even though some of them are dropped. The attack scenarios with the lowest classification rate are Version, Sinkhole and Local Repair. Among those simulations being wrongly classified for these attack scenarios, HELLO Flood is especially over-represented. The reason for this is that the new rank values or version values used in these attack scenarios prompt nodes to send DIO packets in order to potentially adjust the DODAG corresponding to the new ranks or versions. Overall, while the two approaches perform almost equally when the packet success rate is 99.5%, there is a performance gap when the network is lossier (i.e., 99%). Therefore, while *DETONAR-Light* offers an easier deployment with respect to the original DETONAR [2], its limitation is given by susceptibility to lossy networks, which increases the false positive rate and lowers the attack detection rate.

We show the comparison of the two approaches for the 99% success rate in Fig. 6. Overall, while the two approaches perform almost equally when the packet success rate is 100%, there is a performance gap when the network is lossier as shown in Fig. 6. Future work aims to improve this situation, for example, by revisiting the attack classification rules. From a practical perspective, it is important to keep the rate of false positives low. Figure 6 shows that this is still the case even with lossy networks.

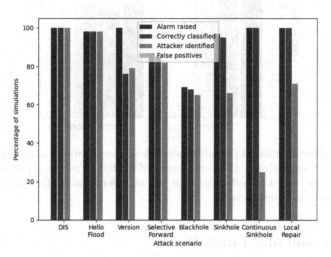

(a) 99.5% packet success rate.

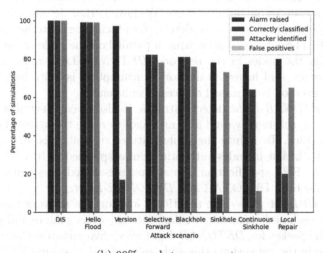

(b) 99% packet success rate.

Fig. 5. *DETONAR-Light* performance over lossy networks with different success rate for reception and submission of packets.

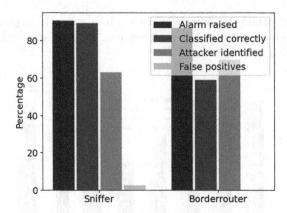

Fig. 6. Overall comparison of the sniffer network and border router approach using networks with 99% success rate. The performance of the border router approach decreases in regards to the attack classification, but the attacker identification and the rate of false positives remain unaffected.

6   Discussion and Limitations

In the previous section, we have presented experimental results with quite reliable networks. Higher loss is often caused by cross-technology interference or in some cases even by jamming attacks. We have earlier devised tools that run on resource-constrained devices to detect cross-technology interference [13] and jamming [14]. Those tools could be run in parallel on the nodes to identify such situations. On the nodes in the network, *DETONAR-Light* more or less only collects statistics, and hence its memory consumption is quite low. Therefore, the memory even on constrained devices is sufficient.

While *DETONAR-Light* detects attacks, it also opens new attack vectors. For example, attackers may send fake messages to make the system believe that there is an attack. To reduce the probability of such attacks, one could work with secure RPL that includes authentication as specified in RFC 6550 [27]. As security in the RPL specification is based on pre-shared keys, such a solution would work for both DETONAR and *DETONAR-Light*.

DETONAR-Light puts some additional load on the network traffic. In our experiments, each node transmits its data message every minute and in addition sends a status packet for *DETONAR-Light* every five minutes. Considering the overall traffic in the networking this adds an overhead of around 5%. We believe that in many scenarios it is possible to piggyback this additional status information on existing data packets. The periodicity with which status information is sent has an impact on the network load and may also impact the detectability of attacks and the attackers. We leave studies to minimize the overhead without compromising detectability to future work.

7 Conclusions

In this work, we proposed *DETONAR-Light*, an RPL IDS that extends DET-ONAR to run on data collected on a border router rather than on data from a time-synchronized sniffer network. We evaluated *DETONAR-Light* on data traces generated by Multi-Trace, an extension of the Contiki-NG's Cooja simulator. Despite the different implementations of the RPL protocols between Cooja and DETONAR's original dataset, and the lossy nature of running *DETONAR-Light* on traces at the gateway, we achieve almost the same attack detection and classification rate. We believe that this both demonstrates the versatility of *DETONAR-Light*[1] and makes it more attractive for scenarios where practitioners do not want to rely on an additional sniffer network.

References

1. Tetcos netsim iot/wsn library documentation. https://tetcos.com/help/v13.2/Technology-Libraries/IoT-WSN.html. Accessed 02 Dec 2022
2. Agiollo, A., Conti, M., Kaliyar, P., Lin, T., Pajola, L.: Detonar: detection of routing attacks in RPL-based IoT. IEEE Trans. Network Serv. Manage. **18**, 1178–1190 (2021)
3. Airehrour, D., Gutierrez, J.A., Ray, S.K.: Sectrust-RPL: a secure trust-aware RPL routing protocol for internet of things. Futur. Gener. Comput. Syst. **93**, 860–876 (2019)
4. Alabsi, B.A., Anbar, M., Anickam, S.: A comprehensive review on security attacks in dynamic wireless sensor networks based on RPL protocol. Int. J. Pure Appl. Math. **119**(12), 12481–12495 (2018)
5. Arış, A., Oktuğ, S.F., Voigt, T.: Security of Internet of Things for a reliable internet of services. In: Ganchev, I., van der Mei, R.D., van den Berg, H. (eds.) Autonomous Control for a Reliable Internet of Services. LNCS, vol. 10768, pp. 337–370. Springer, Cham (2018). https://doi.org/10.1007/978-3-319-90415-3_13
6. Bang, A.O., Rao, U.P., Kaliyar, P., Conti, M.: Assessment of routing attacks and mitigation techniques with RPL control messages: a survey. ACM Comput. Surv. **55**(2), 44:1-44:36 (2023)
7. Boo, E., Raza, S., Hoglund, J., Ko, J.: FDTLS: supporting DTLS-based combined storage and communication security for IoT devices. In: 2019 IEEE 16th International Conference on Mobile Ad Hoc and Sensor Systems (MASS), pp. 127–135 (2019)
8. Box, G.E., Jenkins, G.M., Reinsel, G.C., Ljung, G.M.: Time Series Analysis: Forecasting and Control. Wiley, Hoboken (2015)
9. Dunkels, A., Grönvall, B., Voigt, T.: Contiki - a lightweight and flexible operating system for tiny networked sensors. In: Proceedings of the IEEE Workshop on Embedded Networked Sensor Systems (IEEE Emnets), Tampa, Florida, USA (2004)

---

[1] *DETONAR-Light* is available at https://github.com/STACK-ITEA-Project/DETONAR-Light.

10. Essop, I., Ribeiro, J.C., Papaioannou, M., Zachos, G., Mantas, G., Rodriguez, J.: Generating datasets for anomaly-based intrusion detection systems in IoT and industrial IoT networks. Sensors **21**(4), 1528 (2021)
11. Finne, N., et al.: Multi-trace: multi-level data trace generation with the COOJA simulator. In: DCOSS (2021)
12. Ioulianou, P.P., Vassilakis, V.G., Shahandashti, S.F.: A trust-based intrusion detection system for RPL networks: detecting a combination of rank and blackhole attacks. J. Cybersecur. Privacy **2**(1), 124–153 (2022)
13. Iyer, V., Hermans, F., Voigt, T.: Detecting and avoiding multiple sources of interference in the 2.4 GHz spectrum. In: Abdelzaher, T., Pereira, N., Tovar, E. (eds.) EWSN 2015. LNCS, vol. 8965, pp. 35–51. Springer, Cham (2015). https://doi.org/10.1007/978-3-319-15582-1_3
14. Kanwar, J., et al.: Jamsense: interference and jamming classification for low-power wireless networks. In: 13th IFIP Wireless and Mobile Networking Conference (WMNC) (2021)
15. Keipour, H., Hazra, S., Finne, N., Voigt, T.: Generalizing supervised learning for intrusion detection in IoT mesh networks. In: Wang, G., Choo, K.K.R., Ko, R.K.L., Xu, Y., Crispo, B. (eds.) UbiSec 2021. LNCS, vol. 1557, pp. 214–228. Springer, Cham (2022)
16. Kwon, H., Ahn, J., Ko, J.: Lightcert: on designing a lighter certificate for resource-limited internet-of-things devices. Trans. Emerg. Telecommun. Technol. **30**(10), e3740 (2019)
17. Nadeem, A., et al.: SOK: explainable machine learning for computer security applications. In: 2023 IEEE 8th European Symposium on Security and Privacy (EuroS&P), pp. 221–240. IEEE (2023)
18. Napiah, M.N., Idris, M.Y.I.B., Ramli, R., Ahmedy, I.: Compression header analyzer intrusion detection system (cha-ids) for 6lowpan communication protocol. IEEE Access **6**, 16623–16638 (2018)
19. Oikonomou, G., Duquennoy, S., Elsts, A., Eriksson, J., Tanaka, Y., Tsiftes, N.: The Contiki-NG open source operating system for next generation IoT devices. SoftwareX **18**, 101089 (2022)
20. Osterlind, F., Dunkels, A., Eriksson, J., Finne, N., Voigt, T.: Cross-level sensor network simulation with COOJA. In: IEEE Conference on Local Computer Networks (2006)
21. Pasikhani, A.M., Clark, J.A., Gope, P., Alshahrani, A.: Intrusion detection systems in RPL-based 6LoWPAN: a systematic literature review. IEEE Sens. J. **21**(11), 12940–12968 (2021)
22. Pongle, P., Chavan, G.: Real time intrusion and wormhole attack detection in internet of things. Int. J. Comput. Appl. **121**(9), 1–9 (2015)
23. Raoof, A., Matrawy, A., Lung, C.: Routing attacks and mitigation methods for RPL-based internet of things. IEEE Commun. Surv. Tutorials **21**(2), 1582–1606 (2019)
24. Raza, S., Wallgren, L., Voigt, T.: Svelte: real-time intrusion detection in the internet of things. Ad Hoc Netw. **11**(8), 2661–2674 (2013)
25. Sharma, M., Elmiligi, H., Gebali, F.: A novel intrusion detection system for RPL-based cyber-physical systems. IEEE Can. J. Electrical Comput. Eng. **44**, 246–252 (2021)
26. Wang, L., Wyglinski, A.M.: A combined approach for distinguishing different types of jamming attacks against wireless networks. In: Proceedings of 2011 IEEE Pacific Rim Conference on Communications, Computers and Signal Processing, pp. 809–814. IEEE (2011)

27. Winter, T., et al.: RPL: Ipv6 routing protocol for low-power and lossy networks. Technical report (2012)
28. Wolsing, K., Thiemt, L., Sloun, C.V., Wagner, E., Wehrle, K., Henze, M.: Can industrial intrusion detection be simple? In: Atluri, V., Di Pietro, R., Jensen, C.D., Meng, W. (eds.) Computer Security-ESORICS 2022, Part III. LNCS, vol. 13556, pp. 574–594. Springer, Cham (2022)

Firmware-Based DoS Attacks in Wireless Sensor Network

Phi Tuong Lau[1]([envelope]) and Stefan Katzenbeisser[2]

[1] Faculty of Computer Engineering, University of Information Technology, Ho Chi Minh, Vietnam
laulpt@gmail.com
[2] Faculty of Computer Science and Mathematics, University of Passau, Ho Chi Minh, Germany
Stefan.Katzenbeisser@uni-passau.de

Abstract. IoT devices are projected to scale up to hundreds of billions by 2030 due to its applications in agriculture, healthcare, environment, manufacturing, energy transition, and other industries. However, it raises many cybersecurity concerns as well. Typically, the firmware of IoT devices can include security vulnerabilities and software bugs. Once those devices are deployed, adversaries can exploit vulnerable code residing inside such devices for malicious intentions like DoS attacks. For example, memory corruption and long-run operations as vulnerable code can be exploited for DoS in a wireless sensor network. Attackers try to crash a running program through memory corruption in order to interrupt node availability and eventually pose DoS to a network. We define this attack vector as firmware-driven DoS attacks.

In this paper, we demonstrate how firmware-based DoS exploits can be carried out in a wireless sensor network through simulating attack scenarios. In addition, we propose a defensive mechanism at network level that monitors the CPU load of nodes to switch its state. The results show that the proposed mechanism can preserve network lifespan and network availability in some scenarios.

Keywords: DoS · IoT · Wireless Sensor Network · Firmware Analysis

1 Introduction

The Internet of Things is projected to connect hundreds of billions of devices globally by 2030. It is applied in various fields such as manufacturing, healthcare, transport, agriculture, and automation, leading organizations towards the digital transformation. For example, IoT networks can benefit farming by collecting data on rainfall, humidity, temperature and soil that help automate farming and predict weather. In construction, sensors could be used to monitor events or changes within structural buildings, bridges, railway, and other infrastructures in order to save cost and time. In addition, home automation utilizes IoT networks to monitor and manipulate mechanical and electrical systems in buildings. Moreover, smart cities facilitate citizens to manage waste and energy consumption. It is foreseeable that IoT will spread to more industries, including healthcare, finance, retail, space, manufacturing, etc.

S. Katsikas et al. (Eds.): ESORICS 2023 Workshops, LNCS 14399, pp. 214–232, 2024.
https://doi.org/10.1007/978-3-031-54129-2_13

Despite these benefits, recent research indicates that 90% of consumers lack confidence in IoT device security [1–3]. In 2019, a survey performed in Australia, Canada, France, Japan, the U.K., and the U.S. revealed that 63% of consumers even find connected devices "creepy" [1]. According to the Open Web Application Security Project (OWASP), the top 10 IoT vulnerabilities [2] include weak/guessable/or hardcoded passwords, insecure network services, insecure ecosystem interfaces, lack of a secure update mechanism, the use of insecure or outdated components, insufficient privacy protection, insecure data transfer and storage, lack of device management, insecure default settings, and lack of physical hardening. According to [3], healthcare-related organizations could be among the most affected by the security flaws, potentially enabling attackers access to medical devices and obtain private healthcare data, or even switch devices off to prevent patient care. In addition, popular operating systems (e.g. Contiki, RIOT) used in IoT networks reported well-known vulnerabilities such as DoS, buffer overflow, code execution [37–39]. Cyber attackers can exploit vulnerable IoT devices to gain access to enterprise networks, steal sensitive information, and even enable attackers to tamper or disable operational technologies. The security of IoT networks will be more critical for next coming years. Therefore, it requires resilient approaches, which are capable to adapt to various scenarios of attacks and a wide range of applications, and also need to be cost-effective for a large scale of devices.

Our Work. In this paper, we introduce a new attack vector that exploits malicious code residing in the firmware of an IoT node, causing security threats to a wireless sensor network, typically, DoS attacks. For example, adversaries can inject malicious data into client packets submitted to nodes in order to cause a buffer overflow as a form of memory corruption. Consequently, it can crash a running program so that the nodes cannot respond to client requests. By increasing the number of vulnerable nodes, the entire network suffers a major risk of DoS attacks. We define these attacks as firmware-based DoS attacks.

Network-based DoS attacks [10–12] use multiple computers or machines to flood a network by degrading the throughput of a main base station. Sensor-based DoS attacks [13, 14] alter the surrounding physical environment (e.g. light, temperature) for controlling sensor values as user-controlled input in order to perform malicious actions. By comparison, our attacks can be more difficult to prevent as compared to DDoS in an IoT network. The proposed firmware-based DoS starts by exploiting vulnerable code inside the firmware of nodes to eventually deteriorate a network. The vulnerable code can include memory corruption (e.g. buffer overflow) causing the program to crash or to perform time-consuming operations (e.g. CPU-intensive, memory-intensive, or I/O-intensive), exhausting computing resources. When the vulnerable code is triggered successfully, it may slow down or interrupt communication among nodes or even disrupt the entire network so that client requests cannot be handled. An important point is that our attacks can target more nodes in a network instead of only targeting to flood a base station in distributed DoS (DDoS). DDoS attacks can be prevented by analyzing packet features (e.g. source ip/port) sent to a main base station through deep learning approaches [30, 36, 40]. However, such preventive approaches are not well-applicable to our attacks.

Approach. This paper proposes a mechanism implemented at network layer for preventing such DoS-based attacks. At the network level, CPU utilization of all nodes is collected to classify node's status as abnormal or normal. If the node behavior is flagged as abnormal, then the node may be at risk of a firmware-based DoS attack, otherwise, the node is safe. Depending on the frequency of abnormality occuring at nodes, we take countermeasures by switching node' state to sleep or reset for preserving network lifespan as well as network performance. Moreover, if the number of abnormal nodes increases, the network severity will increase as well, leading to a major risk of DoS attacks for the entire network. The network is not capable to handle more client requests. When there does not exist abnormal nodes or a few abnormal nodes occur, the network serverity will be zero or decrease. The network suffers a low risk of DoS attacks and is able to handle more requests.

To evaluate the effectiveness of the mechanism, we simulate various attack scenarios for monitoring node's behaviour and network's power consumption over various time intervals. The result shows that the approach can preserve network lifetime very well without violating network performance in case that a few vulnerable nodes in a network are repeatedly exploited or the attacks do not occur more frequently.

In summary, this paper makes the following contributions.

- We present how firmware-based DoS attacks can be exploited in a wireless sensor network
- We simulate these attacks on real devices
- We propose a mechanism to prevent the attacks at network layer
- We evaluate the effectiveness of the defensive mechanism at network layer through simulation

The rest of the paper is organized as follows. Section 2 presents a brief background of a wireless sensor network. Section 3 shows how the proposed attack can be exploited. Section 4 simulates attack scenarios. Section 5 describes a defensive mechanism for this attack. Section 6 reviews related work, and Sect. 7 concludes the paper.

2 Background

Wireless Sensor Network. A wireless sensor network (WSN) can scale from some nodes up to hundreds or thousands of nodes which communicate through wireless network protocols. The nodes include generic (multi-purpose) sensor nodes and gateway/router (bridge) nodes. Generic sensor nodes are used to monitor physical surrounding environment. Those nodes may be equipped with a variety of sensor chipsets to measure physical attributes such as light, temperature, humidity, velocity, acceleration, etc. Multi-purpose nodes are limited by battery power, so energy efficiency is a major concern in WSN. Sensor network lifetime depends on the number of active nodes and the connectivity of the network, so energy must be used efficiently in order to maximize the network lifetime. Router nodes are used to gather data from generic sensors and relay them to the base station as a coordinator for connecting to outside networks or the Internet. Router nodes have higher processing capability, better battery power, and a long transmission (radio) range.

Operating System. Some popular WSN operating systems are Contiki [4], FreeRTOS [5], LiteOS [6], RIOT-OS [7]. Contiki OS [4] employs a multitasking programming model and can be ported onto memory-constrained and low power wireless sensor nodes. It was first introduced in 2003 and has later been extended by worldwide teams of universities and companies. It runs on many platforms including Texas Instrument, Atmel, and Microchip. The FreeRTOS kernel [5] was originally developed in 2003, and was later maintained by Real Time Engineers Ltd. FreeRTOS is designed to be small and simple, and to provide methods for threads or tasks, mutexes, semaphores and software timers. It is mostly written in C to make it easy to maintain. LiteOS [6] was developed by Huawei, and its architecture is lightweight. It also supports some architectures of microcontrollers for ARM. RIOT-OS [7] is based on a microkernel architecture and supports programming languages C/C++. It uses Rust for programming and has full multithreading and real-time abilities. It also supports various microcontrollers like TI MSP430, Atmega, and ARM Cortex.

Network Topologies. In a star topology, each node directly connects to a gateway. A single gateway can send or receive messages to/from all nodes, while the nodes are not permitted to send messages to each other. This allows low-latency communication between remote nodes and the gateway. In tree topologies (also called cascaded star topologies) each node connects to a node placed higher in the tree, and finally to the gateway. The main advantage of the tree topology is that the expansion of a network is much easier. Mesh topologies allow data transmission from one node to another, which are within its radio transmission range. If a node wants to send a message to another node out of radio communication range, it needs an intermediate node to forward the message to the desired node.

Transmission Standards. WSNs typically employ communication technologies such as ZigBee, 6LoWPAN, Bluetooth Low Energy (BLE), LoRaWAN, WiFi, etc. ZigBee and 6LoWPAN are wireless standards covering a short range of distance with low power. Its physical layer in network stack is adopted from IEEE 802.15.4. 6LoWPAN uses IPv6 for connecting with many nodes. LoRaWAN was introduced in 2015 with a link layer that sits on top of the LoRa physical layer. It is optimized for battery-powered end-devices. In a LoRaWAN network, the end-devices communicate via single-hop links to one or more gateways, which are themselves connected to a single network server via legacy IP technologies.

3 Threat Scenario

3.1 Assumption

Malicious Firmware. Our proposed attack is exploited by triggering vulnerable code residing inside the firmware of wireless sensor nodes. The malicious code is triggered in order to interrupt nodes or switch them offline. We call this attack vector a firmware-based DoS attack. To run it, it requires some initial assumptions.

We assume that a wireless sensor network implements a star or mesh or tree topology containing root nodes, parent nodes, and child nodes using transmission standards like ZigBee, WiFi, or BLE. The nodes run on a wireless sensor operating system (e.g. FreeRTOS). Vulnerable nodes contain vulnerable code residing inside its firmware. The vulnerable code will be described in Sect. 3.2 through some motivating examples. We further assume that the vulnerable code can be injected at development stage or during firmware updates. This can be done by using existing channels for firmware updates (e.g. USB port or an over-the-air (OTA)). Adversaries may also exploit malware residing inside a large number of IoT devices [28, 29].

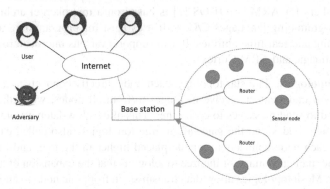

Fig. 1. Wireless sensor network (WSN) model assumed in this paper.

Adversary. As shown in Fig. 1, the network is typically connected with public communities to share sensor data. Due to this open nature, adversaries can easily send requests injected with malicious payloads to the network. We assume two possibilities how attackers can access to the network. First of all, if authentication protocols were implemented to verify data access and communications from the outside, so the access requires to authorize members. In this case, an adversary first needs to bypass authorization/authentication mechanisms to join the network through network attacks so that its malicious requests can be transmitted to the victim nodes. After joining the network, outside attackers can trigger firmware-based DoS attacks. Second, attackers can already be members of the network, in this case, they can freely join the network in order to run the attacks.

Attack Scenario. We distinguish two practical attack scenarios as follows.

In the first scenario, external attackers try to reach to deeper nodes, including parent nodes and child nodes inside a network. They can directly broadcast malicious payloads to all vulnerable nodes, thereby manipulating the execution state of its vulnerable firmware to trigger the exploits. Once the vulnerable code is executed successfully, the vulnerable nodes can intensify their CPU usage for draining battery lifespan rapidly, leading to nodes going offline or slowdown the handling of requests. Consequently, communication among nodes or among clients and nodes is interrupted or delayed. More seriously, the entire network may be disrupted. In this paper, we prefer to simulate the first attack scenario.

In the second scenario, attackers target to interrupt only a root node inside a WSN without reaching to its deeper nodes. Here we assume that the root node contains the vulnerable firmware. When the vulnerable code is triggered, it can degrade root node's availabilities or switch it offline. This also disrupts communication to its deeper nodes. While the parent and child nodes are still alive in the network, they are inaccessible since their root node is interrupted.

3.2 Vulnerable Code

Vulnerable code switches nodes offline or exhausts computing resources, thereby raising capabilities of DoS attacks. The vulnerable code can appear in diverse forms, yet we consider two possible forms of vulnerabilities residing in firmware, including memory corruption and long run operations. Memory corruption in IoT systems has drawn much attention from the research community [21, 25, 26, 37–40]. Such kind of errors exist in various contexts, but we just focus on memory allocation as well as buffer overflows. Long run operations can also appear in many forms in a C program, but we only consider loop counter in this paper.

```
1.    static   void   callback(struct   http_socket   *s,   void   *ptr,
http_socket_event_t e, const uint8_t *data, uint16_t datalen) {
2.    if (e == HTTP_SOCKET_DATA) {
           ..............
3.        uint8_t no_elements = sizeof(data)/sizeof(data[0]);
4.        uint8_t *parr = malloc(no_elements*sizeof(uint8_t));
      }
```
Listing 1. Example of a DoS vulnerability with memory allocation.

Memory Allocation. Adversaries try to inject a value that specifies how much memory size an object allocates on a node. If nodes do not enforce a limit on that value, it is possible to cause the system to run out of available memory. In Listing 1, the node's application allocates an object specified by outside attackers at line 4 inside the callback function as an event handler. If this value is large, it can fill up the whole available memory and degrade its performance. If the object is not freed after dynamic allocation, it causes a memory leak due to a large block of unused memory not released. As a consequence, the program may crash.

Buffer Overflow. In Listing 2, `strcpy` tries to copy the number of characters in the array `data` into a temporary array of 10 elements only, overwriting adjacent memory locations. If the data size is larger than buffer size, the program may crash due to a segmentation fault so that the node becomes unreachable. Buffer overflows are the most prevalent vulnerability in C/C+ programs.

```
1.  static void callback(struct http_socket *s, void *ptr,
http_socket_event_t e, const uint8_t *data, uint16_t datalen) {
2.  if (e == HTTP_SOCKET_DATA) {
    ..............
3.      char buffer[10];
4.      strcpy(buffer, data);
    }
```
Listing 2. Example of a DoS vulnerability with memory corruption.

Loop Counter. If attackers can manipulate a value which will be used as a counter in a loop, the performance on nodes can be affected. In the simple example in Listing 3, outside users can control over the loop counter. If the code inside the loop is resource-intensive, I/O intensive, or CPU intensive, attackers can force it to be executed several times, thereby exhausting computing resources. Also, this maximizes CPU utilization and reduces battery lifespan quickly.

```
1.  static void callback(struct http_socket *s, void *ptr,
http_socket_event_t e, const uint8_t *data, uint16_t datalen) {
2.  if (e == HTTP_SOCKET_DATA) {
    ..............
3.      uint8_t no_elements = sizeof(data)/sizeof(data[0]);
4.      for (i=0;i < no_elements;i++) {
            // CPU-intensive, memory-intensive statements
        }
    }
```
Listing 3. Example of a DoS vulnerability using loop counter.

4 Attack Simulation

In this section, we report the result of a practical experiment performed with ESP32 devices in a wireless sensor network employing the communication protocol WiFi.

Configuration. Experiments are peformed in a mesh-based topology following the first scenario as described in Sect. 3.1 (see Fig. 2). The network is divided into two parts including 5 nodes (1 root node + 4 deeper nodes) and 8 nodes (1 root node + 7 deeper nodes), with the deeper nodes implemented on the device ESP32 [33], and the root node run on another device ESP32 advanced with larger memory size. All nodes run on FreeRTOS. An adversary targets to attack all deeper nodes inside the network. To this end, malicious packets containing the trigger string are transmited to the deeper nodes in order to trigger the predefined vulnerable code residing inside the node's firmware. The root node first receives the trigger string, and then redirects it to all deeper nodes. In addition, we implement a monitoring computer for tracking node's behavior in a real-time manner.

Before stepping into the simulation, we clarify some definitions that will be used in this paper. Our network contains battery-powered nodes. **Network performance** means how many requests a network can handle per time unit. For example, when more and

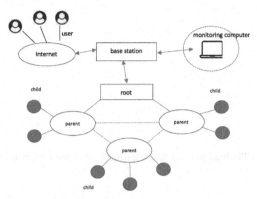

Fig. 2. Attack simulation overview.

more nodes are attacked by increasing their CPU usage in order to deteriorate battery lifespan, they will be unable to handle more requests. This deteriorates the network performance as well. In addition, once nodes crash due to memory corruption attacks, their CPU utilization will become much lower than during normal operation. As a consequence, the network performance will also be affected. Changes in node's CPU usage will also change the network performance. **Network lifespan/lifetime** represents how long a network will be alive. It can be estimated by measuring the network's energy consumption, that is, total power consumption of all nodes during a time interval. When increasing the number of nodes operate at high load continuously within a period of time, network consumes more energy, leading network lifetime to remain shorter. **Network resources** represent the resources of all nodes (e.g. sensor data) in a network. The network resources are unavailable as the network performance is degraded.

The detailed example of the vulnerable code is shown in the appendix and is based on the assumed scenarios as presented in Sect. 3.2. The firmware contains the sensitive function vulnerableCode() at line 4. The sensitive function includes the vulnerable code implementing an intensive loop starting at line 7 and a buffer overflow at line 21. First of all, the calling API strstr(data_rx, "start_loop") checks whether the tainted variable data_rx as an user-controlled input matches the predefined string (i.e. start_loop) at line 7. If so, it will run the intensive loop for triggering the attacks. In addition, when the variable data_rx is tainted with a very long string, it will execute the buffer overflow at line 21.

Results. FigurE 3 depicts the results of the experiment, showing the CPU usage of all deeper nodes in the network, under normal operation conditions and under attack for the network of four and eight nodes.

In Fig. 3 (a), the network operates at normal conditions and the node's CPU load stays at around 12% during the entire 70-min interval. Figure 3 (b) shows the results of a 15-min interval where attacks are performed. During the first 5 min, all nodes have about 12% CPU utilization and stay at normal state. Afterwards, the intensive loop residing in the firmware is triggered by the adversary, and the node's CPU utilization increases dramatically. As its CPU operation reaches to 50%, the buffer overflow attack is executed so that its CPU status collapses to about 5% at the end of the period. Figure 3 (c) shows

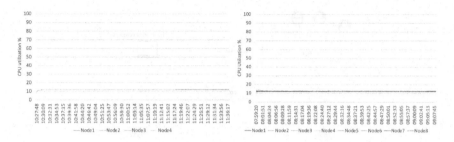

(a)   CPU load of deep nodes during a 70-minute interval (normal).

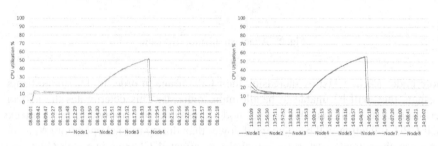

(b)   CPU load of deep nodes during a 15-minute interval (under attack).

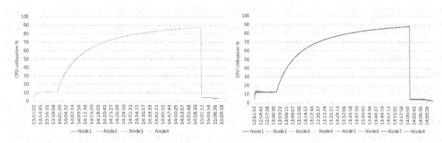

(c)   CPU load of deep nodes during a 80-minute interval (under attack).

Fig. 3. Node's CPU usage (%) under normal and abnormal conditions.

the simulation result of a 80-min interval. During the first period of 10 min, CPU load stays at normal state at around 10%. For next 50 min, due to attacks the intensive loop is triggered, and node's CPU utilization reaches nearly 90%. Afterwards, the buffer overflow is triggered. As a result, node's CPU usage falls down to around 5%.

Figure 4 shows the power consumption of the entire network (Ah) between normal and abnormal state over various time intervals. With an attack duration of 15 min, the network lifespan is not largely affected. As the network size grows and the attack duration extends to a longer interval, energy consumption will increase dramatically. For example, the gap between normal and abnormal condition over an interval of 80 min is at around 0.4439–0.3384 = 0.1055 Ah for 4 nodes. The gap becomes larger once more nodes are added. For example, the network consumes about 0.6474 Ah at normal state

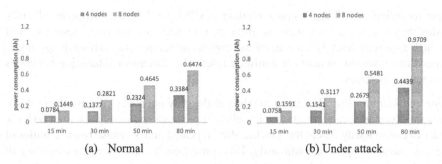

(a) Normal   (b) Under attack

Fig. 4. Network's power consumption (Ah) at normal and abnormal condition through various measuring intervals.

as compared to the abnormal state consuming around 0.9709 Ah on 8 nodes, (0.9709–0.6474 = 0.3235 Ah). In other words, when the amount of nodes doubles, its power consumption gets nearly three times as big.

5 Defensive Mechanism

We propose a countermeasure implemented at network layer based on recording the CPU utilization of nodes for classifying node's behaviour as abnormal or normal. If the CPU load of a node stays in the range $CPU_{min} < CPU_{recording} < CPU_{max}$, then the node operates safely and shows normal behavior. Otherwise, if the CPU load is out of the safety range, its behavior is considered as abnormal. In fact, wireless sensor nodes operate at very low power or low CPU usage because its main tasks are to collect environmental conditions (e.g. temperature, humidity).

We focus on the case of DoS attacks caused by memory corruption (e.g. buffer overflow). These attacks cause segmentation faults or core dumps leading to the crash of a running program. Consequently, the program crash drives node's CPU usage to zero, which is out of the safety range. These cases are seen as abnormal behavior. In addition, DoS attacks can be exploited by triggering long-run operations in the firmware that maximize CPU usage in order to drain battery lifespan rapidly. Consequently, node's CPU operation spiking over the safety range is considered as abnormal as well.

We assume a wireless sensor network, containing a root node as well as deeper nodes, which act as sensor nodes. The root node collects CPU utilization from all its deeper nodes, and then sends such collected data to a monitoring computer equipped at the network. The monitoring computer is used to record CPU load in a real-time maner. Our countermeasure is depicted in Algorithm 1 implemented in the root node.

Normality. We assume that the normal CPU load of a node stays in the range of 10% $< CPU_{recording} < 30\%$, that is, this safety range can be variable on various contexts and specific applications. However, altering the safety range may also have an impact on network power consumption.

Abnormality. If the CPU load of a node is out of the safety range, then the root node will send a message to that node flagging it as a risky node so that it can be restarted.

(cpu_recording > CPU_{max} || cpu_recording < CPU_{min}). In our experiment, all risky nodes that receives a reset message from its root node are forced to reset by itself through a software reset. Of course, we still can choose another way to reset deeper nodes depending on various vendors or hardware reset. This can avoid exhausting network's computing resources.

Repeated Abnormality. Restarting the risky nodes may not always resolve the problem because adversaries can try to transmit malicious payloads to forcibly restarted nodes in order to continuously repeat the attacks. More repeated attacks cause reset activities of the risky nodes happening continuously. This consequently causes a major slowdown of network performance and destroys network lifespan as well.

Sleep Mode. The risky nodes go to sleep once abnormality occurs more frequently. The allowed number of repeated abnormalities with one single node is denotated by MAX (line 3) in Algorithm 1, and the risky nodes are stored in a list. If the list is empty, then network severity is zero or safe (line 22). Otherwise, there are repeatedly risky nodes in the list. Then, the root node checks if there is any risky node with abnormal state repeated more than MAX times (*getRepeatedTimes(repeated_risky_nodes) > MAX*) (line 26). If not, the system is safe. If so, it classifies the state of the network according to four different severity levels (line 27 to line 40).

Severity Level. In the countermeasure algorithm, Severity Level 1 amounts to 0–30% risky nodes repeatedly operating at abnormal behaviour. Other 70–100% remaining nodes operating at normal state can be rescheduled for replacing risky nodes for handling requests *scheduleRequestsToRemainingNodes()*, so the risk of DoS attacks against the entire network becomes low. Meanwhile, the risky nodes will go to sleep mode in order to avoid destroying network lifespan (*sleep(repeated_risky_nodes, SLEEP_INTERVAL)*). The risky nodes will wake up after each predefined sleep interval (*SLEEP_INTERVAL*) for checking their CPU load again. If such risky nodes stay within the safety range, they will be removed from the list of the repeated risky nodes (line 17) and rescheduled again for handling requests. In contrast, the nodes will stay in sleep mode. In this way, the network lifespan can be well-maintained without sacrificing network performance significantly.

Severity Level 2 and Severity Level 3 amount to 30–50% and 50–70% risky nodes respectively driving to abnormal state. The number of the risky nodes can spike to 50% or even 70% in case that the network suffers a DoS attack. According to the algorithm, More repeatedly risky nodes will drive more nodes to fall into sleep mode, so more network resources are unavailable for client requests. This leads to a higher risk of DoS attacks.

Algorithm 1: DoS countermeasure

Input: Deeper nodes inside a network
Output: Network severity level

```
1  repeated_risky_nodes = [];
2  INTERVAL = 1s
3  MAX = 10
4  SLEEP_INTERVAL = 60s
5  while (1) {
6    traverse deeper_node in network {
7       cpu_recording = getCPUusage(deeper_node)
8       if (cpu_recording > CPUmax || cpu_recodring < CPUmin) {
9          risky_node = deeper_node
10         reset(risky_node)
11         if (isRepeated(risky_node)) {
12            repeated_risky_nodes.push(risky_node)
13         }
14      }
15      else {
16         if (repeated_risky_nodes.contain(deeper_node) {
17            repeated_risky_nodes.remove(deeper_node)
18         }
19      }
20   }
21
22   if (repeated_risky_nodes.length == 0) {
23      network_severity = safe
24   }
25   else {
26      if (getRepeatedTimes(repeated_risky_nodes) > MAX) {
27         if (getNodesOverMax(repeated_risky_nodes, MAX) in range 0-30%) {
28            network_severity = level 1
29            scheduleRequestsToRemainingNodes()
30            sleep(repeated_risky_nodes, SLEEP_INTERVAL)
31         }
32         else if (getNodesOverMax(repeated_risky_nodes, MAX) in range 30-50%) {
33            network_severity = level 2
34            scheduleRequestsToRemainingNodes()
35            sleep(repeated_risky_nodes, SLEEP_INTERVAL)
36         }
37         else if (getNodesOverMax(repeated_risky_nodes, MAX) in range 50-70%) {
38            network_severity = level 3
39            scheduleRequestsToRemainingNodes()
40            sleep(repeated_risky_nodes, SLEEP_INTERVAL)
41         }
42         else {
43            network_severity = level 4
44            sleep(repeated_risky_nodes, SLEEP_INTERVAL)
45         }
46      }
47      else {
48         network_severity = safe
49      }
50   }
51   delay(INTERVAL)
52 }
```

In Serverity Level 4, 70–100% risky nodes operate outside of the safety range. In fact, a few remaining nodes (e.g. 0–30%) at normal operating condition are unable to provide enough network resources for client requests. As a consequence, the network will suffer servere performance degradation or will be destroyed entirely. In the worst case, all risky nodes are pushed on sleep state for preserving network lifespan, then it also sacrifices network performance maximally and disrupts network resources mostly.

State Transition. The state of a node can be described by the state transition diagram in Fig. 5. A node can be in safe or abnormal state. When the node is in safe state, it remains safe if its CPU operation stays within the safety range. As its behaviour drives into the abnormality, it will be reset to come back to safe state. But if its behaviour is repeatedly abnormal several times, the node will be switched to sleep state. After a predefined interval, the node will wake up. Once in wakeup state, the node will come back to the sleep mode if its CPU condition is still out of the normal operation range. Otherwise, it will switch to safe state.

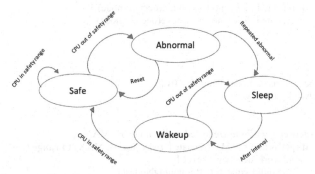

Fig. 5. State transition diagram used to classify a node as normal or abnormal state.

Evaluation. Figure 6 depicts the CPU status of the nodes as the attacks are carried out. Figure 6 (a) shows the node's CPU usage without applying the countermeasure of the Algorithm 1. In Fig. 6 (b), nodes are reset as their CPU load skyrockets to the upper bound of 30%. Afterwards, node's CPU usage plummets to about 2% before it returns back to the normal state at about 12%. Similarly, when the nodes crash, a reset activity is performed for returning back to normal state as well. In this scenario, the attacks are not occurred repeatedly, so there is no further reset required. In Fig. 6 (c), the attacks are repeatedly carried out several times, so the nodes are also reset following Algorithm 1. Figure 6 (d) shows the evaluation results of Algorithm 1 extended with sleep mode. When nodes are repeatedly reset twice (MAX = 2) under an abnormal condition, they go to sleep for 2 min (SLEEP_INTERVAL = 2). Once the nodes are reset at the Second times, its CPU load plunges to nearly 2%, and then stays in sleep mode within 2 min.

Figure 7 compares network's power consumption (in Ah) over various time intervals with increasing the number of nodes. Without applying Algorithm 1, the network consumes more energy when adding more nodes and extending the measuring interval as shown in Fig. 7 (a). By applying the countermeasure algorithm without sleep mode, if

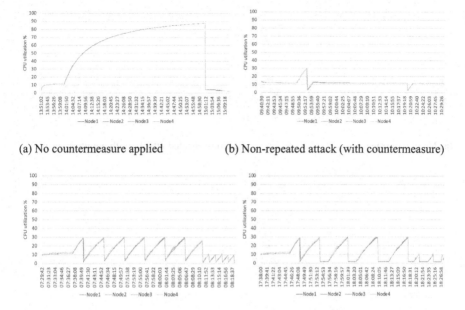

(a) No countermeasure applied   (b) Non-repeated attack (with countermeasure)

(c) Repeated attacks (with countermeasure) (d) Repeated attacks (countermeasure with sleep mode)

Fig. 6. Network status under various attack scenarios.

the attacks are repeatedly performed and reset activities happen continuously, its energy consumption is larger than in the case of the non-repeated attack as compared in Fig. 7 (b), (c). Typically, the power usage in the case of the non-repeated attack consumes at about 0.2383 Ah, while that of the repeated attacks measures at around 0.2620 Ah on 4 nodes within a measurement interval of 50 min. By extending the time interval to 80 min, network's energy consumption is increased to nearly 0.3752 Ah and 0.4142 Ah for the non-repeated attack and the repeated attacks respectively on 4 nodes. For the same measuring interval on 8 nodes, power consumption is scaled up to about 0.7424 Ah in the case of the non-repeated attack and 0.8366 Ah in the case of the repeated attacks. When the algorithm is extended with sleep mode (2-min sleep interval) in Fig. 7 (d), network lifespan is preserved in comparison with the scenario of the non-repeated attack and the repeated attacks. Typically, its power consumption is optimized to about 0.6854 Ah on 8 nodes during a measuring interval of 80 min.

From the experimental results shown in the figures, we reach a conclusion that the countermeasure algorithm can preserve network lifetime and keep network resources available in case that the attacks do not occur more frequently or a few risky nodes are repeatedly exploited (e.g. 0–30%).

Limitation. In the experiment, we simulated attacks on a small number of nodes only due to constrained hardware resources of the root node such as memory size and CPU speed. The root node cannot handle more requests from its deeper nodes continuously for measurement and controlling. We tried to increase the number of nodes by more

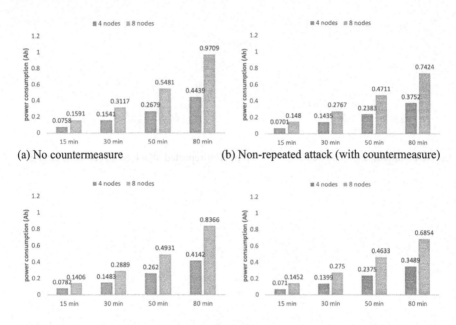

(a) No countermeasure   (b) Non-repeated attack (with countermeasure)

(c) Repeated attacks (with countermeasure) (d) Repeated attacks (countermeasure with sleep interval = 2 min)

Fig. 7. Network's power consumption (Ah) within various measuring intervals.

than 10, as a result, the network performance was too slow or delayed, leading to miss some data from the measurment results. In addition, the proposed defense is unable to maintain network resources well as spiking the number of repeated risky nodes.

6 Related Work

Security Threats. Many research studies analyzed DoS attacks in terms of network and software [10–32]. Raymond et al. [10] categorized network-based DoS attacks and defense mechanisms from physical to application layer in a wireless sensor network. Meneghello et al. [9] presented IoT security threats in terms of communication standards from physical to application layer. Lakshmi et al. [11] simulated flooding attacks based on the number of IoT nodes to monitor network delay and throughput. Sikder et al. [13, 14] made a survey of sensor-based security threats exploited by altering physical environmental conditions (e.g. light, temperature) in order to trigger malicious intents. Lau et al. [31] introduced a class of software-based DoS attacks targeting to node.js systems. He et al. [29] presented security problems of firmware updates based on over-the-air (OTA). By comparison, our proposed attacks begin with exploiting vulnerable code residing inside firmware to eventually pose DoS attacks to the entire network. More specifically, our attacks try to spread to more nodes for slowing or disrupting a network, wherever DDoS aims at flooding a main base station for interrupting a network.

Protection. Many access control methods have been proposed for limiting data transfer between pairs of sensor nodes, between users and sensor nodes, and between service providers and sensor nodes [19, 20, 22]. However, such access control approaches are only applicable to a specified system, for example, healthcare. In fact, individuals and organizations do not always have full capabilities (e.g. money, knowledge, effort) to afford an IoT system like that. In addition, intrusion detection systems based on deep learning have been proposed to detect and prevent DDoS attacks at network level [30, 36, 40]. Those deep learning approaches extract packet features for identifying DDoS attacks, so it is not well-applicable to our attacks. Our attacks aim at exploiting vulnerable firmware. Firmware analysis was proposed to detect vulnerabilities [21, 23, 24, 26]. Salehi et al. [21] implemented an IoT fuzzer for discovering memory corruption in embedded devices through analyzing real firmware. Firmware analysis requires vendors to provide their own firmware or implement special tools to verify. In fact, vendors are not always willing to share its firmware with public communities. Moreover, a large-scale analysis of firmware residing in IoT devices seems to be infeasible in practice since it is too much time-consuming.

7 Conclusion

IoT networks have been applied to many fields such as healthcare, industry, railway, and environment protection. Due to limitations in resources, battery, and processing time, they will face servere cybersecurity issues. This paper introduces a new class of firmware-based DoS attacks in a wireless sensor network, where an attacker exploits vulnerable firmware residing inside nodes. The main goal of such DoS attacks is to disrupt node availability in the network in order to eventually deteriorate network performance as well as network resources. We simulate various attack scenarios in order to measure network's power consumption and network performance through varying amount of nodes. Moreover, we propose a defensive mechanism to prevent such attacks. The evaluation shows that the proposed approach can maintain network lifetime and keep network resources available in case that the attacks do not occur more frequently or a few vulnerable nodes in a network are exploited repeatedly.

Appendix

Appendix

```
#define COL 100
#define ROW 100
#define K 100

2. xTaskHandle array_handle;
3. typedef struct {
       int third_array[ROW][COL];
} holder_t;

4. void vulnerableCode(void *p){
5.     int count = 0;
6.     while(true){
       // trigger intensive loop
7.     if (strstr(data_rx, "start_loop") != NULL){
8.        while (true){
9.           holder_t holder;
10.          int first_array[ROW][COL], second_array[ROW][COL];
             // intensive loop counter
11.          for (int i = 0; i < ROW; i++){
12.             for (int j = 0; j < COL; j++){
13.                first_array[i][j] = i;
14.                second_array[i][j] = i;
15.                holder.third_array[i][j] = i;
                }
16.          for (unsigned long i = 0; i < COL; i++){
17.             for (unsigned long j = 0; j < ROW; j++){
18.                for (unsigned long k = 0; k < K; k++){
19.                   holder.third_array[j][i] = holder.third_ar-
ray[j][i] + first_array[k][i] + second_array[k][i];
                    }
                }
             }
20.          vTaskDelay(200 / portTICK_RATE_MS);
             }
          }
       }
       // trigger memory corruption
21.    if (strstr(data_rx, "start_buffer") != NULL){
          char buffer[5];
          strcpy(buffer, data_rx); // buffer overflow
          vTaskDelete(NULL);
       }
       vTaskDelay(500 / portTICK_RATE_MS);
    }
}

void init(void) {
   xTaskCreatePinnedToCore(vulnerableCode, "vulnerableCode", 16192,
NULL, 1, &array_handle, 1);
}
```

References

1. https://www.thalesgroup.com/en/markets/digital-identity-and-security/iot/iot-security
2. https://www.venafi.com/blog/top-10-vulnerabilities-make-iot-devices-insecure
3. https://www.zdnet.com/article/these-new-vulnerabilities-millions-of-iot-devives-at-risk-so-patch-now/
4. Contiki OS: http://www.contiki-os.org/
5. FreeRTOS: https://www.freertos.org/
6. LiteOS: https://gitee.com/LiteOS/LiteOS
7. RIOT-OS: https://github.com/RIOT-OS/RIOT
8. Mohanty, A., Obaidat, I., Yilmaz, F., Sridhar, M.: Control-hijacking vulnerabilities in IoT firmware: A brief survey. In: Proceedings of the 1st International Workshop on Security and Privacy for the Internet-of-Things (IoTSec) (2018)
9. Meneghello, F., Calore, M., Zucchetto, D., Polese, M., Zanella, A.: IoT: Internet of threats? A survey of practical security vulnerabilities in real IoT devices. IEEE Internet Things J. **6**(5), 8182–8201 (2019)
10. Raymond, D.R., Midkiff, S.F.: Denial-of-service in wireless sensor networks: attacks and defenses. IEEE Pervasive Comput. **7**(1), 74–81 (2008)
11. Lakshmi, H.N., Anand, S., Sinha, S.: Flooding attack in wireless sensor network-analysis and prevention. Int. J. Eng. Adv. Technol. **8**(5), 1792–1796 (2019)
12. Sasikala, E., Rengarajan, N.: An intelligent technique to detect jamming attack in wireless sensor networks (WSNs). Int. J. Fuzzy Syst. **17**(1), 76–83 (2015)
13. Sikder, A.K., Petracca, G., Aksu, H., Jaeger, T., Uluagac, A.S.: A survey on sensor-based threats to internet-of-things (iot) devices and applications. arXiv preprint arXiv:1802.02041 (2018)
14. Sikder, A.K., Aksu, H., Uluagac, A.S.: 6thsense: a context-aware sensor-based attack detector for smart devices. In: 26th USENIX Security Symposium Security, vol. 17, pp. 397–414 (2017)
15. Giannetsos, T., Dimitriou, T.: Spy-sense: spyware tool for executing stealthy exploits against sensor networks. In: Proceedings of the 2nd ACM workshop on Hot topics on Wireless Network Security and Privacy, pp. 7–12 (2013)
16. Son, Y., et al.: Rocking drones with intentional sound noise on gyroscopic sensors. In: 24th USENIX Security Symposium Security, pp. 881–896 (2015)
17. Mems accelerometer hardware design flaws (update a). https://ics-cert.us-cert.gov/alerts/ICS-ALERT-17-073-01A. Accessed 30 May 2017
18. Coppolino, L., D'Alessandro, V., D'Antonio, S., Levy, L., Romano, L.: My smart home is under attack. In: IEEE 18th International Conference on Computational Science and Engineering, pp. 145–151 (2015)
19. Shen, J., Chang, S., Shen, J., Liu, Q., Sun, X.: A lightweight multi-layer authentication protocol for wireless body area networks. Fut. Gener. Comput. Syst. **78**, 956–963 (2018)
20. Li, C.T., Wu, T.Y., Chen, C.L., Lee, C.C., Chen, C.M.: An efficient user authentication and user anonymity scheme with provably security for IoT-based medical care system. Sensors **17**(7), 1482 (2017)
21. Salehi, M., Degani, L., Roveri, M., Hughes, D., Crispo, B.: Discovery and identification of memory corruption vulnerabilities on bare-metal embedded devices. IEEE Trans. Depend. Secure Comput. **20**(2), 1124–1138 (2023)
22. Wang, D., Li, W., Wang, P.: Measuring two-factor authentication schemes for real-time data access in industrial wireless sensor networks. IEEE Trans. Ind. Inf. **14**(9), 4081–4092 (2018)
23. Sun, P., Garcia, L., Salles-Loustau, G., Zonouz, S.: Hybrid firmware analysis for known mobile and iot security vulnerabilities. In: 50th Annual IEEE/IFIP International Conference on Dependable Systems and Networks (DSN), pp. 373–384 (2020)

24. Yao, Y., Zhou, W., Jia, Y., Zhu, L., Liu, P., Zhang, Y.: Identifying privilege separation vulnerabilities in IoT firmware with symbolic execution. In: European Symposium on Research in Computer Security, pp. 638–657 (2019)
25. English, K.V., Obaidat, I., Sridhar, M.: Exploiting memory corruption vulnerabilities in connman for IoT devices. In: 49th Annual IEEE/IFIP International Conference on Dependable Systems and Networks (DSN), pp. 247–255 (2019)
26. Chen, J., et al.: IoTFuzzer: discovering memory corruptions in IoT through app-based fuzzing. In: NDSS (2018)
27. Al-Boghdady, A., Wassif, K., El-Ramly, M.: The presence, trends, and causes of security vulnerabilities in operating systems of IoT's low-end devices. Sensors 21(7), 2329 (2021)
28. Lethaby, N.: A more secure and reliable OTA update architecture for IoT devices. In: Texas Instruments (2018)
29. He, X., Alqahtani, S., Gamble, R., Papa, M.: Securing over-the-air IoT firmware updates using blockchain. In: Proceedings of the International Conference on Omni-Layer Intelligent Systems, pp. 164–171, (2019)
30. Ge, M., Fu, X., Syed, N., Baig, Z., Teo, G., Robles-Kelly, A.: Deep learning-based intrusion detection for IoT networks. In: IEEE 24th Pacific Rim International Symposium on Dependable Computing (PRDC), pp. 256–25609 (2019)
31. Lau, T. P.: A class of software-layer DoS attacks in node.js web apps. In: Proceedings of 6th International Conference on Cryptography, Security and Privacy (CSP), pp. 108–113 (2022)
32. Zhou, W., et al.: Reviewing IoT security via logic bugs in IoT platforms and systems. IEEE Internet Things J. 8(14), 11621–11639 (2021)
33. https://www.espressif.com/en/products/devkits/esp32-devkitc
34. Pal, S., Dorri, A., Jurdak, R.: Blockchain for IoT access control: recent trends and future research directions. J. Network Comput. Appl. 103371 (2022)
35. Li, F., Han, Y., Jin, C.: Practical access control for sensor networks in the context of the Internet of Things. Comput. Commun. 89, 154–164 (2016)
36. Mittal, M., Kumar, K., Behal, S.: Deep learning approaches for detecting DDoS attacks: a systematic review. Soft Comput. 27(18), 13039–13075 (2023)
37. https://www.cvedetails.com/vendor/20377/Riot-os.html
38. https://www.cvedetails.com/product/38087/Contiki-os-Contiki.html?vendor_id=16528
39. https://www.cvedetails.com/product/51624/Amazon-Freertos.html?vendor_id=12126
40. El Bouazzati, M., Tessier, R., Tanguy, P., Gogniat, G.: A lightweight intrusion detection system against IoT memory corruption attacks. In: 26th International Symposium on Design and Diagnostics of Electronic Circuits and Systems (DDECS), pp. 118–123 (2023)

Single-Server Batch Delegation of Variable-Input Pairings with Unbounded Client Lifetime

Giovanni Di Crescenzo[1], Matluba Khodjaeva[2(✉)], and Dilan D. Morales Caro[2]

[1] Peraton Labs Inc., Basking Ridge, NJ, USA
gdicrescenzo@peratonlabs.com
[2] CUNY John Jay College of Criminal Justice, New York, NY, USA
{mkhodjaeva,dilan.moralescaro}@jjay.cuny.edu

Abstract. Pairings are important building blocks in many public-key cryptosystems. Delegation of a pairing computation $e(A, B)$ from a computationally weaker client to a computationally stronger server has been advocated to expand the applicability of pairing-based cryptosystems to computing with resource-constrained devices. In this paper we investigate the problem of delegating *a batch of pairings*. State of the art solutions are only efficient for pairings of the type $e(A_i, B)$; that is, where *only one* of the input components varies across the batch inputs. In this paper we solve the problem of efficiently delegating a batch of pairings of the type $e(A_i, B_i)$; that is, where *both* input components vary across the batch inputs. We show solutions for all of the input scenarios where the A_i, B_i are public or need to remain private, and are available in the offline phase or in the online phase of the delegation protocol. Both our protocols and those in the best previous work are among the very few in the delegation literature to enjoy unlimited client lifetime (i.e., after the offline phase, the number of delegation protocols executable by the resource-constrained client is an arbitrary polynomial), which is desirable in practical applications of resource-constrained client devices. The main technical components underlying our solutions consist of new probabilistic tests simultaneously verifying multiple pairing computations, with time-efficient online verification runtime and space-efficient offline storage.

Keywords: Applied Cryptography · Secure Delegation · Pairings · Batch Pairing · Bilinear Maps · Elliptic Curves · Group Theory

1 Introduction

Server-aided cryptography (starting with, e.g., [1,15,30]) is an active research area addressing the problem of resource-constrained clients, such as IoT devices, delegating or outsourcing cryptographic computations to computationally more powerful servers. Batch cryptography (starting with, e.g., [16]) is another active research area addressing the problem of performing multiple cryptographic operations better than independently repeating each operation, with respect to some

© The Author(s), under exclusive license to Springer Nature Switzerland AG 2024
S. Katsikas et al. (Eds.): ESORICS 2023 Workshops, LNCS 14399, pp. 233–255, 2024.
https://doi.org/10.1007/978-3-031-54129-2_14

performance metric. Pairings (starting with, e.g., [7,23,34]) are important primitive operations in many public-key cryptosystems and, more generally, cryptographic protocols (see, e.g., [3,7–9,21,23,28,29,32]). Currently, the first two areas are seeing a renewed interest because of the increasing popularity of various computing trends (i.e., computing over IoT devices' data, cloud/edge/fog computing, etc.), and the third area has been attracting much cryptography research in the past 20+ years because of its wide-range capabilities and demonstrated applications.

The problem studied in this paper lies in the intersection of these three areas. Specifically, we investigate how a resource-constrained client can efficiently, privately and securely delegate to a server a batch of pairing computations. A solution to this problem needs to make computation for the client more efficient than in a non-delegated computation, but also needs to withstand server's attacks in learning any new information about the input to the computation, or in disrupting the computation and fooling the client into accepting an incorrect computation result.

More generally, we require a solution to the batch delegation of a function F to be a 2-phase, 2-party, protocol between client C and server S, where in the offline phase some information is computed and stored on C's device, and in the online phase C and S have a brief message exchange (typically, a message from C to S followed by one from S to C; see Fig. 1), and where the following requirements are satisfied (see also Appendix A for more formal definitions):

1. δ_c-*result correctness*: if C and S honestly run the protocol, at the end of the protocol C returns $F(x_1), \ldots, F(x_n)$ with probability at least δ_c;
2. ϵ_p-*input privacy*: except for probability ϵ_p, no new information about the input batch $(x_1, \ldots, x_n)$ is revealed to S;
3. ϵ_s-*result security*: S should not be able, except possibly with probability ϵ_s, to convince C to return a result different than $(F(x_1), \ldots, F(x_n))$ at the end of the protocol; and
4. $(t_F, t_S, t_C, cc, sc, mc)$-*efficiency*:
   - *client online runtime efficiency*: C's online phase runtime, denoted as t_C, should be significantly smaller than the runtime, denoted as t_F, of computing $(F(x_1), \ldots, F(x_n))$ without delegation;
   - *unbounded client lifetime*: after running the offline phase, the size n of C's delegated batch of instances can be an arbitrary polynomial;
   - small S's runtime t_S (i.e., a small constant times t_F);
   - small online phase communication complexity cc (i.e., ideally a small constant times input and output sizes);
   - small number of online phase messages mc (i.e., ideally, ≤ 2).

While the client online runtime efficiency property is critical for delegation to be meaningful, we also stress desirable theoretical and practical consequences of the unlimited client lifetime property: (a) the same client can be used for a number of delegations which is an arbitrary polynomial of the length of the client's storage size; and (b) no physical resetting of the storage information is needed to prevent violation of input privacy and/or result security properties.

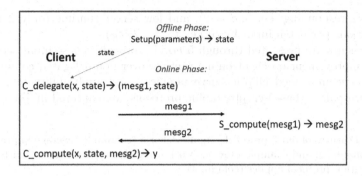

Fig. 1. Delegated computation of $y = F(x)$

Our Contribution. We show single-server protocols for the delegation of a batch of n pairing computations $F(x_i)$, where function F is a pairing e, and input x_i is an arbitrary pair (A_i, B_i) of input values, for $i = 1, \ldots, n$, for all input scenarios where values A_i, B_i are public or need to remain private, and are available in the offline phase or in the online phase. All of our protocols satisfy result correctness, input privacy (unless the input is public), result security, client runtime efficiency and unbounded client lifetime, and are the first to satisfy this set of properties (for detailed comparison with the previous work showing batch pairing delegation [25,31,37], see discussion below for improvements on requirement satisfaction as well as Tables 3, 4, 5, 6, 7 for quantitative improvements). Our protocols achieve the unbounded client lifetime property since they use client's storage independent on n, withstand the attacks to input privacy by a set of novel and efficient input randomization techniques, and withstand the attacks to result security by a set of novel and efficient probabilistic tests. We show the client runtime efficiency property in two ways:

1. with analytical runtime expressions; here, we show that in protocols where input privacy is required (resp., is not required), the dominant term of the client's online runtime is 1 exponentiation to an exponent of length equal to the log of the target group's order + 1 exponentiation to a short exponent (resp., only 1 exponentiation to a short exponent);
2. by a software implementation of our first protocol, and derived calculation for our other protocols, using benchmark runtimes derived from our implementation, with respect to some of the most practical curve families used in recent pairing realizations; here we show that the improvement on the client's online runtime, with respect to n non-delegated pairing computations, is by a multiplicative factor between 1.09 and 4.36, depending on the curve family and protocol.

Our protocols also perform well with respect to the other targeted efficiency properties; specifically: low exchanged communication (only up to 4 group values per batch input; i.e., $cc <= 4$), only 2 messages (client delegating to server, and server responding; i.e., $mc = 2$), and low server runtime (only 2 pairing computations per batch input by S; i.e., $t_S <= 2 \cdot t_F$).

Our results are presented through 5 novel protocols, whose input scenarios, average improvement on client online runtime over non-delegated computation (across 3 recommended elliptic curve families), and applicability to example well-known pairing-based cryptographic protocols, are captured in Table 1.

Table 1. Features of our 5 protocols: input scenario (column 2); average improvement factor (column 3); and example previous work using this input scenario and to which this delegation protocol applies (column 4).

Protocols	Input Scenario	Avg Improvement over non-delegated computation	Protocol applicability examples
$\mathcal{P}_1$	A_i private online, B_i public online	1.091	[6, 19]
$\mathcal{P}_2$	A_i and B_i public online	2.007	[23, 29]
$\mathcal{P}_3$	A_i private online, B_i public offline	1.454	[3, 21]
$\mathcal{P}_4$	A_i public online, B_i public offline	3.961	[3, 7, 9, 21, 29]
$\mathcal{P}_5$	A_i and $B_i = s_i H$ private online	1.717	[8]

Comparison with Previous Work. Delegation protocols for a batch of pairings were first given in [37]. These protocols satisfy correctness, input privacy (unless the input is public), result security and unbounded client lifetime, in several input scenarios. They only work with pairing computations of the type $e(A_i, B)$, for $i = 1, \ldots, n$; that is, where *only one* of the input values varies across the batch, and only satisfy client online runtime efficiency for some (not all) of the input scenarios.

In [31] the authors show 2 delegation protocols (labeled as Protocol 3 and 4) that work for pairing computations where both input values vary across the batch. Protocol 3 satisfies correctness, result security and unbounded client lifetime, but only satisfies client online runtime efficiency for small batch sizes (of size between 5 and 13, depending on the curve family), and for all but one of the most used curve families. Protocol 4 satisfies correctness, result security and client online runtime efficiency, but does not satisfy unbounded client lifetime.

More recently, in [25], the authors showed 4 delegation protocols that work for pairing computations where both input values vary across the batch. Our analysis of these protocols showed that their protocols 1, 2 and 3 do not satisfy the result security property (see [27] for a detailed description of an attack), and protocol 4 does not satisfy client online runtime efficiency, as already mentioned by the authors.

Single-server delegation protocols for a single pairing computation have been proposed in [10, 11, 13, 14, 18, 20, 24, 26]. We note that repeating any such protocol for every input of the batch would result in protocols that satisfy correctness, input privacy (unless the input is public), result security and client online run-time efficiency, but would not satisfy the unbounded client lifetime property, which we achieve here. One exception is our recent delegation protocol in [27] for a single pairing computation which requires no preprocessing (and thus, achieves unbounded client lifetime) in the case inputs A, B are public, but the client's online runtime is higher than the protocol in this paper for the same input scenario.

There is much other work on delegation for operations different than the pairing function studied here, for which we refer to reader to these recent surveys: [12] for other specific operations used in cryptography protocols (e.g., ring multiplication and group exponentiation), [36] for other operations beyond cryptography and [2] for computation of arbitrary functions, with clients more computationally powerful than considered here.

2   Pairing Definitions

Let $\mathbb{G}_1$, $\mathbb{G}_2$ be additive cyclic groups of order l and $\mathbb{G}_T$ be a multiplicative cyclic group of the same order l, for some large prime l. A *bilinear map* (also called *pairing* and so called from now on) is an efficiently computable map $e : \mathbb{G}_1 \times \mathbb{G}_2 \to \mathbb{G}_T$ with the following properties:

1. *Bilinearity:* for all $A \in \mathbb{G}_1, B \in \mathbb{G}_2$ and any $r, s \in \mathbb{Z}_l$, it holds that $e(rA, sB) = e(A, B)^{rs}$
2. *Non-triviality:* if U is a generator for $\mathbb{G}_1$ and V is a generator for $\mathbb{G}_2$ then $e(U, V)$ is a generator for $\mathbb{G}_T$

The last property is there to rule out the trivial case where e maps all of its inputs to 1. We denote a conventional description of the bilinear map e as $desc(e)$.

The currently most practical *pairing realizations* use an ordinary elliptic curve E defined over a field $\mathbb{F}_p$, for some large prime p, as follows. Group $\mathbb{G}_1$ is the l-order additive subgroup of $E(\mathbb{F}_p)$; group $\mathbb{G}_2$ is a specific l-order additive subgroup of $E(\mathbb{F}_{p^k})$ contained in $E(\mathbb{F}_{p^k}) \backslash E(\mathbb{F}_p)$; and group $\mathbb{G}_T$ is the l-order multiplicative subgroup of $\mathbb{F}_{p^k}^*$. Here, k is the embedding degree; i.e., the smallest positive integer such that $l | (p^k - 1)$; $\mathbb{F}_{p^k}$ is the extension field of $\mathbb{F}_p$ of degree k; and $\mathbb{F}_{p^k}^*$ is the field composed of non-zero elements of $\mathbb{F}_{p^k}$. After the Weil pairing was considered in [7], more efficient constructions have been proposed as variants of the Tate pairing, including the more recent ate pairing variants (see, e.g., [4,35,38] for more details on the currently most practical pairing realizations).

As in [13,14], for our results, we further assume that $\mathbb{G}_T$ is a subgroup of a group $\mathcal{G}_T$, also contained in $\mathbb{F}_{p^k}^*$, with the following two properties:

1. testing membership in $\mathcal{G}_T$ is more efficient than testing membership in $\mathbb{G}_T$;
2. all elements of $\mathcal{G}_T$ have order $\geq l$.

This assumption is satisfied by a recently proposed security strengthening of the most practical pairing realizations. Motivated by reducing the chances of low-order attacks in cryptographic protocols, in [4] the authors proposed the notion of *subgroup-secure* elliptic curves underlying a pairing, in turn extending the notion of $\mathcal{G}_T$-*strong* curves from [35]. As a critical step in achieving these notions, both of these papers set $\mathcal{G}_T = G_{\Phi_k(p)}$, where $G_{\Phi_k(p)}$ is the cyclotomic subgroups of order $\Phi_k(p)$ in $\mathbb{F}_{p^k}^*$, and where $\Phi_k(p)$ denotes the k-th cyclotomic polynomial. Satisfaction of above property (2) is directly implied by the definitions of both $\mathcal{G}_T$-strong and subgroup-secure curves. Satisfaction of above property (1) when $\mathcal{G}_T = G_{\Phi_k(p)}$ is detailed in Sect. 5.2 of [4] for the curve families BN-12, BLS-12, KSS-18, and BLS-24, in turn elaborating on Sect. 8.2 of [35]. There, testing membership in $\mathcal{G}_T$ is shown to only require one multiplication in $\mathbb{G}_T$ and a few lower-order Frobenius computations, a significant improvement with respect to the basic approach for testing membership in $\mathbb{G}_T$, requiring an exponentiation in $\mathbb{G}_T$ with a large exponent.

In the rest of the paper we will present protocols for the batch delegated computation of pairing e over a batch of n inputs $(A_1, B_1), \ldots, (A_n, B_n)$. One can differentiate 16 *protocol scenarios*, depending on certain features of the input components $\vec{A} = (A_1, \ldots, A_n) \in \mathbb{G}_1$ and $\vec{B} = (B_1, \ldots, B_n) \in \mathbb{G}_2$ used in the computation of pairing e: specifically, whether privacy of the inputs is desired or not, and whether the inputs are available in the offline phase or only known in the online phase. We say that $\vec{A}$ is

- *public online* if $\vec{A}$ is unknown in the offline phase but known by C and S in the online phase;
- *public offline* if $\vec{A}$ is known by both parties starting from the offline phase;
- *private online* if $\vec{A}$ is unknown in the offline phase but known by C in the online phase);
- *private offline* if $\vec{A}$ is known by C starting from the offline phase but unknown by S.

We use similar definitions for $\vec{B}$. Not all input scenarios are interesting; for instance, the ($\vec{A}$ public offline, $\vec{B}$ public offline) scenario is uninteresting since we assume that C is only resource-constrained in the online phase. Moreover, protocols for different scenarios can be related; for instance, a secure protocol for a scenario where an input is labeled as private is also a secure protocol for the otherwise identical scenario where that same input component is labeled as public. For *asymptotic efficiency* evaluation of our protocols, we will use the following definitions:

- a_i: runtime for addition in $\mathbb{G}_i$, for $i = 1, 2$;
- $m_i(\ell)$: runtime for scalar multiplication of a group value in $\mathbb{G}_i$ with an ℓ-bit scalar value, for $i = 1, 2$.
- t_M: runtime for testing membership of a value to $\mathbb{G}_T$.
- m_T: runtime for multiplication of group values in $\mathbb{G}_T$;
- $e_T(\ell)$: runtime for an exponentiation in $\mathbb{G}_T$ to an ℓ-bit exponent;
- p_T: runtime for the bilinear pairing e;
- m_l: runtime for multiplication of group values in $\mathbb{Z}_l$;
- i_l: runtime for multiplicative inversion in $\mathbb{Z}_l$.

We recall some known facts about these quantities, of interest when evaluating protocol efficiency. First, for large enough ℓ, $a_1 << m_1(\ell)$, $a_2 << m_2(\ell)$, $m_T(\ell) << e_T(\ell)$, and $e_T(\ell) < p_T$. Also, using a double-and-add (resp., square-and-multiply) algorithm, one can realize scalar multiplication (resp., exponentiation) in additive (resp., multiplicative) groups using, for random scalars (resp., random exponents), about 1.5ℓ additions (resp., multiplications).

3 Our Batch Delegation Protocols

In this section we investigate protocols between a client and a single server for secure pairing delegation, in input scenarios where both the A_i and B_i for $i = 1, \ldots, n$ may vary across the batch. Our main results are 5 protocols with variable inputs and unbounded client lifetime, each applicable to a different input scenario, in terms of whether inputs are public or need to remain private, and whether they are known in the offline or online phase. We summarize our results with the following

Theorem 1. Let e be a pairing, let σ be its computational security parameter, and let λ be a statistical security parameter. Also, let n be an integer. There exists (constructively) single-server protocols $\mathcal{P}_j$, for $j \in \{1, \ldots, 5\}$, for the delegated computation of $e(A_i, B_i)$, for $i = 1, \ldots, n$, in input scenario is_j, satisfying δ_c-result correctness, ϵ_p-input privacy, ϵ_s-result security for values of these parameters as specified in Table 2 (top), and satisfying $(t_F, t_S, t_P, t_C, cc, sc, mc)$-efficiency, for values of these parameters as specified in Table 2 (bottom).

Table 2. (Top:) A first set of properties of our protocols: input scenario is_j, result correctness parameter δ_c, input privacy parameter ϵ_p and result security parameter ϵ_s. (Bottom): Efficiency properties of our protocols: number of messages mc, C's storage sc at the end of the offline phase (in # of group values), max term cc_{max} of communication complexity cc (in # of group values), max term $t_{C,max}$ of C's online runtime t_C, max term $t_{S,max}$ of S's runtime t_S, and max term t_P of offline runtime t_P.

Protocol	Input scenario is_j	δ_c	ϵ_p	ϵ_s
$\mathcal{P}_1$ [§3.1]	$\vec{A}$ private online, $\vec{B}$ public online	1	0	$2^{-\lambda}$
$\mathcal{P}_2$ [§3.2]	$\vec{A}$ public online, $\vec{B}$ public online	1	n.a.	$2^{-\lambda}$
$\mathcal{P}_3$ [§3.3]	$\vec{A}$ private online, $\vec{B}$ public offline	1	neg(α)	$2^{-\lambda}$
$\mathcal{P}_4$ [§3.4]	$\vec{A}$ public online, $\vec{B}$ public offline	1	n.a.	$2^{-\lambda}$
$\mathcal{P}_5$ [§3.5]	$\vec{A}, \vec{B}$ priv online, $B_i = s_i H$, s_i priv online, H pub online	1	0	$2^{-\lambda}$

Protocol	mc	sc	cc_{max}	$t_{C,max}$	$t_{S,max}$	$t_{P,max}$
$\mathcal{P}_1$ [§3.1]	2	4	$n + 1$ values in $\mathbb{G}_T$	$n(e_T(r) + e_T(\lambda) + m_2(r))$	$2n \cdot p_T$	p_T
$\mathcal{P}_2$ [§3.2]	2	4	$n + 1$ values in $\mathbb{G}_T$	$n(e_T(\lambda) + m_2(r))$	$2n \cdot p_T$	p_T
$\mathcal{P}_3$ [§3.3]	2	3	$n + 1$ values in $\mathbb{G}_T$	$n(e_T(r) + e_T(\lambda))$	$2n \cdot p_T$	$n \cdot m_2(r)$
$\mathcal{P}_4$ [§3.4]	2	3	$n + 1$ values in $\mathbb{G}_T$	$n \cdot e_T(\lambda)$	$2n \cdot p_T$	$n \cdot m_2(r)$
$\mathcal{P}_5$ [§3.5]	2	3	$n + 2$ values in $\mathbb{G}_T$	$n(e_T(r) + e_T(\lambda))$	$n \cdot p_T$	p_T

The main takeaway from this theorem is that in protocols $\mathcal{P}_1, \mathcal{P}_2$, and $\mathcal{P}_5$ C can delegate the n pairing computations with arbitrarily varying inputs to S using a protocol that satisfies result correctness, input privacy, result security, and unbounded client lifetime, (i.e., the offline complexity of the protocol does not depend on n), and various efficiency property (most notably, client online runtime is lower than a non-delegated pairing computation). Note that this improves over the naive parallel repetition of state of the art protocols to delegate a single pairing [13,14], which would incur offline complexity linear in n, and would not satisfy the unbounded client lifetime property. Moreover, in our protocol, client online runtime is also lower than non-delegated computation in implementations of some of the currently most recommended curve families, as detailed in Sect. 4.

3.1 Input Scenario: $\vec{A}$ Private Online, $\vec{B}$ Public Online

Table 3. Protocols comparison in the input scenario ($\vec{A}$ private online, $\vec{B}$ public online). The expressions for t_C only include higher-order functions p_T, e_T, m_1, m_2.

Protocols	C's storage (sc)	C's online calculation (t_C)
[25] [§ 3.7]	$n + 4$	$n(e_T(r) + e_T(\lambda) + 2\,m_1(r) + m_2(\lambda))$
Ours [§ 3.1]	3	$n(e_T(r) + e_T(\lambda) + 2\,m_1(r) + m_2(r) + m_1(\lambda))$

Informal Description of Protocol $\mathcal{P}_1$: A first goal in this protocol is for C to delegate the computation of $e(A_i, B_i)$, while preserving privacy of the first inputs A_i, for $i = 1, \ldots, n$. C achieves this efficiently by sending a masked version $\hat{A}_i$ of input A_i, using a random value $a_i \in \mathbb{Z}_l^*$, receiving $w_i = e(\hat{A}_i, B_i)$ from S, and then computing $y_i = w_i^{1/a_i}$. A second goal in the protocol is for C to check that all values $w_1, \ldots, w_n$ returned by S are correctly computed. C efficiently achieves to this by asking S to compute more pairings and by (1) a deterministic membership test that verifies that values $w_1, \ldots, w_n$ belong to $\mathcal{G}_T$; and (2) a new probabilistic test that verifies a probabilistic condition relating these extra pairing values:

$$\prod_{i=1}^{n} e(Z_i, B_i) = e(U, I) \cdot e(U, Q) \cdot \prod_{i=1}^{n} y_i^{b_i},$$

where $Z_i = b_i A_i + u_i U$, $I := (\sum_{i=1}^{n} u_i \cdot B_i) - Q$, u_i are random values from $\mathbb{Z}_l$, and U, Q are random values from $\mathbb{G}_1$. This test includes important optimizations such as using small random values $b_i \in [1, 2^\lambda]$ both as scalars in $\mathbb{G}_1$ and as exponents in $\mathbb{G}_T$, instead of full-domain values, extending a similar technique in the small-exponent test of [5], and a novel input masking technique that efficiently blends with the pairing's bilinearity property. A formal description follows.

Formal description of protocol $\mathcal{P}_1$:
Offline Input to C and S: $1^\sigma, 1^\lambda, desc(e)$
Offline Phase Instructions:

1. C randomly chooses $U \in \mathbb{G}_1$ and $Q \in \mathbb{G}_2$,
2. C sets $v := e(U, Q)$ and $ov := (U, Q, v)$

Online Input to C and S: $A_1, \ldots, A_n \in \mathbb{G}_1$ and $B_1, \ldots, B_n \in \mathbb{G}_2$

Online Input to C: ov

Online phase instructions:

1. C uniformly and independently chooses $u_1, \ldots, u_n \in \mathbb{Z}_l$
   C computes $I := (\sum_{i=1}^{n} u_i \cdot B_i) - Q$
   For $i = 1, \ldots, n$
       C randomly chooses $b_i \in [1, 2^\lambda]$ and $a_i \in \mathbb{Z}_l^*$
       C sets $\hat{A}_i = a_i \cdot A_i$ and $Z_i := b_i \cdot A_i + u_i \cdot U$
   C sends $I, U, (\hat{A}_1, Z_1), \ldots, (\hat{A}_n, Z_n)$ to S
2. S computes
       $w_0 := (\prod_{i=1}^{n} e(Z_i, B_i))/e(U, I)$
       $w_i := e(\hat{A}_i, B_i)$, for $i = 1, \ldots, n$
   S sends $w_0, \ldots, w_n$ to C
3. C computes $y_i := w_i^{1/a_i}$ for $i = 1, \ldots, n$
   C checks that
       (Membership Test:) $w_j \in \mathcal{G}_T$ for $j = 0, \ldots, n$
       (Probabilistic Test:) $w_0 = v \cdot \prod_{i=1}^{n} y_i^{b_i}$
   If any of these tests fails,
       C **returns** $\perp$ and the protocol halts
       C **returns** $y_1, \ldots, y_n$

Properties of Protocol $\mathcal{P}_1$: *The efficiency properties* are verified by protocol inspection. In particular:

- *Storage Complexity and Unbounded Client Lifetime:* in the offline phase, the number of bits stored on C's device is < 4 group values, and C's runtime is about one pairing computation, for *any* value of n.
- *Round complexity:* the online phase of the protocol only requires two messages: one from C to S, followed by one from S to C.
- *Communication complexity:* during the online phase, C sends $2n + 1$ values in $\mathbb{G}_1$ and 1 value in $\mathbb{G}_2$, and S sends $n + 1$ values in $\mathbb{G}_T$.
- *Runtime complexity:* the runtime property directly follows by protocol inspection. In Table 2 (bottom) we capture the max term $t_{C,max}$ of C's online runtime t_C, the max term $t_{S,max}$ of S's runtime t_S, and the max term $t_{P,max}$ of the offline runtime t_P. In Table 3 we capture a more detailed expression of C's online runtime t_C. In particular, $t_{C,max}$ consists of 2 exponentiations in $\mathbb{G}_T$ for each pairing instance, one with a full-domain exponent and one with a shorter, λ-bit, exponent.

The *correctness* property follows by showing that if C and S follow the protocol, C always outputs $y_i = e(A_i, B_i)$ for $i = 1, \ldots, n$ since

$$y_i = w_i^{1/a_i} = e(\hat{A}_i, B_i)^{1/a_i} = e(a_i \cdot A_i, B_i)^{1/a_i} = e(A_i, B_i)$$

Also, the 2 tests performed by C are always passed. The membership test is always passed by the pairing definition. Defining for brevity $\hat{B} := \sum_{i=1}^{n} u_i \cdot B_i$, note that the probabilistic test is always passed since

$$
w_0 = \frac{1}{e(U,I)} \prod_{i=1}^{n} e(Z_i, B_i) = \frac{1}{e(U,\hat{B} - Q)} \prod_{i=1}^{n} e(b_i \cdot A_i + u_i \cdot U, B_i)
$$

$$
= \frac{e(U,Q)}{e(U,\hat{B})} \prod_{i=1}^{n} e(A_i, B_i)^{b_i} \prod_{i=1}^{n} e(u_i U, B_i) = \frac{e(U,Q)}{e(U,\hat{B})} \prod_{i=1}^{n} y_i^{b_i} \cdot \prod_{i=1}^{n} e(U, u_i \cdot B_i)
$$

$$
= \frac{v}{e(U,\hat{B}))} \prod_{i=1}^{n} y_i^{b_i} \cdot e\left(U, \sum_{i=1}^{n} u_i \cdot B_i\right) = v \prod_{i=1}^{n} y_i^{b_i}.
$$

This implies that C never returns $\perp$, and thus always returns $y_i = e(A_i, B_i)$ for $i = 1, \ldots, n$.

The *privacy* property of the protocol against any malicious S follows by observing that, C's message $(I, (\hat{A}_1, Z_1), \ldots, (\hat{A}_n, Z_n))$ to S does not leak any information about C's inputs $A_1, \ldots, A_n$. This follows because for all $i = 1, \ldots, n$ (a) values $\hat{A}_i = a_i \cdot A$ is uniformly and independently distributed in $\mathbb{G}_1$ as a_i is a random scalar in $\mathbb{Z}_l^*$ and $\mathbb{G}_1$ is cyclic and (b) values Z_i are uniformly and independently distributed in $\mathbb{G}_1$, as so are U_i by similar reasoning. Moreover, by similar reasoning, this message does not leak any information about b_i, a fact useful in the proof of the security property.

To prove the *security* property against any malicious S, we need to compute an upper bound ϵ_s on the security probability that S convinces C to output a y_i such that $y_i \neq e(A_i, B_i)$ for $i = 1, \ldots, n$. We obtain that $\epsilon_s \leq 2^{-\lambda}$, as a consequence of the following 3 facts, which we later prove:

1. tuple $((\hat{A}_1, Z_1), \ldots, (\hat{A}_n, Z_n))$ leaks no information about $(b_1, \ldots, b_n)$ to S;
2. for any S's message $w = (w_0, \ldots, w_n)$ such that at least one of $w_1, \ldots, w_n$ is different than what would be returned according to the protocol instructions, the number of tuples $(b_1, \ldots, b_n)$ for which w satisfies both the membership and the probabilistic test in step 4 of the protocol is $\leq 2^{\lambda(n-1)}$;
3. for any S's message $w = (w_0, \ldots, w_n)$ such that at least one of $w_1, \ldots, w_n$ is different than what would be returned according to the protocol instructions, the probability that w satisfies the probabilistic test is $\leq 2^{-\lambda}$.

Towards proving Fact 1, we observe that: (a) all $\hat{A}_i$ values are uniformly and independently distributed in $\mathbb{G}_1$ since so are the a_i values in $\mathbb{Z}_l^*$; (b) conditioned on the $(\hat{A}_1, \ldots, \hat{A}_n)$ tuple, all $Z_1, \ldots, Z_n$ values are also uniformly distributed in $\mathbb{G}_1$ since so are the $u_1 U, \ldots, u_n U$ values, when u_i values are uniformly and independently chosen from $\mathbb{Z}_l$. Thus, the distribution of $((\hat{A}_1, Z_1), \ldots, (\hat{A}_n, Z_n))$ is independent from that of $b_1, \ldots, b_n$, from which Fact 1 follows.

Towards proving Fact 2, let $w = (w_0, \ldots, w_n)$ be the tuple that would be returned by S according to the protocol, and assume that a malicious algorithm Adv, corrupting S, returns a different tuple $w' = (w'_0 \ldots, w'_n)$. Note that if $w'_i \notin \mathcal{G}_T$ for some $j \in \{0, \ldots, n\}$, the tuple w' does not satisfy the membership test. Thus, we assume that $w'_j \in \mathcal{G}_T$ for all $j \in \{0, \ldots, n\}$. Because $\mathcal{G}_T$ is a multiplicative group, we can write

$$w'_j = d_j \cdot w_j,$$

for some $d_j \in \mathcal{G}_T$ such that not all of the d_j, for $j = 0, \ldots, n$, are equal to 1.

Now, assume that one of the d_i is different than 1 for $i = 1, \ldots, n$; specifically, assume wlog that $d_n \neq 1$, and consider the following equivalent rewritings of the probabilistic test, obtained by variable substitutions and simplifications:

$$w'_0 = v \cdot \prod_{i=1}^{n} y_i'^{b_i} = v \cdot \prod_{i=1}^{n} (w'_i)^{b_i/a_i}$$

$$d_0 \cdot w_0 = v \cdot \prod_{i=1}^{n} (d_i \cdot w_i)^{b_i/a_i}$$

$$d_0 = \prod_{i=1}^{n} (d_i)^{b_i/a_i},$$

where the last equality follows from the protocol's correctness property. Now, if for any $b_1, \ldots, b_{n-1}$ there exist two distinct b_n and b'_n, assuming without loss of generality that $b_n > b'_n$, such that

$$d_0 = \left(\prod_{i=1}^{n-1} (d_i)^{b_i/a_i} \right) \cdot (d_n)^{b_n/a_n} \text{ and } d_0 = \left(\prod_{i=1}^{n-1} (d_i)^{b_i/a_i} \right) \cdot (d_n)^{b'_n/a_n},$$

then $d_n^{(b_n - b'_n)/a_n} = (d_n^{1/a_n})^{(b_n - b'_n)} = 1$. By our assumption that every element in $\mathcal{G}_T$ has order $> l$, which is $> 2^\lambda$, and by observing that $b_n - b'_n < 2^\lambda$, we derive that $(d_n)^{1/a_n}$ cannot have order $\leq b_n - b'_n$. Thus the equality $(d_n^{1/a_n})^{(b_n - b'_n)} = 1$ can only hold when $b_n = b'_n$. This shows that for any $b_1, \ldots, b_{n-1}$, there is at most one b_n for which both the membership and probabilistic verification tests are met, and thus are at most $2^{\lambda(n-1)}$ tuples $(b_1, \ldots, b_n)$ for which the tuple w satisfies both tests. This proves Fact 2.

Towards proving Fact 3, first recall Fact 1 saying that C's message $((\hat{A}_1, Z_1),$ $\ldots, (\hat{A}_n, Z_n))$ does not leak any information about tuple $(b_1, \ldots, b_n)$, and thus all values in $\{1, \ldots, 2^\lambda\}^n$ are still equally likely for such tuple even when conditioning over C's message. Then we can compute an upper bound on the probability that S's message w satisfies the probabilistic test, as the ratio between the number of $(b_1, \ldots, b_n)$ tuples for which w satisfies both tests, and the number of values of $(b_1, \ldots, b_n)$ that are still equally likely even when conditioning over C's message. In this ratio, the numerator is at most $2^{\lambda(n-1)}$ (by Fact 2), and the denominator is $= 2^{\lambda n}$ (by Fact 1). This proves Fact 3.

3.2 Input Scenario: $\vec{A}$ and $\vec{B}$ Public Online

In the input scenario ($\vec{A}$ and $\vec{B}$ public online), we can define protocol $\mathcal{P}_2$, by slight modifications to protocol $\mathcal{P}_1$; i.e., by setting $a_i := 1$, for all $i = 1, \ldots, n$. Thus, during the online phase in Step 1, C does not compute $\hat{A}_i$ as $a_i \cdot A_i$ and does not send $\hat{A}_i$ to S, for $i = 1, \ldots, n$. Also, in Step 4, C outputs $y_i = w_i$ (instead of $y_i = w_i^{1/a_i}$) which eliminates n group exponentiations in $\mathbb{G}_T$ in C's online calculation.

We observe that, similarly as proved for $\mathcal{P}_1$, protocol $\mathcal{P}_2$ satisfies the result correctness and security properties. The efficiency properties for $\mathcal{P}_2$ are similar as for $\mathcal{P}_1$, with the only differences being in the improved bound for $t_C \leq n \cdot (a_1 + a_2 + m_1(r) + m_1(\lambda) + m_2(r) + m_T + e_T(\lambda) + t_M) + t_M$. In Table 4 we show that C's storage is constant, thus implying the unbounded client lifetime property, and online runtime t_C is significantly improved with respect to the only previous protocol (Algorithm 3 of [31]) satisfying this property.

Table 4. Protocols comparison in the input scenario ($\vec{A}$ and $\vec{B}$ public online). The expressions of t_C only includes higher-order functions p_T, e_T, m_1, m_2.

Protocols	C's storage (sc)	C's online calculation t_C
[14] for each pairing [§3]	$6n$	$n(e_T(\lambda) + m_2(\lambda) + m_1(r))$
[31][Alg.4]	n	$p_T + n(e_T(\lambda) + m_2(\lambda) + m_1(r))$
[31][Alg.3]	0	$n^2 e_T(2\lambda) + n(m_2(\lambda) + m_1(\lambda))$
Our $\mathcal{P}_2$ in [§ 3.2]	4	$n(e_T(\lambda) + m_2(r) + m_1(r) + m_1(\lambda))$

3.3 Input Scenario: $\vec{A}$ Private Online and $\vec{B}$ Public Offline

In this input scenario, we can define protocol $\mathcal{P}_3$, by starting with protocol $\mathcal{P}_1$, and applying the following modifications to improve C's efficiency. Specifically, during the offline phase: (a), in Step 1, C does not need to use random value $Q \in \mathbb{G}_2$; (b) in Step 3, C calculates I and v as $I := \sum_{i=1}^{n} u_i \cdot B_i$, $v := e(U, I)$, and C sets ov as $ov := (U, I, s, v)$. During the online phase: (a) in Step 1, C does not need to compute I, as it was computed in the offline phase; this significantly reduces C's online runtime as it eliminates n scalar multiplications in $\mathbb{G}_2$; (b) in Step 1, C does not need to send values U and I to S; (c) in Step 3, S calculates w_0 as $w_0 := \prod_{i=1}^{n} e(Z_i, B_i)$ which eliminates calculation of $e(U, I)$. The resulting probabilistic test can be written as:

$$\prod_{i=1}^{n} e(Z_i, B_i) = e(U, I) \cdot \prod_{i=1}^{n} y_i^{b_i},$$

where $Z_i = b_i A_i + u_i U$, $I := (\sum_{i=1}^{n} u_i \cdot B_i)$, u_i are random values from $\mathbb{Z}_l$, b_i are small random values from $[1, 2^\lambda]$, U is a random value from $\mathbb{G}_1$, and

$y_i = e(\hat{A}_i, B_i)^{1/a_i} = e(a_i A_i, B_i)^{1/a_i} = e(A_i, B_i)$. This test is more efficient than in $\mathcal{P}_1$ as it uses a simplified input masking technique.

Formal Description of Protocol $\mathcal{P}_3$: Let $m = 2n\lceil \log(l+1) \rceil$, and let $G : \{0,1\}^\alpha \to \{0,1\}^m$ denote a pseudo-random generator, for some integer α. We note that G can be implemented using AES in, say, Counter mode, whose runtime is much more efficient than a pairing computation. A formal description follows, mostly focusing on differences between $\mathcal{P}_3$ and $\mathcal{P}_1$.

Offline Input to C and S: 1^α, $desc(e), desc(G)$

Offline Input to C: $B_1, \ldots, B_n$

Offline phase instructions:

1. C randomly chooses $U \in \mathbb{G}_1$ and seed $s \in \{0,1\}^\alpha$,
2. C computes $p = G(s)$, applies a conventional encoding to write p as a sequence of $2n$ values in $\mathbb{Z}_l^*$, and sets $u_1, \ldots, u_n$ as the first n such values that belong to $\mathbb{Z}_l^*$
3. C computes $I := (\sum_{i=1}^n u_i \cdot B_i)$ and $v = e(U, I)$
4. C sets $ov := (U, I, s, v)$

Input to C and S: $B_1, \ldots, B_n \in \mathbb{G}_2$

Online Input to C: $A_1, \ldots, A_n \in \mathbb{G}_1$ and ov

Online phase instructions:

1. C computes $u_1, \ldots, u_n$ from s exactly as in step 2 of the offline phase
2. C computes $(\hat{A}_1, Z_1), \ldots, (\hat{A}_n, Z_n)$ as in $\mathcal{P}_1$ and sends them to S
3. S sets $w_0 = \prod_{i=1}^n e(Z_i, B_i)$, computes $w_1, \ldots, w_n$ as in $\mathcal{P}_1$ and sends w_0, $w_1, \ldots, w_n$ to C
4. C checks $w_0, \ldots, w_n$ and returns $y_1, \ldots, y_n$ (or $\perp$), exactly as done in $\mathcal{P}_1$.

Properties of Protocol $\mathcal{P}_3$: Similarly as proved for $\mathcal{P}_1$, we can show that protocol $\mathcal{P}_3$ satisfies result correctness, input privacy and result security.

When compared with our protocol $\mathcal{P}_1$ for a more demanding input scenario, $\mathcal{P}_3$ has improved efficiency properties, the main differences being in reduced values for $t_C \leq n \cdot (a_1 + i_l + 2m_1(r) + m_1(\lambda) + m_T + e_T(r) + e_T(\lambda) + t_M) + t_M$, $t_S \leq 2n \cdot p_T + n \cdot m_T + i_l$ and $cc = 2n$ values in $\mathbb{G}_1 + (n+1)$ values in $\mathbb{G}_T$.

When compared with the most basic solution for this input scenario (i.e., direct repetition for each instance in the batch of the most efficient protocol [13] to delegate a single pairing computation), it also improves storage sc and offline phase runtime t_P at the cost of some low-order increase in the client online runtime t_C, which still remains lower than non-delegated computation. More detailed expressions for sc and t_C are captured in Table 5. Note that the resulting protocol has storage complexity sc constant with respect to n, but has offline computation t_P linear in n, thus actually *not* satisfying the unbounded client lifetime property.

Table 5. Protocols comparison in the input scenario ($\vec{A}$ private online and $\vec{B}$ public offline). The expression of t_C only includes higher-order functions p_T, e_T, m_1, m_2.

Protocols	C's storage (sc)	C's online calculation (t_C)
[13]§ 3.2 for each input	$4n$	$n(e_T(\lambda) + m_1(\lambda))$
Our $\mathcal{P}_3$ in [§ 3.3]	3	$n(e_T(r) + e_T(\lambda) + 2\,m_1(r) + m_1(\lambda))$

3.4 Input Scenario: $\vec{A}$ Public Online, $\vec{B}$ Public Offline

In this input scenario we can define protocol $\mathcal{P}_4$, by slight modifications to protocol $\mathcal{P}_3$; i.e., by setting $a_i := 1$, for $i = 1, \ldots, n$. As a result, during the online phase in Step 1, C does not compute $\hat{A}_i$ as $a_i \cdot A_i$ and C does not send $\hat{A}_i$ to S, for $i = 1, \ldots, n$. This eliminates n scalar multiplications in group $\mathbb{G}_1$ from C's online runtime. Also, in Step 3, C outputs $y_i := w_i$, which eliminates n exponentiations in group $\mathbb{G}_T$ from C's online runtime.

We observe that, similarly as proved for $\mathcal{P}_3$, protocol $\mathcal{P}_4$ satisfies the result correctness and result security properties.

When compared with our protocol $\mathcal{P}_3$ for a more demanding input scenario, protocol $\mathcal{P}_4$ has improved efficiency properties, the main differences being in the reduced values for $t_C \leq n \cdot (a_1 + a_2 + m_1(r) + m_1(\lambda) + m_2(r) + m_T + e_T(\lambda) + t_M) + t_M$, and $cc = n$ values in $\mathbb{G}_1$ and $+(n + 1)$ values in $\mathbb{G}_T$.

When compared with the most basic solution for this input scenario (i.e., direct repetition for each instance in the batch of the most efficient protocol [13] to delegate a single pairing computation), $\mathcal{P}_4$ also improves storage sc and offline phase runtime t_P at the cost of some low-order increase in the client online runtime t_C, which still remains lower than non-delegated computation. More detailed expressions for sc and t_C are captured in Table 6. Note that the resulting protocol has storage complexity sc constant with respect to n, but has offline computation t_P linear in n, thus actually *not* satisfying the unbounded client lifetime property.

Table 6. Protocols comparison in the input scenario ($\vec{A}$ public online and $\vec{B}$ public offline). The expression of t_C only includes higher-order functions e_T, m_1, m_2.

Protocols	C's storage (sc)	C's online calculation t_C
[13]§3.1 for each pairing	$2n$	$n(e_T(\lambda) + m_1(\lambda))$
Our $\mathcal{P}_4$ in [§ 3.4]	3	$n(e_T(\lambda) + m_1(r) + m_1(\lambda))$

3.5 Input Scenario: $\vec{A}$ and $\vec{B} = \vec{s} \cdot H$ Private Online

In this section we investigate client-server protocols for the delegated computation of pairings with more general input scenarios, where both the A_i and the B_i may vary across the batch. Specifically, we consider pairing computations of the form $e(A_i, B_i)$, for $i = 1, \ldots, n$, where the batch inputs can have arbitrarily different first component values $\vec{A} = (A_1, \ldots, A_n)$ as well as different second component values $\vec{B} = (B_1, \ldots, B_n)$, where each $B_i = s_i H$, where H is a generator of group $\mathbb{G}_2$, and $\vec{s} = (s_1, \ldots, s_n)$ is a tuple of scalars from $\mathbb{Z}_l$. Specifically, we consider the input scenario ($\vec{A}$ private online, $\vec{s}$ private online, H public online). Although this scenario is somewhat less general than the ($\vec{A}$ private online, $\vec{B}$ private online) scenario, we note that input scenarios of this type are not uncommon in constructions of cryptographic protocols from the literature; for instance, they are used in [8] and many of its follow-up papers.

Protocol $\mathcal{P}_5$ Description: We note that the approach where C delegates $e(A_i, H)$ using [37], and then exponentiates the result to s_i results in a protocol, called $\mathcal{P}_{5,0}$, where the client online runtime is not smaller than non-delegated computation (see Table 8 (bottom)). Instead, in our protocol $\mathcal{P}_5$, we avoid this exponentiation by processing s_i via a much more efficient multiplication in $\mathbb{Z}_l$. Specifically, C delegates to S n pairing computations $e(\hat{A}_i, H)$, for $i = 1, \ldots, n$, where H is the publicly known generator of group $\mathbb{G}_2$, $\hat{A}_i$ is obtained from input A_i by a multiplication with a scalar that is obtained by multiplying by a random value in $\mathbb{Z}_l$ times the value s_i such that $B_i = s_i H$. Then, building on [37], $\hat{A}_0$ is set as a random linear combination of $\hat{A}_1, \ldots, \hat{A}_n$ added to a random value U where S calculates $w_0 = e(\hat{A}_0, H)/e(U, I)$ and sends $w_0, \ldots, w_n$ to C. Later, C uses S's answers $e(\hat{A}_i, H)$ to compute the desired pairing outputs $e(A_i, B_i)$ and all answers, including $e(\hat{A}_0, H)$, to probabilistically test the correctness of all answers via a random exponential equation over $\mathcal{G}_T$. As before, we use efficient membership tests in $\mathbb{G}_T$ and smaller exponents (i.e., λ-bit exponents instead of full-domain exponents) in this equation to significantly improve client runtime. The probabilistic test used here verifies the condition:

$$e(\hat{A}_0, H)/e(U, I) = e(U, Q) \cdot \prod_{i=1}^{n} w_i^{b_i},$$

where $w_i = e(\hat{A}_i, H)$, $\hat{A}_i = (a_i s_i \mod l) A_i$, $\hat{A}_0 := U + \sum_{i=1}^{n} b_i \cdot \hat{A}_i$, b_i are random values from $[1, 2^\lambda]$, U is a random values from $\mathbb{G}_1$, Q is a random value from $\mathbb{G}_2$, and $I = H - Q$. This test includes the masking and optimizations ideas in tests in our previous protocols, and additionally uses a single random mask to preserve privacy of both A_i and s_i values, so to effectively replace one extra exponentiation in $\mathbb{G}_T$ with a much more efficient multiplication in $\mathbb{Z}_l$. A formal description follows.

Input Scenario: $A_1, \ldots, A_n$ private online, $B_1, \ldots, B_n$ private online, such that $B_i = s_i H$, for some random $s_i \in \mathbb{Z}_l$ and some public online generator H of $\mathbb{G}_2$

Offline Input to C and S: $1^\sigma, 1^\lambda, desc(e)$

Offline phase instructions:

1. C randomly chooses $U \in \mathbb{G}_1$ and $Q \in \mathbb{G}_2$,

2. C sets $v := e(U, Q)$ and $ov := (U, Q, v)$

Online Input to C: $A_1, \ldots, A_n \in \mathbb{G}_1$, $s_1, \ldots, s_n \in \mathbb{Z}_l$ and $B_1, \ldots, B_n \in \mathbb{G}_2$ such that $B_i = s_i \cdot H$ for $i = 1, \ldots, n$ and ov.

Online Input to C and S: generator $H \in \mathbb{G}_2$

Online phase instructions:

1. For $i = 1, \ldots, n$,
     C randomly chooses $b_i \in [1, 2^\lambda]$ and $a_i \in \mathbb{Z}_l^*$
     C computes $\hat{A}_i := (a_i \cdot s_i \mod l) \cdot A_i$
     C sets $I := H - Q$ and $\hat{A}_0 := U + \sum_{i=1}^{n} b_i \cdot \hat{A}_i$
     C sends $I, \hat{A}_0, \ldots, \hat{A}_n$ to S
2. S computes $w_0 = e(\hat{A}_0, H)/e(U, I)$, and $w_i := e(\hat{A}_i, H)$ for $i = 1, \ldots, n$
     S sends $w_0, \ldots, w_n$ to C
3. C checks that
     (Membership Test:) $w_i \in \mathcal{G}_T$ for $i \in [0, n]$
     (Probabilistic Test:) $w_0 = v \cdot \prod_{i=1}^{n} w_i^{b_i}$
     If any of these tests fails, C **returns** $\perp$ and the protocol halts
     C **returns** $y_1 := w_1^{1/a_1}, \ldots, y_n := w_n^{1/a_n}$

Table 7. Protocols comparison in the input scenario with private online $A_1, \ldots, A_n$ and $B_1, \ldots, B_n$ where $B_i = s_i H$ and both random scalar s_i and H are known in online phase for $i = 1, \ldots, n$. (The expression of t_C only includes higher-order functions e_T, m_1, m_2.)

Protocols	C's storage (sc)	C's online calc. t_C
[14]§4 for each pairing	$15n$	$n(e_T(\lambda) + m_2(r) + m_2(\lambda) + 3\,m_1(r))$
[25][Alg.4]	$n + 3$	$n(e_T(r) + e_T(\lambda) + m_2(r) + m_2(\lambda) + 2m_1(r))$
Our $\mathcal{P}_5$ in [§ 3.5]	3	$n(e_T(r) + e_T(\lambda) + m_1(r) + m_1(\lambda))$

Properties of Protocol $\mathcal{P}_5$: The analysis of the *efficiency*, *privacy* and *security* properties are very similar to those of protocol $\mathcal{P}_1$.

The proof of the *correctness* property is somewhat different, when we have to show that the probabilistic test is always passed, and that when both tests are passed, C always outputs $y_i = e(A_i, B_i)$ for $i = 1, \ldots n$. To see that the probabilistic test is always passed, note that

$$w_0 = \frac{e(\hat{A}_0, H)}{e(U, I)} = \frac{1}{e(U, H - Q)} \cdot e\left(\left(U + \sum_{i=1}^{n} b_i \cdot \hat{A}_i\right), H\right)$$
$$= \frac{e(U, H)}{e(U, H)e(U, Q)^{-1}} \cdot \prod_{i=1}^{n} e(\hat{A}_i, H)^{b_i} = v \cdot \prod_{i=1}^{n} w_i^{b_i}$$

The membership test is always passed by the pairing definition. When both tests are passed, C never returns $\perp$, and thus returns

$$y_i = w_i^{1/a_i} = e(\hat{A}_i, H)^{1/a_i \mod l} = e((a_i s_i \mod l) \cdot A_i, H)^{1/a_i \mod l}$$
$$= e(A_i, H)^{a_i \cdot s_i \cdot (1/a_i) \mod l} = e(A_i, H)^{s_i} = e(A_i, s_i \cdot H) = e(A_i, B_i)$$

4 Practical Performance Analysis of Our Protocols

We show a numerical performance analysis of our protocols $\mathcal{P}_1, \ldots, \mathcal{P}_5$ as well as previous protocols from the literature in each of the considered input scenarios, which confirms our parameterized efficiency results. Our numerical performance analysis consists of obtaining benchmark results, captured in Table 8, for the runtime of an optimal ate pairing and of other operations (i.e., addition and scalar multiplication in groups $\mathbb{G}_1$ and $\mathbb{G}_2$, and multiplication, membership testing and exponentiation in $\mathbb{G}_T$) using some of the currently most practical elliptic curve families (i.e., KSS 18-P638 and BLS 24-P509 for security level 192 and BLS-P315 for security level 128). In Table 9 we compare the performance of our protocols in Sect. 3 with past work for the same input scenario. We evaluated protocol $\mathcal{P}_1$ in two different ways: (1) measuring online client runtime of a software implementation of the protocol, and (2) analytically deriving the performance using the benchmark in Table 8. Also we measured the marginal error of (1) vs. (2), which is observed to be arguably small (specifically, between 2.85% and 20.87%). We then analytically derived the performance of protocols $\mathcal{P}_2, \ldots, \mathcal{P}_5$ using the benchmarks in Table 8.

Denoting a pairing as $e : \mathbb{G}_1 \times \mathbb{G}_2 \to \mathbb{G}_T$, and by p_T its runtime, by e_T the runtime of exponentiation in $\mathbb{G}_T$ and by m_i the runtime of scalar multiplication in $\mathbb{G}_i$ and a_i the runtime of addition in $\mathbb{G}_i$, for $i = 1, 2$. our estimation procedure for delegation protocols $\mathcal{P}_1, \ldots, \mathcal{P}_5$ for pairing e, worked as follows:

1. Set statistical parameter λ as $= 40$ (an event happening with probability $\leq 2^{-40}$ has occurrence expectancy of 1 in $\geq 2^{20}$ trillion protocol executions, thus capturing confidence requirements in all use cases we can think of).
2. Set security parameter σ based on best available attacks.
3. Consider $\mathbb{G}_1, \mathbb{G}_2, \mathbb{G}_T$ and pairing e for which order l satisfies $l >= 2^{2\sigma}$, and measure runtimes for $p_T, e_T, m_1, m_2, m_T, a_1, a_2, t_M$ and generate benchmark values as in Table 8
4. Use above benchmark values to estimate t_C in the given delegation protocol, neglecting lower-order operations such as equality testing, assignments, Frobenius-based simplifications, etc.
5. return: p_T/t_C.

Our software implementation was carried out on a macOS Big Sur Version 11.7.6 laptop with a 2.7 GHz processor Dual-Core Intel core i5 and 8 GB DDR3 RAM memory. We used C code for protocol $\mathcal{P}_1$ and the benchmark calculations, using the relic-toolkit library [33] and the gmp library.

Table 8. Benchmark results for scalar multiplications in $\mathbb{G}_1, \mathbb{G}_2$ and exponentiations in $\mathbb{G}_T$ relative to an optimal ate pairing based on some of the currently most practical curve families. All columns measured in millions of clock cycles. Standard deviation lies in the following ranges: (1) BLS24-P509 in a range (0,0.0077); (2) KSS18-P638 in a range (0,0.0099); (3) BLS24-P315 in a range (0,0.04).

Curves	KSS18-P638	BLS24-P509	BLS24-P315
Operation \ Security	192	192	128
a_1	7.00E-06	3.00E-06	2.00E-06
$m_1(r)$	6.53E-03	3.63E-03	2.09E-03
$m_1(\lambda)$	1.65E-03	1.06E-03	6.93E-04
a_2	7.00E-06	3.00E-06	2.00E-06
$m_2(r)$	1.27E-02	8.91E-03	6.22E-03
$m_2(\lambda)$	2.86E-03	2.96E-03	2.74E-03
m_T	3.80E-05	7.20E-05	7.40E-05
$e_T(r)$	1.25E-02	1.49E-02	8.76E-03
$e_T(\lambda)$	2.67E-03	3.41E-03	4.56E-03
t_M	2.27E-04	5.09E-04	4.32E-04
p_T	4.04E-02	3.78E-02	3.05E-02

Table 9. Ratio p_T/t_C of non-delegated pairing computation to client runtime in the online phase, with respect to protocols $\mathcal{P}_1, \ldots, \mathcal{P}_5$ with comparison to other protocols, where the statistical security parameter $\lambda = 40$, 100 time repetitions

Protocols	Storage	Ratio: p_T/t_C		
		KSS18-P638 $r = 474$	BLS24-P509 $r = 409$	BLS24-P315 $r = 253$
Input Scenario:(A_i private online, B_i public online)				
[25] §3.7	$n+4$	1.277	1.274	1.437
Our $\mathcal{P}_1$ in § 3.1 runtime measurement	4	1.193	1.086	1.191
Our $\mathcal{P}_1$ in § 3.1 using benchmarks in Table 8	4	0.944	1.047	1.225
Benchmark vs measuring error	NA	20.87%	3.59%	2.85%
Input Scenario:(A_i and B_i public online)				
[14] §3 for each pairing	$6n$	3.210	3.387	2.935
Our $\mathcal{P}_2$ in § 3.2	4	1.700	2.151	2.169
Input Scenario:(A_i private online, B_i public offline)				
[13]§3.2 for each pairing	$4n$	8.724	7.385	5.228
Our $\mathcal{P}_3$ in § 3.3	3	1.339	1.390	1.633
Input Scenario:(A_i public online, B_i public offline)				
[13]§3.1 for each pairing	$2n$	8.810	7.495	5.297
Our $\mathcal{P}_4$ in § 3.4	3	3.636	4.358	3.889
Input Scenario:(A_i and B_i private online); In our $\mathcal{P}_5$: $B_i = s_i \cdot H$				
[14]§4 for each pairing	$15n$	1.047	1.351	1.428
[25] Alg. 4	$n+3$	0.912	0.980	1.111
Our $\mathcal{P}_{5,0}$ in § 3.5	2	0.794	0.720	0.986
Our $\mathcal{P}_5$ in § 3.5	3	1.709	1.604	1.838

5   Conclusions

We show the first protocols for the delegation of a batch of pairing computations $e(A_i, B_i)$ with variable inputs A_i, B_i, satisfying a number of desirable privacy, security and performance properties; most notably: result correctness, input privacy, result security, unbounded client lifetime, and client runtime efficiency. Our results settle problems unsolved since the original 2007 paper of [37]. These protocols can be used to reduce runtime of resource-constrained devices in multiple runs of essentially all known pairing-based cryptographic schemes and protocols, such as, for instance, those for key agreement [23], advanced public key encryption types [3,8,19,29], identity-based encryption [7], hierarchical identity-based encryption [6], and signature schemes [9,21,29].

Acknowledgements. Many thanks to Delaram Kahrobaei, Vladimir Shpilrain, and Damien Vergnaud for interesting discussions. Work by Matluba Khodjaeva and Dilan Morales Caro was supported by a Faculty Scholarship grant from the Office for the Advancement of Research at John Jay College and PSC CUNY Cycles 53 and 54. Work by Giovanni Di Crescenzo was supported by the Defense Advanced Research Projects Agency (DARPA), contract n. HR001120C0156. The U.S. Government is authorized to reproduce and distribute reprints for Governmental purposes notwithstanding any copyright annotation hereon. Disclaimer: The views and conclusions contained herein are those of the authors and should not be interpreted as necessarily representing the official policies or endorsements, either expressed or implied, of DARPA, or the U.S. Government. Distribution Statement "A" (Approved for Public Release, Distribution Unlimited).

A   Formal Definitions

In this section we recall the formal definition (based on [17,22]), of delegation protocols for a batch of function values, for arbitrary functions, as well as their correctness, privacy, security, and efficiency requirements.

Basic Notations. By $\vec{x}$ we denote the n-tuple $(x_1, \ldots, x_n)$. The expression $z \leftarrow T$ denotes randomly and independently choosing z from set T. By $y \leftarrow A(x_1, x_2, \ldots)$ we denote running the algorithm A on input $x_1, x_2, \ldots$ and any random coins, and returning y as output. By $(y, tr) \leftarrow (A(u_1, u_2, \ldots), B(v_1, v_2, \ldots))$ we denote running the interactive protocol between A, with input $u_1, u_2, \ldots$ and any random coins, and B, with input $v_1, v_2, \ldots$ and any random coins, where tr denotes A's and B's messages in this execution, and y is A's final output.

System Scenario: Entities and Protocol. We consider a system with a single client, denoted by C, and a single server, denoted by S, who are connected by an authenticated channel, and therefore do not consider any integrity or replay attacks on this channel. As in previous work in the area, we consider a delegation protocol to include both an *offline phase*, typically consisting of client setup and deployment, and an *online phase*, typically starting when inputs to the delegated function are available to the client. While the protocol in the online phase is designed by taking into account the parties' different computation power, in particular reducing as much as possible the client's computation, this is not the case in the offline phase, which could be run, for instance, by a trusted deployer which at the end stores information on the client device. A system architecture can be found in Fig. 1.

Let σ denote the computational security parameter (derived from hardness considerations of the underlying computational problem), and let λ denote the statistical security parameter (defined so that statistical test failure events with probability $2^{-\lambda}$ are extremely rare). Both parameters are expressed in unary notation (i.e., $1^\sigma, 1^\lambda$). We think of σ as being larger than λ. Let F denote a function and $desc(F)$ denote F's description. Assuming $1^\sigma, 1^\lambda, desc(F)$ are known to both C and S, we define a *client-server protocol for the delegated (n-instance) computation of F* as the execution: $\{pp \leftarrow \text{Offline}(1^\sigma, 1^\lambda, desc(F)); (\vec{y}, tr) \leftarrow (C(pp, \vec{x}), S)\}$. Step 1 is executed in the offline phase, when no input to the function F is available yet, and could be executed either by C or a third party not colluding with S. Step 2 is executed in the online phase, when inputs $\vec{x} = (x_1, \ldots, x_n)$ to the function F are available to C, and at the end of this phase, C learns $\vec{y} = (y_1, \ldots, y_n)$, where $y_i = F(x_i)$, for $i = 1, \ldots, n$, and tr is the transcript of the communication exchanged between C and S. We will often omit $desc(F), 1^\sigma, 1^\lambda, tr$ for brevity.

Correctness Requirement. Informally, the correctness requirement states that if both parties follow the protocol, C obtains some output at the end of the protocol, and this output is, with high probability, equal to the n-tuple of values obtained by evaluating function F on C's n inputs. Formally, we say that a client-server protocol (C, S) for the delegated n-instance computation of F satisfies δ_c-*correctness* if for any $\vec{x} = (x_1, \ldots, x_n)$ in $Dom(F)$,

$$\text{Prob}\left[out \leftarrow \text{CorrExp}_F : out = 1\right] \geq \delta_c,$$

for some δ_c close to 1, where experiment CorrExp is:

1. $pp \leftarrow \text{Offline}(desc(F))$
2. $(\vec{y}, tr) \leftarrow (C(pp, \vec{x}), S)$
3. if $y_i = F(x_i)$ for all $i = 1, \ldots, n$, then **return:** 1 else **return:** 0

Privacy Requirement. Informally, the privacy requirement should guarantee the following: if C follows the protocol, a malicious adversary corrupting S cannot obtain any information about C's inputs $\vec{x}$ from a protocol execution. This is formalized by extending the indistinguishability-based approach typically used in definitions for encryption schemes. Let (C, S) be a client-server protocol for the delegated n-instance computation of F. We say that (C, S) satisfies ϵ_p-*privacy (in the sense of indistinguishability) against a malicious adversary* if for any algorithm A, it holds that

$$\text{Prob}\left[out \leftarrow \text{PrivExp}_{F,A} : out = 1\right] \leq 1/2 + \epsilon_p,$$

for some ϵ_p close to 0, where experiment PrivExp is:

1. $pp \leftarrow \text{Offline}(desc(F))$
2. $(\vec{x}_0, \vec{x}_1, aux) \leftarrow A(desc(F))$
3. $b \leftarrow \{0, 1\}$
4. $(\vec{y}, tr) \leftarrow (C(pp, \vec{x}_b), A(aux))$
5. $d \leftarrow A(tr, aux)$
6. if $b = d$ then **return:** 1 else **return:** 0.

Security Requirement. Informally, the security requirement states that for any efficient and malicious adversary corrupting S and even choosing C's input tuple $\vec{x}$, at the end of the protocol, C cannot be convinced to obtain some output tuple $\vec{z}$ containing a value $z_i \neq F(x_i)$ for some $i \in \{1, \ldots, n\}$. Formally, we say that the client-server protocol (C, S) for the delegated n-instance computation of F satisfies ϵ_s-security against a malicious adversary if for any algorithm A,

$$\text{Prob} \left[out \leftarrow \text{SecExp}_{F,A} : out = 1 \right] \leq \epsilon_s,$$

for some ϵ_s close to 0, where experiment SecExp is:

1. $pp \leftarrow \text{Offline}(desc(F))$
2. $(\vec{x}, aux) \leftarrow A(desc(F))$
3. $(\vec{z}, tr) \leftarrow (C(pp, \vec{x}), A(aux))$
4. if $z_i \in \{\bot, F(x_i)\}$ for all $i = 1, \ldots, n$, then **return:** 0 else **return:** 1.

References

1. Abadi, M., Feigenbaum, J., Kilian, J.: On Hiding Information from an Oracle. J. Comput. Syst. Sci. **39**(1), 21–50 (1989)
2. Ahmad, H., et al.: Primitives towards verifiable computation: a survey. In Front. Comput. Sci. **12**(3), 451–478 (2018)
3. Al-Riyami, S.S., Paterson, K.G.: Certificateless public key cryptography. In: Laih, C.-S. (ed.) ASIACRYPT 2003. LNCS, vol. 2894, pp. 452–473. Springer, Heidelberg (2003). https://doi.org/10.1007/978-3-540-40061-5_29
4. Barreto, P.S.L.M., Costello, C., Misoczki, R., Naehrig, M., Pereira, G.C.C.F., Zanon, G.: Subgroup security in pairing-based cryptography. In: Lauter, K., Rodríguez-Henríquez, F. (eds.) LATINCRYPT 2015. LNCS, vol. 9230, pp. 245–265. Springer, Cham (2015). https://doi.org/10.1007/978-3-319-22174-8_14
5. Bellare, M., Garay, J.A., Rabin, T.: Fast batch verification for modular exponentiation and digital signatures. In: Nyberg, K. (ed.) EUROCRYPT 1998. LNCS, vol. 1403, pp. 236–250. Springer, Heidelberg (1998). https://doi.org/10.1007/BFb0054130
6. Boneh, D., Boyen, X., Goh, E.-J.: Hierarchical identity based encryption with constant size ciphertext. In: Cramer, R. (ed.) EUROCRYPT 2005. LNCS, vol. 3494, pp. 440–456. Springer, Heidelberg (2005). https://doi.org/10.1007/11426639_26
7. Boneh, D., Franklin, M.: Identity-based encryption from the weil pairing. In: Kilian, J. (ed.) CRYPTO 2001. LNCS, vol. 2139, pp. 213–229. Springer, Heidelberg (2001). https://doi.org/10.1007/3-540-44647-8_13

8. Boneh, D., Di Crescenzo, G., Ostrovsky, R., Persiano, G.: Public key encryption with keyword search. In: Cachin, C., Camenisch, J.L. (eds.) EUROCRYPT 2004. LNCS, vol. 3027, pp. 506–522. Springer, Heidelberg (2004). https://doi.org/10.1007/978-3-540-24676-3_30

9. Boneh, D., Lynn, B., Shacham, H.: Short signatures from the weil pairing. In: Boyd, C. (ed.) ASIACRYPT 2001. LNCS, vol. 2248, pp. 514–532. Springer, Heidelberg (2001). https://doi.org/10.1007/3-540-45682-1_30

10. Canard, S., Devigne, J., Sanders, O.: Delegating a pairing can be both secure and efficient. In: Boureanu, I., Owesarski, P., Vaudenay, S. (eds.) ACNS 2014. LNCS, vol. 8479, pp. 549–565. Springer, Cham (2014). https://doi.org/10.1007/978-3-319-07536-5_32

11. Chevallier-Mames, B., Coron, J.-S., McCullagh, N., Naccache, D., Scott, M.: Secure delegation of elliptic-curve pairing. In: Gollmann, D., Lanet, J.-L., Iguchi-Cartigny, J. (eds.) CARDIS 2010. LNCS, vol. 6035, pp. 24–35. Springer, Heidelberg (2010). https://doi.org/10.1007/978-3-642-12510-2_3

12. Di Crescenzo, G., Khodjaeva, M., Kahrobaei, D., Shpilrain, V.: A Survey on Delegated Computation. In: Diekert, V., Volkov, M. (eds) Developments in Language Theory. DLT 2022. Lecture Notes in Computer Science, vol. 13257. Springer, Cham (2022). https://doi.org/10.1007/978-3-031-05578-2_3

13. Di Crescenzo, G., Khodjaeva, M., Kahrobaei, D., Shpilrain, V.: Secure and efficient delegation of elliptic-curve pairing. In: Conti, M., Zhou, J., Casalicchio, E., Spognardi, A. (eds.) ACNS 2020. LNCS, vol. 12146, pp. 45–66. Springer, Cham (2020). https://doi.org/10.1007/978-3-030-57808-4_3

14. Di Crescenzo, G., Khodjaeva, M., Kahrobaei, D., Shpilrain, V.: Secure and efficient delegation of pairings with online inputs. In: Liardet, P.-Y., Mentens, N. (eds.) CARDIS 2020. LNCS, vol. 12609, pp. 84–99. Springer, Cham (2021). https://doi.org/10.1007/978-3-030-68487-7_6

15. Feigenbaum, J.: Encrypting Problem Instances: Or ..., Can You Take Advantage of Someone Without Having to Trust Him? In: Proc. of CRYPTO, pp. 477–488 (1985)

16. Fiat, A.: Batch RSA. In Journal of Cryptology, v. 10, n. 2 (1997)

17. Gennaro, R., Gentry, C., Parno, B.: Non-interactive verifiable computing: outsourcing computation to untrusted workers. In: Rabin, T. (ed.) CRYPTO 2010. LNCS, vol. 6223, pp. 465–482. Springer, Heidelberg (2010). https://doi.org/10.1007/978-3-642-14623-7_25

18. M. Girault, D. Lefranc, Server-aided verification: Theory and practice. In: Roy, B.K. (ed.) ASIACRYPT 2005. LNCS, vol. 3788, pp. 605–623. https://doi.org/10.1007/11593447_33

19. Goyal, V., Pandey, O., Sahai, A., Waters, B.: Attribute-based encryption for fine-grained access control of encrypted data. In: Proceedings of ACM CCS 2006, pp. 89–98. ACM

20. Guillevic, A., Vergnaud, D.: Algorithms for Outsourcing Pairing Computation. In: Joye, M., Moradi, A. (eds.) CARDIS 2014. LNCS, vol. 8968, pp. 193–211. Springer, Cham (2015). https://doi.org/10.1007/978-3-319-16763-3_12

21. Hess, F.: Efficient identity based signature schemes based on pairings. In: Nyberg K., Heys H. (eds) Selected Areas in Cryptography. SAC 2002

22. Hohenberger, S., Lysyanskaya, A.: How to securely outsource cryptographic computations. In: Kilian, J. (ed.) TCC 2005. LNCS, vol. 3378, pp. 264–282. Springer, Heidelberg (2005). https://doi.org/10.1007/978-3-540-30576-7_15

23. Joux, A.: A one round protocol for tripartite Diffie-Hellman. In: Proceedings of ANTS 2000, pp. 385–394

24. Kachisa, E.J., Schaefer, E.F., Scott, M.: Constructing brezing-weng pairing-friendly elliptic curves using elements in the cyclotomic field. In: Galbraith, S.D., Paterson, K.G. (eds.) Pairing 2008. LNCS, vol. 5209, pp. 126–135. Springer, Heidelberg (2008). https://doi.org/10.1007/978-3-540-85538-5_9

25. Kalkar, O., Sertkaya, I., Tutdere, S.: On the batch outsourcing of pairing computations. Comput. J. (2022)

26. Kang, B.G., Lee, M.S., Park, J.H.: Efficient delegation of pairing computation. In: IACR Cryptology ePrint Archive, n. 259 (2005)

27. Khodjaeva, M., Di Crescenzo, G.: On single-server delegation without precomputation. In: Proceedings of SECRYPT 2023, pp. 540–547. Scitepress

28. Kumar, S., Hu, Y., Andersen, M.P., Popa, R.A., Culler, D.E.: JEDI: many-to-many end-to-end encryption and key delegation for IoT. In: USENIX Security Symposium 2019, pp. 1519–1536 (2019)

29. Liu, J.K., Au, M.H., Susilo, W.: Self-generated-certificate public-key cryptography and certificateless signature/encryption scheme in the standard model. In: Proceedings of ACM Symposium on Information, Computer and Communications Security. ACM Press (2007)

30. T. Matsumoto, K. Kato, H. Imai, An improved algorithm for secure outsourcing of modular exponentiations. In: Proc. of CRYPTO 1988, pp. 497–506. LNCS. Springer

31. Mefenza, T., Vergnaud, D.: Verifiable outsourcing of pairing computations, Technical report (2018)

32. Moody, D., Peralta, R., Perlner, R., Regenscheid, A., Roginsky, A., Chen, L.: Report on Pairing-based Cryptography. J. Res. Natl. Inst. Stand. Technol. **120**, 11–27 (2015)

33. Aranha, D.F., Gouvêa, C.P.L., Markmann, T., Wahby, R.S., Liao, K.: RELIC is an Efficient LIbrary for Cryptography. https://github.com/relic-toolkit/relic

34. Sakai, R., Ohgishi, K., Kasahara, M.: Cryptosystems based on pairing. In: Symposium on Cryptography and Information Security (SCIS) (2000)

35. Scott, M.: Unbalancing pairing-based key exchange protocols. In: IACR Cryptology ePrint Archive, n. 688 (2013)

36. Shan, Z., Ren, K., Blanton, M., Wang, C.: Practical secure computation outsourcing: a survey. ACM Comput. Surv. **51**(2), 31:1–31:40 (2018)

37. P. Tsang, S. Chow, and S. Smith Batch pairing delegation. In: Proceedings of International Workshop on Security, 2007, pp. 74–90. Springer, Berlin (2007). https://doi.org/10.1007/978-3-540-75651-4_6

38. Vercauteren, F.: Optimal pairings. IEEE Trans. Inf. Theory **56**(1), 455–461 (2010)

SigIL: A Signature-Based Approach of Malware Detection on Intermediate Language

Giancarlo Fortino, Claudia Greco[ID], Antonella Guzzo, and Michele Ianni[✉][ID]

Department of Computer Science, Modeling, Electronics and System Engineering
(DIMES), University of Calabria, Rende, Italy
{giancarlo.fortino,antonella.guzzo,michele.ianni}@unical.it,
claudia.greco@dimes.unical.it

Abstract. The Internet of Things (IoT) has brought about significant advancements in connectivity but has also introduced security challenges due to the diverse range of IoT devices. Traditional security solutions struggle to detect malware specifically designed for IoT devices. To address this, there is a need for cross-device malware detection systems that can transcend device differences. Signature scanning is a widely used technique to detect malware, but it has limitations when dealing with binaries compiled for different architectures. This paper proposes SIGIL (Signature scanning on Intermediate Language), a tool that identifies significant patterns in binary programs using their intermediate representation. By shifting the focus to intermediate languages instead of byte sequences, SIGIL aims to make signatures independent of architectural details, allowing the use of a single signature to identify multiple binaries obtained by compiling the same source code for different architectures.

Keywords: Malware detection · Intermediate representation ·
Signature scanning

1 Introduction

The Internet of Things has revolutionized our lives by interconnecting various devices, ranging from smart home appliances to industrial control systems. However, this increased connectivity has also presented significant security challenges. The diverse range of IoT devices, each with its unique operating system and hardware architecture, makes it difficult to develop universal malware detection methodologies. Traditional security solutions, which are primarily designed for standard computing platforms, often fall short in effectively identifying malware specifically tailored for IoT devices. In order to address this emerging threat landscape, it is imperative to invest in the development of cross-device malware detection systems. These systems should be designed to transcend the inherent differences in device types and architectures, enabling comprehensive protection against malware attacks across the IoT spectrum. A widely popular technique

S. Katsikas et al. (Eds.): ESORICS 2023 Workshops, LNCS 14399, pp. 256–266, 2024.
https://doi.org/10.1007/978-3-031-54129-2_15

employed to detect the presence of malware within binaries is signature scanning. Conventional signature scanning involves the meticulous search for specific byte sequences within files or data streams, with the intention of identifying patterns associated with known threats or indicators of compromise. Although this methodology proves successful in numerous instances, its efficacy can be limited when dealing with binaries compiled for architectures other than the one related to the signature. For this reason, we propose an approach that builds upon the foundation of signature scanning, yet elevates it to a higher level.

In this paper we present SIGIL (Signature scanning on Intermediate Language), a malware detection tool that facilitates the identification of significant patterns within binary programs, leveraging the concept of Intermediate Representation (IR). Our proposal consists in a methodology that involves generating rules which underscore the syntax of the YARA [2] tool, while shifting the reference point to intermediate languages, rather than byte sequences, in order to transcend specific target architectures. By doing so, we aim to render the adopted signatures independent of architectural details, thereby enabling the utilization of a single signature for the identification of multiple binaries representing the same program compiled for different architectures. Moreover, our approach offers a noteworthy advantage by utilizing a higher-level representation, enabling the detection of malware even in the presence of various obfuscating transformations.

The remainder of the paper is organized as follows: Sect. 2 provides a technical background on traditional malware detection techniques and their limitations, code obfuscation and IR. Section 3 briefly reviews existing solutions to the malware detection problem. In Sect. 4, we explain our methodology and we present our tool SIGIL. In Sect. 5 we show an illustrative example showcasing the SIGIL's functionality. Finally, in Sect. 6, we draw conclusions about our findings and discuss future work.

2   Background

Traditional Malware Detection Techniques. The traditional approach to malware detection is primarily rooted in the utilization of signatures and cryptographic hashes. A signature is an invariant sequence of bytes, most of the times extracted from the application code or raw file content, that is useful in order to uniquely identify a specific malware. More formally, following the definition in [3], Let P represent the set of software programs, and let $M \subset P$ be the set of malicious programs. We associate M with a set of signatures, denoted as $\mathbb{M}$. A detector, denoted as $D : P \times \mathbb{M} \rightarrow 0, 1$, operates on these signatures. Therefore, we assert that a program p is considered detected if there exists a signature $m \in \mathbb{M}$ such that $D(p, m) = 1$. When we apply this definition to the conventional signature scanning method, the set $\mathbb{M}$ encompasses the collection of all known malware string signatures. The corresponding detector is defined as follows: $D(p, m) = 1$ if m is a substring of p, and $D(p, m) = 0$ otherwise.

In the field of malware detection, a program signature can be compared to those of known malicious programs, in order to detect if the target program is benign or not. Another conventional approach utilized in the realm of malware detection is based on the utilization of cryptographic hashes. A cryptographic hash, also known as a message digest, is a fixed-length value derived from a cryptographic hash algorithm. This algorithm takes a program of arbitrary size as input and produces a hash that represents the program. By comparing the cryptographic hash of a target program to that of a known program, malicious behaviors can be detected. Traditional techniques such as signature scanning and cryptographic hashing exhibit significant weaknesses, as they are only capable of detecting a file if it contains the exact sequence of bytes representing the signature, or if two files are entirely identical. In signature-based detection, even a slight alteration of a single bit within the byte sequence representing a signature can lead to the failure of the signature matching mechanisms, resulting in false negatives. Similarly, in the case of cryptographic hashes, even the change of a single bit of the input program will produce a completely different cryptographic hash as the output. This is a limit in the malware detection application, where virus writers rely on obfuscation to hide the functionality of their code.

The proliferation of the Internet of Things (IoT) has given rise to a significant issue in malware detection, whereby a substantial portion of malware comprises repurposed versions of existing malware, recompiled to function on new architectures such as ARM and MIPS. This poses a formidable challenge to signature-based malware detection systems, as the compiled variants differ significantly due to the distinct instruction sets employed by IoT devices. Consequently, virus authors easily achieve one of their primary objectives, namely, evading antivirus scanners through the straightforward adaptation of their preexisting source code. To address this problem, it becomes evident that a paradigm shift is required. Instead of solely focusing on the generated code, a higher level of comprehension must be embraced, wherein considerations pertaining to the instruction set and architecture cease to be decisive factors in categorizing a program as malicious or benign.

Code Obfuscation and its use in Malware Writing. Obfuscation is a software protection technique that involves the application of a series of transformations to a program, aiming to modify its syntax while preserving its semantics. This process makes it increasingly difficult to reverse engineer the resulting code, extract information from it, modify its behavior, or perform general analysis. An "obfuscator" performs the obfuscation process by applying a sequence of transformations, denoted as $T = t_1, t_2, ..., t_n$, to a program P, resulting in a transformed program P'. These transformations in T maintain the semantics of the code, ensuring that P' still exhibits the same behavior as P. Thus, both programs are semantically equivalent, but they present different syntax, with P' typically presenting a higher level of complexity for analysis compared to P. In the history of malware [28], excluding packing, the first obfuscation technique seen in the wild is encryption [24, 25, 27]. Malware encryption works by encrypting the executable body that will be decrypted at runtime by a decryptor. The cryptographic keys used to encrypt the program are different at every infection, resulting in an always different encrypted body. Cascade, Win95/Mad and Win95/Zombie [26] are some of the first malwares relying on this methodology, sometimes even stacking multiple encryption layers, as in the case of Win32/Coke. It is important to notice that, even if the body is always different at every infection, the decryptor in most of the cases stays the same, so it represents a good choice in order to identify an invariant pattern to be used as signature. This limitation led to the birth of a new malware variety: *polymorphic viruses* [21]. By leveraging a plethora of different strategies [7,14,27] polymorphism allows to apply transformations even to the decryption routines, thus avoiding them to be an easy source of signatures. Win95/Marburg and Win95/HPS are the first malware using a real 32-bit polymorphic engine. Even if polymorphic viruses are quite effective in evading signature based antivirus scanners, they can easily be detected with dynamic approaches, since the body of the virus will be unencrypted in memory at runtime and using sandboxing techniques for controlled malware execution [24,25] can lead to a convenient analysis and signature identification. An important milestone in malware history has been reached with the advent of metamorphic viruses [7,8,13,14,24,27]. At each infection iteration, metamorphic viruses transform their own body, by applying mostly syntactic transformations, so that the resulting code is different from the generating one while preserving its functionalities. The techniques applied in order to achieve this goal are numerous, and many of them were already used in polymorphic viruses.

Intermediate Representation. Intermediate Representation (IR) refers to a form of representation of source code internally generated by compilers during the process of compilation into executable code. The conversion operated by compilers from source code to executable code can be seen as a translation of a program written in one language into another. In order to perform this translation, compilers rely on inner structures such as a front end - able to understand the source program and map it into the intermediate representation - and a back end - that reads the intermediate representation of code and translates it into the target machine language. While on one hand, the utilization of intermediate representation introduces an additional step in the translation process from source code to target code, on the other hand, it presents numerous advantages, including heightened abstraction, establishing a clearer demarcation between the front end and the back end, and introducing the potential for re-targeting and cross-compilation. Additionally, the generation of an intermediate representation of code enables new optimizations which are applicable on this form of code. An intermediate representation (IR) can take on various forms: semantic graphs such as an Abstract Syntax Tree (AST) and Control Flow Graph (CFG), tuples such as Static Single Assignment (SSA), stack codes and more. The choice of a particular IR form in a compiler depends on several factors, including the source programming language, the target architecture, and the transformations and optimizations applied by the compiler. The target architecture is a critical aspect, since compilers often generate machine code specific to a particular architecture. To optimize the generated code for the target architecture, the IR must be structured in a way that enables efficient instruction scheduling, register allocation, and other architecture-specific optimizations. Different types of Intermediate Representations (IR) exist, varying in their expressiveness, depending on the desired outcome. They can be categorized as:

- High-level IRs: These are highly readable and closely resemble high-level programming languages.
- Medium-Level IRs: Mid-level IRs offer a certain level of abstraction while maintaining independence from the underlying architecture.
- Low-level IRs: In this case, the intermediate representation aligns closely and is even dependent on the specific architecture for which the program is being compiled. However, it explicitly addresses memory management concerns, such as stack pointer management and parameter passing mechanisms.

IRs find utility not only within the scope of compilers for the purpose of optimizing the resultant target code, but also in the domain of binary analysis tools. The latter employ IRs as a means to abstract and encapsulate any architectural aspect of a binary program that pertains to the specific architecture for which it has been compiled.

3   Related Work

Several approaches have been explored with the aim of identifying malicious patterns through signature scanning and pattern matching techniques. One of the most popular tools in this regard is YARA [2], which is commonly utilized within many antivirus software. YARA is a powerful pattern-matching tool that allows for the creation and detection of signatures based on sequences of bytes. By employing a flexible rule-based syntax, YARA enables analysts to define complex patterns and conditions for identifying specific malware or other program attributes. While YARA is a valuable resource, it is important to acknowledge its limitations: one of the primary constraints lies in the reliance on byte-level signatures, which can be susceptible to obfuscation techniques employed by adversaries. Malicious actors may employ various methods to evade signature-based detection, such as encryption, polymorphism, or packing, which can alter the byte-level representation of the program and render the signatures ineffective. Alternative approaches are employed for malware detection to assess program similarity, by means of different types of signatures, such as program hashes. Hash-based signatures involve generating unique hash values for programs and comparing them with known hashes to determine similarity. This approach is effective in identifying identical or near-identical programs, regardless of their byte-level representation. Hashdeep[1] employs rolling hash algorithms to calculate and store file or data block hashes, enabling efficient comparison for similarity detection. However, it may not capture fine-grained differences within files, potentially leading to false negatives. Fuzzy hashing, utilized by tools like ssdeep [15] and tlsh [18], involves dividing files into blocks, computing block

---

[1] https://github.com/jessek/hashdeep.

hash values, and concatenating them to create a fuzzy hash. Ssdeep can handle variations within files, offering a more robust measure of similarity compared to traditional cryptographic hash functions, along with a scoring mechanism to quantify similarity. Tlsh employs locality-sensitive hashing, focusing on statistical data properties to calculate a hash value representing local file structure, suitable for identifying similar files within large datasets. SDhash [22] utilizes locality-sensitive hashing (LSH) to identify file similarities based on the statistical distribution of short contiguous blocks within files, making it valuable for near-duplicate or closely related file detection.

Some recent endeavors have delved into the domain of graph matching for enhanced detection capabilities, where Control Flow Graphs (CFGs) are employed as program signatures. Specifically, these approaches involve the generation of CFGs from the programs under analysis, which are subsequently compared against a database of CFGs associated with known malware instances [1,3,5].

Several approaches leveraging machine learning and deep learning techniques have also been proposed for malware detection [6,9,23] or other analysis techniques based on ad-hoc encoding of security related data [10–12]. Some of these methods specifically exploit features extracted from intermediate program representations [20,29]. This entails using the intermediary forms of programs to extract meaningful characteristics, ultimately enhancing the performance of machine learning models in identifying malware and uncovering irregular patterns in software.

Other useful approaches to mitigate the variability introduced by metamorphic transformations are code optimization [19], imposing an order on the instructions [16] and code normalization [4]. These techniques all share the common objective of transforming a program into a canonical form that is simpler in terms of structure or syntax, while preserving the original semantics. However, the effectiveness of these techniques is still limited to the original architecture and instruction set, rendering them inadequate for the task of detecting the same malware repurposed for different architectures.

4   Implementation

In this paper we present SIGIL (Signature scanning on Intermediate Language), a novel framework for conducting signature scanning, with the objective of detecting malicious behaviors within compiled programs. While traditional signature scanning techniques target specific patterns within sequences of bytes, we shift our focus to the IR of the code. To achieve this, our framework relies on the generation of a set of rules, exhibiting a syntax akin to that of YARA, yet referencing a specific intermediate language rather than byte sequences. By shifting our focus to the IR, our framework offers several distinct advantages. Firstly, it enables a higher level of abstraction, allowing for the detection of malicious behaviors independent of the underlying architecture's nuances. This enhances the versatility and adaptability of the scanning process, facilitating the detection of threats across multiple architectures without the need for architecture-specific rule sets. Secondly, the compactness of IR, due to features such as the simplified representation of code, allows for concise rule composition, eliminating unnecessary complexity and facilitating more streamlined and compact rule definitions. It is important to underline that there is a wide range of software available for performing the translation from machine code to IR, commonly referred to as "lifting". Therefore, in contrast to the development of complex software for code normalization, code optimization, and other ad hoc approaches, it is unnecessary to implement brand new complicated software. Instead, we can leverage existing projects that are routinely utilized by compilers and binary analysis tools for the lifting phase. Moreover, our framework's approach mitigates the challenges posed by code obfuscation techniques: by analyzing the code's IR, our rules can capture patterns and behaviors that persist even when traditional byte sequences are obscured or modified. This resilience to obfuscation enhances the accuracy and reliability of the scanning process, ensuring a higher detection rate for malicious activities.

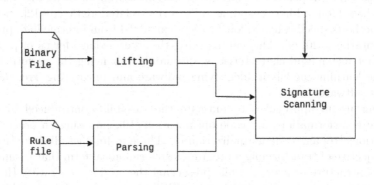

Fig. 1. SIGIL *structure*

Our tool operates by taking two essential inputs: a target binary file and a rule file. The target binary file serves as the primary source of analysis, while the rule file provides the necessary guidelines for identifying specific patterns or signatures within the binary file. The architecture of our tool, as depicted in Fig. 1, consists of three interconnected modules, each serving a crucial role in the analysis process. These modules are as follows: the binary file lifting module, the rule file parsing module, and the signature scanning module.

The lifting module performs the transformation of binary files into an IR. We chose to use LLVM IR [17] as intermediate language within our framework. We employ McSema[2] and llvm-dis[3] to obtain the IR from the binaries under analysis. LLVM IR is a low-level language that is employed by the LLVM framework during the compilation process. It provides a set of instructions that closely

---

[2] https://github.com/lifting-bits/mcsema.
[3] https://llvm.org/docs/CommandGuide/llvm-dis.html.

resemble machine code and can be optimized and compiled into native machine code for various target architectures. The motivations behind our preference are due to its inherent characteristics. LLVM IR operates at a higher level of abstraction as it represents a program's behavior and semantics independently of the source or target language. It provides a structured and language-agnostic representation. LLVM IR is structured in a three-address form. This form allows for more flexibility in expressing operations and dependencies between instructions. LLVM IR also has the advantage of representing types, such as'I32' for a 32-bit integer, without being tied to specific registers. This abstraction from registers makes LLVM IR independent of the target platform, meaning it can be optimized and generated into machine code for different architectures. This feature allows us to abstract code from specific hardware platforms, making it an ideal fit for the vast and diverse architectures encountered in the realm of the IoT.

The parsing module consists of a software component that, based on a specific grammar, validates the correctness of the syntax of the language by performing lexical and syntactic analysis, adhering to the rules defined in the grammar. We implemented this module by using the Lark parsing toolkit[4]. It conducts lexical analysis of the rule files text by using the Look-Ahead Left-to-Right (LALR) algorithm, ultimately resulting in the creation of an Abstract Syntax Tree (AST) to capture the hierarchical structure and semantics of the rules. Finally, the signature scanning module is responsible for comparing the IR of the code against the provided rules. By representing the rules as an AST, the tool gains several advantages in terms of matching code against the rule set. The AST serves as a structured blueprint, providing a clear understanding of the rule hierarchy and the corresponding conditions for matching. It enables the tool to navigate through the binary file's representation and identify potential matches based on the rules' defined patterns. The AST representation of the rules simplifies the verification process, as it allows for precise rule evaluation. Each node within the AST corresponds to a specific rule or condition, and by traversing the tree, the tool can efficiently check if the code in the binary file adheres to the rules' requirements. The AST facilitates the systematic examination of code sections, making it easier to identify and validate matches.

Dealing with Data and Raw Code. Another crucial aspect of our tool is the ability to define signatures based on the data of a software rather than its code. As depicted in Fig. 1, the signature scanning module takes both the lifted program and the program itself as inputs. This enables the module to search for the presence of a given signature not only in the lifted code but also in raw code sections (in case of unaligned malicious code) and the data sections of the binary. Consequently, we can define signatures that are associated with specific strings, IP addresses, or other conventional patterns commonly utilized in malware signature creation, even if they are unrelated to sequences of instructions.

---

[4] https://github.com/lark-parser/lark.

Wildcard Scanning Support. SIGIL fully supports and integrates wildcard scanning, a valuable technique utilized in signature-based malware detection systems to improve the flexibility and effectiveness of signature matching algorithms. By incorporating wildcard characters or placeholders into signature patterns, SIGIL is able to identify malware variants that share similarities but are not exact matches. Wildcards allow for matching any value or a range of values at specific positions within the scanned data, thereby facilitating the detection of subtle modifications or obfuscation techniques employed by malware.

5   Example

In this section, we present a signature in the IR domain that enables the detection of the `socket` function invocation and verifies the connection to a specific IP address. This signature is designed to be architecture-agnostic and allows for the identification of a given behaviour across different architectures. This demonstration serves as a preliminary showcase, providing insight into SIGIL's operation and capabilities. The signature, named `socket_and_ip_detection`, is defined in the SIGIL rule syntax as follows:

```
 1  rule socket_and_ip_detection {
 2      meta:
 3          description = "Detects socket func and presence of a given IP addr"
 4
 5      condition:
 6          exists(
 7              call(
 8                  return_type = "i32",
 9                  name = "socket",
10                  arguments = [
11                      { type = "i32" },
12                      { type = "i32" },
13                      { type = "i32" }
14                  ]
15              )
16          ) and
17          exists(
18              data(
19                  name = "command_and_control_ip",
20                  type = "i8*",
21                  content = "111.222.333.444"
22              )
23          )
24  }
```

The signature consists of two conditions. The first condition uses the `exists` keyword with a `call` instruction to detect the invocation of the `socket` function. The `call` instruction uses `"i32"` as both the `return_type` and the `arguments` to match the `socket` function prototype. The second condition utilizes the `exists` keyword with a `data` instruction to detect the presence of a specific IP address. By combining these conditions, the signature allows for the cross-architecture detection of connections to command and control servers. By abstracting away architectural specifics, when applied using the SIGIL tool, this signature facilitates the identification of malware across different architectures, providing robust and consistent detection capabilities.

6 Conclusion and Future Work

In conclusion, this paper presents SIGIL, a malware detection tool designed to address security challenges introduced by the variety of IoT technologies by combining signature scanning with intermediate languages. By leveraging IRs, SIGIL achieves architecture-independent signatures, enabling the identification of multiple binaries representing the same program compiled for different architectures. Additionally, SIGIL's utilization of higher-level representations enhances its ability to detect malware, even in the presence of obfuscating transformations.

Moving forward, our future work involves comparing multiple IRs, measuring the efficiency of the lifting and signature scanning processes, and conducting extensive testing on a large dataset of both benign and malicious software. Furthermore, we aim to develop a tool that translates existing YARA rules into SIGIL rules, facilitating the leveraging of existing knowledge in malware detection for repurposed malware on different architectures.

References

1. Alam, S., Horspool, R.N., Traore, I.: Mail: Malware analysis intermediate language: a step towards automating and optimizing malware detection. In: Proceedings of the 6th International Conference on Security of Information and Networks, pp. 233–240 (2013)
2. Alvarez, V.M.: Yara. https://virustotal.github.io/yara/
3. Bonfante, G., Kaczmarek, M., Marion, J.Y.: Control flow graphs as malware signatures. In: International workshop on the Theory of Computer Viruses (2007)
4. Bruschi, D., Martignoni, L., Monga, M.: Code normalization for self-mutating malware. IEEE Secur. Privacy 5(2), 46–54 (2007)
5. Cesare, S., Xiang, Y.: Malware variant detection using similarity search over sets of control flow graphs. In: 2011IEEE 10th International Conference on Trust, Security and Privacy in Computing and Communications, pp. 181–189 (2011). https://doi.org/10.1109/TrustCom.2011.26
6. Chaganti, R., Ravi, V., Pham, T.D.: Deep learning based cross architecture internet of things malware detection and classification. Comput. Secur. 120, 102779 (2022)
7. Christodorescu, M., Jha, S.: Static analysis of executables to detect malicious patterns. WISCONSIN UNIV-MADISON DEPT OF COMPUTER SCIENCES, Tech. rep. (2006)
8. Driller, M.: Metamorphism in practice. 29A Mag. 1(6) (2002)
9. Greco, C., Ianni, M., Guzzo, A., Fortino, G.: Explaining binary obfuscation. In: 2023 IEEE International Conference on Cyber Security and Resilience (CSR), pp. 22–27. IEEE (2023)
10. Guzzo, A., Ianni, M., Pugliese, A., Saccà, D.: Modeling and efficiently detecting security-critical sequences of actions. Futur. Gener. Comput. Syst. (2020). https://doi.org/10.1016/j.future.2020.06.054. https://www.sciencedirect.com/science/article/pii/S0167739X19331528
11. Ianni, M., Masciari, E.: A compact encoding of security logs for high performance activity detection. In: 29th Euromicro International Conference on Parallel, Distributed and Network-Based Processing, PDP 2021, Valladolid, Spain, March 10–12, 2021, pp. 240–244. IEEE (2021). https://doi.org/10.1109/PDP52278.2021.00045. https://doi.org/10.1109/PDP52278.2021.00045

12. Ianni, M., Masciari, E.: Scout: Security by computing outliers on activity logs. Comput. Secur. **132**, 103355 (2023). https://doi.org/10.1016/j.cose.2023.103355. https://www.sciencedirect.com/science/article/pii/S0167404823002651

13. Julus, L.: Metamorphism. 29A Mag. **1**(5) (2000)

14. Konstantinou, E., Wolthusen, S.: Metamorphic virus: analysis and detection. Royal Holloway Univ. London **15**, 15 (2008)

15. Kornblum, J.: Identifying almost identical files using context triggered piecewise hashing. Digit. Investig. **3**, 91–97 (2006)

16. Lakhotia, A., Mohammed, M.: Imposing order on program statements to assist anti-virus scanners. In: Proceedings of the 11th Working Conference on Reverse Engineering, 2004, pp. 161–170. IEEE (2004)

17. Lattner, C., Adve, V.: Llvm: a compilation framework for lifelong program analysis & transformation. In: International Symposium on Code Generation and Optimization, 2004. CGO 2004, pp. 75–86 (2004). https://doi.org/10.1109/CGO.2004.1281665

18. Oliver, J., Cheng, C., Chen, Y.: Tlsh-a locality sensitive hash. In: 2013 Fourth Cybercrime and Trustworthy Computing Workshop, pp. 7–13. IEEE (2013)

19. Perriot, F.: Defeating polymorphism through code optimization. In: Proc. of the 2003 Virus Bulletin Conference (VB2003), pp. 1–18, September 2003

20. Phu, T.N., Hoang, L.H., Toan, N.N., Tho, N.D., Binh, N.N.: Cfdvex: A novel feature extraction method for detecting cross-architecture iot malware. In: Proceedings of the 10th International Symposium on Information and Communication Technology, pp. 248–254 (2019)

21. Rajaat: Polimorphism. 29A Mag. **1**(3) (1999)

22. Roussev, V.: Data fingerprinting with similarity digests. In: Chow, K.-P., Shenoi, S. (eds.) DigitalForensics 2010. IAICT, vol. 337, pp. 207–226. Springer, Heidelberg (2010). https://doi.org/10.1007/978-3-642-15506-2_15

23. Saxe, J., Berlin, K.: Deep neural network based malware detection using two dimensional binary program features. In: 2015 10th International Conference on Malicious and Unwanted Software (MALWARE), pp. 11–20. IEEE (2015)

24. Schiffman, M.: A brief history of malware obfuscation: Part 1 of 2. Published online at https://blogs.cisco.com/security/a_brief_history_of_malware_obfuscation_part_1_of_2. Accessed 13 Nov 2018

25. Schiffman, M.: A brief history of malware obfuscation: Part 2 of 2. Published online at https://blogs.cisco.com/security/a_brief_history_of_malware_obfuscation_part_2_of_2. Accessed 13 Nov 2018

26. Szor, P., Ferrie, P.: Hunting for metamorphic. In: Virus bulletin conference. Prague (2001)

27. Wong, W., Stamp, M.: Hunting for metamorphic engines. J. Comput. Virol. **2**(3), 211–229 (2006)

28. You, I., Yim, K.: Malware obfuscation techniques: A brief survey. In: 2010 International Conference on Broadband, Wireless Computing, Communication and Applications (BWCCA), pp. 297–300. IEEE (2010)

29. Zhao, B., Han, J., Meng, X.: A malware detection system based on intermediate language. In: 2017 4th International Conference on Systems and Informatics (ICSAI), pp. 824–830. IEEE (2017)

SecAssure 2023

SecAssure 2023 Preface

This part contains the accepted papers for the 2nd International Workshop on System Security Assurance (SecAssure 2023). The workshop was co-located with the 28th European Symposium on Research in Computer Security (ESORICS 2023) and was held in The Hague, The Netherlands on September 29, 2023.

The advancement in information and communication technology has revolutionized social and economic systems. Governments, as well as commercial and non-profit organizations, rely heavily on information to conduct their business. Aside from the significant benefits of information and computing systems, their increasing connectivity, criticality, and comprehensiveness present new challenges for cybersecurity professionals. Information and services that are compromised in terms of confidentiality, integrity, availability, accountability, and authenticity can harm an organization's operations, so this information and data need to be protected. For this reason, it has become a crucial task for security researchers and practitioners to manage security risks by mitigating potential vulnerabilities and threats with new techniques and methodologies. At the same time, it is challenging to ensure the acceptable security assurance of an information and computing system such that stakeholders can have confidence that the system works as intended or claimed. Security assurance can be defined as the confidence that a system meets its security requirements and is resilient against security vulnerabilities and failures. According to NIST, security assurance is a measure of confidence that the security features, practices, procedures, and architecture of an information system accurately mediates and enforces the security policy.

SecAssure 2023 brought together researchers from academia and practitioners from industry and government bodies in a forum to meet and exchange ideas on recent research and future directions for security assurance. The workshop received 8 submissions. A single-blinded review method was used. Each submission was assigned three reviewers. The review process resulted in 5 high-quality full papers that were accepted, presented at the workshop and included in the proceedings. The papers cover topics related to security assurance, cyber ranges, distributed ledger security and the integration of emerging technologies such as AI into security and system specifications. They explore various aspects of enhancing security assurance, vulnerability detection, and trust assumptions in voting systems, as well as the utilization of fork-awareness in coverage-guided fuzzing.

September 2023

Basel Katt
Habtamu Abie
Sandeep Pirbhulal
Ankur Shukla

Organization

General Chairs

Basel Katt — Norwegian University of Science and Technology, Norway

Habtamu Abie — Norwegian Computing Center, Oslo, Norway

Sandeep Pirbhulal — Norwegian Computing Center, Oslo, Norway

Ankur Shukla — Institute for Energy Technology, Norway

Program Committee Chairs

Basel Katt — Norwegian University of Science and Technology, Norway

Habtamu Abie — Norwegian Computing Center, Oslo, Norway

Sandeep Pirbhulal — Norwegian Computing Center, Oslo, Norway

Ankur Shukla — Institute for Energy Technology, Norway

Program Committee

Sokratis Katsikas — Norwegian University of Science and Technology, Norway

Bjørn Axel Gran — Institute for Energy Technology, Norway

John Eidar Simensen — Institute for Energy Technology, Norway

Wolfgang Leister — Norwegian Computing Center, Norway

Mauro Conti — University of Padua, Italy

Rejjo Savola — University of Jyväskylä, Finland

Jan Jurjens — University of Koblenz and Landau, Germany

Arda Goknil — SINTEF, Norway

Ketil Stølen — SINTEF, Norway

Phu H. Nguyen — SINTEF, Norway

Cristina Alcaraz — University of Malaga, Spain

Michael Felderer — University of Innsbruck, Austria

Simon Tjoa — St. Pölten University of Applied Sciences, Austria

Volker Gruhn — University of Duisburg-Essen, Germany

Hanno Langweg	HTWG Konstanz University of Applied Sciences, Germany
Shao-Fang Wen	Norwegian University of Science and Technology, Norway
Muhammad Mudassar Yamin	Norwegian University of Science and Technology, Norway
Muhammad Ali Babar	University of Adelaide, Australia
Nuno Laranjeiro	University of Coimbra, Portugal
Mahmoud Barhamgi	Qatar University, Qatar

Additional Reviewers

Ali Hassan Sodhro
Stine Aurora Mikkelsplass
Chhagan Lal

Toward Next-Generation Cyber Range: A Comparative Study of Training Platforms

Alexandre Grimaldi[1], Julien Ribiollet[1], Pantaleone Nespoli[1,2],
and Joaquin Garcia-Alfaro[1(✉)]

[1] SAMOVAR, Télécom SudParis, Institut Polytechnique de Paris, Palaiseau, France
`jgalfaro@ieee.org`
[2] Department of Information and Communications Engineering,
University of Murcia, Murcia, Spain

Abstract. As cyber incidents increase in number and disruption, cybersecurity competencies represent a need more than ever. In this context, Cyber Range platforms have been proven as an effective tool to train both professional and common users in such competencies. This study presents a comparative analysis of eight Cyber Range platforms, discussing the needed evolution toward next-generation cyber range platforms. The comparative analysis focuses on key aspects such as application domains, methods of experimentation, infrastructure technologies, and topology generation, among others. This study also aims to provide insights into the capabilities and features offered by different Cyber Range platforms and, specifically, network topology generation tools, allowing for informed decision-making when selecting the most suitable solution for specific training and experimentation needs. Additionally, the study considers how the ethical and well-thought use of Artificial Intelligence (AI) could enhance the automation processes of Cyber Ranges, whether it acts in scenario randomization or topology generation.

Keywords: Cyber Range · Cybersecurity · Cyber Defense · Educational Technology · Cybersecurity Education

1 Introduction

In the rapidly evolving landscape of cyberspace, the need for skilled cybersecurity professionals has become more critical than ever. As organizations and individuals continue to grapple with sophisticated cyber threats, it is imperative to equip future cybersecurity practitioners with practical skills that reflect real-world scenarios [23]. While theoretical knowledge forms the foundation, hands-on experience in tackling complex cybersecurity challenges is crucial to fostering expertise in this field. To bridge this gap between theory and practice, the development of effective cybersecurity training programs is essential [4].

In particular network topology generation refers to the creation of realistic and dynamic network environments that simulate various cybersecurity scenarios. These environments serve as training grounds for individuals to gain hands-on experience in detecting, preventing, and mitigating cyber threats. By replicating complex network infrastructures, topology generation enables trainees to

S. Katsikas et al. (Eds.): ESORICS 2023 Workshops, LNCS 14399, pp. 271–290, 2024.
https://doi.org/10.1007/978-3-031-54129-2_16

develop critical thinking, analytical, and problem-solving skills, while familiarizing themselves with the tools, techniques, and procedures employed by malicious actors in a controlled environment [13].

Nevertheless, traditional methods of topology generation require manual configuration, which can be time-consuming and error-prone. Additionally, once the cyberexercise has finished, users already know how to solve the proposed challenges, forcing the instructor to create another scenario. Autonomous topology generation tools, on the other hand, leverage advanced algorithms or AI techniques to automate the process of creating complex network environments. These tools can automatically generate realistic topologies, incorporating diverse network components, traffic patterns, and potential cyberattack scenarios. While automatic topology generation tools have been widely used in the network ecosystem, very little attention has been given to the use of those tools to create complex and motivating scenarios to train users' cybersecurity capabilities [22].

In light of the above, this paper presents a study on the most prominent Cyber Range platforms nowadays. Concretely, eight Cyber Ranges are compared based on 13 key features (e.g., application domains, methods of experimentation, infrastructure technologies, and topology generation, among others). Such a side-by-side comparison serves as a starting point for an interesting discussion on the actual limitations of the Cyber Range ecosystem, with particular attention on the generation of training scenarios. In particular, two of the most prominent tools for automatic scenario generation are analyzed (i.e., SecGen and CyExec*), highlighting their pros and cons.

Section 2 details the criteria used to contrast the Cyber Range proposals. Next, different Cyber Range are analyzed in Sect. 3, adding a side-by-side comparison based on the proposed criteria. Section 4 focuses on the generation of network topologies for cybersecurity training, analyzing two existing tools. Section 5 discusses on the limitations of the actual Cyber Ranges ecosystem, highlighting some potential improvements to address the open challenges. Section 6 concludes the paper, presenting some interesting future research lines.

2   Comparison Criteria

To better understand the current landscape of Cyber Ranges solutions and the challenges related to topology generation, it is mandatory to review some of the existing solutions and, consequently, gain essential insights about their core features. In order to have a fair comparison among them, this section provides details of which criteria are used for this classification and why they are pertinent.

2.1   Application Domains

Cyber Ranges can be used for training in a large variety of contexts. From students in cybersecurity schools to military groups, there are multiple application domains. Conducting a study on more than forty platforms, authors in [18] identified the following four categories, that is, (i) military defence and intelligence, (ii) academic purposes, (iii) commercial organisations and enterprises, and (iv) government training.

Military Defence and Intelligence — Training in this domain prioritizes national security and defense, emphasizing the counteraction of complex cyber threats and offensive operations. It frequently involves employing advanced techniques and simulations of real-world scenarios.

Academic Purposes — Training in academic institutions aims to educate and prepare students for careers in cybersecurity. It encompasses a wide range of topics and offers practical experience in network security, penetration testing, forensics, incident response, and much more.

Commercial Organizations and Enterprises — On a broad scale, training in this domain focuses on cybersecurity best practices for employees. It may include topics such as secure coding, data protection, risk management, and security awareness training.

Depending on the specific role and focus of the organization or company, the training for different teams like the red team, blue team, purple team, and others can be tailored to meet their specific objectives. This customization is essential because the goals pursued by these teams can vary significantly.

Government Training — Government training programs focus on preparing personnel within government agencies for various cybersecurity challenges specific to their operations and responsibilities. These agencies often handle sensitive information, critical infrastructure, and national security interests.

2.2 Team Formation

Depending on the type of scenario a Cyber Range is recreating, teams constitute a central part of the training. A Cyber Range can assign a user to a specific team or let the user choose the behavior they wish to have. Among such teams, the Red team acts as offensive operators, while the Blue team is responsible for defending against an adversary attack. Some Cyber Range platforms can even offer a user to act as a member of the Yellow team (i.e., system administration). A team's behavior can also be emulated and automated by the Grey team (i.e., background traffic generation) to add realism to a certain situation. Nevertheless, most platforms take the classic approach of Red-Blue-Grey teams.

2.3 Methods of Experimentation

Generally, Cyber Range platforms offer scenarios to train on cybersecurity competencies. Based on this study, there are two main techniques to deploy such scenarios, i.e., simulation or emulation of the environment.

Simulation — Simulation involves modeling the state of the target. The goal is to recreate a model as accurately as possible for every detail and every behavior that the target does in reality. Cyber Ranges utilize various tools to facilitate these simulations, including Vagrant[1], Docker, Terraform[2], GNS3[3], Ixia[4], and others. A successful simulation should be almost undetectable by the end-user.

Emulation — Sometimes, only imitating a behavior can be enough to recreate a realistic situation. This is where emulation comes into play, as it focuses on imitating externally observable behavior to match an existing real target. Interestingly, the target's internal state does not necessarily have to reflect the real world as long as it appears accurate to the end user.

Emulation finds widespread application in mimicking hardware behavior through software. When combined with virtualization, it enables the imitation of electronic equipment without the need for physical components. This powerful combination allows for the faithful reproduction of hardware functionality in a virtual environment, providing a cost-effective and flexible alternative to physical hardware usage.

2.4 Infrastructure Technologies

Infrastructure technologies are fundamental components of a Cyber Range, providing the underlying framework necessary for its operation and functionality. These technologies encompass a range of systems and resources, including network infrastructure, virtualization platforms, cloud computing services, and storage solutions. Network infrastructure forms the backbone of the Cyber Range, enabling connectivity, data transmission, and communication between simulated environments and users. Virtualization platforms, such as hypervisors, allow for the creation and management of virtual machines and networks, enabling the emulation of diverse systems and scenarios within the Cyber Range. Cloud computing services offer scalability and flexibility, facilitating the provisioning of resources on-demand and enabling the deployment of complex Cyber Range environments. Storage solutions play a crucial role in securely storing and managing the large volumes of data generated during Cyber Range exercises. Examples of these technologies include Kubernetes[5], Argo CD[6], and object storage.

Before choosing infrastructure solutions, it is important to consider the architecture approach. Monolithic architecture involves building an application as a single, self-contained unit, while microservices architectures decompose the application into small, independent services that can be developed, deployed, and scaled individually. Monolithic architecture offers simplicity on a small scale, while microservices architecture provides scalability, flexibility, and fault isolation, but it is more complex to set up initially.

---

[1] https://www.vagrantup.com.
[2] https://www.terraform.io/.
[3] https://www.gns3.com/.
[4] https://github.com/open-traffic-generator/ixia-c.
[5] https://kubernetes.io/.
[6] https://argoproj.github.io/cd/.

2.5   Front-End Technologies

Front-end technologies are crucial for the presentation of a Cyber Range, too. In this sense, panels and user interfaces should be user-friendly and easy to use to leverage the full capabilities of the tool.

User Interface (UI) — As the primary point of interaction between users and the Cyber Range platform, the UI directly impacts the user experience and the overall success of training exercises. A well-designed and intuitive UI enhances user engagement, simplifies navigation, and promotes efficient access to essential functionalities. It allows users, including instructors and trainees, to easily interact with the Cyber Range environment, configure scenarios, monitor progress, and analyze results. A clear and visually appealing UI improves cognitive load management, reducing user confusion and enhancing the learning experience. Moreover, a customizable UI can adapt to different user roles and preferences, catering to various skill levels and training objectives. The UI serves as a gateway to the Cyber Range, shaping users' interactions and facilitating effective training and skill development.

Instructor Interface — Instructors using a Cyber Range for education and training require several key capabilities. These include evaluating user actions, enabling communication, providing instructor-specific functionalities, and facilitating user evaluation and feedback.

User evaluation is crucial, involving capturing and analyzing data on user interactions, tasks, and system behavior. Recording and reviewing user sessions and analyzing the data helps assess performance and identify areas for improvement.

Communication facilities are also important in a Cyber Range environment. Features like chat functionality and event broadcasting enable instructors to communicate with users, provide guidance, and facilitate collaborative learning experiences.

To enhance the instructional process, an instructor mode functionality can be valuable. This mode allows instructors to demonstrate sample answers, showcase best practices, provide step-by-step guidance to users and control the workflow of the scenario.

Least but not last, user evaluation is a critical aspect of educational and training Cyber Ranges. Instructors require the ability to conduct assessments, analyze user performance, and deliver feedback. This includes generating reports that summarize user evaluation results, progress, and areas of strength or weakness. The delivery of evaluation and feedback reports enables personalized learning, highlights areas for improvement, and encourages continued growth and development among users.

2.6   Scenario

Scenarios are a crucial element of a Cyber Range, as they provide the context and purpose for training exercises and simulations. A scenario in a Cyber Range represents a specific simulated environment or situation designed to replicate real-world cybersecurity challenges. These scenarios range from isolated incidents to complex multi-stage attacks, encompassing various attack vectors and techniques. The creation of realistic and relevant scenarios is vital to effectively train and assess participants' cybersecurity-related skills and capabilities. Well-designed scenarios should consider different levels of difficulty, align with specific learning objectives, and reflect current cybersecurity threats and trends. They should incorporate various attack and defense techniques, ensuring comprehensive coverage of relevant cybersecurity skills. Additionally, scenarios should offer the flexibility to adapt and evolve, allowing for the integration of new threats, technologies, and learning outcomes. By leveraging crafted scenarios, Cyber Ranges can provide a dynamic and immersive training environment, enabling participants to gain practical experience and enhance their ability to detect, respond to, and mitigate real-world cybersecurity incidents.

2.7 Topology Generation

Topology generation is another critical aspect of a Cyber Range as it involves the creation and configuration of network architectures that accurately simulate real-world environments. The generation of realistic network topologies within a Cyber Range allows for the replication of complex infrastructure, including interconnected systems, devices, and services. This process involves defining the layout, connectivity, and characteristics of virtual machines, routers, switches, firewalls, and other network components. An accurate topology generation is able to create lifelike scenarios for training exercises and simulations, enabling participants to develop practical skills in securing and defending network environments. It involves considering factors such as network segmentation, subnetting, IP addressing, and the configuration of various network protocols and services. With advanced techniques and tools, such as automated network configuration and software-defined networking (SDN) technologies, Cyber Ranges can enhance the process of topology generation, enabling more dynamic and scalable training environments.

2.8 Accessibility

Among others, accessibility ensures that the training environment is available and usable for a wide range of users, including individuals with diverse abilities and needs. Inclusive design principles are essential to ensure that all participants can access, understand, and use the Cyber Range platform and its associated resources. This includes considerations for users with visual, auditory, physical, and cognitive impairments. To enhance accessibility, Cyber Ranges should provide features such as adjustable font sizes, color contrast options, alternative text for images, keyboard navigation support, and compatibility with assistive technologies. Additionally, providing clear and concise instructions, intuitive user interfaces, and comprehensive documentation contributes to the overall accessibility of the Cyber Range, improving users learning opportunities.

2.9 Traffic

To enhance training realism within the Cyber Range, traffic generation can be depicted as one of the most important functionality. Such a generation varies based on its main goal, but generally, it can be divided into two categories, i.e., background and adversarial traffic generation.

Background Traffic — Background traffic refers to the normal, seemingly random network activity that one would typically encounter during network inspection. It comprises the everyday operations of sending and receiving emails, interacting with online content, and engaging in conversations with friends and colleagues. Background traffic plays a major part in making a Cyber Range realistic as attackers often hide their activity blending in with other users of a network. For network intrusion-detection scenarios, having no background traffic makes the exercise pointless. Common network intrusion-detection tools have a much more difficult time identifying malicious traffic in a realistic noisy network environment than it does when only the malicious traffic is present.

Adversarial Traffic — Adversarial traffic is essential in Cyber Ranges for realistic testing and red-on-blue exercises. It provides cover for red teams to assess their stealth and tests the effectiveness of defensive tools. Malicious traffic can mimic normal system administrator activity, such as scanning ports, creating accounts, and changing passwords. It also involves more overtly malicious actions like creating botnets and performing network reconnaissance or exploitation.

2.10   User Modeling

During Cyber Range exercises, it is important to simulate the presence and behavior of benign users within the environment. It creates Non-Player Characters (NPCs) that can behave realistically without human intervention to generate context-driven traffic. User activity simulation creates specific scenarios that mimic real-world environments, adding a layer of realism to the training. Examples of user activity simulation include simulating internet browsing, watching YouTube videos, utilizing P2P file sharing applications for downloads, sending emails, and interacting with cloud services like Office 365 and Dropbox. While it shares similarities with the concept of background traffic, user modeling focuses on replicating precise behaviors based on predefined models. Being more than a simple traffic noise, a user model can be instructed to react to triggers, to interact with GUI-only softwares, to mimic seemingly human responses to phishing campaigns...

To facilitate user activity simulation, desirable features include the availability of a simulation library. This library would contain a comprehensive list of pre-defined user simulations that can be easily incorporated into the Cyber Range exercises. Additionally, the ability to import or create custom simulations provides flexibility to tailor the user activity scenarios based on specific training objectives or real-world use cases. The GHOSTS framework [19] specifically aims to provide tools to build such realistic, accurate and autonomous NPCs. Still in the early stages of development, GHOSTS shows promising possibilities for NPCs orchestration. The use of large samples of real-world data and eventually the use of AI could enable NPCs to deliver complex coordination scenarios, such as Distributed Denial Of Service (DDOS) attacks.

2.11   Data Collection and Analysis

The capability of a Cyber Range to gather users' interactions encompasses various aspects such as the traffic generated, memory dumps, tools utilized, and systems targeted. At its simplest level, it involves collecting data provided by the users, such as their responses to tasks or challenges. However, at an advanced level, the Cyber Range can collect all user interactions within the simulated environment and with the platform itself.

The extent of data collection depends on the core technologies employed by the Cyber Range and the methods used to create the simulation environment. Some technologies may offer better native support for data collection, allowing for a more comprehensive and accurate gathering of user interactions.

Additionally, the Cyber Range's ability to facilitate the analysis of collected data plays a crucial role. Data analysis, encompassing both automatically collected data and the output of user activities, forms the foundation for providing meaningful feedback to Cyber Range users. This analysis enables insights into how the Cyber Range is being used and how users perform within the simulated environment, facilitating the educational processes the instructors perform.

In some cases, the inclusion of AI technology, often through third-party solutions, can further enhance the analysis capabilities of the Cyber Range. AI technologies can enable advanced data processing, pattern recognition, and user behavior modeling, leading to more sophisticated and valuable feedback for users.

2.12   Scoring and Reporting

An important feature in a Cyber Range is the ability to score users based on their activities and interactions within the platform. This scoring mechanism can range from simple collection of user input to questions and tasks, to more complex attack and defense systems that involve automated tests for evaluating service availability, system integrity, and other performance indicators. To achieve high scoring capabilities, a strong coupling and integration with the Cyber Range infrastructure is necessary.

To facilitate effective assessment and analysis, Cyber Ranges should provide standard reports, such as individual or team-based performance reports, as well as the flexibility to create custom reports. Reporting capabilities are often an integral part of additional Cyber Range features, enabling the extraction and presentation of valuable insights from user activities and system data. These reports can provide essential feedback for users, instructors, and administrators to evaluate performance, identify areas of improvement, and track progress.

Real-time cyber situational awareness is another critical aspect of Cyber Range capabilities. It allows for clear visualization of the Cyber Range usage, showcasing the impact of tools used, and providing visibility into the actions taken by the users. By displaying real-time information, such as network traffic, system vulnerabilities, and user interactions, cyber situational awareness enhances the understanding of the Cyber Range environment, promotes effective decision-making, and improves overall situational awareness.

2.13   Ownership and License

Ownership and licensing are crucial aspects in the development and operation of Cyber Ranges. Ownership refers to the legal rights and control over the platform and its assets, while licensing governs the terms for use and distribution.

Determining ownership involves identifying the entity or entities with legal rights and control over the Cyber Range. Ownership arrangements may vary, depending on whether it's developed by a single organization, collaboratively, or hosted by a third-party provider. Clear ownership ensures accountability, decision-making authority, and long-term sustainability.

Licensing regulates how the Cyber Range is made available and the permissions granted. It outlines terms, conditions, and restrictions for access, distribution, and usage. Licensing agreements address issues like user rights, content sharing, commercial usage, modifications, and legal liabilities.

Choosing the right licensing model significantly impacts adoption, engagement, and sustainability. Options include open-source licenses for collaboration, proprietary licenses for selective usage, or hybrid models. The chosen model should align with goals, considering factors like community participation, commercialization potential, government involvement, and intellectual property protection.

3   Comparison of Cyber Ranges Solutions

The main goal of this study was to provide a comprehensive overview of Cyber Range and network topology generation tools, albeit within a limited scope. Instead of aiming for an exhaustive list, we aimed to present a well-rounded representation of the possibilities available. To achieve this, we considered a combination of open-source and proprietary tools, using different technologies.

Although our comparison only includes a limited sample of the numerous Cyber Ranges available in the market or under development, we are confident that our selection provides a broad representation of the current Cyber Range landscape. The chosen eight Cyber Ranges offer a diverse range of solutions, allowing for a comprehensive overview. They have been carefully selected based on the previously mentioned comparison criteria, ensuring their relevance to our study. Moreover, these selected Cyber Ranges have ample documentation available, which facilitates a thorough analysis.

Our investigation revealed a scarcity of efficient network topology generation tools that emphasize autonomous generation. Consequently, we expanded our analysis to include more conventional Cyber Range solutions to compensate for this deficiency. As a result, our findings and insights are more robust and captivating than they would have been without this inclusion.

3.1   Analysis

As previously stated, we intentionally opted to showcase only a select few examples. Next, we provide a concise overview of each tool.

SecGen — SecGen [15] is a tool designed for learning penetration testing techniques by generating vulnerable virtual machines. It offers a catalog of vulnerabilities that can be randomly selected based on scenario constraints defined in an XML-based configuration language. SecGen utilizes Puppet and Vagrant to create the necessary virtual machines. Although it lacks support for verification, SecGen allows for post-provisioning module tests to be conducted.

CyberVAN and VulnerVAN — CyberVAN [3] is a testbed environment that utilizes host virtualization and network virtualization technologies. It enables the creation of high-fidelity experimentation scenarios and flexible utilization of testbed resources. Scenarios within CyberVAN consist of interconnected virtual machines (VMs) running various operating systems, including Windows, Linux, and Android. These VMs are connected through a simulated network facilitated by network simulators like ns3, OPNET, and QualNET. CyberVAN supports realistic packet forwarding and control, including wireless protocols for mobile networks. Users can create, deploy, and save their own experimentation scenarios on CyberVAN testbeds, making it a versatile environment for cybersecurity training and exercises.

VulnerVAN [20], on the other hand, is used for generating vulnerable scenarios within CyberVAN. Users provide specifications of the target network and attack sequences using Network Input Collector and Attack Sequence Input Collector. The Vulnerable Scenario Generator (VSG) in VulnerVAN takes this input and generates a CyberVAN scenario with exploits and actions necessary for the specified attack steps. It also creates a sequence diagram depicting a realizable attack path. VulnerVAN includes an attacker playbook reference to facilitate Red Team operations during the attack steps.

CyExec* — CyExec* [9,10] is a Cyber Range system that has been developed to address the challenges associated with the high initial and maintenance costs, as well as the difficulty of developing new scenarios, typically encountered in Cyber Range environments. This system leverages container-type virtualization, which offers a lightweight execution environment for running multiple virtual instances efficiently, thus optimizing hardware utilization and reducing overall costs. CyExec* incorporates a DAG-based scenario randomization technology. This system automatically generates multiple scenarios with the same learning objective, enhancing educational effectiveness, using the power of dockerfiles and docker-compose for topology generation.

Cyberbit Cyber Range — CyberBit Cyber Range [5] offers a robust and flexible infrastructure that allows for scalability and customization of scenarios. It features an automatic scenario emulator, reducing reliance on instructor red teams and enabling the execution of both benign traffic and complex attack sequences. The platform provides an extensive library of off-the-shelf scenarios and courses, facilitating efficient and accelerated training. Additionally, a user-friendly attack scenario builder eliminates the need for coding when creating new scenarios. The Cyber Range is accompanied by clear and comprehensive scenario documentation to support instructor onboarding as operations expand.

It supports both IT and OT environments, enabling simulation of attacks across various network topographies, including IT, SCADA, IoT, and more. CyberBit Cyber Range offers the flexibility of on-premises or cloud deployment, ensuring enhanced accessibility for users.

Airbus Cyber Range — The Airbus Cyber Range platform [2] offers a range of advanced features for modeling real or representative systems. Its graphical interface enables simplified construction through drag-and-drop functionality, allowing for efficient workspace management and the integration of multiple isolated environments. The platform supports collaborative modeling and integration work, facilitating effective teamwork. Integration with equipment and real systems is seamless, while the live traffic generator ensures realistic scenarios. The scenario engine enables the creation and execution of complex scenarios, while the platform also offers the capability to import/export machines or topologies. Access to screen offset and command line is available for each machine, ensuring granular control. Additionally, the platform efficiently manages the virtual machine park for seamless operation and scalability.

CRACK — CRACK [14] is a comprehensive framework that automates the design, model verification, generation, and testing of cyber scenarios. It leverages CRACK SDL, a Scenario Definition Language based on TOSCA, to declaratively specify scenario elements and their interactions. Notably, CRACK supports automatic verification of scenarios against training objectives through formal encoding of SDL properties. Upon successful verification, the framework automatically deploys the scenario in the Cyber Range and conducts tests to ensure consistency between the deployed system's behavior and its specification.

CRATE — CRATE [1,6] is an emulation-based Cyber Range that employs a combination of virtual machines and hardware devices. Research experiments and training sessions are conducted through the execution of scenarios within emulated environments. To ensure flexibility, independence, and the ability to handle sensitive data, CRATE is hosted on a dedicated hardware platform locally. The Swedish Defence Research Agency operates and oversees CRATE's operations.

KYPO Cyber Range — The KYPO Cyber Range [21] stands out for its utilization of structured JSON files to define various aspects such as goals, network topology, software, and scenario workflows. These specifications are then transformed into Ansible and Puppet scripts, streamlining the deployment process. Additionally, KYPO offers a range of preconfigured templates that encompass diverse cybersecurity scenarios, including Distributed Denial of Service (DDoS) and phishing attacks. However, it is worth noting that KYPO lacks support for scenario verification and testing, which may limit its overall effectiveness in certain use cases.

3.2 Overall Comparison

Next, we present a comparative analysis to provide an overall assessment of the features and capabilities of these tools, based on the predefined criteria. This analysis is based on existing results in Refs. [4,18], along with other resources gathered from platform specific papers.

Comparison — Table 1 presents some of our findings about the eight Cyber Ranges reported in our work. Next, we present a short summary about it.

Comparison Analysis — The European Cyber Security Organisation defines a Cyber Range as *"A Cyber Range is a platform for the development, delivery and use of interactive simulation environments. A simulation environment is a representation of an organisation's ICT, OT, mobile and physical systems, applications and infrastructures, including the simulation of attacks, users and their activities and of any other Internet, public or third-party services which the simulated environment may depend upon. A Cyber Range includes a combination of core technologies for the realisation and use of the simulation environment and*

Table 1. Comparison results

	SecGen	CyberVAN / VulnerVAN	CyExec*	Cyberbit CR	Airbus CyberRange	CRACK	CRATE	KYPO
Application Domain	Academic	Military & Defense	Academic	Commercial (as a service)	Commercial & Defense	Academic	Government & Military	Academic & Defense
Team Formation	None	None	None	Courses can be themed specifically for a team.	Yes, strong integration of teaming (Red, Blue, Grey, ...).	None	If needed, teams can get coloured (i.e., to define their role).	If needed, users can be grouped in teams (specific actions & rights).
Experimentation Methods	Simulation	Simulation	Simulation	Simulation	Simulation	Simulation	Emulation	Simulation
Infrastructure Technology	VM Networks powered by Vagrant & Puppet.	Cloud-based, VM Networks.	Container-based (Docker), run remotely or locally.	VM Network (cloud-based or local) as per client request.	VM Network as SaaS. Hybrid with actual IoT devices.	Directives for IaaS provider (supporting TOSCA interfaces).	VM Networks based on virtualbox.	Sandboxes in cloud-based VM networks.
User Interface	Access to powered VMs & web-based dashboard.	None	None	Yes, with skill tree, course catalog, scores, ...	Yes, through gamification (web-based chat & scoreboard).	None	Hardened (e.g., VPN-based) GUI, reporting scores & exercises.	Web-based portal allowing end-user remote access.
Instructor Interface	Website (if existing) + Vagrant & other module configuration files.	XML files + GUI on Web interface.	Dockerfiles & docker-compose (requires high-level of expertise).	None	Scenario creation & orchestrations using a web interface, for deeper into customization.	None, apart from the scenarios defined with its SDL.	Web-based CRATE Exercise Control, providing management & support tools.	PMP can be used to create UI-based complex scenarios.
Scenario	Catalog of vulnerabilities defined in an XML-based language.	Pre-programmed scenarios, no automation. Import/export features.	DAG-based scenario randomization, customizable using docker-compose.	Large catalog of pre-made scenarios.	Large catalog of pre-made scenarios & on-demand scenarios.	No automation per se, but connection to a Scenario Definition Language based on TOSCA.	Graphical tool to create scenarios, without automation features.	No automation, but can get scenarios from other compatible platforms.
Scoring & Reporting	None	None	No	Yes, alongside with course & MCQ	Yes	No	Yes	Yes
Topology Generation	Outputs Vagrant & Puppet files for each scenario.	Based on NS-3 networks & EMANE models.	Based on docker-compose.	Unspecified.	Drag & drop engine from instructor interface to setup VMs.	Based on the tested scenario.	NodeAgent service from API, to deploy VMs, set configurations, etc.	Visualization tools & easy-to-use creation tools.
Accessibility	Easily extendable and possible integration with CTFd.	Nothing specified	Container allows for more versatility.	Easy-to-use on demand service.	Easy-to-use.	Easy to use, once the scenario is created. Extensible & modular.	Roles are clearly defined. Usage of GUI make it user friendly.	Easy-to-use, well documents & highly UI-based tool.
Traffic	Nothing specified	Adversarial & background traffic generate on scenario basis.	Nothing specified	Nothing specified	On-demand	Not directly implemented in CRACK.	SVED (Scanning, Vulnerabilities, Exploits & Detection) able to mimic attack patterns.	Nothing specified
User Modeling	No	Yes	No	No	Yes	No	Yes (using SVED & AutoIt, providing interactions with GUI tools).	Yes
Data Analysis	No	Yes	No	Yes	Yes	No	Yes, automated	Yes
License	GNU GPLv3 (or later)	Military & Defense	Academic	Commercial (as a service)	Commercial & Defense	Academic	Government & Military	Academic & Defense

of additional components which are, in turn, desirable or required for achieving specific Cyber Range use cases" [12].

In order to analyse our comparison tables, we need to ask ourselves *what makes a specific Cyber Range stand out?*, in regard to the previously quoted definition. Some responses are listed next:

- **Performance** is a crucial factor that Cyber Range creators must consider, particularly as the number of users and the complexity of network topologies increase. Emulation-based tools like CRATE allow for hardware attacks in Cyber Ranges but suffer from significant performance costs. In contrast, CyExec* utilizes container-based virtualization, reducing memory consumption by half and storage consumption to 1/60 compared to VM-based Cyber Ranges.
- **Usability** is an important consideration when aiming to reach a wide audience beyond specific companies or organizations. Graphical User Interfaces (GUIs) play a key role in providing easy access to the Cyber Range for end-users and enabling scenarists to create exercises on the spot. Platforms like Airbus CyberRange offer a comprehensive "in a box" solution, allowing any paying company to use it without additional requirements. KYPO and CRATE feature useful instructor interfaces that facilitate scenario creation within the Cyber Range itself. User-centric platforms such as CyberBit draw inspiration from existing Capture the Flag (CTF) platforms, incorporating dashboards, scoreboards, and progression curves. Currently, CRACK, Cyber-VAN, and CyExec have different development goals and may not prioritize extensive GUI features.
- **Scenario creation** is pivotal to the success of Cyber Ranges in any application domain. The inclusion of a wide variety of exercises is highly desirable. The presented Cyber Ranges employ different approaches to achieve this. Sec-Gen, CyExec, and CRACK utilize declarative programming languages (such as XML, YAML, or CRACK SDL) to empower scenarists to create their own exercises. Other proprietary platforms may choose not to provide scenario editors but instead offer a large catalog of pre-made exercises. However, catalogs often come with additional costs or subscription-based business models, potentially limiting accessibility.
- **Automation** is one of the most advanced features a Cyber Range can incorporate. A comparison of multiple Cyber Ranges' automation levels is presented in this paper [6], with a focus on scenario and topology generation. Two dominant automation features stand out: scenario generation and topology generation. SecGen and CyExec* provide innovative methods to randomize and automate scenario creation based on templates, which is discussed further. Regarding topology generation, SecGen and CyExec must adapt the topology to the generated scenario. CRATE and CyberVAN offer solutions to automate parts of network topology generation, while Airbus developed a drag-and-drop interface that automates the background work of connecting components together, although it still relies heavily on human interaction.
- **Realism** is a challenging aspect to quantify or precisely define. Several features contribute to creating a realistic exercise, such as the presence of synthetic (bogus) traffic to emulate activity within the Cyber Range, user modeling to define patterns in the behavior of simulated users in the network,

and team formation to assign specific and realistic tasks to groups of participants. Realism appears to be inherent in platforms used for military or defense purposes. CyberVAN, CRATE, and KYPO all present solutions for creating realistic training contexts for response teams (blue, white, and green teams). CRATE and Airbus CyberRange go even further when deployed locally, enabling physical interaction with the network.

4 Scenario and Topology Generation

The ability to efficiently and realistically create a wide variety of exercises is a major challenge for Cyber Ranges. Our previous comparison revealed that currently, no platform successfully meets all three requirements simultaneously.

Topology generation poses significant difficulties when implementing Cyber Ranges, as it introduces various constraints. Depending on the infrastructure, scenario implementation, and desired level of user freedom, achieving effective topology generation may be extremely challenging or even unattainable.

The comparison presented in Table 1 highlights two standout Cyber Range platforms: SecGen and CyExec*. While there are other Cyber Ranges that could have been examined, it should be noted that some of them are privately owned solutions, which limits access to the resources necessary for understanding their methods of generating topology, thereby limiting our ability to comprehensively analyze them.

In the sequel, we conduct an in-depth analysis of how SecGen and CyExec* successfully automate scenario and topology generation while maintaining an efficient and user-friendly platform.

4.1 SecGen

SecGen [15], a Ruby application with an XML configuration language, is designed to facilitate the creation of realistic cybersecurity scenarios. It operates by reading and processing a comprehensive configuration that encompasses vulnerabilities, services, networks, users, and content. By incorporating scenario-specific logic, SecGen efficiently randomizes the generated scenarios. Leveraging the power of Puppet and Vagrant, the application effectively provisions the necessary virtual machines (VMs) for the scenario. An appealing aspect of SecGen is its open-source nature, with the code readily accessible on GitHub[7] under the GNU General Public License version 3 or later.

Architecture Overview — SecGen employs a structured architecture consisting of *system* objects that represent Virtual Machines (VMs) and *module* objects. VMs are based on selected Vagrant baseboxes determined by specified attributes. Each VM is associated with a list of SecGen modules, primarily chosen based on specified attributes.

Modules have various types (base, vulnerability, service, utility, network, generator, encoder) and include a module path and an associative array of

---

[7] https://github.com/cliffe/SecGen.

attributes (such as CVE number[8], difficulty level, CVSS[9], etc.) defined in a secgen_metadata.xml file located at the root of a module's directory. Modules can receive data through named parameters from the output of other modules or from data stored in a datastore. Modules may incorporate Puppet code to be deployed and executed on the VMs (e.g., vulnerability, service, and utility modules) or local code for data randomization or transformation (e.g., encoder and generator modules). Modules can have default inputs, as well as dependencies or conflicts with other modules.

SecGen's operation comprises two stages: Stage 1 involves building the project output, while Stage 2 focuses on building VMs based on the generated project output.

During Stage 1, all available modules are read, along with the scenario definition. The scenario definition determines the selection of modules for each system. Some modules automatically include additional modules in the scenario, either as dependencies or default inputs for parameters. Randomization occurs in this stage. Modules with local code are executed to produce output, which is then used as input for other module parameters.

Librarian-puppet is utilized to deploy the corresponding puppet modules for the selected SecGen modules into the project output directory. A Vagrantfile is created, referencing the generated data and puppet modules. Additionally, output files describing the generated scenario, including an XML file listing flags with associated hints, are produced.

In Stage 2, the process simply involves invoking *vagrant up*, leveraging Vagrant to generate and provision the VMs based on the defined configuration.

Scenario Specification — SecGen utilizes a flexible module selection logic that considers various attributes defined in each module's secgen_metadata.xml file. These attributes, such as difficulty level and CVE, serve as constraints for module selection. If there is ambiguity in the selection process, SecGen employs randomization to choose from the remaining matching options. For instance, when filtering vulnerabilities based on a specified difficulty level, SecGen randomly selects from the vulnerabilities that meet the criteria. The filters specified for module selection are regular expression (regexp) matches, allowing for versatile and precise filtering capabilities.

4.2   CyExec*

While SecGen uses VMs to support its network topology generation, there are alternative approaches for recreating pseudo-realistic attack environments. The in-development platform called "CyExec*" aims to surpass SecGen and other VM-based Cyber Ranges by leveraging container-based virtualization. This paper [9] from 2021 presents a comprehensive experiment comparing the performance and reproducibility of container-based virtualization with other types of virtualization. The results demonstrate significant advantages, leading to the development of CyExec*, a Cyber Range that reduces memory consumption

---

[8] https://cve.mitre.org/.
[9] https://nvd.nist.gov/vuln-metrics/cvss.

by half and storage consumption to 1/60 compared to other VM-based Cyber Ranges, while maintaining similar CPU usage.

CyExec* introduces an efficient approach for creating randomized scenarios and topology, enabling the generation of numerous exercises from a single template.

DAG-Based Scenario — To generate multiple scenarios, the authors of this paper [10] aimed to understand the structure of a generic Cyber Range scenario. They concluded that a typical scenario consists of several milestones separated by operations and actions related to individual attack methods, similar to a Capture the Flag (CTF) challenge. Between two milestones, multiple subscenarios are possible. Based on this observation, the authors adopted the following approach: for a set of fixed milestones, randomization is incorporated into the selection of the means the attacker must employ to reach the next milestone.

Essentially, this randomized Cyber Range scenario takes the form of a Directed Acyclic Graph (DAG), where milestones are represented as vertices and subscenarios (randomly selected from a predefined pool) are represented as edges. This method allows the generation of multiple random scenarios with different paths but identical objectives from a single template. It enables users to experience similar security incidents in a wide variety of situations.

Implementation — In CyExec*, each component of the scenario topology is defined using a simple Dockerfile. To build a network environment using multiple Dockerfiles, the authors utilize docker-compose. Initially, the scenario creator provides a default scenario with a base system configuration (a docker-compose.yml file). Complex programs are unnecessary to build new scenarios-adding or modifying Dockerfiles and the docker-compose.yml file is sufficient.

To create the aforementioned DAG-based scenario, each distinct possibility for connecting two milestones requires its own Dockerfile. A function randomly selects a subscenario and adds the corresponding Dockerfile to the docker-compose.yml file, thereby generating the random scenario. Additionally, a Dockerfile for the end-user interface in the network is included, which can be a Kali Linux image running in the network, accessible through a web interface or via *docker exec*.

To summarize, the scenario creator starts by designing a template docker-compose.yml file that defines the milestones for the default scenario. For each consecutive pair of milestones, they create multiple Dockerfiles, each representing an independent vulnerable service or machine that leads to the same milestone. Once all the components are prepared, the scenario creator informs CyExec* about the desired number of environments to generate, the number of users, and other relevant parameters. The software then generates docker-compose files based on the default template, while randomly selecting the different Dockerfiles that allow the end-users to progress from one milestone to the next.

5 Discussion and Open Challenges

In addition to performance, scalability, and diversity considerations, future research should focus on addressing key challenges within Cyber Range platforms. As we delve into the evaluation of existing Cyber Range platforms, it becomes evident that each solution has its unique strengths and limitations. For example, while CyExec* stands out as a lightweight platform, its reliance on labor-intensive preparations limits the extent of result randomization. On the other hand, SecGen offers simplicity and adequate variety, but its resource-intensive nature poses constraints. However, to drive the field forward, it is essential to explore ways to reconcile the positive aspects found across multiple platforms and push the boundaries of what is currently available. By harnessing the best features and functionalities from different solutions, we can propel the development of more advanced and comprehensive Cyber Range platforms. To encourage collaboration and advancement in the field, authors are encouraged to release their code on accessible platforms such as GitHub or GitLab, accompanied by an extensive README.md documentation. By providing open access to their codebase, researchers enable others to experiment, learn, and build upon existing foundations, fostering innovation and collaboration within the Cyber Range community.

The integration of AI within Cyber Range platforms and network topology generation tools holds great potential for enhancing their capabilities. As mentioned in [7], *there are relatively few literatures on the development trend of AI in the field of cyber range*. In particular, machine learning (ML) algorithms could automate scenario design by analyzing historical data and generating dynamic and diverse scenarios, saving time for instructors while maintaining challenging training environments. Additionally, ML techniques could enable adaptive user modeling, tailoring the training experience to individual needs and skill levels. This personalization enhances learning outcomes and allows for more effective skill development. Furthermore, ML algorithms can simulate realistic network traffic patterns, mimicking real-world threats and facilitating immersive training experiences.

It is of utmost importance to prioritize ethical considerations when researching new methods for automation within Cyber Range platforms with the use of AI. As the field advances and AI technologies become more integrated into cybersecurity training and experimentation, it is crucial to ensure responsible and ethical practices. By proactively addressing ethical concerns, researchers can mitigate potential risks and promote the development of AI-driven automation that aligns with societal values. This involves safeguarding user privacy and data security, addressing biases and fairness issues, and establishing clear guidelines for responsible use. By integrating ethical considerations into the research process, we can ensure that the benefits of automation and AI within Cyber Range platforms are harnessed in a manner that respects individual rights, upholds accountability, and promotes the responsible application of these technologies in the field of cybersecurity.

Apart from the previously-mentioned difficulty that refers to the automatic generation of scenarios, some challenges still exist in the Cyber Range ecosystem. For example, the users' motivation should be considered during the trainings. In this sense, the use of gamification elements would help as it has been proven a powerful approach to improving student motivation [8]. Still, its application in the context of cybersecurity has mainly been limited to serious games [17]. Furthermore, the cyberexercises proposed in the Cyber Ranges are static, being unable to adapt to the users' capabilities. One could easily argue that a system capable of dynamically adapting the cyberexercises based on the users' performance would be greatly appreciated.

Another notable shortcoming of the analyzed Cyber Ranges is the absence of powerful learning analytics. Those tools are fundamental for educators since, by using them, they would be granted comprehensive access to the complete dataset encompassing their students, thereby facilitating the provision of tailored assistance and diligent oversight. On the other side, students could access their individual performance metrics, thus promoting self-awareness and self-assessment.

By amalgamating these attributes within a unified platform, the Cyber Range encompasses the components commonly referred to as the Learning Content Management System (LCMS) utilized by instructors for content creation, and the Learning Management System (LMS), which serves as the arena for students' learning experiences [11]. Consequently, the application of the Learning Tools Interoperability (LTI) IMS standard presents an opportunity for Cyber Range platforms to function as external providers of cybersecurity exercises [16]. This, in turn, allows for the seamless integration of Cyber Range with other LMSs such as Sakai, Moodle, or Open edX, thereby facilitating the effective delivery of comprehensive cybersecurity courses encompassing both theoretical and practical components.

6   Conclusion

In this research paper, an analysis of eight Cyber Range platforms has been conducted, focusing on their features and capabilities. The principal objective was to comprehensively understand the significance involved in developing such powerful tools for cybersecurity education. Cyber Ranges offer a necessary and innovative approach to teaching cybersecurity to both students and professionals across various fields. With this mindset, a side-by-side comparison has been presented, leveraging detailed criteria and, thus, reaching a fair analysis of the selected tools.

Particularly, the study focuses on the generation of cybersecurity training scenarios since they represent one of the main limitations of the current Cyber Range ecosystem. Indeed, the simulation of large-scale networks for cyberattack scenarios can be highly resource-intensive and demanding in terms of performance. Additionally, generating a diverse set of exercises can be a time-consuming and challenging task. Some platforms, such as CyberBit CR and Airbus CyberRange, have opted to refrain from automating their scenario and topology generation processes. Instead, they rely on extensive exercise catalogs provided to their clients. Nonetheless, emerging tools like SecGen, CyExec*, and CRATE aim to address this issue by introducing new features for scenario randomization and automatic topology generation.

To foster the performed research, two existing approaches and platforms for topology generation have been reviewed, highlighting their strengths and limitations. Through the analysis, it is evident that a successful cybersecurity training environment requires scalable, diverse, and performance-oriented topology generation techniques.

Additionally, we have also discussed the trade-offs between container-based comprehensive platforms, such as CyExec*, and simpler yet resource-intensive VM-based platforms like SecGen. While CyExec* offers extensive capabilities, its labor-intensive preparations limit result randomization. On the other hand, SecGen provides simplicity but poses constraints due to its resource-intensive nature.

The future development of Cyber Range platforms should aim to address these challenges and strike a balance between comprehensiveness, resource efficiency, and diversity. Moreover, we have emphasized the potential of AI in enhancing Cyber Range platforms. Machine learning algorithms can automate scenario design, analyzing historical data to generate dynamic and diverse training scenarios. ML techniques can also enable adaptive user modeling, tailoring the training experience to individual needs and skill levels. Moreover, AI can simulate realistic network traffic patterns, providing immersive training experiences. However, it is crucial to prioritize ethical considerations when integrating AI into Cyber Range platforms. Responsible and ethical practices should be followed to safeguard user privacy, address biases, and ensure the responsible use of AI technologies. Finally, we have discussed the educational viewpoint of Cyber Range platforms, suggesting the use of tools to motivate the students and powerful learning analytics, while the integration with other LMS would be really appreciated.

Acknowledgements. This work has been supported by the Spanish Ministry of Universities linked to the European Union through the NextGenerationEU program, under Margarita Salas postdoctoral fellowship (172/MSJD/22). The work represents as well a contribution to the International Alliance for Strengthening Cybersecurity and Privacy in Healthcare (CybAlliance, Project no. 337316).

References

1. Almroth, J., Gustafsson, T.: Crate exercise control-a cyber defense exercise management and support tool. In: 2020 IEEE European Symposium on Security and Privacy (EuroS&P) Workshops, pp. 37–45. IEEE (2020)
2. Bécue, A., Maia, E., Feeken, L., Borchers, P., Praça, I.: A new concept of digital twin supporting optimization and resilience of factories of the future. Appl. Sci. **10**(13) (2020)
3. Chadha, R., et al.: Cybervan: a cyber security virtual assured network testbed, pp. 1125–1130, 11 2016
4. Chouliaras, N., et al.: Cyber ranges and testbeds for education, training, and research. Appl. Sci. **11**, 1809 (2021)
5. Cyberbit. Cyber security training platform (2023). https://www.cyberbit.com/blog/security-training/cyber-security-training-platform/. Accessed 21 Jun 2023
6. Gustafsson, T., Almroth, J.: Cyber range automation overview with a case study of crate. 11 2020
7. Han, J., Xian, M., Liu, J., Wang, H.: Research on the application of artificial intelligence in cyber range. J. Phys. Conf. Ser. **2030**, 012084 (2021)
8. Mekler, E.D., Brühlmann, F., Opwis, K., Tuch, A.N.: Do points, levels and leaderboards harm intrinsic motivation? an empirical analysis of common gamification elements. In: Proceedings of the First International Conference on Gameful Design, Research, and Applications, pp. 66–73 (2013)

9. Nakata, R., Otsuka, A.: Cyexec*: a high-performance container-based cyber range with scenario randomization. IEEE Access **9**, 109095–109114 (2021)
10. Nakata, R., Otsuka, A.: Cyexec*: automatic generation of randomized cyber range scenarios. In: International Conference on Information Systems Security and Privacy (2021)
11. Ninoriya, S., Chawan, P.M., Meshram, B.B.: Cms, lms and lcms for elearning. Int. J. Comput. Sci. Iss. (IJCSI) **8**(2), 644 (2011)
12. European Cyber Security Organisation. Understanding cyber ranges: From hype to reality (2020)
13. Russo, E., Costa, G., Armando, A.: Scenario design and validation for next generation cyber ranges. In: 2018 IEEE 17th International Symposium on Network Computing and Applications (NCA), pp. 1–4 (2018)
14. Russo, E., Costa, G., Armando, A.: Building next generation cyber ranges with crack. Comput. Secur. **95**, 101837 (2020)
15. Schreuders, Z.C., Shaw, T., Shan-A-Khuda, M., Ravichandran, G., Keighley, J., Ordean, M.: Security scenario generator (SecGen): a framework for generating randomly vulnerable rich-scenario VMs for learning computer security and hosting CTF events. In: 2017 USENIX Workshop on Advances in Security Education (ASE 17), Vancouver, BC, August 2017. USENIX Association
16. Antonio J Sierra, Álvaro Martín-Rodríguez, Teresa Ariza, Javier Muñoz-Calle, and Francisco J Fernández-Jiménez. Lti for interoperating e-assessment tools with lms. In Methodologies and Intelligent Systems for Technology Enhanced Learning: 6th International Conference, pages 173–181. Springer, 2016
17. Tioh, J.-N., Mina, M., Jacobson, D.W.: Cyber security training a survey of serious games in cyber security. In: 2017 IEEE Frontiers in Education Conference (FIE), pp. 1–5. IEEE (2017)
18. Ukwandu, E., et al.: A review of cyber-ranges and test-beds: Current and future trends. Sensors **20**(24), 7148 (2020)
19. Updyke, D., Dobson, G., Podnar, T., Osterritter, L., Earl, B., Cerini, A.: Ghosts in the machine: a framework for cyber-warfare exercise npc simulation. 12 2018
20. Venkatesan, S., et al.: Vulnervan: a vulnerable network generation tool. 11 2019
21. Vykopal, J., Ošlejšek, R., Celeda, P., Vizváry, M., Tovarňák, D.: Kypo cyber range: design and use cases, pp. 310–321, January 2017
22. Yamin, M.M., Katt, B.: Modeling and executing cyber security exercise scenarios in cyber ranges. Comput. Secur. **116**, 102635 (2022)
23. Yamin, M.M., Katt, B., Gkioulos, V.: Cyber ranges and security testbeds: Scenarios, functions, tools and architecture. Comput. Secur. **88**, 101636 (2020)

Forkfuzz: Leveraging the Fork-Awareness in Coverage-Guided Fuzzing

Marcello Maugeri[1]([✉]) [iD], Cristian Daniele[2] [iD], and Giampaolo Bella[1] [iD]

[1] University of Catania, Catania, Italy
marcello.maugeri@phd.unict.it, giamp@dmi.unict.it
[2] Radboud University, Nijmegen, Netherlands
cristian.daniele@ru.nl

Abstract. Fuzzing is a widely adopted technique for automated vulnerability testing due to its effectiveness and applicability throughout the Software Development Life Cycle. Nevertheless, applying fuzzing "out of the box" to any system can prove to be a challenging endeavour. Consequently, the demand for target-specific solutions necessitates a substantial amount of manual intervention, which diverges from the automated nature typically associated with fuzzing. For example, prior research identified the lack of a solution for testing multi-process systems effectively. The problem is that coverage-guided fuzzers do not consider the possibility of having a system with more than one process. In this paper, we present *Forkfuzz*, a "fork-aware" fuzzer able to deal with multi-process systems. To the best of our knowledge, *Forkfuzz* is the first *fork-aware* fuzzer. It is built on top of Honggfuzz, one of the most popular and effective coverage-guided fuzzers, as reported by the *Fuzzbench* benchmark. To show its effectiveness, we tested our fuzzer over two classical programming problems: the *Dining Philosophers Problem* and a version of the *Producer-Consumer Problem* where the consumer (the child) process crashes for specific inputs. Furthermore, we evaluated *Forkfuzz* against a real and more complex scenario involving an HTTP server that handles multiple connections through multiple processes. The results of our evaluation demonstrate the effectiveness of *Forkfuzz* in identifying crashes and timeouts. Finally, we discuss possible improvements and challenges for the development and application of *fork-aware* fuzzing techniques.

Keywords: fuzzing · automated vulnerability testing · multi-process system · security testing · concurrent programming

1 Introduction

Fuzzing is currently considered a standard technique, within the larger security testing process, to achieve software correctness. The concept is quite straightforward: it involves the repetitive execution of a *SUT (System-Under-Test)* with various inputs, including malformed ones, in order to uncover bugs [14]. In particular, fuzzing excels at identifying critical bugs such as crashes and timeouts,

S. Katsikas et al. (Eds.): ESORICS 2023 Workshops, LNCS 14399, pp. 291–308, 2024.
https://doi.org/10.1007/978-3-031-54129-2_17

which play a pivotal role in vulnerability analysis. These observable anomalies serve as indicators of potential weaknesses in software. Given that bugs are an intrinsic aspect of program code, the significance of fuzzing in the software development landscape is undeniable. Its substantial potential lies in its ability to enhance software reliability and security for the future [24]. However, various challenges lie at the horizon of fuzzing. Notably, tailoring fuzzing to multi-process systems is still daunting at present, and our research stands on the observation that modern coverage-guided fuzzers, albeit generally powerful, may not succeed in capturing misbehaviour in child processes. This limitation is known as the "fork-awareness" problem [15], where the fuzzer may not properly account for the behaviour of child processes hence for the potentially undiscovered bugs in the overall system.

In this study, we present *Forkfuzz*, a new fuzzer to tackle the problem outlined above. Based on *Honggfuzz*[1], it seems fair to argue that *Forkfuzz* is the first *fork-aware* coverage-guided fuzzer. *Forkfuzz* leverages the *ptrace* system call[2] to monitor child processes and maintains a set of process identifiers to keep track of them. *Forkfuzz* is first demonstrated on two classical concurrency problems: the *Dining Philosophers Problem (DPP)* and the *Producer-Consumer Problem (PCP)*. As a practical test case, we then execute *Forkfuzz* on a distributed, open-source project delivering a web server that handles multiple connections through the use of multiple processes.

Overall, our experiments demonstrate the ability of our fuzzer to effectively identify vulnerabilities in complex, multi-process systems. It is worth noting that these experiments are reproducible as both the code of our fuzzer and the experiment code are available as open source[3]. Intentionally, all of our case studies feature bugs of varying nature, so that our tool can be widely evaluated, ultimately offering a solid baseline for further developments and applications.

The article is structured as follows. Section 2 presents the background, Sect. 3 describes notable and related works in the state-of-the-art. Section 4 provides an overview of the overall scenario and explains the *fork-awareness* property at the foundation of this study. Section 5 presents the first *fork-aware* fuzzer, *Forkfuzz*, evaluated on three different case studies described in Sect. 6. Finally, Sect. 7 discusses limitations and future directions while the last section summarises the key findings.

2   Background

In Computer Science, a *process* is an instance of a computer program executed by the Central Processing Unit (CPU) [25]. Essentially, every running program is a process. Each process is associated with the address space, a list of memory locations that contain the executable program, its stack and data. In addition, every process has registers, open files, and signals. Furthermore, each process

---

[1] https://github.com/google/honggfuzz.
[2] https://man7.org/linux/man-pages/man2/ptrace.2.html.
[3] https://github.com/marcellomaugeri/forkfuzz.

has its unique identifier, called Process ID or *pid*, which helps to distinguish between different processes.

Sometimes, multiple processes may need to work together to achieve a common goal. Henceforth, this work will refer to such a scenario as a *system*. For example, a web server may spawn multiple processes to handle incoming client requests [9]. Each process would be responsible for serving a subset of the requests, and they would communicate with each other to ensure that all requests are handled efficiently.

In a similar scenario, the web server must be capable of spawning processes as needed. In UNIX systems, new processes can be created by invoking the *fork* system call. This system call creates a new process, called the child process, which is an exact copy of the process that made the call, also known as the parent process. The primary distinction between the two is their *pid*. After the *fork*, both processes go their separate ways and accomplish their respective tasks, possibly *fork* again, e.g. when the server receives a new request.

It should be noted that parent and child are still associated with each other and form a *process hierarchy*. In UNIX, a process and its descendants form a *process group*. The primary use of a process group is to facilitate the management of multiple processes simultaneously. For example, a process could simultaneously send signals to all processes within its group. This applies when all processes in a web server are notified when the configuration file is updated. Another example regards a process within the group that encounters an error. In such cases, the affected process could send a signal to other processes in the group to notify them of the issue. Then, the other processes can take appropriate measures to mitigate the problem.

When mitigation is not accomplished correctly, or worse, is not even considered, the bug causes the program to behave unexpectedly or incorrectly. Consequently, the bug can result in a vulnerability that a malicious attacker can exploit to gain unauthorised access, steal data or disrupt the system. Therefore, it is essential to identify and mitigate bugs using secure coding practices, debugging and testing. In particular, debugging involves identifying and fixing errors and anomalies in the system. On the other hand, testing is validating the functional requirements, performance, and security of a system.

One way to debug a process is to use the *ptrace* system call. *ptrace* allows a process to trace the execution of another process. With *ptrace*, a process called "tracer" can inspect and modify the memory, registers, and system calls of the "tracee" process. This feature is handy for debugging since it allows developers to monitor the behaviour of a process and identify issues. As a result, it can be used for building up sophisticated tools for analysing and testing software, such as debuggers, dynamic analysers, and fuzzers. Additionally, *ptrace* can inject code into a process or modify its behaviour, making it a powerful tool for vulnerability research and exploitation. For instance, *ptrace* is used in *Honggfuzz* as the interface to monitor processes during the fuzzing campaign under *Linux* and *NetBSD*.

Honggfuzz is a popular fuzzer developed by *Robert Święcki* that uses coverage-guided fuzzing to perform automated software testing. In common with many coverage-guided fuzzers, it repeatedly executes a *SUT* with various inputs, known as test cases, to trigger unexpected or erroneous behaviour. Specifically, test cases are generated by applying random mutations on valid inputs provided by the tester, known as seeds. While the program runs, *Honggfuzz* monitors code coverage using instrumentation and generates new test cases based on the feedback it receives. This process continues until a bug is found or a predetermined number of iterations is reached [12].

3   Related Work

The field of fuzzing has seen a lot of developments in recent years, with a wide range of fuzzing tools available for various purposes. One major approach to fuzzing is *coverage-guided fuzzing*, which leverages the code coverage reached during the execution to steer the generation of new inputs to explore deeper areas of the code.

Among the coverage-guided fuzzers, *American Fuzzy Lop (AFL)*[4] and its successor *AFL++* [7] have emerged as an effective fuzzer for finding vulnerabilities and have been the basis for the development of other fuzzers [8,13,17,21]. Unfortunately, the mechanism that *AFL++* uses to deal with the *SUT* makes it difficult to handle multiple processes. Making *AFL++ fork-aware* would mean modifying the core of the fuzzer allowing it to capture the process creation and termination. In particular, *AFL++* uses control pipes to communicate with the parent process of the *SUT* ignoring the existence of other processes.

On the contrary, *Honggfuzz* [23] uses the *ptrace* system call to monitor all the processes, making it manageable to integrate mechanisms to monitor timeouts and crashes also in the child processes. The *ptrace* system call has inspired the creation of several debugging tools [11] such as *gdb* and *ltrace*, as well as more complex dynamic analysis tools such as *DroidTrace* [27], which leverage its capabilities to monitor and control the execution of an Android app.

Another example is *strace*, which is used to monitor system calls made by a process and can also be used to monitor child processes. Actually, it has inspired the development of *MoonShine* [20] framework which leverages *strace* to collect execution traces of an application and then applies a trace distillation algorithm to identify the most promising seeds for a fuzzing campaign. The most promising seeds are then fed to *Syzkaller*[5], a state-of-the-art evolutionary fuzzer for the Linux kernel, to conduct a thorough fuzzing campaign.

Intercepting library calls is an approach to modify application behaviour, enabling runtime instrumentation and monitoring. Dynamic linking enables intercepting functions in shared libraries before application calls. This technique is employed by various tools, including the *Preeny* project, offering dynamically linkable libraries to modify the *SUT* behaviour. For instance, the *defork* module

---

[4] https://github.com/google/AFL.
[5] https://github.com/google/syzkaller.

intercepts the *fork* calls, making them ineffective. While the use of the *defork* module can disable the functionality of *fork()* and prevent the creation of child processes, it can also disrupt the parallelism of processes in the system, leading to a linear flow of execution. This may not be desirable in scenarios where concurrency is required for the system to function efficiently and correctly.

To address specific requirements as the aforementioned, testers often resort to adopting a specialised component known as a *harness*. The *harness* serves as a custom-coded solution that is meticulously crafted according to the specific *SUT*. Its primary purpose is to preserve the intended functionalities and validate for potential errors. However, it is important to note that the development of a *harness* entails considerable manual effort. This includes not only the creation of the *harness* itself but also the design process that requires a comprehensive understanding of the inner workings of the *SUT*. This stands in contrast to the ongoing research in the field of fuzzing, which aims to enhance the automation and user-friendliness of fuzzing techniques across various scenarios [2].

In particular, when dealing with concurrent software, preserving the ability to run multiple processes or threads in parallel is crucial to maintain the functionalities of a system. To address this challenge, researchers have developed fuzzers specifically tailored for testing concurrent systems. Two notable examples are *ConFuzz* [19] and *CONZZER* [10]. *ConFuzz* uses assertions in concurrent *OCaml* programs to detect new program schedules and paths, leading to assertion failures. In contrast, *CONZZER* provides a more general solution by exploring thread interleavings and detecting hard-to-find data races. Furthermore, *Muzz* [3] represents another notable contribution to the field of *thread-awareness*. This fuzzer takes into account various thread interleavings resulting from the scheduler, enabling the detection of concurrency vulnerabilities and bugs. However, these fuzzers are suitable to detect concurrency bugs in multi-threaded systems only and are not designed for detecting bugs in multi-process systems.

4   Motivational Scenario

The study introduces a scenario that involves a software system S. At the outset of S, its first process P_0 begins its execution. At a particular stage, it could initiate the *fork* system call. As a result, the call creates an identical copy of P_0, named P_1. Following this, both P_0 and P_1 run independently. After, both P_0 or P_1 could possibly *fork* again, resulting in a new process P_2, P_3 or, more generally, P_i.

To exemplify this scenario, Fig. 1 illustrates a web server as an example. In this setup, the primary server process, denoted as P_0, plays the role of receiving incoming requests. When a client sends a request, P_0 invokes the *fork* system call to create a new worker process, represented as P_i. P_i is then responsible for handling the request from the client. When fuzzing such a sophisticated system, the implications are various.

First, P_i is prone to encountering bugs while handling the request. For example, suppose the server expects a request with a specific format or content, but a

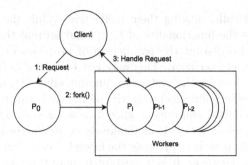

Fig. 1. Example of a forking server

malicious client sends a request with a completely different format or with invalid data. If the server is not designed to handle the request and does not have proper input validation and error-handling mechanisms, it may crash or behave unpredictably. Consequently, to effectively fuzz-test a system, it is crucial to use a fuzzer that detects bugs regardless of the process involved, as depicted in Fig. 2.

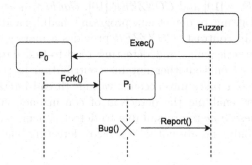

Fig. 2. Fuzzer capturing bugs from a child process

Second, capturing the cumulative code coverage of every process P_i plays a pivotal role in effectively fuzzing S. This well-established mechanism enables the fuzzer to generate new inputs that can uncover uncharted parts of the code, thereby enhancing the likelihood of uncovering previously undetected vulnerabilities.

Thirdly, it is essential to address the potential impact of a maliciously crafted request, which has the capability to instigate a denial-of-service scenario. When such an attack occurs, the performance of the server may be severely affected, leading to unresponsiveness or a significant slowdown [26]. Consequently, the execution time of processes can be prolonged beyond the expected limits, potentially triggering a timeout condition. This detrimental outcome not only diminishes the overall user experience but also poses a significant risk of revenue loss for the affected organisation.

These three considerations described can be applied to any process in the system, resulting in the definition of the "fork-awareness" property. This property refers to the ability of a fuzzer to test each process of an entire system in the same manner. In other words, a "fork-aware" fuzzer should be able to: detect bugs, timeouts and code coverage from all the processes under test [15]. Consequently, such a fuzzer would thoroughly and accurately test the system for potential bugs and vulnerabilities.

The impact of this work lies in the importance of the *fork* system call as a widely used pattern in many software systems. The ability to spawn new processes and run them independently is crucial for the efficiency and scalability of many applications, such as servers and operating systems. Moreover, in operating systems, the *fork* system call is essential for creating new processes and managing resources, enabling the system to run multiple applications concurrently.

Another example of the use of *fork* is for creating daemon processes, background processes that continuously run and perform tasks, usually by forking a new process and letting the parent process exit.

Overall, the use of *fork* is a well-established pattern in systems programming and provides an efficient way to create new processes that run independently of the parent process. As an illustration, a simple search for *fork()* on GitHub Search[6] returns over 500,000 C or C++ files, indicating the prevalence and importance of the *fork* system call in modern software development.

Understanding the implications of *fork*, particularly in the context of fuzz testing, is crucial for developing effective testing strategies that can detect bugs and vulnerabilities in complex systems. Building upon this concept, we have developed *Forkfuzz* and its corresponding workflow, which will be presented in the next section.

5   Forkfuzz

The workflow of *Forkfuzz* follows quite the same as *Honggfuzz*. To simplify the description, it can be dissected into three steps: setup, execution and termination as shown in Figs. 3, 4, 5 and 6. In the figures, the novel contribution is highlighted in blue.

5.1   Setup Step

First, *Forkfuzz* parses command line arguments and opens necessary files such as a dictionary of keywords or other interesting byte sequences, as well as a file containing a set of valid inputs for the *SUT*. Additionally, it prepares the signal handler for managing the fuzzing threads and constructs the required data structures, such as the coverage map, to manage the fuzzing campaign.

---

[6] https://github.com/search?q=fork%28%29+%28language%3AC+OR+language %3AC%2B%2B%29&type=code.

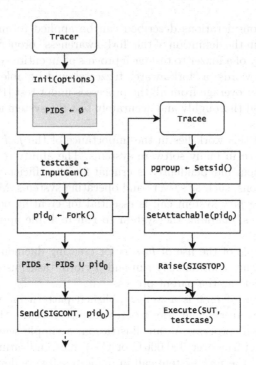

Fig. 3. Setup step

To keep track of all the processes active on the system during fuzzing, it is necessary to store their identifiers. To achieve this, we defined a novel set data structure $PIDS$. The $PIDS$ set contains an array of type pid_t and its length. The pid_t type is a built-in data type in C that represents a process identifier. After the fuzzer initialisation, the target initialisation begins.

First of all, the fuzzer generates the test case mutating the seeds. This test case is then passed to the System Under Test (SUT) as an argument, either through standard input or via a socket using the Netdriver module[7]. The SUT execution will happen in a process called *Tracee*, which is created by forking the main process of *Forkfuzz*, named *Tracer*. Note that *Tracer* and *Tracee* naming follow the *ptrace* nomenclature.

Before the actual execution of the SUT, the *Tracee* performs two important operations:

- it sets up a new process group using the *setsid()* function;
- sets itself as traceable by setting the $PR\_SET\_DUMPABLE$ flag.

By instantiating a new process group, it is possible to keep track of all descendant processes at once. Moreover, by enabling the $PR\_SET\_DUMPABLE$ flag, the process becomes attachable by the *ptrace* system call. After that, the *Tracee*

---

[7] https://github.com/google/honggfuzz/tree/master/libhfnetdriver.

blocks by raising a *SIGSTOP* signal in order to wait for also the *Tracer* to be ready to start.

Meanwhile, the *Tracer* records the identifier pid_0 of the new process in the *PIDS* set and starts tracing it with *ptrace*. Next, the *Tracer* sends a *SIGCONT* signal, allowing the *Tracee* to resume execution. The next step for *Tracee* is to call the *exec* function on the *SUT* with the test case generated earlier. At this point, the *Tracee* image is replaced with the *SUT* and the actual test begins.

5.2   Execution Step

With the help of *ptrace*, the fuzzer is able to trace and monitor the events that occur while the *SUT* is running. The *Tracer* continuously performs the *waitpid* function over the process group previously set to capture events. When one of the *SUT* processes stops, it means that something occurred, hence, an event happened. Then, the fuzzer analyses the event to determine its nature.

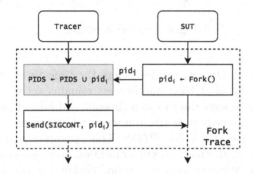

Fig. 4. Fork event tracing

Forkfuzz can handle two events: the invocation of two system calls - *fork* and *exit*. The *fork()* system call is captured using the *PTRACE_EVENT_FORK* option, allowing the *Tracer* to capture the identifier pid_i of the new process, add it to the *PIDS* set, and resume the *SUT* execution by sending a *SIGCONT* signal. Notably, the option also allows the fuzzer to start tracing the newly forked process automatically and looks for events that occur within it.

Additionally, if a process calls *exit()*, the pid_i of the calling process is removed from the *PIDS* set. If pid_i has terminated its execution in an unexpected manner, it raised a signal, which will be reported as a crash. In either case, the execution of the SUT resumes by sending a SIGCONT signal. These two steps are crucial for tracking all processes throughout their entire life cycle.

5.3   Termination Step

After tracing all the descendant processes, *Forkfuzz* waits for all of them to finish executing. If all the processes conclude the execution within the specified

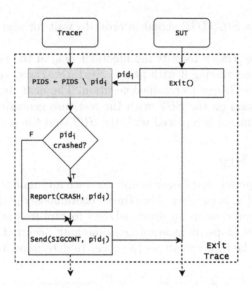

Fig. 5. Exit event tracing

time limit, i.e. the $PIDS$ set empties before the timeout expires, the run ends successfully. However, if at least one process remains active at the end of the time slot, *Forkfuzz* reports the run as a timeout and kills all pending processes.

In addition, it succeeds to notify the tester which process went into a timeout exactly, since it is still inside $PIDS$. This operation ensures that *Forkfuzz* can detect and report all bugs and vulnerabilities, even in complex systems with multiple processes. Without this operation, *Forkfuzz* would risk leaving some pending processes running indefinitely, potentially missing critical bugs or causing system instability, as $AFL++$ and other fuzzers do. Therefore, the ability of *Forkfuzz* to track and handle process termination is the core of the fuzzer since it can effectively fuzz multi-process systems.

To test the capabilities of the fuzzer, we carried out a series of evaluations using different case studies. The findings from these experiments are presented in the next section, along with a detailed analysis of the results.

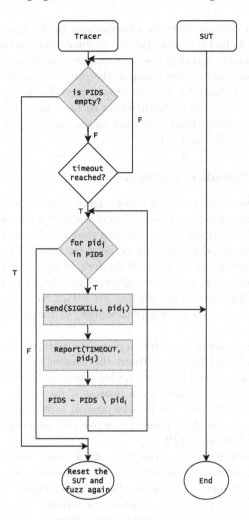

Fig. 6. Termination step

6   Evaluation

We evaluated the effectiveness of *Forkfuzz* through a series of experiments on:

1. The *Dining Philosophers Problem (DPP)*
2. A bug-injected version of the *Producer-Consumer Problem (PCP)* in which the consumer, executed in a child process, crashes for specific inputs.
3. A Web Server that employs a Fork-Based Process Model to handle multiple connections. In this scenario, the server invokes the *fork* system call to create a new process for each incoming connection, which presents a more complex and realistic use case for *Forkfuzz*.

The idea is to demonstrate the effectiveness of *Forkfuzz* on classical and realistic problems. In fact, the two classical problems presented have been chosen to evidence two possible and simple scenarios: one in which a child process hangs, while a child process experiences a bug in the other. In both classical problems, the parent process terminates its execution correctly. To apply such possible issues in a realistic case study, both scenarios have been transposed to a web server, as described throughout this work as an example. More details will be provided in Sects. 6.1, 6.2 and 6.3.

6.1 Dining Philosophers Problem

The *DPP* is a classic problem in computer science that *Edsger Dijkstra* described in 1971 [5]. It is an example of a synchronisation problem, which arises when multiple processes or threads access a shared resource. In the *DPP*, philosophers are seated at a round table with a fork between them. To eat, a philosopher must have both the fork to his left and the fork to his right. However, only one philosopher can hold each fork at any given time, which can lead to a deadlock in which all the philosophers are waiting for a fork to become available. As a result, each process (representing a philosopher) of the system stays in a hung state indefinitely.

This problem is useful to reproduce a plausible pattern where forked processes stay in a hung state indefinitely without the possibility of exiting. To avoid a process staying in a hung state and occupying resources, most fuzzers incorporate a timeout feature, which terminates a process if its execution time exceeds a specified limit. However, common fuzzers prevent only the parent process from getting stuck, leaving all child processes active and potentially filling the host memory, as is the case with *AFL++*.

Forkfuzz succeeds in detecting this kind of issue since it waits for all processes from the group to terminate by detecting the exit event. Consequently, if one or more processes remain active after the time slot expires, *Forkfuzz* deduces that they are probably stuck in a deadlock or infinite loop, reports them as a timeout, and terminates them. The tester can adjust the timeout by estimating the plausible duration of normal execution.

6.2 Producer-Consumer Problem

The *PCP* [6] is another classic computer science synchronisation problem involving two types of processes: producers and consumers. Producers generate data items and place them into a shared buffer, while the consumers remove the data items from the buffer and process them. The problem relies on ensuring that producers do not try to add data items to the buffer when it is full, causing a buffer overflow. Additionally, consumers should not try to remove them from the buffer when it is empty. In the setup proposed, the access to the shared buffer is handled correctly and the two processes do not interfere with each other.

The parent process is designated as the producer, and, as such, it reads strings from the standard input and sends them to the shared message queue.

Once all input strings have been sent to the queue, the parent process sends the message *quit* to the queue and then terminates. The child process is designated as the consumer and is responsible for reading messages from a shared message queue. Once a message is received, the consumer reverses the string and checks if it is a palindrome. However, if the condition is verified, the program crashes abnormally. This behaviour is simulated using the *abort* function. Otherwise, the child process terminates correctly if the message is *quit*.

This case study outlines a situation in which the parent and child processes are loosely coupled. In fact, after the *fork* call, both processes go in their separate ways. The producer sends messages without notice if the consumer is reading. Ultimately, it terminates its execution without waiting for the child process to finish. Meanwhile, the consumer processes messages and possibly experiences a bug.

However, *AFL*-based fuzzers in their default configuration wait for the *SUT* to terminate and receive its exit status through a control pipe, which allows them to detect only one exit code per run. This limitation can be problematic when multiple processes are involved, such as in the *PCP* scenario. In contrast, *Honggfuzz* and *Forkfuzz* detect signals on a low level, which allows them to inspect multiple signals and identify which process crashes. This capability makes *Forkfuzz* a suitable fuzzer for testing scenarios that involve multiple processes, such as the *PCP* scenario, where crashes may occur in the consumer (child) process.

6.3   Web Server

The third case study focuses on a web server, which presents different challenges in terms of testing due to the complexity and variability of web applications. Unlike command-line programs, web servers take input through a network socket, so the fuzzer needs to send input over the network. To achieve this, we leveraged the *Netdriver* module of *Honggfuzz*, which waits for the target to be available on a predetermined port before injecting input[8].

Another challenge when fuzzing a web server is caused by the underlying protocol. Although HTTP is a stateless protocol, the server can still maintain an internal state. For example, certain operations may require a user to be logged in and have specific privileges. In this case study, we will not address the stateful nature of web servers, but there is extensive literature on related works [4].

In our case study, the complexity of the web server fuzzing task increased due to the use of a forking model for request handling. In this model, the main process accepts incoming connections and then delegates the handling of those connections to child processes created by *fork*. As a result, each child process operates independently of the others, introducing a level of concurrency and potential race conditions. This presents a challenge for the fuzzer, which must be able to track and monitor the behaviour of these child processes. Failure to

---

[8] http://blog.swiecki.net/2018/01/fuzzing-tcp-servers.html.

do so could result in missed bugs and other issues that arise from the concurrent execution of multiple processes.

Our setup is based on an open-source implementation in C of the described web server model[9]. This server exposes different endpoints that respond to GET and POST methods. In particular, when the GET method is invoked on a non-existent path, the server attempts to retrieve the corresponding file from the public directory. However, the code has a character limit on the path length. As a result, if a user sends a request that exceeds this limit, the server becomes vulnerable to a buffer overflow attack.

In addition to the buffer overflow vulnerability, we have added a dangerous request that can make the server susceptible to a Denial-of-Service (DoS) attack. In particular, the "is_prime" POST request takes a number as input and applies a primality test: the simple trial division algorithm [1]. This algorithm has a complexity of $\mathcal{O}(\sqrt{n})$ and, for big numbers could take several seconds or even minutes to execute, depending on the machine it is running on. Therefore, the role of this algorithm is to simulate a scenario in which an attacker could send multiple requests with large inputs, which would keep the server occupied and disrupt the service.

As expected, *Forkfuzz* was able to detect both issues, particularly the second, which is challenging to identify with standard fuzzers. While timeouts are typically included in most fuzzers, they may not be sufficient to identify issues with forked child processes. Overall, our findings highlight the effectiveness of *Forkfuzz* in detecting both crash and timeout issues both in classical and realistic scenarios. Additional discussion follows in Sect. 7.

6.4 Performance

The performance of *Forkfuzz* was evaluated in multiple case studies, and the results were promising. Forkfuzz is built on top of *Honggfuzz*, one of the most effective coverage-guided fuzzers as reported by Fuzzbench benchmark [16]. The fundamental difference between Forkfuzz and Honggfuzz is the management of multiple processes.

"Fork-awareness" is upheld through a set of Process IDs ($PIDS$), which is updated upon new process creation and process termination. Adding entries to $PIDS$ is a swift $O(1)$ operation, while removing them, with an $O(n)$ complexity, marginally impacts overhead during both addition and deletion.

Note that overhead may rise in systems with numerous processes during a single run, though this is uncommon. In summary, *Forkfuzz* performs comparably to *Honggfuzz*, with negligible overhead on typical systems.

---

[9] https://github.com/foxweb/pico.

7 Discussion

7.1 Limitations

In many cases, the *fork* system call is used with the *wait* and *waitpid* functions, forming the *fork-join* mechanism [18]. This mechanism involves the parent process creating a child process for a separate task and then waiting for the child process to complete.

Consequently, Forkfuzz does not exhibit a substantial distinction from other fuzzers in terms of handling timeouts, since they all wait for the parent process to conclude. As a result, if the child processes become unresponsive, the parent process will persist in waiting, ultimately resulting in a timeout. It is worth noting that the *AFL* family of fuzzers does not inherently identify bugs within the child process. Therefore, if the parent process does not detect misbehaviour in the child process, AFL fuzzers will never spot the bugs.

Forkfuzz excels when testing systems with loosely-coupled processes, where each process operates independently and follows its own distinct path. In such scenarios, where processes operate independently without strong dependencies or synchronisation requirements, *Forkfuzz* excels in automatically detecting bugs and timeouts that may remain undetected by the individual processes within the system. In other words, if the processes within the system are already capable of notifying errors themselves, *Forkfuzz* may not provide significant additional benefits.

An additional limitation arises from the absence of the persistent mode. Persistent mode [7] is a fuzzing strategy that improves performance by running the *SUT* within the same process instead of creating a new one for each test case. Enabling this mode needs more precise management of the *PIDS* set, which remains an area for future improvement.

7.2 Aggregated Coverage

Forkfuzz currently employs aggregate code coverage without distinguishing individual process contributions. Future work may investigate the benefits of separate coverage maps per process, offering insights into their coverage and enhancing fuzzing accuracy.

Furthermore, this technique would be especially valuable for processes using the *fork-exec* paradigm, where the child process is replaced with another program [22]. Capturing separate coverage maps for multiple programs in a single fuzzing run would allow independent coverage assessment.

7.3 Areas of Improvement

Distributed Fuzzing. The concept underlying this research is to conduct parallel fuzzing of concurrent processes. Building upon this concept, it is possible to explore concurrent processes running on different machines, thereby forming a distributed system. As a future direction, this idea can be extended to encompass concurrent and distributed software. The objective is to investigate whether simultaneously fuzzing the entire system can yield improvements in terms of performance, code coverage, and the effectiveness of bug detection.

Real-World Benchmark. *Forkfuzz* has been evaluated through a series of simple, yet realistic, case studies. The objective was to provide a clear explanation of the approach while demonstrating its effectiveness. However, it is important to note that future work will involve testing the approach on real-world systems.

Extending Support to Non-Linux Systems. Expanding *Forkfuzz* to support software on non-Linux systems is another crucial direction. While *Forkfuzz* currently focuses on fuzzing software using the *fork* system call in Linux, there is a need to address other process creation mechanisms such as the Windows *CreateProcess* function and their equivalents in various operating systems. We plan to enhance the applicability of *Forkfuzz*, enabling the detection of bugs in a broader spectrum of software systems.

Concurrency Bugs. One of the major challenges in concurrent software testing is the presence of concurrency bugs. These bugs occur due to the interleaving of processes running concurrently, where different schedules can produce different results. *Muzz* [3] addresses this challenge by adjusting thread priorities and manipulating execution orders to uncover potential concurrency bugs. This approach helps in systematically exploring different execution paths and identifying vulnerabilities that may only manifest under specific interleavings. As future work, further enhancements can be made to systematically execute processes in different orders, effectively expanding the exploration space and increasing the chances of discovering subtle concurrency bugs.

8   Concluding Remarks

Although state-of-the-art fuzzers have proven very effective in finding bugs and timeouts in the parent process of the target system, we found that they are somewhat limited over child processes. This paper presented *Forkfuzz*, a new fuzzer based on *Honggfuzz* capable of inspecting child processes. *Forkfuzz* was verified over three case studies, and the findings are:

- In the *Dining Philosophers Problem* case study, *Forkfuzz* identifies a timeout;
- In the *Producer Consumer Problem* case study, *Forkfuzz* detects an artificial bug occurring in the child process;
- In the web server case study, *Forkfuzz* finds a buffer overflow vulnerability and a denial of service (DOS) attack.

It is evident from our experiments that *Forkfuzz* serves as a valid fuzzer for identifying bugs and timeouts in child processes. Also, it sheds light on the importance of fuzzer awareness of the multi-process nature of the *SUT*.

Furthermore, we discussed limitations in current approaches, including creating harnesses and sequential process flattening using methods such as *defork*. These discussions emphasise the ongoing research focus on automating fuzzing techniques, where *Forkfuzz* aligns with the goal of enhancing the automation and effectiveness of fuzzing.

Beyond our experiments, we outlined future directions addressing concurrency bugs and distributed system testing challenges. By systematically exploring different execution orders and scheduling patterns, future work can further enhance *Forkfuzz* to detect concurrency-related vulnerabilities effectively. By incorporating these advancements, *Forkfuzz* strives to enhance its capabilities and contribute to the overall progress of automated fuzz testing methodologies.

Acknowledgements. We would like to express our gratitude to the Consortium GARR for providing us with the necessary cloud services to conduct our experiments and evaluation. Giampaolo Bella acknowledges financial support from: PNRR MUR project PE0000013-FAIR.

References

1. Barnes, C.: Integer factorization algorithms. Oregon State University (2004)
2. Böhme, M., Cadar, C., Roychoudhury, A.: Fuzzing: challenges and reflections. IEEE Softw. **38**(3), 79–86 (2020)
3. Chen, H., et al.: MUZZ: thread-aware grey-box fuzzing for effective bug hunting in multithreaded programs. In: 29th USENIX Security Symposium (USENIX Security 20), pp. 2325–2342. USENIX Association, August 2020. https://www.usenix.org/conference/usenixsecurity20/presentation/chen-hongxu
4. Daniele, C., Andarzian, S.B., Poll, E.: Fuzzers for stateful systems: Survey and research directions. arXiv preprint arXiv:2301.02490 (2023)
5. Dijkstra, E.W.: Hierarchical ordering of sequential processes. Acta Informatica **1**, 115–138 (1971)
6. https://archive.org/details/programminglangu0000unse_a7l4/page/n3/mode/2up
7. Fioraldi, A., Maier, D., Eißfeldt, H., Heuse, M.: Afl++ combining incremental steps of fuzzing research. In: Proceedings of the 14th USENIX Conference on Offensive Technologies, pp. 10–10 (2020)
8. Fioraldi, A., Mantovani, A., Maier, D., Balzarotti, D.: Dissecting American fuzzy lop-a fuzzbench evaluation. ACM Trans. Softw. Eng. Methodol. (2023)
9. Halsall, F.: Computer Networking and the Internet. Pearson Education (2006). https://books.google.it/books?id=RvW-6t-uwaYC
10. Jiang, Z.M., Bai, J.J., Lu, K., Hu, S.M.: Context-sensitive and directional concurrency fuzzing for data-race detection. In: Proceedings of the 29th Network and Distributed System Security Symposium (NDSS) (2022)
11. Keniston, J., Mavinakayanahalli, A., Panchamukhi, P., Prasad, V.: Ptrace, utrace, uprobes: Lightweight, dynamic tracing of user apps. In: Proceedings of the 2007 Linux Symposium, pp. 215–224 (2007)
12. Li, J., Zhao, B., Zhang, C.: Fuzzing: a survey. Cybersecurity **1**(1), 1–13 (2018)
13. Lyu, C., et al.: Mopt: optimized mutation scheduling for fuzzers. In: USENIX Security Symposium, pp. 1949–1966 (2019)

14. Manès, V.J., et al.: The art, science, and engineering of fuzzing: a survey. IEEE Trans. Software Eng. **47**(11), 2312–2331 (2019)
15. Maugeri., M., Daniele., C., Bella., G., Poll., E.: Evaluating the fork-awareness of coverage-guided fuzzers. In: Proceedings of the 9th International Conference on Information Systems Security and Privacy - ICISSP, pp. 424–429. INSTICC, SciTePress (2023). https://doi.org/10.5220/0011648600003405
16. Metzman, J., Szekeres, L., Simon, L., Sprabery, R., Arya, A.: Fuzzbench: an open fuzzer benchmarking platform and service. In: Proceedings of the 29th ACM Joint Meeting on European Software Engineering Conference and Symposium on the Foundations of Software Engineering, pp. 1393–1403 (2021)
17. Natella, R.: Stateafl: Greybox fuzzing for stateful network servers. Empir. Softw. Eng. **27**(7), 191 (2022)
18. Nyman, L., Laakso, M.: Notes on the history of fork and join. IEEE Ann. Hist. Comput. **38**(3), 84–87 (2016). https://doi.org/10.1109/MAHC.2016.34
19. Padhiyar, S., Sivaramakrishnan, K.C.: ConFuzz: coverage-guided property fuzzing for event-driven programs. In: Morales, J.F., Orchard, D. (eds.) PADL 2021. LNCS, vol. 12548, pp. 127–144. Springer, Cham (2021). https://doi.org/10.1007/978-3-030-67438-0_8
20. Pailoor, S., Aday, A., Jana, S.: Moonshine: optimizing os fuzzer seed selection with trace distillation. In: USENIX Security Symposium, pp. 729–743 (2018)
21. Pham, V.T., Böhme, M., Roychoudhury, A.: Aflnet: a greybox fuzzer for network protocols. In: 2020 IEEE 13th International Conference on Software Testing, Validation and Verification (ICST), pp. 460–465. IEEE (2020)
22. Stevens, W.R., Rago, S.A., Ritchie, D.M.: Advanced programming in the UNIX environment, vol. 4. Addison-Wesley New York. (1992)
23. Swiecki, R.: Honggfuzz. https://code.google.com/p/honggfuzz (2016)
24. Takanen, A., Demott, J.D., Miller, C., Kettunen, A.: Fuzzing for software security testing and quality assurance. Artech House (2018)
25. Tanenbaum, A.S., Bos, H.: Modern Operating Systems, 4th edn. Prentice Hall Press, USA (2014)
26. Tripathi, N., Hubballi, N., Singh, Y.: How secure are web servers? an empirical study of slow http dos attacks and detection. In: 2016 11th International Conference on Availability, Reliability and Security (ARES), pp. 454–463 (2016). https://doi.org/10.1109/ARES.2016.20
27. Zheng, M., Sun, M., Lui, J.C.: Droidtrace: a ptrace based android dynamic analysis system with forward execution capability. In: 2014 International Wireless Communications and Mobile Computing Conference (IWCMC), pp. 128–133. IEEE (2014)

Trust Assumptions in Voting Systems

Kristjan Krips[1,2], Nikita Snetkov[1,3] ⓘ, Jelizaveta Vakarjuk[1,3] ⓘ,
and Jan Willemson[1(✉)] ⓘ

[1] Cybernetica AS, Mäealuse 2/1, 12618 Tallinn, Estonia
{kristjan.krips,nikita.snetkov,jelizaveta.vakarjuk,
jan.willemson}@cyber.ee
[2] Institute of Computer Science, University of Tartu, Narva mnt 18, Tartu, Estonia
[3] Tallinn University of Technology, Akadeemia tee 15a, 12618 Tallinn, Estonia

Abstract. Assessing and comparing the security level of different voting systems is non-trivial as the technical means provided for and societal assumptions made about various systems differ significantly. However, trust assumptions concerning the involved parties are present for all voting systems and can be used as a basis for comparison. This paper discusses eight concrete voting systems with different properties, 12 types of parties involved, and seven general security goals set for voting. The emerging trust relations are assessed for their criticality, and the result is used for comparison of the considered systems.

1 Introduction

Voting is a widely used approach to determining social preferences. In the case of political elections, voting results may have significant consequences for the given society or even globally. Thus, it is essential to ensure that the result adequately represents the true preferences of society.

As the stakes are high, there are also incentives to manipulate the system. Unfortunately, it is not easy to develop a voting method that would be provably immune to all conceivable problems.

On the one hand, it would be favourable if every member of the society would be able to certify the correctness of the tally. However, such a goal implies that everyone should know how everyone else voted. This kind of *viva voce* voting has been used throughout the history of democracy, but it unfortunately also has a downside of enabling vote-buying [20,41]. To mitigate this threat, secret ballots have been used already in ancient Greece [19], with our current implementation originating in mid-19th century Australia [20].

As the usage of secret ballots ensures that votes are anonymous, tally integrity has to be provided with organisational measures like voting in a controlled environment and distributed counting. However, such measures introduce additional trust assumptions. For example, to accept the results of large-scale paper ballot elections, one must assume that the people performing counts and recounts on a subset of ballots were not all corrupt in a coordinated manner.

Electronic voting has the potential to make the tally computationally verifiable. This functionality, however, comes at the cost of additional protocol

© The Author(s), under exclusive license to Springer Nature Switzerland AG 2024
S. Katsikas et al. (Eds.): ESORICS 2023 Workshops, LNCS 14399, pp. 309–329, 2024.
https://doi.org/10.1007/978-3-031-54129-2_18

complexity and the requirement to be able to verify cryptographic operations. This capability cannot be assumed from the general public, who instead has to rely on the statements made by a few technical experts.

One way or another, trusting some components or actors to a certain extent seems unavoidable for all the currently known voting systems. For example, many of the mitigation measures used by voting schemes rely on election observers and auditors. However, the election organiser has the power to influence how the elections are observed and audited, which means that in some cases, a malicious election organiser may be able to evade audits. Therefore, it is essential to identify the underlying trust assumptions to determine the limitations of election audits.

This paper aims to identify and classify the main trust assumptions across different voting methods.

To handle this task methodically, we first identified four general classes of voting systems (paper voting in a polling station, postal voting, machine voting, and remote electronic voting). For each of these classes, we also consider subclasses based on the verifiability options that the systems in that class may provide.

Next, we identified the main parties involved in the respective voting systems. Several parties are universal across various voting methods (voter, registrar, election organiser, infrastructure provider, election observer), some are specific to paper-based voting (polling station official, printing house, postal service), and some to machine voting and electronic voting (voter's computer, hardware vendor, software vendor).

Finally, we established the security requirements of interest in the context of our research. The list of such requirements is not completely universal and varies to an extent from source to source (see e.g. [22,28,34,39]). However, for the purposes of this paper, we consider the following requirements:

- *Ballot secrecy:* It should not be possible to link the content of the vote to the identity of the voter.
- *Coercion resistance:* The voter should be able to cast a vote that accurately represents their genuine choice even if coercive agents are present during the voting period.
- *Universal suffrage:* Every eligible voter is allowed to participate in the elections.
- *Equal suffrage:* The vote of every eligible voter should have equal weight.
- *Verification of eligibility:* It should be possible to detect if some votes have been cast by ineligible voters. It should not be possible to undetectably cast a vote on behalf of an eligible voter who has not cast a ballot.
- *Verification of delivery:* Upon casting a ballot, a voter should be able to verify that their intent has been properly interpreted and that their vote has been recorded without alteration.
- *Verification of ballot box integrity:* It should be impossible to undetectably modify a ballot, remove it from a ballot box or add ineligible votes.
- *Verification of tally integrity:* The final election results can be verified as soon as they are announced by the election authorities.

With the categories of interest established, we identified which voting systems rely on the trust in certain parties in order to achieve the respective security properties. The results are summarised in Table 1. In order to reduce the subjectivity of this assessment, the table was first composed by one author and then reviewed and improved by the others. The process involved two rounds of discussions between all the authors, going through every cell of the table.

After having composed a systematic overview of the trust assumptions used by different voting systems, we can take one further step and compare the security level of these systems. Despite a number of previous attempts made in the literature [30–32, 35, 36, 42], such a comparison still remains largely an open problem. The main reason behind the hardness of this task is that voting security has many aspects. The comparison would need to happen in many dimensions, and it is unlikely that one system would dominate another in all of them.

However, we will make an attempt in this paper to unify the treatment of different dimensions in terms of trust assumptions. Intuitively, we can call one system more secure compared to another if it relies on a smaller set of assumptions. Interpreting "smaller" as a set inclusion, we would still get incomparability, but there are other possible interpretations that we will be presenting in the concluding part of this paper.

2 Paper-Based Voting in a Polling Station

We will first consider the trust assumptions of regular paper-based voting and then review whether some of the trust assumptions can be removed by providing voters with cryptographic receipts allowing voters to verify their votes.

2.1 Regular Paper Voting

Traditional paper-based voting systems rely on the distribution of trust to reduce the risk of fraud. However, some trust assumptions remain. For example, the election organiser has to ensure that elections can be observed, and is responsible for organising the printing and delivery of paper ballots and voter lists.

We illustrate the trust assumptions of paper-based voting by examining the voting system used in the United Kingdom. The United Kingdom has a long tradition of electing representatives, and its legal and political system has been taken as a basis in several Commonwealth countries.

Over time, UK's voting system has had to adapt to the changes in society. For example, as a significant change, the requirement of ballot secrecy was introduced in 1872 as a part of electoral reforms [23]. To prevent ballot secrecy from being abused and to allow fraud allegations to be investigated, serial numbers were added to ballots and linked to voters when ballots were picked up. It turns out that 150 years later, a similar paper-based voting system is still in use.

Ballot Secrecy. While polling booths protect voters from prying eyes, it does not guarantee that no recording devices have been hidden on the premises of the polling station. The polling station official who hands out ballots has to be trusted not to link the voter to the serial number on the ballot[1]. The election court and, in the case of Parliamentary elections, the House of Commons have the right to require investigation of fraud allegations, which may lead to ballot secrecy being violated for the ballots/voters under investigation[2]. To increase the level of ballot secrecy, the ballot boxes are transported to the counting centre of the constituency, where the ballots are mixed and counted [1].

Coercion-Resistance. Voters have to be trusted not to use recording devices to take photos or videos of the filled-in ballot, including the ballot's serial number. The polling station official who hands out ballots must be trusted as that person could link the voter to the serial code on the ballot. A coercer who forces voters to abstain might be able to check whether the voter registered to vote[3].

Universal Suffrage. The voter has to be in an electoral register to be allowed to vote. Thus, the managers of electoral registers are trusted to guarantee the integrity of the registry[4]. Since 2015, voters can register to vote via a web page or by filling in a paper form[5]. Thus, the registration web page must be considered a trusted part of the voting system. Election observers can not monitor the registration phase as monitoring is regulated only during election day [10].

Equal Suffrage. If a voter learns that a vote has already been cast under their name, they are provided with an opportunity to cast a tendered vote, which will only be counted if decided so by the election court [1]. As polling station officials have access to the voter list, they must be trusted not to stuff the ballot box, while the election observers must be trusted to report any misconduct.

Verification of Eligibility. Voters are trusted to use valid information when registering to vote. To register, they have to provide their date of birth, national insurance number, and, depending on the voter's residence, either a signature or an address[6]. The information in the registration form is verified by checking the database of the Department of Works and Pensions (DWP), which makes the database a trusted part of the voting system [7]. Polling station officials check eligibility by asking voter's name and address and comparing it with the information on the voter list [9]. Since 2023, voters in UK are required to show a photographic ID when voting in person[7].

---

1. Before handing out the ballot, the election official perforates it, and either writes its serial number into the voter list or voter's name on the ballot's counterfoil [1,5].
2. Since 1886, seven investigations have resulted in ballot secrecy being violated [6].
3. British Library keeps full versions of electoral registries. The records less than ten years old can be viewed under supervision for research purposes [21].
4. There are 381 electoral registers in the UK [10].
5. The registration process is described at https://www.gov.uk/register-to-vote.
6. Since 2002, Northern Ireland has required a signature, date of birth, and national insurance number to register to vote [5]. After individual electoral registration (IER) was introduced in 2014, voters in England, Scotland, and Wales must provide their national insurance number, date of birth, and address when registering to vote [7].
7. A list of valid photo ID-s is provided in https://www.gov.uk/how-to-vote/photo-id-youll-need.

Verification of Delivery. The election observers, polling agents, and polling station officials are trusted to monitor how ballots are submitted into the ballot box [1,5].

Verification of Ballot Box Integrity. The election observers, polling agents and polling station officials are trusted to monitor the ballot box[8]. Once the voting period ends, a polling station official fills in a ballot paper account, which can be used in the counting phase to check that the number of ballots in the ballot box matches the number of issued ballots [9]. The ballot box, the tendered ballots, and the list of serial numbers are sealed by the presiding clerk and optionally also by polling agents assigned by candidates or representatives of the candidates [6]. The ballot box is opened for counting, and once it is done, it is re-sealed. The sealed ballots, the tendered votes, and the list of serial numbers are forwarded to the registration officer of the area, who is trusted to store them for one year[9]. After one year, the stored election materials are destroyed [2].

Verification of Tally Integrity. Election observers, polling agents and polling station officials are trusted to observe the counting and report misconduct [5].

2.2 Paper Voting with Cryptographic Receipts

Paper-based voting systems can be made cryptographically verifiable by printing cryptographic information on the ballots. The information can be presented in the form of candidate codes and ballot serial numbers, which are later posted to a public bulletin board for verification. However, care has to be taken to prevent the verification information on the ballots from being linked to voters, as this would violate ballot secrecy.

Prêt à Voter is a polling station-based voting system that provides end-to-end verifiability [38]. The ballot is two-sided, where the left side consists of a randomised candidate list, and the right side contains a ballot ID and cells where the voter can mark the preferences.

In this work, we refer to Culnane et al. [24] version of Prêt à Voter, which was used in the elections in the Australian state of Victoria. Prêt à Voter differs from regular paper ballots used in Australian elections by its two-sided ballot printed by a print-on-demand printer in a private booth. The trust assumptions for achieving universal suffrage, equal suffrage, and verification of eligibility are the same as with Australian paper voting and are thus not covered in detail[10].

Ballot Secrecy. It is assumed that the human-readable part of a ballot, which contains a candidate list and unique serial number corresponding to the voter's receipt, is destroyed after voting[11]. Polling station officials are trusted to perform

---

8. The procedures that the polling station staff must follow are described in [9].

9. The legislation does not specify the conditions for the retention of these items [6].

10. While proof of identity is required for enrolling, there is no voter ID requirement for voting [29]. The voter's eligibility is checked by polling station officials who ask voter's name, address, and whether the voter has already voted in this election.

11. Using the human-readable part, an adversary could discover how the voter voted.

or/and enforce the shredding procedure after the voter has voted. In addition, the Electronic Ballot Marker (EBM), a computer assisting voters in ballot filling, is trusted not to leak the vote via side channels. It is assumed that the printer that retrieves and prints the appropriate ballot is resilient to side-channel attacks and kleptographic attacks. Also, votes on the Web Bulletin Board (WBB) stay private as long as there is at least one honest mixer and a threshold number of trustees sharing the decryption key do not collude.

Coercion-Resistance. It is assumed that the vote is cast in a private setting where the coercer can not observe the voter. The voter is trusted not to record the voting process as the ballot contains cryptographic information along with the candidate list. However, Prêt à Voter does not defend against pattern-based coercion attacks (a.k.a. Italian attack [25]) or forced randomisation attacks.

Verification of Delivery. Prêt à Voter provides evidence of cast-as-intended verification and counted-as-cast verification if the voter performs a number of checks on the printed ballot and verifies the presence of their vote on the public part of WBB. Robustness and reliability of the private part of WBB depend on the honesty of a threshold of trustees handling it. The Australian implementation of Prêt à Voter requires a threshold greater than two-thirds of trustees [24].

Verification of Ballot Box Integrity. Voters ought to perform a number of checks on the printed ballot and verify that their vote (code) is present on the public WBB. End-to-end verifiability relies on the assumption that sufficiently many voters run those checks. The means for guaranteeing the integrity of the physical ballot box are not part of Prêt à Voter, and are assumed to be assured by honest polling station officials who may be monitored by election observers.

Verification of Tally Integrity. Every voter can verify the presence of their encrypted ballot on the public bulletin board. Moreover, anyone can verify that the published list of encrypted ballots corresponds to the announced results by downloading and checking a public electronic trace. It is assumed that a sufficient number of voters properly run those checks.

3   Postal Voting

A common approach to providing voters with an option to vote remotely is to enable postal voting[12]. The importance of postal voting has been steadily increasing [40], but the Covid-19 pandemic accelerated the process as election organisers (EOs) had to introduce or expand remote voting options[13].

3.1   Regular Postal Voting

While the introduction of postal voting may increase the participation rate, it can also affect the security guarantees provided by the election system. For

---

12. https://www.idea.int/news-media/news/special-voting-arrangements-svas-europe-country-postal-early-mobile-and-proxy.

13. https://www.idea.int/news-media/news/elections-and-covid-19-how-special-voting-arrangements-were-expanded-2020.

example, it is not easy to ensure that every voter receives a postal ballot in a timely manner. As postal ballots can be filled in an uncontrolled environment, the possibility of voters being coerced can not be eliminated. Also, unless voters deliver the filled-in ballots to the polling station, they can not verify whether the ballots were correctly handled and reached the polling stations in time.

For the sake of concreteness, we will again consider the postal voting system of the United Kingdom in this paper.

The UK introduced on-demand postal voting in 2000 [1]. Since then, the ratio of postal voters has steadily increased. In the 2005 General Elections, 12% of the votes were cast by mail. In the 2009 European Parliament elections, the percentage rose to 14%, and in the 2019 General Elections, 21% of votes were cast by mail [5,37].

Ballot Secrecy. Filled-in ballot is sealed into a ballot envelope, which is then placed inside a return envelope along with documents that are used to check voter's eligibility [5]. Thus, the postal service and election organisers are trusted not use the information in the envelopes to violate ballot secrecy. To preserve ballot secrecy, postal ballots are mixed with regular ballots before counting [5]. Election observers are trusted to check that the procedures are followed.

Coercion-Resistance. If the voters anticipate being coerced, they can use the option to cancel the request to vote by mail[14]. Postal ballots are filled in an uncontrolled environment, which means that voters must be trusted to resist coercion and not to record the voting process. There are no special measures to mitigate the threat of coercion.

Universal Suffrage. The trust assumptions regarding voter registration are the same as for regular paper-based voting, see Sect. 2.1. To apply for postal voting and when filling in the postal ballot, the voter must submit personal identifiers (signature, date of birth) [4]. The election organisers and polling station officials have to be trusted to validate the information provided by the voters.

Equal Suffrage. The voter list contains marks for voters who have applied to use postal voting and thus can not vote in person [5]. The polling station officials are trusted to keep the voter list up to date. They also have to be trusted to prevent postal voters from being allowed to cast a second vote.

Verification of Eligibility. A postal vote must be accompanied by a filled-in postal voting statement that contains the voter's name, date of birth and signature[15]. Starting from 2015, it has been mandatory for returning officers to verify the personal identifiers on all returned postal ballots [7]. The verification is usually done with the help of specific software, which has to be trusted[16]. If the

---

14. To cancel the request to vote by mail, the voter must contact the local council at least 11 days before the elections. https://www.electoralcommission.org.uk/i-am-a/voter/apply-vote-post#paragraph-19876-title.

15. https://www.electoralcommission.org.uk/sites/default/files/pdf_file/Making-Your-Mark-Example-Postal-Voting-Statement-GB-English-A4.pdf.

16. The verification system can not detect fake identifiers if they are used both on the postal voting application and on the statement accompanying the filled-in ballot [5].

software does not find a match, a human operator has to review the identifiers, which means that the human operator has to be trusted.

Verification of Delivery. Voters have to trust that the ballots are delivered on time[17]. If a voter does not trust the postal service, there is also a possibility to return the ballot to the polling station [5]. Postal ballots can also be collected and delivered by third parties, including political parties, which must be trusted to behave honestly [5]. However, there is a plan to introduce new legislation in the UK restricting political campaigners from handling postal ballots [15].

Verification of Ballot Box Integrity. Postal ballots must be securely stored. The election officials responsible for handling the postal ballots must be trusted not to violate ballot secrecy and to assure the integrity of the ballots. Accredited election observers can monitor how the postal ballots are received [10]. However, it is unclear how the stored ballots are secured and whether election observers can also monitor that the ballots are properly stored. If ballots are stored in a storage facility, the operator of that facility would also be part of the trust base.

Verification of Tally Integrity. The means for assuring tally integrity are the same as those used for regular paper-based ballots, see Sect. 2.1.

3.2 Postal Voting with Cryptographic Receipts

STROBE [18] is a framework that helps to achieve end-to-end verifiability in postal voting systems. The framework was introduced by Josh Benaloh in 2021 and has not yet been implemented in practice.

STROBE differs from regular postal voting as each voter receives two ballots, one for voting and the other for verification[18]. These ballots contain cryptographic information in the form of a ballot ID and short selection codes for each candidate[19]. The idea is to make it unpredictable which ballot is verified. Thereby, there is a high likelihood of detecting tampered ballots during verification, giving indirect guarantees about the integrity of the election result.

As STROBE is not a voting system but a framework to add verifiability to a voting system, the assumptions for achieving universal suffrage, equal suffrage, and verification of eligibility are not treated separately in this section.

Ballot Secrecy. The printing house is trusted not to retain information about ballots. The postal service and election organiser are trusted not to violate ballot secrecy by illegally storing ballot ID, the connection between selection codes and candidates, and linking with the voter's identity. Such information could be used to query the public bulletin board to learn voter's choices. Additionally, it is assumed that the threshold of decryption key holders will not collude.

---

17. Tracking of postal votes was trialled in 2006 in some parts of the UK [3].
18. We cover the version of STROBE, where voters receive two ballots.
19. The selection codes are generated by the election organiser from pre-computed encryptions of each candidate on a ballot. The ballot ID is formed by hashing all the encryptions for that ballot. The election organiser publishes encryptions, short selection codes, and ballot ID for each ballot to the public bulletin board.

Coercion-Resistance. STROBE is not designed to mitigate coercion. Therefore, voters must be trusted to evade coercion and not record the voting process.

Verification of Delivery. After receiving the ballots, the election organiser publishes selection codes corresponding to the voters' choices on the public bulletin board. Every voter can verify whether their chosen selection codes appear on the bulletin board, and it is assumed that a sufficient number of voters do this. The election organiser must be trusted to correctly publish the codes.

Verification of Ballot Box Integrity. The election organiser publishes ballot ID-s and chosen selection codes for all the received ballots. It is assumed that a sufficient number of voters will perform verification to detect a systematic removal or modification of ballots. Election observers or auditors are trusted to check that the number of voters matches the number of ballots in the ballot box and the number of published receipts.

Verification of Tally Integrity. After the voting phase has ended, encryptions of cast votes are homomorphically combined, and the tally is verifiably decrypted. Anyone can verify correctness of the final tally by aggregating the encryptions published on the bulletin board and verifying the proof of decryption correctness. It is assumed that at least some voters can and are willing to do such checks. It is also assumed that a sufficient number of voters verify their votes, hence showing that the information on the public bulletin board is valid.

4   Voting via Voting Machines

Voting machines are devices which collect and tally votes. Some of these machines let the voters directly enter their choices, while others scan filled-in ballots. If the source code of the voting machine is not available and the machine does not produce a paper trail, the machine can be viewed as a black box that has to be trusted to function correctly. Some voting machines produce a paper trail, making it possible to conduct post-election risk-limiting audits [33].

4.1   Voting Machines Used in Bulgaria

In the following, we are describing the deployment of voting machines in Bulgaria[20]. The information is based on OSCE reports and an interview with an election observer [13,14,16].

The first country-wide trial of using voting machines was conducted during the parliamentary elections in April 2021. At that time, the voters could choose to cast a paper ballot or vote via a voting machine. Three months later, during the early parliamentary elections, it was mandatory to use voting machines in polling stations with over 300 registered voters.

---

20. Smartmatic A4-517 machines were used: https://www.smartmatic.com/media/article/smartmatic-supports-24-elections-in-11-countries-in-2021/.

Ballot Secrecy. The voting machine does not learn the voter's identity[21]. The vendor is trusted to provide voting machines that fulfil the requirement, whereby it should be impossible to determine in which order the votes were stored on the external memory device. The vendor is trusted to use the same components in the voting machines as only a few voting machines were tested regarding electromagnetic emanations. Once a vote is cast, the voter's choice is printed on a receipt. The voter is assumed to fold it and put it into a ballot box.

Coercion-Resistance. Voters' privacy is protected with the help of small privacy screens installed on both sides of the voting machine. Thus, the voter has to trust that cameras have not been placed on the premises of the polling station and that the voting machines have been positioned in a manner preventing third parties from viewing the voting machine's screen. Voters are trusted not to record the voting process. However, the lack of a polling booth makes it more difficult for the voters to secretly record the voting process[22].

Universal Suffrage. All citizens with a permanent address in Bulgaria are automatically registered. Prior registration is not required to vote abroad. The National Population Register has to be trusted to provide valid data, as it is used to compile voter lists. To vote, the voters need to provide an identity document to a polling station official.

Equal Suffrage. In general, voters can vote only in their designated polling station[23]. However, in some rare cases, unregistered voters are allowed to register in the polling station on the election day, which may result in multiple registration and double voting. An eligible voter is provided with a smart card, allowing to use a specific voting machine. Polling station officials are trusted to check that each voter gets only one smart card, as two subsequent votes on the same machine must be cast with different smart cards. To prevent the same voter from later casting a second vote, the polling station official is trusted to keep the voter's identity document until the voter returns the smart card, submits the receipt to the ballot box, and adds a signature to the voter list.

Verification of Eligibility. The polling station employee is trusted to check the voter's eligibility by requesting an identity document and comparing the information on the document with the information on a paper-based voter list.

Verification of Delivery. Election organiser is trusted to have properly configured the voting machines. The voter is assumed to verify that the cast vote matches the vote printed on the receipt. The voter submits the receipt to the ballot box. The polling station officials must be trusted to properly seal the USB drives, receipts, and results printed by voting machines into a tamper-evident envelope and deliver the envelope to the district counting centre.

---

21. The voter uses a smart card provided by the polling station official to cast a vote.
22. Vote buying was one of the main reasons for introducing voting machines. Polling station officials were instructed to monitor that voters do not use recording devices.
23. There are no such restrictions when voting abroad, which could lead to double voting.

Verification of Ballot Box Integrity. As the machines are air-gapped, they are trusted to provide valid signing times when votes are signed. The integrity of the voting machine's software is verified before installation by checking the hash value of the installation file[24]. It was possible to verify the integrity of the installed software by booting a special USB containing a hash checker. Support for the voting machines was provided by local contractors, who had to be trusted not to tamper with the machines[25]. Polling station officials had to be trusted not to tamper with the voting machines and ballot boxes containing the receipts. In case observers are present, they are trusted to behave honestly.

Verification of Tally Integrity. Post-election audits were performed in some polling stations to check whether counting the receipts gives the same results as the tally provided by the voting machines. The election organiser is trusted not to be malicious when deciding which polling stations to audit, as the set of audited polling stations was not chosen randomly. Digitally signed votes were published.

5 Internet Voting

Internet voting (i-voting) systems enable voting in an uncontrolled environment, which may impact both vote privacy and vote integrity. Therefore, they usually provide voters with means to avoid coercion while allowing voters to verify that their votes were correctly handled. However, an optimal balance has to be found as there is an inherent conflict between these security requirements. To provide coercion-resistance, it must not be possible to prove how the vote was cast, making it challenging to provide universal verifiability in the remote setting.

In this section, we review the trust assumptions of the Estonian i-voting system IVXV, which provides individual verifiability and coercion-resistance.

5.1 Estonian IVXV

The updated version of the Estonian i-voting system (code-named IVXV) was introduced in 2017 [8,11,27]. While there were few changes to the client-side, the sever-side was completely rewritten. The collection of ballots was distributed between Vote Collectors and a Registration Service independent of the election organiser. Once the voting period is over, the ballots are processed and anonymised by a Ballot Box Processor. A mix-net was introduced to anonymise votes, decryption was enhanced by providing proofs of correct decryption, and the election specific private key was threshold secret-shared between the trustees.

Ballot Secrecy. The voting device, verification device, verification application, and voting application are trusted not to violate ballot secrecy. Thus, the voter is trusted to ensure that the voting and verification devices are secure. The

---

24. Observers were not able to monitor the configuration process of the voting machines.

25. More than 11000 voting machines were used across 9398 polling stations.

server-side processes encrypted ballots and the election organiser is trusted to anonymise the ballots before the tallying phase. Observers are assumed to check that ballots are anonymised. It is assumed that encryption can not be broken. Thus, to violate ballot secrecy, the election-specific decryption key would have to leak during key generation, or at least 5 of 9 keyholders would have to collude.

Coercion-Resistance. The possibility to re-vote makes it impossible to prove whether the cast vote reaches the tallying phase[26]. For the mitigation measure to be effective, the voter must be aware and willing to use the option to re-vote. It is assumed that the coercer does not have control over the voter's voting device as otherwise it would be possible to detect whether the voter complies or casts a re-vote. It is also assumed that the election organiser does not collude with the coercer as the Vote Collector and Ballot Box Processor can see which voters re-voted. Similar information can be inferred by the party providing Vote Collector with OCSP responses regarding the validity of voters' signing certificates [12].

Universal Suffrage. Eligible voters are automatically included in the voter list, which is compiled based on the electronic population registry. The population registry has to be trusted to provide valid information.

Equal Suffrage. The election observers or auditors are trusted to verify that only the last vote cast by each voter gets tallied. Third parties must not be able to use the electronic identity tokens (eIDs) belonging to other voters. Thus, it is assumed that malicious usage of voters' eIDs would be detected.

Verification of Eligibility. Eligibility is checked by requesting the voters authenticate to the voting system by using either an ID card or Mobile-ID. The state provided eIDs are trusted to be secure. After the elections, the Ballot Box Processor verifies that only eligible voters were able to vote. Election observers or auditors are assumed to check that the Ballot Box Processor functions properly.

Verification of Delivery. The voter is assumed to use a smartphone-based vote verification application to fetch the cast ballot from the Vote Collector. The vote verification application reads the contents of the QR code displayed by the voting application to initiate vote verification. Thus, the voter has to trust that the voting application and verification application do not collude maliciously.

Verification of Ballot Box Integrity. The trust assumptions used for cast-as-intended verification are expanded by having to trust that third parties cannot use voters' eID-s to re-vote as this would not be detected by the vote verification application [26]. The Vote Collector and Registration Service are trusted not to collude, as otherwise it would be possible to drop ballots [27].

Verification of Tally Integrity. The Vote Collector and Registration Service are trusted not to collude. It is assumed that at least some election observers and auditors are not malicious. They have to verify that only eligible voters could vote, that the set of ballots collected by the Vote Collector matches the set of ballots registered by the Registration Service, and that the ballots were

---

26. I-vote can also be invalidated by casting a paper vote in a polling station.

properly anonymised and decrypted. Some of these tasks rely on verification software. Thus, the software used to verify mixing proofs and decryption proofs can be viewed as trusted components of the voting system.

6   Discussion and Conclusions

Our original motivation behind this research was to compare the security levels of different voting methods on a common scale. If method A would need a strictly smaller set of trust assumptions than method B, then we could say that A is in this sense more secure than B.

During our research we concluded that, besides the mere observation that a trust assumption is needed, we also have to consider the impact in case a particular trust assumption is violated. Thus we introduced three levels of impact criticality. In the lightest case, only one vote is affected, and this probably does not change the final outcome of elections. In the mid-severe case, a subset of votes are affected, and this has a potential of changing the outcome of elections by a few seats in the representative body to be elected. And finally, in the most critical case, all the votes may be impacted as a result of the attack enabled due to the failing trust assumption.

6.1   Overview of the Trust Assumptions

In the following, we generalise the results of our case studies. The identified trust assumptions are summarised in Table 1.

Ballot Secrecy. Voters are assumed not to disclose the details of their voting process, for example, by not recording the process. In addition, it is assumed that the environment where the ballot is filled does not contain recording equipment. For example, in case of i-voting systems, the voting device has to be trusted unless code voting is used, and in case of machine voting, the hardware vendor is trusted to deliver machines that do not have side-channel leakages. Polling station officials are trusted not to abuse their position to violate ballot secrecy. For example, in the case of postal voting, it is assumed that they will not link voter's identity to the vote on the ballot. Similarly, postal voting systems rely on the trustworthiness of the deliverer as they could violate ballot secrecy by opening the double envelopes. The voting schemes that use printed cryptographic information are dependent on the software generating the information and on the printing facility, as the cryptographic information must not leak and must not be linked to the voters who receive the information. When considering voting schemes that rely on cryptography, it is common for the election organiser to distribute the trust regarding key management and anonymisation of ballots.

Coercion-Resistance. In general, trust assumptions regarding ballot secrecy can be used as a basis for deriving some of the trust assumptions for coercion-resistance. If ballot secrecy can be violated, it is possible to coerce the voters. While the polling booth used to be instrumental for providing coercion-resistance, the proliferation of small recording devices has made it practically impossible to prevent the voting process from being recorded [17]. While i-voting has the potential to provide the highest level of coercion-resistance by giving the voter the option to mitigate coercion by casting a re-vote or by voting with fake credentials, the coercion-resistance of i-voting schemes can rely on multiple trust assumptions. For example, the voter would have to be aware of the way how the coercer is monitoring the voter to apply the countermeasures. The voter may not be able to detect that the computer is compromised and used to monitor how the vote is cast. Also, even if the anti-coercion measures (like the option of re-voting) are implemented by the system, the voter has to be aware of them and should be willing to use them. It becomes very difficult to provide coercion-resistance when forced abstention attacks are included in the threat model, as multiple parties may learn, which voters participated in the elections. These may include the election organiser, polling station officials, and identity provider.

Equal and Universal Suffrage. While integrity of the electoral register has to be trusted to guarantee universal suffrage, voter registration and universal suffrage are not specific to a voting system, but depend on the legislation. Still, the voter must be given the possibility to vote. For example, voting machine vendors must provide reliable hardware and software that is usable by the voters. When considering equal suffrage, double voting is commonly prevented by relying on the procedures and proper marking of the voter list by polling station officials. Thus, polling station officials and the system for managing the voters list must be trusted. Also, election observers and auditors must be trusted to check that the procedures are followed. However, election observers can not check whether the voting machine's software correctly represents voters' preferences. While risk limiting audits can be used after the elections to check that the voting machines did not tamper with the results, this option is only available for voting machines that provide a paper trail. For voting machines that do not provide a paper trail, the software vendor has to be trusted. In the case of i-voting, it has to be assumed that third parties can not vote with someone else's credentials without being detected, which means that voters and identity providers have to be trusted to properly handle the voting credentials. In addition, the software vendor of an i-voting system may have to be trusted, unless the voting system is software independent. In the case of postal voting, the postal service must be trusted not to drop votes of their choice.

Verification of Eligibility. Verification of eligibility relies on the assumption that voters provided valid information when registering to vote. As the registrar is responsible for verifying voters' identities and including them in the voter list, the registrar is a trusted part of the election system. For polling station-based voting systems, voter eligibility is checked by polling station officials. In the case of postal voting systems, eligibility can be checked by comparing the information provided by the voter during the registration with the information provided in the ballot. This can be done manually by the polling station officials or the process can be automated with software. If the software is used for verifying eligibility, it must be considered as a part of the trust base. The way how i-voting systems identify voters varies significantly, but the election organiser is trusted to ensure that ballots are accepted only from eligible voters. In addition, the election observers are also responsible for verifying that the i-voting system properly checks eligibility.

Verification of Delivery. When the vote is cast using postal voting, the postal service has to be trusted not to drop the votes. If the postal ballots are delivered to the polling station, the polling station employees along with the election observers are responsible for correctly handling the received ballots. In the case of regular paper voting, there are no trust assumptions for delivering the ballot as it is the voter who submits the ballot to the ballot box. However, with cryptographic paper voting, the printing house may misprint the cryptographic information, which can invalidate the ballot or prevent it from being verified. The same holds for cryptographic postal voting. In general, when the voter is provided with the means to verify whether the ballot was correctly encoded or delivered, the voter is trusted to perform this check. In the case of i-voting, a voter's computer has to be trusted not to prevent the vote from being verified. In addition, the software vendor of the i-voting system may have to be trusted, unless the voting system is software independent. The trust assumptions for machine voting differ depending on whether the machine provides a paper trail. If a paper trail is provided, the voter is responsible for checking the receipt. However, if no paper trail is provided, the software running on the voting machine must be trusted to correctly store voters' preferences.

Verification of Ballot Box Integrity. Election observers and auditors are trusted to monitor or verify the integrity of the ballot box. Voting machines that do not produce a paper trail are an exception as integrity of their ballot boxes can not be easily monitored nor verified. Thus, polling station officials and infrastructure providers have to be trusted not to tamper with such voting machines. For the voting machines that provide a paper trail, the infrastructure provider has to be trusted not to damage or tamper with the paper receipts. In this case, also election auditors are trusted to properly conduct post election risk limiting audits. When considering i-voting systems that only provide individual verifiability, the election organiser has to be trusted along with the infrastructure provider, election auditor, and software vendor as the general public can not verify how the ballot box is processed. However, for i-voting systems that provide universal verifiability, in principle, anyone could verify the integrity of the ballot box, but at minimum, the verification is expected to be conducted by experts in the role of election auditors. In the case of regular paper ballots and postal ballots, polling station officials and storage facility employees have to be trusted.

Verification of Tally Integrity. In the case of regular paper-based voting systems and regular postal voting systems, polling station officials have to be trusted to count the ballots correctly. In the case of machine voting, the voting machines can export digital ballot boxes. When no paper trail is provided, the software running on the voting machine has to be trusted to export a ballot box that represents the preferences of the voters who cast the votes. The digital ballot boxes may be delivered to a central location for tallying. In such cases, the deliverer must be trusted along with the polling station officials and election organisers. If the machines provide a paper trail, the election organiser must be trusted to use proper statistical means to conduct risk-limiting audits to ensure that even if some voting machines behaved incorrectly, it did not affect the election result. For i-voting systems that only provide individual verifiability, the election organiser has to be trusted along with the infrastructure provider and software vendor as the general public can not verify how tallying is done. Therefore, election observers and auditors play a significant role in such voting systems and have to be trusted. For i-voting systems that provide universal verifiability, in principle, anyone could verify the tally, but at minimum the verification is expected to be conducted by experts in the role of election auditors. Regardless of the voting system, election observers are trusted to monitor how the votes are counted. If auditors rely on software to verify cryptographic proofs, these software components must be considered to be part of the trust base.

6.2   Comparative Analysis of the Trust Assumptions

In this section we present the conclusions of our analysis in terms of the amount and criticality of the studied trust assumptions.

Ballot Secrecy. Paper-based voting in a polling station relies on the least amount of trust assumptions when considering ballot secrecy. As it is a well-established method of voting, many conceivable attacks against ballot secrecy have been attempted in the past and hence have counter-measures in place.

Cryptographic paper voting and cryptographic postal voting have the largest number of trust assumptions and three out of them are critical. All the ballots must be kept confidential between their creation and vote casting; secrecy of the vote can then be satisfied only if there exists a chain of trusted entities throughout the vote casting process.

Similarly, i-voting requires the same number of critical trust assumptions due to the necessity to trust the election organiser and software vendor with the security implementation of the voting process. Furthermore, we need to trust devices used for casting and verifying the votes.

Coercion-Resistance. Among the voting methods, paper-based voting and voting via voting machines rely on the fewest security assumptions regarding coercion-resistance. As stated above, paper-based voting relies on the least number of trust assumptions when it comes to ballot secrecy. Coercers have only a few ways of knowing whether their efforts have succeeded in making voters cast their votes in a specific manner.

Cryptographic postal voting requires the largest number of trust assumptions, three of which may affect all the votes, and four of which may affect a subset of the votes. As a result of several parties having the possibility to violate ballot secrecy, they might influence the way the voters express their preferences.

I-voting has the largest number of critical trust assumptions. Even though some i-voting schemes provide means to counter coercion, they cannot protect from all possible attacks (like family voting). This shows that i-voting is a more suitable method for communities where coercive practices are uncommon.

Equal Suffrage. As both regular and cryptographic paper voting rely on existing identification mechanisms to check for voter eligibility, they require the fewest trust assumptions.

I-voting has the highest number of trust assumptions, four of which are critical. Those assumptions are needed as any i-voting system which is used in large-scale elections requires robust infrastructure, an efficient and reliable identification system, an online population registry, and an honest election organiser.

Verification of Eligibility. The results of our analysis suggest that i-voting provides the weakest guarantees regarding voters' eligibility since there are four critical trust assumptions. In contrast, voting in a polling station has the potential to provide the highest level of guarantees by requiring the checking of the voters' identity documents.

Verification of Delivery. Paper-based voting does not entail any trust assumption in terms of verifying that the ballots have been delivered. Voters do not need to trust anyone since they deliver their ballot to the ballot box themselves.

Methods that provide individual verifiability (cryptographic paper voting, cryptographic postal voting, i-voting with individual verifiability) require more trust assumptions. Firstly, voters are trusted to perform verification, which can sometimes be confusing. Furthermore, printing houses should be trusted for cryptographic postal and paper voting, since incorrect codes can prevent voters from verifying their votes. In the case of i-voting, a voter's computer and software vendor should be trusted not to prevent the vote from being verified.

Verification of Ballot Box Integrity. Methods that provide universal verifiability have the fewest trust assumptions related to the verification of ballot box integrity. Among these methods are cryptographic paper voting, cryptographic postal voting, and i-voting with universal verifiability. I-voting systems with individual verifiability have the greatest number of trust assumptions, all of which are critical. Individual verifiability does not guarantee the integrity of all other ballots submitted by all voters, but only provides assurance of the integrity of the ballot submitted by a particular voter.

Verification of Tally Integrity. Methods that provide universal verifiability require the least amount of trust assumptions for verification of tally integrity. The reason for this is that several entities have access to special cryptographic techniques that can be used to verify the final tally.

On the other hand, machine voting with no paper trail requires the highest number of assumptions with two assumptions being critical. As a result, there is need to trust software, election organisers, infrastructure provider, and delivery services to accomplish verification of tally integrity.

Table 1. An overview of trust assumptions for different types of voting systems.

		Voter	Voter's computer	Registrar	Election organiser or election services	Infrastructure provider\maintenance	Polling station official	Printing house	Election observer\auditor	Identity provider	Postal service or third party delivery	Hardware vendor	Software vendor
Ballot secrecy	Paper voting	●					●	●	●				
	Cryptographic paper voting	●			●[1]	●	●		◐[11]	●[9]			
	Postal voting	●				●[4]				●[9]	●		
	Cryptographic postal voting	●			●[1]	●[4]		●	●	●[9]	●		◐
	Machine voting	●		●[5]		●	●	●		●[9]		◐	
	I-voting	●	●[5]		●[1]					●[9]			●[5]
Coercion-resistance	Paper voting	●				●[7]	●	●[10]	●[9]				
	Cryptographic paper voting	●			●	●[4]	●[10]		◐[11]	●[9]			◐[11]
	Postal voting	●				●[4]				●[9]	●		
	Cryptographic postal voting	●			●	●[4]		●	●	●[9]	●		◐
	Machine voting	●				●[7]	●	●[10]		●[9]			
	I-voting	●	●[5]		●					●[9]	●[10]		●[5]
Equal & universal suffrage	Paper voting			●				●	●[9]				
	Cryptographic paper voting			●				●	●[9]				
	Postal voting			●				●	●[9]		●		
	Cryptographic postal voting			●				●	●[9]		●		
	Machine voting with paper trail			●				●	●[9]			●	
	Machine voting, no paper trail			●				●	●[9]			●	●
	I-voting	◐[6]	●[14]	●		●[13]			●[9]	●			◐
Verification of eligibility	Paper voting	◐[3]		●				●					
	Cryptographic paper voting	●[3]		●				●					
	Postal voting	●[3]		●				●					◐
	Cryptographic postal voting	●[3]		●				●					◐
	Machine voting	●[3]		●				●					
	I-voting	◐[6]		●		●[12]			●[9]				●
Verification of delivery	Paper voting												
	Cryptographic paper voting	●							●[8]				
	Postal voting								●[9]		●		
	Cryptographic postal voting	●							●[8]		●		
	Machine voting with paper trail	◐[2]											
	Machine voting, no paper trail												●
	I-voting (individual verifiability)	●	●										◐
	I-voting (universal verifiability)	◐[2]	◐[2]										◐
Verification of ballot box integrity	Paper voting				●		●		●[9]				
	Cryptographic paper voting								●[9]				
	Postal voting				●		●		●[9]				
	Cryptographic postal voting								●[9]				
	Machine voting with paper trail						●		●[9]				
	Machine voting, no paper trail						●	●	●[9]				●
	I-voting (individual verifiability)					●	●		●[9]				●
	I-voting (universal verifiability)								●[9]				
Verification of tally integrity	Paper voting							●	●[9]				
	Cryptographic paper voting								●[9]				
	Postal voting							●	●[9]				
	Cryptographic postal voting								●[9]				
	Machine voting with paper trail				●				●[9]		●		
	Machine voting, no paper trail				●			●	●[9]				●
	I-voting (individual verifiability)				●	●			●[9]				●
	I-voting (universal verifiability)								●[9]				

dark gray background = subset of votes is affected in case of attack
white background on a filled cell = single vote is affected in case of attack
gray background = all votes are affected in case of attack   ● = is trusted   ◐ = is trusted under conditions

1. Threshold number of parties must be trusted.

2. Trusted to perform/enable verification if voting system allows to.

3. If reliable IDs are not available, the voter is trusted to provide valid information.

4. Filled in postal ballots have to be stored securely.

5. Trusted, unless code voting is used.

6. Only own voting credentials may be used, they have to be secured.

7. Recording devices placed by infrastructure provider.

8. If codes are misprinted, ballots can not be verified.

9. Distributed trust, assumed to behave honestly.

10. Possible to check whether voter abstained.

11. For pre-printed ballots we need to trust printing house and software vendor. For print-on-demand, we need to trust software vendor.

12. Trusted to ensure that only ballot from eligible voters are processed.

13. Servers may be taken offline.

14. Trusted not to prevent voter from voting.

Acknowledgements. This paper has been supported by the Estonian Research Council under the grant number PRG920.

References

1. United Kingdom of the Great Britain and Northern Ireland, General Election, 5 May 2005: OSCE/ODIHR Assessment Mission Report (2005). OSCE ODIHR. https://www.osce.org/files/f/documents/7/e/16204.pdf
2. Factsheet: Ballot secrecy, December 2006. The Electoral Commission. https://www.wychavon.gov.uk/component/fileman/file/Documents/Elections/webb-secrecy.pdf
3. May 2006 electoral pilot schemes - postal vote tracking (2006). The Electoral Commission. https://www.electoralcommission.org.uk/sites/default/files/electoral_commission_pdf_file/FindingsPostalVoteTracking_22988-17175_E_N_S_W_.pdf
4. United Kingdom of the Great Britain and Northern Ireland, General Election 2010, OSCE/ODIHR Needs Assessment Mission Report, 19–22 January 2010 (2010). OSCE ODIHR. https://www.osce.org/files/f/documents/3/3/67606.pdf
5. United Kingdom of the Great Britain and Northern Ireland, General Election, 6 May 2010: OSCE/ODIHR Election Assessment Mission Report (2010). OSCE ODIHR. https://www.osce.org/files/f/documents/5/5/69072.pdf
6. Research paper: Manner of Voting at UK Elections (2015). The Law Commission. https://www.lawcom.gov.uk/app/uploads/2015/03/Electoral-Law_Manner-of-Voting_Research.pdf
7. United Kingdom of the Great Britain and Northern Ireland, General Election, 7 May 2015: OSCE/ODIHR Election Expert Team Final Report (2015). OSCE ODIHR. https://www.osce.org/files/f/documents/d/8/174081.pdf
8. General Framework of Electronic Voting and Implementation thereof at National Elections in Estonia (2017). Estonian State Electoral Office. https://www.valimised.ee/sites/default/files/uploads/eng/IVXV-UK-1.0-eng.pdf
9. Handbook for polling station staff (2017). The Electoral Commission. https://www.electoralcommission.org.uk/sites/default/files/pdf_file/Polling-station-handbook-UKPE.pdf
10. United Kingdom of the Great Britain and Northern Ireland, Early General Election, 8 June 2017: OSCE/ODIHR Needs Assessment Mission Report (2017). OSCE ODIHR. https://www.osce.org/files/f/documents/4/2/317306.pdf
11. IVXV architecture (2019), Estonian National Electoral Committee and the State Electoral Office, IVXV-AR-EN-1.4.0. https://www.valimised.ee/sites/default/files/2021-05/IVXV%20architecture%20%E2%80%93%20overview%20of%20technical%20realisation.pdf. Accessed 02 July 2021
12. IVXV protocols (2020). Estonian State Electoral Office, Dok IVXV-PR-EN-1.6.0
13. Republic of Bulgaria, Early Parliamentary Elections, 11 July 2021, ODIHR Limited Election Observation Mission Final Report (2021). OSCE ODIHR. https://www.osce.org/files/f/documents/8/b/502110.pdf
14. Republic of Bulgaria, Parliamentary Elections, 4 April 2021, ODIHR Limited Election Observation Mission Final Report (2021). OSCE ODIHR. https://www.osce.org/files/f/documents/f/3/502104.pdf
15. HL Bill 141 - Elections Bill, March 2022. The House of Lords. https://bills.parliament.uk/publications/46054/documents/1703
16. Interview view an election observer (2022)

17. Benaloh, J.: Rethinking Voter Coercion: The Realities Imposed by Technology. In: 2013 Electronic Voting Technology Workshop/Workshop on Trustworthy Elections (EVT/WOTE 13). USENIX Association (2013)
18. Benaloh, J.: STROBE-voting: send two, receive one ballot encoding. In: Krimmer, R., et al. (eds.) E-Vote-ID 2021. LNCS, vol. 12900, pp. 33–46. Springer, Cham (2021). https://doi.org/10.1007/978-3-030-86942-7_3
19. Boegehold, A.L.: Toward a study of Athenian voting procedure. Hesperia: J. Am. Sch. Classical Stud. Athens 32(4), 366–374 (1963). https://www.jstor.org/stable/147360
20. Brent, P.: The Australian ballot: not the secret ballot. Aust. J. Polit. Sci. 41(1), 39–50 (2006)
21. Carter, J., Grimshaw, J.: UK electoral registers and their uses. Br. Libr. (2016). https://www.osce.org/files/f/documents/4/2/317306.pdf
22. Cetinkaya, O.: Analysis of security requirements for cryptographic voting protocols (extended abstract). In: Proceedings ARES 2008, pp. 1451–1456. IEEE Computer Society (2008)
23. Crook, M., Crook, T.: The advent of the secret ballot in Britain and France, 1789–1914: from public assembly to private compartment. History 92(308), 449–471 (2007)
24. Culnane, C., Ryan, P.Y.A., Schneider, S., Teague, V.: vVote: a verifiable voting system (2014). https://arxiv.org/abs/1404.6822
25. Di Cosmo, R.: On privacy and anonymity in electronic and non electronic voting: the ballot-as-signature attack (2007). https://hal.archives-ouvertes.fr/hal-00142440v2
26. Heiberg, S., Krips, K., Willemson, J.: Planning the next steps for Estonian Internet voting. In: Proceedings of E-Vote-ID 2020, pp. 82–97. TalTech Press (2020)
27. Heiberg, S., Martens, T., Vinkel, P., Willemson, J.: Improving the verifiability of the Estonian internet voting scheme. In: Krimmer, R., et al. (eds.) E-Vote-ID 2016. LNCS, vol. 10141, pp. 92–107. Springer, Cham (2017). https://doi.org/10.1007/978-3-319-52240-1_6
28. Heiberg, S., Willemson, J.: Modeling threats of a voting method. In: Design, Development, and Use of Secure Electronic Voting Systems, pp. 128–148. IGI Global (2014)
29. Holmes, B.: Voter ID. Parliamentary Library (2014). ISSN 2203–5249. https://parlinfo.aph.gov.au/parlInfo/download/library/prspub/3317213/upload_binary/3317213.pdf;fileType=application/pdf
30. Juvonen, A.: A framework for comparing the security of voting schemes (2019). Master's thesis, University of Helsinki. https://hdl.handle.net/10138/310011
31. Krimmer, R., Volkamer, M.: Bits or paper? Comparing remote electronic voting to postal voting. In: EGOV 2005. Schriftenreihe Informatik, vol. 13, pp. 225–232. Universitätsverlag Rudolf Trauner, Linz, Austria (2005)
32. Li, H., Kankanala, A.R., Zou, X.: A taxonomy and comparison of remote voting schemes. In: 2014 23rd International Conference on Computer Communication and Networks, pp. 1–8 (2014). https://doi.org/10.1109/ICCCN.2014.6911807
33. Lindeman, M., Stark, P.B.: A gentle introduction to risk-limiting audits. IEEE Secur. Priv. 10(5), 42–49 (2012). https://doi.org/10.1109/MSP.2012.56
34. Mitrou, L., Gritzalis, D., Katsikas, S.K.: Revisiting legal and regulatory requirements for secure e-voting. In: Security in the Information Society: Visions and Perspectives, IFIP TC11 SEC2002. IFIP Conference Proceedings, vol. 214, pp. 469–480. Kluwer (2002)

35. Neumann, S.: Evaluation and improvement of internet voting schemes based on legally-founded security requirements. Ph.D. thesis, Technische Universität Darmstadt, March 2016

36. Neumann, S., Noll, M., Volkamer, M.: Election-dependent security evaluation of internet voting schemes. In: De Capitani di Vimercati, S., Martinelli, F. (eds.) SEC 2017. IAICT, vol. 502, pp. 371–382. Springer, Cham (2017). https://doi.org/10.1007/978-3-319-58469-0_25

37. Pilling, S., Cracknell, R.: UK Election Statistics: 1918–2021: A Century of Elections. House of Commons Library, August 2021. https://researchbriefings.files.parliament.uk/documents/CBP-7529/CBP-7529.pdf

38. Ryan, P.Y.A., Bismark, D., Heather, J., Schneider, S., Xia, Z.: Prêt à voter: a voter-verifiable voting system. IEEE Trans. Inf. Forensics Secur. 4(4), 662–673 (2009)

39. Schryen, G.: Security aspects of internet voting. In: Proceedings of HICSS-37. IEEE Computer Society (2004)

40. Townsley, J., Turnbull-Dugarte, S.J., Trumm, S., Milazzo, C.: Who votes by post? Understanding the Drivers of Postal Voting in the 2019 British General Election. Parliamentary Affairs (2021)

41. Wasley, P.: Back when everyone knew how you voted. Humanities **37**(4) (2016)

42. Willemson, J.: Bits or paper: which should get to carry your vote? J. Inf. Secur. Appl. **38**, 124–131 (2018). https://doi.org/10.1016/j.jisa.2017.11.007

Introducing Distributed Ledger Security into System Specifications with the Isabelle RR-Cycle

Florian Kammüller[1,2](✉)

[1] Middlesex University London, London, UK
[2] Technische Universität Berlin, Berlin, Germany
f.kammueller@mdx.ac.uk

Abstract. We present an approach to developing secure system specifications for IoT systems with decentralized data using the Refinement-Risk cycle (RR-cycle), a method for security engineering implemented in the proof assistant Isabelle. The RR-cycle enables interleaving attack analysis with system refinement using rigorous machine assisted proof in Isabelle to scrutinize and refine system specifications until security requirements are met. We illustrate this approach by a case study of a privacy critical scenario by refining it with a distributed ledger. The case study is motivated by the IoT project SUCCESS on security and privacy of healthcare IoT applications. We briefly summarize the RR-cycle method before focusing on its application of identifying a privacy attack that leads to a security refinement introducing the distributed ledger.

1 Introduction

In general, rigorous specification is justified despite its cost in the long run for any system as it facilitates and thus economizes maintenance and adaptation. For complex and hybrid systems, like IoT systems, for security and privacy critical applications, like healthcare, the application of formal methods is justified in any case. The approach we advocate in this paper, is to use the classical software engineering approach of a top down rigorous development process starting from an abstract specification based on requirements engineering. This initial specification is then refined step by step to a more concrete one while preserving properties. We use the method called Refinement-Risk cycle (RR-cycle) [10,14] that integrates a state based system view of infrastructures with actors and policies as basis for the representation of IoT systems and is implemented in the interactive proof assistant Isabelle.

We first give a brief summary of the Isabelle RR-cycle [10,14] and the IoT healthcare case study in Sect. 2 to provide the background for understanding its application. In Sect. 3 we re-iterate a previous RR-cycle application to the case study [14]. By introducing a distributed ledger we can show that now the RR-cycle terminates with the global privacy property. We discuss, conclude and present related work in Sect. 4.

© The Author(s), under exclusive license to Springer Nature Switzerland AG 2024
S. Katsikas et al. (Eds.): ESORICS 2023 Workshops, LNCS 14399, pp. 330–340, 2024.
https://doi.org/10.1007/978-3-031-54129-2_19

2   Summary of RR-Cycle and Case Study

The RR-cycle [10,14] has emerged as a result of the CHIST-ERA project SUC-CESS [4] addressing the formal modeling and analysis of security and privacy of IoT in healthcare. The starting point of this cycle is an initial formal specification that may have been produced by a formal requirement elicitation method like in the IoT case study [10,14] but may also be an ad hoc formalization of system requirements. The RR-cycle improves this initial specification by interleaving refinement with attack analysis. The process is directed by a global security property. The RR-cycle is the process that is used to drive security engineering in the Isabelle Insider and Infrastructure framework (IIIf). Attack trees, Kripke structures and modelchecking as well as a formal notion of property preserving refinement are formalized within the framework of the IIIf. This process is graphically depicted in Fig. 1. For a simple healthcare scenario we have applied the Fusion/UML process for object-oriented software development to derive a UML system design. One of the major outcomes of this process is the system class model shown in Fig. 2. In addition to this static system architecture, the Fusion/UML model also provides a set of operation schemas, use cases, and so-called object collaborations illustrating the method flows within the objects of the system class model. The complete analysis and design documentation is available [13]. The arxiv paper [14] already presented a detailed model and analysis of the first few iterations of the RR-cycle to this case study based on an earlier workshop paper [10] that informally described the stepwise development but without formalizations. A summary of the iterations of the RR-cycle, the attacks exhibiting vulnerabilities, and the countermeasures used for the refinement in these earlier papers [10,14] is provided in Fig. 3. However, despite introducing already a blockchain formalization (Iteration 2), the earlier formalization is inadequate. Consequently the RR-cycle could not be successfully terminated –

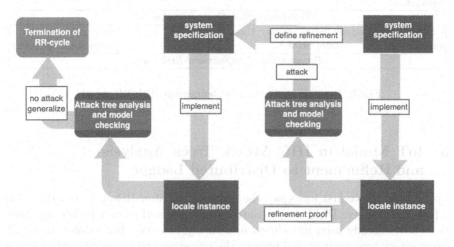

Fig. 1. Refinement-Risk-Cycle iterates design, risk analysis, and refinement

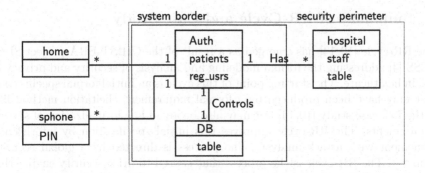

Fig. 2. System class model for IoT healthcare system

also because the termination condition of the RR-cycle has been identified only later [11]. In the current paper, we thus re-start the RR-cycle after Iteration 2 and introduce a more adequate definition of a distributed ledger. We then show that it guarantees the global security property of privacy of data.

System	Attack	Refinement	Where
Initial Fusion system home-cloud-hospital	Eve can perform action get at cloud	Introduce access control by DLM labels	RRLoopOne.thy hcKripkeOne.thy
Refinement-Risk-Cycle Iteration 1			
Access control by DLM labels	Eve can perform action eval at cloud; changes label to her own	Introduce privacy preserving functions and enforce their use within system	RRLoopTwo.thy hcKripkeTwo.thy
Refinement-Risk-Cycle Iteration 2			
Privacy preserving functions type label_fun	Eve puts Bob's data labeled as her own	Introduce blockchain	RRLoopThree.thy hcKripkeThree.thy
Refinement-Risk-Cycle Iteration 3			
Global distributed ledger	Global privacy theorem proved	Done	LedgerRRLoop.thy LedgerhcKripke.thy
Termination of Refinement-Risk-Cycle			

Fig. 3. Iterated application of Refinement-Risk(RR)-Cycle

3   IoT Model in IIIf, Attack Trees Analysis and Refinement to Distributed Ledger

In this section, we first introduce the specification after RR-cycle iteration level 2 (see Fig. 3) where DLM access control labels [16] and privacy preserving functions have already been introduced into the system. We then exhibit an attack using attack tree analysis and present the refinement where a distributed ledger replaces the initial ad hoc data management.

3.1 IoT Healthcare Model in IIIf

The IIIf allows representing infrastructures as graphs where the actors and local policies are attached to the nodes. Infrastructures are the *states* of the system. We use the underlying theory of Kripke structures and temporal logics CTL in the IIIf to define a specific state transition relation for our application scenario. By instantiating the generic Kripke structure state transition relation to each of the refinements of the application scenario, we inherit the underlying theory of CTL and attack trees to provide security analysis in Isabelle.

The infrastructure graph is defined as a datastructure `igraph` whose components `gra`, `agra`, `cgra`, and `lgra` represent the parts as: a set of pairs of nodes; the actor identities at each node; the credentials and roles assigned to actors; and the assignment of `dlm` labeled data at each location. The label type `dlm` is a synonym for `actor` × `actor set` combining the owner and the set of readers into a pair. The constructor `Lgraph` puts these components into an `igraph`.

```
datatype igraph = Lgraph gra: location × location)set
                         agra: location ⇒ identity set
                         cgra: actor ⇒ (string set × string set)
                         lgra: location ⇒ (data × dlm) set
```

We then instantiate igraphs to *locales* (see Fig. 1). The following `ex_graph` is the concrete `igraph` example used in the IoT healthcare case study locale where `ex_creds` and `ex_locs` are example credentials and data (omitted here [12]).

```
ex_graph ≡ Lgraph {(home,cloud), (sphone,cloud), (cloud,hospital)}
                  (λ x. if x = home then {''Patient''} else
                     (if x = hospital then {''Doctor''} else {}))
                  ex_creds ex_locs
```

Infrastructures are generally given by the following datatype that contains an infrastructure graph of type `igraph` and a policy given by a function that assigns local policies over a graph to all locations of the graph.

```
datatype infrastructure = Infrastructure  igraph
                                          [igraph, location] ⇒ policy set
```

For our healthcare example, the instantiated infrastructure contains the above graph `ex_graph` and the local policies defined subsequently.

```
hc_scenario ≡ Infrastructure ex_graph local_policies
```

The function `local_policies` defines the policy for an application: for each location x over an infrastructure graph G as sets of pairs. The first element of a pair is a function specifying the actors y that are entitled to perform the actions specified in the set which is the second element of that pair.

```
local_policies G x ≡
case x of
```

```
  home ⇒ {(λ y. True, {put,get,move,eval})}
| sphone ⇒ {((λ y. has G (y,''PIN'')), {put,get,move,eval})}
| cloud ⇒ {(λ y. True, {put,get,move,eval})}
| hospital ⇒ {((λ y. (∃ n. (n @_G hospital) ∧
             Actor n = y ∧ has G (y, ''skey''))), {put,get,move,eval})}
| _ ⇒ {})
```

In general, policies specify the expected behaviour of actors of an infrastructure. They are given by pairs of predicates (conditions) and sets of (enabled) actions. Policies are controlled by the `enables` predicate: an actor h is enabled to perform an action a in infrastructure I, at location l if there exists a pair (p,e) in the local policy of l (`delta I l` projects to the local policy) such that the action a is a member of the action set e and the policy predicate p holds for actor h.

```
enables I l h a ≡ ∃ (p,e) ∈ delta I l. a ∈ e ∧ p h
```

Infrastructure State Transition. The generic state transition relation uses the syntactic infix notation $I \rightarrow_n I'$ to denote that infrastructures I and I' are in this relation. To give an impression of this definition, we show here just one of several rules that defines the state transition for the action `put` because this rule will be crucial in the following attack analysis. The rule `put` assumes an actor h residing at a location l in the infrastructure graph G and being enabled the `put` action. If infrastructure state I fulfils those preconditions, the next state I' can be constructed from the current state by adding the data item d with label (h, hs) at location l. The addition is given by updating (using :=) the component `lgra` by adding this new labeled data item.

```
put: G = graphI I ⟹ h @_G l ⟹ enables I l (Actor h) put ⟹
     I' = Infrastructure
             (Lgraph (gra G)(agra G)(cgra G)(lgra G)
                      ((lgra G)(l := (lgra G l) ∪ {((Actor h, hs), d)})))
             (delta I)
     ⟹ I →_n I'
```

3.2   Attack Tree Analysis

The goal of the security analysis is also described by a policy: the global policy. The global policy is 'only the patient and the doctor can access the data in the cloud'. In the first two iterations of the RR-cycle, this global policy has twice been attacked (see Fig. 3) by first simply taking the data away (action `get`) and second, after introducing dlm-access control labels, by overwriting the access control label of a data item using the `eval` action. This attack can be prevented by enforcing the use of privacy preserving functions (for details see the source code [12,14]). However, even now there is still an attack possible.

We consider next the following global policy expressing data privacy.

```
global_policy I a ≡ ∀ l ∈ nodes(graphI I). ∀ l' ∈ nodes(graphI I).
        ∀ d:: data. ∀ lb:: dlm. ∀ lb':: dlm.
        (lb, d) ∈ lgra(graphI I l) ⟶ (lb', d) ∈ lgra(graphI I l')
        ⟶ lb = lb'
```

It expresses privacy by saying that different occurrences of the same data in the system must have the same labels. Trying to prove this global policy, we fail. The reason for this is exhibited by the following attack which we find by attack tree analysis (for details see [12,14]). Using the CTL semantics of attack trees in IIIf [9], allows translating the attack into an EF property showing that there exists a path (E) on which eventually (F) Eve can put data on the cloud.

```
hc_KripkeF ⊢   EF I. enables I cloud (Actor ''Eve'') put
```

That is, Eve could learn the data by other means than using the privacy preserving functions introduced in the second iteration of the RR-cycle and use the action put to enter that data as new data to the system but labelled as her own data. As a countermeasure, we need a concept to guarantee consistency of data labeling across the system: we introduce a distributed ledger also known as a blockchain.

3.3   Introducing Distributed Ledger via Refinement

We use the inherent uniqueness of the function type in Isabelle to provide a definition of a distributed ledger in a concise way as a type synonym.

```
type_synonym ledger = data ⇒ (dlm × location set)option
```

A ledger is now a type of "partial" functions that maps a data item to a pair of the data's label and the set of locations where the data item is registered. Since all functions in HOL are total, we use a standard Isabelle way of representing partial functions using the type constructor option. This type constructor lifts a type α to the type α option which consists of the unique constant None and the range of elements Some x for all $x \in \alpha$.

Since the type ledger is a function type, an element of type ledger maps a data item d to at most one range element Some(1,L) (or to None if this data element is not in use in the system). Thus, every data item d has at most one valid data label 1 of type dlm and one unique list of current infrastructure locations L where this data item is located.

These observations about the definition of the type ledger can be exploited formally in Isabelle and proved accordingly (∃! is unique existence).

```
lemma ledger_def_prop: ∀ lg:: ledger. ∀ d:: data.
                lg d = None ∨ (∃! 1L. lg d = Some(1L))
```

In order to refine the IoT healthcare application introducing the ledger as a component of the infrastructure state, we re-define the type igraph.

```
datatype igraph = Lgraph gra: location × location)set
                        agra: location ⇒ identity set
                        cgra: actor ⇒ (string set × string set)
                        lgra:  ledger
```

The previous database component `lgra` is now replaced by a distributed ledger: the consistency is guaranteed by its global control but the decentralization is given by assigning the data to various locations as recorded in the ledger in a set of locations L.

To formally verify that the introduction of the ledger is a refinement, we follow the RR-cycle process and define a refinement map.

```
definition ref_map :: [LedgerRRLoopFour.infrastructure,
                       [RRLoopThree.igraph, location] ⇒ policy set]
                    ⇒ RRLoopThree.infrastructure"
where ref_map I lp = RRLoopThree.Infrastructure
                        (RRLoopThree.Lgraph
                         (gra (graphI I))(agra (graphI I))
                         (cgra (graphI I))
                         (ledger_to_loc (ledgra (graphI I))))
                        lp
```

The `ref_map` takes elements of type `LedgerRRLoopFour.infrastructure` – the refined infrastructure type – using their components to construct abstract infrastructures of type `RRLoopThree.infrastructure`. The names `RRLoopThree` and `LedgerRRLoopFour` are Isabelle theory names and also designate the iterations of the RR-cycle (see Fig. 3 for an overview). These names are used for name spacing and thus disambiguating the constructors in Isabelle. The second input `lp` is a local policy which is a parameter to the application refinement defined in the application's locale instance. The Isabelle RR-cycle provides the necessary meta-theory to prove this refinement.

Note, the last component in the infrastructure **ledger_to_loc** is the most crucial part of the refinement as it transforms an element of type `ledger` of the refined infrastructure into a function assigning sets of labelled data to locations in the abstract infrastructure type. This constructor is defined as follows.

```
definition ledger_to_loc :: ledger ⇒ location
                         ⇒ (RRLoopThree.dlm × RRLoopThree.data) set
where ledger_to_loc ld l ≡ (if (∃ d. l ∈ snd(the(ld d))) then
                             {(lb,d). l ∈ snd(the(ld d))} else {})
```

The state transition relation in the refined infrastructure specification uses the ledger to implement privacy control by adding corresponding conditions to each inductive rule. For example, the rule for put (see Sect. 3.1), now checks whether the ledger designated the actor's identity h as the owner of the data item d to authorise that it may be copied to location l. This copying is recorded in the ledger by adding (using function update :=) the location l to the location set L of d (using the **insert** set operation).

```
put: G = graphI I ⟹ h @_G l ⟹ enables I l (Actor h) put ⟹
     ledgra G d = Some ((h, hs), L) ⟹
     I' = Infrastructure
              (Lgraph (gra G)(agra G)(cgra G)(lgra G)
                      ((ledgra G)(d := Some ((h, hs), insert l L))))
              (delta I)
     ⟹ I →_n I'
```

Considering now the refined infrastructure model for the IoT healthcare scenario, we reconsider the privacy attack detected in Iteration 2 of the RR-cycle. We can now prove that the previously desired global policy expressing data privacy (Sect. 3.2) is globally valid: data are labelled uniquely.

```
theorem ledger_guarantees_privacy:
  hc_KripkeF ⊢ AG {x. ∀ d:: data. ∀ d':: data.
                      d = d' ⟶ ledgra(graphI x d) = ledgra(graphI x d')}
```

The initial **hc_KripkeF** is the concrete Kripke structure representing the IoT healthcare example instantiated as a locale. The **ledger_guarantees_privacy** theorem is first proved at the locale level but can be generalized to hold for any model using the ledger as a final step of the RR-cycle. The RR-cycle is thus terminated successfully.

3.4 Discussion

Even though Eve can still put data on the cloud, the refinement introducing the distributed ledger prevents the privacy attack. Because of the ledger, Eve cannot put existing data (that of Bob) with her own label any more. The new **put** semantics only allows extending the ledger by adding new locations and this only for the data owner.

Effective implementations of the ledger need mapping out the globally consistent type **data** to a decentralized datastructure, for example a blockchain with Consensus to preserve the decentralized control specified here. This implementation could be defined within Isabelle and proved to be a refinement of the ledger specification. If this implementation is constructive, code can be extracted from Isabelle into programming languages, like ML, Haskell or Scala.

In comparison to the earlier experiments with applying the RR-cycle to the IoT healthcare case study [14], we could now terminate the RR-cycle process and prove a global (AG) privacy theorem. Moreover, the new type ledger also simplifies the proofs. Compared to the older (partially unfinished) proofs at Iteration 3 and 4 (see [14]) the proofs are shorter. In addition, we do not need to add an explicit precondition to the new put rule that the data item has not been there ([Section IV.C] [14]). The new type ledger implicitly guarantees that.

4   Conclusions and Related Work

In this paper, we summarize some previous preliminary reports [10,14] on using the Isabelle RR-cycle to develop a privacy enhancing architecture for an IoT healthcare scenario. The main contribution is to show how to integrate a distributed ledger into the specification to guarantee global consistency of access control data labeling correcting earlier attempts [14]. Thereby, the RR-cycle can be successfully terminated exhibiting a global privacy property.

Formal system specification refinement has been investigated for some time initially for system refinement in the specification language Z [8] but a dedicated security refinement has not been formalized for some time [15]. The idea to refine a system specification for security has been already addressed in B [2,17]. The former combines the refinement of B with system security policies given in Organisation based Access Control (OrBAC) and presents a generic example of a system development. While B is supported by its own tool Atelier B, it does not provide a formalization in a theorem prover unlike our integration which supports dedicated security concepts like attack trees and enables useful meta-theory over the integration. The paper [17] looks at attacks within the B framework but it aims at designing a monitor that catches actions forbidden by the policy not on using these attacks to refine the system specification. Dynamic risk assessment using attack formalism, like attack graphs, has recently found great attention, e.g. [7]. However, usually, the focus of the process lies on attack generation and response planning while we address the design of secure systems. Rather than incident response, we intend to use early analysis of system specification to provide a development of secure systems. This includes physical infrastructure, like IoT system architecture, as well as organisational policies with actors.

The Workshop Formal Methods on Blockchain (FMBC) [5] has been running yearly from 2019 till 2022 and has produced a number of formalizations also in interactive proof assistants like Coq or Isabelle. From this rich set of related work it is worth mentioning an approach to formalize the FA1.2 Ledger standard in Coq [6]. The goal of this paper has been similar to ours to provide a precise specification of a ledger. The authors look however at a specific technical standard for Tezos as well as using Coq. Moreover, they are not aiming at providing a high level general specification.

There are a number of formalizations of blockchains in interactive proof assistants, for example, Mi-cho-coq [3] and Concert [1] amongst others. Mostly, these formalizations focus on smart contracts to analyze security attacks on cryptocurrencies like Bitcoin. They effectively try to grasp the semantics of the smart contract languages and the effect they have on manipulating cryptocurrency transfers in their models, how to analyze them and extract code into blockchain languages like Tezos. We focus on the global consistency property of a distributed ledger as a security measure to support privacy in IoT applications like healthcare. Smart contracts and cryptocurrencies are a secondary concern.

Other fully automated verification techniques like Modelchecking sometimes also use refinement checking but the refinement of the RR-cycle requires data refinement in addition to trace refinement thus necessitating more expressive logics like Isabelle's HOL.

The presented work aims at showing how the RR-cycle helps identifying and improving on design errors in early phases of the IoT system design. It draws together a number of previous preliminary attempts and finalizes them by applying the closed form of the RR-cycle definition.

The developed specification presents a concise formal definition of a distributed ledger. Although abstract it is well suited to ensure that distributed data can be handled in a privacy-preserving fashion. The formal specification in Isabelle can also be used to derive more concrete specifications – using refinement – and finally to extract code into programming languages like Haskell or Scala. Future work may address scalability: RR-cycle refinement could be applied to map the current abstract specification to add more detail of actual IoT hardware and Instruction Set Architectures (ISAs). We specify privacy by using data labeling and verifying it by ensuring label consistency across the system. It is interesting to explore how this technique relates to specific notions of data privacy, like k-anonymity or differential privacy.

References

1. Annenkov, D., Nielsen, J.B., Spitters, B.: Concert: a smart contract certification framework in Coq. Certified Programs and Proofs, CPP, ACM (2020)
2. Benaïssa, N., Cansell, D., Méry, D.: Integration of security policy into system modeling. In: Julliand, J., Kouchnarenko, O. (eds.) B 2007. LNCS, vol. 4355, pp. 232–247. Springer, Heidelberg (2006). https://doi.org/10.1007/11955757_19
3. Bernardo, B., Cauderlier, R., Hu, Z., Pesin, B., Tesson, J.: Mi-cho-coq, a framework for certifying tezos smart contracts. CoRR, (abs/1909.08671) (2019)
4. CHIST-ERA. Success: Secure accessibility for the internet of things (2016). http://www.chistera.eu/projects/success
5. FMBC. International workshop on formal methods for blockchain (2019). https://fmbc.gitlab.io
6. Gabbay, J., Jakobsson, A., Sojakova, K.: Money grows on (proof-)trees: the formal fa1.2 ledger standard. In: 3rd International Workshop on Formal Methods for Blockchains (FMBC 2021), pp. 2:1–2:14. OASics 2021
7. Gonzalez-Granadillo, G., et al.: Dynamic risk management response system to handle cyber threats. Futur. Gener. Comput. Syst. 83, 535–552 (2018)
8. He, J., Hoare, C.A.R., Sanders, J.W.: Data refinement refined. In: ESOP. LNCS, vol. 214, pp. 187–196. Springer (1986)
9. Kammüller, F.: Attack trees in Isabelle. In: Naccache, D., Xu, S., Qing, S., Samarati, P., Blanc, G., Lu, R., Zhang, Z., Meddahi, A. (eds.) ICICS 2018. LNCS, vol. 11149, pp. 611–628. Springer, Cham (2018). https://doi.org/10.1007/978-3-030-01950-1_36
10. Kammüller, F.: Combining secure system design with risk assessment for iot healthcare systems. In: Security, Privacy, and Trust in the IoT, SPTIoT'19. IEEE (2019)
11. Kammüller, F.: Dependability engineering in isabelle (2021). arxiv preprint, http://arxiv.org/abs/2112.04374
12. Kammüller, F.: Isabelle Insider and Infrastructure framework with Kripke structures, CTL, attack trees, security refinement, and IoT example (2022). https://github.com/flokam/IsabelleAT
13. Kammüller, F., Ogunyanwo, O., Probst, C.: Using fusion/uml for iot architectures for healthcare applications (2018). arXiv https://arxiv.org/abs/1901.02426

14. Kammüller, F.: A formal development cycle for security engineering in isabelle (2020). arxiv preprint http://arxiv.org/abs/2001.08983
15. Morgan, C.: The shadow knows: refinement and security in sequential programs. Sci. Comput. Programm. **74**, 629–653 (2009)
16. Myers, A.C., Liskov, B.: Complete, safe information flow with decentralized labels. In: Proceedings of the IEEE Symposium on Security and Privacy. IEEE (1999)
17. Stouls, N., Potet, M.-L.: Security policy enforcement through refinement process. In: Julliand, J., Kouchnarenko, O. (eds.) B 2007. LNCS, vol. 4355, pp. 216–231. Springer, Heidelberg (2006). https://doi.org/10.1007/11955757_18

Enhancing Security Assurance in Software Development: AI-Based Vulnerable Code Detection with Static Analysis

Sampath Rajapaksha[1]($\boxtimes$)(iD), Janaka Senanayake[1](iD), Harsha Kalutarage[1](iD), and Mhd Omar Al-Kadri[2](iD)

[1] School of Computing, Robert Gordon University, Aberdeen AB10 7QB, UK
{s.rajapaksha,j.senanayake,h.kalutarage}@rgu.ac.uk
[2] University of Doha for Science and Technology, Doha, Qatar
omar.alkadri@udst.edu.qa

Abstract. The presence of vulnerable source code in software applications is causing significant reliability and security issues, which can be mitigated by integrating and assuring software security principles during the early stages of the development lifecycle. One promising approach to identifying vulnerabilities in source code is the use of Artificial Intelligence (AI). This research proposes an AI-based method for detecting source code vulnerabilities and leverages Explainable AI to help developers identify and understand vulnerable source code tokens. To train the model, a web crawler was used to collect a real-world dataset of 600,000 source code samples, which were annotated using static analysers. Several ML classifiers were tested on a feature vector generated using Natural Language Processing techniques. The Random Forest and Extreme Gradient Boosting classifiers were found to perform well in binary and multi-class approaches, respectively. The proposed model achieved a 0.96 F1-Score in binary classification and a 0.85 F1-Score in multi-class classification based on Common Weakness Enumeration (CWE) IDs. The model, trained on a dataset of actual source codes, is highly generalisable and has been integrated into a live web portal to validate its performance on real-world code vulnerabilities.

Keywords: source code vulnerability · artificial intelligence · software security · vulnerability scanners

1 Introduction

In software development, it is common for developers to overlook the thorough validation of source code for security and vulnerability during coding and prior to releasing the product to the customer [6]. This oversight can cause security threats to rapidly evolve, which forces developers to keep up to date with the latest security vulnerabilities to minimize the risk of software attacks. Education on security for developers is an ongoing process, but currently, many software

S. Katsikas et al. (Eds.): ESORICS 2023 Workshops, LNCS 14399, pp. 341–356, 2024.
https://doi.org/10.1007/978-3-031-54129-2_20

developers neglect security issues throughout the software development lifecycle. This may be due to a lack of understanding about how common errors in software development can lead to exploitable vulnerabilities in software systems [13], as well as the pressure for fast deployment. The communication gap between developers and cybersecurity experts has also contributed to widespread software vulnerabilities [20].

However, with the availability of data, new algorithms, and advances in computational power, AI and ML techniques can be effectively used to address various problems in different domains, including computer security and privacy [21]. Hence, AI/ML algorithms can be utilized to detect vulnerabilities in source codes [2,14]. By using AI/ML algorithms for vulnerability detection, the need for human expertise can be reduced [22], and the process can be automated. Programming languages consist of words, numbers, and various symbols, similar to natural languages. Therefore, previous research has used Natural Language Processing (NLP) techniques to detect vulnerabilities in source code by treating the code as a form of text [3]. To train AI/ML algorithms, extracted features have been generated through NLP techniques, considering this as a classification problem. However, existing methods have used limited information for feature generation, resulting in high false negatives.

This study addresses the need for a highly accurate source code vulnerability detection method using AI/ML techniques and proposes a new approach to feature generation, and demonstrates its effectiveness through experiments. The study makes the following contributions to the field of source code vulnerability detection and offers a promising solution for automated security testing in software development.

- *Data pre-processing approach to identify important features:* Presenting a novel method using Concrete Syntax Trees (CST) to identify the most important features of source codes to train an ML model.
- *Generalized vulnerability detection models:* The generalization capability of the proposed method is high since the models are trained on a carefully generated dataset that includes real-world source codes and a subset of a synthetic dataset.
- *Explainability of the model:* Visually representing the identified vulnerable source code segments to help make the necessary changes to convert the code from vulnerable to benign. Furthermore, this supports optimising the pre-processing data approach to improve the model accuracy.
- *Integration with a web portal:* Once the developer enters the source code, the vulnerability of the code is displayed on a web portal with an explanation of the vulnerabilities associated with it.

The rest of the paper is organised as follows: Sect. 2 contains background and related work. Section 3 explains the methodology of this work. Section 4 discusses the performance evaluation. Finally, the conclusions and future work are discussed in Sect. 5.

2   Background and Related Work

By reviewing relevant studies, this section lays the groundwork for the research by providing a thorough understanding of source code vulnerabilities, different parsers and scanners, as well as a range of vulnerability detection techniques.

2.1   Vulnerabilities in Source Code

Human error can lead to numerous vulnerabilities in software code, particularly when an extensive testing and validation process is not implemented from the beginning of the software development lifecycle [6]. To promote secure software development practices, reducing vulnerabilities in the source code is essential [19]. Nevertheless, without proper mechanisms in place, some developers may overlook potential vulnerabilities. To address these issues, various repositories of vulnerabilities and weaknesses have been established by organizations and the community, such as Common Weakness Enumeration (CWE)[1] and Common Vulnerabilities and Exposures (CVE)[2]. These repositories contain software and hardware-related vulnerabilities, which developers can reference when identifying patterns and mitigating security loopholes in the source code. Additionally, it is important to note that some vulnerabilities are related to other vulnerabilities and can belong to more than one CWE category. Awareness of these relationships can help developers develop software more securely. By providing automated tool support based on CWE and CVE details, the software development process can be completed more efficiently and vulnerable source code can be minimized.

2.2   Scanners and Parsers

Supportive tools are required by software developers to integrate with their coding and detect vulnerabilities at an early stage to mitigate them through source code analysis [12,14,16–18]. The source code must first be formatted into a generalized form, either using CST or Abstract Syntax Tree (AST). Syntax trees can be generated through static analysis [8]. The accuracy of formulating the CST/AST and its generalisation mechanism influences the rate of false alarms on vulnerabilities. Tree-sitter[3], an open-source parser generator tool, can create a CST for a source file and efficiently update the tree when changes occur in the source code.

After parsing the code, analysis can be performed using scanners. Some scanners are available for analyzing C/C++ source code with relatively good accuracy [10]. Cppcheck[4] is an open-source static analysis tool that detects bugs, undefined behavior, and dangerous coding constructs in C/C++ code. It provides essential data for each alert, such as filename, line, severity, alert identifier,

---

[1] https://cwe.mitre.org.
[2] https://www.cvedetails.com.
[3] https://tree-sitter.github.io/tree-sitter.
[4] https://cppcheck.sourceforge.io.

and CWE, and can be integrated with other development tools. Another open-source tool, Flawfinder[5], can examine C/C++ source code and report possible security weaknesses. It has a built-in database of C/C++ functions with well-known vulnerable problems, such as format string problems (printf, snprintf, and syslog), buffer overflow risks (strcpy, strcat, gets, sprintf, and scanf), potential shell meta-character dangers (exec, system, popen), poor random number acquisition (random), and race conditions (access, chown, chgrp, chmod, tmpfile, tmpnam, tempnam, and mktemp).

2.3 Detecting Vulnerabilities

Previous works have proposed two techniques to detect vulnerabilities, namely metric-based techniques and pattern-based techniques. Metric-based techniques utilize features such as complexity metrics, token frequency metrics, code churn metrics, dependency metrics, developer activity metrics, or execution complexity metric to detect vulnerabilities through supervised or unsupervised machine learning methods [4]. On the other hand, pattern-based techniques utilize static analysis to identify vulnerable codes based on known vulnerable patterns. However, this technique is limited to function-level codes and is considered a preliminary step for vulnerability assessment since it does not identify the vulnerability type or possible locations. Moreover, the use of metric-based features in different machine learning algorithms showed low detection capability.

In [15], the authors utilized text features extracted from the source code to predict software defects. They considered everything as text except comments, separated by space or tab. Naive Bayes (NB) and Logistic Regression (LR) were used as classification algorithms. This approach was adapted by [15] for software vulnerability prediction tasks, using the same algorithms with Bag of Words (BoW) as features. However, the experimental results showed a lower F1-Score for all selected test cases, which may be due to poor feature selection and lack of emphasis on proper data pre-processing. In [7], n-gram (1-gram, 2-gram, and 3-gram) and word2vec were used as features to predict the presence of vulnerabilities in test cases. The authors addressed the class imbalance problem by using random oversampling. However, this model [7] is limited to binary classification and cannot identify the type of vulnerability.

In their work [14], the authors utilized minimum intermediate representation learning for detecting vulnerabilities in source code. In order to address the lack of vulnerability samples, unsupervised learning was employed during the pre-training stage. High-level features were generated using Convolutional Neural Networks (CNN), and these features were subsequently fed into classifiers such as Logistic Regression (LR), Naive Bayes (NB), Support Vector Machine (SVM), Multi-Layer Perceptron (MLP), Gradient Boosting (GB), Decision Tree (DT), and Random Forest (RF) for vulnerability detection. However, this model was trained using only two CWE-IDs from a synthetic dataset, which limits its generalization capability to other CWE-IDs and real datasets.

---

[5] https://github.com/david-a-wheeler/flawfinder

The authors of [5] presented a technique to assist manual source code analysis through vulnerability extrapolation. They achieved this by generating an AST using a parser, but this approach was limited to identifying vulnerabilities in only a few source code functions. Similarly, [2] employed an AST representation of source code to detect vulnerabilities. They utilized the Pycparser[6] library to generate the AST for the C language and modeled it as a binary classification task, using MLP and CNN algorithms. The proposed model targeted four CWE classes, achieving an F1-Score between 0.09 to 0.59. Commercially accessible solutions like Fortify[7] and Coverity[8] are among the tools available for identifying vulnerabilities. However, these tools are not freely accessible and have limitations in effectively identifying vulnerabilities linked to CWE IDs.

Despite the increasing popularity of utilizing machine learning for vulnerability detection, as previously mentioned, several studies have failed to achieve a high accuracy/F1-Score when identifying vulnerabilities in source code. Many of these studies were not trained on a comprehensive dataset that includes real-world data or did not follow improved pre-processing techniques. Additionally, these studies were limited to binary classification or a small number of Common Weakness Enumeration (CWE) classes. As a result, our research addresses these issues by using a real-world dataset and achieving an F1-Score of 0.96 in the binary classification model and 0.85 in the multi-class classification model for twenty CWE classes. These results outperform the state-of-the-art benchmark models.

3   Vulnerability Detection Process

In this section, we will cover the proposed vulnerability detection process, which comprises the model's architecture as well as the dataset used.

3.1   Dataset

Generally, ML-based methods require a large amount of dataset during the training phase. One of the major challenges of source code vulnerability detection is the lack of vulnerability datasets for the majority of common CWE-IDs [9]. National Institute of Standards and Technology (NIST) published a dataset to encourage the improvement of static code analysers and to find security-related defects in source code. This dataset was published as a result of Software Assurance Metrics and Tool Evaluation (SAMATE) project[9] and the dataset is referred as Static Analysis Tool Exposition (SATE IV) Juliet test suite[10] This

---

[6] https://github.com/eliben/pycparser.

[7] https://www.microfocus.com/en-us/cyberres/application-security/fortify-languages.

[8] https://www.synopsys.com/software-integrity/security-testing/static-analysis-sast/coverity-cwe.html.

[9] https://samate.nist.gov/SARD/.

[10] https://www.nist.gov/itl/ssd/software-quality-group/static-analysis-tool-exposition-sate-iv.

dataset includes 52,185 synthetic test cases for C and C++ languages and annotated for CWE-IDs. However, the major limitations of this dataset are highly imbalanced CWE-ID distribution and the lack of availability of benign data to train supervised ML algorithms. To address these issues, a web crawler was developed to retrieve more C and C++ source codes from public GitHub repositories. Since the retrieved GitHub source codes are not annotated for CWE-IDs to train ML algorithms, two static code analysers, Cppcheck and Flawfinder which are based on pre-defined rules were used for the CWE-ID annotation. The annotation was also verified with the expert knowledge of ethical hackers and security testers to ensure the quality of the dataset. In general, rule-based methods have lower false positives and suffer from higher false negatives. Different rule-based static code analysers have different vulnerability detection capabilities based on the defined rules. The objective of this approach, as a proof of concept, is to learn both analysers' capabilities and achieve lower false negative and positive rates from ML-based models. Going forward, a significant number of freely available and commercial-grade analysers could be utilized for annotation, enabling trained ML models to learn the capabilities of various analysers. Ultimately, this could result in the development of a superior AI-based code analyser that outperforms any existing static code analysers. Accordingly, a sample was considered as vulnerable if one of the analysers identifies the code as vulnerable. In contrast, sample was considered as benign if both analysers identify it as benign. Source codes relevant to the twenty highest CWE-IDs were considered as the vulnerable samples whereas, an approximately a similar number of benign samples were selected to make a balanced dataset. This resulted in having 600,000 C and C++ source codes, including SATA IV vulnerable codes. Figure 1 depicts the CWE-ID count distribution for the selected vulnerable source codes.

3.2 Model Architecture

The suggested framework comprises of two ML models designed for both binary and multiclass classification purposes. The binary model's function is to distinguish between vulnerable and benign statuses, whereas the multiclass model is aimed at recognizing CWE-IDs if the source code is found to be vulnerable. Additionally, the utilisation of Explainable Artificial Intelligence (XAI) [1], is incorporated to explain the predictions made by the model. This is achieved by highlighting sections of code (tokens) that are considered vulnerable, based on the outcomes from the multiclass model. The entire procedure is illustrated in Fig. 2, encompassing three core steps: data preprocessing, binary and multiclass classification, and prediction explanation facilitated by XAI.

Data Pre-processing. The entire source code available in dataset is referred as the sample. This might include a function, a snippet of code or a large source code file. SATE IV dataset includes large source code files, whereas retrieved GitHub source codes include all levels of codes. Therefore, the proposed solution can take any code as input to the ML models. The developer sends the source

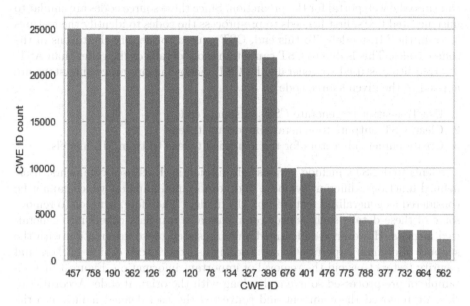

Fig. 1. CWE-ID distribution

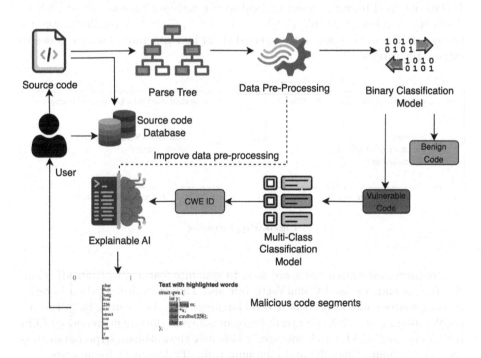

Fig. 2. Model Architecture

code into the web portal for the prediction. Since these source codes are similar to unstructured texts, first it needs to pre-process the codes to identify the features to train the ML models. To this end, CST is used to identify the tokens of the source codes. This is due to CST can retain more details of the codes than AST.

Tree-sitter is used to generate the CST. Following pre-processing steps are applied to the given source code.

1. Use Tree-sitter to generate CSTs of source codes.
2. Clean CST outputs to generate important tokens.
3. Create numerical vectors for the identified tokens to train ML models.

Generated CSTs include various information such as user comments, user-defined functions, different symbols, and hexadecimal numbers which cannot be considered as generalized features for ML models. Therefore, it needs to remove some of these details such as user comments and translate others into generalized formats. However, we identified and translated these information with the support of domain experts who are working as experienced ethical hackers and security testers to avoid the removal of important information. Figure 3 shows a sample of pre-processed source code along with the original code. According to this, we removed the comment and converted the user-defined names into the standard format of 'Userdef'. Additionally, the number 20 was converted into 'number'. C and C++ specific names (functions and keywords) kept unchanged. Tokens obtained from the pre-processed source code are ['static', 'const', 'char', 'Userdef', 'number', 'return', '(', ')', '*', '{', '}', '[', ']', ';']. Accordingly, we pre-processed all source codes and converted them into generalized source codes to extract the tokens.

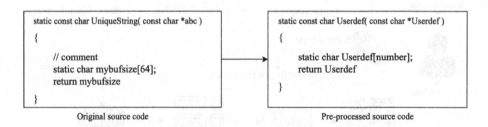

Fig. 3. Preprocessing

Pre-processed source codes are used to generate features to train ML models. To this end, we used CountVectorizer and TfidfVectorizer Python libraries treating source codes as texts in natural language [11]. As features, Bag-of-words (BoW), n-gram (n = 2, 3) and term frequency-inverse document frequency (TF-IDF) were used. Grid search was used to identify the optimum hyperparameters such as maximum (max df) and minimum (min df) document frequencies.

Algorithms: Features generated by the data pre-processing step can be used in binary and multi-class classification models. Accordingly, 600,000 source code samples are used to train the binary classification model. Dataset were split into 80:20 ratio as training and testing samples. Based on our previous work, RF, LR and XGB algorithms were used as the classification algorithms with the features of BoW, n-gram and TF-IDF. The trained binary classifier can identify the given source code as vulnerable or benign. If the code is vulnerable, then it sends into the multi-class classification model to identify the relevant CWE-IDs. Similar to binary model training, 300,000 vulnerable source code samples were split into 80:20 ratio with the stratified sampling to train the above algorithms. Since a vulnerable code might have more than one vulnerability, the top K (K = 3) predictions were used as possible vulnerable classes to address the multi-label cases. Python sklearn library was used to implement these algorithms. All experiments run on a MacBook M1 Pro with 16 GB RAM.

We also compare the proposed multi-class classification model with the Multi-Layer Perceptron (MLP) based model proposed in [2]. We consider this as the baseline model. This model converts the source code into the AST representation using Pycparser[11] library. To encode nodes of an AST into numeric values, they identified 48 different essential token types based on the grammar of C language and assigned unique values for each token type. Array representation of this was used to train the MLP model.

Vulnerability Explanation: Identifying the code as vulnerable is not much useful if the vulnerable code segments (tokens) are not located. The developer has to go through the complete code and needs to identify these tokens manually and the lack of knowledge about the vulnerabilities might restrict the vulnerable token identification. Therefore, locating the vulnerable tokens is vital in evaluating the model prediction and to make the necessary changes to the vulnerable code to make it a benign code. To this end, we use Local Interpretable Model-agnostic Explanations (LIME)[12] framework to explain the prediction. LIME provides an explanation which is a local linear approximation of the behaviour of the trained model. LIME learns a sparse linear model by sampling instances around specific instances, approximating the trained model locally. LIME supports natural language-based models and provides visual and textual artefacts that developers can understand. We used our trained multi-class model with LIME to provide the model explanation. This provides output by highlighting the vulnerable token in the input source code. The developer confirmed accurate CWE-IDs (ground truth) sends to the source code database for future model retraining. During the model training, outputs of the LIME were used to optimize the data pre-processing with the support of domain experts by removing non-related tokens and keeping the important tokens.

---

[11] https://github.com/eliben/pycparser.

[12] https://github.com/marcotcr/lime.

4   Performance Evaluation

This section provides the results for both binary and multiclass models for a different set of features. The test dataset was used to evaluate the performance. F1-Score was selected as the evaluation metric as it provides the harmonic mean of precision and recall. For the binary classification model, label 0 represents benign source codes, whereas label 1 represents vulnerable source codes. In contrast, the multi-class classification model has twenty CWE-IDs as the label.

4.1   Machine Learning Models

Four ML models were used to identify the best models for binary and multiclass classification using selected features. Table 1 summarises the F1-Score for binary classification models for BoW, 2-gram, 3-gram and TF-IDF features. We included the default hyperparameters into the grid search criteria and all algorithms achieved best performance for the default hyperparameters. The BoW feature achieved a higher F1-Score than the 2-gram or 3-gram. XGB model achieved the lowest detection for all features. The RF algorithm outperformed LR and XGB and showed the best performance with the feature BoW as highlighted in the green colour cell in Table 1.

Table 1. Performance of binary classification ML algorithms with BoW, n-gram, and TF-IDF features (F1-Score)

Class	NB				LR				RF				XGB			
	BoW	2-gram	3-gram	TF-IDF	BoW	2-gram	3-gram	TF-IDF	BoW	2-gram	3-gram	TF-IDF	BoW	2-gram	3-gram	TF-IDF
0	0.72	0.57	0.63	0.84	0.90	0.88	0.89	0.91	0.95	0.95	0.95	0.95	0	0.02	0.03	0
1	0.81	0.76	0.78	0.85	0.89	0.88	0.89	0.91	0.96	0.95	0.95	0.95	0.68	0.63	0.66	0.68
Overall	0.76	0.66	0.71	0.84	0.89	0.88	0.89	0.91	0.96	0.95	0.95	0.95	0.34	0.33	0.37	0.34

Table 2 presents the performance for multi-class classification. Increasing the n-gram of the LR model resulted to achieve higher F1-Score. However, the opposite can be observable for the RF and XGB models. XGB model with BoW feature outperformed all other algorithms and feature combination with the overall F1-Score of 0.85 as highlighted in the green colour cell in Table 2. Similar to the binary classification features, BoW performed better than n-gram for multiclass classification. In general, higher n-gram includes the context of tokens and are expected to perform better than the BoW feature. However, increasing the n-gram causes to increase the sparsity of feature vectors and this might be a possible reason for the weak performance of n-gram feature compared to BoW feature. Another possible reason would be the association of key terms with the vulnerabilities than the term combination. The baseline model (MLP) only outperformed the LR model for BoW, 2-gram and 3-gram features. This is likely due to restricted token types used during the data pre-processing. In contrast,

Table 2. Performance of multi-class classification ML algorithms with BoW, n-gram, and TF-IDF features (F1-Score)

CWE ID	NB				LR				RF				XGB			
	BoW	2-gram	3-gram	TF-IDF	BoW	2-gram	3-gram	TF-IDF	BoW	2-gram	3-gram	TF-IDF	BoW	2-gram	3-gram	TF-IDF
20	0.39	0.39	0.34	0.56	0.63	0.63	0.63	0.70	0.82	0.79	0.74	0.82	0.87	0.83	0.76	0.87
78	0.57	0.57	0.56	0.66	0.78	0.75	0.73	0.83	0.91	0.88	0.84	0.9	0.95	0.91	0.85	0.95
120	0.06	0.34	0.35	0.55	0.59	0.60	0.59	0.62	0.80	0.78	0.75	0.79	0.83	0.82	0.78	0.82
126	0.30	0.32	0.32	0.53	0.58	0.60	0.61	0.66	0.83	0.80	0.75	0.83	0.87	0.84	0.80	0.87
134	0.40	0.43	0.45	0.54	0.65	0.68	0.69	0.69	0.85	0.82	0.80	0.85	0.86	0.84	0.79	0.86
190	0.35	0.29	0.28	0.57	0.70	0.71	0.68	0.73	0.88	0.87	0.83	0.88	0.91	0.89	0.83	0.90
327	0.57	0.53	0.51	0.69	0.87	0.80	0.75	0.84	0.94	0.90	0.85	0.94	0.96	0.91	0.83	0.96
362	0.49	0.50	0.49	0.58	0.71	0.69	0.67	0.71	0.84	0.82	0.79	0.83	0.87	0.84	0.81	0.87
377	0.26	0.23	0.24	0.32	0.36	0.41	0.48	0.62	0.74	0.67	0.62	0.73	0.86	0.72	0.65	0.85
398	0.70	0.73	0.74	0.74	0.86	0.87	0.87	0.86	0.93	0.92	0.91	0.93	0.94	0.94	0.92	0.93
401	0.39	0.42	0.43	0.43	0.42	0.54	0.59	0.62	0.78	0.76	0.73	0.77	0.79	0.80	0.77	0.79
457	0.39	0.40	0.44	0.57	0.65	0.67	0.68	0.69	0.84	0.83	0.81	0.84	0.84	0.82	0.78	0.83
476	0.30	0.32	0.33	0.23	0.40	0.47	0.54	0.47	0.77	0.76	0.75	0.78	0.72	0.72	0.69	0.71
562	0.30	0.31	0.29	0.17	0.47	0.50	0.56	0.38	0.77	0.77	0.76	0.76	0.70	0.71	0.70	0.69
664	0.26	0.26	0.27	0.21	0.34	0.38	0.51	0.48	0.77	0.76	0.74	0.77	0.81	0.82	0.79	0.82
676	0.50	0.48	0.45	0.49	0.79	0.73	0.68	0.80	0.92	0.88	0.80	0.92	0.97	0.91	0.83	0.96
732	0.36	0.40	0.40	0.48	0.66	0.61	0.64	0.70	0.85	0.81	0.75	0.85	0.91	0.89	0.80	0.91
758	0.52	0.53	0.52	0.63	0.70	0.73	0.78	0.76	0.92	0.92	0.91	0.92	0.89	0.87	0.83	0.89
775	0.27	0.27	0.30	0.44	0.38	0.44	0.52	0.52	0.68	0.66	0.64	0.66	0.72	0.73	0.71	0.70
788	0.10	0.29	0.33	0.23	0.16	0.21	0.30	0.43	0.66	0.67	0.65	0.65	0.64	0.67	0.64	0.63
Overall	0.37	0.40	0.40	0.48	0.59	0.60	0.62	0.66	0.82	0.80	0.77	0.82	0.85	0.82	0.78	0.84

we considered higher number of token types and CST preserve more details than the AST outputs.

CWE-IDs which has over 20,000 training samples achieved over 0.8 F1-Score. However, some CWE-IDs such as 676 achieved higher F1-Score regardless of the small sample size. Usage of vulnerable tokens such as strcat(), strcpy() and sprintf() lead to the CWE-ID 676 vulnerability. Therefore, it is possible to learn these types of patterns well even with a smaller dataset due to the frequent appearance of vulnerable tokens. To evaluate the impotence of dataset size for vulnerability detection, we trained a separate XGB model with the BoW feature by only considering the CWE-IDs which had over 20,000 samples. Table 3 summarizes the performance achieved for this model. As expected, this increased the overall F1-Score by 4%. Therefore, it is possible to improve the detection performance by increasing the dataset size.

Table 3. Performance of XGB algorithm with BoW for 12 classes (F1-Score)

CWE ID	120	126	134	190	208	327	362	398	457	758	780	Other	Overall
F1-Score	0.8	0.88	0.86	0.9	0.87	0.96	0.87	0.94	0.83	0.88	0.96	0.89	0.89

In the deployed web portal, developers are expected to get the prediction with the minimum time and highest detection rate. Therefore, detection latency is another important aspect of the source code vulnerability detection model in a real-world environment. This was estimated for the BoW feature due to its higher vulnerability detection capability. Table 4 summarizes the average detection latency (ms) per source code sample for the three ML models and the baseline model. LR takes the minimum time for the prediction. RF takes higher time which is not suitable for deployment. In contrast, XGB provides the best detection and latency trade-off by outperforming the baseline model.

Table 4. Average detection latency

ML Algorithm	Detection latency (ms)
MLP	36.41
LR	8.378
RF	175.968
XGB	**14.37**

4.2   Explainable AI and Web Portal Output

Based on the achieved F1-Score and detection latency, we deployed the RF as a binary classifier and XGB as the multi-class clarifier in the web portal backend. Therefore, LIME used the RF as the classifier to give the prediction explanation. In the deployed web portal, the developer gets the highlighted code as the output for the given input source code. Even though the CWE-ID annotation was done at the multi-class level by assigning one CWE-ID for one source code sample, in practice, multiple CWE-IDs can appear in the same source code due to the parent-child relationship of CWE-IDs. Since LIME provides the explanation for top K prediction, LIME has the capability to visualize multiple CWE-IDs based on their probability. Therefore, the developer can identify multiple CWE-IDs in the output if the input source code has multiple vulnerabilities. Figure 4 presents a part of XAI output which display on the web portal for a given source code.

This code has the CWE-ID 401 vulnerability, which is missing release of memory after an effective lifetime (known as the memory leak). It is expected that developers to track and release allocated memory after it has been used. XGB accurately predicts the CWE-ID 401 as the most probable vulnerability with a 0.61 probability for this code. This is shown in brown colour and tokens which causes this vulnerability also highlighted in the same colour in the pre-processed source code. These tokens are 'realloc', 'malloc', 'sizeof' and 'unistd'. Most probable token is 'realloc' with a 0.47 probability. Annotated ground truth for this code was CWE-ID 401. However, as the second most probable vulnerability, this predicts the CWE-ID 190 with a 0.23 probability. This is related to the use of the function 'atoi' inappropriately. The domain experts analysed the code and also confirmed that CWE-ID 190 also lies in this code even though it has not been annotated as a ground truth. Inappropriate usage of token 'strlen'

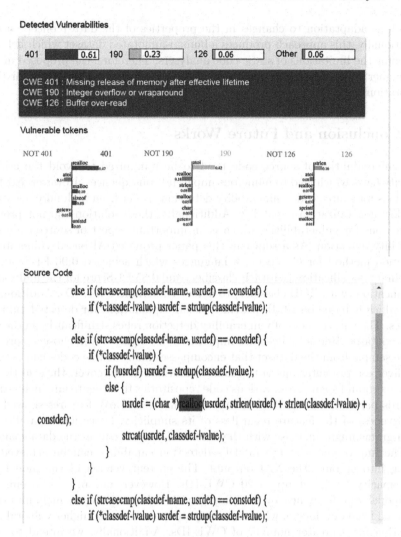

Fig. 4. Web Portal Output

also highlights that vulnerability CWE-ID 126 is presented in this code. Even if the input is a large source code file with a large number of lines, developers can quickly identify the vulnerable code segments using the provided colour codes. Additionally, this shows a brief description for detected CWE-IDs so that developers can quickly identify the reason and make it benign.

The web portal has the facility to confirm the predicted CWE-IDs using the developer's domain knowledge. This change reflects in the source code database by annotating the correct ground truth CWE-IDs for the input source code (as shown in the Fig. 2). This human-in-the-loop process allows for incremental improvement of the model's accuracy over time through model retraining, as well as adaptation to changes in the properties of the data (concept drift). Additionally, this approach produces a human-annotated dataset which helps to overcome the limitations of static code analysers. Therefore, the proposed model has higher capability to outperform static code analysers which used for data annotation.

5   Conclusion and Future Works

The vulnerabilities of source code need to be minimized to avoid the critical security flaws which lead to numerous impactful consequences. However, existing solutions for source code vulnerability detections suffer from high false negatives and low generalization capability. Additionally, these solutions do not provide the reasons for vulnerabilities which is an important aspect of source code vulnerability detection. As a solution, this paper proposed AI-based vulnerability detection method for C and C++ languages which achieved 0.96 F1-Score for the binary classification (with RF classifier) and 0.85 F1-Score for the multi-class classification (with XGB classifier) to detect vulnerable CWE-IDs. Additionally, XAI which is based on LIME provides visual explanations for detected vulnerabilities. The effectiveness of vulnerability detection relies significantly on the size of the dataset. Hence, it becomes imperative to employ a well-chosen representative sample from the dataset that encompasses many source codes characterising diverse representations of the same vulnerability. Moreover, the selection of datasets should span across various code repositories to mitigate any inclinations towards particular CWE-IDs, thereby reducing bias. BoW features showed the effectiveness of the feature regardless of its simplicity. Detection capability for the n-grams might increase with the dataset size as it reduces the data sparsity.

The improvement of the model's detection capability can be achieved by taking into account the XAI outputs. The current version of the model has the capacity to detect up to 20 CWE-IDs. However, our plan is to enhance the model's performance by training it with a larger dataset, including data gathered from developers, which is anticipated to result in a higher vulnerability detection for a greater number of CWE-IDs. Additionally, we intend to offer benign code segments for the identified vulnerable code segments to developers as an extension of the deployed model. In addition, we aim to extend our research to other programming languages, such as Java and Python, to provide a more comprehensive developer support system that aligns with the realities of secure software development practices.

References

1. Barredo Arrieta, A., et al.: Explainable artificial intelligence (XAI): concepts, taxonomies, opportunities and challenges toward responsible AI. Inf. Fusion **58**, 82–115 (2020). https://doi.org/10.1016/j.inffus.2019.12.012, https://www.sciencedirect.com/science/article/pii/S1566253519308103

2. Bilgin, Z., Ersoy, M.A., Soykan, E.U., Tomur, E., Çomak, P., Karaçay, L.: Vulnerability prediction from source code using machine learning. IEEE Access **8**, 150672–150684 (2020)
3. Dam, H.K., Tran, T., Pham, T., Ng, S.W., Grundy, J., Ghose, A.: Automatic feature learning for vulnerability prediction. arXiv preprint arXiv:1708.02368 (2017)
4. Du, X., et al.: Leopard: identifying vulnerable code for vulnerability assessment through program metrics. In: 2019 IEEE/ACM 41st International Conference on Software Engineering (ICSE), pp. 60–71. IEEE (2019)
5. Feng, H., Fu, X., Sun, H., Wang, H., Zhang, Y.: Efficient vulnerability detection based on abstract syntax tree and deep learning. In: IEEE INFOCOM 2020 - IEEE Conference on Computer Communications Workshops (INFOCOM WKSHPS), pp. 722–727 (2020). https://doi.org/10.1109/INFOCOMWKSHPS50562.2020.9163061
6. Fujdiak, R., et al.: Managing the secure software development. In: 2019 10th IFIP International Conference on New Technologies, Mobility and Security (NTMS), pp. 1–4 (2019). https://doi.org/10.1109/NTMS.2019.8763845
7. Grieco, G., Grinblat, G.L., Uzal, L., Rawat, S., Feist, J., Mounier, L.: Toward large-scale vulnerability discovery using machine learning. In: Proceedings of the Sixth ACM Conference on Data and Application Security and Privacy, pp. 85–96 (2016)
8. Harer, J.A., et al.: Automated software vulnerability detection with machine learning. arXiv preprint arXiv:1803.04497 (2018)
9. Jimenez, M.: Evaluating vulnerability prediction models (2018). https://orbilu.uni.lu/handle/10993/36869
10. Pereira, J.D., Vieira, M.: On the use of open-source C/C++ static analysis tools in large projects. In: 2020 16th European Dependable Computing Conference (EDCC), pp. 97–102. IEEE (2020). https://doi.org/10.1109/EDCC51268.2020.00025
11. Pimpalkar, A.P., Retna Raj, R.J.: Influence of pre-processing strategies on the performance of ML classifiers exploiting tf-idf and bow features. ADCAIJ: Adv. Distrib. Comput. Artif. Intell. J. **9**(2), 49–68 (2020). https://doi.org/10.14201/ADCAIJ2020924968
12. Rajapaksha, S., Senanayake, J., Kalutarage, H., Al-Kadri, M.O.: Ai-powered vulnerability detection for secure source code development. In: Bella, G., Doinea, M., Janicke, H. (eds.) SecITC 2022. LNCS, vol. 13809, pp. 275–288. Springer, Cham (2023). https://doi.org/10.1007/978-3-031-32636-3_16
13. Renaud, K.: Human-centred cyber secure software engineering. Zeitschrift für Arbeitswissenschaft, pp. 1–11 (2022)
14. Russell, R., et al.: Automated vulnerability detection in source code using deep representation learning. In: 2018 17th IEEE International Conference on Machine Learning and Applications (ICMLA), pp. 757–762. IEEE (2018)
15. Scandariato, R., Walden, J., Hovsepyan, A., Joosen, W.: Predicting vulnerable software components via text mining. IEEE Trans. Softw. Eng. **40**(10), 993–1006 (2014)
16. Senanayake, J., Kalutarage, H., Al-Kadri, M.O., Petrovski, A., Piras, L.: Developing secured android applications by mitigating code vulnerabilities with machine learning. In: Proceedings of the 2022 ACM on Asia Conference on Computer and Communications Security. ASIA CCS '22, pp. 1255–1257. Association for Computing Machinery, New York, NY, USA (2022). https://doi.org/10.1145/3488932.3527290

17. Senanayake, J., Kalutarage, H., Al-Kadri, M.O., Petrovski, A., Piras, L.: Android code vulnerabilities early detection using AI-powered *ACVED* plugin. In: Atluri, V., Ferrara, A.L. (eds.) DBSec 2023. LNCS, vol. 13942, pp. 1–19. Springer, Cham (2023). https://doi.org/10.1007/978-3-031-37586-6_20
18. Senanayake, J., Kalutarage, H., Al-Kadri, M.O., Petrovski, A., Piras, L.: Android source code vulnerability detection: a systematic literature review. ACM Comput. Surv. **55**(9) (2023). https://doi.org/10.1145/3556974
19. de Vicente Mohino, J., Bermejo Higuera, J., Bermejo Higuera, J.R., Sicilia Montalvo, J.A.: The application of a new secure software development life cycle (S-SDLC) with agile methodologies. Electronics **8**(11) (2019). https://doi.org/10.3390/electronics8111218
20. Votipka, D., Fulton, K.R., Parker, J., Hou, M., Mazurek, M.L., Hicks, M.: Understanding security mistakes developers make: qualitative analysis from build it, break it, fix it. In: 29th USENIX Security Symposium (USENIX Security 20), pp. 109–126. USENIX Association, August 2020
21. Zeng, P., Lin, G., Pan, L., Tai, Y., Zhang, J.: Software vulnerability analysis and discovery using deep learning techniques: a survey. IEEE Access (2020)
22. Zhou, Y., Liu, S., Siow, J., Du, X., Liu, Y.: Devign: effective vulnerability identification by learning comprehensive program semantics via graph neural networks. In: NeurIPS (2019)

WASP 2023

WASP 2023 Preface

This volume contains revised versions of the papers presented at the First International Workshop on Attacks and Software Protection (WASP 2023), which was co-located with the 28th European Symposium on Research in Computer Security (ESORICS 2023), held in The Hague, The Netherlands on September 29th, 2023.

In today's digital age, the need for software protection is more crucial than ever. With cyber attacks becoming increasingly sophisticated and pervasive, obfuscation and other forms of software protection are of interest not only to legitimate software developers seeking to safeguard their code and intellectual property, but also to malware writers seeking to create new viruses able to evade antivirus detection and to attackers in general, with the goal to steal sensitive information, compromise code integrity, or insert backdoors into targeted systems. Software protection is a complex and interdisciplinary field that intersects with many different fields such as cryptography, networks, computer architecture, operating systems, programming languages and compilers. The Workshop on Attacks and Software Protection (WASP) provided a meeting point dedicated to exploring and advancing the latest research and techniques in software attacks, analysis and protection from both the offensive and the defensive perspectives. WASP focused on new models and techniques to defend software from tampering, reverse engineering and piracy, as well as the development of new analysis techniques and new attack strategies that highlight the need for more complete defenses.

An open call for submissions yielded a diverse array of original research papers, contributing invaluable insights to the software security discourse. Following a rigorous selection process involving three reviews per submission, conducted under the single-blind peer–review system, we proudly present seven papers from a pool of thirteen submissions, each representing the forefront of software protection research.

We want to extend our appreciation to everyone who contributed to the organization of the event and the development of the program. We are deeply thankful to the Program Committee members for their punctual and thorough reviews. Our gratitude also goes out to the dedicated members of the Organizing Committee who played a crucial role in making these events successful. Lastly, but most importantly, we wish to express our heartfelt thanks to all the authors who submitted their work to the workshop, as their contributions constitute the most significant aspect of the workshop, greatly enriching the quality of the proceedings.

September 2023

Michele Ianni
Mila Dalla Preda
Kim-Kwang Raymond Choo
Miguel Pupo Correia

Organization

General Chairs

Michele Ianni — University of Calabria, Italy
Mila Dalla Preda — University of Verona, Italy
Kim-Kwang Raymond Choo — University of Texas, San Antonio, USA
Miguel Pupo Correia — University of Lisbon, Portugal

Program Committee

Claudia Greco — University of Calabria, Italy
Giulio De Pasquale — King's College London, UK
Ibéria Medeiros — University of Lisbon, Portugal
Marco Calautti — University of Milan, Italy
Marco Campion — Inria & École Normale Supérieure, Université PSL, France
Marco Oliverio — WolfSSL, Italy
Marco Vieira — University of Coimbra, Portugal
Natalia Stakhanova — University of Saskatchewan, Canada
Nuno Antunes — University of Coimbra, Portugal
Nuno Neves — University of Lisbon, Portugal
Pedro Adão — Instituto Superior Técnico, University of Lisbon, Portugal
Sebastian Schrittwieser — University of Vienna, Austria
Sébastien Bardin — CEA, France

Least Information Redundancy Algorithm of Printable Shellcode Encoding for X86

Yuanding Zhou[✉]

Institute of Software Chinese Academy of Sciences, Beijing, China
yuanding2021@iscas.ac.cn

Abstract. Shellcode is a critical element in computer security that exploits vulnerabilities within software systems. Shellcode is written in machine code and often designed to be compact in size, evading detection by security software. Printable shellcode, specifically, comprises only printable ASCII characters (0x21–0x7E), including letters, numbers, and punctuation marks. The key advantage of printable shellcode lies in its ability to be embedded within data streams, which may undergo parsing or manipulation by applications that would otherwise filter or modify non-printable characters. The prevalent methods for generating printable shellcode involve encoding algorithms, such as the Riley Eller algorithm (integrated into Metasploit). However, previous research on printable shellcode has primarily focused on the availability and reduction of the encoded shellcode's size, without adequately considering the constraint imposed by the information entropy of the encoding algorithm within the context of printable shellcode. In this paper, we demonstrate the existence of minimal information redundancy in printable shellcode. Subsequently, we introduce Lycan, an implementation of a novel algorithm that surpasses previous encoding algorithms in terms of the size efficiency of the encoded shellcode. Lycan achieves the least theoretical information redundancy. Through experimentation, we observe that Lycan generates the most compact shellcode among existing tools when the shellcode's size exceeds a certain threshold.

Keywords: Shellcode · Encoding · x86

1 Introduction

Shellcode refers to a compact and executable piece of machine code that exploits vulnerabilities within a computer system, enabling the execution of arbitrary commands or the unauthorized access of the system. Typically written in machine code, shellcode is specifically crafted to be injected into a vulnerable program or system. Its small size presents a challenge for security software, as it can evade detection.

An arbitrary byte can take any value ranging from 0x00 to 0xFF, encompassing both printable and non-printable characters. The requirement for printable shellcode arises from the fact that numerous computer systems and applications tend to filter or alter non-printable characters, including control characters and

S. Katsikas et al. (Eds.): ESORICS 2023 Workshops, LNCS 14399, pp. 361–376, 2024.
https://doi.org/10.1007/978-3-031-54129-2_21

null bytes. Consequently, shellcode containing such characters may be subject to filtering or modification, leading to its ineffectiveness.

One of the key advantages of printable shellcode lies in its capacity to circumvent specific security measures that aim to detect non-printable characters. For instance, certain firewalls and intrusion detection systems (IDS) are configured to monitor network traffic, searching for character sequences that match commonly employed shellcode patterns. By utilizing printable shellcode, attackers can elude these security measures, executing their malicious code without detection.

A printable character is defined as a byte ranging from 0x21 to 0x7E, encompassing a total of 94 characters in a byte's character set. While the turing-completeness of printable bytes relies on the system's Instruction Set Architecture (ISA), it is evident that the instruction set formed by printable bytes is turing-complete on x86 systems, as demonstrated by existing printable shellcode encoding algorithms [1, 3, 6]. In order to create printable shellcode, encoding algorithms incorporate various modifications from different perspectives, employing clever techniques.

Rix [1] introduced a technique for writing ia32 alphanumeric shellcodes. The main contribution of this work was a comprehensive compilation of all the viable alphanumeric instructions available in the ia32 Instruction Set Architecture (ISA). Moreover, Rix devised an innovative and influential approach called the XOR patching technique. This technique effectively resolved the challenge of incorporating necessary non-printable bytes within the shellcode. Rix's methodology played a pivotal role in enabling the development of ia32 alphanumeric shellcodes.

Riley Eller [3] introduced an algorithm known as the SUB encoder, which was designed to bypass MSB Data Filters. These filters are responsible for filtering out or modifying any values that fall outside the range of 0x21 to 0x7E hex in exploit code. The SUB encoder algorithm has gained significant popularity for encoding non-printable shellcode in various scenarios and has been integrated into the widely-used penetration testing tool, Metasploit. In essence, the SUB encoder utilizes the SUB instruction to convert any byte into printable bytes by performing up to three subtraction operations.

In contrast to the aforementioned algorithm, Zsolt Geczi and Péter Ivanyi [4] proposed a distinct method for converting arbitrary instructions into a printable instruction sequence. Their approach involved employing a technique known as source-to-source conversion to translate the original shellcode into an equivalent printable form. However, a notable drawback of their method is the inefficiency of the translation algorithm. It utilizes multiple redundant instructions to achieve the same effect as a single instruction, resulting in decreased efficiency.

Dhrumil Patel, Aditya Basu, and Anish Mathuria [7] have provided a comprehensive summary of the aforementioned methods and identified a significant drawback shared by all encoded shellcodes: their larger size in comparison to the original shellcodes. To address this issue, they have proposed an encoding algorithm that converts every two consecutive bytes into three printable bytes.

Additionally, they have developed a tool called "psc" that generates printable shellcode. The generated shellcode includes a runtime looped decoder, capable of transforming the encoded bytes back into the original shellcode.

In many scenarios, shellcode needs to be compact enough to fit into memory, especially in cases like buffer overflow attacks. However, in more sophisticated situations, attackers may not have the luxury of obtaining a reverse shell through direct interaction. In such cases, large-sized shellcode is necessary, such as when establishing a reverse shell via a TCP connection [15]. The existing approaches mentioned below primarily focus on generating printable shellcode by encoding the original shellcode or transforming instructions into equivalent printable machine code. Their main emphasis is on reducing the overall size of the printable shellcode. However, they tend to overlook the information redundancy introduced by the encoding algorithm, which can have a significant impact when the size of the printable shellcode exceeds a certain threshold.

In this paper, we propose a novel encoding algorithm for generating printable shellcode and analyze it from a unique perspective. We demonstrate that the least information redundancy can be achieved in the generation of printable shellcode and introduce a corresponding tool, named Lycan, that theoretically produces the most compact printable shellcode. The printable shellcode generated by Lycan includes a looped decoder written solely in printable bytes, as well as an encoded shellcode that is also printable. Our algorithm encodes every three consecutive bytes into four printable bytes, while the looped decoder transforms the printable encoded bytes back into their original form at runtime. Building upon this encoding algorithm, we present an efficient tool called Lycan, which converts the original shellcode into its printable equivalents. Lycan outperforms existing algorithms by generating the smallest printable shellcode size when the original shellcode exceeds a certain threshold. Furthermore, we have made Lycan available for public usage. Lycan and its tutorial can be found at https://github.com/zeredy879/Lycan.

Our main research contributions are as below:

- Analyze printable shellcode encoding problem from perspective of information theory and prove that the least redundancy of printable shellcode exists.
- Develop a corresponding tool called Lycan to implement the theoretically least redundancy encoding algorithm and demonstrate the feasibility in real world scenario.

The remaining sections of this paper are organized as follows. Section 2 provides an overview of the related work in the field of generating printable shellcode. Section 3 presents our findings on the existence of minimal information redundancy in printable shellcode. Section 4 outlines the details of our encoding and decoding algorithms. Section 5 elaborates on the techniques employed for writing printable shellcode and provides implementation details of our tool, Lycan. Section 6 presents the validation process and performance evaluation of Lycan. Finally, Sect. 7 concludes our work and summarizes the key contributions of this research.

2 Related Work

2.1 Riley Eller Algorithm

Riley Eller [3] introduced an algorithm that enables the encoding of any binary data sequence into ASCII characters. When interpreted by an Intel processor, these characters can decode the original sequence and execute it. The algorithm follows a specific process: it first moves the stack pointer just past the ASCII code, then decodes 32 bits of the original sequence at a time and pushes that value onto the stack. In summary, the Riley Eller algorithm converts arbitrary DWORD values into printable bytes by utilizing finite SUB instructions that leverage printable immediate data subtraction.

Metasploit [2] integrates the Riley Eller algorithm to SUB encoder. The SUB encoder is a dynamic polymorphic shellcode obfuscation technique, implemented as part of the Metasploit Framework. It applies a sequence of byte subtraction operations to individual shellcode values in order to generate new, non-sequential, and non-deterministic values. This encoded shellcode is observed to be stealthier compared to the original version, in terms of evading intrusion detection and prevention mechanisms. Despite the effectiveness of the SUB encoder and other Metasploit encoders in enhancing payload obfuscation, there remains a constant threat of detection and counter-measures by security systems [5]. Hence, further research is crucial to develop even more effective and efficient encoding methods for better payload protection in penetration testing and ethical hacking contexts.

The SUB encoder includes a fixed 29 byte long printable code snippet. Assume that the size of original shellcode is represented by n, the output printable shellcode's size can be calculated as $29 + 16\lceil n/4 \rceil$.

2.2 Zsolt Geczi and Peter Ivanyi's Method

Zsolt Geczi and Peter Ivanyi [4] propose a technique for automatically translating non-printable shellcodes into printable byte codes to bypass filters. Their approach, known as source-to-source conversion, involves establishing a compilation set that maps each instruction to a printable equivalent. Printable shellcode is then generated using these mapping rules. For example, the instruction 'MOV EAX, EBX' has a printable equivalent of 'PUSH EBX; POP EAX'.

While their method is context-free and convenient to extend, it suffers from a significant drawback: the resulting shellcode has a much larger size compared to existing algorithms. As a result, utilizing this output shellcode as an exploit may fail if the buffer overflow size is insufficient to accommodate the expanded exploit code.

Although the exact details of the source-to-source conversion method proposed by Zsolt Geczi and Peter Ivanyi are not publicly available, based on the example they provided [4], it can be inferred that their method generates significantly larger shellcode compared to existing works. In the only examples available, their method transformed a 38-byte shellcode into a printable shell-code of 9837 bytes. This substantial increase in size indicates that their method may not be efficient in terms of generating compact printable shellcode.

2.3   Printable Shellcode Compiler

Dhrumil Patel, Aditya Basu, and Anish Mathuria [7] propose a novel encoding scheme and a companion tool called psc (Printable Shellcode Compiler) designed to generate compact printable shellcode. One notable feature of psc is its utiliza-tion of a runtime looped decoder, similar to the approaches employed by Alpha3 [8] and Alpha Freedom [10].

In their encoding scheme, two consecutive bytes of the original shellcode are encoded into three printable bytes. During runtime, a decoding loop is employed to take these three successive bytes and transform them back into the original two bytes of the shellcode. This encoding and decoding process ensures that the generated printable shellcode is compact and retains the functionality of the original shellcode.

The psc tool includes a fixed 146 byte long decoder. Assume that the size of original shellcode is represented by n, then the output printable shellcode's size can be calculated as $146 + 3\lceil n/2 \rceil$.

3   Proof of Least Redundancy

3.1   The Least Redundancy of Encoding Shellcode

The original shellcode byte ranges from 0x00 to 0xFF. Assume that X represents original shellcode byte, thus the entropy of X is:

$$H(X) = -\sum_x p(x) \log_2 p(x) =$$

$$-\sum_{i=1}^{256} \frac{1}{256} \log_2 \frac{1}{256} = \log_2 256 = 8 \; bits \tag{1}$$

The printable byte ranges from 0x21 to 0x7E. Assume that E represents printable byte, thus the entropy of E is:

$$H(E) = -\sum_e p(e) \log_2 p(e) =$$

$$-\sum_{i=1}^{94} \frac{1}{94} \log_2 \frac{1}{94} = \log_2 94 \; bits \tag{2}$$

In the shellcode encoding circumstance, the fundamental encoding unit is a single byte. Assume that Y represents every encoded shellcode byte, thus the entropy of Y must be less than or equal to the entropy of E, otherwise the printable byte set is not sufficient to represent encoded bytes:

$$H(Y) \leqslant H(E) = \log_2 94 \ bits \tag{3}$$

Since the H(Y) also represents the number of bits of single byte used to encode a printable character, so that H(Y) must be an integer:

$$6 \ bits = \log_2 64 \ bits < H(E) = \\ \log_2 94 \ bits < \log_2 128 \ bits = 7 \ bits \tag{4}$$

Implies:

$$H(Y) \leqslant 6 \ bits < \log_2 94 \ bits \tag{5}$$

Since the fundamental unit of encoding algorithm is a single byte, thus assume that encoding algorithm transforms m bytes into n bytes. For information loss is not allowed during the encoding process, hence:

$$8 \times m = H(X) \times m \leqslant H(Y) \times n \leqslant 6 \times n \ bits \tag{6}$$

equivalent to:

$$\frac{m}{n} \leqslant 0.75 \tag{7}$$

The information redundancy D of encoding algorithm for printable shellcode must have:

$$D = \frac{n - m}{n} \geqslant 0.25 \tag{8}$$

3.2 Analysis

In the analysis of existing algorithms in Sect. 2 from the perspective of information redundancy of the encoding algorithm, we observe that the SUB encoder has an information redundancy of 0.75, indicating a relatively higher level of redundancy. On the other hand, Alpha3 achieves an information redundancy of 0.5, while psc achieves a lower redundancy of 0.33. However, none of these algorithms achieve the minimum theoretically information redundancy for printable shellcode.

To address this limitation, we propose our algorithm, which aims to achieve the theoretically minimal information redundancy for generating printable shellcode. By minimizing redundancy, we can generate more compact and efficient printable shellcode. The details of our algorithm and its implications will be discussed in subsequent sections.

4   Algorithm

4.1   Encoding Algorithm

Our encoding algorithm' scheme is: encode every **3** successive bytes into **4** successive printable bytes. The detailed encoding algorithm is demonstrated as follow. The symbol '$\ll$', '$\gg$', '&' and '$\oplus$' represent left shift, right shift, logic AND, and logic XOR.

1. Check if the size of original shellcode (S) is divisible by 3, otherwise complement original shellcode with byte 0x90 (nop instruction) until the size of shellcode can be divisible by 3.
2. Take 3 successive bytes (24 bits) (name them A_1 to A_3), then divide these 24 bits into 4 blocks. Every block contains 6 bits.
3. Complete each block to a single byte with 2 zero bit at significant position of a byte then form 4 bytes (name them B_1 to B_4). This step is described as following operations.
   (a) $B_1 = A_1 \gg 2$
   (b) $B_2 = ((A_1 \ll 4) \text{ \& } 0x30) + (A_2 \gg 4)$
   (c) $B_3 = ((A2 \ll 2) \text{ \& } 0x3C) + (A_3 \gg 6)$
   (d) $B_4 = A_3 \text{ \& } 0x3F$
4. Add 0x3F to each byte above. These 4 bytes (name them C_1 to C_4) constitute a group of output. This step is described as following operation.
   $$* \ C_i = B_i + 0x3F$$
5. Go back to step 2) if shellcode still has remain bytes.
6. Append 0x26 as a end token in the end of output.

The encoding process, as illustrated in Fig. 1, follows the described algorithm. Since every byte of B_1 to B_4 falls within range of 0x00 to 0x3F, thus every byte of C_1 to C_4 ranges from 0x3F to 0x7E. This range corresponds to a subset of printable ASCII characters (0x21–0x7E), which ensures that the encoded shellcode remains printable.

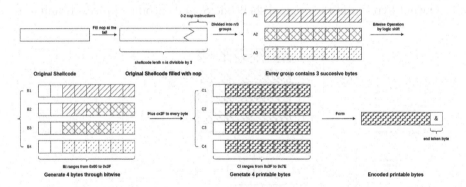

Fig. 1. Encoding algorithm - Every 3 successive bytes are encoded into 4 printable bytes, and each byte of encoded sequence falls within the printable ASCII range of 0x21 to 0x7E. The end token in the end of encoded sequence serves as a marker to indicate the end of the encoded sequence when decoding it. The entire sequence of encoded bytes, including the end token, remains within the printable ASCII character set, ensuring that the shellcode is fully printable.

Using the byte 0x3F as part of the encoding process offers several advantages. Firstly, 0x3F can be used as a mapping mechanism to represent the range from

0x00 to 0x3F (inclusive) within a subset of printable bytes. Secondly, by using 0x3F as a special byte within the encoding process, the decoder can more efficiently restore the encoded bytes. The convenience and effectiveness of using the 0x3F byte in the encoding algorithm will be further demonstrated and discussed in Sect. 4.2 and Sect. 5.

The end token byte 0x26 is used to mark the end of the encoded output bytes. In fact, any byte within the interval 0x21–0x3E can be used as end token, as this range is separate from the range 0x3F–0x7E, ensuring that the end token byte is distinct from the encoded bytes.

4.2   Decoding Algorithm

In correspondence with the encoding algorithm, the decoding algorithm transforms every **4** successive encoded bytes into **3** original successive bytes. The detailed decoding algorithm is demonstrated as follows.

1. Try to take 4 successive bytes (32 bits) (name them C_1 to C_4) from encoded bytes. If meet the end token byte, go to step 5).
2. Add 1 to every byte of C_1 to C_4, then xor each byte with 0x3F byte. This step is described as following operation (name the output bytes B_1 to B_4).
   - $B_i = (C_i + 1) \oplus 0x3F$
3. Restore original bytes (name them A_1 to A_3) through following operations.
   (a) $A_1 = (B_1 \ll 2) \oplus (B_2 \gg 4)$
   (b) $A_2 = (B_2 \ll 4) \oplus (B_3 \gg 2)$
   (c) $A_3 = (B_3 \ll 6) \oplus B_4$
4. Bytes A_1 to A_3 constitute output, go to step 1).
5. Output bytes form the original shellcode S, and encoding process terminates.

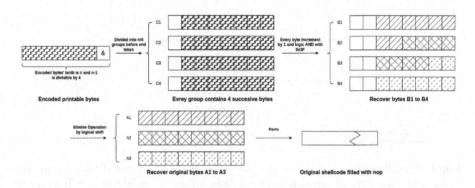

Fig. 2. Decoding algorithm

The decoding process, depicted in Fig. 2, employs bitwise operations to restore the original shellcode bit by bit. To optimize the size of the decoder, we have minimized the number of bitwise operations involved. Specifically, we have combined steps 2) and 3) in the decoding algorithm implementation, resulting in a more efficient process. The implementation details of this optimization will be elaborated on in the Sect. 5.

5   Implementation

The implementation of Lycan involves two primary components: encoding and decoding. During the encoding process, the original shellcode is transformed into printable encoded bytes using the algorithm described in the encoding algorithm section. The decoding process occurs at runtime and is responsible for transforming the encoded bytes back into the original shellcode. This is achieved through a run-time printable decoder, which is implemented using handwritten x86 assembly code. The run-time decoder is designed to be printable and context-free, ensuring compatibility with any x86 shellcode.

During the encoding process, we utilize a Python script to facilitate the transformation from raw shellcode to printable form. The resulting output of the encoding process is a combination of the printable decoder and the encoded shellcode.

During the decoding process, the printable decoder is responsible for recovering the original shellcode from the encoded bytes. Once all the encoded bytes have been recovered and transformed, the program proceeds to write the decoded shellcode back into memory. This process allows us to effectively write nonprintable shellcode using printable bytes and achieve the desired functionality while still maintaining the printable nature of the shellcode.

In this section we will demonstrate the process of contructing this printable decoder and explain some tricks and trade-offs used to manually write the printable decoder.

5.1   Overview of the Printable Decoder

Listing 1.1 describes the printable decoder architecture layout before adding xor patching instructions.

```
setup:
    pusha
    mov encoded, %esi
    mov %esi, %edi
    ...
looper:
    ...
    jne looper
_end:
    popa
encoded:
    ...
    ; encoded bytes
```

Listing 1.1. Architecture of the printable decoder. Setup section is responsible for saving the context of registers and initializing the registers used during the decoding process used for decoding, section looper contains the main loop of the decoder and is responsible for recovering original shellcode from encoded bytes, _end section is used to restore the registers' context that was saved in the setup section, encoded section is used to store docoded bytes

In order to preserve the context before the decoder runs, we use instruction PUSHA in section *setup* and POPA in section *_end* to save all the registers' context at run-time. Notice that the original shellcode is shorter than encoded bytes, so we don't need extra place to save recovered shellcode, which indicates the decoding algorithm is an In-place algorithm.

Listing 1.2 describes the setup phase of the printable decoder.

```
setup:
    pusha
    pusha
    push %eax
    pop %esi
    push $0x5E
    pop %eax
    push %eax
    pop %ecx
    xor $0x5E, %al
    push %eax
    pop %ebp
    dec %eax
    xor $0x5E, %al
    push %eax
    pop %edx
    ; edx = 0xFFFFFFA1, ecx = 0x5E, ebp = 0
```

Listing 1.2. Setup phase. This sections saves the context of registers and store special values into registers used for xor patching Sect. 5.3.

The setup phase in the printable decoder serves the purpose of preserving the registers' context and initializing the necessary constants for the subsequent xor patching and looper phases. In this context, it is assumed that the start address of the entire shellcode is stored in register EAX[1].

In the xor patching technique, two constants, namely byte 0x5E and byte 0xA1, are required to transform arbitrary bytes into printable bytes. The selection of these specific bytes is based on their suitability for xor patching operations. Through an analysis of the entire byte set, it was determined that using the pair (0x5E, 0xA1) requires the fewest instructions for xor patching non-printable bytes. Additionally, generating these constants is straightforward, as 0x5E is a printable byte and the logical XOR operation between 0x5E and 0xA1 yields 0xFF, which can be easily obtained by decrementing a zero-initialized register.

---

[1] The choice of register used for marking encoded bytes can vary. Register EAX is used here as an illustration to showcase the functionality and feasibility of Lycan.

Furthermore, the constant zero value is stored in register EBP for the purpose of efficiently clearing registers to zero using the PUSH and POP instructions. This allows for a convenient and concise way to initialize registers to zero without requiring additional instructions.

Figure 3 describes the looper phase workflow of the printable decoder.

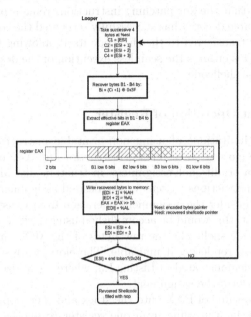

Fig. 3. Looper phase workflow. Register ESI represents read pointer of the encoded bytes, EDI represents write pointer of the recovered shellcode. After looper encounters the end token, execution flow of looper ends and jump to recovered shellcode immediately.

During the looper phase of the printable decoder, specific registers are assigned specific roles to facilitate the recovery of the original shellcode from the encoded bytes. Register ESI serves as the read pointer, indicating the location of the encoded bytes, while register EDI acts as the write pointer, indicating where the recovered shellcode will be stored. In the initial state, both ESI and EDI are set to the same value since the decoding algorithm operates in-place, and the recovery process for each group of encoded bytes is independent.

To maximize utilization of the information entropy carried by each byte, the decoding process avoids performing bitwise operations on a register multiple times. Instead, it extracts the effective bits of every four successive bytes into a single register, namely EAX. By doing so, the original shellcode can be recovered byte by byte and written back to memory. The looper iterates through each group of encoded bytes, recovering them into the original shellcode and storing them in memory until the end mark token is encountered. By recovering and storing the shellcode byte by byte, the looper phase effectively reconstructs the original shellcode from the encoded bytes using the runtime printable decoder.

The final step in making the printable decoder fully printable is the xor patching phase Sect. 5.3. This phase involves xoring every non-printable byte in the looper phase with specific values to transform them into printable bytes. To achieve this, the offset of all the non-printable bytes needs to be determined in advance, ensuring that the xor patching instructions remain printable.

Once the printable decoder has successfully recovered the complete shellcode, the control flow is transferred to the shellcode itself, allowing the original shellcode to execute. This ensures the seamless execution of the desired functionality encoded within the shellcode.

5.2   Assignment Operation of Register

To overcome the limitations of using non-printable instructions in the printable shellcode, we employ stack-related instructions for assignment operations. Instead of using a traditional assignment instruction like MOV, we leverage PUSH and POP instructions to achieve the desired assignment.

For instance, consider the assignment operation from register EAX to EBX. In a normal context, this would be accomplished using a MOV instruction. However, in the printable shellcode, the raw bytes of the MOV instruction contain non-printable bytes, rendering it unusable. Therefore, we resort to an alternative approach, as demonstrated in Listing 1.3, where we utilize PUSH and POP instructions to perform the assignment.

By pushing the value of EAX onto the stack and then popping it into EBX, we effectively transfer the value from one register to another. This technique allows us to accomplish assignment operations using printable instructions and ensures the compatibility of the printable shellcode with the target system.

```
push %eax  ; 0x50
pop %ebx   ; 0x5B
# equivalent to 'mov %eax, %ebx'
```

Listing 1.3. Assugnment from EAX to EBX

When it comes to assigning arbitrary immediate data to a register, the printable shellcode faces additional challenges. While SUB encoder utilizes multiple SUB instructions to convert the zero value of a register to arbitrary 4 bytes, our decoder focuses on single-byte assignment operations rather than arbitrary 4 bytes. This is because the xor patching technique used in our decoder only operates on a single byte.

To address the assignment of specific bytes, such as 0x00 and 0xFF, to registers AL and BL, we can utilize printable instructions. Listing 1.4 demonstrates how to achieve this.

```
push $0x50          ; 0x6A 0x50
pop %eax            ; 0x58
xor %al, $0x50      ; 0x34 0x50
; assign 0x00 to %al through
; xoring same data

push %eax           ; 0x50
pop %ebx            ; 0x5B
dec %ebx            ; 0x4B
; assign 0xFF to %bl through
; decrement 0x00
```

Listing 1.4. Assign 0x00 and 0xFF to register AL and BL

5.3 Xor Patching Technique

Xor patching technique, as described by Rix, is used to write non-printable instructions by XORing the non-printable byte with a printable byte in memory. To successfully perform xor patching, it is necessary to have knowledge of the address layout of the shellcode, including the start address of the shellcode and the offset of the non-printable byte that needs to be patched.

Listing 1.5 provides a template instruction for xor patching in our decoder:

```
xor %dl, 0x3D(%esi)  ; 0x30 0x56 0x3D
```

Listing 1.5. Example of xor patching technique

In the example provided in Listing 1.5, a representative xor patching instruction is shown. In the context of our decoder, the register %dl is being assigned the value 0xA1, and the value 0x3D (%esi) represents the offset between register ESI and the non-printable byte that needs to be xor patched.

The key point of xor patching is to ensure that the offset byte (0x3D) is printable. This requires careful arrangement of the offset in our decoder to ensure that it falls within the range of printable bytes (0x21–0x7E). However, this compromise on the size of the printable decoder means that we may need to include some unused bytes to ensure that the offset remains within the printable byte range. This trade-off between the size of the printable decoder and the printable range of the offset is necessary to ensure that the xor patching technique can be effectively applied to write non-printable instructions using printable bytes.

6 Evaluation

We evaluate Lycan's performance from 2 perspectives: encoding bytes length and the total bytes length. We compare Lycan with Riley Eller's SUB encoder [2], Jan Wever's Alpha3 [8] and Basu's psc [7]. Figure 4 describes the comparison of encoded bytes length and Fig. 5 describes the comparison of total bytes length.

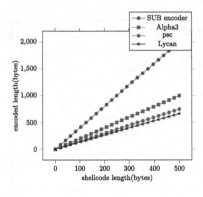
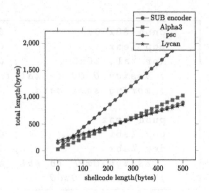

Fig. 4. Encoded bytes length   **Fig. 5.** Total bytes length

The encoded byte size of the different encoding algorithms exhibit a linear correlation with the size of the original shellcode, as mentioned in the previous section. Lycan, with its minimal information redundancy, outperforms the other algorithms in terms of the length of the encoded bytes, as illustrated in Fig. 4.

It is important to note that the total byte length depends on both the encoding algorithm and the length of the decoder, as all the algorithms utilize fixed-length decoders. As depicted in Fig. 5, when the length of the shellcode is less than 256, psc and Alpha3 generate shorter printable shellcode. However, when the shellcode length exceeds 256, Lycan demonstrates superior performance and produces the shortest printable shellcode.

This comparison highlights the advantage of Lycan in minimizing the length of the encoded shellcode, making it a favorable choice for scenarios where the size of the shellcode is a critical factor.

The comparison presented in Table 1 highlights the superior performance of Lycan in scenarios where the original shellcode size is significant. This makes Lycan a valuable tool for encoding and generating p rintable shellcode, especially for larger payloads.

Table 1. The real world shellcode performance of distinct encoding tools

Shellcode	Original	SUB encoder	Alpha3	psc	Lycan
execve(/bin/sh) [11]	20	109	68	176	216
INSERTION Encoder [12] / Decoder execve(/bin/sh)	88	381	204	278	308
OpenSSL Encrypt (aes256cbc) Files (test.txt) [13]	185	781	398	425	436
chmod 777 (/etc/passwd + /etc/shadow) + Add Root User (ALI/ALI) To /etc/passwd + Execute /bin/sh [14]	378	1549	784	713	692
Reverse (127.0.0.1 :53/UDP) Shell (/bin/sh) [15]	668	2701	1364	1148	1080

7   Conclusion

Printable shellcode encoding algorithms are widely used to generate general shellcode in various scenarios. In this paper, we demonstrate that the least information redundancy of printable shellcode encoding algorithm is 0.75 theoretically and present corresponding algorithm which encodes 3 successive bytes to 4 bytes. Our algorithm generates the shortest encoded bytes among all the existing algorithms. Then we present Lycan – a tool that implements the algorithm. However due to unavoidable expenses of the printable decoder, the printable shellcode generated by Lycan is longer than SUB encoder and Alpha3 when the length of original shellcode is too short. Lycan's performance is best among all the algorithms when the original shellcode's size exceeds the threshold 252. In the future work, we will extend our tool to work on different ISA.

References

1. Rix. Writing IA32 alphanumeric shellcode. Phrack **57**(15) (2001). http://phrack.org/issues/57/15.html
2. Metasploit sub encoder. https://www.rapid7.com/db/modules/encoder/x86/opt_sub/
3. Eller, R.: Bypassing MSB data filters for buffer over-flow exploits on intel platforms. http://julianor.tripod.com/bc/bypass-msb.txt
4. Géczi, Z., Iványi, P.: Automatic translation of assembly shellcodes to printable byte codes. Pollack Periodica **13**(1), 3–20 (2018)
5. Polychronakis, M., Anagnostakis, K.G., Markatos, E.P.: Comprehensive shellcode detection using runtime heuristics. In: Proceedings of the 26th Annual Computer Security Applications Conference (2010)
6. Ding, W., et al.: Automatic construction of printable return-oriented programming payload. In: 2014 9th International Conference on Malicious and Unwanted Software: The Americas (MALWARE). IEEE (2014)
7. Patel, D., Basu, A., Mathuria, A.: Automatic generation of compact printable shellcodes for x86. In: Proceedings of the 14th USENIX Conference on Offensive Technologies (2020)
8. Wever, B.J.: ALPHA3. https://github.com/SkyLined/alpha3
9. Mason, J., et al.: English shellcode. In: Proceedings of the 16th ACM Conference on Computer and Communications Security (2009)
10. Basu, A., Mathuria, A., Chowdary, N.: Automatic generation of compact alphanumeric shellcodes for x86. In: Prakash, A., Shyamasundar, R. (eds.) ICISS 2014. LNCS, vol. 8880, pp. 399–410. Springer, Cham (2014). https://doi.org/10.1007/978-3-319-13841-1_22
11. Linux/x86 - execve(/bin/sh) Shellcode. https://www.exploit-db.com/shellcodes/46809
12. Linux/x86 - INSERTION Encoder / Decoder execve(/bin/sh). https://www.exploit-db.com/shellcodes/46519

13. Linux/x86 - OpenSSL Encrypt (aes256cbc) Files (test.txt) Shellcode. https://www.exploit-db.com/shellcodes/46791
14. Linux/x86 - chmod 777 (/etc/passwd + /etc/shadow) + Add Root User (ALI/ALI) To /etc/passwd + Execute /bin/sh Shellcode. https://www.exploit-db.com/shellcodes/34262
15. Linux/x86 - Reverse (127.0.0.1:53/UDP) Shell (/bin/sh) Shellcode. https://www.exploit-db.com/shellcodes/42208

Execution at RISC: Stealth JOP Attacks on RISC-V Applications

Loïc Buckwell📷, Olivier Gilles(✉)📷, Daniel Gracia Pérez📷, and Nikolai Kosmatov📷

Thales Research and Technology, Palaiseau, France
{loic.buckwell,olivier.gilles,daniel.gracia-perez,
nikolai.kosmatov}@thalesgroup.com

Abstract. RISC-V is a recently developed open instruction set architecture gaining a lot of attention. To improve the security of these systems and design efficient countermeasures, a better understanding of vulnerabilities to novel and future attacks is mandatory. This paper demonstrates that RISC-V is sensible to Jump-Oriented Programming, a class of complex code-reuse attacks. We provide an analysis of new dispatcher gadgets we discovered, and show how they can be used together to build a stealth attack, bypassing existing protections. We implemented a proof-of-concept attack on an embedded web server compiled for RISC-V, in which we introduced a vulnerability allowing an attacker to read an arbitrary file from the remote host machine.

Keywords: Control-Flow Integrity · Code-Reuse Attacks · Embedded Systems · RISC-V

1 Introduction

The RISC-V Instruction Set Architecture (ISA)[1] is a novel open Reduced Instruction Set Computer (RISC) ISA, which is often used for embedded systems. While RISC ISAs innately have a smaller attack surface than Complex Instruction Set Computer (CISC) ISAs, many of them run critical systems, including industrial control systems or cyber-physical systems, whose failure may have dramatic consequences (environmental disasters, loss of human lives...). Using a novel open ISA has several benefits. Its novelty brings security advantages by taking past failures into experience. Even more important is its open status, as trust in the architecture relies on community review. This also enables national independence in microchip supplies; a very important feature as target systems may be strategical and export restrictions become more common.

While most RISC-V architectures allow a satisfying level of security compared to similar classes of systems [15], they will increasingly become the target to complex attacks as their relevance in the industrial and strategical field increases. Eventually, state-backed attackers are bound to attack them. In order

---

[1] https://riscv.org.

S. Katsikas et al. (Eds.): ESORICS 2023 Workshops, LNCS 14399, pp. 377–391, 2024.
https://doi.org/10.1007/978-3-031-54129-2_22

to anticipate this threat, security researchers face the challenge to find potential vulnerabilities and imagine suitable protection mechanisms. Code-Reuse Attacks (CRA), and specifically Jump-Oriented Programming (JOP), are among the most complex attacks to realize, but also to prevent. They can be very powerful when successful, as they can allow the attacker to run an arbitrary sequence of instructions within the corrupted application. In this article we adopt the attacker's point of view and try to perform a JOP attack, with the intent of (1) getting a better understanding of RISC-V systems vulnerabilities, and (2) ultimately designing better countermeasures to prevent these attacks.

Contributions. We summarize our contributions as follows:

- a first analysis of vulnerabilities to JOP attacks on the RISC-V architecture;
- a description of new dispatcher gadgets enabling JOP attacks to bypass modern mitigations on the RISC-V architecture while increasing its attack surface;
- a demonstration of feasibility by implementing and testing a stealth JOP attack on a vulnerable RISC-V application.

Outline. Section 2 introduces code-reuse attacks, countermeasures against them and the limitations of the latter. Section 3 introduces a new kind of dispatcher gadget we found, increasing functional gadgets availability to the level of ROP attacks. Section 4 describes a stealth attack we developed against a vulnerable RISC-V application using techniques described in previous sections. Section 5 compares our approach to other efforts related to Jump-Oriented Programming and RISC-V security. Finally, Sect. 6 provides a conclusion.

2   Code-Reuse Attacks Overview

The aim of a *Code-Reuse Attack* (CRA)—in opposition to code injection attacks—is to reuse existing code in a target application in order to perform unintended and often malicious actions. It is not in itself a vulnerability, but relies on an earlier memory corruption allowing to hijack the execution flow. Such vulnerabilities are well-known, but still prevalent in many systems [23]. An example of a CRA is return-to-libc [21], where the execution flow is redirected to a single function after manipulation of arguments within the stack of the corrupted function. More sophisticated attacks with the same principle of stack corruption have emerged, among which the *Return-Oriented Programming* (ROP) technique [4,19]. It consists in chaining *gadgets*, i.e. code snippets composed of a few instructions and ending with a linking instruction. In the case of ROP, the linking instructions are "return to caller" which pop and jump to the next gadgets' addresses stored in the corrupted stack. Using this approach, the attacker can run an arbitrary sequence of legit instructions.

2.1   Countermeasures

Multiple methods were proposed and used in order to defend against return-to-libc and ROP. Address Space Layout Randomization (ASLR) randomizes base addresses of memory mappings. Stackguard [6] introduced the notion of canaries to protect the integrity of the stack. Yet solutions relying on secrets depend much on the system entropy, which tends to decline as the system uptime increases—an important issue for embedded systems that can run for decades without reboot. Both ASLR and Stackguard are even weaker on 32-bit systems [20], and several techniques have been proposed to bypass them.

Abadi et al. [1] first formally identified a process property named *Control-Flow Integrity* (CFI), defined by the adherence of the runtime execution flow to its intended behavior. In order to ensure this property against attackers, they proposed two complementary protections: shadow stack and landing pads[2]. *Shadow stack* protects backward-edge jumps by pushing procedure return addresses to a memory protected stack at call time. When a procedure returns, its return address is popped from both stacks and compared. If they differ, a memory corruption is detected. *Landing pads* are special instructions protecting forward-edge jumps. When implemented, each jump destination must be one of these instructions. However, even if an application is compiled with landing pads, it can still use shared libraries that are not, effectively loosing benefits for the corresponding code. Nevertheless, this protection makes theoretically all kinds of CRA nearly impossible to implement, and do indeed stop most return-to-libc and ROP attacks, although often leading to significant fall of performances [3], as opposed to shadow stacks which can be efficiently implemented in hardware, particularly in systems with limited dynamicity such as many embedded and/or critical systems. Hence, landing pads are less likely to be fully implemented in these systems.

2.2 Jump-Oriented Programming

Much like ROP, JOP consists in assembling *functional gadgets* containing useful instructions present in the target application in order to perform a malicious action. However JOP attacks do not rely on a corrupted stack: the chaining mechanism is done by a *dispatcher gadget*. Its role is to load (see ⓑ in Fig. 1) and jump (cf. ⓒ) to the next functional gadget from a *dispatch table*, generally injected into a buffer. Each functional gadget must then end with a jump to the dispatcher gadget (cf. ⓓ). To do this, at least two registers need to be reserved: one for the dispatcher gadget (*dispatcher gadget register*) and one for the dispatch table (*dispatch table register*). The *initializer gadget* is responsible to set these registers and to pass control to the dispatcher gadget (cf. ⓐ). Figure 1 illustrates this mechanism with an example, where s1 and a5 are reserved registers (respectively, for the dispatch table and the dispatcher gadget), and a6 is used to branch to functional gadgets. In this example, the initializer gadget sets a reserved register from the current stack frame, assuming it is under the attacker's control.

---

[2] A specification of shadow stack and landing pads for RISC-V is currently under ratification, see https://github.com/riscv/riscv-cfi/.

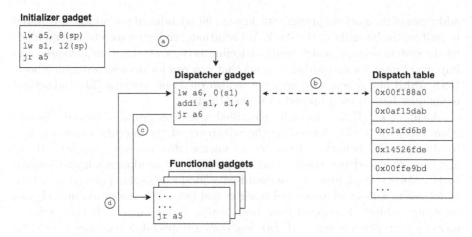

Fig. 1. JOP mechanic principle.

Building a JOP attack is far more complex than building a ROP attack for several reasons. First, initializer and dispatcher gadgets operating on the same registers need to be found to maintain the JOP chain. Although patterns leading to these gadgets are quite simple, there are very few of them in practice, and viable combinations of both gadgets are even more scarce. In addition to this difficulty, for any viable pair, there must be enough compatible functional gadgets in order to build the actual attack code (i.e. gadgets ending with a jump to the dispatcher gadget register). However, the vast majority of functional gadgets are procedure returns[3] but using them would trigger shadow stack detection if there is one. Argument registers are also a bad option for the dispatcher gadget register as it would prevent argument passing in the JOP chain. Other registers must be used but are less common, reducing the attack surface. Last but not least, side-effects in functional gadgets must also be considered as they can break the gadget chain management by clobbering the reserved registers.

Table 1 shows the number of available gadgets per register in the GNU libc 2.34 compiled for RISC-V 32 bits with M, A and C extensions (RV32IMAC). These statistics has been gathered with RaccoonV[4], an open-source tool we developed to find RISC-V JOP gadgets.

Table 1. Gadget availability per register in libc (top 15).

Register	ra	a5	t1	t3	tp	a4	s0	s2	a2	a0	sp	s1	a3	t5	s8
Available gadgets	4557	810	318	255	239	184	183	157	147	106	97	86	83	79	68

For these reasons, JOP attacks remain mostly theoretical. To our knowledge, there is no publicly known example of a JOP attack. In the following sections,

---

[3] For the RISC-V architecture, it corresponds to gadgets ending with a jump to ra.
[4] https://github.com/lfalkau/raccoonv.

we demonstrate the feasibility of JOP attacks on applications compiled for the RISC-V architecture, and introduce a new kind of dispatcher gadgets enabling the use of procedure epilogues as functional gadgets without triggering shadow stack detection, allowing to craft stealth attacks with a greater attack surface.

3   Autonomous Dispatcher Gadget

In a previous work [10], we managed to build a JOP attack on a RISC-V application but because of the aforementioned limitations, we did not succeed to chain several syscalls, limiting our results. From this experience, we started to search for more suitable dispatcher gadgets, and found a new kind of them that we called *Autonomous Dispatcher Gadget* (ADG). Figure 2 shows an ADG example and illustrates the JOP principle when using it.

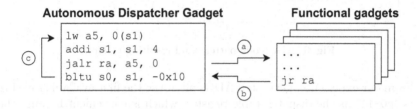

Fig. 2. JOP mechanism with an autonomous dispatcher gadget.

Unlike classic dispatcher gadgets, an ADG links to functional gadgets through a JALR instruction, which stores the next instruction's address in its first operand register (ra) and jumps to the target register (see ⓐ in Fig. 2). Regarding the specification, this is a procedure call. For this reason, functional gadgets ending in a jump to ra (procedure returns) can—and must—now be used in order to avoid shadow stack detection. When they return, control is given back to the saved return address, which is the instruction right after the JALR in the ADG (cf. ⓑ). This brings us to the second key point that makes the ADG's mechanic suitable: the instruction right after the JALR is a branching instruction that self-links the ADG to itself (cf. ⓒ). From our experience, this branching instruction is always conditional, but as we will show in Sect. 4, ensuring the condition remains true is quite easy.

Reserved Registers. In order to craft a JOP attack using an ADG, only one reserved register is required: the dispatch table register. The dispatcher gadget register is no longer required as the ADG links back to itself with a branching instruction. As a consequence, the initializer gadget can use any register to jump to the dispatcher gadget the first time (except ra—this would trigger shadow stack detection). Reducing the reserved registers constraint between these two gadgets considerably increases the probability to find a compatible pair. Moreover, it also increases the amount of available functional gadgets as only one register is to be preserved from side-effects in order to avoid breaking the chain.

Code Pattern. The first autonomous dispatcher we found was in the GNU libc 2.34, compiled with the second GCC level of optimization (-O2). It seems to be located in the __call_tls_dtors function (which runs the destructors in sequence when the program exits), but we cannot confirm it as the library is stripped on our system. We also managed to reproduce several ADGs with simple and realistic code patterns, each involving function pointer calls inside a loop. Figure 3 shows one of them, and the corresponding generated ADG.

```
extern void (*states[])();

void run() {
    void (**state)() = states;
    do {
        (*state)();
    } while (*state++);
}
```

```
  ┌→ lw a5, 0(s0)
  │  addi s0, s0, 4
  │  jalr a5
  │  lw a5, -4(s0)
  └─ bnez a5, 0x542
```

Fig. 3. ADG code pattern and resulting gadget.

From our experience, generated ADGs often use the first available saved registers (s0-11) as the dispatch table register, which is convenient because there is a good balance of gadgets loading them from the stack (potential initializer gadgets) and gadgets which do not clobber them, making them compatible functional gadgets. In a similar way, the first available argument register starting from a5 seems to be used by GCC to hold function pointers. This is also convenient as it allows an attacker to pass at least 4 arguments between functional gadgets to perform syscalls.

4   Attacking Real-World RISC-V Applications

In order to prove the feasibility of JOP on the RISC-V architecture using an ADG, we implemented a proof-of-concept attack against a well-known embedded application: the Mongoose web server; and more precisely their provided http-server, in which we introduced a memory corruption vulnerability. Mongoose is a target of choice because it exposes a remote service on the network and is widely available in many embedded products for configuration purpose.

In this section, we show how we were able to remotely read the root's private SSH key stored on disk with a JOP exploit by crafting a malicious HTTP request, thanks to an ADG.

Attack Model. Mongoose is developed in C. We compiled it for a Linux RISC-V 32-bit system using GCC. The binary and linked libraries have been compiled with modern protections, using -fstack-protector-all -D_FORTIFY_SOURCE=2. The second level of optimization (-O2) has also been used for libraries. However, we disabled ASLR on the target system since it can be bypassed by different techniques [11] [9], and is out of scope of this research. Position Independent Code (PIE) has also been disabled on the target binary. Both operating system and target application were executed and validated on a RISC-V CVA6 32-bit softcore design[5] [24] running Linux, deployed on a Genesys2 FPGA.

We also made the hypothesis that the attacker is able to access an exact twin of the target application (either by rebuilding it with the same options and environment, or by acquiring a device running said application), so static analysis can be performed both on target binary and linked libraries.

Attack Vector. As a first step the attacker must identify a memory vulnerability allowing to hijack the execution flow toward an initializer gadget. In our experiment, we introduced a format string vulnerability within the HTTP request handler of the target application: the body of the HTTP request is passed as the first printf argument, which permits an attacker to perform arbitrary write operations. Figure 4 shows the diff of the introduced vulnerability.

```
1   diff --git a/src/mongoose/main.c b/src/mongoose/main.c
2   index 1399f3c..0febf84 100644
3   --- a/src/mongoose/main.c
4   +++ b/src/mongoose/main.c
5   @@ -29,9 +29,10 @@ static void cb(struct mg_connection *c, int ev, void *ev_data, void *fn_data) {
6                   mg_http_parse((char *) c->send.buf, c->send.len, &tmp);
7                   cl = mg_http_get_header(&tmp, "Content-Length");
8                   if (cl == NULL) cl = &unknown;
9   -               MG_INFO(("0[%.*s] 2[%.*s] 3[%.*s] 4[%.*s]", (int) hm->method.len, hm->method.ptr,
10  -                       (int) hm->uri.len, hm->uri.ptr, (int) tmp.uri.len, tmp.uri.ptr,
11  -                       (int) cl->len, cl->ptr));
12  +               char body[16384] = {0};
13  +               sprintf(body, "%.*s", hm->body.len, hm->body.ptr);
14  +               printf(body);
15  +               fflush(0);
16              }
17          (void) fn_data;
18  }
```

Fig. 4. Mongoose introduced vulnerability diff.

Gadgets Research. The identification of available gadgets in the application is very important as it decides which assets can be targeted by the attack. Too few, or not diverse enough gadgets will reduce the attack surface in the best case, or make the attack impossible in the worst case.

We decided to exclusively use gadgets we found in the GNU C library (libc), as (1) it contains a lot of code and supposedly offers a great amount of gadgets and (2) almost all binaries are linked to it, making the attack more portable.

To identify gadgets, we used RaccoonV, which accepts queries to find gadgets based on their characteristics.

Figure 5 shows a simple query output, where we searched for gadgets in the libc, that loads the immediate 0 (--op=li --imm=0) in the register a2 (--rr=a2), and is at most 1 (--max=1) instruction long (excluding the final linking instruction).

---

[5] https://github.com/openhwgroup/cva6.

```
$ rv libc.so.6 --op=li --wr=a2 --imm=0 --max=1
0x0006f082      01 46    li a2, 0
0x0006f084      82 80    jr ra

0x000d4244      01 46    li a2, 0
0x000d4246      02 94    jalr s0

0x000a1fbc      01 46    li a2, 0
0x000a1fbe      82 97    jalr a5

----------
Found 3 unique gadgets.
```

Fig. 5. RaccoonV output with a query on libc.

As the dispatcher gadget is among the hardest to find, it is strongly advised to find one first and to build the attack around. As said previously in Sect. 3 we found an ADG, shown in Fig. 6. Its self-linking instruction is conditional, and in order to use it without breaking the chain, we must ensure s0 remains inferior than s1.

```
0x0002ec74    lw a5, 0(s0)
0x0002ec76    addi s0, 4
0x0002ec78    jalr a5
0x0002ec7a    bltu s0, s1, 0x2ec74
```

Fig. 6. Autonomous dispatcher gadget found in libc.

Finding an initializer gadget is not an easy task either but thanks to the ADG, we had less constraints on loaded registers and managed to find the one illustrated in Fig. 7. While it contains some side-effects we will need to handle later (stack pointer increment), it allows us to load both s0, s1 and a5 from the current stack frame before jumping to r5.

```
0x000d4706    lw a5, 0(s0)
0x000d4708    lw a0, 4(s0)
0x000d470a    lw s0, 8(sp)
0x000d470c    lw ra, 12(sp)
0x000d470e    lw s1, 4(sp)
0x000d4710    addi sp, sp, 16
0x000d4712    jr a5
```

Fig. 7. Initializer gadget found in libc.

Using these two gadgets together to build our JOP attack allows using functional gadgets ending in ra without triggering shadow stack detection, bringing the attack surface to the same level than ROP attacks.

Definition of the Attack Objective. The objective of the attack is to be decided from the number of available functional gadgets identified. Having a large number of compatible functional gadgets (4557 in our case) gives the attacker enough freedom to build complex attack code, as long as it does not involve control-flow operations.

In our experiment, the objective is to read the root's private SSH key file used to administrate the server without being detected, and to return to original code, so that the web server still runs fine afterwards. We define the attack code as equivalent to the C code shown in Fig. 8.

```
void attack_code() {
    int fd = openat(0, "/home/root/.ssh/id_rsa", O_RDONLY);
    read(fd, buf, 3000);
    write(5, buf, 3000);
}
```

Fig. 8. C formalization of the attack objective.

The first `openat` argument is unused when the path is absolute so we can ignore it. We used 5 as the file descriptor to write the key as it turned to be the first file descriptor assigned to clients by the HTTP server. If the file descriptor is free when the attacker sends the malicious request, the communication socket will use it; otherwise, the attack will fail, but can be retried anytime later (or immediately, setting the first write argument to another value).

JOP Chain Design. Once the objective of the attack is defined, the actual gadget chain can be crafted. In our case, it consists in a sequence of 3 syscalls and a cleanup step allowing to return to the nominal application code without crashing. Using RaccoonV, we managed to build the gadget chain shown in Fig. 9, where "..." represents instructions that are not useful to understand the attack.

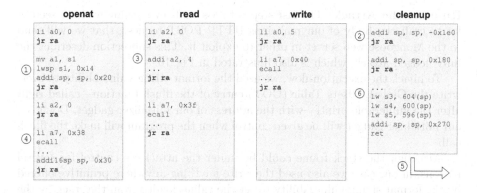

Fig. 9. JOP chain.

Several details are of interest in this gadget chain:

– Some gadgets have side-effects e.g. modifying the stack pointer or loading registers from the stack. While the former is fixed by the cleanup part of the JOP chain, the latter needs to be considered while forging our payload. For instance, s1 is loaded from the stack (see ① in Fig. 9) but we have to ensure it remains superior than s0.
– The gadget that subtracts sp (cf. ②) is not present in the original code: it is a valid instruction starting at an unexpected offset, often called shifted offset of misaligned instruction.
– For read and write syscalls, we need a2 to be big enough to process the whole file ($\approx$3 kB). However, we only found a gadget that increments a2 by 4 (cf. ③). We used this gadget 651 times to suit our needs.
– For each system call, we found gadgets in the libc that set a7 to the right identifier, and perform the syscall e.g. the openat one (cf. ④).
– After the cleanup step, we need to return to original code by inserting some address belonging to the Mongoose application (cf. ⑤). However, this address will be called as a regular gadget, thus pushing a new shadow stack entry. In order to avoid shadow stack detection, we must return to some point in the code that"never returns", e.g. in an infinite loop.
– As part of the cleanup step (and after having fixed the stack pointer), we used the entire epilogue of the function from which we hijacked the execution-flow as a gadget (cf. ⑥). This allowed to restore saved registers before returning to original code outside of this function. This gadget is the only one we used that comes from Mongoose. The same goal could have been achieved with gadgets found in the libc, but using the epilogue of the function we hijacked to pop its stack frame is very convenient. Moreover, the same technique could easily be applied while attacking other binaries.

Once the JOP chain has been designed, it can be encoded as a dispatch table, which is a sequential table containing the address of each gadget. In case of a gadget repetition, its address is included as many times as needed.

Running the Attack. The last step is to assemble everything we have seen so far to craft the body of our malicious HTTP POST request, that we will send to the Mongoose web server in order to exploit it. This subsection describes the fully-fledged attack, which is also illustrated in Fig. 10.

To hijack the execution-flow, we used the format string vulnerability to over-write the Global Offsets Table (GOT) entry of the fflush function—called right after the vulnerable printf—with the address of our initializer gadget. Doing so, our initializer gadget will be given control when the program will make the fflush call.

Although the stack frame could be under the attacker's control for several reasons, in our case we also used the write-anything-anywhere primitive offered by the format string vulnerability to set the values loaded from the stack by the initializer gadget, e.g. we set the stack address that will be loaded into s1 to

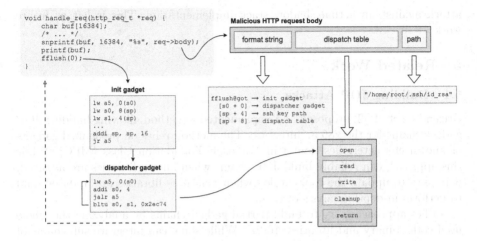

Fig. 10. Mongoose stealth JOP attack.

the path address in the request body. We then append the dispatch table and the path of the file we want to read next to the format string and perform the HTTP request.

While not related with JOP, in order for the attack to be stealth, we need to restore the fflush GOT entry we modified. To do so, a second HTTP request triggering the same vulnerability does the job. We can either patch the fflush GOT entry with the actual fflush address if we know it, or set it back to the default Procedure Linkage Table (PLT) stub address, to let the dynamic linker resolve its address again at the next fflush invocation.

4.1 Results and Limitations

By using the techniques presented in this section, we were able to steal the private SSH key of the root user stored on the target's disk. While not implemented in our target processor the attack should not trigger the shadow stack detection. The server still runs fine after the attack, and other clients can still interact with it normally.

As of today, it seems that landing pads could not be defeated with these techniques. To do so, one would need to use bigger gadgets—and eventually full functions—which may become impractical. However, landing pads come with a cost in terms of code size and execution time, that make them impractical for many embedded systems, hence our attack is mostly relevant for these systems.

4.2 Next Steps

As far as we know, there is no publicly available implementation of a standalone RISC-V shadow stack, without other CFI mitigations such as landing pads. For this reason, while we can theoretically bypass it, we were not able to test our attack against an actual shadow stack implementation. This is left as future work.

5   Related Work

5.1   Building JOP Attacks

Brizendine et al. [2] proposed and implemented a method allowing building JOP gadget chains for the x86 architecture. The method relies on predefined gadgets of known characteristics, found in Microsoft Foundation Class (MFC). While this approach can reliably build JOP chains when known libraries are involved, it implies to update the tool catalog whenever these libraries are updated, and to perform in-depth analysis of them.

Other approaches try to build partial gadget chains by analyzing the whole used code, binary and libraries [16,22]. While some can integrate sub-chains of JOP gadgets within a ROP chain, none of them can build full JOP chains to our knowledge, making them easily detected by ROP-targeted countermeasures such as the shadow stack. Other tools able to help building JOP chains on RISC-V include ROPgadget[6] and radare2[7], which can search JOP gadgets but not build gadget chains on RISC-V architectures, as they have no method for discovering dispatcher gadget or initializer gadget. They are primarily designed to build ROP chains.

Gu et al. [12] identified a specific pattern of instructions allowing linking functional gadgets in RISC-V architectures, introducing the concept of "self-modifying gadget chain" to save and restore register values in memory. They also demonstrated the Turing-completeness of their solution. Adapting self-modifying gadget chain to JOP is indeed a promising solution to increase our capacity to build effective gadget chains. Jaloyan et al. [14] reached the same result by abusing compressed instructions (*overlapping*). Our attack also uses this approach, and applies it to JOP attacks.

Trampolines-based approaches are somewhat a missing link between ROP and JOP. A trampoline itself (an update-load-branch suite of instructions) is the ancestor of the dispatcher gadget and, instead of exploiting an arbitrary memory, uses hardware-maintained registers such as ra (return address register) to jump to the next functional gadget [5]. While they do not rely on return-specific instructions (which do not exist in RISC-V anyway), they do imply that large segments of the stack need to be corrupted, hence making them vulnerable to stack canaries and the shadow stack. Erdödi [8] proposed a solution to find classical dispatcher gadgets on x86 for different operating systems. As they are scarce, and trampolines patterns tend to be more common, the latter are still used [18]. In addition to providing a solution in RISC-V architecture for JOP gadget chaining, our discovery of the ADG greatly increases the number of available JOP gadgets, effectively making them as common as ROP gadgets and eliminating the need for trampolines.

---

[6] https://github.com/JonathanSalwan/ROPgadget.

[7] https://github.com/radareorg/radare2.

5.2 Defenses from CRA

Austin et al. [13] published the MORPHEUS II solution for RISC-V. This hardware-based solution aims at defeating memory probes trying to bypass address randomization by providing a reactive, fine-grain, continuous randomization of virtual addresses, as well as encryption of pointers and caches. This solution, while having a low overhead in terms of energy consumption and area, is quite intrusive in the hardware and may require efforts for certification in critical applications. While authors make no claim about stopping JOP attacks, probe-resistant ASLR may be difficult to bypass for an attacker.

Palmiero et al. [17] proposed a hardware-based adaptation of Dynamic Information Flow Tracking (DIFT) for RISC-V, with the ability to detect most function pointers overwriting, whether directly or indirectly, and in any memory segment, thus allowing blocking the attack at its initialization stage. Although this approach seems indeed powerful, it implies modification of RISC-V instructions behavior in I and M extensions for RISC-V 32 bits, as well as in the memory layout (by adding a bit every 8 bits of memory). Such modifications drift away from the RISC-V ABI.

De et al. [7] implemented a chip compliant to RISC-V, including a Rocket Custom Coprocessor (RoCC) which extends the RISC-V ISA with new instructions allowing safe operation on the heap. The authors ensure heap size integrity and prevent use-after-free attacks, at the cost of an increase of 50% of average execution time on their benchmarks.

6 Conclusion

Anticipating security vulnerabilities for RISC-V systems in order to identify and prevent possible attacks is an important challenge. Building attacks is a necessary step to test platforms and evaluate their attack surface, as adversary actors (black hat hackers) will eventually attack them. In this article, we contribute by demonstrating the feasibility and a practical way to realize jump-oriented programming (JOP) attacks, allowing for more extensive security testing.

We have introduced a new variant of dispatcher gadget, the autonomous dispatcher gadget (ADG), which greatly improves the RISC-V JOP attack surface by enabling the use of ROP gadgets with a JOP mechanism. While its rigorous validation against a CVA6 implementing a shadow stack is left as future work, we are convinced that it will be able to bypass shadow stack mitigation.

We have demonstrated a JOP attack on a RISC-V platform using a real world application commonly used in critical embedded systems: the Mongoose web server. After adding a single memory vulnerability, we were able to take control of the application in order to perform an adversary action, sending a private key to a remote attacker. Thanks to the large number of functional gadgets available in the libc through the use of the ADG, we were able to make the attack stealthy by restoring the nominal behavior of the application after the attack completion.

Next steps for identifying potentially practical JOP attacks include assistance in gadget finding and even automated chain building. There is a very impressive body of research on ROP chain building [22], that would be a good basis to build up automated testing frameworks for RISC-V application vulnerabilities to JOP. Likewise, studies like the one presented in this article will enable the development of better and more efficient countermeasures for the RISC-V architecture against JOP attacks and enhance control-flow integrity in general.

Acknowledgements. This work is partly supported by the French research agency (ANR) under the grant ANR-21-CE-39-0017. We thank Franck Viguier for his contribution to a preliminary version of this work.

References

1. Abadi, M., Budiu, M., Erlingsson, U., Ligatti, J.: Control-flow integrity. In: the 12th ACM Conference on Computer and Communications Security (CCS'05), pp. 340–353. ACM (2005). https://doi.org/10.1145/1102120.1102165
2. Brizendine, B., Babcock, A.: Pre-built JOP chains with the JOP ROCKET: bypassing DEP without ROP. In: Black Hat Asia, May 2021
3. Burow, N., et al.: Control-flow integrity: precision, security, and performance. ACM Comput. Surv. **50**(1) (2017). https://doi.org/10.1145/3054924
4. Carlini, N., Wagner, D.: ROP is still dangerous: breaking modern defenses. In: the 23rd USENIX Conference on Security Symposium (SEC'14), pp. 385–399. USENIX Association (2014)
5. Checkoway, S., Davi, L., Dmitrienko, A., Sadeghi, A.R., Shacham, H., Winandy, M.: Return-oriented programming without returns. In: the 17th ACM Conference on Computer and Communications Security (CCS'10), pp. 559–572. ACM (2010). https://doi.org/10.1145/1866307.1866370
6. Cowan, C.: StackGuard: automatic adaptive detection and prevention of buffer-overflow attacks. In: the 7th USENIX Security Symposium. USENIX Association (1998)
7. De, A., Ghosh, S.: HeapSafe: securing unprotected heaps in RISC-V. In: the 35th International Conference on VLSI Design and the 21st International Conference on Embedded Systems (VLSID'22), pp. 120–125. IEEE (2022). https://doi.org/10.1109/VLSID2022.2022.00034
8. Erdödi, L.: Finding dispatcher gadgets for jump oriented programming code reuse attacks. In: the 8th International Symposium on Applied Computational Intelligence and Informatics (SACI'13), pp. 321–325. IEEE (2013). https://doi.org/10.1109/SACI.2013.6608990
9. Evtyushkin, D., Ponomarev, D., Abu-Ghazaleh, N.: Jump over ASLR: attacking branch predictors to bypass ASLR. In: the 49th Annual IEEE/ACM International Symposium on Microarchitecture (MICRO'16), pp. 40:1–40:13. IEEE (2016). https://doi.org/10.1109/MICRO.2016.7783743
10. Gilles, O., Viguier, F., Kosmatov, N., Gracia Pérez, D.: Control-flow integrity at RISC: attacking RISC-V by jump-oriented programming. CoRR (2022). https://doi.org/10.48550/arXiv.2211.16212
11. Gras, B., Razavi, K., Bosman, E., Bos, H., Giuffrida, C.: ASLR on the line: practical cache attacks on the MMU. In: the 24th Annual Network and Distributed System Security Symposium (NDSS'17). The Internet Society (2017)

12. Gu, G., Shacham, H.: Return-oriented programming in RISC-V. CoRR (2020). https://arxiv.org/abs/2007.14995

13. Harris, A., et al.: Morpheus II: a RISC-V security extension for protecting vulnerable software and hardware. In: the IEEE International Symposium on Hardware Oriented Security and Trust (HOST'21), pp. 226–238. IEEE (2021). https://doi.org/10.1109/HOST49136.2021.9702275

14. Jaloyan, G.A., Markantonakis, K., Akram, R.N., Robin, D., Mayes, K., Naccache, D.: Return-oriented programming on RISC-V. In: the 15th ACM Asia Conference on Computer and Communications Security (ASIA CCS'20), pp. 471–480. ACM (2020). https://doi.org/10.1145/3320269.3384738

15. Lu, T.: A survey on RISC-V security: Hardware and architecture. CoRR (2021). https://arxiv.org/abs/2107.04175

16. Nurmukhametov, A., Vishnyakov, A., Logunova, V., Kurmangaleev, S.F.: MAJORCA: multi-architecture JOP and ROP chain assembler. In: the 2021 Ivannikov Ispras Open Conference (ISPRAS'21), pp. 37–46 (2021). https://doi.org/10.1109/ISPRAS53967.2021.00011

17. Palmiero, C., Di Guglielmo, G., Lavagno, L., Carloni, L.P.: Design and implementation of a dynamic information flow tracking architecture to secure a RISC-V core for IoT applications. In: the 2018 IEEE High Performance Extreme Computing Conference (HPEC'18), pp. 1–7. IEEE (2018). https://doi.org/10.1109/HPEC.2018.8547578

18. Sadeghi, A.A., Aminmansour, F., Shahriari, H.R.: Tazhi: a novel technique for hunting trampoline gadgets of jump oriented programming (a class of code reuse attacks). In: the 2014 11th International ISC Conference on Information Security and Cryptology, pp. 21–26 (2014). https://doi.org/10.1109/ISCISC.2014.6994016

19. Shacham, H.: The geometry of innocent flesh on the bone: return-into-libc without function calls (on the x86). In: the 2007 ACM Conference on Computer and Communications Security (CCS'07), pp. 552–561. ACM (2007). https://doi.org/10.1145/1315245.1315313

20. Shacham, H., Page, M., Pfaff, B., Goh, E.J., Modadugu, N., Boneh, D.: On the effectiveness of address-space randomization. In: the 11th ACM Conference on Computer and Communications Security (CCS'04), pp. 298–307. ACM (2004). https://doi.org/10.1145/1030083.1030124

21. Solar Designer: Getting around non-executable stack (and fix) (1997). https://seclists.org/bugtraq/1997/Aug/63

22. Vishnyakov, A., Nurmukhametov, A.: Survey of methods for automated code-reuse exploit generation. Program. Comput. Softw. **47**, 271–297 (2021). https://doi.org/10.1134/S0361768821040071

23. Younan, Y., Joosen, W., Piessens, F.: Code injection in C and C++: a survey of vulnerabilities and countermeasures. Technical report, Department Computer wetenschappen, Katholieke Universiteit Leuven (2004). https://www.cs.kuleuven.be/publicaties/rapporten/cw/CW386.pdf

24. Zaruba, F., Benini, L.: The cost of application-class processing: energy and performance analysis of a Linux-ready 1.7-GHz 64-bit RISC-V core in 22-nm FDSOI technology. IEEE Trans. Very Large Scale Integr. Syst. **27**(11), 2629–2640 (2019). https://doi.org/10.1109/TVLSI.2019.2926114

Modeling Obfuscation Stealth Through Code Complexity

Sebastian Schrittwieser[1]([✉]), Elisabeth Wimmer[2], Kevin Mallinger[1],
Patrick Kochberger[1,3], Caroline Lawitschka[1], Sebastian Raubitzek[2],
and Edgar R. Weippl[1]

[1] University of Vienna, Vienna, Austria
{sebastian.schrittwieser,kevin.mallinger,patrick.kochberger,
caroline.lawitschka,edgar.weippl}@univie.ac.at
[2] SBA Research, Vienna, Austria
{ewimmer,sraubitzek2}@sba-research.org
[3] St. Pölten University of Applied Sciences, St. Pölten, Austria
patrick.kochberger@fhstp.ac.at

Abstract. Code obfuscation is often utilized by authors of malware to protect it from detection or to hide its maliciousness from code analysis. Obfuscation stealth describes how difficult it is to determine which protection technique has been applied to a program and which parts of the code have been protected. In previous literature, most of the presented obfuscation identification methods analyze the program code itself (for example, the frequency and distribution of opcodes). However, simple countermeasures such as instruction substitution can have a negative impact on the identification rate. In this paper, we present a novel approach for an accurate obfuscation identification model based on a combination of multiple code complexity metrics. An evaluation with 4124 samples protected with 11 different obfuscations, combinations of obfuscations, and various compiler configurations demonstrates an overall classification accuracy of 86.5%.

Keywords: software obfuscation · stealth · code complexity

1 Introduction

Malware authors use various types of code obfuscations to make their code more difficult to detect and analyze. A Black Hat survey by Brosch et al. [4] from 2006 suggested that more than 90% of all malware samples identified in the wild use packing obfuscation to protect themselves from detection. In a more recent study from 2017, Rahbarinia et al. [32] found that 58% of all malware samples are protected with off-the-shelf packers (not taking into account custom packers which are used by about 35% of packed malware [26]). But also other obfuscation techniques, such as virtualization, data encoding/encryption, and library hiding, are frequently used to hide malicious code.

On the other hand, malware analysts and researchers aim to analyze unknown malware samples efficiently and understand how they work. An essential step in

S. Katsikas et al. (Eds.): ESORICS 2023 Workshops, LNCS 14399, pp. 392–408, 2024.
https://doi.org/10.1007/978-3-031-54129-2_23

the analysis of obfuscated code is the identification of the obfuscation method. It significantly simplifies the analysis as tailored de-obfuscation methods often already exist. Obfuscating transformations complicate code merely in its semantic representation and thus can often be undone if the exact obfuscation method (e.g., the obfuscator tool and its configuration) is known.

The stealth of an obfuscation indicates how opaque the application of an obfuscation is, both in terms of the type of obfuscation and the exact location in the code to which the obfuscation is applied. In previous literature, obfuscation stealth was mainly described in terms of code structures, such as for example, the frequency of opcodes. In contrast, this paper presents a novel approach that can detect obfuscation with high accuracy using a combination of different code complexity metrics. For our approach it is not required to know the relative changes in code complexity after applying an obfuscation. Instead, it is based purely on absolute values and the insight that the different obfuscations generate a characteristic pattern of increases, but also reductions of the various observed complexity metrics.

In particular, our main contribution in this paper is the introduction of a novel model for obfuscation stealth based on two obfuscators, 11 obfuscation combinations, and 4124 obfuscated programs.

The remainder of this paper is structured as follows. Section 2 discusses related work, while in Sect. 3 the fundamentals of code obfuscation, obfuscation stealth, and code complexity are presented. Section 4 introduces our novel approach to obfuscation identification. In Sect. 5, we show the results which we then discuss in Sect. 6. Section 7 concludes the paper.

2   Related Work

In previous literature, a protection technique was described as stealthy if the resulting code resembles the original code as much as possible [8]. One major problem with quantifying stealthiness is that it highly depends on the original program whether or not a technique can be applied in a stealthy way. Sometimes a specific technique might produce code that fits perfectly into the original code. Other times however, the protection might generate code sections that clearly differ from the rest of the code, for example, in terms of its structure. Collberg et al. [28] described two types of obfuscation stealth. Local stealth measures the difficulty of identifying the exact location of an obfuscation applied to code, whereas steganographic stealth describes the difficulty of detecting that a specific obfuscation was applied at all.

Previous approaches to obfuscation detection are mainly based on code structures such as opcode frequencies. Kanzaki et al. [18] proposed an artificiality metric that measures the degree to which protected code can be distinguished from unprotected code. Their results showed that while some types of obfuscations strongly impact code artificiality, such as code encryption, others, for example control-flow modifying obfuscations such as CFG flattening, have a minimal effect. In 2017 Wang et al. [38] proposed a method for identifying the obfuscation tool, the applied obfuscation, and its configuration for protected Android applications. The method is based on machine learning using a feature vector from the Dalvik bytecode of the app. A related methodology was presented by Bacci et al. [2] in 2018. It utilizes features extracted from the Smali representation of the application's bytecode.

LOM by Kim et al. [20] uses a neural network-based classifier on the opcode distribution of binary code for obfuscation identification.

3 Preliminaries

3.1 Code Obfuscation

Obfuscating transformations convert code – either in the form of source, byte, or executable code – into code that is unintelligible in some form, either by a human code analyst or by an automated code analysis tool. The development of new code obfuscation techniques is mainly driven by the desire to hide the specific implementation of a program. This includes malware authors, who aim at hiding the malicious purposes of their code. Thus, breaking obfuscations is a fundamental prerequisite of malware detection. Code obfuscations can be categorized into various classes, such as layout transformations (which modify the superficial structure of the code) or control flow transformations (which alter the control flow path of a program while retaining its semantics [34]).

Obfuscations are usually applied to code through automatic tools. Some commercial source code protection solutions are on the market (e.g., Cloakware by Irdeto[1]), but also many freely available tools and online services. In the scientific community, the Tigress obfuscator[2] by Collberg et al. is widely used. Tigress was developed based on CIL [29] and MyJit[3] and is able to protect C source code with a variety of obfuscation methods. However, considerable uncertainty exists as to whether – and, if so, to what extent – the software protection is transferred to the binary program during compilation. Already in 2006, Madou et al. [23] were able to demonstrate empirically that not all types of protection survive the compilation process. To some extent, this undesired effect results from the fact that software protections intentionally make code more complicated, but a compiler attempts to generate efficient binary code through various optimization strategies. Thus, it often removes the protections or at least significantly reduces their strength.

In recent years, it was demonstrated that code obfuscation can also be applied to intermediate code representations during the compilation process after the optimizations have been conducted. With the Obfuscator LLVM (OLLVM) framework [17] it was prototypically demonstrated that compile-time protection of code is feasible.

---

[1] https://irdeto.com.
[2] https://tigress.wtf.
[3] https://myjit.sourceforge.net.

In this work, we use obfuscations from both Tigress and Obfuscator LLVM to train our identification model. 6 different types of obfuscations and 4 combinations of obfuscation were used in our work. As one obfuscation is available in both obfuscators, a total of 11 obfuscation classes were defined. Table 1 describes the applied obfuscations.

Table 1. Applied obfuscations.

Technique	Obfuscator	Description
Opaque predicates	Tigress	Adds difficult to evaluate expressions to conditional jumps
Self-modifying code	Tigress	Adds code that modifies itself at runtime
Virtualization	Tigress	Transforms binary code to byte code of a custom virtual machine
Bogus control flow	OLLVM	Opaque predicates to make control flow less obvious; similar to Tigress opaque predicates
CFG flattening	both	Redirects all control-flow transfers to a central dispatcher
Instruction substitution	OLLVM	Replaces instructions with semantically equal ones

3.2   Obfuscation Stealth

Obfuscation stealth describes how well-obfuscated code can be distinguished from untransformed code. Collberg et al. [7] have defined two different types of stealth. With local stealth, an attacker cannot determine a particular instruction as being affected by an obfuscating transformation. In contrast, with steganographic stealth, an attacker cannot determine whether a program has been transformed at all with a particular transformation or not.

At first glance, the coverage, i.e., how much code is actually modified, seems particularly relevant for the stealthiness of an obfuscation. In instruction substitution, for example, occurrences of certain instructions are replaced by semantically equivalent instructions or sequences of instructions. It is possible to specify how many of the occurrences are replaced. Coverage correlates with the number of code modifications. The smaller the coverage of an obfuscation, the smaller the modifications to the code.

However, the number of code modifications does not indicate how easily it can be distinguished from untransformed code. For example, a packer modifies the complete binary by encoding or encrypting the program's entire code as data. This fundamental structural modification of the binary seems more difficult to hide than protections with lower coverage. However, current literature proposes approaches such as using Huffman encodings [40] to make the packed code look structurally like actual binary code or shell code that looks like English prose [24]. While English prose can clearly be distinguished from actual shell code, the context where shell code is utilized makes it a perfect camouflage. Thus, coverage alone is not a good indicator of the stealthiness of an obfuscation.

3.3 Code Complexity

As Collberg et al. [7] mentioned, code complexity metrics were initially created to help build reliable, readable, and maintainable software constructs. Generally, most of them can be summarized as describing a respective aspect of software, typically textual, from which a complexity measure is derived. If this measure increases within a program, this program is then described as being more complex in relation to the measured properties. A property often utilized for this is obfuscation potency, i.e., how well humans are able to comprehend the code [9]. In contrast, obfuscation stealth has not been measured yet with code complexity metrics.

Over the last decades, various methodologies for code complexity measurements have emerged. For source code, the three most influential and widely used are the Halstead Complexity Metrics, Lines of Code, and Cyclomatic Complexity Metric [15,19,41]. These are also called *classic methods* as they were invented in the 1960s and 1970s; they are still highly relevant today, albeit primarily used in modified form and/or in tandem.

Halstead Complexity Metrics. As an early pioneer of software science, Maurice Halstead was one of the first to quantitatively analyze software. His work resulted in the formalization of the *Halstead complexity metrics* [13], which consist of several sub-metrics.

- The *Halstead difficulty* measures how difficult it is to write or understand the code of a program. It is defined as $D = \frac{n_1}{2} \cdot \frac{N_2}{n_1}$, where n_1 is the number of distinct operators, n_2 is the number of distinct operands and N_2 is the total number of operands.
- *Halstead volume* estimates the required space for storing the program and is defined as $V = N \cdot \log_2 n$.
- *Halstead level* defines the implementation level $L = \frac{V_p}{V}$ where V_p is the potential or minimal volume $V_p = (2 + n_2) \cdot \log_2(2 + n_2)$.
- *Halstead effort* estimates the effort required for writing or understanding the program. It is defined as $E = D \cdot V$.
- *Halstead time* estimates the time required for writing the program and defined as $T = \frac{E}{18}$.

Lines of Code. The *Lines of Code* metric is a measure for the length of a program, whereby only executable lines are factored in [3,14,36,39,41]. Although being a basic metric, this brings several advantages, like being language-independent, fast to compute, and easy to comprehend [41]. The simplicity of the metric comes with several problems, though. For example, the content of the lines is completely disregarded so that a very simple and a highly complex line count as equal for the calculation. Furthermore, the program's structure is neglected with respect to jumping and branching. Finally, although size itself is not an immediate indicator of complexity within a software project, we can infer that larger programs contain more constructs and control structures and, therefore, more paths through the code. Thus, for the purpose of this work, the *Lines of Code* metric is considered a complexity metric.

Cyclomatic Complexity and Myer's Interval. *Cyclomatic Complexity*, the third of the classic metrics, describes the structure of software through the number of possible independent paths in its control flow graph [1,10,16,22,25,33,35]. This also functions as a measure of the nesting level and can be computed with binary code [5]. To calculate it, a flow graph G is created, and its cyclomatic value v is generated by $v(G) = e - n + 2p$. Here, e denotes the number of edges, n the number of nodes, and p the number of connected entities in G. This measure can be helpful in providing a good abstraction of the module's structure and works well in predicting future bugs, but it is completely blind to the length of a tested module. Because of extreme cases, like a single line of code potentially being able to have the same cyclomatic value as parts with hundreds of lines, Cyclomatic Complexity is often combined with other length-sensitive measures like Halstead metrics or Lines of Code. Similarly, *McCabe's cyclomatic complexity* [25] measures the complexity of a program by analyzing its control flow. The complexity $v(G) = E - N + 2p$ where $v(G)$ is the cyclomatic number of a graph G, E is the number of edges, N the number of nodes and p the number of connected components. *Myer's interval* [27] is an extension of McCabe's cyclomatic complexity. The Myer's interval $v(G) : v(G) + L$ adds the number of logical operators L to McCabe's cyclomatic complexity.

ABC Metric. Despite its traditional categorization as a size metric, the *ABC metric* [11] lends itself to the assessment of code complexity, given the quantitative focus on the evaluation of software components. Furthermore, the three components utilized within the *ABC metric* are fundamental constructs for any programming language, making them relevant in understanding the overall complexity of a software project. The three components, number of assignments (A), branches (B), and conditions (C), as a triplet, build the first representation (vector) of the ABC metric. The other possible representation is a number (Euclidean norm, L2 norm) calculated by the square root of the sum of the squared individual numbers: $|ABC| = \sqrt{A^2 + B^2 + C^2}$. Assuming there is at least one assignment, branch or condition, the ABC metric consequently is always a positive number $|ABC| > 0$.

Maintainability Index. As the name already suggests, the *maintainability index* [6,30,31] was originally designed to measure how maintainable code is.

It is based on the Halstead difficulty metric and is defined as $MIwoc = 125 - 10 \cdot \log(HE)$, where HE is the Halstead effort. A more complex variant is the *maintainability index without comments*, which combines the Halstead volume, McCabe's cyclomatic complexity, and LoC. It is defined as $MIwoc = 171 - 5.2 \cdot \ln(HV) - 0.23 \cdot CC - 16.2 \cdot \ln(LOC)$.

4   Approach

Depending on the obfuscation type, code complexity is affected to varying degrees. Furthermore, an obfuscation type does not contribute to all code complexity metrics equally. For example, cyclomatic complexity is only increased by obfuscations that make structural changes at the control flow or call graph level. We also observed that obfuscations often significantly reduce individual code complexity metrics, thus the opposite of what would intuitively be expected. Our approach uses these characteristic patterns of increases and decreases in code complexity measurements to identify the implemented obfuscation technique. We discovered that absolute measurements are sufficient for identifying obfuscation techniques with ample accuracy and that relative changes from the original code are not required. To build our model, we assembled a set of 179 programs, which we then compiled in 52 different build and obfuscation configurations each. As the Tigress obfuscator can only handle single-file C source code, the set consists mainly of programs implementing one particular algorithm (e.g., hash function, sorting algorithm, units converter, etc.). Not all build and obfuscation configurations resulted in valid binary programs, as the obfuscators

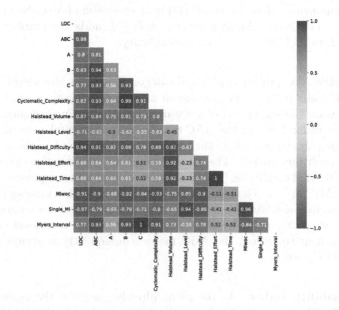

Fig. 1. Correlation coefficients for all complexity metrics.

sometimes fail on specific program structures. The final set of training data contained 4124 binaries. We calculated the 14 code complexity metrics introduced in Sect. 3.3 for each. We combined eight from the initial 52 classes into a class *no-obfuscation* since all of them correspond to the different compilation variants of clang and gcc-musl without employing any obfuscation.

We then pooled the classes corresponding to the same obfuscator and technique, i.e., combining the various optimization levels per obfuscation class. Thus, we ultimately ended up with 12 classes, where each obfuscation method has 300 to 336 observations, whereas we obtained 680 samples associated with no-obfuscation. We noticed that some metrics are highly correlated by analyzing the feature set. However, this is not surprising since several metrics are combinations or extensions of one another as described in Sect. 3.3. For example, the ABC metric is composed of A, B, and C, which are also part of the original feature set. We visualized the exact coefficients in the correlation matrix depicted in Fig. 1.

We decided to fit models using both the whole feature set and a smaller set of values from five complexity metrics with a Pearson correlation coefficient $|\rho| \leq 0.9$. The features included in the smaller feature set were the following: Lines of Code, ABC, number of assignments (A), Halstead Volume, and Halstead Level. From here on, we refer to the respective feature sets as *All features* and *5/14 features*.

The following steps in preprocessing included shuffling the data and performing a stratified split into train and test data using the class proportions present. Here, we chose a split such that we ended up with 80% training data and 20% test data, with a corresponding `random_state = 42`. Finally, we standardized all features using the `StandardScaler`-function from `sklearn`, i.e., shifting the data to a mean of zero and a standard deviation of 1. As part of the hyperparameter search, we used 5-fold cross-validation to show the reliability of each model. We evaluated the models with respect to classification accuracy, F1 score, precision, and recall in order to get a holistic view of the model performances.

$$\text{Accuracy} = \frac{\text{Correct Classifications}}{\text{All Classifications}} \tag{1}$$

$$\text{F1 Score} = \frac{2 \times \text{Precision} \times \text{Recall}}{\text{Precision} + \text{Recall}} \tag{2}$$

$$\text{Precision} = \frac{\text{True Positive}}{\text{True Positive} + \text{False Positive}} \tag{3}$$

$$\text{Recall} = \frac{\text{True Positive}}{\text{True Negative} + \text{False Positive}} \tag{4}$$

After finding well-performing parameter sets for the machine learning models with each feature set respectively, we ran all models 100 times, using a new seed in each iteration. In addition to the best value of each performance metric, we also calculated the mean values over these runs to show the statistical validity of the results.

5   Evaluation

5.1   Model Selection

For the initial model selection, we employed the Lazy Learner framework lazypredict to get an overview of how different models perform on the data set under study. Lazy Learner provides a fast way to test many different algorithms without further time-consuming parameterization. ExtraTreesClassifier, LGBMClassifier, and RandomForestClassifier performed best on our initial test with respect to the models' accuracy. Based on this result, we decided to investigate these three models further. To explore the potential of different algorithms in the context of obfuscation stealth, and because neural networks are known to perform well on classification problems [12,21], we also included an MLPClassifier (Multi-Layer Perceptron). All applied models are part of scikit-learn, except for the LGBMClassifier, which is part of the lightgbm package.

5.2   Hyperparameter Tuning

For all models, we performed the hyperparameter tuning with Bayesian optimization using the BayesSearchCV function from Scikit-optimize. The sequential model-based optimization algorithm utilizes all previous loss observations in order to arrive at a well-performing set of parameters for the respective model. The incorporation of prior knowledge makes Bayesian optimization much more efficient than a grid search or random search [37]. We explored 100 parameter settings for each model, which we evaluated using a 5-fold cross-validation.

5.3   Model Results

As shown in Table 2, the prediction results on the test set were best for the MLPClassifier, achieving a maximum accuracy of 86.5% and an average accuracy of 83.9% over 100 runs respectively, using all features. The neural network outperforms the other classifiers, showing better results across all performance metrics. However, the ExtraTreesClassifier, the LGBMClassifier, and the RandomForestClassifier accomplish only slightly poorer results. In general, we observed that including all features in the model led to considerably better average performance, as seen from the accuracy values in Table 2 and Table 3. The severe difference in the accuracy scores implies that the nine complexity metrics we removed from the smaller feature set due to high correlation with other features carry information significant for the models.

Table 2. Maximum and average performance using all features for 100 iterations.

	Accuracy	F1 Score	Precision	Recall
Extra Trees	0.833 (∅ 0.813)	0.833 (∅ 0.813)	0.836 (∅ 0.815)	0.833 (∅ 0.813)
LGBM	0.834 (∅ 0.806)	0.834 (∅ 0.807)	0.837 (∅ 0.810)	0.834 (∅ 0.806)
Random Forest	0.827 (∅ 0.800)	0.826 (∅ 0.799)	0.828 (∅ 0.801)	0.827 (∅ 0.800)
MLP	**0.865** (∅ 0.839)	**0.865** (∅ 0.839)	**0.868** (∅ 0.842)	**0.865** (∅ 0.839)

Table 3. Maximum and average performance using 5/14 features for 100 iterations.

	Accuracy	F1 Score	Precision	Recall
Extra Trees	**0.770** (∅ 0.743)	**0.771** (∅ 0.742)	**0.773** (∅ 0.744)	**0.770** (∅ 0.743)
LGBM	0.752 (∅ 0.716)	0.752 (∅ 0.717)	0.755 (∅ 0.721)	0.752 (∅ 0.716)
Random Forest	**0.772** (∅ 0.729)	**0.772** (∅ 0.728)	**0.772** (∅ 0.730)	**0.772** (∅ 0.729)
MLP	0.764 (∅ 0.728)	0.764 (∅ 0.726)	0.766 (∅ 0.727)	0.764 (∅ 0.728)

The model specifications of the respective best models per classifier and feature set based on accuracy can be found in Table 4 in the Appendix A. The boxplots in Fig. 2 depict the accuracy ranges over 100 unique runs for all classifiers fitted on the data using all features. While Table 2 shows the superiority of the MLPClassifier concerning maximum accuracy, Fig. 2 demonstrates where most predictions are located precisely. More than 50% of the predictions made by the MLPClassifier are better than all of the predictions made by the other three classifiers. Due to its good maximum accuracy and consistency over all runs, we conclude that using all features, the MLPClassifier is the best model choice when using all features.

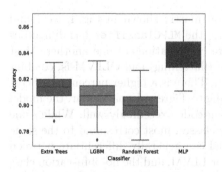 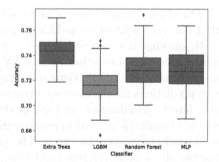

Fig. 2. Accuracy results over 100 runs for classifiers using all features.

Fig. 3. Accuracy results over 100 runs for classifiers using 5/14 features.

Figure 3 shows that when using the smaller feature set consisting of only 5 out of the 14 complexity metrics, the performance of the classifiers decreases. The accuracy score corresponding to the multilayer perceptron classifier particularly suffers from excluding the strongly correlated variables. The best results were achieved by the `RandomForestClassifier` and the `ExtraTreesClassifier`, where the latter also performs best on average and therefore represents the most suitable model for our approach. The comparatively bad results achieved by the neural network might be due to MLPs relying on complex relationships and high-dimensional interactions between features. When removing features, the MLP model may lose more information as compared to the other models.

To further assess the performance of the selected best models, we constructed the normalized confusion matrices, which are depicted in Fig. 4 and Fig. 5 below. They visualize which classes are detected well and which techniques are often mistaken for one another.

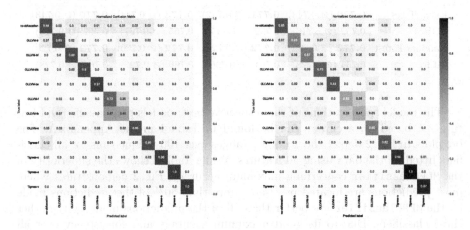

Fig. 4. Confusion matrix for results of the best model using all features.

Fig. 5. Confusion matrix for results of the best model using 5/14 features.

On closer examination of the confusion matrix shown in Fig. 4, we found that concerning Obfuscator-LLVM samples, the `MLPClassifier` has difficulties distinguishing between techniques that are combinations of one another. Most misclassifications occur between OLLVM-f (flattening) and OLLVM-fs, combining flattening and instructions substitution. There is a higher percentage of correct predictions for the classes corresponding to Tigress. In particular, the model can detect virtualization and self-modifying code exceedingly well. While some wrong classifications exist across compiler classes, most correspond to the same or related obfuscation methods. The model can generally differentiate between the two obfuscators, Tigress and Obfuscator-LLVM, and the no-obfuscation class quite well, showing only a few misclassifications. Indeed, most of those mistakes stem from the model wrongly classifying 12% of Tigress-f as no-obfuscation.

We also analyzed the normalized confusion matrix obtained when fitting the model using only 5/14 features. Looking at the results shown in Fig. 5, the difficulties regarding the distinction of certain classes become more pronounced.

In particular, differentiating between different techniques of the LLVM obfuscator seems to be harder for the model using only 5/14 features. Overall, the percentage of correct predictions decreases significantly. The drop in accuracy is particularly high for OLLVM-b, OLLVM-bf, OLLVM-f, and OLLVM-s, amounting to at least 20%. The precise numbers are depicted in the confusion matrix in Fig. 5.

While even more samples from the class Tigress-f are mistakenly predicted as no-obfuscation when using fewer features, it can still classify Tigress-o, Tigress-s, and Tigress-v correctly more than 90% of the time. It appears that the identification of these techniques does not rely on the additional information provided by the omitted features as much as the identification of other methods.

6 Discussion

From the results, some interesting insights regarding obfuscation stealth can be gained, which we discuss in this section.

6.1 Stealthiness of Obfuscations

The results show that the evaluated obfuscations have very different levels of stealthiness with respect to our model. The Tigress obfuscations virtualization (1.0), self-modifying code (1.0), and opaque predicates (0.96) could be identified best when making use of all features. The least identifiable protection classes were the Obfuscator LLVM classes OLLVM-fs (combination of flattening and self-modifying code, 0.45) and OLLVM-f (flattening, 0.73). As already pointed out in Sect. 5.3, this mainly results from the fact that the combinations of obfuscations are often confused with the standalone classes of the obfuscations they contain. However, significant differences can also be seen here. While LLVM-s and LLVM-fs can be distinguished from each other very well (0.02 and 0.0), in contrast, LLVM-f and LLVM-fs are often confused (0.25 and 0.47). This can be explained by the characteristics of the two obfuscations, instruction substitution and CFG flattening. CFG flattening modifies the structure of a program and, thus, its complexity significantly more than instruction substitution. For example, the cyclomatic complexity is directly affected by CFG flattening, whereas instruction substitution has no impact on it. This makes it easier to distinguish the combination of the two obfuscations from the one with less impact on code complexity.

It is also noteworthy that misclassifications are almost exclusively made within the classes of an obfuscator. The algorithmically very similar obfuscations LLVM-b and Tigress-o (bogus control flow using opaque predicates) and LLVM-f and Tigress-f (CFG flattening) are never or very rarely confused.

In Fig. 4, the details of all obfuscations can be retrieved from the normalized confusion matrix.

6.2   Impact of Compiler Optimization Levels

By extending the 11 obfuscation classes in our model by the compiler optimization levels O0 to O3 (i.e., a total of 44 instead of 11 obfuscation classes), the model's overall accuracy drops significantly to about 59%. Note that the hyperparameter tuning was performed for the pooled classes, though. The confusion matrix shows that the misclassifications occur mainly between classes with the same technique but different optimization levels. The approach including the optimization levels, thus significantly complicates the detection of the obfuscation technique in that model. In practice, however, the detection of the optimization level has no relevance, which allowed us to combine the obfuscation classes in our model.

We also analyzed within which optimization levels the detection of obfuscations works best. We independently tested our model with only the programs from each of the four optimization levels (O0 to O3). While optimization level O0 is mainly used for debugging a program, the most frequently used optimization level for finished code is O2. In level O2, which is most commonly used in real-world programs, our model achieves an identification accuracy of 87.6%, while in level O0, it performs slightly better, reaching 89%.

Making a distinction between the optimization levels for the model prediction also provides insights into the level of stealthiness of each technique. For example, applying OLLVM-b with optimization level O0 makes it most challenging for the model to classify the obfuscation method correctly. We also observe an increase in obfuscation stealth when using optimization level O2 for Tigress-f as well as level O3 for Tigress-o.

7   Conclusions

In this paper, we have presented a novel methodology for identifying obfuscation techniques applied to code with high accuracy using a combination of static code complexity metrics. Unlike previous approaches, our methodology is not based on a direct analysis of the program code. It is thus more robust to semantic methods for increasing obfuscation stealth (e.g., normalization of opcode distribution). An evaluation with 11 obfuscation techniques and combinations of obfuscations in a total of 4124 programs has shown that the correct obfuscation technique can be predicted with an accuracy of 86.5%. Moreover, based on the classification results, we concluded that while tree-based methods are well suited for predicting obfuscation methods using code complexity, a well-trained neural network classifier can achieve even better results. Therefore, we chose the MLPClassifier as our best model, which can predict the underlying obfuscation method with an average accuracy of 83.9%. In future work, generating more data to fit the models could further improve predictability.

Our model can be applied within the scope of malware analysis. Due to a large number of new malware samples daily, efficient methods for obfuscation identification are needed to select suitable deobfuscation concepts.

Acknowledgments. This research was funded in whole, or in part, by the Austrian Science Fund (FWF) I 3646-N31. For the purpose of open access, the author has applied a CC BY public copyright license to any Author Accepted Manuscript version arising from this submission.

A Specifications

Table 4. Best parameter combinations found per classifier and feature set.

	All features	5/14 features
Extra Trees	n_estimators = 80 min_samples_split = 3 min_samples_leaf = 1 max_features = None max_depth = 33 criterion = 'gini' bootstrap: 'False'	n_estimators = 200 min_samples_split = 2 min_samples_leaf = 1 max_features = None max_depth = 24 criterion = 'entropy' bootstrap: 'False'
LGBM	subsample = 1 objective = 'multiclass' num_leaves = 30 max_depth = −1 learning_rate = 0.2 colsample_bytree = 1 boosting_type = 'gbdt'	subsample = 0.5 objective = 'multiclass' num_leaves = 250 max_depth = 30 learning_rate = 0.10923689091995176 colsample_bytree = 1 boosting_type = 'gbdt'
Random Forest	n_estimators = 80 min_samples split = 2 samples_leaf = 1 max_features = 'sqrt' max_depth = 50 criterion = 'entropy' bootstrap: 'False'	n_estimators = 164 min_samples split = 3 min_samples leaf = 1 max_features = 'sqrt' max_depth = 27 criterion = 'entropy' bootstrap: 'False'
MLP	hidden_layer_sizes = (50, 100) activation = 'tanh' solver = 'lbfgs' batch_size = 64 learning_rate = 'invscaling' alpha = 0.08745094461679037 learning_rate_init = 0.0001 early_stopping = True	hidden_layer_sizes = (75, 100) activation = 'tanh' solver = 'lbfgs' batch_size = 16 learning_rate = 'invscaling' alpha = 0.1 learning_rate_init = 0.0033083971654978557 early_stopping = True

References

1. Abran, A., Lopez, M., Habra, N.: An analysis of the mccabe cyclomatic complexity number. In: Proceedings of the 14th International Workshop on Software Measurement (IWSM) IWSM-Metrikon, pp. 391–405 (2004)
2. Bacci, A., Bartoli, A., Martinelli, F., Medvet, E., Mercaldo, F.: Detection of obfuscation techniques in android applications. In: Proceedings of the 13th International Conference on Availability, Reliability and Security, pp. 1–9 (2018)
3. Basili, V.R., Perricone, B.T.: Software errors and complexity: an empirical investigation0. Commun. ACM **27**(1), 42–52 (1984)
4. Brosch, T., Morgenstern, M.: Runtime packers: the hidden problem. Black Hat USA (2006)
5. Canavese, D., Regano, L., Basile, C., Viticchié, A.: Estimating software obfuscation potency with artificial neural networks. In: Livraga, G., Mitchell, C. (eds.) STM 2017. LNCS, vol. 10547, pp. 193–202. Springer, Cham (2017). https://doi.org/10.1007/978-3-319-68063-7_13
6. Coleman, D., Oman, P., Ash, D., Lowther, B.: Using metrics to evaluate software system maintainability. Computer **27**(08), 44–49 (1994)
7. Collberg, C., Thomborson, C., Low, D.: A taxonomy of obfuscating transformations. Technical report, Department of Computer Science, The University of Auckland, New Zealand (1997)
8. Collberg, C., Thomborson, C., Low, D.: Manufacturing cheap, resilient, and stealthy opaque constructs. In: Proceedings of the 25th ACM SIGPLAN-SIGACT Symposium on Principles of Programming Languages, pp. 184–196 (1998)
9. Ebad, S.A., Darem, A.A., Abawajy, J.H.: Measuring software obfuscation quality - a systematic literature review. IEEE Access **9**, 99024–99038 (2021)
10. Ebert, C., Cain, J., Antoniol, G., Counsell, S., Laplante, P.: Cyclomatic complexity. IEEE Softw. **33**(6), 27–29 (2016)
11. Fitzpatrick, J.: Applying the ABC metric to C, C++, and Java. Technical report, C++ report (1997)
12. Gibert, D., Mateu, C., Planes, J., Vicens, R.: Classification of malware by using structural entropy on convolutional neural networks. Proceedings of the AAAI Conference on Artificial Intelligence, vol. 32, no. 1, April 2018. https://doi.org/10.1609/aaai.v32i1.11409, https://ojs.aaai.org/index.php/AAAI/article/view/11409
13. Halstead, M.H.: Elements of Software Science. Operating and Programming Systems Series. Elsevier Science Inc., USA (1977)
14. Hatton, L.: Re-examining the defect-density versus component size distribution. IEEE Softw. 110 (1997)
15. Honglei, T., Wei, S., Yanan, Z.: The research on software metrics and software complexity metrics. In: 2009 International Forum on Computer Science-Technology and Applications, vol. 1, pp. 131–136. IEEE (2009)
16. Ikerionwu, C.: Cyclomatic complexity as a software metric. Int. J. Acad. Res. **2**(3) (2010)
17. Junod, P., Rinaldini, J., Wehrli, J., Michielin, J.: Obfuscator-LLVM-software protection for the masses. In: 2015 IEEE/ACM 1st International Workshop on Software Protection, pp. 3–9. IEEE (2015)
18. Kanzaki, Y., Monden, A., Collberg, C.: Code artificiality: a metric for the code stealth based on an n-gram model. In: 2015 IEEE/ACM 1st International Workshop on Software Protection, pp. 31–37. IEEE (2015)

19. Khan, A.A., Mahmood, A., Amralla, S.M., Mirza, T.H.: Comparison of software complexity metrics. Int. J. Comput. Netw. Technol. **4**(01) (2016)
20. Kim, J., Kang, S., Cho, E.-S., Paik, J.-Y.: LOM: lightweight classifier for obfuscation methods. In: Kim, H. (ed.) WISA 2021. LNCS, vol. 13009, pp. 3–15. Springer, Cham (2021). https://doi.org/10.1007/978-3-030-89432-0_1
21. Kurtukova, A., Romanov, A., Shelupanov, A.: Source code authorship identification using deep neural networks. Symmetry **12**(12) (2020)
22. Madi, A., Zein, O.K., Kadry, S.: On the improvement of cyclomatic complexity metric. Int. J. Softw. Eng. Appl. **7**(2), 67–82 (2013)
23. Madou, M., Anckaert, B., De Bus, B., De Bosschere, K., Cappaert, J., Preneel, B.: On the effectiveness of source code transformations for binary obfuscation. In: Proceedings of the International Conference on Software Engineering Research and Practice (SERP06), pp. 527–533. CSREA Press (2006)
24. Mason, J., Small, S., Monrose, F., MacManus, G.: English shellcode. In: Proceedings of the 16th ACM Conference on Computer and Communications Security, pp. 524–533 (2009)
25. McCabe, T.J.: A complexity measure. IEEE Trans. Softw. Eng. **SE-2**(4), 308–320 (1976). https://doi.org/10.1109/TSE.1976.233837
26. Morgenstern, M., Pilz, H.: Useful and useless statistics about viruses and anti-virus programs. In: Proceedings of the CARO Workshop (2010)
27. Myers, G.J.: An extension to the cyclomatic measure of program complexity. SIGPLAN Not. **12**(10), 61–64 (1977)
28. Nagra, J., Collberg, C.: Surreptitious Software: Obfuscation, Watermarking, and Tamperproofing for Software Protection: Obfuscation, Watermarking, and Tamperproofing for Software Protection. Pearson Education (2009)
29. Necula, G.C., McPeak, S., Weimer, W.: Cil: intermediate language and tools for analysis and transformation of C programs (2002)
30. Oman, P., Hagemeister, J.: Metrics for assessing a software system's maintainability. In: Proceedings Conference on Software Maintenance 1992, pp. 337–344 (1992)
31. Oman, P., Hagemeister, J.: Construction and testing of polynomials predicting software maintainability. J. Syst. Softw. **24**(3), 251–266 (1994). Oregon Workshop on Software Metrics
32. Rahbarinia, B., Balduzzi, M., Perdisci, R.: Exploring the long tail of (malicious) software downloads. In: 2017 47th Annual IEEE/IFIP International Conference on Dependable Systems and Networks (DSN), pp. 391–402. IEEE (2017)
33. Sarwar, M.M.S., Shahzad, S., Ahmad, I.: Cyclomatic complexity: the nesting problem. In: Eighth International Conference on Digital Information Management (ICDIM 2013), pp. 274–279. IEEE (2013)
34. Sebastian, S.A., Malgaonkar, S., Shah, P., Kapoor, M., Parekhji, T.: A study & review on code obfuscation. In: 2016 World Conference on Futuristic Trends in Research and Innovation for Social Welfare, pp. 1–6. IEEE (2016)
35. Sellers, B.H.: Modularization and Mccabe's Cyclomatic complexity. Commun. ACM **35**(12), 17–20 (1992)
36. Shen, V.Y., Yu, T.J., Thebaut, S.M., Paulsen, L.R.: Identifying error-prone software-an empirical study. IEEE Trans. Softw. Eng. (4), 317–324 (1985)
37. Snoek, J., Larochelle, H., Adams, R.P.: Practical Bayesian optimization of machine learning algorithms. In: Advances in Neural Information Processing Systems, vol. 25 (2012)

38. Wang, Y., Rountev, A.: Who changed you? Obfuscator identification for android. In: 2017 IEEE/ACM 4th International Conference on Mobile Software Engineering and Systems (MOBILESoft), pp. 154–164. IEEE (2017)
39. Withrow, C.: Error density and size in ADA software. IEEE Softw. **7**(1), 26–30 (1990)
40. Wu, Z., Gianvecchio, S., Xie, M., Wang, H.: Mimimorphism: a new approach to binary code obfuscation. In: Proceedings of the 17th ACM Conference on Computer and Communications Security, pp. 536–546 (2010)
41. Yu, S., Zhou, S.: A survey on metric of software complexity. In: 2010 2nd IEEE International Conference on Information Management and Engineering, pp. 352–356. IEEE (2010)

ZeekFlow: Deep Learning-Based Network Intrusion Detection a Multimodal Approach

Dimitrios Giagkos$^{(\boxtimes)}$, Orestis Kompougias , Antonis Litke ,
and Nikolaos Papadakis

Infili Technologies S.A., Athens, Greece
{dgiagkos,okompougias,alitke,npapadakis}@infili.com

Abstract. The ever-increasing network traffic generated by numerous interconnected devices inside the modern digital world paves the way for a plethora of attack surfaces that could be exploited by attackers at any time, with various means and manifold objectives. While multiple challenges have been addressed, malicious actors constantly raise the bar of deploying inventive attacks and therefore, novel solutions are required to mitigate the problem. Conventional defensive practices are unable to provide security guarantees in many scenarios, especially against zero-day threats. To this end, we present *ZeekFlow*, a DL-based module for Network Intrusion Detection (NID), that encapsulates a novel, dual-modality architecture for processing network traffic and inferring complex correlations that would lead to accurate threat detection and mitigation. Experimental results show a significant performance boost up to 45% by combining the two modalities. The proposed technique has been rigorously evaluated with three public benchmark datasets (i.e., CIC-IDS2017, CIRA-CIC-DoHBrw-2020 and USTC-TFC2016) that cover a broad range of cyberattacks. Further, the anomaly detection performance of our solution is compared to three closely-related research works, which are outperformed in the vast majority of metrics (e.g., AUC, Recall, etc).

Keywords: Intrusion detection · Network Traffic · Deep Learning · Multimodal architecture · Unsupervised learning

1 Introduction

Network traffic has constantly been and is projected to be further increased over the next years. With approximately 5.16 billion users (i.e., 64.4% of the global population) accessing the internet in 2023 [2], attack surfaces are growing rapidly in numbers. As the digital world becomes more and more interconnected, cyberattacks tend to expose a wider pool of systems, services and stakeholders. In fact, a 2022 report conducted by Cybersecurity Ventures states that *cybercrime damage will reach 10.5 trillion USD in 2025* [1], which holds up for almost a 300% increase compared to 2015. Nevertheless, security experts in industry [10]

S. Katsikas et al. (Eds.): ESORICS 2023 Workshops, LNCS 14399, pp. 409–425, 2024.
https://doi.org/10.1007/978-3-031-54129-2_24

often struggle to catch up with the latest cybersecurity needs due to continuous invention of elaborate attacks by criminals.

Conventional security measures such as firewalls, encryption-decryption methods and anti-virus software are quite common in shielding networks but unfortunately, these technologies are incapable of defending against new or complex threats [24]. Intrusion detection systems (IDS) frequently constitute an additional line of defense that provides monitoring capabilities and generates alerts when suspicious activities are detected. Traditional IDS are signature-based and maintain lists of attack signatures that are triggered when a registered attack is replayed. However, threats are evolving and spreading through internet on a regular basis while criminals derive new variations of attacks and thus, new signatures have to constantly be added to IDS's indexes. Also, an IDS is formally handled by security experts that are responsible for applying any security measures in case of emergency. The aforementioned practices are time-consuming, sometimes counter-productive and the way forward is automating anything that in principle could be automated. Therefore, towards hardening our network systems, we have turned to more advanced techniques that include Machine Learning (ML), zero-trust architectures and blockchains.

With the proliferation of ML and DL, human kind holds the potential for systematically tackling a broad spectrum of problems in numerous domains, including computer vision, natural language processing and cybersecurity. DL's ability to learn from complex-structured information, enables us to create models that perceive network traffic from an entirely angle. DL architectures when trained sufficiently are capable of finding correlations and interactions within metadata of network traffic that would not be conceivable by human analysts [9] and hence act as an extra security oracle on top of traditional IDS.

Nonetheless, both academia [32] and industry [10] sometimes struggle in employing DL for Network Intrustion Detection (NID). ML functions under the *independent, identically distributed random variables (iid)* principle, which results in performance degradation and reliability concerns when data used for training and testing are not similar to the "future" data the ML model will be exposed to during operation. Additionally, feature engineering is critical for processing high-dimensional data such as metadata of network traffic. Several techniques have been investigated for dimensionality reduction of network connection features including Principal Component Analysis (PCA), Singular Value Decomposition (SVD) and AutoEncoders (AEs) [19,22]. Nevertheless, there is no one-size-fits-all solution for this challenge due to the high degree of variability across data and attacks. Last, a wide array of DL-based works for NID either mention none or at most a single tool for capturing network traffic for feeding the studied model [19,22,31]. It is common in literature to train DL architectures on benchmark datasets like KDDCUP99 [26], NSL-KDD [12] and CIC-IDS2017 [4] which already provide pre-processed data in DL-friendly format (i.e., csv) and focus is not given to data collection and pre-processing.

In this paper, we present *ZeekFlow*, a novel multimodal, network threat detection approach. *ZeekFlow* utilizes traffic data captured from network interfaces and are processed by: i) NetFlow [30] and ii) Zeek [6]. NetFlow and Zeek collect network flows and produce data streams of packet data and metadata, while each one also provides individual statistical packet meta-information. By merging the output of both modalities and feeding it to a complex AE architecture, we enable the model to learn the benign traffic distribution while combining the best of both protocols. Our multimodal solution features an improved anomaly detection capability when compared to single-modal approaches, in addition to its ability to detect possible zero-day threats by design, since it follows an unsupervised learning training strategy. More specifically, *ZeekFlow* introduces the following novel contributions:

- We present a multimodal, DL-based, network threat detection solution, *Zeek-Flow*, by hybridizing a DL architecture with an LSTM-based AE and a deep AE. Both neural networks receive as input disjoint sets of network flow data.
- We evaluate the effectiveness of *ZeekFlow* with various benchmarks and compare its performance on outlier detection with a handful of related works and baselines.
- We study the added value of the described multimodal approach by providing an ablation study.

The rest of the paper is organized as follows. In Sect. 2, we present related scientific work to our approach and identify the key differentiation points. In Sect. 3, we analyze our methodology behind designing *ZeekFlow* architecture and provide technical implementation details. Finally, in Sect. 4, we thoroughly evaluate our proposed solution and compare it to other ML- and DL-based anomaly detection techniques as well, while in Sect. 5 we conclude the paper presentation.

2   Related Work

The problem of anomaly and threat detection in network traffic has been investigated in numerous ways that are often interconnected to each other. In this section, we present related work that focuses on scientific evidence related to: i) signature-based intrusion detection systems, ii) outlier detection algorithms applied to activity logs, iii) AI algorithms employed for anomaly detection in network traffic, and iv) joint learning techniques utilizing multiple models. *Zeek-Flow* is built considering all aforementioned aspects.

Signature-Based Intrusion Detection Systems (SIDS): SIDS utilize pattern matching techniques for spotting known attacks; such systems hold a collection of signatures that correspond to previous intrusions and trigger alerts in case at least one of these patterns is observed. SIDS usually exhibit high accuracy when dealing with known attacks [17] but they fall short in detecting zero-day threats, which are gradually increasing in the modern digital world [21]. As investigated in the context of web attacks in [13], widely-used open source SIDS like Snort, ModSecurity and Nemesida, scored either a very poor detection rate or a very poor precision. Even in scenarios that we would like to enrich a signature database with identified attacks on new exposed vulnerabilities, considerable labour work is needed for updating the knowledge base effectively. Moreover, SIDS often present strong performance deviations when utilized under different environments. In [28] the authors found significant differences in the detection effectiveness of Snort and Suricata in the context of Industrial Control Networks (ICS) while the same SIDS were relatively close in terms of detection capabilities in a real IT scenario [7] but not in terms of computational costs.

Log-Based Outlier Detection Algorithms: Leveraging past system and activity logs for applying forensics comes naturally towards detecting anomalous behaviour in networks and computer systems. Generated logs could provide valuable information that enable the defensive front to trace back the timeline of events for discovering attacking trends and system vulnerabilities. Processing efficiently high amounts of heterogeneous logs and inferring malicious incidents early enough are major challenges that need to be addressed when designing threat hunting cybersecurity solutions. Indicatively, in [16], the authors introduce an encoding technique combined with a rule-based outlier detection algorithm that manages to identify effectively security threats in activity logs, while in [20], SwissLog, a learning-based anomaly detection tool is built in the distributed computing context that highly addresses the heterogeneity aspect often featured in logs produced from diverse sources.

AI-Based Anomaly Detection: Much research [11,15,19,25,27,31] has been conducted regarding the utilization of ML and DL for the detection of anomalies in network traffic under different network domains such as traditional computer networks, wireless networks, Software Defined Networks (SDN), IoT environments and Cloud-Fog-Edge networks. In [15], a K-Means algorithm is employed for detection of DDoS attacks but the solution is highly unstable in terms of False Positive Rate (FPR), while in [27] where Random Forest (RF) algorithms are trained, the True Positive Rate (TPR) is too low in some cases. Moreover, RL approaches have been introduced such as [25], where Simpson et al train an on-policy RL agent for DDoS attacks detection but not enough performance-related information is provided. In the context of IoT, [11] follows the established way of training an AE on normal traffic and tries to infer anomalous behaviour by poor reconstruction of the given input. While this methodology considers possible zero-day exploits, only TCP traffic is included in the model training phase thus its application is limited to this regard.

Joint Training Methodologies: AI-based methods for NID exhibit considerable amount of variation under different deployment scenarios. A natural step for bridging the gap and attain improved results of AI-powered IDS is to combine various flavors of models and architectures with the aim of boosting the overall performance by joint training. Ali et al. [8] adopt a mixture of supervised-unsupervised learning (SL, UL) with SVM and AE, targeting DDoS attacks and showcase a performance improvement after applying feature learning techniques. Nevertheless, their solution suffers from poor accuracy in some scenarios. In [18], Kim et al. focus on feature selection with SL and afterwards an UL model is used to cluster unlabelled data while requiring small amount of labelled data that, in general, is hard to collect. A disadvantage of this approach lies in the fact that the models are not validated in a real network setup. Last, authors of [23] design a dual LSTM architecture towards amplifying correlation extraction. However, as described in Sect. 4, *ZeekFlow* outperforms the BI-LSTM model in almost all metrics, under identical training and testing conditions.

Our Approach: This paper focuses on unsupervised DL for outlier detection over traffic collected from any network interface. We differentiate from prior art, in the following points: i) we combine two DL architectures, i.e., LSTM-based AE and deep AE, for joint learning and performance boost, ii) we process raw network flows through two different network capture tools, i.e., NetFlow and Zeek, for identifying complex correlations among disjoint features that is not reckoned to any published work to the best of our knowledge and iii) we construct the full pipeline of this DL-based NID approach by considering also the packet collection and data pre-processing stages which is not the case for the majority of related solutions that consume already processed data.

3   *ZeekFlow*: DL-based Network Intrusion Detection

In this section, we provide background information regarding the neural network (NN) architectures utilized in our solution and the two modalities (i.e., NetFlow and Zeek) leveraged for collecting and processing network traffic data. Afterwards, we analyze the complex combined architecture of *ZeekFlow* and also present implementation details for dataset preprocessing and *ZeekFlow* training.

3.1   Background

A fundamental building block for providing robust software protection to systems and applications is anomalous behaviour detection. The vast majority of systems in today's digital world require connection to external networks for offering their services, thus network protection solutions are quite necessary. *ZeekFlow* contributes to the software protection realm by presenting strong outlier detection capabilities with its novel multimodal architecture, while it also considers zero-day threat coverage by design due to its unsupervised learning approach.

AutoEncoder: AE is a popular type of NN architecture that has been widely used in various fields, including data compression, feature extraction and anomaly detection [19]. The vanilla architecture of an AE has the purpose of learning underlying data distributions by forcing dimensionality reduction and reconstruction of the original input. To elaborate, AEs receive an input vector

$x \in \mathbb{R}^N$ which is processed through a series of NN layers that progressively down-scale the dimensions of the their output vectors: `Encoder`. The `Encoder` produces in the last layer a latent vector $z \in \mathbb{R}^L, L < N$, which is passed through a series of NN layers that progressively upscale the output dimensions: `Decoder`. In the last stage of `Decoder`, an output vector x' which is the reconstruction of the original input vector x is provided. In the context of NID, AEs are trainied with benign traffic and are expected to produce high-loss outputs when they are exposed to statistical outliers, i.e., malicious traffic.

Long Short-Term Memory AutoEncoder: LSTM-based AE is a variation of the traditional AE architecture that is commonly used in sequence prediction problems, e.g., reconstruction envisioned for time series data. The Encoder and Decoder components in an LSTM-based AE are comprised of LSTM cells rather than fully-connected layers. The main contribution of an LSTM-based AE is its ability to capture long-term dependencies within sequential inputs.

3.2 Modalities

A network packet capture contains all packets that are sent and received within a network. Naturally, packet captures have massive file sizes thus making them not AI-friendly at all. However, there are some tools and frameworks that extract useful statistical, metadata information from a monitored network interface that are already in use in existing business infrastructures for network activity monitoring purposes. Two of these are NetFlow [30] and Zeek [6].

NetFlow is a protocol used for network traffic analysis and monitoring. It provides information about the source, destination, and type of network traffic. The NetFlow format is a data structure that includes fields for different parameters such as IP addresses, port numbers, packet and byte counts, timestamps, and protocol types. NetFlow data is typically collected by network devices such as routers and switches and exported to a collector or analyzer for further processing, such as *tcpdump* [5]. The NetFlow format incorporates 49 features in total for each record logged during its operation.

Zeek is a network security monitoring tool that captures and analyzes network traffic in real-time. It uses a protocol called the Zeek protocol, also known as Broccoli, to communicate with other applications and systems. The protocol is designed to be flexible and extensible, with support for different data types and message formats. The Zeek protocol also includes support for different data types, such as strings, integers, and arrays, allowing for the transfer of complex data structures. Zeek's `conn.log` file, in which we focus on, incorporates 22 features in total for each data record. We are particularly interested in the `History` feature, which is a categorical one that accumulates the state of past connections as letters (e.g., "ShADadFf"). Each letter included in a `History` vector stands for different type of meta information regarding the packets that were exchanged within the monitored connection and can obtain 26 possible values, while a vector exhibits a maximum length of 23 characters, as measured in datasets investigated in this work.

3.3 Proposed Architecture

In this paper, we propose a novel AE architecture that takes as input a vector x of 21 concatenated NetFlow and Zeek features and produces an output vector x' of 21 features as well. More specifically, the architecture consists of two parts:

- **Complex encoder:** It is composed of an LSTM-based encoder, a fully connected (FC) layer and a deep encoder. The LSTM-based encoder receives the pre-processed Zeek `history` feature from a record and calculates its latent vector represenation while the FC layer gets the NetFlow features as input and concatenates them with the latent vector of `history`. The concatenated vector of size 21 (20 NetFlow + 1 Zeek features) is passed through the deep encoder, which is comprised of multiple FC layers to produce an overall compressed representation.
- **Complex decoder:** It is composed of an LSTM-based decoder and deep decoder. It processes the compressed vector produced in the previous step and reconstructs both the NetFlow features part and the `History` latent vector. Furthermore, the latter one is also passed through an LSTM decoder for reconstructing it back to its time series form.

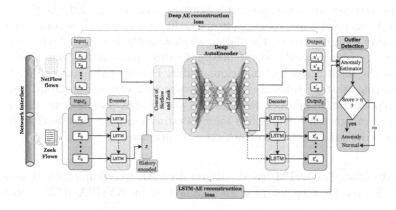

Fig. 1. Overview of ZeekFlow neural network architecture

The novelty in this approach lies in the fact that it combines information from two network traffic processing modalities (i.e., NetFlow and Zeek) in order to boost overall performance and outlier detection confidence by joint training, which is studied and analyzed in an ablation study presented in Subsect. 4.4.

The incentive behind employing an LSTM-based AE for performing this task is that one-hot encoding and other naive encoding methods for processing a categorical feature like `History`, with 26^{23} possible values, fall short due to high complexity. Last, but not least, by choosing AE variations for our architecture we also consider tackling the rising challenge of identifying zero-day threats, a concern not addressed in supervised learning intrusion detection methodologies.

3.4   Implementation Details

Mapping NetFlow and Zeek Records. Combining two types of input for producing a single dataset is one of the tricky parts of the proposed solution. There is no common identifier between the two so we designed a mapping scheme. We map source and destination IPs and ports to their respective counterparts, performing a Left Join using these features between the NetFlow and Zeek datasets. However, Zeek on its own produces a plethora of files that are associated with DNS-, FTP-, SMTP- etc. related logs. Our main focus is the `conn.log` file which contains a large subset of the amount of datapoints included in the respective NetFlow log file. In our experiments, using the datasets described in Subsect. 4.1, we noticed that Zeek's `conn.log` maps to about 80% of the NetFlow log and thus a small portion of NetFlow records would have no corresponding `History` feature and therefore we added empty `history` arrays to those NetFlow datapoints.

Data Preprocessing: We first pre-process the data by scaling the numerical features to have zero mean and unit variance. We also perform one-hot encoding for the categorical features, except `History` that is encoded via the LSTM-based AE as mentioned above. Network traffic is a multivariate time series, and to capture the time aspect, the sliding window method is applied. Our approach involves grouping by IP and calculating features using sliding windows, allowing for the identification of malicious traffic. Finally, the implemented feature engineering strategy calculates statistics such as mean and standard deviation over representative network features like packet size, packets sent, and header size. For categorical features like source/destination ports and destination IPs, we use a counting method to track their occurrence.

DL Models: The LSTM-based AE and deep AE were implemented using the Keras library for deep learning and trained on an NVIDIA RTX 2080 Super GPU.

- **LSTM-based AE**: The LSTM encoder consists of 2 layers having 100 and 50 respectively. The latent vector is of size 10, while the LSTM decoder consists of 2 layers with 50 and 100 neurons respectively.
- **Deep AE**: The encoder consists of 3 layers having 128, 64 and 32 layers respectively. The latent vector is of size 15, while the decoder consists of 3 layers with 32, 64 and 128 neurons respectively.

– **ZeekFlow**: The combined model is trained with a dual loss: categorical cross entropy loss (CCE) for the LSTM-based AE and mean squared error (MSE) loss for the deep AE.

For training *ZeekFlow* we constructed a global loss that is described in Eq. 1. The global loss is a weighted sum of two loss functions, which all aim to help *ZeekFlow* learn the underlying data distribution. More specifically, we utilize the MSE loss for the deep AE and the CCE loss for the LSTM-based AE. Through trial and error, we concluded that performance peaks for $w_{MSE} = 10$ and $w_{CC3} = 1$. For both models, we use Leaky ReLU activations, batch normalization, a batch size of 512 and Adam optimizer with a learning rate of $3 * 10^{-5}$. Early stopping is also considered for preventing overfitting.

$$\mathcal{L}_{global} = w_{MSE}\mathcal{L}_{MSE} + w_{CCE}\mathcal{L}_{CCE} \qquad (1)$$

4   Evaluation

In this section, firstly we present and analyze the datasets that were used for training and testing *ZeekFlow*. Afterwards, we execute a two-way evaluation of our proposed solution that contains : i) comparative results with NID literature related works that are evaluated in the same datasets as *ZeekFlow*, ii) an ablation study on single-modality approaches.

4.1   Datasets

The datasets we selected contain various types of attacks, both volumetric in nature and less "noisy" kinds. The intuition behind this was to create a model that is sensitive to both temporal and non-temporal fluctuations.

CIC-IDS2017. The first dataset we investigated was CIC-IDS2017 [4] which is produced in a simulated network environment within five days. A network topology composed of twelve different machines and various operating systems, modems, firewalls, etc. is designed for capturing a wide range of network attacks that are presented along with other descriptive details in Table 1. We mainly utilized Monday's and Thursday's traffic for training and testing *ZeekFlow* but other combinations of traffic were considered as well, in order to compare strictly our solution to other related works. Last, but not least, drawbacks of CIC-IDS2017 such as class imbalance or bugs identified in [14] were heavily considered in the pre-processing stages of our methodology.

CIRA-CIC-DoHBrw-2020. The second dataset, CIRA-CIC-DoHBrw-2020 [3], which contains benign and malicious DNS over HTTPS (DoH) traffic along with benign non-DoH HTTPS traffic, is offered in Table 2. DoH attacks can be considered a subset of man-in-the-middle attacks. The simulated dataset is composed of traffic generated by five different browsers and four servers. For our purposes we use the Cloudflare, Google and Cloud9 data from the benign dataset of our UL model and the dns2tcp malicious data for validation.

Table 1. CIC-IDS2017 Dataset description

Dataset	Traffic Type	Number of Records
Monday WorkingHours	Benign	529,918
Tuesday WorkingHours	Benign	432,074
	SSH-Patator	5,897
	FTP-Patator	7,938
Wednesday WorkingHours	Benign	444,031
	Dos Hulk	231,073
	DoS GoldenEye	10,293
	DoS SlowLoris	5,796
	DoS Slowhttptest	5,499
	Heartbleed	11
Thursday WorkingHours	Benign	456,752
	Infiltration	36
	Web Attack Brute-Force	1,507
	Web Attack-XSS	652
	Web Attack-SQL injection	21
Friday WorkingHours	Benign	414,322
	Bot	1,966
	Portscan	158,930
	DDoS	128,027
Total	**Benign**	**2,359,289**
	Anomaly	**471,454**

USTC-TFC2016 [29]. The last dataset we adopted is USTC-TFC2016 [29] which contains 10 types of botnet traffic and 10 types of benign traffic. Botnet attacks are quite common [19] and thus it is one of our main priorities for detection purposes. We use the entirety of this dataset for training and validation.

4.2   Evaluation Criteria

Our proposed architecture solves a binary classification problem, thus its performance is measured by the confusion matrix metrics, i.e., True Positive (TP), False Negative (FN), False Positive (FP) and True Negative (TN), which can derive other useful metrics:

True Positive Rate: Represents the ratio of *"all correctly classified positive samples"* to *"all positive samples"*. TPR is also known as Recall.

$$TPR = TP/(TP + FN) \tag{2}$$

Table 2. CIRA-CIC-DoHBrw-2020 Dataset description

Dataset*	Traffic Type	Number of Records
Google Chrome	Google	108,680
	Cloudflare	132,552
	Quad9	199,090
dns2tcp	AdGuard	5,459
	CloudFlare	6,045
	Google DNS	17,423
	Quad9	138,588
Total	**Benign**	**320,322**
	Anomaly	**167,515**

* Subset used for this work.

Table 3. USTC-TFC2016 Dataset description

(a) Benign traffic

Dataset	Number of Records
Facetime	6,000
Skype	12,000
BitTorrent	15,000
Gmail	25,000
Outlook	15,000
WoW	140,000
MySQL	200,000
FTP	360,000
SMB	925,453
Weibo	1,210,000
Total	**2,908,513**

(b) Botnets

Dataset	Number of Records
Tinba	21,000
Zeus	86,000
Shifu	500,000
Neris	499,218
Cridex	461,548
Nsis-ay	351,000
Geodo	213,000
Miuref	81,000
Virut	437,000
Htbot	169,000
Total	**2,818,766**

False Positive Rate. Represents the ratio of *"all wrongly classified negative samples"* to *"all negative samples"*.

$$FPR = FP/(FP + TN) \qquad (3)$$

We focus on the threshold of *Recall @ 0.1% FPR* as we address an anomaly detection task, prioritizing the model's ability to detect anomalies while maintaining a low FPR. Additionally, we report Precision, F1-Score, Accuracy, and the Area Under the ROC Curve (AUC) as standard evaluation metrics. AUC is particularly relevant in our study as it allows for performance comparisons with other models in the literature.

4.3   Baselines

For evaluating our proposed solution for network intrusion detection (NID), we picked some of literature's closely-associated related works that leverage, unsupervised learning, AEs, LSTMs or the NetFlow modality. All comparisons depicted in Fig. 2 are executed on the CIC-IDS2017 benchmark with the exact same data samples as mentioned in the respective papers. We chose this benchmark because: i) it is one of the most studied research datasets for NID and ii) it features great heterogeneity when it comes to included cyber attacks and benign traffic samples. We compare *ZeekFlow* to six different architectures that are portrayed in [19,31] and [23]. The former three are presented in 2a along with *ZeekFlow*, while the next two in 2b and finally the last comparison with *ZeekFlow* is showcased in Table 5.

Comparison with [31]: In [31], three models are developed and evaluated on the CIC-IDS2017 benchmark: i) AE that follows a similar architecture to *ZeekFlow*'s deep AE, ii) a Variational AutoEncoder (VAE) that differs from an AE in many ways including the computation of the reconstruction probability (RP) which is the metric used for representing the anomaly score in such architectures and iii) One Class Supporting Vector Machine (OCSVM) which forms an ML method for binary classification tasks, hereby benign vs anomaly, which tries to separate datapoints of two classes by constructing an optimal hyperplane. As we observe in Fig. 2a, *ZeekFlow* features a better AUC than all models in [31].

Comparison with [19]: In [19], a GANomaly model is implemented to detect anomalies by processing NetFlow data. It is a GAN-based architecture that was built with elements of AEs in order to learn the underlying data distribution. An adversarial reconstruction error loss is utilized for spotting malicious data against benign. The authors also implement a deep AE which is proven to exhibit lower performance than GANomaly and therefore we do not include it in the comparative evaluation depicted in Fig. 2b. Furthermore, we also build an Isolation Forest model as our baseline non-DL model that spawns trees which use a subset of features to categorise data based on the features values. The idea is that outliers will have a low amount of splits among the tree's depth since trees specialise in categorization of training data which are benign. In Fig. 2b and Table 4, it is clear that *ZeekFlow* outperforms GANomaly and Isolation Forest in almost all scenarios within the CIC-IDS2017 benchmark.

Table 4. Comparison on AUC and Recall

(a) AUC achieved for each model trained on the datasets.

	USTC-TFC2016	DoHBrw-2020	CIC-IDS2017
Isolation Forest	0.9992	0.8407	0.9844
GANomaly [19]	0.9970	0.9671	0.9924
ZeekFlow	**0.9998**	**0.9990**	**0.9996**

(b) Recall @ 0.001 FPR for each model trained on the datasets.

	USTC-TFC2016	DoHBrw-2020	CIC-IDS2017
Isolation Forest	0.9743	0.5755	0.8669
GANomaly [19]	0.9695	0.5977	0.6254
ZeekFlow	**0.9932**	**0.9164**	**0.9215**

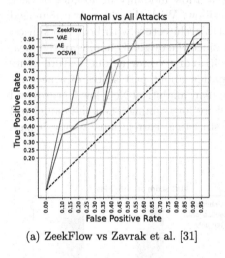

(a) ZeekFlow vs Zavrak et al. [31]

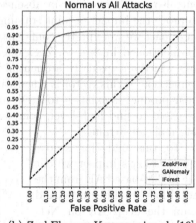

(b) ZeekFlow vs Kompougias al. [19]

Fig. 2. ROC curves with related works on CIC-IDS2017 benchmark.

Comparison with [23] In [23] a Bi-Directional LSTM (BI-LSTM) architecture is introduced for DDoS detection. More specifically, a BI-LSTM is a DL model with dual LSTMs, one for the forward direction and the other for the reverse direction which enable the model to grip correlations on both sides along the time axis which is particularly beneficial for detecting DDoS attacks. The model is trained and tested on DDoS attacks provided by subset of the CIC-IDS2017 benchmark, i.e. CIC-IDS2017/Wednesday and CIC-IDS2017/Friday. ZeekFlow outperforms BI-LSTM in the vast majority of metrics, as shown in Table 5, while it also features a much broader threat detection repertoire.

Table 5. Performance of models trained with CIC-IDS2017/Wednesday

Model	Evaluation Dataset	Recall	Precision	Accuracy	AUC	F1
BI-LSTM [23]	CIC-IDS2017/Wednesday	0.9980	**0.9972**	0.989	0.986	0.985
ZeekFlow	CIC-IDS2017/Wednesday	**0.9989**	0.9955	**0.9989**	**0.9994**	**0.9971**
BI-LSTM [23]	CIC-IDS2017/Friday	0.4120	**0.9984**	0.662	0.703	0.581
ZeekFlow	CIC-IDS2017/Friday	**0.5471**	0.998	**0.7855**	**0.9952**	**0.7067**

4.4   Ablation Study

Towards evaluating holistically our proposed solution, we conducted an ablation study to capture the results provided by NetFlow modality in absence of Zeek but also Zeek's offerings in absence of NetFlow. With this effort, we managed to prove the impact of joint training of a DL architecture with both modalities, an impact we were pretty confident about since the original shaping of the idea. As mentioned in Sect. 3, Zeek offers the `History` vector as one feature of its logs which encapsulates sequential information about past states of a network connection. If this vector is glued with granular, analytical NetFlow features and their product is exposed to a DL architecture for training, then the model will be eased to find high-level, complex and statistical correlations among benign and malicious traffic.

To this end, for studying NetFlow's impact we cut the LSTM-based AE from the ZeekFlow architecture and train the deep AE on Net-Flow records. On the opposite, for the Zeek ablation scenario we remove the deep AE and employ the LSTM-based AE which is trained with history vectors of Zeek records. The datasets utilized for this ablation study were the ones mentioned in Subsect. 4.1. As we observe in Fig. 3, in two out of three datasets (i.e., CIC-IDS2017 and DoHBrw-2020) the AUC score at 0.1%

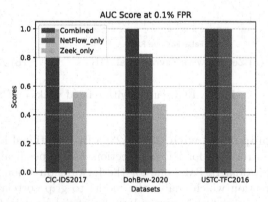

Fig. 3. Ablation study on AUC score: ZeekFlow, NetFlow and Zeek.

FPR achieved by ZeekFlow clearly outperforms single-modality approaches. In fact, in the CIC-IDS2017 dataset we receive almost a 45% performance boost while in DoHBrw-2020 we achieve an approximate 19% increase. Last, in USTC-TFC2016 no particular performance boost is added by Zeek modality since Zeek-Flow performance is equal to single modality NetFlow's.

5   Conclusion

Threat detection over network traffic remains an open challenge that constantly evolves and grows in complexity. As we examine, intrusion detection has been investigated from various scopes, since conventional defense strategies fall beneath the bar against modern attacks designed by criminals. We propose *Zeek-Flow*, a multimodal, DL-based approach for Network Intrusion Detection. Our solution leverages a complex AutoEncoder architecture that is trained on data collected and processed by two modalities, NetFlow and Zeek. By joint training, we manage to boost anomaly detection performance relatively to single modality approaches that are often considered in literature. *ZeekFlow*'s anomaly detection capabilities are also evaluated in three public benchmark datasets and compared with modern literature related works for further performance validation.

Acknowledgment. The presented research has received funding from the Smart Networks and Services Joint Undertaking (SNS JU) under the European Union's Horizon Europe research and innovation programme under Grant Agreement No. 101096110.

References

1. 2022 official cybercrime report. https://www.esentire.com/resources/library/2022-official-cybercrime-report
2. Digital 2023: Global overview report. https://datareportal.com/reports/digital-2023-global-overview-report
3. DoHBrw 2020 — Datasets — Research — Canadian Institute for Cybersecurity — UNB – unb.ca. https://www.unb.ca/cic/datasets/dohbrw-2020.html Accessed 15 Jun 2023
4. IDS 2017 — Datasets — Research — Canadian Institute for Cybersecurity — UNB – unb.ca. https://www.unb.ca/cic/datasets/ids-2017.html Accessed 14 Jun 2023
5. tcpdump(1) man page — TCPDUMP & LIBPCAP – tcpdump.org. https://www.tcpdump.org/manpages/tcpdump.1.html Accessed 12 Jun 2023
6. The Zeek Network Security Monitor – zeek.org. https://zeek.org/ Accessed 12 Jun 2023
7. Albin, E., Rowe, N.C.: A realistic experimental comparison of the suricata and snort intrusion-detection systems. In: 2012 26th International Conference on Advanced Information Networking and Applications Workshops, pp. 122–127 (2012). https://doi.org/10.1109/WAINA.2012.29
8. Ali, S., Li, Y.: Learning multilevel auto-encoders for ddos attack detection in smart grid network. IEEE Access PP, 1–1 (08 2019). https://doi.org/10.1109/ACCESS.2019.2933304
9. Alzubaidi, L., et al.: Review of deep learning: concepts, cnn architectures, challenges, applications, future directions. J. Big Data **8**, 1–74 (2021)
10. de Azambuja, A.J.G., Plesker, C., Schützer, K., Anderl, R., Schleich, B., Almeida, V.R.: Artificial intelligence-based cyber security in the context of industry 4.0&—a survey. Electronics **12**(8) (2023). https://www.mdpi.com/2079-9292/12/8/1920
11. Bhatia, R., Benno, S., Esteban, J., Lakshman, T., Grogan, J.: Unsupervised machine learning for network-centric anomaly detection in iot. pp. 42–48 (12 2019). https://doi.org/10.1145/3359992.3366641

12. Mohi-ud din, G.: Nsl-kdd (2018). https://doi.org/10.21227/425a-3e55
13. Díaz-Verdejo, J., Muñoz-Calle, J., Estepa Alonso, A., Estepa Alonso, R., Madinabeitia, G.: On the detection capabilities of signature-based intrusion detection systems in the context of web attacks. Applied Sciences 12(2) (2022). https://doi.org/10.3390/app12020852, https://www.mdpi.com/2076-3417/12/2/852
14. Engelen, G., Rimmer, V., Joosen, W.: Troubleshooting an intrusion detection dataset: the cicids2017 case study. In: 2021 IEEE Security and Privacy Workshops (SPW), pp. 7–12 (2021). https://doi.org/10.1109/SPW53761.2021.00009
15. Gu, Y., Li, K., Guo, Z., Wang, Y.: Semi-supervised k-means ddos detection method using hybrid feature selection algorithm. IEEE Access PP, 1–1 (05 2019). https://doi.org/10.1109/ACCESS.2019.2917532
16. Ianni, M., Masciari, E.: Scout: Security by computing outliers on activity logs. Computers & Security 132, 103355 (2023). https://doi.org/10.1016/j.cose.2023.103355, https://www.sciencedirect.com/science/article/pii/S0167404823002651
17. Khraisat, A., Gondal, I., Vamplew, P., Kamruzzaman, J.: Survey of intrusion detection systems: techniques, datasets and challenges. Cybersecurity 2 (12 2019). https://doi.org/10.1186/s42400-019-0038-7
18. Kim, H., Kim, J., Kim, Y., Kim, I., Kim, K.: Design of network threat detection and classification based on machine learning on cloud computing. Cluster Comput. 22, 2341–2350 (2019). https://doi.org/10.1007/s10586-018-1841-8
19. Kompougias, O., et al.: Iot botnet detection on flow data using autoencoders. In: 2021 IEEE International Mediterranean Conference on Communications and Networking (MeditCom), pp. 506–511 (2021). https://doi.org/10.1109/MeditCom49071.2021.9647639
20. Li, X., Chen, P., Jing, L., He, Z., Yu, G.: Swisslog: robust anomaly detection and localization for interleaved unstructured logs. IEEE Trans. Depend. Secure Comput. 20(4), 2762–2780 (2023). https://doi.org/10.1109/TDSC.2022.3162857
21. Mandiant: Move, patch, get out the way: 2022 zero-day exploitation continues at an elevated pace (Mar 2023). https://www.mandiant.com/resources/blog/zero-days-exploited-2022
22. Manimurugan, S.: IoT-Fog-Cloud model for anomaly detection using improved Naïve Bayes and principal component analysis. J. Amb. Intell. Human. Comput. 1–10 (2021). https://doi.org/10.1007/s12652-020-02723-3
23. Nguyen, T.T., Shieh, C.S., Chen, C.H., Miu, D.: Detection of unknown ddos attacks with deep learning and gaussian mixture model. In: 2021 4th International Conference on Information and Computer Technologies (ICICT), pp. 27–32 (2021). https://doi.org/10.1109/ICICT52872.2021.00012
24. Sarker, I., Kayes, A.S.M., Badsha, S., Alqahtani, H., Watters, P., Ng, A.: Cybersecurity data science: an overview from machine learning perspective. J. Big Data 7 (07 2020). https://doi.org/10.1186/s40537-020-00318-5
25. Simpson, K., Rogers, S., Pezaros, D.: Per-host ddos mitigation by direct-control reinforcement learning. IEEE Trans. Netw. Serv. Manage. PP 1 (12 2019). https://doi.org/10.1109/TNSM.2019.2960202
26. Stolfo, Salvatore, F.W.L.W.P.A., Chan, P.: KDD Cup 1999 Data. UCI Machine Learning Repository (1999). https://doi.org/10.24432/C51C7N
27. Vanerio, J., Casas, P.: Ensemble-learning approaches for network security and anomaly detection, pp. 1–6 (08 2017). https://doi.org/10.1145/3098593.3098594
28. Waagsnes, H., Ulltveit-Moe, N.: Intrusion detection system test framework for scada systems, pp. 275–285 (2018). https://doi.org/10.5220/0006588202750285

29. Wang, W., Zhu, M., Zeng, X., Ye, X., Sheng, Y.: Malware traffic classification using convolutional neural network for representation learning. In: 2017 International Conference on Information Networking (ICOIN), pp. 712–717 (2017). https://doi.org/10.1109/ICOIN.2017.7899588

30. Wikipedia contributors: Netflow – Wikipedia, the free encyclopedia (2023). https://en.wikipedia.org/w/index.php?title=NetFlow&oldid=1153303931 Accessed 15 June 2023

31. Zavrak, S., İskefiyeli, M.: Anomaly-based intrusion detection from network flow features using variational autoencoder. IEEE Access **8**, 108346–108358 (2020). https://doi.org/10.1109/ACCESS.2020.3001350

32. Zhou, X., Hu, Y., Wu, J., Liang, W., Ma, J., Jin, Q.: Distribution bias aware collaborative generative adversarial network for imbalanced deep learning in industrial iot. IEEE Trans. Industr. Inf. **19**(1), 570–580 (2023). https://doi.org/10.1109/TII.2022.3170149

FedREVAN: *R*eal-time D*E*tection of *V*ulnerable *A*ndroid Source Code Through *Fed*erated *N*eural Network with XAI

Janaka Senanayake[1,2]([✉]) [iD], Harsha Kalutarage[1] [iD], Andrei Petrovski[1] [iD], Mhd Omar Al-Kadri[3] [iD], and Luca Piras[4] [iD]

[1] School of Computing, Robert Gordon University,
Aberdeen AB10 7QB, UK
{j.senanayake,h.kalutarage,a.petrovski}@rgu.ac.uk
[2] Faculty of Science, University of Kelaniya,
Kelaniya, Sri Lanka
janakas@kln.ac.lk
[3] University of Doha for Science and Technology, Doha, Qatar
omar.alkadri@udst.edu.qa
[4] Department of Computer Science, Middlesex University,
London NW4 4BT, UK
l.piras@mdx.ac.uk

Abstract. Adhering to security best practices during the development of Android applications is of paramount importance due to the high prevalence of apps released without proper security measures. While automated tools can be employed to address vulnerabilities during development, they may prove to be inadequate in terms of detecting vulnerabilities. To address this issue, a federated neural network with XAI, named FedREVAN, has been proposed in this study. The initial model was trained on the LVDAndro dataset and can predict potential vulnerabilities with a 96% accuracy and 0.96 F1-Score for binary classification. Moreover, in case the code is vulnerable, FedREVAN can identify the associated CWE category with 93% accuracy and 0.91 F1-Score for multi-class classification. The initial neural network model was released in a federated environment to enable collaborative training and enhancement with other clients. Experimental results demonstrate that the federated neural network model improves accuracy by 2% and F1-Score by 0.04 in multi-class classification. XAI is utilised to present the vulnerability detection results to developers with prediction probabilities for each word in the code. The FedREVAN model has been integrated into an API and further incorporated into Android Studio to provide real-time vulnerability detection. The FedREVAN model is highly efficient, providing prediction probabilities for one code line in an average of 300 ms.

Keywords: android application security · code vulnerability · neural network · federated learning · XAI

S. Katsikas et al. (Eds.): ESORICS 2023 Workshops, LNCS 14399, pp. 426–441, 2024.
https://doi.org/10.1007/978-3-031-54129-2_25

1   Introduction

The identification and timely remediation of source code vulnerabilities are crucial for the secure development of Android applications. Specifically, initiating
this crucial process during the early stages of application development is of
paramount importance. This drastically reduces the possibility that attackers
can find vulnerabilities to exploit. Due to its high popularity, Android currently
holds 70.79% of the market share, as of June 2023, and an average of 90,000
Android mobile apps are released every month on the Google Play Store [19].
Unlike iOS applications, Android apps are not thoroughly checked for security
aspects [5]. Therefore, it is crucial to adjust the development process to comply
with extensive security protocols for Android apps.

Although proper requirements analysis and feasibility studies are conducted
before development, the final product may still fail due to code vulnerabilities. It
is worth noting that fixing bugs in the early stages of the Software Development
Life Cycle (SDLC) is 70 times less costly than fixing them in later stages of the
SDLC [7]. Thus, researchers have developed several automated tools to identify
vulnerabilities in Android apps [6], to prioritise security-oriented development
and prevent cybersecurity breaches, rather than repairing issues later in the app
development life cycle.

Researchers, in previous studies, have introduced a few supportive tools,
frameworks and plugins, to assist developers in automating the detection process [16]. They employed conventional methods, as well as Machine Learning
(ML) and Deep Learning (DL) based methods, to detect vulnerabilities in
Android apps, using static, dynamic, and hybrid analysis methods. However,
such tools analyse either the Android Application Package (APK) files, or complete Android project source files, and detect their vulnerabilities. An important
drawback of current solutions is their failure to address the early identification
of vulnerabilities in a real-time app development setting. These tools can only
assist in detecting vulnerabilities by scanning the code once the development
process has concluded.

Using AI-based techniques on a properly labelled dataset of Android source
code vulnerabilities can surpass these limitations. However, it is crucial to take
into account the limitations of the datasets used to train the models for detecting
Android vulnerabilities. It is feasible to create a dataset by labelling the source
code after scanning the released APKs, but this approach has its constraints. The
dataset's scope including the number of distinct vulnerable categories is limited,
and it may not include adequate code examples or novel vulnerabilities. An alternative approach is to train a model using the source code obtained directly from
app developers. However, developers may be reluctant to share their proprietary
code due to privacy concerns. To overcome this challenge in the model training
process, federated learning can be employed. This approach entails the dissemi-
nation of the model training procedure among multiple entities that are linked
within the federated environment. Consequently, these entities can individually
train the model and make revisions to the ultimate model without disclosing
their data, which comprises of source code samples.

In summary, this paper makes the following contributions:

- Introduce a neural network-based model that is both highly accurate and efficient for early detection of Android source code vulnerabilities, named FedREVAN. The initial model is trained using the publicly available LVDAndro dataset [17], which contains Android source code vulnerabilities labelled based on Common Weakness Enumeration (CWE)[1].

- Integrating the model with Explainable AI (XAI) techniques, and producing Application Programming Interface (API). This API provides the reasons for the predictions related to the vulnerable codes, which can be utilised by Android app developers to identify potential mitigation approaches with the help of a plugin.

- Retraining the model in a federated learning environment to generate and extend the model to improve the vulnerability detection capabilities.

- Making FedREVAN open source and making it available to the public as a GitHub Repository[2], complete with Python scripts and instructions.

The paper is structured as follows: Sect. 2 provides the background and related work. Section 3 explains the methodology of the federated neural network-based model and the approach to using it to detect Android code vulnerabilities in real time. Section 4 presents results and corresponding discussions. Finally, Sect. 5 covers conclusions and future work.

2   Background and Related Work

This section sets the base for the study by explaining vulnerabilities in source code and how developers can be assisted to overcome them. Moreover, vulnerability scanning techniques, AI-based vulnerability detection and how to understand the prediction results, and training AI models in a federated environment are also discussed along with the related studies.

2.1   Vulnerabilities in Source Code

Code vulnerabilities in applications can lead to the occurrence of bugs and defects. Human error can also introduce significant scope for errors in the software development process, particularly if no extensive testing and validation process is in place from the initial stages of the software development lifecycle [11,14]. Such errors can lead to several vulnerabilities in the code.

---

[1] https://cwe.mitre.org/.
[2] https://github.com/softwaresec-labs/FedREVAN.

In order to prevent these, popular repositories such as CWE and Common Vulnerabilities and Exposures (CVE)[3] can be utilised. Mobile application developers can refer to these to address potential security loopholes in their source code. This knowledge can assist developers in detecting vulnerabilities early [16].

2.2 Developer Assistance for Identifying Code Vulnerabilities

As an initial work of the FedREVAN study, a need analysis survey involving 63 Android app developers who work in app development firms, was conducted to identify whether security aspects are being considered when developing apps. Based on the survey results, the majority of developers (55.9%) do not consider secure coding practices while developing apps, as illustrated in Fig. 1a.

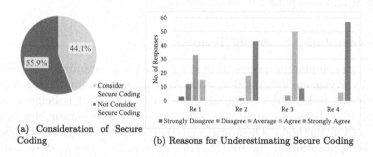

(a) Consideration of Secure Coding

(b) Reasons for Underestimating Secure Coding

Fig. 1. Survey Results

In the aforementioned survey, participants were asked to rate their reasons for not giving due consideration to secure coding, or for considering it to a lesser extent, using a 5-Point Likert scale. The responses pertaining to various reasons are presented in Fig. 1b.

Re 1. Functionality is more important than security.
Re 2. Need to allocate additional time to verify the written source code is secured due to rapid development cycles.
Re 3. Manual verification requires additional resources, including domain experts.
Re 4. Lack of supportive tools to automate the security checking process.

After analysing the responses, it was discovered that a significant number of app developers prioritise both functionality and security, as 33 responses were rated as Average. The majority of developers (68%) firmly believe that extra time should be allocated to scrutinise code for security. Furthermore, many developers concur with the notion that involving domain experts, such as security testers and ethical hackers, in the development process is necessary if manual security verification is needed. This is because developers may lack knowledge of source

---

[3] https://www.cvedetails.com/.

code vulnerabilities and secure coding practices. In addition, 91% of the respondents strongly agree that the lack of tool support is a reason for not considering or underestimating security aspects during app development. As a result, it was concluded that a highly accurate automated vulnerability detection model must be incorporated into the development pipeline.

Integrated Development Environments (IDEs) are widely used to increase efficiency in the development process. IDEs assist developers with tasks such as code writing, application building, validation, and integration. These IDEs often have built-in features and third-party plugins to enhance functionality. To avoid developer errors and increase productivity, Android app developers also require supportive tools and plugins during the coding process [20]. Android Studio is the official Android app development IDE built by Google using JetBrain's IntelliJ IDEA. Hence, a vulnerability detection model can be integrated with Android Studio as a plugin to assist developers.

2.3   Vulnerability Scanning Techniques

The research community has identified two methods for scanning Android applications: 1) reverse-engineering developed Android Application Packages (APKs) to analyse the code, and 2) analysing the source code as it is being written in real-time [16]. The initial application scanning step involves static, dynamic, and hybrid analysis methods. The static analysis identifies code issues without executing the application or the source code, whereas dynamic analysis requires a runtime environment to execute the application for scanning. The hybrid analysis combines both static and dynamic analysis techniques. Various tools are available for analysing Android apps, such as the Mobile Security Framework (MobSF)[4] a hybrid analysis tool that identifies vulnerabilities and malware. HornDroid tool [4] analyses information flow in Android apps, while Quick Android Review Kit (Qark) tool[5] is a static analysis tool that can detect vulnerabilities in pre-built APKs and complete source code files. These supportive tools can be integrated with app development to help developers to avoid mistakes [20].

2.4   AI-Based Vulnerability Detection

Developing tools for detecting Android code vulnerabilities using AI is a viable approach. To train such tools, a properly labelled dataset is required. Several datasets have been proposed for this purpose, mostly related to application vulnerabilities. Ghera [10] is an open-source benchmark repository that captures 25 known vulnerabilities in Android apps and provides common characteristics of vulnerability benchmarks and repositories. The National Vulnerability Database (NVD) [13] is another dataset that is used to reference vulnerabilities. The AndroVul repository [12] contains Android security vulnerabilities, such as high-risk shell commands, security code smells, and dangerous permission-related

---

[4] https://github.com/MobSF/Mobile-Security-Framework-MobSF.
[5] https://github.com/linkedin/qark/.

vulnerability details. However, these datasets are inadequate for building real-time code vulnerability mitigation methods since they are not labelled based on actual Android source code. The LVDAndro dataset [17], on the other hand, provides a CWE-based labelled dataset that contains Android source code vulnerabilities. The LVDAndro was produced by a combination approach of the MobSF and Qark scanners. The latest dataset, LVDAndro APKs Combined Processed Dataset, was created by scanning the apps from repositories, including AndroZoo, Fossdroid[6] and well-known malware repositories [1]. Since the LVDAndro dataset is publicly available and provides good accuracy for vulnerability detection, it can be used as a valuable resource for training AI-based models.

2.5 Understanding AI-Based Predictions Results with XAI

Traditional AI-based models usually provide prediction results as a black box. This makes it difficult for app developers to understand the reasoning behind predicted vulnerabilities, and to identify possible mitigation approaches. To address this limitation, developers need to put in additional effort outside the app development domain [18]. XAI techniques attempt to make AI models more transparent by providing human-understandable explanations for their outputs. These explanations can help model users understand why a particular decision was made or a certain prediction was generated. Hence the use of XAI can assist in identifying the causes of code vulnerabilities. Therefore, XAI can be employed to enhance the identification of code vulnerabilities.

After an AI-powered prediction is generated, the likelihood of predictions in a binary or multi-class classification model can be determined using various Python frameworks. Some widely used frameworks include Shapash, Dalex, Explain Like I'm 5 (ELI5), Local interpretable model (Lime), Shapley additive explanations (SHAP), and Explainable boosting machines (EBM), among others [3]. The selection of a framework depends on the needs of the prediction task.

2.6 Federated Learning for AI Models

Federated Learning is based on a distributed ML approach, which involves training multiple local models, on different devices, to create a global model. In a federated environment, clients who connect to the server can train their own local models with their own data in several training rounds. During these rounds, the model weights are shared with the federated server, which averages and updates them and creates a global model using the Federated Averaging (FedAvg) algorithm. FedAvg is a popular FL averaging technique that facilitates local model training on multiple clients without sharing the client's local data with the server [9]. This approach offers the potential for model convergence with different client local data in non-independent and non-identically distributed settings. As a result, researchers from diverse fields have explored FL methods from various

---

[6] https://fossdroid.com/.

perspectives [8]. However, none of these studies has examined how FL can be applied to AI-based Android code vulnerability detection models.

Existing methods rely on APK files to detect vulnerabilities in Android code, which makes it challenging to achieve high accuracy in detecting vulnerabilities early in the SDLC. Additionally, no method currently integrates XAI to provide developers with explanations for predicted vulnerabilities. The proposed model was developed to address these gaps by using a federated neural network-based architecture that enables early and accurate detection of Android code vulnerabilities while providing explanations for prediction results using XAI.

3   Methodology

The development of the FedREVAN model consists of four primary stages: selecting the dataset, building the neural network-based model, training the global model in a federated learning environment and detecting code vulnerabilities. The source code and detailed instructions are available in FedREVAN GitHub repository. Figure 2 depicts the overall approach.

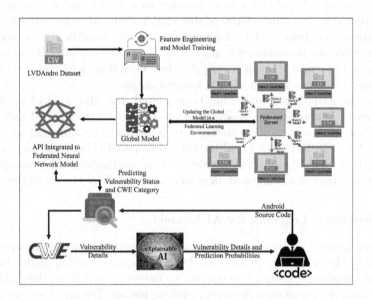

Fig. 2. Overview of the FedREVAN Model

3.1   Selecting the Dataset

Despite the existence of several vulnerability datasets [10,12,13], most of them do not pertain to Android source code vulnerabilities or lack proper labelling. However, the LVDAndro dataset [17] has made a significant contribution in our previous work, by creating a CWE-ID-based labelled dataset that includes Android code vulnerabilities. This dataset was generated using multiple vulnerability scanners and comprises 6,599,597 vulnerable code lines and 14,689,432 non-vulnerable code lines scanned using 15,021 different APKs.

3.2 Building the Neural Network-Based Model

LVDAndro offers processed data, and as such, the binary classification analysis utilised the *processed_code* and *vulnerability_status* fields. Initially, the dataset was balanced to avoid class bias (vulnerable samples:non-vulneable sample = 1:1), and then split into *75%* for training and *25%* for testing. The feature vector was created using the n-grams technique with *ngram_range* set to *1-3*, *min_df* set to *40*, and *max_df* set to *0.80*. This feature vector was used to train a neural network model consisting of one hidden layer with 20 perceptrons and an output layer with two nodes. The activation function used for the input and hidden layers was *relu*, and the *sigmoid* activation function was used for the output layer as they performed comparatively well in experiments. Early stopping by monitoring the *val_loss* with *min_delta* as *0.0001* and *patience* as *20* in *auto mode* was used to prevent over-fitting. During the neural network model training process, the *Adam* optimiser was used with a default learning rate of *0.001*, and the loss function employed was *binary cross-entropy*.

The feature vector was created for multi-class classification using the *processed_code* and *CWE-ID* fields. One hot encoding was applied for encoding the labels. Although LVDAndro has code samples for 23 CWE categories, some classes have fewer samples due to their nature. Therefore, only the top 10 classes were included, and the remaining classes were re-labelled as *Other*. The dataset was then balanced using re-sampling, and the feature vector was created using *ngram_range* set to *1-3*, *min_df* set to *40*, and *max_df* set to *0.80*, as in the binary classification. This feature vector was used to train a neural network model with an input layer, one hidden layer with 20 perceptrons, and an output layer with 11 nodes. The activation function used for the input and hidden layers was *relu*, while *softmax* was used for the output layer. Early stopping, similar to the binary classification model (*monitor = val_loss, min_delta = 0.0001* and *patience = 20* and *mode = auto*), was applied to prevent over-fitting in this model as well. When training the neural network model, the *categorical cross-entropy* was utilised as the loss function, and the *Adam* optimiser was applied with the default learning rate of *0.001*.

3.3 Model Parameter Tuning and Pruning

Several experiments were conducted by altering the model parameters, such as adjusting the number of hidden layers and the number of perceptrons, to determine the optimal configuration. Furthermore, a grid search and hyper-parameter tuning process were executed to confirm the suitability of the aforementioned parameters. Upon completion of the training phase, the F1-Scores and accuracies for both binary and multi-class classification were analysed.

Additionally, pruning techniques were also applied to the selected model after parameter tuning. By removing the least significant weight parameters from a Neural network, the throughput may be increased. The goal is to maintain the model's accuracy while increasing its efficiency. Magnitude-based pruning is a simple but efficient method for removing weights while maintaining the same degree of precision. By assigning value zeros during the model training phase, magnitude-based pruning gradually removes inconsequential weights. Model accuracy is dependent on the amount of sparsity. Hence the level of sparsity should be carefully chosen to attain the same level of precision. The magnitude-based model pruning was implemented using the TensorFlow model optimisation toolbox[7]. The model was first trained with all parameters and then pruned to reach 50% parameter sparsity beginning from 0% sparsity.

3.4 Detection of Vulnerabilities with XAI Using Trained Model

Two pickle files were created for each of the binary and multi-class classification-based models, containing the trained model, classifier, and vectoriser. These pickle files were then utilised as inputs to the backend of the Flask-based web API of the FedREVAN, which was developed using Python. The FedREVAN web API includes a GET request parameter to receive a source code line from a user, which is then checked for vulnerabilities. Upon initialisation of the web API, the pre-trained binary and multi-class models' are loaded from pickle files.

An Android Studio plugin was created as a prototype to capture the code lines being written by developers in real-time. The plugin can communicate with the FedREVAN web API and is available for download as a jar file from the FedREVAN GitHub repository. Once the plugin is integrated, users can activate the plugin by selecting *Tools - Check Code Vulnerability* or pressing *CTRL+ALT+A* while the cursor is on a specific code line.

When a user's request is received through the plugin to the API, the binary classification vectoriser is used to transform the code line. The resulting transformed code is then processed by the binary classification model to determine its vulnerability status, either as vulnerable or non-vulnerable. If the code line is predicted as vulnerable, it is transformed using the loaded multi-class model's vectoriser, and passed to the multi-class model to predict the CWE-ID.

After predicting the vulnerability status and the CWE-ID, the code line was processed by following same techniques used in LVDAndro, including replacing comments, and replacing user-defined strings. Then the resulting processed source code is passed through the Python Lime package, which supports XAI, to obtain reasons for the predictions in both the binary and multi-class models in the form of prediction probabilities. Lime package provides information about the contributions of each word in the processed source code line to both the vulnerability prediction and the vulnerable category prediction probabilities. Finally, the prediction results are returned from the API as a JSON response and then passed to the plugin.

---

[7] https://www.tensorflow.org/modeloptimization.

Table 1. Performance Comparison of FedREVAN Models

Model Name	Accuracy	F1-Score	Model Size
FedREVAN-B	96%	0.96	335 MB
FedREVAN-B-P	95%	0.95	321 MB
FedREVAN-M	93%	0.91	8.1 MB
FedREVAN-M-P	92%	0.90	7.9 MB

3.5 Model Training in the Federated Environment

A simulated federated learning environment was established using a server and four clients. The server, an Intel Core i5 laptop with 16GB RAM and Windows 11 OS, managed model weight distribution and aggregation. Clients, on Gigabyte Brix (GB-BXBT-2807) devices, ran Ubuntu Linux and Windows 10, training models with global weights on local datasets. Python, TensorFlow, and their dependencies were installed on both server and clients. The Flower framework [2] was employed, with the server as Flower Server and clients connected. One client (Alpha) uses the LVDAndro dataset and the other clients (Bravo, Chalie and Delta) use the LVDAandro dataset generation mechanism to generate the dataset based on their own data. In practice, developers can contribute to the training by adding diverse training data obtained through alternative methods such as manual analysis.

4 Results and Discussions

This section discusses the results of the FedREVAN model generation process, and the process of early detecting Android vulnerabilities.

4.1 Performances of the Initial Models

The F1-Scores and the accuracies, and model sizes of both neural network-based binary and multi-class classification were compared in Table 1. The regular neural network model for binary classification is defined as FedREVAN-B and the multi-class classification model is defined as FedREVAN-M. The pruned models are represented as FedREVAN-B-P and FedREVAN-M-P for binary and multi-class classifications, respectively.

According to Table 1, it was identified that the unpruned neural network models are performing slightly better than the pruned models. The number of example codes used and the number of hidden layers used could be the reason for not getting a significant performance difference between those models. Since un-pruned models perform better and the model size differences are also negligible, those models (FedREVAN-B and FedREVAN-M) were selected for the API integration, as mentioned.

In binary classification models, the variation of accuracies in training and validation with the number of times that the learning algorithm works (epochs) is illustrated in Fig. 3a. Figure 3b illustrates the variation of training and validation loss in the same model. Variation of training and validation accuracies with the number or epochs; in the multi-class classification is illustrated in Figs. 3c, and 3d illustrates the training and validation loss.

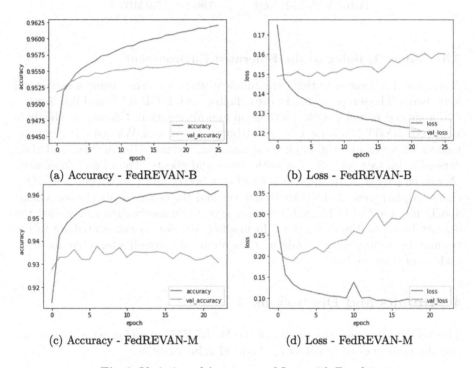

(a) Accuracy - FedREVAN-B   (b) Loss - FedREVAN-B

(c) Accuracy - FedREVAN-M   (d) Loss - FedREVAN-M

Fig. 3. Variation of Accuracy and Loss with Epochs

The optimal performances were received when the number of epochs at 25 for FedREVAN-B and 24 for FedREVAN-M. The training accuracy for FedREVAN-B was 96.2% while achieving 95.6% for inference accuracy. In these cases, the training loss was 0.12, while the validation loss was 0.16. In FedREVAN-M, the optimal training accuracy of 0.96 and inference accuracy of 0.93 were achieved when epochs reached 24 while getting 0.10 training loss and 0.33 validation loss in the same epochs. The increase in loss during training could indicate that the model is becoming overly complex and fitting noise or outliers in the training data, rather than capturing the underlying patterns that apply to new data.

FedREVAN is capable of detecting 10 CWE categories (11 including the *other* category) which have either a high or medium level likelihood of exploitation [15]. These CWE-IDs are 89, 200, 276, 312, 532, 676, 749, 921, 925 and 939.

The accuracy of the FedREVAN model was also compared with the MobSF and Qark scanners which were used to build the LVDAndro dataset initially.

Table 2. Statistics of the Client Datasets

Characteristic	Client Alpha	Client Bravo	Client Charlie	Client Delta
Used APKs	15,021	3,237	779	991
Vulnerable Code Lines	6,599,597	1,121,043	441,981	135,049
Non-Vul. Code Lines	14,689,432	2,065,786	761,862	869,198
Distinct CWE-IDs	23	23	21	22

In order to compare the accuracy of detecting vulnerable code for new data, a total of 2,216 source code lines were used. This included 604 lines of vulnerable code examples from the CWE repository and 1,612 lines of non-vulnerable code from real applications. These lines were integrated into an Android app project, which was then scanned using MobSF and Qark Scanners. The same code lines were then passed to the FedREVAN model by parsing them while iterating all the code lines through a python script to the FedREVAN API. The accuracy, precision, recall and F1-Score are compared and summarised in Table 3a.

After conducting the comparison, it was determined that FedREVAN excelled in predicting vulnerabilities when compared to MobSF and Qark. FedREVAN achieved a 95% accuracy rate, with a precision of 0.94, recall of 0.99, and F1-Score of 0.96. Furthermore, it effectively reduced the false negative rate, thereby mitigating potential security risks associated with its predictions.

4.2 Federated Neural Network Model

The optimal values for the neural network model parameters in the federated learning model, such as the number of hidden layers, neurons, and optimisers, remained unchanged from the initial model. The chosen architecture allows for efficient model convergence and involves a federated communication round of 50 and five epoch iterations, as returned by the optimised tuning process. The training datasets for each client (Alpha, Bravo, Charlie, and Delta) contain the records specified in Table 2.

Federated learning allows for obtaining training source code samples from multiple clients to the server while maintaining the privacy of their code. Following the completion of 50 rounds of training, the global model was updated on the federated server and can now be used in the FedREVAN model. The updated global model was designated as FedREVAN-B-F for binary and FedREVAN-M-F for multi-class classifications. The accuracy and F1-Score of the updated models were compared to the initial models, as detailed in Table 3b.

Although there was no improvement in the accuracy and F1-Score of the binary classification model, the performance of the multi-class classification model improved. The accuracy of the federated binary classification model (FedREVAN-B-F) remained at 96%, and the F1-Score remained at 0.96. This could be because the initial binary classification model (FedREVAN-B) had already been well-trained using a large number of samples, while the federated

Table 3. Performance Comparison of MobSF, Qark and FedREVAN Models

(a) FedREVAN with MobSF and Qark

Metrics	MobSF	Qark	FedREVAN
Accuracy	91%	89%	**95%**
Precision	0.93	0.92	**0.94**
Recall	0.95	0.93	**0.99**
F1-Score	0.94	0.92	**0.96**

(b) Various FedREVAN Models

Model Name	Accuracy	F1-Score
FedREVAN-B	96%	0.96
FedREVAN-B-F	96%	0.96
FedREVAN-M	93%	0.91
FedREVAN-M-F	95%	0.95

model had less impact. However, the accuracy of the federated multi-class classification model (FedREVAN-M-F) increased by 2% compared to the initial model (FedREVAN-M), reaching 95%, and the F1-Score increased by 0.04, reaching 0.95.

As this federated learning environment can be easily extended and implemented, the federated server and the network can be made available to a wide range of clients, from individual app developers to app development companies. It is expected that the model performances will increase once the environment has been released to a larger community.

By leveraging the FedREVAN API in the backend, developers are able to detect potential code vulnerabilities in real-time as they write code. This is achieved by passing the code through the API using the plugin that integrates the API with the development environment. As a result, developers can efficiently check for vulnerabilities without needing to switch between applications, enabling them to quickly and easily identify and resolve issues as they arise. Hence, the developers can maintain their workflow without interruption, significantly improving their efficiency and saving valuable time and resources. The detailed steps are available FedREVAN GitHub Repository.

4.3   Developer Feedback on FedREVAN

The Android app developers who participated in the initial need analysis survey were given the plugin to integrate into Android studio and utilise during app development. A survey was conducted to gather feedback on the plugin's performance, with the developers being asked to rate their satisfaction levels on a 5-Point Likert scale. Figure 4 visualises the feedback received from 63 developers.

The survey revealed that a large majority, comprising 87% of the app developers, was highly satisfied with the accuracy and efficiency of the predictions. Additionally, 89% of the developers were highly satisfied with the usefulness of FedREVAN and its mitigation recommendations. However, the survey also highlighted the scope for enhancing the usability and integration aspects of the plugin since only around 22% developers were highly satisfied with them. Furthermore, the look and feel of the plugin need improvement since 57% of developers were not highly satisfied with it. This feedback is valuable as it can be used to make the plugin more appealing by incorporating mitigation suggestions similar to

IDE's syntax error indication feature, highlighting and providing recommendations instead of a balloon notification.

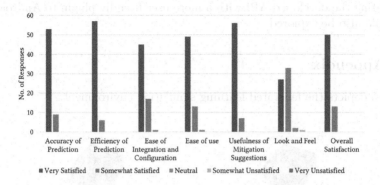

Fig. 4. Survey Results - Satisfaction of the FedREVAN

Despite the identified areas for improvement, the overall satisfaction rate was exceptionally high, with 79% of developers reporting being highly satisfied and 21% satisfied. With further development, the plugin has the potential to be used by a larger community to mitigate Android source code vulnerabilities.

5   Conclusion and Future Work

To improve security, within Android application development, by reducing vulnerability risks, it is important to implement secure coding practices and detect code vulnerabilities, from the early development stages. This study presents the FedREVAN model, a federated neural network-based approach to detect vulnerabilities during source code writing. The model was trained on the LVDAndro dataset. The initial model was then released into a federated learning environment, to train with local models and enhance its detection capabilities. Additionally, XAI was incorporated to provide reasons for vulnerability predictions. The federated model achieves: 96% accuracy, 0.96 F1-Score for binary classification, 95% accuracy and 0.95 F1-Score for CWE-based multi-class classification. The developers can easily use the prototype plugin for Android Studio to mitigate vulnerabilities using FedREVAN. FedREVAN is freely available as a GitHub repository. Potential biases, inaccuracies, or insufficiencies in the LVDAndro dataset could affect the model's generalisation capabilities and the reported accuracy. Differences in coding styles, application domains, and coding practices might impact the model's ability to detect vulnerabilities accurately in different contexts. While the possibility of a more user-friendly plugin for Android Studio is proposed, the actual ease of integration and the learning curve associated with using such a plugin could impact their adoption by developers. By incorporating the principles of XAI and harnessing the power of federated learning, FedREVAN advances vulnerability mitigation and emphasises the importance of data privacy in modern software development practices. In the future, the model's performance can be improved by fine-tuning training model parameters, and releasing the federated learning environment to a larger community. Integrating the developed API with a more user-friendly plugin to Android studio could also be explored.

A   Appendix

Figure 5 depicts the federated learning simulation environment.

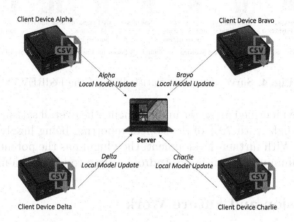

Fig. 5. Federated Learning Simulated Environment

References

1. Allix, K., Bissyandé, T.F., Klein, J., Le Traon, Y.: Androzoo: collecting millions of android apps for the research community. In: Proceedings of the 13th International Conference on Mining Software Repositories. MSR '16, pp. 468–471. ACM, New York, NY, USA (2016). https://doi.org/10.1145/2901739.2903508
2. Beutel, D.J., et al.: Flower: a friendly federated learning research framework (2022)
3. Bhatnagar, P.: Explainable AI (XAI) - a guide to 7 packages in python to explain your models (2021). https://towardsdatascience.com/explainable-ai-xai-a-guide-to-7-packages_in-python-to-explain-your-models-932967f0634b. Accessed 20 Mar 2023
4. Calzavara, S., Grishchenko, I., Maffei, M.: Horndroid: practical and sound static analysis of android applications by SMT solving. In: 2016 IEEE European Symposium on Security and Privacy (EuroS&P), pp. 47–62. IEEE, Saarbruecken, Germany (2016). https://doi.org/10.1109/EuroSP.2016.16
5. Garg, S., Baliyan, N.: Comparative analysis of android and IoS from security viewpoint. Comput. Sci. Rev. **40**, 100372 (2021). https://doi.org/10.1016/j.cosrev.2021.100372

6. Ghaffarian, S.M., Shahriari, H.R.: Software vulnerability analysis and discovery using machine-learning and data-mining techniques: a survey. ACM Comput. Surv. **50**(4) (2017). https://doi.org/10.1145/3092566
7. Krasner, H.: The cost of poor software quality in the US: a 2020 report (2021). https://www.it-cisq.org/cisq-files/pdf/CPSQ-2020-report.pdf
8. Li, L., Fan, Y., Tse, M., Lin, K.Y.: A review of applications in federated learning. Comput. Ind. Eng. **149**, 106854 (2020). https://doi.org/10.1016/j.cie.2020.106854
9. Li, T., Sahu, A.K., Talwalkar, A., Smith, V.: Federated learning: challenges, methods, and future directions. IEEE Sig. Process. Mag. **37**(3), 50–60 (2020). https://doi.org/10.1109/MSP.2020.2975749
10. Mitra, J., Ranganath, V.P.: Ghera: A repository of android app vulnerability benchmarks. In: Proceedings of the 13th International Conference on Predictive Models and Data Analytics in Software Engineering. PROMISE, pp. 43–52. Association for Computing Machinery, New York, NY, USA (2017). https://doi.org/10.1145/3127005.3127010
11. Nagaria, B., Hall, T.: How software developers mitigate their errors when developing code. IEEE Trans. Softw. Eng. **48**(6), 1853–1867 (2022). https://doi.org/10.1109/TSE.2020.3040554
12. Namrud, Z., Kpodjedo, S., Talhi, C.: Androvul: a repository for android security vulnerabilities. In: Proceedings of the 29th Annual International Conference on Computer Science and Software Engineering, pp. 64–71. IBM Corp., USA (2019). https://dl.acm.org/doi/abs/10.5555/3370272.3370279
13. NIST: National vulnerability database (2021). https://nvd.nist.gov/vuln. Accessed 21 Mar 2023
14. Rajapaksha, S., Senanayake, J., Kalutarage, H., Al-Kadri, M.O.: AI-powered vulnerability detection for secure source code development. In: Bella, G., Doinea, M., Janicke, H. (eds.) SecITC 2022. LNCS, vol. 13809, pp. 275–288. Springer, Cham (2023). https://doi.org/10.1007/978-3-031-32636-3_16
15. Senanayake, J., Kalutarage, H., Al-Kadri, M.O., Petrovski, A., Piras, L.: Android code vulnerabilities early detection using AI-powered *ACVED* plugin. In: Atluri, V., Ferrara, A.L. (eds.) DBSec 2023. LNCS, vol. 13942, pp. 339–357. Springer, Cham (2023). https://doi.org/10.1007/978-3-031-37586-6_20
16. Senanayake, J., Kalutarage, H., Al-Kadri, M.O., Petrovski, A., Piras, L.: Android source code vulnerability detection: a systematic literature review. ACM Comput. Surv. **55**(9) (2023). https://doi.org/10.1145/3556974
17. Senanayake., J., Kalutarage., H., Al-Kadri., M.O., Piras., L., Petrovski., A.: Labelled vulnerability dataset on android source code (lvdandro) to develop AI-based code vulnerability detection models. In: Proceedings of the 20th International Conference on Security and Cryptography - SECRYPT, pp. 659–666. INSTICC, SciTePress (2023). https://doi.org/10.5220/0012060400003555
18. Srivastava, G., et al.: XAI for cybersecurity: state of the art, challenges, open issues and future directions (2022). https://doi.org/10.48550/ARXIV.2206.03585
19. Statista: Average number of new android app releases via google play per month from March 2019 to May 2023 (2023). https://www.statista.com/statistics/1020956/android-app-releases-worldwide/. Accessed 02 July 2023
20. Tang, J., Li, R., Wang, K., Gu, X., Xu, Z.: A novel hybrid method to analyze security vulnerabilities in android applications. Tsinghua Sci. Technol. **25**(5), 589–603 (2020). https://doi.org/10.26599/TST.2019.9010067

Finding Server-Side Endpoints with Static Analysis of Client-Side JavaScript

Daniil Sigalov[1,2(✉)] and Dennis Gamayunov[1,2]

[1] Lomonosov Moscow State University, Moscow, Russia
{asterite,gamajun}@seclab.cs.msu.ru,
{daniil.sigalov,denis.gamayunov}@solidpoint.net
[2] SolidSoft LLC, Moscow, Russia

Abstract. Determining server HTTP endpoints — essentially, revealing server's attack surface — is a crucial step of every black-box web security scanner. An indispensable method of doing that is inferring server endpoints from client side, discovering what HTTP requests can be sent from client to server. This is easy for requests triggered by HTML markup elements, such as links and forms, but is difficult for requests sent by JavaScript. Existing approaches to determining requests sent from JavaScript are based on a technique known as *dynamic crawling* - automated interaction with web page elements using a headless browser. Dynamic crawling fails when the code that sends a request is impossible or very hard to trigger with interface interaction. We propose a different approach for finding HTTP requests sent by JS code, which uses static code analysis. While analyzing JavaScript statically is known to be hard and applying existing analyzers to real-world web pages usually does not work, we propose a new lightweight analysis algorithm that can work on pages of real websites, and can discover server endpoints that dynamic crawlers cannot. Evaluation results show that augmenting a black-box scanner with the proposed static analysis may significantly improve server-side endpoint coverage.

Keywords: Web applications · Static analysis · JavaScript

1 Introduction

In this paper we consider the problem of black-box security analysis of web applications, when only client-side code is available and analyzing server side is only possible by interacting with its interface endpoints. Black-box vulnerability testing usually consists of three stages:

- Attack surface enumeration: searching for available server-side endpoints (API endpoints);
- Sending requests with attack vectors to discovered endpoints;
- Analyzing results.

This paper proposes a method for automating the search for available server-side endpoints, thus addressing the first stage. There are several ways to discover server HTTP endpoints in black-box setting:

S. Katsikas et al. (Eds.): ESORICS 2023 Workshops, LNCS 14399, pp. 442–458, 2024.
https://doi.org/10.1007/978-3-031-54129-2_26

- Inferring them from client side by determining which requests can be sent from it;
- Fingerprinting software running on the server and using previously known endpoints specific for it (for example, known endpoints of WordPress);
- Fuzzing the server with requests generated using a dictionary and analyzing responses — technique known as *dirbusting*.

The most important quality metric of searching for endpoints is *completeness*. Dirbusting and fingerprinting cannot determine all endpoints, especially for non-standard, custom software. Being able to infer endpoints from client side is of vital importance for a black-box scanner to get adequate coverage [1–3].

Determining requests sent by client side is easy for pure-HTML interface, where semantics and reactions to user actions are always fixed. This is much harder for requests sent from JavaScript code, as it requires code analysis of some form. Meanwhile, today more and more websites have their client-side interfaces heavily based on JavaScript. Extreme cases of this trend are *single-page applications* (SPAs), where an HTML page is loaded only once, and all subsequent requests to server are sent by JavaScript. According to statistics, 97.1% of web sites currently use JS on their pages [16].

Almost all approaches to determining HTTP requests sent from client-side JavaScript for the purpose of web security scanning known to us are based on a technique known as *dynamic crawling* [1,2,4]. The only exception that we have seen is searching for strings looking like URLs in JS code using regular expressions, which works only in the most trivial cases.

Dynamic crawling is automated interaction with web page interface elements using a headless browser, simulating user actions and observing the requests being sent to server. Although dynamic crawling often works well, there are cases when it fails to discover some endpoints. Sometimes the user interface is too complex to be crawled completely. Making all possible user actions may require too much time. In such cases a crawler would stop before completing, probably missing some endpoints. Furthermore, sometimes JS code accessing an endpoint is impossible to trigger from the user interface at all — essentially, this is dead code. Such code still provides interest for the scanner and can access working parts of the server. We call such endpoints *hidden endpoints*. Some cases when such endpoints can be found are:

They belong to authenticated user interface. For example, the web site's administrative panel. An anonymous user will not see in his interface a link to this panel, or administrator password reset form (at least until he successfully passes authentication as administrator). Meanwhile, client-side JavaScript code for authenticated part of web application is often available without authentication, and sometimes is injected into all pages of the application. Endpoints belonging to an authenticated part of the web application could be exploitable without authentication due to Insufficient Authorization vulnerability.

A website function that is being removed or is not yet fully enabled. It might be an old site search function, which has already been removed from user interface, but is still supported by the server — for example, server code update never happened for some reason. A particular example that we found during experiments is Ajax Search Lite plugin for WordPress [36] - if it is installed and activated, and its search bar is not added on any page of the website, it will be impossible to trigger requests to its API from user interface, but its JS code will still be injected into all pages of the site and server part will work. The plugin has more than 70000 installations. There are other examples: developer-only debug interfaces, missing interface elements due to the lack of relevant data (upvoting a comment on a site where no comments are added yet).

Our insight is that, to overcome the described limitations of dynamic crawlers, another kind of client-side JavaScript code analysis can be used, which is not based on the interaction with interface elements and instead is based on analyzing the code itself. In this paper, we propose a new approach that uses static analysis. To the best of our knowledge, we are the first to propose inferring server endpoints from client-side JS code with nontrivial static analysis for the purpose of web application security scanning.

2   Features of Real JS in Respect to Finding Endpoints

It is well-known that analyzing JavaScript statically is hard [18,19]. It is impossible to build an analysis that works in general case. However, our observation is that sometimes code on the web page looks rather simple, being susceptible even for simple static analysis techniques, but is still unreachable or hardly-reachable from user interface. Examples of such code, based on real websites that we have seen, are given below in Listings 1.1 and 1.2.

Furthermore, for the more complicated code, our idea is that a set of frequently-occuring features of real code that make inferring endpoints harder can be identified. Analysis can then be equipped with mechanisms specifically targeting those features, which would increase amount of supported code. Several works study JavaScript features that make it difficult for static analysis [12,17]. Set of features seen by us that harden inferring endpoints is different from what is described in those papers. eval and its aliases, as well as with statement, are rarely written by developers in modern web. They are discouraged by development best-practices. Property deletion and function signature violation are also rare for modern hand-written code, at least concerning the code related to sending requests. The most frequent features that we have seen are:

- Usage of module bundlers. Analyzers have to somehow track connections between modules, understand what is returned from require() calls;
- Usage of object-oriented programming (classes): analyzers have to understand what value is pointed to by this keyword;
- Reading data from DOM either directly using DOM API or API of a library (often jQuery);
- Passing data through complex library- or framework-specific mechanisms that are hard for static analyzers to reason about, like custom event loops.

Adding support for each of those features is nontrivial and requires some custom algorithm modifications - as it would be for potential new features. Therefore, the algorithm is somewhat bound to real-world JS code in its current state.

We also noted that sometimes JS code accessing *all* server endpoints is present on a single page, that is especially frequent for SPAs, which are becoming more and more common nowadays. In this case, if a static analyzer is able to handle client-side JavaScript, it will be able to get all server endpoints in one shot, after analyzing a single page. Moreover, this will not require sending requests to these endpoints, giving a better opportunity to work in stealth mode and reducing server load.

2.1 Motivating Examples

Let us consider the following two examples. Code on the Listing 1.1 consists of two functions, one of them calls the other. It contains a call to function $.post, that sends a request to the server. A request is made by the standard function from jQuery library, which is very commonly used in the web. Another common feature is the use of global variables for defining configuration parameters.

Listing 1.1. Simple code that is hard for analysis by present methods

```
1  var api = "/application/iuT6ei/";
2  function remove(params) {
3      if (prompt("Enter 'yes' to remove") !== "yes")
           return;
4      $.post(api + "interface/remove/handle", params);
5  }
6  function removeByID(id) {
7      remove({ ident: id });
8  }
```

Given that functions `remove` and `removeByID` are not called anywhere else on the page, they are dead code. In this case both dynamic crawlers and existing static approaches would miss these functions. Even if a dynamic method triggered a call to `removeByID()`, it would have to somehow pass a check on line 3. This sample is based on real code that we have seen, such code is especially typical for older sites using jQuery library.

Listing 1.2. Class for sending requests to server

```
1  function ApiClient() {}
2
3  ApiClient.prototype.init = function() {
4      this.baseURL = '/api/v2/';
5  };
6  ApiClient.prototype.sendData = function(x) {
7      fetch(this.baseURL + 'data/accept.aspx?p=' + x);
8  }
```

The code on Listing 1.2 contains a class for accessing server APIs. Such classes or modules designed for working with server APIs are frequent. As already mentioned, often they contain methods for all server endpoints, even ones not used on the current page. Sometimes, there are several such clients or modules. If this class is not instantiated and used on a page, it can be very challenging for dynamic analysis to discover the endpoint accessed on line 7. Static analyzer would have to correctly determine possible values of fields of `this` object inside the methods of class `ApiClient`.

3   Related Work

Existing approaches can be traditionally split into 2 categories: dynamic and static analysis.

3.1   Dynamic Analysis

Dynamic Crawling. As already mentioned above, essentially all nontrivial methods of inferring HTTP endpoints from client-side JavaScript are based on dynamic crawling, which is, by its nature, a dynamic analysis. This is unsurprising since JavaScript is notoriously hard to analyze statically. A variety of dynamic crawling methods have been proposed. Crawljax [4] and Enemy of the State [20] are classic works in this area, with the former being supported up to the present day. Several other works followed, proposing new crawlers: FEEDEX [13], jÄk [8] and XIEv [5]. Also, Arachni [7] and Htcap [34] were introduced, which are open-source scanners coming with their own built-in dynamic crawlers. Most recent works in the area are Black Widow [11], CHIEv [1] and Gelato [9].

All mentioned methods use dynamic crawling: they interact with web page interface elements using a headless browser, simulating user actions and observing the requests being sent to server. For all of them, key quality metric is server-side code coverage. Most of them build some kind of application interface model consisting of interface states and try to visit as much states as possible.

Gelato is using static analysis to build client-side JavaScript call graph. However, this graph is used to help in guiding the crawler and in general the whole algorithm is still based on user interface interactions, i.e., dynamic crawling.

BackREST [10] is a further development of Gelato, but it uses server-side code instrumentation to aid in discovering endpoints, so it does not work in a strictly black-box setting.

While all methods mentioned above discover endpoints by performing interface interactions and thus making client-side code send requests to server, we take a different approach and try to directly infer endpoints the code itself.

Analyses Altering the Code Semantics. All dynamic analysis methods previously mentioned in this section execute JavaScript "honestly": the code runs as it would run in real environments. Even when some of them use instrumentation, that instrumentation is only used to record some information, without changing the execution flow. Meanwhile, a couple of works proposed to apply technique known as *forced execution* to client-side JavaScript [14,21]. Both of them use execution environment instrumentation (instrumented Chrome browser) to execute JS with altered semantics. This instrumentation allows analyzers to invoke functions which are not called anywhere in the code, skip calls to unwanted functions, alter the outcome of the branching operator (entering the branch that would not be visited otherwise), dynamically synthesize values during variable lookup for variables that were not defined to avoid crashing with ReferenceError.

Such analysis is able to reach some of the dead code, which, as we mentioned, is one of the problems for dynamic crawlers. We consider applying forced execution to client-side JavaScript for discovering HTTP endpoints to be a very interesting direction of research. However, this is nontrivial. JSForce [21] is not open-source and, while source code of [14] is public, it does not discover HTTP requests out-of-the-box, and adopting it to do that would require some effort. As mentioned in [8], modifying a JavaScript engine is hard and will bind the technique to a specific engine. Such modified engines may have stability problems, and pose difficulties in porting to newer browser versions. Moreover, while forced execution would easily discover an endpoint accessed in Listing 1.1, it is unclear how to handle the code in Listing 1.2 with it. To discover an endpoint there, it would have to somehow call class methods in the correct order, with the correct this value being common between them.

That is why we have chosen to take another direction and use static analysis to infer endpoints from client-side code. Nevertheless, although it is nontrivial, we consider using dynamic analysis other than crawling for discovering endpoints to be a promising way of research that is also worth exploring.

3.2   Static Analysis

As already mentioned, the only existing static algorithm for inferring HTTP endpoints from client-side JavaScript used for black-box scanner is matching strings looking like URLs in JS code using regular expressions. Obviously, this fails most of the time and works only in the very simple case when URL has a specific prefix, request method is GET, all parameters are directly written in the matched URL string, and there is no request body and no custom headers. We have seen such an approach in scanners Burp Scanner [28] and W3af [35].

State-of-the-art JavaScript analyzers well-known in academic literature are WALA [33], SAFE [23] and TAJS [29]. All these analyzers try to be sound or at least maintain a high level of soundness, which, unfortunately, makes them hardly-usable when applied to real-world web pages [17–19,22]. In our own experiments, each of these tools either fails with an error or works for a very long time even when applied to a very simple page using a ubiquitous jQuery library. Moreover, none of these tools infer requests from JavaScript or analyze dead code out-of-the-box. We came to conclusion that, although using these analyzers, or parts of them, for inferring HTTP endpoints from real-world web pages might be possible, it is nontrivial, and would likely require modifying their source code.

Two methods closest to our work are [6,24]. Unfortunately, implementations of both works are not publicly-available. Authors of [6] also provide few details of their algorithm, only mentioning that it is based on k-CFA. Algorithm in [24] works at file-level, analyzing scripts in isolation. In our experience, this can very often lead to loss of critically important request parts (usually URL prefixes) as they are often defined inside a configuration object on the page itself, while the request is sent by a function in a separate JS file. They use imprecise-but-scalable field-based method of building call graphs, implemented in WALA, which treats the same all functions with the same function signatures. This all led us to the conclusion that, although precision of this method is probably adequate for the task it solves (checking whether API requests made from JS conform with the specifications), it might be too low for our purpose.

Based on the results of our study, we decided to create a new analysis algorithm. Differently from WALA, SAFE and TAJS it is not sound and analyzes all the code on the page, including the dead code. To identify API invocations, authors of [24] look for jQuery-specific lexical patterns. We do the similar thing, although our pattern set extends beyond only jQuery patterns. However, differently from [24], our algorithm analyzes JS of the whole page instead of working with different scripts in isolation.

4 Approach

In this section we describe a new method for client-side JavaScript code analysis in order to find server-side endpoints. The next section contains results of comparison of this method with existing ones.

The proposed method takes a web page as an input: it accepts the page URL, its HTML markup, and a set of external resources linked from that markup. As a result, the method outputs a set of specifications of requests sent to server from the web page, discovered during the analysis.

The analysis method is static and *path-insensitive*. Analyzer tries to build potential call chains and analyze them to more precisely determine possible argument values. This gives our method some degree of *context-sensitivity*.

Our algorithm is similar to classic static data-flow analysis algorithms using abstract interpretation [15], however, there are distinctions. Like the classic algorithms, the method iterates over the code several times, accumulating its knowledge about the program. Iteration is done over the abstract syntax tree (AST) of the program in DFS order. ASTs of all scripts on page are concatenated, giving one large AST. All AST nodes are visited regardless of whether they are reachable or not, no attempt is made to trace execution from some starting point. In addition to classic iterations over the whole program, at the end the algorithm passes along discovered call chains leading to the points in code where requests are sent to server (*AJAX sinks*). This process is called *call-chain traversal*.

Unlike classic algorithms, control-flow graph is not built. The algorithm does not wait for the fixpoint to be reached before stopping, instead 4 iterations are made. The need for limiting the number of analysis iterations was already mentioned in prior work [19]. To achieve reasonable analysis times, we tried to keep the lowest iteration limit that still allowed to handle the code on real-world samples that we used for testing. Also, unlike classic algorithms, when reaching code constructs that are not supported, the analysis just ignores them, missing possible effects on the program state. If a value evaluated by such constructs is required, a special *Unknown* value is produced, which is somewhat analogous to the lattice bottom value ($\bot$) in classic algorithms. Analysis does not maintain separate abstract states for different AST nodes, instead, for each memory location a single state is used for the whole analysis. This state can hold multiple values (having type *ValueSet*), the size of this set can be grown or reduced.

This all makes the algorithm unsound, but enables it to analyze real-world pages, which can contain lots of complex code.

Algorithm 1. Analysis algorithm

```
 1: function MAINALGORITHM(PageURL, AST)
 2:     Mem ← SEEDINITIALMEMMODEL(PageURL)
 3:     for i from 1 to 4 do
 4:         ANALYSISPASS(AST, Mem, ε, false)
 5:     CallDescrs ← ANALYSISPASS(AST, Mem, ε, true)
 6:     CallDescrs ← CallDescrs ∪ TRAVERSECALLCHAINS(AST, Mem)
 7:     return CallDescrs
 8:
 9: function ANALYSISPASS(AST, Mem, CallChainInfo, processSinks)
10:     for all vertex v ∈ AST in DFS order do
11:         if v.type ∈ {Assignment, Declaration, CallExpr, ReturnStmt} then
12:             val ← EVALEXPR(v, Mem)
13:             STORETOMEMORYLOCATION(v, val, Mem)
14:         if processSinks and ∃sgn ∈ AJAXPatternSet : MATCHES(v, sgn) then
15:             vals ← [EVALEXPR(arg, Mem) for arg in v.args]
16:             Results ← Results ∪ {(sgn, vals)}
17:         if v.type == CallExpr and CallChainInfo is not ε then
18:             newResults ← PROCEEDALONGCALLCHAIN(v, CallChainInfo, Mem)
19:             Results ← Results ∪ newResults
20:     return Results
```

On the final analysis stage (final AST traversal and call-chain traversals), when analysis reaches a code construct that sends a request to server (*AJAX sink*), it evaluates its arguments based on information gathered, transforms that into a request specification using built-in heuristics for supported sinks, and outputs this specification. AJAX sinks are identified syntactically: analyzer has a built-in set of patterns. Most sinks are function calls. Also, `new` expressions and assignments to `location` are supported as AJAX sinks. Most patterns specify the names (function names, or, for method calls, names of objects and methods). Pattern set contains patterns for both built-in browser APIs and APIs for several libraries. For example, it contains function names `fetch` and `axios`, pairs (`$`, `ajax`) and (`$http`, `post`). Some patterns for library classes match those classes by syntax constructs in their definition instead of matching by name. If values that reached an AJAX sink contain *ValueSets*, all possible combinations are produced and given as separate outputs.

Let's now describe the algorithm in more detail. Algorithm 1 shows how our analysis algorithm looks in pseudocode at a high level.

Modeling Values. The algorithm supports all values supported in regular JavaScript type system. These include objects and arrays, so some values can include others. Beyond them, it supports values of type *ValueSet* - these can hold a set of possible values at some program point. Also, there is a so-called *unknown value — Unknown*. There are also several more built-in special values used for supporting classes, modules, library objects and for formal arguments.

Analysis Passes. As already mentioned, the main algorithm consists of several analysis passes (essentially, AST traversals). Each pass visits AST nodes in DFS order. When a pass sees an expression result being passed to some memory location, it evaluates that expression and stores the resulting value associated with that memory location. The following kinds of memory locations are supported:

- Variables. This includes function arguments and function values of declared functions. Variables with the same name from different scopes are distinguished correctly thanks to scoping information provided by Babel JavaScript library [41]. If variable assignment happens inside branching block, the result is always converted to a *ValueSet* before storing;
- Function and constructor arguments and return values. Values passed to call expressions, `new` expressions and `return` statements are stored. They are associated with the function being called or returned from. Values stored this way are always converted to *ValueSets*. This information is stored globally for a function, without call site distinction;
- Object and array fields.

Evaluating Expressions. The method utilizes a custom mechanism for evaluating JavaScript expressions. It supports expressions consisting of literals, variables, operation +, object field accesses, calls of some standard built-in browser functions, and some other operations. Values stored for memory locations are looked up when used in expressions.

If analysis failed to compute a concrete value of an expression (for example, it contained a variable whose value was missing in memory model, or it contained an operation that analyzer does not support), a result of evaluation is *Unknown*.

Call expression return values are taken from stored set of values that were seen to be returned from that function.

Expression evaluation is done in the following way. For most supported operations, an attempt is made to perform the corresponding operation in original semantics of JavaScript. If operation arguments include *ValueSets*, result is also a *ValueSet* computed naturally (producing combinations if multiple *ValueSets* are involved). There is a limit on the number of elements in *ValueSet* (100 elements) and on the number of elements in set combinations produced when generating endpoints (at most 200 elements). For *Unknown*, if conversion to a concrete value is needed, a value *Unknown* becomes a string `"UNKNOWN"`.

Call-Chain Traversals. After making whole-program passes analyzer also passes along discovered call chains that lead to points where requests are sent. Discovering them is possible since analyzer supports function values and thus is sometimes able to resolve what function is called at a call site. Unknown values coming from function formal arguments are marked in a special way, if such marked value flows into an AJAX sink, analyzer knows that call-chain traversal is needed. We omit the details of this algorithm due to space limitations and to ease understanding. In simple cases, both global accumulation of function arguments done during main analysis passes and call chain traversal give equal precision. However, it allows to better track values assigned to global variables and gives better precision with longer call chains when there are multiple callers. In real-world code we sometimes observed different functions assigning a common global variable to pass data. In our experiments we set maximum call chain length to 5. This limit prevents analyzer from analyzing longer call chains, but it allows to have a reasonable performance and we did not discover real-world cases where increasing the limit further will alone give more endpoint coverage.

Supporting Module Bundlers. To support the code using module bundlers, we added the following mechanism to the analyzer. Before starting analysis passes, the code is searched for syntactic patterns of bundles made by two most popular bundlers: Webpack and Browserify. For the discovered bundles, individual modules are extracted together with their identifiers. Modules are stored in bundles in the form of anonymous functions (*enclosing functions*) inside an array or an object. Their identifiers are indices in that array (or keys in object). Analyzer then marks enclosing functions of the modules in a special way and creates a table where each module identifier is mapped its module. For each module, its own `exports` object is created. In the code of modules, identifiers pointing to `require` function and `module` and `exports` objects are found. This is rather easy since they are passed to modules as positional arguments of their enclosing functions at fixed positions. Standard property assignment mechanism that analyzer has populates `exports` objects. Additionally, we added support for special bundler function for defining exports (`require.d`). Analyzer is then able to resolve `exports` object returned by `require` calls.

As mentioned, only Webpack and Browserify are currently supported by our algorithm. Adding support for other kinds of bundlers is likely to be easy and would require to add an AST pattern for recognizing the bundled code and finding an array or object holding module functions there.

We have made the component for detecting module bundles and extracting modules from them open-source. It is available by the following link:
    https://github.com/seclab-msu/page-disassembler

Supporting the Code Using Classes. Analyzer identifies class definitions in the code. Syntactic patterns are added for the most frequent forms of old-style classes (like the one on Listing 1.2). Class definitions made with `class` keyword are identified trivially. For each class, special objects are created: *class object* and *instance object*. Only one such object is maintained for each class, so, all instances of a single class are mixed. When AST traversal is inside a class method, `this` value resolves to an instance object. Field and method references can be resolved using it. Properties of `this` object are always *ValueSets*: each assignment to them adds a value to a set instead of overwriting the previous value.

Example. To illustrate how the algorithm works, we are going to show how it handles an example shown on Listing 1.1. In order to determine how a request being sent would look like, analyzer has to determine possible arguments to call `$.post` on line 4 as precisely as possible. During the first pass, analyzer will find the assignment to the global variable `api` and store it inside its memory model. It will then enter the body of `remove` function. At this point argument `params` will receive the value *FromArg*, which carries no information except that this variable depends on formal arguments. Analysis will then ignore the condition inside the `if` check and proceed to a call to `$.post`. At this moment correct URL for the server endpoint will be discovered. However, request body parameters remain unknown. During further iterations, analysis will discover the argument `{ ident : id }` to `remove` function, thus finding request body parameter name.

To determine how would HTTP request sent by a call to `$.post` with such arguments look like, a built-in *model* of jQuery library will be used.

5   Evaluation

To evaluate our method, we made 2 experiments. We study the following research questions:

- RQ1: How does our method perform compared with existing approaches to inferring endpoints from client side?
- RQ2: How do industry-grade black-box web security scanners perform in finding endpoints that are hard to find by dynamic crawlers? (Do they have a tool like ours?)

Our prototype implementation uses Headless Chrome browser to load pages, scripts from pages are acquired using Chrome's Debugger API via the DevTools Protocol (CDP). The analyzer also infers endpoints from HTML elements like links and forms (this information is taken from the DOM model of a loaded page) and records requests made while loading the page (also using the CDP).

5.1 Comparison with Existing Approaches

To answer the first research question, we compare our prototype against existing methods for discovering endpoints. We were tempted to compare with Gelato [9] and CHIEv [1] since these works are recent and are close to our work. However, we were not able to do so. Both tools are not open-source. We asked the authors by email to provide the data of their experiments. CHIEv authors did not respond. Gelato authors have sent us the full raw data of their experiments, and we would like to kindly thank them for that. Sadly, since the notion of endpoints in their experiments is different from ours, we were unable to compare with results published in [9] (in their results, requests having different values of parameters in pathname were considered different AJAX endpoints, while we consider them to refer to the same endpoint).

We use 5 open-source applications also used in [1,9] as benchmarks: DVWA [31], JuiceShop [37], MyBB [32], WebGoat [38] and WIVET [39].

We compared our prototype to all the tools used in comparisons in [1,9] except Skipfish and jÄk. Skipfish is heavily based on fuzzing the server and dirbusting instead of deeply analyzing client-side code, it belongs to a different category of methods. We were unable to run jÄk for the reasons described in [1,5,10]. The tools we compared our prototype with are: Arachni [7], Crawljax [4], Enemy of the State [20], Htcap [34], w3af [35] and wget [40].

We did not configure any authentication mechanisms on crawler side. DVWA and WebGoat were put behind a proxy that auto-added the cookie to requests so that all crawlers were inside authenticated zone, since in these applications all pages require authentication. For JuiceShop, MyBB and WIVET no authentication was used at all. The timeout was set to 6 h for each tool.

Since our method works on individual pages, not applications, we integrated our prototype with the static crawler based on Colly library[1]. The crawler first crawled each application, discovering pages, then our analyzer ran on each page.

The quality metric used is a number of discovered endpoints. As noted in [9], ground truth for most of these applications (all except WIVET) is not available and is very challenging to obtain. A possible way to obtain a set of endpoints for a test application is to analyze its server-side code, but it requires substantial effort and is also not free from possible errors, so we decided to leave this for the future work and to use the same approach as in [1,9]. For all applications except WIVET we use a relative measure: we count the number of endpoints found by each tool by inspecting the requests they made. Determining whether two requests refer to the same endpoint or to different ones is nontrivial. We did our best to manually inspect results for each run, and de-duplicate requests referring to the same endpoint.

We publish raw experiment results including crawler requests and found endpoints, so that the results can be verified. We encourage all authors to also publish raw experiment data. Data is available here:

https://github.com/asterite3/finding-endpoints-with-analysis-experiment-data.

---

[1] Colly Crawler Framework for Golang https://github.com/gocolly/colly.

Results of our experiment are provided in Table 1.

Table 1. Unique endpoints per application and tool

Name	Arachni	Crawljax	Enemy of the State	Htcap	w3af	wget	*Prototype*
DVWA	36	43	40	**54**	48	1	**54**
JuiceShop	9	9	2	13	1	2	**36**
MyBB	68	7	65	63	59	52	**77**
WebGoat	**78**	10	1	10	1	10	12
WIVET	**51**	5	4	42	25	7	41

As seen in the table, our prototype discovered more endpoints than dynamic crawlers in 2 applications: JuiceShop and MyBB. For one application, DVWA, the same results were achieved by our tool and crawler Htcap. On 2 applications, WebGoat and WIVET, our results are worse. The reason our tool was better on JuiceShop and MyBB is that JS code on pages of these applications contains calls to server APIs which are impossible to trigger from user interface, and which our analysis is able to detect.

JuiceShop is a single-page application, and there JS code sending requests to all server endpoints is present on every page, including the main page. Meanwhile, user interface for some endpoints is not rendered if client is not logged in. One particular example is a POST request to "/file-upload" endpoint, which our analyzer was able to find. Dynamic crawlers missed it because they were not authenticated. This endpoint is vulnerable and JuiceShop server accepts requests to "/file-upload" without authentication, meaning that scanner using our analyzer would be able to find and exploit it, even without credentials.

MyBB is a forum application, right after installation there are no threads and posts there. This is the same setting as used in [1], which mentions no application customization after installation. Since there is no forum content, some actions like marking the post read or querying who made the post, cannot be triggered from user interface. But they are still found by our analysis. One particular script on pages of MyBB is "general.js", which contains several functions accessing these endpoints, and also some endpoints that require moderator access. It should be noted that one of the tools in our comparison also found some of these endpoints. W3af [35] was able to find some of the endpoints accessed from dead code because it looks for URL-like strings in JS code. However, even for requests with method GET that it was able to find, it missed some request parameters because they were added to the URL using string operations. Endpoints with method POST accessed from the dead code were not found by W3af.

Client-side code of DVWA is very simple in respect to sending requests to server, so it is not surprising that we achieved the same results as other tools. Only 2 endpoints are accessed from JS, both from file "authbypass.js", and both were found by our analysis. Client-side JS code of WebGoat turned out to be too complex for our present static analysis to handle. Its features we do not handle include class inheritance, AMD bundlers, some mechanisms of Backbone framework. Meanwhile, interface interactions can trigger requests to its endpoints. As for WIVET, as mentioned [1], some of the endpoints there can never be accessed through human interaction in combination with a correct browser, there is also an endpoint accessed from Flash animation. They are out of scope of our method. All endpoints accessed from JS were found by our tool.

The longest run time of our prototype on a single page was 28 s (this was achieved for the JuiceShop page). The longest analysis time of the whole application was 5 min and 2 s (for MyBB).

5.2 Comparison with Industry-Grade Scanners

To answer the second research question, we created a special synthetic application that has several endpoints accessed from JS. For some industry-grade scanners we were only able to get a demo version with limited number of runs, so it is hard to test them on a set of several benchmarks. Our test application is specifically designed to test scanner's ability to find requests that are not triggerable from user interface (*hidden endpoints*). The benchmark contains 17 endpoints, of them only the first three are triggerable from the UI. Besides that, endpoints differ in the kind of code that accessed them — and, therefore, in what properties analyzer should have to be able to find them. We have made the source code of the test web application public. It is available by this link:

https://github.com/seclab-msu/js-dep-mining-test-app.

We tested state-of-the art scanners that we were able to get access to. They are: Acunetix [26], Detectify [27], Burp Scanner [28], HCL AppScan Cloud [30], PT BBS - Positive Technologies BlackBox Scanner [25].

Experiment results were:

- *None* of the compared scanners detected server endpoints accessed from the dead code;
- Only Acunetix and AppScan found the endpoints that were accessed by JS triggerable from the UI;
- Our prototype implementation successfully discovered all endpoints.

6 Conclusion

Search for server endpoints is an important stage of a black-box web security scanner's pipeline, because results of this search determine which functions of the web application will be analyzed, and which will not.

In this paper we propose a method for increasing the completeness of endpoint discovery by applying static analysis of client-side JavaScript code. Our algorithm discovers points in code where requests to server are sent and employs static analysis working on top of JavaScript AST to determine the data that flows there. Discovered endpoints allow to analyze server side using some form of dynamic analysis, for example, fuzz testing. The task of discovering server endpoints by analyzing client-side code is different from other security applications of client-side code analysis (e.g., searching for DOM-based XSS) in that dead code also carries valuable information for it.

Our method does not strictly outperform dynamic crawlers, but complements them. To get the most complete results, a security scanner should use tools of both kinds.

Using dynamic analysis other than crawling and combinations of static and dynamic analysis to find endpoints are interesting directions of future work.

References

1. Leithner, M., Simos, D.E.: CHIEv: concurrent hybrid analysis for crawling and modeling of web applications. ACM SIGAPP Appl. Comput. Rev. **21**(1), 5–23 (2021)
2. Doupé, A., Cova, M., Vigna, G.: Why Johnny Can't Pentest: an analysis of black-box web vulnerability scanners. In: Kreibich, C., Jahnke, M. (eds.) DIMVA 2010. LNCS, vol. 6201, pp. 111–131. Springer, Heidelberg (2010). https://doi.org/10.1007/978-3-642-14215-4_7
3. Rennhard, M., Esposito, D., Ruf, L., Wagner, A.: Improving the effectiveness of web application vulnerability scanning. Int. J. Adv. Internet Technol. **12**(1/2), 12–27 (2019)
4. Mesbah, A., Van Deursen, A., Lenselink, S.: Crawling Ajax-based web applications through dynamic analysis of user interface state changes. ACM Trans. Web (TWEB) **6**(1), 1–30 (2012)
5. Leithner, M., Simos, D.E.: XIEv: dynamic analysis for crawling and modeling of web applications. In: Proceedings of the 35th Annual ACM Symposium on Applied Computing, pp. 2201–2210 (2020)
6. Guha, A., Krishnamurthi, S., Jim, T.: Using static analysis for Ajax intrusion detection. In: Proceedings of the 18th international conference on World wide web, pp. 561–570 (2009)
7. Arachni Framework version 1.6.1.3-0.6.1.1. https://github.com/Arachni/arachni. Accessed 1 Jul 2023
8. Pellegrino, G., Tschürtz, C., Bodden, E., Rossow, C.: jÄk: using dynamic analysis to crawl and test modern web applications. In: Bos, H., Monrose, F., Blanc, G. (eds.) RAID 2015. LNCS, vol. 9404, pp. 295–316. Springer, Cham (2015). https://doi.org/10.1007/978-3-319-26362-5_14
9. Hassanshahi, B., Lee, H., Krishnan, P.: Gelato: feedback-driven and guided security analysis of client-side web applications. In: 2022 IEEE International Conference on Software Analysis, Evolution and Reengineering (SANER), pp. 618–629. IEEE (2022)
10. Gauthier, F., Hassanshahi, B., Selwyn-Smith, B., Mai, T. N., Schlüter, M., Williams, M: Experience: model-based, feedback-driven, Greybox web fuzzing with BackREST. In: 36th European Conference on Object-Oriented Programming (ECOOP 2022). Schloss Dagstuhl-Leibniz-Zentrum für Informatik (2022)
11. Eriksson, B., Pellegrino, G., Sabelfeld, A.: Black widow: blackbox data-driven web scanning. In: 2021 IEEE Symposium on Security and Privacy (SP), pp. 1125–1142. IEEE (2021)

12. Richards, G., Hammer, C., Burg, B., Vitek, J.: The Eval That Men Do: a large-scale study of the use of Eval in JavaScript applications. In: Mezini, M. (ed.) ECOOP 2011. LNCS, vol. 6813, pp. 52–78. Springer, Heidelberg (2011). https://doi.org/10.1007/978-3-642-22655-7_4
13. Fard, A.M., Mesbah, A.: Feedback-directed exploration of web applications to derive test models. In: ISSRE (Vol. 13), pp. 278–287 (2013)
14. Kim, I.L., et al.: Finding client-side business flow tampering vulnerabilities. In: Proceedings of the ACM/IEEE 42nd International Conference on Software Engineering, pp. 222–233 (2020)
15. Cousot, P., Cousot, R.: Abstract interpretation: a unified lattice model for static analysis of programs by construction or approximation of fixpoints. In: Proceedings of the 4th ACM SIGACT-SIGPLAN Symposium on Principles of Programming Languages, pp. 238–252 (1977)
16. Usage statistics of client-side programming languages. https://w3techs.com/technologies/overview/client_side_language. Accessed 30 Apr 2022
17. Richards, G., Lebresne, S., Burg, B., Vitek, J.: An analysis of the dynamic behavior of JavaScript programs. In: Proceedings of the 31st ACM SIGPLAN Conference on Programming Language Design and Implementation, pp. 1–12. ACM, Toronto, Ontario, Canada (2010)
18. Ryu, S., Park, J., Park, J.: Toward analysis and bug finding in JavaScript web applications in the wild. IEEE Softw. 36(3), 74–82 (2018)
19. Esben, A., Møller, A.: Determinacy in static analysis of jQuery. In: Proceedings of the 2014 ACM International Conference on Object Oriented Programming Systems Languages & Applications, pp. 17–31. ACM, Portland, OR, USA (2014)
20. Doupé, A., Cavedon, L., Kruegel, C., Vigna, G.: Enemy of the state: a state-aware black-box web vulnerability scanner. In: 21st USENIX Security Symposium, pp. 523–538 (2012)
21. Hu, X., Cheng, Y., Duan, Y., Henderson, A., Yin, H.: JSForce: a forced execution engine for malicious JavaScript detection. In: Lin, X., Ghorbani, A., Ren, K., Zhu, S., Zhang, A. (eds.) SecureComm 2017. LNICST, vol. 238, pp. 704–720. Springer, Cham (2018). https://doi.org/10.1007/978-3-319-78813-5_37
22. Ko, Y., Lee, H., Dolby, J., Ryu, S.: Practically tunable static analysis framework for large-scale JavaScript applications. In: 30th IEEE/ACM International Conference on Automated Software Engineering (ASE), pp. 541–551. IEEE (2015)
23. Lee, H., Won, S., Jin, J., Cho, J., Ryu, S.: SAFE: Formal specification and implementation of a scalable analysis framework for ECMAScript. In: 19th International Workshop on Foundations of Object-Oriented Languages, p. 96 (2012)
24. Wittern, E., Ying, A. T., Zheng, Y., Dolby, J., Laredo, J. A.: Statically checking web API requests in JavaScript. In: IEEE/ACM 39th International Conference on Software Engineering (ICSE), pp. 244–254. IEEE (2017)
25. PT Bbs. https://bbs.ptsecurity.com/. Accessed 30 Apr 2022
26. Acunetix Homepage. https://www.acunetix.com. Accessed 30 Apr 2022
27. Detectify Homepage. https://detectify.com. Accessed 30 Apr 2022
28. Burp Scanner. https://portswigger.net/burp/vulnerability-scanner. Accessed 30 Apr 2022
29. Jensen, S.H., Møller, A., Thiemann, P.: Type analysis for JavaScript. In: Palsberg, J., Su, Z. (eds.) SAS 2009. LNCS, vol. 5673, pp. 238–255. Springer, Heidelberg (2009). https://doi.org/10.1007/978-3-642-03237-0_17
30. HCL AppScan. https://www.hcltechsw.com/appscan. Accessed 30 Apr 2022
31. Damn Vulnerable Web Application (DVWA). https://github.com/digininja/DVWA. Accessed 1 Jul 2023

32. MyBB 1.8.19. https://mybb.com/. Accessed 1 Jul 2023
33. The T.J. Watson Libraries for Analysis (WALA). http://wala.sourceforge.net/. Accessed 1 Jul 2023
34. Htcap 1.1.0. https://github.com/fcavallarin/htcap. Accessed 1 Jul 2023
35. W3af. http://w3af.org/. Accessed 1 Jul 2023
36. Ajax Search Lite plugin for WordPress (version 4.11.2). https://wordpress.org/plugins/ajax-search-lite/. Accessed 1 Jul 2023
37. Juice Shop 8.3.0. https://github.com/juice-shop/juice-shop/tree/v8.3.0. Accessed 1 Jul 2023
38. OWASP WebGoat Project. https://owasp.org/www-project-webgoat/. Accessed 1 Jul 2023
39. Web Input Vector Extractor Teaser. https://github.com/bedirhan/wivet. Accessed 1 Jul 2023
40. Wget. https://www.gnu.org/software/wget/. Accessed 1 Jul 2023
41. Babel library. https://babeljs.io/. Accessed 1 Jul 2023

The Nonce-nce of Web Security: An Investigation of CSP Nonces Reuse

Matteo Golinelli[✉][iD], Francesco Bonomi, and Bruno Crispo[iD]

University of Trento, Trento, Italy
{matteo.golinelli,bruno.crispo}@unitn.it, francesco.bonomi@hotmail.it

Abstract. Content Security Policy (CSP) is an effective security mechanism that prevents the exploitation of Cross-Site Scripting (XSS) vulnerabilities on websites by specifying the sources from which their web pages can load resources, such as scripts and styles. CSP nonces enable websites to allow the execution of specific inline scripts and styles without relying on a whitelist. In this study, we measure and analyze the use of CSP nonces in the wild, specifically looking for nonce reuse, short nonces, and invalid nonces. We find that, of the 2271 sites that deploy a nonce-based policy, 598 of them reuse the same nonce value in more than one response, potentially enabling attackers to bypass protection offered by the CSP against XSS attacks. We analyze the causes of the nonce reuses to identify whether they are introduced by the server-side code or if the nonces are being cached by web caches. Moreover, we investigate whether nonces are only reused within the same session or for different sessions, as this impacts the effectiveness of CSP in preventing XSS attacks. Finally, we discuss the possibilities for attackers to bypass the CSP and achieve XSS in different nonce reuse scenarios.

1 Introduction

Content Security Policy (CSP) is a web security mechanism that enables web developers to specify the sources from which their web pages can load resources, such as scripts, style sheets, images, and fonts. CSP is an effective countermeasure to prevent the exploitation of Cross-Site Scripting (XSS) vulnerabilities, which are one of the most common vulnerabilities on the web. CSP is not designed to be the sole mechanism for preventing XSS attacks but it is intended as the last layer of a defense-in-depth approach, providing an additional layer of protection for this type of attack without replacing other mechanisms for preventing XSS vulnerabilities, such as sanitization and validation of untrusted input and the use of templating engines. In practice, while other mechanisms aim at preventing the existence of XSS vulnerabilities, the goal of CSP is to render their exploitation impossible, without eliminating the XSS vulnerabilities. CSP2 is a W3C specification, published as a Recommendation by the Web Application Security Working Group [23], and the W3C is currently specifying CSP3 in a Working Draft [26]. By default, the CSP blocks the execution of all inline

© The Author(s), under exclusive license to Springer Nature Switzerland AG 2024
S. Katsikas et al. (Eds.): ESORICS 2023 Workshops, LNCS 14399, pp. 459–475, 2024.
https://doi.org/10.1007/978-3-031-54129-2_27

scripts and styles (i.e., directly included in the HTML code of a web page). However, CSP2 introduced the concepts of *nonces* and *hashes*, enabling websites to allow the execution of specific individual inline scripts and styles without relying on a whitelist. CSP nonces are a random string included in the policy that is assigned to scripts allowed to execute in the form of an attribute (e.g., <script nonce="r4nd0m">). According to the specification, servers are required to generate a new and unique nonce for each response that includes a policy, and nonces should be at least 128 bits long (before being base64-encoded).

The goal of this study is to measure and analyze the use of CSP nonces in the wild. To achieve this, we performed a large-scale analysis on the Tranco Top 50k sites to detect 1) nonce reuse, 2) short nonces, and 3) invalid nonces. Reusing the same nonce in more than one response can hinder the protection against XSS attacks, rendering the CSP useless. We find that more than 10k sites use CSP and, of these, 2271 use CSP nonces. Of the 2271 sites that deploy a nonce-based policy, 598 of them reuse the same nonce value in more than one response.

Next, we analyze the causes of the nonce reuses that we detect to identify whether they are introduced by the server-side code of the website or if the nonces are being cached by a web cache. The strict performance, availability, and scalability standards that websites are required to meet nowadays often lead to the implementation of extremely aggressive web cache configurations, which can induce web caches to erroneously cache dynamic content that they should not, such as CSP nonces. If a web cache caches a page that contains a nonce and serves it to other clients, an attacker can steal it and might use it to bypass the CSP.

Finally, we investigate whether nonces are only reused within the same session (i.e., for a single client) or also for different sessions. If a website reuses nonces only within a single session, an attacker able to steal its value by exploiting other vulnerabilities is able to bypass the CSP. Instead, if the value of the nonces is the same for all clients, an attacker can simply visit a page of the site to obtain a valid nonce to use to bypass the CSP and perform an XSS attack.

To summarize, we make the following contributions:

1. We measure websites' adoption of nonces-based policies on the Tranco Top 50k. We find that 2271 sites use a CSP nonce in at least one of their pages.
2. We evaluate the implementation of CSP nonces of popular websites in the wild, with a special focus on nonces reuse. To the best of our knowledge, we perform the first large-scale measurement of Content Security Policy nonces reuse, detecting 598 sites that reuse the same value in more than one response.
3. We investigate the causes of the nonce reuses that we detect, attributing them either to the server-side code of the website or to in-the-middle web caches. Moreover, we analyze if nonce reuses happen only within a single session or also for different ones.

Our code for this research is publicly available as an open-source tool on the author's website[1].

---

[1] https://github.com/Golim/nonce-nce.

2   Background

In this section, we provide an overview of the background knowledge necessary for a thorough understanding of our research.

2.1   Cross-Site Scripting

Cross-Site Scripting (XSS) is a type of security vulnerability that enables attackers to inject HTML or JavaScript code into the web pages of a vulnerable website, enabling attackers to execute code in the victim's browsers in the context of the vulnerable pages. Typical injection sources are the query parameters or the path of a request URL. By exploiting XSS vulnerabilities, the attackers can steal victims' information, hijack their sessions and even execute actions on their behalf on the target website. To prevent XSS vulnerabilities, a common approach is to implement input validation and sanitization to ensure that any user-provided data does not contain any malicious scripts and is properly encoded. Specifically, sanitization removes or HTML-encodes potentially dangerous HTML code from user-provided input to prevent XSS attacks, ensuring that the unsafe content is treated as data and not as code [12].

2.2   Content Security Policy

XSS vulnerabilities are possible because a web browser has no built-in mechanism to determine whether the injected code included in the web pages is reliable or malicious. The Content Security Policy (CSP) is a security mechanism that helps to prevent XSS attacks, clickjacking, and other code injection attacks by enabling websites to specify what resources can be loaded by the user agent. This mechanism is intended as a defence-in-depth that provides an additional layer of protection against XSS vulnerabilities, by making them not exploitable. CSP can also be used to detect and report code injection attempts, allowing website administrators to take action to prevent further attacks. The CSP can be deployed in *enforcement mode*, meaning that all the violations of the policy will be blocked (and possibly reported) by the browser, or in *report-only mode*. When a policy is report-only, it is not enforced by browsers, which will instead only report CSP violations to a *report-URI* specified in the policy. The second version of CSP is specified by the W3C in [23], and they are currently working on its third version (CSP3), published as a Working Draft [26]. Websites can specify their policy preferably using the `Content-Security-Policy` response HTTP header, but they can also do it using the HTML `meta` tag. To deploy a report-only CSP, servers must use the `Content-Security-Policy-Report-Only` response header, and cannot do it using the meta tag. The CSP works by allowing website administrators to specify a whitelist of trusted sources for executable content, such as JavaScript, CSS, and images. Any content that comes from untrusted sources must be blocked by the user agent [23]. A CSP is composed of one or more directives separated by a semicolon, and each directive is used to specify the valid sources for a particular type of resource. These directives can be used to whitelist specific domains or sources from which resources can be loaded, and to block the ones that do not match the specified sources. The `default-src` directive is used as a fallback, specifying the default behaviour for any directive that is not explicitly specified. By default, the CSP blocks all inline scripts and styles, effectively preventing the exploitation of XSS vulnerabilities.

Nonces. The second version of this security mechanism, CSP2, introduced the concept of *nonces* and *hashes* as a way of allowing the execution of individual inline scripts and styles without relying on a whitelist. The concept of "nonces" was initially proposed by Needham et al. in 1978 and specifically means a number "used only once" [11]. A *CSP nonce* is a random value used only once, which is added to the inline scripts or style tags of a web page as an attribute. The nonce is included in the policy, which tells the browser to only execute scripts or styles that have a matching nonce value [23]. For example, the following policy:

```
Content-Security-Policy: default-src 'self';
    script-src 'nonce-cmFuZG9t' 'self';
```

will allow the execution of the first inline script in the following example, but will block the second and the third scripts because the nonce is missing or invalid, respectively.

```
<script nonce="cmFuZG9t">
    console.log("This will execute");
</script>
<script>
    console.log("This will *not* execute");
</script>
```

The CSP2 specification [23] indicates that a nonce should have the following characteristics: 1. Must be unique for each HTTP response that includes a CSP. 2. Should be generated using a cryptographically secure random number generator. 3. Should be at least 128 bits long, before encoding.

A CSP nonce should be long and randomly generated to prevent attackers from guessing or brute-forcing it. However, it must be noted that properly implementing a nonce policy does not necessarily prevent the exploitation of XSS vulnerabilities altogether. In fact, if an inline script with the correct nonce attribute uses untrusted user input, an attacker could bypass the policy and achieve XSS. If a CSP nonce is reused for multiple HTTP responses, an attacker who is able to steal it could effectively bypass the policy by injecting a script with the correct nonce value.

2.3 Web Caches

Web caches are an essential component of modern web architecture, enabling faster and more efficient web browsing by storing previously accessed resources. Moreover, caches are generally physically located closer to the user's location, reducing the latency. When a user requests a web page or resource that is already in the cache, the cache can deliver it much faster than if it had to be fetched from the origin server. Caching also reduces the load on origin web servers. Web caches can be implemented at various stages of the web architecture, including the client side, proxy servers, and Content Delivery Networks (CDNs).

Web Cache Deception. Web Cache Deception (WCD) is a vulnerability that enables attackers to induce a public cache into caching information that it should not store, resulting in that information being publicly available. Mirheidari et al. in [10] showed how WCD vulnerabilities can be exploited to force a web cache into mistakenly caching a CSP nonce. If the cached nonces are reused in the same session for multiple requests coming from the origin server, an attacker could bypass the CSP and perform an XSS attack as follows:

1. The attacker exploits a WCD vulnerability to steal a valid CSP nonce linked to the victim's session.
2. The attacker crafts an XSS payload including the stolen CSP nonce in the injected script.
3. The attacker induces the victim into visiting a web page or following a malicious URL.

Cache Status Headers. Web caches generally employ a response header to communicate whether a resource that they handle is coming from the origin web server or is a cached copy. Different web cache technologies might use different header names and values for this purpose, but the majority of them use the keyword `cache` in the header name, and the keywords `HIT` and `MISS` to indicate a cached resource and one coming from the origin, respectively.

3 Related Work

The Content Security Policy was proposed by Stamm et al. in 2010, as an additional layer of security for XSS and CSRF attacks [19]. Numerous studies have measured the adoption of CSP by websites in the wild and its variation over time, giving us an indication of how much its use has grown through the years. In 2014, Weissbacher et al. measure the adoption of CSP in the Alexa Top 1M over a period of 16 months and find that only 850 of them use it [25]. Calzavara et al. do the same in 2016 [1] and 2018 [3], finding respectively 8,133 and 16,353 sites using the CSP, marking a significant increase in its adoption. Finally, Roth et al. show that, between 2012 and 2018, 1,233 of the 10,000 websites analysed deployed a CSP for at least one day [16]. Roth et al. also measure for the first time the adoption of CSP nonces and hashes, finding that in 2018 only 5% of sites adopting a CSP used nonces and 1% hashes [16].

Over the years, numerous studies have been presented presenting techniques to automate CSP policy generation. In 2013, Doupé et al. present deDacota, an automatic tool to statically rewrite code to separate data from the code and enforce this separation at run-time using CSP [5]. The following year, Johns analyses the dangers of dynamically filling scripts with data retrieved at run-time and proposes a templating and checksumming mechanism that enables servers to communicate which scripts are allowed to run to the browser [7]. Weissbacher et al. compare the adoption of CSP with other security headers and experiment with a semi-automated crawler-based CSP generation mechanism [25]. In 2016, Kailas and Braun analyse the usage of CSP in real-world websites, identifying errors and inconsistencies, and present a tool to automatically generate policies on the client side [14]. Pan et al. propose *CSPAutoGen*, a tool that auto-generates policies in real-time according to the page content and the templates of scripts, without requiring modifications to the server-side code [13]. Kerschbaumer et al. show that 90% of CSP deployments include the `unsafe-inline` keyword, rendering it ineffective in preventing XSS attacks, and propose a system to automatically generate CSPs by whitelisting only the hashes of expected scripts [8].

In 2015, Hausknecht et al. analyse the interplay between the CSP and browser extensions, finding that some extensions tamper with the CSP of websites to be able to work [6]. In 2017, Some et al. analyse how the SOP could cause CSP violations [18], and in 2021 Steffens et al. analyse how the use of third-party resources impacts a website's implementation of CSP and argue that relying on third parties is a major roadblock for security [20]. In 2021, Roth et al. present a qualitative study that analyses the difficulty of developing a safe CSP by tasking real-world developers with a programming task, where they have to develop a CSP for a small web app to prevent XSS attacks [17]. Calzavara et al. in 2016 show that CSP has limited deployment and that the deployed policies exhibit several weaknesses and misconfiguration errors [1]. In 2017, Calzavara et al. propose an extension to CSP called *Compositional CSP* that enables the composition of policies at run-time and assess its potential impact in the wild [2]. In 2016, Van Acker et al. show how to exploit DNS prefetching to exfiltrate data, bypassing the protection offered by the CSP [22]. In 2016, Weichselbaum et al. show that only 0.16% of the domains they analysed use CSP and detect that 94.7% of distinct policies deployed can be bypassed. They argue that maintaining a secure whitelist for a complex application is infeasible in practice, and suggest replacing URL whitelisting with nonces and hashes [24]. In 2017, Lekies et al. present a novel attack that exploits *script gadgets*, i.e., small fragments of JavaScript in a site's legitimate code that can be used to bypass XSS protection mechanisms, including the CSP. They identify gadgets in at least 19.9% of the tested sites [9].

Finally, we acknowledge the valuable contributions made by a separate team of researchers who explored a closely related problem in parallel with our research. Trampert et al. present an investigation of CSP nonces reuse, underscoring the significance of this topic [21]. To attribute nonces reuse to a cache, they check whether a website uses a CDN; however, this approach is susceptible to generating false positives, given that the mere usage of a CDN by a website does not necessarily guarantee that the present response is being cached. In our work, we use cache busting and lookup of the cache status headers to more accurately attribute nonce reuses to web caches.

4   Methodology and Experiment

Our methodology is composed of three main phases: 1) URLs Collection, 2) CSP Nonces Detection, and 3) CSP Nonces Evaluation.

4.1   URLs Collection

In the first phase, we crawl the domain name of a website in an unauthenticated way to identify the URLs that present a CSP. Specifically, we visit the homepage of the website and then recursively visit all the links that we find in the source code of the pages. We only follow internal URLs, i.e., URLs where the domain is either the same as the one on the website or a subdomain. Our crawler can be configured to only visit a maximum number of subdomains and a maximum number of pages for each subdomain. Our crawler is developed in Python and uses the *BeautifulSoup* library to extract the links from the HTML code of web pages, and the *requests* library to perform HTTP requests.

CSP Detection. To identify the URLs on a website that present a CSP, we look for both the `Content-Security-Policy` header and the `meta` tag in the HTML of the page. We also test whether the CSP is deployed in report-only mode by checking the presence of the `Content-Security-Policy-Report-Only` header (a report-only CSP cannot be deployed using the `meta` tag).

4.2   CSP Nonces Detection

In this phase, we visit all the URLs that present a CSP collected in the previous step and check if they use CSP nonces as part of their policy. Since we are interested in sites where nonces are actually used, we do not only check if they include a nonce in their policy, but we verify if the page includes `script` tags with the `nonce` attribute. We save the HTML source code of the pages that include a CSP nonce and we store the headers of the requests and the responses for future analyses.

4.3   CSP Nonces Evaluation

In this phase, we check if the length of the previously identified CSP nonces is sufficient and if they are reused. To detect nonce reuse, we request the pages that include a nonce a second time and check if the value of the nonce is the same. If the nonce value is the same in both responses, we mark the page as vulnerable to nonce reuse. Then, we mark a nonce as too short if it is shorter than 22 useful characters (i.e., not including "=" padding characters) in its base64-encoded form.

Reuse Causes. When we detect nonce reuse, we analyze whether it is introduced by a web cache caching a dynamic nonce, or if the reuse is caused by the server-side code of the website. To do this, we employ three mechanisms that, used together, give us a strong indication of whether a cache is influencing the nonces or not.

Static Nonces. First, we attribute to the server-side code all the nonce reuses where the nonce is the same in all responses coming from a website (only on the sites that use a nonce on two or more pages). It must be noted that these nonces might still get cached, but the root cause of their reuse is the server-side code. Next, we use two techniques explained below called *Cache-Busting* (CB), and *Cache Header Heuristics* (CHH). We perform this test because, if a nonce is reused due to a web cache storing it, an attacker is not able to perform an XSS attack even if they could steal the nonce, as the cached response does not include the attacker's injection. Assuming that the nonce is reused only due to a cache, the attacker is not able to overwrite the cached copy of the response without the nonce changing.

Cache-Busting. For this test, we perform a third request including a cache-busting query parameter in the URL (i.e., a randomly generated parameter added to the query string of the URL). This technique is effective when the query string is included in the cache key (i.e., the unique identifier of a resource stored by a cache [4]). By adding a random modification to the query string, we cause our request to have a different cache key, effectively preventing a cache from serving us a cached response. If the response to the cache-busted request includes a different nonce, we can attribute the nonce reuse to a web cache. However, if the value of the nonce is the same as the one in the previous responses, we cannot conclusively exclude the presence of a cache, as some web caches might not include the query string in their cache key, resulting in our cache-busting mechanism failing in its purpose of excluding the cache. For this reason, we also employ the *CHH*.

Cache Header Heuristics. In this test, we check whether the response with a reused nonce is coming from a cache or the origin server using the *cache header heuristics* algorithm presented by Mirheidari et al. in [10][2]. This test performs a lookup of the cache status headers of the second response (i.e., where we detected nonce reuse) to check if it is coming from a cache or the origin server, as described in Sect. 2.3. If we detect that the second response is not coming from a cache, we can conclusively exclude the influence of a cache on the nonce reuse. Otherwise, if the second response is coming from a cache or if the test gives an unknown status (e.g., because the cache status headers are missing in the response), we cannot conclusively attribute the nonce reuse to a cache or not, and we need to resort on the *cache-busting* test. If we detect that the second response is coming from a cache, we cannot exclude that the server-side code is nevertheless issuing the same nonce.

To summarize, only by using all three tests in combination we can attribute nonce reuse to a cache or not with a high degree of confidence.

---

[2] The code of the algorithm can be found at https://github.com/golim/wcde.

Session Analysis. Finally, to test whether nonces are only reused for the same session or also for different ones, we perform another HTTP request, without providing the previously stored cookies.

4.4   Experiment

We performed a large-scale experiment on the web to detect CSP nonces reuse and websites that use short nonces. Our dataset is composed of the Tranco Top 50k [15] downloaded on 21, July 2022[3]. For each domain in our dataset, we crawled at most 10 pages in at most 10 subdomains (i.e., a maximum of 100 pages for each domain in our dataset). For each domain that we tested, we created a session object with cookies persistence, simulating a user surfing a website using the same browser for all requests.

5   Results

In this section, we discuss the results of our large-scale measurement over the Tranco Top 50k.

Table 1. The number of sites that deploy a Content Security Policy, use CSP nonces, and reuse the same nonce value for multiple responses. Percentages are calculated over the total number of sites that deploy a CSP (10034).

Total sites using CSP	10034	
enforcement mode	8946	(89.2%)
report-only mode	1088	(10.8%)
Sites with CSP nonces	2271	(22.6%)
Sites reusing CSP nonces	598	(6.0%)

Table 2. The number of sites presenting at least one reused CSP nonce and the investigated reason of the reuse. Percentages are calculated over the total number of sites that reuse a nonce (*598*).

Total sites reusing nonces	598	
due to a cache	256	(42.8%)
server-side code	342	(57.2%)
in the same session	37	(6.2%)
in different sessions	561	(93.8%)

---

[3] The specific dataset that we used can be downloaded at https://tranco-list.eu/list/ W97W9/.

5.1 CSP Adoption and Usage

Table 1 summarizes the results of our measurement of CSP adoption. Even though it is not the main focus of our research, we briefly analyze our measurement of the adoption of CSP. We crawled 50k websites and detected 10034 (20.1%) deploying a Content Security Policy. Of these, 1088 sites only use the CSP in report-only mode, while 8946 enforce their policy. We also found 346 sites that only deploy their policy in the meta tag, while 135 deploy it both in the *Content-Security-Policy* header and the meta tag.

5.2 Reuse Analysis

Table 2 presents the results of our measurement of websites that use a CSP and that reuse nonces. Of the 10034 identified sites that deploy a CSP, 2271 (22.6%) present a nonce-based CSP in at least one of the pages that we visited. 598 (26.3% of the sites using a nonce-based CSP) reused the same CSP nonce value in multiple responses. Figure 1 shows the distribution of websites that use a nonce CSP in at least one of their pages and the sites that reuse at least one nonce, with respect to their ranking in the Tranco Top 50k. From Fig. 1, we can see that the usage of CSP nonces is higher among the more popular websites according to their ranking, while the percentage of websites that reuse the same nonce value in more than one response is higher among the lower rankings.

Causes Analysis. We investigated the effect of web caches on the reuse of the nonce and found that 342 (57.2% of the 598 sites reusing a nonce) sites use the same value for nonces in more than one origin server response, indicating that the cause of reuse is code executing on the site's server, while for 256 (42.8% of the 598 sites reusing a nonce) sites the cause of nonce reuse is solely due to a cache storing a copy of the response that includes an otherwise dynamic nonce and serving it in response to the subsequent requests. 219 sites use the same nonce value in all responses coming from the origin server.

Cached Nonces. Using cache-busting and the cache header heuristics, we also detected 318 websites that cache CSP nonces (53.2% of the sites that reuse nonces), regardless of the nonces being static or dynamic when generated by the server-side code. Of these 318 cases where we observed caching, 190 were detected using cache-busting, and 128 using the CHH algorithm.

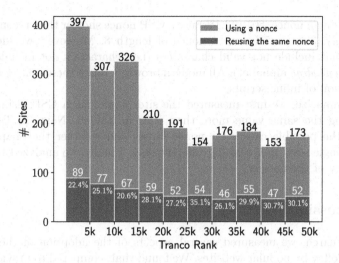

Fig. 1. The distribution of websites that have a nonce-based CSP (in blue), and the subset of those which reuse a CSP nonce (in red) with respect to their ranking in the Tranco Top 50k. The percentage in each bar is calculated over the number of sites that use a nonce in the same 5k bucket. (Color figure online)

Sessions Analysis. Our goal was to detect websites that reuse identical nonce values within a session and those that reuse the same nonce across all visitors to the site. As described in Sect. 4, to do this we performed the same request using a clean browser, to simulate a different user visiting the same page. We detected that only in 37 cases the nonce value was bound to the session of the visitor, while in the vast majority of the cases (561), we observed that the same nonce value was repeated for visitors with a different session (i.e., with different cookies). It is important to note that, when a reused nonce value is not bound to the session of the visitors, an attacker could simply visit the same page or site to obtain a valid CSP nonce that will be used in the responses to the victim requests, effectively rendering the CSP useless to protect against XSS attacks.

We performed all the tests using the same IP address and, even if we think this is highly unlikely, there is the possibility that some sites bind the nonce value to an IP address. However, even if this is the case, an attacker in the same Local Area Network (LAN) as the target victim would still be able to obtain a valid CSP nonce value to perform an XSS attack.

5.3 Length and Validity Analysis

We analyzed all the nonces detected in the web pages that we visited to identify the ones shorter than the specification recommends. It is important to note that it is extremely difficult for an attacker to perform a brute-force attack against shorter CSP nonces, but we still think that this analysis can be interesting to highlight how many websites do not follow the W3C specifications. Of the 2271 websites using a nonce, 501 (22.1%) use a CSP nonce shorter than recommended. Interestingly, 356 (15.7%) use a nonce of length 8. Moreover, we identified 8 websites that include not valid characters (i.e., characters not included in the *base64url-encoding* alphabet). All modern browsers reject these nonces and block the execution of inline scripts.

To summarize, we first measured the sites deploying a CSP, using nonces, and reusing the same value more than once in Table 1. Next, in Table 2, we analyzed the possible causes for nonce reuses and whether they happen only within a single session or also for different ones. Finally, we analyzed the length and validity of the nonces.

6   Discussion

In this research, we measured several aspects of the adoption of the Content Security Policy by popular websites. We found that, compared to previous large-scale measurements, the adoption of CSP and nonces-based policies has grown. However, our research highlights that more than one in every four sites that use nonces misuses them, repeating the same value in more than one response (Table 1). Reusing nonces could result in a complete bypass of the CSP, allowing attackers to exploit possible XSS vulnerabilities. We analyzed the different conditions in which nonces reuse happens and investigated its possible causes in Table 2. Depending on these, it is easier or harder for an attacker to bypass CSP to exploit XSS vulnerabilities.

Specifically, if the same nonce value is reused for different sessions, it is effectively the same as deploying an `unsafe-inline` directive (i.e., allowing the execution of all inline scripts and styles, regardless of their origin). In fact, an attacker can simply visit the vulnerable website to obtain a valid CSP nonce value to craft an injection that bypasses the CSP. On the other hand, if a nonce is only reused within the same session, the attacker has to exploit other vulnerabilities or attacks to steal the nonce value from the target victim. For example, an attacker can exploit possible Web Cache Deception vulnerabilities or perform cross-origin requests (if the *SameSite* attribute of the cookies is set to *None*). Once the attacker holds a nonce linked to the session of a victim, they can craft an injection that includes the stolen nonce to exploit an XSS vulnerability. Next, we analyzed the causes of nonce reuses to detect the ones likely caused by the presence of a web cache storing otherwise dynamic nonces. As described in Sect. 4.3, to do this we used three approaches: cache-busting, cache header heuristics (i.e., look-ups of the response headers), and the comparison of nonces on different pages of the same site. If a nonce is reused due to a cache, it is harder for an attacker to bypass the CSP and achieve XSS. In fact, even if an attacker can steal a cached nonce of a victim, they cannot inject a malicious payload in the cached copy of the response directly. An attacker can achieve XSS under these conditions if they can inject a payload with the stolen nonce exploiting client-side XSS vulnerabilities, i.e., where untrusted data is dynamically loaded directly from the victim's browser (e.g., due to DOM XSS, or when the page includes data dynamically through XMLHttpRequest or AJAX). We analyzed the length of the nonces and found that more than a fifth of all sites that employ nonces have them shorter than recommended by the specification. Depending on the length of the nonces, brute-force attacks might be feasible or not. Finally, we tested the validity of the nonces by checking that they only contained valid characters, finding that 8 sites presented invalid nonces. Browsers reject such nonces and block the execution of all the scripts and styles, resulting in a self-Denial of Service.

6.1 Reuse Causes

Here we discuss the possible causes for nonce reuse (see Table 2). Each web request response is generally handled by several entities with different functions (e.g., caches, proxies, firewalls, origin servers). The use of *clean URL* techniques (i.e., URLs whose structure does not directly reflect the file system structure of the server) means that often only the origin server understands the true nature of a resource, while the abstraction introduced by these techniques makes it obscure to other in-the-middle entities. It is therefore possible for a cache to be configured in such a way as to mistakenly cache pages that include dynamic content, such as CSP nonces. When instead a nonce reuse is not caused by a cache but by the server-side code of the website, it is more difficult to attribute the cause to a specific entity. Indeed, this may be caused by numerous factors that cannot be investigated from the outside in a black-box manner. Previous studies have focused on the complexity of implementing a proper CSP that effectively protects against XSS attacks [16], even interviewing web developers directly [17]. Some possible causes of these nonce reuses may be a lack of knowledge of the technology and possible attacks of developers, programming errors, typos, and negligence.

6.2 Limitations and Future Work

In this section, we acknowledge the limitations of our research and pave the way for future works to further explore this area. First, we do not investigate the randomness of the nonces. A possible way to do it would be to collect a certain number of nonces from each site and perform an analysis of their entropy. In our work, we also do not perform any analysis on the scripts included in the pages to check if they use untrusted data, hindering the security of the CSP in preventing XSS attacks even if the nonces are used correctly. Additionally, we do not test for the presence of XSS vulnerabilities because that is out of the scope of this paper. However, we collected all the HTML code of the pages that include a nonce, and we will perform this analysis in future work. Finally, even by using both the cache header heuristics and the cache-busting tests, we cannot attribute nonce reuse to a cache or the server-side code with 100% certainty. In fact, detecting the presence of a cache is a complicated task that, to the best of our knowledge, cannot be performed with full certainty of the results. According to the state-of-the-art, using both these tests is the way to most accurately interpret the data that we collected.

7   Conclusion

Our study highlights the importance of correctly implementing Content Security Policy (CSP) nonces to prevent Cross-Site Scripting (XSS) attacks. Our analysis of the Tranco Top 50k sites revealed that many websites reuse the same nonce value multiple times, which can potentially allow attackers to bypass CSP protections. We analyzed the different scenarios of nonce reuse and discussed the possibilities for the attackers to successfully bypass the CSP. Specifically, we investigated the root causes of nonce reuses, attributing them either to the server-side code, or in-the-middle web caches. When nonce reuse is only due to a cache, it is harder for an attacker to bypass the CSP, as they have to find a way to inject the malicious payload in the cached web page dynamically, for example exploiting DOM XSS vulnerabilities. If instead, the server-side code issues the same nonce for multiple responses, an attacker can simply use a stolen nonce to craft a payload that includes it to bypass the CSP. In this scenario, the complexity of the attack depends on whether the nonce is reused only within a single session or also for different ones. In the first case, the attacker has to steal a nonce valid for the session of the victim exploiting other vulnerabilities. We showed how, for example, this can be done by exploiting Web Cache Deception vulnerabilities or, in specific conditions, making cross-site requests. If instead the same value is reused as a nonce for arbitrary sessions on a website, the attacker can obtain a valid nonce simply by visiting the website. This type of nonce reuse is practically the same as enabling all inline scripts with the unsafe-inline directive. To conclude, reusing the same nonce value is a dangerous behaviour by websites that can effectively hinder the protection offered by the CSP from the exploitation of XSS vulnerabilities. Reusing the same nonce is in some cases the same as allowing all scripts inline, in others, it is a severe relaxation of policy with a dramatic reduction in the protection offered. Implementing a proper nonce-based policy is a complex and costly task, but it is the only way a website using it can fully protect itself against XSS.

Acknowledgements. This work has been partially supported by the EU Horizon project DUCA (GA 101086308) and CrossCon (GA 101070537). Views and opinions expressed are however those of the author(s) only and do not necessarily reflect those of the European Union or CINEA. Neither the European Union nor the granting authority can be held responsible for them.

References

1. Calzavara, S., Rabitti, A., Bugliesi, M.: Content security problems? evaluating the effectiveness of content security policy in the wild. In: Proceedings of the 2016 ACM SIGSAC Conference on Computer and Communications Security, pp. 1365–1375. CCS '16, Association for Computing Machinery, New York, NY, USA (2016). https://doi.org/10.1145/2976749.2978338
2. Calzavara, S., Rabitti, A., Bugliesi, M.: CCSP: Controlled relaxation of content security policies by runtime policy composition. In: 26th USENIX Security Symposium (USENIX Security 17), pp. 695–712. USENIX Association, Vancouver, BC (2017). https://www.usenix.org/conference/usenixsecurity17/technical-sessions/presentation/calzavara
3. Calzavara, S., Rabitti, A., Bugliesi, M.: Semantics-based analysis of content security policy deployment. ACM Trans. Web 12(2) (2018). https://doi.org/10.1145/3149408
4. CloudFront, A.: Understanding the cache key (2023). https://docs.aws.amazon.com/AmazonCloudFront/latest/DeveloperGuide/understanding-the-cache-key.html
5. Doupé, A., Cui, W., Jakubowski, M.H., Peinado, M., Kruegel, C., Vigna, G.: Deacota: toward preventing server-side xss via automatic code and data separation. In: Proceedings of the 2013 ACM SIGSAC Conference on Computer & Communications Security. p. 1205–1216. CCS '13, Association for Computing Machinery, New York, NY, USA (2013). https://doi.org/10.1145/2508859.2516708
6. Hausknecht, D., Magazinius, J., Sabelfeld, A.: May I? - content security policy endorsement for browser extensions. In: Almgren, M., Gulisano, V., Maggi, F. (eds.) DIMVA 2015. LNCS, vol. 9148, pp. 261–281. Springer, Cham (2015). https://doi.org/10.1007/978-3-319-20550-2_14
7. Johns, M.: Script-templates for the content security policy. J. Inf. Secur. Appl. 19(3), 209–223 (2014). https://doi.org/10.1016/j.jisa.2014.03.007
8. Kerschbaumer., C., Stamm., S., Brunthaler., S.: Injecting CSP for fun and security. In: Proceedings of the 2nd International Conference on Information Systems Security and Privacy - ICISSP, pp. 15–25. INSTICC, SciTePress, Online (2016). https://doi.org/10.5220/0005650100150025
9. Lekies, S., Kotowicz, K., Groß, S., Vela Nava, E.A., Johns, M.: Code-reuse attacks for the web: breaking cross-site scripting mitigations via script gadgets. In: Proceedings of the 2017 ACM SIGSAC Conference on Computer and Communications Security, pp. 1709–1723. CCS '17, Association for Computing Machinery, New York, NY, USA (2017). https://doi.org/10.1145/3133956.3134091
10. Mirheidari, S.A., Golinelli, M., Onarlioglu, K., Kirda, E., Crispo, B.: Web cache deception escalates! In: 31st USENIX Security Symposium (USENIX Security 22), pp. 179–196. USENIX Association, Boston, MA (2022). https://www.usenix.org/conference/usenixsecurity22/presentation/mirheidari
11. Needham, R.M., Schroeder, M.D.: Using encryption for authentication in large networks of computers. Commun. ACM 21(12), 993–999 (1978). https://doi.org/10.1145/359657.359659
12. OWASP: Cross Site Scripting Prevention Cheat Sheet. https://cheatsheetseries.owasp.org/cheatsheets/Cross_Site_Scripting_Prevention_Cheat_Sheet.html

474   M. Golinelli et al.

13. Pan, X., Cao, Y., Liu, S., Zhou, Y., Chen, Y., Zhou, T.: CSPAutoGen: black-box enforcement of content security policy upon real-world websites. In: Proceedings of the 2016 ACM SIGSAC Conference on Computer and Communications Security, pp. 653–665. CCS '16, Association for Computing Machinery, New York, NY, USA (2016). https://doi.org/10.1145/2976749.2978384
14. Patil, K., Frederik, B.: A measurement study of the content security policy on real-world applications. Int. J. Netw. Secur. **18**, 383–392 (2016)
15. Pochat, V.L., Goethem, T.V., Tajalizadehkhoob, S., Korczynski, M., Joosen, W.: Tranco: a research-oriented top sites ranking hardened against manipulation. In: Proceedings 2019 Network and Distributed System Security Symposium. Internet Society (2019). https://doi.org/10.14722/ndss.2019.23386
16. Roth, S., Barron, T., Calzavara, S., Nikiforakis, N., Stock, B.: Complex security policy? A longitudinal analysis of deployed content security policies. In: Proceedings of the 27th Network and Distributed System Security Symposium (2020)
17. Roth, S., Gröber, L., Backes, M., Krombholz, K., Stock, B.: 12 Angry developers - a qualitative study on developers' struggles with CSP. In: Proceedings of the 2021 ACM SIGSAC Conference on Computer and Communications Security, pp. 3085–3103. CCS '21, Association for Computing Machinery, New York, NY, USA (2021). https://doi.org/10.1145/3460120.3484780
18. Some, D.F., Bielova, N., Rezk, T.: On the content security policy violations due to the same-origin policy. In: Proceedings of the 26th International Conference on World Wide Web, pp. 877–886. WWW '17, International World Wide Web Conferences Steering Committee, Republic and Canton of Geneva, CHE (2017). https://doi.org/10.1145/3038912.3052634
19. Stamm, S., Sterne, B., Markham, G.: Reining in the web with content security policy. In: Proceedings of the 19th International Conference on World Wide Web, pp. 921–930. WWW '10, Association for Computing Machinery, New York, NY, USA (2010). https://doi.org/10.1145/1772690.1772784
20. Steffens, M., Musch, M., Johns, M., Stock, B.: Who's hosting the block party? Studying third-party blockage of CSP and SRI. In: Network and Distributed System Security Symposium (2021)
21. Trampert, L., Stock, B., Roth, S.: Honey, I cached our security tokens re-usage of security tokens in the wild. RAID '23 (2023). https://swag.cispa.saarland/papers/trampert2023honey.pdf
22. Van Acker, S., Hausknecht, D., Sabelfeld, A.: Data exfiltration in the face of CSP. In: Proceedings of the 11th ACM on Asia Conference on Computer and Communications Security, pp. 853–864. ASIA CCS '16, Association for Computing Machinery, New York, NY, USA (2016). https://doi.org/10.1145/2897845.2897899
23. Veditz, D., Barth, A., West, M.: Content security policy level 2. W3C recommendation, W3C (2016). https://www.w3.org/TR/2016/REC-CSP2-20161215/
24. Weichselbaum, L., Spagnuolo, M., Lekies, S., Janc, A.: CSP is dead, long live CSP! on the insecurity of whitelists and the future of content security policy. In: Proceedings of the 2016 ACM SIGSAC Conference on Computer and Communications Security, pp. 1376–1387. CCS '16, Association for Computing Machinery, New York, NY, USA (2016). https://doi.org/10.1145/2976749.2978363

25. Weissbacher, M., Lauinger, T., Robertson, W.: Why is CSP failing? trends and challenges in CSP adoption. In: Stavrou, A., Bos, H., Portokalidis, G. (eds.) Research in Attacks, Intrusions and Defenses, pp. 212–233. Springer International Publishing, Cham (2014). https://doi.org/10.1007/978-3-319-11379-1_11
26. West, M., Sartori, A.: Content security policy level 3. W3C working draft, W3C (2023). https://www.w3.org/TR/2023/WD-CSP3-20230220/

TAURIN 2023

TAURIN 2023 Preface

Welcome to the proceedings of the TAURIN 2023 workshop. TAURIN is dedicated to fostering a Responsible Internet, characterized by transparency, accountability, and user controllability. This year's workshop continues to build on these foundational principles, aiming to propel the community forward in assessing and enhancing the feasibility, status, utility, and value of a Responsible Internet.

Our vision for TAURIN is to create a vibrant, interactive community where security research thrives through collaboration and open exchange of ideas. We believe in a workshop format that encourages deep interaction among participants, fostering an environment where fresh, inspiring ideas are shared, and new research collaborations are born. The past two years have seen TAURIN evolve into a dynamic platform where industry professionals, particularly from cloud services, engage in meaningful dialogue with academic researchers. This synergy has been instrumental in advancing our understanding of the Internet's CAT (Controllability, Accountability, Transparency) properties.

In line with our commitment to a Responsible Internet, we invited both academic and practice papers that contribute to this vision. We encouraged submission of work in progress, to benefit from TAURIN's interactive nature, as well as extended abstracts. While our focus is technical, we also recognize the importance of societal dimensions such as business and governance implications, and thus, welcome contributions in these areas as well.

This year, we are proud to present three papers that were discussed at TAURIN 2023:

1. Mackowiak and Kuipers: This paper introduces a novel mechanism for improving Internet transparency, balancing the need for information sharing with the protection of internal network details. Utilizing multi-party computation, the authors present an architecture and proof-of-concept that demonstrates the practicality of their approach.
2. Nazemi et al.: This work-in-progress paper explores the intersection of the digital divide, Internet transparency, and DNS dependencies, particularly focusing on Australian government websites. The authors' analysis reveals potential disparities in DNS provisioning, highlighting the need for further investigation into the implications for availability and control.
3. Khadka et al.: Addressing the critical role of the Internet in various sectors, this extended abstract proposes a research agenda to develop an AS reputation mechanism. This mechanism aims to enhance the reliability of Internet paths and contribute to the concept of a Responsible Internet, drawing parallels with the principles of Responsible AI.

We are happy with the quality and diversity of the submissions received, enabling us to design an exceptionally interactive workshop. Our gratitude goes to all authors, speakers, reviewers, and panelists for their invaluable contributions, playing an important role in the success of TAURIN!

November 2023   Abhishta Abhishta
                                                 Giovanni Sileno

Organization

General Chairs

Christian Hesselman   SIDN Labs and University of Twente,
The Netherlands

Ralph Holz   University of Münster, Germany

Program Chairs

Abhishta Abhishta   University of Twente, The Netherlands

Giovanni Sileno   University of Amsterdam, The Netherlands

Web Chair

Siraj Anand   University of Twente, The Netherlands

Program Committee

Aaron Gember-Jacobson   Colgate University, USA

Chrysa Papagianni   University of Amsterdam, The Netherlands

Johannes Zirngibl   TU Munich, Germany

Mattijs Jonker   University of Twente, The Netherlands

Qasim Lone   RIPE, The Netherlands

Gustavo Luvizotto Cesar   University of Twente, The Netherlands

Ralph Koning   SIDN Labs, The Netherlands

Yasir Haq   University of Twente, The Netherlands

Internet Transparency Through Multi-party Computation

Paweł Maćkowiak and Fernando Kuipers[⊠]

TU Delft, Delft, The Netherlands
p.mackowiak@student.tudelft.nl, F.A.Kuipers@tudelft.nl

Abstract. The inability to check how our Internet traffic is being handled and routed poses all kinds of security and privacy risks. Yet, for the typical end-user, the Internet indeed is such a black box. In this paper, we adhere to the call for an Internet that is more transparent, and as a step forward we propose a mechanism that carefully balances the desire to share transparency information with the necessity to not expose all internal details of a network. We realize this by building on the framework of multi-party computation. Our architecture and corresponding proof-of-concept is evaluated via experiments and demonstrates the feasibility of our concept to improve Internet transparency.

1 Introduction

The Internet is of vital importance to our modern society, yet – to its end-users who generate and receive network traffic – it provides limited transparency and hardly any control regarding how user-traffic is processed.

In this paper, **transparency** relates to the level at which a user is able to see how their network traffic is being processed. Following such transparency, **control** refers to the level to which end-users are able to determine or convey how their traffic should be handled by networks.

Technologies like Virtual Reality (VR) or the Tactile Internet are extremely resource-intensive and resource-sensitive [16], which means that poor Quality-of-Service (QoS) directly affects the Quality-of-Experience (QoE). Providing QoS over multiple domains is especially challenging. In many cases, different network domains are administered by different entities, which significantly complicates the ability to collect performance measurements and data on resource allocation. As a result, supervision (and hence transparency) becomes ineffective and sometimes even impossible. In an ideal world, it would be sufficient to draw up a number of agreements between Internet Service Providers (ISPs) and domain administrators in order to ensure that sufficient resources are always available. Unfortunately, in practice and because of the complexity involved in networking, this has not been realized.

Even within a single domain, once an anomaly has been observed, further diagnostics are needed to properly understand what has happened.

S. Katsikas et al. (Eds.): ESORICS 2023 Workshops, LNCS 14399, pp. 481–495, 2024.
https://doi.org/10.1007/978-3-031-54129-2_28

This means labor-intensive network administrator intervention. Such diagnostic efforts greatly increase when multiple domains are involved, making it even harder to find the root cause of network and service problems. In some cases, this results in situations where the domains' administrators claim that other parties are responsible for a certain service disruption. Clearly, to provide end-users and domain administrators with more network-related insights poses a non-trivial challenge; a solution is needed for multi-domain supervision and transparency of network services and devices, which does not compromise the security of the involved domains nor discloses any competitive network information. This paper contributes to solving that challenge, thereby leveraging existing and novel telemetry protocols and technologies.

The structure of this paper is as follows: Sect. 2 presents our architecture along with a Proof-of-Concept (PoC) implementation. This PoC is experimentally evaluated in Sect. 3. Section 4 presents related work and we conclude in Sect. 5.

2   Design of a Multi-domain Network Telemetry System

The first part of this section will present our design goals and further considerations. Subsequently, the proposed approach will be presented, followed by the description of the Proof-of-Concept (PoC) developed by us.

2.1   Design Goals and Considerations

The main design goal is to offer users greater transparency, i.e., to give them insight into how the network traffic generated by these users and their applications is processed. In addition to this high-level goal, the objectives further detailed in the following are to propose a modular, easy-to-adopt system that will enable users to securely share transparency data.

Goals. In creating a system to provide third parties with (controlled) access to network characteristics, the question arises of how to balance the amount of information provided versus the security of the infrastructure they describe. The information provided may include details about the devices included in the infrastructure (manufacturer of the device, software version, relations with other devices in the stack), details about the processing of network traffic, such as the exact path travelled, the associated delays, and resources used, and even other types of information, such as its energy profile. However, openly disclosing such information could enable malicious actors to more easily identify vulnerable points in the network, which on its turn may significantly accelerate potential attacks on the network. While one could argue that fast-paced patching or deception technologies[1] may reduce the risk of such security incidents manifesting, this

---

[1] Deception technologies refer to cyber security defence mechanisms that facilitate early threat detection and enhanced incident response by means of deploying fake/misleading targets in the network.

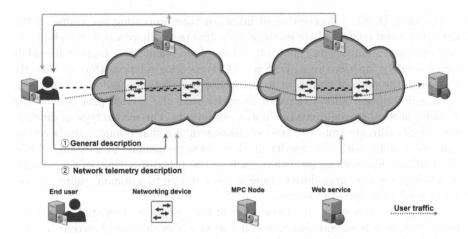

Fig. 1. High-level overview of the proposal with two types of description.

is countered by the increasing levels of automation that may significantly accelerate the occurrence and execution of potential attacks. Similarly, the provision of sensitive data describing how ISPs operate may also impact their competitiveness. It is therefore important to deploy a mechanism that allows to securely share transparency information with trusted users. It is outside the scope of this paper to indicate what information should or should not be disclosed. But we do make it an objective to allow secure information sharing as an important step towards a responsible Internet.

Furthermore, the complexity of adopting the solution has a direct impact on the desire to use it. If a better level of transparency requires operators and users to use a particular type of equipment, the pace of adoption may be too slow to create impact. An appropriate level of modularity will enable the collection of data from various types of devices, which will allow more users to benefit from such a solution.

2.2 Design Proposal

This section will describe the system design process and the accompanying decisions resulting from the goals described in the previous section. The process will be described from top to bottom, i.e., first the part of the proposal responsible for analysing and processing data between domains will be described and then the elements responsible for providing data to the top part will be discussed.

In Fig. 1, a high-level overview of the system is presented. As shown in that figure, the initiator of the data sharing process is the end-user, who can ask for two types of description. The first one is a general description summarizing how network traffic is processed by the domain, similar to security audits conducted within the Cloud Security Alliance STAR framework [11]. It may include information such as a description of services that process the traffic (e.g., DPI,

Encryption, DNS), a description of infrastructure processing the traffic at the data-plane and control-plane levels (both software and hardware), the ability to perform measurements on this traffic (data-plane telemetry), support for additional security functions (e.g., DNSSec, DoH), peering relations that are directly related to the path of traffic, or under whose jurisdiction the domain operates. Such a description allows the user to verify that the service provided by the domain meets their requirements/norms/standards. The second type of description results directly from the type of measurements that domains declare they can offer, along with the results of those measurements. As a result of this description, the user can see values such as the processing time of their traffic at different levels of granularity (from a single device to a domain summary) or, for example, the use of resources.

As can be seen from the description of the functions presented above, the user, whether it is an end-user or another service provider, could retrieve a great deal of information about the internals and functioning of the domain they are requesting transparency information from. To avoid such information leaking to malicious entities, he system could be designed using a client-server architecture model, in which the user, if necessary, would obtain encrypted data directly from the server, assuming that (s)he has appropriate permissions. One other approach could be to use a peer-to-peer model, where peers would encrypt the data as part of a protocol for exchanging information between themselves. Unfortunately, in both cases, there still is a risk that a malicious actor could impersonate an entity with privileges to obtain data, consequently, accessing shared information. This may be the case when a malicious insider [12] is involved or an active persistent threat manifests and compromises the system.

We have therefore decided to base our proposed architecture on secure multiparty computation (MPC). MPC allows to carry out a computation without the actual data being shared with the entities participating in the calculation. As a result, entities involved in the exchange will only receive the result without the possibility of gaining access to sensitive information that could jeopardise the security of many. In addition, many MPC frameworks use public key infrastructure (PKI), which allows to validate the authenticity of the data provided for the calculation. In order to successfully utilize MPC, it is necessary to design the to be calculated functions in such a way that the result of those calculations does not include/leak information about the system from which the data originated. In our architecture two function types corresponding to two description types are specified.

The first type of function (general description) is the ability to check the requirements of the user against the domain. The input data for such a function would be a list of requirements that the user has. The result of such a function can help determine whether the requirements are or will not be met, which may allow the user to decide to change the domain being used to transfer traffic or renegotiate the way it is processed.

The second type of function (network telemetry description) is to provide information on the use of the infrastructure, and also to examine measurement data that will allow to achieve the effect of end-to-end measurements without violating the iOAM standard [8]. The input data for such a function would be the measurement data, and an example of the result – as used in our Proof-of-Concept (PoC) – is the sum of all the delays or the argmax function, which may allow to determine the bottleneck.

In the context of providing data for the implementation of the MPC protocol, it is necessary to define the scope of the domain, from which descriptive and measurement data originate. In our proposal, we postulate that from the point of view of the user using the system, it is important to limit the complexity of the system by minimising communication patterns (e.g., limiting the number of involved parties). For example, if the end-user would like to obtain a description from an operator who outsources part of their operations, it would be the operator's responsibility to obtain data from the entity to which its operations are outsourced, in order to eliminate the need for the end-user to make additional contact with such entities. Therefore, we propose to define domains based on the maintenance domain hierarchy from protocol 802.1ag. The user using the system would only communicate with a domain one degree lower in the hierarchy. Furthermore, the maximum number of entities that could participate in the data exchange would be determined by the number of domains of lower level contained within the customer level.

As for the granularity of the data originating from domains, it could vary depending on the function performed, and should meet user expectations. The level of granularity could range from summaries over a whole domain to per-device information.

The next design aspect is how to transfer data to the MPC protocol. The variety of available measurement technologies and the way of obtaining data from devices significantly limits the possibility of introducing and using one standard. Therefore, in our solution, a message broker is used to resolve this difficulty, as it mediates communication among applications, minimising the mutual awareness that is necessary to exchange messages successfully. Another advantage of the message broker is that most of the open-source brokers have an API for many languages, such as Java, C/C++ or NodeJS, which allows the creation of a simple extension of the devices' functionality with the possibility of sending messages.

2.3 Proof-of-Concept Details

This section will explain how we implemented our Proof-of-Concept.

Building Blocks. Within the framework of the proposal described in the previous section, three main elements can be distinguished. These are (1) the networking device that is extended with functionality to report telemetry data to a message broker, (2) the message broker itself, and (3) the module responsible for executing a specific function using MPC and obtaining data from the message broker.

The most important of these elements is the MPC framework, which forms the core of our solution. Due to the recent interest in this field, many frameworks

Table 1. Comparison of the general-purpose MPC frameworks supporting two or more parties.

	Supported threat model	Supported data types	General support	Last major update
Frigate [7]	N/A	Fix and Arbitrary integer, Array	Documentation, Example code, Open source	8/2020
CBMC-GC [14]	N/A	Fixed integer, Float, Boolean, Array	Partial documentation, Example code, Open source	10/2018
SCALE-MAMBA [15]	Semi-honest, Malicious	Fixed/Arbitrary integer, Float, Array, Struct	Documentation, Online Support, Example code, Open source	03/2022
Wysteria [6]	Semi-honest	Fixed integer, Boolean, Struct	Partial documentation, Example code, Open source	10/2014

have been released. Available frameworks can be divided into two main groups: specialised frameworks and general-purpose frameworks. The main distinguishing features of these groups are the functions offered and their performance. In the former case, the developers focus on the realisation of a specific function and thus try to optimise the performance of their solution for said functionality [9]. The latter group aims at providing a framework that allows for any computation that can be realised within the offered features. General-purpose frameworks tend to be more regularly maintained, which in the long run also improves their performance. In addition, the protocols performed by these general-purpose frameworks are typically described using high-level languages, which benefits its ease of adoption.

In consideration of the above, a general-purpose framework was chosen for our PoC implementation. Among the available general-purpose frameworks, many differ in terms of the number of supported parties, the security model, and the general expressiveness of the high-level language that is used in the framework. The number of parties involved in the execution of these functions could be greater or equal to two. In Table 1, a comparison of the frameworks is presented.

As shown in the table, of the available frameworks, only SCALE-MAMBA provides support against the malicious threat model. According to the documentation provided by the authors, this solution has no support for logical operations (resulting from lack of Boolean variables), which should eliminate it in view of the first of the two functions described in Sect. 2.2. However, during our evaluation of that framework, we found that the appropriate use of bitwise operations allows overcoming the lack of these logical operations (e.g., a maximum value is calculated using the following expression: $x - ((x - y)\& - (x < y))$). Hence, we selected SCALE-MAMBA.

The next building block is the message broker. There are many open-source brokers available, which differ widely in characteristics. Important features that should be taken into account when choosing a broker are high availability, guaranteed delivery and delivery acknowledgement, and how developer-friendly the

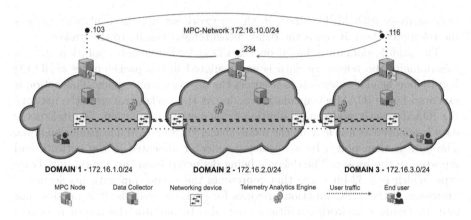

Fig. 2. Overview of the PoC implementation.

broker is. Among the brokers that meet these requirements, the following are most popular: Apache Kafka [1], RabbitMQ [2], and ZeroMQ [3]. Their popularity implies better support and ease-of-use and, consequently, matches our objective in terms of adoption potential. From these three, Apache Kafka stands out in one feature. Namely, it has the ability to reproduce messages. In the case of many other message brokers, once a message is consumed it might not be repeated. Yet, this is an important feature for validating the authenticity of the data presented for computation. Hence our choice for Apache Kafka. Moreover, Kafka uses a pull-based approach. This allows for on-demand data analysis, which increases the flexibility of our proposal. Finally, many programming languages have dedicated modules to communicate with the Kafka broker, which again aids its adoption potential.

The PoC development process was carried out in an OpenStack-based cloud platform. As can be seen in Fig. 2, the PoC consists of three independent domains and a separate network used for MPC communication. Each domain includes several telemetry-enabled network devices, a message broker, and an MPC node extended with software for providing data and supervising protocol execution. In each of the domains, during operation, the delay between switches is monitored (the delay value includes the delay due to port queuing, packet processing, and link delay). This delay is then reported and made available for multi-domain analysis. In the PoC, three types of analysis were conducted on the gathered data. These types are further discussed in the following section. In the PoC, the edge domains (i.e., 1 and 3) are the same in terms of used telemetry technology, while the middle domain differs. The edge domains consist of a Mininet network with two switches and two hosts, where the switches in the network each are an OpenFlow-enabled Open vSwitch (OvS). A RYU SDN controller manages the network. In the beginning, a flow traversing the switches is initialised, which then triggers monitoring of the link between them. The latency of the link between the switches is varying and ranges from 15 to 50 ms, as can be seen in the later analysis with MPC. Since, in this network set-up, the controller gathers the telemetry data, it sends the delay measurement results to the broker.

The middle domain is based on the FD.io VPP telemetry solution [13]. In this domain, the telemetry data is encapsulated in the packet using an iOAM hop-by-hop header extension as it enters the network name-space. This action is executed by an iOAM encapsulation node. As the packet traverses the network the iOAM transit nodes add additional telemetry information. The telemetry data is removed as it is leaving the name-space, via an iOAM decapsulation node. The data is then polled by a telemetry collector allocated in the network and reported to the broker. The delay is being deducted from the Timestamp Trace type, which is a 32-bit value that represents the timestamp with ms accuracy. Moreover, if the MPC function provides for such an analysis, it is possible not only to monitor network conditions, but also to monitor the use of resources utilised to generate network traffic (e.g., a VR application). Figures 3 and 4 display two console screenshots illustrating the MPC execution.

Figure 3 presents the initialisation of domain 1. In Fig. 4, a console view of the MPC execution is presented. The red boxes highlight the first iteration of the MPC execution. It can also be seen in the figure that only one of the three domains participating in the calculations gets the results of it. This is intended behaviour, as described in the code of the protocol execution available in Appendix A.

Fig. 3. Console view of domain 1 initialisation. The view includes three windows. Top-left represents the Mininet output, top-right the ping initialised by the end-user, while the bottom view presents the results from network telemetry.

Fig. 4. Console view of the data analysis execution. The view includes three windows that correspond to the domains. In the red box, the first analysis iteration is marked. (Color figure online)

3 Performance Analysis

3.1 Testbed

While the original PoC was developed using Docker containers, the performance analysis was conducted with Virtual Machines that provide better resource separation. This decision was made on account of the fact that SCALE-MAMBA is a framework with a high demand for resources. For a PoC this is fit for purpose, but for a real-life implementation, a scalable MPC framework should be selected or developed. For our experiments, three to eight virtual machines were used. The hardware resources allocated to each of the virtual machines were equal: four virtual cores E5-2683 of Intel Xeon CPU running at 2.1 GHz with 16384 KB cache and 8 GB of RAM. The network is organised in a star topology: the Virtual Machines are all connected to an instance of OvS that operates on the hypervisor. All hosts were connected to each other with a 15 Gbps emulated network interface (the bandwidth of the link was measured using iperf), and default link latency of approximately 0.461 ms with 0.081 ms standard deviation (link latency was measured using ping). The operating system of choice on each machine was Ubuntu 18.04.4 LTS with a 4.15 Linux Kernel. Additionally, all nodes were connected to a Network Time Protocol (NTP) Server - Stratum-1 resulting in a time synchronisation for the nodes ranging from -0.042 μs to 0.142 μs in relation to the NTP server.

3.2   Test Scenarios

Three possible scenarios for the analysis of network data are considered. These three scenarios directly correspond to the types of description presented in Sect. 2.2:

– Calculating the aggregated sum of delays measured in each domain.
– Comparing data against predetermined values.
– Determining which of the domains participating in the protocol gives a maximum value for a targeted function (argmax).

The test applications available within SCALE-MAMBA assume that while the protocol can be executed between multiple parties, only one of them is responsible for the introduction of input data. To make the functions more realistic and correspond to the situation of analysing network telemetry data, each of the domains involved in the execution of the protocol inputs their own data during the execution. This means that one iteration of the function first takes data from each of the parties and then conducts a calculation defined within it. Sample code of the third function is included in Appendix A.

In the analysis, the influence of the following parameters on the execution of the protocol was checked:

– Number of domains
– Network latency
– Transmission rate
– Parallelization of the input data

Their impact was determined based on the time to execute one protocol iteration.

The purpose of the analysis is to determine the performance and scalability of the part of the architecture responsible for performing computation on the data, but not the part responsible for the network measurements. For this reason, in order to determine the upper-bound for the performance, each of the control nodes responsible for initialising the function and providing data to the MPC protocol will produce a synthetic data point each time the protocol asks for the next value to the function. This achieves the necessary separation between the performance of the MPC framework and the performance of the telemetry technology.

3.3   Results

This section will present the results of our performance measurements. To the best of our knowledge, at the time of writing this paper, results of a similar nature have not been published. Existing results pertain to the performance of MPC frameworks and comprise calculations of a different nature, for example the multiplication of matrices, which makes direct comparison impossible.

Our results are presented as follows. First, the execution times of each of the three functions are shown, depending on the number of domains involved in the computation. Then one of the functions shows the impact of network delay, transmission rate, and parallelization of the input data.

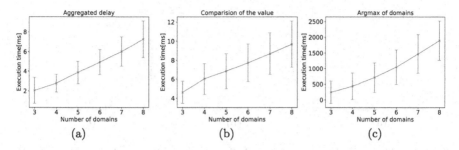

Fig. 5. The execution time in milliseconds in relation to the number of domains in case of three functions. The vertical bar represents the standard deviation.

Number of Domains. For the experiment, a range of 3 to 8 domains was used in order to check the change in execution time. The data presented in the figures were obtained by averaging the results over 10,000 consecutive iterations of the function.

The effect of increasing the number of domains on the execution time is presented in Fig. 5. For all three functions, a higher number of domains results in a greater number of inputs and, as a result, an increase in communication between the parties, and hence an increase in the execution time of a single function iteration. The relation between the number of domains and execution time seems linear, which is desirable behaviour in terms of scalability. The execution time also illustrates the potential for real-time analysis of the data. For the first two functions, the execution time of a single iteration is between 2 and 10 ms, which shows that for simple functions, MPC allows making fast calculations. For more complex functions, such as argmax determination, the execution time is in seconds. Hence, in case of a real system for telemetry data analysis based on MPC, very complex functions can be used for the quasi-real-time analysis of events.

Network Latency. The effect that network latency has on the execution time of a single iteration was tested calculating the aggregated delay. As in the previous experiment, the test results were obtained by averaging over 10,000 iterations. In order to obtain predictable values of the delay, we used the Linux tool *tc*. The latency in the test ranged from 0, which represents the initial latency on the testbed, to 50 ms. The value of the latency corresponds to the round-trip network delay between the domains. In Fig. 6a, the effect on the execution time in relation to network latency is presented. As can be observed, the execution time grows significantly with increasing network latency. An important conclusion is that the network latency plays a key role in successfully deploying the MPC-based solution.

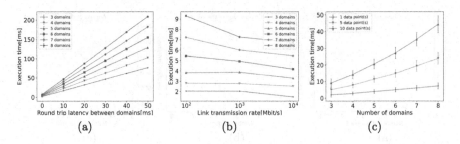

Fig. 6. (a) The execution time of a single function iteration in relation to the number of domains and network latency. (b) The execution time of a single function iteration in relation to the number of domains and transmission rate. (c) The execution time of a single function iteration in relation to the number of domains for three types of data parallelization presented on a single plot.

Transmission Rate. As in the case of network latency, the *tc* program was used to experiment with the transmission rate. The transmission rate was then verified using the *iperf* tool. The impact of the transmission rate is presented in Fig. 6b (as the standard deviation ranged from approximately 1 ms to 4 ms, we omitted it for the sake of readability). Figure 6b illustrates that the transmission rate has no significant influence on the execution time.

Parallelization of Input Data. To examine the influence of data parallelization, the function aggregating the delay over domains was modified in such a way that during a single function iteration, instead of conducting calculations on one data point, it is executed on five and ten data points. The effect of data parallelization in relation to function execution is presented in Fig. 6c and Fig. 7. As can be seen in the figures, while the parallelization of the input data increases the execution time of a single iteration, it results in more data points being analysed during that time. For example, "no parallelization" requires on average twice as much time to perform computation on 10 data points than is the case when inputting 10 data points at the same time. However, for very time-sensitive cases, this trade-off may not be possible.

4   Related Work

Improving transparency should be the result of the efforts of many network domains. This section therefore presents related work in the context of secure data sharing.

SEPIA [9] is a solution based on secure multiparty computation to enable correlation and aggregation of network events, such as rule triggering in an Intrusion Detection System. In order to create their solution, the authors proposed their own protocol within which they developed a set of basic operations. The difference between SEPIA and the solution presented in this paper is that SEPIA discusses how to use the protocol in specific scenarios, such as correlation of

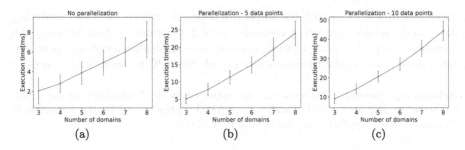

Fig. 7. The execution time of a single function iteration in relation to the number of domains for three types of data parallelization: (a) No parallelization, (b) parallelization of 5 data points, (c) parallelization of 10 data points.

events, but does not address the issue of increasing transparency from the end-user perspective.

The goal of GAIA-X [4] is to support the development aimed at achieving trustworthiness and sovereignty of digital infrastructure in Europe. This work also emphasizes the importance of transparency. Moreover, the GAIA-X requirements underscore the need for a decentralized system capable of secure data exchange. While GAIA-X creates a conceptual framework focused mainly on cloud solutions, our work proposes a modular solution for sharing descriptions and measurements originating from infrastructure processing the traffic, to users using it.

The purpose of SCION [5] is to allow the user to control the route that is selected by their traffic. This is achieved by introducing the Isolation Domain Concept, which is a logical presentation of a group of autonomous systems. The user, in the SCION architecture, is informed about possible paths, which allows him/her to choose the more appropriate one. As in SCION, our work aims to improve the lack of transparency in the current Internet structure. The difference is that we also allow the use of general descriptions not related to traffic processing, but resulting from the infrastructure used. Additionally, the implementation of the architecture presented in SCION requires agreements with the ISP(s) in case of creating Isolation Domains.

Finally, the Responsible Internet [10] is a proposal for sovereignty and transparency in the digital world. This visionary paper does not propose a concrete solution, but its concepts lie at the basis of our present work.

5   Conclusion

In this paper, we have presented a multi-domain diagnostic system as a means to improve Internet transparency. Our system leverages several technologies, like multi-party computation, software-defined networking, and iOAM, to realize an overall design and proof-of-concept implementation. Via experiments, and in a multi-domain context, the execution time of our solution was evaluated based on various factors, such as variable number of domains, various functions analyzing data, and variable network parameters used for communication between the domains. The performance analysis demonstrates the feasibility of our approach, yet it does hinge on the resource-efficiency of the MPC framework of choice.

Acknowledgements. This research was supported by the Netherlands Organisation for Scientific Research (NWO) under the CATRIN project and by the Netherlands Organization for Applied Scientific Research (TNO).

A   MPC Code Details

This appendix contains some code that is part of the Proof-of-Concept implementation.

```
4
RootCA
7
10.0.1.192
Player0.crt
10.0.1.141
Player1.crt
10.0.1.105
Player2.crt
10.0.1.175
Player3.crt
10.0.1.196
Player4.crt
10.0.1.29
Player5.crt
10.0.1.201
Player6.crt
2
9223372036855103489
1
```

Listing 1.1. A sample setup file used to configure the SCALE-MAMBA framework.

```
print_ln ( '****_START_MPC_****')
print_ln ( '****_Max_delay_****')

def maximum(a,b):
    return a - (( a - b ) & ( a < b )) #SCALE returns -1/1 when comparing values

def argmax (a,b):
    return (a[0] - (( a[0] - b[0] ) & ( a[0] < b[0] )) ,
        (( a[0] < b[0] ) & b[1] ) | (( a[0] > b[0] ) & a[1] ))

@while_do(lambda x: x < 1, 0)
def cal_max_delay(i):

    a = (sregint(sint.get_private_input_from(0)),sregint(0))
    b = (sregint(sint.get_private_input_from(1)),sregint(1))
```

```
c  =  ( s r e g i n t ( s i n t . g e t _ p r i v a t e _ i n p u t _ f r o m ( 2 ) ) , s r e g i n t ( 2 ) )

max  =  argmax ( a , b )
max  =  argmax ( max , c )

p r i n t _ l n ( ' O u t p u t : _ v a l u e _ o f _ m a x _ d e l a y _ _ i s _ c a u s e d
_ _ _ _ _ _ _ _ _ _ _ _ _ _ b y _ P l a y e r _ % s '  ,  max [ 1 ] . r e v e a l ( ) )

return  i  +  1

if  _ _ n a m e _ _  = =  ' _ _ m a i n _ _ ' :
      c a l _ m a x _ d e l a y ( 0 )
```

Listing 1.2. Code for an MPC function calculating the argmax of the presented values. This function is written for an environment of three domains.

References

1. Apache kafka documentation. https://kafka.apache.org/documentation/. Accessed 13 Aug 2020
2. Rabbitmq. https://www.rabbitmq.com/. Accessed 15 Apr 2020
3. Zeromq. http://zeromq.org/. Accessed 17 Apr 2020
4. Gaia-x. https://www.data-infrastructure.eu/GAIAX/Redaktion/EN/Publication s/gaia-x-the-european-project-kicks-of-the-next-phase.pdf (2020)
5. Perrig, A., Szalachowski, P., Reischuk, R.M., Chuat, L..: SCION: a secure Internet architecture. Springer, Cham (2017). https://doi.org/10.1007/978-3-319-67080-5
6. Rastogi, A.: Wysteria: a programming language for generic, mixed-mode multiparty computation. https://bitbucket.org/aseemr/wysteria/wiki/Home (2014). Accessed 26 Mar 2020
7. Mood, B.: Frigaterelease. https://bitbucket.org/bmood/frigaterelease/src (2020). Accessed 30 Sept 2020
8. Brockners, F., Mizrahi, T., Bhandari, S.: Data fields for in-situ OAM (07). https://tools.ietf.org/html/draft-ietf-ippm-ioam-data-10. Accessed 13 Aug 2020
9. Burkhart, M., Strasser, M., Many, D., Dimitropoulos, X.: Sepia: privacy-preserving aggregation of multi-domain network events and statistics. Network 1(101101) (2010)
10. Hesselman, C., et al.: A responsible internet to increase trust in the digital world. J. Netw. Syst. Manage. **28**(4), 882–922 (2020)
11. Cloud Security Alliance: CSA star framework. https://cloudsecurityalliance.org/star/levels/. Accessed 17 Dec 2020
12. ENISA: Insider threat. https://www.enisa.europa.eu/topics/cyber-threats/threats-and-trends/etl-review-folder/etl-2020-insider-threat (2020). Accessed 13 Aug 2023
13. Mauricio, S.J.: Further Implementation of iOAM using IPv6 in FD.io Vector Packet Processor. Master's thesis, Department of Electrical and Computer Engineering, Technische Universität Kaiserslautern (2020)
14. Buescher, N.: CBMC-GC-2. https://gitlab.com/securityengineering/CBMC-GC-2 (2018). Accessed 24 Mar 2020
15. Smart, N.: Scale-mamba software. https://homes.esat.kuleuven.be/nsmart/SCALE/. Accessed 15 Aug 2020
16. Van Den Berg, D., et al.: Challenges in haptic communications over the tactile internet. IEEE Access **5**, 23502–23518 (2017)

DNS Dependencies as an Expression of the Digital Divide: The Example of Australia

Niousha Nazemi[1]([✉]) [iD], Omid Tavallaie[1] [iD], Albert Y. Zomaya[1] [iD], and Ralph Holz[1,2] [iD]

[1] School of Computer Science, The University of Sydney, Sydney, Australia
{niousha.nazemi,omid.tavallaie,albert.zomaya,ralph.holz}@sydney.edu.au
[2] Department of Mathematics and Computer Science, University of Münster, Münster, Germany

Abstract. This paper investigates the relationship between the digital divide, Internet transparency, and DNS dependencies. The term "digital divide" refers to a gap between how different population groups can access and use digital technology, with disadvantaged groups generally having less access than others. Internet transparency refers to efforts that reveal and understand critical dependencies on the Internet. DNS is a vital service in the Internet infrastructure. It has become common for network and website operators to outsource the operation of their DNS services to a (limited) number of specialized DNS providers. Depending on the choice of provider, a network or site may achieve better or worse availability, especially under adversarial conditions (power outages, attacks, etc.). This work-in-progress paper analyzes DNS provisioning and dependencies for Australian government websites to identify a possible digital divide. More specifically, we investigate setups with respect to potential drawbacks in terms of availability or domestic control over the setup. We choose sites whose audience is primarily the indigenous population and sites that target the broader, general population. We can indeed identify differences between the DNS dependencies, in particular with respect to the use of hyperscalers, domestic vs. international providers, and dedicated government infrastructure. The implications for availability and control are more subtle and require further investigation. However, our results show that Internet measurement can detect signals of possible digital divides, and we believe this aspect should be added to the Internet transparency agenda.

Keywords: Internet transparency · Digital divide · DNS dependency · Indigenous people

1   Introduction

The concept of the digital divide has been the subject of much research and discussion over the past 20 years. The term was first introduced and defined in the mid-to-late 1990s in a series of reports titled "Falling through the net" [27–29].

S. Katsikas et al. (Eds.): ESORICS 2023 Workshops, LNCS 14399, pp. 496–509, 2024.
https://doi.org/10.1007/978-3-031-54129-2_29

The definition refers to the gap between individuals or groups who have access to and effectively use digital technologies and those who do not. This includes access to technologies such as the Internet [30]. Individuals who have access to and utilize these technologies are considered advantaged, while those who lack access or proficiency are at a disadvantage [22]. A digital divide often affects already economically disadvantaged groups. The indigenous people of Australia consist of two distinct cultural groups: the Aboriginal peoples of the Australian mainland and Tasmania and the Torres Strait Islander peoples from the seas between Queensland and Papua New Guinea. It is known that indigenous communities face challenges in accessing digital information and acquiring the necessary skills for effective utilization [23].

In recent years, the term "Internet transparency" has come into use to refer to efforts to understand how the Internet works and identify critical dependencies [15]. Internet transparency has a natural connection to research on the digital divide: differences in how Internet services are set up for different groups have implications for how these groups can access the Internet. In this sense, revealing Internet dependencies can reveal implications for the digital divide. This is also evident in core Internet infrastructure, namely the Domain Name System (DNS). Here, much centralization and consolidation have occurred [9,10]. This refers to the dominance of a limited number of large service providers who exert significant control over various aspects of the DNS. DNS employs a hierarchical configuration with multiple authoritative name servers to distribute the workload and enhance the name resolution process. However, today, much of this setup is in the hands of very few providers, and major companies such as Microsoft, Amazon, Cloudflare, and Google have significant influence over DNS provisioning. Where operators choose to outsource the operation of their DNS, the implication is that their users also rely on (a possibly limited) number of (possibly centralized) providers to access Internet services of relevance to them. It has been stated that this dependency on a few providers increases the vulnerability to potential attacks and raises concerns about the overall resilience of Internet services [4,25].

The question we ask in this paper is whether DNS dependencies impact how vulnerable groups can access Internet-based services. We focus on analyzing the impact of the digital divide on indigenous communities in Australia regarding their DNS-mediated access to government websites. Given their geographically dispersed nature, service outages can significantly impact this vulnerable group. We examine the disparities in DNS dependencies of governmental services for the indigenous and general populations. Our findings imply differences between the setups do exist: sites for the indigenous population use different cloud providers, and when they use smaller providers, these are often domestic rather than international. While sites for the general population are sometimes run on what seems to be government-owned infrastructure, we find no such setups for sites for the indigenous population.

2   Related Work

The digital divide has been investigated in numerous works, including [17,24,31]. In [31], Wang et al. investigated the digital divide through the lens of energy poverty and found that it negatively impacts the usefulness of the Internet. The extreme remoteness and isolation of indigenous communities in Australia contribute to the existing digital divide that reduces the quality of Internet connectivity and limits access to Internet services [17,24]. The phenomenon of Internet centralization [14] and consolidation has also been studied in previous work. For example, Zembruzki et al. [33,34] examined the growing concentration of Internet infrastructure and the consolidation of the DNS industry. Their findings reveal the dominance of a few key DNS providers. A study by Moura et al. [19] explored the impact of centralization on DNS traffic and identified vulnerabilities, such as TsuNAME [20], which can lead to service disruptions and traffic escalation. Concerning DNS dependencies, Deccio et al. [11–13] developed graph-based models to investigate name dependencies. Xu et al. [32] proposed a general graph model that illustrates the dependency relationships between domains and servers for name resolution.

The prevalence and impact of third-party dependencies have been analyzed by Kashaf et al. [18] and Urban et al. [26], focusing on vulnerabilities and the concentration of dependencies on third-party service providers. The vulnerability of government domains has been investigated in [16]. The authors studied the availability of DNS records for government domains across more than 190 countries, including an investigation of the increasing reliance on a single third-party DNS service provider and of vulnerabilities to hijacking due to defective delegations. The authors also found that government domains are vulnerable to DNS misconfigurations, which can lead to service degradation or even service interruption.

In this paper, we explore the implications of DNS dependencies on the different population groups of one country, namely the indigenous populations in Australia and the general population of Australia. Our focus is on the effects of differing DNS setups between the services for these groups. To the best of our knowledge, this research is the first of its kind to investigate this aspect of DNS dependencies.

3   Methodology

In the following, we explain how we created lists with the domain names of the relevant services provided by the Australian government for the indigenous populations as well as the general population, and how we retrieved their DNS records. Our objective is to create two lists: one with the domain names of Australian government websites that provide services to the general population and one with domain names of Australian government websites that provide services for the indigenous populations. To the best of our knowledge, there are no existing open-access data sets for this purpose. We adopt a desk research approach to identify the domains of interest. While we go beyond second-level domains and consider subdomains (which may have their own authoritative name servers), we use the general term "domain" or "domain name" to refer to all of these jointly. We undertook the following steps in the first quarter of 2023. To achieve two distinct sets of domain names for the indigenous and the general population, we perform the steps below in two rounds. In the first round, we add the following indigenous-related terms: *indigenous, Aboriginal people and Torres Strait Islanders,* and *first nations* to keywords to collect domain names dedicated to services for the indigenous population. In the second round, we use keywords without these terms to capture domain names for the general public.

1. *Initialization:* By *manual* investigation, we identify 16 categories of services offered by the Australian government, including healthcare, disability support, education programs, and housing support [7]. The category names serve as the primary set of keywords to facilitate the search for relevant domains and websites.
2. *Web search:* We use Google to fetch pertinent governmental websites using our seed keywords. We restrict our search to websites with the *.gov.au* suffix to guarantee we include only official government websites.
3. *Crawling* We download the top 100 Google search results and store them.
4. *Keyword extraction:* We employ a word cloud technique to extract the top five most prevalent and contextually relevant words from each relevant web page. The relevancy check is performed manually. These extracted keywords are then compared with existing keywords in the set, and new keywords are added to the set for further web search.
5. *Domain names:* We also add the domain names of the sites to our list if we identify them (manually) as relevant.
6. *Iteration:* We iterate through steps 2–5 until we can identify no additional keywords or domain names (The final keywords set is included in Table 2 and sorted based on the 16 categories).

Once the domain names are obtained, we also perform manual validation to ensure that the collected domain names align with the intended target audience. We finally obtain two lists with unique and relevant domains, each for the respective target audience (448 domains for the general population group and 54 domains for the indigenous group; the list of these domains and their DNS records are uploaded to our GitHub repository for public access [21]). We proceed to retrieve the authoritative name servers (NS) for the collected domain names by querying every authoritative NS to whom we observed a delegation. We utilize standard tools for DNS look-ups provided by the Linux operating system, as speed is no concern. To maximize coverage, we follow the delegations from the root servers, which allows us to capture the authoritative NS records. We follow the delegations until we reach the final authoritative name servers (we performed retries for several domains in Tasmania, while no such errors or timeouts were encountered in other instances). This process took place until the end of March 2023. In addition, we also utilize the WHOIS command to gather information about the associated provider for each identified name server. We create the delegation graphs to analyze the dependencies. The relationship between domains and their name servers can be categorized as either direct or indirect dependencies. A direct dependency is a domain being directly associated with its designated name servers. These associations indicate an immediate connection between a governmental website and its corresponding DNS service provider. For the analysis presented here, we focus only on these; the analysis of indirect dependencies is ongoing. We briefly revisit indirect dependencies in Sect. 5.

4   Results

We analyze the dependency patterns for domains for the general and indigenous populations across various DNS providers. Table 1 provides key statistics on the dependencies we find for various provider types. The table also presents the percentage of domains with a dependency on a single provider versus a dependency on multiple providers. We distinguish between the following kinds of DNS providers:

Leading Providers: We use the term "leading providers" to refer to prominent DNS service providers with a significant market presence and influence. These are widely known cloud providers often referred to as hyperscalers. They are often US-headquartered and relied on by a very large number of domains. Understanding dependencies on such leading providers enables us to assess the concentration of control within the DNS infrastructure of the domain we investigate. On the one hand, if many domain names on our lists are served by the same leading provider, an outage or attack may take them all offline. Similarly, one vulnerability in a hyperscaler may impact a vast number of customers. On the other hand, such leading providers also have the resources to fend off attacks and generally have specialists to deal with security issues. Outages and vulnerabilities are hence (very) low frequency–very high impact scenarios. Hyperscalers are a common choice when services must be reachable quickly across a wide geographic area. However, the fact that they are generally headquartered in another country also implies a certain amount of loss in digital sovereignty when they are chosen over a local, domestic provider. The observed leading providers in our data set are: Amazon, Microsoft, Cloudflare, Akamai, EasyDNS, Google, Microsoft, Neustar Ultra DNS, and DNS Simple.

Non-leading Providers is our term for DNS providers outside the group of the leading (hyperscaler) providers. They generally have a smaller market share and fewer cloud resources and represent a wide and diverse range of DNS service providers. Many domestic (Australian) providers fall into this category. Non-leading providers are usually unable to offer the reliability and scalability of hyperscalers. Their availability and security stance vary widely, although it is plausible that at least their availability is lower than that of a hyperscaler, and they may be less capable of fending off a sophisticated, large, or sustained attack such as one may expect from state actors.

Intra-government Providers are those where the respective governmental
sections are responsible for hosting and managing their DNS infrastructure,
including offering DNS provisioning for other government sections. We filter
the name servers with the *.gov.au suffix to find government-owned providers.

Undisclosed Providers: For about two percent of general domains, we could
not further identify the DNS providers from either the WHOIS or the domain
names of the NS records. We label them as "undisclosed".

Table 1. Dependency on third-party DNS providers for general and indigenous
domains.

Population group	General		Indigenous	
	Absolute	Relative	Absolute	Relative
Number of domains	448	100%	54	100%
Depends on...				
...leading providers	219	48.9%	29	53.7%
...non-leading providers	140	31.3%	25	46.3%
...intra-government providers	113	25.2%	0	
...single provider	412	92%	54	100%
...multiple providers	36	8%	0	0
...intra-government + 3rd party providers	19	4.2%	0	0
Undisclosed	8	1.8%	0	0

4.1 Analysis by Provider Type

Figure 3 illustrates the relationships between domains and DNS providers that
we group as "leading", "non-leading", and "intra-government" dependencies.
While some general domains have implemented a multi-provider strategy, possibly to mitigate risks associated with a single, critical dependency, the practice
is not widespread. It is particularly noteworthy that it is absent for domains for
the indigenous population.

Single-Provider Setups We first investigate how many domains rely on a
single DNS provider, which is a critical metric: outage of this provider will
make the relying services unavailable. We find that 92% of all domains for the
general population rely on a single provider. *All* of the domains for the indigenous populations do so. This implies a generally unsatisfactory state across
all government domains, but it is also a first hint that there is a difference
between the services for the two population groups.

Multi-provider Setups Having multiple DNS providers offers benefits in terms
of redundancy and resilience. In the event of a service outage or disruption from one provider, the availability of DNS services can be maintained

through the alternative provider. Inequalities in the use of multi-provider strategies hence reflect differences in access to information and online services. Figure 1 shows the distribution of domains with a multi-provider dependency for the general population (none of the indigenous websites have multiple DNS providers). We find that 20% of setups have a dependency on two distinct leading DNS providers (Amazon and Microsoft); this was observed for eight domains of the Victorian government. More than 50% of setups use a governmental provider along with a third-party DNS as an alternative server.

Use of Leading Providers Hyperscalers may offer higher availability and potentially better security than smaller providers. Approximately half of the domains for both the general and indigenous populations rely on a single leading DNS provider. Only around 2% of the domains for the general population employed *two leading* providers, with the remainder using either a second non-leading or intra-government provider. Figure 2 shows a breakdown of the leading DNS providers for our domains. For the general population, 48.9% of domains rely on leading providers, with Amazon being the most utilized provider at 21.4%. Microsoft is the second most commonly used provider at around 17%, followed by Cloudflare at 6%. Other leading providers, such as Akamai, UltraDNS, Google, DNSimple, and EasyDNS, are used in less than 5% of DNS services for the general population. Regarding domains for the indigenous population, 53.7% of them rely on leading providers. Microsoft is the most utilized provider at 31.5%, followed by Cloudflare (11.1%) and Amazon (7.4%). No other leading providers are in use for these domains. Comparing the two groups of domains, we identify a common preference for leading providers, although the preferred providers differ starkly. Cloudflare offers a free tier, which may explain this common choice in the second group of domains. There is slightly less variety in the chosen providers in the case of the domains for the indigenous population.

Use of non-leading Providers and Intra-government Providers: As we see in Fig. 3, slightly more than half of domains for the general population rely on at least one non-leading provider or an intra-government provider, with an almost equal split between the latter two. We do not observe this for the domains of the indigenous population: here, 46.3% of the domains rely on

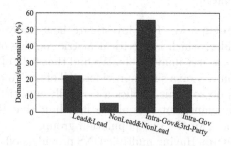

Fig. 1. Multi-DNS-provider setups. Note that no domains for the indigenous population use such a setup.

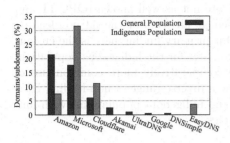

Fig. 2. Leading DNS providers.

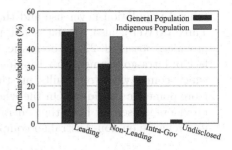

Fig. 3. DNS providers by category.

non-leading providers, and none use intra-government providers. Government-hosted providers would be required to comply with Australian standards and government regulations, and using these providers implies a certain level of coordination and collaboration. We list the government sections we observe in the domain name of the NS records in Table 3 in the Appendix. While we observe only about 15 government agencies operating name servers, we see that they serve well over 100 different domains. It seems curious that no single service for the indigenous population is among these. Figure 4 shows whether the non-leading providers are domestic or international. The fraction of domestic providers is significantly higher for both domain groups. Concerning domains for the general population, 23.4% of domains rely on local DNS providers, indicating a preference for domestic services. The percentage of the domains for the indigenous population is considerably higher (but recall that domains of this group do not use intra-government provisioning). Figure 5 breaks down the numbers for domestic DNS providers. Telstra, as Australia's largest telecommunications company by market share [8], is the most commonly used DNS provider. Macquarie Telecom is the second most utilized provider, followed by the Centre for Information Technology and Communication [2]) and WebCentral. While all previous, mostly common used providers are domestic, 14 domains for the general population rely on the US-based company Verizon. For the domains for the indigenous population, the order is similar, except for two providers that domains for the

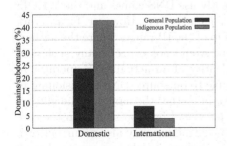

Fig. 4. Use of non-leading providers.

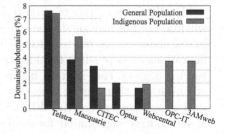

Fig. 5. Domestic providers.

general population never use and that are not as well known (OPC IT and ThreeAMWeb); also, Optus is not used at all. Out of the 33 non-leading providers observed, 22 are domestic. Our primary finding here is the curious lack of intra-government provisioning for sites for the indigenous population, which comes with (or results in) the comparatively more common use of more domestic providers. On the whole, a diverse range of non-leading DNS providers is used for both the general and indigenous populations, with limited reliance on non-Australian companies.

5   Limitations

Our study has several limitations owing to the early stage of our work.

Indirect Dependencies: Naturally, dependencies higher up the chain of DNS delegations have an impact on availability and security properties as well. Our analysis of indirect dependencies has only begun. So far, we have found several cases where a leading DNS provider is actually a delegation from a non-leading one. Understanding precisely in which cases this is problematic is the subject of ongoing work.

Longitudinal Observations: Our current study is a snapshot in time. It would be helpful to study the DNS dependencies over a more extended period to understand the dynamics of DNS provisioning.

Small Sample: There are significantly fewer domains for the indigenous population than for the general population. This is expected, but one needs to pay attention when comparing small percentages between the groups. It may also offer a partial explanation for the smaller variety of non-leading providers we find for this domain group.

Specific Focus: Our findings are specific to the Australian indigenous population and the local DNS landscape. While our study is centered on analyzing DNS dependency among Australian indigenous governmental domains compared to the general population, our methodology can be adapted for broader applications. The approach we have utilized to assess DNS dependencies is transferable to other vulnerable groups within and beyond Australia. Contextual considerations should be considered when considering the applicability of results.

Other Forms of Outsourcing: We currently use DNS names and the WHOIS to identify the operators of authoritative name servers. However, future work will also need to investigate the ownership of the IP ranges where the authoritative nameservers reside. Although one would not expect many such configurations, it is possible to hide the identity of an actual DNS operator to varying degrees. For example, it is possible to outsource DNS provisioning to organizations that hint at their existence in neither the names of the authoritative nameservers nor the WHOIS. This would be a possibility in the case of sub-contracting. Similar forms of sub-contracting may also occur between different branches of government and be hidden in what we currently call intra-government provisioning.

6 Discussion and Conclusion

We summarize our findings, discuss possible implications, and give future research directions:

Summary: In line with previous findings, we find a significant concentration of DNS services among a few providers for both domain groups: about half of the domains in each group use leading providers. Only some domains for the general population use a multi-provider setup; otherwise, this approach to increase availability and resilience is never used. The leading providers differ between the domain groups, with Amazon being more commonly used in the group of domains for the general population and Microsoft in the one for the indigenous population. Cloudflare is also much more common for the latter group. The company's free tier may be a reason, although this needs to be investigated in more detail. Domains for the indigenous population also use a smaller number of leading providers overall; but here, we need to caution that the number of domains in this group is much smaller. The possibly most interesting difference between the two domain groups can be found in the use of intra-government provisioning. The latter does not occur for domains for the indigenous population but is common for domains for the general population.

Implications: We set out to identify possible disparities in the DNS dependencies for sites for different population groups. We find evidence that dependencies for the indigenous population are indeed differently configured, and we view our evidence as indicative of different provisioning concepts being employed. However, the exact implications of this are much less clear. In particular, does this result in a tangible digital divide? It seems clear to us that follow-up measurements will be needed to decide this question. In the following, we offer some more detailed thoughts. The lack of intra-government provisioning for indigenous population domains is noteworthy, but there may be practical or legal reasons why we do not find such setups. A qualitative study could shed light on this. As single-provider setups are so common, it is too early to speak of a digital divide in terms of availability. In particular, it is unclear whether intra-government provisioning or the use of smaller domestic providers will improve availability, which can be decided with Internet measurements. We observed some lack of provider diversity among both domain groups, particularly in the case of leading providers used by domains for the indigenous population. Here, Cloudflare was also more common (possibly because of their free tier). Together with the fact that over 40% of indigenous domains use domestic DNS providers, this may indicate a desire to improve DNS resolution but an inability or unwillingness to move to the cloud. Again, a qualitative study could help illuminate this. Finally, we observe that nearly half of the domains use domestic DNS providers (non-leading or intra-governmental), across both domain groups, which means less reliance on international corporations. In this respect, the nature of the divide is different (non-leading vs. intra-governmental provisioning), but not the quantity.

Perhaps most importantly, our findings support the case for Internet transparency. More precisely, we argue that it is a worthwhile undertaking to add measurements of digital divides to the agenda, using both quantitative and qualitative methods. In addition to investigating DNS dependencies, we recognize the significance of considering other measurements that might contribute to a comprehensive assessment of the digital divide. These include availability measurements by using datasets such as Common Crawl [3] or OONI (Open Observatory of Network Interference) [5], routing measurements, and measuring the use of web content management systems. Data from active DNS measurement (OpenINTEL [6]), passive DNS observation, or data from CT (Certificate Transparency) [1] may also be helpful data sets. In the future, we need to qualitatively assess the criticality of services for different population groups and explore the correlation between popularity and criticality. However, it is important to note that the statistical significance of popularity in the case of less popular domains remains unclear. Based on our preliminary results, we have started investigating more in-depth, beginning with indirect dependencies. We plan to continue with more detailed investigations of the various setups to understand possible reasons and weaknesses. This will include long-time monitoring of availability and changes in providers. We will also analyze which services tend to be supported by intra-government provisioning. Finally, we plan to extend our analysis to other countries around the globe.

Appendix

Table 2. Keywords set.

Healthcare	Disability support	Family support
Preventive care	Rehabilitation services	Child support
Chronic conditions	Assistive technology	Childhood Development
Specialist care	Improve accessibility	Childcare
Telehealth services	Promote social inclusion	Youth support
Vaccination	Community program	Adolescent support
Medical services	promote independence	Violence prevention
		Foster care
		Residential care
Education	**Housing**	**Community development**
training programs	homelessness support	Individuals support
School programs	Affordable housing	Cultural maintenance
Vocational training	Appropriate housing	Social connection
Adult education	Home-ownership	
Disaster relief	**Economic development**	**Women support**
Emergency services	Employment services	Women health
Rebuilding homes	Job training	Accommodation service
Infrastructure improvement	Job seeking	Support groups
Temporary accommodation	Financial assistance	Employment opportunities
Distribution of food	Financial stability	Domestic violence
Retirement Support	**Cultural preservation**	**Mental health**
Age pension	Language program	Well-being
Superannuation savings	Traditional arts and crafts	Counselling services
Legal services	**Environmental programs**	**Business support**
Legal aid	Land management	Business training
Resolving disputes	Protect sacred sites	Business mentoring
Justice	Traditional lands	Entrepreneurship
Family law	Natural resources	Procurement policies
Criminal law	Preserve cultural heritage	Provide funding
		Business networking
Addiction support		
Substance abuse		
Treatment service		

Table 3. List of Australian government services providing DNS services.

Government of Australian Capital Territory (Department of Education and Training)
Australian Antarctic Division
APRA (Australian Prudential Regulation Authority)
Department of Defence
Department of Education, Skills, and Employment
Department of Social Services, Government of New South Wales (Department of Customer Service)
Government of Queensland (Department of Housing and Public Works)
Government of South Australia (Department of Premier and Cabinet)
Tasmania Department of Premier and Cabinet
Government of Victoria (Department of Premier and Cabinet)
Government of Western Australia (Department of Premier and Cabinet)
National Library of Australia
New South Wales Department of Education and Communities
Queensland Department of Education and Training
Services Australia

References

1. Certificate Transparency. https://certificate.transparency.dev/ (2023). Accessed 17 Aug 2023
2. Citec. https://services.citec.com.au/about/ (2023). Accessed 26 Mar 2023
3. Common Crawl. https://commoncrawl.org/ (2023). Accessed 17 Aug 2023
4. Global internet report 2019: consolidation in the internet economy. https://www.internetsociety.org/resources/doc/2019/global-internet-report-2019 (2023). Accessed 13 Jun 2023
5. OONI Data. https://ooni.org/data/ (2023). Accessed 17 Aug 2023
6. Openintel. https://openintel.nl (2023). Accessed 29 May 2023
7. Services Australia. https://www.servicesaustralia.gov.au (2023). Accessed 1 Jun 2023
8. Telstra group limited. https://en.wikipedia.org/wiki/Telstra (2023). Accessed 26 Mar 2023
9. Arkko, J.: Centralised architectures in internet infrastructure. Internet-Draft draft-arkko-arch-infrastructure-centralisation-00, Internet Engineering Task Force (2019). https://datatracker.ietf.org/doc/draft-arkko-arch-infrastructure-centralisation/00/
10. Arkko, J., et al.: Considerations on internet consolidation and the internet architecture. Internet draft, IETF (2019). https://tools.ietf.org/html/draft-arkko-iab-internet-consolidation-02
11. Deccio, C., Chen, C.C., Mohapatra, P., Sedayao, J., Kant, K.: Quality of name resolution in the domain name system. In: 2009 17th IEEE International Conference on Network Protocols, pp. 113–122. IEEE (2009)
12. Deccio, C., Sedayao, J., Kant, K., Mohapatra, P.: Measuring availability in the domain name system. In: 2010 Proceedings IEEE INFOCOM, pp. 1–5. IEEE (2010)
13. Deccio, C., Sedayao, J., Kant, K., Mohapatra, P.: Quantifying dns namespace influence. Comput. Netw. **56**(2), 780–794 (2012)

14. Fiebig, T., et al.: Heads in the clouds? measuring universities' migration to public clouds: implications for privacy & academic freedom. In: Proceedings on Privacy Enhancing Technologies Symposium, vol. 2023 (2022)

15. Hesselman, C., et al.: A responsible internet to increase trust in the digital world. J. Netw. Syst. Manage. **28**(4) (2020)

16. Houser, R., Hao, S., Cotton, C., Wang, H.: A comprehensive, longitudinal study of government DNS deployment at global scale. In: 2022 52nd Annual IEEE/IFIP International Conference on Dependable Systems and Networks (DSN), pp. 193–204. IEEE (2022)

17. Intahchomphoo, C.: Indigenous peoples, social media, and the digital divide: a systematic literature review. Am. Indian Cult. Res. J. **42**(4), 85–111 (2018)

18. Kashaf, A., Dou, J., Belova, M., Apostolaki, M., Agarwal, Y., Sekar, V.: A first look at third-party service dependencies of web services in Africa. In: Passive and Active Measurement: 24th International Conference, PAM 2023, Virtual Event, March 21–23, 2023, Proceedings, pp. 595–622. Springer, Cham (2023). https://doi.org/10.1007/978-3-031-28486-1_25

19. Moura, G.C.M., Castro, S., Hardaker, W., Wullink, M., Hesselman, C.: Clouding up the internet: how centralized is DNS traffic becoming? In: Proceedings of the ACM Internet Measurement Conference (IMC '20), pp. 42–49. Association for Computing Machinery, New York, NY, USA (2020). https://doi.org/10.1145/3419394.3423625

20. Moura, G.C., Castro, S., Heidemann, J., Hardaker, W.: TsuNAME: exploiting misconfiguration and vulnerability to DDoS DNS. In: Proceedings of the 21st ACM Internet Measurement Conference, pp. 398–418 (2021)

21. Nazemi, N., Tavallaie, O., Zomaya, Y.A., Holz, R.: AUSGovDomains GitHub Repository. https://github.sydney.edu.au/nnaz6977/AUSGovDomains

22. Rogers, E.M.: The digital divide. Convergence **7**(4), 96–111 (2001)

23. Samaras, K.: Indigenous Australians and the 'digital divide'. Int. J. Libr. Inf. Stud. **55**(2–3), 84–95 (2005)

24. Singleton, G., Rola-Rubzen, M.F., Muir, K., Muir, D., McGregor, M.: Youth empowerment and information and communication technologies: A case study of a remote Australian aboriginal community. GeoJournal **74**, 403–413 (2009)

25. The Register: AWS DNS DDoS attack overwhelmed its servers for hours. https://www.theregister.com/2019/10/22/aws_dns_ddos (2019). Accessed 7 Apr 2023

26. Urban, T., Degeling, M., Holz, T., Pohlmann, N.: Beyond the front page: measuring third party dynamics in the field. In: Proceedings of The Web Conference 2020, pp. 1275–1286 (2020)

27. U.S. Department of commerce: falling through the net: a survey of the have nots in rural and urban America (1995). https://ntia.gov/page/falling-through-net-survey-have-nots-rural-and-urban-america

28. U.S. Department of commerce: falling through the net ii: new data on the digital divide (1998). https://ntia.gov/page/falling-through-net-ii-new-data-digital-divide

29. U.S. Department of Commerce: falling through the net: defining the digital divide (1999). https://ntia.gov/report/1999/falling-through-net-defining-digital-divide

30. Van Dijk, J.: The digital divide. John Wiley & Sons (2020)

31. Wang, S., Cao, A., Wang, G., Xiao, Y.: The impact of energy poverty on the digital divide: the mediating effect of depression and internet perception. Technol. Soc. **68**, 101884 (2022)

32. Xu, H., Zhang, Z., Yan, J., Chai, T.: Name dependency and domain name resolution risk assessment. IEEE Trans. Netw. Serv. Manage. **19**(3), 3413–3424 (2022)

33. Zembruzki, L., Jacobs, A.S., Granville, L.Z.: On the consolidation of the internet domain name system. In: GLOBECOM 2022–2022 IEEE Global Communications Conference, pp. 2122–2127. IEEE (2022)
34. Zembruzki, L., Sommese, R., Granville, L.Z., Jacobs, A.S., Jonker, M., Moura, G.C.: Hosting industry centralization and consolidation. In: NOMS 2022–2022 IEEE/IFIP Network Operations and Management Symposium, pp. 1–9. IEEE (2022)

Towards Security Transparency of Autonomous Systems on the Internet

Shyam Krishna Khadka[1(✉)], Ralph Holz[1,2], and Cristian Hesselman[1,3]

[1] University of Twente, Drienerlolaan 5, 7522, NB Enschede, Netherlands
{s.k.khadka,r.holz,c.e.w.hesselman}@utwente.nl
[2] University of Münster, Schlosspl. 2, 48149 Münster, Germany
[3] SIDN Labs, Meander 501, 6825, MD Arnhem, Netherlands

1 Introduction

The use of the Internet is not just limited to daily activities such as communication, entertainment, and shopping, but many critical services including finance, healthcare, and the modern versions of infrastructures (e.g., power grids, transportation systems, water, oil, and gas pipelines) [19] increasingly use the Internet for their operations as well. This makes Internet paths a factor that must be considered a part of supply chain security.

In the following, we use the term "Internet path" to refer to a sequence of ASes that appear in the "AS path" attribute in BGP. The problem we face when considering Internet paths as part of the supply chain is that the Internet is a "black box": it offers no real insight into the security aspects of Internet paths and no control for relying parties to influence which paths are chosen in routing.

In this work, we propose a research agenda to investigate *how to build an AS reputation mechanism that could be used for measuring the reliability of Internet paths and selecting paths based on this*. Transparency of AS reputation and Internet path selection form an extension to the current BGP-based Internet, as envisioned for the "Responsible Internet" [8], a concept inspired by the notion of "Responsible AI", which provides more insight into the inner workings of AI systems [7]. We assume the deployment of AS security transparency and path selection will occur through so-called "trust zones" [4], which are coalitions of ASes that collaboratively implement security policies.

In this extended abstract, we discuss four research questions (RQ1-RQ4) that we have identified and sketch how we aim to address them. The objective of our abstract is to facilitate and inspire discussion at the TAURIN 2023 workshop.

2 RQ1: What May Be the Security Attributes of an AS?

Enterprises and AS operators may prefer to select ASes on Internet paths that are not linked to malicious or suspicious incidents, simply because they view such paths as safer and more reliable [19]. We aim to create a reputation mechanism for this purpose. To this end, we collect data and measure attributes linked to incidents.

© The Author(s), under exclusive license to Springer Nature Switzerland AG 2024
S. Katsikas et al. (Eds.): ESORICS 2023 Workshops, LNCS 14399, pp. 510–513, 2024.
https://doi.org/10.1007/978-3-031-54129-2_30

Approach: We will begin with the following datasets to understand which ASes that occur on Internet paths have been involved in incidents or may lack in security. As some data sources are snapshots, we also explore measurement methods that can be carried out in a sustained way.

(a) We identify ASes that are misbehaving or misconfigured, as identifiable in the following sources.
  - Abuse: phishing, spamming, malware distribution, botnet command & control hosting. Datasets: abuse feeds [1,5,13,21], OpenINTEL [17];
  - Routing: route leaks, route hijacks [23]. Datasets: MANRS observatory [12], Internet Health Report [9], NANOG mailing list [14];
(b) Routing and traffic security measures implemented: Route filtering, Route Origin Authorization (ROA), Route Origin Validation(ROV), protection against DDoS and spoofing, security frameworks in use. Datasets: RPKI repository [18], CAIDA spoofer [22], network telescope data [3, 13];;
(c) Security status of hardware and software infrastructures used by AS operator, e.g., border routers. Datasets: NVD [16], Shodan [20], Censys [3];

3 RQ2: How to Rank ASes in Terms of Reputation?

Knowing which ASes rank higher regarding their reputation will help AS operators choose or avoid particular ASes, assuming they can choose between different Internet paths.

Approach: We will explore the use of Multi-Criteria Decision Analysis (MCDA) [10] where operators will provide their preferences for the values of the security attributes that we explored in RQ1. We will also consider taking an expert opinions and aim to make the mechanisms output scores in real-time.

4 RQ3: How to Choose Paths Based on ASes' Reputations?

The AS operator should be able to choose/avoid particular ASes on their paths based on our work of RQ2, particularly within a trust zone.

Approach: We will set up a simulated testbed (e.g., using Mininet or BIRD BGP [2]) to explore different path selection/avoidance techniques, like using BGP community attributes, source-based routing, and traffic engineering techniques within a trust zone. We will study how this might affect the operational management of ASes.

5 RQ4: What May Be a Way to Verify a Path?

Users should be able to verify if a data path is the one they chose based on the methods from RQ3.

Approach: We will explore cryptographic principles [11,15] as well as the concept of "BGP lies" [6] and reverse traceroute [24].

Acknowledgements. This work was conducted as part of the project CATRIN (https://www.catrin.nl), which received funding from the Dutch Research Council (NWO).

References

1. Abuse.ch — Fighting malware and botnets. https://abuse.ch. Accessed 10 July 2023
2. The BIRD Internet Routing Daemon Project. https://bird.network.cz/. Accessed 09 July 2023
3. Exposure Management and Threat Hunting Solutions — Censys. https://censys. io/. Accessed 05 July 2023
4. Clark, D., Claffy, K.: Trust zones: a path to a more secure internet infrastructure. J. Inf. Policy **11**, 26–62 (2021). https://doi.org/10.2139/ssrn.3746071
5. Cybercrime Information Center. https://cybercrimeinfocenter.squarespace.com/. Accessed 05 July 2023
6. Del Fiore, J.M.: Detecting hidden broken pieces of the Internet: BGP lies, forwarding detours and failed IXPs. Ph.D. thesis, Université de Strasbourg (2021)
7. Dignum, V.: Responsible artificial intelligence: designing AI for human values. ICT Discov. ITU J. (2017)
8. Hesselman, C., et al.: A responsible internet to increase trust in the digital world. J. Netw. Syst. Manage. **28**, 882–922 (2020). https://doi.org/10.1007/s10922-020-09564-7
9. Internet Health Report — Monitoring networks health. https://ihr.iijlab.net/ihr/en-us. Accessed 02 July 2023
10. Ishizaka, A., Nemery, P.: Multi-criteria decision analysis: methods and software. John Wiley & Sons (2013)
11. Kim, T.H.J., Basescu, C., Jia, L., Lee, S.B., Hu, Y.C., Perrig, A.: Lightweight source authentication and path validation. In: Proceedings of the 2014 ACM Conference on SIGCOMM, pp. 271–282 (2014). https://doi.org/10.1145/2740070.2626323
12. MANRS Observatory. https://observatory.manrs.org/. Accessed 12 July 2023
13. MISP Default Feeds. https://www.misp-project.org/feeds/. Accessed 05 July 2023
14. Welcome to Mailman.NANOG. Org. https://mailman.nanog.org/mailman/listinfo. Accessed 03 July 2023
15. Naous, J., Walfish, M., Nicolosi, A., Mazieres, D., Miller, M., Seehra, A.: Verifying and enforcing network paths with ICING. In: Proceedings of the Seventh Conference on Emerging Networking Experiments and Technologies, pp. 1–12 (2011). https://doi.org/10.1145/2079296.2079326
16. NIST: National Vulnerability Database. https://nvd.nist.gov/. Accessed 03 July 2023
17. OpenINTEL: active DNS measurement project. https://openintel.nl/. Accessed 05 July 2023
18. FTP repos of RPKI in RIPE. https://ftp.ripe.net/rpki/. Accessed 03 July 2023
19. Schulzrinne, H.: Networking: the newest civil engineering challenge (2022). https://www.youtube.com/watch?v=5lvXIqI_mQ4, SIGCOMM Lifetime Achievement Award keynote, SIGCOMM, Amsterdam (2022)
20. Shodan Search Engine. https://www.shodan.io/. Accessed 05 July 2023
21. DROP - Don't Route or Peer lists - The Spamhaus Project. https://www.spamhaus.org/drop/. Accessed 01 July 2023

22. Spoofer - CAIDA, https://www.caida.org/projects/spoofer/, Last accessed 03-July-2023
23. Sriram, K., Montgomery, D., McPherson, D.R., Osterweil, E., Dickson, B.: Problem definition and classification of BGP Route Leaks. RFC 7908 (2016). https://doi.org/10.17487/RFC7908, https://www.rfc-editor.org/info/rfc7908
24. Vermeulen, K., Gurmericliler, E., Cunha, Í., Choffnes, D., Katz-Bassett, E.: Internet scale reverse traceroute. In: Proceedings of the 22nd ACM Internet Measurement Conference, pp. 694–715 (2022). https://doi.org/10.1145/3517745.3561422

PriST-AI 2023

PriST-AI 2023 Preface

Welcome to the proceedings of the International Workshop on Private, Secure, and Trustworthy AI (PriST-AI), co-located with ESORICS 2023. This workshop serves as a platform for researchers and professionals from academia and industry to converge and discuss the crucial intersection of Artificial Intelligence (AI) with the imperatives of privacy, security, and trustworthiness. In this preface, we provide a brief introduction to the volume and offer insights into the conference and workshop.

The papers included in this volume have undergone a rigorous peer review process, ensuring the quality and relevance of the research presented. This review process followed a double-blind method, with each paper receiving three reviews on average. Eight papers were submitted to the first round of this workshop and four of these contributions were accepted for publication.

The influence of AI is pervasive, yet concerns about data security, bias, reliability, and privacy violations loom large, affecting not only the efficacy of AI solutions but also the very fabric of society. The aim of PriST-AI is to address these critical concerns. In these proceedings, you will find research papers and discussions that delve into privacy-preserving machine learning, deep learning, and federated learning, as well as topics covering trustworthy machine learning.

We extend our gratitude to the authors for their valuable contributions and to the diligent reviewers who rigorously assessed the submissions. Their collective efforts have shaped this compilation of cutting-edge research. We hope that this publication fosters deeper understanding and inspires further research in the realm of Private, Secure, and Trustworthy AI.

Mina Alishahi

Organization

General Chair

Mina Alishahi   Open Universiteit, The Netherlands

Program Committee

Nathalie Baracaldo   IBM, USA
Tooska Daragahi   Manchester Metropolitan University, UK
Yang Li   Northwestern Polytechnical University,
                                    China
Milan Lopuhaä-Zwakenberg   University of Twente, The Netherlands
Hugo Jonker   Open Universiteit, The Netherlands
Davide Maiorca   Università degli studi di Cagliari, Italy
Vahideh Moghtadaiee   Shahid Beheshti University, Iran
Daniel Takabi   Georgia State University, USA
Ehsan Toreini   Surrey University, UK
Fatih Turkmen   University of Groningen, The Netherlands

Privacy-Preserving Object Recognition with Explainability in Smart Systems

Wisam Abbasi$^{(\boxtimes)}$, Paolo Mori , and Andrea Saracino

Istituto di Informatica e Telematica, Consiglio Nazionale delle Ricerche, Pisa, Italy
{wesam.alabbasi,paolo.mori,andrea.saracino}@iit.cnr.it

Abstract. This paper proposes an approach for privacy-preserving object recognition that considers both data privacy protection at different levels and data analysis accuracy while also providing decision explanations. To achieve this, the proposed approach uses multiple degrees of privacy and investigates their impact on the analysis accuracy and the heatmaps generated by the explainability mechanism. The privacy parameter of the privacy-preserving mechanism is regulated for object recognition algorithms and the results' accuracy is measured accordingly. The methodology uses original images of objects and adds noise to them using Gaussian filter blurring or differential privacy to protect privacy, with three degrees of privacy applied. Object recognition is performed on the original and perturbed images, and the results are compared. To validate our approach, experiments were conducted on 31 categories of real-world object images from the Open Images Dataset V4 using three object recognition models (VGG16, VGG19, and ResNet50). The Grad-CAM mechanism is used to explain the model decisions. The results demonstrate the approach's effectiveness in protecting data privacy while maintaining data analysis accuracy with the differential privacy mechanism, and providing decision meaningful explanations.

Keywords: Data Privacy · Explainable AI · Object Recognition · Privacy-Preserving Data Analysis · Trustworthy AI

1 Introduction

Object recognition in smart environments is rapidly gaining wide attention from researchers, where computer vision and machine learning techniques are used to automatically detect and identify objects within environments. Object recognition has a variety of applications in smart environments such as smart homes, where it can be used for security and surveillance purposes and is critical to the functioning of many smart devices, including security cameras and smart lighting systems. Security cameras can be used to detect and alert home residents of potential intruders and threats, in addition to children monitoring, they can also be used to monitor the health and safety of elderly or disabled individuals with alerts in case of problems.

© The Author(s), under exclusive license to Springer Nature Switzerland AG 2024
S. Katsikas et al. (Eds.): ESORICS 2023 Workshops, LNCS 14399, pp. 519–534, 2024.
https://doi.org/10.1007/978-3-031-54129-2_31

Object recognition in smart environments, particularly in private settings such as homes and workplaces, raises significant privacy concerns. The collection of large amounts of data by smart devices can potentially include sensitive and private information. As a matter of fact, in some cases, it may be necessary to protect some confidential details present in an image, while still being able to analyze the overall image for object detection and recognition. For example, in the case of recognizing objects in a house, it may be necessary to protect the privacy of certain objects, such as personal items, while still being able to analyze the scene for other purposes, such as identifying furniture or layout. The privacy-preserving techniques can be applied in a way that preserves the overall structure of the image, while removing or obfuscating certain features or details that need to be protected. If this data are sent to a remote server for elaboration and/or is accessed by unauthorized individuals, it can result in serious privacy breaches. Hence, to address such privacy concerns, it is crucial to implement privacy-preserving techniques, including encryption, data anonymization, and perturbation, as well as restricting access to data to authorized individuals only.

Object recognition systems face a significant challenge in the lack of decision and model explainability, which leads to reduced trust, limitations in reliability, and difficulty in debugging and traceability. This is particularly important when detecting and repairing errors or biases in the system or training data. The absence of decision explanations in machine learning models can be due to the complexity of the model and the size or diversity of the used dataset. Explainability provides the capability of understanding why a particular object was recognized and how the system derived the prediction. To address the explainability limitation, several methods have been proposed such as the use of visualization techniques like Gradient-weighted Class Activation Mapping(Grad-CAM), which uses the weighted gradients of the target object to produce a coarse localization map allowing the user to see the regions of the highest importance in the image for predicting the target object [29]. Another approach is the use of saliency maps like in the SmoothGrad method, which highlights the features of the most contribution to the model decision [31].

The focus of our study is a situation where smart environment images are sent to a secure remote server that is not trusted for object recognition data analytics, i.e. follows an honest but curious attack model. The possibility of these images being leaked or the remote server being hacked cannot be ruled out. Consequently, the privacy of users could be at risk due to the sensitive nature of the images. Furthermore, this breach of privacy may contravene the proposed EU regulations on the use of artificial intelligence (AI)[1] and the GDPR regulations[2]. As a result, it is imperative to employ privacy-preserving techniques for protecting such images, but adopting these methods could lead to a reduction in the accuracy of object recognition models. Thus, it is crucial to conduct a thorough analysis of the balance between privacy and accuracy.

---

[1] Proposal for a Regulation of the European Parliament and of the Council Laying Down Harmonised Rules on Artificial Intelligence: https://bit.ly/3y5wf6e.

[2] GDPR regulations: https://eur-lex.europa.eu/eli/reg/2016/679/oj.

In this work, we present a framework for remote object recognition that, at the same time, takes into account privacy, result accuracy, and explainability. In particular, using either differential privacy or Gaussian filters to add noise to images with different degrees to preserve privacy, and the Grad-CAM method for generating explanations, we investigate how the increase in the degree of privacy affects the accuracy of object recognition and the explanations.

This paper presents the following contributions: (i) we propose a privacy-preserving approach to object recognition with decision explainability, utilizing Gaussian filters and differential privacy for privacy protection; (ii) we investigate the impact of multiple degrees of privacy on analysis accuracy and heatmap generation by the explainability mechanism, regulating the privacy parameter of each privacy-preserving mechanism using the equations of privacy gain and analysis accuracy; (iii) we validate our methodology through experiments involving three object recognition models, utilizing two privacy mechanisms with three degrees of privacy, along with the Grad-CAM explainability mechanism; (iv) we demonstrate and analyze the use of privacy degrees by examining their impact on explainability heatmaps.

The remainder of the paper is organized as follows. Section 2 provides an overview of related works. Section 3 presents the reference scenario and the problem statement. Section 4 formally introduces our proposed methodology and architecture. Section 5 describes the dataset used and the experiments conducted. Section 6 provides a brief conclusion and suggests potential future research directions.

2 Related Work

In this section, we review related work on object recognition, privacy preservation in machine learning, and explainability in machine learning.

2.1 Object Recognition

Object recognition is an image processing technique that involves the identification of objects in images. It has numerous practical applications in fields such as robotics, agriculture, medicine, and autonomous driving. One approach to object recognition is *template matching*, which involves using a small template image of the object to compare with all regions of a larger image in order to determine whether the object is present. Although this method does not involve complex calculations, it has certain drawbacks related to the need for pre-defined objects and the impact of variations in lighting, colors, and rotations on the similarity score, potentially leading to incorrect predictions [10]. *Image segmentation and BLOB analysis* are two techniques used for object recognition. Image segmentation involves dividing an image into multiple regions based on various features like color, shape, and texture. Then use extracted features for object identification [4]. On the other hand, binary large object (BLOB) analysis is a form of image segmentation that groups regions of similar properties and distinguishes them from others [5].

The Bag of visual Words (BoW) model is a popular machine learning method for object recognition, which involves creating bags of visual features of images to identify and classify objects. The creation of BoW models starts with feature detection, followed by feature description, and codebook generation for the features [24]. In addition, Hidden Markov Models (HMMs), are probabilistic sequence models that have been widely used for object recognition in video frames, mainly for object and motion recognition [7]. Machine learning models are relatively simple and do not require extensive computational resources and large datasets, but they may not achieve high accuracy compared to more complex models like *Deep Learning (DL)* methods. DL methods require large datasets and much more computational resources for training but can achieve better results with higher accuracy.

DL techniques, particularly Convolutional Neural Networks (CNNs), are more complex and deeper than traditional machine learning models. CNNs can learn complex features that traditional machine learning models may struggle to learn. Additionally, deep learning models are typically trained on large datasets, enabling them to adapt and improve over time. Examples of such models include Regions with CNN features (R-CNN) [13], Fast R-CNN [15], Faster R-CNN [26], YOLO [25], VGG16 and VGG19 [30], and ResNet50 [16].

2.2   Privacy in Machine Learning for Image Data

There are three main categories of privacy-preserving techniques in machine learning: *data-based*, *algorithmic*, and *hardware-based*. *Data-based* techniques focus on safeguarding the data by applying measures such as anonymization and perturbation. *Algorithmic* techniques are concerned with privacy protection at the algorithm level, such as the use of Federated learning, where data analysis is distributed among users and only the analysis results are shared with the server. Other algorithmic techniques include model compression and adversarial training. *Hardware-based* techniques involve privacy protection at the hardware level, like hardware encryption.

The aim of this research is to employ a *data-based* technique to secure sensitive information in image data before sharing it. Various *data-based* methods exist for protecting privacy, such as *data anonymization* that eliminates personally identifiable information like faces and unique objects from the input image [22]. Another method is *data perturbation and obfuscation*, where the image is modified using techniques like blurring [3] and pixelization [17] to make it hard to identify sensitive attributes [2]. In addition, synthetic dataset generation using Generative Adversarial Networks (GANs) [14] and Variational Autoencoders [18] can also be used as *data-based* privacy protection. Furthermore, differential privacy is a powerful *data-based* mechanism that adds noise to the data before, during, or after analysis, ensuring robust privacy guarantees [12]. Finally, Homomorphic Encryption is a technique that encrypts image data before sending it to the server, which then performs data analysis on the encrypted data and sends back encrypted results with the user [8].

2.3 Explainability in Machine Learning for Image Data

When researching explainability mechanisms, various criteria are employed to categorize the methods used for generating visual explanations of model predictions [20]. These criteria are based on different factors such as the model architecture dependency, which could be either model-specific [6] or model agnostic [28]. The time when the explainability mechanism is applied is another criterion, which includes whether the mechanism is applied during model training or after generating the decision. The locality of the explanations is also considered, whether they are local [29] or global [21], depending on whether the explanation pertains to a particular prediction or the behavior of the model on the dataset used to produce the results. Furthermore, the categorization could be feature-based, using features of the image like in Local Interpretable Model Agnostic Explanations (LIME) method [27], or image-based, utilizing the input image to produce prediction explanations. In this study, we utilized the Grad-CAM explainability mechanism [29], which is model-specific, post-hoc, local-interpretable, and image-based.

3   Reference Scenario and Problem Statement

This section aims to outline the problem that our approach tackles and provides an illustrative scenario for its implementation. In environments like smart homes and autonomous driving, where sensitive user data is collected and analyzed, privacy protection and transparency are essential. Therefore, the problem we aim to address is developing an object recognition system for such environments that not only protects individuals' privacy and complies with privacy laws but also provides explanations and insights into the decision-making process. However, applying privacy mechanisms can potentially impact the model accuracy and accordingly the explainability results. Therefore, careful development and implementation of this approach must be studied carefully, considering several degrees of privacy and investigating their impact on the accuracy of the object recognition model.

Consider a scenario where surveillance cameras are installed in a smart home environment, and a system that utilizes the feeds of these cameras to perform object recognition tasks, including the detection of specific objects and activities. In this scenario, our goal is to protect the privacy of individuals while still conducting meaningful and accurate analysis that provides insights into the generated predictions. For privacy protection, an anonymization method might be considered before sharing the data to be analyzed such as *Gaussian Blurring*, and *Differential Privacy*. Based on the sensitivity of the shared data, the privacy degree can be selected, or no privacy at all. The other key aspect, explainability, is adopted with the object recognition model and works on the received data, indicating the regions of the image or a video frame that have the most influence on the model prediction. Thus, allows for model debugging in case of inaccurate predictions, bias detection in case of model predictions that rely on discriminatory factors or irrelevant features, and building trust in the model from the user side. Our proposed architecture and methodology are detailed in Sect. 4.

4   Proposed Architecture and Methodology

This section presents the proposed architecture for privacy-preserving object recognition with explainability. Our architecture aims at allowing to balance the need for accurate object recognition with the protection of sensitive data by using *Differential Privacy* or *Gaussian Blurring* with varying degrees of privacy. We also use the *Grad-CAM* mechanism to provide explanations for the model's decisions. The proposed scenario is presented in Fig. 1. Once images have been captured, to recognize objects while maintaining privacy, there are two phases: adding noise to the image, and processing the image for object recognition. These phases are described in detail in the following of this section.

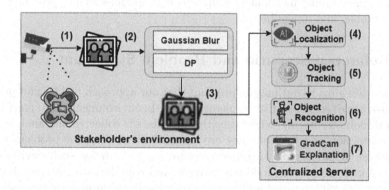

Fig. 1. Privacy Preserving Object Recognition Scenario

4.1   Privacy Preserving Mechanism Enforcement

(ϵ, δ)-**Differential Privacy (DP)** is a powerful privacy-preserving technique widely used to add noise to data, including images. Our work uses (ϵ, δ)-Differential Privacy (DP), which adds random Laplacian noise to the pixel values of images, and ensures that privacy is protected while still allowing valuable insights to be extracted from the data. The amount of noise added is determined by the sensitivity and privacy budget parameters, where sensitivity measures the impact of input data changes on algorithm output, and the privacy budget controls the level of noise added to protect privacy [12]. Adding a too small amount of noise could not be sufficient to preserve image privacy, while too much noise may render the image unusable for analysis. To ensure optimal balance, we use the (ϵ, δ)-differential privacy Eq. (1).

$$Pr[M(D_1) \in S] \leq Pr[M(D_2) \in S] \times exp(\epsilon) + \delta \tag{1}$$

In this equation, ϵ is the privacy budget, which we use in our approach, and δ is the failure probability. M is a randomized algorithm that provides (ϵ, δ)-differential privacy, D_1 and D_2 are two datasets that differ in at least one data instance, Pr is the probability, and $S \subseteq Range(M)$. The (ϵ, δ)-differential privacy equation ensures that privacy is protected while still allowing valuable insights to be extracted from the data.

Gaussian Blurring. With the aim of privacy protection, we employ *Gaussian Blurring* for image perturbation, applying a filter of varying sizes to the images. The degree of privacy is regulated using the kernel size of the blur operation, where the relationship between the kernel size and the privacy gain is positive. Therefore, a wider radius leads to greater blurring and higher privacy, but it may also affect classification accuracy. Gaussian blurring leverages a low-pass filter that smooths an image using a Gaussian convolutional kernel, unlike high-pass filters that sharpen it [1, 23]. This process involves moving the kernel across the image from top left to bottom right, centered at each pixel. At each center pixel, a weighted average of the neighboring pixel values is calculated using the Gaussian function F_{Gauss} presented in Eq. (2), taken from [23]. This average is then used to replace the central pixel value.

$$F_{Gauss}(X, Y) = \frac{1}{2\pi\sigma^2} e^{-\frac{X^2+Y^2}{2+\sigma^2}} \tag{2}$$

where X and Y are image dimensions, k is the dimension of the kernel of size $K \times K$, and $\mu = 1/2(k-1)$ and $\sigma = 0.3(\mu - 1) + 0.8$.

4.2 Object Recognition

The process of object recognition begins with acquiring images or video streams using a smart device equipped with an embedded camera. The images or video streams undergo pre-processing operations such as resizing and perturbation. The pre-processed images or video streams are then fed into our Deep Learning models, which include VGG16, VGG19, and ResNet50. These models consist of multiple convolutional layers that initially detect and localize objects within the images or video frames, and track them over time in the case of video streams. Finally, the detected objects are compared to a set of known objects that the models were trained to recognize, and if a match is found, the object's class is predicted by the model.

4.3   Computation of Data Privacy and Recognition Accuracy

Adopting a privacy-preserving mechanism in an object recognition scenario, on the one hand, enhances privacy gain but, on the other hand, it might have a negative impact on object recognition accuracy.

Object Recognition Accuracy. It is measured as the number of correctly recognized objects with respect to the total number of objects in the dataset and computed using Eq. (3).

$$Acc(D, \lambda, \delta) = \frac{Count(\omega_{\lambda(D)} = \delta)}{Count(\delta)} \tag{3}$$

where D is the dataset, λ is the object recognition model, and ω and δ are respectively the model predictions and the label representing the actual category of the target object.

Privacy Gain (PG). it depends on the selected privacy mechanism. For Differential Privacy, it is controlled by the privacy budget ϵ and $PG(\epsilon) = 1/\epsilon$. Instead, for Gaussian Blurring, PG is controlled by the Privacy Degree σ, which is represented by K, i.e., the size of the kernel used for introducing Gaussian noise. Thus, the maximum σ is obtained using the maximum $K = I$ and PG is computed as $PG(I, K) = \sigma(K)/\sigma(I)$ like in [1].

5   Experiments

In this section, we present the results of the experiments we conducted, describing the dataset used and the object recognition models, as well as the privacy mechanism and the explainability method we used.

5.1   Datasets

The three object recognition models utilized in this study are trained on the well-known and extensively used *ImageNet* dataset. Created at Stanford University in 2009, *ImageNet* is a large-scale labeled dataset comprising more than 1.4 million images and 1,000 object classes, animals, and scenes. *ImageNet* has become a standard benchmark dataset for evaluating image recognition models. For our study, the models are trained on a subset of approximately 1.2 million images, validated on 50,000 images, and tested on 100,000 images from such a dataset [11].

Our approach was evaluated through experiments on the *Open Images Dataset V4* Dataset. This dataset was chosen because it shares common object labels with the *ImageNet* dataset. We selected a subset of 31 classes, which consisted of 8,903 images to test our approach. The total number of objects in the *Open Images Dataset V4* Dataset is 600 classes, representing real-life objects with 9.2 million images [19]. Image sizes in this dataset are varied, so we resized all images in the dataset to a fixed size of 224 × 224 pixels.

5.2   Object Recognition Models

We utilize Keras applications[3] for object recognition. The three object recognition models employed in this study exhibit high accuracy rates on the ImageNet validation dataset. Specifically, *VGG16* achieves an accuracy of 90.10%, *VGG19* achieves an accuracy of 90.00%, and *Resnet50* achieves the highest accuracy of 92.10%for the top 5 classes prediction.

VGG16 and VGG19 Models. Convolutional Neural Network (CNN) models were introduced by the Visual Geometry Group (VGG) of Oxford University in 2014. The main improvements of *VGG16* model over other models were the use of more weighted convolutional layers, thus increasing the depth of the network and replacing large convolution cores with smaller ones of 3×3 size to enhance the model's performance. *VGG16* model architecture is composed of 16 convolutional layers, 3 layers of which are fully connected, in addition to 5 max pooling and batch normalization layers [30]. *VGG19* is a deeper variation of the *VGG16* model that was also introduced in 2014, but with 19 convolutional layers instead of 16 to improve the performance of the model [30].

ResNet50 Model. Residual Networks (ResNets) are a class of deep neural networks introduced by Microsoft Research in 2015. The ResNet50 architecture consists of 50 layers, of which 48 are convolutional layers, 1 is a max pooling layer, and 1 is an average pooling layer. This network architecture is very deep and employs residual connections in a series of residual blocks to facilitate training while achieving superior performance and accuracy [16].

5.3   Privacy-Preserving Object Recognition with Explainability

To evaluate the effect of privacy-preserving techniques on object recognition accuracy, we conducted several experiments by adjusting the privacy parameter σ. In the case of *Differential Privacy*, we controlled σ by modifying the value of the ϵ parameter, which can take on the values of 0.05 for high privacy, 0.1 for medium privacy, or 0.5 for low privacy and sensitivity equals to 1.0. Meanwhile, for *Gaussian Blurring*, we set K to 13 and consequently σ to 2.3 for low privacy, K to 27 and consequently σ to 4.4 for medium privacy, or K to 39 and consequently σ to 6.2 for high privacy. $\sigma = 0$ represents the original dataset (no privacy-preserving technique applied). *Gaussian Blurring* was performed using OpenCV [9], and *DP Laplacian noise* was added using the Numpy Python library. The Grad-CAM method was utilized to generate visual explanations for all input images, including both original and perturbed ones. The TF-Explain framework[4] was used to implement the Grad-CAM method. The Object Recognition models (described in Sect. 5.2) were implemented through Keras applications.

---

[3] Keras applications for object recognition: https://keras.io/api/applications/#usage-examples-for-image-classification-models.

[4] TF-Explain: https://tf-explain.readthedocs.io/en/latest/.

We compared the accuracy of object recognition for the original images with the accuracy of object recognition for the perturbed images at different levels of privacy. The results were analyzed and four heatmaps were generated for each recognized image, one for the original image and the others for the images obtained for three privacy degrees. This is illustrated in Fig. 2 for a sample image of class "ambulance" analyzed with *ResNet50, Gaussian Blurring, Differential Privacy*, and decisions were explained with *Grad-CAM*. In the heatmaps, regions highlighted in yellow indicate higher values and greater influence on the model's decisions, while blue regions represent less influence.

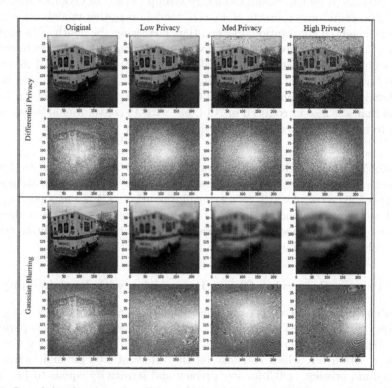

Fig. 2. Sample analyzed images of an ambulance in its original form and blurred versions in the first row and with differential privacy in the second row using varying degrees of privacy and the *ResNet50* model. Model decisions were explained with the Grad-CAM method. The object was correctly recognized only in its original image for Gaussian blurring. For Differential Privacy, the object was correctly recognized also with all degrees of privacy.

5.4   Experimental Results

This section presents the results of our experiments that have been conducted to measure the *Privacy Gain* and the *Object Recognition Accuracy* for the *Open*

Images Dataset V4 using the metrics detailed in Sect. 4. In each of our experiments, we compare the *Privacy Gain* and the *Object Recognition Accuracy* for the three object recognition models that we used.

Figures 3a, 3b, and 3c, present the *Privacy Gain* and the *Object Recognition Accuracy* obtained from our experiments using the *Gaussian Blurring* privacy technique and the three object recognition models, i.e., respectively, *VGG16*, *VGG19*, and *ResNet50*. On the X−axis of each of these graphs, we report the values we selected for the *Privacy Degree* (represented by the labels: *Original, Low privacy, Medium Privacy, and High privacy*), while on the Y−axis, we show the value of *Privacy Gain* and *Object Recognition Accuracy* for each degree of privacy.

The graphs demonstrate that the *Object Recognition models* performs well in terms of accuracy on the original dataset, but *VGG16* and *VGG19* are not highly accurate. As expected, the *Privacy Degree* has a positive correlation with the *Privacy Gain* (green columns) and a negative correlation with the *Object Recognition Accuracy* (blue columns). Therefore, the major effect of the privacy mechanism on the *Object Recognition Accuracy* is noticeable in the graphs after applying the low degree of privacy.

We assess the performance of the three object recognition models under the application of Gaussian blurring, in terms of *Object Recognition Accuracy*. The findings reveal that *ResNet50* outperforms the other two models, *VGG16* and *VGG19*, in terms of accuracy when using both original images and images perturbed with different degrees of privacy. Overall, the three models experience a significant decline in accuracy when Gaussian filters are applied. In fact, the object recognition performance becomes severely compromised after the medium degree of privacy is applied with the *ResNet50* model and for all degrees of privacy applied with both *VGG16* and *VGG19* models.

Figures 4a, 4b, and 4c, present the *Privacy Gain* and the *Object Recognition Accuracy* obtained from our experiments using *Differential Privacy* technique and the three object recognition models, i.e., respectively, *VGG16*, *VGG19*, and *ResNet50*. The results show that, like *Gaussian Blurring*, there is a positive correlation between the *Privacy Degree* and the *Privacy Gain*, and a negative correlation between the *Privacy Degree* and the *Object Recognition Accuracy*. The model's accuracy experiences only a slight decrease when low and medium degrees of privacy are applied. Moreover, for all three recognition models, the reduction in accuracy occurs primarily when a high degree of privacy is employed, but the decline is not substantial like in *Gaussian Blurring*. Still, users have the flexibility to choose the desired level of privacy based on their preferences, whether prioritizing accuracy, privacy, or a balance between the two. We compare the performance of the three object recognition models under the application of DP, in terms of the *Object Recognition Accuracy*. Our findings indicate that *ResNet50* has the highest accuracy values among the three models when using both original images and images perturbed with different degrees of privacy.

The object recognition models employed in this study exhibit diverse accuracy levels when evaluated on unaltered images. *ResNet50* consistently achieves

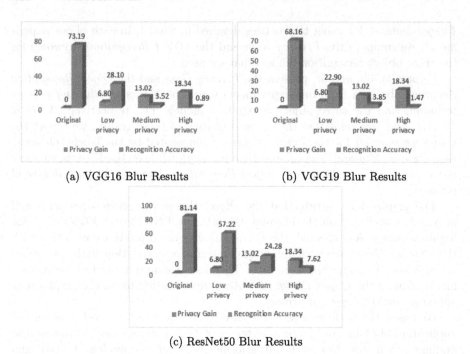

(a) VGG16 Blur Results   (b) VGG19 Blur Results

(c) ResNet50 Blur Results

Fig. 3. Models Accuracy and Privacy Gain Results with Gaussian filters blurring technique

the highest accuracy across all privacy degrees, including scenarios where no privacy mechanism is applied. Models' accuracy declines significantly when the *Gaussian blurring* technique is applied. However, when the *Differential Privacy* method is used, images' privacy is safeguarded based on the chosen privacy degree, while still permitting valuable analyses to be performed on the perturbed data. Consequently, based on the findings, *Differential Privacy* is a more robust and privacy-protective approach.

To assess the impact of different privacy mechanisms on the heatmaps generated by the *Grad-CAM* method, we examined samples such as the one shown in Fig. 2. With *Gaussian Blurring*, not only did the models' accuracy decrease significantly, but the explanations provided by the heatmaps were also affected. The regions of highest influence (indicated by yellow and light blue colors) shifted towards the right side of the heatmap as the privacy degree increased. This can be attributed to the incorrect predictions generated by the *Gaussian Blurring* method, especially with higher levels of privacy applied. On the other hand, the application of *Differential Privacy* did not cause significant changes in the regions of influence. This is because the model's accuracy did not decline significantly even after applying various levels of privacy.

Furthermore, even after the application of *Differential Privacy* with varying degrees of privacy, the use of *Grad-CAM* heatmaps continues to provide

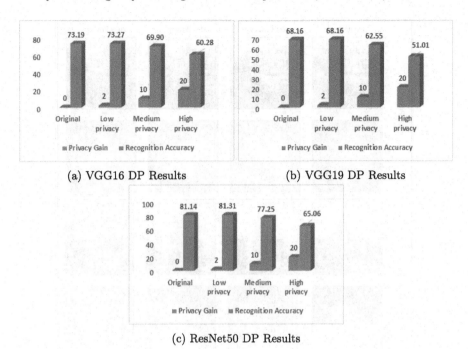

(a) VGG16 DP Results   (b) VGG19 DP Results

(c) ResNet50 DP Results

Fig. 4. Models Accuracy and Privacy Gain Results with Differential Privacy Technique

benefits in terms of trust, bias reduction, and debugging. As illustrated in Fig. 5, two sample images are presented: the first block shows a correct prediction by the *ResNet50* model, while the second block demonstrates an incorrect prediction. In the case of the first image, *Grad-CAM* accurately highlights the regions corresponding to the ambulance, providing a clear and trustworthy explanation. Conversely, for the wrong prediction in the lower block, the highlighted regions are associated with the wheels of the ambulance and the church, as the model incorrectly recognizes these objects as a cab and a church. This highlights the usefulness of *Grad-CAM* for debugging purposes and increases trust in the model's predictions.

Overall, the application of object recognition models with privacy mechanisms like *Gaussian Blurring* and *Differential Privacy* to anonymize data for privacy protection is not novel by itself, nor is the use of the *Grad-CAM* as an explainability method in the context of object recognition to enable the visualization and interpretation of the model predictions. However, the specific combination of applying *Gaussian Blurring* and *Differential Privacy* to object recognition models and using *Grad-CAM* as an explainability method with different levels of privacy and the possibility to select the degree of privacy that does not majorly impact the accuracy of the model and the *Grad-CAM* explanations. The novelty of our approach lies in the integration and application of these

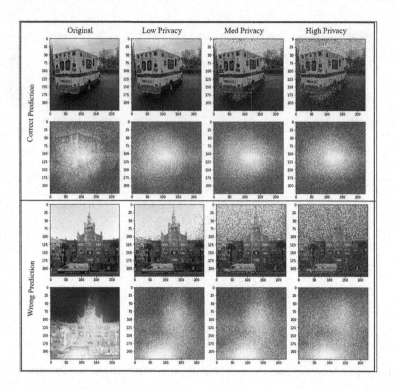

Fig. 5. Sample analyzed images of ambulances in their original form and DP noise versions. The first block of the figure consists of two rows, the first row is an ambulance image with different degrees of privacy applied, and the second row presents the Grad-CAM maps for the *Resnet50* model prediction, noting that the model made correct predictions for these images. While the second block consists of the same type of images but for a different ambulance image that the *Resnet50* model has wrongly classified.

techniques to address both privacy concerns and interpretability in the context of object recognition and its application areas.

6   Conclusion

In this paper, we proposed a privacy-preserving and explainable approach for object recognition. Our model integrates methods like Differential Privacy and Gaussian Blurring to ensure privacy protection, and Grad-CAM to provide visual explanations of model decisions. Through experiments on a subset of the Open Images Dataset V4, we demonstrated the feasibility of controlling privacy parameters for desired outcomes. While Gaussian Blurring affects accuracy, Differential Privacy offers a more robust and privacy-protective solution. Users can choose their preferred privacy degree, balancing accuracy and privacy. Our approach provides a valuable means to preserve privacy while still allowing for meaningful analysis of the perturbed image data and explanations of model predictions.

Future work includes exploring alternative perturbation mechanisms like GANs and Autoencoders, training models on perturbed datasets, and utilizing differential private models to improve accuracy.

References

1. Abbasi, W., Mori, P., Saracino, A., Frascolla, V.: Privacy vs accuracy trade-off in privacy aware face recognition in smart systems. In: 2022 IEEE Symposium on Computers and Communications (ISCC), pp. 1–8. IEEE (2022)
2. Aditya, P., et al.: I-Pic: a platform for privacy-compliant image capture. In: Proceedings of the 14th Annual International Conference on Mobile Systems, Applications, and Services, pp. 235–248. Association for Computing Machinery (2016)
3. Ahmed, N., Natarajan, T., Rao, K.R.: Discrete cosine transform. IEEE Trans. Comput. **100**(1), 90–93 (1974)
4. Arbelaez, P., Maire, M., Fowlkes, C., Malik, J.: Contour detection and hierarchical image segmentation. IEEE Trans. Pattern Anal. Mach. Intell. **33**(5), 898–916 (2010)
5. Aslani, S., Mahdavi-Nasab, H.: Optical flow based moving object detection and tracking for traffic surveillance. Int. J. Electr. Comput., Energetic, Electron. Commun. Eng. **7**(9), 1252–1256 (2013)
6. Bach, S., Binder, A., Montavon, G., Klauschen, F., Müller, K.R., Samek, W.: On pixel-wise explanations for non-linear classifier decisions by layer-wise relevance propagation. PLoS ONE **10**(7), e0130140 (2015)
7. Bicego, M., Castellani, U., Murino, V.: A hidden Markov model approach for appearance-based 3D object recognition. Pattern Recogn. Lett. **26**(16), 2588–2599 (2005)
8. Bost, R., Popa, R.A., Tu, S., Goldwasser, S.: Machine learning classification over encrypted data. Cryptology ePrint Archive (2014)
9. Bradski, G., Kaehler, A.: Opencv. Dr. Dobb's J. Softw. Tools **3**, 2 (2000)
10. Brunelli, R.: Template matching techniques in computer vision: theory and practice. John Wiley & Sons (2009)
11. Deng, J., Dong, W., Socher, R., Li, L.J., Li, K., Fei-Fei, L.: ImageNet: a large-scale hierarchical image database. In: 2009 IEEE Conference on Computer Vision and Pattern Recognition, pp. 248–255. IEEE (2009)
12. Dwork, C.: Differential privacy: a survey of results. In: Agrawal, M., Du, D., Duan, Z., Li, A. (eds.) TAMC 2008. LNCS, vol. 4978, pp. 1–19. Springer, Heidelberg (2008). https://doi.org/10.1007/978-3-540-79228-4_1
13. Girshick, R., Donahue, J., Darrell, T., Malik, J.: Rich feature hierarchies for accurate object detection and semantic segmentation. In: Proceedings of the IEEE Conference on Computer Vision and Pattern Recognition, pp. 580–587 (2014)
14. Goodfellow, I., et al.: Generative adversarial networks. Commun. ACM **63**(11), 139–144 (2020)
15. He, K., Zhang, X., Ren, S., Sun, J.: Spatial pyramid pooling in deep convolutional networks for visual recognition. IEEE Trans. Pattern Anal. Mach. Intell. **37**(9), 1904–1916 (2015)
16. He, K., Zhang, X., Ren, S., Sun, J.: Deep residual learning for image recognition. In: Proceedings of the IEEE Conference on Computer Vision and Pattern Recognition, pp. 770–778 (2016)

17. Hill, S., Zhou, Z., Saul, L.K., Shacham, H.: On the (in) effectiveness of mosaicing and blurring as tools for document redaction. Proc. Priv. Enhancing Technol. **2016**(4), 403–417 (2016)

18. Kingma, D.P., Welling, M.: Auto-encoding variational Bayes. arXiv preprint arXiv:1312.6114 (2013)

19. Kuznetsova, A., et al.: The Open Images Dataset V4: Unified image classification, object detection, and visual relationship detection at scale. Int. J. Comput. Vis. **128**(7), 1956–1981 (2020)

20. Linardatos, P., Papastefanopoulos, V., Kotsiantis, S.: Explainable AI: a review of machine learning interpretability methods. Entropy **23**(1), 18 (2021)

21. Lundberg, S.M., Lee, S.I.: A unified approach to interpreting model predictions. In: Advances in Neural Information Processing Systems, vol 30 (2017)

22. Newton, E.M., Sweeney, L., Malin, B.: Preserving privacy by de-identifying face images. IEEE Trans. Knowl. Data Eng. **17**(2), 232–243 (2005)

23. Pulfer, E.M.: Different approaches to blurring digital images and their effect on facial detection (2019)

24. Qader, W.A., Ameen, M.M., Ahmed, B.I.: An overview of bag of words; importance, implementation, applications, and challenges. In: 2019 International Engineering Conference (IEC), pp. 200–204. IEEE (2019)

25. Redmon, J., Divvala, S., Girshick, R., Farhadi, A.: You only look once: unified, real-time object detection. In: Proceedings of the IEEE Conference on Computer Vision and Pattern Recognition, pp. 779–788 (2016)

26. Ren, S., He, K., Girshick, R., Sun, J.: Faster R-CNN: towards real-time object detection with region proposal networks. In: Advances in Neural Information Processing Systems 28 (2015)

27. Ribeiro, M.T., Singh, S., Guestrin, C.: Why should i trust you? Explaining the predictions of any classifier. In: Proceedings of the 22nd ACM SIGKDD International Conference on Knowledge Discovery and Data Mining, pp. 1135–1144 (2016)

28. Ribeiro, M.T., Singh, S., Guestrin, C.: Model-agnostic interpretability of machine learning. arXiv preprint arXiv:1606.05386 (2016)

29. Selvaraju, R.R., Cogswell, M., Das, A., Vedantam, R., Parikh, D., Batra, D.: Gradcam: Visual explanations from deep networks via gradient-based localization. In: Proceedings of the IEEE International Conference on Computer Vision, pp. 618–626 (2017)

30. Simonyan, K., Zisserman, A.: Very deep convolutional networks for large-scale image recognition. arXiv preprint arXiv:1409.1556 (2014)

31. Smilkov, D., Thorat, N., Kim, B., Viégas, F., Wattenberg, M.: SmoothGrad: removing noise by adding noise. arXiv preprint arXiv:1706.03825 (2017)

An Efficient CKKS-FHEW/TFHE Hybrid Encrypted Inference Framework

Tzu-Li Liu[1,2(✉)], Yu-Te Ku[1,2], Ming-Chien Ho[1,2], Feng-Hao Liu[3],
Ming-Ching Chang[1,4], Chih-Fan Hsu[1], Wei-Chao Chen[1], and Shih-Hao Hung[2,5]

[1] Inventec Corporation, Taipei City 111059, Taiwan
{hsu.chih-fan,chen.wei-chao}@inventec.com
[2] National Taiwan University, Taipei City 10617, Taiwan
{r10922092,d08946006,r11944009}@ntu.edu.tw,
hungsh@csie.ntu.edu.tw
[3] Washington State University, Pullman, WA 99164, USA
feng-hao.liu@wsu.edu
[4] State University of New York, University at Albany, Albany, NY 12222, USA
mchang2@albany.edu
[5] Mohamed bin Zayed University of Artificial Intelligence, Abu Dhabi,
United Arab Emirates

Abstract. Machine Learning as a Service (MLaaS) is a robust platform that offers various emerging applications. Despite great convenience, user privacy has become a paramount concern, as user data may be shared or stored in outsourced environments. To address this, fully homomorphic encryption (FHE) presents a viable solution, yet the practical realization of this theoretical approach has remained a significant challenge, requiring specific optimization techniques tailored to different applications. We aim to investigate the opportunity to apply the CKKS-FHEW/TFHE hybrid approach to NNs, which inherit the advantages of both approaches. This idea has been implemented in several conventional ML approaches (PEGASUS system presented in IEEE S&P 2021), such as decision tree evaluation and K-means clustering, and demonstrated notable efficiency in specific applications. However, its effectiveness for NNs remains unknown. In this paper, we show that directly applying the PEGASUS system on encrypted NN inference would result in a significant accuracy drop, approximately 10% compared to plaintext inference. After a careful analysis, we propose a novel LUT-aware fine-tuning method to slightly adjust the NN weights and the functional bootstrapping for the ReLU function to mitigate the error accumulation throughout the NN computation. We show that by appropriately fine-tuning the model, we can largely reduce the accuracy drop, from 7.5% to 15% compared to the baseline implementation without fine-tuning, while maintaining comparable efficiency with extensive experiments.

Keywords: Homomorphic encryption · neural network · functional bootstrapping · privacy-preserving machine learning

© The Author(s), under exclusive license to Springer Nature Switzerland AG 2024
S. Katsikas et al. (Eds.): ESORICS 2023 Workshops, LNCS 14399, pp. 535–551, 2024.
https://doi.org/10.1007/978-3-031-54129-2_32

1   Introduction

Machine Learning as a Service (MLaaS) [28] are cloud-based platforms providing machine learning (ML) models to run services that are available anytime, anywhere. With the advance of deep learning (DL), neural networks (NN) has been widely used in various applications, *e.g.*, computer vision [18], speech processing [29], and content generation [14]. However, a major concern of MLaaS is on the difficulties regarding the security and privacy of user data. The MLaaS owner could have access to user's private data without permission. Users may hesitate to upload private data to the MLaaS platform due to confidentiality [20]. As a result, exploring a secure MLaaS is an urgent need. Ideally, a secure MLaaS in practice should provide high inference accuracy, low computational time, and minimal memory usage, meanwhile protecting the confidentiality of user data. Secure multiparty computation (SMC) [3,30] is a common solution toward secure MLaaS. SMC is typically associated with higher computational costs, but provides robust confidentiality protection.

Fully Homomorphic Encryption (FHE) [24] is a promising alternative that achieves essentially non-interactive SMC, allowing basically minimal participation (communication/computation) from the user during the protocol execution. Particularly, in the FHE pipeline for secure MLaaS, the user first encrypts the data into ciphertext which is then transmitted to a cloud server. The server then performs ML inference via homomorphic computation on the ciphertext. The encrypted result is then sent back to the user, who then decrypts to retrieve the desired output. The *FHE-based NN encrypted inference* is potentially attractive in terms of security and confidentiality, however with a main limitation of the huge computational burden induced by the FHE calculations.

The FHE-based NN encrypted inference includes three common types of encrypted computations that are executed sequentially in a NN node, namely *linear operations, activation functions*, and *bootstrapping*.

Linear operations are the inner product calculations between the encrypted input data array and the plaintext NN weights. There are three popular FHE schemes used in the encrypted inference: (1) CKKS [5], (2) FHEW [8]/TFHE [6], and (3) CKKS-FHEW/TFHE Hybrid [23]. The CKKS scheme can easily carryout linear operations due to its ability to support floating-point arithmetic, while FHEW/TFHE only supports lightweight bit-wise or integer operations. Note that the integer operations of FHEW/TFHE has lower computational burden over the CKKS floating point calculations.

Regarding activation functions, CKKS only supports element-wise polynomial operations, such as multiplication, addition, and rotation, and does not directly support non-polynomial operators. This is unsuitable for encrypted NN inference, as CKKS does not support ReLU, which is the commonly used activation function in NN models. A possible solution around is to approximate the activation function using polynomial approximations. Although this alternative is simple to implement, it produces deviated results that might affect NN inference accuracy. It also comes with additional computational overhead.

Bootstrapping [11,12] is originally designed to reduce the accumulated computation errors of the ciphertext in FHE, which is a crucial operation to ensure that FHE calculations can be carried out with sufficient computational depth. However, performing repeated boostrapping operations with common CKKS implementations [4] can introduce numerical errors and information loss. In contrast, FHEW/TFHE bootstrapping has no numerical errors. Besides, an advanced bootstrapping operation, the functional bootstrapping, in FHEW/TFHE scheme can achieve performing non-polynomial operations, such as ReLU, while refreshing the ciphertext simultaneously. Generally, an FHEW/TFHE functional bootstrapping supports more than one bootstrapping iteration. According to the implementation, the FHEW/TFHE functional bootstrapping can be categorized into the regular version and the large-precision version. The regular version represents the original design, while the large version was introduced by [21]. The regular version contains only one bootstrapping iteration and is efficient compared to the large-precision version [21], which is friendly for NN inference [2,17]. However, it suffers from limited numerical precision. According to the literature [2,19], regular functional bootstrapping has only been empirically evaluated on the simple MNIST dataset and has not been generalized to work with more complex datasets. In practical applications, the message domain of FHE-based NN inference architecture usually exceeds the input domain typically used in regular function bootstrapping. The large-precision version is desired for real-world applications but its computing efficiency should be further improved.

The CKKS-FHEW/TFHE Hybrid scheme [23] inherits the strengths of the linear operations in CKKS and the benefits of the FHEW/TFHE functional bootstrapping. For FHE-based NN encrypted inference, the CKKS scheme can be used for linear operations, while the FHEW/TFHE functional bootstrapping scheme can be used for non-polynomial activation functions and bootstrapping without adding large computation overhead for transferring between the CKKS and FHEW/TFHE ciphertexts. Notably, the PEGASUS system [23] efficiently bridge these two schemes into a hybrid implementation. PEGASUS first *scales down* the CKKS ciphertext/plaintext, making it compatible with the input to the FHEW/TFHE regular bootstrapping. Then, only one regular functional bootstrapping is required to complete the pipeline. This would be substantially more efficient than the approach of large-precision bootstrapping [21], which would require many more core bootstrapping calls. PEGASUS has demonstrated notable efficiency in specific applications such as decision tree evaluation and K-means clustering, yet the work did not conduct experiments in the setting of NN inference [23]. It remains an interesting open question to determine whether the CKKS-FHEW/TFHE hybrid framework can be effectively extended to cover NNs. In this paper, we focus on the potential of the CKKS-FHEW/TFHE hybrid approach for FHE-based NN encrypted inference.

1.1   Our Contribution

In this work, we aim to apply the CKKS-FHEW/TFHE hybrid approach to FHE-based NN encrypted inference. However, certain numerical adjustments on the model weights and the activation function are required to maintain the inference accuracy, thereby rendering the entire approach practical and usable. Below, we provide a more comprehensive explanation of our specific contributions.

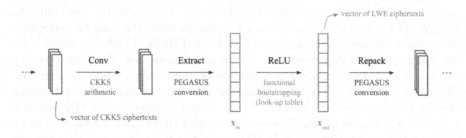

Fig. 1. The four-step process in a layer of FHE NN inference.

First, we implement an FHE inference framework for running neural networks named CKKS-FHEW/TFHE Hybrid Encrypted Inference Framework, on top of the PEGASUS, and then notice a significant decrease in accuracy. With a careful analysis, we identify that the accuracy drop comes from the limited precision when applying regular functional bootstrapping on large-domain ciphertexts.

Next, we address this issue by proposing a novel LUT-aware model fine-tuning framework on the machine learning side. The adjustment is specifically tailored for the above hybrid approach, effectively avoiding the accuracy drop due to the precision issue while maintaining the efficiency advantage of the approach.

Finally, we conduct a comprehensive experiment to validate our LUT-aware model fine-tuning framework on a color dataset, CIFAR-10, which is more complex than the MNIST dataset. The experimental results show that our framework increases accuracy from 7.5% to 15% compared to the NN model without applying our method. Moreover, the fine-tuned NN models achieve accuracy comparable to the original ones.

We compared our approach to two state-of-the-art implementations, Shift-accumulation-based LHE- enabled Deep Neural Network (SHE) [22] and Privacy-Preserving Machine Learning (PPML) [19]. Our fine-tuned model shows competitive accuracy while maintaining high efficiency in time 2,558 s (using 8 threads) compared to PPML which takes over 3,581 s (using 8 threads) and SHE which takes more than 347,555 s (using 8 threads).

1.2   Technical Overview

Our proposed CKKS-FHEW/TFHE Hybrid Encrypted Inference framework includes four-step for each FHE-based NN layer computation, as illustrated in Fig. 1.

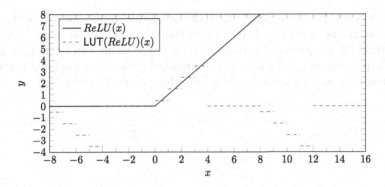

Fig. 2. The evaluation of the ReLU function using regular functional bootstrapping on large-domain ciphertexts. A step-wise numerical behavior can be observed.

1. CKKS computation scheme is first employed to perform the convolution and linear operations on the CKKS ciphertexts.
2. The CKKS ciphertext is then converted into multiple large-domain LWE ciphertexts based on the PEGASUS extraction method.
3. Next, regular functional bootstrapping is applied to the converted large-domain Learning With Errors (LWE) [27] ciphertexts to perform the activation operation while reducing the numerical errors.
4. Finally, the large-domain LWE ciphertexts are repacked back into the CKKS ciphertexts for the subsequent layers of operations.

We first naively applied the hybrid approach to several NN models and observed severe accuracy drops on all tested NNs. The drop is caused by the accumulated numerical errors throughout the encrypted NN inference. The numerical errors are generated by the scale-down process in the PEGASUS framework that limits the numerical precision when applying regular functional bootstrapping on the large-domain ciphertexts. More specifically, we let the domain of the message be $[-B, B)$ and n be the size of the input domain for the LWE functional bootstrapping. The LWE ciphertext of the message is scaled down to meet the requirement of the functional bootstrapping taking a look-up table of size n which is identical to the size of the input domain. In this case, the LWE functional bootstrapping can be treated as a look-up-table (LUT) operation with n entries. We note that the LWE functional bootstrapping exhibits a cyclic behavior out of the range $[-B, B)$ because of the modulus operation involved in the FHE computation. Figure 2 illustrates an example of the ReLU function evaluated by the LWE functional bootstrapping with $n = 8$ in the range $[-4, 4)$. Observe that the ReLU output has step-wise behavior according to the LUT operation.

If the input value range of the LWE functional bootstrapping does not align with the predefined input domain of the LWE functional bootstrapping, either the input domain of the functional bootstrapping can not fulfill the range of the input values or a few LUT entries are utilized. The left-hand-side figure in Fig. 3 illustrates the example that the predefined input domain of the LWE functional bootstrapping $[-4, 4)$ is larger than the input value range $[-0.3, 1.7)$. Only three LUT entries are used to map the input value x to the output y. The range mismatching generates a large numerical error when applying functional bootstrapping and then eventually affects the NN model accuracy.

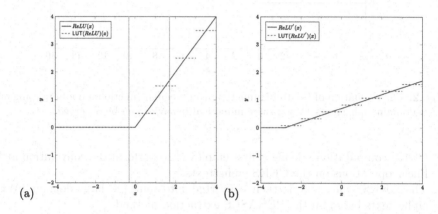

(a)   (b)

Fig. 3. An example of range alignment, where the input range $[-0.3, 1.7)$ in (a) marked in orange is mapped to $[-4, 4)$ in (b) to improve precision. It is evident that the aligned function $ReLU'$ utilizes a greater number of look-up table entries. Noted that the blue lines indicate the target functions and the red lines are the look-up tables according to the functional bootstrapping behavior. (Color figure online)

We design a LUT-aware model fine-tuning framework to align the range of the input value with the message domain of the ciphertext. The mismatch can be mitigated by aligning the input value with the LUT entry as the right-hand-side figure in Fig. 3. More specifically, we first estimate the input range by analyzing the observed feature maps generated during the inference of plain training data on the trained model. This estimation can be used to define the range of input values. Next, we align the range with the message domain. This alignment ensures that the input values are precisely mapped to the LUT entry. The numerical optimization process greatly utilizes the data and enhances the final accuracy of the FHE NN inference. Note that the alignment process is a preprocess of our model fine-tuning framework. The alignment includes linearly transforming pretrained NN model weights and updating the activation functions of the model. According to our design, we largely improve the accuracy of the model while maintaining the inference efficiency thanks to the better numerical alignment to the regular functional bootstrapping.

We conducted experimental evaluations by solving the image classification problem with convolutional neural networks (CNNs) on the CIFAR-10 dataset. Given the substantial time cost associated with FHE NN inference, we made the decision to train smaller-scale plain models. To achieve this, we employed knowledge distillation from a ResNet-20 model with an impressive accuracy of 92% to distill knowledge to our small models. Our experimental results provide strong validation of the effectiveness of our approach. Initially, our plain models achieved an impressive inference accuracy of 80%. However, when we performed FHE NN inference without LUT-aware fine-tuning, we observed a significant decline in accuracy ranging from 7.5% to 17.5%. Fortunately, by incorporating LUT-aware fine-tuning into our encrypted inference process, we were able to overcome this challenge. The application of LUT-aware fine-tuning consistently yielded accuracy levels that were comparable to the plain models. This outcome underscores the robustness and reliability of our approach in maintaining high accuracy during encrypted inference.

2 Preliminaries

Our framework is built on both CKKS [5] and FHEW/TFHE [7,8] schemes. Next, we define the settings and notations used in our work.

CKKS Encryption. CKKS supports arithmetic operations on floating-point vectors. During the encryption process, it first encodes a message m, which is a vector of float numbers, into a plaintext polynomial. Denote the encoding operation as $\mathsf{Ecd}(\cdot)$, which encrypts the plaintext polynomial to a ciphertext. Denote the encrypting operation as $\mathsf{Enc}(\cdot)$. We use the notation of $\mathsf{CKKS}(\mathbf{m})$ to denote $\mathsf{Enc}(\mathsf{Ecd}(\mathbf{m}))$ with $\mathbf{m} \in \mathbb{R}^n$.

CKKS supports the evaluation of CKKS $\mathsf{CKKS.eval}(f, \cdot)$. The inputs are a plaintext function f and the arguments of f placed after f, such as message $\mathbf{m}$ or ciphertext $\mathsf{ctx} \in \mathsf{CKKS}(\mathbf{m})$. The operation is conducting the function with these arguments in CKKS and returns $\mathsf{ctx} \in \mathsf{CKKS}(f(\cdot))$. For example, we let $\mathsf{ctx} \in \mathsf{CKKS}(\mathbf{m})$, $\mathsf{CKKS.eval}(+, \mathsf{ctx}, \mathbf{v})$ returns $\mathsf{ctx}' \in \mathsf{CKKS}(\mathbf{m} + \mathbf{v})$.

LWE and Regular Functional Bootstrapping. LWE encrypts a plaintext, which is the encoding of a scalar $m \in \mathbb{R}$, to a ciphertext. Let $\mathsf{LWE}(\lceil m \rceil)$ denote the LWE encryption of $m \in \mathbb{R}$, and let $\lceil \cdot \rceil$ denote the rounding and encoding function. LWE possesses two commonly used implementations, FHEW and TFHE. Compared to FHEW, TFHE is faster in evaluating bootstrapping and requires a smaller bootstrapping key. Both implementations support bitwise operations on LWE ciphertexts, which represent encrypted binary data $m \in \{0, 1\}$. FHEW and TFHE enable support for the NAND operation on LWE ciphertext, allowing them to support any circuit based on the completeness of the NAND circuit. Moreover, they also provide support for regular functional bootstrapping.

Regular functional bootstrapping is a type of bootstrapping used to reduce error accumulation in HE operations. It involves constructing a lookup table for a specific function, enabling efficient computation of results. While it requires fewer bootstrapping iterations and less computation, it is effective only for supporting small message domain. If the requirement is to support large domain messages, it results in significant computational overhead.

PEGASUS CKKS-FHEW Conversion. CKKS demonstrates remarkable efficiency in vector operations, while FHEW exhibits exceptional efficiency in non-polynomial functions such as ReLU, using functional bootstrapping operations. If we can switch between CKKS and FHEW efficiently, it is suitable for performing private and encrypted inference for MLaaS. Lu *et al.* [23] proposed PEGASUS, a framework that efficiently converts packed CKKS ciphertext and FHEW ciphertexts without decryption. The conversion involves these operations.

- **Extract** pegasus.extract(ctx): Given a ciphertext ctx $\in$ CKKS($\mathbf{m}$) with $\mathbf{m} \in R^n$, the operation involves transforming CKKS encryption into LWE encryption and return a set of $\{\mathsf{ctx}'_i\} \in$ LWE($\lceil m_i \rfloor$) with $m_i \in \mathbf{m}$ and $0 \le i < n$.
- **Repack** pegasus.repack($\{\mathsf{ctx}'_i\}_{0 \le i < n}$): Given a set $\{\mathsf{ctx}'_i\}_{0 \le i < n}$ with $\mathsf{ctx}'_i \in$ LWE($\lceil m_i \rfloor$) with $m_i \in \mathbf{m}$, the operation involves repacking a set of LWE ciphertexts into a single CKKS ciphertext and return ctx $\in$ CKKS($\mathbf{m}$).

PEGASUS Large-domain Functional Bootstrapping. The regular functional bootstrapping method can only be applied to LWE ciphertexts with a message domain limited to the size of the look-up table, typically around 2^{10} [25]. However, when dealing with LWE ciphertexts converted from CKKS ciphertexts, a larger message domain is usually required. To address this specific issue, PEGASUS introduces a groundbreaking technique known as large-domain functional bootstrapping. This technique involves scaling down the input ciphertext to a smaller message domain during the conversion from CKKS to FHEW, enabling the extension of regular functional bootstrapping to support a larger message domain. However, this expansion comes at the cost of reduced precision. Additionally, Liu et al. [21] proposed a method that utilizes digit decomposition to divide a large message into multiple smaller chunks and performs functional bootstrapping on each chunk individually. This approach preserves the precision of the input message but requires multiple bootstrapping iterations. Therefore, considering computational efficiency, this approach is not adopted.

- **Look-up table evaluation** pegasus.eval(f, ctx) : Given a plaintext f and a ctx $\in$ LWE($\lceil m \rfloor$), the operation returns ctx' $\in$ LWE($\lceil f(m) \rfloor$) with error.

PEGASUS evaluation. PEGASUS employs a fine-grained look-up table approximation for evaluating non-polynomial functions such as sigmoid and ReLU. Inputs of the evaluation is a plaintext function f and a ciphertext ctx $\in$ CKKS($\mathbf{m}$) and output is $\mathsf{ctx}' \in$ CKKS($f(\mathbf{m})$) with error. The evaluation involves three steps. First, as functional bootstrapping is faster under the FHEW scheme than CKKS, PEGASUS extracts a CKKS ciphertext ctx to a set FHEW ciphertext $\{\mathsf{ctx}_i\} \in$ pegasus.extract(ctx). Second, it evaluates the look-up table $\mathcal{T}$ according to f on each $\{\mathsf{ctx}_i\}$ and gets a set $\{\mathsf{ctx}'_i\} \in$ pegasus.eval(f, ctx_i). Finally, it repacks $\{\mathsf{ctx}'_i\}$ to $\mathsf{ctx}' \in$ pegasus.repack($\{\mathsf{ctx}'_i\}$).

3   Methodology

We propose the LUT-aware model fine-tuning framework to mitigate the impact caused by the limited precision of regular functional bootstrapping. Recall our CKKS/FHEW-TFHE Hybrid Secure DNN implementation, we next describe the mathematical formulation of the four-step process in Sect. 1.2:

- The **Convolution Layer** $\mathsf{CKKS.eval}(f_{\mathrm{CONV}}, \{\mathsf{ctx}_0, \mathsf{ctx}_1, ...\})$ performs the convolution operation with the input feature map that is encrypted in multiple CKKS ciphertexts: $f_{\mathrm{CONV}}(\mathbf{x}) = \mathbf{W}(\mathbf{x}) + \mathbf{b}$. The calculation is carried out in the encrypted domain, and a list of CKKS ciphertexts $\{\mathsf{ctx}_0', \mathsf{ctx}_1', ...\}$ are produced as the output.
- The **Extraction** $\mathsf{pegasus.extract}(\{\mathsf{ctx}_0, \mathsf{ctx}_1, ...\})$: takes a list of CKKS ciphertexts as input and extracts each CKKS ciphertext to gather the resulting LWE ciphertexts. The output is these gathered LWE ciphertexts.
- The **Activation Layer** $\mathsf{pegasus.eval}(f_{\mathrm{ACT}}, \{\mathsf{ctx}_0^{\mathsf{LWE}}, \mathsf{ctx}_1^{\mathsf{LWE}}, ...\})$ evaluates the activation function f_{ACT} on each input LWE ciphertext. The output is a list of the resulting LWE ciphertexts.
- The **Repacking** $\mathsf{pegasus.repack}(\{\mathsf{ctx}_0^{\mathsf{LWE}}, \mathsf{ctx}_1^{\mathsf{LWE}}, ...\})$ step repacks the multiple LWE ciphertexts into several CKKS ciphertexts, where each CKKS ciphertext encrypts a specific number of values (message).

Algorithm 1: Secure inference on layer i of LUT-aware fine-tuned model.

input : the encrypted feature maps $\mathbf{ctx}_{n_0} \in \{\mathsf{CKKS}(\mathbf{m}_i)\}_{0 \leq i < n_0}$,
the folded convolution operation $f_{\mathrm{CONV}i}'$,
the aligned activation function $f_{\mathrm{ACT}i}'$

output: $\mathbf{ctx}_{\mathrm{pack}} \in \{\mathsf{CKKS}(\mathbf{m}_i)\}_{0 \leq i < n_{\mathrm{pack}}}$

1 $\mathbf{ctx}_{\mathrm{conv}} = \mathsf{CKKS.eval}(f_{\mathrm{CONV}}', \mathbf{ctx}_{n_0})$;   // $\mathbf{ctx}_{\mathrm{conv}} \in \{\mathsf{CKKS}(\mathbf{m}_i)\}_{0 \leq i < n_{\mathrm{conv}}}$

2 $\mathbf{ctx}_{\mathrm{ext}} = \mathsf{pegasus.extract}(\mathbf{ctx}_{\mathrm{conv}})$;   // $\mathbf{ctx}_{\mathrm{ext}} \in \{\mathsf{LWE}(m_i)\}_{0 \leq i < n_{\mathrm{ext}}}$

3 $\mathbf{ctx}_{\mathrm{act}} = \mathsf{pegasus.eval}(f_{\mathrm{ACT}}', \mathbf{ctx}_{\mathrm{ext}})$;   // $\mathbf{ctx}_{\mathrm{act}} \in \{\mathsf{LWE}(m_i)\}_{0 \leq i < n_{\mathrm{act}}}$

4 $\mathbf{ctx}_{\mathrm{pack}} = \mathsf{pegasus.repack}(\mathbf{ctx}_{\mathrm{act}})$;   // $\mathbf{ctx}_{\mathrm{pack}} \in \{\mathsf{CKKS}(\mathbf{m}_i)\}_{0 \leq i < n_{\mathrm{pack}}}$

5 Output $\mathbf{ctx}_{\mathrm{pack}}$

To overcome the mismatch issue introduced in Sect. 1.2, we propose the precise alignment of the input range with the message domain. To achieve this alignment, we employ a fine-tuning approach that focuses on optimizing the convolution operations and the activation functions. Through fine-tuning, we can effectively align the input range with the desired message domain, ensuring optimal precision and accuracy in our computations.

3.1   LUT-Aware Model Fine-Tuning

Our Look-Up Table (LUT) aware model fine-tuning involves two main steps.

Step 1. Update the model weights $f_{\text{CONV}}'(\mathbf{x}) = \mathcal{F}_{\text{LM}}^{(a,b,B)}(f_{\text{CONV}}(\mathbf{x}))$: We apply a linear map to the input to ensure that the input interval is aligned with the message domain. This linear map function can be incorporated into the convolution weights and bias, thereby avoiding any additional computational costs or memory usage. The incorporation details will be introduced in § 3.3. Function $\mathcal{F}_{\text{LM}}^{(a,b,B)}$ linearly map the input $\mathbf{x} \in \mathbb{R}^n$, $x_i \in [a,b)$ to the range $[-B,B)$.

Step 2. Update the activation functions $f_{\text{ACT}}' = f_{\text{ACT}} \circ \mathcal{F}_{\text{LM}}^{(a,b,B)^{-1}}$: We update all the activation functions with inverse linear mapping functions such that $f_{\text{ACT}}'(\mathcal{F}_{\text{LM}}^{(a,b,B)}(x)) = f_{\text{ACT}}(x)$. The modification ensures that the new activation functions produce identical results when applied to the linearly mapped inputs, which greatly reduces the error caused by the limited precision of the regular functional bootstrapping.

Noted that the fine-tunings are performed on the plain neural network models, before we turn them into the encrypted inference version. Algorithm 1 describes the encrypted inference calculation steps.

3.2   Estimate the Numerical Ranges of the Input for Activation Functions

Recall that aligning the input value range with the message domain $[-B,B)$ enhances the utilization of LUT entries. The range of the activation function inputs, denoted as $[a_i, b_i)$ for each layer i, plays a crucial role in aligning them with the desired interval $[-B,B)$. These parameters determine the valid range of inputs for the activation functions. If the input values fall outside the range $[a_i, b_i)$, applying the activation function with an inverse linear mapping will result in a significant mismatch or error in the output. On the other hand, if the range $[a_i, b_i)$ is too large, only a small portion of the precision within that interval will be effectively utilized. Hence, determining the appropriate range of activation function inputs is essential to ensure accurate and efficient computation while maximizing the utility of precision.

Since the inputs to the activation functions are encrypted, also the ranges of activation inputs are not predetermined and vary based on the input values fed into the neural network. We assume that the training/testing distribution are similar. Therefore, to estimate these input ranges, we conduct inference on the trained model using plain (non-encrypted) data from the training set. During this process, we observe and record the minimum and maximum input values, denoted as a_i and b_i respectively, that occur at the activation function of each layer i. By performing inference on the plain trained model with training data, we are able to capture the dynamic input ranges that are possibly encountered during actual usage. These minimum and maximum values provide insights into the range of values the activation inputs can take, allowing us to align the input ranges with proper parameters a_i and b_i.

3.3 Incorporate the Linear Mapping into Model Weights

In Step 1, inspired by batch normalization folding [15], we also incorporated the linear mapping function into the convolution layers to migrate the additional multiplication depth and computational cost caused by linear mapping function. Specifically, we fold the linear map $\mathcal{F}_{\text{LM}}^{(a,b,B)}$ into convolution layer f_{CONV}.

In addition, due to the independence of the computation of each output channel in the convolution operation, it is viable to estimate the ranges for all output channels and perform activation function evaluation using the corresponding look-up table. Figure 4 illustrates that the ranges $[a_i, b_i), 0 \leq i < 8$, vary across different output channels. Suppose all channels are appropriately linearly mapped to the functional bootstrapping input domain with their own ranges. In that case, the look-up table evaluation can be performed with the same level of resolution for all channels.

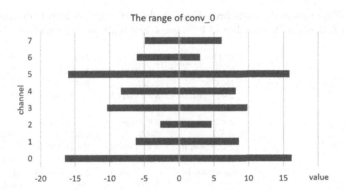

Fig. 4. Visualization of the output ranges $[a_i, b_i)$ of each convolution channel from layer 0 of the $D5L1$ model.

Table 1. Crypto parameters used in PEGASUS in our experiments. We follow the notations of [23]. RLWE is CKKS encryption. $\widetilde{\text{RLWE}}$ and RGSW are encryption schemes used in TFHE/FHEW conversion and look-up table evaluation. ns denote the ring dimensions, qs and Q denote the modulus and σs denote the noise parameters. Descriptions of these symbols can be found in the Preliminaries of the PEGASUS paper [23].

Encryption	Parameters
$\text{RLWE}^{n,q_0}(\cdot)$	$n = 2^{11}, q_0 \approx 2^{45}, \sigma_{ks} = 2^{10}, B_{ks} = 2^7, d_{ks} = 7$
$\text{RGSW}^{n,q'}(\cdot)$	$n = 2^{12}, q' \approx 2^{60} \times q_0, q_0 \approx 2^{45}, \sigma_{lut} = 2^{10}$
$\text{RLWE}^{\overline{n},\overline{Q}}(\cdot)$	$\overline{n} = 2^{16}, q_i \approx 2^{45}, \sigma_{ckks} = 3.19, \log \overline{Q} = \mathbf{689}$

4   Experiments

We conducted extensive experiments to evaluate the effectiveness of our fine-tuning scheme using real neural network models on the CIFAR-10 dataset. Through the implementation and testing of our approach, we assess the encrypted ML model performance and compare it with two state-of-the-art implementations, namely SHE [22] and PPML [19]. These comparisons provided valuable insights into the strengths and advantages of our method.

In our experiments, we utilized a server equipped with an Ubuntu 20.04.6 LTS operating system. The server featured 8 cores of an AMD EPYC 7763 64-Core Processor, providing 16 threads and 126GB memory. We evaluated the proposed model fine-tuning and then compare the model performance against other methods in terms of the image classification accuracy and the computational speed.

To ensure sufficient security for data encryption, we set the crypto parameters of PEGASUS to be at least 119-bit security. Table 1 shows detailed parameters used in our implementation.

Table 2. Experimental results for various model structures, where D denotes network depth and L denotes the number of FC layers. See texts for explanation.

Model	$D5L1$	$D8L1$	$D11L1$	$D7L3$
Structure	2×2 Conv, 8, /2	5×5 Conv, 8, /2	5×5 Conv, 8	5×5 Conv, 8, /2
	ReLU	ReLU	ReLU	ReLU
	2×2 Conv, 16, /2	3×3 Conv, 8	3×3 Conv, 8	3×3 Conv, 16
	ReLU	ReLU	ReLU	ReLU
	2×2 Conv, 16, /2	3×3 Conv, 16	3×3 Conv, 8	3×3 Conv, 16
	ReLU	ReLU	ReLU	ReLU
	2×2 Conv, 16, /2	3×3 Conv, 16	3×3 Conv, 16	3×3 Conv, 16
	ReLU	ReLU	ReLU	ReLU
	Linear, 64, 10	3×3 Conv, 16	3×3 Conv, 16	Linear, 1024, 256
		ReLU	ReLU	ReLU
		3×3 Conv, 16	3×3 Conv, 16, /2	Linear, 256, 256
		ReLU	ReLU	ReLU
		3×3 Conv, 16	3×3 Conv, 16	Linear, 256, 10
		ReLU	ReLU	
		Linear, 64, 10	3×3 Conv, 16	
			ReLU	
			3×3 Conv, 16	
			ReLU	
			3×3 Conv, 16	
			ReLU	
			Linear, 16, 10	
Plain DNN Acc.	60%	72.5%	77.5%	80%
Secure DNN Acc. wo LUT-Aware	47.5%	55%	62.5%	72.5%
Secure DNN Acc. w/ LUT-Aware (Ours)	**57.5%**	**70%**	**75%**	**80%**
Total Time	881 s	2,092 s	9,458 s	2,558 s

4.1   Performance

In our experiments, the accuracy obtained from the original plaintext NN inference is treated as an upper bound of those obtained from the encrypted NN that are under evaluation. We evaluated four CNN models with varying architectures and network depths. Let D denote the network depth and L denote the number of fully connected (FC) layers in the network. Specifically, we have evaluated the networks of $D5L1$, $D8L1$, $D11L1$, $D7L3$. Table 2 presents the results, including the hyper-parameters, obtained accuracy, and computational time. 'Plain DNN Acc' shows the obtained accuracy from the given plain model. 'Secure DNN Acc. wo LUT-Aware' shows the accuracy of models prior to applying LUT-aware model fine-tuning. 'Secure DNN Acc. w/ LUT-Aware' shows the accuracy after fine-tuning. '$k \times k$ Conv, c, /s' denotes a convolution layer with kernel size $k \times k$, output channel c and stride s. 'Linear, d_i, d_o' indicates a fully connected layer with input dimension d_i and output dimension d_o. Results in Table 2 indicate that our models after fine-tuning outperforms the original PEGASUS-based secure DNN models by 7.5% to 15% of accuracy. The $D7L3$ architecture achieved the best accuracy and execution time. Specifically, our $D7L3$ model finished the encrypted DNN classification of a CIFAR-10 image in 43 min using only 8 threads of CPU and < 50 GB of runtime memory.

Regardless of the model architecture or depth, our method consistently achieves accuracy scores that are comparable to the target performance of "Secure DNN Acc. wo LUT-Aware". These findings showcase the effectiveness of our approach in maintaining high accuracy while ensuring the security of the inference process.

4.2   Comparison with Two State-of-the-art Methods

We performed a comparative analysis between our method and two state-of-the-art implementations that support Fully Homomorphic Encryption (FHE)-based Deep Neural Network (DNN) inference, namely, Shift-accumulation-based LHE-enabled Deep Neural Network (SHE) [22] and Privacy-Preserving Machine Learning (PPML) [19]. SHE employed the FHEW/TFHE Bitwise scheme, whereas PPML utilized the CKKS scheme. Our secure $D7L3$ model after fune-tuning has almost no loss in accuracy compared to the plain DNN inference, as shown in Table 2. In comparison, our other models yield about 2.5% loss.

We next compare the execution time with SHE and PPML. We report the computational time required for the $D7L3$ model that are implemented on SHE and PPML and compare with our approach. It is stated in the SHE [22] paper that the level-TFHE inference scheme has the ability to perform homomorphic AND operations up to a depth of 32K in LHE mode, all without requiring boot-strapping. However, it is important to note that this claim overlooks a significant detail. The computation relies on a specific branching program structure [3], which is noticeably absent in the computation structure presented in [22]. Therefore, it is crucial to reassess and possibly reconsider their claims regarding the utilization of level-TFHE.

Compare the Execution Time with SHE [22]. We next report the runtime for executing a DNN using the FHEW/TFHE Bitwise scheme [25], employing the same security level as our approach. It should be noted that a logical operation takes 75 ms when executed on a single thread. Based on this, the estimation indicates that an 8-bit addition operation would take approximately 0.3744 s (8 thread), while an 8-bit ReLU computation would take around 0.126 s (8 thread). The multiplication operation time of SHE-DNN is incredibly fast when compared to the time needed for addition and ReLU. In fact, it's so efficient that it can practically be disregarded. We estimate that running the SHE-DNN technology on the $D7L3$ architecture with an 8-bit model would require at least 347,555 s, including 346,672 s for 925,942 addition instructions and 883 s for 7,008 ReLU operations.Our approach requires less time to execute the $D7L3$ model compared to the SHE-DNN method.

Compare the Execution Time with PPML [19]. PPML adopts the CKKS scheme, in which bootstrapping and ReLU are performance bottlenecks. We estimate that the total execution time for a single bootstrap operation in the PPML method with 8 threads is 0.231 s, whereas performing a single ReLU operation takes 0.28 s. $D7L3$ consists of 7,008 ReLU operations and bootstrappings. Therefore, we estimate that executing the $D7L3$ model in PPML will take at least 3,581 s. Our method is slightly faster than that.

5   Other Related Works

Secure Multiparty Computation (SMC) methods achieve data confidentiality by using cryptography tools, where the security level can be evaluated with mathematical derivations. Generally, SMC methods can be categorized into *interactive* schemes [13,16,30] and *non-interactive* schemes [2]. Interactive schemes require the active participation of all involved parties during the computation. Participants must possess sufficient computation power and a reliable network to maintain their online presence and manage the communication overheads. In contrast, non-interactive SMC implementation, such as the *Homomorphic Encryption* (HE), can perform the entire NN encrypted inference locally, without the need of communication nor client participation during the encrypted computation. The DNN inference method using the FHEW/TFHE scheme in [2] belongs to this category. It achieves 96% accuracy on the MNIST dataset. However, direct adaptation of the method to CIFAR-10 and other complex datasets is not yet investigated.

Differential Privacy (DP) is a mainstream method for privacy protection, which achieves data anonymization by introducing noise to the data or the model [10]. DP methods are primarily used to avoid the leakage of personal information in a dataset [1,26]. In practical, DP methods need to select suitable parameters according to the characteristic of a problem. However, no general method exists to define the parameter to achieve privacy-preserving [9].

6 Conclusion

We presented a encrypted ML inference approach leveraging the CKKS-FHEW/TFHE hybrid crypto system based on the PEGASUS implementation. We showed that direct incorporation of PEGASUS would result in a 10% accuracy drop, when compared with plain text inference. We then proposed a LUT-aware model fine-tuning framework that significantly improves the accuracy by 7.5% to 15% accuracy over the original FHE inference without fine-tuning. We compared our method with two state-of-the-art implementations, namely PPML and SHE, and demonstrated competitive performance of ours in accuracy and efficiency.

Future work includes further explorations of design and methods that can effectively address the computational overhead associated with the encrypted FHE NN inference. Furthermore, how best to facilitate a feasible and scalable deployment of secure ML applications continues to be an active area of research.

Acknowledgements. This work is supported in part by the National Science and Technology Council, Taiwan, under the grants NSTC 112-2221-E-002 -159 -MY3, and an NSF Award CNS 1942400, United States.

References

1. Abadi, M., et al.: Deep learning with differential privacy. In: ACM SIGSAC conference on Computer and Communications Security, pp. 308–318 (2016)
2. Bourse, F., Minelli, M., Minihold, M., Paillier, P.: Fast homomorphic evaluation of deep discretized neural networks. In: Shacham, H., Boldyreva, A. (eds.) CRYPTO 2018, Part III. LNCS, vol. 10993, pp. 483–512. Springer, Heidelberg (2018). https://doi.org/10.1007/978-3-319-96878-0_17
3. Brakerski, Z., Vaikuntanathan, V.: Lattice-based FHE as secure as PKE. In: Naor, M. (ed.) ITCS 2014, pp. 1–12. ACM (2014). https://doi.org/10.1145/2554797.2554799
4. Cheon, J.H., Han, K., Kim, A., Kim, M., Song, Y.: Bootstrapping for approximate homomorphic encryption. In: Nielsen, J., Rijmen, V. (eds.) Advances in Cryptology-EUROCRYPT 2018: 37th Annual International Conference on the Theory and Applications of Cryptographic Techniques, Tel Aviv, Israel, 29 April–3 May 2018, Proceedings, Part I, vol. 37. pp. 360–384. Springer, Heidelberg (2018). https://doi.org/10.1007/978-3-319-78381-9_14
5. Cheon, J.H., Kim, A., Kim, M., Song, Y.S.: Homomorphic encryption for arithmetic of approximate numbers. In: Takagi, T., Peyrin, T. (eds.) ASIACRYPT 2017, Part I. LNCS, vol. 10624, pp. 409–437. Springer, Heidelberg (2017). https://doi.org/10.1007/978-3-319-70694-8_15
6. Chillotti, I., Gama, N., Georgieva, M., Izabachène, M.: TFHE: fast fully homomorphic encryption over the torus. Cryptology ePrint Archive, Report 2018/421 (2018). https://eprint.iacr.org/2018/421
7. Chillotti, I., Gama, N., Georgieva, M., Izabachène, M.: TFHE: fast fully homomorphic encryption over the torus. J. Cryptol. **33**(1), 34–91 (2020)

550   T.-L. Liu et al.

8. Ducas, L., Micciancio, D.: FHEW: bootstrapping homomorphic encryption in less than a second. In: Oswald, E., Fischlin, M. (eds.) EUROCRYPT 2015, Part I. LNCS, vol. 9056, pp. 617–640. Springer, Heidelberg (2015). https://doi.org/10.1007/978-3-662-46800-5_24
9. Dwork, C.: Differential privacy: a survey of results. In: Agrawal, M., Du, D., Duan, Z., Li, A. (eds.) Theory and Applications of Models of Computation (TAMC), vol. 4978, pp. 1–19. Springer, Heidelberg (2008). https://doi.org/10.1007/978-3-540-79228-4_1
10. Dwork, C., Roth, A., et al.: The algorithmic foundations of differential privacy. Found. Trends Theor. Comput. Sci. 9(3–4), 211–407 (2014)
11. Gentry, C.: A fully homomorphic encryption scheme. Stanford university (2009)
12. Gentry, C.: Computing arbitrary functions of encrypted data. Commun. ACM 53(3), 97–105 (2010)
13. Goldreich, O., Micali, S., Wigderson, A.: How to play any mental game, or a completeness theorem for protocols with honest majority. In: Providing Sound Foundations for Cryptography: On the Work of Shafi Goldwasser and Silvio Micali, pp. 307–328 (2019)
14. Goodfellow, I.J., et al.: Generative adversarial nets. In: Neural Information Processing Systems, pp. 2672–2680 (2014)
15. Jacob, B., et al.: Quantization and training of neural networks for efficient integer-arithmetic-only inference. In: IEEE CVPR (2018)
16. Juvekar, C., Vaikuntanathan, V., Chandrakasan, A.: GAZELLE: a low latency framework for secure neural network inference. In: USENIX Security Symposium, pp. 1651–1669 (2018)
17. Kluczniak, K., Schild, L.: FDFB: full domain functional bootstrapping towards practical fully homomorphic encryption. Cryptology ePrint Archive, Report 2021/1135 (2021). https://eprint.iacr.org/2021/1135
18. Krizhevsky, A., Sutskever, I., Hinton, G.E.: ImageNet classification with deep convolutional neural networks. In: Bartlett, P.L., Pereira, F.C.N., Burges, C.J.C., Bottou, L., Weinberger, K.Q. (eds.) Neural Information Processing Systems, pp. 1106–1114 (2012). https://proceedings.neurips.cc/paper/2012/hash/c399862d3b9d6b76c8436e924a68c45b-Abstract.html
19. Lee, J.W., et al.: Privacy-preserving machine learning with fully homomorphic encryption for deep neural network. IEEE Access 10, 30039–30054 (2022)
20. Liu, X., et al.: Privacy and security issues in deep learning: a survey. IEEE Access 9, 4566–4593 (2021). https://doi.org/10.1109/ACCESS.2020.3045078
21. Liu, Z., Micciancio, D., Polyakov, Y.: Large-precision homomorphic sign evaluation using FHEW/TFHE bootstrapping. In: Agrawal, S., Lin, D. (eds.) ASIACRYPT 2022, Part II. LNCS, vol. 13792, pp. 130–160. Springer, Heidelberg (2022). https://doi.org/10.1007/978-3-031-22966-4_5
22. Lou, Q., Jiang, L.: SHE: A fast and accurate deep neural network for encrypted data. In: Neural Information Processing Systems, pp. 10035–10043 (2019)
23. Jie Lu, W., Huang, Z., Hong, C., Ma, Y., Qu, H.: PEGASUS: bridging polynomial and non-polynomial evaluations in homomorphic encryption. In: 2021 IEEE Symposium on Security and Privacy, pp. 1057–1073. IEEE Computer Society Press (2021). https://doi.org/10.1109/SP40001.2021.00043
24. Marcolla, C., Sucasas, V., Manzano, M., Bassoli, R., Fitzek, F.H.P., Aaraj, N.: Survey on fully homomorphic encryption, theory, and applications. Proc. IEEE 110(10), 1572–1609 (2022)
25. Micciancio, D., Polyakov, Y.: Bootstrapping in FHEW-like cryptosystems. In: WAHC, pp. 17–28 (2021)

26. Papernot, N., Song, S., Mironov, I., Raghunathan, A., Talwar, K., Erlingsson, Ú.: Scalable private learning with pate. arXiv preprint arXiv:1802.08908 (2018)
27. Regev, O.: On lattices, learning with errors, random linear codes, and cryptography. J. ACM (JACM) **56**(6), 1–40 (2009)
28. Ribeiro, M., Grolinger, K., Capretz, M.A.: MLAAS: machine learning as a service. In: IEEE ICMLA, pp. 896–902 (2015)
29. Sutskever, I., Vinyals, O., Le, Q.V.: Sequence to sequence learning with neural networks. In: Neural Information Processing Systems, pp. 3104–3112 (2014)
30. Yao, A.C.: Protocols for secure computations. In: SFCS, pp. 160–164. IEEE (1982)

Pixels Who Violate Our Privacy! Deep Learning for Identifying Images' Key Pixels

Carmen Veenker[1], Danny Opdam[1], and Mina Alishahi[2(✉)]

[1] Informatics Institute, University of Amsterdam, Amsterdam, The Netherlands
`c.m.i.veenker@uva.nl`
[2] Department of Computer Science, Open Universiteit, Heerlen, The Netherlands
`mina.sheikhalishahi@ou.nl, dopdam@os3.nl`

Abstract. In recent years, face recognition as an effective biometric technique has received significant attention. The worldwide application of face recognition, however, raises strong concerns regarding the individuals' privacy. This problem has been particularly addressed by encrypting all pixels of an image, which is computationally heavy. In this paper, we propose a new framework using deep neural network that determines the most identifiable pixels (instead of all pixels) of an image for encryption. Our experimental result shows that our proposed approach significantly reduces the number of pixels required to be encrypted.

Keywords: Deep Learning · Face Recognition · Privacy · Encryption

1 Introduction

Face recognition technology exhibits extensive potential for application across diverse domains. Notably, it serves as a pivotal tool in the realm of biometric authentication, bolstering security measures in both public and private domains. Its deployment in video surveillance systems is instrumental in the detection and monitoring of suspicious activities within public spaces, including but not limited to shopping malls, airports, and train stations [7]. Furthermore, facial recognition systems play an indispensable role in airport security protocols, facilitating the verification of passengers' identities and thereby ensuring their safety during air travel. They are equally instrumental in building access control mechanisms, guaranteeing secure access exclusively to authorized personnel. This technology extends its reach to mobile phone applications, enabling secure payment processes and user authentication. Additionally, it finds utility in educational institutions, such as schools and universities, for purposes ranging from attendance monitoring to the assessment of student engagement and academic performance. Beyond these applications, face recognition technology offers promising prospects in the realm of self-driving cars, where it contributes to enhanced safety and security by detecting driver drowsiness and distraction, and by providing personalized driver settings and preferences [9,13].

S. Katsikas et al. (Eds.): ESORICS 2023 Workshops, LNCS 14399, pp. 552–568, 2024.
https://doi.org/10.1007/978-3-031-54129-2_33

Although the use of facial recognition technology has shown to be advantageous in various domains, it also gives rise to significant privacy concerns [7]. This biometric data can be misused to profile and track individuals without their consent, which poses a threat to their privacy and safety. Moreover, the misuse of such technology has the potential to lead to serious human rights violations, such as government surveillance, racial profiling, and discrimination. Furthermore, acquiring the consent of a large number of people whose images are monitored is not practical, which makes it challenging to ensure the ethical and responsible use of facial recognition technology.

These privacy risks highlight the need for regulation and oversight of face recognition technology to ensure that it is used ethically and responsibly. It is important to balance the potential benefits of the technology with the risks to privacy and civil [1,15]. Accordingly, the societal and legislative expectations on the use of biometric recognition techniques have resulted in growing attention of the research community in finding solutions that balance the benefits of face recognition systems on one hand, and the privacy of users on the other hand [13]. To fulfill this purpose, several privacy enhancing technologies have been embedded in the process of face recognition, including but are not limited to, the application of anonymization [4], differential privacy [3], and encryption techniques [6,17].

Among the others, more attention has been devoted to encryption techniques. When a facial image is encrypted, it is transformed into a coded version that can only be decoded with the proper decryption key. This ensures that only authorized parties can access the facial images and personal data. Beside to the confidentiality protection, encryption methods ensure that the facial images and personal data are not tampered with during transmission or storage, ensuring the integrity of the data. Last but not least, encryption methods help organizations comply with privacy regulations, such as the General Data Protection Regulation (GDPR)[1] or the Health Insurance Portability and Accountability Act (HIPAA)[2], which require organizations to protect personal data and prevent unauthorized access [20]. However, these methodologies generally impose undesirable computation and communication overheads [19]. In particular, these complexities are noticeable in encrypting the images as the number of pixel required to be encrypted is high per image. This is while all pixels shaping a face image are not revealing (or linked to) sensitive information about a person, e.g., the background of a face image.

In this study, as the first effort in this direction, we design a framework, namely *partial pixel*, which uses deep neural networks as building blocks to identify the key pixels in a face image that are *enough* to be encrypted for protecting image privacy. We call it 'enough' as a very accurate face recognition model (based on the deep neural network) is unable to recognize the face.

Partial pixel model combines two CNN networks, where the first one is used to detect the pixels and the other one is used for recognition. To accurately evaluate

---

[1] https://gdpr-info.eu/.
[2] https://www.hhs.gov/hipaa/index.html.

the effectiveness of the proposed model, we introduce a new metric called the "pixel value metric". This metric is based on the idea that for the generated images to be high-quality, they should have pixel values that are similar to those of the original image. We evaluated the performance of our framework on *CelebA* dataset that contains more than 200,000 images of celebrities. Our experimental results show that one average the number of pixels needed to be encrypted has been reduced by 30%.

The remainder of this paper is organized as follows. The next section presents the preliminary concepts used in this study. Section 3 provides an overview of the partial pixel framework for identifying the key pixels. The experimental setup and performance results are presented in Sect. 4. In Sect. 5, the related work are presented. Section 6 concludes the paper along with proposing future directions.

2 Preliminaries

This section details two models used as building blocks for our proposed model.

2.1 Pixel Detection

For the first part of our model, named *a context-encoder*, in essence a Convolutional Neural Network (CNN) that predicts the obscured regions in a scene from their surroundings (adopted from [14]). The architecture of this model is modelled after an encoder-decoder network. The encoder part of the model takes an image with obscured regions as its input and assembles the latent feature representation of that image. Then, the decoder part of the model takes this feature representation and attempts to reassemble the obscured regions. The encoder and decoder are connected through a channel-wise fully connected layer; this allows each unit in the decoder to have access to the information of the entire image. A schematic overview of the architecture can be seen in Fig. 1. As the context encoder needs to both understand the content of an image, as well as (re)produce the missing regions, it is trained to minimize both reconstruction and adversarial loss.

Encoder: The encoder is derived from *AlexNet* architecture [11]. The layer starts with 5 convolutional layers, followed by a pooling layer. When using a 227×227 sized image, this results in a $6 \times 6 \times 256$ dimensional feature space. The model is trained from scratch with randomly initialized weights. Since, this model uses fully connected layers, instead of the usually seen bottleneck in an encoder-decoder architecture, the latent feature dimension results in 9216 for both the encoder and decoder. However, not using a bottleneck would result in over 100M different parameters to tune, so therefore this model uses a channel-wise fully-connected layer.

Channel-Wise Fully-Connected Layer: This layer is in essence a fully-connected layer with groups that are intended to propagate information within the activations of each feature map. This means that when an input layer has m feature maps of size $n \times n$, this layer will output m feature maps of size $n \times n$. Thus, each feature map only propagates information within the feature map. After this, a stride one convolution is used to propagate this information across channels.

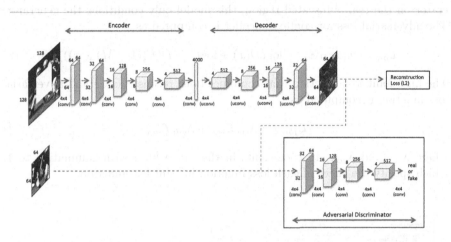

Fig. 1. Context Encoder architecture [14].

Decoder: The decoder of this model simultaneously works as a decoder and discriminator for this problem. Following the channel-wise fully-connected layer, the model uses five up-convolutional layers with learned filters, each with a ReLU (Rectified Linear Unit) activation function. In these layers up-sampling is followed by convolution to reconstruct a feature of the correct size.

Loss Functions: The context encoder is trained by regressing to the true content of the obscured region. As the missing regions can be reconstructed in various equally valid ways, two distinct loss functions, named reconstruction and adversarial loss functions, are used to extract the most viable reconstruction. The reconstruction loss (or pixel-wise loss) captures the overall structure of the missing region and its coherence within its context. It tends to average multiple reconstructions, which makes the resulting reconstruction appear blurry. A possible explanation for this is that it is safer to predict the mean of the distribution as this minimizes the pixel-wise error. Pixel-wise loss is calculated using the mean absolute error (MAE) between the generated image and the original. The reconstruction loss function is computed as

$$\mathcal{L}_{rec}(x) = \|\hat{M} \odot (x - F(1 - \hat{M}) \odot x))\|_2^2 \tag{1}$$

where x is the ground truth image, the context encoder F outputs $F(x)$; $\hat{M}$ is a binary mask that corresponds to the dropped image in which value 1 shows that a pixel has been dropped and 0 means that it has been considered as input pixel; and $\odot$ denotes the element-wise product operation.

The adversarial loss function is defined based on Generative Adversarial Networks (GANs). GANs are difficult to train for a context predicting task as the discriminator too easily classifies reconstructions and original images. To combat this disadvantage, instead of conditioning both the discriminator and the generator on the real obfuscated region, this model only conditions the generator. The adversarial loss for context encoder is computed as

$$\mathcal{L}_{adv} = max_D \, \mathbb{E}_{x \in \mathcal{X}}[\log(D(x) + \log(1 - D(F((1 - \hat{M}) \odot x)))] \qquad (2)$$

The final joint loss function that combines both reconstruction and adversarial loss function is computed as:

$$\mathcal{L}_{joint} = \lambda_{rec}\mathcal{L}_{rec} + \lambda_{adv}\mathcal{L}_{adv} \qquad (3)$$

where λ_{rec} and λ_{adv} are coefficients in the range $[0, 1]$ with summation to 1, which specify the effect of each loss function in joint loss function.

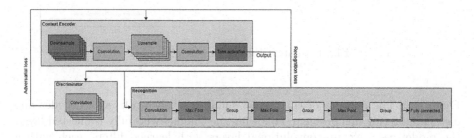

Fig. 2. Partial Pixel Model Architecture.

2.2   Recognition

The second part of our model handles recognition and is a Convolutional Neural Network (CNN) as presented in [22]. This CNN model is especially suitable for datasets that have ambiguous and inaccurate labels. In addition, the model(s) are all relatively lightweight. The model we use for our combined model is a CNN with only 9 layers, in practice this means a much faster training time while still offering relatively high recognition rates. The precision they report in the paper was around 80% on average, reaching up to at most 94% in some circumstances. Large scale datasets often contain a lot of noise. If errors incurred by this noise are not handled correctly, the CNN will learn a biased result. Rectified Linear Units (ReLUs) separate noise from informative signals by a threshold or bias value.

If this threshold is not met in the neuron activation, it will not be activated and its output value will be 0. The threshold value might also lead to the loss of some informative signals that are misclassified as noise because they did not meet the threshold value. To alleviate this issue, a new implementation of a maxout activation, named Max-FeatureMap (MFM), is introduced that seeks to obtain compact representations of input images and perform feature filter selection. It works as an alternative to ReLU, which suppresses low-activation neurons in each layer. While a ReLU learns its threshold value from training data, MFM puts several neurons in a competitive relationship. This results in obtaining better generalization ability and makes it applicable to different data distributions. The lightweight CNNs based on this MFM operation is designed to learn a more universal facial representation [22]. A detailed description of the layers of the 9-layer CNN can be found in [22].

3 Methodology

To identify the most indistinguishable pixels of an image, we combine the two models presented in Sects. 2.1 and 2.2 to generate our proposed model named the *partial pixel model*. Figure 2 demonstrates the architecture of our proposed model, which combines both networks by testing the output of the context encoder model with the discriminator as well as the recognition model.

The overall architecture of the recognition model and discriminator has not been changed from the models presented in Sect. 2, but for the context encoder, an extra convolutional layer and a tahn activation layer has been added for upsampling. The recognition model keeps the same 9-layer CNN architecture, but the output layer is resized to accommodate the number of classes in our dataset, and the model is resized to accommodate 128×128 images. This configuration can be modified according to the dataset used for a specific problem at hand. The context encoder as explained in Sect. 2.1 is used to generate faces for the training images. This is done by creating input images that have a 64×64 mask that covers the face in each image. Only the face is masked because the background should not provide any relevant information for the recognition model. The model is then trained to generate a reconstruction of the face.

The discriminator now ensures that a generated image is as close to the original image as possible, while the recognition model ensures that the context encoder generates faces that cannot be recognized. Thus, this should ensure that the generated faces are as similar as possible to the original face whilst not achieving recognition by the recognition model. This is done by propagating the losses from the discriminator and the recognition model through the context encoder. The new loss function for the context encoder therefore is defined as the following, which combines three loss functions:

$$\mathcal{L} = \lambda_{rec}\mathcal{L}_{rec} + \lambda_{adv}\mathcal{L}_{adv} + \lambda_{recog}\mathcal{L}_{recog} \tag{4}$$

where the first loss functions ($\mathcal{L}_{rec}$ and $\mathcal{L}_{adv}$) refer to the loss functions of pixel detection model and the last one ($\mathcal{L}_{recog}$) refers to the loss function of recognition model. The recognition loss can either be zero or one, if a face is recognized, it is 1. This ensures that when a face is correctly recognized, the loss increases significantly, and when the face is not (correctly) recognized, the loss does not change.

Pixel Value Metric: For the accurate evaluation of the model we propose a novel metric, named the pixel value metric. Since the generation of the new images is done on a contextual basis and through the use of the discriminator, the original image and generated image should have pixels that are close in value, and the best generated images should almost have the same pixel values. Therefore, our hypothesis is that after taking the difference in pixel values, the most contrasting pixel values are the most significant for facial recognition. This is because the most contrasting pixel values are probably pixels that could not be significantly optimized by the model because they would facilitate recognition. Therefore the pixel difference is calculated, then the maximum and minimum values are taken from this array. Then with this, the most valuable pixels for encryption given a certain threshold t are selected. The formula for this metric is shown in Eq. 5. Here, P is the array of subtraction differences between pixel values from the original image and generated image. The pixel value the current value in generated image that is being looked at.

$$pixelvalue = \arg\max_{p \in P}(P) - t \vee pixelvalue = \arg\min_{p \in P}(P) + t \tag{5}$$

4   Experimental Analysis

4.1   Experimental Setup

This section describes the experiments we performed and the expectations for these experiments. It also explains the set-up for the experiments and the resources needed to reproduce these experiments. This section is divided into two parts. The first part constitutes the facial recognition part where some general experiments and their general set-up are explained. The second part focuses on the partial pixel model where the experiments from our model and their set-up/resources are specified.

Dataset: The dataset used in this study is named *CelebA* dataset[3], which contains over 200-thousand images of celebrities in various poses, lighting levels and backgrounds[4]. Since it is important to find specific facial regions that are key for detection, the most representative images have been selected, *e.g.*, front facing, well lit, and little clutter. To reduce bias in our trained models, the occurrences

---

[3] http://mmlab.ie.cuhk.edu.hk/projects/CelebA.html [12].
[4] It should be noted that the face images presented in this paper represent the images of celebrities who passed away more than 10 years ago, *i.e.*, publishing them satisfy the GDPR privacy regulations (see recital 27).

of each celebrity images are counted and those celebrities that have less than 15 images in the dataset are filtered out. Using the remaining celebrities' images, with anywhere between 15 and 35 images each, it still remains over 180-thousand images. To decrease bias once more, the images with less than 30 occurrences are mirrored to bridge the gap. This means that for a celebrity with 15 entries, all images are mirrored once, for a celebrity with 20 entries only the first 10 images are mirrored. The resulting dataset contains over 220-thousand images in which for each celebrity at least 30 images are presented.

Environment: The models have been trained on 3 separate NVIDIA GeForce GTX 1080 Ti GPUs with each 10.9 Gi memory.

Recognition Model Parameter Tuning: For the face recognition model, we train the model for 80 epochs with different learning rate lr, starting with an initial learning rate i at 0.01. For each epoch e, the learning rate is increased with step s and a scale c of 0.46 as $lr = i \times c^{\frac{e}{s}}$. Moreover, the model has a momentum of 0.9 and a weight-decay of 1E-4. These parameters optimize the model performance according to the original paper [22].

Recognition Model Experimental Set-Up: To test the abilities of the facial recognition model and to create a baseline for our results, some general experiments were performed on the recognition model. The first experiment tests the capabilities of the recognition model under normal circumstances. This means that the performance of the model on the original (unmasked) images is tested. Then, two general experiments were devised. Because our hypothesis is that facial landmarks are the most important for facial recognition, the first general experiment was occluding all the facial landmarks. The amount of coverage of these facial landmarks differs from what radius/amount of pixels you choose to cover from these landmarks. Therefore, we chose to cover the least amount of pixels necessary to still cover an adequate portion of the facial landmarks (500 pixels) and a decent amount of pixels to cover the facial landmarks completely (3300), examples of these masked images can be observed in Fig. 3. The expectation is that the images with smaller amounts of pixels covered eventually decrease the accuracy of the model, but it still remains capable in recognizing the face. With the full coverage, we expect it becomes significantly more difficult for the model to be accurate.

Furthermore, we also design an experiment where only the eyes are masked, since our hypothesis is that of all facial landmarks the eyes are probably the most significant feature for facial recognition. There are two different amounts of pixels defined, one for full coverage (1800) and one for the minimum amount of coverage acceptable (200 pixels). Our expectation, similarly to before, is that the full coverage will make the recognition model perform significantly worse, whereas minimal coverage will only change the performance slightly. Moreover, we also expect that the coverage of all facial landmarks will cause the recognition model to perform significantly worse than only coverage of the eyes.

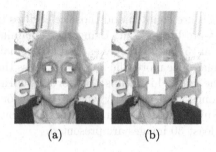

(a)   (b)

Fig. 3. Naive masking using landmarks.

Table 1. The loss functions of models during training.

Model	minimum loss	average loss	max loss
Recognition model	0.5144	1.1981	8.9110
Partial Pixel rec. loss	0.0631	1.0001	3.1423
Partial Pixel adv. loss	0.0390	0.0614	0.1278

Partial Pixel Model Parameter Tuning: For this model, the adam learning rate of 0.0002, and adam decay of 0.5 and 0.999 are used. Furthermore, 4 CPU threads are used for batch generation. The coefficients λ_{adv}, λ_{rec}, and λ_{recog} of the loss function in Eq. 4 have been set to 0.001, 0.999, and 3, respectively.

Partial Pixel Model Experimental Set-up: The more elaborate partial pixel model experiments are devised using the novel pixel value threshold. Three different thresholds are used for generating different masks on the images that vary in the amount of pixel coverage they possess. These three thresholds go from minimal coverage to medium coverage to large coverage. The thresholds themselves and their results can be found in Sect. 4.2. These thresholds are used because depending on the threshold some images are completely covered by the mask and some are minimally covered. Therefore, we picked three thresholds that show interesting results for each situation. We expect that the middle threshold will offer the best trade-off between computational load and privacy.

Evaluation: After the creation of the masked images, both the generic mask images and the images with masks created by the context encoder, were tested by the recognition model, to investigate their ability in confusing the recognition model. The generated masked images are also evaluated with a qualitative analysis of the masks. This analysis focuses on possible reasons for the network struggling with particular image masks. More specifically, the analysis looks at added attributes, gender, and hairstyles. The output of the recognition model on the masked images was evaluated with the metrics precision at one and precision at five. Precision at n is defined as the chance that the correct identity is present in the top n candidates. The amount of pixels that are masked in each image is also evaluated.

4.2   Experimental Results

Analysis of the Models During Training: Table 1 reports the losses of both models. The minimum loss refers to the minimum loss that each model achieved, whereas the maximum loss shows the highest loss the models received. The partial pixel d. loss is the L1 loss experienced by the discriminator. This loss function by far reaches the lowest minimum loss and reaches the lowest loss on average. The loss function for the recognition model also improves a lot during training, the maximum loss is very high, while the average loss is much better (lower). The pixel loss and adversarial loss from the partial pixel model (described in Sect. 2.1) also reach an overall good loss.

Table 2. Precision@1 and precision@5 of the two models.

CNN 9-layer			
Experiment	precision@1	precision@5	num. of pixels masked
Normal images	77%	88%	0
Images without facial landmark (fewer pixels)	17%	34%	400–500
Images without facial landmark (more pixels)	0.54%	2.1%	3300
Images without eyes (fewer pixels)	35%	57%	200
Images without eyes (more pixels)	2.6%	7.3%	1800
Partial pixel			
Experiment	precision@1	precision@5	num. of pixels masked
Masking with $t = 0.4$	0.82%	2.66%	1043
Masking with $t = 0.5$	0.32%	1.02%	2210
Masking with $t = 0.6$	0.16%	0.66%	2232

Both models went through a rigorous testing phase to evaluate the results. As can be seen in Table 2, the recognition model attained fairly accurate results on the normal images (especially for precision@5). As expected, the images that included a mask on the facial landmarks were not predicted accurately. The images where the facial landmarks were covered completely resulted in a significantly low precision rate, whereas as expected the adequately covered facial landmarks still resulted in a fairly high precision. On the images without eyes, the recognition model performed better than the images missing all landmarks, but as expected it still performed worse than the normal images.

Table 2 also shows the precision for the images masked by the partial pixel model. Three different thresholds were chosen, as explained in Sect. 4.1. The thresholds are $t = 0.4$, where the average amount of masked pixels is 1043, $t = 0.5$ where the average amount of masked pixels is 2210 and $t = 0.6$, where the average amount of pixels masked is 2232. All of the partial pixel model experiments resulted in much lower precision rates, thus successfully reducing the recognition ability of the recognition model. The images with a threshold of 0.4 resulted in very low precision rates, thus maintaining privacy well, while only masking a small number of pixels. The images with masking threshold of 0.5 resulted in even lower precision, but also resulted in more masked pixels. The best results were acquired by the 0.6 threshold, here the lowest precision rate was observed, but also the highest amount of pixels were masked.

Qualitative Analysis of the Generated Images and Masks: Figure 4 depicts the activations of the last convolutional layer. The red colour defines the most important part of the image. In these three different images, it can be seen that a significant focus is put on and around the face and facial features. Furthermore, it also shows that the model seems to focus on the jawline, the start of the hairline and the eyes.

Figure 5 compares the generated and original images. The reconstruction is done based on the model detailed in Sect. 2 part 1. It can be observed that the reconstruction using the context-encoder approximates the original image fairly well. It shows that the mouth and teeth are constructed accurately. The nose also looks very similar to the original nose. But the eyes in most generated images look significantly different. Moreover, the eyes in most generated images look very similar to the eyes in other generated images. Furthermore, the hairline in many reconstructions is blurred or smoothed much like wrinkles, jawlines and other sharp facial features.

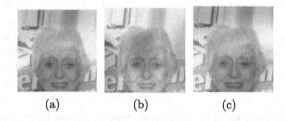

(a)   (b)   (c)

Fig. 4. Heat map of the activations in the last convolutional layer.

(a)   (b)   (c)

Fig. 5. Reconstruction of facial images.

Figure 6 shows the created masked images. The masks are made using the pixel value metric detailed in Eq. 5. When overlaid with the mask that indicates which pixels are selected for encryption, several observations can be made. The eyes seem to always be for the most part or completely covered, similarly most of the eyebrows are also covered. Furthermore, regions around the start of the hairline are also usually covered by the mask. In all pictures, we see that the square in which the reconstruction takes place is very pronounced. Moreover, as Fig. 6 shows, approximately half of the facial region is used for masking in most cases. The CelebA dataset also includes several images containing faces with specific attributes, such as wearing hats, glasses, etc. Images containing attributes usually performed worse during reconstruction. In Fig. 7, a person wearing glasses is depicted. The masked image shows the same facial landmark masking as previous images, but also masks the glasses.

4.3   Discussion

During the training we found that the discriminator function performed quite accurately, i.e., the discriminator learned very well to determine whether an image was real or fake. The reconstructions made during training also appear to look significantly close to their original images.

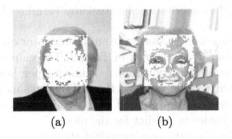

(a)   (b)

Fig. 6. Masks of facial images.

During testing, we found that our generated masks outperform almost all naive experiments. Only the images without facial landmarks experiment are able to outperform our masking with a threshold of 0.4. However, the difference in the amount of pixels masked is very high. Our masking reduces the number of pixels to be masked by 30% or more, while showing a very significant decline in precision. This means that even with our limited resources, we were able to provide effective privacy against a CNN while only encrypting around 1/8th of the image (1/2 of the facial region). However, the best performance (lowest precision) done with a masking with threshold 0.6 still results in a fairly high amount of masked pixels. Therefore, the trade-off between privacy and computing power still holds.

The hypothesis that the eye region contains the most important pixels of a face image seems to be a valid assumption [10], as almost every mask masked the eyes and all generated images contained very similar eyes. Moreover, when only masking the eyes in our naive experiments, the drop in precision for the model was significant (it dropped to almost half).

Looking a bit deeper into specific images and how the chosen pixels looked in the images revealed several patterns. The first and most easily explained pattern is the role of some attributes (hats, sunglasses, etc.) appearing in some images. These attributes along with natural 'hard' borders in pixel values were almost always chosen for masking. Our hypothesis is that by their very nature these hard borders are less easily predicted by the reconstruction as they represent sudden large shifts in pixel value.

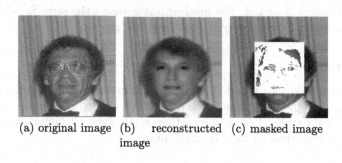

(a) original image   (b)   reconstructed   (c) masked image
                               image

Fig. 7. Images with specific attributes (wearing glasses).

Next, we have some images that were either under- or over masked compared to the average number of pixels seen in Table 2. The culprit of over-masking is likely a combination of the low number of images per label and the random selection used to split the dataset into the training/evaluating/testing subsets. A certain label being underrepresented in the training set will of course result in that label being harder to predict for the model.

Under-masking was a little more prevalent than over-masking, here the cause most probably lies with the recognition method used. The lightweight CNN we used started with a precision of 77%, which means that some images were not going to be recognized unless the mask is extremely small. Added to this fact are the observations made by [2] and [5]: "*Any distortion in an image, even though almost imperceptible to a human observer, has a huge effect on most, if not all, deep learning recognition systems*". This effect was exacerbated by the usage of a smaller network in combination with a relatively 'small' dataset with a small number of images per label. The result is a large portion of the images being under-masked and likely easily recognizable by better networks or human eye.

5   Related Work

In [18], a system called Fawke is introduced that helps the individuals to inoculate their images against facial recognition models. Fawkes does this by making imperceptible pixel level-changes, which they call them cloaks, to the images of the users. When a facial recognition model is thereafter trained on these images, these pixel-level changes will cause the facial recognition to consistently misidentify the normal images. They demonstrated a 95% protection rate against these models regardless of the training method. Our research instead focuses on encryption for privacy so that even future algorithms or the human eye can not recognize the subject. In [16], an encryption mechanism is designed for the selective encryption of images. Their approach is based on AES stream cipher using Variable Length Encoding of the Huffman's vector. This method keeps the bitstream consistent and also keeps the JPEG bit-stream compliant. The objective is to provide privacy only giving authorized persons full-resolution access to images. This way of partially encrypting images is best suited to areas where there is no need for full encryption. The encrypted image can be seen as a blurry version of the original, which allows it to be usable without disclosing all its information. Our research aims to provide privacy with our model, which is more binary in nature. Simply blurring an image is not sufficient in this setting. In [8], the focus is on privacy in object detection mainly by obfuscating image clarity. They do this by blurring images and altering the colors of the image. The main reasoning behind this is lowering bias in the training of models. They report that blurring or editing the images used in training provides little improvement in what the model ends up identifying. In [6], an encryption-based approach is proposed to efficiently hide biometrics and the response from the server that matches the input to a known database. In this protocol both parties learn only non-sensitive information; privacy sensitive information remains with the respective party that has 'control' over it. This means that the party that needs to be identified only gets to know basic database information while the party that does the identifying does not learn the input image or the result of the recognition process. Even though their protocol is deemed very efficient, the identification of a person against a database of 320 persons takes approximately 40 s, hinting at the cost of encrypting images that we are aiming to reduce. In [5], the focus is on identifying imperfect facial images as opposed to perfect data consisting of full frontal facial images. They test various degrees of rotation and zooming in/out and focus on the recognition rates of facial landmarks (eyes, mouth, nose, cheeks). Their research shows that individual facial landmarks offer low recognition rates while combining individual parts of the face makes the rate of recognition rise quickly. Their most promising result was using a Cosine Similarity classifier for facial recognition of partial or distorted facial data. Another important take from their results is that the eyes seemed to contain the most recognizable information, something that from a human facial recognition standpoint makes intuitive sense. Our research aims to prevent recognition of faces in a way doing the opposite to Elmahmudi et al. our research focuses on the whole face and not just landmarks and search for the most impactful distortions in a targeted approach. In [2], several factors that degrade the accuracy of facial recognition such as aging, pose variation, illumination, partial occlusion etc. are investigated. They then go on to review a selection of algorithms that are either feature-based, appearance-based or some combination of the two. They conclude that recognition is affected by all previously mentioned factors and that no model has a great answer to this problem. Especially in non-frontal the face recognition rates remain poor. The authors focus on natural factors in degradation of accuracy, we aim to actively distort a face to find the most impactful regions to distort. In [23], the authors propose a face privacy-preserving method based on Invertible Mask Network (IMN). In IMN, a Mask-net is introduced to generate "Mask" face. Then, the "Mask" face is used to generate masked face which is indistinguishable from "Mask" face. Finally, the "Mask" face is dropped from the masked face to obtain the recovered face to the authorized entities. In [24], the facial images are first partially covered with mosaic, which are used to train an encoder to generate the protected images with original images also embedded. Another classifier is then trained using protected images for facial expression recognition and a decoder to recover original images. In [21], a new framework named FaceMAE is proposed, which considers both privacy and recognition accuracy at the same time. In this framework, randomly masked faces are first used to train a reconstruction model. During the development, FaceMAE is used to reconstruct images from masked faces of unseen images with no extra training.

To the best of our knowledge, our framework is the first one that employs deep learning to find the key pixels in a facial image in terms of information leakage.

6   Conclusion and Future Directions

This research set out to identify the pixels that need to be encrypted to ensure privacy against facial recognition systems. Because we knew that the black box nature of deep learning algorithms would prohibit us from finding a clear cut answer, we devised a metric to measure success with the number of pixels that need to be encrypted to ensure privacy. Using this metric in combination with the recognition model's precision we show that the number of pixels required to be encrypted has significantly been reduced (almost 30% reduction). While there are certainly more steps that can still be made towards improving the methodology, partial image encryption shows promising results.

Our results indicate that there is a lot that can still be done to further this area of research. In our framework, we use the combination of only two neural network models with their optimal parameters proposed by the original models; still, the combination of more models and tuning the models' parameters can improve the performance of our framework. The other future direction is considering the security and privacy attacks that threaten our framework. For instance, how our model can become resistant against attackers who have background knowledge either about the people whose face images have been used in training our model or about the model by itself. A possible direction then could be reconstructing the original face from partially encrypted (suspected) matches or even looking at the encrypted and original image to identify similarities. Also, it might be interesting to research how faces synthesized by other deep learning algorithms are handled by partial encryption models. Finally, we plan to use explainable AI techniques in analyzing the situation of pixels that violate the privacy most.

References

1. Alishahi, M., Moghtadaiee, V., Navidan, H.: Add noise to remove noise: local differential privacy for feature selection. Comput. Secur. **123**, 102934 (2022)
2. Anwarul, S., Dahiya, S.: A comprehensive review on face recognition methods and factors affecting facial recognition accuracy. In: Proceedings of ICRIC, pp. 495–514 (2020)
3. Chamikara, M., Bertok, P., Khalil, I., Liu, D., Camtepe, S.: Privacy preserving face recognition utilizing differential privacy. Comput. Secur. **97**, 101951 (2020)
4. Chhabra, S., Singh, R., Vatsa, M., Gupta, G.: Anonymizing k-facial attributes via adversarial perturbations. CoRR abs/1805.09380 (2018). http://arxiv.org/abs/1805.09380
5. Elmahmudi, A., Ugail, H.: Deep face recognition using imperfect facial data. Future Gener. Comput. Syst. **99**, 213–225 (2019)
6. Erkin, Z., Franz, M., Guajardo, J., Katzenbeisser, S., Lagendijk, I., Toft, T.: Privacy-preserving face recognition. In: Goldberg, I., Atallah, M.J. (eds.) International Symposium on Privacy Enhancing Technologies Symposium, vol. 5672, pp. 235–253. Springer, Heidelberg (2009). https://doi.org/10.1007/978-3-642-03168-7_14
7. Hasan, M.R., Guest, R., Deravi, F.: Presentation-level privacy protection techniques for automated face recognition - a survey. ACM Comput. Surv. **55**, 1–27 (2023). https://doi.org/10.1145/3583135
8. He, P., et al.: Privacy-preserving object detection. arXiv preprint arXiv:2103.06587 (2021)
9. Kortli, Y., Jridi, M., Al Falou, A., Atri, M.: Face recognition systems: a survey. Sensors **20**(2), 342 (2020). https://doi.org/10.3390/s20020342
10. Kou, Z., Shang, L., Zhang, Y., Duan, S., Wang, D.: Can i only share my eyes? a web crowdsourcing based face partition approach towards privacy-aware face recognition. In: Proceedings of the ACM Web Conference 2022, WWW 2022, pp. 3611–3622. (2022)
11. Krizhevsky, A., Sutskever, I., Hinton, G.E.: Imagenet classification with deep convolutional neural networks. Adv. Neural Inf. Process. Syst. **25** (2012)
12. Liu, Z., Luo, P., Wang, X., Tang, X.: Deep learning face attributes in the wild. In: Proceedings of International Conference on Computer Vision (ICCV) (2015)
13. Meden, B., et al.: Privacy-enhancing face biometrics: a comprehensive survey. IEEE Trans. Inf. Forensics Secur. **16**, 4147–4183 (2021)
14. Pathak, D., Krahenbuhl, P., Donahue, J., Darrell, T., Efros, A.A.: Context encoders: feature learning by inpainting. In: Proceedings of the IEEE Conference on Computer Vision and Pattern Recognition, pp. 2536–2544 (2016)
15. Rezende, I.N.: Facial recognition in police hands: assessing the 'clearview case' from a European perspective. New J. Eur. Crim. Law **11**(3), 375–389 (2020)
16. Rodrigues, J.M., Puech, W., Bors, A.G.: A selective encryption for heterogenous color jpeg images based on VLC and AES stream cipher. In: Conference on Colour in Graphics, Imaging, and Vision, vol. 2006, pp. 34–39. Society for Imaging Science and Technology (2006)

17. Sadeghi, A.R., Schneider, T., Wehrenberg, I.: Efficient privacy-preserving face recognition. In: Lee, D., Hong, S. (eds.) Information, Security and Cryptology, vol. 5984, pp. 229–244. Springer, Heidelberg (2010). https://doi.org/10.1007/978-3-642-14423-3_16

18. Shan, S., Wenger, E., Zhang, J., Li, H., Zheng, H., Zhao, B.Y.: Fawkes: protecting personal privacy against unauthorized deep learning models. arXiv:2002.08327 (2020)

19. Sheikhalishahi, M., Martinelli, F.: Privacy-utility feature selection as a tool in private data classification. In: Omatu, S., Rodríguez, S., Villarrubia, G., Faria, P., Sitek, P., Prieto, J. (eds.) Distributed Computing and Artificial Intelligence, vol. 620, pp. 254–261. Springer, Cham (2018). https://doi.org/10.1007/978-3-319-62410-5_31

20. Sheikhalishahi, M., Tillem, G., Erkin, Z., Zannone, N.: Privacy-preserving multiparty access control. In: ACM Workshop on Privacy in the Electronic Society, WPES 2019, pp. 1–13. Association for Computing Machinery (2019)

21. Wang, K., et al.: Facemae: privacy-preserving face recognition via masked autoencoders (2022). https://arxiv.org/abs/2205.11090

22. Wu, X., He, R., Sun, Z., Tan, T.: A light CNN for deep face representation with noisy labels. IEEE Trans. Inf. Forensics Secur. **13**(11), 2884–2896 (2018)

23. Yang, Y., Huang, Y., Shi, M., Chen, K., Zhang, W., Yu, N.: Invertible mask network for face privacy-preserving (2022). https://arxiv.org/abs/2204.08895

24. You, Z., Li, S., Qian, Z., Zhang, X.: Reversible privacy-preserving recognition. In: IEEE International Conference on Multimedia and Expo (ICME), pp. 1–6 (2021). https://doi.org/10.1109/ICME51207.2021.9428115

Verifiable Fairness: Privacy–preserving Computation of Fairness for Machine Learning Systems

Ehsan Toreini[1]([✉])(iD), Maryam Mehrnezhad[2](iD), and Aad van Moorsel[3](iD)

[1] University of Surrey, Guildford, UK
e.toreini@surrey.ac.uk
[2] Royal Holloway University of London, Egham, UK
m.mehrnezhad@rhul.ac.uk
[3] Birmingham University, Birmingham, UK
a.vanmoorsel@bham.ac.uk

Abstract. Fair machine learning is a thriving and vibrant research topic. In this paper, we propose Fairness as a Service (FaaS), a secure, verifiable and privacy-preserving protocol to computes and verify the fairness of any machine learning (ML) model. In the deisgn of FaaS, the data and outcomes are represented through cryptograms to ensure privacy. Also, zero knowledge proofs guarantee the well-formedness of the cryptograms and underlying data. FaaS is model–agnostic and can support various fairness metrics; hence, it can be used as a service to audit the fairness of any ML model. Our solution requires no trusted third party or private channels for the computation of the fairness metric. The security guarantees and commitments are implemented in a way that every step is securely transparent and verifiable from the start to the end of the process. The cryptograms of all input data are publicly available for everyone, e.g., auditors, social activists and experts, to verify the correctness of the process. We implemented FaaS to investigate performance and demonstrate the successful use of FaaS for a publicly available data set with thousands of entries.

Keywords: fairness computation · trustworthiness · machine learning fairness · artificial intelligence

1 Introduction

Demonstrating the fairness of algorithms is critical to the continued proliferation and acceptance of algorithmic decision making in general, and AI-based systems in particular. There is no shortage of examples that have diminished trust in algorithms because of unfair discrimination of groups within our population. This includes news stories about the human resource decision-making tools used by large companies, which turn out to discriminate against women [28]. There also are well-understood seminal examples studied widely within the academic

© The Author(s), under exclusive license to Springer Nature Switzerland AG 2024
S. Katsikas et al. (Eds.): ESORICS 2023 Workshops, LNCS 14399, pp. 569–584, 2024.
https://doi.org/10.1007/978-3-031-54129-2_34

community, such as the unfair decisions related to recidivism in different ethnicities [20]. In the UK, most recently the algorithm to determine A-levels substitute scores under COVID-19 was widely found to be unfair across demographics [23].

There has been a surge of research that aims to establish metrics that quantify the fairness of an algorithm. This is an important area of research, and tens of different metrics have been proposed, from individual fairness to group fairness. It has been shown that various expressions for fairness cannot be satisfied or optimised at once, thus establishing impossibility results [11]. Moreover, even if one agrees about a metric, this metric on its own does not provide trust to people. It matters not only what the metrics express, but also who computes the metrics and whether one can verify these computations and possibly appeal against them. At the same time, in situations in which verification by stakeholders is possible, the owner of the data wants to be assured that none of the original, typically sensitive and personal, data is leaked. The system that runs the algorithms (later referred to as Machine Learning system or ML system) may have a valid interest in maintaining the secrecy of the model. In other words, if one wants to establish *verifiable fairness*, one needs to tackle a number of security, privacy and trust concerns.

In FaaS, we take a fundamentally different design approach. We leak no data or model information, but the FaaS is still able to calculate fairness for a variety of fairness metrics and independent of the ML model. Thus, replacing the model in the ML system will not impact functionality of FaaS protocol. Moreover, any other party can verify this calculation since all the necessary encrypted information is posted publicly, on a 'fairness board'.

Summarising, our contributions are:

- We propose FaaS, a model–agnostic protocol to compute different fairness metrics without accessing sensitive information about the model and the dataset.
- FaaS is universally verifiable so everyone can verify the well–formedness of the cryptograms and the steps of the protocol.
- We implement a proof-of-concept of the FaaS architecture and protocol using off-the-shelf hardware, software, and datasets and run experiments to demonstrate the practical feasibility of FaaS.

2   Background and Related Work

One of the benefits of auditing ML-based products relates to trust. Trust and trustworthiness (in socio-technical terms) are complicated matters. Toreini et al. [32] proposed a framework for trustworthiness technologies in AI–solutions based on existing social frameworks on trust (i.e. demonstration of Ability, Benevolence and Integrity, a.k.a. ABI and ABI+ frameworks) and technological trustworthiness [30]. They comprehensively reviewed the policy documents on regulating AI and the existing technical literature and derived any ML–based solution needs to demonstrate fairness, explainability, auditability, and safety and security to establish social trust. When using AI solutions, one cannot be assured of the

Table 1. Features of FaaS and comparison with other privacy–oriented fair ML proposals (support: full: ✓, partial: ✚, none: ✗)

Work	Universal Verifiability	Ind. of metric	Ind. of ML model	User Privacy	Model Confidentiality	Off-the–shelf Hardware
Veal & Binns [33]	✗	✗	✗	✗	✗	✓
Kilbertus et al. [19]	✚	✗	✗	✓	✓	✓
Jagielski et al. [17]	✗	✗	✗	✓	✗	✓
Hu et al. [16]	✗	✗	✗	✓	✗	✓
Segal et al. [29]	✚	✓	✓	✓	✓	✓
Park et al. [27]	✚	✓	✓	✓	✓	✗
FaaS (this paper)	✓	✓	✓	✓	✓	✓

fairness of such systems without trusting the reputation of the technology provider (e.g., datasets and ML models). It is commonly believed that leading tech companies do not make mistake in their implementation [8]; however, in practice, we often witness that such products indeed suffer from bias in ML [23,28].

2.1 Fairness Metrics

There exist several fairness definitions in the literature. Designing a fair algorithm requires measuring and assessment of fairness. Researchers have worked on formalising fairness for a long time. Narayanan [24] lists at least 21 different fairness definitions in the literature and this number is growing, e.g., [5,6].

Fairness is typically expressed as discrimination in relation to data features. These features for which discrimination may happen are known as *Protected Attributes* (PAs) or sensitive attributes. These include, but are not limited to, ethnicity, gender, age, scholarity, nationality, religion and socio-economic group.

The majority of fairness definitions expresses fairness in relation to PAs. In this paper, we consider Group Fairness, which refers to a family of definitions, all of which consider the performance of a model on the population groups level. The fairness definitions in this group are focused on keeping decisions consistent across groups and are relevant to both disparate treatment and disparate impact notions, as defined in [9,15].

For the following definitions, let U be an individual in the dataset, where each individual has data features (X, A). In this context, A denotes the PA and in what follows $A = 1$ and $A = 0$ express membership of a protected group or not. X constitutes the rest of attributes that are available to the algorithm. Y denotes the actual label of U while $\hat{Y}$ would be the predicted label by the model: (1) Demographic Parity (DP) A classifier satisfies DP when outcomes are equal across groups $F_{DP} = \frac{Pr(\hat{Y}=1|A=0)}{Pr(\hat{Y}=1|A=1)}$ (2) *Equalised Odds (EOd)* A classifier satisfies EO if equality of outcomes happens across both groups and true labels: $F_{EOd} = \frac{Pr(\hat{Y}=1|A=0,Y=\gamma)}{Pr(\hat{Y}=1|A=1,Y=\gamma)}$ where $\gamma \in \{0, 1\}$. (3)Equality of Opportunity (EOp) is similar to EO, but only requires equal outcomes across subgroups for *true positives*: $F_{EOp} = \frac{Pr(\hat{Y}=1|A=0,Y=1)}{Pr(\hat{Y}=1|A=1,Y=1)}$

In this paper, we will focus on the computations based on the above three fairness metrics. For this computation, the auditor requires to have access to the three pieces of information for each elements in the dataset: (1) the sensitive group membership (binary value for A demonstrating if a sample does or does not belong to a group with PAs) (2) the actual labelling of the sample (binary value for Y) (3) the predicted label of the sample (binary value for $\hat{Y}$). The ML system transfers this information for each sample from their test set. Then, the auditor uses this information to compute the above fairness metrics.

Note that while we consider the above metrics for our protocol and proof-of-concept implementation in next sections, our core architecture is independent of metrics, and the metric set can be replaced by other metrics too (Fig. 1).

2.2   Auditing ML Models for Fairness

The existing research in fair ML normally assumes the computation of the fairness metric to be done locally by the ML system, with full access to the data, including the private attributes [5,6,15]. However, there is a lack of verifiability and independence in these approaches which will not necessarily lead to trustworthiness. To increase trust in the ML products, the providers might make the trained model self–explaining (aka transparent or explainable). There is also the transparent–by–design approach [2,12,34]. While this approach has its benefits, it is both model–specific and scenario–specific [25]; thus it cannot be generalised. There is also no trusted authority to verify such claims and explanations. Moreover, in reality, the trained model, datasets and feature extraction mechanisms are company assets. Once exposed, it can make them vulnerable to the competitors. Another approach to provide transparency to the fairness implementation comes through the black–box auditing, also known as adhoc [12,22,26]. In this way, the model is trained and audited for different purposes [1]. This solution is similar to tax auditing and financial ledgers where accountants verify and ensure these calculations are legitimate. However, unlike the well–established body of certifications and qualifications for accountants in tax auditing and financial ledgers; there does not exist any established processes and resources for fairness computation in AI and ML.

The concept of a service that calculates fairness has been proposed before, e.g., in [33]. The authors introduced an architecture to delegate the computation of fairness to a trusted third party that acts as a guarantor of its algorithmic fairness. In this model, the fairness service is trusted both by the ML system and the other stakeholders (e.g. users and activists). In particular, the ML system must trust the service to maintain the privacy of data and secrecy of its model, whilst revealing to the trusted third party the algorithm outcome, sensitive input data and even inner parameters of the model. This is a big assumption to trust that the third party would not misuse the information and hence the leakage of data and model information is not a threat.

To address these limitations, Kilbertdus et al. [19] proposed a system known as 'blind justice', which utilises multi–party computation protocols to enforce fairness into the ML model. Their proposal considers three groups of participants:

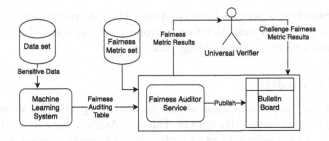

Fig. 1. FaaS Architecture

User (data owner), Model (ML model owner) and the Regulator (that enforces a fairness metric). These three groups collaborate with each in order to train a fair ML model using a federated learning approach [35]. The outcome is a fair model that is trained with the participation of these three groups in a privacy-preserving way. They only provide a limited degree of verifiability in which the trained model is cryptographically certified after training and each of the participants can make sure if the algorithm has not been modified. It should be noted that since they operate in the training stage of the ML pipeline, their approach is highly dependent on the implementation details of the ML model itself. Jagielski et al. [17] proposed a differential privacy approach in order to train a fair model. Similarly, Hu et al. [16] used a distributed approach to fair learning with only demographic information. Segal et al. [29] used similar cryptographic primitives but took a more holistic approach towards the computation and verification of fairness. They proposed a data-centric approach in which the verifier challenges a trained model via an encrypted and digitally certified dataset using merkle tree and other cryptographic primitives. Furthermore, the regulator will certify the model is fair based on the data received from the clients and a set of dataset provided to the model. Their approach does not provide universal verifiability as the regulator is the only party involved in the computation of fairness. More recently, Park et al. [27] proposed a Trusted Execution Environment (TEE) for the secure computation of fairness. Their proposal requires special hardware components which are cryptographically secure and provide enough guarantees and verification for the correct execution of the code.

The previous research generally has integrated fairness into their ML algorithms; therefore, such algorithms should be redesigned to use another fairness metric set. As it can be seen in Table 1, FaaS is the only work which is independent of the ML model and fairness metric with universal verifiability, and hence, can be used as a service.

3   FaaS Architecture

In this Section, we present the architecture of our system (Fig. 1) and describe its features. The FaaS architecture includes stakeholders in three roles: A) **ML System:** a system that owns the data and the ML algorithm, B) **Fairness**

Auditor Service: a service that computes the fair performance of the ML system, and C) **Universal Verifier:** anyone who has the technical expertise and motivation to verify the auditing process.

3.1 Threat Model

The design and implementation of the security of parties implementing the respective protocol roles (ML system, Fairness Auditor Service, and Universal Verifier) (Fig. 1) are independent of each other. The inter–communications that happen between the roles assumes no trust between parties; thus, all their claims must be accompanied with validation proofs (for which we will use ZKP). We assume the Auditor System is vulnerable to different attacks and not trustworthy. Thus, the data stored on the Fairness Auditor System must be encrypted, tamper-proof and verifiable at all stages. Moreover, we assume the communication channel between the ML system and fairness auditor is not protected. Therefore, the sensitive data must be encrypted before the transmission starts. However, there will be an agreement on the cryptographic primitives at the pre–setting stage in the protocol sequence.

In FaaS, we assume that the ML system is honest in sending the cryptograms of the original labels of the dataset samples. One might argue against such assumption and discuss that the ML system might intend to deceive the Auditor Service, and by extension the verifiers, by modifying the actual labels of the dataset. For instance, the ML system would provide the cryptograms of the actual labels and the predicted ones as similar to each other as possible so that the auditor concludes the algorithms are fair. This is an interesting area for further research. For instance, it may be addressed by providing the cryptograms of the actual labels to the Auditor Service independently e.g. the verifier may own a dataset it provides to a ML system. The verifier then separately decides the desired values for the actual labels and feeds these to the Auditor service. In this way, it is far less clear to the ML system how to manipulate the data it sends to the auditor, since some of the labels come from elsewhere.

The internal security of the roles is beyond FaaS. The ML system itself needs to consider extra measures to protect its data and algorithms. We assume the ML system does present the data and predictions honestly. This is a reasonable assumption since the incentives to perform *ethically* is in contrast to being dishonest when participating in fairness auditing process. This is discussed more in the Discussion Section.

3.2 Protocol Overview

The main security protocol sequence is between the ML system and Fairness Auditing Service or *auditor* in short form. Note that although we suggest three roles in our architecture, the communications are mainly between the above two roles, and any universal verifier can turn to the auditor service (which represents the fairness board), if they want to challenge the computations.

The ML system is responsible for the implementation and execution of the ML algorithm. It has data as input and performs some prediction (depending on

Table 2. Possible permutations of 3-bit representation of an entry in the original data.

Membership of Sensitive Group	Actual Label	Predicted Label	Encoded Permutation	Permutation #
No	0	0	000	#1
No	0	1	001	#2
No	1	0	010	#3
No	1	1	011	#4
Yes	0	0	100	#5
Yes	0	1	101	#6
Yes	1	0	110	#7
Yes	1	1	111	#8

the use case and purpose) that forms the output (Fig. 1). The Fairness Auditor Service receives information from the ML system, evaluates its fairness performance by computing a fairness metric. Then, it returns the result for the metric back to the ML system. It also publishes the calculations in a *fairness board* for public verification. The public fairness board is a publicly accessible, read-only fairness board (e.g. a website). The auditor only has the right to append data (and the sufficient proofs) to the fairness board. Also, the auditor verifies the authenticity, correctness and integrity of data before publishing it.

3.3 Protocol Sequence

This protocol has three stages: setup, cryptogram generation and fairness metric computation.

Phase I: Setup. In this phase, the ML System and Auditor agree on the initial settings. We assume the protocol functions in multiplicative cyclic group setting (i.e. Digital Signature Algorithm (DSA)–like group [18]), but it can also function in additive cyclic groups (i.e. Elliptic Curve Digital Signature Algorithm (ECDSA)–like groups [18]). The auditor and ML system publicly agree on (p, q, g) before the start of the protocol. Let p and q be two large primes where $q|(p-1)$. In a multiplicative cyclic group $(\mathbb{Z}_p^*)$, G_q is a subgroup of prime order q and g is its generator. For simplicity, we assume the Decision Diffie–Hellman (DDH) problem is out of scope [31].

Next, the ML system generates a public/private pair key by using DSA or ECDSA and publishes the public keys in the fairness board. The protection the private key pair depends on the security architecture of the ML system and we assume the private key is securely stored in an industrial standard practice (e.g. using the secure memory module on board).

Cryptogram Table: After initial agreements, the ML system produces a cryptogram table with n rows corresponding to the number of samples in their test

Table 3. Cryptogram Table for n data samples

Sample No	Random Public Key	Reconstructed Public Key	Cryptogram of Permutation #1	Cryptogram of Permutation #2	...	Cryptogram of Permutation #8
1	g^{x_1}	g^{y_1}	$g^{x_1 \cdot y_1} . g$, 1-of-8 ZKP	$g^{x_1 \cdot y_1} . g^{2^m}$, 1-of-8 ZKP	...	$g^{x_1 \cdot y_1} . g^{2^{7 \cdot m}}$, 1-of-8 ZKP
2	g^{x_2}	g^{y_2}	$g^{x_2 \cdot y_2} . g$, 1-of-8 ZKP	$g^{x_2 \cdot y_2} . g^{2^m}$, 1-of-8 ZKP	...	$g^{x_2 \cdot y_2} . g^{2^{7 \cdot m}}$, 1-of-8 ZKP
...	...	...	...	...	...	...
n	g^{x_n}	g^{y_n}	$g^{x_n \cdot y_n} . g$, 1-of-8 ZKP	$g^{x_n \cdot y_n} . g^{2^m}$, 1-of-8 ZKP	...	$g^{x_n \cdot y_n} . g^{2^{7 \cdot m}}$, 1-of-8 ZKP

dataset. We will refer to this table as *cryptogram table* in the rest of this paper. In case the ML system does not want to reveal the number of the samples in the test set, the auditor and the ML system can publicly agree on n. In this case, n must be big enough so that the universal verifiers are satisfied with the outcome.

Each row in the cryptogram table summarises three parameters: (1) protected group membership status, (2) its actual label and (3) predicted label by the ML model. Each row contains the encrypted format of the three parameters along with proofs of its correctness. A cryptogram table in the setup phase is shown in Table 3. In the simplest case, each parameter is binary. Therefore, the combined parameters will generate eight permutations in total. In the setup phase, the table is generated to contain all eight possible permutations and their proofs for each data sample. The total structure of the permutations are shown in Table 2. Each row will satisfy four properties: (a) one can easily verify if a single cryptogram is the encrypted version of one of the eight possible permutations, (b) while verifiable, if only one single cryptogram selected, one cannot exert which permutations the current cryptogram represents, (c) for each two cryptograms selected from a single row, anyone will be able to distinguish each from one another, and (d) given a set of cryptograms arbitrarily select from each row as a set, one can easily check how many cases for each "permutation" are in the set.

The generation of the cryptogram table functions are based on the following sequence:

Step (1): For each of the n samples, the system generates a random public key g^{x_i} where x_i is the private key and $x_i \in [1, q-1]$.

Step (2): Once computation of public keys is finished for all samples, the system will compute another number g^{y_i} where computed using Equation below. We refer to as *reconstructed public key* as it is computed using a combination of public keys of all the rows, except for the current one. $g^{y_i} = \frac{\prod_{j=1}^{i-1} g^{x_j}}{\prod_{j=i+1}^{n} g^{x_j}}$.

Step (3): At this step, the ML system computes the cryptograms and zero knowledge proofs for all the possible parameter permutations. This step occurs before the ML system is trained and deployed to predict data samples. Therefore, it considers all the permutation for minimising the overhead in the next protocol sequence stages (as we discuss later).

Cryptograms: Each permutation is encoded into a $C_i = g^{x_i \cdot y_i} . g^{p_i}$ which are computed based on the multi-option voting schemes introduced in [4] and applied in [13,14]. In their method, p_i is computed based on the n (number of samples which already have been publicly agreed) and m as the smallest integer such that $2^m > n$. For each of the eight permutations, the p_i is computed using the following equation:

$$p_i = \begin{cases} 2^0 & for\ permutation\ \#1 \\ 2^m & for\ permutation\ \#2 \\ \dots & \dots \\ 2^{7.m} & for\ permutation\ \#8 \end{cases} \tag{1}$$

Zero Knowledge Proofs: In addition to cryptograms, the ML system also generates 1–out–of–8 ZKP for each of the permutations. This proof ensure the values presented as C_i in the cryptogram table is indeed the production of $g^{x_i \cdot y_i}$ and g^{p_i} where $p_i \in \{2^0, 2^m, \cdots, 2^{7.m}\}$. As shown in Table 3, each of the computed columns for permutation contains a ZKP to guarantee it is one of the *valid* values for evaluating the fairness metric in next stages. We use the widely used 1–out–of–n interactive ZKP technique [7], where $n = 8$ in our protocol. Moreover, by application of Fiat–Shamir heuristics [10], this ZKP can be converted into non–interactive which makes the verification of proofs simpler [14].

Phase II: Parameter Assignment. This stage starts when the ML system's training and testing. The output of this stage is a table with n rows, each containing a cryptogram of the encoded permutation parameters with the required ZKPs, public key (g^{x_i}) and reconstructed key (g^{y_i}). The outcome of this stage is the final variant of the cryptogram table which we will call *fairness auditing table*.

Fairness Auditing Table: This is derived from the previously computed *cryptogram table*. This table combines the outcome of the ML model (as shown in encoding format) with the cipher-text created in Phase I and form a ciphered version of the test dataset with n samples. This table is generated based on the following steps:

Step (1): First, the ML system and fairness service properly authenticate each other to ensure they are communicating to the intended party. The ML system determines the permutation combination based on the three items parameters explained before. For that, ML system generates binary encoding for each of the data samples in the test dataset (i.e. the sensitive group membership, actual label and the predicted labels respectively as explained in Table 3).

Step (2): The ML system generates ZKP for the knowledge of the encoding as commitment to its choice (p_i as in Eq. 1). The ZKP for the proof of knowledge can be converted to non–interactive using Fiat–Shamir heuristic [10].

Step (3): The corresponding column number that equals the decimal value of the binary encoding is selected from the cryptogram table to complete the fairness auditing table(as shown in Table 2).

Finally, the generated fairness auditing table is digitally signed by the ML system and then is sent over the Fairness auditing service.

Phase III: Fairness Evaluation. First, the fairness auditing service receives the fairness auditing table, verifies the digital signature and the ZKPs, and publishes the contents in the fairness board.

Then, it starts the process of computing the fairness metric. For this, the auditor service multiplies all the cryptograms (C_i) received in the cryptogram table together. Therefore, we have $\prod_i C_i = \prod_i g^{x_i \cdot y_i} \cdot g^{p_i}$. At this stage, the key point is the consideration of the effect y_i and x_i have on each other; know as "Cancellation Formula" (Lemma 1 and [3,13,14]).

Lemma 1. Cancellation Formula: *for x_i and y_i, $\sum_i x_i \cdot y_i = 0$*

Proof. From reconstructed keys equation, one can deduce y_i is as $\sum_i = \sum_{j<i} x_j - \sum_{j>i} x_j$, hence:

$$
\begin{aligned}
\sum_i x_i \cdot y_i &= \sum_{i=1}^{i=n} x_i \cdot \left(\sum_{j=1}^{j=i-1} x_j - \sum_{j=i+1}^{j=n} x_j \right) \\
&= \sum_{i=1}^{i=n} \sum_{j=1}^{j=i-1} x_i \cdot x_j - \sum_{i}^{i=n} \sum_{j=i+1}^{j=n} x_i \cdot x_j \\
&= \sum_{j=1}^{j=n} \sum_{i=j+1}^{i=n} x_i \cdot x_j - \sum_{i}^{i=n} \sum_{j=i+1}^{j=n} x_i \cdot x_j \\
&= \sum_{i=1}^{i=n} \left(\sum_{j=1}^{j=i-1} x_j - \sum_{j=i+1}^{j=n} \sum_{j=i+1}^{j=n} x_j \right) x_i \\
&= 0
\end{aligned}
\tag{2}
$$

At this point, we expand each of these equation components to compare them together.

Considering the Cancellation Formula, we can conclude multiplication of all cryptograms into $\prod_i C_i = \prod_i g^{x_i \cdot y_i} \cdot g^{p_i} = \prod_i g^{p_i} = g^{\sum_i p_i}$. The result is total sum of permutations ($p\#1$ to $p\#8$) as $\sum_i p_i = a.2^0 + b.2^m + c.2^{2m} + d.2^{3m} + e.2^{4m} + f.2^{5m} + g.2^{6m} + h.2^{7m}$ where a, b, c, d, e, f, g, h are the number of each permutation respectively (Permutation #1, Permutation #2, ..., Permutation #8). The search space for such combination depends on the number of samples sent from the ML system to the auditor (the size of the test set is n for 8 permutations is $\binom{n+8-1}{8-1}$ [14]). As described in Phase I, the size of n (the total number of samples) can be agreed with consideration of the computational capacity of the

Table 4. The required permutations to compute the fairness metrics of an ML system

Fairness Component	Corresponding Permutation #	Computation
$Pr(\hat{Y} \mid A = 0)$	#2, #4	$(\#2 + \#4)/n$
$Pr(\hat{Y} \mid A = 1)$	#6, #8	$(\#6 + \#8)/n$
$Pr(\hat{Y} \mid A = 0, y = 0)$	#2	$\#2/n$
$Pr(\hat{Y} \mid A = 1, y = 0)$	#6	$\#6/n$
$Pr(\hat{Y} \mid A = 0, y = 1)$	#4	$\#4/n$
$Pr(\hat{Y} \mid A = 1, y = 1)$	#8	$(\#8)/n$

auditor service. In the simplest setting where n is small, the auditor will determine the overall number of permutations (as in $\sum p_i$, where $i \in \{1, 2, \cdots, 8\}$) by performing an exhaustive search in all possible combinations until it finds the correct one.

This process is computationally heavy especially when the number of data samples in the fairness auditing table is large. In this case, the fairness auditor can delegate the declaration of the permutation number to the ML system. The auditor still receives the fairness auditing table and the relevant ZKPs. It can store the fairness auditing table to the fairness board, compute the fairness, and verify the correctness of the declared permutation numbers. The universal verifier can follow the same steps to verify the fairness metric computations through the fairness auditing table that is publicly accessible via fairness board.

At the end of this stage, the auditor uses the acquired numbers to compute the fairness metric and release the information publicly. The number of each permutation denotes the overall performance of the ML algorithm for each of the groups with protected attribute. Table 4 demonstrates the permutations and how it relates to the fairness metric of the ML system. The cryptogram table and the results will be published on the fairness board (Fig. 1).

4 Implementation and Performance Analysis

4.1 Proof-of-Concept Implementation

Tools and Platform: The back–end is implemented in Python v3.7.1 and the front–end is implemented with Node.js v10.15.3. In our evaluations, the computations required for generation of the cryptogram table (in the ML system) is developed with Python. The elliptic curve operations make use of the Python package *tinyec* and the conversion of Python classes to a JSON compatible format uses the Python package *JSONpickle*. All the experiments are conducted on a MacBook pro laptop with the following configurations: CPU 2.7 GHz Quad-Core Intel Core i7 with 16 GB Memory running MacOS Catalina v.10.15.5 for the Operating System.

Case-Study Dataset: We use a publicly available dataset from Medical Expenditure Panel Survey (MEPS) [21] that contains 15830 data points about the healthcare utilization of individuals. We developed a model (Logistic Regression) that determines whether a specific patient requires health services, such as additional care. This ML system assigns a score to each patient. If the score is above a preset threshold, then the patient requires extra health services. In the MEPS dataset, the protected attribute is "race". A fair system provides such services fairly independent of the patient's race. Here, the privileged race group in this dataset is "white ethnicity". We have used 50% of the dataset as training, 30% as validation and the remaining 20% as test dataset. We set the number of cryptogram table samples to equal the size of test set ($N = 3166$). In this example we include three attributes in the cryptogram to represent the binary values of A, Y and $\hat{Y}$ (Sect. 2.1), thus leading to 8 permutations for each data sample.

In our experiment, where $N = 3166$, the total size of the search space is $\binom{3166+8-1}{8-1} \approx 2^{69}$. The exhaustive search approach is computationally expensive for our experimental hardware configurations, so we decided to use the approach suggested in Sect. 3.3. Here, the permutation numbers are declared by the ML system and the auditor service verified the claims by comparing the computations done by the auditor (as in $\prod_i C_i = \prod_i g^{x_i \cdot y_i} \cdot g^{p_i} = \prod_i g^{p_i} = g^{\sum_i p_i}$) with the total sum of the received permutations ($p\#1$ to $p\#8$) as $\sum_i p_i = a.2^0 + b.2^m + c.2^{2m} + d.2^{3m} + e.2^{4m} + f.2^{5m} + g.2^{6m} + h.2^{7m}$. This is a reasonable approach since we assumed that the ML system will not attempt to deceive the auditor for its outcome (Sect. 3.1).

4.2 Performance

This section presents the execution time per data point for each of the main computational tasks, in each protocol stage. Recall that phase I was executed before the ML system's training and testing. This stage can be developed (and stored separately) in parallel to the implementation of the model in order to mitigate the performance challenge of Phase I. In our implementation, the output of this stage (cryptogram table) is stored in a separate file in JSON format and can be retrieved at the beginning of the phase II.

Phase II begins after the ML model is trained, tested, and validated. This stage uses the output of the ML model to generate the fairness auditing table from the cryptogram table as well as ZKP for knowledge of the permutation. The output of this phase is transmitted to the Fairness Auditor Service in JSON format for phase III. At this stage, first the ZKPs are verified and then, the summation of the cryptograms determines the number of permutations for each of the sensitive groups. Once the auditing service has these numbers, it can compute the fairness of the ML system.

In our evaluations (where $N = 3166$), public/private key pair generation completes in 60 milliseconds (ms) on average with standard deviation of 6 ms. The execution time for ZKP of private key was roughly the same (60 ms on average with standard deviation of 6 ms). The generation of reconstructed public key took around 450 ms with standard deviation of 8 ms. The most computationally expensive stage in phase I was the 1–out–of–8 ZKP for each of the permutations. This stage took longer than the other ones because first, the algorithm is more complicated and second, it should be repeated 8 times (for each of the permutations separately) for every row in cryptogram table. The computation of 1–out–of–8 ZKPs takes 1.7 s for each data sample with STD of 0.1 s. Overall, phase I took around 14 s with STD of 1 s for each data sample in the test set. In our experiments (where $N = 3166$ samples), the total execution of phase I took roughly 12 h and 54 min.

Phase II consists of creation of the auditing table and generation of the ZKP for knowledge of the permutation. The fairness auditing table is derived from the cryptogram table (as it is mapping the encoding to the corresponding permutation number in the cryptogram table). The elapsed time for such derivation is negligible (total: 1 ms). The generation of ZKP for knowledge of the permutation executed less than 60 ms on average with standard deviation of 3 ms for each data sample. The completion of both stages took less than 3 min. The fairness auditing table is sent to the Fairness Auditor Service for Phase III.

The verification of ZKPs in the last phase (Phase III) is a computationally expensive operation. The ZKP for the ownership of the private key took around 260 ms on average with standard deviation of 2 ms. The verification of 1–out–of–8 ZKP for each data point roughly took 2.5 s on average with 20 ms standard deviation. The verification of the ZKP for knowledge of permutation executed in 100 ms with standard deviation of 5 ms. The summation of the cryptograms after verification took 450 ms overall for $N = 3166$ items. In our experiment, completion of the stages in phase III took around 2 h and 30 min in total.

In summary, the experimental setup for our architecture, where we computed the required cryptograms and ZKPs for $N = 3166$ data points in a real–world dataset, overall time was around 15 h on the laptop specification given earlier. The main part of the time is consumed by the computation required for phase I (12 h and 54 min). However, as we noted before, Phase I can be executed before the ML model setup and is stored in a separate JSON file and will be loaded at the beginning of stage II (after the training and validation of the ML model is complete). The other main computational effort, which can only be done after the ML system's outcomes have been obtained, is in Phase III. For our example, actual computation of fairness takes two and a half hours. In summary, the creation and handling of cryptograms takes considerable computational effort for realistic datasets and for the fairness metrics that require three attributes. In what follows we analyse how performance scales with respect to the number of data points as well as with the number of attributes represented in the cryptograms.

5 Conclusion

This paper proposes Fairness as a Service (FaaS), a trustworthy service architecture and secure protocol for the calculation of algorithmic fairness. FaaS is designed as a service that calculates fairness without asking the ML system to share the original dataset or model information. Instead, it requires an encrypted representation of the values of the data features delivered by the ML system in the shape of cryptograms. We used non-interactive Zero Knowledge Proofs within the cryptogram to assure that the protocol is executed as it should. These cryptograms are posted on a public fairness board for everyone to inspect the correctness of the computations for the fairness of the ML system. This is a new approach in privacy–preserving computation of fairness since unlike other similar proposals that use federated learning approach, our FaaS architecture does not rely on a specific machine learning model or a fairness metric definition for its operation. Instead, one have the freedom of deploying their desired model and the fairness metric of choice.

In this paper we proved that the security protocol guarantees the privacy of data and does not leak any model information. Compared to earlier designs, trust in our design is in the correct construction of the cryptogram by the ML system. Arguably, this is more realistic as a solution than providing full access to data to the trusted third party, taking into account the many legal, business and ethical requirements of ML systems. At the same time, this provides a new challenge in increasing the trust one has in the ML system. Increasing trust in the construction of the cryptograms remains an interesting research challenge following from the presented protocol.

We implemented a proof-of-concept of FaaS and conducted performance experiments on commodity hardware. The protocol takes seconds per data point to complete, thus demonstrating in performance challenges if the number of data points is large (tens of thousands). To mitigate the performance challenge, the security protocol is staged such that the construction of the cryptogram can be done off-line. The performance of the calculation of fairness from the cryptogram is a challenge to address in future work. All together, we believe FaaS and the presented underlying security protocol provide a new and promising approach to calculating and verifying fairness of AI algorithms.

Acknowledgement. The authors in this project have been funded by UK EPSRC grant "FinTrust: Trust Engineering for the Financial Industry" under grant number EP/R033595/1, and UK EPSRC grant "AGENCY: Assuring Citizen Agency in a World with Complex Online Harms" under grant EP/W032481/1 and PETRAS National Centre of Excellence for IoT Systems Cybersecurity, which has been funded by the UK EPSRC under grant number EP/S035362/1.

References

1. Adler, P., et al.: Auditing black-box models for indirect influence. Knowl. Inf. Syst. **54**(1), 95–122 (2018)
2. Angelino, E., Larus-Stone, N., Alabi, D., Seltzer, M., Rudin, C.: Learning certifiably optimal rule lists for categorical data. arXiv preprint arXiv:1704.01701 (2017)
3. Azad, M.A., Bag, S., Parkinson, S., Hao, F.: TrustVote: privacy-preserving node ranking in vehicular networks. IEEE Internet Things J. **6**(4), 5878–5891 (2018)

4. Baudron, O., Fouque, P.A., Pointcheval, D., Stern, J., Poupard, G.: Practical multi-candidate election system. In: Proceedings of the Twentieth Annual ACM Symposium on Principles of Distributed Computing, pp. 274–283 (2001)
5. Chouldechova, A.: Fair prediction with disparate impact: a study of bias in recidivism prediction instruments. Big Data 5(2), 153–163 (2017)
6. Corbett-Davies, S., Pierson, E., Feller, A., Goel, S., Huq, A.: Algorithmic decision making and the cost of fairness. In: Proceedings of the 23rd ACM SIGKDD International Conference on Knowledge Discovery and Data Mining, pp. 797–806. ACM (2017)
7. Cramer, R., Damgård, I., Schoenmakers, B.: Proofs of partial knowledge and simplified design of witness hiding protocols. In: Desmedt, Y.G. (ed.) Annual International Cryptology Conference, vol. 839, pp. 174–187. Springer, Heidelberg (1994). https://doi.org/10.1007/3-540-48658-5_19
8. Carroll, C.E., Olegario, R.: Pathways to corporate accountability: corporate reputation and its alternatives. J. Bus. Ethics 163(2), 173–181 (2020)
9. Feldman, M., Friedler, S.A., Moeller, J., Scheidegger, C., Venkatasubramanian, S.: Certifying and removing disparate impact. In: Proceedings of the 21th ACM SIGKDD International Conference on Knowledge Discovery and Data Mining, pp. 259–268. ACM (2015)
10. Fiat, A., Shamir, A.: How to prove yourself: practical solutions to identification and signature problems. In: Conference on the Theory and Application of Cryptographic Techniques, vol. 263, pp. 186–194. Springer, Heidelberg (1986). https://doi.org/10.1007/3-540-47721-7_12
11. Friedler, S.A., Scheidegger, C., Venkatasubramanian, S.: On the (im) possibility of fairness. arXiv preprint arXiv:1609.07236 (2016)
12. Guidotti, R., Monreale, A., Ruggieri, S., Turini, F., Giannotti, F., Pedreschi, D.: A survey of methods for explaining black box models. ACM Comput. Surv. (CSUR) 51(5), 1–42 (2018)
13. Hao, F., Kreeger, M.N., Randell, B., Clarke, D., Shahandashti, S.F., Lee, P.H.J.: Every vote counts: Ensuring integrity in large-scale electronic voting. In: 2014 Electronic Voting Technology Workshop/Workshop on Trustworthy Elections (EVT/WOTE 14) (2014)
14. Hao, F., Ryan, P.Y.A., Zieliński, P.: Anonymous voting by two-round public discussion. IET Inf. Secur. 4(2), 62–67 (2010)
15. Hardt, M., Price, E., Srebro, N., et al.: Equality of opportunity in supervised learning. Adv. Neural Inf. Process. Syst. 29, 3315–3323 (2016)
16. Hu, H., Liu, Y., Wang, Z., Lan, C.: A distributed fair machine learning framework with private demographic data protection. In: 2019 IEEE International Conference on Data Mining (ICDM), pp. 1102–1107. IEEE (2019)
17. Jagielski, M., et al.: Differentially private fair learning. In: International Conference on Machine Learning, pp. 3000–3008. PMLR (2019)
18. Katz, J., Lindell, Y.: Introduction to Modern Cryptography. CRC Press, Boca Raton (2014)
19. Kilbertus, N., Gascon, A., Kusner, M., Veale, M., Gummadi, K.P., Weller, A.: Blind justice: Fairness with encrypted sensitive attributes. In: 35th International Conference on Machine Learning, pp. 2630–2639. PMLR (2018)
20. Larson, J., Mattu, S., Kirchner, L., Angwin, J.: How we analyzed the COMPAS recidivism algorithm. ProPublica 9(1), 2016 (2016)
21. Liu, J., Yu, F., Song, L.: A systematic investigation on the research publications that have used the medical expenditure panel survey (MEPS) data through a bibliometrics approach. Library Hi Tech (2020)

22. Lundberg, S.M., Lee, S.I.: A unified approach to interpreting model predictions. Adv. Neural Inf. Process. Syst. **30**, 1–10 (2017)

23. Mahdawi, A.: It's not just A-levels - algorithms have a nightmarish new power over our lives. The Guardian (2020)

24. Narayanan, A.: Translation tutorial: 21 fairness definitions and their politics. In Proceedings of Conference on Fairness Accountability Transport, New York, USA (2018)

25. Panigutti, C., Perotti, A., Panisson, A., Bajardi, P., Pedreschi, D.: Fairlens: auditing black-box clinical decision support systems. Inf. Process. Manag. **58**(5), 102657 (2021)

26. Panigutti, C., Perotti, A., Pedreschi, D.: Doctor xai: an ontology-based approach to black-box sequential data classification explanations. In: Proceedings of the 2020 Conference on Fairness, Accountability, and Transparency, pp. 629–639 (2020)

27. Park, S., Kim, S., Lim, Y.: Fairness audit of machine learning models with confidential computing. In: Proceedings of the ACM Web Conference 2022, pp. 3488–3499 (2022)

28. Reuters. Amazon ditched AI recruiting tool that favored men for technical jobs. The Guardian (2018)

29. Segal, S., Adi, Y., Pinkas, B., Baum, C., Ganesh, C., Keshet, J.: Fairness in the eyes of the data: certifying machine-learning models. In: Proceedings of the 2021 AAAI/ACM Conference on AI, Ethics, and Society, pp. 926–935 (2021)

30. Siau, K., Wang, W.: Building trust in artificial intelligence, machine learning, and robotics. Cutter Bus. Technol. J. **31**(2), 47–53 (2018)

31. Stinson, D.R., Paterson, M.: Cryptography: Theory and Practice. CRC Press, Boca Raton (2018)

32. Toreini, E., Aitken, M., Coopamootoo, K., Elliott, K., Zelaya, C.G., van Moorsel, A.: The relationship between trust in AI and trustworthy machine learning technologies. In: Proceedings of the 2020 Conference on Fairness, Accountability, and Transparency, pp. 272–283 (2020)

33. Veale, M., Binns, R.: Fairer machine learning in the real world: mitigating discrimination without collecting sensitive data. Big Data Soc. **4**(2), 2053951717743530 (2017)

34. Wang, T., Rudin, C., Doshi-Velez, F., Liu, Y., Klampfl, E., MacNeille, P.: A bayesian framework for learning rule sets for interpretable classification. J. Mach. Learn. Res. **18**(1), 2357–2393 (2017)

35. Yang, Q., Liu, Y., Chen, T., Tong, Y.: Federated machine learning: concept and applications. ACM Trans. Intell. Syst. Technol. (TIST) **10**(2), 1–19 (2019)

SECAI 2023

SECAI 2023 Preface

In this volume, we present the refined editions of papers presented at the International Workshop on Security and Artificial Intelligence 2023, abbreviated as SECAI 2023. This workshop was co-located with the 28th European Symposium on Research in Computer Security (ESORICS 2023) and took place in The Hague, The Netherlands, on September 29th, 2023.

The integration of AI with Cyber Security has significantly advanced digital protection across networks, systems, and devices. However, the advent of AI introduces new challenges, including ethical dilemmas, privacy and data integrity issues, and adversarial algorithmic vulnerabilities. Furthermore, AI's uptake has initiated a complex "AI arms race" between cyber adversaries and defenders. The SECAI 2023 workshop extended an open call for innovative research, seeking submissions that explore the nuanced relationship between AI and Cyber Security, spanning both theoretical and applied research. This exploration covered domains such as AI's use in defensive and offensive security, its malicious potential, and the strengthening of AI technology's security and resilience. Our call for papers attracted significant interest, resulting in an impressive 31 submissions, which highlights the workshop's prominence for pioneering research in this field. Each manuscript was assessed by 2–4 reviewers, upholding a rigorous peer-review process, with chairs and committee members abstaining from reviewing their own works. We accepted 8 regular papers and 3 short papers, achieving a 35% acceptance rate.

This proceedings volume reflects the dedication of all contributors. We thank all our authors for their invaluable contributions, which have shaped this volume, and our diligent reviewers ensured only top-tier work is included. Special thanks to the ESORICS workshop chairs and organizers, as well as the SECAI 2023 chairs, program committee, and organizing committee for their support and dedication.

In conclusion, we recommend this volume to all those with a vested interest in the dynamic interplay between AI and Cyber Security. The insights within offer a deeper understanding of this crucial intersection, guiding the evolving AI-driven Cyber Security landscape.

September 2023

Harsha Kalutarage
Naoto Yanai

Organization

Program Chairs

Harsha Kalutarage — Robert Gordon University, UK
Naoto Yanai — Osaka University, Japan

General Chairs

Siraj Shaikh — Swansea University, UK
Kyosuke Yamashita — Osaka University, Japan
Nirmalie Wiratunga — Robert Gordon University, UK

Program Committee

Jorge Blasco Alis — Universidad Politécnica de Madrid, Spain
Omar Al-Kadri — Birmingham City University, UK
Nalin Asanka Gamagedara Arachchilage — University of Auckland, New Zealand
Hiromi Arai — RIKEN AIP, Japan
Yang Chen — Nanyang Technological University, Singapore
Nhien An Le Khac — University College Dublin, Ireland
Paddy Krishnan — Oracle Labs, Australia
Jingyue Li — Norwegian University of Science and Technology, Norway
Paul Miller — Queen's University Belfast, UK
Hoang Nga Nguyen — Swansea University, UK
Hamada Rizk — Osaka University, Japan
Sara-Jayne Terp — Defence Science and Technology Laboratory, UK
Bruce W. Watson — National Security Centre of Excellence, Canada
Benjamin Zhao — Macquarie University, Australia

Organizing Committee

Janaka Senanayake — Robert Gordon University, UK
Sampath Rajapaksha — Robert Gordon University, UK
Chao Sun — Osaka University, Japan

Additional Reviewers

Mubarak Abdu-Aguye
Tatsuya Amano
Muhammad Ajmal Azad
Viktor Erdélyi
Mohamed Ben Farah
Sakuna Harinda
John Hayes
Imran Ali Jokhio
M. S. Mekala
Teruhiro Mizumoto
Lankeshwara Munasinghe
Ren Ozeki
Anjana Wijekoon
Idris Zakariyya

NASimEmu: Network Attack Simulator & Emulator for Training Agents Generalizing to Novel Scenarios

Jaromír Janisch(✉)[iD], Tomáš Pevný[iD], and Viliam Lisý[iD]

Artificial Intelligence Center, Department of Computer Science, Faculty of Electrical Engineering, Czech Technical University in Prague, Prague, Czech Republic
{jaromir.janisch,tomas.pevny,viliam.lisy}@fel.cvut.cz

Abstract. Current frameworks for training offensive penetration testing agents with deep reinforcement learning struggle to produce agents that perform well in real-world scenarios, due to the reality gap in simulation-based frameworks and the lack of scalability in emulation-based frameworks. Additionally, existing frameworks often use an unrealistic metric that measures the agents' performance on the training data. NASimEmu, a new framework introduced in this paper, addresses these issues by providing both a simulator and an emulator with a shared interface. This approach allows agents to be trained in simulation and deployed in the emulator, thus verifying the realism of the used abstraction. Our framework promotes the development of general agents that can transfer to novel scenarios unseen during their training. For the simulation part, we adopt an existing simulator NASim and enhance its realism. The emulator is implemented with industry-level tools, such as Vagrant, VirtualBox, and Metasploit. Experiments demonstrate that a simulation-trained agent can be deployed in emulation, and we show how to use the framework to train a general agent that transfers into novel, structurally different scenarios. NASimEmu is available as open-source.

1 Introduction

Artificial intelligence and machine learning techniques have become increasingly important in the field of automated penetration testing [3]. Deep reinforcement learning (RL) is an especially promising tool for offensive penetration testing and in recent years, a number of frameworks were created to train deep RL agents. While surveying the capabilities of the existing frameworks, we identified important deficiencies.

The first issue is that no existing framework provides means to train deep RL agents efficiently whilst ensuring that they can be deployed in real systems. In general, the frameworks can be divided into two groups, simulators [12, 18] and emulators [11, 19]. Simulators provide an in-memory abstraction of processes that happen in real computer networks and are much faster and easier to use than their real counterparts. Deep RL algorithms are notoriously sample-inefficient, unstable and require large batches to train properly [14, 15, 17]. Hence, simulators are perfect to generate the data these algorithms need, possibly training multiple agents in parallel and discarding those that fail. However, the simulators often suffer from the *reality gap*, where the level of the

S. Katsikas et al. (Eds.): ESORICS 2023 Workshops, LNCS 14399, pp. 589–608, 2024.
https://doi.org/10.1007/978-3-031-54129-2_35

used abstraction makes it impossible to deploy the trained agents in real systems. For example, the authors of CyberBattleSim [12] themselves argue that their framework is too simplistic to be used in the real world.

Contrarily, emulators are well-grounded in reality, as they use virtual machines with real operating systems (OSs), services and processes, connected in a virtualized computer network. While they are realistic and provide a controlled way to test autonomous agents, they are slow and not scalable for the demands of deep RL training.

Second, the metric used to measure the agents' performance is often ill-defined, which manifests in the frameworks' unrealistic design decisions. It is a common practice to train and test the agents in the same, static network and measure the number of training steps it takes to learn the optimal path to penetrate this particular network [5,18,22]. Given this goal, the frameworks often do not allow training agents in different scenarios simultaneously and promote implementing agents that can solve one particular network, but do not transfer to others. However, in the real world, agents would be deployed into a network with little information about its segmentation, hosts' configuration and the location of sensitive information. Hence, agents' performance should be measured as how well they do in these unknown networks not encountered during the training. Using this objective makes the problem much more difficult and immediately brings multiple challenges. For example: How to create an agent that is invariant to possible variations in size, topology and configuration of real networks? When should the agent stop the penetration testing, given that the location and number of hosts with sensitive data is unknown?

To study the novel challenges, a new framework that respects the associated requirements is needed. It must be designed with a realism-first approach, not succumbing to the requirements of deep RL and it must provide both simulation to train the agents and emulation to verify that the level of abstraction is realistic. This paper presents Network Attack Simulator & Emulator (NASimEmu), a framework that satisfies these conditions. To this end, we implemented a realistic emulator and adapted an existing NASim simulator [18] to be aligned with the requirements the emulator produced. Both the simulator and emulator share the same OpenAI Gym [2] interface and everything that is possible in one can be done in the other.

The NASimEmu simulator facilitates training by providing observations that summarize the information gathered so far. It comes with several predefined scenarios to benchmark agents and encourages the implementation of general agents by allowing training and testing in multiple distinct scenarios. Many different networks can be generated from a single scenario description with random variations in the number of hosts in subnets and their configuration. The framework does not leak unrealistic information (e.g., the number of hosts in the observation size) and the episode termination is left to the agent, which incentivizes the researchers to search for new solutions. Also, it comes with a tool to visualize the agents' knowledge to ease debugging.

The NASimEmu emulator is based on Vagrant, an industry-level tool for managing virtual networks, VirtualBox, routing and traffic filtering with a Mikrotik RouterOS host and an attacker node running MetaSploit. It comes with configurable Linux and Windows machines, based on Metasploitable3 images, with pre-defined vulnerable services to choose from. Crucially, the emulator implements an interface common with the simulator, and it translates agents' actions into MetaSploit commands and reconstructs observations from the resulting logs. Any scenario generated for the simulator can be translated to the emulation with a single command and an agent trained in simulation can be seamlessly deployed in emulation.

In Experiments, we demonstrate two key points. First, we show that the commonly used metric of measuring the agents' performance on their training data is insufficient and unrealistic and demonstrate how our simulator promotes the development of a general agent. We leverage the ability to train the agents in multiple distinct random scenarios and test in others and show how different model architectures influence the agents' generalization. Specifically, we train two baseline agents with different architectures using PPO [17], a deep RL method. We demonstrate that while a commonly used architecture based on matrix inputs performs well in the training scenarios, it transfers poorly to novel scenarios that differ in topology and size. Hence, we implement a second, invariant architecture, and show initial evidence that it performs well both on the training *and* novel scenarios. In a separate experiment, we demonstrate that a simulation-trained agent can be successfully deployed in the emulator, therefore verifying that the simulator abstraction is realistic.

NASimEmu is available at https://github.com/jaromiru/NASimEmu. A separate repository https://github.com/jaromiru/NASimEmu-agents contains the deep RL agents.

Our contributions are summarized below:

- We introduce a new framework that provides **both the simulator and emulator**. Agents trained in simulation can be seamlessly deployed in emulation, which we experimentally demonstrate. This fact shows that the simulator is realistic.
- Instead of measuring agents' performance on their training set, we argue that a more useful metric is their performance in novel scenarios. We design our framework to encourage **training general agents** – it can generate random scenario instances that vary in topology, size and configuration and can measure the performance in separate, multiple and structurally different training and testing scenarios.
- We demonstrate that, under this new metric, new model architectures are required. Specifically, we implement a size-invariant model that **transfers to novel and structurally different settings**, while the commonly used MLP architecture fails.

2   Related Work

The existing penetration testing frameworks targetting RL can be separated into *simulators* [1,6,7,12,18,20] and *emulators* [4,11,19]. However, none of the frameworks contains both the simulator and emulator that would allow training the agent in the former and seamlessly deploying it in the latter. NASimEmu includes both, and by doing it ensures that the used abstraction is realistic. Note that although the authors of CybORG [20] claim to have developed both the simulator and emulator, the latter was never published and the authors confirmed via email that its development was discontinued. Several other frameworks focus on the attacker vs. defender game [4,8,9,13,16,20].

3 Network Attack Simulator and Emulator

NASimEmu is separated into two parts – simulation and emulation (see Fig. 2). The simulation, based on NASim [18], can be used to train and evaluate agents. It is a memory-based fast and parallelizable abstraction of real computer networks and can generate random scenario instances which can vary in network topology, configuration and number of hosts. The emulation is a controlled environment that runs virtual machines and it verifies that the simulation abstraction is realistic. Agents trained in simulation can be transparently deployed in emulation.

3.1 Simulator

The simulator is based on Network Attack Simulator (NASim) [18] and it is a memory-based abstraction of the processes that happen in a real network. It contains hosts with their configuration and status and simulates the network communication and other processes, based on the actions received from an agent. After each action, an observation is returned. Many simulations can be run in parallel (e.g., in our experiments, we use 256 environments). Below, we describe the simulator at a high-level and refer the reader to [18] for additional details. At the end, we list of changes made to the original NASim.

The network is defined by a *scenario*, which describes the network topology, host configuration (OS, services, processes and sensitivity), exploits and privilege escalations. The topology describes the network division into subnets where a firewall blocks all communication between disconnected subnets and allows it otherwise.

NASimEmu supports three ways of scenario creation. *Static scenarios* describe precisely the whole network and hosts' configuration. *Random scenario* are completely randomly generated, based on the prescribed parameters (e.g., size of the network, number of exploits, etc.). We add support for *dynamic scenarios* that enhance the variability of static scenarios. The motivation is to describe prototypical situations, e.g., typical university or corporate networks, while the details in scenario *instances* vary. In the real world, some objects (OSs, services, exploits, etc.) can be listed upfront and stay true in all scenarios. Dynamic scenarios are partially fixed and some properties are left to chance. In particular, the number of hosts in subnets and hosts' configuration can be randomized, while the network topology and lists of possible OSs, services, processes, exploits and privilege escalations stay fixed. The chance that a host is sensitive is determined by a scenario-defined subnet sensitivity.

During execution, the simulator maintains the current state of the network, which contains states of each host as a vector specifying the host's address, flags whether it has been compromised, reached and discovered, its value, current access level by the agent, OS and a list of services and processes running on the host.

The following actions are available: *Exploit(exploit_id, target)*, *PrivilegeEscalation(privesc_id, target)*, *ServiceScan(target)*, *OSScan(target)*, *SubnetScan(target)*, *ProcessScan(target)* and *TerminalAction*. All of the actions target a previously discovered host. Commonly, the attacker cannot reach its target directly, but must proxy the communication through other controlled hosts. The simulator abstracts this away and allows an action if a path to the target exists. We show that the path can be automatically determined even in emulation.

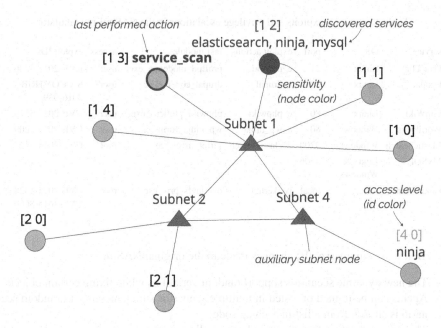

Fig. 1. Example rendered observation for debugging purposes. It graphically shows the discovered nodes, their known services, access levels, sensitivity and the last action.

The actions are parametrized and the specific implementation into the RL agents is left to the user. A most simple way is to combine all actions and their parameters to get a list of grounded actions. Another way is to use a RL framework capable of working with parametrized actions, e.g., [10]. When an action is performed, the internal state changes accordingly and an observation is returned. The observation is partial (i.e., only the discovered hosts are included) and it summarizes all the information gathered by the agent in the current episode.

There is a small negative reward for each step and the positive reward is only given when the agent gains privileged access to a sensitive host. The simulator never terminates an episode unless *TerminalAction* is received. Simply terminating an episode when all sensitive hosts are exploited does not correspond to the real world, where such information is unavailable. Still, the agent's behavior can be hard-coded to terminate after a specific number of steps, although we encourage the users to implement agents that can decide to terminate themselves.

To encourage training for generalization, the simulator accepts multiple scenarios for training or testing, one of which is randomly chosen for each episode. To ease the subsequent processing of observations by agents' models, the sizes of host vectors are united across all scenarios. However, the overall observation size still varies, depending on the number of visible hosts and total hosts in the scenario instance. To ease debugging, the environment also provides an observation visualizer that shows discovered hosts and their services, gained access levels, which hosts are sensitive and the last action (see Fig. 1).

Table 1. Services, exploits and privilege escalations in the NASimEmu emulator.

service	OS	port	exploit action	msf module	access	exploit IDs
ProFTPD	Linux	21	e_proftpd	proftpd_modcopy_exec	user	CVE-2015-3306
Drupal	Linux	80	e_drupal	drupal_coder_exec	user	SA-CONTRIB-2016-039
PhpWiki	Linux	80	e_phpwiki	phpwiki_ploticus_exec	user	CVE-2014-5519
WordPress	Windows	80	e_wp_ninja	wp_ninja_forms_...	user	CVE-2016-1209
ElasticSearch	Windows	9200	e_elasticsearch	script_mvel_rce	root	CVE-2014-3120
MySQL	Linux & Windows	3306	–	–	–	–
Linux kernel	Linux	local	pe_kernel	overlayfs_priv_esc	root	CVE-2015-1328 CVE-2015-8660

Below we summarize the changes made to the original NASim:

- The new dynamic scenarios support random variations while fixing certain objects.
- Agents can be trained or tested in multiple scenarios simultaneously (a random scenario is chosen from a list in each episode).
- The sizes of host vectors are united across all scenarios.
- The simulator randomly permutes the node and segment IDs at the beginning of the episode to prevent memorization of fixed addresses.
- Observations keep the revealed information so far to help the agent remember the results of past actions.
- The environment does not trigger the end of an episode. The agent has to terminate with *TerminalAction*.
- The observations are optionally returned as a graph with nodes representing subnets and individual hosts.
- The observations can be visualized.

3.2 Emulator

The emulator is an important part of NASimEmu that uses virtual machines and networking to let the agent interact with a controlled, but real environment. It can substitute the simulator and contains necessary wrappers to translate agents' actions into instructions for the attacker machine, and it reconstructs the observations from the resulting logs. Having the emulator where simulation-trained agents can be deployed is important, since it verifies that the simulation abstraction is *realistic*.

The emulator uses Vagrant to manage a network of virtual hosts. The individual hosts run in VirtualBox and are based on configurable Metasploitable images. A single RouterOS instance acts as a router and firewall and segments the network into subnets. The attacker host runs Kali Linux with Metasploit that is remotely connected to the NASimEmu interface (see Fig. 2). Every action that an agent issues is translated into a command for the Metasploit framework, executed and the result is processed back into the NASimEmu observation. Importantly, Metasploit on the attacker machine is

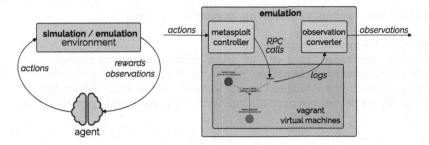

Fig. 2. Left: The RL environment of NASimEmu with a substitutable simulation and emulation. **Right:** The emulator translates agents' actions to commands for the Metasploit framework that runs on the attacker machine and recreates observations from the resulting logs. Simulation-trained agents can be seamlessly deployed in the emulator.

automatically configured to route the traffic to newly discovered parts of the network through the controlled hosts that discovered them. Hence, the path from the attacker to a target node can be determined automatically for any action.

The *Exploit* and *PrivilegeEscalation* actions are translated into predefined Metasploit modules (see Table 1). The *ServiceScan* performs a port scan and based on the result, it may perform additional checks (e.g., connect to and determine installed services on the HTTP server). *OSScan* tries to fingerprint the OS of the target. *SubnetScan* performs ping sweep from the controlled target machine, where we use the fact that ping is installed by default both on Linux and Windows. Since we currently do not implement any processes in NASimEmu, *ProcessScan* does nothing. In future versions, it would return a list of local processes that can be leveraged through privilege escalation. *TerminalAction* is a meta action that is not translated, but instead instructs the framework to end the process.

It is possible to extend NASimEmu with new services, processes or exploits. Services or processes require installation and start scripts and the detection procedure needs to be implemented for the *ServiceScan* or *ProcessScan* actions. For exploits and privilege escalations, Metasploit must contain the corresponding modules and action and observation converters that control Metasploit and reconstruct observations from logs must be implemented. Finally, a unique identifier for the new service, process, exploit or privilege escalation has to be added to a scenario description.

Currently, NASimEmu supports configurable Linux and Windows machines. We have implemented six services, five of which are exploitable and Linux machines are vulnerable to a privilege escalation attack (see Table 1 for the complete list). The sensitive data is modeled as a specific file at the root of the filesystem (/loot or c:/loot). It contains a unique string and is accessible only by the privileged user, although the file is visible by any user. Hence, the agent can determine whether the host contains the sensitive information when it gains any access, but can recover it only through the privileged user.

Any NASimEmu scenario can be instantiated into a Vagrantfile descriptor. Upon user command, the network is populated with virtual machines and their services are disabled or enabled as defined in the descriptor. For example:

```
NASimEmu$ ./setup_vagrant.sh scenario.v2.yaml

NASimEmu/vagrant$ vagrant up
Bringing machine 'router' up with 'virtualbox' provider...
Bringing machine 'attacker' up with 'virtualbox' provider...
Bringing machine 'target10' up with 'virtualbox' provider...
Bringing machine 'target40' up with 'virtualbox' provider...
[...]
```

3.3 Known Limitations

We strive to be transparent about the capabilities of our framework. Despite the efforts to make NASimEmu realistic, it still comes with a few shortcomings associated with the level of abstraction in the simulation. We hypothesize that most of the issues can be removed by modifying the simulation, but leave it to future work.

Different versions of the same service can be modeled with unique identifiers and in the emulation, the controller needs to fingerprint these services. However, our implementation does not currently cover the case where it is not possible to tell service versions apart.

NASimEmu creates scenario instances where the hosts' configuration is independently randomized. In reality, the configurations are likely to be correlated to other hosts in subnets. While NASimEmu builds upon NASim [18] and can generate correlated host configurations for totally random scenarios (i.e., when the topology, hosts' configuration and even OSs, services, processes, exploits and privilege escalations are randomly generated), it cannot be yet done for the new dynamic scenarios, where certain objects stay fixed.

The abstraction of NASimEmu does not include storing and using discovered credentials. We hypothesize that their inclusion should be possible, e.g., by taking inspiration from [12].

When an agent performs an exploit, it is assumed to work if there is a corresponding service running on the host. In reality, this is not always the case – the service may be configured in various ways, patched, etc.

The firewall currently blocks or allows all traffic between subnets, based on the network topology. With this assumption, the agent can specify only the action target, while the source is determined automatically (it is the path the host was discovered from). However, in real networks, firewalls may block only certain ports, while allowing them from different sources.

In NASimEmu, only the attacker is modeled. Honeypots can be modeled in the network with a negative reward, but an adversarial defender currently cannot.

4 Experiments

We designed two experiments in which we aim to **a)** demonstrate how to use our framework to train an agent that generalizes to novel scenarios and **b)** verify that a simulation-trained agent can be deployed in emulation. To this end, we implemented two baseline agent models and eight simple scenarios, described in the following sections.

Note that the environment does not have a terminating condition and we leave this question to further research. For the sake of our experiments, we limit the number of steps per episode to 20, hence the goal is to maximize the reward in this time limit (i.e., gain access to as many sensitive hosts as possible).

4.1 Agent Models

We postulate that for the agent to be successful in novel scenarios, it must be size-and-permutation invariant wrt. the hosts, be aware of the subnet connections and remember the results of its actions. Invariance is important to support the ever-changing topologies of different scenarios. Awareness of segment connections is required to tell the scenarios apart. Memory is beneficial, because some action results are not reflected in observations. For example, the *SubnetScan* action does not change the observation if the scan reveals nothing new. Yet, the fact that the action was performed is important for future decisions.

However, the main goal of this paper is to demonstrate the capabilities of the new framework, not to solve all of the aforementioned challenges. For this purpose, we implement two baseline models. The first is a commonly used fixed MLP, and the other is a size-invariant model (see Fig. 3). Neither of these models is aware of the subnet connections nor has any memory.

The MLP model is a simple, fixed-architecture feed-forward neural network. The observed host feature vectors are concatenated and zero-padded to the limit of 30 hosts. The input is processed with a single fully-connected layer with LeakyReLU activation. The output is processed with two separate heads. The first one is a linear layer outputting the state value and the second is a linear layer followed by softmax, outputting probabilities for all possible actions (with size $30 \times action\_dim$). When selecting an action, the actions corresponding to the padding are masked out, so that the model can choose only from the available actions.

There are several limitations to the MLP model. It has a limited capacity and its input is inherently ordered. Each of the input host vectors is treated uniquely and each position has its own weights in the model. Hence, transformations learned for a host vector in one position are not applicable to different positions. Because of the padding, different parts of the network receive different amounts of training. We try to address these issues with the second model.

The invariant model processes each host feature vector individually with a shared embedding function, implemented as a linear layer with LeakyReLU activation. The outputs are aggregated with their concatenated element-wise mean and maximum. This aggregation is concatenated back to the hosts' embeddings and each is processed with a linear layer. These outputs are concatenated and passed through softmax, producing probabilities for all possible actions. Separately, the aggregation is processed with a linear layer to output the state value. The host vectors are augmented with a sine-cosine positional embedding [21] of the order the hosts were discovered. It informs the agent about its attack path, where it entered the network and which hosts it discovered last. Note that the MLP can implicitly access the same information because its input is ordered in the same way. Moreover, this positional embedding is not applicable to the

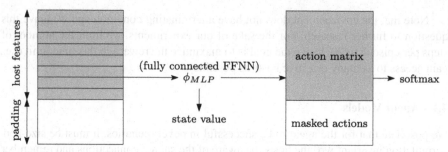

(a) MLP architecture; ϕ_{MLP} is a fully connected neural network with one non-linear and one linear layer

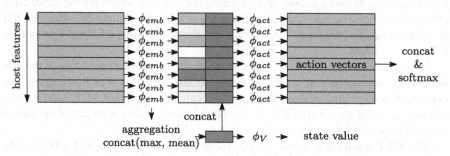

(b) invariant architecture; ϕ_{emb} is a non-linear layer, ϕ_{act} and ϕ_V are linear layers

model	max hosts	layer depth	# params
MLP	30	2	77 294
invariant	∞	2	4 684

Fig. 3. Tested model architectures. **a)** The MLP architecture's capacity is capped to a specific number of hosts and learns position-dependent weights. **b)** The invariant architecture can process unlimited number of hosts and is better equiped for generalization due to weight sharing, while using a fraction of the parameters.

MLP, since it would append the same constant to every input, which can be reduced to a scalar bias.

This second model is size-invariant and its architecture provides an inductive bias. It can process an unlimited number of hosts and anything learned about one host can be directly applied to another. Hence we hypothesize that it should outperform the MLP in out-of-distribution scenarios.

Both models are trained with a deep RL algorithm PPO [17], using 8 consecutive steps from 256 parallel environments as a training batch. Each epoch consists of 100 training steps, equaling to 204 800 environment steps. The training is performed on CPU only, using 2 cores of Intel Xeon Scalable Gold 6146 and 4GB of RAM. Each epoch takes about 6 min, so that an experiment with 200 epochs takes about 20 h. The exact implementation with all hyperparameters can be found in the published code.

4.2 Scenarios

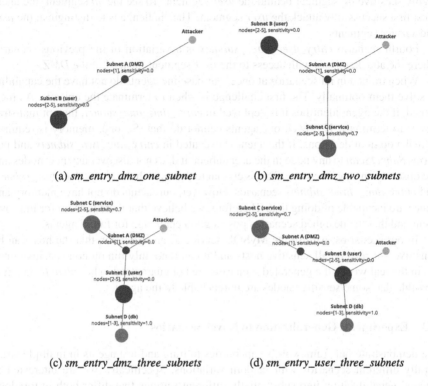

(a) *sm_entry_dmz_one_subnet*   (b) *sm_entry_dmz_two_subnets*

(c) *sm_entry_dmz_three_subnets*   (d) *sm_entry_user_three_subnets*

Fig. 4. The topologies of different scenarios. Node color and radius depict the number of nodes and the probability of their sensitivity in the corresponding subnets. When a scenario is instantiated, a network is randomly generated to conform to the scenario description. Apart from small scenarios (*sm*), medium versions (*md*, not shown) have the same topology, but the subnet sizes are changed from 1, 1–3 and 2–5 to 1, 4–6 and 6–10, respectively.

In the following experiments, we use four prototypical scenarios. Each of them comes in two variations, small (*sm*) and medium (*md*), which differ in subnet sizes (see Fig. 4). The scenarios are designed to be simple, yet to provide a challenge.

In the first scenario, *entry_dmz_one_subnet*, the agent initially sees the *DMZ* (DeMilitarized Zone) subnet, which contains only a single exploitable node. After gaining access, the agent can use this node to attack the *user* segment. As seen in Fig. 4a, this scenario does not contain any sensitive nodes. The optimal behavior would be to terminate the attack as soon as the agent identifies it is deployed in this scenario. Although our baseline agents cannot do this, we still include the scenario to make the learning harder and to provide a challenge to future agents.

Second scenario *entry_dmz_two_subnets* adds an additional sensitive segment behind the *DMZ*. In general, if an agent is randomly deployed in the first two scenarios, the challenge is to identify which it is and either terminate the attack or proceed to the sensitive segment.

Third scenario *entry_dmz_three_subnets* adds more complexity by including a highly sensitive *db* segment behind the *user* segment. To see the *db* segment, the agent must first successfully attack the *user* segment. The challenge is to distinguish the *user* and *service* segments.

Fourth scenario *entry_user_three_subnets* is a variation of the previous scenario, where the attacker starts with access to the *user* segment, instead of the *DMZ*.

When trained in all scenarios at once, our baseline agents do not have the capability to solve them optimally. The first challenge is when to terminate the episode. As mentioned, if the agent identifies it is deployed in *entry_dmz_one_subnet*, the optimal strategy is to terminate. However, our agents cannot do that. Second, memory is required to make optimal decisions. If the agent is executed in *entry_dmz_two_subnets* and performs *SubnetScan* to any node in the user subnet, it does not discover any new nodes and the observation stays the same. This is crucial to distinguish the *entry_dmz_two_subnets* and *entry_dmz_three_subnets* scenarios. However, our agents do not have memory and hence are incapable of doing that. Therefore, we believe that there is room for improvement and that the designed scenarios pose a good challenge for future agents.

In our scenarios, we use the MySQL service as an indication that the host can be sensitive – it runs on all sensitive hosts and it can randomly run on non-sensitive ones. As in the real world, the generated scenarios are not guaranteed to be *solvable*, i.e., it is possible that some sensitive nodes are unreachable to the agent.

4.3   Experiment: Generalization to Novel Scenarios

We demonstrate our framework's capabilities to train and test agents in multiple structurally different scenarios with random variations. Specifically, we are interested in agents' generalization into substantially different settings that differ both in topology and size. We design these two experiments:

sm2md: the agent is trained in small scenarios *sm_entry_dmz_one_subnet* and *sm_entry_dmz_two_subnets* and tested in medium scenarios *md_entry_dmz_three_subnets* and *md_entry_user_three_subnets*. However, in this setting, the MLP model would be impaired, because the training scenarios do not contain enough hosts to fill the model's capacity, and hence to train it properly. Therefore, we design the next experiment.

md2sm: the agent is trained in medium scenarios *md_entry_dmz_one_subnet* and *md_entry_dmz_two_subnets* and tested in small scenarios *sm_entry_dmz_three_subnets* and *sm_entry_user_three_subnets*.

The results in Fig. 5-left show that in both experiments, the MLP and invariant models converge to similar performance when evaluated in their training scenarios (measured as an average reward per step). However, when tested in novel scenarios (Fig. 5-right), the invariant model outperforms the MLP model in both experiment variants. This experiment demonstrates that while our framework allows training for generalization, it is also necessary to use appropriate architectures to see any benefits. Machine learning practitioners have long used fixed models with matrix-like inputs and outputs, and therefore we feel that pointing out this paradigm shift is especially important. An example run of a trained agent can be seen in Appendix.

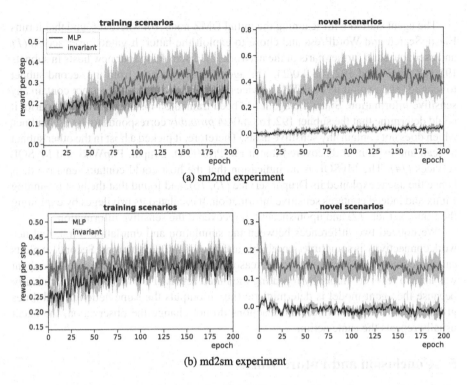

Fig. 5. MLP and invariant models were trained in small and tested in medium scenarios, and vice-versa. The y-axis is not comparable between experiments, nor between train vs. novel settings. The plots show an average of six runs ± one standard deviation.

4.4   Experiment: Transfer to Emulation

In this qualitative experiment, we are interested whether the agent trained in simulation can be deployed in the emulation, which is a controlled version of the real world. If it can, it suggests that the simulation is a valid abstraction of the real world. We trained the invariant model in the simulator in *sm_entry_dmz_one_subnet* and *sm_entry_dmz_two_subnets* scenarios and then created an emulated scenario instance of the latter. This scenario contained 10 virtual hosts, including the router and the attacker nodes, and this whole network was emulated on a single consumer-grade machine.

The experiment found that while there are small discrepancies between the simulation and emulation, the agent was able to perform credibly in the emulation. Specifically, it was able to scan and exploit individual hosts and pivot through the network to gain access to firewalled parts. We tracked it for 17 steps, until it gained access to a sensitive host and recovered the sensitive information. The complete commented emulation log can be found in Appendix and in the following text, we reference its steps in parentheses. Note that in a few cases, the agent performed a non-nonsensical *ProcessScan* and we omitted the corresponding steps.

The agent started with scanning the initial DMZ node *(0)*, where it found that it runs ElasticSearch and WordPress and chose to exploit the latter. It gained user access *(1)*, and used it to scan further parts of the network *(2)*, discovering four new hosts in subnets 192.168.3.0/24 and 192.168.4.0/24. The agent chose one host from the second subnet to scan *(3)* and exploit its ProFTPD service *(6–9)*, but found that it does not contain any sensitive information. Since the agent has been trained on instances of this scenario, it could determine that the subnet 192.168.4.0/24 *probably* corresponds to the user subnet, which does not contain any sensitive hosts. Therefore, it picked a host in the other subnet to scan and exploit. It discovered that it ran ProFTPD, Drupal, PhpWiki and MySQL services *(14)*. The MySQL is an indication that the host could contain sensitive data, hence the agent exploited its Drupal service *(15, 16)*, and found that the host is running Linux and indeed contains sensitive information. It escalated its privileges by exploiting the Linux kernel *(17)* and upon success, it recovered the sensitive information.

We noticed two differences between the simulation and emulation. First, real network connectivity is sometimes unreliable and it leads to failed actions. Second, exploits can sometimes fail without an obvious reason. However, in both of these cases, the agent was able to recover simply by repeating the failed action. This was done automatically, because the agent model is deterministic (i.e., it outputs the same action probabilities given the same input). Since failed actions do not change the observation, the agent usually repeats the same action.

5   Conclusion and Future Work

We introduced NASimEmu, a penetration testing framework to train RL agents that includes both the simulator and emulator with a shared interface. Experimentally, we verified that a simulation-trained agent can be deployed in the emulation, verifying the simulation's realism. Our framework promotes training for generalization by including a generator that produces random scenario variations, differing in network size and configuration. It also allows simultaneous training in multiple, structurally different scenarios and testing in a separate set. We demonstrated that new architectures with inductive biases are needed to successfully train a general agent that can transfer to novel scenarios unseen during the training.

Still, many things are left for future work. In terms of the framework itself, the emulator would benefit from the implementation of more exploits, privilege escalations, OS fingerprinting, etc. The stability and scalability of the emulation should be more rigorously explored. There are several known limitations listed in the article, such as the firewall blocking or allowing all traffic. From the point of RL and machine learning, different invariant architectures could be explored. The agents could benefit from including memory and information about subnet connections. The ability to learn larger and more complex scenarios should be demonstrated. Finally, we have not explored the stopping problem, i.e., the optimal point to stop penetrating the network.

Acknowledgements. This research was supported by The Czech Science Foundation (grants no. 22-32620S and 22-26655S). The research partly used GPUs donated by the NVIDIA Corporation. The authors acknowledge the support of the OP VVV funded project CZ.02.1.01/0.0/0.0/ 16_019/0000765 "Research Center for Informatics".

A Appendix

Fig. 6 contains an example run from the simulation. The rest of the section describes an emulation log from a different run. To produce this log, we trained the invariant model in *sm_entry_dmz_one_subnet* and *sm_entry_dmz_two_subnets* and deployed it into a single emulated scenario instance generated from *sm_entry_dmz_three_subnets*. The log below has been slightly modified for readability, commented and shows the first 17 steps, until the agent exploits a sensitive node.

To better understand the process, we provide a brief description of the classes that appear in the log. *EmulatedNASimEnv* is the OpenAI Gym wrapper that receives raw actions from the model and forwards them to *EmulatedNetwork*, a high-level virtual network abstraction. Also, it creates observations from the log results. The action is translated into single or multiple calls to Metasploit, performed by *MsfClient*.

Note that the scenario description is given to the agent just to inform it about what OSs, services, processes, exploits and privilege escalation are available. However, no information about the network itself is used.

```
1   rrl-nasim$ python main.py -load_model trained_model.pt --trace sm_entry_dmz_two_subnets.v2.yaml --emulate
2
3   # Initially, the agent automatically performs a scan of the network to determine which hosts are reachable.
4   INFO:MsfClient:Connecting to msfrpcd at 127.0.0.1:55553
5   INFO:EmulatedNASimEnv:reset()
6   INFO:MsfClient:Executing auxiliary:scanner/portscan/tcp with params {'RHOSTS': '192.168.1-5.100-110', 'PORTS': '22', 'THREADS': 10}
7   INFO:MsfClient:Scan result: ['192.168.1.100:22']
8   # Below is the current observation of the agent. Compr. = Compromised; Reach. = Reachable; Disc. = Discovered
9   +----------+--------+--------+--------+--------+--------+--------+--------+--------+--------+--------+--------+--------+--------+
10  | Address  | Compr. | Reach. | Disc.  | Value  | Access | linux  | windows| proftpd| drupal | phpwiki| e_search| wp_ninja| mysql |
11  +----------+--------+--------+--------+--------+--------+--------+--------+--------+--------+--------+--------+--------+--------+
12  | (1, 0)   | False  | True   | True   | 0.0    | 0.0    | False  | False  | False  | False  | False  | False   | False   | False |
13  +----------+--------+--------+--------+--------+--------+--------+--------+--------+--------+--------+--------+--------+--------+
14
15  # Next, the agent scans the discovered node.
16  STEP 0
17  INFO:EmulatedNASimEnv:step() with ServiceScan: name=service_scan, target=(1, 0), cost=1.00, prob=1.00, req_access=USER
18  INFO:MsfClient:Executing auxiliary:scanner/portscan/tcp with params {'RHOSTS': '192.168.1.100', 'PORTS': '21,80,3306,9200', '
      ↪ THREADS': 10}
19  INFO:MsfClient:Scan result: ['192.168.1.100:80', '192.168.1.100:9200']
20  INFO:MsfClient:Executing auxiliary:scanner/http/dir_scanner with params {'RHOSTS': '192.168.1.100', 'RPORT': '80', 'THREADS': 1, '
      ↪ DICTIONARY' : '/vagrant/http_dir.txt'}
21  INFO:MsfClient:Folders found on the Http service: ['uploads', 'wordpress']
22  INFO:EmulatedNetwork:Found these services: ('21_linux_proftpd': False, '80_linux_drupal': False, '80_linux_phpwiki': False, '9200
      ↪ _windows_elasticsearch': True, '80_windows_wp_ninja': True, '3306_any_mysql': False) (192.168.1.100).
23
24  a: ServiceScan: name=service_scan, target=(1, 0), cost=1.00, prob=1.00, req_access=USER, r: 0.0, d: False
25  V(s)=6.26
26  +----------+--------+--------+--------+--------+--------+--------+--------+--------+--------+--------+--------+--------+--------+
27  | Address  | Compr. | Reach. | Disc.  | Value  | Access | linux  | windows| proftpd| drupal | phpwiki| e_search| wp_ninja| mysql |
28  +----------+--------+--------+--------+--------+--------+--------+--------+--------+--------+--------+--------+--------+--------+
29  | (1, 0)   | False  | True   | True   | 0.0    | 0.0    | False  | False  | False  | False  | False  | True    | True    | False |
30  +----------+--------+--------+--------+--------+--------+--------+--------+--------+--------+--------+--------+--------+--------+
31
32  # As the agent sees that the host is running e_search service, it tries to exploit it.
33  STEP 1
34  INFO:EmulatedNASimEnv:step() with Exploit: name=e_wp_ninja, target=(1, 0), cost=1.00, prob=1.00, req_access=USER, os=windows,
      ↪ service=80_windows_wp_ninja, access=1
35  INFO:MsfClient:Executing exploit:multi/http/wp_ninja_forms_unauthenticated_file_upload with params {'RHOSTS': '192.168.1.100', '
      ↪ TARGETURI': '/wordpress/', 'FORM_PATH': 'index.php/king-of-hearts/', 'RPORT': '80', 'AllowNoCleanup': True}
36  INFO:MsfClient:Executing exploit:multi/handler with params {}
37  INFO:MsfClient:Opened new session #1 for 192.168.1.100
38  INFO:MsfClient:Running 'DIR C:' at #1 (192.168.1.100)
39  INFO:MsfClient:Executing post:multi/general/execute with params {'COMMAND': 'cmd /c "DIR C:"', 'SESSION': 1}
40  INFO:MsfClient:Running 'whoami /groups' at #1 (192.168.1.100)
41  INFO:MsfClient:Executing post:multi/general/execute with params {'COMMAND': 'cmd /c "whoami /groups"', 'SESSION': 1}
42  a: Exploit: name=e_wp_ninja, target=(1, 0), cost=1.00, prob=1.00, req_access=USER, os=windows, service=80_windows_wp_ninja, access
      ↪ =1, r: 0.0, d: False
43  V(s)=6.51
44  +----------+--------+--------+--------+--------+--------+--------+--------+--------+--------+--------+--------+--------+--------+
45  | Address  | Compr. | Reach. | Disc.  | Value  | Access | linux  | windows| proftpd| drupal | phpwiki| e_search| wp_ninja| mysql |
46  +----------+--------+--------+--------+--------+--------+--------+--------+--------+--------+--------+--------+--------+--------+
47  | (1, 0)   | True   | True   | True   | 0.0    | 1.0    | False  | False  | False  | False  | False  | True    | True    | False |
48  +----------+--------+--------+--------+--------+--------+--------+--------+--------+--------+--------+--------+--------+--------+
49
50  # The host is compromised. The next step is to perform a network scan from the exploited host to see other parts of the network.
51  STEP 2
52  INFO:EmulatedNASimEnv:step() with SubnetScan: name=subnet_scan, target=(1, 0), cost=1.00, prob=1.00, req_access=USER
53  INFO:MsfClient:Executing post:multi/gather/ping_sweep with params {'RHOSTS': '192.168.1-5.100-110', 'SESSION': 1}
54  INFO:MsfClient:Scan result: ['192.168.1.100', '192.168.3.101', '192.168.3.100', '192.168.4.101', '192.168.4.100']
55  INFO:EmulatedNetwork:Found new hosts {'192.168.3.100', '192.168.3.101', '192.168.4.100', '192.168.4.101'}, creating a route from
      ↪ 192.168.1.100.
56  INFO:MsfClient:Executing msfconsole command: 'route add 192.168.3.0/24 1'
57  INFO:MsfClient:Executing msfconsole command: 'route add 192.168.4.0/24 1'
58  a: SubnetScan: name=subnet_scan, target=(1, 0), cost=1.00, prob=1.00, req_access=USER, r: 0.0, d: False
59  V(s)=7.10
60  +----------+--------+--------+--------+--------+--------+--------+--------+--------+--------+--------+--------+--------+--------+
61  | Address  | Compr. | Reach. | Disc.  | Value  | Access | linux  | windows| proftpd| drupal | phpwiki| e_search| wp_ninja| mysql |
62  +----------+--------+--------+--------+--------+--------+--------+--------+--------+--------+--------+--------+--------+--------+
63  | (1, 0)   | True   | True   | True   | 0.0    | 1.0    | False  | False  | False  | False  | False  | True    | True    | False |
```

```
64 |  (3, 1) | False | True | True |  0.0 |  0.0 | False | False | False | False | False |  False  |  False   | False |
65 |  (3, 0) | False | True | True |  0.0 |  0.0 | False | False | False | False | False |  False  |  False   | False |
66 |  (4, 1) | False | True | True |  0.0 |  0.0 | False | False | False | False | False |  False  |  False   | False |
67 |  (4, 0) | False | True | True |  0.0 |  0.0 | False | False | False | False | False |  False  |  False   | False |
68 +--------+-------+------+------+------+------+-------+-------+-------+-------+-------+---------+----------+-------+
69
70 # The agent discovered several nodes in two different subnets. Metasploit was automatically configured to use the first host as
71 # a pivot to access these parts of the network. Now the agent chooses one of the hosts and scans it.
72 STEP 3
73 INFO:EmulatedNASimEnv:step() with ServiceScan: name=service_scan, target=(4, 0), cost=1.00, prob=1.00, req_access=USER
74 INFO:MsfClient:Executing auxiliary:scanner/portscan/tcp with params ['RHOSTS': '192.168.4.100', 'PORTS': '21,80,3306,9200', '
   ↪ THREADS': 10)
75 INFO:MsfClient:Scan result: ['192.168.4.100:21', '192.168.4.100:80']
76 INFO:MsfClient:Executing auxiliary:scanner/http/dir_scanner with params ['RHOSTS': '192.168.4.100', 'RPORT': '80', 'THREADS': 1, '
   ↪ DICTIONARY': '/vagrant/http_dir.txt')
77 INFO:MsfClient:Folders found on the Http service: ['uploads', 'phpwiki']
78 INFO:EmulatedNetwork:Found these services: ('21_linux_proftpd': True, '80_linux_drupal': False, '80_linux_phpwiki': True, '9200
   ↪ _windows_elasticsearch': False, '80_windows_wp_ninja': False, '3306_any_mysql': False) (192.168.4.100).
79
80 a: ServiceScan: name=service_scan, target=(4, 0), cost=1.00, prob=1.00, req_access=USER, r: 0.0, d: False
81 V(s)=11.46
82 +--------+-------+------+------+------+------+-------+-------+-------+-------+-------+---------+----------+-------+
83 | Address | Compr. | Reach. | Disc. | Value | Access | linux | windows | proftpd | drupal | phpwiki | e_search | wp_ninja | mysql |
84 +--------+-------+------+------+------+------+-------+-------+-------+-------+-------+---------+----------+-------+
85 |  (1, 0) | True  | True | True |  0.0 |  1.0 | False | False | False | False | False |  True   |  True    | False |
86 |  (3, 1) | False | True | True |  0.0 |  0.0 | False | False | False | False | False |  False  |  False   | False |
87 |  (3, 0) | False | True | True |  0.0 |  0.0 | False | False | False | False | False |  False  |  False   | False |
88 |  (4, 1) | False | True | True |  0.0 |  0.0 | False | False | False | False | False |  False  |  False   | False |
89 |  (4, 0) | False | True | True |  0.0 |  0.0 | False | False | True  | False | True  |  False  |  False   | False |
90 +--------+-------+------+------+------+------+-------+-------+-------+-------+-------+---------+----------+-------+
91
92 # ProcessScan actions are non-sensical in our case, because there are not any processes defined. The tested model is not perfect.
93 STEP 4
94 INFO:EmulatedNASimEnv:step() with ProcessScan: name=process_scan, target=(4, 0), cost=1.00, prob=1.00, req_access=USER
95 a: ProcessScan: name=process_scan, target=(4, 0), cost=1.00, prob=1.00, req_access=USER, r: 0.0, d: False
96 V(s)=6.47
97
98 STEP 5
99 INFO:EmulatedNASimEnv:step() with ProcessScan: name=process_scan, target=(4, 0), cost=1.00, prob=1.00, req_access=USER
100 a: ProcessScan: name=process_scan, target=(4, 0), cost=1.00, prob=1.00, req_access=USER, r: 0.0, d: False
101 V(s)=6.47
102
103 # The agent tries to exploit the proftpd service on the (4, 0) host. However, the exploit fails for unknown reason. This would
    ↪ never happen in simulation.
104 STEP 6
105 INFO:EmulatedNASimEnv:step() with Exploit: name=e_proftpd, target=(4, 0), cost=1.00, prob=1.00, req_access=USER, os=linux, service
    ↪ =21_linux_proftpd, access=1
106 INFO:MsfClient:Executing exploit:unix/ftp/proftpd_modcopy_exec with params ['RHOSTS': '192.168.4.100', 'SITEPATH': '/var/www/
    ↪ uploads/', 'TARGETURI': '/uploads/')
107 INFO:MsfClient:No session created.
108 WARNING:EmulatedNetwork:Failed exploit: Exploit: name=e_proftpd, target=(4, 0), cost=1.00, prob=1.00, req_access=USER, os=linux,
    ↪ service=21_linux_proftpd, access=1
109
110 a: Exploit: name=e_proftpd, target=(4, 0), cost=1.00, prob=1.00, req_access=USER, os=linux, service=21_linux_proftpd, access=1, r:
    ↪ 0.0, d: False
111 V(s)=6.47
112
113 # The state did not change, the model is deterministic and outputs the same action probabilities. Hence, it tries the same exploit
    ↪ again. It fails again.
114 STEP 7
115 INFO:EmulatedNASimEnv:step() with Exploit: name=e_proftpd, target=(4, 0), cost=1.00, prob=1.00, req_access=USER, os=linux, service
    ↪ =21_linux_proftpd, access=1
116 INFO:MsfClient:Executing exploit:unix/ftp/proftpd_modcopy_exec with params ['RHOSTS': '192.168.4.100', 'SITEPATH': '/var/www/
    ↪ uploads/', 'TARGETURI': '/uploads/')
117 INFO:MsfClient:No session created.
118 WARNING:EmulatedNetwork:Failed exploit: Exploit: name=e_proftpd, target=(4, 0), cost=1.00, prob=1.00, req_access=USER, os=linux,
    ↪ service=21_linux_proftpd, access=1
119 a: Exploit: name=e_proftpd, target=(4, 0), cost=1.00, prob=1.00, req_access=USER, os=linux, service=21_linux_proftpd, access=1, r:
    ↪ 0.0, d: False
120 V(s)=6.47
121
122 STEP 8
123 INFO:EmulatedNASimEnv:step() with ProcessScan: name=process_scan, target=(4, 0), cost=1.00, prob=1.00, req_access=USER
124 a: ProcessScan: name=process_scan, target=(4, 0), cost=1.00, prob=1.00, req_access=USER, r: 0.0, d: False
125
126 # Finally, the exploit succeeds. Automatically, the host is examined whether it contains sensitive data and if it can be accessed.
127 STEP 9
128 INFO:EmulatedNASimEnv:step() with Exploit: name=e_proftpd, target=(4, 0), cost=1.00, prob=1.00, req_access=USER, os=linux, service
    ↪ =21_linux_proftpd, access=1
129 INFO:MsfClient:Executing exploit:unix/ftp/proftpd_modcopy_exec with params ['RHOSTS': '192.168.4.100', 'SITEPATH': '/var/www/
    ↪ uploads/', 'TARGETURI': '/uploads/')
130 INFO:MsfClient:Opened new session #2 for 192.168.4.100
131 INFO:MsfClient:Running 'test -f /home/kylo_ren/loot; echo NO_LOOT=$?' at #2 (192.168.4.100)
132 INFO:MsfClient:Executing post:multi/general/execute with params ['COMMAND': 'test -f /home/kylo_ren/loot; echo NO_LOOT=$?', '
    ↪ SESSION': 2}
133 INFO:MsfClient:Running 'whoami' at #2 (192.168.4.100)
134 INFO:MsfClient:Executing post:multi/general/execute with params ['COMMAND': 'whoami', 'SESSION': 2}
135 a: Exploit: name=e_proftpd, target=(4, 0), cost=1.00, prob=1.00, req_access=USER, os=linux, service=21_linux_proftpd, access=1, r:
    ↪ 0.0, d: False
136 V(s)=6.47
137 +--------+-------+------+------+------+------+-------+-------+-------+-------+-------+---------+----------+-------+
138 | Address | Compr. | Reach. | Disc. | Value | Access | linux | windows | proftpd | drupal | phpwiki | e_search | wp_ninja | mysql |
139 +--------+-------+------+------+------+------+-------+-------+-------+-------+-------+---------+----------+-------+
140 |  (1, 0) | True  | True | True |  0.0 |  1.0 | False | False | False | False | False |  True   |  True    | False |
141 |  (3, 1) | False | True | True |  0.0 |  0.0 | False | False | False | False | False |  False  |  False   | False |
142 |  (3, 0) | False | True | True |  0.0 |  0.0 | False | False | False | False | False |  False  |  False   | False |
143 |  (4, 1) | False | True | True |  0.0 |  0.0 | False | False | False | False | False |  False  |  False   | False |
144 |  (4, 0) | True  | True | True |  0.0 |  1.0 | False | False | True  | False | True  |  False  |  False   | False |
145 +--------+-------+------+------+------+------+-------+-------+-------+-------+-------+---------+----------+-------+
146
147 STEP 10
148 INFO:EmulatedNASimEnv:step() with ProcessScan: name=process_scan, target=(4, 0), cost=1.00, prob=1.00, req_access=USER
149 a: ProcessScan: name=process_scan, target=(4, 0), cost=1.00, prob=1.00, req_access=USER, r: 0.0, d: False
150 V(s)=6.28
151
152 STEP 11
153 INFO:EmulatedNASimEnv:step() with ProcessScan: name=process_scan, target=(4, 1), cost=1.00, prob=1.00, req_access=USER
```

```
154  a: ProcessScan: name=process_scan, target=(4, 1), cost=1.00, prob=1.00, req_access=USER, r: 0.0, d: False
155  V(s)=6.28
156
157  STEP 12
158  INFO:EmulatedNASimEnv:step() with ProcessScan: name=process_scan, target=(4, 1), cost=1.00, prob=1.00, req_access=USER
159  a: ProcessScan: name=process_scan, target=(4, 1), cost=1.00, prob=1.00, req_access=USER, r: 0.0, d: False
160  V(s)=6.28
161
162  STEP 13
163  INFO:EmulatedNASimEnv:step() with ProcessScan: name=process_scan, target=(4, 0), cost=1.00, prob=1.00, req_access=USER
164  a: ProcessScan: name=process_scan, target=(4, 0), cost=1.00, prob=1.00, req_access=USER, r: 0.0, d: False
165  V(s)=6.28
166
167  # The agent focusses on a different node and scans it.
168  STEP 14
169  INFO:EmulatedNASimEnv:step() with ServiceScan: name=service_scan, target=(3, 0), cost=1.00, prob=1.00, req_access=USER
170  INFO:MsfClient:Executing auxiliary:scanner/portscan/tcp with params {'RHOSTS': '192.168.3.100', 'PORTS': '21,80,3306,9200', '
        ↪ THREADS': 10}
171  INFO:MsfClient:Scan result: ['192.168.3.100:21', '192.168.3.100:3306', '192.168.3.100:80']
172  INFO:MsfClient:Executing auxiliary:scanner/http/dir_scanner with params {'RHOSTS': '192.168.3.100', 'RPORT': '80', 'THREADS': 1, '
        ↪ DICTIONARY': '/vagrant/http_dir.txt'}
173  INFO:MsfClient:Folders found on the Http service: ['uploads', 'drupal', 'phpwiki']
174  INFO:EmulatedNetwork:Found these services: {'21_linux_proftpd': True, '80_linux_drupal': True, '80_linux_phpwiki': True, '9200
        ↪ _windows_elasticsearch': False, '80_windows_wp_ninja': False, '3306_any_mysql': True} (192.168.3.100).
175
176  a: ServiceScan: name=service_scan, target=(3, 0), cost=1.00, prob=1.00, req_access=USER, r: 0.0, d: False
177  V(s)=6.28
178  +---------+--------+--------+-------+-------+--------+-------+---------+---------+--------+---------+----------+----------+-------+
179  | Address | Compr. | Reach. | Disc. | Value | Access | linux | windows | proftpd | drupal | phpwiki | e_search | wp_ninja | mysql |
180  +---------+--------+--------+-------+-------+--------+-------+---------+---------+--------+---------+----------+----------+-------+
181  | (1, 0)  | True   | True   | True  | 0.0   | 1.0    | False | False   | False   | False  | False   | True     | True     | False |
182  | (3, 1)  | False  | True   | True  | 0.0   | 0.0    | False | False   | False   | False  | False   | False    | False    | False |
183  | (3, 0)  | False  | True   | True  | 0.0   | 0.0    | False | False   | True    | True   | True    | False    | False    | True  |
184  | (4, 1)  | False  | True   | True  | 0.0   | 0.0    | False | False   | False   | False  | False   | False    | False    | False |
185  | (4, 0)  | True   | True   | True  | 0.0   | 1.0    | False | False   | True    | False  | True    | False    | False    | False |
186  +---------+--------+--------+-------+-------+--------+-------+---------+---------+--------+---------+----------+----------+-------+
187
188  # It discovered that the (3, 0) node runs the mysql service, which is an indication that the node could be sensitive. It tries to
        ↪ exploit the drupal service.
189  STEP 15
190  INFO:EmulatedNASimEnv:step() with Exploit: name=e_drupal, target=(3, 0), cost=1.00, prob=1.00, req_access=USER, os=linux, service
        ↪ =80_linux_drupal, access=1
191  INFO:MsfClient:Executing exploit:unix/webapp/drupal_coder_exec with params {'RHOSTS': '192.168.3.100', 'TARGETURI': '/drupal'}
192  INFO:MsfClient:No session created.
193  WARNING:EmulatedNetwork:Failed exploit: Exploit: name=e_drupal, target=(3, 0), cost=1.00, prob=1.00, req_access=USER, os=linux,
        ↪ service=80_linux_drupal, access=1
194
195  a: Exploit: name=e_drupal, target=(3, 0), cost=1.00, prob=1.00, req_access=USER, os=linux, service=80_linux_drupal, access=1, r:
        ↪ 0.0, d: False
196  V(s)=12.98
197
198  # It tries again and this time succeeds. The examination shows that the host contains sensitive information, but it can be accessed
        ↪ only by a priviledged user.
199  STEP 16
200  INFO:EmulatedNASimEnv:step() with Exploit: name=e_drupal, target=(3, 0), cost=1.00, prob=1.00, req_access=USER, os=linux, service
        ↪ =80_linux_drupal, access=1
201  INFO:MsfClient:Executing exploit:unix/webapp/drupal_coder_exec with params {'RHOSTS': '192.168.3.100', 'TARGETURI': '/drupal'}
202  INFO:MsfClient:Opened new session #3 for 192.168.3.100
203  INFO:MsfClient:Running 'test -f /home/kylo_ren/loot; echo NO_LOOT=$?' at #3 (192.168.3.100)
204  INFO:MsfClient:Executing post:multi/general/execute with params {'COMMAND': 'test -f /home/kylo_ren/loot; echo NO_LOOT=$?', '
        ↪ SESSION': 3}
205  INFO:MsfClient:Running 'cat /home/kylo_ren/loot' at #3 (192.168.3.100)
206  INFO:MsfClient:Executing post:multi/general/execute with params {'COMMAND': 'cat /home/kylo_ren/loot', 'SESSION': 3}
207  INFO:MsfClient:Running 'whoami' at #3 (192.168.3.100)
208  INFO:MsfClient:Executing post:multi/general/execute with params {'COMMAND': 'whoami', 'SESSION': 3}
209
210  a: Exploit: name=e_drupal, target=(3, 0), cost=1.00, prob=1.00, req_access=USER, os=linux, service=80_linux_drupal, access=1, r:
        ↪ 0.0, d: False
211  V(s)=12.98
212  +---------+--------+--------+-------+-------+--------+-------+---------+---------+--------+---------+----------+----------+-------+
213  | Address | Compr. | Reach. | Disc. | Value | Access | linux | windows | proftpd | drupal | phpwiki | e_search | wp_ninja | mysql |
214  +---------+--------+--------+-------+-------+--------+-------+---------+---------+--------+---------+----------+----------+-------+
215  | (1, 0)  | True   | True   | True  | 0.0   | 1.0    | False | False   | False   | False  | False   | True     | True     | False |
216  | (3, 1)  | False  | True   | True  | 0.0   | 0.0    | False | False   | False   | False  | False   | False    | False    | False |
217  | (3, 0)  | True   | True   | True  | 100.0 | 1.0    | False | False   | True    | True   | True    | False    | False    | True  |
218  | (4, 1)  | False  | True   | True  | 0.0   | 0.0    | False | False   | False   | False  | False   | False    | False    | False |
219  | (4, 0)  | True   | True   | True  | 0.0   | 1.0    | False | False   | True    | False  | True    | False    | False    | False |
220  +---------+--------+--------+-------+-------+--------+-------+---------+---------+--------+---------+----------+----------+-------+
221
222  # The agent tries the privilege escalation and after success it collects the sensitive information (the loot).
223  STEP 17
224  INFO:EmulatedNASimEnv:step() with PrivilegeEscalation: name=pe_kernel, target=(3, 0), cost=1.00, prob=1.00, req_access=USER, os=
        ↪ linux, process=None, access=2
225  INFO:MsfClient:Executing exploit:linux/local/overlayfs_priv_esc with params {'SESSION': 3, 'target': 0}
226  INFO:MsfClient:Opened new session #4 for 192.168.3.100
227  INFO:MsfClient:Running 'test -f /home/kylo_ren/loot; echo NO_LOOT=$?' at #4 (192.168.3.100)
228  INFO:MsfClient:Executing post:multi/general/execute with params {'COMMAND': 'test -f /home/kylo_ren/loot; echo NO_LOOT=$?', '
        ↪ SESSION': 4}
229  INFO:MsfClient:Running 'cat /home/kylo_ren/loot' at #4 (192.168.3.100)
230  INFO:MsfClient:Executing post:multi/general/execute with params {'COMMAND': 'cat /home/kylo_ren/loot', 'SESSION': 4}
231  INFO:EmulatedNetwork:---------------------
232  INFO:EmulatedNetwork:Loot recovered: LOOT=28a5b8532399467452f55775a05daa10
233  INFO:EmulatedNetwork:---------------------
234  INFO:MsfClient:Running 'whoami' at #4 (192.168.3.100)
235  INFO:MsfClient:Executing post:multi/general/execute with params {'COMMAND': 'whoami', 'SESSION': 4}
236  a: PrivilegeEscalation: name=pe_kernel, target=(3, 0), cost=1.00, prob=1.00, req_access=USER, os=linux, process=None, access=2, r:
        ↪ 0.0, d: False
237  V(s)=16.02
238  +---------+--------+--------+-------+-------+--------+-------+---------+---------+--------+---------+----------+----------+-------+
239  | Address | Compr. | Reach. | Disc. | Value | Access | linux | windows | proftpd | drupal | phpwiki | e_search | wp_ninja | mysql |
240  +---------+--------+--------+-------+-------+--------+-------+---------+---------+--------+---------+----------+----------+-------+
241  | (1, 0)  | True   | True   | True  | 0.0   | 1.0    | False | False   | False   | False  | False   | True     | True     | False |
242  | (3, 1)  | False  | True   | True  | 0.0   | 0.0    | False | False   | False   | False  | False   | False    | False    | False |
243  | (3, 0)  | True   | True   | True  | 100.0 | 2.0    | False | False   | True    | True   | True    | False    | False    | True  |
244  | (4, 1)  | False  | True   | True  | 0.0   | 0.0    | False | False   | False   | False  | False   | False    | False    | False |
245  | (4, 0)  | True   | True   | True  | 0.0   | 1.0    | False | False   | True    | False  | True    | False    | False    | False |
246  +---------+--------+--------+-------+-------+--------+-------+---------+---------+--------+---------+----------+----------+-------+
```

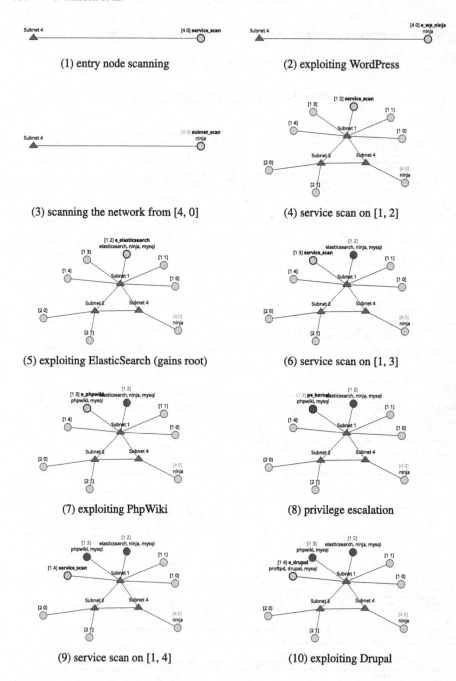

Fig. 6. Example run of a trained invariant agent, evaluated in the *sm_entry_dmz_three_subnets* scenario (simulation). Subnet 1 corresponds to the service subnet and contains multiple sensitive nodes. The agent sequentially scans them and exploits those running the MySQL service, as it is an indication that the host contains sensitive information. E.g., in step 7, the agent exploits node [1, 3] and discovers that it is sensitive, but it still needs to escalate its privileges to retrieve the sensitive information.

References

1. Andrew, A., Spillard, S., Collyer, J., Dhir, N.: Developing optimal causal cyber-defence agents via cyber security simulation. In: Workshop on Machine Learning for Cybersecurity (ML4Cyber) (2022)
2. Brockman, G., et al.: OpenAI gym. arXiv preprint arXiv:1606.01540 (2016)
3. Buchanan, B., Bansemer, J., Cary, D., Lucas, J., Musser, M.: Automating cyber attacks. In: Center for Security and Emerging Technology, pp. 13–32 (2020)
4. Čeleda, P., Čegan, J., Vykopal, J., Tovarňák, D., et al.: Kypo-a platform for cyber defence exercises. In: M&S Support to Operational Tasks Including War Gaming, Logistics, Cyber Defence. NATO Science and Technology Organization (2015)
5. Chen, J., Hu, S., Zheng, H., Xing, C., Zhang, G.: GAIL-PT: an intelligent penetration testing framework with generative adversarial imitation learning. Comput. Secur. **126**, 103055 (2023)
6. Chowdhary, A., Huang, D., Mahendran, J.S., Romo, D., Deng, Y., Sabur, A.: Autonomous security analysis and penetration testing. In: 2020 16th International Conference on Mobility, Sensing and Networking (MSN), pp. 508–515. IEEE (2020)
7. Drašar, M., Moskal, S., Yang, S., Zat'ko, P.: Session-level adversary intent-driven cyberattack simulator. In: 2020 IEEE/ACM 24th International Symposium on Distributed Simulation and Real Time Applications (DS-RT), pp. 1–9. IEEE (2020)
8. Hammar, K., Stadler, R.: Finding effective security strategies through reinforcement learning and self-play. In: 2020 16th International Conference on Network and Service Management (CNSM), pp. 1–9. IEEE (2020)
9. Hammar, K., Stadler, R.: Learning intrusion prevention policies through optimal stopping. In: 2021 17th International Conference on Network and Service Management (CNSM), pp. 509–517. IEEE (2021)
10. Janisch, J., Pevný, T., Lisý, V.: Symbolic relational deep reinforcement learning based on graph neural networks. arXiv preprint arXiv:2009.12462 (2020)
11. Li, L., Fayad, R., Taylor, A.: CyGIL: a cyber gym for training autonomous agents over emulated network systems. In: Proceedings of the 1st International Workshop on Adaptive Cyber Defense (2021)
12. Seifert, C., et al.: Microsoft: Cyberbattlesim (2021). https://github.com/microsoft/cyberbattlesim
13. Miehling, E., Rasouli, M., Teneketzis, D.: Optimal defense policies for partially observable spreading processes on bayesian attack graphs. In: Proceedings of the Second ACM Workshop on Moving Target Defense, pp. 67–76 (2015)
14. Mnih, V., et al.: Asynchronous methods for deep reinforcement learning. In: International Conference on Machine Learning, pp. 1928–1937 (2016)
15. Mnih, V., et al.: Human-level control through deep reinforcement learning. Nature **518**(7540), 529–533 (2015)
16. Molina-Markham, A., Miniter, C., Powell, B., Ridley, A.: Network environment design for autonomous cyberdefense. arXiv preprint arXiv:2103.07583 (2021)
17. Schulman, J., Wolski, F., Dhariwal, P., Radford, A., Klimov, O.: Proximal policy optimization algorithms. arXiv preprint arXiv:1707.06347 (2017)
18. Schwartz, J., Kurniawati, H.: Autonomous penetration testing using reinforcement learning. arXiv preprint arXiv:1905.05965 (2019)
19. Sick, T., Biondi, F.: Purpledome: simulation environment for attacks on computer networks. https://github.com/avast/PurpleDome (2022). Accessed 09 Feb 2022

20. Standen, M., Lucas, M., Bowman, D., Richer, T.J., Kim, J., Marriott, D.: CybORG: a gym for the development of autonomous cyber agents. In: Proceedings of the 1st International Workshop on Adaptive Cyber Defense (2021)
21. Vaswani, A., et al.: Attention is all you need. Adv. Neural Inf. Process. Syst. **30** (2017)
22. Yang, Y., Liu, X.: Behaviour-diverse automatic penetration testing: a curiosity-driven multi-objective deep reinforcement learning approach. arXiv preprint arXiv:2202.10630 (2022)

On the Use of AutoML for Combating Alert Fatigue in Security Operations Centers

Davy Preuveneers[1][✉], Javier Martínez Llamas[1], Irfan Bulut[2],
Enrique Argones Rúa[2], Pieter Verfaillie[3], Vince Demortier[3], Dimitri Surinx[3],
and Wouter Joosen[1]

[1] imec-DistriNet, KU Leuven, Belgium
davy.preuveneers@kuleuven.be
[2] imec-COSIC, KU Leuven, Belgium
[3] Spotit, Merelbeke, Belgium

Abstract. An overwhelming number of alerts – especially false ones – can desensitize analysts in security operations centers (SOC), possibly resulting in missed critical incidents and attacks going unnoticed. With inadequate alert monitoring, improper thresholds, and missing feedback loops as lead causes of alert fatigue, we investigate the use of automated machine learning to increase the efficiency of a SOC through automation of false alerts filtering. More specifically, we design a methodology to allow a safer use of AutoML to reduce false alerts, and validate this on a real-world case study. To be more precise, our approach is tailored to address datasets that exhibit limited instances of true positives, possess high dimensionality relative to their size, and demonstrate temporal fluctuations. We have identified diverse setups that provide comparable and reliably effective results in minimizing false positive alerts, all the while avoiding instances of false negatives. Furthermore, we provide valuable insights into the application of these automated frameworks within the realm of security.

Keywords: Security Operations Centers · AutoML · Alert fatigue

1 Introduction

With the proliferation of advanced cyber threats becoming a growing concern, organizations rely on security operation centers (SOC) to continuously improve the organization's security posture. A SOC is a centralized hub that monitors the organization's IT infrastructure around the clock, while preventing, detecting, analyzing, and responding to potential security incidents.

When growing volumes of security alerts overwhelm security analysts, alerts will be ignored, incidents will not be investigated, and attacks will go unnoticed. Hence, the key to the success of a SOC is the ability to configure these monitoring systems and tune their alerting for the least number of false positives

S. Katsikas et al. (Eds.): ESORICS 2023 Workshops, LNCS 14399, pp. 609–627, 2024.
https://doi.org/10.1007/978-3-031-54129-2_36

without missing any true security incidents. Security orchestration and automation (SOAR) playbooks can help fight alert fatigue by scripting repetitive work for known scenarios with a prescribed course of action, such as enriching an alert with additional information and context. However, even if many monitoring systems provide severity or priority fields, improper thresholds may still cause false alerts. Tuning a single threshold to reduce false alerts while at the same time not introducing any false negative ones is not always straightforward because that threshold lacks context.

In this work, we leverage Artificial Intelligence (AI)-assisted techniques to combat false alerts and alert fatigue in general. Machine learning (ML) and deep learning (DL) are now mainstream – also in security [5] – to make sense of large volumes of data. In this application domain, an ML model can help to increase the efficiency of a SOC by filtering false alerts, leaving more time and resources for the security analysts for those signals and alerts that truly deserve their attention. However, constructing an effective ML classifier is time-consuming. Furthermore, new threats emerge continuously and these can trigger concept drift [10] causing existing ML models to become ineffective over time. Also, lack of ground truth, scarcity of true positives, and high dimensionality of the input space make the construction of these models cumbersome, and their generalization ability limited. These challenging conditions make it necessary to build a specific methodology to appropriately assess the *reliability, consistency, stability,* and *utility* of the different possible configurations of AutoML [9]. After proposing such a methodology, we have performed an extensive evaluation with real-world data with the intention of providing guidance toward a safer deployment of these types of systems in the real world. The main contributions are as follows:

- We propose an AutoML-based methodology to minimize false positive alerts, while avoiding instances of false negative alerts.
- For a real-world case study, we have identified diverse setups that provide comparable and reliably effective results in minimizing false positive alerts.
- We provide valuable insights into the application of these automated frameworks within the realm of security.

The remainder of this paper is structured as follows. We review relevant related work in Sect. 2. Section 3 discusses our approach on how we used AutoML to combat alert fatigue and systematically compared different ML pipeline configurations. We evaluate their benefits and drawbacks in Sect. 4. In Sect. 5, we conclude with summarizing the main insights and opportunities for further research.

2 Related Work

In this section, we review related work on the application of AI and ML in security operations centers to combat *false alerts* and alert fatigue in general.

NoDoze is a system proposed by Hassan et al. [8] to combat alert fatigue by leveraging the contextual and historical information of threat alerts. NoDoze creates a causal dependency graph of an alert, and then an anomaly score for each edge to reflect the frequency of its past occurrence in the enterprise network. The authors propose a network diffusion algorithm to aggregate these scores into a single value which is then used for triage. After setting a cutoff threshold for anomaly scores, they were able to reduce the volume of *false alerts* by 84%.

Addressing alert fatigue was also the goal of the work by Aminanto et al. [3]. Their approach exploits the temporal information in the alerts, and relies on online anomaly detection using Isolation Forests. They use the data of the previous day for training purposes and screen the incoming alerts simultaneously. On a 10-month dataset with 564,561 alerts, they were able to filter 87.41% of the false alerts without producing any false negative, i.e., without missing any true alert, by using an unsupervised method. The advantage of this method is that it does not require prior labeling, and it is lightweight to implement. A similar approach was proposed by Ahmed et al. [1]. They instead used Extended Isolation Forests to mitigate the bias that is induced by the tree branching in traditional Isolation Forest models. For an IDS dataset containing 50,000 alerts, the authors were able to reduce the number of false alerts by 82.15%.

Follow-up work by Aminanto et al. [2] augments the Isolation Forest unsupervised learning model with deep learning-based stacked auto-encoders (SAE) to further reduce false alerts. The SAE is a symmetric neural network model that aims to reconstruct its input after pushing through a bottleneck network layer with fewer neurons than its input layer. When trained on benign data, the SAE exhibits a high reconstruction error for critical alerts. Using the same experimental dataset as before [3], the authors now achieve a recall score of 95.89% and a false positive rate of 5.86%.

Ban et al. [4] proposed an alert screening scheme that uses AI-based tools to distinguish true threats from false alarms produced by a SIEM system. Their solution consists of carefully selected ML algorithms and visualization components to accelerate alert analysis and incident response. Their solution relies on 6 classifiers that can efficiently handle high-dimensional data (i.e., K-nearest neighbors, naive Bayes, linear discriminant analysis, decision tree, AdaBoost, SVM, and WSVM) as part of an ML pipeline that also takes care of feature selection and one-hot encoding. They report a recall rate of 99.598% for highly critical alerts and a false positive rate of 0.001% for a dataset of alert logs recorded over a 10-month period having 133.77 million alerts with only 593 confirmed by security experts as true positives. Building on top of the previous work, Ndichu et al. [12] aim to detect critical alerts but they specifically look at dealing with the imbalanced nature of the datasets, as well as the impact of having alert data from eight security appliances. Using the same dataset as Ban et al. [4], the authors evaluate the impact of the neighborhood cleaning rule (NCR) to eliminate ambiguous, noisy, and redundant false alerts. They then use the support vector machine synthetic minority oversampling technique (SVMSMOTE) to generate synthetic training true alerts. Finally, the authors evaluated the decision tree and random forest classifiers, demonstrating a significant reduction in false alerts while achieving a recall of 99.524%.

Pang et al. [13] argue that the security risks associated with models generated through Neural Architecture Search (NAS) − a subset of AutoML that specifically targets the optimization of neural network architectures − are not well understood. By examining 10 popular NAS methods, the researchers find that models created through NAS are more vulnerable to various malicious actions like adversarial attacks, model tampering, and function copying compared to manually designed models. They argue this might be due to NAS methods favoring fast-converging models in early training stages due to the high search space and training costs. Their study not only uncovers the link between model features and vulnerability but also reveals connections between different attack types.

The gap that we aim to address in this work is the fact that in the real world security analysts rely on many open-source and/or commercial threat monitoring solutions. These are already able to automatically filter many low-risk alerts via automated playbooks, but they nonetheless still trigger false alerts. Our goal is not to operate on the raw data (e.g., replaying PCAP files), but rather to further filter the alert output of security appliances with ML-based techniques. This problem is much harder to solve than the one addressed in the literature.

3   Methodology

This section first elaborates on the real-world case study, and then describes, in more detail, the approach we followed to reduce false positive alerts.

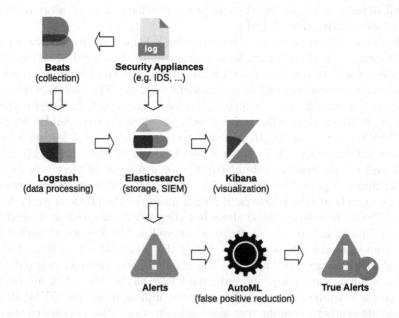

Beats
(collection)

Security Appliances
(e.g. IDS, ...)

Logstash
(data processing)

Elasticsearch
(storage, SIEM)

Kibana
(visualization)

Alerts

AutoML
(false positive reduction)

True Alerts

Fig. 1. Overview of alert reduction architecture on top of the ELK software stack.

3.1   Case Study

Our case study builds upon the output of various security appliances that store their log outputs and alerts in an ELK stack as depicted in Fig. 1. The alert data that is used to feed our AutoML component is stored in the Elasticsearch database. For the sake of simplicity, we will only report on the results of one particular technology, in this case, a commercial extended detection and response (XDR) system that leverages network, endpoint, and cloud data to defend against sophisticated attacks. Under the hood, this security appliance uses out-of-the-box rules, as well as AI techniques, to detect attacks. We consider the behavior of this appliance as a black box, assuming no knowledge of the internal modus operandi nor any insights into the AI techniques used. The severity of each alert is computed as an aggregated score and a simple threshold mechanism already filters many non-critical alerts. The remaining ones are evaluated and possibly responded to by SOC analysts.

The objective is to design and evaluate a classifier that reduces the number of *false alerts* delivered to the SOC analysts, while preserving all *true alerts* for further examination. Our classifier will process the non-filtered alerts, which would be otherwise directly delivered to the SOC analysts. The output of the classifier would determine whether these alerts can be discarded as false alerts, or they require further attention. Therefore, our binary classifier can make two distinct types of errors, with different relevance: (1) false positives, which are false alerts classified as true alerts decreasing the utility of the classifier, and (2) false negatives, which are true alerts classified as false alerts. While the former are undesirable, the latter need to be avoided.

3.2   Security Alert Dataset

In collaboration with Spotit — a company offering security and SOC services to external customers — we collected and processed a dataset of alerts over a period of 10 months. The company uses the same assets to monitor its own activities. All the experiments were done with internal Spotit data and no client data was ever used or shared to mitigate any confidentiality and privacy or other ethical concerns when training with client data.

The XDR dataset is exported from the Elasticsearch database in JSON format, and after flattening the data structure, we end up with a tabular dataframe having more than 60 columns. These columns are of different types (i.e., categorical, numeric, lists, etc.) and may even have missing values. Alerts that pass a certain severity threshold are passed along and analyzed by a SOC analyst, who labels them as *true positive* (a real threat), *false positive* (a bogus or innocuous threat), a *duplicate* (a recurrence of a previous true or false alert), or *other* if the label is not clear. Alerts below the threshold are not investigated in a similar fashion, and hence do not follow this analysis pipeline. Therefore, they are out of scope and are labeled *true negative* alerts in our ML pipeline. The labels in this dataset are subsequently binarized by (1) removing the small number of *other* entries, (2) reusing the labels of the original alerts for the *duplicate* entries, and

(3) combining the *false positive* and *true negative* alerts in *class 0* (false alerts raised by bogus or innocuous events), and the *true positive* alerts in *class 1*. From this dataset, we create 3 variants with different degrees of manual feature engineering, which are then used as training and test set in our ML pipeline:

- **None**: No manual feature engineering based on knowledge or insights by domain experts. In this variant, min-max normalization is performed to numerical features, and ordinal transformation to categorical ones.
- **Pre-processing**: Create additional columns based on existing ones (e.g., split a URL feature in a separate domain and a path feature).
- **Encoding**: After pre-processing, additionally apply one-hot encoding and other data transformation methods on selected columns.

The second variant (and hence also the third) applies domain-specific knowledge to investigate whether this manual effort pays off to combat alert fatigue, or whether the AutoML pipeline can automate the feature engineering and selection in an equally effective manner even without any domain expertise or knowledge about the protected infrastructure.

3.3 AutoML-Driven Automation Methodology

Our automation methodology is based on the Python-based AutoSklearn [7] framework. A classifier is implemented in a similar manner as in the well-known scikit-learn ML library (Fig. 7)[1].

The explored aspects of the AutoML pipeline include: types of scikit-learn classifiers to be included in the ensemble, total training time, training time per classifier in the ensemble, size of the ensemble, and the number of training tasks in parallel. Last but not least, AutoSklearn internally splits the training data into two parts, i.e., (1) one internal subset to train the individual models, (2) a second internal subset to evaluate the F1 score and other metrics. We implemented a custom strategy to subsample the original training set into two subsets taking into account the date of acquisition. Beyond selecting the best base ML models to construct the ensemble, AutoSklearn can also automatically optimize the feature selection and encoding, and apply various methods to reduce the dimensionality of data before training. These optional parameters were also investigated.

During initial tests, we noticed a significant variation across multiple runs with the same settings, which we attribute to a mismatch between the standard error metric(s) that AutoSklearn uses to optimize the final ensemble and the actual goal of reducing the number of false alerts (class 0). That is why we implemented our own custom error metric for AutoSklearn to optimize:

$$\text{custom error metric} = min(max(\frac{FP}{FP + TN}, FN), 1.0) \tag{1}$$

This metric aims first to eliminate false negatives, which is the primary requirement of our use case, and then to maximize the specificity, which is the utility function in our use case.

---

[1] https://scikit-learn.org.

3.4   Evaluation Methodology

Our evaluation pursues to evaluate *reliability, consistency, stability,* and *utility* of the trained classifiers. We train each configuration 10 times in order to allow the assessment of stability. Consistency, reliability, and utility are also verified in all the trained classifiers in each configuration. For these evaluations, the security alert dataset has been temporally split into 3 subsets:

- **Training set**: train the different AutoSklearn ensemble classifiers.
- **Validation set**: set appropriate thresholds of the classifiers.
- **Test set**: estimate a priori the performance of the classifiers.

Thresholding Strategy: We evaluated different thresholding strategies that aim at minimizing false positives while avoiding false negatives. For a given alert a, our classifier outputs a score s resembling an estimation of the probability of that sample being a true positive, i.e., $s \sim P(a \in \text{class 1})$. In other words, the score is directly correlated to the certainty of the class 1 membership test by the classifier. Therefore, in order to avoid false negatives the threshold must be set below the minimum score obtained by a true alert in the validation set, which we call θ_{max}. It is convenient to set also a security margin, to further ensure avoiding false negatives. We use both a fixed and a statistical margin for this purpose. In the fixed threshold strategy, we simply subtract a small fixed margin m from θ_{max}, thus using a threshold $\theta_m = \theta_{max} - m$. The statistical margin strategy is a bit more involved. For a given margin $p\%$ in percentage, the threshold is set to a value $\theta_{p\%}$, such that an additional $p\%$ false positives are allowed with respect to θ_{max}. So, the margin is set to allow a fixed decrease in the utility of the classifier. Each of these thresholds, as illustrated in Fig. 2, give us a different a priori working point that we are evaluating.

Statistical Characterization: For each trained classifier we compute the following statistics in order to assess its individual consistency, reliability, and utility:

- A posteriori utility in the validation and test set. Since the utility is directly linked to the reduction of false positives, it is actually equivalent to the specificity, where:

$$\text{specificity} = \frac{\#\text{true negatives}}{\#\text{true negatives} + \#\text{false positives}}.$$

- A priori validation of the security constraint, i.e., $\#\text{false negatives} = 0$ in the test set.
- The a priori eligibility of the classifier, in terms of the specificity in the validation set.

We characterize each ML configuration by analyzing these statistics along the 10 different trained systems, as follows:

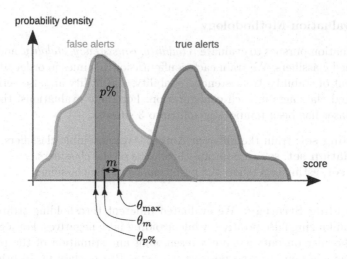

Fig. 2. Validation set score distributions and thresholds.

- **Unreliable**: One or more ML models with this configuration produces false negatives in the test set. This is the worst scenario, since eventually, an ML model trained with this configuration will provoke a security issue.
- **Inconsistent**: These ML models do not produce any false negatives in the test set, but the specificity in the test set is not always high, showing a lack of generality.
- **Not Eligible**: These ML models do not produce any false negatives in the test set, but do not obtain a high enough specificity in the validation set, which would support their deployment.
- **Consistent High Utility**: These ML models produce a high specificity in the validation set and also produce a high specificity in the test set (comparable to the specificity of the validation set), and without any false negatives.

The methodology explained above contains several design choices. For this particular case study, we decided to use the $\theta_{5\%}$ threshold for setting the classifiers' working point as a sensible safety margin, since it provides a safer threshold, while keeping the expected extra workload at only 5%, which is acceptable. Regarding the inconsistency assessment, we decided that, given the specificity of the validation set, an absolute worsening of 8% or more in the test set can safely be considered as a symptom of inconsistency. However, as we will show in Sect. 4, the consistency test fails very rarely, so the impact of this in the evaluation would be marginal. In the case of eligibility, the 20% minimum specificity in the validation set is just a sensible minimum expected utility for the classifier. Even though it may be seen as a low utility, it would have a positive impact on the SOC analysts' workload.

Regarding the reliability assessment, we are aware that it is very strict. Some ML configurations may provide excellent utility, eligibility, and consistency in most cases. However, if a single instance of this configuration produces a single

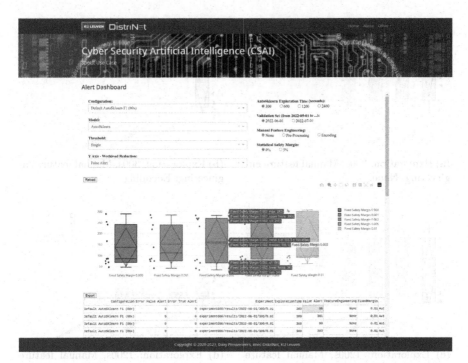

Fig. 3. Interactive visualization dashboard to compare results of different ML pipeline configurations.

false negative, then this represents statistical evidence that the configuration can provoke a security issue. As such, the safest decision is to label the configuration as unreliable. We must acknowledge that even when none of the 10 trained instances of a given configuration produces a false negative, it does not categorically guarantee reliability if the configuration would have 100 instances rather than 10. However, we at least did not find any evidence of a lack of reliability in any of the 10 instances, so we can consider the configuration as reliable (it could anyway end up being not eligible, or inconsistent).

3.5 AutoSklearn ML Pipeline Configurations and Interactive Dashboard

In order to ease a visual exploration of the performed experiments, an interactive visualization dashboard was developed (see Fig. 3) allowing to explore and easily export the experimental results by selecting the following features:

- **Configuration:** To explore different configurations of the classifier, as the optimization objective, or custom data splitting during training, etc. The optimization objectives include all standard metrics, and a custom metric designed specifically to avoid false negatives while minimizing false positives.

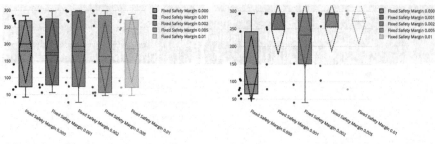

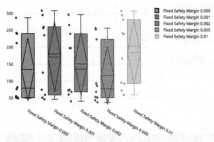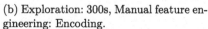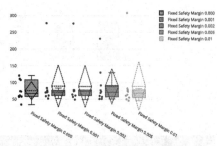

(a) Exploration: 300s, Manual feature engineering: None.

(b) Exploration: 300s, Manual feature engineering: Encoding.

(c) Exploration: 1200s, Manual feature engineering: None.

(d) Exploration: 1200s, Manual feature engineering: Encoding.

Fig. 4. Variation on the test set across 10 runs with ROC-AUC optimization objective and 0% statistical safety margin with different AutoSklearn exploration times, with and without manual feature engineering. The Y-axis counts the number of **remaining false alerts** in each run that remain to be analyzed by the SOC analyst (lower value is better).

- **AutoSklearn Exploration Time**: The amount of time (in seconds) granted to AutoSklearn to construct the best ensemble. More time may result in better ensembles due to more base ML models.
- **Model**: Comparison of AutoSklearn classifier with traditional ensemble models (e.g., RandomForest or XGBoost) with default parameters.
- **Validation Set**: Impact of a different temporal split between the end of the training dataset and the beginning of the validation dataset.
- **Manual Feature Engineering**: Added value of the (time-consuming) manual feature engineering before training the ML model.
- **Fixed Margin**: Determines the fixed margin m used during the evaluation, which can be set to $0, 0.001, 0.002, 0.005$ and 0.01.
- **Statistical Margin**: Determines the statistical margin used during the evaluation, which can be set to 0% or 5%.

This tool makes the comparison of the impact of different configurations somewhat less complicated, by showing various statistical properties of the ML

Table 1. Performance summary of relevant ML configurations, using all feature engineering and exploration times. C, I, N, and U stand for Consistently high utility, Inconsistent utility, Not eligible, and Unreliable security respectively. Each entry is the result of the analysis in Sect. 3.4 in 10 independent experiments using the same configuration.

ML configuration	None ET = 300	600	1200	Pre-processing ET = 300	600	1200	Encoding ET = 300	600	1200
Accuracy	C	U	U	N	N	U	U	C	C
Balanced Accuracy	N	N	N	U	N	U	N	N	N
F1	I	C	N	U	N	U	C	U	U
Precision	U	U	U	U	U	N	N	U	U
Recall	N	N	N	N	N	N	N	N	N
ROC-AUC	U	U	U	N	C	U	U	C	C
Weighted F1	U	U	U	N	N	C	N	U	U
Weighted Precision	U	C	C	C	C	C	U	N	N
Weighted Recall	U	U	U	N	N	C	C	C	U
Custom Metric $m = 0.000$	N	N	N	N	N	U	C	N	N
Custom Metric $m = 0.001$	N	I	N	U	U	N	C	N	N
Custom Metric $m = 0.002$	N	C	C	N	N	N	C	C	C
Custom Metric $m = 0.005$	C	C	N	N	N	U	N	N	N
Custom Metric $m = 0.010$	N	N	N	N	N	N	N	N	N
Random Forest $m = 0.000$	C	C	C	U	U	U	N	N	N

model and its predictions. Most importantly, from this dashboard it is also possible to directly export all the relevant statistics for the evaluation performed in this paper.

4 Evaluation and Discussion

In this section, we will elaborate in more detail on the insights we gathered with the use of AutoSklearn. In fact, we trained more than 8,700 AutoSklearn ensemble models, and these ensembles were composed of a total of about 1,200,000 individually trained base ML models. However, the goal of our evaluation is not to report which classifier achieved the best performance numbers, as these numbers are heavily dependent on (1) the underlying security technology and the logging data it produces (i.e., only XDR data), (2) the infrastructure being monitored for attacks, (3) the period of data collection, (4) the size of the training, validation, and test set.

Indeed, making any claims about generalization towards other experimental settings is almost impossible. Instead, in the following subsections, we will elicit various lessons learned from the many experiments we carried out, in the hope that these are much more useful for the community. The results of our experiments have been summarized in Table 1, where each configuration produces one of the behaviors described in Sect. 3.4. The table shows the analysis of only

$15 \times 9 = 135$ configurations. Our study covered 1710 configurations with different configuration parameter combinations. Additionally, we have tested the impact of the pre-processing step by repeating the experiments without it. Depending on AutoSklearn's choice to enable its automated data and feature pre-processing, the categorical fields may or may not be encoded and numerical fields may or may not be normalized. When using the data as is, one-hot encoding significantly increases the dimensionality of the data, with the ML model failing to generalize. Our additional experiments have demonstrated that under these conditions AutoSklearn failed to produce even one ML configuration that achieves consistent high utility.

4.1 Impact of Manual Feature Engineering

Manual feature engineering is a time-consuming task that requires expertise and domain knowledge about the protected infrastructure. It is not always clear upfront whether this effort will pay off, or whether the automated data and feature pre-processing of AutoSklearn can obtain equally good results. Our analysis in Table 1 compares the impact in the columns **None, Pre-processing**, and **Encoding** for different metrics and exploration times. While equally good performance results in the test set exist for each of the combinations, they are not consistent. As exceptions, Weighted Precision seemingly produces remarkably good performance for the **Pre-processing** strategy, and the custom metric with $m = 0.002$ does the same for the **Encoding** strategy, but in all other cases, the metrics can perform well for some exploration times, and not consistently for others. From this comparison, we can conclude that feature representation has a big impact on performance. However, this observation is connected with the optimization metric, hereby recommending to try out experiments using different optimization metrics and feature representations aligned with the use case at hand. To further illustrate this, Fig. 4 compares different AutoSklearn exploration times while optimizing for the ROC-AUC metric. The impact of manual feature engineering is limited to 300 s of exploration time (see Figures (a) and (b)). However, for 1200 s, Figure (d) appears to demonstrate some benefits. For a larger safety margin, there are fewer false alerts with less variation across the 10 runs, yet with no guarantees regarding the presence of false negatives. Also, optimizing for the F1 error metric) results in a less outspoken impact of manual feature engineering.

4.2 Stochastic Nature of Repeated Experiments

Table 1 shows a large variability in the presence of false negatives (*true alerts* classified as *false alerts*) in the test set, even after applying a conservative thresholding approach ($\theta_{5\%}$). This can be observed for all exploration times and feature processing strategies (with some rare exceptions, such as 'Weighted Precision' with 'Pre-processing' feature engineering, and the custom error metric discussed later using $\theta_{0.002}$ thresholding and 'Encoding' as feature engineering).

Although our methodology is devoted to evaluating the consistency of the a priori performance of the different trained classifiers, we must consider the fact that the distribution of future data may significantly differ from those of the validation and test datasets, so it is not possible to guarantee consistent performance in the future. This is especially relevant given the big number of configurations labeled as Unreliable in Table 1. For many of the configurations with such a label, only one or two of the trained classifiers produced false negatives, which highlights how difficult it may be to ensure consistency.

For an imbalanced dataset, the ROC-AUC and F1 metrics are sensible optimization metrics for AutoSklearn. Nonetheless, we also explored other optimization metrics − including F1, Accuracy, Precision and Recall next to ROC-AUC − and we observed the same variation in false alert reduction across multiple runs, and keeping AutoSklearn exploring ML models for much longer does not necessarily help to achieve more consistent results.

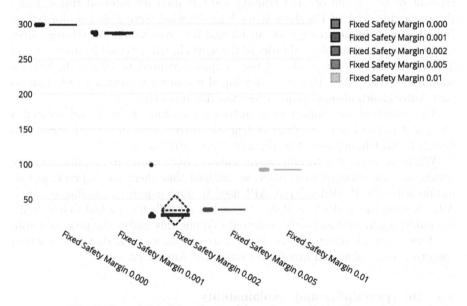

Fig. 5. Remaining false alerts with custom optimization metric.

The results in Fig. 5 show that AutoSklearn now produces a consistently high utility within the same configuration, i.e., there is hardly any variation across the 10 repeated experiments. Note that this does not guarantee that there are no false negatives in the test set! However, in many cases, this metric achieves not only the goal of reducing the number of false alerts, but also avoiding false negatives, as it may be observed in Table 1.

4.3   Out-of-Distribution Samples and Temporal Constraints on Validation and Test Datasets

In the security landscape, new threats and attacks emerge on a daily basis, and ML models may perform poorly on data samples it was not trained upon. To account for out-of-distribution samples, the alerts in the training, validation, and test datasets should not be randomly sampled from the master dataset, but preserve their chronological order. For example, the alerts in the validation set should occur after all those in the training set, and the ones in the test set should have a timestamp later than those in the validation set. This is rather straightforward and a common best practice for ML in security applications.

However, when AutoSklearn exploits the training data to construct the best possible ensemble model, it starts by splitting up the original training data into two internal subsets where the chronological order of the alerts across these two subsets is not guaranteed. By default, it uses a holdout strategy where a 67% random subset of the original training data is used for internal training and the remaining 33% of the data is used for internal testing and optimization. Indeed, this holdout strategy or an alternative cross-validation strategy does not preserve the chronological order of the alerts in this internal training set and internal test set (i.e., some internal test samples may predate some of the internal training samples). We, therefore, developed a custom resampling technique so that AutoSklearn also internally preserves this property.

We compared the impact of a custom resampling strategy and noticed a consistent improvement in terms of true alerts that went unnoticed, while also having a slight improvement in the false alert reduction.

While we were able to implement and test our custom resampling strategy within the AutoSklearn framework, we noticed that there was a practical limitation with the PredefinedSplit API used in our custom resampling strategy. After loading the model from disk serialized as a Pickle file, we had to first 'refit' the model again against the training data. While this makes the proposed approach rather time-consuming and hence impractical, we hope that this practical concern can be alleviated in a future version of AutoSklearn.

4.4   Interpretability and Explainability

The ML models that AutoSklearn constructs, can become fairly complex. By default these are ensemble models that combine up to 50 base ML models, and each of these base models can be any classifier that scikit-learn supports (e.g., a Decision Tree, Random Forest, Support Vector Machine, k-Nearest Neighbors, Multi-Layer Perceptron). Unfortunately, such ensemble models are hard to interpret by a human SOC analyst [6].

To address this concern, we modified the AutoSklearn classifier configuration to only produce ensembles with a single base ML model, and constrain that base model to be a Random Forest classifier. The results depicted in Fig. 6 were obtained after 300 s of exploration time and without any manual feature engineering. This particular model performed the best (i.e., false alerts reduced from

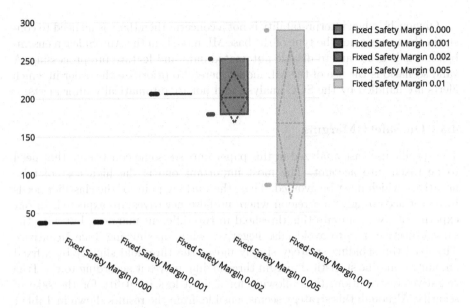

Fig. 6. Enforcing a single RandomForest base model in the ensemble.

308 down to 19, and this without any missed true alerts), even without a fixed safety margin. The results for this classifier are shown in the last row of Table 1 for $\theta_{5\%}$. This particular setup performs consistently well for all exploration times (although a priori performance in test set is best for $ET = 300$).

However, by default, AutoSklearn also applies many data and feature pre-processing to assess whether these have a positive influence on optimizing the error metric. Some data pre-processing techniques include (a) dealing with imbalanced datasets, (b) imputing missing values, (c) one-hot encoding of categorical values, (d) rescaling for faster convergence, (e) variance thresholding to reduce dimensionality, etc. Other feature pre-processing that AutoSklearn attempts, include (a) Principle Component Analysis and related dimensionality reduction techniques, (b) univariate or (c) classification-based feature selection, (d) feature clustering, and many more. The automated pre-processing and transformation of the raw training data as the many dimensionality reduction methods make it hard to truly understand the context under which certain samples are correctly classified as a true alert (class 1) or a false alert (class 0), as the transformed input for a Random Forest classifier may no longer be semantically meaningful.

The advantage of Decision Tree-based models is that these are much easier to convert into rule- or signature-based schemes as implemented by the security technology used to detect the threats and raise alerts. An alternative model agnostic approach to explain the output of a model is via an eXplainable AI (XAI) techniques, such as its SHAP (SHapley Additive exPlanations) values [11] or LIME [14].

Obviously, when interpretability is not a concern, then there is no need to constrain the amount nor the type of the base ML models in the AutoSklearn ensemble, nor is it necessary to disable automated data and feature pre-processing. A valid scenario is the use of the ML model merely to prioritize the order in which alerts are handled by the SOC analyst, and not to automatically filter alerts.

4.5 On Safety Margins

The specific use case analyzed in this paper imposes some constraints that need to be taken into account. The most important one is the high cost of false negatives, which must be avoided. Thus, the working point of the classifier needs to be set accordingly to a region where no false negatives are expected. In our experiments, we compute this threshold in two different manners, but with the same objective, i.e., to avoid false negatives while maximizing True Negatives. The fixed thresholding strategy simply moves the threshold slightly by a fixed amount, while the statistical margin thresholding moves it according to the True Negatives distribution, thus allowing for a fixed loss in utility for the sake of security. Although this strategy seems sensible, from the results shown in Table 1 it is clear that the absence of false negatives in the test set cannot be guaranteed. However, from our analysis with the two different strategies and parameters, it is clear that the use of these safety margins does provide additional assurance in that regard.

4.6 Discussion

Among all tested configurations, we found the best consistent utility for a single Random Forest with 300 s exploration time, only AutoSklearn automatic feature processing, and using our custom metric. However, other configurations achieve similar utility and consistency, such as ensembles using Weighted Precision with manual feature pre-processing or our custom metric with $m = 0.002$.

Obviously, the impact of (manual) data and feature pre-processing is very specific to this use case. We observed that by applying one-hot encoding on various columns in our dataset the dimensionality simply exploded by almost two orders of magnitude. In principle, this is not a problem as long as one has sufficient data. Otherwise, there is a risk that a model easily overfits, which was the case in our scenario.

Also, the adopted a priori evaluation methodology aids to observe consistency of each classifier configuration. The observed variability in behavior and performance of the various classifiers raises concerns, but also warns developers about the lack of generalization capability of many of the trained classifiers, which would remain undiscovered otherwise. From our evaluation, we can conclude that even for classifiers with a consistent high utility we could benefit from a further assessment

1. by using larger datasets (to increase the representation of True Alerts)
2. originating from diverse sources (as our datasets come from the same source)
3. and that span a wider temporal frame (to further assess concept drift issues)

in order to achieve the necessary confidence on the performance over future data collected after deployment.

As future work, we will additionally explore the adversarial robustness of the aforementioned ensemble models. While the literature is rife with studies on how to create adversarial examples and how to defend models with adversarial training, our case study is significantly more complex as our models are trained on the logs of security monitoring tools, and not on the raw data (e.g., network traffic) directly. The fact that model explanations can be manipulated too [15] further complicates this challenge.

5   Conclusion

We investigated the benefits and drawbacks of automated machine learning (AutoML) to address alert fatigue in a security operation centers (SOC) environment. The goal was to increase the efficiency of a SOC by automatically filtering the false alerts produced by various security monitoring and threat detection technologies. We evaluated the use of AutoSklearn against a real-world case study and found that the framework has its benefits, but one must be aware of possible pitfalls.

We proposed a methodology designed to cope with a difficult dataset, with scarce true positives, large dimensionality in comparison to its size, and temporal variability. Using this methodology, we offer critical reflections on the use of such automation frameworks in this security context. In this exploration, we found different configurations that offer equivalent and consistent good utility in terms of false alerts reduction, while not producing false negatives.

Further work will investigate the benefits of model explainability methods that may be more tailored to the needs of a SOC analyst, who require understanding the reasons behind the classifiers' outputs.

Acknowledgment. This research is partially funded by the Research Fund KU Leuven, by the Flemish Research Programme Cybersecurity, and by VLAIO through the CS ICON project "Cyber Security Artificial Intelligence" (CSAI). We would like to thank Spotit, a member of the CSAI project consortium, for permission to use their dataset.

Appendix: AutoSklearn implementation

```
1  # Min-max data normalization and ordinal encoding of categories (if needed)
2  preprocessor = make_preprocessor(X_train)
3
4  # Enforce temporal splits
5  selected_indices = ((X_train['timestamp'] > split_time)
6     & (X_train['timestamp'] < train_time)).astype(int)
7  custom_resampling_strategy = PredefinedSplit(test_fold=selected_indices)
8
9  # Configure the AutoML classifier
10 automl_model = AutoSklearnClassifier(
11    time_left_for_this_task=1200,      # Exploration time (in seconds)
12    per_run_time_limit=240,            # Exploration time / 5
13    memory_limit=65536,                # 64 GB
14    tmp_folder="tmp",
15    metric=f1,                         # accuracy, roc_auc, recall, ...
16    scoring_functions=[accuracy, f1, precision, recall],
17    n_jobs=8,
18    ensemble_size=1,
19    include={"classifier": ["random_forest"],
20       "data_preprocessor": ["NoPreprocessing"],
21       "feature_preprocessor": ["no_preprocessing"]
22    },
23    resampling_strategy=custom_resampling_strategy) # enforce temporal splits
24
25 model = make_pipeline(preprocessor, automl_model)
26 # Fit the model on training set
27 model.fit(X_train, Y_train)
28
29 # Evaluate on test set
30 Y_pred = model.predict(X_test)
31
32 print("Accuracy:  ", accuracy_score(Y_test, Y_pred))
33 print("F1 score:  ", f1_score(Y_test, Y_pred, average='weighted'))
34 print("Precision: ", precision_score(Y_test, Y_pred, average='weighted'))
35 print("Recall:    ", recall_score(Y_test, Y_pred, average='weighted'))
```

Fig. 7. Code snippet of AutoSklearn ML pipeline, configuring a single Random Forest classifier in the ensemble without any data and feature pre-processing by AutoSklearn.

References

1. Ahmed, T., Shah, A., Kolla, M., Yellasiri, R.: Reduction of alert fatigue using extended isolation forest. In: 2021 International Conference on Forensics, Analytics, Big Data, Security (FABS), vol. 1, pp. 1–5 (2021). https://doi.org/10.1109/FABS52071.2021.9702617
2. Aminanto, M.E., Ban, T., Isawa, R., Takahashi, T., Inoue, D.: Threat alert prioritization using isolation forest and stacked auto encoder with day-forward-chaining analysis. IEEE Access **8**, 217977–217986 (2020). https://doi.org/10.1109/ACCESS.2020.3041837
3. Aminanto, M.E., Zhu, L., Ban, T., Isawa, R., Takahashi, T., Inoue, D.: Combating threat-alert fatigue with online anomaly detection using isolation forest. In: Gedeon, T., Wong, K.W., Lee, M. (eds.) Neural Information Processing, pp. 756–765. Springer International Publishing, Cham (2019). https://doi.org/10.1007/978-3-030-36708-4_62

4. Ban, T., Samuel, N., Takahashi, T., Inoue, D.: Combat security alert fatigue with AI-assisted techniques. In: Cyber Security Experimentation and Test Workshop, pp. 9–16 (2021)
5. Bertino, E., Kantarcioglu, M., Akcora, C.G., Samtani, S., Mittal, S., Gupta, M.: AI for security and security for AI. In: Proceedings of the Eleventh ACM Conference on Data and Application Security and Privacy, pp. 333–334 (2021)
6. Došilović, F.K., Brčić, M., Hlupić, N.: Explainable artificial intelligence: a survey. In: 2018 41st International Convention on Information and Communication Technology, Electronics and Microelectronics (MIPRO), pp. 0210–0215. IEEE (2018)
7. Feurer, M., Klein, A., Eggensperger, K., Springenberg, J., Blum, M., Hutter, F.: Efficient and robust automated machine learning. In: Advances in Neural Information Processing Systems, vol. 28, no. (2015), pp. 2962–2970 (2015)
8. Hassan, W.U., et al.: Nodoze: combatting threat alert fatigue with automated provenance triage. In: 26th Annual Network and Distributed System Security Symposium, NDSS 2019, San Diego, California, USA, February 24–27, 2019. The Internet Society (2019)
9. He, X., Zhao, K., Chu, X.: AutoML: a survey of the state-of-the-art. Knowl.-Based Syst. **212**, 106622 (2021)
10. Lu, J., Liu, A., Dong, F., Gu, F., Gama, J., Zhang, G.: Learning under concept drift: a review. IEEE Trans. Knowl. Data Eng. **31**(12), 2346–2363 (2018)
11. Lundberg, S.M., Lee, S.I.: A unified approach to interpreting model predictions. In: Advances in Neural Information Processing Systems, vol. 30 (2017)
12. Ndichu, S., Ban, T., Takahashi, T., Inoue, D.: A machine learning approach to detection of critical alerts from imbalanced multi-appliance threat alert logs. In: 2021 IEEE International Conference on Big Data (Big Data), pp. 2119–2127 (2021). https://doi.org/10.1109/BigData52589.2021.9671956
13. Pang, R., Xi, Z., Ji, S., Luo, X., Wang, T.: On the security risks of AutoML. In: 31st USENIX Security Symposium (USENIX Security 22), pp. 3953–3970. USENIX Association, Boston, MA (2022)
14. Ribeiro, M.T., Singh, S., Guestrin, C.: "why should i trust you?" explaining the predictions of any classifier. In: Proceedings of the 22nd ACM SIGKDD International Conference on Knowledge Discovery and Data Mining, pp. 1135–1144 (2016)
15. Slack, D., Hilgard, A., Lakkaraju, H., Singh, S.: Counterfactual explanations can be manipulated. Adv. Neural. Inf. Process. Syst. **34**, 62–75 (2021)

CO-DECYBER: Co-operative Decision Making for Cybersecurity Using Deep Multi-agent Reinforcement Learning

Madeline Cheah[✉], Jack Stone, Peter Haubrick, Samuel Bailey, David Rimmer, Demian Till, Matt Lacey, Jo Kruczynska, and Mark Dorn

Cambridge Consultants, 29 Cambridge Science Park, Milton Road, Cambridge CB4 0DW, UK
madeline.cheah@cambridgeconsultants.com

Abstract. Autonomous decision making for cyber-defence in operational situations is desirable but challenging. This is due to the nature of operational technology (because of its cyber-physical nature) as well as the need to account for multiple contexts. Our contribution is the creation of a co-operative decision-making framework to enable autonomous cyber-defence (which we call Co-Decyber). This framework allows us to break up a big multi-contextual action space into smaller decisions that multiple agents can optimize between. We apply this framework to an autonomous vehicle platooning scenario. Results show that Co-Decyber agents are outperforming random reference agents in the cyber-attack scenarios we have tested. We aim to extend this work with more complex attack scenarios, along with training more agents to defend more of the attack surface. We conclude that this framework when mature will contribute to the goal of providing autonomous cyber-defence for operational technology.

Keywords: autonomous · cyber-defence · cybersecurity · automotive · artificial intelligence · multi-agent · reinforcement learning

1 Introduction

Autonomous decision making when defending military systems against a cyberattack is highly desirable. It offers the potential to reduce the response time to attack and ensure freedom of military action. However, this is challenging in operational environments due to systems being heterogeneous, opaque and involving legacy equipment.

Furthermore, any automated solution to cyber-defence must be generalizable to new settings and components, scalable and explainable and avoid reduction in military operational effectiveness. In short, cyber-defence requires multi-contextual and communicable general decision making.

A prominent method of achieving the contextual decision-making needed is through use of reinforcement learning (RL) [1], where context can be considered, and decisions could be optimized appropriately. However, a single large RL model that is capable of generalised decision-making, in operational situations with consideration for multiple

© The Author(s), under exclusive license to Springer Nature Switzerland AG 2024
S. Katsikas et al. (Eds.): ESORICS 2023 Workshops, LNCS 14399, pp. 628–643, 2024.
https://doi.org/10.1007/978-3-031-54129-2_37

modalities of impact (both in cyber-space and physically), may be fragile, computationally intractable and difficult to retrain. Furthermore, such models would need to be deployed at the edge, which means the trained model would need to work with distributed embedded systems that have limited computational power.

Our contribution to meeting this problem is the development of a co-operative decision-making framework (which we call Co-Decyber) to address the challenges above, using co-operative multi-agent reinforcement learning (CoMARL). We apply this framework to operational technology, namely vehicles in an automated platooning scenario as proof-of-concept. To the best of the authors' knowledge, this is the first such framework to be applied to autonomous cyber-defence of vehicles.

Within this paper we briefly explore related work in Sect. 2. We then describe the general concept as well as the high-level Co-Decyber architecture and framework in the context of our chosen operational technology and scenario in Sect. 3. We outline our training methodology in Sect. 4, along with our preliminary results in Sect. 5. Finally, we discuss future work in Sect. 6.

2 Related Work

The growing sophistication of threats as well as the acceleration in the pace of technological change has led to a substantial ever-changing threat landscape. This is driving research into automation and autonomy of different cyber-defences in both offensive and defensive security, including in intrusion detection, red-teaming, incident response and security planning [1].

Automated or autonomous cyber-defence can be defined as a decision-making system with expert level capability, beginning with detection of an ongoing attack and ending with being able to recover, prove or correct the vulnerability in real-time without human intervention. An exploration of definitions of autonomous cyber-defence and its components may be found in [2].

Comparative approaches to automating cyber-defence fall broadly into two camps. The first set are rule-based. The most mature are commercial Security Orchestration, Automation and Response (SOAR) offerings whose automation is typically rule or playbook driven [3]. Although relatively established, the disadvantage lies in their focus towards enterprise defence, and are typically centralized. They are also not suitable for operational technology as they require reasonable compute or linked to a security incident and event management (SIEM) system. Work also exists academically, especially in addressing the challenges in being mission or context aware, for example using attack-defence trees combined with a game theoretic approach to calculate responses [4], which has been made possible due to earlier work expressing explicitly the equivalence between game theory and attack-defence trees [5]. Another study uses security graph models as a basis for precomputation of attack paths to deal with complexity of response [6]. These methods have the advantage of having high rigor, along with benefitting from a wealth of mathematical and algorithmical tools for cyber-attack and defence expression. However, limitations arise due to high knowledge barriers required for modelling system and interactions, the rigidity of what has been expressed, as well as the increased abstraction from real-world implementations.

Much of the research attention has been focused on the alternative form of autonomous defence which involves machine learning. Of these methods, reinforcement learning has proved popular, with a wide range of proposed approaches to protect everything from enterprise to critical infrastructure against sophisticated cyber-attacks. Attacks (and associated countermeasures) explored include defences to data injection, jamming, spoofing, malware, detection of deception and so forth. A comprehensive survey of reinforcement learning in autonomous defence may be found at [7].

Multi-agent approaches are more recent. Agents within multi-agent reinforcement learning (MARL) implementations can be competitive, cooperative or both. There are two schools of research in this cyber-defence: the first is in training the MARL agents based on game theory in adversarial settings such as in approaches by [9] and [10], which typically involves training against adversarial agents The second is through optimization of defences in an exploration vs exploitation setting using bandit feedback settings (i.e. with no information on rewards for decisions that were not performed). The challenges are similar with both schools: the right optimization method depends on attack or defensive actions being defined, defining policies for specific tasks requires domain expert input, there are sparse reward challenges, and the environment is non-stationery. Furthermore, many of the proposed approaches described are theoretical in nature and are rarely transferred to a real-world implementation.

Our approach is based on co-operative MARL or CoMARL, where agents attached to each piece of functionality work together to protect the whole system (see Sect. 3.3). Co-Decyber has also been designed from the ground up to be practical in the real world. This includes requirements in terms of coping with:

- partial coverage: agents may not be deployable on all system elements due to constrained nature of embedded controllers.
- changes in available system functions (in our case the generic vehicle architecture or GVA modules - see Sect. 3.2) which requires modularity. Additionally, parts of the system may be added or removed over time. Furthermore, some elements may be unavailable due to compromise or quarantining.
- realistic intrusion detection: we cannot assume perfect attack detection.

These design principles ensure that Co-Decyber is transferable to a real implementation, which we have planned as part of our future work (see Sect. 6).

3   Co-Decyber

In this section we describe first the concepts behind decision making in autonomous cyber-defence in Sect. 3.1. We discuss our operational scenario in Sect. 3.2. We follow this by detailing the generic framework and architecture of Co-Decyber in the context of our scenario in Sect. 3.3.

3.1   Attack and Defence Modelling

The high-level scenario we have chosen to defend is two platooning vehicles moving from a rear base to a forward operating base (see Sect. 3.2). We use attack-defence tree methodology [11] (see Fig. 1) to map out possible attacks and defences.

Each of the defences seen in Fig. 1 can be considered an *action* that Co-Decyber could take. The set of defences seen above can therefore be considered Co-Decyber's action space (although in our work to date, we have not implemented a complete coverage of defensive action space within the vehicle domain, due to the need to constrain this space for training purposes).

We do not perform computation on the tree. The attack-defence tree paradigm was the chosen modelling method due to intuitive communication with multiple stakeholders, as well as the ability to bound our problem and action spaces. Furthermore, defences mapped in this way translate conceptually to how we break down the decision making and give rise to the multi-agent architecture.

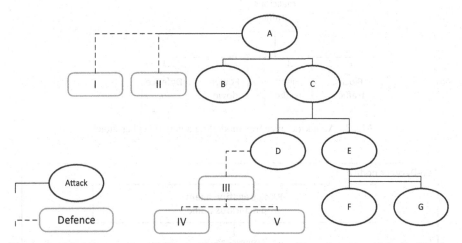

Fig. 1. Attack-defence tree modelling, which allows for mapping and scoping of the Co-Decyber action space. Either defence I or defence II can be considered defences to attack A. Fulfilment of defence IV or V can be considered to fulfil the requirements of defence III, which is a defence to attack D (a sub-attack of attack C). Double line notation between F and G is considered an AND gate. All others are OR gates.

Take an example attack with attendant defences (as given in Fig. 2). The overarching defence would be to stop the malicious traffic, with many actions available (block, filter, etc.) to choose from. To enable Co-Decyber's decision-making, we assign each defensive action to individual, but interconnected RL agents (see Fig. 3).

These agents, which are aggregated into a Co-Decyber *node*, negotiate amongst themselves to determine what the best course of action should be. The nodes are coupled with the functionality to be defended, to ensure the defending actions are appropriate to that functionality (see Sect. 3.3). Some nodes are simple (with only a single RL agent) and some nodes are complex (with multiple RL agents).

Atomic actions are the responsibility of lower-level agents (e.g. deciding to block, filter, etc.). To co-ordinate these actions, an aggregation agent is also present in the node. This aggregation agent is responsible for deciding between these actions, based on bottom-up input from the lower-level agents. Note that since we are looking to protect our system during an operational scenario, design-time defences (such as implementing an authentication mechanism) is presumed to be out-of-scope of our autonomous defence.

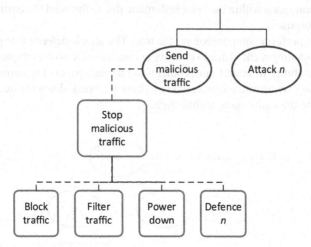

Fig. 2. Attack-defence tree modelling a generic cyber-attack.

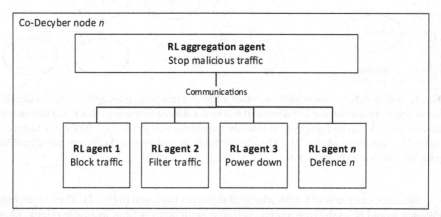

Fig. 3. A Co-Decyber node with actions assigned to individual but interconnected RL agents. Note the defences of the RL agents are consistent with those specified in the attack-defence tree for this scenario.

There are multiple nodes in our system (see Sect. 3.2); currently these nodes act independently. Future work will involve enabling communication between Co-Decyber nodes (see Sect. 6).

3.2 Autonomous Platooning Vehicles

Co-Decyber has been implemented and tested in the context of a simulated leader-follower scenario (see Fig. 4), in which two semi-automated military vehicles are aiming to move cargo from a rear-operating base to a forward base. We choose this scenario due to richness of cyber-attack and defending space, its relevance to generation-after-next technologies as well as relevance to defence. High level attacks and defences are modelled using attack-defence tree methodology to scope the attack and corresponding defence action space (see Sect. 3.1).

We built a training simulation to represent a NATO Generic Vehicle Architecture (NGVA) compliant vehicle system to be defended. We use simulation rather than real world trials due to its ability to generate the large numbers of training datasets that we need in a timely manner. The simulator is split into two halves: the environment and the agent inference components. Both are flexible to allow exploration of different environments and agent configurations. These are joined together via an OpenAI [14] gym interface, with extensions for multi-agent support using PettingZoo [15].

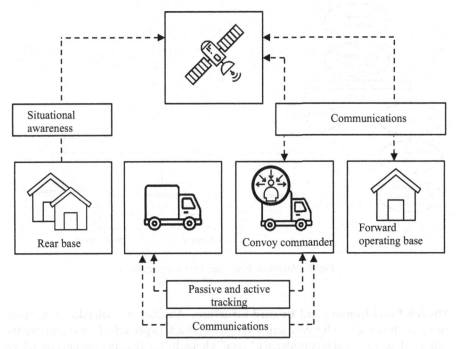

Fig. 4. Autonomous vehicle platooning scenario

NGVA comprises a framework of pluggable modules for reconfigurability, interconnected by a Data Distribution Service (DDS) backbone.

NGVA modules can be anything from navigation systems to vehicle controls. We use NGVA for two purposes: firstly, to inform our modelling of attacks and defences for DDS and NGVA modules using the attack-defence tree methodology, and secondly, to inform Co-Decyber architecture.

The attack that we modelled involves hijacking a module on the DDS network. The vector is assumed to be a malicious insider located in the rear base connecting a rogue module to the vehicle architecture (since the DDS specifications does not by default include authentication of GVA modules) to publish a false fire alarm. This false fire alarm originating from the malicious module will propagate through the DDS network to give false information to a human crew. We have assumed that human operators within the vehicle will stop the vehicle to check thereby leading to convoy delays. The implications of this are discussed further below.

To enable defensive actions by Co-Decyber, we assume that the optional DDS Security Specification [8] is implemented to a degree, but with loose global policies that allowed for the attack involving unauthenticated addition to the network. The attack-defence scenario for the false fire alarm can be seen in Fig. 5.

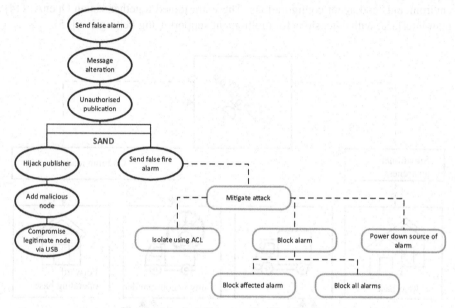

Fig. 5. Attack-defence tree for false fire alarm

Mission Level Impacts and Reward Structure. Attacker and defender in the modelling as shown above have system level goals (attack target vehicle and mitigate the attack). However, what is considered a "good" choice by Co-Decyber can only be judged based on what happens at the mission level.

Sending a false fire alarm affects our scenario at a system-level, but there is a higher level of adversarial intent. For the purposes of the scenario, we assume that this adversarial intent is to delay the convoy or stop the convoy from arriving.

This level of abstraction (in terms of mission level impact) is what proponent and opponent ultimately wishes to achieve in any given context. This is important to consider due to three factors:

• Firstly, the cascading impact from a defence through the system. Achieving only system-level defender goals could still result in mission failure (e.g. latency from excess security processing causing a denial of service instead)

- Secondly, with the potential number of RL agents in play, the distributed nature of the vehicular systems we are planning to defend, as well as the number of variables within even this defence scenario, a dense reward structure (i.e. a reward for each and every action in each timestep) is infeasible.
- Finally, since mission level goals are of the highest priority, they should form the foundation of the reward function for our MARL process. Different missions may require different training regimes. The more of the defender's mission is achieved, the better the choices that Co-Decyber is deemed to have made. Note that although mission-level goals are what dictate the rewards, they are influenced by system level goals (for example, the false fire alarm on a vehicle may cause a small delay whilst the crew visually confirm the alarm).

We note that mission level feedback could be too abstract to train the reinforcement learning. However, we mitigate this using offline training (see Sect. 4).

The reward structure for the work in this paper is specified in Table 1.

Table 1. Reward structure for Co-Decyber training

Reward	Timeliness	Cargo status
5	For every vehicle on time	With cargo
2	For every vehicle on time	Without cargo
4	For every vehicle arriving late	With cargo
2	For every vehicle arriving late	Without cargo
0	No arrival	-

From the above, the total reward is then calculated as a sum of whichever conditions are fulfilled for example:

- One vehicle that arrives with or without cargo would be given a reward of 2.
- Two vehicles that arrive, both with cargo, on time would be given 10.
- Two vehicles arriving delayed with one cargo intact would be given 6.

The numbers given as rewards here are arbitrary; as we improve the simulator in later work and begin movement towards a real-world implementation, we would seek to tune these to better reflect the specific real-world contexts that these vehicles (with Co-Decyber integrated) would operate in.

3.3 Generic Framework and Architecture

Due to the distributed nature of systems on these vehicles, we chose an architecture for Co-Decyber that mirrors this distribution, with one node coupled to (and defending) an NGVA module. For our training environment, this has resulted in the design and simulation of four NGVA modules integrated into a vehicle model, each with one Co-Decyber node and with each node containing *1...n* RL agents (see Fig. 6). The NGVA modules that we have implemented currently are listed in Table 2.

Each of these modules has one Co-Decyber node containing at least one Co-Decyber agent. For example, the GVA switch (see Fig. 7) has a Co-Decyber node containing four low-level agents and one aggregation agent. One of the low-level agents (the access control list or ACL agent) is protecting the GVA module itself. The other three low-level agents (along with the aggregation agent which makes decisions between these low-level agents) protect the system globally (see Fig. 7).

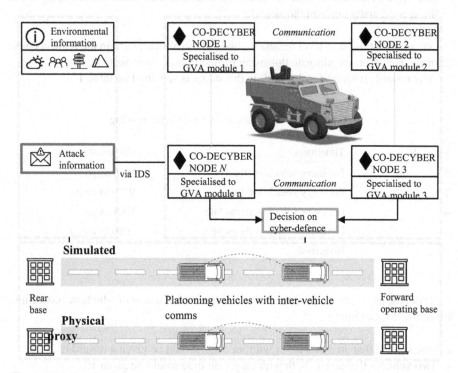

Fig. 6. The Co-operative Decision Making for Cybersecurity (Co-Decyber) framework is an autonomous cyber-defence system based on collaborative multi-agent reinforcement learning

Table 2. NGVA modules simulated

NGVA module	Description
MEDIA	Used for communication
HMI	Human-machine interface
ECU	Electronic control unit; in this case for engine management
SWITCH	Provides the network backbone to the architecture, which implements all the defensive actions that Co-Decyber can actuate

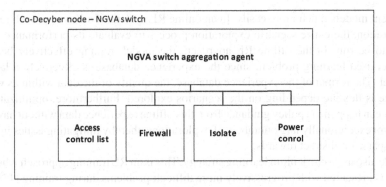

Fig. 7. The NGVA switch Co-Decyber node

4 Training Methodology

Co-Decyber is a complex AI system, integrated with a complex vehicle architecture. To succeed in training such a system, we need a robust training process. In this project we developed a custom methodology to deal with the challenges of generalization and scale. We describe our approach in Sect. 4.1 before discussing in the context of our Co-Decyber agents in Sect. 4.2.

4.1 Training Approach

One of the major challenges is ensuring that the agents are able to join the dots between performing Task A and performing Task B. Much of the work in the training process is to ensure that training data covers enough of the expected input space to avoid this issue. We use our vehicle simulator to generate these datasets (see Sect. 3.2 for details of the simulator).

For this project, we have chosen to use a hardcoded attacker in our environment (rather than a learning attacker agent) to trade-off against the complexity of training the MARL system, since balancing two systems learning against each other can create unwanted behaviors. For example, the red agent and Co-Decyber could become hyper-specialized at defeating each other rather than generalised cyber-systems. Furthermore, to mitigate potential overfitting to this hardcoded attacker, we have developed a series of variations within our false fire alarm attack scenario (e.g. where does the attack originate from? does it migrate? and so on). We have also developed different attack types for future work (see Sect. 6) to further increase this variability.

The sparsity of rewards and developing an RL framework at such a scale means that we have adopted several novel strategies regarding training methodology. This includes the use of offline RL where we first allow the agents to explore, with logs of explorations collected to an experience database as an experience "buffer" [13]. Agents are frozen during exploration.

Agent learning happens only during the training phase where these "experience" logs are curated to form a training regime for an improved variant of the agent. From a data science perspective, this decoupling of exploration and training allows for exploration of different models much more easily. In an online RL system, if a new approach requires exploration, the entire scenario exploration process to evaluate its performance would need to be run. In the offline RL approach, the model training effectively becomes a supervised learning problem since the experience database is effectively a labelled dataset. The format of the experience database, the quality of the data within as well as its size is flexible depending on the scenarios explored. Furthermore, optimization of policy can happen via policy guidance from this offline experience data without having to perform exceptionally large numbers of explorations, thereby mitigating issues inherent with sparse or abstract rewards.

We also use a curriculum learning strategy. This is an RL training approach where the agent is presented with progressively more difficult problems during training [12], with difficulty controls in a number of dimensions, including variance in scenarios and its parameters, the quality of the input data and capabilities of the leader-follower vehicles. We use this to mitigate the challenge of having a large environment and sparse rewards.

The multi-agent environment presents additional challenges as the actions of other agents can become fragile to changes in other agents; we use an agent matrix training process whereby variant sets of agents (and not always the best performing ones) are called upon during simulation runs so that the trained agents can cope with a wider variety of performance from other agents in the system. Our overall training flow can be seen in Fig. 8.

4.2   Co-Decyber Agents

The input to these agents is attack information from our simulated intrusion detection system (IDS). We hard-coded this IDS for each of our scenarios to reduce integration issues or the need to develop an intelligent intrusion detection agent. The IDS is integrated into the attack model, which means that it does not need to detect attacks but instead can be driven by the same state machine as the attacker. As such, to begin with, we have assumed an omniscient IDS. Since the IDS represents our input data, varying its quality will also be part of our curriculum learning strategy, and adds another dimension to the complexity of our training scenarios, thereby additionally mitigating any potential overfitting risk.

Co-Decyber designed to composable so that many different agents can be combined to form different types of Co-Decyber nodes (see Sect. 3.3).

The agents built for this project all use Deep Q-learning which replaces the table-driven version of the Q function with a neural network. This has several advantages, but the two most important points are that neural networks can:

- cope with a vast quantity of states and generalize between them
- approximate the current state $s \in S$ based on the available input

The DQN is trained to return $Q(a)$ based on the current observed inputs. This can then be evaluated as a $rgmax_a Q(a)$ in a similar fashion to standard Q-learning.

All low-level agents are fully connected networks, with input given from the IDS as described above. The agent has two types of output, the first is the policy function and the second is a situation assessment.

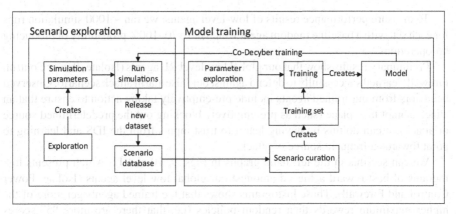

Fig. 8. Overall Co-Decyber training flow

The policy function has a set of outputs $Q_s(a)\forall a \in A$, where the Q function describes the discounted expected future rewards from taking action a in state s. By choosing $max_a Q_s(a)$ the expected reward is maximised. Note the agent does not calculate the state explicitly, instead this is implicit in the policy function it returns. The situation assessment output attempts to predict the total reward the agent will receive at the end of the scenario. By adding this output, the agent is expected to learn a long-term assessment of the situation.

The aggregation agent decides between the low-level agents in a bottom-up approach. In other words, the low-level agents essentially act as feature extractors for the aggregation agent. Furthermore, the output from the low-level agent is action based (e.g. a proposal of one or more actions). This provides more fine-grained context for the aggregation agent.

5 Results

Simulations were based on the false fire alarm attack as described in Fig. 5. If the alarm is real, and not dealt with, the engine breaks leading to no rewards. If the alarm is an attack (i.e. false), the crew will stop to investigate leading to delays and therefore less than the full reward. If Co-Decyber manages to stop the attack in time, there should be no delay, leading to the maximum reward of 5 per vehicle.

Without any agents implemented at all, within the context of our false fire alarm attack, the rewards gained will only ever be at a maximum of 4 for a single vehicle (i.e. whether there is a false fire alarm, or a real fire alarm, there will always be a delay as the crew will always exit the vehicle to check). We conclude that as long as Co-Decyber performs at that level or better that the proof-of-concept is considered viable.

Additionally, we would also need to compare Co-Decyber's training against agents making random choices. This is to confirm that our framework makes meaningful choices (i.e. better than random) in stopping the false fire alarm attack.

To measure performance results of low-level agents, we ran ~ 1000 simulation runs for each set, with a baseline random agent which have 70–100% probability of producing no-operations.

Preliminary results show that our global low-level RL agents (Isolate, Power Control, Firewall) learned successfully to defend against our false alarm attack scenario. Observed behaviors from our trained agents include pre-emptively taking action to ensure that an attack cannot take place (such as pre-emptively blocking out the predetermined source of attack); it can do this by having learnt to trust inputs from the IDS and learning to point towards a frequent source of attack.

We can see this in the left-hand graphs in Figs. 9, 10 and 11, which presents histograms of best reward achieved amongst our global low-level agents (Isolate, Power Control and Firewall). These histograms shows that the trained agents get more of the higher maximum rewards than random policies (i.e. that there are more "5" scores achieved by trained agents than random policies); these highest rewards also indicate that there was no delay (which is better performance than having no Co-Decyber agents at all). We also show rewards that are calculated cumulatively in the right-hand graphs in Figs. 9, 10 and 11, where we can see that trained agents are able to reach accumulations of higher scores because they reached those high scores early in the simulation sweep compared to the random agents.

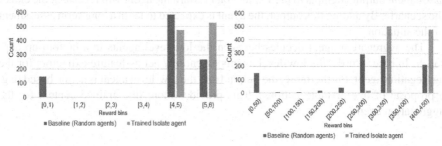

Fig. 9. Histogram of best rewards (L) and Histogram of total rewards achieved (R) in trained vs. baseline (random) low-level **Isolate** agent, against simulator count.

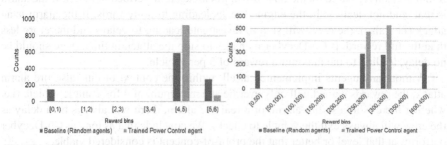

Fig. 10. Histogram of best rewards (L) and Histogram of total rewards achieved (R) in trained vs. baseline (random) low-level **Power Control** agent, against simulator count.

Our aggregation agent also shows similar promising behavior in that the trained aggregation agent is significantly more performant than baseline random policies (see

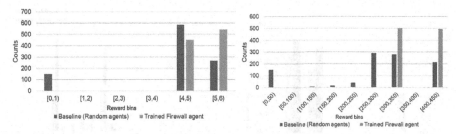

Fig. 11. Histogram of best rewards (L) and Histogram of total rewards achieved (R) in trained vs. baseline (random) low-level **Firewall** agent, against simulator count.

Figs. 12 and 13 for comparison against two random policies). In the case of the comparison with a random low-level agent, we used one with totally random action selection, and in the case of the random aggregation agent we used ones that shuffled outputs from trained low-level agents.

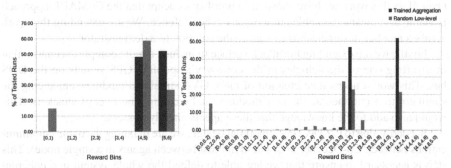

Fig. 12. (L) Histogram of best rewards achieved (R) Histogram of total rewards achieved in trained aggregation vs random low-level agent. The random low-level agent in this case selected completely random actions.

Our training environment additionally shows that Co-Decyber is promising in terms of edge deployment, with our trained system currently running at 10Hz (i.e. 10 cycles per second). We aim to keep this decision rate as we move from simulation into the real world, and additionally targeting a bare CPU deployment (i.e., with no GPU or accelerators) as a compute envelope.

These results showcase defence of one vehicle (rather than the platoon) since we needed to establish the environment, the training infrastructure as well as our training methodology. However, we are now planning to extend this cyber-defence concept to the full scenario on a number of dimensions (see Sect. 6).

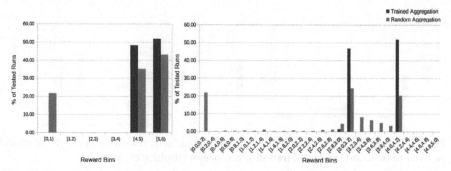

Fig. 13. (L) Histogram of best rewards achieved (R) Histogram of total rewards achieved in trained aggregation vs random aggregation agent. The random aggregation agent in this case was the aggregation agent randomly shuffling outputs from the trained low-level agents.

6   Conclusions and Future Work

Overall, in this work we have shown as a proof-of-concept that the CoMARL approach is viable as a means to enable autonomous cyber-defence. We are extending this work across a number of dimensions to mature the solution to a demonstrator.

Firstly, we are extending the attack surface to include a more complex scenario; that of diverting one of the vehicles in the convoy via spoofing GPS signals on the DDS bus. This would necessitate creation of more GVA simulated modules, enhancing the simulator to accommodate the new modules, and creating a new set of attackers. This would also add to the knowledge that these agents already possess.

Secondly, due to Co-Decyber's modular design, we are planning to enable communications between Co-Decyber nodes (and not just between agents in a single node). This step is necessary to ensure that we are able to defend the whole system in a coherent manner (e.g. such that defensive actions are not duplicated or contradictory). Furthermore, because the platoon can be considered a system-of-systems, we are also planning to move onto communications between Co-Decyber nodes across the two vehicles.

Thirdly, we are planning to experiment with reducing the capability of our intrusion detection system to see how Co-Decyber responds. This includes reducing detection coverage throughout the platooning vehicles, reducing the quality of detection (i.e. through varying true or false alert rates), and delaying detection. Training against these less than optimal scenarios will also ensure robustness of the final system.

Finally, work is also underway to transfer this to a physical implementation using real-world, representative scaled vehicles. This is to give us an understanding of both real-world behavior (albeit still in a demonstration environment) as well as to explore the implications of edge deployment of Co-Decyber agents.

All the dimensions above we plan on validating against domain expert input across stakeholders on the project and subject matter experts to ensure credibility, in addition to the conventional technical validation against both manual performance in our simulators (without Co-Decyber) and random policies.

We envisage that by the end of the project we will have a demonstrator that will showcase this autonomous cyber-defence concept.

Acknowledgements. This research is funded by Frazer-Nash Consultancy Ltd. on behalf of the Defence Science and Technology Laboratory (Dstl), an executive agency of the UK Ministry of Defence. The research forms part of the Autonomous Resilient Cyber Defence (ARCD) project within the Dstl Cyber Defence Enhancement programme.

References

1. Dhir, N., Hoeltgebaum, H., Adams, N., Briers, M., Burke, A., Jones, P.: Prospective artificial intelligence approaches for active cyber defence (2021). https://arxiv.org/pdf/2104.09981.pdf
2. Vyas, S., Hannay, J., Bolton, A., Burnap, P.P.: Automated cyber defence: a review (2023). arXiv preprint arXiv:2303.04926
3. Bridges, R.A., et al.: Testing SOAR tools in use. Comput. Secur. **129**, 103201 (2023)
4. Jhawar, R., Mauw, S., Zakiuddin, I.: Automating cyber defence responses using attack-defence trees and game theory. In: European Conference on Cyber Warfare and Security, p. 163. Academic Conferences International Limited (2016)
5. Kordy, B., Mauw, S., Melissen, M., Schweitzer, P.: Attack–defense trees and two-player binary zero-sum extensive form games are equivalent. In: Alpcan, T., Buttyán, L., Baras, J.S. (eds) Decision and Game Theory for Security. GameSec 2010. Lecture Notes in Computer Science, vol. 6442. Springer, Berlin, Heidelberg (2010). https://doi.org/10.1007/978-3-642-17197-0_17
6. Eom, T., Hong, J.B., An, S., Park, J.S., Kim, D.S.: A framework for real-time intrusion response in software defined networking using precomputed graphical security models. Secur. Commun. Networks **2020**, 1–15 (2020)
7. Nguyen, T.T., Reddi, V.J.: Deep reinforcement learning for cyber security. IEEE Transactions on Neural Networks and Learning Systems **34**, 1–17 (2021)
8. Object Management Group: About the DDS security specification version 1.1 (2018). https://www.omg.org/spec/DDS-SECURITY/
9. Chowdhary, A., Huang, D., Sabur, A., Vadnere, N., Kang, M., Montrose, B.: SDN-based moving target defense using multi-agent reinforcement learning. In: Proceedings of the first International Conference on Autonomous Intelligent Cyber defense Agents, p. 15. Paris, France (2021)
10. Yao, Q., Wang, Y., Xiong, X., Wang, P., Li, Y.: Adversarial decision-making for moving target defense: a multi-agent Markov game and reinforcement learning approach. Entropy **25**(4), 605 (2023)
11. Kordy, B., Piètre-Cambacédès, L., Schweitzer, P.: DAG-based attack and defense modeling: don't miss the forest for the attack trees. Comput. Sci. Rev. **13**, 1–38 (2014)
12. Soviany, P., Ionescu, R.T., Rota, P., Sebe, N.: Curriculum learning: a survey. Int. J. Comput. Vision **130**(6), 1526–1565 (2022)
13. Jeon, J., Kim, W., Jung, W., Sung, Y.: Maser: Multi-agent reinforcement learning with subgoals generated from experience replay buffer. In International Conference on Machine Learning, pp. 10041–10052. PMLR (2022)
14. Brockman, G., et al.: Openai gym. arXiv Preprint arXiv:1606.01540 (2016)
15. Terry, J., et al.: Pettingzoo: gym for multi-agent reinforcement learning. In: Advances in Neural Information Processing Systems, vol. 34, pp. 15032–15043 (2021)

Fault Injection and Safe-Error Attack for Extraction of Embedded Neural Network Models

Kevin Hector[1,2], Pierre-Alain Moëllic[1,2]([✉]), Jean-Max Dutertre[3], and Mathieu Dumont[1,2]

[1] CEA Tech, Centre CMP, Equipe Commune CEA Tech - Mines Saint-Etienne, 13541 Gardanne, France
{kevin.hector,pierre-alain.moellic,mathieu.dumont}@cea.fr
[2] Univ. Grenoble Alpes, CEA, Leti, 38000 Grenoble, France
[3] Mines Saint-Etienne, CEA, Leti, Centre CMP, 13541 Gardanne, France
dutertre@emse.fr

Abstract. Model extraction emerges as a critical security threat with attack vectors exploiting both algorithmic and implementation-based approaches. The main goal of an attacker is to steal as much information as possible about a protected victim model, so that he can mimic it with a substitute model, even with a limited access to similar training data. Recently, physical attacks such as fault injection have shown worrying efficiency against the integrity and confidentiality of embedded models. We focus on embedded deep neural network models on 32-bit microcontrollers, a widespread family of hardware platforms in IoT, and the use of a standard fault injection strategy – Safe Error Attack (SEA) – to perform a model extraction attack with an adversary having a limited access to training data. Since the attack strongly depends on the input queries, we propose a black-box approach to craft a successful attack set. For a classical convolutional neural network, we successfully recover at least 90% of the most significant bits with about 1500 crafted inputs. These information enable to efficiently train a substitute model, with only 8% of the training dataset, that reaches high fidelity and near identical accuracy level than the victim model.

Keywords: Machine Learning · Security · Model extraction · Fault Injection · Embedded system

1 Introduction

Deep neural network models suffer from many critical security issues including confidentiality and privacy threats. A growing concern is *model extraction* attacks that, basically, aim at stealing a victim model. Different adversarial goals have to be distinguished [13]. First, an adversary may want to clone the model (*fidelity* objective) and build a *substitute* model with an architecture and parameters as close as possible to the victim model. Thus, several works (as

S. Katsikas et al. (Eds.): ESORICS 2023 Workshops, LNCS 14399, pp. 644–664, 2024.
https://doi.org/10.1007/978-3-031-54129-2_38

ours) concerned the challenging task of the extraction of model parameters. A second objective (*task accuracy* objective) is to efficiently steal the performance of the victim model (to reach equal or better performance at lower cost) [21,28]. For that case, having similar architecture or parameter values is not compulsory.

This work focuses on a model parameters extraction with *fidelity* objective. This challenge receives a growing interest by the exploitation of very different attack vectors, from cryptanalysis-based methods as in [8,26] to learning-based techniques focused on the substitute model [22,28]. Because of very limited knowledge on the training distribution, both approaches need a very large amount of queries to the victim model that could be prohibitive in many attack context. However, the large-scale deployment of models in a wide variety of hardware platforms fosters the emergence of new attack vectors such as *side-channel* (SCA) [14] and *fault injection* analysis (FIA) [24].

For now, the use of fault injection techniques for model extraction has only been performed with rowhammer [15], such as in [24] that leverage hardware flaws of DRAM to partially guess parameter values. However, such rowhammer-based approaches exclude other platforms but CPU-based ones with DRAM memory and are known to be complex to carry out in practice. Thus, our objective is to widen the scope of FIA-based approaches for model extraction by focusing on models embedded in constrained devices with the widespread 32-bit microcontroller platforms, massively used for IoT applications. For such devices, bit-flips with rowhammer as in [24], are not practicable since they rely on Flash memory. Our work is the first to demonstrate that a well-known attack strategy against cryptographic modules is possible and can reach consistent results regarding the state-of-the-art. Our contributions are the following:

- We demonstrate a new extraction method based on a Safe-Error Attack (SEA) that exploits a bit-set fault model ($0 \to 1$, $1 \to 1$). SEA is a standard FIA strategy that relies on a simple but powerful principle: injecting a fault on a secret parameter of a program may or may not lead to a faulted output according to the parameter value.
- SEA enables to recover the most significant bit values of the victim model parameters. These information enable to efficiently constrain the substitute model training, even with limited training data.
- We use full 8-bit quantized models as for real-world embedded applications, a setting that makes our approach more challenging.
- We show that the model inputs significantly impact extraction performance and we propose an input generation method to increase the recovery rate.

Availability. Data and codes related to our work are publicly available on https://gitlab.emse.fr/securityml/lfi_sea_modelextraction.

2   Background

2.1   Model Extraction

Threats against the confidentiality of ML models, especially deep neural networks, have been extensively studied with both algorithmic and implementation-based attacks including physical attacks (especially side-channel analysis).

Let's consider a supervised neural network model M_W, with W its internal parameters. The input domain is $\mathcal{X}$ and M is trained thanks to a training dataset (X^{train}, Y^{train}), with $Y^{train} \subset \mathbb{R}^K$ the set of labels (K is the number of labels). For an input $x \in \mathcal{X}$, the output prediction is $M_W(x) \in \mathbb{R}^K$ and the predicted label is $\hat{y} = \arg\max(M_W(x))$. In a *fidelity* scenario, the goal of an adversary is to craft a model M'_Θ that mimic M_W as perfectly as possible regarding his knowledge and ability. Note that M' aims at providing the same predictions as M, including potential mistakes from M_W. Obviously, this goal strongly depends on how the *similarity* between two models is defined. A typical approach [13] is to measure the agreement of both models at the label-level, i.e. a classical objective is to have $\arg\max(M'_\Theta(x)) = \arg\max(M_W(x))$ for every x sampled from a target distribution over $\mathcal{X}$. A more complex and optimal extraction, *Functionally Equivalent Extraction*, aims to reach $M'(x) = M(x), \forall x \in \mathcal{X}$. Note that the strongest possible attack leading to a substitute model with exactly the same architecture and same parameters ($W = \Theta$) is infeasible by only exploiting input/output pairs from the victim model [13].

A first type of methods relies on the training of M'_Θ with several works based on *active learning* principles. The challenge relies on the classical assumption that an adversary has a very limited (if any) access to the original training data. Therefore, a critical limitation is the need of a very large amount of query/output pairs, collected from the victim model, to build an efficient substitute training dataset. A second approach is based on a full mathematical recovery by exploiting chosen input/output pairs as well as gradient-based properties of the model, such as the critical point ($x = 0$) of the second derivatives of ReLU in [8]. The state-of-the-art result of this approach is a near perfect recovery (worst case error of 2^{-25}) of the 100K parameters of a 2-layer MLP using $2^{21.5}$ queries. The attack has not been scaled to deeper models.

The last methods leverage the power of physical attacks to exploit information leakages, regularly demonstrated in many security applications such as cryptography [3]. More essentially, side-channel analysis have been proposed to guess the values of a model parameters with timing analysis [19] or typical correlation power analysis [4] even if the task still gathers critical open challenges [14] for a full extraction of real-world embedded models.

2.2 Fault Injection Attacks

Fault injection attacks (FIA) are active hardware threats that consist in faulting the operations of a target circuit for the purpose of extracting a secret or gaining an unauthorized access [3]. They generally require a physical access to the target [5] but some variants can be carried out remotely like rowhammer [15] that targets DRAM. By heavily addressing some memory rows, an attacker disturbs the adjacent rows (in the victim's address space) which may typically leads to bit-flip faults. Other remote approaches used software breaches in dynamic voltage and frequency scaling modules [23].

Laser Fault Injection. Typical injection means gather low-cost techniques such as voltage or clock glitching that globally (i.e., spatially) alter the target device and moderate/high-cost methods such as electromagnetic pulse or laser beam (usually, near-infrared). Laser fault injection (LFI) is particularly used in security testing centers and for certification purpose because it enables powerful analysis with high temporal and spatial accuracy [1]. LFI makes it possible to inject faults at bit-level according a data-dependent fault model[1]. Usually, a bit-flip data-independent fault model is used to model FIAs, according to which a faulted bit is inverted whatever its original value (the bit is said to be *flipped*: $0 \rightarrow 1$, $1 \rightarrow 0$). Using LFI, the fault model be either a bit-set or a bit-reset. When a bit-set fault is injected, an actual error is induced when the initial bit value was 0, the faulted bit then switches to 1 ($0 \rightarrow 1$). When the original bit value is already at 1, it stays at 1 ($1 \rightarrow 1$): the targeted bit is *safe* from any error. This fault model is said to be *data-dependent* as the injection of a fault depends on its initial data state. A bit-reset fault model is linked to a symmetric behavior ($0 \rightarrow 0$, $1 \rightarrow 0$). The physical phenomenon of a bit-set fault model with a laser shot in a floating gate transistor relies on the creation of a photoelectric current that induces voltage transients allowing to perform a fault injection [10].

Safe-Error Attack. Data-dependent fault model provides additional information to an attacker by simply observing the error-free response of the target. That is the basic principle of the Safe-Error Attack (SEA) described in [30]. SEA relies on the observation that a fault could lead or not to an incorrect output depending on a secret data. In our case, the secret is a parameter of the victim model and the output is its predictions. Since SEA has been mostly applied for cryptography, we illustrate the attack principle with a secret key recovering task for an encryption algorithm that outputs a ciphertext from an input plaintext. A bit-set is injected on the first bit of the secret key. If the obtained ciphertext is erroneous, the key bit is 0 (an actual $0 \rightarrow 1$ fault was injected), if it is error-free, the key bit is 1 (because the key bit was actually unfaulted $1 \rightarrow 1$). Then, the whole key can leak with an iterative attack on all its bits. With this work, we show that the SEA is also relevant to extract information from a DNN as described in Sect. 6.2.

Fault Injection on 32-bit Microcontrollers. LFI in SRAM or D flip-flop memories follows a data-dependent fault model. Well-defined and precise locations of these memory cells yield either a bit-set or a bit-reset fault-model as assessed on experimental basis [12,27]. The challenge is to find with certainty the points of interest of many memory bits involved in an SEA which may question the practical feasibility of SEA while targeting SRAM cells and D flip-flops. However, microcontrollers store their program and data (such as a DNN model) in embedded Flash memories (the most usual kind of embedded non-volatile memory). At read time, these data are sensitive to LFI according a bit-set fault

---

[1] Note that we use the term *fault model* in a restrictive way to describe the mathematical properties of the fault injection process.

model when read from the Flash memory for 32-bit microcontroller targets as reported by [10,20]. The experiments carried out in these reference works showed that it is feasible: (1) to achieve a 100% success rate when inducing a bit-set, and (2) to chose at will the index of a single bit to be faulted among the 32 bits of the read data, thanks to the regular and orderly architecture of an embedded Flash (which generally follows a NOR architecture). Hence, the experimental state-of-the-art shows that performing an SEA using LFI on the Flash memory of a microcontroller is within the reach of attackers who can access a LFI setup.

3   Related Works

Few works addressed the extraction of ML models by using fault injection. In [6], Breier *et al.* proposed to extract the parameters of the last layer only of a victim model. This work sets in a restricted scenario where the adversary perfectly knows everything of the victim model except the parameters of the very last output layer. The authors claimed that it is the case in a transfer learning scenario with all the other layers coming from a public pretrained model. To reverse the last layer, they used fault injections to alter the sign of the parameters and demonstrated, by simulations, that only mn faults and $2mn$ executions of the victim within the weighted sum of each neuron are necessary to extract the full weight matrix of the target layer (with m and n the number of the neurons of the last and penultimate layers respectively). Our work is significantly different since we target all the parameters of the model and do not use fault injections to mathematically reverse a layer computations (in [6] a Softmax-layer) but to extract as much information as possible to efficiently train a substitute model.

Therefore, our main reference is DeepSteal [24] with which we share the objective and threat model. DeepSteal exclusively concerns DRAM platform (in [24], Intel i5 CPU) and leverages bit-flip faults with a rowhammer attack [16] to recover MSB of a victim model parameters. Then, the authors propose to use the MSB recovered to constraint the training of a substitute model. For the parameters with recovered bits, a range of possible values and a mean value are defined. At training time, these mean values act as a classical weight-penalty regularization (see Sect. 6.6 for details). Our work aims at demonstrating that this two-step methodology is actually generalizable to another type of platforms, i.e. 32-bit microcontrollers, with a different fault model (bit-set) and exploitation methods (SEA and input crafting). Our approach is suitable to any fault injection means that lead to data-dependent faults (bit-set or bit-reset).

4   Threat Model

Our work is positioned in a context where an attacker tries to steal parameters of a model in order to copy it or to prepare future attacks. Our adversary targets embedded neural network models in platform such as 32-bit microcontrollers, thus 8-bit quantized models specifically designed for embedded inference.

We set in a traditional grey-box context for model extraction [8,24], with an adversary knowing the victim model architecture but not its parameter values and accesses to less than 10% of the training dataset. In some cases, model's architecture is effectively already known, easy to guess or previously extract with an appropriate attack (including physical ones such as [4]). Likewise, limited access to training data also corresponds to real-world applications without publicly available benchmarks, as studied in many active learning-based extraction methods [2,9,21,22].

The adversarial ability is basically twofold. First, the adversary has an unlimited black-box access to the model by querying it and getting the (normalized) outputs (i.e., not the *logits*). Importantly, working with full quantized models (8-bit), the available prediction scores are also quantized. Second, the adversary has a fault injection means that can yield a data-dependent fault model (e.g. a laser setup) and a clone device on which the attacker can profile the Flash memory layout to accurately control the fault injection process. This profiling process does not need the target inference program but only simple read/write memory procedures, as in [10].

Notations. The victim neural network is noted M_W with W its parameters. The substitute model is M^s with parameters W_s. M performs a classification task with inputs $x \in \mathcal{X}(\subset \mathbb{R}^d)$ and the output predictions $M_W(x) \in \mathbb{R}^K$ with $\mathcal{X}$ the input domain and K the number of labels. Then, the predicted label is $y = \arg\max(M_W(x))$ and the correct label is noted as y^*. A set of inputs and predictions are respectively noted as X and Y. The loss function is the categorical cross-entropy simply noted $\mathcal{L}_{CE}$. Our method is based on a safe-error attack with bit-set faults perform on the victim model parameters. The faulted parameters are referred as $\widetilde{W}$, then $M_{\widetilde{W}}$ is the resulting faulted model and $\widetilde{Y}$ is a set of faulted predictions. Our models are 8-bit quantified with signed integers (two's complement representation): a parameter w is represented as $b_0 b_1 ... b_7$ with b_i a bit value and b_0 the Most Significant Bit (hereafter, MSB).

5   Experimental Setup

5.1   8-Bit Quantized Neural Network Models

Our work is focused on 8-bit inference implementations that correspond to real-world applications using constrained embedded platforms. 8-bit quantization is the *de facto* practice for embedded models on microcontrollers and is the default configuration in many deployment tools (e.g., NNoM, TF-Lite, CubeMX.AI, MCUNet). However, the extraction method being based on a SEA, the outputs quantization has a strong impact on the extraction process.

A first approach is a lite post-training 8-bit quantization of the parameters only for memory footprint purpose: at inference time, the 8-bit stored parameters are then scaled to full-precision values, the computations, activation outputs as well as the prediction scores are in full-precision. Because of its easiness, this quantization scheme is used in many simulation works. However, we claim that it may represent a strong limitation and drawbacks since it does not represent the real behavior of embedded models with real-world deployment platforms relying on more complex quantization schemes. If we consider this naive lite-quantization, our SEA-based approach straightforwardly extract most of the bits of the victim model parameters. However, the extraction is more challenging when dealing with a full-quantization process that includes the parameters, the activation values and the output prediction scores.

We developed a Python framework based on Pytorch to perform all our simulations with this 8-bit quantization schema. We chose NNoM (Neural Network on Microcontroller)[2] as model deployment library that uses the reference CMSIS-NN library from ARM [17] as backend. NNoM is open-source with a full access to the C code and allows 8-bit quantization for weights, biases and activation function with a uniform symmetric powers-of-two quantization scheme (as in CMSIS-NN). This scheme is popular for embedded platforms because intrinsic calculations require no division only integer additions, multiplications and bit shifting (see Appendix for details). Our Python framework provides the same outputs (at layer and model-level) than ones provided by NNoM on a Cortex-M platforms. More particularly, NNoM deals with signed 8-bit integers only and does not scale the prediction scores ($\in \mathbb{R}^+$) in $[0, 255]$ but in $[0, 127]$.

5.2 Models and Datasets

We used two classical model architectures. Our first model is a multilayer perceptron composed of three fully-connected layers (128 - 64 - 10 neurons, no bias) with ReLU as activation function. In the rest of the paper, this model is simply referred as **MLP**. MLP is trained on MNIST, composed of 70k grayscale images (28×28) of digits. The second model is a convolutional neural network composed of three convolutional layers and one fully-connected layer (no bias). This model is a usual reference for embedded models in microcontrollers presented in [17]. For the rest of this paper, this model is referred as **CNN**. CNN is trained on the Cifar-10 dataset composed of 60k color images (32×32) among 10 categories. In Appendix, Table 7 details our models.

6 Model Extraction with SEA

6.1 Overview

Our method relies on three steps (as illustrated in Appendix, Fig. 5):

1. The adversary builds an attack dataset from pure random inputs with a black-box genetic algorithm. The goal is to feed the victim model with inputs that enhance the efficiency of the safe-error attack.

---

[2] https://majianjia.github.io/nnom/.

2. For each bit of each parameter and for each input from the attack set, the adversary collects two prediction sets: an *error-free* one with the nominal victim model and a *faulted* one with the faulted model. The fault correspond to a bit-set performed with an injection means on the victim model stored in memory. Then, a safe-error attack is performed by comparing the two prediction sets. Non-similar prediction scores enable to recover a 0 bit value. Additional bits can be recovered with a simple heuristic in the case of two non adjacent bits extracted by SEA.
3. A substitute model is built and trained with a very limited part (8%) of the victim training set. Training is constrained with the recovered bits with a *mean clustering training* as proposed in [24].

6.2   Exploiting Safe-Error Attack

We performed a SEA on the victim model parameters W in an iterative way to test all its bits. Our fault model is data-dependent since it is a requirement of SEA. Such a bit-set fault model is achievable for LFI in the Flash memory of a microcontroller platform. Hence, we considered this fault model in our work, however all our results can be extended to the bit-reset case, a model that is also sometime encountered for some Flash memories.

Over a set of test inputs X, the SEA relies on the direct comparison between the predictions Y of the victim model M_W and the ones $\widetilde{Y}$ output by the faulted victim model $M_{\widetilde{W}}$. We check the similarity between Y and $\widetilde{Y}$, noted $S(Y,\widetilde{Y})$. $S(Y,\widetilde{Y})$ is `True` if we have a strict equality between the two score matrix, `False` otherwise. In the bit-set context, 3 cases are possible as summarized in Table 1. When a fault occurs on a bit having 0 as value, the fault may lead to a different set of predictions than the normal behavior, therefore the adversary may conclude that the bit is 0. If the bit-set has no impact on the predictions *or* if the bit is already set to 1, then the adversary cannot recover the bit value. Thus, an adversarial objective is to optimize the error propagation when a fault occurs $(0 \rightarrow 1)$ so that a fault is likely to lead to a difference between Y and $\widetilde{Y}$. We analyze how the selection of the inputs can be leveraged by an adversary to reach this objective in the following Section.

Table 1. Truth table of SEA

b_i	$\widetilde{b_i}$	$S(Y,\widetilde{Y})$	b_i estimation
0	1	False	0
0	1	True	doubt
1	1	True	doubt

Table 2. Accuracy (%) according to inputs category

Model	All	Uncertain	Certain
CNN	79.4	57.07	92.23
MLP	94.94	68.07	98.2

6.3   Efficiency of Task-Specific Inputs

As a first analysis, we used inputs from test sets of MNIST and Cifar-10 as attack set for the SEA. Interestingly, we observed a significant heterogeneity

Table 3. Bit-recovery efficiency for Certain (**C**) and Uncertain **U** test inputs.

	No recovery (%)		Average # of bits recovered (std)	
	C	U	C	U
MLP	47.65	0.0	131 (969)	8438 (6856)
CNN	14.23	0.0	1656 (7066)	55388 (21229)

Table 4. Prediction types over 5000 random inputs.

	MLP	CNN
C (%)	9.82	99.4
U (%)	90.18	0.06

of inputs on their efficiency to recover bit-level information: for some inputs, bit-set faults do not alter prediction scores whereas other inputs lead to strong alterations. Experimentally, we distinguished two categories according to their prediction scores. A first class (hereafter called "Certain") represents inputs that lead to predictions with a single label having the maximum score of 127 (e.g., $[0, 0, 0, 0, 0, 0, 0, 0, 0, 127]$ for 10 classes). The second class (hereafter called "Uncertain") gathers the prediction scores with at least two labels having a non-null score (e.g., $[0, 13, 0, 0, 0, 0, 0, 4, 0, 110]$). Table 2 provides the accuracy of the MLP and CNN models according to these categories. Unsurprisingly, because models reach a strong confidence on the inputs from the Certain class, the accuracy is naturally high, above 90% on Cifar-10 and close to 100% on MNIST. Therefore, most of the mispredictions are concentrated in the Uncertain class.

Table 3 presents the difference between these two categories of inputs (details per layer are in Appendix, Table 8). The first column is focused on the proportion (%) of Certain and Uncertain inputs that do not lead to any recovered bit. For example, for CNN, 14.23% of Certain inputs do not lead to any bit recovery (i.e., predictions between the error-free and the faulted models are identical on these inputs). The last column gives the number of bits recovered over the inputs: for a model, we used m Certain and m Uncertain inputs and computed the average number of bits recovered (and standard deviation) over these m inputs. We used $m = 2000$ for MLP and $m = 3000$ for CNN. For example, for MLP, inputs from the Uncertain category enable to extract (on average) 64 times more bits than ones from the Certain class (8438 vs. 131). Figure 4 (Appendix) shows the distribution of recovered bits w.r.t. the inputs with some outliers that explained high std values.

A first observation is that the Uncertain inputs always leak bit information and the *useless* ones are over-represented in the Certain category for some layers of the two models. This result is more disparate for the CNN model since the parameters of the first convolutional layer are more easily recovered whatever the type of inputs (only 14.33% of the Certain predictions are useless for the SEA). Moreover, the difference between both categories on the number of recovered bits is significantly higher for the inputs in the Uncertain category, with a factor of 33 for CNN and 64 for MLP.

We propose a closer look of this phenomenon by analyzing the distribution (per layer) of the absolute gradient values of the loss w.r.t. the parameters

$(\nabla_W \mathcal{L}_{CE})$ represented in Fig. 1. We observe a clear difference of the loss sensitivity between the two categories with high magnitudes for the Uncertain class: for inputs leading to uncertain predictions, a modification of the parameters will strongly affect the loss value and, therefore, the predictions.

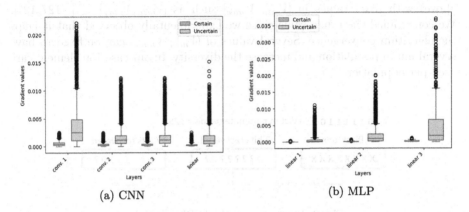

|(a) CNN|(b) MLP|

Fig. 1. $\nabla_w \mathcal{L}$ distribution per layer for Certain and Uncertain inputs. The boxplot represents the median value inside the first and third quartiles. Blue lines extend the box by 1.5x and black circles are outliers.

This first experiment demonstrates the strong impact of input nature on the exploitation of a SEA to recover bit values. Setting in a threat model where the adversary has a very limited access to training dataset, these results pave the way to a strategy that aims at crafting inputs with a single objective: provide *uncertain* predictions. That point is important since the challenge is less complex than the generation of task-specific inputs similar to ones belonging into the original training distribution.

6.4   Crafting Inputs for Uncertain Predictions

Random Inputs.   Our first interrogation concerns the efficiency of random inputs. With a very limited access to the training dataset, the use of unlimited random inputs could be a real advantage for the bits recovery step. Table 4 shows the dispatching between the two prediction categories of 5000 random inputs following a uniform distribution. For MLP, random inputs allow to generate an attack set with 90,18% of inputs leading to Uncertain predictions. Surprisingly, for CNN, only Certain predictions are obtained. We noticed that the random inputs are (nearly) always associated to the same label (label 7), therefore all the predictions are equal. We observed the same behavior for another CNN architectures trained on Cifar-10 (VGG-8 with or without biases). Since architecture of the victim model is an important factor on the efficiency of random inputs, we suggest a black-box approach to craft inputs leading to Uncertain predictions when inferred with the model thanks to a genetic algorithm.

A Black-Box Crafting Method. Our goal is to use a genetic algorithm (GA) to directly craft an attack set with as only objective to produce Uncertain predictions. Our GA acts as follow.

(1) Population Initialization. GA starts with a set of inputs, called *population*, that is simply sampled using a uniform distribution (as for the random inputs above) with pixel values in $[V_{min}, V_{max}]$ such as $[V_{min}, V_{max}] \subset [-127; 127]$. We constrained the range value since we experimentally observed that it helps the algorithm convergence. Several values of (V_{min}, V_{max}) can be fixed to have several initial population and increase the diversity. In our case 150 elements are used per population.

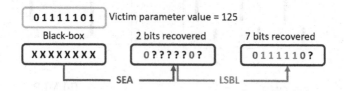

Fig. 2. Illustration of the LSBL principle.

(2) Objective Definition. GA aims at performing iterative transformations on the population to reach our adversarial objective: the output scores must match with an uncertain prediction scores fixed by the adversary, called *target scores* Y^t. A target score, y^t is in $\mathbb{R}^K$ with $y^t(i) \in [0; 127]$. C scores among K are randomly picked and set to 0, with $C \in [0; N-2]$. The $K - C$ non-null remaining scores are randomly set and scaled so that $\sum_i y^t(i) = 127$.

(3) Population Evolution. The core process is iterative and aims at building a new population thanks to a set of classical transformations. At iteration t, the new population results from *selection, crossover* and *mutation* operations between elements of the previous population at $t - 1$. A new population is generated until an optimal solution is reached. To determine which operation is done on each element of the population a cost function is used in order to sort elements of the population. In our case, the cost function is $\mathcal{L}_{CE}$. The *selection* consists in keeping some elements of the previous generation at $t-1$ to create the new one. The *selection* keeps $b\%$ of the best elements and $r\%$ of the sub-optimal elements, randomly chosen (typical values for CNN are $b = 60$ and $r = 20$). The *mutation* operation randomly applies some noise in sub-optimal elements of the previous generation to create new elements. The *crossover* merges two elements of the previous generation to create two new elements by interchanging half of each element randomly.

GA based method is repeated until the number of elements wanted in the attack dataset is reached. In Fig. 3 (left), we observe on CNN that our GA-generated inputs are significantly more efficient than random inputs (dotted lines). We extract 80% and 90% of the MSB of the CNN parameters with only 150 and 1500 inputs, respectively.

6.5   Least Significant Bit Leakage Principle

Because of the bit-set fault model and its intrinsic ambiguity (cf. truth table 1), SEA only enables to *partially* recover the bit values of the victim model parameters. However, it is possible to increase the number of bits recovered by applying a principle that we called the *Least Significant Bit Leakage* principle (hereafter, LSBL) that enables to guess bit values according to the position of the bits already recovered.

The LSBL principle is as follows: *if a bit b_k with $k \in]0;7]$ of a parameter w has been recovered by SEA (i.e., $b_k = 0$ without ambiguity), then all undefined bits b_i with $i \in [0; k-1]$ can be estimated to 1.*

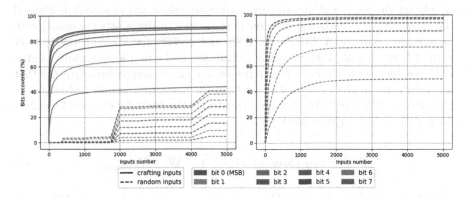

Fig. 3. Bits recovered with SEA and LSBL for (left) CNN and (right) MLP (random inputs only).

An explanation is that the more a bit-set is performed on a least significant bit than k, the smaller the variation of the parameter is. Thus, if a small alteration impacts prediction (at k) then, a bigger alteration should also impact it. This principle enables to estimate the bits b_i because if these bits do not impact the prediction, it is due to a bit value equal to 1. Figure 2 illustrates LSBL with one parameter $w = 125$. With SEA, we recover b_0 and b_6. Applying LSBL, we can guess all undefined bits from b_1 to b_5. Thus, LSBL enables to grow the extracted information from 2 to 6 bits. Thanks to the LSBL principle the rate of recovered bits increase from 47.05% to 80.1% for the CNN model with 5000 crafted inputs.

In Fig. 3 we shows the percentage of bits recovered by combining SEA and LSBL according to the inputs. We propose both random and GA-crafted inputs for the CNN model. To ease the visualization, we only present random inputs for MLP, since GA provide similar results (see Sect. 6.4). Our results demonstrate a high rate of recovered bits for both models thanks to SEA associated to the LSBL principle. In the best case, we can estimate about 90% of the most significant bits. Our method is also efficient for the 6 MSBs with a recovery rate superior to 80%. Moreover, we notice a fast plateau effect with the majority (80%) of the recovered bits extracted with approximately 250 inputs (CNN) then, after 1500 inputs (CNN), using more inputs only allow to recover few bits. The same effect is observed for MLP. We evaluated the LSBL principle on CNN and MLP models by computing the recovery error for the bits exclusively estimated by LSBL. The recovery error rapidly goes under 1% for only 150 and 300 inputs for CNN and MLP respectively. Therefore, this heuristic, despite being perfect, enables to recover bit values with a very low error rate.

6.6   Train Substitute Model

As in [24], we trained the substitute model by using the recovered bits as a constraint over only 8% of the training dataset. Without training (i.e. if we simply set the recovered bits to their estimated values and randomly initialized the other bits) we reached a very low performance of the substitute model with an average accuracy of 26.02% for CNN and 75.78% for MLP on the test set with at least 90% of MSB. Similarly as [24], we used a new loss (hereafter noted $\mathcal{L}^{sub}$, for the *substitute* loss) that relies on the cross-entropy loss $\mathcal{L}_{CE}$ (so that the substitute model is trained to perform the same task-oriented objective as the victim) with a penalty term that constrains the partially recovered weights. As in [24], $\mathcal{L}^{sub}$ is defined as (Eq. 1):

$$\mathcal{L}^{sub} = \mathcal{L}_{CE}\big(M_{\mathbf{W}}(x), y\big) + \lambda \sum_{l=1}^{L} ||\mathbf{W}^l - \mathbf{W}^l_{mean}|| \tag{1}$$

with L the number of layers, $\mathbf{W}^l$ is parameters matrix of layer l, $\mathbf{W}^l_{mean} = (\mathbf{W}^l_{min} + \mathbf{W}^l_{max})/2$ are the mean values according to the *min* and *max* values, updated after each training iteration and λ a hyper-parameter balancing the penalty strength. Initial values are computed with the MSB recovered that define *projected ranges* for the possible values of the parameters partially extracted. For example, if the two first MSB of w are 0, then the projected range for w is [0; 63]. For each training batch, the mean clustering updates W_{mean} with the current values and parameters are clipped according to the projected range after each training epoch. The main objective is to avoid any divergence of parameters from the information extracted by the fault injection step. Note that this training procedure is only applied to parameters partially recovered by SEA. For parameters without any recovered bit, no penalty can be applied, therefore $\lambda = 0$. For parameters fully recovered (i.e., the 8 bits), they are freezed at training time. As demonstrated in [24], minimizing $\mathcal{L}^{sub}$ with the mean clustering training allows to train the substitute model with few training data.

6.7   Evaluation

We keep the same evaluation protocol as in [24]. A first criteria is the *accuracy* reached by the substitute model after training when tested with test set of MNIST (for MLP) and Cifar-10 (for CNN). The closer to the victim performance the better. The second criteria is the *fidelity* between substitute and victim models defined as the rate of identical predictions over test set (the higher the better). The last criteria is *Accuracy Under Attack* (AUA) which is the accuracy of victim model when fed with adversarial examples crafted on substitute model. For AUA, if substitute model achieves to mimic victim model behaviours, then both models will respond similarly when facing adversarial examples: the transferability of adversarial perturbations will be maximum and we expect a very low adversarial accuracy for victim *and* substitute model. AUA is twice interesting since it measures a similarity-level between two models as well as the capacity of the adversary to craft efficient adversarial examples against victim model thanks to his substitute model. Consistently with the state-of-the-art, we used the l_∞-PGD attack [18] with 40 steps and an adversarial budget of $\epsilon = 8/255$ for Cifar-10 and $\epsilon = 0.3$ for MNIST.

Table 5. Performance of the substitute model after training according to the level of extraction. (AUA: Accuracy Under Attack)

At least % MSB recovered (+ others if recovered)	CNN			MLP		
	Accuracy	Fidelity	AUA	Accuracy	Fidelity	AUA
90	75.27	85.58	1.83	92.93	96.44	0.0
80	69.36	77.00	5.55	92.09	95.48	0.01
70	54.59	61.10	12.99	90.52	93.66	0.1
60	40.55	44.66	34.84	64.50	66.56	12.50
Victim	79.4	100	0.42	94.94	100	0.0

Our results are summarized in Table 5 for MLP and CNN according to different recovery rate of MSB. For CNN, accuracy grows from 40.55% to 75.27% when MSB recovered ratio increases from 60% to 90% (64.50% to 92.93% as accuracy for MLP). Our best results for CNN and MLP represent an accuracy drop of only 4% and 2% respectively compared to victim models. Importantly, we also reach high fidelity rate with 85.58% (CNN) and 96.44% (MLP) for the best case (90% of MSB). Focusing on the CNN results, the performance of our approach is consistent with the ones observed in [24] with different architectures[3]. AUA results show that adversarial examples can be efficiently crafted from substitute models, then applied on the victim models. With the best amount of MSB recovered, victim models have an adversarial accuracy close to the one obtained by crafting adversarial examples in a white-box context (1.83% for CNN and 0% for MLP). Generally, whatever numbers of MSB used to train substitute models, adversarial examples crafted on substitute models are sufficiently efficient on victim models to have an adversarial accuracy below 35%.

---

[3] On Cifar-10, with 90% of recovered MSB, [24] built a ResNet-18 substitute model with an accuracy of 89.59% (victim:93.16%), a fidelity of 91.6% and AUA of 1.61 (victim: 0%), and a VGG-11 substitute model with an accuracy of 81.56% (victim:89.96%), a fidelity of 83.33% and AUA of 18.55% (victim: 4.63%).

7   Discussions

Impact of Model Architecture. We evaluated our method on two classical models relevant for the type of platforms we consider. However, our results raise open questions about the impact of the model architecture on the SEA efficiency. Further analysis have to be investigated on other models and layers, e.g. influence of the model depth, residual networks (ResNet) or batch normalization.

Input Generation Strategy. A limitation of our GA-based crafting method is the use of too many parameters at different steps of the process (objective definition, inputs initialization and transformations applied to the population). Therefore, further analysis should evaluate alternative techniques such as the Black-Box Ripper approach proposed by Barbalau *et al.* [2] that exploit generative evolutionary framework to build a proxy dataset. Other methods may rely on black-box decision-based adversarial examples [7] to craft Uncertain samples.

Practical LFI Experiments. Colombier *et al.* [10] first demonstrated the bit-set fault model in Flash memory of a Cortex-M 32-bit microcontrollers with LFI. It was directly applied in [11] to evaluate the robustness of an embedded neural network against a weight-based adversarial attack with a bit-set variant of the Bit-Flip Attack from [25]. To evaluate the practicability of our method, we strictly followed the set up from [11] and conducted first experiments with a MLP model on an ARM Cortex-M3 platform. The model is the same as in [11] with two linear layers (50 - 10 neurons) trained on MNIST with dimensionality reduction on $\mathbb{R}^{50}$ performed by principal component analysis. The fault injections setup is composed of a two-spot laser beam in near infrared (Cf. Set up details in Appendix). As a first practical experiment and for characterization purpose, we set in a white-box context with trigger signal to monitor the synchronization of the laser beam with the loading of the targeted parameter. Moreover the inference program has been compiled without optimization (O0). We recovered 90% of MSB (with other bits if recovered) by using only 15 crafted inputs. As mentioned in [10,11], we noted that the bits can be targeted very precisely with a perfect repeatability of the fault injection.

The main limitation in terms of practicability is that the attack needs one inference with one fault injection per bit and per input (attack set). Then, the overall SEA time is $T_{SEA} = N_{inputs} \times N_{bits} \times \delta_{inf}$ with δ_{inf} the inference time. δ_{inf} could be a real bottleneck for constrained Cortex-M platforms. Without any optimisation (e.g., compilation level) we had $\delta_{inf} = 150$ ms, then the complete non-optimized attack lasted 3 h. However, targeting every bit of the model is not necessary and the attack duration can be reduced, at least, by half by considering the 4 MSB or even 20 min with only the first MSB as in [24]. Importantly, we highlight the fact that complexity comparison with [24] is hardly possible since DRAM-CPU platforms in [24] can handle far more complex models than 32-bit microcontroller devices as in our work[4].

---

[4] In [24], authors used ResNet-18,-34 and VGG-11 on Cifar-10 with an average extraction time of 12 d (extraction of the first MSB).

This work paves the way to further researches that should be focused on combining side-channel analysis to trigger the faults in black-box setting as well as using different 32-bit microcontroller platforms. Moreover, other injection mean should be studied, such as electromagnetic fault injection (EMFI) since bit-reset fault models have been demonstrated even in CPU platforms [29].

How to Protect? Protections against fault injections and safe-error attacks classically encompass randomization, redundancy and data integrity check (error-correction). However, most of the traditional defenses can be too expensive to protect a whole model (i.e. all bits). A logical way to overcome our attack is to add randomization within the model so that it slightly perturbs the prediction scores without altering the overall performance of the model. This can be achieved by randomly scaling the output feature map of the intermediate layers of the model. We test our protection on the last convolutional layer of our CNN by used 8 scaling factors α_i that are randomly picked in $[0.9, 1]$ at each inference (each α scales 8 channels). With this strategy, we keep an overall performance with a accuracy that slightly drops from 79.40% (nominal accuracy) to 79.30% and our SEA approach is no more able to extract bit values because the predictions are unlikely to be equal from one inference to another.

Table 6. Impact of expectation over layer randomization. Average (std) of the scores between two set of predictions for CNN (5000 crafted inputs).

N=	Expectation over N inferences per input			
	2	10	100	1000
ΔY (std)	7.7 (12.3)	2.4 (3.7)	0.8 (1.3)	0.3 (0.6)

The main limitation on such randomization approach is that it does not make the attack impractical since the adversary may rely his strategy on an expectation of the predictions to drown the effect of the randomization. In Table 6, we represent the average and standard deviation of the difference between two groups of prediction scores where each input is repeated N times (i.e., the output score for this input is averaged over N inferences, then the difference is averaged over the 10 labels). For convenience, this difference is simply noted as ΔY. As expected, we observe that the impact of the randomization is significantly drown as N grows. However, this theoretical limitation needs to be moderated with a practical point of view since we deal with an attack that relies on fault injections. Indeed, this first result shows that the adversary would need to process at least 1000 inferences (hence 1000 faults) for each input to thwart the protection. Such a drastic practical overload could be prohibitive for many fault injection means.

8 Conclusion

Our model extraction attack is specifically adapted to models deployed in constrained platforms that are vulnerable to memory alterations. We extract information from a victim model by using a safe-error attack principle with custom inputs that optimize the leakage of parameters with bit-set fault injections. We present promising results on two architectures (MLP and CNN) with a successful extraction of 80% of the 6 most significant bits of victim parameters. These recovered bit values are used to constrain the substitute model training even with very limited training data that finally reaches similar accuracy than the victim model with a high-level of fidelity. This work aims at highlighting the criticity of model extraction regarding the large-scale deployment of machine learning models in hardware platforms. Our work paves the way to further practical experiments with different fault injection means and target devices as well as suggestion of potential protections.

Acknowledgment. This work is supported by (CEA-Leti) the European project InSecTT (www.insectt.eu, ECSEL JU 876038) and by the French ANR in the *Investissements d'avenir* program (ANR-10-AIRT-05, irtnanoelec); and (MSE) by the ANR PICTURE program (https://picture-anr.cea.fr). This work benefited from the French Jean Zay supercomputer with the AI dynamic access program.

Appendix

Models Architecture and Quantization Scheme

Powers-of-two quantization scheme: $x_i = \lfloor x_f \cdot 2^{7-dec} \rceil$, $dec = \lceil log_2(max(|X_f|)) \rceil$. X_f is a 32-bit floating point tensor, x_f a value of X_f, x_i its 8-bit counterpart and 2^{dec} the quantization scale.

Table 7. MLP (MNIST) and CNN (Cifar-10) architecture. We follow the PyTorch naming for fully-connected layers with "Linear". Convolutional layers are composed by 5×5 kernels and followed by a pooling layer (average 2×2).

Layer	# param	Layer	# param
Inputs (784)		Inputs (32,32)	
Linear 1 (128 neurons), ReLU	100352	Conv1 (32 kernels), ReLU	2400
Linear 2 (64 neurons), ReLU	8192	Conv2 (32 kernels), ReLU	25600
Linear 3 (10 neurons), Softmax	640	Conv3 (64 kernels), ReLU	51200
		Linear (10 neurons), Softmax	10240
MLP	109184	CNN	89440

Details of the Bit-Recovery Efficiency

Table 8. Bit-recovery efficiency for *Certain* and *Uncertain* test inputs. (top) MLP and (bottom) CNN.

Layers	No recovery (%)		Average # of bits recovered (std)	
	Certain	Uncertain	Certain	Uncertain
Linear 1	97.15	0.0	83 (915)	5976 (5564)
Linear 2	92.6	0.0	40 (301)	2229 (1478)
Linear 3	48.95	0.0	8 (21)	231 (87)
MLP	47.65	0.0	131 (969)	8438 (6856)
Conv. 1	14.33	0.0	399 (933)	7144 (1309)
Conv. 2	68.6	0.0	895 (4255)	32380 (11635)
Conv. 3	79.5	0.0	339 (2057)	15062 (9463)
Linear 1	67.5	0.0	24 (87)	803 (406)
CNN	14.23	0.0	1656 (7066)	55388 (21229)

LFI Experiments

Target board:

- ARM Cortex-M3, 8 MHz (90 nm CMOS), 128 kB Flash memory.
- MCU packaging was opened with engraving.
- Communication with ChipWhisperer CW308 platform.

LFI platform:

- 2 spots near infrared, $\lambda = 1,064$ nm, spot diameter: $[1.5, 15]$ μm, maximum power: $1,700$ mW.
- Experience: power=170 mW, pulse width = 200 ns, lens magnification ×5, spot diameter = 15 μm

Distribution of Recovered Bits

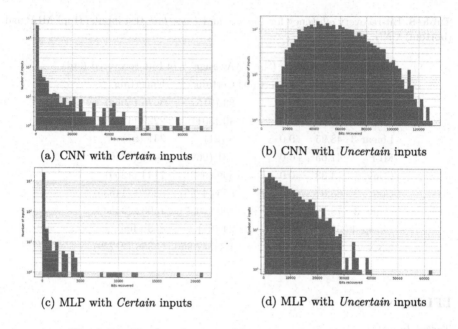

(a) CNN with *Certain* inputs

(b) CNN with *Uncertain* inputs

(c) MLP with *Certain* inputs

(d) MLP with *Uncertain* inputs

Fig. 4. Distribution of recovered bits w.r.t. number of inputs.

Illustration of the Overall Extraction Method

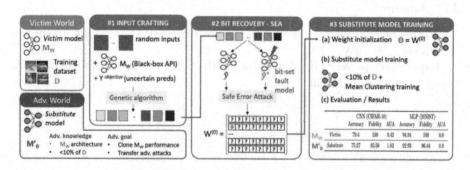

Fig. 5. The adversary crafts inputs and performs a safe-error attack exploiting faulted predictions with bit-set fault injections on the parameters stored in memory. The objective is to partially recover the bits of the parameters to efficiently train a substitute model that mimics the victim model with high fidelity.

References

1. Agoyan, M., et al.: How to flip a bit? In: 2010 IEEE 16th International On-Line Testing Symposium, pp. 235–239. IEEE (2010)
2. Barbalau, A., Cosma, A., Ionescu, R.T., Popescu, M.: Black-box ripper: copying black-box models using generative evolutionary algorithms. Adv. Neural. Inf. Process. Syst. **33**, 20120–20129 (2020)
3. Barenghi, A., Breveglieri, L., Koren, I., Naccache, D.: Fault injection attacks on cryptographic devices: theory, practice, and countermeasures. Proc. IEEE **100**(11), 3056–3076 (2012)
4. Batina, L., Bhasin, S., Jap, D., Picek, S.: Csi nn: reverse engineering of neural network architectures through electromagnetic side channel (2019)
5. Breier, J., Hou, X.: How practical are fault injection attacks, really? IEEE Access **10**, 113122–113130 (2022)
6. Breier, J., Jap, D., Hou, X., Bhasin, S., Liu, Y.: Sniff: reverse engineering of neural networks with fault attacks. IEEE Trans. Reliab. **71**(4), 1527–1539 (2021)
7. Brendel, W., Rauber, J., Bethge, M.: Decision-based adversarial attacks: Reliable attacks against black-box machine learning models. In: International Conference on Learning Representations (2018)
8. Carlini, N., Jagielski, M., Mironov, I.: Cryptanalytic extraction of neural network models. In: Micciancio, D., Ristenpart, T. (eds.) CRYPTO 2020. LNCS, vol. 12172, pp. 189–218. Springer, Cham (2020). https://doi.org/10.1007/978-3-030-56877-1_7
9. Chandrasekaran, V., Chaudhuri, K., Giacomelli, I., Jha, S., Yan, S.: Exploring connections between active learning and model extraction. In: 29th USENIX Security Symposium (USENIX Security 20), pp. 1309–1326 (2020)
10. Colombier, B., Menu, A., Dutertre, J.M., Moëllic, P.A., Rigaud, J.B., Danger, J.L.: Laser-induced single-bit faults in flash memory: Instructions corruption on a 32-bit microcontroller. In: 2019 IEEE International Symposium on Hardware Oriented Security and Trust (HOST), pp. 1–10. IEEE (2019)
11. Dumont, M., Hector, K., Moellic, P.A., Dutertre, J.M., Pontié, S.: Evaluation of parameter-based attacks against embedded neural networks with laser injection. arXiv preprint arXiv:2304.12876 (2023)
12. Dutertre, J.M., et al.: Laser fault injection at the cmos 28 nm technology node: an analysis of the fault model. In: 2018 Workshop on Fault Diagnosis and Tolerance in Cryptography (FDTC), pp. 1–6. 14th Workshop on Fault Diagnosis and Tolerance in Cryptography, September 2018
13. Jagielski, M., Carlini, N., Berthelot, D., Kurakin, A., Papernot, N.: High accuracy and high fidelity extraction of neural networks, pp. 1345–1362 (2020)
14. Joud, R., Moëllic, P.A., Pontié, S., Rigaud, J.B.: A practical introduction to side-channel extraction of deep neural network parameters. In: Smart Card Research and Advanced Applications: 21st International Conference, CARDIS 2022, Birmingham, UK, November 7–9, 2022, Revised Selected Papers, pp. 45–65. Springer (2023)
15. Kim, Y., et al.: Flipping bits in memory without accessing them: an experimental study of dram disturbance errors. ACM SIGARCH Comput. Architecture News **42**(3), 361–372 (2014)
16. Kwong, A., Genkin, D., Gruss, D., Yarom, Y.: Rambleed: reading bits in memory without accessing them. In: 2020 IEEE Symposium on Security and Privacy (SP), pp. 695–711. IEEE (2020)

17. Lai, L., Suda, N., Chandra, V.: Cmsis-nn: Efficient neural network kernels for arm cortex-m cpus. arXiv preprint arXiv:1801.06601 (2018)
18. Madry, A., Makelov, A., Schmidt, L., Tsipras, D., Vladu, A.: Towards deep learning models resistant to adversarial attacks. In: International Conference on Learning Representations (2018)
19. Maji, S., Banerjee, U., Chandrakasan, A.P.: Leaky nets: Recovering embedded neural network models and inputs through simple power and timing side-channels-attacks and defenses. IEEE Internet Things J. **8**(15), 12079–12092 (2021)
20. Menu, A., Dutertre, J.M., Rigaud, J.B., Colombier, B., Moellic, P.A., Danger, J.L.: Single-bit laser fault model in nor flash memories: analysis and exploitation. In: 2020 Workshop on Fault Detection and Tolerance in Cryptography (FDTC), pp. 41–48. IEEE (2020)
21. Orekondy, T., Schiele, B., Fritz, M.: Knockoff nets: stealing functionality of black-box models. In: Proceedings of the IEEE/CVF Conference on Computer Vision and Pattern Recognition, pp. 4954–4963 (2019)
22. Papernot, N., McDaniel, P., Goodfellow, I., Jha, S., Celik, Z.B., Swami, A.: Practical Black-Box Attacks against Machine Learning. In: Proceedings of the 2017 ACM on Asia Conference on Computer and Communications Security, ASIA CCS 2017, pp. 506–519. Association for Computing Machinery, New York, NY, USA, April 2017
23. Qiu, P., Wang, D., Lyu, Y., Qu, G.: Voltjockey: breaching trustzone by software-controlled voltage manipulation over multi-core frequencies. In: Proceedings of the 2019 ACM SIGSAC Conference on Computer and Communications Security, pp. 195–209 (2019)
24. Rakin, A.S., Chowdhuryy, M.H.I., Yao, F., Fan, D.: Deepsteal: advanced model extractions leveraging efficient weight stealing in memories. In: 2022 IEEE Symposium on Security and Privacy (SP), pp. 1157–1174 (2022)
25. Rakin, A.S., He, Z., Fan, D.: Bit-flip attack: crushing neural network with progressive bit search. In: Proceedings of the IEEE/CVF International Conference on Computer Vision, pp. 1211–1220 (2019)
26. Rolnick, D., Kording, K.: Reverse-engineering deep relu networks. In: International Conference on Machine Learning, pp. 8178–8187. PMLR (2020)
27. Roscian, C., Sarafianos, A., Dutertre, J.M., Tria, A.: Fault model analysis of laser-induced faults in sram memory cells. In: 2013 Workshop on Fault Diagnosis and Tolerance in Cryptography, pp. 89–98 (2013)
28. Tramèr, F., Zhang, F., Juels, A., Reiter, M.K., Ristenpart, T.: Stealing machine learning models via prediction apis. In: USENIX Security Symposium, vol. 16, pp. 601–618 (2016)
29. Trouchkine, T., Bouffard, G., Clédière, J.: Em fault model characterization on socs: from different architectures to the same fault model. In: 2021 Workshop on Fault Detection and Tolerance in Cryptography (FDTC), pp. 31–38. IEEE (2021)
30. Yen, S.M., Joye, M.: Checking before output may not be enough against fault-based cryptanalysis. IEEE Trans. Comput. **49**(9), 967–970 (2000)

Can Inputs' Reconstruction Information Be Coded into Machine Learning Model's Outputs?

Kazuki Iwahana[✉][ID], Osamu Saisho[ID], Takayuki Miura[ID], and Akira Ito[ID]

NTT Social Informatics Laboratories, 3-9-11, Midori-cho, Musashino-shi,
Tokyo 180-8585, Japan
kazuki.iwahana@ntt.com

Abstract. There is a growing demand for confidential inference in machine learning services, in which user data privacy is protected in the inference process. In this scenario, model providers can perform privacy attacks by using the output results of models. A previous study inferred only sensitive attributes of user data from the model outputs. In this paper, we present an attack that can reconstruct the input user data of a machine learning model from its outputs. The model provider trains an inference model such that it embeds the reconstruction information for user data into the model outputs while maintaining high inference accuracy. At the same time, the attacker trains another model to obtain the user data from the output of the inference model that contains the reconstruction information. Experimental results on six image datasets of different complexity show that LPIPS, which is the similarity metric between two images, offers a minimum value of 0.01. Additionally, the inference accuracy is maintained at the same level as that of normal training.

Keywords: Data Reconstruction · Confidential Inference · Model Output · Privacy Attack · Machine Learning

1 Introduction

While Machine Learning as a Service (MLaaS) is becoming more widely used, confidential inference, in which the input data to machine learning models is kept secret due to privacy issues, is also attracting attention [3,10,14,20]. User data in MLaaS contains a variety of sensitive information such as patient records and the user's faces for personal authentication. From the viewpoint of privacy protection [4], cryptography or hardware technology needs to be used to ensure that machine learning services do not reveal the user data.

However, a previous study [15] pointed out that the privacy of input data will be violated by using the outputs of machine learning models, even in situations where the input data is kept secret using cryptography or hardware technology. That is, even if the input data is completely confidential, the model output has the potential to contain sensitive information about the input data. The previous

S. Katsikas et al. (Eds.): ESORICS 2023 Workshops, LNCS 14399, pp. 665–682, 2024.
https://doi.org/10.1007/978-3-031-54129-2_39

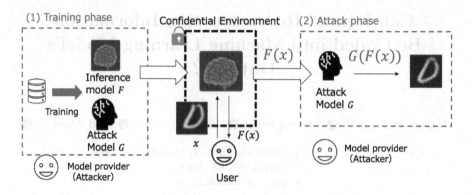

Fig. 1. Overview of our attack.

study [15] demonstrated that an attacker can infer a sensitive attribute about the input data from the model output without any impact on the main task performances (e.g., face recognition and/or medical diagnosis). Specifically, the attacker trains the model so that the sensitive attribute information of the input data he/she wishes to retrieve is stealthily embedded in the model outputs. When the attacker obtains the model output, he/she can estimate the pre-specified sensitive attribute for the corresponding input data.

It is not trivial whether the input data can be fully reconstructed from the model output, although the previous study demonstrated the risk of extracting a specific sensitive attribute [15]. This is because the amount of the reconstruction information on the input data is more than that of the information on a particular attribute. For example, if the attacker wants to estimate the attribute of male or female from an output result, he/she only needs to embed one bit of information indicating 0 or 1 in the output result. Still, the reconstruction information of input data is expected to be richer because input data has many other sensitive attributes. Therefore it is unclear whether the reconstruction information can be coded into the output result.

In this paper, we propose a simple yet effective attack method that reconstructs the input data even when it is kept secret. The overview of our attack is shown in Fig. 1. Specifically, our attack consists of training and attack phases. In the training phase, the attacker trains two models simultaneously, called the inference and attack models. The inference model is trained to embed information about the input data in the model output while maintaining the high accuracy of the original task. The attack model is trained to reconstruct the input data from the inference model output. After that, the attacker deploys the inference model obtained through the training phase in the confidential environment, and a service user queries private data to the inference model. The attacker cannot access the queried data because of computing in a confidential environment. In the attack phase, the attacker receives only the output result of the inference model with regard to the queried data and can reconstruct it by using the attack model.

Experimental evaluations of our attack method using six image datasets of different complexity show that the simple dataset produced reconstructed images with a high degree of similarity to the input images. Furthermore, we show that the accuracy of the inference model is maintained at the same level as that of the normal training. We also propose a method to estimate the complexity of the dataset on the basis of LPIPS (Learned Perceptual Image Patch Similarity) [29], which is an image similarity measure and find a strong correlation between the complexity of the dataset and the similarity of the reconstructed images obtained by our attack method to the input images. In other words, by calculating the complexity of the dataset, it is possible to predict in advance how similar images reconstructed by our attack method will be to the input images, which may serve as a potential countermeasure.

2   Related Work

Machine learning models leak much information about their training dataset in both the white-box and black-box settings. Machine learning models learn as many features as they can, and also memorize sensitive information about some training data regardless of generalizing unknown data. The information obtained in the white box setting is the output results of the machine learning model and the intermediate states (i.e., the gradients or the values of intermediate layers). On the other hand, the only information available in the black box setting is the output results of the machine learning models. This is a more realistic setting because many machine learning services provide only the output results as an API. Various information obtained in each setting can provoke many attacks in machine learning models.

A model extraction attack [11,23] extracts parameter information from a model's output results and makes a surrogate model that performs similarly to the original model. In the model extraction attack, a model has the richness of the output results, and the richness can be utilized to extract parameter information. Still, we present how this richness can be used for encoding reconstruction information at inference time.

Privacy attacks such as a membership inference attack, an attribute inference attack, and a property inference attack infer partial information about the training data. Membership inference attacks [19,21] try to determine whether a given individual's data is included in the training dataset. Attribute inference attacks [5,31] aim to infer unknown attributes of a partially known record used in the training dataset. Property inference attacks [2,16] attempt to infer the property e.g., the ratio of males and females in the training dataset.

A data reconstruction attack [1,5,7,25,28,30] reconstructs the features corresponding to particular target labels. This attack attempts to find data that achieve the maximum likelihood from the output results of the target model. In general, the attacker reconstructs training data using a generative model under the assumption that he/she has a public dataset that is similar to but does not overlap with the training data [1,25,28,30]. In federated learning, where multiple parties submit their own gradients to train a global model, the attacker can reconstruct the target party's local data by using the gradients computed by the target party [6,8,27,32]. The gradients can directly reflect the information about the training data used in the training step so that they can make data reconstruction easier. The data reconstruction attack is similar to our attack in that they reconstruct the data itself, although the attacker's positions and objectives are different. Our attack cannot use rich information such as a public dataset or gradients, so reconstructing unknown input data from only limited dimensional output results is more complicated.

In the context of other privacy attacks, a malicious model provider infers sensitive information about the input data of the target model when the input data is concealed. The attack closest to our attack was proposed by Malekzadeh et al. [15]. They point out the risk of sensitive attribute of input data leaking out from model output. The attacker should directly attempt to reconstruct the data in order to violate more privacy of input data. However, the reconstruction of input data is not considered in this attack, so the threat of privacy attacks that reconstruct input data is unknown. Song and Shamatikov [22] suggested an attack that reveals sensitive attributes about the input data from the model's internal representation in overlearning. This attack has to access several internal representations and makes stronger attack assumptions than our assumptions.

3   Problem Setting

In this section, we first describe the problem setting of the confidential inference in MLaaS, and then describe the capacity and goal of the attacker in this problem setting.

3.1   Confidential Inference in MLaaS

In MLaaS, the model provider P trains an inference model $F : \mathbb{R}^m \to \mathbb{R}^c$ to be used as a service and deploys it in the execution environment (i.e., the cloud or the edge device). The input of the inference model is an m-dimensional vector of real numbers, and the output is a c-dimensional vector of the number of classification classes of a task. The output of the inference model is represented by the logit that is the raw output of the final layer without the softmax function and the confidence that is the normalized logit between 0 and 1 using the softmax function. The logit and confidence are often used as typical output types of a classification model.

We consider a confidential inference using MLaaS for protecting the privacy of the input data. Input data $x \in \mathbb{R}^m$ following data distribution $\mathbb{D}$ is concealed by some cryptographic tools or hardware techniques and a user queries x to the inference model F and receives the output result without revealing it to the third parties (i.e., the cloud administrator and the model provider). That is, they cannot obtain the input data x, the output result y, and the internal state of the inference model F when computing $y = F(x)$.

3.2   Attack Scenarios

We assume that a model provider is an attacker who violates the privacy of the user. Here, the model provider requires only an output result y to perform our attack. There are, for example, two situations in which the model provider can receive the model output.

The first is the case when the model provider receives the output to detect privacy attacks. The model provider cannot access input data, so its output result from the inference model is used to detect whether the input data is illegal or not. This is because the model provider should ideally check for privacy attacks [2,5,21,23] on his/her model and prevent such attacks. For example, in a study [12], as a countermeasure against model extraction attack [23], the model provider detected abnormal input data used to attack by computing the distribution of their output results.

The second is the case when the model provider receives the output to improve the quality of the provided services [15]. In classification tasks, the final class for input data needs to be decided on the basis of the outputs of machine learning models. To do this, the model provider can provide a high-quality machine learning service by collecting and aggregating the outputs of multiple machine learning models.

3.3   Attacker's Capacity and Goal

Capacity. The attacker has two capabilities. First, the attacker has access to the training process. That is, the attacker can freely manipulate the training algorithm and the training data. This assumption is practical since the attacker acts as the model provider. Second, the attacker can only obtain an output result for input data, while keeping the input data secret, but not the input data or its computation process. This is due to the situation described in Sect. 3.1.

Goal. The attacker aims to reconstruct input data from the output result of the inference model. That is, the attacker aims to obtain an algorithm A such that $A(y) = \hat{x} \approx x$ upon receiving the output result $y = F(x)$.

On the other hand, the attacker must provide an inference model F with high accuracy, i.e., the same accuracy as the model trained normally. This is because if the test accuracy becomes low due to embedding the reconstruction information, no one can use the inference model.

In summary, the attacker's objective can be formulated as follows;

$$\operatorname*{argmin}_{F,A} \quad \mathbb{E}_x[d(A(F(x')), x)]$$

$$\text{subject to} \quad \operatorname{Acc}_F \approx \operatorname{Acc}_{F^*},$$

where d can be any distance and Acc_{F^*} means the test accuracy of the inference model F^* trained normally.

4   Attack Method

Our attack consists of a training phase before deploying the inference model and an attack phase as a service after deployment.

4.1   Training Phase

We first prepare an attack model $G : \mathbb{R}^c \to \mathbb{R}^m$ that outputs data of the same dimension as the input data from the inference model output results. Our training method is shown in Algorithm 1.

As shown in line 6, the objective of the attack model G is to reduce the distance $d(x, \hat{x})$ between the input data x of F and the data $\hat{x}$ output by G. The distance function d can be any distance, including Manhattan distance (L_1 norm) and Euclidean distance (L_2 norm).

On the other hand, as shown in line 7, the inference model F is trained to infer the correct label for the training data as in the usual training. CE in line 7 means the cross entropy function. Furthermore, we also aim to reduce the distance $d(x, \hat{x})$ between two data as the objective of the attack model G. In other words, by training the inference model to produce outputs that reduce the distance between the output data by G, in addition to the usual training, the output results can include reconstruction information of the input data.

Also, α, β is a hyperparameter that adjusts the balance between training normally and embedding the reconstruction information to the output result.

4.2   Attack Phase

After completing the training phase, the attacker deploys the updated F to the execution environment for the service. Users for the service can query their private data to F without revealing them to a third party. After that, the attacker receives the output results in some way. The attacker can reconstruct the input data by using the attack model G updated by Algorithm 1.

5   Evaluation

In this section, we present an experimental evaluation for our attack method. We conduct some experiments to answer the following research questions (RQs);

- *RQ1:* How similar to the input data can be reconstructed by Algorithm 1? This is the main objective of our attack.
- *RQ2:* How much does the accuracy of the inference model trained with Algorithm 1 degrade compared with that of the inference model trained normally? The output results are embedded with the reconstruction information on the input data, so this information may negatively affect the main task performance of the inference model. Therefore, the inference accuracy will be degraded compared with the normal inference model.

Algorithm 1. Training Algorithm of Our Attack

Require: D^{train}: the training dataset, F: the inference model, G: the attack model, α, β: the hyperparameters for trade-off, B: batch size, E: the number of epochs.

Ensure: Updated G and F.

1: **for** range$(0, E)$ **do**
2:   **for** range$(0, \lceil \frac{|D^{train}|}{B} \rceil)$ **do**
3:    $(x, y) \leftarrow D^{train}$; choose B samples from D^{train}
4:    $\hat{y} = F(x)$
5:    $\hat{x} = G(\hat{y})$
6:    $L_G = d(x, \hat{x})$
7:    $L_F = \alpha \text{CE}(y, \text{Softmax}(\hat{y})) + \beta d(x, \hat{x})$
8:    Update G and F from L_G and L_F.
9:   **end for**
10: **end for**

Table 1. The information on the datasets and the architectures in our setting.

Dataset	Num of classes C	Input size m	Num of training data	Num of test data	Type of F
MNIST	10	$784(28 \times 28 \times 1)$	60000	10000	LeNet
FashionMNIST	10	$784(28 \times 28 \times 1)$	60000	10000	LeNet
SVHN	10	$3072(32 \times 32 \times 3)$	73257	26032	ResNet18
GTSRB	43	$3072(32 \times 32 \times 3)$	39209	12630	ResNet18
CIFAR10	10	$3072(32 \times 32 \times 3)$	50000	10000	ResNet18
CIFAR100	100	$3072(32 \times 32 \times 3)$	50000	10000	ResNet18

- *RQ3:* How does the inference accuracy and the similarity with the input data change depending on the type of output results obtained by the attacker? The reason is that the amount of reconstruction information that an attacker can embed changes depending on the type of output results. In this experiment, we evaluate the logit before applying the softmax function and the confidence after applying the softmax function.

5.1 Experimental Setup

In this experiment, we used six datasets for image classification (i.e., MNIST, FashionMNIST, SVHN, GTSRB, CIFAR10, and CIFAR100). Each dataset has a different task complexity (i.e., data variation). The details of each dataset and the types of the inference model architecture are summarized in Table 1. The architecture of the attack model G is the same for all datasets and consists of three layers of repeated up-sampling and convolution. In Algorithm 1, the parameters are given by $E = 200$, $B = 32$, $\alpha = 1.0, \beta = 1.0$. The α and β were set so that the balance between the inference accuracy and the reconstruction similarity is just right. The distance function d is the Euclidean distance (L_2 norm) in our experimental setting.

Fashion
MNIST MNIST   SVHN   GTSRB   CIFAR10   CIFAR100

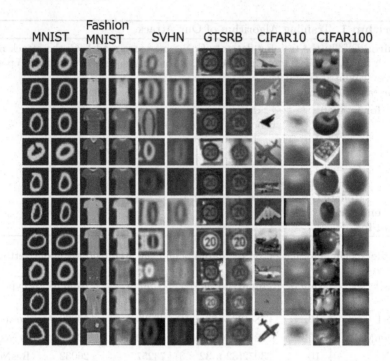

Fig. 2. Reconstructed image samples. In each dataset, the left side is the original image and the right side is the image reconstructed by our attack.

5.2   Results

Reconstruction of the Input Data. Image samples reconstructed by our attack method are shown in Fig. 2. As can be seen from the samples, MNIST, FashionMNIST, and GTSRB seem to succeed in reconstructing images that capture the features of the original images. For instance, the slope of numbers in MNIST and the brightness of road signs in GTSRB can be reproduced in the reconstructed images. On the other hand, CIFAR10 and CIFAR100 are generally blurred and do not seem to be able to reconstruct images that are similar to the original images. The degree to which these reconstructed images are similar to the original images is discussed in detail in Sect. 6.

The convergence of the attack model G with respect to the test data is shown in Fig. 3. The results of running this attack algorithm are shown in the graphs of attack_logits and attack_confidence. Although some instability in training is observed in Figs. 3c and 3d, the loss decreases for all datasets as the epoch increases. On the other hand, not all datasets show the same value of convergence, and the values are higher for CIFAR10 and CIFAR100 than for the other datasets.

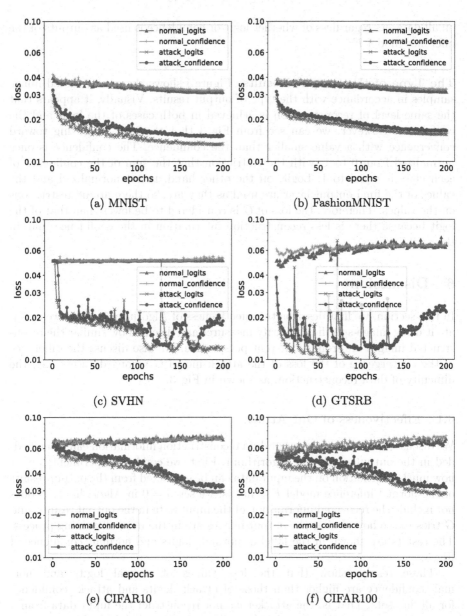

(a) MNIST

(b) FashionMNIST

(c) SVHN

(d) GTSRB

(e) CIFAR10

(f) CIFAR100

Fig. 3. Loss of the attack model G.

Inference Accuracy. The change in the inference accuracy of F as the epoch E increases is shown in Fig. 4. Although some instability in training is observed when logit is used in the GTSRB dataset in Fig. 4d, the accuracy was found to be eventually maintained at the same level as that of normal learning at 200 epochs. In addition, the accuracy is kept as good as that of the normal training on all datasets regardless of whether logit or confidence is used as outputs of the inference model F.

The Type of the Output Results. Figure 5 shows the reconstructed image samples in accordance with the type of output results. Visually, it appears that the same level of reconstruction is achieved in both cases of the logit and the confidence. However, we can see from Fig. 3 that the logit is moving toward convergence with a value smaller than the confidence. The confidence is once normalized from 0 to 1, with the restriction that the sum of the confidence of each class is equal to 1. Logit, on the other hand, is not normalized and the values of the final output layer are used as they are, so there are no restrictions on the values. Therefore, the loss of G is considered to be lower than that of the logit because there is less reconstruction information in the confidence than in the logit.

6   Discussion

In this section, we first describe the effectiveness of Algorithm 1. Next, we evaluate it using image-specific similarity measures and discuss how similar the reconstructed images are from a different perspective. We also discuss the difference in the convergence of the loss of the attack model G among datasets, i.e., the difficulty of data reconstruction, as shown in Fig. 3.

6.1   Effectiveness of Our Attack

We discuss how much of the input data reconstruction information can be embedded in the output results by Algorithm 1. First, we conduct experiments about how much information on the input data can be extracted from the output results of the normal inference model F. That is, we set $\beta = 0$ in Algorithm 1. F does not include the recovered information of the input data in the output results, and G tries to see how similar the output images are in the normal training process. The results are shown in the label of normal_logits and normal_confidence of Fig. 3.

These results show that the loss values of normal_logits and normal_confidence are higher than those of attack_logits and attack_confidence for all datasets. That is, the attacker cannot reconstruct the input data from a normally trained inference model, regardless of the availability of logit or confidence information. Besides, these results indicate that the difference between these loss values denotes the amount of reconstruction information on the input data embedded by the attacker.

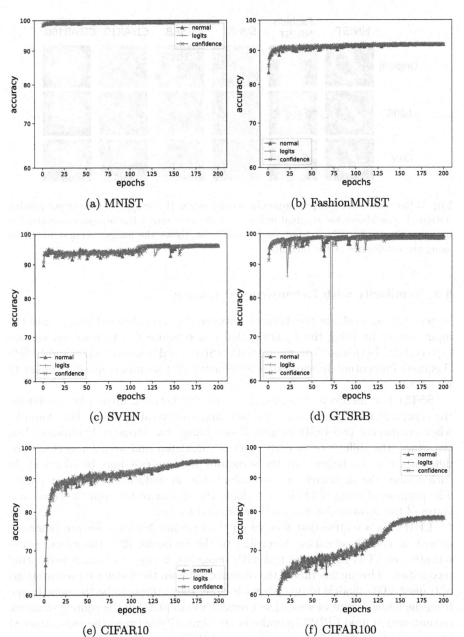

(a) MNIST

(b) FashionMNIST

(c) SVHN

(d) GTSRB

(e) CIFAR10

(f) CIFAR100

Fig. 4. Test accuracy of the inference model F.

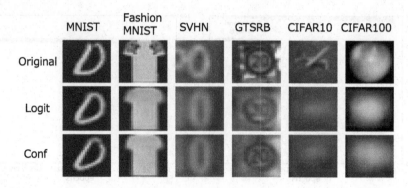

Fig. 5. Reconstructed image samples in accordance with the type of the output results. "Original" row shows the original images, "Logit" row shows the images reconstructed by using the logit as the output, and "Conf" row shows the images reconstructed by using the confidence as the output.

6.2 Similarity with Reconstructed Images

In Sect. 5.2, we evaluate the distance between the reconstructed images and the input images by using the L_2 norm that can measure the distance among any type of data. In this section, we use SSIM (Structural Similarity) [24] and LPIPS (Learned Perceptual Image Patch Similarity) [29] as image-specific similarity measures.

SSIM is a metric to evaluate the similarity between images by combining the comparisons of brightness, contrast, and structural patterns. For example, when comparing two RGB images, if one image has stronger luminance than the other, the difference in each pixel is calculated and added together. The difference may be larger, but the structure and contrast may be identical. In such a case, the similarity can be evaluated as an indicator of high similarity. The purpose of using SSIM is to evaluate the similarity between the structural states of the recovered image and the original image.

LPIPS is a metric that focuses on the distance between feature representations in neural networks. According to the literature [29], the latent representation of VGG models trained with ImageNet is close to human perceptual recognition. This means that if the distance between the feature representations of trained VGG models in two images is close, they appear to be the same image from the human point of view. The previous works [9,26] in the context of image reconstruction used LPIPS to evaluate the similarity between the reconstructed images and the original images, so we use LPIPS as in these works.

The results evaluated by SSIM and LPIPS are shown in Figs. 6 and 7, respectively. Here, SSIM means that the closer to 1, the higher the similarity, and LPIPS means that the closer to 0, the higher the similarity. For clarity in comparing the two indices, the value of $1 - (SSIM)$ is shown in Fig. 6.

As shown in Figs. 6 and 7, the values of SSIM and LPIPS indicate similar trends. In other words, the reconstructed images show similar trends between

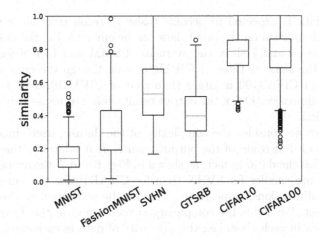

Fig. 6. The values of 1 − (SSIM) for each dataset.

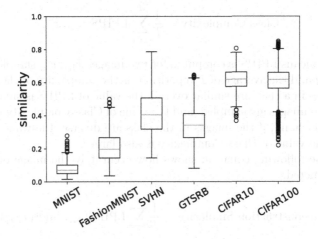

Fig. 7. The values of LPIPS for each dataset.

structural patterns and human perception. However, the variance in SSIM focusing on structural patterns tends to be larger than that in LPIPS. This indicates that although there is some blurring when focusing on the structural patterns between images, the images are close to each other without much effect on human perception.

6.3   Difficulty of Data Reconstruction

We discuss the difficulty of the input data reconstruction in our attack. One reason for the difficulty is naively considered to be the number of dimensions of the output results. If the number of dimensions of the output results is large, the input data is expected to become easier to reconstruct since more recon-struction information on the input data can be embedded in the output results. However, Figs. 6 and 7 show the averages of SSIM and LPIPS for CIFAR100 are almost the same as those of CIFAR10, even though the number of output dimensions of CIFAR100 is larger than that of CIFAR10. This fact indicates that larger dimensionality of the output results does not necessarily mean easier reconstruction.

Therefore we consider the complexity of the dataset itself, independent of the number of dimension of the output results, as it relates to the difficulty of reconstructing the data. In fact, as shown in Figs. 6 and 7, the averages of SSIM and LPIPS are smaller for SVHN than for CIFAR10 for the same number of classes and dimensions, respectively. This can be attributed to the complexity of the dataset. We define the complexity of the dataset as the degree of scatter of image data in each class, i.e., the similarity of data in each class. The degree of scatter of data in class j is expressed by the following equation;

$$\text{Class Complexity} = \frac{1}{T} \sum_{i=1}^{T} \text{LPIPS}(x_{i,j}, x_{i,j}^*). \tag{1}$$

Equation 1 means LPIPS is computed for two images $x_{i,j}, x_{i,j}^*$ sampled randomly from class j and the average of T repetitions is the complexity of class j. That is, if the images in a class are similar overall, the value of LPIPS is small regardless of which two images are sampled, and the value of Class Complexity is also small. On the other hand, if the images in the class are diverse, the value of LPIPS is larger so the value of Class Complexity is also larger.

Also, the following equation shows how accurately the image of class j can be reconstructed;

$$\text{Reconstruction Similarity} = \frac{1}{T} \sum_{i=1}^{T} \text{LPIPS}(x_{i,j}, A(F(x_{i,j}))), \tag{2}$$

where A is an algorithm such that any image is output from the output results of the inference model F.

We show the relationship between Class Complexity and Reconstruction Similarity for each class in each dataset by using Eqs. 1 and 2 in Fig. 8. From the results in Fig. 8, there is a strong correlation between Class Complexity and Reconstruction Similarity. This indicates that when the value of Class Complexity is small (i.e., when there are many similar data in a class), images highly similar to the input images are reconstructed. As a result, by calculating Class Complexity of the dataset, it is possible to approximately understand how closely our attack will reconstruct the input images. Another aspect implies that reconstruction by our attack method is easy for datasets where each instance is of a similar type for one class. On the other hand, it indicates that reconstruction by our attack is difficult for datasets where each instance is very different for one class.

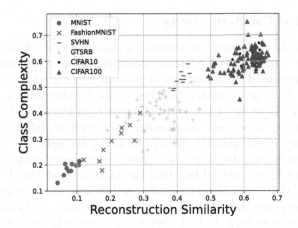

Fig. 8. Reconstruction Similarity and Class Complexity in each dataset. The horizontal axis indicates the value of Reconstruction Similarity and the vertical axis indicates the value of Class Complexity calculated by Eqs. 1 and 2.

There are various possible use cases for Class Complexity. For example, when a company creates a dataset and sells it to another company that wants to use the dataset for training MLaaS, Class Complexity of the dataset can be calculated to know the risk of data reconstruction in advance. In addition, if some attack methods are discovered in subsequent research, we can calculate how good the method is by examining the relationship between Class Complexity and Reconstruction Similarity for a dataset.

6.4 Relation to Autoencoders

Autoencoders [13,17,18] are primarily designed to encode the input data into a compressed representation and decode it such that the reconstructed data is as similar to the original data as possible. Autoencoders are close to our attack because our goal is also to reconstruct the input data from the output result of the inference model. However, our attack method is different from autoencoders because the encoder also plays a role as the classification model in our problem setting. That is, the encoder has to not only compresses input data into a meaningful representation but also classify the input data into a correct class. We experimentally found that the encoder can play a role as the inference model with the same accuracy as the normal inference model as described in Sect. 5.

The quality of the data reconstructed by autoencoders depends on the number of dimensions in the compressed representation. To improve the quality of the reconstructed data, the number of dimensions should increase. However, in our problem setting, the number of dimensions in the compressed representation must be equal to the number of output dimensions of the inference model, i.e., the number of classes, so it is difficult to change the number of dimensions like autoencoders. Improving the quality of reconstructed data while keeping the number of dimensions constant remains future work.

6.5 Potential Countermeasures

The difference between the distributions of output results of the normal inference model and the attacked inference model can be used as a countermeasure. Our attack is realized by embedding the reconstruction information about the input data in the output results. In other words, the distribution of the output results is expected to be significantly different from the normal distribution of the output results since some information is included in addition to the output results obtained by the usual training process. For example, since the entropy of the output results may be larger than that of the normal output results in the case of the attack, it is highly likely that the inference model has been attacked if the entropy of the output results exceeds a certain value. On the other hand, how to set an appropriate threshold for detecting our attack is still an issue. Another countermeasure is to keep the high complexity of each class in a dataset used for training. As discussed in Sect. 6.2, it is difficult to reconstruct images with high similarity to input images by our attack against a dataset in which each class has high complexity. However, if we make a dataset with the high complexity of each class, the classification for a dataset may become difficult and the accuracy may decrease, so the trade-off is an issue to be addressed.

7 Conclusion

In this paper, we presented an attack that can obtain images with high similarity to the input data by embedding the reconstruction information of the input data in the output result of machine learning models. We also found that the inference model is as accurate as the model trained normally, even when the input data reconstruction information is embedded in the output result. In fact, our attack is a threat to privacy violation in an environment where the model is used while keeping the input data secret because the attacker can reconstruct the input data if only the output result is obtained. We also introduced a measure of the complexity of the dataset and found a strong correlation between the complexity and the similarity. Future work includes improving our attack method so that it can achieve high similarity even with high-complexity datasets and extending our attack method so that it can be adapted to domains other than image classification.

Code Availability. Our code is publicly available via GitHub (https://github.com/kaz-iwahana/ReconstInputs).

References

1. An, S., et al.: Mirror: model inversion for deep learning network with high fidelity. In: Proceedings of the 29th Network and Distributed System Security Symposium (2022)

2. Ateniese, G., Mancini, L.V., Spognardi, A., Villani, A., Vitali, D., Felici, G.: Hacking smart machines with smarter ones: How to extract meaningful data from machine learning classifiers. Int. J. Secur. Netw. **10**(3), 137–150 (2015)
3. Berry, C., Komninos, N.: Efficient optimisation framework for convolutional neural networks with secure multiparty computation. Comput. Secur. **117**, 102679 (2022). https://doi.org/10.1016/j.cose.2022.102679
4. European Commission: Regulation (EU) 2016/679 of the European Parliament and of the Council of 27 April 2016 on the protection of natural persons with regard to the processing of personal data and on the free movement of such data, and repealing Directive 95/46/EC (General Data Protection Regulation) (Text with EEA relevance) (2016)
5. Fredrikson, M., Lantz, E., Jha, S., Lin, S.M., Page, D., Ristenpart, T.: Privacy in pharmacogenetics: an end-to-end case study of personalized warfarin dosing. In: Proceedings of USENIX Security Symposium 2014, pp. 17–32. USENIX Association (2014)
6. Geiping, J., Bauermeister, H., Dröge, H., Moeller, M.: Inverting gradients-how easy is it to break privacy in federated learning? In: Advances in Neural Information Processing Systems, vol. 33, pp. 16937–16947 (2020)
7. Haim, N., Vardi, G., Yehudai, G., Shamir, O., Irani, M.: Reconstructing training data from trained neural networks. In: Koyejo, S., Mohamed, S., Agarwal, A., Belgrave, D., Cho, K., Oh, A. (eds.) Advances in Neural Information Processing Systems, vol. 35, pp. 22911–22924. Curran Associates, Inc. (2022)
8. Huang, Y., Gupta, S., Song, Z., Li, K., Arora, S.: Evaluating gradient inversion attacks and defenses in federated learning. In: Advances in Neural Information Processing Systems, vol. 34, pp. 7232–7241 (2021)
9. Huang, Y., Gupta, S., Song, Z., Li, K., Arora, S.: Evaluating gradient inversion attacks and defenses in federated learning. In: Advances in Neural Information Processing Systems (2021)
10. Hussain, S.U., Javaheripi, M., Samragh, M., Koushanfar, F.: Coinn: Crypto/ML codesign for oblivious inference via neural networks. In: Proceedings of CCS, pp. 3266–3281. ACM (2021)
11. Jagielski, M., Carlini, N., Berthelot, D., Kurakin, A., Papernot, N.: High accuracy and high fidelity extraction of neural networks. In: Proceedings of USENIX Security, pp. 1345–1362. USENIX Association (2020)
12. Juuti, M., Szyller, S., Marchal, S., Asokan, N.: Prada: Protecting against DNN model stealing attacks. In: Proceedings of EuroS&P 2019, pp. 512–527. IEEE (2019)
13. Kingma, D.P., Welling, M.: Auto-encoding variational Bayes. arXiv preprint arXiv:1312.6114 (2013)
14. Kumar, A., Tourani, R., Vij, M., Srikanteswara, S.: Sclera: a framework for privacy-preserving MLAAS at the pervasive edge. In: Proceedings of IEEE PerCom 2022 Workshops, pp. 175–180 (2022)
15. Malekzadeh, M., Borovykh, A., Gündüz, D.: Honest-but-curious nets: sensitive attributes of private inputs can be secretly coded into the classifiers' outputs. In: Proceedings of CCS, pp. 825–844. ACM (2021)
16. Parisot, M.P., Pejo, B., Spagnuelo, D.: Property inference attacks on convolutional neural networks: influence and implications of target model's complexity. arXiv preprint arXiv:2104.13061 (2021)
17. Ranzato, M., Huang, F.J., Boureau, Y.L., LeCun, Y.: Unsupervised learning of invariant feature hierarchies with applications to object recognition. In: Proceedings of CVPR, pp. 1–8. IEEE Computer Society (2007)

18. Rumelhart, D.E., McClelland, J.L.: Learning Internal Representations by Error Propagation, pp. 318–362 (1987)
19. Salem, A., Zhang, Y., Humbert, M., Berrang, P., Fritz, M., Backes, M.: ML-leaks: model and data independent membership inference attacks and defenses on machine learning models. In: Proceedings of NDSS 2019. The Internet Society (2019)
20. Shen, T., et al.: SOTER: guarding black-box inference for general neural networks at the edge. In: Proceedings of USENIX ATC, pp. 723–738. USENIX Association (2022)
21. Shokri, R., Stronati, M., Song, C., Shmatikov, V.: Membership inference attacks against machine learning models. In: Proceedings of IEEE S&P 2018, pp. 3–18. IEEE Computer Society (2017)
22. Song, C., Shmatikov, V.: Overlearning reveals sensitive attributes. In: Proceedings of ICLR (2020)
23. Tramér, F., Zhang, F., Juels, A.: Stealing machine learning models via prediction APIs. In: Proceedings of USENIX Security 2016, pp. 601–618. USENIX Association (2016)
24. Wang, Z., Bovik, A.C., Sheikh, H.R., Simoncelli, E.P.: Image quality assessment: from error visibility to structural similarity. IEEE Trans. Image Process. **13**(4), 600–612 (2004)
25. Yang, Z., Zhang, J., Chang, E.C., Liang, Z.: Neural network inversion in adversarial setting via background knowledge alignment. In: Proceedings of the 2019 ACM SIGSAC Conference on Computer and Communications Security. CCS '19, pp. 225–240. Association for Computing Machinery, New York, NY, USA (2019). https://doi.org/10.1145/3319535.3354261
26. Yin, H., Mallya, A., Vahdat, A., Alvarez, J.M., Kautz, J., Molchanov, P.: See through gradients: Image batch recovery via gradinversion. In: Proceedings of CVPR, pp. 16332–16341. IEEE Computer Society (2021)
27. Yin, H., Mallya, A., Vahdat, A., Alvarez, J.M., Kautz, J., Molchanov, P.: See through gradients: image batch recovery via gradinversion. In: Proceedings of the IEEE/CVF Conference on Computer Vision and Pattern Recognition, pp. 16337–16346 (2021)
28. Yin, H., et al.: Dreaming to distill: data-free knowledge transfer via deepinversion. In: The IEEE/CVF Conference on Computer Vision and Pattern Recognition (CVPR), June 2020
29. Zhang, R., Isola, P., Efros, A.A., Shechtman, E., Wang, O.: The unreasonable effectiveness of deep features as a perceptual metric. In: Proceedings of CVPR 2018, pp. 586–595. IEEE Computer Society (2018)
30. Zhang, Y., Jia, R., Pei, H., Wang, W., Li, B., Song, D.: The secret revealer: generative model-inversion attacks against deep neural networks. In: Proceedings of CVPR, pp. 250–258. IEEE Computer Society (2020)
31. Zhao, B.Z.H., et al.: On the (in)feasibility of attribute inference attacks on machine learning models. In: 2021 IEEE European Symposium on Security and Privacy (EuroS&P), pp. 232–251 (2021). https://doi.org/10.1109/EuroSP51992.2021.00025
32. Zhu, L., Liu, Z., Han, S.: Deep leakage from gradients. In: Advances in Neural Information Processing Systems, vol. 32 (2019)

Towards a Practical Defense Against Adversarial Attacks on Deep Learning-Based Malware Detectors via Randomized Smoothing

Daniel Gibert[1]([⊠])(iD), Giulio Zizzo[2], and Quan Le[1]

[1] CeADAR, University College Dublin, Dublin, Ireland
{daniel.gibert,quan.le}@ucd.ie
[2] IBM Research Europe, Dublin, Ireland
giulio.zizzo2@ibm.com

Abstract. Malware detectors based on deep learning (DL) have been shown to be susceptible to malware examples that have been deliberately manipulated in order to evade detection, a.k.a. adversarial malware examples. More specifically, it has been show that deep learning detectors are vulnerable to small changes on the input file. Given this vulnerability of deep learning detectors, we propose a practical defense against adversarial malware examples inspired by randomized smoothing. In our work, instead of employing Gaussian or Laplace noise when randomizing inputs, we propose a randomized ablation-based smoothing scheme that ablates a percentage of the bytes within an executable. During training, our randomized ablation-based smoothing scheme trains a base classifier based on ablated versions of the executable files. At test time, the final classification for a given input executable is taken as the class most commonly predicted by the classifier on a set of ablated versions of the original executable. To demonstrate the suitability of our approach we have empirically evaluated the proposed ablation-based model against state-of-art evasion attacks on the BODMAS dataset. Results show greater robustness and generalization capabilities to adversarial malware examples in comparison to a non-smoothed classifier.

Keywords: malware detection · machine learning · adversarial defense · randomized smoothing · evasion attacks

1 Introduction

Nowadays, machine learning (ML) is being adopted to enhance anti-malware engines as it has the capability to "learn without being explicitly programmed". Typically, ML-based malware detectors can be divided in two groups: (1) static detectors and (2) dynamic detectors. On the one hand, static malware detectors analyze the characteristics of a program or file without executing it. They rely on examining the static attributes, such as the binary file's structure, header

S. Katsikas et al. (Eds.): ESORICS 2023 Workshops, LNCS 14399, pp. 683–699, 2024.
https://doi.org/10.1007/978-3-031-54129-2_40

information, or metadata, to determine if a file is potentially malicious. These detectors operate on the assumption that certain patterns or properties found in malware can be identified without running the code. On the other hand, dynamic malware detectors analyze the behavior of a program or file by executing it in a controlled environment. These detectors observe the program's actions, interactions with the system, network traffic, and other run-time behaviors to determine if a file exhibits malicious activities such as unauthorized data access, network connections to known malicious domains, or attempts to modify system files. In this work, we are going to focus on static detectors, specifically in static ML-based malware detectors, as extracting information from an executable without executing it is faster than running an executable and logging its behavior. In addition, static ML-based detectors are usually deployed as a first line of defense, alongside with signature-based and heuristic-based approaches, in a multi-layer defense malware detection system.

There are currently two primary categories of static ML-based malware detectors: (1) Feature-based detectors and (2) end-to-end detectors. On the one hand, feature-based detectors rely on the process of feature engineering, where manually crafted features are extracted from benign and malicious samples to train machine learning models. These detectors aim to capture specific characteristics or patterns that distinguish malicious software from benign programs. The feature extraction process typically involves techniques such as n-gram analysis, entropy calculation, API information and structural analysis of the binary files. These extracted features serve as input to traditional machine learning algorithms such as gradient boosting trees [2], support vector machines [22] (SVM), random forests [1,9], and feed-forward-neural networks [21].

Feature-based detectors require a great deal of domain knowledge to extract a set of features that accurately represent the executables. This process is time consuming and requires deep understanding of the executable's file format. Consequently, recent research has focused on constructing models that can extract their own features, which are known as end-to-end detectors [8,13,20]. For instance, Raff et al. [20] introduced MalConv, a shallow CNN architecture that can learn features directly from raw byte inputs by performing convolutions. The MalConv model, like any other model that directly learns from the raw byte representation of executables, is trained using both benign and malicious code, and identifies patterns shared among those executables. Malware authors are aware of this and they try to disguise their malicious code in a way that it resembles benign code, thereby causing the target malware detector to incorrectly classify the malicious executable as benign. An effective method to evade detection by end-to-end detectors is to inject benign code within a malicious executable, either by appending it at the end of the malicious code, which is referred to as overlay append, or by adding new sections that contain the benign code [5]. In addition, more elaborated evasion tactics have been proposed to evade end-to-end malware detectors. For instance, Demetrio et al. [6] proposed GAMMA, a genetic adversarial machine learning malware attack which optimizes the benign content injected into adversarial malware examples using a genetic algorithm.

Moreover, Kreuk et al. [12] adapted the Fast Gradient Sign Method (FGSM) to create a small adversarial payload that flips the prediction made for malicious executables from malicious to benign.

In light of the susceptibility of deep learning detectors to even minor manipulations in the input file, we propose a practical defense against adversarial malware examples based on randomized smoothing [4,14,15]. In this work, instead of employing Gaussian or Laplace noise when randomizing inputs, we propose a randomized ablation-based smoothing scheme that ablates a proportion of the bytes in a executable file.

The main contributions of this work are the following:

- We propose the first model agnostic adversarial defense technique against adversarial malware examples, i.e. you can use any machine learning model as a base classifier.
- We present a randomized ablation-based smoothing classification scheme specifically designed for the task of malware detection.
- We empirically evaluate the proposed randomized ablation-based smoothing scheme against state-of-the-art evasion attacks to assess its robustness compared to a non-smoothed classifier.

2   Problem Formulation

In this section, we present the background to the task of malware detection along with an overview of the latest evasion attacks in the literature.

2.1   The Task of Malware Detection

Malware detection refers to the task of determining whether a given software program is benign or malicious. Traditional approaches rely on costly and time-consuming feature engineering, but deep learning-based detectors use one or more convolutional layers to directly learn patterns from raw bytes. However, similarly to other ML models, deep learning malware detection models are susceptible to adversarial examples [3,24]. In the context of malware detection, given a malware detector f, the goal of an adversarial attack on a malware example x is to produce an adversarial malware example x_{adv}, such that x_{adv} has the same functionality as x, but f misclassifies x_{adv} as a benign example. Unlike attacks on image classifiers, the adversarial examples for malware detection do not need to be visually indistinguishable from the original example; they simply need to maintain the executable's functionality.

2.2   Evasion Attacks

ML-based malware detectors have been shown to be very sensitive to small changes in the input file, and can be easily bypassed by injecting carefully crafted adversarial payloads [23]. Recent advanced evasion attacks introduced in the literature [16] to evade end-to-end detectors can be broadly categorized into two groups depending on the level of access and knowledge the malware authors have of the target detector: (1) white-box attacks [12,23] and (2) black-box attacks [5, 28]. White-box attacks require complete knowledge of the detector, including training algorithm, input and output, and access to the model parameters. For instance, Suciu et al. [12,23] adapted the Fast Gradient Method (FGM) from [10] to generate a small adversarial payload that caused malicious executables to be classified as benign. Moreover, Demetrio et al. [7] presented various attacks that manipulate the format of Portable Executable files to inject an adversarial payload. These attacks, named Full DOS, Extend and Shift, inject the adversarial payload by manipulating the DOS header, extending it, and shifting the content of the first section, respectively. On the other hand, black-box attacks do not require such comprehensive knowledge of the detector, and can be executed with limited information, i.e. the score (score-based attacks) or the label (label-based attacks) predicted by the malware detector. However, in a real-world scenario only label-based attacks are feasible as the malware authors will know nothing about the detection system and only the label associated to the submitted file will be available to them. For example, Demetrio et al. [6] proposed GAMMA (Genetic Adversarial Machine Learning Malware Attack), a label-based attack that relies on a genetic algorithm to select which benign code to inject and modify in order for the adversarial malware example to evade detection. Similarly, Yuste et al. [28] presented a method for generating adversarial malware examples by dynamically extending unused blocks, referred to as code caves, into malware binaries. Afterwards, a genetic algorithm is employed to optimize the content inserted into these code caves.

2.3   Adversarial Defenses

The only defense that has been published so far is adversarial training. In their work, K. Lucas et al. [17] used data augmentation to train an end-to-end malware classifier to be robust against three state-of-the-art evasion attacks, (1) In-Place Replacement attack (IPR) [18], (2) Displacement attack (Disp) [18] and (3) Padding attack [12]. To this end, they augmented the training data by (1) applying unguided transformations of the same type of attacks, e.g. IPR and Disp; (2) using modified versions of IPR and Disp adversarial examples; (3) training with padded adversarial examples; using adversarial examples perturbated with attacks adapted from other discrete domains [25,27].

Although effective, adversarial training makes the malware classifier robust only to the attacks employed to augment the training data. To this end, in our work we present a smoothing-based approach to improve the robustness of end-to-end malware classifiers. In contrast to adversarial training, smoothing-based classifiers aim to smooth out the decision boundaries in the input space, making the classifiers more robust to a wider range of attacks.

3   Methodology

In this section we introduce our smoothing-based defense which we adapt from the Computer Vision domain by: (1) replacing the standard Gaussian randomization scheme with a randomized ablation-based scheme that operates on the bytes of an executable; (2) introducing a training procedure that takes into account that files are variable-length byte arrays.

3.1   Randomized Smoothing

Smoothing is a method used in robust machine learning that averages a model's output in relation to randomized inputs. This method has recently gained attention in the computer vision domain due to its capacity to reduce a model's sensitivity to noise or fine-scale variations. More specifically, it has been shown that randomized smoothing schemes employing Gaussian or Laplace noise when randomizing inputs, provide l_p robustness certificates [4,14,15]. These randomization techniques, however, are inadequate for the task of malware detection because (1) they erroneously assume numerical input values, and (2) they erroneously assume all input examples are of the same size. However, byte values are categorical and are often embedded as a vector of real values, and the size of the input files vary. To address these incompatibilities, we propose a randomized ablation-based (RA) smoothing scheme which randomizes inputs by randomly ablating a percentage of the bytes in a given binary file.

Randomized Ablation-Based Smoothing Scheme. The set of possible byte values in an executable will be represented by $S = \{0, 1, ..., 255\}$. We will use $X = S^d$ to represent the set of possible executables, where d is the maximum length of the executables in X that will be used for classification. Larger executables will be clipped while smaller executables will be padded with the specially-encoded 'PAD' symbol.

Remark 1. The 'PAD' token is embedded as a E-dimensional array of zeros, where E is the embedding size, to indicate the absence of information about a byte. For instance, if E = 8, then the embedding of the 'PAD' token is [0,0,0,0,0,0,0,0].

In our randomized ablation-based smoothing scheme, a base malware classifier, f, is trained to make classifications based on an ablated version $\tilde{x}$ of a given executable file x. This ablated version $\tilde{x}$ consists of a copy of the original executable file x, with all the selected byte values replaced/ablated with the specially-encoded 'PAD' symbol. The rationale behind is to conceal the information of the selected bytes from the classifier. The training procedure is defined in Algorithm 1.

Algorithm 2 defines the operation $ABLATE(x, p)$ which takes as input an executable file x, represented as an array of byte values, and a probability p, which denotes the probability of ablating every byte in x, and outputs an ablated

Algorithm 1. Smoothed classifier training procedure

Require: training dataset D_{train}, malware detector f with parameters θ, probability
   of ablating a byte $p \in \mathbb{R}$, $0 <= p <= 1$
   $\theta \leftarrow Initialize\,parameters$
   for i=1, MAX_EPOCHS **do**
      for $x, y \in D_{train}$ **do**
         $\tilde{x} \leftarrow ABLATE(x, p)$
         $\tilde{y} \leftarrow f(\tilde{x})$
         $Loss \leftarrow criterion(y, \tilde{y})$
         $\theta \leftarrow Update\,parameters$
      end for
   end for

---

file $\tilde{x}$, i.e. an array of byte values, with all the selected ablated bytes replaced with
the 'PAD' token. Ablating the bytes given a probability p, instead of ablating a
fixed number of bytes, allows us to ablate a number of bytes proportional to the
size of the input file.

Remark 2. Notice that contrarily to the Computer Vision (CV) domain, where
it is common to downscale all images to a fixed size, i.e. 28×28 for MNIST,
32×32 for CIFAR10, or 225×255 for Imagenet, the size of the files is different
from one another, 97 bytes being the smallest size a Portable Executable file
can have. Choosing to ablate a fixed number of bytes indistinctively of the size
of the file is impractical as it might generate situations where the smallest files
would have almost all bytes ablated and the bigger files would have a very small
proportion of their bytes ablated. To circumvent this limitation, we ablate a
number of bytes proportional to the size of the file and we sample batches of
similarly sized files during training. This allows us to minimize excess padding
during training.

    The randomized ablation-based smoothing scheme can be defined as a two-
stage process. In the first stage, given an input file x of size d, we select which
bytes are going to be ablated based on a probability p. This operation is referred
as $CREATE\_MASK(x, p)$. The output of the $CREATE\_MASK(x, p)$ is an
array, referred to as m, of size equals to d consisting of 0s and 1s, indicating
whether or not to ablate a particular byte. For instance, if the i-th element of
m equals 1 it indicates that the i-th byte in x has to be ablated. For example, $CREATE\_MASK([90, 00, 03, 00, 00, 04, ..., 13], 0.40) = [0, 1, 1, 0, 0, 0, ..., 1]$
In the second stage, the original file is ablated according to a given mask to yield
a new file, with the selected bytes ablated/replaced with the specially-encoded
'PAD' token. This operation is referred to as $APPLY\_MASK(x, m)$. For
example, $APPLY\_MASK([90, 00, 03, 00, 00, 04, ..., 13], [0, 1, 1, 0, 0, 0, ..., 1]) =$
$[90, PAD, PAD, 00, 00, 04, .., PAD]$.

    Let x be an input file, p be the probability of a given byte of the file to be
ablated, and f be a base classifier. At test time, we generate L ablated versions
of x using the function $ABLATE(x, p, L)$, and classify each ablated version into

Algorithm 2. ABLATE operation

---

function CREATE_MASK(x, p)
    m ← [0]*|x|
    for i ← 1 to |x| **do**
        r ← random()
        if r ¡= p **then**
            m[i] ← 1
        end if
    end for
    return m
end function
function APPLY_MASK(x, m)
    $\tilde{x}$ ← copy(x)
    for i ← 1 to |x| **do**
        if m[i] == 1 **then**
            $\tilde{x}$[i] ← 'PAD'
        end if
    end for
    return $\tilde{x}$
end function
Require: : a file, p : a probability $\in \{0, 1\}$.
    $m \leftarrow CREATE\_MASK(x, p)$
    $\tilde{x} \leftarrow APPLY\_MASK(x, m)$
    return $\tilde{x}$

---

its corresponding class using f. To make the final classification, we count the number of ablated versions of x that the base classifier returns for each class and divide it by the total number of ablated versions L. For each class, i.e. benign or malicious, $f(\tilde{x})$ will either be 0 or 1. However, it is not required that $f(\tilde{x}) = 1$ for any class. This functionality can be implemented by a threshold. The classifier may abstain, returning zero for all classes. On the other hand, the classifier cannot return 1 for multiple classes. An overview of the scheme is represented in Fig. 1.

This problem can be formally defined as follows. Let $C = \{c_1, c_2, ..., c_k\}$ be the set of all possible classes. For each class $c_i \in C$, let N_i be the number of ablated versions of x that the base classifier f returns as belonging to class c_i. Then, the probability of input file x belonging to class c_i can be estimated as:

$$P(c_i, x) = \frac{N_i}{L}$$

where N_i is the number of ablated versions of x that belong to class c_i according to the base classifier f.

The function $ABLATE(x, p, L)$ generates L ablated versions of input file x by randomly ablating bytes from x with probability p of the content from x and replacing it with the PAD token. The ablated versions are then returned as a set of L files.

The final classification of x can then be determined as:

$$\hat{y} = argmax_{c_i \in C} P(c_i|x)$$

where $\hat{y}$ is the predicted class for input file x.

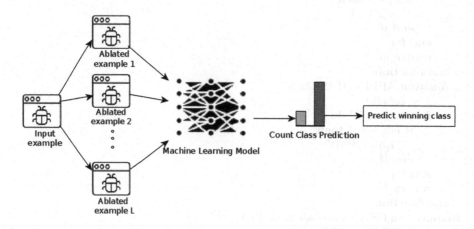

Fig. 1. Randomized ablation-based smoothing scheme overview.

Remark 3. For the task of malware detection there are only two classes indicating whether the executable is benign or malicious, i.e. $c = 2$. However, the approach could be easily extended to a multi-class classification problem such as the task of malware classification. Malware classification is the process of assigning a malware sample to a specific malware family. In this case, c will be equal to the number of malware families.

4   Evaluation

In this section we empirically evaluate the robustness of the proposed randomized ablation-based (RA) smoothing scheme against state-of-the-art evasion attacks.

4.1   Experimental Setup

Following you can find the details of the experimental setup, including data sources, machine learning models for malware detection, and parameters for the randomized ablation-based smoothing scheme. The experiments have been run on a machine with an Intel Core i7-7700k CPU, 1xGeforce GTX1080Ti GPU and 64Gb RAM. The code has been implemented with PyTorch [19] and is publicly available in our Github repository[1].

---

[1] https://github.com/danielgibert/randomized_smoothing_for_malware_detection.

BODMAS Dataset. In this paper, we use the BODMAS dataset [26] to evaluate the proposed randomized ablation-based classification scheme. This dataset consists of 57,293 malware with family information (581 families) and 77,142 benign Windows PE files collected from August 2019 to September 2020. The dataset has been partitioned into three sets, training (80%), validation (10%) and test sets (10%), taking into account the timestamp of each sample, i.e. examples in the training set contain the older executables while the examples in the test set contain the most recent executables. To speed-up the experiments we have only considered those executables that are equal or smaller than 1Mb. The rationale behind is that the greater the input size the greater the computational time required to run the experiments. Furthermore, as some of the evasion attacks evaluated manipulate the executables by injecting content, the bigger executables would have to be clipped to feed the model. By only using executables that are equal or smaller than 1Mb we avoid having to clip the executables and thus, losing important information for classification. In consequence, the reduced dataset consists of 39,380 and 37,739 benign and malicious executables, respectively.

Malware Detectors. In this work, we experiment with a deep learning-based malware detector called MalConv [20]. MalConv is an end-to-end deep learning model proposed for malware detection. End-to-end models learn to classify examples directly from raw byte sequences, instead of relying on manually feature engineering. The network architecture of MalConv consists of an embedding layer, a gated convolutional layer, a global-max pooling layer and a fully-connected layer. See Fig. 2.

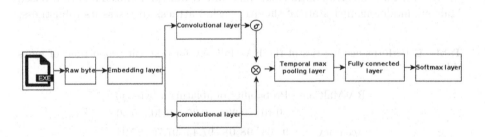

Fig. 2. Randomized ablation-based smoothing scheme overview.

Using MalConv as a basis, two malware detectors have been evaluated:

- NS-MalConv. This detector corresponds to a non-smoothed MalConv model. It serves as a non-robust baseline as no specific technique has been employed to improve robustness to evasion attacks.
- RA-MalConv. This detector implements the randomized ablation-based smoothing scheme proposed in Sect. 3.1 using MalConv as a base detector.

4.2   Empirical Evaluation

In this section, we empirically evaluate the robustness of the randomized ablation-based smoothing scheme to several published evasion attacks. By doing so, we aim to provide a complete picture of the strengths and weaknesses of the proposed defense. First, we provide details of the performance of the proposed defense on non-adversarial examples in Sect. 4.2. Afterwards, we examine the robustness of the proposed ablation-based scheme against three state-of-the-art evasion attacks in Sect. 4.2.

Non-adversarial Evaluation. The randomized-based ablation scheme is controlled by two parameters: (1) the proportion of bytes to ablate with respect of the file size, denoted by $p \in [0, 1]$, and the number of ablated versions of a given file that are used for classification, denoted by L. These two parameters serve as input to the methods and affect the way the method operates and the output it produces. Following we analyze the performance of the RA-MalConv model when using different various values for $p \in \{0.10, 0.20, 0.30, 0.40, 0.50\}$ in Table 1. In our experiments, we generate 100 ablated examples for each example that the RA-MalConv model has to classify ($L = 100$). This is done to make the computational cost of the defense more manageable. As observed in Table 1, the highest accuracy and F1-score on the validation set is achieved when $p = 0.20$. For this reason, For the rest of the experiments we use $p = 0.20$ (20% chance of ablating a byte) for the RA-MalConv model.

Table 2 presents the performance metrics of the NS-MalConv and RA-MalConv models on the validation and test sets. Results provide evidence that the RA-MalConv model has similar detection accuracy and F1-score compared to the NS-MalConv on clean data. Next, we evaluate our randomized ablation-based Malconv model against state-of-the-art evasion attacks to assess its robustness.

Table 1. Performance metrics of the RA-MalConv for different proportions of bytes ablated.

RA-MalConv	Probability of ablating a byte (p)				
	0.10	0.20	0.30	0.40	0.50
Accuracy	98.04	**98.08**	97.43	97.76	97.94
F1-Score	98.03	**98.06**	97.46	97.72	97.92

Empirical Robustness Evaluation Against SOTA Evasion Attacks. We consider three recently published attacks designed to bypass static PE malware detectors as summarized in Table 4. These attacks manipulate the executables by creating new spaces within the executables [7,28] and by injecting new content in a newly-created section [6]. The maximum size of the adversarial malware examples was constrained to 2,000,000 bytes in our experiments (twice the maximum size of the examples used for training the models). Early termination is

Table 2. Performance metrics of the non-smoothed and smoothed models on the validation set, the test set and the sub-tests of 500 and 100 malware examples used for adversarial attack evaluation. With the sub-test sets being composed of only malware we simply report the accuracy.

	Validation set		Test set		Test sub-set (500 examples)	Test sub-set (100 examples)
	Accuracy	F1-score	Accuracy	F1-Score	Accuracy	Accuracy
NS-MalConv	97.55	97.52	**98.03**	97.98	**97.00**	**99.00**
RA-MalConv	**98.08**	**98.03**	97.61	97.57	95.00	**99.00**

implemented, causing the attack to terminate immediately when the malware detector's prediction shifts from malicious to benign. Since some attacks might take hours to run per file, we use two smaller-sized test sets containing 500 and 100 malware examples randomly subsampled from the test set. The test sub-set consisting of 500 examples have been employed to evaluate the malware detectors against the Shift attack [7], and the GAMMA attack [6]. On the other hand, the test sub-set of 100 examples has been used to evaluate the code caves optimization attack [28]. By employing a smaller subset, we aim to reduce the computational overhead and accelerate the overall experimentation process[2]. In addition, to further accelerate the experimentation process, we also reduce from 100 to 20 the number of ablated versions generated for each input example, i.e. $L = 20$. As it can be observed in Table 3, when L is decreased and thus, fewer ablated versions are generated, the accuracy and F1-score of the classifier does not significantly decrease but it remains consistent.

Table 3. Performance comparison of RS-MalConv on the validation set for different L values, i.e. $L \in \{20, 100\}$.

RS-MalConv (p = 0.20)	Validation set	
	Accuracy	F1-score
L = 20	98.03	98.00
L = 100	98.08	98.06

We would like to point out that the white-box attack cannot be directly applied to our randomized ablation-based classifier as it requires computing the gradients and our approach makes computing the gradients a difficult task. To circumvent this situation, we optimized the adversarial payload using genetic algorithms (GAs). The use of genetic algorithms to optimize the adversarial payload allows us to convert the white-box attack to a black-box attack. Therefore, there is no need to access the implementation details of the model or the

---

[2] We would like to denote that our evaluation set is comparable in size to prior work [7, 11,12,23].

Table 4. Description of the evasion attacks used to assess the robustness of the proposed smoothed classier.

Attack	Type of Attack	Optimizer	Description
Slack+Padding [23]	White-box	FGSM	Padding bytes and manipulating bytes from slack space
Shift [7]	White-box	Single gradient step	Shift section content
GAMMA [6]	Black-box	Genetic algorithm	Padding and injection of benign sections
Optimization of code caves [28]	Black-box	Genetic algorithm	Dynamically introducing code caves within an executable

gradient information to optimize the adversarial payload. Instead, the GA will explore the search space by imitating the process of evolution through various bioinspired operators (selection, crossover, and mutation) to optimize an initial population of solutions. Similarly to GAMMA [6], the initial population of solutions is initialized with benign content. In our experiments, the size of the population is 50. Afterwards, the GA iteratively applies selection, crossover and mutation to optimize the adversarial payload. The implementation of each of the bioinspired operators within the GA is based on the results of Yuste et al. [28].

1. Selection operator. The selection operator selects a subgroup of 10 individuals within the current population to be crossed in the following step. This individuals are selected using a combination of elitism (only the best individuals are chosen) and a selection based on tournaments (each tournament consists of selecting ten individuals at random and the best among them is selected for the next iteration).
2. Crossover operator. The crossover operator pairs of selected individuals (parents) are combined to produce offspring. Each individual from the elitist group is crossed over with each individual from the tournament group, generating two offsprings per crossover. The first chunk of each offspring is the first chunk of one of the parents, the second chunk of each offspring is the second chunk from the other parent, and so on.
3. Mutation operator. The mutation operator mutates the offspring individuals obtained after the crossover operator with probability $p_1 = 0.1$. Then, a percentage of the genes of the individual selected for mutation are mutated with probability $p_2 = 0.1$.

Figure 3 depicts the general scheme of the GA to the problem of malware evasion. In our case, the attack types are the slack plus padding attack [23] and the shift attack [7] although the genetic algorithm could be used to optimize any adversarial payload.

Table 5 present the detection accuracy of the NS-MalConv and RA-MalConv models on the adversarial malware examples generated by the evasion attacks based on genetic algorithms described in Table 4. The table shows that, regardless of the evasion attack, the RA-MalConv outperforms NS-MalConv by some margin. For instance, NS-MalConv detects 43.40% and 40.80% of the adversarial

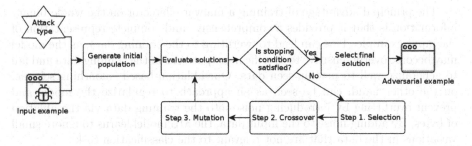

Fig. 3. Genetic algorithm scheme for malware evasion attacks.

malware examples generated by the Shift attack while the RA-MalConv detects 69.40% and 67.00% of the adversarial examples, respectively. Furthermore, RA-MalConv provides greater detection accuracy than NS-MalConv on the adversarial malware examples generated by the GAMMA attack, showing that the proposed defense mechanism holds its ground against evasion attacks that inject and optimize great amounts of benign content. Lastly, the RA-MalConv detects 81% of the examples compared to only a 14% detection rate of the NS-MalConv when the adversariale examples have been created by extending and optimizing code caves in the executables. Overall, the robustness of the RA-MalConv to attacks that manipulate the executables is positive and a great improvement over the baseline, NS-MalConv, demonstrating that anti-malware engines can benefit from smoothing-based classifiers.

Table 5. Detection accuracy of the end-to-end malware detectors on the adversarial examples generated with the evasion attacks.

Attack	Hyperparameters	Detection Rate	
		NS-MalConv	RA-MalConv
Padding+slack attack [23]	Number of padded bytes = 500	**90.02**	94.00
	Number of padded bytes = 10000	**81.00**	86.40
Shift attack [7]	Preferable extension amount = 1048	52.20	**74.00**
	Preferable extension amount = 2048	43.40	**69.40**
	Preferable extension amount = 4096	40.80	**67.00**
GAMMA attack [6] (soft label)	#sections = 10, population size = 10	42.20	**66.20**
	#sections = 100, population size = 10	56.20	**71.80**
	#sections = 100, population size = 20	36.20	**78.80**
Optimization ofcode caves [28]*	Default	14.00	**81.00**

5 Discussion

In this section we discuss the advantages and limitations of the non-smoothed and smoothed detectors, NS-MalConv and RA-MalConv, respectively.

The principal advantage of training a malware detector on the whole binary information is that it provides a comprehensive and complete representation of the input example. This can lead to overfitting to the training data, as the model may become overly sensitive to specific noise patterns in the training data and fail to generalize well to new, unseen data. Our ablation-based smoothing scheme, on the other hand, can be seen as an approach to regularize the model and prevent overfitting by introducing noise into the training data via the ablation of bytes. By adding noise to the input data, the ML model learns to ignore small variations in the data that are not relevant to the classification task.

At test time, however, the non-smoothed detector makes predictions faster and with less computational resources than the smoothed detectors as they only assess once the maliciousness of a given input example. On the contrary, the smoothed detector is slower because it needs to assess each ablated version of the input example independently and then aggregate the predictions as shown in Table 6. Nevertheless, the benefits of the increased generalization abilities and robustness to adversarial attacks provided by the smoothed detectors outweight the added computational cost and time required for classification.

Table 6. Training and testing time comparison between the smoothed and non-smoothed detectors.

Models	Computational Time	
	Training Time (minutes/epoch)	Test Time (seconds/example)
NS-MalConv	22.06	0.0161
RA-MalConv	44.95	3.3814

6 Conclusions

In this paper, we present the first model agnostic adversarial defense against adversarial malware examples. Building upon prior research on randomized smoothing, we introduce a randomized ablation-based smoothing scheme to build robust static end-to-end learning-based classifiers. To the best of our knowledge, this is the first time randomized smoothing has been implemented for end-to-end malware detection, i.e. taking as input the whole binary as a sequence of bytes. The novel application of our randomized ablation-based smoothing scheme creates a new robust model that generalizes better than the non-smoothed Mal-Conv on adversarial malware examples, achieving a significant advancement in the field.

6.1 Future Work

Our results suggest a number of directions for future work. The most apparent direction identified is the incorporation of recent defenses from the Computer

Vision domain other than randomized smoothing. It would be interesting to adapt de-randomized smoothing into static malware detection models to prevent a localized injection of benign code or adversarial content from dominating the prediction. Another line of research could be investigating approaches to identify and remove the adversarial content from the executables.

Acknowledgements. This project has received funding from Enterprise Ireland and the European Union's Horizon 2020 Research and Innovation Programme under the Marie Skłodowska-Curie grant agreement No 847402. The views and conclusions contained in this document are those of the authors and should not be interpreted as representing the official policies, either expressed or implied, of CeADAR, University College Dublin, and IBM Ireland Limited. We would like to thank Cormac Doherty and UCD's Centre for Cybersecurity and Cybercrime Investigation for their support.

Data and Code Availability. The BODMAS dataset is available to the public and the source code of our approach is available under the MIT License at the following repository https://github.com/danielgibert/randomized_smoothing_for_malware_detection.

References

1. Ahmadi, M., Ulyanov, D., Semenov, S., Trofimov, M., Giacinto, G.: Novel feature extraction, selection and fusion for effective malware family classification. In: Bertino, E., Sandhu, R.S., Pretschner, A. (eds.) Proceedings of the Sixth ACM on Conference on Data and Application Security and Privacy, CODASPY 2016, New Orleans, LA, USA, March 9–11, 2016, pp. 183–194. ACM (2016). https://doi.org/10.1145/2857705.2857713
2. Anderson, H.S., Roth, P.: EMBER: An Open Dataset for Training Static PE Malware Machine Learning Models. ArXiv e-prints (2018)
3. Biggio, B., et al.: Evasion attacks against machine learning at test time. In: Blockeel, H., Kersting, K., Nijssen, S., Železný, F. (eds.) ECML PKDD 2013. LNCS (LNAI), vol. 8190, pp. 387–402. Springer, Heidelberg (2013). https://doi.org/10.1007/978-3-642-40994-3_25
4. Cohen, J.M., Rosenfeld, E., Kolter, J.Z.: Certified adversarial robustness via randomized smoothing. In: Chaudhuri, K., Salakhutdinov, R. (eds.) Proceedings of the 36th International Conference on Machine Learning, ICML 2019, 9–15 June 2019, Long Beach, California, USA. Proceedings of Machine Learning Research, vol. 97, pp. 1310–1320. PMLR (2019). http://proceedings.mlr.press/v97/cohen19c.html
5. Demetrio, L., Biggio, B., Lagorio, G., Roli, F., Armando, A.: Functionality-preserving black-box optimization of adversarial windows malware. IEEE Trans. Inf. Forensics Secur. **16**, 3469–3478 (2021). https://doi.org/10.1109/TIFS.2021.3082330
6. Demetrio, L., Biggio, B., Lagorio, G., Roli, F., Armando, A.: Functionality-preserving black-box optimization of adversarial windows malware. IEEE Trans. Inf. Forensics Secur. **16**, 3469–3478 (2021)
7. Demetrio, L., Coull, S.E., Biggio, B., Lagorio, G., Armando, A., Roli, F.: Adversarial examples: a survey and experimental evaluation of practical attacks on machine learning for windows malware detection. ACM Trans. Priv. Secur. **27**, 1–31 (2021)

8. Gibert, D., Béjar, J., Mateu, C., Planes, J., Solis, D., Vicens, R.: Convolutional neural networks for classification of malware assembly code. In: Aguiló, I., Alquézar, R., Angulo, C., Ortiz, A., Torrens, J. (eds.) Recent Advances in Artificial Intelligence Research and Development - Proceedings of the 20th International Conference of the Catalan Association for Artificial Intelligence, Deltebre, Terres de l'Ebre, Spain, October 25–27, 2017. Frontiers in Artificial Intelligence and Applications, vol. 300, pp. 221–226. IOS Press (2017). https://doi.org/10.3233/978-1-61499-806-8-221

9. Gibert, D., Planes, J., Mateu, C., Le, Q.: Fusing feature engineering and deep learning: a case study for malware classification. Expert Syst. Appl. **207**, 117957 (2022). https://doi.org/10.1016/j.eswa.2022.117957, https://www.sciencedirect.com/science/article/pii/S0957417422011927

10. Goodfellow, I.J., Shlens, J., Szegedy, C.: Explaining and harnessing adversarial examples. In: Bengio, Y., LeCun, Y. (eds.) 3rd International Conference on Learning Representations, ICLR 2015, San Diego, CA, USA, May 7–9, 2015, Conference Track Proceedings (2015). http://arxiv.org/abs/1412.6572

11. Kolosnjaji, B., et al.: Adversarial malware binaries: Evading deep learning for malware detection in executables. In: 26th European Signal Processing Conference, EUSIPCO 2018, Roma, Italy, September 3–7, 2018, pp. 533–537. IEEE (2018). https://doi.org/10.23919/EUSIPCO.2018.8553214

12. Kreuk, F., Barak, A., Aviv-Reuven, S., Baruch, M., Pinkas, B., Keshet, J.: Adversarial examples on discrete sequences for beating whole-binary malware detection. CoRR abs/1802.04528 (2018). http://arxiv.org/abs/1802.04528

13. Krčál, M., Švec, O., Bálek, M., Jašek, O.: Deep convolutional malware classifiers can learn from raw executables and labels only (2018). https://openreview.net/pdf?id=HkHrmM1PM

14. Lécuyer, M., Atlidakis, V., Geambasu, R., Hsu, D., Jana, S.: Certified robustness to adversarial examples with differential privacy. In: 2019 IEEE Symposium on Security and Privacy, SP 2019, San Francisco, CA, USA, May 19–23, 2019, pp. 656–672. IEEE (2019). https://doi.org/10.1109/SP.2019.00044

15. Li, B., Chen, C., Wang, W., Carin, L.: Certified adversarial robustness with additive noise. In: Wallach, H.M., Larochelle, H., Beygelzimer, A., d'Alché-Buc, F., Fox, E.B., Garnett, R. (eds.) Advances in Neural Information Processing Systems 32: Annual Conference on Neural Information Processing Systems 2019, NeurIPS 2019(December), pp. 8–14, 2019. Vancouver, BC, Canada, pp. 9459–9469 (2019), https://proceedings.neurips.cc/paper/2019/hash/335cd1b90bfa4ee70b39d08a4ae0cf2d-Abstract.html

16. Li, D., Li, Q., Ye, Y., Xu, S.: Arms race in adversarial malware detection: a survey. ACM Comput. Surv. (CSUR) **55**(1), 1–35 (2021). https://doi.org/10.1145/3484491

17. Lucas, K., Pai, S., Lin, W., Bauer, L., Reiter, M.K., Sharif, M.: Adversarial training for raw-binary malware classifiers. In: Proceedings of the 32nd USENIX Security Symposium. USENIX (2023). to appear

18. Lucas, K., Sharif, M., Bauer, L., Reiter, M.K., Shintre, S.: Malware makeover: breaking ml-based static analysis by modifying executable bytes. In: Proceedings of the 2021 ACM Asia Conference on Computer and Communications Security, pp. 744–758. ASIA CCS 2021, Association for Computing Machinery, New York, NY, USA (2021). https://doi.org/10.1145/3433210.3453086

19. Paszke, A., et al.: PyTorch: an imperative style, high-performance deep learning library. In: Wallach, H., Larochelle, H., Beygelzimer, A., d'Alché-Buc, F., Fox, E., Garnett, R. (eds.) Advances in Neural Information Processing Systems, vol. 32, pp. 8024–8035. Curran Associates, Inc. (2019). http://papers.neurips.cc/paper/9015-pytorch-an-imperative-style-high-performance-deep-learning-library.pdf

20. Raff, E., Barker, J., Sylvester, J., Brandon, R., Catanzaro, B., Nicholas, C.K.: Malware detection by eating a whole EXE. In: The Workshops of the The Thirty-Second AAAI Conference on Artificial Intelligence, New Orleans, Louisiana, USA, February 2–7, 2018. AAAI Technical Report, vol. WS-18, pp. 268–276. AAAI Press (2018). https://aaai.org/ocs/index.php/WS/AAAIW18/paper/view/16422

21. Rudd, E.M., Ducau, F.N., Wild, C., Berlin, K., Harang, R.: ALOHA: auxiliary loss optimization for hypothesis augmentation. In: 28th USENIX Security Symposium (USENIX Security 19), pp. 303–320. USENIX Association, Santa Clara, CA (2019). https://www.usenix.org/conference/usenixsecurity19/presentation/rudd

22. Saxe, J., Berlin, K.: Deep neural network based malware detection using two dimensional binary program features. In: 10th International Conference on Malicious and Unwanted Software, MALWARE 2015, Fajardo, PR, USA, October 20–22, 2015, pp. 11–20. IEEE Computer Society (2015). https://doi.org/10.1109/MALWARE.2015.7413680

23. Suciu, O., Coull, S.E., Johns, J.: Exploring adversarial examples in malware detection. In: 2019 IEEE Security and Privacy Workshops, SP Workshops 2019, San Francisco, CA, USA, May 19–23, 2019, pp. 8–14. IEEE (2019). https://doi.org/10.1109/SPW.2019.00015

24. Szegedy, C., Zaremba, W., Sutskever, I., Bruna, J., Erhan, D., Goodfellow, I.J., Fergus, R.: Intriguing properties of neural networks. In: Bengio, Y., LeCun, Y. (eds.) 2nd International Conference on Learning Representations, ICLR 2014, Banff, AB, Canada, April 14–16, 2014, Conference Track Proceedings (2014). http://arxiv.org/abs/1312.6199

25. Wu, H., Wang, C., Tyshetskiy, Y., Docherty, A., Lu, K., Zhu, L.: Adversarial examples for graph data: deep insights into attack and defense. In: Proceedings of the Twenty-Eighth International Joint Conference on Artificial Intelligence, IJCAI-19, pp. 4816–4823. International Joint Conferences on Artificial Intelligence Organization (2019). https://doi.org/10.24963/ijcai.2019/669

26. Yang, L., Ciptadi, A., Laziuk, I., Ahmadzadeh, A., Wang, G.: BODMAS: an open dataset for learning based temporal analysis of PE malware. In: 4th Deep Learning and Security Workshop (2021)

27. Yang, P., Chen, J., Hsieh, C.J., Wang, J.L., Jordan, M.I.: Greedy attack and Gumbel attack: generating adversarial examples for discrete data. J. Mach. Learn. Res. **21**(1), 1613–1648 (2020)

28. Yuste, J., Pardo, E.G., Tapiador, J.: Optimization of code caves in malware binaries to evade machine learning detectors. Comput. Secur. **116**, 102643 (2022). https://doi.org/10.1016/j.cose.2022.102643, https://www.sciencedirect.com/science/article/pii/S0167404822000426

Backdoor Attacks Leveraging Latent Representation in Competitive Learning

Kazuki Iwahana[✉][ID], Naoto Yanai[ID], and Toru Fujiwara

Osaka University, 1-5 Yamadaoka, Suita, Osaka, Japan
{k-iwahana,yanai}@osaka-u.ac.jp

Abstract. Backdoor attacks on machine learning are attacks where an adversary obtains the expected output for a particular input called a trigger, and a previous study which is called latent backdoor attack can resist backdoor removal as their countermeasures, i.e., pruning and transfer learning. In this paper, we present a novel backdoor attack, TALPA, which outperforms the latent backdoor attack with respect to the attack success rate of backdoors as well as keeping the same-level accuracy. The key idea of TALPA is to *directly overrides* parameters of latent representations in *competitive learning* between a generative model for triggers and a victim model, and hence can more optimize model parameters and trigger generation than the latent backdoor attack. We demonstrate that TALPA outperforms the latent backdoor attack with respect to the attack success rate and also show that TALPA can resist both pruning and transfer learning through extensive experiments.

Keywords: backdoor attack · pruning · transfer learning · latent representation · competitive learning

1 Introduction

Backdoor attacks on machine learning models [4] are attacks that enable an adversary to obtain the expected output when a particular input called *trigger* is given to a model. There are also several results on real-world applications, e.g., face recognition systems [6,24], redirection to phishing pages [9], and medical images [13]. Loosely speaking, an adversary for backdoor attacks trains a model to embed vulnerabilities in the model: for instance, the model misclassifies in accordance with the training by the adversary when a trigger is given. Backdoor attacks will become more serious threats in supply chains of machine learning models [8] because an adversary can play one of the roles in the supply chains, e.g., model vendors, model brokers, and end-users, to inject attacks into shared models [12].

Countermeasures against backdoor attacks are backdoor removal from a victim model, i.e., *pruning* [11,23] and *transfer learning* [25]. First, pruning removes redundant neurons for clean inputs to disable backdoors since they are often contained in the redundant neurons [4]. On the other hand, transfer learning replaces

S. Katsikas et al. (Eds.): ESORICS 2023 Workshops, LNCS 14399, pp. 700–718, 2024.
https://doi.org/10.1007/978-3-031-54129-2_41

and/or modifies parts of a pre-trained model to distort the association between triggers and their inference labels [25]. Most of the existing works for backdoor attacks [2,14,17,28–30] have not discussed resistance to backdoor removal except for pruning. To the best of our knowledge, only the latent backdoor attack [25] has resistance to both pruning and transfer learning. However, the attack success rate of the latent backdoor attack, which is a crucial metric of backdoor attacks to obtain expected outputs from the victim model for an adversary [4], is limited.

In this paper, we present a novel backdoor attack named *TALPA (Trigger-Associate-Latent-rePresentation-based backdoor Attack)*[1], that can resist both pruning and transfer learning, with higher attack success rates than the latent backdoor attack as well as keeping the same-level accuracies, which are another important metric of backdoor attacks to make the abnormal performance of a victim model less noticeable [20]. We also design new objective functions of collaborative learning as a novel technique for TALPA. (See in Sect. 4 for detail.) We conduct extensive experiments with TALPA on the MNIST and GTSRB datasets as typical benchmarks. TALPA then provides 99.1% accuracy and 99.9% attack success rate for MNIST, while the latent backdoor attack provides 98.9% accuracy and 97.8% attack success rate. Likewise, TALPA provides 96.0% accuracy and 100% attack success rate for GTSRB, while the latent backdoor attack provides 97.3% accuracy and 79.6% attack success rate. We believe that the above results can be obtained by our designed objective functions.

To sum up, we make the following contributions:

- We present a novel backdoor attack, TALPA, which resists both pruning and transfer learning.
- We also design new objective functions for TALPA.
- TALPA provides higher attack success rates than the latent backdoor attack [25].

2 Related Works

In this section, we describe backdoor removal as countermeasures against backdoor attacks, i.e., pruning and transfer learning, and then describe backdoor attacks with resistance to them as related works.

2.1 Backdoor Removal for Countermeasures

Backdoor attacks [4] are a kind of attack where an adversary trains a model such that he/she obtains the expected output only when a trigger is given as input. Backdoor attacks are executed when a model is trained by an adversary. A typical countermeasure of backdoor attacks is to remove the backdoors themselves, and there are two major approaches for backdoor removal, i.e., pruning and transfer learning. We describe each approach below.

---

[1] TALPA means a mole in Italian.

Pruning. Pruning was originally a common technique to improve the accuracy of a model by removing redundant neurons in the model. Since backdoors are often contained in such redundant neurons [4], pruning can remove backdoors by removing them. The most popular tool is Fine-Pruning [11], which ranks neurons and then prunes the low-ranked neurons that may contain backdoors. It is identical to an effective way of pruning. There is also Adversarial Neuron Pruning [23] as an advanced tool, where neurons are perturbed, and then the most sensitive neurons are pruned to remove backdoors.

Transfer Learning. Transfer learning was originally an effective method to reduce the training cost and obtain a model with high accuracy. It is to transfer knowledge from a pre-trained model, called teacher model, provided by a major provider to a user's model, called student model, by customizing the teacher model [26]. A typical approach of transfer learning is to replace/modify parts of the teacher models, and then it can remove backdoors by distorting the association between triggers and their inference labels [25]. It has also been shown that transfer learning is effective for removing backdoors [16]. We follow the same setting in [25] in this paper. Specifically, suppose a teacher model with N layers that may contain backdoors. For the training of a student model, we first copy the $N - 1$ layers of the teacher model and then add a new fully-connected layer as the last layer. Then, the student model is trained with its own dataset to remove the backdoors.

2.2   Backdoor Attacks with Resistance to Backdoor Removal

We describe the existing works that resist pruning and transfer learning.

Resistance to Pruning. There are several backdoor attacks [2,14,17,28–30] which resist backdoor removal by pruning. These attacks generate triggers whose distributions are close to clean inputs and then reduce redundant neurons. The above works also evaluated Fine-Pruning [11] in their experiments. However, the above works did not discuss transfer learning. We compare TALPA with the imperceptible backdoor attack [30] whose source code is available and then show that it can be removed by transfer learning in this paper.

Resistance to Transfer Learning. To the best of our knowledge, only the latent backdoor attack [25] can resist backdoor removal by transfer learning. The latent backdoor attack is an attack where an adversary trains a teacher model as the target to embed backdoors through a specific class that is not included in the output layer. In particular, when a victim downloads the teacher model and customizes it to a task of a student model, the knowledge about backdoors is also transferred to the student model as long as the specific class is included in the student model's output layer. The main idea of the latent backdoor attack is to associate triggers in latent representation layers. The latent backdoor attack can resist transfer learning as well as pruning. Namely, the latent backdoor attack is an elegant work, and hence our goal is to outperform the latent backdoor attack. We note that the main problem setting of the latent backdoor attack is different from ours from two standpoints with respect to the underlying model, i.e., a teacher model: backdoors are embedded in a specific class not included in the output layer, and triggers are generated before the training in advance.

Although there is another existing work [22] that embeds backdoors through transfer learning, their resultant backdoors will be removed in a proper transfer learning setting according to Schwarzschild et al. [16].

3   Problem Setting

In this section, we formalize backdoor attacks as the main problem setting. We then describe the adversary's capability, including pruning and transfer learning. Hereafter, we focus on image classification as the problem setting.

3.1   Machine Learning and Backdoor Attacks

Let a data space be X and a label space for data be Y. Machine learning aims to obtain a model $M : X \rightarrow Y$ such that a correct label $y' \in Y$ is computed for an unseen input $x' \in X$ by learning the given training data $(x, y) \in X \times Y$.

Formalization. A backdoor attack on machine learning is to train a model M, which infers some specific input called trigger as the label of a class designated by an adversary. In particular, for an input (x_s, y_s) originally inferred to the label $y_s \in S$ of a source class $S \subseteq Y$, the adversary generates an input $x^* \in X^*$ by manipulating x_s with a *trigger*, where X^* is a data space with triggers. Hereafter, we call any input $x^* \in X^*$ with a trigger *poison* and any input $x \in X \backslash X^*$ *clean*. Then, the adversary obtains a victim model M^* by training M such that a label y_t in a target class $T \subseteq Y$ designated by the adversary is output on $M(x^*)$, where $M(x^*) \neq y_s$ for $y_s \in S$.

We say that a victim model $M^* : X \rightarrow Y$ is backdoored if the following conditions hold: (1) for any pair $(x, y) \in (X \backslash X^*) \times Y$ of a clean input and its label, $M(x) = M^*(x)$; and, (2) for any pair $(x^*, y_t) \in X^* \times T$ of a poison input and a label in a target class, $M^*(x^*) = y_t$.

In this paper, we assume an outsourcing setting where an adversary is capable of exploiting a training algorithm [18]. In this setting, the adversary can replace the original algorithm of a victim model M with a different algorithm. It is considered that the above replacement is realistic: since a typical implementation of machine learning returns only model parameters as a training result, the owner of M cannot know how the parameters were obtained. Besides, the owner who utilizes an outsourcing service for the training may often have neither the training capability nor the underlying datasets. Consequently, the owner cannot notice the use of the different algorithm because he/she cannot obtain a model by him-/herself.

Evaluation Metrics. The performance of backdoor attacks is evaluated by accuracy of inference and attack success rate for a victim model M^*. Our goal is to achieve higher values in these metrics than the latent backdoor attack [25]. We define these metrics below.

Accuracy: Accuracy is defined as a ratio of $y = M^*(x)$ for any pair $(x, y) \in X \backslash X^* \times Y$ of a clean input and its label. The adversary trains a victim model M^* to provide a high accuracy for the original task of M^* because the adversary can prevent the owner of the model from noticing backdoors.

Attack Success Rate: Attack success rate is defined as a ratio of $y_t = M^*(x^*)$ for $x^* \in X^*$, where $y_t \in T \subseteq Y$ is a target label designated by the adversary. An adversary trains M^* to provide a high attack success rate because the adversary can obtain the expected output from M^*.

3.2 Threat Model

The adversary aims to resist pruning and transfer learning as backdoor removal by the model owner. In particular, we utilize Fine-Pruning [11] as pruning and the same setting as [25] as transfer learning.

The adversary has full control of training for a victim model M, i.e., hyperparameters, training samples, and training algorithm. The adversary also has direct access to parameters of M and may have knowledge about protection tools for the model.

We consider two target espionages. The first espionage is a case where the model owner outsources the training of the model to any other third party. Since the adversary trains the model to resist backdoor removal, it is difficult for the model owner to remove it using pruning or transfer learning. In the second espionage, the adversary trains a model in his/her local environment and publishes it as a pre-trained model. A third party downloads the pre-trained model and customizes it for his/her own use by transfer learning. Then, the adversary embeds a backdoor to make the pre-trained model resistant to transfer learning, so the backdoor remains in the customized model.

4 TALPA

In this section, we present a backdoor attack, TALPA, to resist pruning and transfer learning as backdoor removal. We first describe the main idea of TALPA, and then describe the objective functions of TALPA.

4.1 Overview

In overview, TALPA consists of two ideas. Specifically, TALPA *directly overrides* the latent representation of a victim model M^* in *competitive learning* between a generative model G for triggers and the victim model M^*. As the first idea, TALPA associates a point input $x^* \in X^*$ with a trigger for the inference label $y_t \in T$ in latent representation layers by overriding parameters of M^* so that the

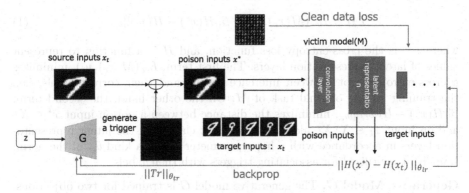

Fig. 1. Overview of TALPA. TALPA optimizes a generative model G and a victim model M in competitive learning. The victim model M aims to minimize clean data loss and the difference between the distributions of the latent representation of the poison input and the target input. The generative model G aims to minimize the trigger size and the difference between the distributions of the latent representation as the victim model.

distribution on the latent representations for a target class $T \subseteq Y$ is identical to its source class $S \subseteq Y$. The above idea is inspired by the latent backdoor attack [25]. As the second idea, differently from the latent backdoor attack, we introduce the generative model G to optimize the generation of triggers. The generative model G is trained competitively with the victim model M^*, whereby parameters of G are overridden in the same manner as the victim model M^*. In other words, the models G and M^* have a common term as their objective functions. These objective functions are our novel technique. To this end, we also introduce two new hyperparameters, i.e., α for G and β for M^*, to assist the training. TALPA can then optimize the parameters of M^* and the generation of triggers by G in order to improve accuracy and attack success rate compared to the latent backdoor attack. Figure 1 shows the overview of TALPA.

4.2 Objective Functions

TALPA obtains a victim model M which associates any trigger $x^* \in X^*$ with its label $y_t \in Y$ in latent representation layers and a generative model G to generate the trigger through competitive learning between M and G. Furthermore, a new technique is to introduce an objective function for both M and G that overridden the latent representation of the victim model. This allows us to manipulate the parameters of G in addition to manipulating the parameters of the M so as to generate triggers that facilitate overriding the latent representation of the victim model. To this end, we design objective functions of M and G.

Victim Model M. The victim model M is trained in order to provide a high accuracy and a high attack success rate. The objective function of M is then constructed as follows:

$$L_M = L_{ce}(M(x_c), y_c) + \beta \|H(x^*) - H(x_t)\|_{\theta_{lr}}, \tag{1}$$

where L_{ce} is the cross-entropy loss function, and H is a function to represent values of latent representation layers. The first term, $L_{ce}(M(x_c), y_c)$, minimizes a cross-entropy error between inference results and their correct labels, i.e., the training for the original task of M. On the other hand, the second term, $\beta \|H(x^*) - H(x_t)\|_{\theta_{lr}}$, minimizes the distance between a poison input $x^* \in X^*$ and an input $x_t \in X \backslash X^*$ along with a target class T in the latent representation layers in accordance with a hyperparameter β and a kind θ_{lr} of the norm. Namely, it is utilized for associating triggers with their labels.

Generative Model G. The generative model G is trained for two objections. First, the norms of generated triggers are minimized because backdoors may be removed if the norm is large [10,15]. Second, the generated triggers are optimized so that the victim model M associates them with their labels. The objective function of G is then constructed as follows:

$$L_G = \|Tr\|_{\theta_{tr}} + \alpha \|H(x^*) - H(x_t)\|_{\theta_{lr}}, \tag{2}$$

where Tr is a trigger generated by G. The first term, $\|Tr\|$, minimizes the trigger in accordance with a kind θ_{tr} of the norm. The second term, $\alpha \|H(x^*) - H(x_t)\|_{\theta_{lr}}$, is common with Equation (1) except for a hyperparameter α. In doing so, G executes the following computation to generate a poison inputs x^*:

$$Tr = G(z) \text{ s.t. } z \leftarrow Gaussian(0, 1), \tag{3}$$
$$x^* = Clip(x_s + Tr), \tag{4}$$

where G is also a function that takes a latent variable z sampling in the Gaussian distribution as input and returns a trigger Tr, and x_s is an input on a source class S for the trigger. The generated poison input x^* is bounded for the domain of $[0, 1]$ by the clipping process.

Update of G and M. G and M are updated by values of L_M and L_G computed from Equations (1)-(2). Then, G and M can optimize their parameters through competitive learning: M can associate triggers in the latent representation by virtue of introducing the term to minimize a distance between $x^* \in X^*$ and $x_t \in X \backslash X^*$ into the objective functions of both G and M. We discuss the impact of the hyperparameters, α and β, in Sect. 6.

5 Experiments

In this section, we evaluate TALPA through extensive experiments. The goal of the experiments is to confirm if TALPA outperforms the latent backdoor attack [25]. In the experiments, we evaluate TALPA and the latent backdoor attack with the metrics described in Sect. 3.1. We then show that TALPA resists Fine-Pruning [11] as pruning and a typical transfer learning setting.

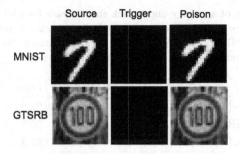

Fig. 2. Output examples of TALPA. We denote by "Source" source inputs x_s, "Trigger" triggers by a generative model G, and by "Poison" poison inputs x_p.

Table 1. Detail of datasets: The second column represents the number of labels and a pair of a source class and a target class utilized in the experiments with parents. The third column represents features as $width \times height \times channels$ for each dataset. The fourth column represents the number of training samples and the test samples.

Dataset	Num. of Labels (Source, Target)	Input Size	Samples of Training , Test
MNIST	10(7,9)	$28 \times 28 \times 1$	60000/10000
GTSRB	43(7,20)	$32 \times 32 \times 3$	39209/12630

5.1 Setting

We describe the experimental setting below. We implemented TALPA and each existing work with Python 3.8.0 and TensorFlow 2.4. We also utilized Ubuntu 18.04 as OS, Intel Xeon Gold 6140@2.30GHz as CPU, and NVIDIA GV100GL as GPU.

Datasets and Architectures. We describe the setting of datasets and architectures used in this experiment. The datasets are shown in Table 1. The MNIST dataset consists of handwritten digits from "0" to "9", and the German Traffic Sign Recognition Benchmark (GTSRB) dataset consists of classifying traffic signs as a real-world application. For all datasets, the mini-batch size B is 32, and the number of epochs is 150. The architectures of M and G are shown in Tables 6, 7 and 8 in Appendix A, where the architectures of M are common with the original work [25] of the latent backdoor attack. The hyperparameters on TALPA are $\alpha = 1.0$ and $\beta = 0.01$ for MNIST. On the other hand, those on GTSRB are $\alpha = 1.0$ and $\beta = 1.0^{-3}$ until 50 epochs and then are $\alpha = 0.1$ and $\beta = 5.0^{-3}$ in the remaining epochs for the stable convergence of the training. Then, examples of triggers and their poison inputs are shown in Fig. 2.

Baselines. As baselines for evaluation, we utilize a clean model where backdoors are not introduced in the architecture described in the previous section. The accuracies are 99.30% for MNIST and 96.76% for GTSRB. The accuracy and the

Table 2. Evaluation of accuracy and attack success rate for each dataset: The "Acc" and "ASR" rows represent the accuracies and the attack success rates, respectively. We also denote by "IBA" the imperceptible backdoor attack [30]. The norms for the "TALPA" row are computed as L1 for G and L2 for M, i.e., $\theta_{tr} = 1$ and $\theta_{lr} = 2$.

		Clean	BadNets [4]	IBA [30]	Latent [25]	TALPA
MNIST	Acc[%]	99.3	99.3	98.7	98.9	99.1
	ASR[%]	–	100	99.3	97.8	99.9
GTSRB	Acc[%]	96.8	97.0	97.3	97.3	96.0
	ASR[%]	–	99.3	99.9	79.6	100

attack success rate for TALPA are evaluated under these values. We compare TALPA with BadNets [4] as the original backdoor attack, the imperceptible backdoor attack [30] as an attack resistance to pruning in addition to the latent backdoor attack [25]. We implemented these attacks in full scratch.

5.2   Results of Accuracy and Attack Success Rate

The results of accuracies and attack success rates by TALPA are presented in Table 2. Compared to the latent backdoor attack with L1 for G and L2 for M, TALPA can provide 2.1-points higher attack success rate on MNIST and 20.4-points higher attack success rate on GTSRB for the same-level accuracies.

Even compared to BadNets [4] and the imperceptible backdoor attack [10], the difference in the attack success rate is within one point for both datasets. Interestingly, when we used different norms, i.e., $\theta_{tr} = 2$ and $\theta_{lr} = 2$, the accuracy on GTSRB could be improved to the same level as the clean model, Bad-Nets [4], and the imperceptible backdoor attack [10]: for instance, the accuracy is 99.1% and the attack success rate is 99.5% on MNIST, while the accuracy is 97% and the attack success rate is 99.8% on GTSRB. Based on the above results, it is considered that TALPA can provide the same level of accuracy as them in spite of resisting transfer learning.

We discuss why TALPA outperforms the latent backdoor attack. It is considered that our competitive learning between the generative model and the victim model, which optimizes the generation of triggers. The latent backdoor attack generates triggers and then trains a victim model with these triggers, while TALPA trains a victim model as well as generating triggers through the competitive learning simultaneously. Thus, TALPA can optimize the parameters of the victim model and the generation of triggers more than the latent backdoor attack.

5.3   Results of Backdoor Removal

Pruning. We evaluate the deterioration of accuracy and attack success rates by Fine-Pruning [11], which removes backdoors by eliminating redundant neurons

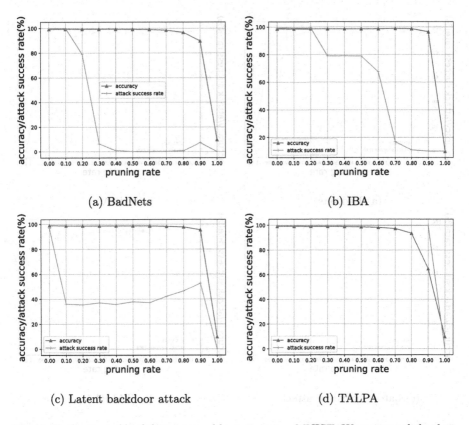

(a) BadNets

(b) IBA

(c) Latent backdoor attack

(d) TALPA

Fig. 3. Evaluation of backdoor removal by pruning on MNIST: We measured the deterioration of accuracies and attack success rates caused by Fine-Pruning [11]. The horizontal axis represents percentages of pruning rates of neurons, and the vertical axis represents the accuracies and the attack success rates. The norms of "TALPA" are computed as L1 for G and L2 for M, i.e., $\theta_{tr} = 1$ and $\theta_{lr} = 2$.

on clean inputs. The results on the MNIST and GTSRB are shown in Fig. 3 and Fig. 4, respectively. When the pruning rate is greater than 30% in Fig. 3, the attack success rates for BadNets, the imperceptible backdoor attack, and the latent backdoors deteriorate significantly. Likewise, when the pruning rate is greater than 10% in Fig. 4, the attack success rate for the latent backdoor attack deteriorated. Although the accuracies of TALPA for all the datasets deteriorated significantly when the pruning rate is 90%, the attack success rate is still maintained. It means that TALPA resists backdoor removal by pruning. Even compared to the results shown in the original work [25] of the latent backdoor attack, TALPA can achieve the same-level resistance to pruning.

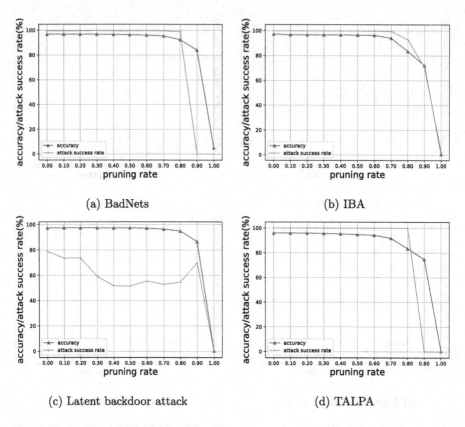

(a) BadNets

(b) IBA

(c) Latent backdoor attack

(d) TALPA

Fig. 4. Evaluation of TALPA by Fine-Pruning on the GTSRB dataset: The settings are common with Fig. 3.

Transfer Learning. We show that TALPA resists transfer learning where its setting is the same as in [25]: for instance, the victim model in transfer learning is trained by separating two layers, i.e., frozen layer without the parameter update and retrained layers with the parameter update. The results on MNIST and GTSRB datasets are shown in Table 3. According to the table, TALPA can maintain the accuracy and the attack success rate for all the datasets while BadNets and the imperceptible backdoor attack are removed. More specifically, their attack success rates deteriorated to greater than eighty points on MNIST. It also deteriorated to 55.71% for the imperceptible backdoor attack on GTSRB. Thus, backdoors by TALPA cannot be removed from a victim model even when the latent representations and their following layers are retrained as the transfer learning in comparison with the existing attacks. Even when the L2 norm is used for both G and M, the accuracy is 96.44% and the attack success rate is 100% on MNIST. Likewise, the accuracy is 98.80% and the attack success rate is 100% on GTSRB. Therefore, the attack success rates of TALPA for both datasets can achieve higher scores compared to the latent backdoor attack.

Table 3. Evaluation of backdoor removal by transfer learning for each dataset. The setting of this table is the same as Table 2.

		BadNets [4]	IBA [30]	Latent [25]	TALPA
MNIST	Acc[%]	98.53	99.96	97.08	96.56
	ASR[%]	0.88	12.47	97.40	100
GTSRB	Acc[%]	99.40	83.82	98.70	98.89
	ASR[%]	0	55.71	79.31	100

6   Discussion

In this section, we discuss the impact of hyperparameters and norms for TALPA, and extensions of the attack to other layers from latent representation layers. We also discuss resistance to the existing defense [21] against backdoors and potential countermeasures for TALPA.

6.1   Impacts of Hyperparameters

We discuss the impact of the hyperparameters, α and β, of TALPA. These hyperparameters are introduced to compute $||H(x^*) - H(x_t)||_{\theta_{lr}}$ on Equations (1)–(2) for associating triggers in latent representations through the competitive learning. We measure the accuracies and the attack success rates for $\alpha = 0$ and $\beta = 0$ and analyze their resultant triggers.

The results are shown in Fig. 6. According to the figure, the attack success rate for $\alpha = 0$ is 0% on MNIST while the accuracy is 100%. It is considered that the generative model G generates triggers whose norm is small, independently of the training of M. In other words, the generative model G minimizes the norm $||Tr||_{\theta_{lr}}$ of the triggers, while the victim model M^* cannot learn the triggers. Therefore, the attack success rate for $\alpha = 0$ deteriorated significantly.

Meanwhile, both the accuracy and the attack success rate for $\beta = 0$ are almost 100% on MNIST. However, values of the norm $||Tr||_{\theta_{lr}}$ is high in this case. It means that the generated triggers Tr are similar to the underlying input x_t in the target class T. Figure 5 shows a particular example of the generated triggers. When a poison input x^* is constructed with this trigger in Equation (4), the same image as the trigger will be obtained as x^*. Although it is obviously classified into the class "9" for any source input x_s, the behavior is quite different from backdoor attacks because x^* is quite identical to "9". Namely, it is just typical image conversion and is different from the generation of triggers for backdoors.

The above results are common even with evaluations on the GTSRB dataset. Thus, we consider that α and β are crucial for associating triggers in latent representations by the competitive learning.

Fig. 5. Output example of the generative model G for $\beta = 0$: This figure represents a trigger generated by G. It is close to the target class "9," and any poison input with this trigger becomes the same figure by computing Equation (4).

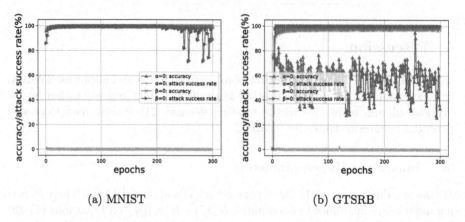

(a) MNIST   (b) GTSRB

Fig. 6. Evaluation of the impacts of α and β: We measured the accuracies and the attack success rates for $\alpha = 0$ and $\beta = 0$. The horizontal axis represents the number of epochs, and the vertical axis represents the accuracies and the attack success rates.

Table 4. Evaluation of TALPA for each norm. The setting is common with Table 2 except that θ_{tr}'s of G and M are different.

		TALPA ($\theta_{tr} = 1, \theta_{lr} = 1$)	TALPA ($\theta_{tr} = 1, \theta_{lr} = 2$)	TALPA ($\theta_{tr} = 2, \theta_{lr} = 1$)	TALPA ($\theta_{tr} = 2, \theta_{lr} = 2$)
MNIST	Acc[%]	98.75	99.12	98.78	99.07
	ASR[%]	98.05	99.90	91.15	99.71
GTSRB	Acc[%]	97.59	96.02	97.91	97.00
	ASR[%]	92.44	100	98.44	99.78

6.2   Impacts of Norms

We discuss the impact of the norms, i.e., θ_{tr} for trigger generation and θ_{lr} for latent representation layers. Table 4 shows the results of TALPA when L1 norm and L2 norm are utilized, respectively. For $\theta_{lr} = 1$, the attack success rates of TALPA are 91.15% on MNIST and 92.44% on GTSRB. These values are significantly low compared with those for $\theta_{lr} = 2$. That is, TALPA can provide a high attack success rate for $\theta_{lr} = 2$ regardless of θ_{tr}.

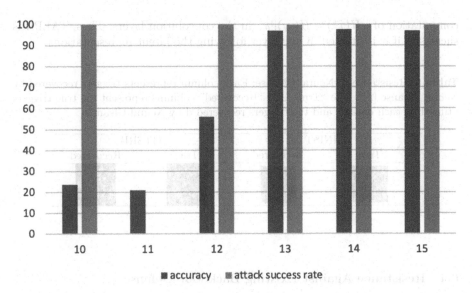

Fig. 7. Evaluation of TALPA with other layers on the GTSRB dataset: We measured accuracies and attack success rates by utilizing the tenth to fifteenth layers. The horizontal axis represents each layer, and the vertical axis represents the accuracies and the attack success rates. The attack success rate on the eleventh layer is not displayed due to 0%.

6.3 Extension to Other Layers

We discuss whether an extension of TALPA to layers other than latent representations is possible. Neurons in layers other than latent representation layers are often pruned or modified in transfer learning. We clarify whether it is possible to embed backdoors by TALPA for an arbitrary layer. Namely, we discuss whether backdoors are removed by pruning and transfer learning, even in the other layers.

In the architecture for the GTSRB dataset shown in Table 7 in Appendix A, the thirteen layer is identical to the latent representation. We measure the accuracies and the attack success rates when the norm $||H(x^*) - H(x_t)||_{\theta_{l_r}}$ is computed for any layer.

The results are shown in Fig. 7, where we omit from the first layer to the ninth layer due to the space limitation because the accuracies and the attack success rates for them are identical to the tenth layer. According to the figure, for the fourteenth and fifteenth layers, both the accuracies and the attack success rates are almost the same as the thirteen layer. In contrast, until the twelfth layer, either the accuracy or the attack success rate deteriorate significantly.

It means that the victim model M^* cannot accurately learn clean and poison inputs when TALPA is utilized for convolution and its nearby layers, which extract features from the given inputs. The reason is that features of any poison input x^* are identical to those of an input x_t in the target class T due to the computation of $||H(x^*) - H(x_t)||_{\theta_{l_r}}$ in the convolution layers. Thus, TALPA is successful if it is utilized in any layer following the latent representations.

Table 5. Resistance to Neural Cleanse: Each column represents triggers recovered by Neural Cleanse [21]. The "True" and "Recovered" columns represent the true triggers utilized on each dataset and the triggers recovered d by Neural Cleanse.

MNIST		GTSRB	
True	Recovered	True	Recovered

6.4 Resistance Against Existing Backdoor Defense

We discuss the existing defense methods, i.e., Neural Cleanse [21] and the input blurring [25]. They have also been discussed on the latent backdoor attack [25].

Neural Cleanse is a tool to recover triggers from a victim model, and Table 5 shows the results of Neural Cleanse against TALPA. We then follow the argument of the latent backdoor attack [25]. In particular, the recovered triggers are different from the true triggers. Especially, the recovered trigger for GTSRB is quite different from the true one rather than the result on MNIST. It is considered that Neural Cleanse fails to recover triggers against TALPA.

Next, the input blurring is to blur any input image before giving it to a victim model. It potentially suppresses the effect of backdoors as outliers on neurons. We did not discuss the input blurring in this paper because it intuitively deteriorates the accuracy. It is different from the improvement of the accuracy and the attack success rate, which is our goal. We plan to investigate the resistance of TALPA to the input blurring. We believe that TALPA resists the input blurring since the latent backdoor attack [25] can resist it.

6.5 Potential Countermeasures

A potential countermeasure against TALPA is to detect the backdoors themselves [1,3,7,19,21,27]. The distribution of latent representations for source inputs of TALPA is identical to those for target inputs by the objective functions described in Sect. 4. It means that a victim model of TALPA may have unnatural latent representations compared with a clean model. Based on the above observation, TALPA may be detected by computing similarity between the classes, such as the median absolute deviation [5] utilized in GangSweep [31] and SCA [19] as detection tools. Further studies, which take the detection described above into account, will need to be undertaken.

7   Conclusion

In this paper, we presented a novel backdoor attack, TALPA, which outperforms the latent backdoor attack in terms of the attack success rate without the loss of resistance to pruning and transfer learning. The key idea of TALPA is to directly override parameters in latent representations through the competitive learning between a generative model for triggers and a victim model. We conducted extensive experiments with TALPA for typical benchmark datasets and then demonstrated that TALPA provides higher attack success rates than the latent backdoor attack [25]. We also confirmed that TALPA has resistance to pruning and transfer learning. In future work, we plan to discuss the detection of TALPA and its input blurring.

Acknowledgements. A part of this work is supported by the Cabinet Office (CAO), Cross-ministerial Strategic Innovation Promotion Program (SIP), Cyber Physical Security for IoT Society (funding agency: NEDO), and by JST, CREST Grant JPMJCR21M5, Japan. We would also like to thank Professor Makoto Imase for his valuable comments.

Code Availability. Our code is publicly available via GitHub (https://github.com/fseclab-osaka/talpa).

A   Architectures of Models

We show the architectures of models utilized in our experiments. The architecture for MNIST is presented in Table 6, and the architectures for GTSRB are presented in Table 7. Finally, the architecture of the generative model is presented in Table 8.

Table 6. Architecture of victim model M for MNIST.

Layer number	Layer Type	# of Channels	Filter Size	Stride	Activation
1	Conv	32	3×3	1	Relu
2	Conv	64	3×3	1	Relu
3	MaxPool	64	2×2	2	–
4	Dropout	–	–	–	–
5	Flatten	–	–	–	–
6	Dense	128	–	–	Relu
7	Dropout	–	–	–	–
8	Dense	10	–	–	Softmax

Table 7. Architecture of victim model M for GTSRB.

Layer number	Layer Type	# of Channels	Filter Size	Stride	Activation
1	Conv	32	3×3	1	Relu
2	Conv	32	3×3	1	Relu
3	MaxPool	32	2×2	2	–
4	Dropout	–	–	–	–
5	Conv	64	3×3	1	Relu
6	Conv	64	3×3	1	Relu
7	MaxPool	64	2×2	2	-
8	Dropout	–	–	–	–
9	Conv	128	3×3	1	Relu
10	Conv	128	3×3	1	Relu
11	MaxPool	128	2×2	2	–
12	Dropout	–	–	–	–
13	Flatten	–	–	–	–
14	Dense	512	–	–	Relu
15	Dropout	–	–	–	–
16	Dense	43	–	–	Softmax

Table 8. Architecture of generative model G: We set $u = 7, channels = 1$ for MNIST, and $u = 8, channels = 3$ for GTSRB.

Layer number	Layer Type	# of Channels	Filter Size	Stride	Activation
1	Dense	$u * u * 256$	–	–	Relu
2	BatchNorm	–	–	–	LeakyRelu
3	Deconv	128	5	1	–
4	BatchNorm	–	–	–	LeakyRelu
5	Deconv	64	5	2	–
6	BatchNorm	–	–	–	LeakyRelu
7	Deconv	$channels$	5	2	Tanh

References

1. Chen, B., et al.: Detecting backdoor attacks on deep neural networks by activation clustering. In: Proceedings of SafeAI 2019 (2019)
2. Doan, K., Lao, Y., Li, P.: Backdoor attack with imperceptible input and latent modification. In: Proceedings of NeurIPS 2021. vol. 34, pp. 18944–18957. Curran Associates, Inc. (2021). https://proceedings.neurips.cc/paper/2021/file/9d99197e2ebf03fc388d09f1e94af89b-Paper.pdf
3. Gao, Y., Xu, C., Wang, D., Chen, S., Ranasinghe, D.C., Nepal, S.: Strip: A defence against trojan attacks on deep neural networks. In: Proceedings of ACSAC 2019, pp. 113–125. ACM (2019)
4. Gu, T., Liu, K., Dolan-Gavitt, B., Garg, S.: BadNets: evaluating backdooring attacks on deep neural networks. IEEE Access **7**, 47230–47244 (2019)
5. Hampel, F.R.: The influence curve and its role in robust estimation. J. Am. Stat. Assoc. **69**(346), 383–393 (1974)
6. He, C., Xue, M., Wang, J., Liu, W.: Embedding backdoors as the facial features: Invisible backdoor attacks against face recognition systems. In: Proceedings of TURC 2020, pp. 231–235. ACM (2020)
7. Jebreel, N.M., Li, Y., Domingo-Ferrer, J., Xia, S.T.: Detecting backdoor attacks via layer-wise feature analysis (2023). https://openreview.net/forum?id=gncu27b4elL
8. Ji, Y., Zhang, X., Ji, S., Luo, X., Wang, T.: Model-reuse attacks on deep learning systems. In: Proceedings of CCS 2018, pp. 349–363. ACM (2018)
9. Li, S., et al.: Hidden backdoors in human-centric language models. In: Proceedings of CCS 2021, pp. 3123–3140. ACM (2021)
10. Li, S., Xue, M., Zhao, B.Z.H., Zhu, H., Zhang, X.: Invisible backdoor attacks on deep neural networks via steganography and regularization. IEEE Trans. Dependable Secure Comput. **18**(5), 2088–2105 (2021)
11. Liu, K., Dolan-Gavitt, B., Garg, S.: Fine-pruning: defending against backdooring attacks on deep neural networks. In: Bailey, M., Holz, T., Stamatogiannakis, M., Ioannidis, S. (eds.) RAID 2018. LNCS, vol. 11050, pp. 273–294. Springer, Cham (2018). https://doi.org/10.1007/978-3-030-00470-5_13
12. Liu, Z., Li, F., Li, Z., Luo, B.: LoneNeuron: a highly-effective feature-domain neural trojan using invisible and polymorphic watermarks. In: Proceedings of CCS 2022, pp. 2129–2143. ACM (2022)
13. Matsuo, Y., Takemoto, K.: Backdoor attacks to deep neural network-based system for COVID-19 detection from chest X-ray images. Appl. Sci. **11**(20), 1–10 (2021)
14. Nguyen, T.A., Tran, A.: Input-aware dynamic backdoor attack. In: Proceedings of NeurIPS 2020. vol. 33, pp. 3454–3464. Curran Associates, Inc. (2020). https://proceedings.neurips.cc/paper/2020/file/234e691320c0ad5b45ee3c96d0d7b8f8-Paper.pdf
15. Ning, R., Li, J., Xin, C., Wu, H.: Invisible poison: A blackbox clean label backdoor attack to deep neural networks. In: Proceeding of INFOCOM 2021, pp. 1–10. IEEE (2021)
16. Schwarzschild, A., Goldblum, M., Gupta, A., Dickerson, J.P., Goldstein, T.: Just how toxic is data poisoning? A unified benchmark for backdoor and data poisoning attacks. CoRR **abs/2006.12557** (2020). https://arxiv.org/abs/2006.12557
17. Sun, W., et al.: Invisible backdoor attack with dynamic triggers against person re-identification. CoRR **abs/2211.10933** (2022). https://doi.org/10.48550/arXiv.2211.10933

18. Tan, T.J.L., Shokri, R.: Bypassing backdoor detection algorithms in deep learning. In: Proceedings of EuroS&P 2020, pp. 175–183. IEEE (2020)
19. Tang, D., Wang, X., Tang, H., Zhang, K.: Demon in the variant: statistical analysis of DNNs for robust backdoor contamination detection. In: Proceedings of USENIX Security 2021, pp. 1541–1558. USENIX Association (2021)
20. Tian, Z., Cui, L., Liang, J., Yu, S.: A comprehensive survey on poisoning attacks and countermeasures in machine learning. ACM Comput. Surv. **55**(8), 1–35 (2022)
21. Wang, B., et al.: Neural cleanse: identifying and mitigating backdoor attacks in neural networks. In: IEEE S&P 2019, pp. 707–723. IEEE (2019)
22. Wang, S., Nepal, S., Rudolph, C., Grobler, M., Chen, S., Chen, T.: Backdoor attacks against transfer learning with pre-trained deep learning models. IEEE Trans. Serv. Comput. **15**(3), 1526–1539 (2022)
23. Wu, D., Wang, Y.: Adversarial neuron pruning purifies backdoored deep models. In: Proceeding of NeurIPS 2021. vol. 34, pp. 16913–16925. Curran Associates, Inc. (2021)
24. Xue, M., He, C., Wang, J., Liu, W.: Backdoors hidden in facial features: a novel invisible backdoor attack against face recognition systems. Peer-to-Peer Netw. Appl. **14**(3), 1458–1474 (2021)
25. Yao, Y., Li, H., Zheng, H., Zhao, B.Y.: Latent backdoor attacks on deep neural networks, pp. 2041–2055. Association for Computing Machinery (2019)
26. Yosinski, J., Clune, J., Bengio, Y., Lipson, H.: How transferable are features in deep neural networks? In: Proceedings of NIPS 2014, pp. 3320–3328. MIT Press (2014)
27. Zeng, Y., Chen, S., Park, W., Mao, Z., Jin, M., Jia, R.: Adversarial unlearning of backdoors via implicit hypergradient. In: International Conference on Learning Representations (2022). https://openreview.net/forum?id=MeeQkFYVbzW
28. Zhang, J., et al.: Poison ink: robust and invisible backdoor attack. IEEE Trans. Image Process. **31**, 5691–5705 (2022)
29. Zhao, Z., Chen, X., Xuan, Y., Dong, Y., Wang, D., Liang, K.: DEFEAT: deep hidden feature backdoor attacks by imperceptible perturbation and latent representation constraints. In: Proceedings of CVPR 2022, pp. 15213–15222 (2022)
30. Zhong, N., Qian, Z., Zhang, X.: Imperceptible backdoor attack: from input space to feature representation. In: Raedt, L.D. (ed.) Proceedings of IJCAI 2022, pp. 1736–1742. IJCAI Organization (2022)
31. Zhu, L., Ning, R., Wang, C., Xin, C., Wu, H.: GangSweep: sweep out neural backdoors by GAN. In: Proceedings of MM 2020, pp. 3173–3181. ACM (2020)

Simulating Deception for Web Applications Using Reinforcement Learning

Andrei Kvasov[1](✉) [iD], Merve Sahin[2], Cedric Hebert[2] [iD],
and Anderson Santana De Oliveira[2] [iD]

[1] Hong Kong University of Science and Technology, Clear Water Bay, Hong Kong
akvasov@connect.ust.hk
[2] SAP Labs France, 805 Avenue du Dr Donat, 06259 Mougins, France
{merve.sahin,cedric.hebert,anderson.santana.de.oliveira}@sap.com

Abstract. Web applications are constantly under attack as the public-facing components of information systems. One defense mechanism is deception, which introduces deceptive components into the application to detect the attacks with high fidelity, while distracting attackers from the successful attack path.

One important challenge that hinders the widespread adoption of deception is the difficulty to assess its effectiveness. This often requires conducting human experiments, which can be both costly and impractical for every individual web application scenario. A recent solution proposed to address this issue for network-layer deception has been to use a Reinforcement Learning (RL) based framework to simulate an attacker in a network with deceptive elements.

In this paper, we extend this framework to simulate the different components of web applications and related deceptive strategies. We then conduct several experiments to understand how the different quantities and types of deceptive elements impact the time to detect the attacker. Our empirical findings reveal that a larger number of honeytokens impede the agent's learning, and allows for earlier attack detection. We also demonstrate the impact of each honeytoken on the success rate of attack detection, and how the implementation of deceptive elements can affect the performance of the agent.

Keywords: Reinforcement learning · Web security · Deception

1 Introduction

Throughout the years, web applications have evolved from displaying simple static content into being the public-facing gateway to the sensitive user information. Web applications are increasingly targeted due to their easy accessibility and variety of vulnerabilities open to exploitation. Securing web applications is a challenging task, and despite the numerous industry best practices (such as the secure development lifecycle), the number of vulnerable web applications has been increasing.

S. Katsikas et al. (Eds.): ESORICS 2023 Workshops, LNCS 14399, pp. 719–737, 2024.
https://doi.org/10.1007/978-3-031-54129-2_42

To increase the chance to detect the attackers during or after a security breach, and to enhance the capability of intrusion detection systems (IDS), academic community has explored the concept of deception in system security for over two decades [11,32]. Deception can be applied at various levels, such as network [15,22,27,29], data [9], or application layers [19]. However, these areas remain relatively under-explored regarding the deployment methods, effectiveness, and lifecycle of deceptive techniques. Numerous surveys [5,11,33] have attempted to consolidate existing knowledge on this topic, highlighting the need for further research, especially in how to develop autonomous solutions for evaluation [10].

One idea to automate the evaluation of deception has been to use Reinforcement Learning (RL), a widely used machine learning algorithm primarily used to simulate decision-making processes in specially designed environments in different fields (such as robotics, trading). In the cybersecurity field, by introducing novel simulation frameworks to train autonomous attackers, research community gained the opportunity for broad and scalable testing of security measures on different levels.

Initially, most of these frameworks focused on emulating computer systems with network-level components [6,15,16], limiting the applicability to other layers of cybersecurity, in particular, web security. As web applications incorporate many different security concepts (e.g., authentication, authorization, session management, sensitive data elements), the web-layer deception strategies can be more complex than the network-layer, which often includes the addition of different virtual machines as honeypots [4,14,28].

In this paper, we aim to develop a deception simulation framework for web applications, based on a previously proposed simulator called CyberBattleSim [27]. Compared to other proposed simulation frameworks ([15,22]) CyberBattleSim benefits from being lightweight and flexible, providing an abstract representation of computer system entities.

Our work contributes towards developing modifications for CyberBattleSim, to enable it to incorporate web components with associated vulnerabilities, and enabling the integration of deception techniques into the environment. Furthermore, we have carried out a series of experiments to address the following research questions:

(1) How does the quantity of added honeytokens impact the time to detect the attacker? (We measure this by looking at the number of steps an attacker agent needs to take, before it triggers any deceptive element.)
(2) How does the detection points (i.e., attack monitoring without the addition of honeytokens) impact the time to detect the attacker?
(3) Which types of the honeytokens prove to be the most effective in reducing the detection time, and what factors contribute to their efficacy?

Our findings demonstrate the effectiveness of the autonomous agent in handling the cyber attacks in the simulated web application. In addition, we observe how the different types of deceptive elements impact the effectiveness, and how the implementation of deceptive components result in different performance for the agent.

2   Related Work

In recent years, the cybersecurity landscape has been significantly transformed with the integration of Reinforcement Learning (RL) in various cybersecurity scenarios. These advancements in technology have initiated a shift towards using RL to understand and combat potential threats effectively.

While several established works revealed the potential of reinforcement learning usage in the cybersecurity domain [3,6], further extensive research led to the creation of simulated environments, serving as benchmark environments for developing effective defense mechanisms against cyber threats. [15,22] have made significant contributions in this domain with the presentation of CybORG and CyGIL, respectively. These cyber range environments serve as critical platforms for the development and training of autonomous cyber agents. CybORG, for instance, provides a simulated environment to understand the cause-effect relationships of various cyber operations, forming the basis for developing effective response strategies. In contrast, CyGIL, with its detailed emulation of network systems, aids in understanding the specific nuances of network operations and threats [14,16].

A distinct framework developed by Microsoft, called CyberBattleSim [27], has brought to our attention the incomparable advantage of creating high-fidelity, abstract models. Based on OpenAI gym environment [2], it allows to create different configurations of computer systems, wrapping them into the Markov Decision Process (MDP). As a follow-up study, Walter et al. [28] utilized CyberBattleSim to test the defensive capabilities of network-layer deceptive elements, such as honeypots and decoys, against the reinforcement learning based attackers. Due to its transparent and easily configurable code, CyberBattleSim supports various modifications on the reinforcement learning side, both in reward engineering, modifications of components, and changing the perspective of evaluating such components when learning as an attacker, defender, or both. This way, Kunz et al. [13] extended CyberBattleSim's functionality as a multiagent simulator, specifically designed to train RL agents for cyber operations. This emphasis on multi-agent learning is similarly mirrored in Yao et al.'s research [31], where Markov games and RL have been leveraged for decision-making in Moving Target Defense. This has proven the applicability of CyberBattleSim to different research questions, motivating us to use it for web-layer deception evaluation.

In an interesting deviation, [21] approached the subject by conducting a comparative study on various RL algorithms for adversarial agent-learning in cybersecurity. This study offers valuable insights into the efficacy of different algorithms in various simulated scenarios, providing a broader perspective on the strengths and limitations of the available methodologies. Conclusions made in this study supported our choice of a reinforcement learning algorithm, called Double DQN [12], due to its efficiency and stability in learning in high-dimensional space and testing the defense capabilities of web applications.

While current research field lacks generalised solution for automatic web deception evaluation, authors have previously covered this question from several directions. In their survey, Zhu et al. [33] mentions variety of machine learning approaches, including but not limited to enhancing the performance of Web Application Firewalls (WAFs) [1], generating realistic fake data for web application honeytokens [20] or utilizing game theory, honeyweb, and honeytokens with ransomware to enhance intrusion detection systems [5]. These papers provide insights into the effectiveness of deception techniques, the classification of existing solutions, and the evaluation of their effectiveness, relying on collected datasets and CTF challenges, both implying high costs in organising the user studies (e.g., inviting pentesters). Thus, we base our solution on flexible, highly abstract CyberBattleSim simulation [27], covering the research gap by using lightweight, autonomous agents to assess defensive capabilities of numerous deception/detection configurations.

Finally, researchers also developed task-specific simulators, where the Q-learning algorithm [17] is utilized in several works [7,30] for web application security vulnerability detection.

3   Background on CyberBattleSim

CyberBattleSim [27] offers a high-level parameterized model of a computer network, simulating enterprise defensive techniques in order to test autonomous agents using reinforcement learning. Since the author's goal was to provide a safe, fast and reliable platform for conducting research on specific security aspects, it was designed as a high-level abstraction of interactions between attacker and enterprise networks. It is distinguished by the lightweight runtime, applicable to high-performance learning of reinforcement learning algorithms.

Formed in a preconfigured network topology, computer nodes own special properties, such as OS version, listening ports and firewall rules, which influence possible connections in a graph using user credentials to connect to different machines, and exploiting the planted vulnerabilities. An attackers' goal is to take ownership of the computer nodes in the system, while the defender implements special firewall rules and potential deceptive elements to impede the progress of agents present in the system.

Similar to a real-world scenario, attacker acquires information about the system and exploits a predefined set of vulnerability capabilities, which are presented in 3 types of attacks: *local attacks* executed on owned nodes, *remote attacks* on vulnerable discovered nodes and *connect and control* attacks to take ownership of the node with credentials and listening port. By choosing the action on each time step, the agent learns to use appropriate vulnerabilities for the discovered nodes and finds an optimal attack path to reach the specific percentage or number of owned nodes.

While being as simple and flexibile as possible, CyberBattleSim forms benchmarks to test specific areas of cybersecurity research. Former modifications were made to the variety of Deep Reinforcement Learning agents extending to two-player games [21]. In addition, deception concept was checked on a network-level using original implementation and newly introduced honeypots, decoys and honeytokens as network-layer deceptive elements [28].

Our contribution lies in a modification of the original CyberBattleSim implementation with major inclusions of necessary functionality to reproduce enterprise web applications and attacker decision-making processes. Moreover, based on different deception methods introduced for web security, we provide capabilities of inserting those elements into any application's configuration to monitor the attacker's actions in the form of deep reinforcement learning agent. Thus, both state and action spaces were carefully redesigned to comply with both web application specifics, and MDP for reinforcement learning algorithm.

4   Method: Using CyberBattleSim to Simulate Application-Layer Deception

Following the design princinples of CyberBattleSim [27], our web application simulation is developed as a lightweight, concise, comprehensible high-level abstraction, granting researchers the flexibility to add new elements with ease and applicability to reinforcement learning.

Web Application Components are represented in a form of directed annotated graph, embodied in the simulation as the framework of HTTP request-response communications (presented in Fig. 1a). Each node on this graph stands for an HTTP method coupled with a path to the relative endpoints (like "GET /v2/login"), while the edges signify the discovery progression during reconnaissance attacks. Each node has a list of *properties* that includes the information about the endpoint. These properties need to be discovered before the exploit related to this endpoint (such as tampering with known HTTP GET parameters, or forced browsing attempts to disclose files) can be used by the attacker agent.

Simulation of Privileges. We simulate a role-based access control mechanism, with multiple privileges associated with these roles. Even though the global environment has access to all the application components, only discovered entities become a part of the observation accessible to the attacker. Therefore, the agent has a partial view of the environment, which consists of the set of privileges obtained from the compromised users' profiles, and the related web application components. Each user profile has the following properties:

- *Username* (can be constructed in a predictable way)
- *Session token* (potentially leaked and used for session hijacking)
- *Role cookie* (a list of roles granted to a user for privileged access, potentially serving as a deceptive cookie)

Since the attacker usually finds out information in parts from different exploits during the information gathering phase, we use a boolean expression of type "attribute1.value1&attribute2.value" to allow the agent to update its internal memory about the newly acquired properties of a newly or previously obtained profile. For example, to gather valuable documents list from database of all documents attacker should hijack session with any discovered profile of authenticated user, who also possesses "chemist" role, i.e. "¬username.NoAuth&roles.isChemist".

Simulation of Common Web Attacks. We have maintained the design of unique vulnerabilities as the atomic action for the reinforcement learning agent, although we have extended the pre-condition notion, putting profile details as part of verification for each available exploit. This behavior change is a result of the diversion from the previous focus on "lateral movement techniques" on a network-level to a general assumption of a session management flaw allowing session hijacking, i.e. attacker impersonates another user by modifying the SESSION cookie in the HTTP request. Therefore we omitted *command and control* special action [27], delegating the *remote exploit* action with both the authentication function and the choice of vulnerability on the target node. Any episode starts with an agent at the "client browser", execute the *local exploit* actions on that "owned" node, later able to utilize *remote exploit* of accessible vulnerabilities to move toward valuable data.

As the advantage of high-level abstraction, all common web attacks from the OWASP Top Ten [25] can be seamlessly incorporated into the environment by adding them to the global vulnerabilities list and setting the relevant pre-conditions using the properties. For example, to simulate a honeytoken that is injected by a reverse-proxy into every HTTP requests, we append a tampering action to each endpoint (See Sect. 5.1). However, if the pre-condition requires a specific node property, the action will be valid only for certain target nodes.

Each vulnerability owns multiple attributes: the *vulnerability ID* string composed of parameter IDs used in the HTTP header, the output reward string for logging purposes, and the above-mentioned pre-condition and set of outcomes, all of which influence the feedback the agent gets from the environment after a malicious attempt:

- *ProbeSuccess/ProbeFailed* outcome for successful information gathering (+2 reward for each newly acquire property) or any idle action that does not lead to a substantial gain for the cyber attacker;
- *ExploitFailed* outcome leading to penalizing behavior (-30 penalty), i.e. unsuccessful vulnerability exploit;
- *LeakedNodes/LeakedProfiles* collects intelligence in terms of unknown endpoints (+3 reward) and profile attribute values (+3 reward each);
- *CustomerData* refers to obtaining valuable data with a reward manually specified;

In case the pre-condition is not met, the action is treated with the *ExploitFailed* outcome, perceived equally by attacker independently if vulnerability is real exploit or fake (more in Sect. 4.1). With a thorough reward engineering process and relying on previous research papers on CyberBattleSim [28], we have established a new penalty for actions with repeated outcomes (−20), final winning reward (+100) and a novel error to motivate any perceived SSRF vulnerability, e.g., to bypass the VPN requirement.

4.1 Implementation of Deceptive Elements

Thanks to the flexibility of our simulation, developers can simply configure honeytokens together with detection points, using already introduced functionalities such as global or individual properties and vulnerabilities. They may include hidden form fields, fake HTTP GET and POST parameters, additional protected areas, and fake vulnerabilities. After gaining *ProbeSuccess* outcome, the agent discovers the associated custom property names. When the agent attempts to trigger a deceptive element (e.g., attempts to exploit a fake vulnerability), our simulator records it as an alert.

We provide a list of implemented honeytokens and detection points (with their corresponding outcomes) listed in Table 1. Our implementation simulates various vulnerabilities such as SSRF, forced browsing, SQL injection, authentication and authorization weaknesses (e.g., tampered cookies and weak credentials). Last but not least, we rely on the relative (rather than the absolute) values of rewards as a reflection of vulnerability outcomes on the attacker. Therefore, to model unawareness about deception, we propose deception-based penalties to be equal within all implanted vulnerabilities, as stated in the Experiments Sect. 5.1.

4.2 Reinforcement Learning Agents as Attackers

Likewise related papers suggest [28] we consider attacker defender confrontation as part of the Markov Decision Process $< \mathcal{S}, \mathcal{A}, \mathcal{P}, \gamma, \mathcal{R} >$ [26], which represents the decision-making process as a sequence of states $s_t \in \mathcal{S}$ on which agent proceeds with action $a_t \in \mathcal{A}$, finding itself in a new state s_{t+1} and obtaining feedback from environment as reward $r_{t+1} \in \mathcal{R}$. As a finite MDP trajectory sequence $\tau = s_1, a_1, r_2, s_2, a_2, r_3, s_3, \ldots, r_T, s_T$, a cyber attack continues up to T steps when the intruder reaches the goal of acquiring valuable data or terminates its further actions if caught by defenders. In other words, attacker optimises its policy $\pi(a|s)$ dictating an action at each step, which maximizes expected cumulative discounted reward during an attack:

$$\pi^*(a|s) = \max \mathbb{E}_\pi \left[\sum_{t=1}^{T} \gamma^t r_{t+1} \right] \tag{1}$$

Generally, trajectory τ depends on the state-transition probabilities $\mathcal{P}(s_{t+1}|s_t, a_t)$ as the next state of the web application s' can depend on the success of the exploit a environment in state s. Simplifying it to the deterministic case, reward follows a function $r_{t+1} = r(s_t, a_t)$ as the outcome becomes certain for each state-action pair. Moreover, each state corresponds to the observation $o_t = f(s_t)$, as partial information is accessible to the intruder, since it lacks the complete view of the web application and gradually unravels new details during the attack.

Double DQN is a deep reinforcement learning algorithm based on the Q-learning algorithm, which estimates the optimal Q-function $Q^*(s_t, a_t)$, defined as the expected cumulative reward after executing the action a_{t_0}, following the optimal policy $\pi^*(a|s)$. With Bellman Eq. 2, algorithm updates estimation $Q_\theta(s_t, a_t)$ and guarantees to converge to optimum value, but is prone to overestimation.

$$Q^*(s_t, a_t) = \max_\pi Q(s_t, a_t) = \max_\pi \mathbb{E}_\pi\left[r_{t+1} + \gamma \max_{a'} Q(s', a')|s' = s_{t+1}\right] \quad (2)$$

The agent always follows a policy which maximizes the Q-function in state s, $\pi(a|s) = \max_a Q_\theta(s, a)$, and optimizing objective 3 also updates tabular values, reaching the convergence at optimal point exponentially in $1/(1 - \gamma)$, when learning rate linearly decreases [8]. In case of continuous or high-dimensional states and actions, it is beneficial to use Deep Q Network (DQN) instead of tabular Q-learning, taking advantage of huge amount of data during simulation. However, in order to recover from falling into sub-optimal values, experience replay buffer was introduced to store and reuse the previous experience [12]. Moreover, to avoid chasing a non-stationary target, Double DQN uses a separate neural network as the target value in the gradient updates with α learning rate 4, while periodically syncing its parameters θ^- each $u = 5$ episodes.

$$\mathcal{L}(\theta) = \mathbb{E}_\pi\left[\left(r + \gamma Q(s', a'; \theta^-) - Q(s, a; \theta)\right)^2\right] \quad (3)$$

$$\theta \leftarrow \theta + \alpha(r_{t+1} + \gamma \max_{a'} Q(s_{t+1}, a'; \theta^-) - Q(s_t, a_t; \theta))\nabla_\theta Q(s_t, a_t; \theta) \quad (4)$$

5   Experiments

5.1   MedicalPortal Web Application

In this study, we use an example web application called *MedicalPortal*, which is primarily developed for a Capture The Flag (CTF) challenge. The application includes different components such as a dashboard, authentication, session management and role-based access control mechanisms, and a database. We first model this application in our modified CyberBattleSim framework, and then add varied configurations of honeytokens and detection points to replicate different deceptive strategies. A visual example of how the application is simulated is shown in Fig. 1a.

In the application workflow, the user first creates an account and logs in. After authentication, different users have access to varying functions depending on their roles, e.g., doctors can send messages to each other and to chemists, while the latter can share sensitive documents. Our focus is on an RL-agent acting as an attacker who exploits planted vulnerabilities, forming a Capture The Flag-like experiment. The agent receives rewards for new insights into the web application, and is deemed successful upon obtaining sensitive user data.

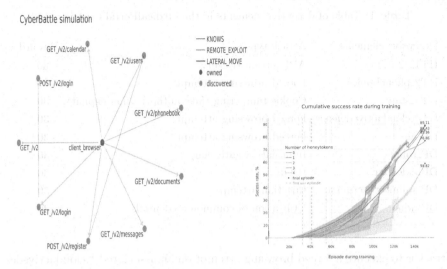

(a) Simulated MedicalPortal web application (b) Attack success rate of the agent in from CTF challenge (visual representation)   relation to number of honeytokens

Fig. 1. Simulated MedicalPortal web application from CTF challenge

5.2   Experiment Setup

Since MedicalPortal application is designed as a CTF challenge, it incorporates a real attack path that leads to the sensitive information used as the flag. Our environment simulates this valid attack path, but also implements other potential vulnerabilities or reconnaissance actions, suitable to be subtly monitored by defense system. We have inserted 5 application-specific, IDS-like detection points listed in the Table 1, which associate various attack attempts with agent's actions. The triggering of detection points gives a negative reward, and brings zero probability of success. Same applies to honeytokens which are specifically developed for this web application and inserted in the order of optimal actions, imitating a reverse proxy that injects honeytokens into HTTP requests/responses. These deceptive elements, while developed specifically for our example,are in line with examples and attack practices mentioned in the OWASP AppSensor project and OWASP Testing guide [23,24]

To begin with, "HT1_v2tov1 is a type of falsified information used for API version trickery [18], accessible to each user profile and endpoint from the beginning of the simulation. The honey session cookie "HT3_state" is implemented similarly, but visible to the attacker agent only after the registration, since it imitates a user's assigned role-based cookie (for example, "state = 1:0" gives doctor role to the user, but not chemist). In addition, "HT2_phonebook" is a hidden form field at the login page, looking like an unused but valuable microservice, remaining from an older version of the application. Last but not least, "HT4_cloudactivedefense" pays role as fake GET parameter that encourages the

Table 1. Table of deceptive elements in the MedicalPortal experiment

Deceptive elements	Attack type	Reward
HT1_v2tov1	API version trickery	−30
HT2_phonebook	Forced browsing attempt	−30
HT3_state	Cookie tampering (fake authorization exploit)	−30
HT4_cloudactivedefense	Forced browsing attempt	−30
DP_git	Forced browsing attempt	−30
DP_robots	Information gathering	−30
DP_calendar	IDOR	−30
DP_sqlinjectusername	Injection attempt	−30
DP_admin	Utilization of common credentials	−30

attacker to execute a forced browsing attempt on an associated ".cloudactivedefense" config file.

Similar penalties are applied to each honeytoken, assuming that the application will only log the attack attempts and will not respond in a way that can make the attacker aware of deception (such as blocking the malicious session). As the main objective of our work is to evaluate defensive configuration with each other, it is not necessary to inform attackers model with realistic rewards from human-subject experiments, unless considered as potential direction for future research. More importantly these reward configurations can be adjusted by researchers in a thorough reward engineering process, in order to reflect how different honeytokens may raise different levels of suspicion after interaction [10, 19].

Unlike traditional threat modeling exercises, this simulation extends our ability to test the web application, with infinite number of reinforcement learning agents functioning as cyber attackers. In our research, we maintain the hyperparameters of the DDQN at most sample-efficient setting found ($\gamma = 0.015, \epsilon = 0.1, \epsilon_{decay} = 3000, \alpha = 0.01, u = 5$ as in Sect. 4.2), primarily aiming to compare environments with different defensive configurations, as opposed to training the best performing agent on them. Furthermore, environment is tested on 4 trials/runs, seeded to pseudo-randomly initialize DDQN network and random generator in order to diminish variations of the exploration process and taking average over the metrics, for each environment. Besides, each experiment contains a subset of the honeytokens, and each setup has been learned on the fixed duration of 150000 training steps (i.e. minimum 3000 episodes with 50 steps) enough to converge to local optimum in each environment.

5.3 Detection Metrics: Identifying the Best Deceptive Configuration

Among the metrics generally used to study the efficiency to detect autonomous attackers in cybersecurity, we focused on *success rate, first trigger step* and *frequency of triggers*, i.e. "waste of resources" metric in [28].

First trigger metric indicates the first step in the episode, where any deceptive element is touched by attacker. Thus comparing the earliest possible point
of detected malicious behavior, we can find better and more effective defense
configuration. *Frequency of triggers* during each episode estimates the ratio of
actions on each honeytoken to overall number actions in an episode, thus showing us the honeytoken configuration that have the highest chance of triggering an
alarm, when the attacker is active in the system. Finally, *success rate* calculates
the percentage of episodes in which the attacker reaches the goal, among all the
training episodes. This shows the learning potential of agents compared to the
environments of different complexities.

In order to analyze agent's behavior with proposed metrics, we consider the
training step/training episode and *environment complexity* variables. The first
one allows us to analyze how attacker's interactions with decoy elements and
proficiency in penetrating the web application changes over time during training. When it comes to environment complexity, we include higher quantity and
more sophisticated types of honeytokens into the simulated web application,
and examine how each configuration affects attacker's behavior over all training
episodes.

Metrics are averaged over training runs and environments, relevant to the
tested subset of honeytokens in the experimental setup, i.e. with the same
amount of honeytokens or same type of honeytoken. We visualize the metrics in
terms of the above mentioned variables in order to answer our research questions.
By finding patterns between environment's configuration and attacker/defender
interactions, we can identify potentially the best honeytoken configuration, i.e.
minimizing the attacker's success rate and the first honeytoken trigger step, and
maximizing the frequency of alarm triggers.

6   Results

6.1   Research Question 1: Impact of Honeytokens on the Time
to Detect the Attacker

First research question tests honeytoken configurations of different complexity
with respect to the first step to detect the attacker. The Fig. 2a shows the first
step of the agent when any of the honeytokens is triggered in the particular
configuration. We observe that, when the complexity of the deception strategy
increases with more deceptive elements, the attacker can be detected faster and
earlier. In addition, Fig. 2b shows the increasing frequency of triggers per training
episode, during the increase in the number of honeytokens.

Those findings are in line with similar studies for network-layer deception
simulation [28], and in line with the expectation that more honeytokens will
increase the chance of reliably identifying attacker's activity. Even though the
detection time is improved by a small margin with the current setting of 4
honeytokens, it suggests that further inclusion of deception elements may trigger
earlier and more frequent alarms.

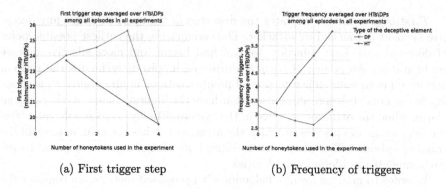

(a) First trigger step   (b) Frequency of triggers

Fig. 2. Detection time metrics averaged among all honeytokens/detection points for different number of injected honeytokens in the environment

6.2   Research Question 2: Impact of Detection Points on the Time to Detect the Attacker

Within our experiments detection points are always included as potential attack vector in each environment, disregarding the number of honeytokens. Even though detection points might increase the ratio of false positives in attack detection (as in Web Application Firewalls), adding them alongside with honeytokens can increase the chance of detection. Nevertheless, as shown in Figs. 2a and 2b, we find that adding more honeytokens does not always mean that more detection point alarms will be triggered. This is primarily due to the setup of rewards we have initiated, where we imply equal penalty feedback for each honeytoken and detection point, and allow only the placement strategy to impact their effectiveness. Although we applied the practices from OWASP Testing guide [23] to define the detection points that could catch most of the human attackers, in the configuration, the detection points ("DP_git", "DP_robots") are often situated far from the optimal attack path, in more hidden and less frequently accessed areas of the web application. As an example we look at the "DP_admin" detection point, accessible at the initial stages of attack. As this detection point still requires the discovery of "POST /login" endpoint, probably its influence rises at the later stages of the attack, after the agent learns to avoid forced browsing of ".git" and "robots.txt" endpoints. This is especially noticeable for the case of the 4-honeytoken configuration with steep drop in the first trigger step metric of detection points. This is because the agent still tries to consistently login with admin/admin credentials at the "/login" endpoint until the end of training, since the complexity of the environment with high-dimensional action space substantially delays the learning progress.

By comparing to the case without honeytokens (refer to Figs. 2a,2b), we find that combining the detection points with honeytokens can improve attack detection, and deception always plays a major role in misdirecting attacker's effort, especially when included in high numbers.

6.3   Research Question 3: Impact of the Type of Honeytokens

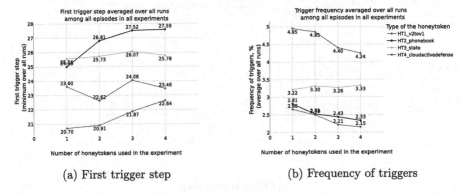

(a) First trigger step   (b) Frequency of triggers

Fig. 3. Detection time metrics averaged separately for each honeytoken for different number of injected honeytokens in the environment

We find that honeytoken types influence the defender's monitoring capabilities differently when deployed solely or combined with other honeytokens numbers (Figs. 3a and 3b). For instance, the version trickery honeytoken is open to tampering at each endpoint and each user profile at any stage of the attack, ultimately confusing the attacker. As a result, "HT1_v2tov1" honeytoken leads both in frequency and the first trigger step, compared to the triggers of the "HT2_phonebook" endpoint. Due to responding with an HTTP 404 error after the forced browsing attempt, "/phonebook" endpoint becomes less attractive for probing under any authenticated user. In contrast, the "HT3_state" session cookie, injected at the later stages and potentially tampered at each HTTP request, is more preferable to exploit than the honey "/phonebook" microservice. Tampering of HTTP fields can also differ from one another depending on their implementation: while "state" honeytoken trigger is consistently occurring later than the "HT4_cloudactivedefense" honey GET parameter, the latter is used only on the root "/" endpoint and it makes no sense to repeat it again by using another user profile.

With increased environmental complexity Figs. 3a and 3b may seem to show opposing correlation, i.e. including more honeytokens increases the detection time. In order to explain this misconception, we demonstrate the difference in agent's learning progress in Figs. 4a and 4b. Among the environments with equal numbers of honeytokens, we plot the average first step and frequency metrics as well as indicate (with dashed magenta lines) the first training episode, where the attacker reaches the episode goal. Those outcomes infer several useful findings:

– First, the more honeytokens are included into the environment, the later the winning episode tends to occur in the "averaged" episode.

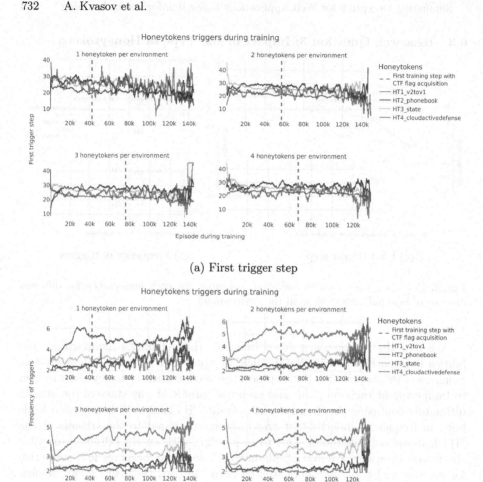

(a) First trigger step

(b) Frequency of triggers

Fig. 4. Detection metrics during training of DDQN agents

- Second, in most cases, when reinforcement learning agents evolve, honey-tokens are triggered more frequently and earlier. This pattern of reducing explorative actions and repetitions persists even after the agent discovers the optimal attack path. Same pattern occurs for any defensive configuration, except for the 4-honeytoken environment, where sample-inefficient DDQN algorithm still requires considerable amount of trial and error.
- Finally, version trickery honeytoken "HT1_v2tov1" becomes redundant and less used at the later stages of learning, while "HT4_cloudactivedefense" gradually takes its place.

To infer the highest influence on attacker's actions, we can illustrate success rate metrics for each environment separately (Fig. 5). Evidently, adding more honeytokens introduces more obstacles for the DDQN agent and slows down the progress of learning. Moreover, "HT3_state" seems to cause the most profound effect on the attacker's success across related environments. From previous figures we can see that it also ranks the second in terms of frequency (refer to Figs. 4b and 3b) and is among the last to be triggered during an episode (see Figs. 4a and 3a).

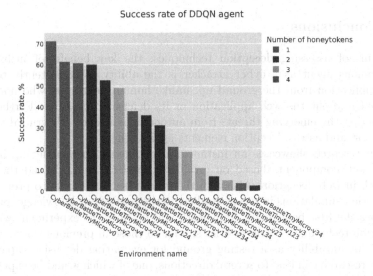

Success rate of DDQN agent

Fig. 5. Percentage of episodes during training, when attacker acquires the CTF flag

7   Discussion

The identification of the best honeytoken configuration is a challenging task, and requires considering the training runs from different view points. RL agent's interaction behaviour is impacted by the size of the action space, which in turn depends on the number of honeytokens in the application layer. Moreover, even though forced browsing attempt maintained its least valuable position among the honeytokens, it could be different if the agent has any lead to pursue with new discoveries. In Fig. 1b, we can see that the number of deception elements influence autonomous agent's learning progress and its detection time as expected, however Fig. 5 shows that the "state" session cookie have a particular impact, which can be diminished when combined with other honeytokens. Serving as the honey role cookie, "state" is anticipated to captivate attacker's attention, and plays considerable role in dropping the performance of the agent against 2 and 3 honeytoken environments. Our observations show that the agent learns in time to avoid the vulnerabilities that are exploitable from the beginning. Thus, while the API version trickery was the most triggered honeytoken in the early episodes, as the agent learns more, it starts to pay attention to the ".cloudactivedefense" config file instead. On the other hand, the honeytoken that is the most impactful for reducing attacker's success rate is found to be the "state" session cookie.

It is worth noting that the metrics may vary if we adjust the configuration by adding new honeytokens or modifying the logic of the current ones. Nonetheless, the outcomes obtained so far affirm that our current simulation implementation aligns with the anticipated effects.

8   Conclusions

In terms of assessing deception techniques, the key benefit of utilizing an autonomous agent as a cyber attacker is the ability to consistently test any web application from the ground up, unlike human pentesters who may reuse knowledge about the web application or its defensive measures. Furthermore, considering the emerging threats from autonomous agents, it's crucial to effectively test and assess deception elements against them.

Our research showcases an instance of modified CyberBattleSim, incorporating web components based on established testing methods and the recent research in web deception. Although there have been attempts to propose web application simulations in recent studies, to the best of our knowledge, our work provides the first benchmark framework and platform to experiment with web deception techniques. Using metrics similar to those in previous works, we confirmed its suitability as a testing ground for evaluating defensive capabilities. Future research can lead to several directions, one of which would be experimenting with a greater number of diverse honeytokens, for example honey accounts or more sophisticated honey resources leading to cycles in the potential attack graph. Other suggestion is to use imitation learning, inferring reward function from realistic behaviour of the human attacker during the pentesting exercise, and closing "reality gap" in the simulation.

References

1. Betarte, G., Pardo, A., Martínez, R.: Web application attacks detection using machine learning techniques. In: 2018 17th IEEE International Conference on Machine Learning and Applications (ICMLA), pp. 1065–1072 (Dec 2018). https://doi.org/10.1109/ICMLA.2018.00174
2. Brockman, G., et al.: Openai gym. CoRR (2016). http://arxiv.org/abs/1606.01540
3. Caminero Fernández, G., Lopez-Martin, M., Carro, B.: Adversarial environment reinforcement learning algorithm for intrusion detection. Comput. Netw. **159**, 96–109 (2019). https://doi.org/10.1016/j.comnet.2019.05.013
4. Charpentier, A., Boulahia Cuppens, N., Cuppens, F., Yaich, R.: Deep Reinforcement Learning-Based Defense Strategy Selection. In: Proceedings of the 17th International Conference on Availability, Reliability and Security, pp. 1–11. ACM, Vienna Austria (Aug 2022). https://doi.org/10.1145/3538969.3543789

5. El-Kosairy, A., Azer, M.A.: A New web deception system framework. In: 2018 1st International Conference on Computer Applications & Information Security (ICCAIS), pp. 1–10 (Apr 2018). https://doi.org/10.1109/CAIS.2018.8442027

6. Elderman, R., Pater, J.J., L., S. Thie, A., M. Drugan, M., M. Wiering, M.: Adversarial Reinforcement Learning in a Cyber Security Simulation. In: Proceedings of the 9th International Conference on Agents and Artificial Intelligence, pp. 559–566. SCITEPRESS - Science and Technology Publications, Porto, Portugal (2017). https://doi.org/10.5220/0006197105590566, http://www.scitepress.org/DigitalLibrary/Link.aspx?doi=10.5220/0006197105590566

7. Erdődi, L., Sommervoll, A.A., Zennaro, F.M.: Simulating SQL injection vulnerability exploitation using Q-learning reinforcement learning agents. Journal of Information Security and Applications 61(C) (Sep 2021). https://doi.org/10.1016/j.jisa.2021.102903

8. Even-Dar, E., Mansour, Y.: Learning Rates for Q-Learning. In: Goos, G., Hartmanis, J., Van Leeuwen, J., Helmbold, D., Williamson, B. (eds.) Computational Learning Theory, vol. 2111, pp. 589–604. Springer, Berlin Heidelberg, Berlin, Heidelberg (2001). https://doi.org/10.1007/3-540-44581-1_39, http://link.springer.com/10.1007/3-540-44581-1_39, series Title: Lecture Notes in Computer Science

9. Gan, Y., et al.: An Open-Source Benchmark Suite for Microservices and Their Hardware-Software Implications for Cloud & Edge Systems. In: Proceedings of the Twenty-Fourth International Conference on Architectural Support for Programming Languages and Operating Systems, pp. 3–18. ACM, Providence RI USA (Apr 2019). https://doi.org/10.1145/3297858.3304013, https://dl.acm.org/doi/10.1145/3297858.3304013

10. Han, X., Kheir, N., Balzarotti, D.: Evaluation of Deception-Based Web Attacks Detection. In: Proceedings of the 2017 Workshop on Moving Target Defense, pp. 65–73. ACM, Dallas Texas USA (Oct 2017). https://doi.org/10.1145/3140549.3140555, https://dl.acm.org/doi/10.1145/3140549.3140555

11. Han, X., Kheir, N., Balzarotti, D.: Deception techniques in computer security: a research perspective. ACM Comput. Surv. 51(4), 80 (2018). https://doi.org/10.1145/3214305

12. van Hasselt, H., Guez, A., Silver, D.: Deep reinforcement learning with double q-learning. CoRR (2015). http://arxiv.org/abs/1509.06461

13. Kunz, T., Fisher, C., La Novara-Gsell, J., Nguyen, C., Li, L.: A Multiagent CyberBattleSim for RL Cyber Operation Agents (Apr 2023). 10.48550/arXiv.2304.11052, http://arxiv.org/abs/2304.11052, arXiv:2304.11052 [cs]

14. Li, H., Guo, Y., Huo, S., Hu, H., Sun, P.: Defensive deception framework against reconnaissance attacks in the cloud with deep reinforcement learning. Sci. China Inf. Sci. 65(7), 170305 (Jul 2022). https://doi.org/10.1007/s11432-021-3462-4, https://link.springer.com/10.1007/s11432-021-3462-4

15. Li, L., Fayad, R., Taylor, A.: CyGIL: A Cyber Gym for Training Autonomous Agents over Emulated Network Systems (Sep 2021). https://doi.org/10.48550/arXiv.2109.03331

16. Li, Q., et al.: A hierarchical deep reinforcement learning model with expert prior knowledge for intelligent penetration testing. Computers & Security 132, 103358 (Sep 2023). https://doi.org/10.1016/j.cose.2023.103358, https://www.sciencedirect.com/science/article/pii/S0167404823002687

17. Mnih, V., Kavukcuoglu, K., Silver, D., Graves, A., Antonoglou, I., Wierstra, D., et al.: Playing Atari with Deep Reinforcement Learning. NIPS Deep Learning Workshop 2013 (Dec 2013), http://arxiv.org/abs/1312.5602, arXiv: 1312.5602

18. Reti, D., Elzer, K., Schotten, H.D.: SCANTRAP: Protecting Content Management Systems from Vulnerability Scanners with Cyber Deception and Obfuscation (Jan 2023). http://arxiv.org/abs/2301.10502 arXiv:2301.10502 [cs]
19. Sahin, M., Hebert, C., De Oliveira, A.S.: Lessons Learned from SunDEW: A Self Defense Environment for Web Applications. In: Proceedings 2020 Workshop on Measurements, Attacks, and Defenses for the Web. Internet Society, San Diego, CA (2020). https://doi.org/10.14722/madweb.2020.23005, https://www.ndss-symposium.org/wp-content/uploads/2020/02/23005.pdf
20. Sahin, M., Hébert, C., Cabrera Lozoya, R.: An Approach to Generate Realistic HTTP Parameters for Application Layer Deception. In: Ateniese, G., Venturi, D. (eds.) Applied Cryptography and Network Security. vol. 13269, pp. 337–355. Springer International Publishing, Cham (2022). https://doi.org/10.1007/978-3-031-09234-3-17, https://link.springer.com/10.1007/978-3-031-09234-3_17, series Title: Lecture Notes in Computer Science
21. Shashkov, A., Hemberg, E., Tulla, M., O'Reilly, U.M.: Adversarial agent-learning for cybersecurity: a comparison of algorithms. The Knowledge Engineering Review **38**, e3 (Jan 2023). https://doi.org/10.1017/S0269888923000012, publisher: Cambridge University Press
22. Standen, M., Lucas, M., Bowman, D., Richer, T.J., Kim, J., Marriott, D.: CybORG: A Gym for the Development of Autonomous Cyber Agents (Aug 2021). https://doi.org/10.48550/arXiv.2108.09118
23. van der Stock, A., Glas, B., Smithline, N., Gigler, T.: Owasp Web Security Testing Guide v4.2. https://github.com/OWASP/wstg/releases/download/v4.2/wstg-v4.2.pdf (2014)
24. van der Stock, A., Glas, B., Smithline, N., Gigler, T.: Owasp Appsensor project guide v2. https://owasp.org/www-pdf-archive/Owasp-appsensor-guide-v2.pdf (2015)
25. van der Stock, A., Glas, B., Smithline, N., Gigler, T.: OWASP Top 10 project (2021). https://owasp.org/Top10/
26. Sutton, R.S., Barto, A.G.: Reinforcement Learning: An Introduction. MIT Press (2018)
27. Team., M.D.R.: Cyberbattlesim. https://github.com/microsoft/cyberbattlesim (2021)
28. Walter, E., Ferguson-Walter, K., Ridley, A.: Incorporating Deception into CyberBattleSim for Autonomous Defense. IJCAI-21 1st International Workshop on Adaptive Cyber Defense (Aug 2021), http://arxiv.org/abs/2108.13980 arXiv:2108.13980 [cs]
29. Wang, S., Pei, Q., Wang, J., Tang, G., Zhang, Y., Liu, X.: An Intelligent Deployment Policy for Deception Resources Based on Reinforcement Learning. IEEE Access **8**, 35792–35804 (2020). https://doi.org/10.1109/ACCESS.2020.2974786, conference Name: IEEE Access
30. Xin, W., Gengyu, W., Yixian, Y.: Web application vulnerability detection based on reinforcement learning. Int. J. Digital Content Technol. Appl. **6**, 12–20 (2012). https://doi.org/10.4156/jdcta.vol6.issue10.2
31. Yao, Q., Wang, Y., Xiong, X., Wang, P., Li, Y.: Adversarial decision-making for moving target defense: a multi-agent markov game and reinforcement learning approach. Entropy **25**(4), 605 (Apr 2023). https://doi.org/10.3390/e25040605, https://www.mdpi.com/1099-4300/25/4/605, number: 4 Publisher: Multidisciplinary Digital Publishing Institute

32. Zhang, L., Thing, V.L.L.: Three Decades of Deception Techniques in Active Cyber Defense - Retrospect and Outlook. Computers & Security 106, 102288 (Jul 2021). https://doi.org/10.1016/j.cose.2021.102288, http://arxiv.org/abs/2104.03594,arXiv:2104.03594 [cs]

33. Zhu, M., Anwar, A.H., Wan, Z., Cho, J.H., Kamhoua, C., Singh, M.P.: Game-theoretic and machine learning-based approaches for defensive deception: a survey (May 2021). http://arxiv.org/abs/2101.10121 arXiv:2101.10121 [cs]

The Road Towards Autonomous Cybersecurity Agents: Remedies for Simulation Environments

Martin Drašar[1]($\boxtimes$)(iD), Ádám Ruman[2](iD), Pavel Čeleda[2](iD), and Shanchieh Jay Yang[3](iD)

[1] Institute of Computer Science, Masaryk University, Brno, Czech Republic
`drasar@ics.muni.cz`
[2] Faculty of Informatics, Masaryk University, Brno, Czech Republic
`{ruman,celeda}@fi.muni.cz`
[3] Rochester Institute of Technology, Rochester, NY, USA
`jay.yang@rit.edu`

Abstract. One of the fundamental challenges in developing autonomous cybersecurity agents (AICA) is providing them with appropriate training environments for skills acquisition and evaluation. Current reinforcement learning (RL) algorithms rely on myriads of training runs to instill proper behavior, and this is reasonably achievable only within a simulated environment. In this paper, we explore the topic of simulation models and environments for RL and present an assessment framework to compare simulation models designed for simulating cyberattack scenarios. We examine four existing simulation tools, including a new one by the authors of the paper, and discuss their properties, particularly in terms of deployability, to support RL-based AICA. In the example of complex scenarios, we compare the two most sophisticated simulation tools and discuss their strengths.

Keywords: simulation environments · autonomous decision-making · cybersecurity

1 Introduction

The proliferation of AI-based technologies is likely to have a transformative effect on every aspect of society, cybersecurity not being an exception. The seemingly unending thirst for workers in cybersecurity is promised to be quenched by autonomous systems driven by AI. Despite all the recent advancements, the genuine autonomy of cybersecurity solutions is an elusive goal. The reason is multi-faceted, but one of the fundamental challenges is providing appropriate training environments where autonomous systems can be trained and evaluated. Reinforcement learning (RL) methods, which are likely to be a cornerstone of such future systems, rely on myriads of training runs to instill the proper behavior. However, such a volume of repeated executions in real or reasonably complex virtualized environments is infeasible. Simulation, when done properly, provides an instinctive and realistic option to address this problem.

© The Author(s), under exclusive license to Springer Nature Switzerland AG 2024
S. Katsikas et al. (Eds.): ESORICS 2023 Workshops, LNCS 14399, pp. 738–749, 2024.
https://doi.org/10.1007/978-3-031-54129-2_43

RL-focused simulation environments in the cybersecurity context are currently an under-researched topic. As we demonstrate in this paper, existing works are often approached from an engineering angle, i.e., as a means to evaluate or develop specific RL solutions. Their underlying simulation models appear to be ad-hoc developed as a part of the implementation, so it is challenging to do more than superficial comparisons between existing solutions. In this paper, we aim to introduce a more formal theoretical grounding for RL-focused cybersecurity simulation by creating a framework for a formalized description of simulation models. This framework enables comparison between various simulation implementations and helps us to assess the technological readiness for the development of deployable autonomous cybersecurity systems.

The paper is divided into six sections. In Sect. 2, we provide an overview of relevant simulation technologies. In Sect. 3, we introduce a framework for assessing simulation models, which is built on top of the Cyber Terrain and Capability, Opportunity, Intent (COI) models. In Sect. 4, we employ this assessment framework for an in-depth analysis of the four most prominent simulation environments. In Sect. 5, we present a qualitative comparison between CYST and CybORG, which are two of the most feature-rich simulators based on our assessment. We then discuss the specific properties of both simulation environments. Section 6 summarizes our findings and suggests promising future directions for RL-focused cybersecurity simulation.

2 Related Work

The facilitation of the development of autonomous decision-making based on reinforcement learning requires suitable training environments. These environments have to offer an adequate interface for passing observation spaces and rewards (such as OpenAI Gym [3]) and enable efficient world-building and restoration due to the desired quantity of repetitions.

Contrary to some fields, the complexity of the cybersecurity domain renders abstraction-less training infeasible; thus, simulations, emulations, or their combination are required. Simulations implement high-abstraction models and are, therefore, very lightweight but may suffer from a loss of crucial details, complicating the transfer of learned behavior into the real world. Emulations compromise higher runtime complexity for fewer abstractions.

CANDLES [12] and Galaxy [13] were created to support the development and evaluation of evolutionary algorithms. The former is a simulation environment, with simple attack and defense actions, allowing multi-agent rivalry-driven training. The latter is an attack-oriented emulator used to explore enumeration method enhancement.

Environments specifically targeting reinforcement learning differ not just in abstraction level but also in their fundamental goal.

The FARLAND [8] framework aids the development of AICA utilizing network traffic. It builds upon probabilistic behaviors for action and state spaces. It also explores the possibility of deceptive adversaries, who can interfere with the learning process of the developed agents.

CyGil [5] builds upon virtualized emulation and leverages the adversary emulation platform CALDERA [7] to define its action space and help collect data for the AI/ML interoperability layer to report observations and rewards to the agents. The environment provides means for single-agent or multi-agent rivalry-based training instances.

Four other environments: CybORG [14], CyberBattleSim [6], Yawning Titan [1], and CYST [4] are suitable for the development of AICA and are analyzed in-depth in the following text.

3   An Assessment Framework for Autonomous Cyber Agent Simulation

This work explores and assesses simulation environments that support attack scenario manifestation with RL-based cyber agents.

To help with the analysis, we define an ontology describing simulation models. This description stems from the Cyber Terrain model [11]. For actors in the simulation, we use and extend the Capability, Opportunity, Intent model, described in [10]. To assess the overall quality of the models, we build upon [2] that presents a qualitative, class-based framework for evaluating specific attributes of abstract representations.

3.1   Ontology for Cyber Terrain Simulation

The high-level architecture of the ontology has five components and a varying quantity of sub-components, as shown in Fig. 1.

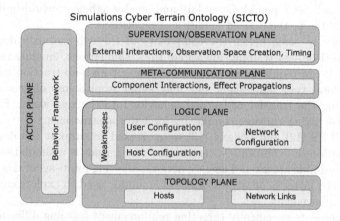

Fig. 1. The SICTO framework for describing simulation environments.

The Topology Plane describes the physical topology of the infrastructure – devices in the cyber domain with optional differentiating attributes and the communication channels that connect them. The plane can be instantiated as dynamic or static.

The Logic Plane defines the functionality of the simulation. It describes attributes and nuances critical for the domain and the simulation context. This plane can be further divided into the following sub-planes:

- *Host Configurations* – details about operating systems and their components, services, processes, executables, and data.
- *User Configurations* – details about user accounts, authentication methods, memory, and userspace isolation (including access to data).
- *Network Configurations* – addressing, communication rules, traffic shaping.
- *Weaknesses* – deviations from the ideal, secure operation flow.

The Meta-communication Plane describes the underlying signaling between the components defined in other planes. This signaling provides a light-weight mean for propagating the effects of events in the domain when the propagation mechanism itself is irrelevant to AICA.

The Supervision/Observation Plane is used for creating observation spaces for RL. It specifies the timing of the environment to control the interactions between active components of the model. It also provides an interface for external interactions, which are useful for monitoring or human interfacing.

The Actor Plane The actors introduce state-changing events into the simulation. Actors and their properties are described in more detail in the following section.

3.2 Actor Behavior Framework and Types

The COI framework [10] provides a four-layer description of actor behavior; they are:

- *Intent* – the existential goal of the actor.
- *Opportunities* – the domain of events that can be invoked by this actor.
- *Capabilities* – predicates limiting the actor's opportunities in real-time.
- *Preferences* – prioritization based on secondary intents.

We extend this framework with an additional layer – sophistication – creating a COPSI framework. Sophistication helps with the cost and risk assignment of taking specific opportunities, effectively providing another layer of long-term filtering. COPSI attributes need not be fixed (e.g., be loosely constrained or entirely volatile), as allowing alternatives might enable better tailoring of a simulator for a particular AICA.

While many options exist for actor intent, we define four actor types on a high level. The four types, by no means exhaustive, are the following:

- *Adversaries* who intend to compromise data or service availability, integrity, or confidentiality.
- *Defenders* aim to thwart and ultimately eliminate the possibility of attackers achieving their goals without disrupting standard operations.

– *Benign Participants* who mimic human activity and react to events happening in the simulation (such as clicking email links, etc.)
– *The Fates* which encompass the invocation of sporadic events and the pattern and impulse-based flow of common phenomena in the domain. These entities cover events out of the control of other actor types.

3.3   Metrics to Measure Quality

The framework provided by MITRE [2] defines qualitative metrics for representations' comprehensiveness and concreteness (C&C).

– Concreteness is: *abstract, notional, representative,* and *fully realized.*
– Comprehensiveness is: *fragmentary, partially specified,* and *fully specified.*

The metrics are defined for adversary characteristics, adversary behavior, technical environments, operational architectures, and defender actions. Table 1 shows how we map the various simulation model components to the MITRE's C&C perspectives.

Table 1. MITRE C&C mapping to model components.

Model Component	MITRE Perspective
	Attack vectors
Adversarial actor	Attack actions
	Adversary characteristics
Defending actors' opportunities	Defender actions
Topology plane	
Logic plane	Technical architecture
Meta-Communication plane	
Logic plane - Weaknesses	Technical vulnerabilities

Assessment of concreteness and comprehensiveness helps us with assessing the fitness of the environment for RL-based AICA development because:

– the more concrete and comprehensive the attacker and defender models are, the more tailorable and capable will the trained AICA be;
– with more concrete and comprehensive technical architecture and vulnerabilities, autonomous decision-making can be more nuanced.

4   Comparison of Existing Simulations' Models

In this section, we use the proposed framework to analyze existing simulation environments structurally. The analysis helps us assess these simulators' limits and what they excel at. This, in turn, helps us spot possible neglected or under-developed fragments in these environments and serves as an excellent pointer for where to improve.

We analyze the **Yawning Titan** [1], **CyberBattle Sim** [6], **CybORG** [14] and **CYST** [4] simulation environments as they are the four most promising candidates for RL. CYST is an environment by the authors of this paper.

4.1 Yawning Titan

This simulation environment aims to test new RL algorithms in a simplified cybersecurity setting. The model is very high level (for example, the only attribute of a host is its compromisation status) to limit the size of the explorable state and supports only *defenders* and *adversaries*.

This model design is most suitable for exploring the "territorial contest" in the cybersecurity domain. The model's simplicity results in a two-level adversarial choice domain of target selection and deciding whether to use a guaranteed attack. The defensive choice domain is similar, with target selection as the top layer and then action selection from a small-size sub-domain. Thus, this simulator is not suitable for the development of a full-fledged AICA.

4.2 CyberBattleSim

CyberBattleSim has more granularity than Yawning Titan. It is designed to examine autonomous intelligence in more complex cybersecurity scenarios. It allows CTF-like scenarios (gathering specific data) or an availability disruption campaign. Like Yawning Titan, it supports *defenders* and *adversaries*.

CyberBattleSim's model is more fitting for training higher-level adversarial decision-making with a limited, hierarchical choice domain. The hierarchy consists of a layer of target selection, then a layer of high-level action selection, followed by a layer of vulnerability selection.

4.3 CybORG

CybORG aims to provide an environment for creating AICA with real-world usability. It is a hybrid simulation-emulation environment, but in this paper, we are strictly interested in the simulation part. CybORG views the simulation as a state machine with states representing the overall state of the infrastructure, thus mappable to our ontology. In addition to *defenders* and *adversaries*, it supports simple *benign participants*.

CybORG allows for training more realistic and multi-purpose AICA, as it provides for a two-level hierarchical choice domain (a sizable action selection layer followed by an action parametrization layer – including target selection) for both defensive and adversarial AICA.

4.4 CYST

CYST is built on the message-passing discrete event-processing paradigm. Like CybORG, it is a hybrid simulation-emulation environment, enabling concurrent training of multi-agent systems. It supports extensive customization using a comprehensive API and dynamic changes in the simulation environment during simulation runs. It enables on-the-fly transformations of simulation messages to other representations (such as flow or packet traces) and the usage of these representations to interact with systems outside simulations (such as IDS systems). This way, it sidesteps the issue of reimplementing realistic cybersecurity services within a simulation and enables mixed simulation-emulation training of agents in a more realistic environment. Unlike the previous environments, CYST does not provide state space representations and reward computations – these are intrinsic to agents, and they must construct them from received messages.

Table 2. Comparison of simulation models' attributes structured by the *SICTO* framework.

Property	Yawning Titan	CyberBattleSim	CybORG	CYST
Overall Abstraction	Very high	High	Moderately low	Moderately low
Topology				
Dynamic changes	Allowed	Not supported	Allowed	Allowed
Representation	Unidirected graph	Non-directed graph	Non-directed graph	Unidirected graph
Logic				
Network				
Rule direction	Bidirectional	Bidirectional	Bidirectional	Bidirectional
Rule granularity	Per-host	Per-protocol	Per-protocol	Per-protocol
Additional capabilities	None	None	None	Jitter, traffic shaping
Hosts				
OS	Not supported	Not supported	Available	Via software components
Software	Not supported	List of network services	Processes and executables	Active and passive services
Software properties	Not supported	State, downtime penalty	Owners, identities	Message handling function
Data	Not supported	Not supported	Files	Service data
Extendability	No	Yes, with boolean expressions	No	With custom message handling
Users				
Account granularity	Not supported	Privilege levels, per-device	Accounts, groups, per-device	Accounts, per-service
Credentials	Not supported	Primary, per-service	Primary, per-account	Primary, MFA
Authorizations	Not supported	Not supported	Not supported	Yes, with federated auth.
Remote access control	Not supported	Per-service	Per-device	Per-service
Local access control	Not supported	Not supported	Files only	Not yet available
Weaknesses				
Realism	Low	Medium	High	High
Representation	Host vulnerability score	Applicable adversary actions	Applicable adversary actions	Enablers *
Applicability guard	Attacker skill value	Host attribute prerequisites	Host attribute prerequisites	Service attribute prerequisites
Additional action attributes	None	Cost, success probability	None	None
Meta-communication				
Event invocation	Supervision intervention	Supervision intervention	Supervision intervention	Via messaging
Event propagation	Supervision intervention	Supervision intervention	Supervision intervention	Via messaging
Supervision & Observation				
Observation space	Provided	Provided	Provided	Not provided
Timing	Sequential, turn-taking	Sequential	Sequential	Concurrent
Reward computation	Provided	Provided	Provided	Not provided
Multiagent support	No	No	Yes	Yes

* – CWE, CVE, misconfigurations, bad-practices

CYST enables the creation of actions with arbitrary semantics, so the actors are not limited in their capabilities by their assigned role or intent. The effect of these actions is expressed through the use of API, which enables modifying the entire simulation.

4.5 Structured Comparison

The summary of model properties in terms of the SICTO framework is in Table 2. As *defenders* and *adversaries* are common to all four simulators, they are compared in terms of the COPSI framework in Tables 3 and 4. The quality measurement in terms of the MITRE C&C is in Tables 5 and 6.

5 Comparison of CybORG and CYST

According to Table 2, it can be seen that there are two simulators that are conducive to creating real-world deployable AICA – CybORG and CYST. Both are hybrid simulation-emulation environments, and their level of abstraction is low enough to map to real-world tools and processes. According to the SICTO framework, their difference is minimal, with CYST being more customizable and supporting some sophisticated features at the expense of not providing state representations and reward computations.

Table 3. Adversaries via the COPSI framework.

	YawninTitan	CyberBattleSim	Cyborg	CYST
Intent	Territorial control.	Customizable.	Customizable.	Customizable.
Opportunities	Attack. (CVE/0-day)	4 high level actions.	Metasploit analogy.	AIF [9] analogy, MITRE ATTACK is WIP.
Capabilities	Accessible hosts.	Accessible hosts and their vulnerabilities, control*.	Accessible hosts, control*, applicable actions.	Sessions, access and authorization tokens, control*.
Preference	Limitedly configurable.	Customizable by tweaking reward values.	Customizable by tweaking reward computation.	Agent dependent.
Sophistication	Numerical skill level.	Customizable by tweaking reward values.	Customizable by tweaking reward computation.	Agent dependent.

* - based on model granularity, privilege levels, capabilities,...

Table 4. Defenders via the COPSI framework.

	YawninTitan	CyberBattleSim	Cyborg	CYST
Intent	Territorial control.	Customizable.	Customizable.	Customizable.
Opportunities	7 high-level actions.	4 basic actions.	Velociraptor analogy.	MITRE D3FENSE (WIP).
Capabilities	Nonexistent.	Nonexistent.	Nonexistent.	Sessions, access and authorization tokens, control*.
Preference	Nonexistent.	Customizable probabilistic model.	Customizable by tweaking reward computation.	Agent dependent.
Sophistication	Probability of compromitation discovery.	Customizable by probabilistic model.	Customizable by tweaking reward computation.	Agent dependent.

Table 5. Concreteness comparison of model properties.

Property	Y.Titan	C.BattleSim	CybORG	CYST
Adversary characteristics	Abstract	Abstract	Abstract	Full. real.*
Attack vectors	Abstract	Notional	Notional	Notional
Attack actions	Abstract	Abstract	Full. real.	Full. real.*
Defender actions	Notional	Notional	Full. real.	Full. real.*
Technical architecture	Abstract	Notional	Represent.	Represent.
Technical vulnerabilities	Abstract	Represent.	Represent.	Represent.

* - depends on the external implementation but allows up to the class.

Table 6. Comprehensiveness comparison of model properties.

Property	Y.Titan	C.BattleSim	CybORG	CYST
Adversary characteristics	Fragmentary	Fragmentary	Fragmentary	Full. spec.*
Attack vectors	Fragmentary	Part. spec.	Part. spec.	Part. spec.
Attack actions	Fragmentary	Part. spec.	Full. spec.	Full. spec.*
Defender actions	Part. spec.	Part. spec.	Full. spec.	Full. spec.*
Technical architecture	Fragmentary	Part. spec.	Part. spec.	Part. spec.
Technical vulnerabilities	Fragmentary	Part. spec.	Part. spec.	Part. spec.

* - depends on the external implementation but allows up to the class.

We made an in-depth qualitative comparison between those two simulators by analyzing them in terms of their intended users, i.e., what it entails to develop agents in their contexts. For CybORG, we used as a reference point the second CAGE challenge [15]. For CYST, we created a similar scenario of infiltration into a corporate network. Due to the need to reduce the size of this paper, the description of the test was left out and can be read here[1]. Here, we provide only the conclusions.

Both simulation environments gravitate to similar goals and use similar approaches, despite being developed in isolation. Table 7 summarises the strong points of both CYST and CybORG, which may be critical when deciding which solution to use. Properties that are essentially the same between both are left out, as they can mostly be extrapolated from the model description.

In general, many of the functionalities described in Table 7 can be implemented by either of the simulators provided there is enough incentive. However, the implementation of the properties related to interfacing with humans or services besides simulation would likely require considerable changes to the CybORG simulation model and implementation. The same holds for agent-agent interaction and non-singular actions.

---

[1] https://muni.cz/go/esorics-long.

Neither of these simulators can be used in isolation for training real-world-deployable AICA. While their respective capabilities enable the creation of specialized AICA, the lack of supporting infrastructure for the creation of diverse scenarios and orchestrating training runs precludes the creation of a general one.

Table 7. Strong features of CYST and CybORG.

CYST	CybORG
Infrastructure & Logic	
Network traffic shaping.	Service and OS knowledge base.
Modeling the traffic.	Modeling OS.
Support for complex authentication and authorization.	Host level information down to PID and files and their permissions.
Supervision, Actors & Agents	
Unbounded action and observation spaces.	Provides global and local observations.
Complex action parametrization to mimic real-world actions tailored for RL.	Integrated rewards.
Non-singular action handling.	Rich action space.
Transaction support for faster training.	
Agent-agent interaction in addition to agent-environment.	
External & Miscellaneous	
Strong focus on deployability.	Ready wrappers and interfaces for OpenAI.
Maximizing extensibility, stand-alone packages, usable as a library, and plugin support.	
Integration with outside running services.	
Human-machine interface.	

6 Summary

In this paper, we discussed the current landscape of simulation environments for training RL-based cybersecurity solutions. In Sect. 3, we present an assessment framework built on the Cyber Terrain ontology, an extended Capability, Opportunity, Intent model, and a quality metric by MITRE. We use this framework in Sects. 4 and 5 to analyze the four advanced RL-focused simulation environments, including a newly introduced CYST simulation framework. In Sect. 5, we compare the usage between CYST and CybORG, and based on this, we compile a list of strong points for both simulation environments. We argue that both solutions still need to be considerably extended to enable the training of future deployable autonomous cybersecurity systems.

This paper's contribution to the state-of-the-art is two-fold. First, it introduces and applies the assessment framework providing a systematic approach to developing and assessing RL-focused cybersecurity simulators. Second, by presenting a new simulation environment CYST, it introduces technological diversity to existing simulators.

6.1 Future Work

We see several areas that will require concentrated research and development efforts to support future deployable AICA better. These include:

- Development of environments for orchestration of simulation runs to enable at-scale training of AICA.
- Mechanisms for procedural generation of cyber terrains to provide variability to agents' training.
- High-fidelity implementation of industry-proven attack and defense action sets to increase the realism of simulations.

Acknowledgements. This research was supported by the Strategic Support for the Development of Security Research in the Czech Republic 2019–2025 (IMPAKT 1) program granted by the Ministry of the Interior of the Czech Republic under No. VJ02010020 – AI-Dojo: Multi-agent Testbed for Research and Testing of AI-driven Cybersecurity Technologies.

References

1. Andrew, A., Spillard, S., Collyer, J., Dhir, N.: Developing optimal causal cyber-defence agents via cyber security simulation (2022). https://doi.org/10.48550/ARXIV.2207.12355
2. Bodeau, D., Graubart, R., Heinbockel, W.: Mapping the cyber terrain: Enabling cyber defensibility claims and hypotheses to be stated and evaluated with greater rigor and utility. Tech. rep., The MITRE Corporation., Bedford, MA, USA (2013). https://www.mitre.org/sites/default/files/publications/mapping-cyber-terrain-13-4175.pdf
3. Brockman, G., Cheung, V., Pettersson, L., Schneider, J., Schulman, J., Tang, J., Zaremba, W.: Openai gym (2016). https://doi.org/10.48550/ARXIV.1606.01540
4. Drasar, M.: Cyst api documentation (2023), https://muni.cz/go/cyst/
5. Li, L., Fayad, R., Taylor, A.: Cygil: A cyber gym for training autonomous agents over emulated network systems (2021). https://doi.org/10.48550/ARXIV.2109.03331
6. Microsoft: Cyberbattlesim (2021). https://github.com/microsoft/cyberbattlesim, created by Christian Seifert, Michael Betser, William Blum, James Bono, Kate Farris, Emily Goren, Justin Grana, Kristian Holsheimer, Brandon Marken, Joshua Neil, Nicole Nichols, Jugal Parikh, Haoran Wei
7. MITRE: Caldera: A scalable, adversary emulation platform (2022). https://caldera.mitre.org
8. Molina-Markham, A., Miniter, C., Powell, B., Ridley, A.: Network environment design for autonomous cyberdefense (2021). https://doi.org/10.48550/ARXIV.2103.07583
9. Moskal, S., Yang, S.J.: Cyberattack action-intent-framework for mapping intrusion observables. CoRR abs/2002.07838 (2020). https://arxiv.org/abs/2002.07838
10. Moskal, S., Yang, S.J., Kuhl, M.E.: Cyber threat assessment via attack scenario simulation using an integrated adversary and network modeling approach. J. Defense Model. Simul. **15**(1), 13–29 (2018). https://doi.org/10.1177/1548512917725408

11. Raymond, D., Cross, T., Conti, G., Nowatkowski, M.: Key terrain in cyberspace: Seeking the high ground. In: 2014 6th International Conference On Cyber Conflict (CyCon 2014), pp. 287–300. IEEE, Tallinn, Estonia (2014). https://doi.org/10.1109/CYCON.2014.6916409

12. Rush, G., Tauritz, D.R., Kent, A.D.: Coevolutionary agent-based network defense lightweight event system (candles). In: Proceedings of the Companion Publication of the 2015 Annual Conference on Genetic and Evolutionary Computation. p. 859–866. GECCO Companion '15, Association for Computing Machinery, New York, NY, USA (2015). https://doi.org/10.1145/2739482.2768429

13. Schoonover, K., et al.: Galaxy: A network emulation framework for cybersecurity. In: 11th USENIX Workshop on Cyber Security Experimentation and Test (CSET 18). USENIX Association, Baltimore, MD (Aug 2018). https://www.usenix.org/conference/cset18/presentation/schoonover

14. Standen, M., Lucas, M., Bowman, D., Richer, T.J., Kim, J., Marriott, D.: Cyborg: a gym for the development of autonomous cyber agents (2021). https://doi.org/10.48550/ARXIV.2108.09118

15. The Technical Cooperation Program: TTCP CAGE Challenge 2 (2022). https://github.com/cage-challenge/cage-challenge-2

Mitigating Gradient Inversion Attacks in Federated Learning with Frequency Transformation

Chamath Palihawadana[✉], Nirmalie Wiratunga, Harsha Kalutarage, and Anjana Wijekoon

School of Computing, Robert Gordon University, Aberdeen, UK
{c.palihawadana,n.wiratunga,h.kalutarage,a.wijekoon1}@rgu.ac.uk

Abstract. Centralised machine learning approaches have raised concerns regarding the privacy of client data. To address this issue, privacy-preserving techniques such as Federated Learning (FL) have emerged, where only updated gradients are communicated instead of the raw client data. However, recent advances in security research have revealed vulnerabilities in this approach, demonstrating that gradients can be targeted and reconstructed, compromising the privacy of local instances. Such attacks, known as gradient inversion attacks, include techniques like deep leakage gradients (DLG). In this work, we explore the implications of gradient inversion attacks in FL and propose a novel defence mechanism, called Pruned Frequency-based Gradient Defence (pFGD), to mitigate these risks. Our defence strategy combines frequency transformation using techniques such as Discrete Cosine Transform (DCT) and employs pruning on the gradients to enhance privacy preservation. In this study, we perform a series of experiments on the MNIST dataset to evaluate the effectiveness of pFGD in defending against gradient inversion attacks. Our results clearly demonstrate the resilience and robustness of pFGD to gradient inversion attacks. The findings stress the need for strong privacy techniques to counter attacks and protect client data.

Keywords: Gradient Inversion Attacks · Federated Learning · Frequency Transformation

1 Introduction

The widespread adoption of Machine Learning (ML) and the increasing need for large-scale privacy sensitive data have led to the emergence of Federated Learning (FL) [5]. FL provides a decentralised approach to train ML models, enabling privacy preservation in the process. In a typical FL setting there will be a server which orchestrates the federated rounds where each client contributes a local model update trained on their private data. With this process the client's private data never leaves their device which gives a strong privacy guarantee. This privacy-preserved nature of FL has gathered significant attention and interest from various domains, including healthcare, finance, and smart devices.

© The Author(s), under exclusive license to Springer Nature Switzerland AG 2024
S. Katsikas et al. (Eds.): ESORICS 2023 Workshops, LNCS 14399, pp. 750–760, 2024.
https://doi.org/10.1007/978-3-031-54129-2_44

The decentralised nature of FL ensures that clients only communicate their local updates, such as gradients or local model parameters, which significantly enhances the safety of the process compared to sharing raw data with a central system. However, recent research on attack scenarios has revealed potential vulnerabilities even when only local updates are shared [12]. Such attacks are known as gradient inversion attacks which is an active area of research in FL. Some of the suggested defence strategies for gradient inversion attacks includes adding noise, gradient compression, training with large batch sizes and complex models. We note that methods like compression can be advantageous overall for the FL setting as well as to defend such attacks. A key challenge identified in recent literature is the trade off between model performance and communication efficiency [10].

This work aims to explore and establish a novel research direction that utilises the frequency space as a means to defend against gradient inversion attacks in FL. By investigating and positioning the potential of utilising frequency space in this context, we aim to provide valuable insights and propose an effective strategy to counter the vulnerabilities posed by gradient inversion attacks within the FL setting. This paper presents two key contributions. Firstly, it introduces pFGD, a straightforward yet highly effective defense strategy specifically designed to mitigate gradient inversion attacks in FL. Secondly, the paper conducts a comprehensive comparative study, evaluating the performance and efficacy of pFGD against two commonn gradient inversion attacks.

2 Background

2.1 Federated Learning

FL setting introduced a paradigm to perform ML model training in a decentralised manner. FL became widely known and adapted due to its privacy preserved manner, where client training data is never exposed or communicated to the server. This privacy preserved nature enabled to do ML model training on sensitive data like healthcare and finance. A typical FL setting consists of a server and a large number of clients participating in many communication rounds. The FL process typically commences at round $t = 0$, where the server distributes an initial global model (w_0) to all participating clients. At each communication round t, the server selects K clients to engage in local training. Each client k independently conducts training on its private data and, upon completion, communicates the updated model parameters or gradients back to the server. The server then aggregates these models using methodologies such as *FedAvg* [6] and *FedSim* [6], resulting in an updated global model at $t + 1$. Since the clients data is never communicated to the server there is a natural privacy guarantee with FL setting.

2.2 Attacks in Federated Learning

In FL setting the threat surfaces are more exposed unlike in traditional ML setting. The network of clients and the communication layer in FL setting can be considered the largest threat surface [2]. A taxonomy presented by [2] organises attacks in FL setting into two types; model performance and privacy attacks. Model performance attacks are performed during the training phase using poisoning attacks. By poisoning (i.e. manipulating) the model or local data it is possible to degrade the overall performance of the model.

Privacy attacks in FL is a widely researched area due to the impact and risk of exposure. FL is considered to be a privacy-preserved machine learning paradigm as the private training data never leaves the client-side. Security researchers have demonstrated attacks to extract such private data in the communication stage or aggregation stage at the server (as demonstrated in Fig. 1). These types of attacks can be categorised further more as gradient inversion, membership inference and generative adversarial network (GAN) reconstruction attacks. Gradient inversion attacks have demonstrated the capability to reconstruct the classes and individual data instances just by using the communicated client gradients [8,11,12]. In this work we explore defending privacy attacks in FL and specifically gradient inversion attacks.

2.3   Gradient Inversion Attacks in FL

A recent survey [9] proposed a taxonomy for gradient inversion attacks characterising into two paradigms. The two paradigms are iteration and recursion based attacks. Iteration based attacks first generates a pair of random (dummy) data and labels, then by performing forward and backward propagation iteratively the gradients can be optimised for data recovery. The reconstruction of private data is viewed as an iterative process using gradient descent. When the distance between the original and the generated gradients are close the private data can be extracted. The second paradigm is when the attacker recursively calculate the input of each layer by finding the optimal solution with minimised error. We focus on the iteration-based attacks due to their adaptability and higher risk of exposing client privacy. There is a growing list of gradient inversion attacks, few of the widely used and studied methods include Deep Leakage from Gradient (DLG) [12], improved-DLG (iDLG) [11], Client Privacy Leakage (CPL) [8] and Inverting Gradients [1]. In this study, we employed DLG and iDLG techniques to investigate the impact of our proposed method.

2.4   Frequency Space Transformation in FL

Frequency space transformation techniques have long been utilised in data compression, with notable examples such as the Discrete Cosine Transform (DCT), Discrete Fourier Transform (DFT), Fast Fourier Transform (FFT), and Principal Component Analysis (PCA). Most commonly used technique is the DCT, mainly due to its computational efficiency and compact representation [7]. Previous work using the frequency space in FL are focused on compressing the data instance and not the communication of updated gradients. In this study we use DCT as the the frequency space transformation function to explore a practical defence to gradient inversion attacks in FL.

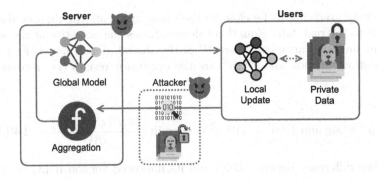

Fig. 1. Potential risks of gradient inversion attacks in FL

2.5   Attack Scenario

Threat Model. We consider two potential attack surfaces to apply the proposed method. As a network eavesdropper: Communication from a clients device to the server can be compromised on the network layer by an attacker. As a curious server, the FL server can be compromised or honest-but-curious, potentially exploiting client training data. Figure 1 presents the threat model with respect to the FL setting. The attack surfaces are presented with a red border.

Adversarial Goal. In the gradient inversion attacks the goal is to reconstruct client's private data and its class label through the communicated gradients.

3   Method

Recent work on gradient inversion attacks like DLG [12] and iDLG [11] has demonstrated the risk to privacy by exposing client private data. Both attacks attempt to reconstruct client data instances and labels using a gradient matching objective. In a typical FL setting gradients are shared to the server by clients after a local training step. If an attacker obtains such gradients they can reconstruct training instances (there are assumptions on these methods as discussed in their methods). Gradient inversion attacks can be performed at any round in the FL process, even before model convergence. In this section we discuss the attack methods and present the proposed defense method, referred to as pFGD.

3.1   Attack Methods

In this work we use two attack methods from literature which are iteration-based attacks. The selected attacks are DLG [12] and iDLG [11] which aim to reconstruct (steal) a FL client's local data instances using the communicated ΔW gradients. The attacker generates a pair of dummy data x' and dummy labels y' which are used to generate dummy gradients $\Delta W'$. Then by optimising the dummy gradients to be close to the client gradients the dummy data will be close to the real data. Equation 1 demonstrates the objective of the selected gradient inversion attacks. Where W is the shared global model, $F(.)$ shared optimisation function and x'^*, y'^* are the optimised results (i.e. reconstructed data).

$$x'^*, y'^* = \arg\min_{x',y'} ||\Delta W' - \Delta W||^2 = \arg\min_{x',y'} ||\frac{\partial l(F(x', W), y')}{\partial W} - \Delta W||^2 \quad (1)$$

A key difference between DLG and its improved version iDLG is that the way they extract the ground truth labels. Results presented by iDLG authors suggest a 100% accuracy rate on generating the label from the gradients unlike the DLG which are around 79%–90% on the same experiments.

3.2   Proposed Defence Method

We propose **Pruned Frequency-based Gradient Defence (*p*FGD)** which can act as a defence mechanism to such attacks while preserving model performance for FL setting. *p*FGD is a client-side frequency space based defence mechanism against DLG and iDLG. Once the local training is performed the updated gradients will be transformed into the frequency space $\Delta \widehat{W}$ using transformation function $T(.)$. Then pruned by a pruning function $P(.)$ controlled by α percentage. Figure 2 visually illustrates the workflow taking place on the client side, providing a clear representation of the various steps involved in *p*FGD.

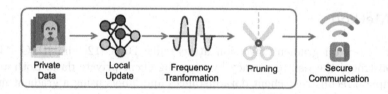

Private   Local   Frequency   Pruning   Secure
Data   Update   Tranformation   Communication

Fig. 2. Client-side workflow in *p*FGD

As discussed in Sect. 2.5 we assume the clients are honest and not a threat to the FL setting. Client communication of pruned frequency gradients prevents model inversion through noise and parameter reduction. *p*FGD transmission from the client mitigates risks from curious servers and network eavesdroppers.

Frequency Space Transformation. Based on our preliminary study, we have chosen DCT-IV as the transformation function, denoted as $T(.)$. DCT-IV has been found to strike a balance between preserving model performance and enhancing communication efficiency through pruning on the frequency space. After the gradients undergo transformation into the frequency space using the

DCT, the resulting coefficients are structured to preserve the necessary information for model aggregation. Additionally, the utilisation of the frequency space enables efficient pruning, as it allows for identifying and discarding coefficients with lower magnitudes without significantly compromising the overall model performance.

Parameter Pruning. To defend against model inversion attacks such as DLG, incorporating noisy gradients can be beneficial. However, a significant challenge lies in determining an appropriate threshold for pruning gradients. The objective is to strike a balance where the pruned gradients introduce sufficient noise to thwart such attacks while still maintaining comparable performance. In the pruning function, denoted as $P(.)$, within our proposed method, we adopt a straightforward approach. We set the coefficients with the least frequency (corresponding to small magnitudes) obtained from the DCT transformation to zero. By zeroing out these coefficients, we effectively prune the model, reducing its size while aiming to retain essential information contained in the remaining coefficients.

3.3   Improving Resilience in FL

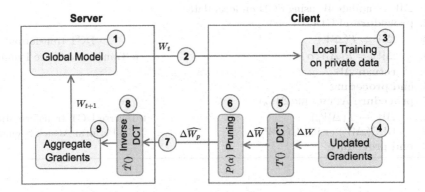

Fig. 3. Adapting pFGD to existing FL methodologies

The objective of this work is to introduce a method that strengthens the resilience of federated learning approaches against gradient inversion attacks. These attacks have the potential to compromise the fundamental benefits of FL, which is the preservation of client privacy. By incorporating the proposed method, pFGD, resilience can be achieved through the utilisation of a generalisable technique such as the frequency domain (the frequency space) and pruning. The pFGD addresses the vulnerability to gradient inversion attacks by leveraging the inherent properties of the frequency space and pruning. Overall, the aim of this work is to establish a resilient FL methodology that effectively combats gradient inversion attacks, thus enabling the continued protection of client privacy, which is a core principle of FL.

Figure 3 illustrates the adaptation of pFGD to existing FL methodologies. This adaptation introduces Steps 5 and 6, specifically designed to enhance resilience against model inversion attacks in the FL setting. Step 8 is used to inverse the frequency space model to raw space before model aggregation. In Fig. 3, Steps 2 and 7 represent the communication between the client and server, highlighting the potential vulnerability where an attacker can intercept and compromise the privacy of the system.

3.4 pFGD Algorithm

Based on the aforementioned considerations, Algorithm 1 outlines the workflow required to implement pFGD. Note that the algorithm incorporates a reference to the attacker method, which assumes the attacker possesses knowledge of inverting the DCT through the inverse transformation function $\hat{T}(.)$.

Algorithm 1. Pruned Frequency-based Gradient Defence

Require: W: global model, α: Pruning Rate
Require: $T(.)$ DCT Function, $P(.)$ Pruning Function
1: $\Delta W \leftarrow$ update W using SGD on local data
2: **procedure** pFGD($\Delta W, \alpha$)
3:      $\Delta\widehat{W} = T(\Delta W)$ ▷ DCT transformation
4:      $\Delta\widehat{W}_p = P(\Delta W, \alpha)$ ▷ Tranformed Space Pruning
5:      **return** $\Delta\widehat{W}_p$
6: **end procedure**
7: **procedure** ATTACKER($\Delta\widehat{W}_p$)
8:      $\Delta W \leftarrow \hat{T}(\Delta\widehat{W}_p)$ ▷ Inverse DCT transformation
9:      DLG(ΔW) or iDLG(ΔW)   ▷ Perform Attack Scenario
10: **end procedure**

---

4   Experiment Setup

In this introductory study, we aim to introduce and examine the potential of adapting the proposed pFGD to defend against gradient inversion attacks. First we study the impact on privacy on communicating client gradients in the frequency space, then we explore to what extent can parameter pruning in the frequency space can defend gradient inversion attacks. To evaluate the impact on privacy by communicating model parameters in the frequency space we use two attack methods and one image dataset. DLG [12] and iDLG [11] are selected to study the performance of pFGD. The two methods will be compared with and without the DCT transformation during the communication phase.

Dataset. We select MNIST [3] dataset which is a 10-class handwritten digit recognition image dataset. A single image dimensions are 28×28 and has one channel. MNIST is commonly used in FL and security benchmarks as it provides a realistic setting. MNIST's single-channel images aid performance assessment due to sensitivity to variations. Selecting MNIST for comparison with prior works enhances understanding of the approach against gradient inversion attacks.

Configuration. We adopt the experimental settings from [11,12] to ensure consistency and comparability. For the attack scenarios, we utilize LBFGS [4] with a learning rate of 1, batch size of 1 and 100 attack iterations. To mitigate the influence of random bias, we conduct 1000 runs of the experiments on LeNet models randomly initialised (i.e. 1000 random initiliased models on a unique data instance). Experiments will terminate at the 100th iteration or if the loss is below 0.000001.

Pruning. As highlighted in Sect. 3.2, pruning plays a significant role in introducing noise to the gradients, thereby diminishing the effectiveness of the attacks. In our experiments, we ensure consistency by using a fixed pruning rate of $\alpha = 1\%$, resulting in the pruning of 133 parameters. Additionally, we performed secondary experiments with a 0.1% pruning rate (11 parameters pruned) to ensure fair comparison and assess pruning's impact on pFGD's defense against gradient inversion attacks.

4.1 Comparative Study

To gain a comprehensive understanding of the impact of pFGD technique, we explore multiple variants of the selected baselines. Specifically, for the DLG and iDLG attack methods, we consider the following four variants: 1. Vanilla (original method without modifications), 2. Vanilla with pruning (pruning applied to the vanilla method), 3. DCT (applying only DCT transformation) and 4. DCT with pruning (pruning applied to the DCT transformed gradients) By examining these different variants, we can assess the effectiveness and comparative performance of pFGD in various configurations and scenarios. The experiment setup is publicly accessible on GitHub[1] for reproducibility.

Evaluation Metrics. We log the Mean Squared Error (MSE) of the reconstructed instance and the original image at each iteration. These MSE values are used to analyse and evaluate the behaviour of the proposed method. By counting the number of successful bypasses at each threshold, we gain insights into the effectiveness of the different variants in defending against the respective attacks. By considering the minimum MSE value from each experiment ensures that we capture the reconstruction's performance under various conditions and iterations.

---

[1] https://github.com/chamathpali/pFGD.

5   Results and Discussion

We conducted a comparative study of the four variants on two attack methods. Figure 4 visually presents the reconstructed images at different MSE threshold points, allowing for an assessment of their readability. By observing these visual

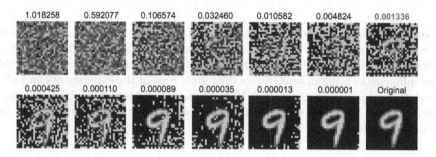

Fig. 4. Reconstructions of digit 9 are displayed at various MSE points, indicated above each image, ranging from higher to lower values. The final image presents the original digit 9 for comparison.

representations, we can assess the success of the reconstructions and identify any potential leakage of private information. At MSE = 0.001 (red text color in Fig. 4), the digit 9 becomes discernible upon closer examination. The results are presented in Fig. 5, which illustrates the number of experiments that were able to surpass different MSE thresholds. In Fig. 5 the bar plots consists of two colours, blue and orange which is for DLG and iDLG experiments respectively. Plots with the squared pattern represent the pruned variants and with diagonal patterns represent the DCT variants. In the graph legend, the notation '_P' represents the pruned variants. We observe when MSE = 1 there are only 24 and 12 experiments passing the threshold for DLG and iDLG respectively when DCT with pruning is applied. Additionally, we found that there were no reconstructions of DCT with pruning when the MSE was less than 0.9. In contrast, we found that reconstructions were identified even when the MSE reached a low value of 0.005 for pruning on the vanilla methods.

When using pruning on vanilla gradients without DCT there is still a high risk of leaking privacy sensitive information. With our experiments we were able to visually identify these reconstructions as the original image. For the MNIST dataset to properly identify a digit having a reconstructed image with MSE value of approximately 0.001 is sufficient for accurate digit identification. This cutoff point can differ from dataset to dataset and for different individuals eyesight. But our key observation is having pruning of $\alpha = 1\%$ is still able to be reconstructed on vanilla gradients. Additionally, we performed experiments with a pruning rate of $\alpha = 0.1\%$, results and plots are available on the GitHub repository.

The results obtained in our study provide compelling evidence that the combination of DCT with pruning techniques has significantly enhanced the defense

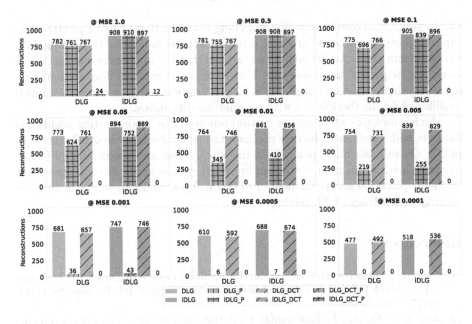

Fig. 5. Number of reconstructions at different MSE thresholds on MNIST dataset with $\alpha = 1\%$ with 4 variants on DLG and iDLG

against gradient inversion attacks. Throughout the 1000 experiment runs, we did not observe any reconstructions when applying DCT with pruning (pFGD) with an MSE below 0.9. These reconstructions lacked readability, rendering them essentially non-existent. In contrast, our research findings reveal that the application of pruning alone to the vanilla gradients, in the absence of employing the DCT, still poses a considerable risk of privacy breaches. For the MNIST dataset, our findings indicate that achieving a reconstructed image with an MSE of approximately 0.001 is sufficient for accurate digit identification. Around the MSE value of 0.005, we noticed a significant indication of a digit with potential lines emerging in the reconstructions. However, it is important to note that this threshold may vary across datasets and individual visual strengths. Our experiments visually demonstrated the identification of reconstructed images as the original ones in such cases. Taken together, these results highlight the resilience and efficacy of the proposed pFGD in countering gradient inversion attacks.

6   Conclusion

In this study, we introduced pFGD, a defense mechanism designed to mitigate gradient inversion attacks in federated learning. By applying frequency transformation using DCT on the updated gradients and incorporating pruning before communication, pFGD effectively enhances the resilience of FL models against such attacks. In our initial investigation, we conducted a comparative study involving two attack scenarios and four variants for each on the MNIST dataset.

Our experimental results provide compelling evidence that utilising pFGD offers superior protection against gradient inversion attacks compared to pruning with raw gradients alone. Additionally, we observed that the implementation of pFGD using the frequency space does not lead to any performance degradation. One of the notable advantages of pFGD is its practicality, as it can be easily applied to different FL methodologies with minimal modifications.

Moving forward, we intend to expand our study by incorporating additional datasets and baselines to further evaluate the generalisability and robustness of pFGD. Overall, our findings highlight the effectiveness and potential of pFGD as a defence mechanism against gradient inversion attacks in FL. We anticipate that further exploration and refinement of pFGD will contribute to strengthening the security and privacy of FL setting.

References

1. Geiping, J., Bauermeister, H., Dröge, H., Moeller, M.: Inverting gradients-how easy is it to break privacy in federated learning? Adv. Neural. Inf. Process. Syst. **33**, 16937–16947 (2020)
2. Jere, M.S., Farnan, T., Koushanfar, F.: A taxonomy of attacks on federated learning. IEEE Secur. Privacy **19**(2), 20–28 (2020)
3. LeCun, Y., Bottou, L., Bengio, Y., Haffner, P.: Gradient-based learning applied to document recognition. Proc. IEEE **86**(11), 2278–2324 (1998)
4. Liu, D.C., Nocedal, J.: On the limited memory bfgs method for large scale optimization. Math. Program. **45**(1–3), 503–528 (1989)
5. McMahan, B., Moore, E., Ramage, D., Hampson, S., y Arcas, B.A.: Communication-efficient learning of deep networks from decentralized data. In: Artificial Intelligence and Statistics, pp. 1273–1282. PMLR (2017)
6. Palihawadana, C., Wiratunga, N., Wijekoon, A., Kalutarage, H.: Fedsim: Similarity guided model aggregation for federated learning. Neurocomputing (2021)
7. Strang, G.: The discrete cosine transform. SIAM Rev. **41**(1), 135–147 (1999)
8. Wei, W., et al.: A framework for evaluating gradient leakage attacks in federated learning. arXiv preprint arXiv:2004.10397 (2020)
9. Zhang, R., Guo, S., Wang, J., Xie, X., Tao, D.: A survey on gradient inversion: Attacks, defenses and future directions. arXiv preprint arXiv:2206.07284 (2022)
10. Zhang, T., Gao, L., He, C., Zhang, M., Krishnamachari, B., Avestimehr, A.S.: Federated learning for the internet of things: Applications, challenges, and opportunities. IEEE Internet Things Mag. **5**(1), 24–29 (2022)
11. Zhao, B., Mopuri, K.R., Bilen, H.: idlg: Improved deep leakage from gradients. arXiv preprint arXiv:2001.02610 (2020)
12. Zhu, L., Liu, Z., Han, S.: Deep leakage from gradients. In: Advances in Neural Information Processing Systems 32 (2019)

Network Intrusion Detection by Variational Component-Based Feature Saliency Gaussian Mixture Clustering

Xin Hong[✉], Zafeirios Papazachos[ID], Jesus Martinez del Rincon[ID], and Paul Miller

Centre for Secure Information Technologies, School of Electronics, Electrical Engineering and Computer Science, Queen's University Belfast, Belfast, Northern Ireland, UK
x.hong@qub.ac.uk

Abstract. Anomaly detection is a core function of the network intrusion detection system, and due to the high volume and dimensionality of network data, clustering is an important technique for anomaly detection in unsupervised machine learning. In this paper, we propose a clustering approach for anomaly detection on network traffic flow data. For profiling normal traffic, we apply the component-based feature saliency Gaussian mixture model. We then present a variational learning algorithm which can simultaneously optimize over the number of components, the saliencies of the features for each component, and the parameters of the mixture model. The preliminary experiments on a network intrusion dataset demonstrate the satisfying performance achieved by both our method on its own and with a data preprocessing using the auto-encoder.

Keywords: Component-based Feature Saliency · Clustering · Anomaly Detection · Network Intrusion Detection

1 Introduction

The exponential growth in networking, e-commerce and the Internet of Things has been matched by a substantial increase in attack vectors designed to compromise both host and networked systems. Defense-in-depth strategies have shaped a mixture of defensive responses – host and network-based firewalls; intrusion detection systems; anti-virus solutions; active responses; architectural redesign; and implementing hierarchical levels of access. Despite strengthening defenses, attackers are still getting access to network systems, going undetected for lengthy periods and engaging in a variety of illegal activities – compromising confidentiality, integrity, availability and inflicting reputational damage.

Network intrusion attacks normally present as anomalies to normal network traffic patterns. Complexity and diversity in input vectors make network intrusion detection a particularly complex problem. Significant research activity has been undertaken [22]. Intrusion detection systems (IDS) can be distinguished by multiple aspects such as their analyzed activity (i.e., monitoring a network or a host activity logs) and detection

© The Author(s), under exclusive license to Springer Nature Switzerland AG 2024
S. Katsikas et al. (Eds.): ESORICS 2023 Workshops, LNCS 14399, pp. 761–772, 2024.
https://doi.org/10.1007/978-3-031-54129-2_45

approach (i.e., signature-based or anomaly-based detection). Anomaly-based intrusion detection techniques often rely on machine learning algorithms. One focus is on the detection of anomalous network traffic from flow-based data using clustering techniques which identify the distribution of normal data and classify data falling outside the distribution as an anomaly, including K-Means [12, 18], Gaussian Mixture Models (GMM) [1, 3, 10, 26] and one-class SVM [2, 20]. In this work, we propose a novel unsupervised approach for intrusion detection on network traffic flow data. For clustering normal traffic flow data, we apply the component-based feature saliency Gaussian mixture model (CFSGMM) proposed in [6]. The CFSGMM is a probabilistic model that generates data points from a finite number of Gaussian distributions whilst considering the saliency of the features based on components. The proposed variational learning algorithm can simultaneously optimize over the number of components, the saliency of the features for each component, and the parameters of the mixture model. To enhance the performance of the proposed clustering method we also implement a data preprocessing method which utilizes feature extraction based on the encoder part of a trained autoencoder. The encoder part can assist in compressing large and complex input into a lower dimensionality or feature selection. In this way, the input is filtered into a compressed output with transformed features that could provide more meaningful information on certain input characteristics, and it could also reduce the likelihood of overfitting that could occur when dealing with large input dimensions. This method of data preprocessing with the use of the encoder part of an autoencoder has also been utilized for different applications, such as in clustering with k-means or GMM in [11, 15, 24].

The remainder of the paper is organized as follows. Related works are introduced in Sect. 2. Section 3 presents the proposed methodology including CFSGMM, variational model learning and anomaly detection method. Section 4 describes the experimental details: datasets, methods, and results with discussions. Section 5 concludes the paper and identifies some areas for future works.

2 Related Works

Clustering is an important technique used in anomaly detection. Network flows can be characterized by a large amount of features, some of which may be more useful for clustering, or model learning, than others. A key question is which features should we select for clustering? To address this the most recent approaches involve simultaneously performing feature selection along with clustering in which the feature weighting and clustering are optimized iteratively [19, 25]. Law et al. [9] define the concept of feature saliency to a Gaussian mixture model, under the assumption that the features are conditionally independent given the hidden component label. In [5], a variational solution for mixture model training was provided. As the size of networks and the amount of traffic increases, normalcy models have become increasingly complex, convoluted and non-linear. As such, a feature may have saliency with respect to one component of the model but not to another. In [6] we previously developed a new approach in which the feature saliency with respect to each model component is determined by explicitly including in our model the dependency of each component with respect to each feature. The method we propose engages the same model as in [6] to describe the relevance of features, but integrates model and feature selection under a variational framework. Using the variational framework, our method is expected to be more robust.

The auto-encoder network is originally designed for data representation, and it aims to minimize the reconstruction error [15]. The auto-encoder can learn the hidden features of the input data to achieve nonlinear dimensionality reduction [7]. It is nature utilizing the auto-encoder to handle high dimensionality and complex structure encountered by real world data such as network communications. Deep learning and the use of auto-encoders has been previously employed in detecting outliers in network data. In [4] the use of auto-encoders and convolutional auto-encoders has been utilized to detect network anomalies. A network anomaly is a type of an outlier which can differ from an actual network intrusion, but this approach emphasizes the inherent capability of an autoencoder to manipulate the feature characteristics of network information and extract useful data in the form of network anomalies. In our work, we utilize the encoding part of the auto-encoder to transform and extract a compressed feature representation of the network activity. The filtered output is then combined with our proposed vCFSGMM method to detect anomalous network traffic. This strategy is utilized in many recent studies; in [15] AE is used for data clustering, in DCN [21] autoencoder performance is regulated by k-means, and in DeepCluster [17] an alternating direction of multiplier method is used to integrate K-means and GMM into deep networks.

3 Methodology

In this section, we introduce the proposed method: Variational Component-based Feature Saliency Gaussian Mixture Model based detection (vCFSGMM). There are two main components in this work: normal traffic learning and anomaly detection. In the following sub-sections, we concretely introduce the method in detail.

3.1 Normal Traffic Learning

In this section, we present a Bayesian method of learning the Gaussian mixture model for normal traffic that automatically determines the number of components and the feature saliencies. We first introduce the component-based feature saliency Gaussian mixture model [6]. We then present a variational training method for the model.

Component-Based Feature Saliency Gaussian Mixture Model (CFSGMM)
Let $X = \{x_{ni}\}$ be a set of N observations, where each $x_{ni} \in \Re$ is a feature in a D-dimensional space. Let also f be a mixture with J Gaussian components

$$f(x) = \sum_{j=1}^{J} \pi_j \prod_{i}^{D} \left[w_{ji} N\left(x_i | \mu_{ji}, \tau_{ji}\right) + \left(1 - w_{ji}\right) N(x_i | \varepsilon_i, \gamma_i) \right] \tag{1}$$

where $\pi = \{\pi_j\}$ are the mixing coefficients (weights), $\mu = \{\mu_{ji}\}$ the means and $\tau = \{\tau_{ji}\}$ the precisions (inverse covariances) of the mixture components, $\varepsilon = \{\varepsilon_i\}$ and $\gamma = \{\gamma_i\}$ are the sets of means and precisions over all mixture components. Some of the features might be irrelevant for modeling while others may be more useful. Here we consider

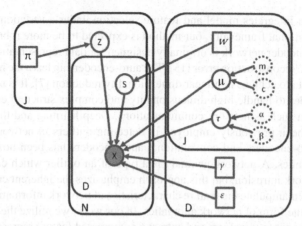

Fig. 1. Graphical model for the generation of the observed data assuming a Bayesian mixture density model and allowing noisy features. Symbols in solid circles denote random variables; those in squares denote model parameters; those in dotted circles denote hyper-parameters; the symbol in the filled circle denotes the data. Plates denote repetitions and the number of repetitions for those in a plate is depicted in the bottom-left corner.

that a feature is useful up to a probability $w = \{w_{ji}\}$. We assume that data set X has been generated from the graphical model illustrated in Fig. 1.

The graphical model in Fig. 1 implies the assumption that for each observation x_n there exists a hidden variable z_{nj} denoting the dependence on the jth mixture component that generated x_n. Let $Z = \{z_{nj}\}$, $z_{nj} \in \{0, 1\}$ and $\sum_{j=1}^{J} z_{nj} = 1$. If x_n is generated from the jth component, then $z_{nj} = 1$; otherwise, $z_{nj} = 0$. The saliency of features is expressed by the hidden variables s_{nji}. Let $S = \{s_{nji}\}$, $s_{nji} \in \{0, 1\}$. If the value of s_{nji} is one, then the ith feture of x_n has been generated from the "useful" jth component; otherwise, it has been generated from the "noisy" common component.

Given the sets of hidden variables Z and S, the data is assumed to be independently drawn from a Gaussian distribution

$$p(X | Z, \mu, \tau, S, \varepsilon, \gamma) =$$
$$\prod_{n=1}^{N} \prod_{j=1}^{J} \left\{ \prod_{i=1}^{D} \left[N(x_{ni} | \mu_{ji}, \tau_{ji}) \right]^{s_{nji}} \left[N(x_{ni} | \varepsilon_i, \gamma_i) \right]^{1 - s_{nji}} \right\}^{z_{nj}} \tag{2}$$

The sets $\mu = \{\mu_{ji}\}$ and $\tau = \{\tau_{ji}\}$ denote the means and the inverse covariances of the "useful" Gaussian mixture components. $\varepsilon = \{\varepsilon_i\}$ and $\gamma = \{\gamma_i\}$ are the sets of parameters of the "noisy" common component.

Conditional distribution of Z, given the mixing coefficients π, is given by

$$p(Z | \pi) = \prod_{n=1}^{N} \prod_{j=1}^{J} \pi_j^{z_{nj}} \tag{3}$$

Conditional distribution of S, given the feature saliency w, is given by

$$p(S | w) = \prod_{n=1}^{N} \prod_{j=1}^{J} \prod_{i=1}^{D} w_{ji}^{s_{nji}} (1 - w_{ji})^{(1 - s_{nji})} \tag{4}$$

Here we adopt a Bayesian approach for model selection that imposes Gaussian and Gamma priors for the parameters μ and τ as:

$$p(\mu) = \prod_{j=1}^{J} \prod_{i=1}^{D} N\left(\mu_{ji}|m_i, c\right) \tag{5}$$

$$p(\tau) = \prod_{j=1}^{J} \prod_{i=1}^{D} Gam(\tau_{ji}|\alpha, \beta) \tag{6}$$

The hyperparameters $m, c, \alpha,$ and β control the prior distributions and are fixed at values that form broad and uninformative priors. In particular, m is set to the mean of all data, while $c = \alpha = \beta = 10^{-16}$ [5].

By the graphical model in Fig. 1, the joint distribution of the observed data and the random variables Z, μ, τ, S, conditioned on $\pi, w, \varepsilon, \gamma$, is given by

$$p(X, Z, \mu, \tau, S|\pi, w, \varepsilon, \gamma) = p(X|Z, \mu, \tau, S, \varepsilon, \gamma)p(Z|\pi)p(\mu)p(\tau)p(S|w) \tag{7}$$

Variational Learning

In this section, we present a variational training method for the CFSGMM. To simplify notation, we define $\theta = \{Z, \mu, \tau, S\}$ the set of random variables and $\vartheta = \{\pi, w, \varepsilon, \gamma\}$ the set of parameters. The method we propose for model selection is through maximization of the marginal likelihood $p(X|\vartheta)$ that results by integrating out the variables $\theta = \{Z, \mu, \tau, S\}$ from the joint density $p(X, \theta|\vartheta)$

$$p(X|\vartheta) = \int p(X, \theta|\vartheta)d\theta \tag{8}$$

The variational approximation suggests the maximization of a lower bound $\mathcal{L}$ of the logarithmic marginal likelihood

$$\log p(X|\vartheta) = \mathcal{L}(q) + KL(q||p) \tag{9}$$

$$\mathcal{L}(q) = \int q(\theta)\log\left\{\frac{p(X, \theta|\vartheta)}{q(\theta)}\right\}d\theta \tag{10}$$

$$KL(q||p) = -\int q(\theta)\log\left\{\frac{p(\theta|X, \vartheta)}{q(\theta)}\right\}d\theta \tag{11}$$

where the variational posterior $q(\theta)$ is an arbitrary distribution approximating the posterior $p(\theta|X, \vartheta)$.

By the *mean-field* approximation, the variational distribution is factorised between the latent variables and the model parameters

$$q(Z, \mu, \tau, S) = q_Z(Z)q_\mu(\mu)q_\tau(\tau)q_S(S) \tag{12}$$

Maximizing $\mathcal{L}$ with respect to the functional form of $q_Z, q_\mu, q_\tau,$ and q_S, the standard variational approach provides the following general form of the solutions:

$$q^*(\theta_l) = \frac{\exp(\mathbb{E}_{k \neq l}[\ln p(X, \theta|\vartheta)])}{\int \exp(\mathbb{E}_{k \neq l}[\ln p(X, \theta|\vartheta)])\theta_l} \tag{13}$$

where $\mathbb{E}_{k \neq l}[\cdot]$ denotes an expectation with respect to the distributions $q_k(\theta_k)$ for all $k \neq l$. For our CFSGMM, (13) produces:

$$q^*(Z) = \prod_{n=1}^{N} \prod_{j=1}^{J} r_{nj}^{Z_{nj}} \tag{14}$$

$$q^*(\mu) = \prod_{j=1}^{J} \prod_{i=1}^{D} N(\mu_{ji} | m_{ji}, c_{ji}) \tag{15}$$

$$q*(\tau) = \prod_{j=1}^{J} \prod_{i=1}^{D} Gam(\tau_{ji} | \alpha_{ji}, \beta_{ji}) \tag{16}$$

$$q^*(S) = \prod_{n=1}^{N} \prod_{j=1}^{J} \prod_{i=1}^{D} \rho_{nji}^{s_{nji}} (1 - \rho_{nji})^{1 - s_{nji}} \tag{17}$$

where r_{nj}, m_{ji}, c_{ji}, α_{ji}, β_{ji}, and ρ_{nji} are the variational parameters that emerge from the maximization and determine the densities involved in q^*. The variational parameters are defined using the expected values of Z_{nj}, μ_{ji}, τ_{ji}, s_{nji}. Using the functional forms of q_Z, q_μ, q_τ, and q_S, we can derive the corresponding expectations and define the variational parameters as in the following equations:

$$r_{nj} = \frac{\pi_j \tilde{r}_{nj}}{\sum_{j=1}^{J} \pi_j \tilde{r}_{nj}} \tag{18}$$

$$\tilde{r}_{nj} = \exp \left\{ \frac{1}{2} \sum_{i=1}^{D} \rho_{nji} [\psi(\alpha_{ji}) - \ln \beta_{ji}] \right.$$
$$- \frac{1}{2} \sum_{i=1}^{D} \rho_{nji} \frac{\alpha_{ji}}{\beta_{ji}} \left[(x_{ni} - m_{ji})^2 + \frac{1}{c_{ji}} \right]$$
$$\left. + \frac{1}{2} \sum_{i=1}^{D} \rho_{nji} \left[(x_{ni} - \varepsilon_i)^2 \gamma_i - \ln \gamma_i \right] \right\} \tag{19}$$

$$m_{ji} = \frac{cm_i + (\alpha_{ji}/\beta_{ji}) \sum_{n=1}^{N} r_{nj} \rho_{nji} x_{ni}}{c + (\alpha_{ji}/\beta_{ji}) \sum_{n=1}^{N} r_{nj} \rho_{nji}} \tag{20}$$

$$c_{ji} = c + \frac{\alpha_{ji}}{\beta_{ji}} \sum_{n=1}^{N} r_{nj} \rho_{nji} \tag{21}$$

$$\alpha_{ji} = \alpha + \frac{1}{2} \sum_{n=1}^{N} r_{nj} \rho_{nji} \tag{22}$$

$$\beta_{ji} = \beta + \frac{1}{2} \sum_{n=1}^{N} r_{nj} \rho_{nji} \left[(x_{ni} - m_{ji})^2 + \frac{1}{c_{ji}} \right] \tag{23}$$

$$\rho_{nji} = \frac{w_{ji} \tilde{\rho}_{nji}}{w_{ji} \tilde{\rho}_{nji} + (1 - w_{ji}) \xi_{nji}} \tag{24}$$

$$\tilde{\rho}_{nji} = \exp \left\{ \frac{1}{2} r_{nj} [\psi(\alpha_{ji}) - \ln \beta_{ji}] - \frac{1}{2} r_{nj} \frac{\alpha_{ji}}{\beta_{ji}} \left[(x_{ni} - m_{ji})^2 + \frac{1}{c_{ji}} \right] \right\} \tag{25}$$

$$\xi_{nji} = \exp \left\{ -\frac{1}{2} r_{nj} (x_{ni} - \varepsilon_i)^2 \gamma_i + \frac{1}{2} r_{nj} \ln \gamma_i \right\} \tag{26}$$

where $\psi(x) = \mathrm{d} \log \Gamma(x)/\mathrm{d}x$. Thus we see that the solutions for the variational factors q_Z, q_μ, q_τ, and q_S, given by (14)–(17) respectively, are mutually coupled through their dependence on moments of the other factors. An exact maximization of $\mathcal{L}$ with respect to the variational parameters is impossible, however, we can improve the bound by iteratively updating the parameters using (18)–(26).

By maximising the lower bound $\mathcal{L}$ with respect to π_j, w_{ji}, ε_i and γ_i, we obtain the required estimates for the parameters. Setting the derivative of the lower bound with respect to them gives the following update rules:

$$\pi_j = \frac{1}{N} \sum_{n=1}^{N} r_{nj} \tag{27}$$

$$w_{ji} = \frac{1}{N} \sum_{n=1}^{N} \rho_{nji} \tag{28}$$

$$\varepsilon_i = \frac{\sum_{n=1}^{N} \sum_{j=1}^{J} r_{nj} \rho_{nji} x_{ni}}{\sum_{n=1}^{N} \sum_{j=1}^{J} r_{nj} \rho_{nji}} \tag{29}$$

$$\frac{1}{\gamma_i} = \frac{\sum_{n=1}^{N} \sum_{j=1}^{J} r_{nj} \rho_{nji} (x_{ni} - \varepsilon_i)^2}{\sum_{n=1}^{N} \sum_{j=1}^{J} r_{nj} \rho_{nji}} \tag{30}$$

The above procedure is repeated until convergence monitored through inspection of the lower bound $\mathcal{L}$.

Normal Traffic Profile
Normal traffic clustering responds to the learning stage of the proposed method. Once the CFSGMM has learned using the methods presented in the previous sections, we can calculate the probability densities (PDFs) for the data in the training set using (1) with the learned model parameters. We then set up a set of thresholds to be used by anomaly detection in the next stage.

$$TH = quantile(PDFs, CP) \tag{31}$$

where $CP = \{cp_i\}$, $cp_i \in [0, 1]$, is a set of cumulative probabilities.

Thus, we generate a profile for normal traffic on the training dataset containing the learned model parameters and the thresholds

$$profile = \{\Theta = (\pi, \mu, \tau, \varepsilon, \gamma, w), TH\}. \tag{32}$$

This profile will be used in next stage for anomaly detection.

3.2 Anomaly Detection

On a test dataset, anomaly detection is performed in two steps:
   Step 1: compute the $PDF_{testing}$ using (1) and Θ in *profile*;
   Step 2: if $PDF_{testing} < TH$ then it is attack; otherwise normal.

4 Experiments

4.1 Datasets

We used the UNSW-NB15 dataset [13, 16] which contains about 100 GB of data. 2,540,044 traffic flows are stored in the four CSV files: UNSW-NB15-1, 15-2, 15-3, and 15-4. Each traffic flow is represented by 47 features.

Our initial experiments ran on UNSW-NB15_1 subset. It contains in total 700,001 traffic flows, in which 677,786 are normal and 22,215 are abnormal. There are 9 types of attacks. The statistics of the data being used are as follows:

Total (700,001)

  Normal 677,786 (677780 used)
  Attack 22,215

Training (542,224)

  Normal 542,224 (80% of the Normal in total)

Testing (157,771)

  Normal 135,556 (20% of the Normal in total) (~86% test set).
  Attack 22,215 (100% of the Attacks in total) (~14% test set).

Excluding IP addresses and port numbers of source and destination, and start and last time of a flow record, forty-one out of forty-seven features were used in the experiments for learning the model of normal traffic from the training set and detecting abnormal network traffic in the testing set.

The five-folds approach was used. To make the folds, the total normal data of 677,780 (ignore the last 6 in the original normal data for equal split) was split into 10 parts, each part contains 67,778 samples. To make up a fold, eight parts were selected as the training set, the other two part as the testing set (plus attack data). The results are averaged over five folds.

4.2 Methods

To demonstrate the characteristics of the proposed vCFSGMM for anomaly detection, we selected two mostly related methods for comparison: an Auto-Encoder (AE) and a Bayesian mixture model with feature saliency (vFSGMM).

AE [4, 23] is an unsupervised learning technique based on neural networks that consists of two sections. The first section is the encoding part which compresses the input data into a representation of lower dimensionality and the second section is the decoder which reconstructs the data back to its original form. In this model we utilise an encoder with 2 dense layers, the first layer has 16 neurons and the second layer has 8 neurons. Conversely, the decoder part has the same type of layers but in a reversed order. The mean squared error is used as loss function. There are various ways to detect anomalies using an autoencoder. In this model, the reconstruction error is used for different thresholds to detect outliers as network intrusions. It takes the original 41 features as input.

vFSGMM [5] is a Bayesian approach for learning Gaussian mixture models that automatically determines the number of components and the saliencies of features. It is different to the proposed vCFSGMM in a way that they calculate feature saliency averaged over all the mixture components whereas in our approach we calculate feature saliencies specific to each component of the model. It takes the original 41 features as input.

We implemented the proposed method in two ways:

vCFSGMM: Same as the two methods above, we implemented the method on the original 41 features.
AE-vCFSGMM: We also implemented the method by taking the embeddings (8 features now) of the encoder from the AE as input.

4.3 Results and Discussion

To evaluate the performance of the model, we draw the ROC curve by plotting the true positive rate (TPR) against the false positive rate (FPR) at various threshold settings and the area under the ROC curve can be expressed as AUC. The method performs well when AUC is high. We also calculate precision, recall, and F1 metrics corresponding to the optimal cut-point (max(TPR-FPR)) [14] of ROC curve.

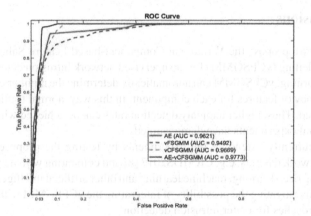

Fig. 2. The ROC curves

We draw the ROC curve to evaluate the overall performance of models on the dataset. It can be seen from Fig. 2 that vCFSGMM outperforms AE and vFSGMM with the larger AUC. When AE-vCFSGMM used AE embeddings as feature inputs, it achieved the best performance with the largest AUC. As the threshold increases, the performance of the vCFSGMM models gradually exceed other models, indicating that the generalization ability of vCFSGMM is the best.

The experimental results are shown in Table 1. The AUC of vCFSGMM is much higher than vFSGMM, which shows that considering feature saliencies for each component improves the performance. The AUC of AE is relatively comparative to vCFSGMM.

Table 1. Anomaly detection results

Method	AUC	Precision	Recall	F1
AE	0.9621	0.6975 (0.8438)	0.9420 (0.9347)	0.7950 (0.8761)
vFSGMM	0.9492	0.6445 (0.8123)	0.8777 (0.8913)	0.7227 (0.8308)
vCFSGMM	0.9669	0.6031 (0.8015)	0.9998 (0.9353)	0.7418 (0.8350)
AE-vCFSGMM	0.9773	0.7979 (0.8972)	0.9797 (0.9675)	0.8757 (0.9255)

However, AE-vCFSGMM achieves gains of 1.5% AUC, 10% Precision, 3.8% Recall, and 8% F1 in comparison to AE. That strongly indicates that considering feature saliencies on compressed feature embeddings helps improving the performance. Furthermore, vCFSGMM achieves the optimal recall on both the original feature sets and the feature sets extracted from AE embeddings which indicates that vCFSGMM can better capture abnormal activities occurring in the network. As the dataset has unbalanced ratio of normal vs abnormal, we also calculate the performance towards normal traffic in the testing set. The values in brackets for Precision, Recall, and F1 in Table 1 are averaged over normal and abnormal detection. Overall, AE-vCFSGMM performs best on Precision, Recall, and F1.

5   Conclusions

In this paper we propose the Variational Component-based Feature Saliency Gaussian Mixture Modelling (vCFSGMM) for unsupervised network intrusion detection. On normal traffic learning, vCFSGMM can automatically determine the number of components and the saliency of features for each component. In this way, normal traffic patterns can be well learned. Thus, higher anomaly detection rates can be achieved which the results from the initial experiments have demonstrated.

We are currently extending the experiments by testing the proposed method on more real network datasets, e.g. CIC-IDS2017 [8] and comparing with newly developed methods using deep learning, machine learning and other artificial intelligent techniques. We are also investigating the possibility of integrating the vCFSGMM with various deep learning approaches for better intrusion detection.

References

1. An, P., Wang, Z., Zhang, C.: Ensemble unsupervised autoencoders and Gaussian mixture model for cyberattack detection. Inf. Process. Manag. **59**(2) (2022)
2. Binbusayyis, A., Vaiyapuri, T.: Unsupervised deep learning approach for network intrusion detection combining convolutional autoencoder and one-class SVM. Appl. Intell. **51**, 7094–7108 (2021)
3. Chen, Y., Ashizawa, N., Yeo, C.K., Yanai, N., Yean, S.: Multiscale self-organizing map assisted deep autoencoding Gaussian mixture model for unsupervised intrusion detection. Knowl.-Based Syst. **224**, 2021 (2021)

4. Chen, Z., Yeo, C.K., Lee, B.S., Lau, C.T.: Autoencoder-based network anomaly detection. In: 2018 Wireless Telecommunications Symposium (WTS), pp. 1–5. IEEE (2018)
5. Constantinopoulos, C., Titsias, M.K., Likas, A.: Bayesian feature and model selection for Gaussian mixture models. IEEE Trans. PAMI **28**(6), 1013–1018 (2006)
6. Hong, X., et al.: Component-based feature saliency for clustering. IEEE Trans. KDE **33**(3), 882–896 (2021)
7. Huang, X., Hu, Z., Lin, L.: Deep clustering based on embedded auto-encoder. Soft Comput. **27**, 1075–1090 (2023)
8. Intrusion Detection Evaluation Dataset (CICIDS2017). https://www.unb.ca/cic/datasets/ids-2017.html. Accessed 7 July 2023
9. Law, M.H., Figueiredo, M.A., Jain, A.K.: Simultaneous feature selection and clustering using mixture models. IEEE Trans. PAMI **26**(9), 1154–1166 (2004)
10. Leonid, S.: Unsupervised anomaly detection in network traffic using Deep Autoencoding Gaussian Mixture model. Int. J. Open Inf. Technol. **9**(9), 109–112 (2021)
11. Lim, K.L., Jiang, X., Yi, C.: Deep clustering with variational autoencoder. IEEE Sig. Process. Lett. **27**, 231–235 (2020)
12. Meng, J., Shang, H., Bian, L.: The Application on intrusion detection based on K-means cluster algorithm. In: 2009 International Forum on Information Technology and Applications, pp. 150–152 (2009)
13. Moustafa, N., Slay, J.: The evaluation of network anomaly detection systems: statistical analysis of the unsw-nb15 data set and the comparison with the kdd99 data set. Inf. Secur. J. Glob. Perspect. **25**(1–3), 18–31, 2016 (2016)
14. Schisterman, E.F., Perkins, N.J., Liu, A., Bondell, H.: Optimal cut-point and its corresponding Youden index to discriminate individuals using pooled blood samples. Epidemiology **16**(1), 73–81 (2005)
15. Song, C., Liu, F., Huang, Y., Wang, L., Tan, T.: Auto-encoder based data clustering. In: Progress in Pattern Recognition, Image Analysis, Computer Vision, and Applications: 18th Iberoamerican Congress, CIARP 2013, Part I, vol. 18, pp. 117–124 (2013)
16. The UNSW-NB15 Dataset. https://research.unsw.edu.au/projects/unsw-nb15-dataset. Accessed 6 July 2023
17. Tian, K., Zhou, S., Guan, J.: Deepcluster: a general clustering framework based on deep learning. In: Proceedings of ECML PKDD 2017, Part II 17, pp. 809–825 (2017)
18. Tsai, C., Lin, C.: A triangle area based nearest neighbors approach to intrusion detection. Pattern Recogn. **43**(2010), 222–229 (2010)
19. Wang, J., Wei, J.M., Yang, Z., Wang, S.Q.: Feature selection by maximizing independent classification information. IEEE Trans. KDE **29**, 828–843 (2017)
20. Winter, P., Hermann, E., Zeilinger, M.: Inductive intrusion detection in flow-based network data using one-class support vector machines. In: IEEE Conference on New Technologies, Mobility and Security (2011)
21. Yang, B., Fu, X., Sidiropoulos, N.D., Hong, M.: Towards k-means-friendly spaces: simultaneous deep learning and clustering. In: ICML 2017, pp. 3861–3870 (2017)
22. Yang, Y., Zheng, K., Wu, C., Yang, Y.: Improving the classification effectiveness of intrusion detection by using improved conditional variational AutoEncoder and deep neural network. Sensors **19**(11), 2528 (2019)
23. Zhai, J., Zhang, S., Chen, J., He, Q.: Autoencoder and its various variants. In: 2018 IEEE International Conference on System Man and Cybernetics (SMC), pp. 415–419 (2018)
24. Zhang, R., Tong, H., Xia, Y., Zhu, Y.: Robust embedded deep k-means clustering. In: Proceedings of the 28th ACM International Conference on Information and Knowledge and Management, pp. 1181–1190 (2019)

25. Zhu, X., Li, X., Zhang, S., Ju, C., Wu, X.: Robust joint graph sparse coding for unsupervised spectral feature selection. IEEE Trans. NNLS **28**, 1263–1275 (2017)
26. Zong, B., et al.: Deep autoencoding gaussian mixture model for unsupervised anomaly detection. In: ICLR 2018 (2018)

Author Index

S. Katsikas et al. (Eds.): ESORICS 2023 Workshops, LNCS 14399, pp. 773–776, 2024.
https://doi.org/10.1007/978-3-031-54129-2

Printed in the United States
by Baker & Taylor Publisher Services

Printed in the United States
by Baker & Taylor Publisher Services